HUDSON T. HARTMANN
Department of Pomology
University of California at Davis

WILLIAM J. FLOCKER
Department of Vegetable Crops
University of California at Davis

ANTON M. KOFRANEK
Department of Environmental Horticulture
University of California at Davis

PLANT SCIENCE

Growth, Development, and Utilization of Cultivated Plants

PRENTICE-HALL, INC.   Englewood Cliffs, New Jersey 07632

Library of Congress Cataloging in Publication Data

HARTMANN, HUDSON THOMAS
   Plant science.

   Includes bibliographies and index.
      1. Plants, Cultivated.   2. Botany, Economic.
I. Flocker, William Jack, joint author.
II. Kofranek, Anton M., joint author.   III. Title.
SB91.H37 1981   633   80-19117
ISBN 0-13-681056-X

*This book is dedicated
to Dr. William J. Flocker,
a devoted teacher of many thousands of students
in his plant science courses at the University of California.
He was an enthusiastic participant
in the preparation of this book
but did not live to see it published.*

Printed in the United States of America
10 9 8 7 6 5 4 3 2 1

Editorial/production supervision by Joan L. Lee
Interior and cover design and page layout
by Judith Winthrop
Manufacturing buyer: John Hall
Botanical art by Alyne Lavoie-Ruppanner
Technical art by Ken Davis
*All photographs, unless otherwise credited,
are the property of the authors.*

PRENTICE-HALL INTERNATIONAL, INC., *London*

PRENTICE-HALL OF AUSTRALIA PTY. LIMITED, *Sydney*

PRENTICE-HALL OF CANADA, LTD., *Toronto*

PRENTICE-HALL OF INDIA PRIVATE LIMITED, *New Delhi*

PRENTICE-HALL OF JAPAN, INC., *Tokyo*

PRENTICE-HALL OF SOUTHEAST ASIA PTE. LTD., *Singapore*

WHITEHALL BOOKS LIMITED, *Wellington, New Zealand*

Contents

4

Origin, Domestication, and Improvement of Cultivated Plants *56*

5

Propagation of Plants *79*

6

Vegetative and Reproductive Growth and Development *116*

7

Photosynthesis, Respiration, and Translocation *145*

8

Soil and Soil Water 166

9

Soil and Water Management
and Mineral Nutrition 195

10

Climatic Influences
on Crop Production 222

11

Biological Competitors
of Useful Plants 238

12

Harvest, Preservation, Transportation, Storage, and Marketing *268*

II

AN OVERVIEW OF THE FRUIT CROPS AND ORNAMENTAL PLANTS *291*

13

Cultural Practices in Orchards and Vineyards *293*

14

Flowering and Fruiting in Fruit Crops *320*

28

Vegetable Crops Grown for Underground Parts 573

29

Temperate Zone Fruit and Nut Crops 589

30

Subtropical Fruit and Nut Crops 610

31

Tropical Fruit and Nut Crops 621

Preface

This book is intended primarily as a text for plant science courses at the lower division university level and in community colleges. It is written so as to be easily understood by students who have little or no botanical background. Basic botanical, soils, climate, and plant protection topics are covered in the first part of the book, as background for the subjects considered later.

The book covers thoroughly the fundamentals of the botany of higher plants that are basic to a good understanding of plant science. The book also emphasizes the principles involved in the response of plants to environmental stresses and how these stresses can be modified. This emphasis will help students understand both the behavior of plants in agricultural and horticultural situations, and how to modify environmental influences to increase plant production. Because the purpose of growing most plants is to provide food, shelter, or esthetic enjoyment, the book also covers modern methods of harvesting, transporting, preserving, and marketing crops.

In addition to the fundamentals of plant structure, growth, and development, this book covers in detail the principles and methods of growing the various fruit, vegetable, and agronomic crops and of obtaining maximum production. The categories of ornamentals, including lawns and landscaping, are also discussed thoroughly; eight chapters in the book cover ornamentals from the standpoint of both the commercial producer and the home gardener. Most important, the book discusses the principles governing the flowering of common greenhouse ornamentals, to help students grow them successfully in college greenhouses. An additional chap-

ter covers the methods by which foliage and flowering plants can be grown and maintained properly under home conditions.

The final unit in the book gives encyclopedic coverage of the world's important agronomic, vegetable, and fruit crop plants, detailing their origin and cultural and harvesting requirements.

At the end of each chapter are extensive lists of references to international plant science literature, either as specific research references or as supplementary readings. The appendix contains a lengthy table giving the food values of major crop products.

By selectively covering various sections and chapters of this book, the instructor can use it as a text for a general plant science course or for horticulture or agronomy courses. He or she can also emphasize particular crops important in a given locality. This book can also serve as a comprehensive reference for students, research and extension workers, and the home gardener.

The text is organized in three major units. The first, consisting of 12 chapters, deals with plant structure, classification, and growth and reproduction, and with use of plant products. This section of the book would be appropriate for use in a basic plant science course. The second and third units supplement the first. The second unit, consisting of 10 chapters, covers horticultural crops—fruits and ornamentals—and would be emphasized in a horticulture course. This unit would be particularly useful for urban horticulture, in beautifying school grounds, city parks, and city homes. The third unit, consisting of 9 chapters, includes material on the cereal, sugar, oil, forage, fiber, and vegetable crops. It should be emphasized in a course directed toward these subject areas.

Unit I begins with an introductory chapter that describes the importance of plants to the survival and well-being of the earth's animal population, including humans. The following three chapters cover the structure and the classification of plants, giving information on where and how the important crop plants originated and were domesticated, and how new kinds of plants are developed by plant breeders. Another chapter covers all the methods of propagating plants—valuable material for courses that require students to propagate and grow plants in the school greenhouses. The next six chapters deal with the physiology of plants and their responses to the environment, including controls agriculturists have adopted to protect crop plants from their biological enemies.

Unit II deals with the horticultural crops: first, in two chapters, tree fruits, grapes, brambles, and strawberries; then, in eight chapters, ornamentals, shade trees, woody shrubs, production and use of greenhouse flowering plants, houseplants, bedding plants, and the bulbous kinds of plants. The final two chapters in this unit cover the fundamentals of growing lawns and the basic principles of home and community landscaping.

Unit III, in nine chapters, gives encyclopedic coverage of the world's important food, forage, and fiber crops. Included are cereal and sugar crops; oil, forage, and fiber crops; vegetables grown for their fruits or seeds; vegetables grown for their leafy parts; and vegetables grown for their underground parts. Fruit crops are discussed in three categories: temperate zone, subtropical, and tropical plants. The discussion of each crop includes information on the origin of the species, cultural and environmental requirements, cultivars, harvesting and storage, and common pest and disease problems. Unit III is a valuable reference; together with the literature citations for each crop, it enables the reader to study in depth any of the crops covered in the unit.

To aid in the use of this book as a text, the chapters in Unit I include chapter summaries and review questions to emphasize important points. In addition, the book contains an extensive glossary as well as an English-metric conversion chart. In view of the nearly universal adoption of the metric system of measurement, values in this book are given first in metric units, followed by the English system equivalents in parentheses.

The Latin plant names used in this book generally conform to those listed in *Hortus Third* (Macmillan, 1976).

Dr. John Madison of the University of California at Davis, who is a world authority on turfgrasses and lawns and has written many articles and two books on the subject, prepared Chapter 21, Lawns and Turfgrasses. We deeply appreciate his help.

The authors have called upon many scientific workers in the United States and other countries to review chapters and parts of chapters in this book. They gave their time most generously and greatly assisted us in assuring accuracy in the subject matter presented. The responsibility, however, for the final version of the text is the authors'. The following persons reviewed chapters or parts of chapters: C. Alley, D. Allison, O. Bacon, V. Ball, C. A. Beasley, D. Beck, J. Beutel, I. Biran, J. W. Boodley, R. S. Bringhurst, J. C. Carpenter, C. A. Conover, J. C. Crane, B. Degan, A. A. De Hertogh, F. De Vos, D. Durkin, C. Elmore, H. English, M. Farhoomand, H. I. Forde, E. J. Fortanier, W. C. Galinat, G. Galletta, M. Gerdts, E. M. Gifford, W. Griggs, R. L. Haaland, A. H. Halevy, J. H. Harrington, R. W. Harris, C. O. Hesse, P. J. Ito, L. K. Jackson, E. Keep, D. E. Kester, H. C. Kohl, H. B. Lagerstedt, R. W. Langhans, P. Larsen, R. A. Larson, R. A. H. Legro, A. T. Leiser, L. N. Lewis, O. A. Lorenz, G. D. Madden, J. H. Madison, J. W. Mastalerz, S. Mayak, R. Mayer, M. Miller, Y. Mor, Julia Morton, D. B. Murray, H. Y. Nakasone, H. Ooka, K. Opitz, D. K. Ourecky, J. L. Paul, J. Popenoe, A. R. Rees, C. Rick, J. M. Robinson, N. Ross, K. Ryugo, R. M. Sachs, C. A. Schroeder, D. H. Scott, J. G. Seeley, W. Sims, L. A. Spomer, G. L. Staby, C. R. Stocking, W. B. Storey, V. T. Stoutemyer, R. M. Thornton, R. Warner, S. Weinbaum, W. Y. Yee, and N. Zieslin.

UNIT

I

PLANTS: STRUCTURE, CLASSIFICATION, GROWTH, REPRODUCTION, AND UTILIZATION

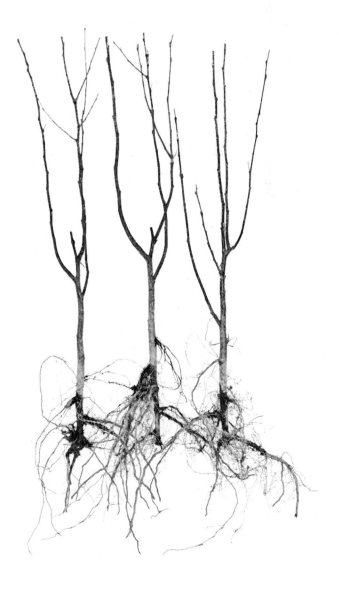

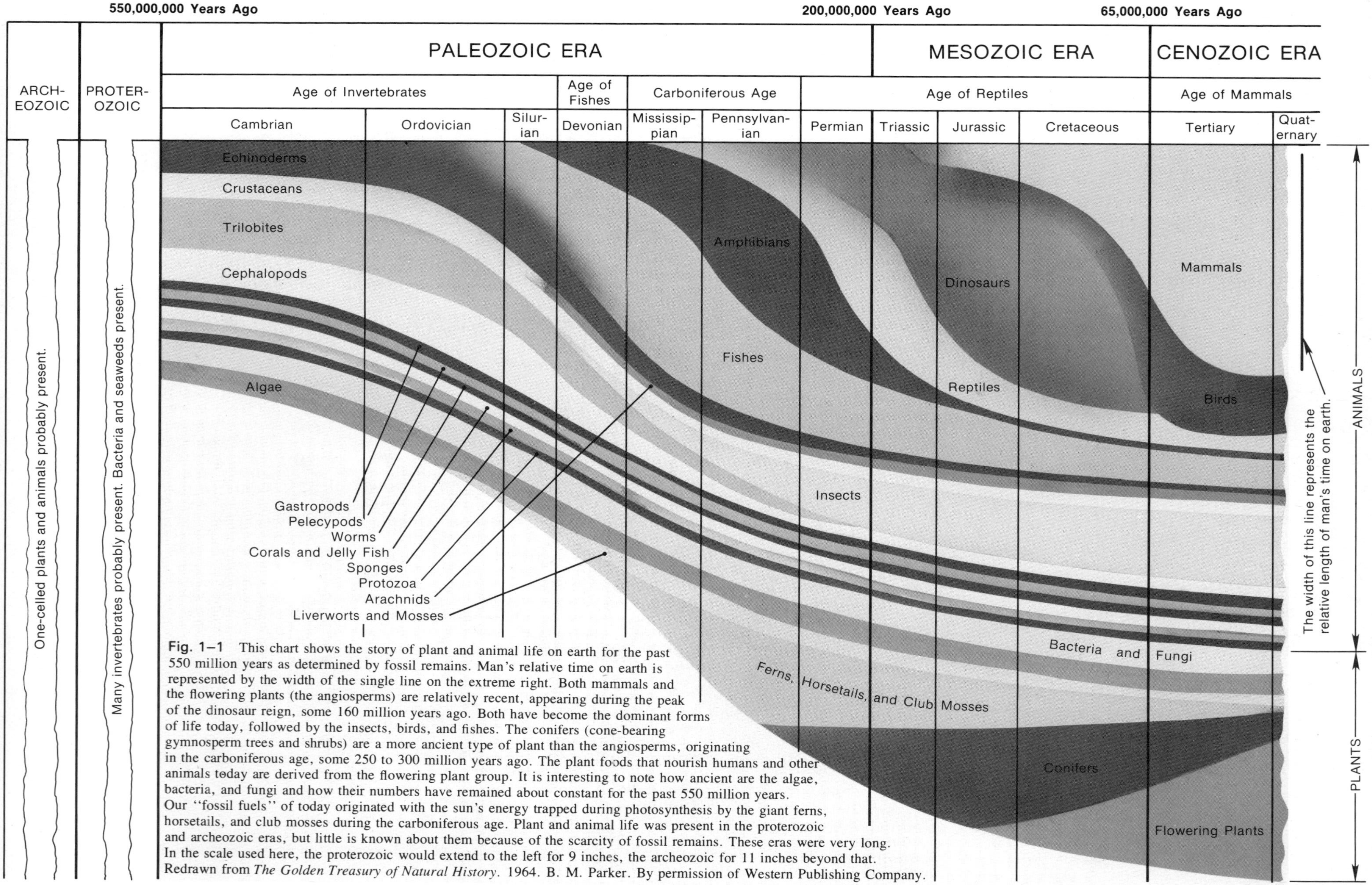

ARCH-EOZOIC | PROTER-OZOIC | PALEOZOIC ERA | MESOZOIC ERA | CENOZOIC ERA

550,000,000 Years Ago   200,000,000 Years Ago   65,000,000 Years Ago

ANIMALS — PLANTS

The width of this line represents the relative length of man's time on earth.

PALEOZOIC ERA

Age of Invertebrates | Age of Fishes | Carboniferous Age

Cambrian | Ordovician | Silurian | Devonian | Mississippian | Pennsylvanian | Permian

MESOZOIC ERA — Age of Reptiles

Triassic | Jurassic | Cretaceous

CENOZOIC ERA — Age of Mammals

Tertiary | Quaternary

Echinoderms
Crustaceans
Trilobites
Cephalopods
Algae
Gastropods
Pelecypods
Worms
Corals and Jelly Fish
Sponges
Protozoa
Arachnids
Liverworts and Mosses
Insects
Fishes
Amphibians
Reptiles
Dinosaurs
Birds
Mammals
Ferns, Horsetails, and Club Mosses
Bacteria and Fungi
Conifers
Flowering Plants

Many invertebrates probably present. Bacteria and seaweeds present.

One-celled plants and animals probably present.

Fig. 1–1 This chart shows the story of plant and animal life on earth for the past 550 million years as determined by fossil remains. Man's relative time on earth is represented by the width of the single line on the extreme right. Both mammals and the flowering plants (the angiosperms) are relatively recent, appearing during the peak of the dinosaur reign, some 160 million years ago. Both have become the dominant forms of life today, followed by the insects, birds, and fishes. The conifers (cone-bearing gymnosperm trees and shrubs) are a more ancient type of plant than the angiosperms, originating in the carboniferous age, some 250 to 300 million years ago. The plant foods that nourish ancient humans and other animals today are derived from the flowering plant group. It is interesting to note how ancient the algae, bacteria, and fungi are and how their numbers have remained about constant for the past 550 million years. Our "fossil fuels" of today originated with the sun's energy trapped during photosynthesis by the giant ferns, horsetails, and club mosses during the carboniferous age. Plant and animal life was present in the proterozoic and archeozoic eras, but little is known about them because of the scarcity of fossil remains. These eras were very long. In the scale used here, the proterozoic would extend to the left for 9 inches, the archeozoic for 11 inches beyond that. Redrawn from *The Golden Treasury of Natural History.* 1964. B. M. Parker. By permission of Western Publishing Company.

The Role of Higher Plants in the Living World

If we could look back some 150 million years to the middle of the geologic period known as the Mesozoic era, the world would not appear entirely strange to us. Among plants, we might recognize some members of the angiosperms,[1] to which belong our present-day grasses, flowers, vegetables, and shrubs and most of our modern trees. In the animal kingdom, by contrast, we would confront those ancient reptiles known as dinosaurs. The careful observer also might note the existence of some small primitive mammals—to which we human beings can trace our own beginnings. Thus both forms of life dominant today originated during the height of the dinosaur reign. It is still a matter of conjecture why the dinosaurs became extinct, but we do know that mammals flourished during the subsequent Cenozoic era, beginning about 65 million years ago. We can trace the evolution of the human race back some two million years to *Australopithecus,* our closest hominid ancestor. *Homo erectus,* the first true human, appeared almost one million years ago, and the modern human species, *Homo sapiens,* came much later, toward the end of the Pleistocene epoch, some 250,000 years ago.

Again looking at the plant kingdom we see the equally impressive evolution of angiosperms over the past 90 million years into those species that humans and other animals live with and depend upon for food, fiber, and shelter. It should be noted, however, that many important timber trees and ornamentals belong to an even more ancient group of plants known as gymnosperms.[2] These cone-bearing trees of our forests, for example, had their beginnings some 300 million years ago, toward the end of the Paleozoic era. Nonetheless, the evolution of human culture and that of the higher plant forms are in general parallel. For example, fossil records show that such plants that we know today as palms, hickories, oaks, beans, breadfruit, magnolias, grapes, and tulip trees were among the angiosperms that flourished some 60 to 70 million years ago. These kinds of plants would have been well established and would have provided sources of food and shelter when the ancient peoples appeared (see Fig. 1–1).

The first food crops for humans were cereals such as wheat and barley, cultivated about 7500 years ago in the eastern Mediterranean region. An agricultural type of existence spread to the European continent some 6000 years ago, replacing a nomadic hunting existence (see Table 4–1). There is evidence that corn was first cultivated in what is now Mexico about 5000 years ago, followed about 1500 years later by potatoes in South America and rice in the Far East. Some of our present-day fruit crops—grapes, figs, olives, dates, pomegranates, and mulberries—were being cultivated in the eastern Mediterranean when history was first being recorded (see Ch. 4).

[1]Derived from the Greek words for "vessel" and "seed."

[2]Derived from the Greek words for "naked" and "seed."

THE DEPENDENCE OF ANIMALS UPON PLANTS FOR THEIR SURVIVAL

It is startling to realize that if animals ceased to exist on earth plants would continue not only to survive but also to thrive very well. However, if plants ceased to exist, all forms of animal life, including human life, would soon disappear. They would simply starve to death. It is true, however, that without humans our highly prized cultivated plants—most of them developed and maintained by our intense interest in them—would disappear within several crop generations. Replacing the beautiful ornamentals, the tasty fruits and vegetables, and the highly productive cereal grains would be wild grasses, thistles, and certain shrubs and trees. They would be able to survive in the natural environment without human aid by their production of seeds and their tolerance of prevailing insects and diseases. The variability that would appear in surviving seedlings would enable some of them to grow in a given, perhaps harsh, environment, while others would perish.

Food Sources from Plants

To understand the importance of plants to the continued existence of animal life on earth, it is necessary to examine the fundamental chemical reaction known as photosynthesis. Photosynthesis takes place in the leaves and other green parts of plants, specifically in the chloroplasts within the green cells. Carbon dioxide absorbed from the air combines with water taken in by the plants' roots from the soil to form organic food materials known appropriately as carbohydrates. An important byproduct of this reaction is the free oxygen the plant releases into the atmosphere. The basic energy source for this process is the visible light rays from the sun. (See Ch. 7 for an in-depth discussion of photosynthesis.)

Once carbohydrates are formed, the plant is able to add nitrogen, absorbed by the roots from the soil, to form proteins and subsequently, by means of further chemical reactions, to produce fats and oils. All these nutrients—carbohydrates, proteins, fats, and oils—are used by plants to sustain their own growth. Scientists refer to living things that produce their own food as *autotrophic*. However, these nutritive materials can also be utilized as food by humans and other animals, which are *heterotropic*—dependent upon plants for their food. Without nutritive materials from plants, such as cereal grains, seeds, fruits, leafy plant parts, and tuberous roots and stems, animals would have no way to sustain life.

Plants are thus essential to humans and other animals because they produce food through the photosynthetic process. Selection of the kinds of plants for the human food supply becomes a history of agricultural development, going back into prehistoric times (see Ch. 4). Obviously the particular kinds of plants selected vary among the agricultural regions of the world. They are the ones best suited to a given set of climatic conditions and are the most efficient in producing food materials (see Ch. 10).

Only a few species of plants feed the world's peoples either directly or indirectly through animals (see Fig. 1–2). These plants, which are all angiosperms, are:

1. Cereal crops—wheat, rice, maize (corn), barley, oats, sorghum, rye, and millet. (Over half the world's food supply comes from the photosynthetic activity of these crops.)
2. Roots and tubers—potatoes, sweet potatoes, and cassavas.
3. Oil crops—soybeans, corn, peanuts, palm, coconuts, sunflower, olive, and safflower.
4. Sugar—sugar cane and sugar beets.
5. Fruit crops—for example, bananas, oranges, apples, pears.
6. Vegetable crops—tomatoes, lettuce, carrots, melons, asparagus, and so forth. (Fruits and vegetables add to the variety and palatability of our daily meals and supply much-needed vitamins and minerals, even though by volume they do not contribute a great deal.)

Table 1–1 shows some of the common crops ranked in relation to the calories and proteins produced per unit of land area. Not all of the total production of food materials becomes available for human consumption. Much is lost during harvesting, transportation, and

Table 1–1 Some Important Food Crops Ranked According to Calorie and Protein Production per Unit of Land Area

Rank	Calories Produced per Unit Area	Protein Produced per Unit Area
1	Sugar Cane	Soybeans
2	Potato	Potato
3	Sugar Beets	Corn
4	Corn	Peanuts
5	Rice	Sorghum
6	Sorghum	Peas
7	Sweet Potato	Beans
8	Barley	Rice
9	Peanuts	Barley
10	Winter Wheat	Winter Wheat

Source: USDA, IR-1 Potato Introduction Station. Sturgeon Bay, Wisconsin.

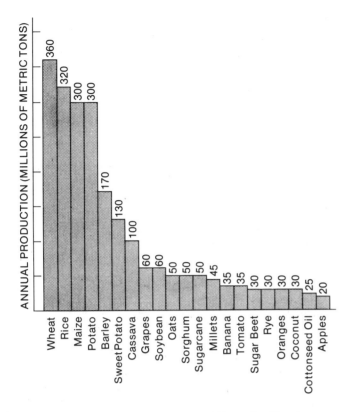

Fig. 1–2　The major crops feeding the world's peoples. Note the predominant positions of wheat, rice, maize (corn), and potato. *Source:* Harlan, J. 1976. The plants and animals that nourish man. *Sci. Amer.* 235(3):89–97.

products—steaks, chops, eggs, processed meats, and dairy products. This shift in food consumption patterns, part and parcel of the modern world's "rising expectations," coupled with the tremendous increase in world population (see Fig. 1–3), is taxing the world's food-

Fig. 1–3　The world's food production can no longer keep pace with the trend in the world's population increase. By 1975 there were an additional 200,000 new mouths to be fed every 24 hours. *Source:* Canby, T. Y. Can the world feed its peoples? *Nat. Geog.* 148(1):2–31. 1975. © National Geographic Society.

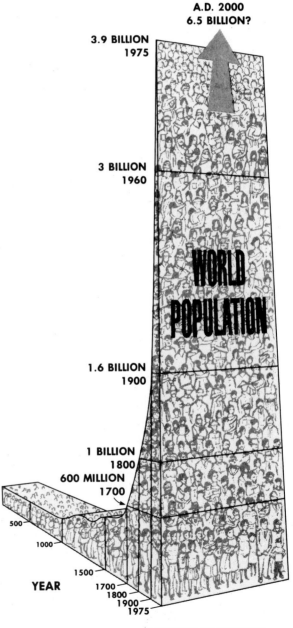

marketing, primarily from attacks by insects, diseases, birds, and rodents (see Ch. 11). Also, some of the production is saved to be used as seed for future plantings. A different kind of energy loss occurs when plants are used to produce human food in the form of animal products. For example, it takes about 10 kilograms (22 pounds) of grain (which could be consumed by humans directly) to produce 1 kilogram (2.2 pounds) of beef. A bushel of corn consumed as whole corn meal would meet the daily energy and protein requirements of 23 people, but when this same bushel is fed to chickens and consumed as eggs, it meets the energy requirements of only two persons and the protein requirements of eight. Nevertheless, meat, milk, and eggs are important in the human diet since they contain proteins of the best quality (balanced quantities of essential amino acids), as well as some of the necessary minerals and vitamins.

Assessing the world's food situation involves another factor besides the utilitarian one of meeting needs, and that is the economic factor. When the people of a country become more affluent, they want and can afford to purchase a greater proportion of their protein requirements in the form of the more palatable animal

producing capacity to its limits. Oceans, polar waste-lands, and deserts cover most of the land surface and are unsuitable for agricultural production. Much of the world's best agricultural land is already under cultivation. There is little remaining land to be developed, and much highly productive fertile land is disappearing under concrete for highways and for suburban housing.

Agricultural research has made new cultivars[3] of high-yielding wheat and rice available to highly populated developing countries; engineers in these countries have constructed new irrigation systems and new fertilizer factories. However, the technological advances in food production since the 1930s have been greatly overshadowed by the soaring increase in world population. Actually the world's food-producing capacity is close to its limits yet a large percentage of the world's population remains undernourished. The World Food Conference in Rome in 1974 estimated that of the world's 4 billion people, over 1 billion got just enough food to stay alive. These underfed populations are mostly in the tropical regions where human fertility rates are high, per capita income is low, and monetary investment in agricultural production sorely lacking. Two or three consecutive years of drought or floods in the major grain-producing countries could result in famine over much of the earth.

Oxygen from Plants

Oxygen (O_2) is released as a byproduct of photosynthesis by both higher and lower forms of green plants. This oxygen is derived from the decomposition of water (H_2O) during carbohydrate manufacture in the plant (see Ch. 7).

All living things require oxygen in order to exist. Oxygen is necessary for the process of respiration, which takes place continuously in the cells of both plants and animals. Respiration may proceed at a very slow rate, but if it stops completely, the cells die. During respiration oxygen combines with sugars or fats in living cells to release carbon dioxide (CO_2), water and energy (see Ch. 7).

The oxygen essential to life is all about us in the earth's atmosphere. At sea level, oxygen makes up about 21 percent of the atmosphere. It originated very early in the history of plant life on earth, coming from certain oxygen-generating plant forms and making possible the beginnings of higher plant and animal life, which depend upon free oxygen for their metabolic processes. It is believed that some 3 billion years ago (scientists speculate that the earth itself originated about 4.5 billion years ago) the first oxygen-producing photosynthetic cells appeared in the oceans, subsequently causing oxygen to appear in

the atmosphere. About 1 billion years ago, with a rapid increase in the oxygen-generating phytoplankton (minute free-floating green plants) in the oceans, the atmospheric oxygen increased from 1 to 2 percent. Finally about 20 million years ago, as the ocean surfaces extended (thus increasing the phytoplankton) and more plants grew on the land, the oxygen content of the atmosphere increased to its present level. Today about 90 percent of the earth's atmospheric oxygen is provided by the phytoplankton in oceans and lakes, and the remainder is supplied by the various land plants.

Some of the oxygen produced by the early plant forms—mainly phytoplankton—upon reaching the stratosphere high above the earth was converted by photochemical action to ozone (O_3). It formed a layer that screened out damaging high-energy ultraviolet radiation from the sun. The reduction in such damaging radiation permitted a more rapid build-up of phytoplankton (and hence oxygen) in the upper, sunlit parts of the oceans and lakes. Today this ozone layer in the upper atmosphere provides life on earth with a protective screen against lethal doses of ultraviolet radiation from the sun, about as it did 500 million years ago.

FOSSIL FUELS FROM PLANTS

During the Carboniferous period about 300 million years ago, photosynthesis in plants trapped energy from the sun in the form of carbon compounds. This was the beginning of the so-called **fossil fuels** (coal, oil, and gas), concentrated energy sources that have played such a dramatic role in recent years in increasing the comforts and living standards of modern populations. The plants from which these fuels originated were huge tropical seed ferns and giant nonflowering trees growing in warm and humid climates that favored rapid growth. The low, swampy forests were successively covered with water, then buried by minor changes in the levels of the seas. These strata of buried organic remains were compressed through geologic action and also underwent chemical changes to form the concentrated petroleum and coal fuels so much in demand today.

PLANT PARTICIPATION WITH ANIMALS IN FOOD CHAINS

Green plants are "primary producers," in that they constitute the base of all food chains in the various communities of plants and animals that form distinct ecosystems. Food chains occur on land and in the oceans, lakes, and rivers. A given ecosystem basically comprises

---

[3]Cultivar = **culti**vated **var**iety (see p. 47, Ch. 3).

three levels: (1) green plants as primary food-manufacturing organisms; (2) plant-consuming, or herbivorous, organisms; and (3) flesh-consuming, or carnivorous, organisms.

Food chains transfer energy. The energy available to support life is found in green plants, the primary producers. At each level or link in a food chain there is some loss of energy, however. An example of an aquatic food chain going through several levels is

algae (a green plant) $\longrightarrow$ crustacean $\longrightarrow$ insect $\longrightarrow$
minnow $\longrightarrow$ trout $\longrightarrow$ otter

A simple land-based food chain is

grass $\longrightarrow$ cattle $\longrightarrow$ man

In all such food chains, plants play the essential role as the initial energy producer. Without plants the other organisms in the chain would disappear.

THE ROLE OF PLANTS IN PREVENTING SOIL EROSION

Imagine for a moment torrential rains falling on a landscape of rolling hills completely denuded of plants. It is easy to visualize the increasing worthlessness of such a landscape as it slowly erodes into the rivers, lakes, and oceans. The fertile topsoil disappears, uncovering a rocky base of little value to humans or animals. However, plants help prevent such erosion because their roots act as webs to hold the soil in place. In addition, their leaves and branches slow the force of the falling water, permitting it to trickle down and become stored in the depths of the soil, gravel, and rocks rather than running in torrents over the surface. Also, as the grasses, shrubs, and trees age and die, their decomposing roots, stems, and leaves add to the soil's mass, forming a humus material that constitutes a favorable environment for the germination of seeds and growth of seedlings. For eons the presence of plants on the earth's surface has protected the fragile topsoil layer, which is the natural habitat for the roots of both naturally occurring and cultivated plants, from the wearing effects of rain and whipping winds. (For a more detailed discussion of plants and soil conservation, see Ch. 9.)

OTHER BENEFITS RECEIVED FROM PLANTS

In addition to providing food and fuel, replenishing the earth's supply of oxygen, and helping prevent soil erosion, plants contribute in numerous ways—some highly visible, others often unnoticed—to the well-being of higher forms of life.

Wood and Wood Products from Timber Trees

The world's forests have provided wood for human shelter since the dawn of civilization. For centuries wood has also served as a source of fuel for warmth and for cooking. Fortunate indeed are those countries endowed by nature with luxuriant stands of tall timber trees. Unlike coal, gas, and oil, wood is a renewable natural resource. With proper management, forests can be enlarged and made more productive by proper tree selection and care. It is essential that the importance of wood for a nation's future be realized and that forests not be exploited for the immediate profits of the day. Protection of its forests from the ravages of fire is a nation's prime responsibility.

Lumber comes from only a few species of trees. These have been classified somewhat roughly into the "softwoods" and the "hardwoods." The softwoods are by far the more important type of lumber trees. The leading softwood species are all conifers (cone-bearing). In the United States the following softwoods account for about 75 percent of the total timber harvest:

Douglas fir
western hemlock
ponderosa pine
spruces
redwood
true firs (*Abies* spp.)
yellow pines (longleaf,
  slash, loblolly)

The remaining 25 percent of U.S timber production is accounted for by the following hardwoods:

oaks (red and white)
maples
hickory
sweet gum

Wood, of course, is used for purposes other than building homes and other structures. For example, in the United States about 3 billion cubic feet of wood per year is used in the manufacture of paper. Even though a great many kinds of synthetic materials are now available, modern industry still creates a wide variety of objects from wood, from furniture to fine violins. Virtually all cultures have become expert in making the most intricate and beautiful objects from wood.

Textiles from Fiber-Producing Crops

Although thread, and ultimately cloth, can be made from almost any plant fiber, cotton (*Gossypium* spp.) is by far the most important plant from which clothing, bedding, and many other cloth products are manufactured. The use of spun yarn made from the mass of fibers attached to the seed of the cotton plant has been traced back to about 3000 B.C. in the Indus Valley of what is now Pakistan. (See Ch. 25 for a discussion of cotton production.)

The flax plant *(Linum usitatissimum),* next in importance among plants traditionally used to make cloth, produces fibers in the bark of its stem that are used to make linen cloth. Actually flax was used more frequently than cotton in cloth making until the late eighteenth century, when new spinning and weaving inventions gave great impetus to the cotton industry.

Hemp *(Cannabis sativa)* is also an ancient crop used widely in earlier days for making rope of high tensile strength from the fibers in the bark of its stem. Also the source of marijuana, *Cannabis* culture has now been relegated to a highly controlled or illegal status in many countries.

Other plants having stem fibers sufficiently long and strong to justify commercial use are ramie *(Boehmeria nivea)* and jute *(Corchorus capsularis).* The latter is used largely in making burlap.

The synthetic fibers, such as nylon, acrylics, and polyesters, made by chemical polymerization, have continually gained in popularity until, by 1969, the combined production of synthetics exceeded that of natural fibers.

Drugs and Medicines

Before the era of modern drugs, many of them now synthetically produced, extracts of large numbers of plants were known to elicit certain reactions from the human body when applied in the prescribed manner. Among the plants that have been used for medicinal purposes are the following:

Chinchona spp. Quinine is extracted from the bark of these plants and is well known for its antimalarial properties. Millions of people have benefited from this plant, particularly in regions where malaria-transmitting mosquitoes flourish.

Papaver somniferum. The opium poppy has been grown since ancient times. The extracts from its fruits are known to have been used in early Egyptian civilization. While the alkaloids morphine, codeine, and heroin, all derived from the opium poppy, have brought relief to millions of persons suffering from pain, opium has also trapped other millions into a strong addiction and has caused untold social problems.

Erythroxylum coca. The leaves of this small tree or shrub produce an anesthetic drug, cocaine, that has been widely used as a local pain killer. Like opium cocaine has habit-forming properties, and its overuse has resulted in problems for those addicted to it.

Digitalis purpurea. The common foxglove plant produces from its dried leaves several substances that are widely used today in treating certain heart conditions.

Nicotiana tabacum. The tobacco plant has been in commerce since the arrival of Columbus and other early explorers on the North and South American continents. There they found the natives using tobacco in much the same manner as it is used today—drying and curing the leaves, which are then processed for smoking, chewing, or snuffing. Nicotine and related alkaloids from the tobacco leaf provide stimulant, habit-forming effects that have given tobacco worldwide popularity. Medical studies have accumulated overwhelming evidence that habitual tobacco usage is associated with increased death rates, primarily from lung cancer, coronary artery disease, chronic bronchitis, and emphysema.

Colchicum autumnale. The autumn crocus produces an alkaloid—colchicine—in its dried corms and seeds that is used medicinally to lessen the frequency and severity of attacks of gout, an extremely painful disease of the joints caused by excessive levels of uric acid in the body. This is one of the oldest diseases described in medical literature, and colchicine is one of the oldest therapeutics.

Rauwolfia serpentina. This small shrub, grown mostly in India, produces in its roots the drug reserpine, frequently prescribed today in the treatment of high blood pressure.

This listing is, of course, merely illustrative of the drugs derived from plants. Throughout history humans have experimented with native plants by tasting, rubbing, chewing, and swallowing their parts or their extracts. Undoubtedly, some highly poisonous plants such as the poison hemlock (infamous as the method of Socrates' execution), the castor bean, and fruits of the yew eliminated the experimenters. On the other hand, extracts of *Coffea arabica* (coffee) and *Camellia sinensis* (tea) provide caffeine, a mild stimulant. Drinks prepared from these extracts have been used and enjoyed daily for many years by millions of people.

Latex, Pitch, Waxes, Essential Oils, Perfumes, and Spices

The vegetative parts of living plants can be thought of as chemical factories, using as their raw materials water and mineral elements taken in by the roots, carbon dioxide absorbed by the leaves, plus energy from the sun. From these materials many products are produced, some in copious amounts, that can be extracted or drained off to provide us with some extremely useful materials. Some important examples are:

LATEX FROM THE RUBBER TREE

It is said that Columbus, in his voyages to the New World during the fifteenth century, saw the native people throwing about resilient balls that had been made from the extract of a tree. Later, during the explorations of the sixteenth, seventeenth, and eighteenth centuries, this gummy material produced from an exudate of a native tropical South American tree *(Hevea brasiliensis)* was brought back to Europe and became familiar to Europeans. Not much was done with the latex material until about the middle of the nineteenth century, when it was discovered that by heating it and adding sulfur, many useful products—including the pneumatic tire—could be fashioned from it. Rubber soon became one of the indispensable products of modern civilization. In the early 1900s huge rubber plantations were developed, largely through the efforts of the British and Dutch in Ceylon (now Sri Lanka), Dutch East Indies (now Indonesia), and Malaya, also in Central America and the West Indies. Still later, American companies developed rubber plantations in West Africa.

The inner bark of the rubber tree produces in latex vessels a material containing about 30 percent rubber, the rest mostly water. Cutting through these latex vessels to the right depth—not deep enough to injure the growing layer (the cambium)—and then attaching a container to the tree allows the latex to flow and be caught for processing. This latex base, from which many rubber products have been made, has been of inestimable value to civilization.

Before World War II most applications that called for a resilient material used natural rubber. During the war, however, the Allies lost access to most of the world's rubber-producing regions. This stimulated the consuming countries to manufacture synthetic rubber, mainly from petroleum and coal, in great quantities. By the mid-1960s the synthetic product had largely replaced natural rubber.

PITCH, TURPENTINE, AND RESIN

From the resin canals in the trunks of various cone-bearing trees, such as longleaf pine *(Pinus palustris)* and slash pine *(Pinus elliottii)*, comes an exudate known in the crude state as "pitch," obtained by tapping or chipping into the tree's trunk. Pitch was used in earlier days to caulk wooden ships. Distillation separates pitch into resin (often called rosin) and turpentine, both of which are widely used in the manufacture of varnishes. In colonial times in the United States, both materials were an important source of income for the residents of the Carolinas and later for those of Florida and Georgia.

ESSENTIAL OILS, PERFUMES, AND SPICES

The practice of obtaining plant extracts with a pleasing odor—to improve the taste of foods, to aid in food preservation, and to adorn the body—dates to antiquity. When the pharaohs were ruling ancient Egypt, perfumes were commonly used. Cleopatra undoubtedly used perfumes to help charm Marc Antony and Julius Caesar. In the early days of colonial expansion by the English, Spanish, Dutch, and Portuguese, empires rose and fell on the search for spices and perfumes produced by plants in faraway countries. These extracts were highly prized symbols of wealth and prosperity among the ruling classes, and no effort or outlay of money was spared to obtain them.

Perfume-producing materials much in demand included rose oil from the flowers of *Rosa damascena* in the Balkans, Asia Minor, and India; jasmine from the flowers of *Jasminum grandiflorum* in southern France and India; geranium oil from the foliage of the *Pelargonium* species; citronella from the leaves of *Cymbopogon nardus* in Java; and patchouli oil from *Pogostemon cablin* in southeast Asia and the Philippines.

Valued spices were black pepper from the dried fruits of *Piper nigrum* in China and India; vanilla from the pods of the climbing orchid, *Vanilla planifolia*, in Aztec Mexico and the islands off the southeast coast of Africa; cloves from the dried flower buds of *Caryophyllus aromaticus* in the East Indies; nutmeg from the seeds of *Myristica frangrans* grown in the West Indies, Sri Lanka, and Indonesia; and cinnamon from the dried inner bark of *Cinnamomum zeylanicum* found in Sri Lanka and the Malabar coast of India.

Plants for Aesthetic Purposes

Modern civilization, with its needs for food, shelter, and clothing satisfied and with ever-increasing leisure time, takes great satisfaction in the aesthetic value of plants. Many people greatly enjoy tending and watching their houseplants, working with the flowers and vegetables in their gardens, and observing the year-by-year increase in the size of their shrubs and fruit trees. The therapeutic value of working among plants surrounded by a restful garden and peaceful green lawns has no doubt permitted many a person to survive the rigors of today's hectic, high-speed urban existence. Plants in their natural habitat—the forest trees, the native shrubs, and the wildflowers—preserved for public enjoyment in innumerable county, state, and national parks and forests, provide great pleasure and relaxation.

BENEFITS FROM LOWER FORMS OF PLANT LIFE

So far we have reviewed the contributions of higher plant forms to human well-being. However, we must not fail to recognize that nongreen plants—bacteria and many fungi—are very much involved in the living processes of our world. Although certain pathogenic (disease-producing) bacteria and fungi have often threatened human existence, many species of lower plants are extremely beneficial.

If we start listing the activities of beneficial bacteria and fungi, the list soon seems neverending. A few examples prove illustrative.

REMOVAL OF DEAD PLANT AND ANIMAL MATTER   Since both bacteria and fungi obtain their energy from the breakdown of animal or plant tissue, living or dead, their decomposition activities save us from being surrounded by great heaps of dead plants and animals. Furthermore, their actions make the products of decomposition available once again as nutrient materials for living plants and aquatic animals.

NITROGEN FIXATION FROM THE ATMOSPHERE   Nitrogen is an essential component of the proteins in living plant and animal tissues. Although the earth's atmosphere consists of approximately 79 percent nitrogen, as such the gas cannot be used by most living things. Nitrogen enters into the food chains primarily through the absorption of nitrates or similar forms by the roots of plants. The almost inexhaustible supply of atmospheric nitrogen cannot be used by the higher plants until it is first converted to a "fixed" form, as nitrates. Certain microorganisms, such as some blue-green algae and some free-living bacteria are "nitrogen fixers." Other nitrogen-fixing bacteria live symbiotically with certain higher plants—in the root nodules of legumes such as

clover, alfalfa, soybeans, and in some trees such as the gingko and alder. There are also industrial processes for nitrogen fixation. Development of these began around 1914, and by 1950 nitrogen fertilizers produced commercially far exceeded the amount that could have been obtained in the natural fixation processes. However, the commercial nitrogen fixing processes consume huge quantities of energy, which may lead to a limit in their usage in the future.

FOOD PRESERVATION THROUGH FERMENTATION PROCESSES   Before the widespread use of mechanical refrigeration in food preservation (and even today) cooks and food preparation experts relied on bacterial action as a natural preservative. For example, shredded cabbage, to which has been added the proper microorganisms, can be preserved through fermentation, a process that increases the acid level and prevents spoilage. The cabbage is then known as sauerkraut. Surplus milk can be stored in the form of cheese after the milk has been treated in the proper manner with certain fungi and bacteria (members of the plant kingdom). Fermentation activities of yeasts, a lower plant form, can transform apple juice into hard cider or grape juice into wine by producing a weak alcohol solution from the sugars in the juices. (See p. 597 for a discussion of how wines are made through fermentation.)

ANTIBIOTICS   An outstanding example of a useful product derived from a lower plant is penicillin, a substance that has strong antibacterial action. The discovery in 1929 of the antibiotic properties of the fungus *Penicillium notatum* marks a major milestone in medical history.

These few examples make it obvious that the lower plant forms—the algae, bacteria, yeasts, and fungi—are intimately involved in a great many of the important life processes.

SUMMARY

The presence of plants on earth is essential for the survival of animal life as we know it today. Plants provide us with food to eat and replenish our supply of oxygen to breathe, and the remains of plants that lived eons ago make possible the operation of automobiles, trucks, and industrial equipment from fossil fuels. Plants are the sole energy source for entire ecosystems that bind various plant and animal forms together in a given environment. The roots, stems, and leaves of a wide array of plants have prevented our precious topsoil from being lost to wind and rain. Throughout history we have depended heavily on wood and wood products for building houses, making paper, and constructing furniture. The lower forms of plants include many beneficial species whose activities contribute greatly to our well-being and prosperity. Other plants, both small and large, have for thousands of years been the source of useful medicines, spices, oils, and latex materials. Besides these utilitarian benefits people derive great enjoyment just from living among plants, both indoors and outdoors.

REVIEW QUESTIONS

1–1. If animals were to disappear from the earth how would this affect plants? If plants were to disappear from the earth how would this affect animals?

1–2. One group of plants and one group of animals are now dominant over other groups on earth. What are these two groups and how far back can their existence be traced?

1–3. What are the four major food crops feeding the world's peoples?

1–4. Approximately how long ago did an agricultural type of existence begin to replace the nomadic hunting-fishing existence among the ancient civilizations?

1–5. Both plants and animals must have oxygen in order to exist. What is the primary source of free oxygen on earth?

1–6. Explain what is meant by the term *fossil fuels* that are so important in present day living. From what did these fuels originate?

1–7. What is meant by the term *food chain?* Give an example of a food chain from its starting point to the last link in its energy cycle.

1–8. Explain how plants can combat soil erosion particularly in hilly areas.

1–9. Give three examples of how the activities of lower plant forms are beneficial to mankind.

1–10. Cite three examples of medicines derived from plants that have proved beneficial to human well-being.

1–11. Which are considered to be the most ancient type of plants, the gymnosperms or the angiosperms? What is the evidence for determining the answer to this question?

1–12. What are by far the most ancient kinds of plant life?

1–13. In terms of the greatest amount of both calories and proteins produced per unit area, which crop ranks the highest?

1–14. Name four kinds of plants important in the production of cloth and fibers.

SUPPLEMENTARY READING

BIANCHINI, F., and F. CORBETTA. 1977. *Health plants of the world (Atlas of medicinal plants)*. New York: Newsweek Books.

The biosphere. 1970. San Francisco: W. H. Freeman & Company Publishers.

BRANDON, S. G. F., ed. 1970. *Ancient empires*. New York: Newsweek Books.

BROUK, B. 1975. *Plants consumed by man*. New York: Academic Press, Inc.

CALDWELL, M. M. 1979. Plant life and ultraviolet radiation: some perspective in the history of the earth's UV climate. *Bioscience* 29(9):520–25.

CANBY, T. Y. 1975. Can the world feed its people? *Nat. Geog.* 148(1):2–31.

CHRISPEELS, M. J., and D. SADAVA. 1977. *Plants, food, and people*. San Francisco: W. H. Freeman & Company, Publishers.

DASMANN, R. F. 1976. People: from ecosystem to biosphere. In *Environmental conservation*. 4th ed. New York: John Wiley.

DEATHERAGE, F. E. 1975. *Food for life*. New York: Plenum.

EBELING, W. 1979. *The fruited plain: the story of American agriculture*. Berkeley: University of California Press.

EVANS, L. T., ed. 1975. *Crop physiology*. London: Cambridge University Press.

FAO. 1977. *The fourth world food survey*. Rome: Food and Agriculture Organization of the United Nations.

HARLAN, J. R. *Crops and man*. 1975. Madison, Wis.: American Society of Agronomy, Crop Science Society of America.

———. 1976. The plants and animals that nourish man. *Sci. Amer.* 235(3):88–97.

HEISER, C. B., JR. 1973. *Seed to civilization*. San Francisco: W. H. Freeman & Company Publishers.

HOWELL, F. C. 1965. *Early man*. New York: Time-Life Books.

LAPEDES, D. N. 1977. *McGraw-Hill encyclopedia of food, agriculture and nutrition*. New York: McGraw-Hill.

LEWIS, W. H., and M. P. F. ELVIN-LEWIS. 1977. *Medical botany: plants affecting man's health*. Somerset, N.J.: John Wiley.

PARRY, J. W. 1969. *Spices,* vol. 1. New York: Chemical Publishing Company.

PULLAR, E. 1979. A history of old herbals. *American Horticulturist* 58(5):28–33.

REED, C. A., ed. 1977. *Origins of agriculture.* Chicago: Aldine-Atherton.

REGAL, P. J. 1977. Ecology and evolution of flowering plant dominance. *Science* 196 (4290):622–29.

SAUER, C. O. 1969. *Agricultural origins and dispersals.* 2nd ed. Cambridge: Massachusetts Institute of Technology Press.

SUMNER, J. 1979. Ancient angiosperms. *Horticulture* 57(9):36–42.

WORTMAN, S., and R. W. CUMMINGS, JR. 1978. *To feed this world.* Baltimore: The Johns Hopkins University Press.

Structure of Higher Plants

The world abounds with plants that enrich our lives. Some plants and their parts can be identified and appreciated from their external structure, but their internal structure and functions are often overlooked. For example, the beauty of an orchid blossom is greatly admired, but just as impressive are the parts of a cell as seen through a microscope and the intricacies of cell division after such processes are understood. The purpose of this chapter is to develop an understanding of the internal and external structures of the higher plants.

An approach that will capitalize on what is already known is to follow a plant from seed germination to full size and then to observe the formation of fruits and seeds. We can then appreciate how the plant grows and develops and, at the same time, acquire the vocabulary necessary to understand the growth processes of plants. This approach will allow us to study both the external form of the plant, or its **morphology,** and its internal structure, or **anatomy.**

Our major food, fiber, wood, and ornamental plants belong to two main classes—the **gymnosperms,** represented mainly by the narrow-leaved, evergreen trees; and the **angiosperms,** usually broad-leaved, flowering plants. The angiosperms are by far the most common in everyday life. Angiosperms are divided into two subclasses: the **monocotyledons,** which have an embryo with one cotyledon, and the **dicotyledons,** which have an embryo with two cotyledons. These names are often shortened to **monocot** and **dicot.** We begin by examining the life cycle of a common monocot, corn (Fig. 2–1), and a common dicot, the bean (Fig. 2–4).

Fig. 2–1 Structure of the seed and seedling of corn (*Zea mays*), a monocotyledonous plant.

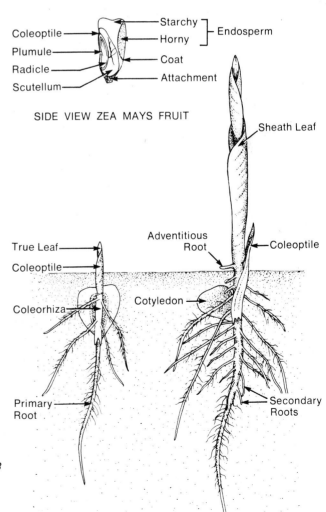

THE LIFE CYCLE OF A CORN PLANT

When a corn seed is planted in moist soil, it imbibes (absorbs) water from the soil. Germination begins with the emergence of the **radicle** (the primary root) and the **plumule** (the primary shoot). These two enlarging axes constitute the primary body of the plant.

The radicle grows downward through a protective sheath, the **coleorhiza,** from which the primary root develops and the secondary roots branch. A mature corn plant can develop roots 2 m (6.1 ft) deep. **Adventitious roots** (roots other than those that develop from the radicle) grow from the shoot axis just at or above the soil surface (Fig. 2–2): These roots, also called anchor, brace, or prop roots, branch out in the soil to give added support to the plant.

The emerging plumule is protected by a sheathlike leaf, the **coleoptile,** that envelops the main stem. As the true foliage leaves develop, the main stem continues to produce sheathing leaves that encircle the stems at each node. The growth of the stem is complex and will be discussed in detail in Chapter 6.

When the corn plant has reached a given size and produced a set number of leaves, female flowers, known as **pistillate flowers** or ears, appear at the base (axil) of one or more clasping leaves. Later the male flowers, known as **staminate flowers** or tassels, develop at the top of the plant. Figure 2–3 shows both kinds of flowers. Blown by the wind, pollen grains from the tassels fall

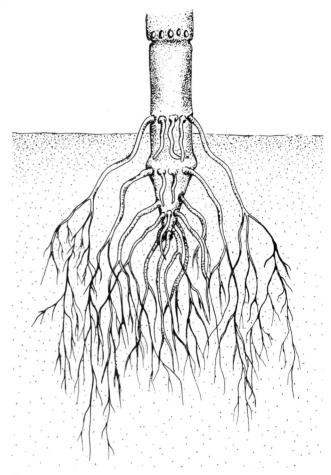

Fig. 2–2   Adventitious or anchor roots developing above the soil from the lower stem of a corn plant.

Fig. 2–3   *Left:* A pollen-bearing corn tassel (staminate flower). *Right:* The ear (pistillate flower), which produces the corn grain.

upon and pollinate the long pistillate filaments (silks) and subsequently fertilize the ovaries, which become the individual corn kernels borne on a stalk (cob) (see Fig. 5–1). Each ovary develops into a fruit, called a **caryopsis,** that encloses the true seed. After the kernels mature and dry, the seeds are harvested and stored over the winter. They can be sown when weather conditions are favorable for germination, and the life cycle repeats itself.

THE LIFE CYCLE OF A BEAN PLANT

After a bean seed has been sown in moist soil, it imbibes water and swells. The seed coat bursts and the radicle emerges (Fig. 2–4). The radicle grows downward and

the hook of the bean, known as the **hypocotyl,** emerges above the soil, carrying the two cotyledons with it. Between the cotyledons lies a growing point (**apical** or **shoot meristem**) flanked by two opposite primary foliage leaves. The stem region just above the cotyledons is called the **epicotyl** (Fig. 2–4). Under favorable conditions the shoot apical meristem rapidly produces two trifoliate leaves on opposite sides of the stem. Also the cotyledons, which have been supplying much of the reserve food for this initial growth, shrivel and drop off. The plant's green leaves are now capable of manufacturing food for future growth of the seedling. All the leaves the bean plant produces are trifoliate, and flowers begin to develop in the axils of about the fourth set of leaves and in each succeeding set. These flowers can pollinate themselves; thus fruits (pods) develop as long as environmental conditions are favorable. The seeds mature

Fig. 2–4   Structure of the seed and seedling—in several growth stages—of the bean (*Phaseolus vulgaris*), a dicotyledonous plant.

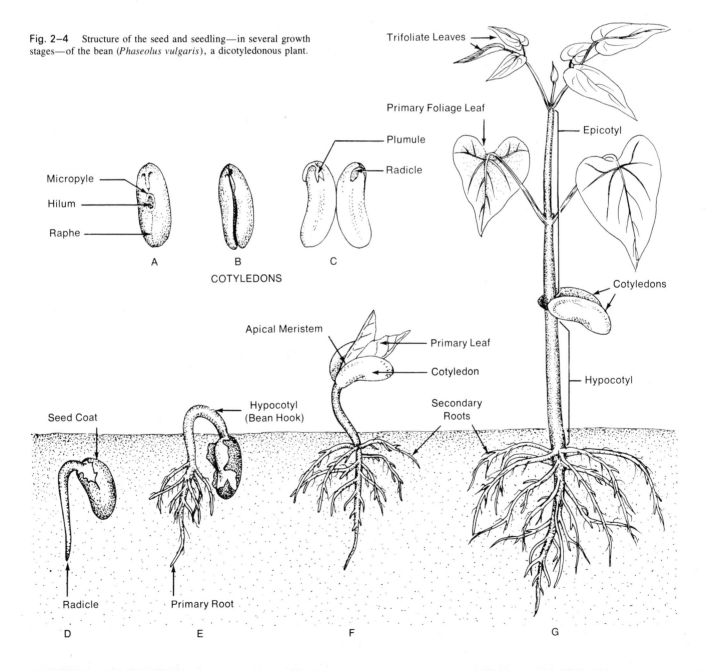

and dry within the pod, and they can be sown to produce another generation of bean plants.

The life cycles of plants like the corn and bean are more or less familiar to most us from our own observations, but to enlarge our knowledge about plants, we must consider the largely unfamiliar areas of plant anatomy and morphology.

THE CELL

The **plant cell** is the basic unit of the plant, the smallest structural and physiological element capable of dividing and replicating itself. The tissues of the plant develop through an orderly process of cell division and differentiation. **Cytology** is the branch of biology that studies the components of cells and their functions. Past cytological studies were conducted with light microscopes, which cannot visualize all the many details of the cell structure. Recently electron microscopes have revealed more information about the organelles within the protoplasm.

Cells vary greatly in size. The smallest must be measured in micrometers (1/1000 of a millimeter) but some fiber cells are several centimeters long. The name

cell comes from Robert Hooke's discovery in 1665 of small "compartments" in the bark of the cork oak. He called these cells, because they reminded him of the small plain sleeping rooms used by monks in a monastery. Hooke calculated that there were about 1259 million cells in 16.4 cm³ (1 in³) of bark.

CELL STRUCTURE

There are two types of cells. **Prokaryotic cells** have no separate cell units; that is, the nucleus is not enclosed in a membrane. These cells, considered primitive, are found in bacteria and blue-green algae. **Eukaryotic cells** have compartmentalized discrete parts, bounded by membranes, with definite structures and functions. These parts, called **organelles,** are the nucleus, mitochondria, the endoplasmic reticulum, dictyosomes, plastids, and microbodies (Fig. 2–5). Eukaryotic cells are characteristic of all plants except bacteria and blue-green algae, so the following discussion pertains only to this type of cell.

The plant cell is basically composed of a **cell wall,** the **protoplast,** and various **inclusions,** which are such nonliving portions as the **vacuoles.**

Fig. 2–5   Photomicrograph of a plant cell showing the various parts and organelles. × 6000

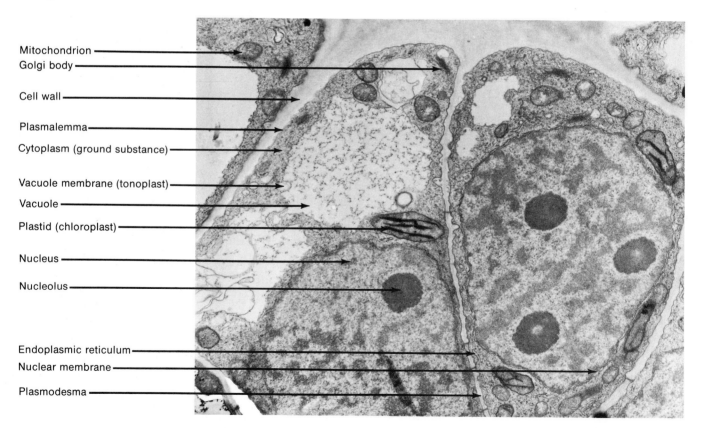

- Mitochondrion
- Golgi body
- Cell wall
- Plasmalemma
- Cytoplasm (ground substance)
- Vacuole membrane (tonoplast)
- Vacuole
- Plastid (chloroplast)
- Nucleus
- Nucleolus
- Endoplasmic reticulum
- Nuclear membrane
- Plasmodesma

The Protoplast

The **protoplast,** the organized living unit of the cell, is a complex material composed of membranes, particles, and various organelles, each of which has a given function in the nutrition, growth, and reproduction of the cell. The protoplasm is divided into the **cytoplasm** and the smaller **nucleus.**

CYTOPLASM

The cytoplasm is the part of the protoplast outside the nucleus. It is a viscous fluid surrounded by a semipermeable membrane called the **plasmalemma** (or the **plasma membrane**) and is located adjacent to the cell wall. Cytoplasmic movement in active leaf cells is clearly visible under a light microscope. The cytoplasm contains a complex network of membranes connected to the plasmalemma by the **endoplasmic reticulum** (ER). Some ERs have **ribosomes** on their surfaces; ribosomes are involved in protein synthesis. The endoplasmic reticula are associated with the plasmodesmata, which are cytoplasmic connections from cell to cell through cell walls.

Plastids of several types are located within the cytoplasm. The colorless **leucoplasts** serve as storage bodies for oil, starch, and proteins. **Chromoplasts** may or may not contain chlorophyll. Those without chlorophyll may contain oils or, in the case of carrot roots, carotenoid substances. Chromoplasts with chlorophyll are called **chloroplasts** and are responsible for photosynthesis in leaves and in some stems. Most chloroplasts also contain other pigments and large quantities of proteins and lipids. Enclosed by a double membrane, the chloroplasts contain cylindrical grana (green granules with parallel lamellae) stacked like plates.

Mitochondria are colorless, rod-shaped or bowl-like bodies that are smaller than plastids. Like the chloroplasts and the nucleus they are surrounded by a double membrane. The mitochondria are sites of respiration and are also involved in protein synthesis. They produce energy-rich compounds such as adenosine triphosphate (ATP) (see Ch. 7). Mitochondria are more numerous in young cells than in older ones.

THE NUCLEUS

The **nucleus** in stained microscopic sections shows as a dense, dark spherical body enclosed by a double membrane known as the **nuclear envelope** and containing one or more **nucleoli.** Within the nucleus are the chromosomes, so named because they are easily stained with dyes. These rod-shaped bodies are responsible for both genetic control and regulation of the reproductive process within the cells. The genetic information passed on to the dividing cells during mitotic division (see Ch. 4) is carried by the compound deoxyribose nucleic acid (DNA). This genetic information controls protein synthesis on the ribosomes outside the nucleus. Endoplasmic reticulum connects the nucleus to other cell parts. DNA is also found outside the nucleus in the mitochondria and in the chloroplasts, thereby giving these bodies a heredity role independent of the nucleus.

VACUOLES

Vacuoles are cavities filled with cell sap contained within a membrane called a tonoplast. In actively dividing cells, vacuoles are very small, but they can account for up to 90 percent of the volume of mature cells. Vacuoles contain dissolved materials, blue or red pigments (anthocyanins), sugars, organic acids, and various inclusions of crystals and inorganic salts. Vacuoles provide water storage space within the cells.

The Cell Wall

The **cell wall** protects the protoplasm and in some specialized cells may act as support-forming tissue. The cell wall is nonliving, made up of cellulose, pectic substances, and lignins. Between cells lies an intercellular layer called the **middle lamella,** which contains many of the mucilaginous pectic compounds that hold adjacent cell walls together. Adjacent to the middle lamella is the **primary wall,** which is composed mostly of cellulose. This elastic but strong material is the chief constituent of most plant cell walls. The **secondary wall** layer, which lies within the primary wall and is formed by the cytoplasm only after the primary wall is complete, is usually thicker than the primary wall when fully developed. The secondary wall is also composed of cellulose, but in addition it may contain lignins, suberins, or cutins. Lignins are closely associated with the cellulose and give it added strength, as well demonstrated by wood fibers. Because cell walls are stable in water they are responsible for the transfer and containment of large quantities of water. Most cell walls contain thin areas called **pits.** Strands of protoplasm known as **plasmodesmata** extend through the pits and connect cells, allowing the transfer of material between them. Water and dissolved materials also move from cell to cell through the pits by diffusion.

PLANT TISSUES

Large tracts of organized cells of similar structure that perform a collective function are referred to as **tissues.** Tissues of various types combine to form complex plant organs such as leaves, flowers, fruits, stems, and roots.

In all plants, both young and mature, two basic kinds of tissues can be distinguished. One kind is the **meristem,** or **meristematic tissue.** These comprise actively dividing cells that develop and differentiate into yet other tissues and organs. Cells in the meristematic tissues have thin walls and dense protoplasts. Meristematic tissues are found in the root and shoot tips, just above the nodes (**intercalary meristems**) and, in woody perennials, as cylinders in the shoots and roots (the **cambium layer**).

The second kind of tissue is those that develop from the meristems and have differentiated fully. These are the **permanent tissues** of which there are two kinds: the **simple,** which includes the epidermis, parenchyma, schlerenchyma, and collenchyma; and the **complex,** which includes the xylem and phloem.

Meristematic Tissues

The common categories of meristematic tissues are:

Apical meristems
 Shoot
 Root
Subapical meristems
Intercalary meristems
Lateral meristems
 Vascular cambium
 Cork cambium

APICAL MERISTEMS

Shoot meristems, frequently referred to as shoot apical meristems, are the termini of the above-ground portions of the plant (see Fig. 2–6). They are responsible for producing new buds and leaves in a uniform pattern at the terminus of the stem and laterally along stems. The pattern of leaves and lateral buds that form from the shoot meristems vary with the species of plant. For example, in the maples *(Acer),* ashes *(Fraxinus),* and in members of the mint (LABIATAE) and olive (OLEACEAE) families, the leaves and buds are opposite—at a 180° angle—to one another. On the other hand, in the oaks *(Quercus)* and walnuts *(Juglans),* for example, the leaves and buds alternate from one side of the stem to the other, and in the pines *(Pinus)* they form a spiral pattern.

The shoot apical meristem produces epidermis, cortex, primary xylem and phloem, and the central pith, tissues that form the primary structure of the stem. The shoot apex can eventually develop terminal inflorescences (floral groupings) instead of continuing to produce leaves and lateral buds as, for example, in the chrysanthemum, poinsettia, and sunflower.

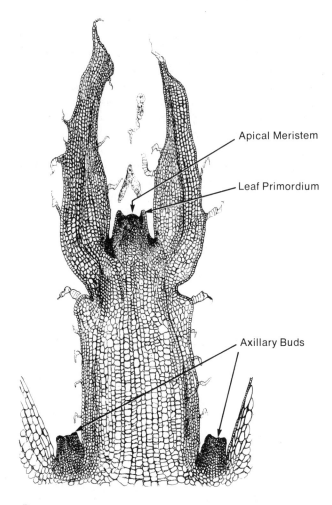

Apical Meristem

Leaf Primordium

Axillary Buds

Fig. 2–6 Longitudinal section of a shoot tip showing the apical meristem. Cell division in this region, along with cell elongation, is responsible for shoot growth. Buds in the axils of leaves also have meristematic regions at their tips that can develop into shoots. Should the apical meristem die or be broken off, an axillary bud can become the new shoot tip and continue shoot growth.

Some shoot meristems always remain vegetative and continue to produce leaves and lateral buds, as in many vines such as the grape. In such cases flowers or inflorescences are borne in the axils of lateral leaves somewhat behind the terminal growing point. Many trees also have this growth pattern; the dominant meristem (central leader) enables the plant to grow upright and gain height. In this case individual flowers or inflorescences are usually borne on side branches in the axils of leaves at some distance below the apex. These growth and flowering characteristics are known for most cultivated plants, and gardeners, orchardists, and foresters use that knowledge to prune trees and other plants to make them grow in the manner they wish.

Root meristems, located at the various termini of the roots, are the growing points for the root system. Some plants have a dominant **tap root,** which develops downward, together with limited lateral root growth (see Fig. 2–7). Examples of plants with tap roots are carrots, beets, and turnips, all well-known root crops. Other species with tap roots include oaks, pecans, alfalfa, and cotton. Many plants, however, do not have a dominant tap root. Instead the roots branch in many directions creating a **fibrous root** system (Fig. 2–7). Examples of these are the grasses, grain crops, and many kinds of shallow-rooted trees.

The root meristem lies just behind the root cap, which protects the meristem as the root pushes through the soil. These root cap cells are constantly being destroyed, but the apical root meristem produces more to replace them. The root meristem produces the primary tissues—that is, protoderm, ground meristem, and procambium—that later become the epidermis, cortex, and vascular cylinder of the mature root.

SUBAPICAL MERISTEMS

The **subapical meristem** produces new cells in the region a few micrometers behind an active shoot or apical meristem. The subapical meristematic region has long been thought of as a region where cells only elongate and expand. Cells do, indeed, expand in this region and thus increase internode length, thus adding to the growth in height of the plant. However, since new cells also form in this subapical region, it is a true meristem. The activity of the subapical meristem can be seen particularly in certain plants that lack tall stems when they are first producing leaves and that grow as a rosette. Examples are beets, carrots, China asters, lettuce, mustard, and turnips. These plants form rosettes of leaves on very short internodes. Later, when the shoot apical meristem initiates flowers, the stem below the flower elongates rapidly (bolts) because of the activity of the subapical meristem. During the period of fast growth, cells divide as well as elongate. The division and elongation together account for the rapid stem growth below the terminal flower buds.

INTERCALARY MERISTEMS

The **intercalary meristems** are active tissues that have been separated from the shoot terminal meristem by regions of more mature or developed tissues. The separation occurs at an early stage of development, and therefore the separated cells retain their ability to divide. The best examples of intercalary meristems are found in monocots and especially in the grasses (p. 455). The active meristematic cells just above the nodes in the lower region of the leaf sheath divide and develop (expand and elongate) rapidly. Grass leaves elongate at the base in a like manner (see Ch. 21).

LATERAL MERISTEMS

The **lateral meristems,** which produce secondary growth, are cylinders of active cell division starting somewhat below the apical or subapical meristems and continuing through the plant axis. These meristems are the **vascular cambium**—which produces new xylem (water and mineral conducting elements) and new phloem (photosynthate conducting elements)—and the **cork cambium**—which chiefly produces bark, the protective covering of old stems and roots (Fig. 2–8). Stem

Fig. 2–7 Two types of root systems. *Left:* Fibrous root system of a cereal plant. *Right:* Tap root system as developed by the carrot plant (*Daucus carota*).

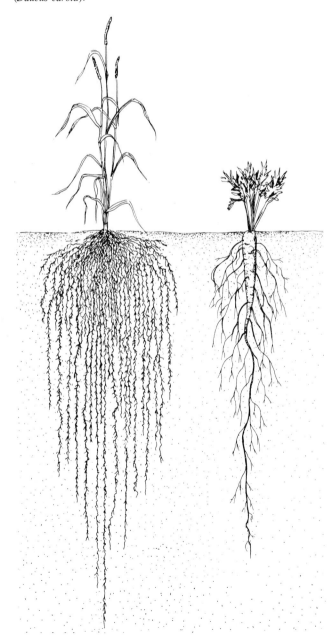

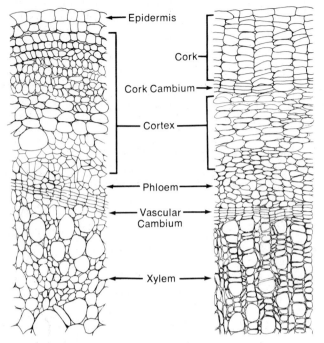

girth of woody perennial plants and trees increases mainly by the activity of these lateral meristems. The number of growth rings indicates the tree's age (Fig. 2–9). Measuring the width of the annual growth rings in the stems is one way to determine the rapidity of lateral growth of a tree. Long-lived trees such as the redwood (*Sequoia*) and certain pines, such as the bristle cone pine (*Pinus aristata*), increase greatly in size by lateral growth, but short-lived summer plants such as marigolds (*Tagetes*), tomatoes (*Lycopersicon*), and peppers (*Capsicum*) develop only a limited girth of the lower stem before the frost destroys them. Tomatoes, however, are perennials, and if they are grown in the frostfree tropics, vascular and cork cambial growth turns the lower stem into a small trunk.

Permanent Tissues

Permanent tissues can be classified into simple and complex tissues. The **simple tissues** are uniform, composed of only one type of cell. Examples are epidermis, parenchyma, sclerenchyma, collenchyma, and cork. **Complex tissues** are mixed, containing different kinds of cells. Examples are xylem and phloem.

Fig. 2–8   *Left:* Cross-section of the stem of a young dicotyledonous plant showing the tissues of the meristematic region. The epidermis lies on the outside. The dividing cells of the vascular cambium layer, producing phloem to the outside and xylem to the inside, account for the thickening of the stem as it grows older. *Right:* Cross-section of an older dicot stem where a cork cambium has developed. This meristematic layer produces the cork cells (bark), which protects the inner, more tender tissues.

Fig. 2–9   Section of a three-year-old stem of pine (*Pinus*) showing the annual rings by the end of the third summer. The porous, fast-growing spring wood is followed by the more dense, slower-growing summer wood.

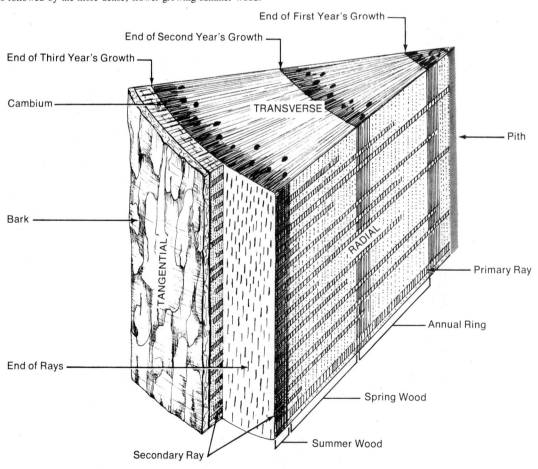

SIMPLE TISSUES

The **epidermis** is a single exterior layer of cells that protects stems, leaves, flowers, and roots. The outside surface of epidermal cells is usually covered with a waxy substance called cutin, which prevents water loss. The epidermis of leaves is usually colorless except for the guard cells of the stomata, which contain chlorophyll and are green. Some leaf epidermal cells are elongated into hairs and are called trichomes (Fig. 2–10). The root epidermis lacks cutin. It develops protuberances called root hairs, which actively absorb water from the soil.

Parenchyma tissue is made up of living thin-walled cells with large vacuoles and many flattened sides. This is the principal tissue of the cylindical zone under the epidermis extending inward to the phloem. This region is called the **cortex.** Parenchyma tissue, however, is not confined to stems but can be found in all plant parts. Parenchyma in leaves is active in photosynthesis. Parenchyma cells, when wounded, are capable of becoming meristematic and then proliferating to heal wounds and to regenerate other kinds of tissues.

Sclerenchyma tissue is composed of thick-walled cells found throughout the plant. These are usually lignified cells devoid of protoplasts when mature; that is, they are nonliving. Sclerenchyma cells are common in stems and bark and are also found as stone cells in, for example, pear fruits and walnut shells.

Collenchyma tissue gives support to young stems, petioles, and the veins of leaves. The walls and corners of the cells are thickened, primarily by cellulose, to provide reinforcement.

Cork tissue occurs commonly in the bark of maturing stems, the trunks of trees, and potato skins. The cell walls are waterproofed with a waxy material called suberin. Cork cells soon lose their protoplasts and die but continue to retain their shape.

COMPLEX TISSUES

Xylem is a structurally complex tissue that conducts water and dissolved minerals from the roots to all parts of the plant. The cells found in the xylem may be vessels, tracheids, fibers, and parenchyma. **Vessels** are long tubes made up of short vessel members that are united after the end walls of the cells have dissolved (Fig. 2–11). **Tracheids** are long, tapered, dead cells that conduct water through pits (Fig. 2–11). Tracheids contribute significant strength and support to the stems of gymnosperms. **Fibers** are thick-walled sclerenchyma cells that provide support. The parenchyma cells in xylem are arranged in vertical files and act as food storage sites. Not all these cell types occur in the xylem tissue of any one plant species; usually one or two are absent.

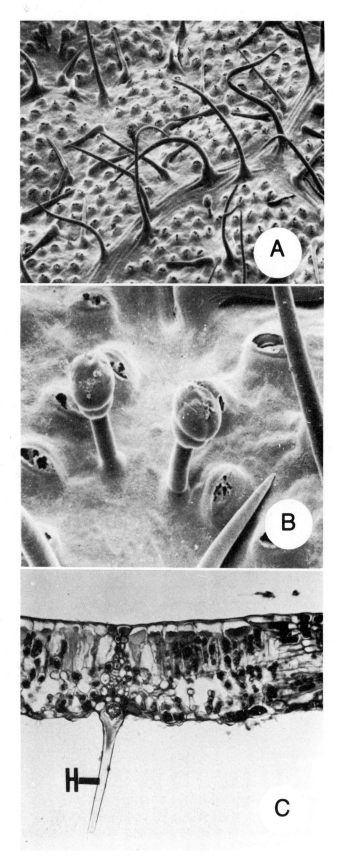

Fig. 2–10 Leaf surfaces of three different species showing the epidermal cells with the trichome protuberances. *Source:* Meyer, R. E., and S. M. Meola. 1978. Morphological characteristics of leaves and stems of selected Texas woody plants. USDA Tech. Bull. 1564.

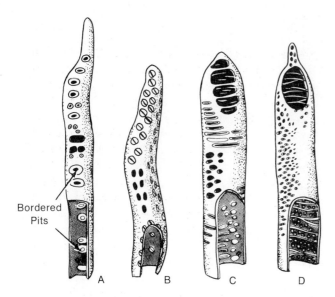

Bordered
Pits

Fig. 2–11 Types of tracheids and vessel elements found in xylem tissue. *Left to right:* Tracheid in pine (*Pinus*); tracheid in oak (*Quercus*); vessel element in magnolia (*Magnolia*); vessel element in basswood (*Tilia*). *Source:* Weier, T. E., C. R. Stocking, and M. G. Barbour. 1974. *Botany, an introduction to plant biology.* 5th ed. New York: John Wiley. State University of New York College of Environmental Science and Forestry.

Phloem conducts food and metabolites from the leaves to the stem, flowers, roots, and storage organs. A complex tissue, phloem comprises sieve tubes, sieve tube members, companion cells, fibers, and parenchyma. **Sieve-tube members** are long slender cells with porous ends called **sieve plates** (Fig. 2–12). Sieve tube members occur only in angiosperms. The equivalent cell in gymnosperms is the **sieve cell,** which is like the sieve-

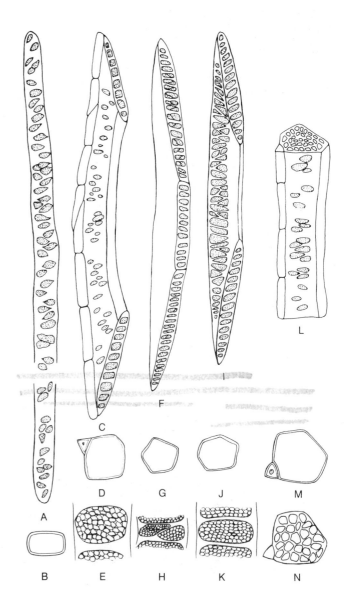

Fig. 2–12 Sieve cells, sieve-tube elements, and companion cells in side view and cross-section, showing detail structure of sieve plates.
  A, B: From Canadian hemlock (*Tsuga canadensis*); only one-third of cell shown.
  C, D, E: From tulip tree (*Liriodendron tulipifera*). *C, D,* with companion cells attached; *E,* detail of sieve plate.
  F, G, H: From apple *(Malus pumila); H,* detail of sieve plate.
  I, J, K: From black walnut (*Juglans nigra*); *K,* part of sieve plate in detail.
  L, M, N: From black locust (*Robinia pseudo-acacia*), with companion cells attached; *N,* detail of sieve plate.
  Source: Eames, A. J., and L. H. McDaniels. 1947. *An introduction to plant anatomy.* New York: McGraw-Hill.

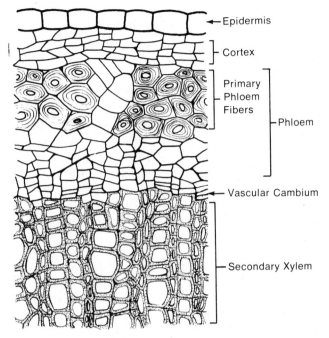

Fig. 2–13 Cross-section through stem of flax (*Linum*) showing thick-walled strengthening phloem fibers. *Source:* Esau, K. 1965. *Plant anatomy.* 2nd ed. New York: John Wiley.

tube element except that it lacks a sieve plate. **Companion cells** aid in metabolite conduction and are closely associated with sieve-tube members (Fig. 2–12). **Phloem fibers** are thick-walled cells that provide stem support (Fig. 2–13). The parenchyma cells in the phloem serve as storage sites.

THE PLANT BODY

The various tissues are united in a structured and organized pattern to form organs such as roots, stems, leaves, flowers, fruits, and seeds. These make up the plant body. When a plant first begins to grow from seed, the original organs are the radicle and plumule. These organs form the primary plant body. As the plant continues to grow, the primary organs develop into mature organs made up of permanent tissues.

Roots

Roots are responsible for absorbing and conducting water and mineral nutrients and for anchoring and supporting the plant. In addition, some roots, as in sugar beets and carrots, act as storage organs for photosynthesized food. The roots of some plants develop secondary xylem from cambial activity and an abundance of

parenchyma cells, which are able to store photosynthates and water. Dissolved mineral nutrients and water required for growth are absorbed by the root hairs, which are extensions of the epidermal cells (Fig. 2–14).

A few kinds of trees develop aerial roots from the underside of branches. Once these roots reach the soil and penetrate it, they become functional as ground roots. Good examples of this are the strangler fig *(Ficus aurea)* and the banyan tree *(Ficus benghalensis)* of the tropics. Some of the strangest roots are those in certain tropical orchids *(Cattleya, Phalaenopsis, Aerides,* and *Vanda)*. The roots contain chlorophyll for photosynthesizing food; they cling to rocks or tree surfaces and are fully exposed to receive light. Frequent rains and mist supply the moisture and nutrients necessary for growth.

The root system is a significant portion of the entire dry weight of any plant, about one-quarter to one-third of the total, depending on the storage or fibrous nature of the root. Measuring the total root system of a single mature rye plant showed that the plant had about 600 km (380 miles) of roots! Many of the functional roots of woody plants extend only into the top 1 m (3 ft) of soil. The depth that tree roots penetrate depends largely on the species of tree and on the structure and water status of the soil.

After the radicle or primary root emerges from the seed, it continues to grow principally as a tap root, or it may develop branch roots and form a fibrous root system

Fig. 2–14 Section of epidermis of a young root showing three stages (bottom to top) in the development of root hairs.

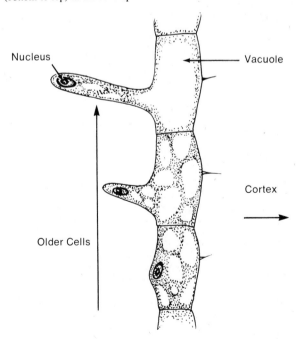

(Fig. 2–7). The tap root usually grows downward, and the branch roots grow downward or horizontally. The tap root can be encouraged to branch at an early stage by removing or breaking the apical root meristem. This often happens when some seedlings are transplanted into the garden; for example, the tap roots of tomatoes are broken when the young plants are removed from the container, and the roots become fibrous (p. 19). When young trees are transplanted from the nursery, the tap root is cut and the roots branch after the tree is transplanted into the home garden or commercial orchard.

The meristematic region of a root is composed of small, thin-walled cells with dense protoplasm that produce primary tissue at a rapid rate. Behind this active meristematic region lies the zone of elongation. Here the cells expand, especially in length, new protoplasm forms, and the size of the vacuoles increases. The apical meristem and the region of elongation take up only a few millimeters of each root. Behind the region of elongation is the region of maturation, where the enlarged cells differentiate into the tissues of the primary body. In the epidermis of this young region the cells protrude and elongate and begin to form root hairs (Fig. 2–15). New root hairs arise in the newly developed region to replace old root hairs destroyed as the roots penetrate the soil.

The root apical meristem produces tissues different from those produced by the shoot apical meristem. The root meristem gives rise to the **root cap, epidermis, cor-**

Fig. 2–15   *Right:* Developmental occurrences in the root tip, showing the various components and their relative location. *Left:* Cross-section of a young root showing the parts of the primary plant body and their location. *Source:* Weier, T. E., C. R. Stocking and M. G. Barbour. 1974. *Botany, an introduction to plant biology.* 5th ed. New York: John Wiley.

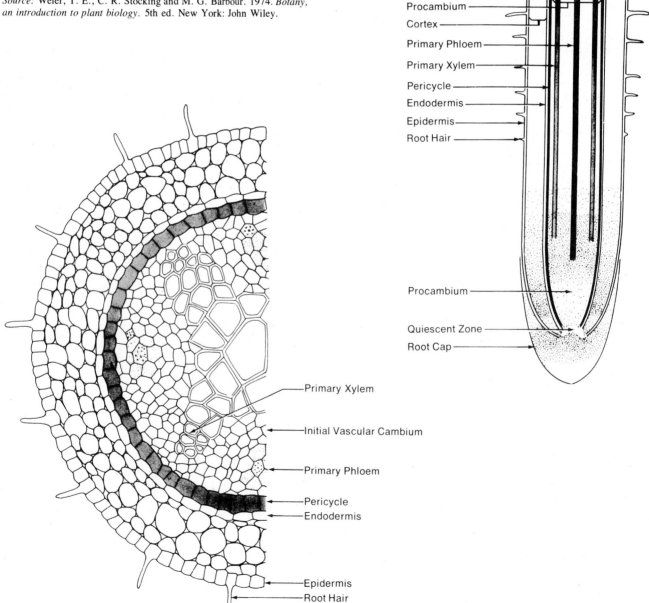

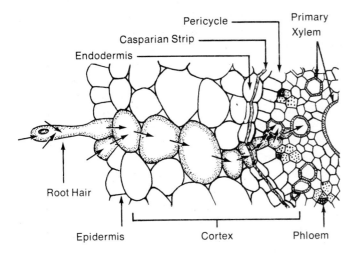

Pericycle —— Primary Xylem
Casparian Strip ——
Endodermis ——

Root Hair

Epidermis   Cortex   Phloem

Fig. 2–16   Cross-section of a young wheat (*Triticum*) root showing the path of entrance of soil solution into the root from a root hair to the tracheary elements of the xylem. *Source:* Esau, K. 1965. *Plant anatomy.* 2nd ed. New York: John Wiley.

tex, and **central vascular cylinder.** The root cap is a thimble-shaped group of cells that protect the actively dividing meristem as it penetrates the soil (Fig. 2–15). These moist cells are sloughed off as the root comes in contact with sharp soil particles; the meristem forms new cells on the inner part of the cap to replace the damaged or lost cells. The meristem produces long rows of cells under the root cap. One of these becomes the **protoderm** that gives rise to the epidermis, or outer layer, of the root. The **ground meristem,** the tissue layer that gives rise to the cortex just below the epidermis is usually thicker than the ground meristem found in stems. The cortical region is mainly composed of storage parenchyma cells, which have large intercellular spaces. A single layer of inner cortical cells forms the **endodermis,** a tissue found only in the root and not the stem. Each thin-walled endodermal cell is completely encircled by a narrow, thickened band of waterproofed material known as the **Casparian strip.** The solution of water and nutrients entering the root from the soil cannot penetrate the Casparian strip. For the soil solution to enter the inner tissue (pericycle) of the root, it must pass through the permeable endodermal cell walls and the protoplast (Fig. 2–16).

THE PROCAMBIUM LAYER

The **procambium layer** gives rise to various tissues of the vascular cylinder. These include the **pericycle,** which is the outermost layer of cells of the central core and lies just inside the endodermis. The pericycle develops from a single parenchyma cell layer on the outer

portion of the procambium. The pericycle is a meristematic region producing lateral (branch) roots that grow outwardly through the cortex and epidermis. It may also give rise to vascular and cork cambium. The procambium layer also produces a vascular cylinder of primary phloem and xylem, vascular cambium, and, in some species, pith. The pericycle and the vascular cylinder collectively are called the **stele.** The primary xylem is a central mass of tissue that may extend as arms beyond the primary phloem (Fig. 2–15). A layer of procambium cells separates these two primary tissues; this layer is the meristematic region for any new vascular tissue that subsequently forms.

As the root grows in girth and the plant matures, a continuous ring of secondary phloem forms outside the vascular cambium and the primary phloem becomes less important than at earlier growth stages. The cambium layer develops from the procambium and from pericycle cells outside the primary xylem. The primary xylem with its extending arms remains, but it is encircled by secondary xylem formed by the adjacent vascular cambium. Annual rings develop in the secondary plant body of the root as it grows in girth, much as in stems except for the star-shaped primary xylem at the core of the root. The cork cambium formed from pericycle produces a corky layer outwardly from the vascular system.

Adventitious roots form at any place on plant tissue other than the radicle of a germinating seed and its extensions. Adventitious roots arise from meristematic cells adjacent to vascular bundles (in herbaceous dicot stems) or from cambium or young phloem cells in young stems of woody perennials. This production of adventitious roots is the basis for propagation by stem cuttings (see Ch. 5). Adventitious roots can arise from plant parts other than stems, such as from leaf petioles or leaf blades or even from old root pieces. Plant parts to be rooted are usually detached from the parent plant and placed under favorable environmental conditions for rooting but in the propagation procedure known as layering, adventitious roots are induced to form on plant parts still attached to the parent plant (see Ch. 5). Adventitious roots also develop on intact plants, as in the corn plant (see Fig. 2–2).

Stems

The main stem and its branches are the skeletal scaffold of the plant, supporting the leaves, flowers, and fruits. The leaves and herbaceous green stems manufacture food, which is transported to the roots, flowers, and fruits through the phloem. Figure 2–17 illustrates the

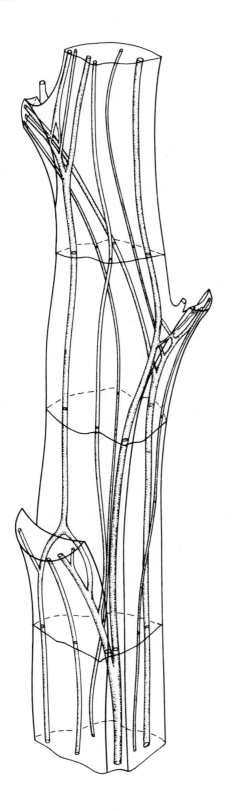

Fig. 2–17 Three-dimensional skeletal section through the stem of a potato plant showing the primary vascular system extending through the stem with branches into the cutaway leaf petioles. *Source:* Eames, A. J., and L. H. McDaniels. *An introduction to plant anatomy.* 1947. New York: McGraw-Hill.

complexity of the primary vascular system. The greater part of the vascular system consists of xylem and phloem. The secondary xylem also serves as the major structural support in woody perennial plants. In trees and other woody plants, the stems also have lateral meristems of vascular and cork cambium, which produce new tissues that add girth, strength, and protection.

The stem develops from three primary tissues produced by the apical meristem: the protoderm, the ground meristem, and the procambium. These give rise to the epidermis, cortex, and vascular cambium, respectively.

The **epidermis,** which is usually a single layer of surface cells, protects the stem. Epidermal cells are usually cutinized on their outer surface to retard desiccation. The epidermis of leaves and young stems has pores, the stomata, that allow for the exchange of gases.

The **cortex** lies just beneath the epidermis and encircles the inner core of the vascular tissue. The cortex comprises parenchyma, collenchyma, sclerenchyma, and secretory cells, with parenchyma cells the most numerous. Some parenchyma cells have chloroplasts and are called chlorenchyma. Parenchyma cells have the ability to divide and form new tissue when wounded, thus providing a protective mechanism for the stem. Collenchyma is the outer cell layer of the cortex adjacent to the epidermal layer. These cells may be thickened at the corners, and their walls contain cellulose, hemicellulose, and pectin. This tissue, therefore, adds strength to the stem. Sclerenchyma cells have thick lignified walls. They can form long fibers, which are the source of strength in mature stems. Secretory cells produce resinous substances and are commonly found, for example, in the resin ducts of pine trees.

The **vascular system** of seed-bearing plants consists of the pericycle, phloem, vascular cambium, xylem, pith rays, and pith. The arrangement of these complex tissues in the vascular system differs among three broad groups of plants: (1) the gymnosperms and the woody dicotyledonous angiosperm perennials (which live for long periods), such as trees and shrubs; (2) the herbaceous dicotyledonous plants, such as potato, petunia and phlox; and (3) the monocotyledonous plants, such as corn and date palms. These three groups are discussed separately below to distinguish among their different internal stem structures and growth patterns.

WOODY PERENNIALS (DICOTYLEDONOUS ANGIOSPERMS AND THE GYMNOSPERMS)

All the cells and tissues originate from a terminal shoot meristem that forms protophloem and protoxylem (primary tissue) (Fig. 2–18). As the stem grows

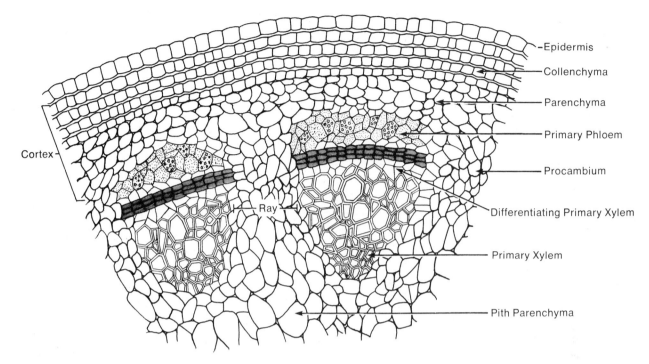

Fig. 2–18   Cross-section of a young woody plant stem toward the end of primary growth showing the various tissues present.

Epidermis
Collenchyma
Parenchyma
Primary Phloem
Procambium
Differentiating Primary Xylem
Primary Xylem
Pith Parenchyma
Cortex
Ray

in length, the secondary tissues form from the vascular cambium. The secondary phloem develops toward the outside of the stem by the vascular cambium and the secondary xylem forms inwardly. These growing secondary and permanent tissues crush the primary tissues until they become difficult to see. Secondary xylem is actively produced by the vascular cambium in the early spring and less actively in late summer. This xylem tissue becomes the early (porous) and late (dense) wood that form the annual growth rings in trees. The vessels or tracheids formed during the spring flush of growth are larger than those formed during the summer (Figs. 2–19, 2–20, and 2–21). The narrow-leaved evergreen trees belonging to the gymnosperms are usually referred to as the softwoods or nonporous wood trees (Fig. 2–19). The xylem of gymnosperms consists mainly of tracheids (Fig. 2–11). The broad-leaved angiosperm trees are called hardwoods or porous wood (Fig. 2–21); the xylem tissue is made up mostly of vessel elements (Fig. 2–11).

Both the gymnosperms and the woody perennial angiosperms grow in girth each year when the cells of the vascular cambium divide, forming annual rings of xylem. A stem nearing the end of its first season of growth is mostly xylem. The phloem as it is crushed by the expanding xylem is constantly being renewed by the vascular cambium. The phloem is a relatively thin layer of complex tissue protected by the bark or cork layer.

Fig. 2–19   Three dimensional view of the wood of a softwood forest species: (1) cross-sectional face; (2) radial face; (3) tangential face; (4) annual ring; (5) early wood; (6) late wood; (7) wood ray; (8) fusiform ray; (9) vertical resin duct; (10) horizontal resin duct; (11) bordered pit; (12) simple pit. *Source:* U.S. Forest Products Laboratory, Madison, Wis.

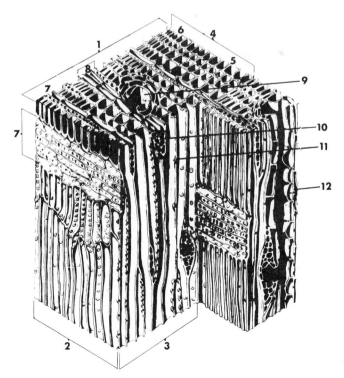

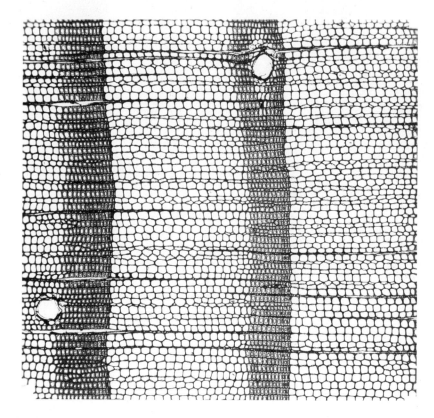

Fig. 2–20 Cross-section through the stem of a softwood forest species, the loblolly pine (*Pinus taeda*), showing the growth rings made up of early (spring) and late (summer) wood. *Source:* U.S. Forest Products Laboratory, Madison, Wis.

Fig. 2–21 Three-dimensional view of the wood of a hardwood forest species: (1) cross-sectional face; (2) radial face; (3) tangential face; (4) annual ring; (5) early wood; (6) late wood; (7) wood ray; (8) vessel; (9) perforation plate. *Source:* U.S. Forest Products Laboratory, Madison, Wis.

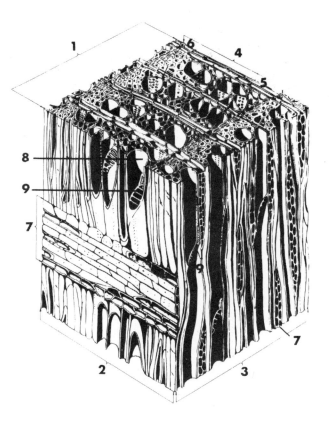

Fig. 2-22 The rough, thick bark of the cork oak (*Quercus suber*), which is commercially stripped for cork products.

Fig. 2-23 The bark of a birch tree (*Betula verrucosa*) showing the lenticels.

The cork cambium (phellogen), which is a meristematic tissue, provides cells that grow both outward and inward. The outward cells become cork cells; the inward, phelloderm. The cork cells become suberized and are, therefore, resistant to entry or loss of water. The cork cells soon die but retain their insulating characteristics against desiccation, disease, insects, and extreme temperatures. The unusually thick bark of the cork oak (*Quercus suber*) is stripped for a multitude of commercial uses (Fig. 2-22).

In young twigs and small trunks of many kinds of trees and shrubs, pore openings (lenticels) allow the inward and outward diffusion of gases (Fig. 2-23).

HERBACEOUS DICOTYLEDONOUS PLANTS

The early stem growth of plants in this category is much like the early growth of woody dicot stems. The vascular bundles (fascicles) of an herbaceous dicot usually remain separated and distinct; they are arranged in a single circle in the stem (Fig. 2-24). A larger proportion of the herbaceous stem is cortex and pith than xylem or phloem. Stem strength comes from the pericycle fibers adjacent to the phloem or from collenchyma or sclerenchyma tissue just beneath the epidermis (Fig. 2-24).

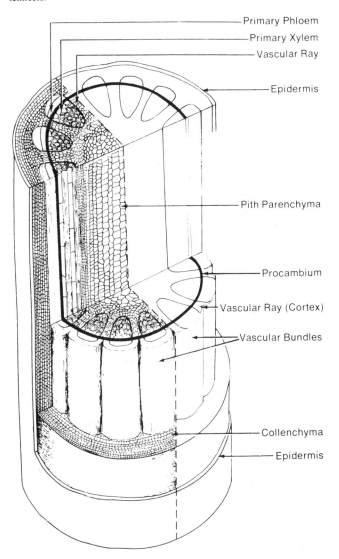

Primary Phloem
Primary Xylem
Vascular Ray
Epidermis
Pith Parenchyma
Procambium
Vascular Ray (Cortex)
Vascular Bundles
Collenchyma
Epidermis

Fig. 2-24 Three-dimensional cutaway view of the stem of an herbaceous dicot plant showing the vascular bundles.

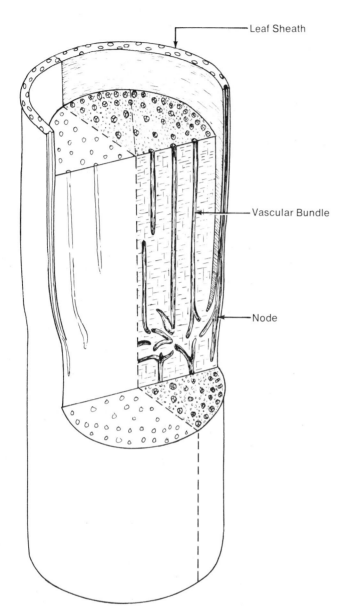

Leaf Sheath

Vascular Bundle

Node

HERBACEOUS MONOCOTYLEDONOUS PLANTS

Stem growth originates from an apical meristem that produces vascular bundles scattered throughout the parenchyma (Fig. 2–25). The vascular bundles form most frequently near the epidermis. The sclerenchyma cells near the epidermis and thick-walled cells surrounding the bundles provide the principal support in monocot stems. Monocots, as Figure 2–25 shows, have no continuous cambium and, therefore, lack secondary growth. Stem diameter from the base to the apex is usually more uniform in monocot stems than in dicot stems with secondary vascular growth.

WOODY PERENNIAL MONOCOTYLEDONOUS PLANTS

In trees such as date and coconut palms (PALMAE) the thickness at the stem apex increases by the activity of a primary thickening meristem. In the trunk below the terminal growing point parenchyma cells continue to divide and enlarge allowing for lateral stem enlargement. This is termed **diffuse secondary growth** since no actual lateral meristem is involved.

Stem Forms

When most people think of the stem of a plant, they envision the upright portion that bears branches, leaves, flowers, and fruits. Stems come in other forms, too. For example, certain fruit trees such as apples, cherries, plums, and pears bear flowers and fruits each spring on the same shortened stems called spurs (Fig. 13–8). Stems can also grow horizontally, as in a pumpkin or cucumber vine. Some species of plants have underground stems; only a small portion of the stem shows above ground for a relatively short period in the spring.

Fig. 2–25 *Left:* Three-dimensional cutaway view of the stem of an herbaceous monocot (solid stem) showing the scattered vascular bundles. *Lower left:* Enlarged view of vascular bundle. *Lower right:* Enlarged cross-section area.

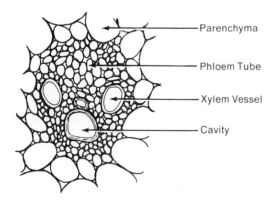

Parenchyma

Phloem Tube

Xylem Vessel

Cavity

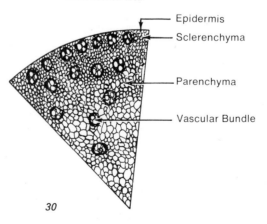

Epidermis

Sclerenchyma

Parenchyma

Vascular Bundle

Fig. 2–26   Potato plant at time of harvest. The tubers are stem structures (rhizomes) growing below ground whose ends have stored sufficient photosynthate to swell into tubers.

tuber as it accumulates starches and sugars from photosynthesis in the leaves (Fig. 2–26). Just like other stems the white potato tuber has buds (eyes) that sprout when planted to form new above-ground stems.

A **rhizome** is an underground stem that grows horizontally. Examples of plants with rhizomatous stems are cannas, certain irises, certain bamboos (Fig. 5–33), and some grasses, such as quack grass and Johnson grass.

Stolons are stems that grow horizontally above ground. Sometimes called runners, stolons can develop roots in the soil at every node or at every other node (strawberry). Examples of species with stolons are ajuga and Bermuda grass.

Corms are thickened compressed stems that grow underground (Fig. 2–27). Buds on corms sprout to produce upright stems, which bear leaves and flowers. Gladiolus, crocus, freesia, and ixia are some examples.

Bulbs are highly compressed underground stems to which numerous storage leaves (scales) are attached. These highly developed stems provide a means for some species to survive the cold of winter and the dry soil of summer. One or more buds on the bulb sprout in the spring to produce an elongated stem with leaves and flowers. Through photosynthesis, the leaves produce carbohydrates, which are translocated to the bulb for storage. The storage of food in bulbs is a mechanism to enable the species to survive through periods of unfavorable climatic conditions. Hyacinths, lilies, onions, and tulips are examples of bulbous plants.

Stem **tubers** are enlarged, fleshy, tips of underground stems. The white potato, as discussed above, is a good example (Fig. 2–26).

These are the so-called bulbous plants (Ch. 20). The white (Irish) potato plant *(Solanum tuberosum),* ready for harvest, exemplifies two kinds of stems: the above-ground stem that bears the leaves and flowers, and an under-ground stem (rhizome), whose end swells into a

Fig. 2–27   A gladiolus corm, which is thickened compressed stem tissue, toward the end of the growing season. The spring-planted corm (below) has shrivelled with a new corm (above) forming above the old corm. New small cormels are forming at the base of the new corm.

Leaves

Leaves develop in a complex series of events closely associated with stem development. Some of these developmental events are still not clearly understood. Leaves are initiated by the apical shoot meristem. Their prescribed pattern, position, and shape are influenced to some extent by their environment. For example, the leaves of cacti are adapted to growth in the desert, whereas leaves of ferns are adapted for growth in a rain forest. Most monocots, such as the grasses and palm trees, have strap-shaped leaves with parallel veins and interveinous connections between major veins. The veins contain sheaths of vascular bundles including xylem and phloem elements. **Palisade** and **spongy mesophyll parenchyma cells,** containing chlorophyll for photosynthesis, surround these veins (Figs. 2–28 and 2–29).

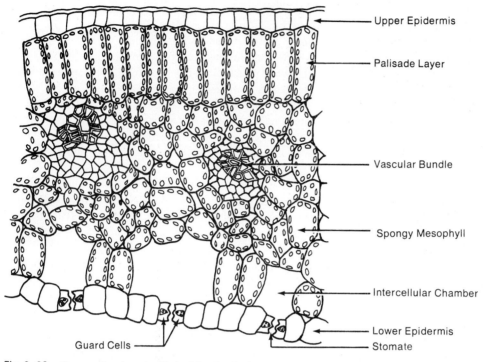

Fig. 2–28. Cross-section through a lily leaf showing the tissues involved in photosynthesis, transpiration, and translocation.

Fig. 2–29 Three-dimensional cutaway view of an apple leaf showing the relation of cells in the various tissues. *Source:* Eamcs, A. J., and L. H. McDaniels. 1947. *An introduction to plant anatomy.* 2nd ed. New York: McGraw-Hill.

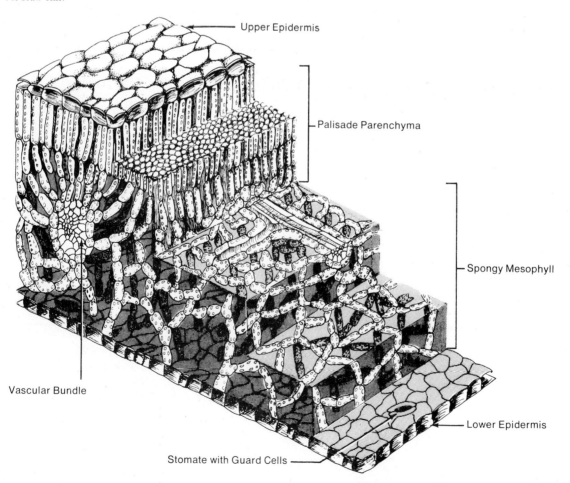

The leaves of dicotyledonous plants vary considerably in size and shape (Fig. 2–30). Practically all have veins arranged in the shape of nets. The large primary veins divide into smaller secondary veins. The veins are made up of xylem and phloem connected to all segments of the leaf. The spongy mesophyll parenchyma (Figs. 2–28 and 2–29) contains the intercellular spaces through which carbon dioxide, oxygen, and water pass. The outside layer or skin of the leaf is made up largely of epidermal cells. In this epidermal layer are found openings or pores called **stomata,** each surrounded by two **guard cells.** There generally are more stomata in the lower epidermal layer of the leaf than in the upper epidermal

Fig. 2–30   Types of leaf patterns with their descriptive names. Leaf form is useful in identifying plants.

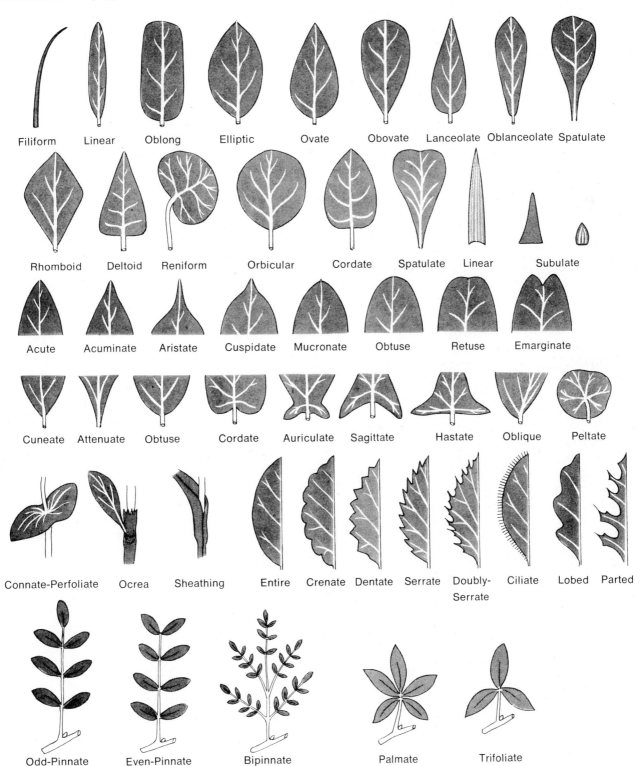

Filiform   Linear   Oblong   Elliptic   Ovate   Obovate   Lanceolate   Oblanceolate   Spatulate

Rhomboid   Deltoid   Reniform   Orbicular   Cordate   Spatulate   Linear   Subulate

Acute   Acuminate   Aristate   Cuspidate   Mucronate   Obtuse   Retuse   Emarginate

Cuneate   Attenuate   Obtuse   Cordate   Auriculate   Sagittate   Hastate   Oblique   Peltate

Connate-Perfoliate   Ocrea   Sheathing   Entire   Crenate   Dentate   Serrate   Doubly-Serrate   Ciliate   Lobed   Parted

Odd-Pinnate   Even-Pinnate   Bipinnate   Palmate   Trifoliate

layer. (Water lilies, however, are an exception to this generality.)

The primary function of leaves is photosynthesis (see Ch. 7); a secondary function is transpiration. The **guard cells,** which occur in pairs on both sides of the stomata, control the opening and closing of the stomata through which carbon dioxide, one of the raw materials for photosynthesis, enters the plant, and oxygen, a product of photosynthesis, is released. Water also enters or escapes through the stomata. The loss of water from the leaf by evaporation, a process called **transpiration,** helps regulate the leaf temperature. Some plants have modified leaf surfaces that affect the rate of transpiration. The leaves of some plants, such as cabbage, have a thick waxy surface (cuticle) that greatly reduces water loss. In leaves of other plants the epidermal cells produce elongated hairs that reduce the wind velocity at the leaf surface, thus reducing the transpiration rate. Some kinds of plants, especially those native to hot dry climates, such as the olive tree, minimize water loss by having stomata sunken deep in the epidermal layer.

Plants often have leaves modified to perform functions other than photosynthesis and transpiration. For example, the leaf stipules of the black locust *(Robinia pseudoacacia)* are modified to become thorns that aid in protecting the plant. Some viny plants like the grape have leaves modified in the form of tendrils that help support the vine when trained on trellises.

In most dicotyledonous plants the leaf is made up of the **blade,** the flat thin part; the stemlike **petiole,** which attaches the blade to the stem; and, in some plants, the **stipules** at the base of the petiole. Some leaf blades are attached directly to the stem and lack a petiole or stipules. These are termed **sessile** leaves.

Leaf shapes among the many plant species vary greatly, and a special morphological terminology describes the leaf shape, margin, tip, and base. Some of the more common leaf types are shown and named in Figure 2–30. Leaves are usually classified as **simple** (a single leaf) or **compound** (one with three or more leaflets). Distinguishing between simple and compound leaves can be difficult. The best test is to examine the base of the petiole. A true leaf has a bud in this location; a leaflet does not. A compound leaf resembling a feather is termed **pinnate;** one resembling the palm of a hand, **palmate.** A **trifoliate** compound leaf has three leaflets, as in the bean plant.

The shapes of simple leaves are described as linear, oblong, elliptical, lanceolate, deltoid, and so forth. The shapes of the tips and bases of simple leaves are also categorized as cordate (heart-shaped), sagittate (arrow-shaped), auriculate (ear-lobed), and sheathing, as in the grasses (Fig. 21–2). Leaf edges or margins range from entire (smooth), dentate (toothlike), serrate (sawlike) to lobed (rounded edges). These leaf characteristics aid in plant identification, as we will see in Chapter 3.

All gymnosperms native to North America and Europe have needlelike leaves and are evergreen. Some gymnosperms native to other parts of the world, particularly Australia, are broad-leaved plants.

Buds

Plant stems produce buds generally in the axils of leaves at the nodes or terminally on shoots. Buds do not occur on roots. A **bud** can be defined as an undeveloped shoot or flower, composed largely of meristematic tissue, and generally protected by modified leaf scales. There are: (1) vegetative buds, which develop into a shoot; (2) flower buds, which open to produce a flower or flowers; and (3) mixed buds, which open to produce both shoots and flowers. Cutting through a bud longitudinally reveals the miniature parts of either a stem growing point or, in a flower bud, all the miniaturized parts of a flower.

Buds are especially prominent in winter on deciduous plants when the leaves have fallen. Just below each bud a leaf scar, where the leaf petiole detached, is visible. Buds may occur opposite each other on a stem or in an alternate arrangement around the stem.

Buds are initiated by terminal growing points as shoots elongate during the growing season. Some buds continue to grow shortly after they are formed, developing into shoots. The growing points in other buds remain dormant until the following spring. Some buds may remain latent for long periods of time and become embedded in enlarging stem tissue.

Buds of deciduous woody species usually go into a physiological resting or quiescent state shortly after they are formed in the summer and stay that way until they are subjected to low-temperature winter chilling, which overcomes their resting condition and enables them to resume growth the following spring (see Ch. 14). Buds of tropical and subtropical plants, however, generally do not develop such a resting condition.

Flower buds form by the differentiation of vegetative buds into flower parts. This change is shown microscopically for the cherry in Figure 14–1. The subsequent growth activities of the meristematic regions of a vegetative bud are described in detail on page 18.

Flowers

In the angiosperms specialized floral leaves borne and arranged on the stem are adapted for sexual reproduction; these are the **flowers.** After fertilization (Ch. 6) portions

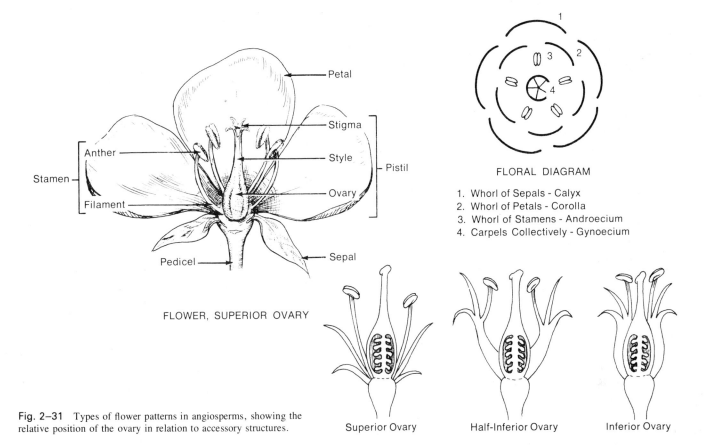

Petal

Stigma

Style — Pistil

Anther

Stamen

Ovary

Filament

Pedicel

Sepal

FLOWER, SUPERIOR OVARY

FLORAL DIAGRAM

1. Whorl of Sepals - Calyx
2. Whorl of Petals - Corolla
3. Whorl of Stamens - Androecium
4. Carpels Collectively - Gynoecium

Superior Ovary   Half-Inferior Ovary   Inferior Ovary

Fig. 2–31 Types of flower patterns in angiosperms, showing the relative position of the ovary in relation to accessory structures.

of the flower develop into a **fruit,** which bears the **seed(s).**

The flowers may be borne at the apex of a stem, as in the sunflower, rose, and poinsettia, or in the axils of the leaves lower down on the stem, as in the tomato,

fuchsia, and many of the temperate zone fruit trees. Flowers or inflorescences vary in shape and form among the species, a fact that aids in identifying a plant's species, genus, and family (see Ch. 3). As with stems, botanists classify flowers in a specialized morphological terminology. Examples are shown in Figures 2–31 and 2–32.

Fig. 2–32 Some typical inflorescences.

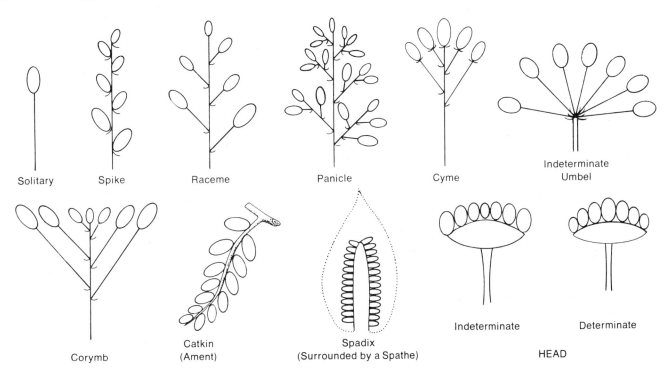

Solitary   Spike   Raceme   Panicle   Cyme   Indeterminate Umbel

Corymb   Catkin (Ament)   Spadix (Surrounded by a Spathe)   Indeterminate   Determinate

HEAD

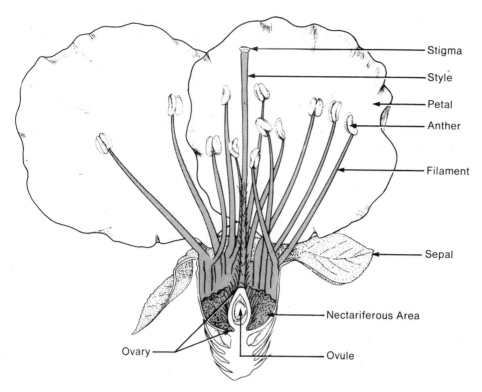

Fig. 2–33   The typical complete flower of the apricot, showing a
superior ovary with a simple pistil. *Source:* USDA.

Fig. 2–34   The typical complete flower of the apple, showing an inferior
ovary with a compound pistil. *Source:* USDA.

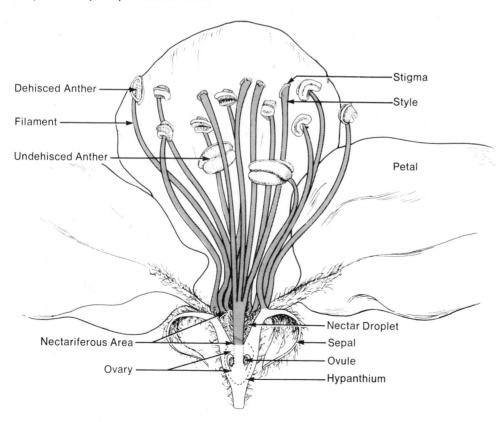

COMPLETE FLOWERS

Complete flowers have four parts—sepals, petals, stamens, and pistil—which are usually borne on a receptacle (Fig. 2–31). The **sepals** are the leaflike scales that encircle the other flower parts, as in the carnation and rose. Most often the sepals are green but sometimes they are the same color as the petals, as in tulips and lilies. The sepals may fold back (rose) (Fig. 17–29) or remain upright (carnation) as the petals grow and emerge. The sepals collectively are called the **calyx.** The **petals** are the next whorl of floral leaves inward from the sepals. The collective term for petals is **corolla.** The petals are usually brightly colored, and they often contain **nectaries** that secrete nectar to attract insects, which pollinate the flowers (Ch. 6). Collectively sepals and petals are called the **perianth.**

The next whorl of floral organs in a complete flower is the male parts, or **stamens.** Each stamen consists of a **filament** and an **anther;** the anther produces the **pollen.** Collectively a group or whorl of stamens is the **androecium.**

The **pistil,** the central female component of the flower, is composed of three parts: the **stigma,** the receptive surface that receives the pollen; the **style,** a tube connected to the stigma; and the **ovary,** attached to the lower end of the style. The ovary contains undeveloped **ovules** that are attached to a **placenta;** the ovules develop into **seeds** after pollination and fertilization (Ch. 6). The pistil can be **simple** (i.e., has but one carpel) or **compound** (i.e., has two or more fused carpels). Collectively the carpels are known as the **gynoecium.** The apricot and the apple (Figs. 2–33 and 2–34) are examples of complete flowers with a simple and a compound pistil, respectively.

The stamens and pistils are considered the essential parts of the complete flower for sexual reproduction. The sepals (calyx) and the petals (corolla) are accessory flower parts.

INCOMPLETE FLOWERS

Incomplete flowers lack one or more of the four parts: sepals, petals, stamens, or pistil. Flowers with both stamens and pistils are called **perfect flowers.** Flowers with stamens only and no pistils are called **staminate** flowers; those with pistils but no stamens are called **pistillate** flowers. Staminate or pistillate flowers are by definition **imperfect** flowers. Plants having both staminate and pistillate flowers borne on the same plant are termed **monoecious** (e.g., alder, corn, walnut) (Fig. 2–35). If the pistillate and staminate flowers are borne on separate individual plants (male and female plants) the

Fig. 2–35   Flowers of a monoecious species, the walnut. Female flowers (*left*) and male flowers or catkins (*right*) are borne in separate structures on the same plant.

species is called **dioecious.** Examples are date palm, gingko, pistachio, and asparagus.

Some flowers, like the tulip, are borne singly on a stalk and are called **solitary,** but others are arranged in multiples or in clusters known as **inflorescences.** Some of these types of flower clusters are illustrated in Figure 2–32. The **corymb** is a short, flat-topped flower with an indeterminate cluster that continues to produce flowers until conditions become unfavorable; the lower flowers open first. An example is the cherry. The **cyme** resembles the corymb, except that the central or topmost flower is the first to open. Examples are chickweed and strawberry. The **raceme** is a single elongated indeterminate arrangement of stalked flowers, found in the mustard and cole crops (CRUCIFERAE), for example. The **spike** is an elongated, simple, indeterminate inflorescence with sessile (no stalk) flowers, as in wheat, oats, and gladiolus. The **catkin** is a spike with only pistillate or staminate flowers exemplified by alder, poplar, walnut, and willow. The **panicle** is an indeterminate branching raceme found in many of the grasses. The **umbel** is an indeterminate, often flat-topped, cluster of flowers that are of equal length and arise from a common point, as in carrots, dill, and onions. A **head** is a short dense spike; daisies and sunflowers have heads. A **spadix** is a complete densely flowered structure surrounded by a spathe (very characteristic of the ARACEAE family).

Fruits

A fruit is a matured ovary plus associated parts; it is generally a seed-bearing organ, but there are parthenocarpic fruits which are seedless (see p. 130). The fruit protects the seed in some plants and helps disseminate it. For example, the seeds of fleshy fruits like peaches or plums occur inside their pits, which are discarded by animals or humans eating the fruit. The seeds in the discarded pits may eventually germinate and grow. One might tend to think of all fruits as fleshy organs, but there are many dry fruits such as nuts, capsules, legume pods, and grains. Fruits develop after pollination and fertilization (Ch. 6). Flowers are self-pollinated or cross-pollinated by wind or insects. The pollen grows from a pollen grain on the stigma through the style and fertilizes the egg, causing the fruit to develop (see Fig. 6–15). Fruits may consist of a single carpel, as in beans and peas, or a combination of several carpels, as in apples (Fig. 2–34) and tomatoes. The fruit matures quickly, in a matter of weeks in the case of some summer annuals and strawberries, or it requires as long as nine months as with oranges. The ovary wall, which is called the **pericarp,** can develop into different structures. The peel of an orange is part of the pericarp. The pod of a pea, or the shell of a sunflower seed, and the skin, flesh, and pit of a peach are all derived from the ovary wall or pericarp.

SIMPLE FRUITS

Simple fruits have a single ovary formed from one flower. The most common classification of simple fruits categorizes them as fleshy, semifleshy, or dry by the texture of the mature pericarp.

FLESHY FRUITS The entire pericarp and accessory parts develop into succulent tissue.

Berry. A pulpy fruit from one or more carpels that develops few to many seeds. Examples are bananas, dates, grapes, peppers, tomatoes, and papayas.

Hesperidium. A fruit with several carpels containing a leathery rind with inner pulp juice sacs or vesicles; for example, orange, lemon, lime, and grapefruit.

Pepo. A fruit formed from an inferior ovary that develops from multiple carpels bearing many seeds. The pericarp is a thick and usually hard rind. Cucumbers, melons, squashes, and watermelons are examples.

DRY-FLESHY FRUITS Some parts of the pericarp become dry and the other portions remain succulent.

Drupe. This is a simple fruit derived from a single carpel. The exocarp (the outer layer) becomes the thin skin; the mesocarp (the middle layer) becomes thick and fleshy; the endocarp (the inner layer) becomes hard and stony and is often referred to as the pit (and often erroneously as the "seed"). Peaches, plums, cherries, apricots, almonds, and olives are examples of drupe fruits.

Pome. This is a simple fruit made up of several carpels. The outer (and edible) portion forms from an accessory structure, the **hypanthium** of the flower, which surrounds the multiple carpels. Apple (Fig. 2–34), pear, and quince are examples.

DRY FRUITS (PAPERY OR STONY) The entire pericarp is dry at maturity.

Dehiscent fruits. These fruits split at maturity to expose the seeds.

Capsule. The fruits form from two or more carpels, each of which produce many seeds. Splitting can occur in several different ways. Iris, poppy, and jimson weed are examples.

Follicle. The fruits form from a single carpel that splits along one suture. *Delphinium* and *Helleborus* are examples.

Silique. Fruits form from two carpels with a septum between. The two halves separate longitudinally, exposing the seeds. Mustard, lunaria, and stocks are examples.

Indehiscent fruits. These fruits do not split open when mature.

Achene. Simple, one-seeded, thin-walled fruit attached to an ovary wall. Very often achenes are mistaken for seeds as in the case of strawberry "fruits" (Fig. 2–36), the so-called seeds of the rose-hip, and sunflower fruits.

Caryopsis (grain). A one-seeded fruit with a thin pericarp surrounding and adhering tightly to the true seed. Corn, rice, wheat, and barley are examples.

Nut. A one-seeded fruit with a thick, hard, stony pericarp. Oak (acorn), chestnut, filbert, and hickory are examples.

Samara. A one-seeded (elm) or a two seeded (maple) fruit with a winglike structure formed from the ovary wall. Ash is another example.

Schizocarp. A fruit formed from two or more carpels that split at maturity to yield two one-seeded halves. Carrots, dill, and parsley are examples.

AGGREGATE AND MULTIPLE FRUITS

Aggregate and **multiple fruits** form from several ovaries. The true fruits are attached to or contained within a receptacle or an accessory structure.

Aggregate fruits develop from many ovaries on a single flower. The strawberry, for example, has many achenes (true fruits), each attached to a single fleshy receptacle (Fig. 2–36). The many achenes of the rose-hip develop inside the receptacle. The blackberry and raspberry are similar to the strawberry except that individual small drupes, instead of achenes, are attached to the fleshy receptacle.

Multiple fruits develop from many individual ovaries fused into a single structure borne on a common stalk. The fig "fruit" we eat is made up of small drupes (the true fruits) contained inside a fleshy receptacle. The whole structure is termed a **syconium** (see Fig. 30–2). The pineapple is a large accessory structure covered with seedless (parthenocarpic) berries. Mulberries are multiple drupelets borne on a fleshy receptacle.

Seeds

Seeds vary considerably in size, shape, structure, and mode of dissemination. The seeds contained in samaras take to the air on their small wings. The downy tufts of milkweed and dandelion seeds enable them to be carried great distances on wind currents. The coconut is known to have floated to new land masses on ocean currents. Some seeds are attached to barbs or hooks or are contained within burrs or siliques that can catch in clothing or animal fur and be transported great distances. Squirrels and other rodents bury nuts, many of which germinate later. Birds and other animals disseminate seeds by eating the fruit and passing resistant seeds through their digestive tract. Some kinds of seeds are forcefully expelled from dehiscing dried fruits as they mature. These varied means of seed dissemination aid in species survival by promoting plant growth in new locations with possibly different environments.

A seed is a mature ovule. The three basic parts are: the embryo, the food storage tissue (endosperm, cotyledons, or perisperm), and the seed coats. Chapter 6 covers the development of the seed in detail.

The **embryo** is a miniature plantlet formed within the seed from the union of the male and female gametes during fertilization (see Fig. 6–15). Basically the embryo has two growing points: the **radicle**, which is the embryonic root, and the **plumule**, which is the embryonic shoot. One or two **cotyledons** are located between these two growing points on the root-shoot axis.

Food can be stored in the endosperm, cotyledons, or perisperm in the form of starch, fats, or proteins. Stored food in the cereal grains is largely endosperm. Seeds having a large portion of their food stored as endosperm are called **albuminous** seeds. Those seeds with no endosperm or only a thin layer surrounding the embryo are called **exalbuminous** seeds. Such seeds store food either in fleshy cotyledons, as in beans, or rarely in the perisperm (developed nucellus), as in beets.

The **seed coverings** are usually tough, preventing damage to the enclosed embryo. They are also relatively impervious to water to save the embryo from desiccation, but again there are exceptions. There may be one or two seed coats (**testa**), which form from the **integuments,** the outer layers of the ovule (see Fig. 6–15). In such dry fruits as achenes, samaras, and schizocarps, the fruit adheres closely to the seed coat; consequently the

Fig. 2–36 Strawberry "fruit." The true strawberry fruits on the left (*A*) are the small achenes borne on the surface of the large fleshy receptacle (*B*). The complete edible part is shown in *C*.

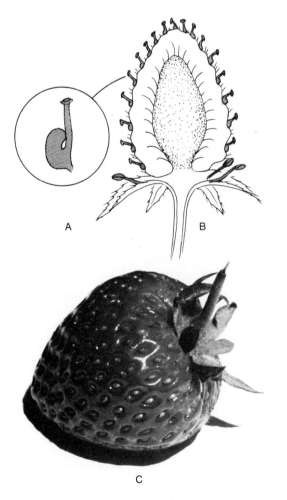

A   B

C

39

true fruit is usually called a "seed." The pits or stones of such drupe fruits as peaches and apricots are often called "seeds"; however, they are actually the hardened inner wall (endocarp) of the pericarp that surrounds the seed.

The scar that remains after breaking the seed from the stalk is called the **hilum,** and the small opening near the hilum is the **micropyle.** The ridge on the seed is the **raphe** (Fig. 2–4).

SUMMARY

The plant is basically composed of cells. These consist of a more or less rigid cellulose cell wall enclosing a protoplast, which is made up of a nucleus and a vacuole surrounded by a viscous material—the cytoplasm. The nucleus contains the chromosomes, which control the heredity in the plant. The cytoplasm contains various kinds of inclusions and organelles important in the functioning of the cell and the plant. These include the plastids—like chloroplasts and leucoplasts—mitochondria, dictyosomes, endoplasmic reticula—with their ribosomes—and other microbodies. Plasmodesmata, which are cytoplasmic strands, connect the protoplasts of adjacent cells through pores in the cell walls.

The cells of the plant are organized into various kinds of tissues. There are the meristematic tissues, composed of cells capable of dividing and redividing, thus enabling the plant to grow in size. Meristematic tissues are located at the root and shoot tips, laterally on stems (buds), and in a cylindrical layer—the cambium—in the stem and roots of woody plants. In addition, a cork cambium layer produces corky bark on the outside of the stems of woody plants. The other tissues in the plant can be classified as simple (composed of only one kind of cell) and complex (composed of two or more kinds of cells). The simple tissues are the epidermis (a protective outer cell layer surrounding the plant body), parenchyma (an ubiquitous kind of cell often functioning in food storage), and sclerenchyma and collenchyma (sturdy cells giving strength and rigidity to the plant). The principal complex tissues are the xylem (a vascular tissue that mainly conducts water and dissolved mineral nutrients from the roots upward throughout the plant), and the phloem (also a vascular tissue conducting food materials, chiefly sugars, manufactured during photosynthesis throughout the plant).

The tissues are organized into various organs that make up the plant body: roots, stems, leaves, buds, flowers, fruits, and seeds. Roots develop either as exten-

sions of the radicle, the lower growing point of a germinating seed, or as adventitious roots, arising from meristematic cells in stems or leaves. Stems of the plant can develop in various ways, depending on the kind of plant, to become either fragile, short-lived herbaceous stems or the strong woody stems of great height and girth of the forest trees. Stems assume many unusual forms. Some are horizontal, trailing along the ground, at or below the surface. Some are greatly compressed into short rounded structures, as in the bulbous plants. Some are even found growing well below ground as in the Irish potato.

The leaves of plants are extremely varied in size and shape. They are all laid down by the terminal meristematic cells on shoot tips. Buds on stems result from the cessation of growth of shoots in which a living group of quiescent meristematic cells remains surrounded by protective coverings—bud scales. These buds subsequently resume growth when conditions are favorable. Some of the vegetative growing points in buds differentiate into other structures to form immature flower parts. These flower buds may also remain quiescent until they resume growth and open into flowers.

Flowers occur in an almost infinite array of sizes and shapes, depending on the kind of plant. They are necessary for sexual reproduction in plants. The male (stamens) and female (pistils) parts are essential, but other parts—sepals and petals—are also found in most kinds of flowers. Some species have the male flowers and the female flowers on separate plants (dioecious), some have separate male and female flowers on the same plant (monoecious), but most kinds of plants have the male and female parts in the same flower (perfect flowers).

Fruits can occur in almost as many varied forms as the flowers, and from fleshy and watery to completely dry. They develop (usually) from a flower which has been pollinated and fertilized, and they result from the developed ovary and (sometimes) associated parts.

Seeds are found in mature fruits, resulting from matured ovules. The seeds are made up of three parts: the embryo (from the fertilized egg), the endosperm (from fertilization of endosperm nuclei), and the seed coats (from the development of the integuments, the outer layers of the ovule). In some kinds of seed (beans) the embryo develops large fleshy cotyledons, which are the food storage organs and the endosperm becomes rudimentary. In other kinds of seeds (cereal grains) the cotyledon is rudimentary with the food storage in the highly developed endosperm.

2–1. There are a number of organelles in the cytoplasm of plant cells. Name four.

2–2. What part of the cell contains the genetic information controlling the plant's growth and development?

2–3. In what organelles in plant cells is photosynthesis carried on?

2–4. What is meant by the term *meristem*?

2–5. Name the location of the five meristematic regions in plants.

2–6. Name two complex tissues in plants and describe their function.

2–7. Name four simple tissues in plants and describe their location.

2–8. How can you distinguish between roots and stems by their external appearance?

2–9. Describe the tissues you would see in a cross-section of the two-year-old stem of a woody perennial plant.

2–10. How would stem cross-sections of a one-year-old woody dicot perennial plant and a one-year-old herbaceous dicot plant differ in appearance?

2–11. How does the appearance of a stem cross-section of a herbaceous monocot plant differ from that of a herbaceous dicot plant?

2–12. Describe the cells and tissues in a section through a leaf from the upper to the lower sides.

2–13. What are the two types of buds in plants and what would you see under a microscope in a longitudinal section through each of them?

2–14. What is the difference between complete and incomplete flowers? Between perfect and imperfect flowers?

2–15. What does the term *monoecious* mean in relation to flowers? *Dioecious?*

2–16. Fruits are matured _____, whereas seeds are matured _____.

2–17. The pit or stone of a peach is actually what tissue?

2–18. The so-called seeds found on the surface of strawberries are actually a type of fruit. What kind are they?

2–19. Seeds have three essential parts. Name them.

2–20. Food storage in seeds occurs in two kinds of structures. What are they?

SUPPLEMENTARY READING

EAMES, A. J., and L. H. MACDANIELS. 1947. *An introduction to plant anatomy*. 2nd ed. New York: McGraw-Hill.

ESAU, K. 1960. *Anatomy of seed plants*. 2nd ed. New York: John Wiley.

——. 1965. *Plant anatomy*. 2nd ed. New York: John Wiley.

FOSTER, A. S., and E. M. GIFFORD, JR. 1974. *Comparative morphology of vascular plants*. 2nd ed. San Francisco: W. H. Freeman & Company Publishers.

FULLER, H. S., and D. D. RITCHIE. 1971. *General botany*. 5th ed. New York: Barnes & Noble.

HARTMANN, H. T., and D. E. KESTER. 1975. *Plant propagation: principles and practices*. 3rd ed. Englewood Cliffs, N.J.: Prentice-Hall.

HAYWARD, H. E. 1948. *The structure of economic plants*. New York: Macmillan.

O'BRIEN, T. P., and M. E. MCCULLY. 1969. *Plant structure and development, a pictorial and physiological approach*. New York: Macmillan.

ROST, T. L., M. G. BARBOUR, R. M. THORNTON, T. E. WEIER, and C. R. STOCKING. 1979. *Botany. A brief introduction to plant biology*. New York: John Wiley.

WEIER, T. E., C. R. STOCKING, and M. G. BARBOUR. 1974. *Botany, an introduction to plant biology*. 5th ed. New York: John Wiley.

WILSON, L., and W. E. LOOMIS. 1967. 4th ed. *Botany*. Holt, Rinehart & Winston.

Naming and Classifying Plants

Since there are over 500,000 different kinds of plants, some method of classifying and naming them had to be developed. The process of developing plant names started over 4000 years ago. It, no doubt, began with simple names that referred to the plant's use, growing habit, or other visible attribute. One example is the milkweed—so named because its sap (latex) is milky in appearance. One difficulty with such names is that often they are used only locally. People in one place know the plant by one name while elsewhere the same plant is known by a different name. The weed *Tribulus terrestris* is known as the "puncture vine" in some areas because the seeds have sharp spines that puncture tires or bare feet; another common name for the same plant in other areas is "goat-head" because the shape of the seed resembles a goat's head. As plant knowledge expanded and the exchange of this knowledge became desirable, it was obvious that a uniform and internationally acceptable system was needed to name and classify plants.

There are many ways to classify plants and any system depends on how the classification is to be used. Some classifications relate directly to specific environmental requirements of the plant for satisfactory growth. For example, such a classification could categorize plants as to their climatic requirements.

CLIMATIC AND RELATED CLASSIFICATIONS

Farmers obviously have to be able to identify and name crops. But this alone is not enough. They also have to distinguish which of the many crops suit their climate.

Most farmers in the United States are working in the temperate zone. For example, some fruit and nut crops grown in the temperate zone are almond, apple, apricot, cherry, peach, pear, pecan, and plum (Ch. 29). Fruit growers in a tropical region would have an entirely different choice of crops, such as cocao, cashew and macadamia nuts, banana, mango, papaya, and pineapple (Ch. 31). The fruits of the subtropical region, which lies between the temperate zone and the tropics, cannot withstand the cold winters of the temperate zone or the heat of the tropics. Some of these subtropical plants are citrus, date, fig, olive, and pomegranate (Ch. 30). Thus, by using climate as a criterion, plants can be classified into distinct groups.

Agronomic crops like grains, forage, fiber, and oil crops and the vegetable and ornamental plants can also be classified by their temperature requirements. For example, some annuals have specific climatic requirements for growth and flowering and are distinguished as winter or summer annuals. Winter annuals are planted in the fall and bloom early the following spring. Summer annuals are planted in the spring and bloom through the summer and fall.

Some crops grow best in certain seasons and are thus classified. For example, warm-season plants such as corn, beans, tomatoes, peppers, watermelons, petunias, marigolds, zinnias, and bermuda grass grow best where monthly temperatures average 18°C to 27°C (65°F to 80°F), while broccoli, cabbage, lettuce, peas, flowering bulbous plants, snapdragons, cyclamen, and bluegrass are cool-season crops growing best at average monthly temperatures of 15°C to 18°C (60°F to 65°F). Plants can be classified by the seasons in which they are most likely to flower and fruit or when the quality of the product can be expected to be at its maximum. Numerous flower and vegetable cultivars can be classified as early, midseason, or late maturing.

Vegetables are classified into groups according to their edible parts. Some are grown for fruits and seeds, such as the tomato, bell pepper, string bean, pea, and corn (Ch. 26). Many are grown for their shoots or leafy parts such as asparagus, celery, spinach, lettuce, and cabbage (Ch. 27). Others are grown for their underground parts (either roots or tubers), such as the carrot, beet, turnip, and potato (Ch. 28).

Ornamentals are sometimes classified by use—that is, as houseplants, greenhouse plants, garden plants, street trees, and various classes of landscape plants. Houseplants, which have become very popular, are often classified according to their foliage, flowers, or growth habits. Common foliage plants, which stay green all year, are the philodendrons, dieffenbachias, and ferns, to name a few. Blooming of some flowering plants may be only seasonal, as in the lily and poinsettia, but the African violet and chrysanthemum are available in flower the year round. Plants outside the home are typically classified by use; for example, such bedding plants as petunias, marigolds, and zinnias, and landscape plants like trees and shrubs.

Fig. 3–2   A grove of coast redwood (*Sequoia sempervirens* D. Don, Endl.) trees along Highway 101 in northern California. The camper truck is dwarfed by these majestic trees.

Fig. 3–1   Jeffrey pine (*Pinus jeffreyi* Grev. and Balf.) tree growing in the Sierra Nevada mountains of northern California near Lake Tahoe. This tree is about 2 m (6.5 ft) in diameter at breast height (DBH), the point where lumber trees are measured. *Source:* Robert A. H. Legro.

The forester classifies trees into two broad groups: the hardwoods and softwoods. Some hardwood types are oaks *(Quercus),* maples *(Acer),* birch *(Betula),* and beech *(Fagus).* Some softwood trees are pines *(Pinus)* (Fig. 3–1), firs *(Abies),* redwood *(Sequoia)* (Fig. 3–2), cedars *(Cedrus),* and spruce *(Picea).* Trees are also classified according to the hardiness zones in which they can survive (see Fig. 10–4). Some are able to withstand very low temperatures during the winter, whereas others are subject to frost damage and therefore must be grown in a subtropical climate (Ch. 15).

COMMON AND BOTANICAL NAMES

Most plants are generally known by their common names because common names are often easier to remember, pronounce, and use. Maple or elm trees growing along the streets are referred to by common names in everyday conversation. Common names often evolve because of certain plant characteristics. *How Plants Get Their*

Names (1) gives many interesting examples of plant names.

A common name has value in conversation only if both persons know exactly what plant is being discussed. This is most likely when persons are from the same community and the common name of the plant cannot be mistaken for another. But take the case of the jasmine, a plant known all over the world and prized for fragrance, flavoring (tea), and landscaping. Many common plant names contain the word *jasmine,* but such plants do not resemble one another and may not even be closely related botanically. Some of the so-called jasmines are listed below, with the botanical (italicized) name following the common name, according to *Hortus Third (3).*

Star jasmine *(Jasminum gracillimum)*

Star jasmine *(Jasminum multiflorum)*

Star jasmine *(Jasminum nitidum)*

Star jasmine *(Trachelospermum jasminoides)*

Angel wing or windmill jasmine *(Jasminum nitidum)*

Blue jasmine *(Clematis crispa)*

Cape jasmine *(Gardenia jasminoides)*

Chilean jasmine *(Mandevilla laxa)*

Cinnamon jasmine *(Hedychium coronarium)*

Crape jasmine *(Tabernaemontana divaricata)*

Japanese or primrose jasmine *(Jasminum mesnyi)*

Night jasmine *(Cestrum nocturnum)*

Night jasmine *(Nyctanthes arbor-tristis)*

Paraguay jasmine *(Brunfelsia australis)*

These are only some of the 27 plants listed in *Hortus Third* under the common name of jasmine. Four "star jasmines" are listed but all have different botanical names. There are also two kinds of night jasmine, depending on locality: *Cestrum nocturnum* from the West Indies and *Nyctanthes arbor-tristis* from southeast Asia.

It is obvious from these examples that common names have their limitations for universal written or verbal communication. There are too many and they are too variable to serve most scientific purposes.

DEVELOPMENT OF BOTANICAL CLASSIFICATIONS

Theophrastus (370–285 B.C.), a student of Aristotle, classified plants by their texture or form. He also classified many as herbs, shrubs, and trees. He noted the annual, biennial, and perennial growth habits of certain plants, and described differences in flower parts that enabled him to group plants for purposes of discussion. He is known as the Father of Botany for these significant contributions *(8).* Many botanists between the fourteenth and eighteenth centuries prepared plant classifications.

Carl von Linné (1707–1778), better known as Carolus Linnaeus, devised another system of categorizing plants, which was published in the second edition of *Hortus uplandicus* in 1732. An enlarged study describing 935 genera, *Genera plantarum* (1737), led to the modern taxonomy or classification of plants. Linnaeus was knighted in 1753 in recognition of his early work *(9).* While his classification based on the sexual parts of the flower is not used today, his nomenclature remains the conventional system.

Kingdom

In today's system of classification all living things are divided into groupings called taxa, of which there are eight. The first, called the kingdom, divides all living things into two major groupings: the animal kingdom or the plant kingdom. Because of disagreement among botanists, some now list two, three, or even four kingdoms—each scientist having some justification for doing so. Upon casual examination, it appears simple to distinguish living organisms as either plants or animals, but upon close examination of the one-celled plants and animals (*Chlamydomonas*—a green algae—*Euglena, Amoeba,* and *Paramecium*), the distinction becomes difficult and debatable. If one considers all plants and animals from the microscopic to the mammoth, one finds that only a few characteristics can be used to distinguish plants from animals—and that there are exceptions. First, most animals are mobile, while most plants are stationary. However, there are exceptions even to this: ocean sponges are stationary animals, while many bacteria (considered by most to be plants) are mobile in water. Second, most plants have the green pigment chlorophyll and hence the remarkable ability to use light to synthesize complex sugars and starch molecules from simple inorganic substances. In contrast, animals rely on ready-made food, feeding on plants or other animals, which, in turn, have fed on plants. Here too are exceptions; some plants are not green and contain no chlorophyll. Certain bacteria and fungi are examples, as is the parasitic weed, dodder *(Cuscuta)* (see Fig. 11–11). Third, the cell walls of plants are rigid and usually made of cellulose. On the other hand, animals lack rigid cell walls and have flaccid cell membranes. Fourth, cellulose is not synthesized by any animal and hence is distinctive of plants. A fifth feature, but one with many exceptions, is the manner of growth. Many plants have unlimited growth and an indefinite number of parts, whereas the growth of animals is limited. Fairly accurate limits can be set on the size of a mouse or an elephant, but many kinds of trees grow to various heights. Also, an animal has a definite number of parts; that is, arms, legs, eyes, and so forth. The number of leaves, stems, buds, flowers of the same kind of plant usually varies from individual to individual.

Division

In 1883 A. W. Eichler divided the plant kingdom into four divisions or phyla, according to their structural characteristics:[1]

1. Thallophyta—these include the algae, bacteria, and fungi. Some taxonomists put the fungi in a separate division. The most familiar plants in this community are the mushrooms and bread molds. The thallophytes are not differentiated into stems and leaves and essentially have no protective coverings for the reproductive cells.

2. Bryophyta—the small green plants without true roots or flowers. The name comes from the Greek word *bryon,* which means moss, and this division includes the mosses, liverworts, and hornworts. These are widely distributed over the earth, particularly in wet places, but none are cultivated for human use.

3. Pteridophyta—green plants with vascular tissue, true roots, and usually distinct leaves and stems. They do not have true flowers and, therefore, produce no seeds. They reproduce themselves by spores found on the underside of leaves. This group includes the psilophytes, club mosses, horsetails, and ferns. They are cultivated mainly as ornamentals.

4. Spermatophyta—seed-producing plants that bear true flowers. Practically all of the economically important plants used for food, feed, fiber, shelter, or recreation belong to this group.

Some taxonomists have expanded the four basic divisions to as many as 28. Taxonomy, or the study of plant classification, is dynamic and changes often as new knowledge becomes available. These classifications can be studied in detail in various botany textbooks *(4, 12, 13)* or plant taxonomy books.

Each division can be further separated into classes. For example, the Spermatophyta division can be divided into the classes gymnosperms and angiosperms. Classes can be divided further into subclasses that include, for example, in the angiosperm class—the monocotyledonous and dicotyledonous plants (Ch. 2). From this point, plants are grouped into **orders** and then into **families, genera,** and finally into **species.** The species is, in general, the working unit for the botanist, agronomist, and horticulturist. A species can be defined as a group of individual plants usually interbreeding freely and having many characteristics in common.

PLANT IDENTIFICATION AND NOMENCLATURE

The family is usually the highest taxon[2] commonly included in plant identification or study. Students of plant science are usually required to learn the family, genus, and species of some plants as well as their common names.

Since the early Christian era, naturalists wrote their books in Latin, which was the language of all educated people in Europe. Thus Linnaeus used names of Latin form. Most of the names he gave, which describe morphological characteristics of the plants, came from Latin words but some were derived from Greek and Arabic.

The names are usually phonetic and often give a clue to the plant's characteristics, its native habit, or for whom it is named. Such derivatives are numerous; many are cited by Bailey *(1, 2, 3).* Names that refer to leaves include *folius, phyllon,* or *phylla,* usually as suffixes. The names can also have prefixes, such as *macro* or *micro.* Thus words are created, such as *macrophylla* (large leaf), *microfolius* or *microphylla* (small leaf), *illicifolius* (holly leaf), and *salicifolius* (willow leaf). The Latin for flower is *flora;* add the prefix *grand* and it becomes *grandiflora* (large flower), as in *Magnolia grandiflora* L., the southern magnolia (Fig. 3–3). Shapes or growing habits of plants can be described with *altus* or *alta* (tall), *arboreus* (treelike), *compactus* (dense), *nanus* or *pumilus* (dwarf), *repens* or *reptans* (creeping), and *scandens* (climbing). Names based on flower or foliage color include *albus,* or *leuco* (white), *argentus* (silver), *aureus* or *chryso* (gold), *rubra, rubens,* or *coccineus* (red), and *croceus, flavus,* or *luteus* (yellow). Species names sometimes reflect the plant's place of origin. Examples are *australis* (southern), *borealis* (northern), *canadensis* (from Canada), *chinensis* or *sinensis* (from

---

[1]This is one of the older plant classifications, but it is still useful because of its simplicity and adaptibility to the needs of practical plant science.

[2]A group of plants with similar characteristics of any rank (plural: taxa).

Fig. 3–3 The southern magnolia (*Magnolia grandiflora* L.). The name *grandiflora* is more than justified; the flower measures 15 cm (6 in) across.

China), *chilensis* or *chileonsis* (from Chile), *japonica*, *nipponica*, or *nipponicus* (from Japan), *campestris* (field), *insularis* (island), and *montanus* (mountain).

Each plant has a two-word, or binomial, name[3] given in Latin. The first name refers to the plant's genus, the second to its species. The Latin binomial name is international and understood universally if a standard reference such as *Hortus Third (3)* or other accepted reference *(8, 10, 11, 14)* is used. Sometimes Linnaeus took names, like *Narcissus,* from classical mythology, or devised names to honor other scientists, like *Rudbeckia,* adapted from Linnaeus' botany professor Rudbeck.

Complete Linnaean names have a third element—the authority, or the abbreviated name of the scientist who named the species. Consider the name for the common white (Irish) potato, *Solanum tuberosum* L. The "L." means Linnaeus, and his initial appears commonly because Linnaeus named so many species. Books and journals often omit the authority for brevity and simplicity, but it is important in situations where different botanists have used different binomials for the same plant. In such cases, the botanical or scientific name that was published first takes precedence.

Wild or naturally occurring plants are named under the rules of the *International Code of Botanical Nomenclature (7)*. Cultivated plants are named according to the

same principles but are covered by the *International Code of Nomenclature of Cultivated Plants (5)*. Some of the basic rules of nomenclature follow.

The generic name always begins with a capital letter; it is underlined when written by hand or typewriter and italicized in print. Thus, the genus name for potato is *Solanum.* The specific epithet *tuberosum* is likewise underlined or italicized. The specific epithet usually begins with a lower case letter except it *may be* capitalized if it is a person's name or the vernacular name of a region, but it is always correct if written entirely in lower case. Therefore, many of the older species names are frequently capitalized (e.g., *Pinus Jeffreyi* Grev. and Balf. or *Pinus jeffreyi* Grev. and Balf.).

To complete the binomial name, the authority for describing and naming the plant is given after the genus and species; thus, *Solanum tuberosum* L. In this text, unless otherwise specified, both the binomials and the authorships agree with those given in *Hortus Third (3)*, which is a recent and widely recognized compilation of the cultivated plants for the United States and Canada. These authority names are often abbreviated. Each taxonomy book has a list of the full names of these authorities.

When several plants in the same genus are listed, the genus name is given in full for the first plant, then shortened to the first initial (which is always capitalized) for the other plants in the list. As an example, the apricot, the European plum, and the peach are all members of the genus *Prunus.* Listed as scientific binomials, they would be *Prunus armeniaca, P. domestica,* and *P. persica,* respectively. This procedure should not be used if there is any chance of confusion with another genus with the same first initial.

Occasionally the plant genus is known but the exact species is not known because it is difficult or impossible to identify. In such a case, the genus name is given and followed by the lower-case letters "sp." for species (singular) and "spp." for species (plural). The singular and plural spelling of *species* is the same. An example is *Prunus* spp. The "spp." usually refers to all of the many species in the genus. However, the "sp." refers to a definite plant whose specific epithet is not known. The "sp." or "spp." is never underlined or italicized.

Botanical Variety

Sometimes the botanical binomial name is not sufficient to identify a distinct **botanical variety** that occurs in the wild. A plant group can be so different from the general species described originally that it warrants a botanical

---

[3]The binomial is a binary combination of the name of the genus followed by a single specific epithet. If an epithet consists of two or more words, these are to be united or hyphenated [Article 23, *International Code of Nomenclature of Cultivated Plants (5)*]. Although the second word of the binomial is technically the "specific epithet," many persons refer to that second name as the "species." This shorter and therefore more convenient form is the one used in this text.

variety classification below that of species. An example of this is *Buxus microphylla* Sieb. and Zucc. var. *japonica* Rehd. and Wils., which is native to Japan. The "var." stands for *varietas*, Latin for "variety." Another botanical variety originated in Korea; it is *Buxus microphylla* var. *koreana* Nakai. These botanical varieties are sufficiently different to warrant unique names and authorities to distinguish them from one another. In this case the name of the variety *japonica* or *koreana* is underlined or italicized. When a varietas epithet is formed from a surname, it may or may not be capitalized depending on the personal preference of the author. However, the trend is to not capitalize them, as recommended by the International Code *(5, 7)*.

Cultivar

Many kinds of plants that are valuable in agriculture must be able to be propagated with little or no genetic change in the offspring. These cultivated varieties are different than botanical varieties and are called **cultivars**, a contraction of *culti*vated *vari*ety. There are two main categories of cultivars—the clones and the lines. If propagated by vegetative methods they are called *clones;* if by seeds (under certain specified conditions) they are called *lines*. The word *cultivar* is abbreviated "cv." and the plural is "cvs." A cultivar is often a distinct variant selected by someone who believed it was uniquely different from any plant already in cultivation. The flower color may have changed from red to white because of a mutation, as in some carnations. Perhaps a plant has fewer spines or thorns than does the ordinary species; an example is a Chinese holly (*Ilex cornuta* Lindl. and Paxt.) found to have few or no spines. It was named *Ilex cornuta* cv. Burfordii. The cultivar name is always capitalized but never underlined or italicized. The term "cv." after *cornuta* may be dropped in favor of single quotes around the cultivar name. Either way of expressing the cultivar name is acceptable, and both can be used in the same article. Either single quotes or the term "cv." are used, but never both. Tables or lists usually use "cultivar" or "cv." in the heading to avoid single quotes around each cultivar name.

Many annual flowers, vegetables, grains, and forage crops are cultivars that are propagated by seed. Others are F_1 hybrids, uniform and nonuniform assemblages (described in Ch. 4). An example is *Petunia* × *hybrida* Hort. Vilm.-Andr.—the hybrid garden petunia. A breeder may develop a new strain that is believed to warrant a cultivar name such as 'Fire Chief' or 'Pink Cascade'. The parent plants can be maintained and crossed to produce the same F_1 hybrid cultivar year after year (p. 76). Many vegetables and flowering annuals are maintained as cultivars in this manner, with the parents maintained to produce new crops of seed each year for planting. Cultivars of fruit trees, grapes, and woody ornamentals are usually maintained as true to type clones by vegetative propagation methods (Ch. 5).

Categories of Cultivars *(5, 6)*

Cultivars can be differentiated into those that are sexually reproduced and those that are asexually reproduced. Within these two groups, cultivars differ by origin, genetic nature, or conditions of reproduction, depending upon the category.

ASEXUALLY REPRODUCED CULTIVARS

Clones

(a) A **clone** is a group of plants originating from a single individual and reproduced by vegetative means, such as by cuttings, layers, or grafts (see Ch. 5). Examples of clones are 'Elberta' peach, 'King Alfred' daffodil, and 'Bliss Triumph' potato.

(b) **Apomictic cultivars** (or **apomicts**) are biologically unique kinds of plants that reproduce by seed but are asexual because of complete or partial apomixis (see p. 92).

SEXUALLY REPRODUCED CULTIVARS

These are propagated by seed. Specific production programs geared to the genetic characteristics of individual cultivars may be necessary to maintain their genetic identity. Chapter 5 describes such programs.

Lines

(a) A **line** is a group of self-fertilizing plants that maintains its genetic identity from generation to generation naturally. Examples are 'Rosy Morn' petunia, 'Marglobe' tomato, and 'Marquis' wheat.

(b) An **inbred line** is a group of naturally cross-fertilizing plants maintained as self-fertilizing lines through artificial restraints on cross-pollination. These are generally used to produce hybrid cultivars.

Uniform assemblages Hybrid line cultivars are groups of plants grown from seed produced by cross-pollinating two or more parental breeding stocks maintained either as inbred lines or as clones. Examples of hybrid cultivars are 'Granex' onion, derived from crossing two onion inbred lines, and 'U.S. 13' corn, produced by consecutive crossing of four inbred lines.

Nonuniform assemblages (a) A cultivar may consist of a seedling mixture of cross-fertilized individuals that, as a group, may be more or less variable genetically but that possess one or more common phenotypic characteristics. For example, *Phlox drummondi* 'Sternenzauber' is a mixture of different color forms, but all have the same star-shaped corolla.

(b) A **synthetic cultivar** is a special category of seedling mixture that combines separately developed seedling lines. An example is 'Ranger' alfalfa, a cultivar derived from intercrossing among five seed-propagated lines previously developed and maintained in isolation.

Group

The group category is used for some vegetables and some ornamentals such as lilies, orchids, roses, and tulips. It is a category below the species and not used as frequently as the cultivar category. A group includes more than one cultivar of a particular kind of plant. For example, when there are evident differences among plants of the same species, they can be further categorized by a group name. When a species has many cultivars, cultivars that are similar are categorized into groups. For example, cultivars of *Brassica oleraceae* can be grouped into the Acephala Group, the Alboglabra Group, the Botrytis Group, or the Capitata Group, depending upon their morphological characteristics. These groups have the same botanical name—*Brassica oleracea*. The name of the group is written within parenthesis between the species name and the cultivar name, as *Brassica oleraceae* (Capitata) 'King Cole', and the group name is always capitalized.

Hybrid

Some plants hybridize naturally and some plants can be hybridized intentionally (see p. 76). In either case the resulting plants do not resemble the original species, and a botanist could have difficulty identifying the new plant or progeny. There could be slight or major variations within a population of these plants. An example of this is *Abelia grandiflora* Andre. Flower color, leaf and flower size, and growth habit of plants in this species vary considerably, and it is difficult to tell whether a particular plant is truly *Abelia grandiflora* Andre as originally described. The famous horticultural taxonomist Alfred Rehder at Harvard University's Arnold Arboretum studied a diverse population of this species, and claimed the plant was a hybrid or cross and therefore should really be classified *Abelia × grandiflora* (Andre) Rehd. This nomenclature tells other horticulturists or botanists that this species is truly variable and does not warrant the species name given to it earlier. The multiplication sign × between the genus and species denotes that this plant is a hybrid or hybridizes quite freely and therefore is variable, or that it is a progeny of an intentional cross. When two species cross (hybridize), the result is called an **interspecific cross.** (A species within the plant population must be stable in certain characteristics to be given a species-level name.) In this example, the new authority appearing at the end of the binomial is now Redh., but the original authority is placed in parentheses to identify the person who originally described the plant as a species as *Abelia grandiflora* Andre.

An × appearing before the genus name means that the plant results from crossing plants in two genera—an intergeneric cross. An example is × *Cupressocyparis leylandii (Chamaecyparis nootkatensis × Cupressus macrocarpa),* a fast-growing evergreen tree.

The family is a group of closely related genera. The relationship can be based on certain plant structures or on chemical characteristics, such as the presence of latex in the milkweed family ASCELPIADACEAE, but flower structure is the usual basis for association. The nightshade family SOLANACEAE contains not only *Solanum* (potato) but also *Lycopersicon* (tomato), *Capsicum* (pepper), *Nicotiana* (tobacco), *Datura* (deadly nightshade), *Petunia,* and many others. This is a large family (about 90 genera and more than 2000 species), most of which are native to the tropics. All species in this family have similar flower structures; the similarities between a tobacco, a tomato, and a potato flower, for instance, are readily seen. Figure 3–4 shows the similarity between potato and tomato flowers.

Fig. 3–4   Side and front views of potato (upper) and tomato (lower) flowers. These views show the similarities of the flowers of plants in the same family, SOLANACEAE. *Source:* Moira Tanaka.

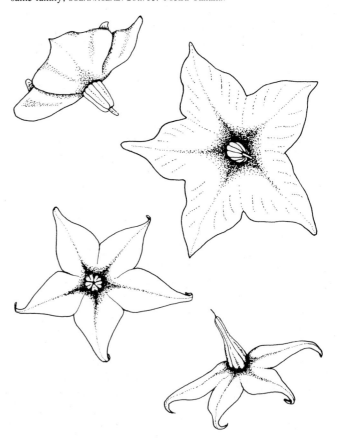

The first letter of family names is always capitalized and the names are sometimes underlined or italicized. The family names are usually written entirely in capital (upper-case) letters, the method used in this text. Most families names end with -*aceae* (pronounced ace-ay-ee) attached to a genus name; for example. SOLANACEAE, ROSACEAE, AMARYLLIDACEAE, LILIACEAE, and MAGNOLIACEAE. Eight families, however, do not follow this standard rule. For the sake of uniformity, new names have been proposed for these families. Either name may be used. The new names appear in parentheses following the old names.

COMPOSITAE (ASTERACEAE)

CRUCIFERAE (BRASSICACEAE)

GRAMINEAE (POACEAE)

GUTTIFERAE (CLUSIACEAE)

LABIATAE (LAMIACEAE)

LEGUMINOSAE (FABACEAE)

PALMAE (ARECACEAE)

UMBELLIFERAE (APIACEAE)

PLANT IDENTIFICATION KEY

Starting on p. 51 is a simplified key used to identify some commonly known seed-bearing plants (Spermatophyta).

To use a key one needs to know the vocabulary of plant structure (see Ch. 2). Examine the plant in question to decide if its characteristics fit in one category or the other offered by the key. Keying plants is a process of elimination by making yes or no decisions to characteristics offered in the key—rejecting those that do not apply (dichotomy). Keys must be complete to assure accuracy, so that there is no question about whether one should pursue one branch of the dichotomous key or its alternative.

To use this simplified key, consider like pairs of numbers and make a choice based on examining plant parts. Eliminate the alternative that does not pertain to the plant in question, and then proceed to the next pair of numbers directly under the proper choice. As an example, the first choice in this key is to determine whether the seeds of the plant being identified are borne naked, as in the cone-bearing plants of the gymnosperms (Fig. 3–5), or enclosed in an ovary, as in the angiosperms. Once this yes or no decision has been made, the next step is to compare the next pair of descriptions directly under the previously chosen characteristic. If the seeds are enclosed within an ovary, the plant in question is an angiosperm and the next pair of numbers to compare is 8.

Fig. 3–5 Cones of the sugar pine (*Pinus lambertiana* Dougl.) in closed and open conditions. When the cones dry, the winged seeds, shown on the 17.8 cm (7 in) ruler, are released and can be disseminated by the wind.

Note that the two 8's are separated by several pairs of subsidiary descriptions. A choice between the two 8's must be made before proceeding further. If the plant in question has parallel-veined leaves and the seeds have one cotyledon, the plant belongs to the monocotyledon subclass. This procedure is followed until the plant to be identified "fits" a given set of plant characteristics. Table 3–1 traces the identity of a wild strawberry species by means of a key.

Table 3–1 The Use of a Simplified Key to Trace the Identity of an Unknown Plant

	Observation	Classification
Kingdom	The living organism is obviously a plant. It has all the attributes of a plant with none of those of the animal kingdom.	Plant
Division	The plant bears distinct flowers and seeds.	Spermatophyta
Class	Seeds are borne in an ovary.	Angiospermae
Subclass	Leaves are net-veined. Seeds have two cotyledons.	Dicotyledonae
Order	Flower petals separate, corolla present.	Rosales
Family	Habit terrestrial, stamens numerous, pistils more than one. Leaves alternate. Sepals and petals usually four or five.	ROSACEAE
Genus	Ovaries superior. Herbaceous, stemless plants producing runners.	*Fragaria*
Species	Leaves thick, bluish-white on the underside. Achenes sunken in pits on receptacle.	*chiloensis* (wild strawberry native to west coast of N. and S. America)

A slight variation of this key appears on p. 460 (Ch. 21) for the identification of turfgrasses; the number at the end of the phrase in that case indicates the next number to pursue.

Certain plant parts might not be available—perhaps because they are not in season—when needed to identify the plant. An example of this occurs in the simplified key. In the family ROSACEAE (the second item), both flowers and fruit are needed to be certain of making the correct choice. In the case of strawberries, both fresh flowers and fruits can be obtained at the same time; however, it is not possible to have flowers and fruits at the same time for the apricot or the pear (Fig. 3–6). In such cases it might be necessary to preserve flowers for future examination or simply describe them thoroughly in the spring when they are abundant, and then wait for the fruit to develop in order to accurately determine its characteristics.

This simple key illustrates how choices are made between two characteristics—eliminating alternatives that are not pertinent in order to finally identify the plant in question. Much of the upper portion of the key can be ignored by a trained taxonomist or a good botany student because to them it is easy to identify a gymnosperm or an angiosperm. The family characteristics are determined by observing and studying certain flower characteristics. Sometimes it is difficult but necessary to distinguish between an inferior or superior ovary (the characteristic that divides the LILIACEAE from the AMARYLLIDACEAE

Fig. 3–6   An inflorescence of the pear (*Pyrus communis* L.) showing the five petals and the many stamens typical of the ROSACEAE. Mature fruits do not develop for another four months.

families; see Fig. 2–31), but one finds these determinations easier after some experience is gained. Once the family is known, the correct genus and species is identified by referring to taxonomic books with detailed keys *(2, 8, 11, 14)*.

Obviously one must be familiar with plant parts and structures (Ch. 2) to use a botanical key and determine the identity of the plant. Figures 2–30, 2–31, and 2–32 illustrate some plant parts and their shapes that are useful in plant identification.

Fig. 3–7   The inflorescence of a cycad (*Dioon edule* Lindl.) native to Mexico. The inflorescence is about 23 cm (9 in) tall. The pinnate leaves might lead one to erroneously call this plant a palm.

Fig. 3–8   The fruits of *Taxas baccata* L. 'Lutea'. The single seed (arrow) is within the cup-like fruit, which is poisonous. *Source:* Robert A. H. Legro.

A Simplified Key for Identifying Some Seed-Bearing Plants (Spermatophyta)

1. Ovules and seeds borne naked on scales in cones without typical flowers (Fig. 3–5); trees or shrubs, often evergreen. Gymnospermae
    2. Plant foliage palmlike. CYCADACEAE (Fig. 3–7)
    2. Plant foliage not palmlike
        3. One seed in a cup-shaped, drupelike fruit. TAXACEAE (Fig. 3–8)
        3. Many seeds in a dry woody cone
            4. Leaves alternate and single
            4. Leaves alternate and in clusters; needle-shaped
                5. Cone-scale without bracts with two to nine seeds
                5. Cone-scales in axils of bracts, flattened, with two seeds. PINACEAE
                    6. Cones upright on top of branchlets. *Abies*
                    6. Cones not upright on branchlets. *Pinus*
                        7. Twigs not grooved. White pines or soft pines
                        7. Twigs grooved. Pitch or hard pines
1. Plants with seeds borne in an ovary (base of pistil) with typical flowers (Fig. 2–31). Herbs, trees, and shrubs. Angiospermae
    8. Leaves usually parallel veined, flower parts usually in multiples of three. One seed-leaf or cotyledon. Do not form annual rings when increasing in stem girth. Monocotyledonae (Fig. 2–25)
        9. Plant with palmlike leaves. PALMAE
            10. Leaves fanlike (Fig. 2–30)
            10. Leaves featherlike. Feather and fishtail palms
                11. Lower feathery leaves not spinelike
                11. Lower feathery leaves spinelike, fruit fleshy with long grooved seed. *Phoenix* spp.
                    12. Plant is a tree with shoots at base, trunk about 50 cm (20 in) in diameter. Fruit edible. *Phoenix dactylifera,* date palm
                    12. Plants not as above. Other *Phoenix* spp.
        9. Plants without palmlike leaves
            13. Perianth none or rudimentary
                14. Stems solid, CYPERACEAE
                14. Stems mostly hollow. GRAMINEAE (Fig. 21–2)
                    15. Plants woody, bamboolike. Bamboos
                    15. Plants herbaceous, not bamboolike
                        16. Grasses that produce sugar. *Saccharum* spp.
                        16. Grasses that produce little sugar
                            17. Small grains and their kin (rice, wheat, etc.)
                            17. Cornlike plants and their kin
                                18. Plants monoecious. *Zea mays,* corn
                                18. Plants not monoecious. *Sorghum* spp.
            13. Perianth present
                19. Pistils several, not united. APONOGETONACEAE
                19. Pistils one, carples united, ovary and fruit superior. AMARYLLIDACEAE
                    20. Anthers six, stem a fibrous rhizome. *Agapanthus* spp.
                    20. Anthers six, stem a corm or bulb (Fig. 20–1). *Allium* spp.
                        21. Leaves large, usually hollow and cylindrical. Bulb rounded and large. *Allium cepa,* onion (Fig. 28–3)
                        21. Leaves large, usually hollow and cylindrical. Bulb slightly thicker than neck. *Allium fistulosum*
    8. Leaves usually without parallel venation, two cotyledons. Herbs, trees, and shrubs with stems increasing in thickness with cambium cells, which form annual rings in woody plants. Dicotyledonae (Fig. 2–9)
        22. Corolla absent or not apparent, calyx present or lacking
        22. Corolla present, calyx usually forming two series of calyxlike bracts
            23. Petals united
            23. Petals separate
                24. Ovary inferior or partly so
                24. Ovary superior
                    25. Stamens few, not more than twice as many as petals
                    25. Stamens numerous, more than twice as many as petals
                        26. Habit aquatic. NYMPHAEACEAE, water lilies (Fig. 3–9)
                        26. Habit terrestrial
                            27. Pistils more than one, filaments of stamens united into a tube. MALVACEAE
                                28. Style—branches slender, spreading at maturity, seeds kidney-shaped. *Hibiscus* spp.
                                28. Styles united, ovary several carpels, calyx deciduous, seed angular. *Gossypium* spp.
                                    29. Staminal column long, anthers compactly arranged on short filaments. *G. barbadense,* sea-island
                                    29. Staminal column short, anthers loosely arranged and of varying lengths. *G. hirsutum,* upland cotton (Fig. 3–10)

27. Pistil more than one, filaments not united into a tube. ROSACEAE
    30. Ovaries superior (Fig. 2–31), fruit not a pome
        31. Pistils one, leaves simple and entire. *Prunus* spp.
            32. Fruit soft and pulpy. *P. armeniaca,* apricot
            32. Fruit dry and hard. *P. Mume,* Japanese apricot
        31. Pistils two to many, leaves compound (at least basal leaves)
            33. Plants woody shrubs. *Rosa* spp.
                34. Styles not extended beyond mouth of hip. Stamens about one-half as long as styles. *R. odorata.*
                34. Styles extend beyond mouth of hip, stamens about as long as styles. *R. multiflora*
            33. Plants herbaceous. *Fragaria* spp.
                35. Underside of leaves are bluish white. *F. chiloensis,* wild strawberry (Fig. 3–11)
                35. Underside of leaves are green. Other *Fragaria* spp.
    30. Ovaries inferior (Fig. 2–31), fruit a pome
        36. Fruit with stone cells. *Pyrus* spp., pears
        36. Fruit without stone cells. *Malus* spp., apples

Fig. 3–9 Water lilies (*Victoria amazonica* Sowerby) at the Botanical Gardens, Tervuren, Belgium. These lily pads are about 1 m (3 ft) in diameter. *Source:* Robert A. H. Legro.

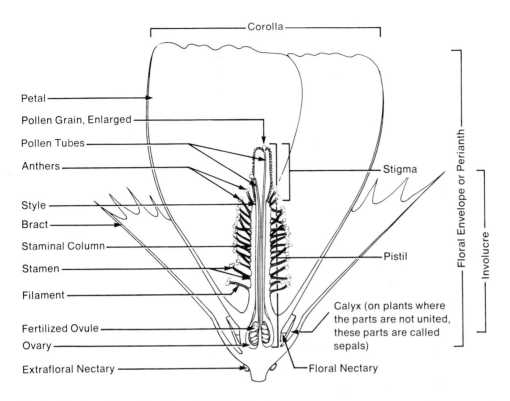

Fig. 3–10 Cotton (*Gossypium hirsutum* L.) flower in a longitudinal section. *Source:* USDA.

Fig. 3–11 A strawberry flower in a longitudinal section. Also shown is an individual achene. *Source:* USDA.

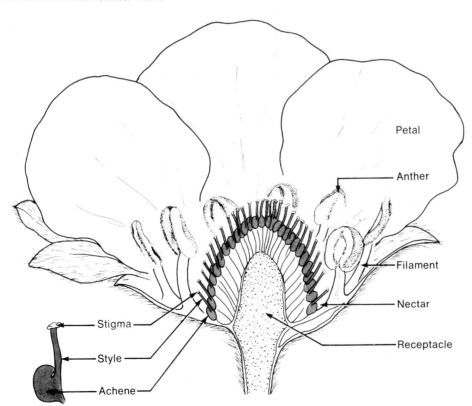

SUMMARY

There are many ways to name and classify plants and the way they are classified generally depends upon the classification's use. For example, a farmer may classify plants according to the climatic zones in which each plant grows best while a landscape architect would arrange various plants according to their respective flower or leaf color, plant size, or plant shape. One can find plant classifications based on the plant's edible portion, the plant's use, the plant's life habits, and many other ways.

The most useful and most widely accepted classification is the botanical or scientific classification. Carolus Linnaeus is often called the father of taxonomic botany and zoology because he proposed the binomial system of nomenclature. Latin was the chosen language because of its unchanging nature with time and usage. The botanical groupings that have been developed are the kingdom, phyla (divisions), classes, subclasses, orders, families, genera, species, and sometimes botanical varieties or cultivated varieties (cultivars). People working with or studying plants are usually concerned with the taxa of family, genus, and species. Families are botanical groupings in which the plants have been classified on similar flower and other morphological and chemical characteristics. The family names are capitalized and for the most part their names end in the letters -ACEAE (e.g., ROSACEAE or SOLANACEAE). Genera are groups of species with similar morphological characteristics and are more closely related to each other. The names are capitalized and are italicized. The species is the next lower group and contains plant populations with still more specific morphological characteristics. The species names (specific epithets) are generally not capitalized but are italicized. Together the genus and species are known as the botanical binomial. The complete name should include the identity of the authority who first described and named the plant. Thus, the complete and proper botanical name for the common white (Irish) potato is *Solanum tuberosum* L. The letter L. is the accepted abbreviation for the authority who first described the plant.

Today the *International Code of Botanical Nomenclature* outlines the rules for naming wild plants and the *International Code of Cultivated Plants* outlines the rules for categorizing cultivated varieties (cultivars).

REVIEW QUESTIONS

3–1. List some useful ways plants are commonly classified.

3–2. A botanist who identifies and classifies plant species is working in the field of (a) anatomy, (b) ecology, (c) morphology, (d) physiology, (e) taxonomy.

3–3. Why is Latin the language for naming plants?

3–4. Define the word *taxon* and list eight taxa in order. Start with the most general and end with the most specific.

3–5. Every described plant has been given a name, consisting of two words. This name is called the plant's binomial classification. In the name for corn, *Zea mays,* to which taxon does each word belong?

3–6. Plants with parallel leaf veins are in the subclass _____.

3–7. Each plant family consists of many _____ and each _____ consists of many species.

3–8. The two subclasses of gymnospermae are monocots and dicots. True or false?

3–9. From what words is the word *cultivar* derived?

3–10. Explain the difference between a cultivar and a botanical variety.

3–11. What does a multiplication sign between the genus and the species signify?

3–12. Most plant family names end with a special suffix. What is that suffix?

3–13. Which of the following names are divisions of the plant kingdom? (a) Angiospermae, (b) Bryophyta, (c) Gymnospermae, (d) *Allium*

3–14. Angiosperms are plants that produce seeds borne in an ovary, have true flowers, and produce either parallel- or net-veined leaves. True or false?

3–15. List six ways plants differ from animals.

3–16. Cereal grains are grasses; thus they belong to the subclass _____ and the family _____.

3–17. Indicate whether each of the following plants is a monocot or dicot: corn, beans, wheat, onions, pine, peas, asparagus, peach, lettuce, rice, apple.

REFERENCES

1. Bailey, L. H. 1963. *How plants get their names.* New York: Dover.

2. ——. 1974. *Manual of cultivated plants.* 14th ed. New York: Macmillan.

3. ———, E. Z. Bailey, and staff of L. H. Bailey Hortorium. 1976. *Hortus third.* New York: Macmillan.

4. Bold, H. C. 1977. *The plant kingdom.* 4th ed. Englewood Cliffs, N.J.: Prentice-Hall.

5. Gilmour, J. S. L., ed. 1969. *International code of nomenclature of cultivated plants.* Utrecht, Netherlands: International Bureau of Plant Taxonomy and Nomenclature of the International Association for Plant Taxonomy.

6. Hartmann, H. T., and D. E. Kester. 1975. *Plant propagation: principles and practices.* 3rd ed. Englewood Cliffs, N.J.: Prentice-Hall.

7. Lanjouw, J., ed. 1966. *International code of botanical nomenclature.* Utrecht, Netherlands: International Bureau for Plant Taxonomy and Nomenclature of the International Association for Plant Taxonomy.

8. Lawrence, G. H. M. 1951. *Taxonomy of vascular plants.* New York: Macmillan.

9. Lawrence, G. H. M. 1955. *An introduction to plant taxonomy.* New York: Macmillan.

10. McClintock, E., and A. T. Leiser. 1979. An annotated checklist of woody ornamental plants. Univ. of Calif. Div. Agr. Sci. Publ. 4091.

11. Rehder, A. 1954. *Manual of cultivated trees and shrubs hardy in North America.* New York: Macmillan.

12. Rost, T. L., M. G. Barbour, R. M. Thornton, T. E. Weier, and C. R. Stocking. 1979. *Botany, a brief introduction to plant biology.* New York: John Wiley.

13. Weier, T. E., C. R. Stocking, and M. G. Barbour. 1974. *Botany: an introduction to plant biology.* 5th ed. New York: John Wiley.

14. Willis, J. C. 1966. *A dictionary of flowering plants and ferns.* 7th ed. London: Cambridge University Press.

Origin, Domestication, and Improvement of Cultivated Plants

ORIGIN OF CULTIVATED PLANTS

Most of the crop plants important today were cultivated in a primitive way long before recorded history *(1)*. Agriculture began some 10,000 years ago when ancient peoples selected certain plant types they found growing about them and thus enlarged their food sources beyond hunting and fishing. Most of these early food plants are still cultivated but in much improved forms. Others that were unknown to early humans have been added over the centuries to make up our present day selection of food plants. Then, much later, as people became more concerned about the aesthetics of their environment, they also added shade trees, shrubs, flowering plants, and lawn grasses to the list of cultivated plants.

Several botanists have brought together fascinating information on the subject of where and when crops originated that now feed the world's peoples and their livestock and other domestic animals. The Swiss botanist Alphonse DeCandolle wrote *Origin of Cultivated Plants (6)*, published first in 1833 and in a second edition in 1886. Later, the famous Russian plant geneticist Nikolai Vavilov studied the origin of cultivated plants from about 1916 to 1936. His work included many plant collecting expeditions to various regions of the world, resulting in hundreds of thousands of plant collections. The results of his studies were published in *The Origin, Variation, Immunity, and Breeding of Cultivated Plants,* translated from the Russian and published in English in 1951 *(31)*. Vavilov concluded from his studies that the various cultivated plants originated in eight independent centers: (1) central China, (2) India, (3) Indochina and the Malay Archipelago, (4) the Turkey-Iran region, (5) the Mediterranean area, (6) the Ethiopia-Somaliland area of east Africa, (7) Mexico and Central America, and (8) the Peru-Ecuador-Bolivia and the Brazil-Paraguay area of South America. Many archeological studies carried out in later years generally confirm Vavilov's locations for these centers.

More recent studies and theories on the origins and movements of the world's agricultural crops have been summarized by Carl Sauer in *Agricultural Origins and Dispersals (25)*, by Jack Harlan in *Crops and Man (10)*, and by Barbara Bender in *Farming in Prehistory (2)*.

Sauer proposes that the cradle of world agriculture was in Southeast Asia, in the area of present-day Thailand, some 10,000 years ago. This region at 10°N latitude probably would have had abundant rainfall and a warm to hot climate, good conditions for plant cultivation. He believes, too, that the founders of agriculture were a sedentary, well-fed people with some skills that would lead them to try new practices in growing plants. According to Sauer, agriculture must have started in woody areas with a diversity of plant materials rather than in large river valleys subject to periodic flooding. He proposes that propagation of plants in much early agriculture was done by vegetative methods (see p. 89), which immediately fix superior plant forms, rather than by seed propagation where improvement is long-term.

Harlan disagrees with Vavilov's concept that agriculture originated in definite centers. He agrees that there were some definite centers, but he also points out that many plant species originated at the same time over wide geographical areas (see Fig. 4–1)—what Harlan

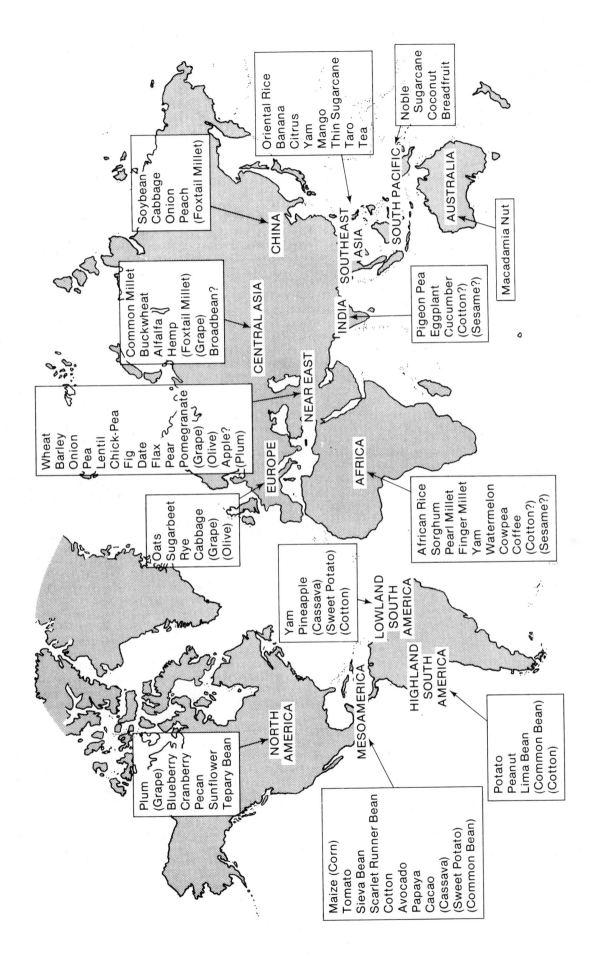

Fig. 4–1 Regions of the world where major food crops were domesticated. Crops that apparently originated in several different areas are shown in parentheses. Question marks after the name indicate doubt about the location of origin. *Source:* Harlan, J. R. 1976. The plants and animals that nourish man. *Sci. Am.* 235(3):88–97.
© September 1976 by Scientific American, Inc. All rights reserved.

calls "noncenters" *(9)*. Harlan believes that these non-centers were based on three large independent systems: one in the Near East and Africa, one in China and Southeast Asia, and one in southern Mexico and South America *(9, 10, 11, 12)*.

Bender *(2)* focuses on the important period some 11,000 years ago when humans made the gradual transition from hunting and gathering to producing food, which profoundly changed human culture.

DOMESTICATION OF PLANTS

Toward the end of the Ice Age, technically the Pleistocene epoch of the Cenozoic era, some 11,000 to 15,000 years ago, when the glaciers were in full retreat and early humans were wandering about the earth, the stage was being set for the initiation of food production (Table 4–1). Before this time, tool-using hunter-gatherers had been on earth for some 4 million years. Then—only about 400 generations ago—there was a gradual transition to food-producing activities. Interesting questions are why it took so long for humans to become food producers and why such activities began in various parts of the world—Southwest and Southeast Asia, middle America, and western South America—at about the same time.

There is definite evidence from archeological sites that agricultural villages existed about 8000 to 9000 B.C. in the area of Southwest Asia known as the Fertile Crescent. It extends from the alluvial plains of Mesopotamia (now Iraq) across Syria and down the eastern coast of

Table 4–1 Beginnings of Agricultural Development in the Old and New World

The Postglacial Time Scale Date	Climatic Changes in Northern Europe	Old World Cultural Stages	New World Cultural Stages
10,000 B.C.	Last glacial stage (Würm-Wisconsin ice)	Late Paleolithic hunting cultures (Cro-Magnon, etc.)	
9,000 B.C.	Retreat of the glaciers (Preboreal period, cold dry)	Mesolithic fishing, hunting, collecting cultures	
8,000 B.C.			Hunting cultures established (Folsom Man, etc.)
7,000 B.C. 6,000 B.C.		**?Agricultural beginnings**	
	Boreal period (Warm dry)		
5,000 B.C.	Altantic period (warm moist)	**Neolithic agriculture established and spreading**	
4,000 B.C.		Beginnings of civilization (Egyptian—Sumerian)	
3,000 B.C.		Neolithic agriculture in northern Europe	
2,000 B.C.			**American agricultural beginnings**
	Subboreal period (colder dry)	Babylonian Empire Invasions: Aryans to India; Medes and Persians to S.W. Asia and Mesopotamia	
1,000 B.C.		Rise and flowering of Greek civilization	
B.C.—A.D.	Sub-Atlantic period (cool moist)		Early Mexican and Mayan civilizations
		Roman empire	
		Invasions: Goths, Huns	Decline of Mayans
		Rise of Islam	
		Norsemen to America	
1,000 A.D.		Mongol and Tartar invasions	Aztecs and Incas
		Voyages of discovery and colonization by Europe	
2,000 A.D.		Industrial revolution and modern period	

Source: Dasmann, R. F. 1976. Environmental conservation. 4th ed. New York: Wiley.

the Mediterranean sea to the Nile Valley of Egypt. Radiocarbon dating suggests that plants and animals were being domesticated at several places in this area at least by 5000 to 6000 B.C. There is evidence from site excavations that einkorn wheat, emmer wheat, barley, lentil, chickpeas, oats, and vetch were being cultivated, as well as dates, grapes, olives, almonds, figs, and pomegranates *(35)*. Recent excavations at Jarmo in Iraqi Kurdistan, at ancient Jericho in the Jordan Valley, and many other sites in the Fertile Crescent have supplied much of the evidence to support these conclusions *(30)*.

An indigenous savanna type of agriculture apparently was developing from domesticated native plants about 4000 B.C. in a belt across central Africa (see Fig. 4–1). This area was the first home of the human race, as we understand it now. The genus *Homo* originated here over two million years ago, and here most of human evolution has occurred. Some important world crops brought under cultivation in this area include coffee, sorghum, millet, cowpeas, yams, oil palm, and cola.

The Chinese center of agricultural origins became important about 4000 B.C. according to radiocarbon dating. Crops domesticated include millet, chestnuts, hazelnuts, peaches, apricots, mulberries, soybeans, and rice. The West did not learn of the all-important rice plant until about 350 B.C., and the peach was unknown outside China until about 200 A.D.

A farming culture in Southeast Asia and what is now Indonesia apparently had domesticated rice around 6000 B.C. Other important crops appearing under cultivation later in this area were sugar cane, coconut, banana, mango, citrus, breadfruit, yams, and taro.

In the New World, evidence from archeological sites shows agricultural beginnings in two areas. One is present-day southern Mexico and Central America, where plant cultivation began about 5000 to 7000 B.C. The plants grown were early forms of maize (corn), sweet potato, tomato, cotton, pumpkin, peppers, squash, runner beans, papaya, avocado, and pineapple.

The second American region is a broad ''noncenter'' of agricultural origins stretching from Chile northward to the Atlantic Ocean and eastward into Brazil. There is evidence that both the snap and lima beans were cultivated here by about 6000 B.C. or earlier. Other important cultivated crops from this region are the potato, peanut, cacao, pineapple, cashew, papaya, avocado, Brazil nut, peppers, tobacco, guava, tomato, yam, manioc, and squash.

No major cultivated crop originated in the area of present-day United States. Agriculture here relies in a large measure on introduced crops. There are, however, many minor native American fruit and nut crops, such as

the American grapes and plums, the pecan, chestnut, hickory nut, hazelnut, black walnut, persimmon, blueberry, raspberry, blackberry, and cranberry. The sunflower (which has long been an important oil crop in the U.S.S.R. and Eastern Europe) originated in the United States, as did hops, the tepary bean, Jerusalem artichoke, and some grasses. Many plants now used as ornamentals, mostly in improved forms, and many of the world's great timber tree species also originated in the United States.

The only food crop to originate in the entire continent of Australia was the macadamia, or Queensland nut.

Methods of Plant Domestication

When ancient peoples started to domesticate plants— that is, propagating and growing plants under their own control—they would have had the choice of vegetative propagation or seed propagation (both described in Ch. 5). The first method is the more obvious, immediate, and direct approach to selecting and maintaining superior plant forms.

VEGETATIVE OR ASEXUAL PROPAGATION METHODS

It is probably no coincidence that some of the oldest cultivated woody plants are the easiest to propagate by such vegetative methods as hardwood cuttings. These plants include the grape, fig, olive, mulberry, pomegranate, and quince *(34)*.

An observant person in prehistoric days would probably have noticed among a wild stand of seedling grapevines, for example, one single plant standing out from the others in its heavy production of large, high-quality fruits. From past experience, too, the person might have known that a piece of the grape cane stuck into the ground in early spring would take root and produce a new plant just like the original. The next logical step, of course, would be to break off and plant many cane pieces (cuttings) from this one very desirable grape plant, then to protect them against animals and the competition of weeds. This action would establish a vineyard based on cultivating a superior seedling and disregarding all seedlings with inferior characteristics.

Many of the tree fruit species—fig, almond, quince, apple, pear, cherry, pomegranate, and walnut—are native to such areas of the Near East as the Soviet states of Georgia and Armenia on the southern slopes of the Caucasus Mountains. In these regions one may still observe the various stages in the evolution of fruit growing. There are forests consisting entirely of seedling wild trees of these species, showing great variability in many characteristics. One may also see trees in which the local farmers have grafted the superior wild types onto inferior seedlings, making use of them only as rootstocks. Also while clearing the brush and forests to make space for grain fields, the farmers have left superior individual wild apple, pear, and cherry seedlings in the fields for harvesting.

Many types of ancient plants brought under domestication by early people could have been—and probably were—easily maintained and increased by unsophisticated vegetative methods. Such plants would have included the potato and sweet potato, propagated by dividing the tubers (see p. 112); banana, bamboo, and ginger, propagated by cutting up rhizomes (see p. 113); pomegranate, quince, fig, olive, and grape, propagated by stem cuttings; filbert, propagated by layering; and pineapple and date, propagated by a form of suckering (see p. 111).

SEED OR SEXUAL PROPAGATION METHODS

Domestication of seed-propagated plants, such as the cereal crops, by the ancient agriculturists probably began as the purposeful harvesting of wild grass seeds, some of which were sown to produce the next year's crop. This established two population types for the next harvest—one that was not harvested and reseeded itself, and one that was sown from the harvested seed. In cereals this procedure immediately starts to separate the "shattering" types (the seed separates from the head) from the "nonshattering" types. Most of the seeds that shatter fall to the ground, while nonshattering seeds are harvested and can be resown. Thus, seed with the desirable nonshattering trait is easily obtained without intentional selection. The mere practice of harvesting sets up a selection pressure for improved forms.

Planting the harvested seeds close together in a cultivated plot kept free of competing weeds also automatically selects for the stronger, more vigorous plants. In some species, seedlings derived from the larger seeds—those having a considerable amount of stored foods—are likely to germinate and grow rapidly, thus suppressing seedlings arising from the smaller seeds with low vitality. The harvested crop would, therefore, come from the more vigorous plants producing the desirable large grains, and the plants producing the smaller, inferior grains would be eliminated. Thus seedling competition sets up an automatic selection pressure for an improved form.

By these procedures, early peoples unconsciously developed superior forms of their cereal crops. Other desirable characteristics arising from selection pressures were loss of seed dormancy, increased flower numbers and larger inflorescences, and a trend toward determi-

nate rather than indeterminate growth.[1] These superior characteristics in the cultivated races over the wild types can usually be obtained with only small genetic differences between the two.

EXAMPLES OF IMPROVEMENT IN SOME IMPORTANT CROP PLANTS[2]

The following examples illustrate patterns in plant improvement, beginning with (1) the harvest of crops from wild plants by primitive humans followed by (2) selection of superior types from prehistoric eras to the present time, and going on to (3) modern methods of plant breeding that can dramatically increase crop yield and quality by applying genetic principles to developing improved cultivars. It should be realized that the present, improved cultivars of such important crops as wheat, corn, rice, potato, sweet potato, and all fruit crops have been so adapted to conform to human cultural practices that they all now completely depend upon our care for their continued existence.

WHEAT (*Triticum aestivum* and *T. turgidum* Durum group) (*7, 16*) (see p. 502)

Wheat is the most widely cultivated plant in the world today and the chief cereal, used worldwide for making bread. Present wheats evolved from wild wheat-like grass plants found and cultivated by ancient humans in the Near East region about 7000 B.C. Native wheatlike plants can still be found in this area. Even in early prehistoric times, wheat probably improved naturally by spontaneous hybridizations, by chromosome doubling, and by mutations to increase fertility. Wheat species occur in a series with increasing chromosome numbers (polyploidy): First is the small primitive diploid einkorn wheat (7 pairs of chromosomes); second is the much larger tetraploid emmer wheat (14 pairs of chromosomes); and third is the hexaploid bread wheats (21 pairs of chromosomes), the ones grown today. (See Table 23–2.) Humans probably had no role in this early advancement of wheat. From the Near East these early wheat forms were taken into ancient Egypt, the Balkans, and central Europe. The Spanish brought wheat to the Americas, and eventually the United States, Canada, and Argentina became the world's largest wheat producers. A chance in-

[1]In determinate growth, shoot elongation stops when flowers form on the shoot terminals. In indeterminate growth, elongation continues after flowering.

[2]For a discussion of the genetic terminology used in this section, see the section "Some Basic Genetic Concepts in Plant Improvement" at the end of this chapter.

troduction of 'Turkey Red' wheat into central Kansas by a small group of Mennonite immigrants from Russia in 1873 established the basis for the tremendous hard red winter wheat industry of the central Great Plains area of the United States.

The two major wheat species today are *Triticum aestivum,* used for flour in making breads and pastries, and *T. turgidum* (Durum group), used for such products as macaroni, spaghetti, and noodles. In the twentieth century, plant breeders, through hybridization and selection, have produced perhaps a thousand cultivars of bread wheat alone designed for certain climates, for high productivity, special milling properties, and particularly for disease resistance. Wheat cultivars resistant to the devastating stem rust disease must continually be developed to cope with the mutating stem rust pathogen.

Today's plant breeders, too, have developed dwarf forms of wheat, which can carry heavy yields without falling over (lodging) when heavily fertilized. Some of these new dwarfed cultivars were developed by Norman E. Borlaug, working at the Rockefeller Foundation's International Maize and Wheat Improvement Center in Mexico. Borlaug won the Nobel peace prize in 1970 for his work. Certain of these cultivars have been so successful with fertilizers and irrigation in Pakistan and India, that both countries have almost become self-sufficient in wheat production.

Wheat plants are self-pollinated, allowing farmers to save their seeds for future planting. F_1 hybrid wheat for increased plant vigor and yields has not been developed to the extent it has with corn, owing to difficulties arising from the wheat's flower structure. Wheat has perfect (bisexual) flowers, making cross-pollination difficult, whereas corn has the male and female flowers separate on the same plant and is cross-pollinated easily (see p. 81).

CORN (*Zea mays*) (20) (see p. 488)

Corn (or maize) originated in the New World about 5000 to 6000 B.C., but its earliest history is still a mystery. Maize is known only as a domestic plant. There is no wild form except, apparently, teosinte. The economic life of the ancient American civilizations—the Aztecs, Mayas, and Incas—depended on corn. At the time of Columbus' expeditions to the New World, corn was being grown by Indian tribes from Canada to Chile. Corn probably originated in several places in both Mexico and South America. An early form of corn still growing in South America is shown in Figure 4–2.

A number of hypotheses have been advanced to explain the origin of corn: (1) It developed from "pod corn," a type in which each individual kernel is enclosed

Fig. 4–2 Improvement in corn (maize) from a primitive type (*left*) still growing on the eastern slope of the Andes mountains in South America, to modern hybrid corn (*right*). The primitive type corn contains a valuable trait—multiple-aleurone layers in the grain—that is being transferred by plant breeders to modern dent corn. This example illustrates the need for maintaining germplasm of seemingly worthless plant types. *Source:* USDA.

in floral bracts—as in the other cereals; (2) it originated from teosinte, corn's closest relative, by gradual selection under the influence of harvesting by humans; (3) corn, teosinte, and *Tripsacum* (a primitive cereal) descended along independent lines directly from a common ancestor; or (4) there is the tripartite theory that (a) cultivated corn originated from pod corn, (b) teosinte is a derivative of a hybrid of corn and *Tripsacum,* (c) the majority of modern corn cultivars are the product of an admixture with teosinte or *Tripsacum* or both.

Corn, even today, is an extremely variable species, from the color of the grains to the size and shape of the grains and ears (Fig. 4–2). Corn mutates easily, forming new types. The Indians of America must have made considerable conscious selection of corn for so many types to be introduced to European agriculture following the New World explorations.

The development of hybrid corn in the 1930s (see p. 81) is one of the most outstanding achievements of modern agriculture (see Fig. 5–1). High-yielding F_1 corn hybrids were developed for different climatic zones. In 1935, 1 percent of the corn planted in the United States was of the hybrid type. By 1970 virtually all corn produced in the United States was of the hybrid type. The planting of hybrid cultivars, along with fertilizers, irrigation, and mechanization, has more than doubled production, giving yields as high as 18 to 20 metric tons per hectare (about 300 bushels per acre). Corn is now one of the world's chief food crops for both humans and domesticated animals, but it would not survive in nature without man's attention and cultivation.

RICE (*Oryza sativa*) (13, 16) (see p. 491)

Rice is the basic food for more than half the world's population and one of the oldest cultivated crops (see Ch. 23). It is believed to have originated in Southeast Asia about 5000 years ago, or even earlier, and it spread to Europe and Japan by the second century B.C.

There are about 25 species of *Oryza*, but *O. perennis*, widely distributed throughout the tropics, is probably the one from which cultivated rice was developed. Primitive humans most likely collected seeds and cultivated the wild types. During cultivation of rice, mutations, plus hybridization with other *Oryza* species, probably occurred, leading to improved forms with larger grains and nonshattering fruit stalks. Rice was first cultivated in America along the coast of South Carolina about 1685. Four rice experiment stations were established by the U.S. government in the early 1900s. From breeding work at these stations, many superior cultivars have been introduced to the rice-growing areas of the United States (see p. 492).

Much of the rice harvested in Asia still comes from old, unproductive types grown under primitive conditions. The Ford and Rockefeller Foundations established the International Rice Research Institution (IRRI) in the Philippines in 1962, bringing together scientists from eastern and western nations for the purpose of improving rice culture. This group of researchers has developed by hybridization new high-yielding dwarf cultivars (IR-8, IR-20, IR-26, IR-28, IR-36) that will not fall over (lodge) when heavily fertilized. These cultivars have dramatically increased yields, and some are highly resistant to insects and disease pathogens native to the Far East, South America, and Africa. In 1967 the International Center for Tropical Agriculture in Colombia brought the technology for growing the new dwarf rice cultivars to Latin America. By 1974 these modern dwarf rice cultivars accounted for more than 99 percent of the irrigated rice acreage in Colombia. Yields increased from 3.0 to 5.4 metric tons per hectare, and Colombia's annual rice production climbed from 680,000 metric tons in 1966 to 1,632,000 metric tons in 1975 on the same land area.

SOYBEAN (*Glycine max*) (see p. 511)

Sometimes called the "Cinderella crop," the soybean has risen spectacularly to prominence in the United States in recent years, with an increase in production from 135,000 metric tons (5 million bushels) in 1925 to about 54 million tons (2 billion bushels) in 1978. This great increase is due, in part, to the availability of more productive, disease-resistant cultivars. From about 1910 to 1950, a massive number of new strains and seed lots of soybeans have been introduced into the United States from the Orient, its native home, largely by USDA plant explorers. From these diverse sources of germplasm, hybridization programs have developed many superior cultivars. Much of this work has been done at the USDA Regional Soybean Laboratory at Urbana, Illinois, in cooperation with various Midwest agricultural experiment stations. These cultivars give high yields, proper bean maturity for the particular area, strong erect plants that hold their seeds until harvest, and high disease resistance and bean quality. The soybean is particularly well adapted to the United States' Midwest "corn belt" and the southeastern states, which together account for more than 70 percent of the world's soybean production.

SUGAR BEET (*Beta vulgaris*) (see p. 498)

The modern sugar beet is a plant developed entirely by human efforts in plant breeding. It is our only major food crop that was not grown in some primitive form in ancient times. It was developed only some 200 years ago in Europe as a source of sugar to compete with the then very expensive cane sugar. The German chemist Andreas Marggraf found in 1747 that the kind of sugar in cultivated garden beets was the same chemically as that in cane sugar. Breeding and selection increased the sugar content in the root from about 2 percent to about 16 to 20 percent, with yields of around 45 MT/ha (20 T/ac) of roots per acre.

In the early part of the nineteenth century, Napoleon encouraged the development and production of the sugar beet industry in France to free that country from the British monopoly on cane sugar. By the end of the nineteenth century, sugar beets were being grown in North America, and they have now become an important temperate zone crop in many areas of the United States and southern Canada. All production phases are now completely mechanized, permitting the sugar beet to compete favorably with the tropical sugar cane plant. To maintain profitable production, however, plant breeders have had to continue to develop sugar beet cultivars resistant to virus and fungus diseases.

POTATO (*Solanum tuberosum*) (13) (see p. 580)

Potatoes are one of the big four crops that feed the world's population. Wild potato species are widespread in South America, particularly in the Andes Mountain region. Potatoes were probably cultivated by primitive peoples in this area more than 4000 years ago, but they became a more productive crop over the years with selection of superior types. The potato was cultivated over the length of the Andes Mountain area at the time the Spanish explorers arrived. They carried it back to the European continent about 1575 where today 90 percent of the world's potato crop is grown.

The potato plant produces pink, white, or blue flowers that develop into small green berries containing seeds. The seeds, when planted, produce new types of potato plants much different from the parent plant and from each other in many respects. In the early days of potato culture, the South American Indians undoubtedly selected superior plant types resulting from natural crosses. Once one single such superior plant was obtained, it could be perpetuated and increased in great numbers as a clone (see p. 89) by tuber division (see p. 112). Some of these superior selections propagated by vegetative methods over the years became commercially successful cultivars. It was noted, however, that certain of these cultivars would degenerate after many generations of such asexual propagation and yield only weak unproductive plants. It was observed, too, that sowing seeds from such plants gave progeny plants with changed characteristics, including renewed vigor and productivity. It is now known that these clonal cultivars had become infected with viruses that passed along through the tubers to the new plants generation after generation. Such viruses did not pass through the seed to the new seedling plant, so that its growth was no longer inhibited by the virus.

In modern commercial potato growing, the planting stock ("seed" tubers) is produced under carefully observed conditions in regions where any viruses can readily be detected and the infected stock discarded. The grower who plants only "certified" stock can be reasonably sure that his fields will not be infected with viruses or other pathogens and will be true to type. In the United States, certified "seed" potatoes are produced by commercial growers in the northern states and inspected strictly by state government agencies.

Many potato cultivars now being grown have been developed by plant breeders who have introduced superior characteristics into an existing cultivar. An example is resistance to *Phytophthora infestans* (late blight)—from *Solanum demissum,* a wild potato species, obtained from collections in Mexico. Many cultivars are being grown today for different purposes and for different climatic zones. New cultivars are constantly being introduced by plant breeders and older ones discarded. In the United States, 'Russet Burbank' is still the leading cultivar, although about 12 other prominent ones are also grown.

TOMATO (*Lycopersicon lycopersicum*) (28) (see p. 548)

The cultivated tomato originated from wild forms in the Peru-Ecuador-Bolivia area of the Andes Mountains in South America. Prehistoric Indians carried it to Central America and Mexico. Early explorers introduced the tomato to Europe about 1550, and it was brought back west, to the Carolinas, in North America, about 1710. Thomas Jefferson grew tomatoes on his plantation about 1780. In those days most people considered the tomato poisonous, but in the United States it started gaining acceptance as a food plant about 1825. The early Indians undoubtedly improved the tomato by planting seeds taken only from the best fruits on the most productive plants. This selection process continued in the early days of tomato culture in Europe and the United States. Early cultivars introduced by U.S. seed companies were Stone and Globe in 1870, Ponderosa in 1891, and Earliana in 1900. In the early 1900s the USDA and the state experiment stations began breeding tomato cultivars to include specific characteristics. Marglobe was introduced by the USDA in 1925 and Rutgers by New Jersey in 1934. Some tomato cultivars more recently introduced, such as Better Boy, carry resistance to fusarium wilt, verticillium wilt, and nematodes. Cultivars developed especially for machine harvesting have square-shaped, firm-fleshed fruits that all ripen at one time. Vigorous, highly productive F_1 hybrids, marketed both as seeds and as bedding plants, are the most recent developments by seed companies.

Fruit Crops

The major fruit crops are all heterozygous (see p. 71). They do not "come true" when propagated by seed, so vegetative propagation must be used to maintain an improved seedling selection (see Ch. 5). In ancient times most kinds of fruit—other than those propagated vegetatively very easily, such as bananas, grapes, figs, pomegranates, and olives—were probably seed propagated and the variability in offspring accepted by farmers. Later, however, as more sophisticated methods of vegetative propagation were developed, such as budding and grafting, it would have been found that certain superior individual fruit plants could be maintained and increased by these methods. Nevertheless, considerable seed propagation of fruit species was undoubtedly practiced in the early days of fruit growing.

APPLES (*Malus pumila*) (see p. 590)

The early U.S. colonists planted many seedling apple trees, probably because it was easier to bring seeds taken from their favorite apple trees in their native homes rather than material for grafting. As a result, they continued to increase their apple orchards by planting seedlings. In these early days much of the apple crop was preserved as cider, for which fruit from seedling trees was quite satisfactory. Certain individual seedling trees, no doubt, were much superior to the others and formed the starting point for vegetative propagation and the origin of the many hundreds of apple cultivars grown in the United States up to the early part of the twentieth century. These numbers dwindled, however, until by the 1970s, when only 13 cultivars accounted for over 90 percent of the apples produced in the United States. The most important cultivars were Delicious, Golden Delicious, McIntosh, Rome Beauty, Jonathan, Winesap, York, and Stayman. Although apple breeding programs have been conducted by the USDA and by some state agricultural experiment stations, all the major apple cultivars now being grown originated as chance seedlings many years ago. For example, the 'McIntosh' apple was found growing as a seedling tree near Dundela, Ontario, Canada by John McIntosh in 1796. The 'Delicious' apple started as a single chance seedling on Jesse Hiatt's farm near Peru, Iowa about 1870. The 'Golden Delicious' also originated as a chance seedling on the A. H. Mullin farm in Cass County, West Virginia about 1910. However, more recent cultivars released from breeding programs at the New York Agricultural Experiment Station—such as Cortland, Empire, Macoun, and Jonagold, are starting to find grower and consumer acceptance.

PEARS (*Pyrus communis*) (see p. 600)

In pears, too, cultivars originating as chance seedlings have dominated the markets. The Bartlett (Williams Bon Chretien) originated in England as a chance seedling in 1796 and has been the world's leading pear cultivar ever since. Other leading pear cultivars in the United States, such as Beurre d'Anjou and Beurre

Bosc, originated in Belgium as open-pollinated seedlings of cultivars then grown there. No pear cultivar from a controlled breeding program in the United States has become commercially important, although European pear breeders have developed several superior cultivars that produce well in France, Italy, and Belgium.

PEACHES AND NECTARINES
(*Prunus persica*) (see. p. 598)

In contrast to the apples and pears, the important peach and nectarine cultivars grown today are the products of public and private plant breeding programs. Plant breeders have provided the consuming public with truly outstanding peaches and nectarines, in contrast to the small-fruited, nonproductive cultivars of earlier days that got their start as chance seedlings. Some of the many present-day peach cultivars resulting from breeding programs throughout the United States are Dixired, Redhaven, Triogem, Redglobe, Richhaven, and Erlired. New nectarine cultivars from breeding programs, such as LeGrand, Late LeGrand, and Sungrand have completely replaced older cultivars.

STRAWBERRIES (*Fragaria* × *Ananassa*)
(see p. 606)

Today's garden strawberry first originated in France about 1720 as a natural hybrid between two native American *Fragaria* species (see p. 605). From this and subsequent hybridizations, a number of cultivar selections were made and maintained vegetatively by runners (see p. 111) in the early days of strawberry culture in Europe. An early amateur horticulturist in England, Thomas A. Knight, crossed these two *Fragaria* species and, from the seedlings, developed the Elton and the Downton cultivars, the latter being used extensively as a parent in later hybridizations. Other amateur horticulturists in Europe and the United States became involved in strawberry breeding and developed many of the cultivars grown during the mid-1800s.

The USDA initiated a strawberry breeding program in 1919, from which came the Blakemore, for 20 years the most widely grown cultivar in the United States. However, many of these early cultivars were susceptible to viruses, verticillium wilt, and other diseases and were low in productivity, so that about 1945 the entire U.S. strawberry industry was falling into a precarious position.

Since World War II a parade of new strawberry cultivars has been replacing older ones, coming from USDA and several state strawberry breeding programs and from similar programs in other countries. New cultivars have been developed for specific climatic regions and for such characteristics as adaptability of fruits to be used for freezing or for fresh shipping, resistance of plants to viruses and fungi and to winter cold, and fruit appearance and flavor. Although some 70 strawberry cultivars are now grown commercially in the United States, only about 10 are truly popular. These are Tioga, Tufts, Hood, Heidi, Florida Ninety, Headliner, Midway, Surecrop, and Guardian.

PLANT IMPROVEMENT PROGRAMS

From the time of Neolithic man up to the early 1900s, plant improvement consisted mostly of selecting seeds from those individual plants in a mixed population that had the wanted characteristics. The seed was planted and from that population seeds were again taken from the most desirable plants, and so on. While improvements resulted, this method offered no way to transfer desirable characteristics from one line to another.

A product of the twentieth century, public and private plant breeding programs have had a tremendous beneficial impact on our food supply and range of ornamental plants. Public and private programs have produced a great many new superior cultivars for almost all cereal, vegetable, forage, fruit, and ornamental crops. The Austrian monk Gregor Mendel demonstrated in the 1860s the genetic mode of plant inheritance. Based on his work and utilizing the expertise of trained geneticists, the modern breeding programs have produce an array of new cultivars for many crops. These have been bred for such characteristics as resistance to disease, insects, and cold and for productivity, flavor, and nutritive value.

The USDA and most state agricultural experiment stations in the United States maintain such programs, often with a separate department of plant breeding. Most other countries also have plant breeding programs, often specializing in certain crops.

Recent innovations by plant breeders include the development of F_1 hybrid corn (see p. 81) and new vegetable and flower cultivars. Most of the new vegetable and flower lines are far superior to previous cultivars in vigor and in insect and disease resistance; the new vegetable cultivars are also superior in flavor, appearance, and productivity. F_1 hybrid vegetables available to today's gardeners include tomato, muskmelon, cucumber, cabbage, carrot, onion, cauliflower, watermelon, broccoli, peppers, squash, and sweet corn. F_1 hybrid flowers available are marigolds, geraniums, *Dianthus,* petunias, zinnias, *Impatiens,* snapdragons, and pansies. These are often sold as bedding plants rather than seeds, because of the expense of the F_1 hybrid seed. Practical production of F_1 hybrid vegetable and flower seeds often requires some

form of inherited male sterility to be introduced into one of the parental lines.

By developing plants that show strong resistance to insects and disease, plant breeders are lessening the need for insecticides and fungicides *(23)*. This, in the long run, would be the best method of pest control. For example, potato cultivars have been developed that are resistant to the late blight disease *(Phytophthora infestans),* which was responsible for the nineteenth-century Irish potato famine. Other potato cultivars have been developed that are resistant to the golden nematode, permitting potatoes to be produced in soils infested by these worms without expensive soil fumigation. Wheat breeders must continually develop new wheat cultivars resistant to stem rust *(Puccinia graminis tritici)* because this fungus continually changes to attack formerly resistant cultivars.

Plant breeders have a useful procedure for obtaining improved plant forms by spontaneous or induced mutations resulting from chromosome or gene changes. These changes can be induced by chemical treatment with colchicine or by irradiation with gamma rays (from radioactive cobalt 60) *(22)*. For instance in California, seeds of the rice cultivar Calrose were exposed to gamma rays from cobalt 60, producing mutated dwarf plants that were found to be highly resistant to lodging (falling over) when the crop is maturing and the heads are becoming heavy.

In one instance plant breeders have gone beyond just improving native plants. They have created a new manmade cereal, triticale by hybridizing the ancient grains, wheat and rye. The name *triticale* derives from the genus names of these two grains: *Tritium* and *Secale* (see Ch. 23). The hybrid combines the high yield and protein content of wheat with the winter hardiness of rye. The triticale plant is disease resistant and thrives in some unfavorable soils and climates. It may have potential as a new food source in countries dependent on cereals. About 400,000 hectares (990,000 acres) are being grown on five continents. Hungary alone grows about 70,000 hectares (173,000 acres).

A cross between wheat and rye was first attempted in 1875 in Scotland. A few seeds germinated from this cross and produced plants, but their seeds were sterile. Continued efforts in Europe brought limited success. It was not until the 1950s and 1960s that real success appeared, through a joint project by the University of Manitoba in Canada and the International Maize and Wheat Improvement Center in Mexico. There are now research and promotional programs in some states in the United States. And there is some possibility that triticale will become a man-made grain that will help feed millions of people, although it is now being used primarily for livestock feed. The yield of triticale is about the same as wheat, the seeds are fertile, the crop matures early, and it is disease resistant.

Genetic engineering to produce plants designed at the gene level is an interdisciplinary effort by cell biologists, biochemists, and geneticists. The techniques of *in vitro* cell culture manipulation are well developed, and they offer great promise for crop improvement. These techniques are already being used to free plants of viruses by shoot tip cultures and to propagate plants rapidly by inducing root and shoot formation on tiny tissue explants (see p. 92).

By 1975, work in various cell biology laboratories showed that new or improved plants could possibly be developed without hybridization through the mechanisms of the flower *(5)*. Fusing together protoplasts (see p. 17) from cells of different plants (cell hybridization) under aseptic conditions in a test tube may develop entirely new plants with new combinations of chromosomes. An example of this might be the fusion of barley and soybean protoplasts to produce a leguminous grain crop that could supply its own nitrogen, extracted from the air, by the bacteria-containing nodules on the roots. It has long been known that a single cell—for example, of carrot—held under the proper conditions can be made to grow into a whole new carrot plant. The DNA (see p. 70) in the nucleus of a single cell has all the genetic information needed to direct the reproduction of the complete new plant.

The fusing together of two cells of different plants is called parasexual hybridization, and it requires the removal of cell walls to give naked protoplasts. The removal can be done by enzymes that dissolve the cell walls. Protoplasts of onions, oats, and tobacco have been fused. However, such fused protoplasts must divide by mitosis (see p. 90) and establish cell division patterns before a new hybrid plant can develop. Protoplast fusion was accomplished in 1972 at the Brookhaven National Laboratory at Long Island, New York with naked protoplasts from two tobacco species *(5)*. The fused protoplasts divided, forming a mass of callus (undifferentiated) cells which, when placed in the proper aseptic nutritive medium containing certain hormones, produced shoots and roots and grew into a new hybrid plant that showed the characteristics of both parents. This early accomplishment stimulated similar studies in other laboratories with many other plant species.

For many years *in vitro* manipulation of plant tissue has resulted in cellular cloning and the rapid multiplication of plants (micropropagation). An example is the proliferation of cells from excised orchid shoot tips to result in rapid, large-scale commercial propagation *(21)*.

In another development in genetic engineering, anther and pollen culture in sterile media at the proper stage can result in haploid (1n) plants (see p. 72). These plants may be induced to double their chromosomes by colchicine treatments and produce homozygous plants. This development could have far-reaching implications in establishing "pure lines" of normally heterozygous cultivars.

SEARCHING FOR AND MAINTAINING NEW GERMPLASM[3]

There is no assurance that we are at present cultivating all the useful food and ornamental plants in existence on earth, or that all the germplasm containing useful genes has been found. Plant explorers have long roamed the world and they continue their searches *(8)*. They have found many plants that have subsequently made a major impact on the world's agriculture, often in different parts of the world from the plants' native regions. Accessible plants have always been moved about over the world by explorers on land and sea, armies, immigrants, and travelers. Plants moved into a new region often perform much better than they did in their original home. For example, the coffee plant *(Coffea arabica)* is native to the Ethiopian area of eastern Africa. It never developed into much of a crop there, but when moved to Brazil and Colombia in South America, the coffee tree prospered so well that these countries now produce the bulk of the world's coffee supply.

A number of prominent plant explorers have contributed much to the wealth of available plant materials *(18)*. During a 70-year period, starting with Captain Cook's voyage from England in 1768, a series of plant exploration trips brought back tremendous numbers of exotic plants from all over the world to English gardens, particularly to the famed Royal Botanic Gardens at Kew, a suburb of London. Sir Joseph Banks, director of Kew Gardens for 48 years, was a prime mover behind these early English expeditions *(18)*. He himself set out from England with Cook in the *Endeavor* in 1768 to bring back great numbers of herbarium specimens and drawings of hitherto unknown plants from the Pacific world. Francis Masson, probably the first professional plant explorer, was sent out from Kew in 1772 with Captain Cook to South Africa, where he collected a great array of seeds, bulbs, and plants of the native species.

David Douglas started his plant collecting trips to the North American continent in 1823. Douglas lived

---

[3]The protoplasm of the sexual reproductive cells containing the units of heredity (chromosomes and genes).

only 35 years, but he probably introduced more trees and plants to English gardens, principally by seed, than any plant explorer before or since. His introductions came chiefly from the North American Pacific Coast. The great timber tree, the Douglas fir, is named after him.

Many of the early plant collecting trips were less than successful because the plants did not survive the long trip back. A London physician who was an amateur horticulturist, Nathanial Ward, invented the Wardian case early in the 1800s. The case was a small glass-enclosed box containing soil in the bottom. Plants kept in the Wardian case could survive long sea voyages, permitting the importation of species never before received alive. Large, magnificent, ornate glasshouses were built in England about this time to house the many tropical and subtropical plants brought back by the plant hunters.

California's wine grape industry can be traced back to Colonel Agoston Haraszthy who was growing grapes in northern California in the 1850s. In 1862, under the auspices of the state's governor, he traveled to the wine-producing countries of Europe and collected about 200,000 cuttings of many grape cultivars and brought them back to California, providing the basis for the newly developing wine industry.

N. E. Hansen was sent to Russia in 1897 by the U.S. Secretary of Agriculture to search for cold resistant fruit and cereal plants suitable for growing in the severe winter areas of the United States' central Great Plains. In 1898 the USDA established the Seed and Plant Introduction Section to handle the material Hansen collected. Mark Carleton, a wheat specialist for the USDA, also went to Russia in 1898 and 1900 as a plant explorer to collect wheat. The types he collected formed the basis of the hard wheat industry in the U.S. northern Great Plains *(18)*.

David Fairchild, a famous plant explorer himself, was involved in the introduction of many thousands of kinds of plants into the United States in his capacity as director of the USDA Office of Foreign Seed and Plant Introduction from 1897 to 1928 *(8)*. The Fairchild Tropical Garden, established at Coconut Grove, Florida is a tribute to his lifelong dedication to introducing new plants of economic value.

The USDA sent Frank Meyer on plant exploring trips through the farms, gardens, forests, and deserts of Asia from about 1900 to 1915, giving the United States a great many valuable new economic plants. Many of his introductions arrived as cuttings or budwood.

Joseph F. Rock, a botanist at the University of Hawaii, conducted many extensive plant exploring trips for a number of years starting about 1910. He was supported by the National Geographic Society. Rock's knowledge of both botany and the Chinese language made him a valuable explorer in Asian countries. He brought back many desirable fruit and ornamental species that have made great contributions to the world's agriculture.

E. H. Wilson was sent to China, Japan, and Korea on several plant collecting expeditions from 1899 to 1918 by British nurserymen to obtain new plant material. He sent back as seeds, bulbs, and cuttings many handsome ornamentals that are now widely grown. Later Wilson became involved in the administration of Harvard's Arnold Arboretum at Boston.

In 1956 the USDA Agricultural Research Service set up a joint program with Longwood Gardens, Kennett Square, Pennsylvania that sponsored 12 collecting trips to search for new ornamental species. And in 1972 USDA geneticists stationed at Utah State University collected seeds of forage grasses and legumes in Iran and Turkey *(7)*. Many of these were species never before known or cultivated in the United States. Such materials were collected for the purpose of acquiring new germplasm to enhance range grass breeding and cytogenetic studies in the United States, for the ultimate purpose of improving range grass pasture lands. Plant collecting trips to the native home of certain desirable plant types are still being made.

Plant explorers usually have a definite goal for their expeditions. They may be looking for an entirely new plant species to serve as a crop in a particular climatic region of their own country. Safflower came to the northern Great Plains of the United States this way, and it has proven most profitable. Plant explorers may also be searching for new germplasm for existing crops. Closely related types can be used by plant breeders to introduce, for example, genes for insect or disease resistance or improved vigor or quality into cultivars already being grown.

To eliminate duplication of effort among countries engaged in plant exploration and to maintain some record of what is being collected and where it is being maintained, the Food and Agriculture Organization of the United Nations (FAO) has set up a clearinghouse procedure *(32)*.

Moving plant materials about the world can also introduce devastating insect or disease pests into a country where they have never before appeared. For example, the chestnut blight fungus *(Endothia parasitica)* was inadvertently introduced on imported plant material to the New York area from the Orient in the late 1800s. By about 1935 this fungus had practically eliminated all stands of the beautiful native American chestnut trees *(Castanea dentata)* from the eastern United States. To guard against introduction of such pests, most countries have set up elaborate inspection, fumigation, and quarantine procedures (see p. 244, Ch. 11 for a description of how this problem is handled in the United States). Plant material can be introduced as seeds, bulbs or corms, rooted cuttings, or as scions or budwood for grafting or budding onto related growing plants. Seeds are the easiest to ship and pose the least danger of carrying pathogens. Rooted plant parts with soil particles around the roots are particulary suspect since the soil may contain nematodes or soil-borne diseases. Vegetative plant material coming into the United States is usually fumigated, then held under postentry quarantine for as long as two years before distribution to nurseries is permitted.

Shipment of plant material is now easy and highly successful because of polyethylene wrapping materials, refrigeration, and frequent worldwide air flights. This is in contrast to the earlier days when only slow ship transport, often through hot tropical seas, was possible.

Preservation of Desirable Germplasm

A concerted worldwide effort is needed to ensure the survival of the earth's endangered plant species so as to preserve genetic diversity *(14)*. Such gene pools are needed for developing improved crops in the future, for introducing beneficial genes into existing crops from close relatives, for maintaining attractive plants and trees valued for their aesthetic purposes, and for keeping plants intact as part of ecosystems where their presence is necessary to the survival of other plant and animal species. The genetic diversity of plants, as well as animals and microbes, is of fundamental importance to our survival on earth. Food and other agricultural crops are derived from the genetic diversity of natural plant populations.

To help prevent eradication of many plant species, the U.S. Congress in 1973 passed the Endangered Species Act, which directed the Smithsonian Institution to prepare a list of endangered plant species and to recommend measures for saving them. As many as one in ten plant species is now extinct or endangered because of the encroachment of agricultural operations, the removal of rare plants by plant collectors, and the general destruction of vegetation from various causes. Such endangered germplasm can be saved and stored for future use as seeds *(15)* or as living plants in special protected locations.

In the United States, the National Plant Germplasm System is already established and functioning *(3)*. The system is a coordinated network of institutions, agencies, and research units working cooperatively to introduce, maintain, evaluate, catalog, and distribute all types of plant germplasm. Financial support comes from the USDA and from state agricultural experiment stations as well as from commercial plant breeding and seed trade organizations. The general mission of the system is to provide plant scientists with the germplasm needed to carry out their work, for example, in breeding new cultivars resistant to certain insects, diseases, smog, or high soil salinity.

The basic elements of the United States' National Plant Germplasm System are:

1. The USDA Germplasm Resources Laboratory at Beltsville, Maryland. This is a national focal point and clearinghouse for exchanges of plant germplasm with foreign countries. All incoming accessions are cataloged here and assigned Plant Introduction (P.I.) numbers.

2. Three USDA Plant Introduction Stations, at Glenn Dale, Maryland; Savannah, Georgia; and Miami, Florida.

3. Four State-Federal Regional Plant Introduction Stations, at Pullman, Washington; Ames, Iowa; Geneva, New York; and Experiment, Georgia.

4. The State-Federal Potato Introduction Station at Sturgeon Bay, Wisconsin.

5. The USDA National Seed Storage Laboratory at Fort Collins, Colorado. Established in 1958, facilities at Fort Collins can store up to 180,000 lots of seeds in one-pint cans at 4.5°C (40°F) and 32 percent relative humidity. Provisions are being made to increase this capacity to a million or more seed lots. Only seeds of plant types that will reproduce true from seed can be stored in the Fort Collins facility. This rule excludes seeds of heterozygous fruits and ornamentals that are generally propagated by vegetative methods. Germination tests are run on all incoming seeds, and all data are stored on computer cards to facilitate retrieval of seeds of the crops having certain characteristics. Seed germination percentage is determined at five-year intervals and deteriorating seeds are replenished with fresh seeds if possible. The stored seeds are generally not distributed unless they are unavailable elsewhere, and then only to research scientists.

6. A large group of federal and state plant germplasm curators located throughout the United States.

The activities of the National Plant Germplasm System are:

1. **Introduction** of plant materials into useful scientific channels is done by planned foreign and domestic exploration trips, by exchanges with foreign agencies, or by traveling scientists. There may also be useful domestic germplasm that should be maintained—for example, mutations, species hybrids, or germplasm resistant to a certain insect or disease—which may be valuable for future crop development. These, along with introduced foreign material, are eligible to enter the National Germplasm System.

2. **Maintenance** of this potentially valuable germplasm for future research programs is the responsibility of the regional and inter-regional plant introduction stations, the National Seed Storage Laboratory, and the curators of collections of specific crops.

3. **Evaluation** of the plant genetic resources is done by initial screening and subsequent tests in the field, greenhouse, and laboratory by cooperating state, federal, and private scientists.

4. **Distribution** of plant germplasm is made free of charge to all qualified scientists and institutions requesting it, in sufficient amounts to enable them to initiate their research program.

A National Plant Germplasm Committee represents the elements in the System, advising on policy and coordinating activities to meet the immediate and long-term national goals of agriculture in the United States.

BROADENING THE BASE OF AGRICULTURAL PRODUCTION

The world's peoples are largely fed today by only about 20 crops (see p. 4). Reliance on so few crops could lead to a catastrophic famine if but a few of them were obliterated by insect or disease attacks or by climatic changes *(33)*. The ravage of U.S. corn plantings by the corn blight disease in 1972 is an example of such a possibility.

In an attempt to broaden the base of agricultural plants in the tropics and to promote interest in neglected but seemingly useful tropical plants with economic potential, the U.S. National Academy of Science promoted a compilation of plants nominated by plant scientists around the world and published an account of 36 plants selected from the 400 proposed *(24)*. Each plant was described along with its special requirements, research

needs, selected readings, research contacts, and germplasm sources.

All 36 plants were thought to have considerable potential but most have not been cultivated out of their own limited region of origin. Among the cereals, for example, the report cited an almost completely neglected grain species in the genus *Amaranthus,* native to Central America, that has very high levels of protein and the essential amino acid lysine, which is usually deficient in plant proteins. Among the vegetables studied, the wax gourd *(Benicasa hispida)* gives three crops a year of a large melonlike fruit that can be stored for 12 months without refrigeration. The mangosteen *(Garcinia mangostana)* is perhaps the world's best-tasting fruit, but it is little known outside the very humid tropics of Southeast Asia.

SOME BASIC GENETIC CONCEPTS IN PLANT IMPROVEMENT

To understand why the characteristics of parent plants do or do not appear in the seedling offspring and to see how genetic manipulation can improve plants, you need some knowledge of genetic processes and the structures controlling inheritance in plants.

Chromosomes

Some plants consist entirely of living cells whereas others, such as woody perennials, are made up of both living and dead cells (see Ch. 2). The living cell consists of a **cell wall** containing a fluid, the **cytoplasm,** in which the **nucleus** is suspended, along with many other structures. The nucleus contains the **chromosomes,** which carry most of the genetic information and transmit that information from one generation of cells to the next. The number of chromosomes is the same in all the vegetative cells of an entire plant species. This is usually the **2n,** or **diploid,** chromosome number (although higher numbers—tetraploid or octaploid, for example—also occur). In the sex cells—the egg and sperm—the number is reduced by half and is termed the **haploid,** or **1n,** chromosome number.

Although usually constant for a given species, the number, size, and appearance of chromosomes vary considerably between different plant species. The chromosomes can be counted by microscopic examination of the nucleus at a stage just before cell division. The chromosome numbers are known for most plant species. For example, the diploid chromosome number for alfalfa

(Medicago sativa) is 32; for barley *(Hordeum vulgare)*, 14; for corn *(Zea mays)*, 20; and for sugar beet *(Beta vulgaris)*, 18.

Chromosomes change in appearance during cellular development and division, but basically each is a long, threadlike structure consisting of **deoxyribonucleic acid (DNA)** plus associated **ribonucleic acids (RNA)** and various proteins. DNA can replicate itself and it can transmit information to other parts of the cell. DNA is a polymer—a very large molecule made up of many repeating units, but the repeating units called **nucleotides** can vary. DNA, the active genetic material, is a very large molecule composed of two spiral strands (see Fig. 4–3). The "backbone" of these strands is composed of

sugar residues (S) linked by **phosphates** (P) on each side. A sugar residue on one strand is connected with a sugar residue on the other by two **bases** that are linked to each other by **hydrogen bonds** (Fig. 4–3). These bases are **cytosine** (C), **guanine** (G), **adenine** (A), and **thymine** (T). The sugar residues in each strand are held tightly together by the phosphate radicals, but the two spiral strands are bound together more loosely by the hydrogen bonds.

One of the characteristics of DNA that makes it possible for the chromosomes to transmit genetic information from one cell generation to the next is its ability to replicate itself. This ability arises from the double-strand structure of the molecule and the properties of the

Fig. 4–3 *Left:* Schematic diagram of the DNA molecule showing the helical structure and the base pairing. Lower detailed view shows the alternate attachment of sugars (S) and phosphates (P) on each strand. Connecting the two strands are the base pairs adenine (A)–thymine (T) and guanine (G)–cytosine (C), which are held together by hydrogen bonds and attached to the sugars on each strand.
Right: During cell division and chromosome splitting, the DNA molecule replicates itself by unraveling, separating at the hydrogen bonds. Then each strand quickly becomes a new double strand just like the original, with each base attracting to itself its complementary base (A=T and G=C).
Source: (left) from McElroy and Swanson. 1976. *Modern cell biology.* 2nd ed. Englewood Cliffs, N.J.: Prentice-Hall.
(right) Wright, J. W. 1976. *Introduction to forest genetics.* New York: Academic Press.

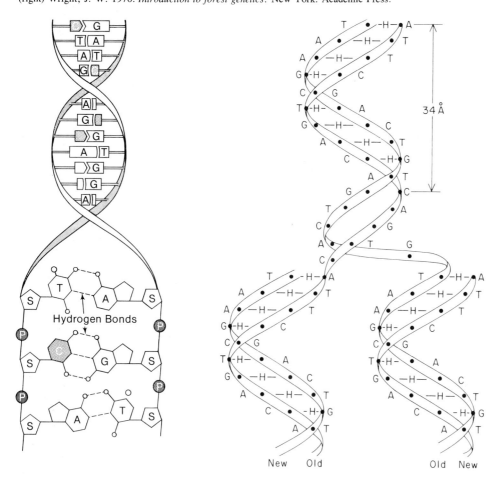

four bases. Adenine and thymine are held together by two hydrogen bonds (A = T). Their molecular structure is such that only they can join together. In the same manner, only cytosine and guanine can join together, and they are held by three hydrogen bonds (C ≡ G). When the chromosome divides during cell division, the two spiral strands of the DNA molecule unravel and separate at the position of these hydrogen bonds. Every base (cytosine, guanine, adenine, or thymine) attached to each strand attracts its complementary base, so that each single strand immediately becomes a new double strand exactly the same as the original double strand (see Fig. 4–3).

Although DNA includes the self-perpetuating **genetic code,** a related substance—ribonucleic acid (RNA)—actually controls the growth processes in the cell. DNA and RNA have certain differences. DNA is double-stranded whereas RNA is a single strand. RNA sugars have one more oxygen atom than DNA sugars. RNA has uracil (U) as a base in place of thymine (T). The DNA molecule acts as a template from which a complementary strand of RNA is formed (in the same manner by which a complementary strand of DNA forms from a single strand).

The form of RNA that carries the genetic instructions as a complementary copy of the DNA series of bases is called **messenger RNA.** Still another form of RNA—**transfer RNA**—is presumed to bring the amino acids to the ribosomes to construct the proteins.

Genes

A gene[4] structurally is a sequence of triplet organic bases (cytosine, guanine, adenine, and thymine) along a DNA molecule. The gene is the ultimate hereditary unit that functions as a certain part of a chromosome determining the development of a particular characteristic in an organism. Thus, one gene (or several interacting genes) may determine plant height, leaf shape, flower color, or fruit size. Genes are much too small to be seen, even with an electron microscope. There are, of course, a great many genes in each cell of the higher plants; they number in the thousands. Any individual gene may have a large effect or a small effect. Some genes act independently whereas others act only in conjunction with other genes.

Since genes are arranged along the chromosome, genes on the same chromosome are **linked**—that is,

---

[4] Virus particles are believed to be similar to or identical with genes. Since viruses can be isolated and easily studied, much knowledge of gene structure is obtained from the study of viruses.

genes on the same chromosome move from one cell generation to the next as a unit. Linkage is not perfect, however; sometimes during meiosis (reduction cell division), chromosomes break and exchange parts, as we will soon study in more detail.

Homologous Chromosomes

In each vegetative cell there are pairs of each individual chromosome. These are called **homologous chromosomes** and are properly defined as such if they each have the same gene or genes affecting the same traits at corresponding positions. Genes are termed **alleles** to each other if they occupy the same position on homologous chromosomes and affect the same trait. If a plant had the genetic constitution ABCDEFG/abcdefg on a certain pair of homologous chromosomes, the genes A and a would be alleles, B and b would be alleles, and so forth.

Allelic genes can be dominant or recessive to each other. A **dominant gene,** A, is one that causes a certain characteristic to be expressed whether the plant is **homozygous,** AA—both alleles the same—or **heterozygous,** Aa—the two alleles different. A **recessive gene** causes the character it controls to be expressed only if both alleles are recessive, aa. (By convention, capital letters express dominant genes, while lower-case express recessive genes.)

Mitosis

Cell division in the shoot and root tips, axillary buds, leaf primordia, and the vascular cambium—all of which increases plant size—is called **mitosis** (see Fig. 5–4, p. 90). These vegetative cells usually contain two sets of homologous chromosomes—the 2n or diploid number. During cell division, the chromosomes split longitudinally, replicating to produce two chromosomes that are identical to each other. One of each pair goes to one daughter cell, and one to the other. An equatorial plate, as it is called, develops between them to form a new cell wall and thus two new cells, each with its full complement of chromosomes—and genes. So each daughter cell has a genotype identical to that of the mother cell.

Meiosis and Fertilization

Meiosis refers to the type of cell division, sometimes called **reduction division,** that occurs in the flower to form—in the angiosperms—the cells from which the pollen grains and the embryo sac (which contains the egg) develop (see Figs. 4–4 and 4–5). In this type of cell

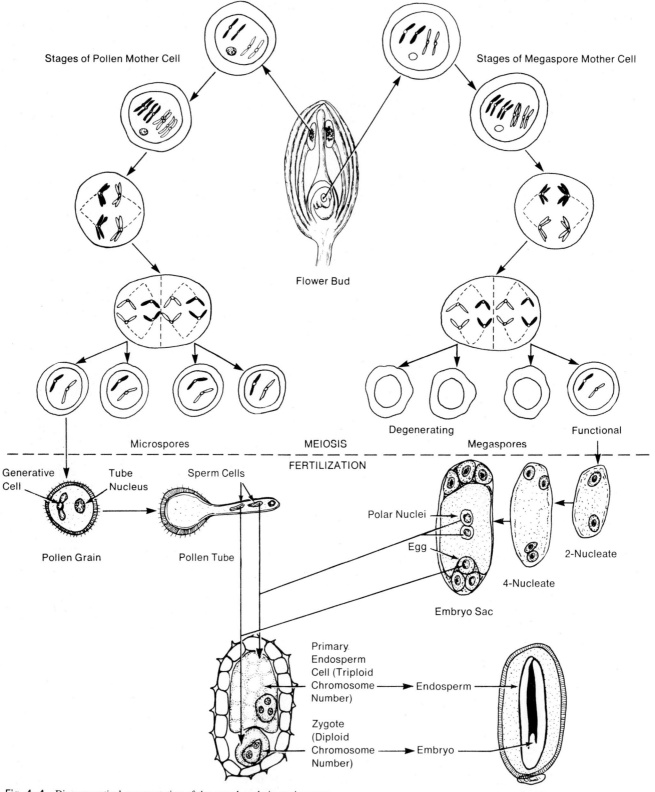

Stages of Pollen Mother Cell

Stages of Megaspore Mother Cell

Flower Bud

Microspores

MEIOSIS

Degenerating

Functional

Megaspores

FERTILIZATION

Generative Cell

Tube Nucleus

Sperm Cells

Polar Nuclei

Egg

2-Nucleate

Pollen Grain

Pollen Tube

4-Nucleate

Embryo Sac

Primary Endosperm Cell (Triploid Chromosome Number) → Endosperm → Endosperm

Zygote (Diploid Chromosome Number) → Embryo → Embryo

Seed

Fig. 4–4 Diagrammatical representation of the sexual cycle in angiosperms.
Meiosis occurs in the flower bud in the anther (male) and the pistil (female) during
the bud stage. During this process the pollen mother cells and the megaspore mother cells,
both diploid, undergo a reduction division in which homologous chromosomes segregate to different cells.
This is followed immediately by a mitotic division which produces four daughter cells, each with half the chromosomes of the mother cells.
In fertilization a male gamete unites with the egg to produce a zygote, in which the diploid chromosome number is restored.
A second male gamete unites with the polar nuclei to produce the endosperm.
Source: Hartmann, H. T. and D. E. Kester. 1975. *Plant propagation.* 3rd ed. Englewood Cliffs, N.J.: Prentice-Hall.

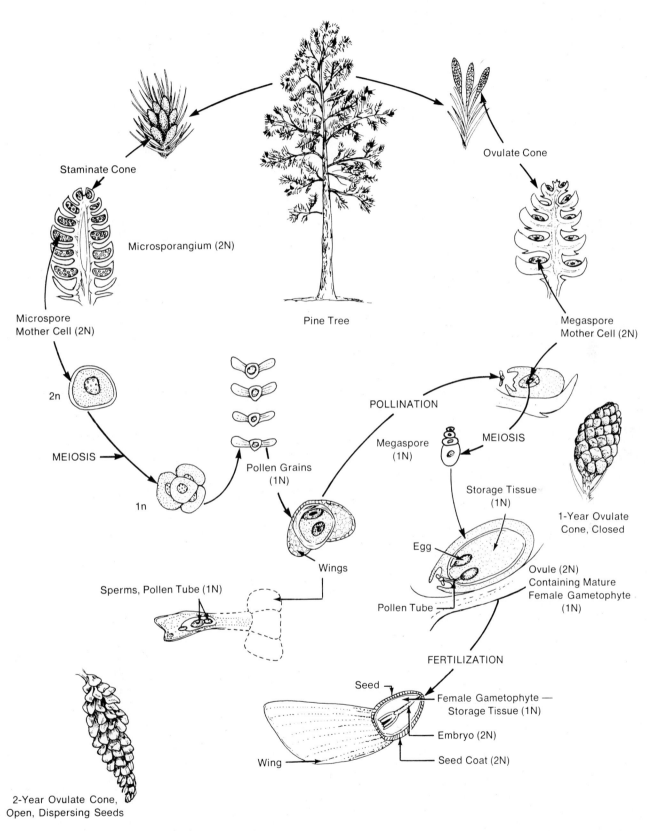

Fig. 4–5 Diagrammatical representation of the sexual cycle in a gymnosperm (pine), showing meiosis and fertilization. *Source:* Hartmann, H. T. and D. E. Kester. 1975. *Plant propagation.* 3rd ed. Englewood Cliffs, N.J.: Prentice-Hall.

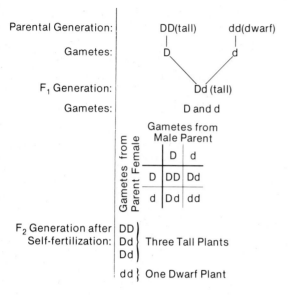

Parental Generation: DD(tall)   dd(dwarf)

Gametes: D   d

F₁ Generation: Dd (tall)

Gametes: D and d

Gametes from
Male Parent

		D	d
Gametes from Parent Female	D	DD	Dd
	d	Dd	dd

F₂ Generation after
Self-fertilization: DD }
                       Dd } Three Tall Plants
                       Dd }

                       dd } One Dwarf Plant

Parental generation: YYgg (white nectarine)   yyGG (yellow peach)

Gametes: Yg   yG

F₁ Generation after
Cross-Fertilization: YyGg (white peach)

                                    YG
Gametes: Yg
                                    yG
                                    yg

Gametes from Male Parent

	YG	Yg	yG	yg
YG	YYGG	YYGg	YyGG	YyGg
Yg	YYGg	YYgg	YyGg	Yygg
yG	YyGG	YyGg	yyGG	yyGg
yg	YyGg	Yygg	yyGg	yygg

(Gametes from Female Parent)

F₂ Generation after
Self-Fertilization: 1 YYGG
                       2 YyGG
                       2 YYGg } Nine White Peaches
                       4 YyGg

                       1 YYgg
                       2 Yygg } Three White Nectarines

                       1 yyGG
                       2 yyGg } Three Yellow Peaches

                       1 yygg } One Yellow Nectarine

---

division, the homologous chromosomes separate from each other without replicating, one going to one daughter cell and one to the other, thus reducing the number of chromosomes—the 1n or haploid number. During pairing of the two sets of homologous chromosomes, **crossing over** can occur. The chromosomes may break at the same locus on each so that they may rejoin after exchanging segments. Thus, if the original gene sequence on the homologous chromosomes was ABCDEFGHI/abcdefghi and crossing over occurred between E and F, then the gene sequence for this particular chromosome appearing in the pollen grain or egg cell would be ABCDEfghi or abcdeFHGI. This gene alteration would, of course, be expressed in altered characteristics of the new plants.

In **fertilization** in angiosperms, one male gamete (1n) from the pollen grain unites with a female gamete—the egg (1n)—to form the zygote (2n), which develops into the embryo and finally the new plant (see Figs. 4–4, 4–5, and 6–13). The manner in which these gametes can segregate and reunite to form new combinations is illustrated for both a monohybrid and a dihybrid cross in Figure 4–6. Also during fertilization in the angiosperms, one male gamete (1n) unites with the two polar nuclei (1n each) in the embryo sac to form a food storage tissue, the endosperm (3n), that can serve as a nutritive material for the developing embryo. The seed coats, developing by mitosis from the female parent, cover both the endosperm and the embryo. In gymnosperms, the endosperm tissue—more correctly termed the female gametophyte—is 1n tissue, rather than 3n as in the angiosperms (see Fig. 4–5).

Fig. 4–6 *Above:* Inheritance involving a single gene pair in a monohybrid cross (one characteristic involved). In garden peas tallness (D) is dominant over dwarfness (d). A tall pea plant is either homozygous (DD) or heterozygous (Dd). Segregation occurs in the F₂ generation to produce three genotypes (see p. 75) (DD, Dd, dd) and two phenotypes (see p. 75) (tall and dwarf). *Below:* Inheritance in a dihybrid cross (two characteristics involved) involving peach (*Prunus persica*). Fuzzy skin (G) of a peach is dominant over the glabrous (i.e., smooth) skin of the nectarine (g). White flesh color (Y) is dominant over yellow flesh color (y). In the example shown, the phenotype of the F₁ generation is different from either parent. Segregation in the F₂ generation produces nine genotypes and four phenotypes. *Source:* Hartmann, H. T. and D. E. Kester. 1975. *Plant propagation.* 3rd ed. Englewood Cliffs, N.J.: Prentice-Hall.

Mutations

As plants grow, hundreds of thousands of cells may be dividing constantly. At each cell division, DNA must replicate itself—the double strand must untwist, the millions of nucleotide triplets must be reproduced exactly on new single strands, and the single strands must then twist around each other to form new double strands. It is a marvel that this complicated process takes place on such a grand scale. With so many cells involved, however, errors can and do occur during replication. When they do they are called **mutations,** and the altered genes may possibly result in changes in the characteristics of the plant—although most mutations have such slight effects that they go unnoticed. The great majority of mutations are deleterious, but some are not and they provide a source of variability that aids the plant breeder in developing new cultivars. Mutation rates can be vastly increased by treatment with ionizing radiation and by certain chemicals. Mutations that occur during the formation of pollen grains and egg cells and appear in the plant's seedling offspring are particularly important to the plant breeder.

In addition to gene mutations, hereditary modifications can also be caused by gross changes in chromosome number or structure. This can involve the doubling of chromosome numbers, the addition or subtraction of an entire chromosome, or some other structural change in a chromosome. Such gross chromosome changes may cause pronounced changes in the plant's characteristics.

Polyploidy

Polyploidy is a condition in which individual plants have more than two sets of homologous chromosomes in their somatic (vegetative) cells. Beyond the normal diploid (2n) number, plants may be triploid (3n), tetraploid (4n), pentaploid (5n), hexaploid (6n), and so forth. Polyploid plants may arise by duplication of the chromosome sets from a single species—**autoploidy**—or by a combination of chromosome sets from two or more species—**alloploidy.** The latter is the more common type of polyploidy in nature. Many of the cultivated crop species evolved in nature as polyploids, as shown in Table 4–2 for oats, wheat, and tobacco.

Cytoplasmic Inheritance

While most inherited characteristics are transmitted by the genes in the nucleus, certain characteristics in some herbaceous plants can be controlled by cytoplasmic factors, which are contributed only by the female parent. Male sterility in corn is due, in part, to a cytoplasmic factor and is used to produce hybrid seed without the laborious procedure of hand detasseling (see p. 81).

Genotype and Phenotype

The term **genotype** refers to the genetic makeup of the plant—its genetic constitution—the kinds of genes it has on the chromosomes and the order in which they are situated. **Phenotype** refers to the plant's appearance, behavior, and chemical and physical properties. The phenotype is also influenced by the environment. A plant may have genes for very vigorous growth but when grown under a deficiency of soil nitrogen, for example, its inherent vigor is not expressed. However, the genes still control the plant's characteristics even if an environmental factor drastically alters the phenotype. Therefore, if seeds are taken from stunted plants grown under deficient soil nitrogen conditions and planted in rich fertile soil, the plants again show the strong, vigorous growth called for by their genotype.

Table 4–2

Common name	Species	Somatic chromosome number
Sand oats	*Avena strigosa*	14
Slender wild oats	*Avena barbata*	28
Cultivated oats	*Avena sativa*	42
Einkorn	*Triticum monococcum*	14
Emmer	*Triticum dicoccum*	28
Common wheat	*Triticum aestivum*	42
Wild tobacco	*Nicotiana sylvestris*	24
Cultivated tobacco	*Nicotiana tabacum*	48

The art of hybridizing plants is not difficult. With a few supplies and some practice, any home gardener can assist nature in rearranging genes to produce completely new genotypes resulting in plants with new characteristics *(19)*.

The first step is to select the plants to be the parents. Success is more likely if both are in the same species, although quite often crosses between plants in two different species—but in the same genus—can succeed.

The second step is to be sure that the flowers on the plant selected as the female parent are not pollinated by their own pollen or by some stray unwanted pollen brought in by insects or wind. This is best accomplished by carefully cutting off the petals and the stamens (filament plus anther) just before the flowers open and before the anthers start to shed their pollen.

The third step is to cover the emasculated flower—which now contains only the pistil, made up of the ovary, the style, and the stigma—with a pollen-tight cloth or paper bag to keep out unwanted pollen. The material should be opaque to reduce light and prevent heat build-up in the bag: A clear polyethylene bag if exposed to the sun would trap so much heat that the tender flower tissues would be injured.

The fourth step is to collect pollen from flowers of the desired male parent (Fig. 4–7). The flowers are closely observed to determine the stage when the anthers begin to open and shed pollen. At this point, placing a small envelope under the anthers and tapping lightly can yield a considerable amount of pollen.

The fifth step is to place the collected pollen on the stigmas of the emasculated flowers (Fig. 4–7). The stigma is receptive when it is fresh looking and has a sticky surface. This period may last only one to three days. Pollination is done by removing the bag covering the flower and applying pollen quickly with a small brush, a cork, or a rubber pencil eraser dipped into the pollen supply. The bag should then be put back over the flower to keep out unwanted pollen. If the pollen is dry, as is the case with wind-pollinated plants, pollen can be placed in an atomizer and blown into the closed bag through a hole punched in a corner. Again, to keep out unwanted pollen, the hole should be sealed immediately. The cross-pollinated flowers should be tagged to identify the parents. After blooming is complete, the bags can be removed.

The sixth step is to collect the fruits when they are mature and extract the seeds and plant them, still maintaining their identity by careful labeling. In woody perennial species, the seeds may have dormancy problems and germination may require certain treatments (see p. 84).

When the hybrid seedling emerges its vegetative characteristics as well as those of the flowers and resulting fruits should be noted. Particularly desirable hybrids can be saved and others discarded. Stocks of outstanding new hybrid plants can often be built up rapidly by vegetative propagation methods, such as rooting cuttings (see p. 92). For those species that breed true to type (homozygous) and are self-pollinated, seeds from the new hybrid can be saved and planted.

Fig. 4–7   Hybridizing peaches. *Above:* Collection of pollen from peach flowers. The anthers are scraped from the unopened flowers and dried, allowing the pollen to escape. The pollen is then stored in small vials for use later. *Below:* Hand pollination of a peach flower. The pollen is placed on the stigma of an emasculated (anthers removed) flower with the tip of a cork.

SUMMARY

Most of the crop plants grown today were cultivated in some primitive form before earliest recorded history. The dawn of agriculture is believed to have occurred some 10,000 years ago in various parts of the world—Southwest and Southeast Asia, middle America, and western South America. Early peoples could have used both vegetative and sexual methods in domesticating crops from the wild forms. The crops we know today were gradually improved to increase yield and improve quality over long time spans, first by rather simple selection processes then, starting in the early part of the twentieth century, by the much more spectacular methods of Mendelian genetics. Starting in the 1970s, genetic engineering, as practiced by cell biologists, biochemists, and geneticists, has been genetically designing crop plants to fit various environmental situations. Plant explorers over the years have combed the largely uninhabited areas of the world and brought back numerous plants to the populated regions. In many cases the introduced plants have been utilized as important food crops and ornamental flowers, shrubs, and trees. Concern has developed worldwide over the preservation of endangered plant forms. Steps have been taken to preserve these plant types either as seeds or as growing plants in germplasm "banks" for use by present-day and future plant breeders. Plant breeders can improve existing plant types by employing basic genetic concepts.

REVIEW QUESTIONS

4–1. How long ago and in what parts of the world did agriculture begin?

4–2. Where is the Fertile Crescent and what does this term mean?

4–3. What cultivated crops originated in the area of the present-day United States?

4–4. What is the advantage of using vegetative methods over sexual methods in domesticating cultivated crops from the wild forms? Conversely, what advantage is there in using sexual methods in crop improvement?

4–5. What big advantage does sexual reproduction of plants have over vegetative reproduction under conditions of a changing environment?

4–6. Why has the production of hybrid corn been so much more successful than the production of hybrid wheat?

4–7. How were cereal grain crops improved before the advent of the principles of Mendelian genetics in the early 1900s?

4–8. What is meant by the term *genetic engineering?*

4–9. Name five famous plant explorers.

4–10. What programs are now in effect in the United States to preserve valuable plant material in the living state?

4–11. In which regions did most of the world's food crops originate—the temperate zones or the tropical and subtropical zones? What is a possible reason for your answer?

SUPPLEMENTARY READING

BROERTJES, C. 1978. *The application of mutation breeding methods in the improvement of vegetatively propagated plants.* Amsterdam: Elsevier.

JANICK, J., and J. N. MOORE, eds. 1975. *Advances in fruit breeding.* West Lafayette, Ind.: Purdue University Press.

REED, H. S. 1942. *A short history of the plant sciences.* Waltham, Mass.: Chronica Botanica.

SPRAGUE, G. F., D. E. ALEXANDER, and J. W. DUDLEY. 1980. Plant breeding and genetic engineering: a perspective. *BioScience* 30(1): 17–21.

REFERENCES

1. Baker, H. G. 1978. *Plants and civilization.* 3rd ed. Belmont, Calif.: Wadsworth.

2. Bender, B. 1975. *Farming in prehistory.* London: John Baker.

3. Burgess, S., ed. 1971. *The national program for conservation of crop germplasm.* USDA/ARS and State Agr. Exp. Sta. Dir. Assoc.

4. Carlson, P. S., and J. C. Polacco. 1975. Plant cell cultures: genetic aspects of crop improvement. In P. H. Abelson, ed. *Food, politics, economics, nutrition, research,* Washington, D.C.: American Association for the Advancement of Science.

5. Carlson, P. S., H. H. Smith, and R. Dearing. 1972. Parasexual interspecific hybridization. *Proc. Nat. Acad. Sci.* 69:2292–94.

6. DeCandolle, A. 1886. *Origin of cultivated plants.* 2nd ed. Reprinted 1959. New York: Hafner.

7. Dewey, D. R., and K. H. Asay. 1975. The crested wheatgrasses of Iran. *Crop Sci.* 15:844–49.

8. Fairchild, D. 1938. *The world was my garden.* New York: Scribner's.

9. Harlan, J. R. 1971. Agricultural origins: centers and non-centers. *Science* 174:468–74.

10. ———. 1975. *Crops and man.* Madison, Wisc.: American Society of Agronomy and Crop Science Society of America.

11. ———. 1975. Our vanishing genetic resources. In P. H. Abelson, ed., *Food, politics, economics, nutrition, research.* Washington, D.C.: American Association for the Advancement of Science.

12. ———. 1976. The plants and animals that nourish man. *Sci. Am.* 235(3):88–97.

13. Heiser, C. B., Jr. 1973. *Seed to civilization.* San Francisco: W. H. Freeman & Company Publishers.

14. Jain, S. K., and M. N. Gagnon, eds. 1977. Germplasm. *Calif. Agr.* (special issue) 31(9).

15. James, E. 1967. Preservation of seed stocks. *Adv. Agron.* 19:87–106.

16. Jennings, P. 1976. The amplification of agricultural production. *Sci. Am.* 235(3):180–94.

17. Klose, N. 1950. *America's crop heritage.* Ames: Iowa State College Press.

18. Lemmon, K. 1969. *The golden age of plant hunters.* Cranbury, N.J.: A. S. Barnes.

19. McGourty, F. Jr., ed. *Breeding plants for home and garden, plants & gardens,* vol. 30, no. 1. Brooklyn, N.Y.: Brooklyn Botanic Garden.

20. Mangelsdorf, P. C. 1974. *Corn: Its origin, evolution, and improvement.* Cambridge, Mass.: Harvard University Press.

21. Murashige, T. 1974. Plant propagation through tissue cultures. *Ann. Rev. Plant Physiol.* 25:135–66.

22. Nabors, M. W. 1976. Using spontaneously occurring and induced mutations to obtain agriculturally useful plants. *BioScience* 26(12):761–68.

23. Pardee, W. D. 1976. Plant breeding in New York. *N.Y. Food and Life Sci. Quart.* 9(1):10–15.

24. Ruskin, F. R., ed. 1975. *Underexploited tropical plants with promising economic value.* Washington, D.C.: National Academy of Science.

25. Sauer, C. O. 1969. *Agricultural origins and dispersals.* Cambridge, Mass.: M.I.T. Press.

26. Shepherd, K. W., and G. M. E. Mayo. 1975. Genes conferring specific disease resistance. In P. H. Abelson, ed. *Food, politics, economics, nutrition, research.* Washington, D.C.: American Association for the Advancement of Science.

27. Skrdla, W. H. 1972. New crops—food for the future? *HortScience* 7(2):156–59.

28. Stoner, A. K. 1976. Tomatoes—Andes Mountains to American tables. *Am. Hort.* 55(2):8–13, 37.

29. Sutton, S. B. 1976. A plant hunter in China. *Horticulture* 54(2):56–63.

30. Ucko, P. J., and G. W. Dimbleby, eds. 1969. *The domestication and exploitation of plants and animals.* Chicago: Aldine.

31. Vavilov, N. I. 1951. *The origin, variation, immunity, and breeding of cultivated plants.* K. S. Chester, trans. Waltham, Mass.: Chronica Botanica.

32. Whyte, R. O. 1958. *Plant exploration, collection and introduction.* FAO Agricultural Studies No. 41. Rome: Food and Agriculture Organization of the United Nations.

33. Wilkes, G. 1977. Breeding crisis for our crops: Is the gene pool drying up? *Horticulture* 55(4):53–59.

34. Zohary, D., and P. Spiegel-Roy. 1975. Beginnings of fruit growing in the Old World. *Science* 187(4174):319–27.

Propagation of Plants

Plants are propagated by either sexual (seed) or asexual (vegetative) methods. Some kinds of plants are almost always propagated by one method or the other; other kinds can be propagated successfully either way. The various ways of propagating plants are outlined in Table 5–1.

Table 5–1 Methods of Propagating Plants, with Typical Examples

I. *Sexual*
 A. Propagation by seed—annual, biennial, and many perennial plants
II. *Asexual (vegetative)*
 A. Propagation by apomictic embryos (see p. 92)—citrus, mango
 B. Propagation by cuttings
  1. Stem cuttings
   a. Hardwood—fig, grape, quince, rose, willow, poplar
   b. Semihardwood—lemon, rhododendron, camellia, holly
   c. Softwood—lilac, pyracantha, weigela, crepe myrtle
   d. Herbaceous—begonia, coleus, chrysanthemum, sugar cane
  2. Leaf cuttings—*Begonia rex,* sansevieria, African violet
  3. Leaf-bud cuttings—blackberry, hydrangea, *Kalanchoe*
  4. Root cuttings—phlox, daphne, horseradish
 C. Propagation by grafting
  1. Root grafting
   a. Whip graft—apple, pear
  2. Crown grafting
   a. Whip graft—Persian walnut
   b. Cleft graft—camellia, grape
  3. Top grafting
   a. Cleft graft—various fruit trees
   b. Bark graft—various fruit trees
   c. Whip graft—various fruit trees
 D. Propagation by budding
  1. T-budding—stone and pome fruit trees, rose
  2. Patch budding—walnut and pecan
 E. Propagation by layering
  1. Tip—trailing blackberry, black raspberry
  2. Simple—honeysuckle, spirea, grape, filbert
  3. Mound or stool—apple rootstocks, gooseberry
  4. Air (pot or Chinese)—India rubber plant, litchi
 F. Propagation by runners—strawberry,
 G. Propagation by suckers—red raspberry, blackberry
 H. Propagation by separation
  1. Bulbs—hyacinth, lily, narcissus, tulip
  2. Corms—gladiolus, crocus, freesia
 I. Propagation by division
  1. Stem tubers—white potato
  2. Tuberous roots—sweet potato, dahlia
  3. Rhizomes—iris, canna
 J. Micropropagation
  1. Shoot-tip culture—orchid, carnation, asparagus, chrysanthemum
  2. Tissue culture—rhododendron
  3. "Embryo" culture—orchid

CHOICE OF PROPAGATION METHODS

In propagating plants we are often interested in starting with one or a few plants and producing many more—maybe hundreds of thousands more—all just like the original. A successful propagation method is one that will transmit all the characteristics of the original mother plant to all the daughter plants. If the desirable characteristics of the mother plant are lost or changed during the propagation procedures, that particular method is unsatisfactory for that type of plant. It is then necessary to use another propagation procedure that will preserve these characteristics.

It is important to realize that the kinds of agricultural and ornamental plants being grown today are ones having particularly desirable characteristics. As Chapter 4 pointed out, such plants originated from a mother plant or plants found growing in the wild or in cultivated plant populations or from mutations or from breeding programs conducted by government agencies or private plant breeders. With the appropriate propagation procedures, such plants can become the starting point for populations of many millions of individuals, all just like the original mother plant. As explained in Chapter 3, the groups of plants that people have developed and cultivate have been given cultivar names, for example, Redhaven peach, Bing cherry, Big Boy tomato, Pawnee wheat, Acala 4-42 cotton, Imperial Blue pansy, Golden Cross Bantam sweet corn, Peace rose, Ranger alfalfa, etc. The propagation methods used for increasing the populations of these groups of plants must do so without changing their characteristics.

There are several kinds of cultivars. If the plant group will reproduce "true" by seeds—with no characteristics changed—the cultivar is termed a **line** (see Ch. 3). A line is homozygous[1] and, if self-pollinated (or if cross-pollination is prevented), seed propagation will give daughter plants like the mother plant. Many of the world's leading economic plants—the cereals, the vegetables, and the garden flowers—are made up of groups of these lines. They are seed propagated and will faithfully maintain their characteristics when propagated in this manner. Many forest species, although seed propagated, are not considered lines because of their higher level of variability. They are known by their species names, such as Douglas fir *(Pseudotsuga menziesii),* ponderosa pine *(Pinus ponderosa)*, or coast redwood *(Sequoia sempervirens)*.

In addition to lines, there are other types of seed-propagated cultivars, such as **inbred lines**—used to produce hybrid cultivars—and **hybrids**—as in hybrid corn (see Fig. 5–1).

Many groups of plants are heterozygous[2] rather than homozygous. These include fruit and nut species, many forage crops and woody ornamentals. These plants have many dissimilar genes controlling their characteristics. During embryo formation in the seed, these genes segregate and recombine in a great many different ways so that the resulting plants differ from each other and from their parent. With these plants, seed propagation cannot maintain the characteristics of the female parent and cannot be used as a successful propagation procedure. With such heterozygous plants, vegetative (asexual) propagation is usually used. A piece of vegetative tissue—a section of a stem, root, or leaf—is placed in a suitable environment, such as a warm, humid rooting frame in the greenhouse. In time, the piece of tissue may regenerate the missing part: a stem piece forms roots, a root piece forms shoots, a leaf forms both shoots and roots. By these means, new plants form that are exactly the same genetically as the plant from which the piece of vegetative tissue was taken; therefore the new plant has all the same characteristics as the parent. The flower is not involved, allowing no opportunity for genetic change (unless, perhaps, a mutation has occurred, which does happen, but rarely). When such vegetative propagation is used, cultivars, even though heterozygous, can be perpetuated generation after generation, involving hundreds of thousands or more individual plants. Cultivars originating from a single plant and maintained in this manner by vegetative propagation are called **clones.**

The vegetative procedures just described—where a piece of tissue regenerates the missing part—is termed **cutting propagation.** There are a number of other, somewhat more complicated vegetative propagation methods, such as grafting (p. 100), budding (p. 104), layering (p. 108), and runners (p. 111).

SEXUAL PROPAGATION

In the sexual reproduction of plants, a seed must be produced in a flower. Seed formation is preceded by a type of cell division termed **meiosis** or reduction division, in which the number of chromosomes in the cells is reduced

---

[1]Having similar genes of a Mendelian pair present in the same cell as, for example, a dwarf pea plant with genes (tt) for dwarfness only.

[2]Having different genes of a Mendelian pair in the same cell as, for example, a tall pea plant with genes for tallness (T) and genes for dwarfness (t).

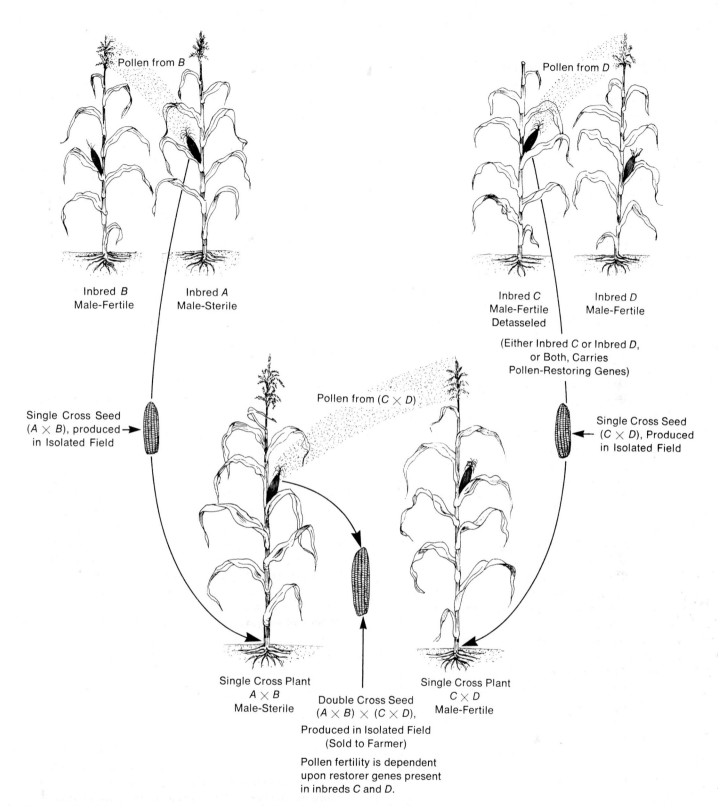

Pollen from B

Pollen from D

Inbred B
Male-Fertile

Inbred A
Male-Sterile

Inbred C
Male-Fertile
Detasseled

Inbred D
Male-Fertile

(Either Inbred C or Inbred D,
or Both, Carries
Pollen-Restoring Genes)

Single Cross Seed
(A × B), produced →
in Isolated Field

Pollen from (C × D)

Single Cross Seed
← (C × D), Produced
in Isolated Field

Single Cross Plant
A × B
Male-Sterile

Double Cross Seed
(A × B) × (C × D),

Produced in Isolated Field
(Sold to Farmer)

Pollen fertility is dependent
upon restorer genes present
in inbreds C and D.

Single Cross Plant
C × D
Male-Fertile

Fig. 5–1 Hybrid seed corn production by the utilization of cytoplasmic
male sterility in production of single cross and double cross. In this
example only one inbred, A, is male sterile. The cytoplasmic male sterility
is transmitted to the single cross A × B. Pollen-restoring genes carried by
the inbreds C or D give pollen fertility to the double cross (A × B) × (C × D) also.
Source: USDA.

by half to form the male sperm cell and the female egg. The egg and sperm combine during fertilization in the ovule to form the zygote that develops into the embryo. These processes are illustrated in Figures 4–4 and 4–5.

Seed Production

If a cultivar—Great Lakes head lettuce, Calrose rice, or Kombar barley, for example—is to be maintained by seed propagation, careful control of the seed source is essential. If the cultivar is homozygous and self-pollinated, seed purity is generally assured. If the cultivar is homozygous but will cross-pollinate with other cultivars or with other species, then the plants used to produce the seeds must be separated by distances of at least several hundred feet from other plants with which they are likely to cross to prevent pollen contamination and loss of genetic purity.

With certain plants propagated by seed, some variability may be tolerated, or it may even be desirable. Examples are reforestation projects, tree and shrub plantings in shelter belts, plantings for wildlife cover, and plant breeding projects.

Most states in the United States and many other countries have established seed certification programs to protect and maintain the genetic quality of cultivars. Government agencies set standards for seed, particularly for such field and forage crops as soybeans, rice, wheat, oats, alfalfa, and clovers. Isolation standards for the seed-producing fields are established, as are requirements for roguing or culling out off-types, diseased plants, and weeds. Field inspections and final seed testing are included in such programs. Thorough cleaning of seed harvesting equipment between seed lots is required.

Seed certification programs in the United States recognize four classes of seeds in agronomic crops, such as cotton, alfalfa, soybeans, and cereal grains:

1. *Breeder seed.* This is produced only in small amounts and is under the control of the plant breeder. It is planted to produce foundation seed. Breeder seed is labeled with a white tag.
2. *Foundation seed.* This is multiplied from breeder seed; it is available only in limited amounts and is planted to produce registered seed. It is controlled by public or private foundation seed stock organizations. Foundation seed is also labeled with a white tag.
3. *Registered seed.* This is the seed source for growers of certified seed and is under the control of the registered seed producers. It is the progeny of either breeder or foundation seed. It is labeled with a purple tag.

4. *Certified seed.* This seed is available in large quantities and is sold to farmers for general crop production. It is labeled with a blue tag. Certified seed is of known genetic identity and purity.

Genetic quality of vegetable and flower seeds, however, is largely regulated by the seed companies, which maintain careful control over their seed plantings and continually test seed purity in special test gardens.

The production of plants from **hybrid seeds** has been one of the outstanding scientific breakthroughs in agricultural history. The use of hybrid seed has more than doubled the yield of both sweet corn and field corn. In the United States, virtually all corn is now produced from hybrid seed. This method of producing hybrid corn seed (see Chs. 4 and 23) was developed in 1918, but it was not used commercially until about 1935 (Figs. 2–3 and 5–1). Hybrid barley and alfalfa cultivars have also been released, and almost all grain sorghum produced in the United States comes from hybrid seed. Considerable research and millions of dollars have been expended by public and private agencies in trying to develop practical methods of producing hybrid seeds of wheat to increase yields, but these are still without the spectacular success achieved with corn. Wheat flowers are not structured for easy cross-pollination, as are the flowers of corn.

The use of F_1[3] hybrid seeds of several of the herbaceous bedding plants—petunias, zinnias, pansies, and marigolds—has made possible much superior flower types and plant vigor, and has given a great boost to the bedding plant industry. Hybrid seeds have greatly increased yields and quality of such vegetable crops as tomato, squash, cucumber, muskmelon, cauliflower, and broccoli.

A seed production industry has developed since about 1935, and it has made outstanding contributions to the increased production of world crops. Working with government and private plant breeders and seed certification agencies, the seed industry has supplied the channels for rapid seed increase and distribution while safeguarding genetic cultivar purity. Many progressive farmers in North America have become accustomed to using certified seed obtained from recognized seed producers rather than relying on their own or a neighbor's ''bin-run'' seed of dubious quality.

Seed Formation

Seeds originate as the final product of a plant's sexual reproduction system (see p. 131, Ch. 6). Figures 2–31,

---

[3]F_1 hybrid is the first generation offspring of a cross between two individuals differing in one or more genes.

2–32, and 6–13 illustrate the parts of the flower and show which parts develop into the various parts of the seed.

A seed has three essential parts:

1. The **embryo,** which develops into the new plant.
2. **Food storage material,** which is available to nourish the embryonic plant. This may be either endosperm tissue or the fleshy cotyledon(s), a part of the embryo itself.
3. **Seed coverings,** which are usually the two seed coats but may include other parts of the ovary wall.

The parts of the seed as they develop from the parts of the flower are:

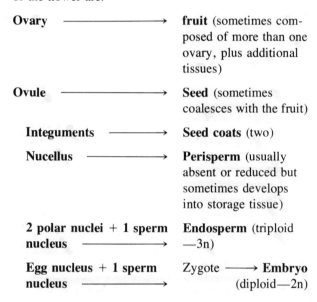

Ovary ⟶ **fruit** (sometimes composed of more than one ovary, plus additional tissues)

Ovule ⟶ **Seed** (sometimes coalesces with the fruit)

Integuments ⟶ **Seed coats** (two)

Nucellus ⟶ **Perisperm** (usually absent or reduced but sometimes develops into storage tissue)

2 polar nuclei + 1 sperm nucleus ⟶ **Endosperm** (triploid —3n)

Egg nucleus + 1 sperm nucleus ⟶ Zygote ⟶ **Embryo** (diploid—2n)

After pollination and fertilization (see p. 131, Ch. 6) are completed, many changes occur in the flower to produce the fruit and the seed. Fruits and seeds appear in innumerable forms, depending upon the species (see Ch. 2), but they all contain the same three essential parts listed above.

Seed Storage and Viability Testing

For a seed to germinate, the embryo must be alive. In some plants, such as the hard-seeded legumes, the embryo generally remains alive for a great many years. In others, such as the willow, maple, and elm, the embryos are very short lived, remaining viable for only a few days or months. Seeds of other kinds of plants range between these extremes, the length of embryo viability often depending upon seed storage conditions. For example, seeds stored in a sealed container under refrigeration at 0° to 4°C (32° to 40°F) and at low relative humidity (e.g.,

15 percent, which would give a seed moisture level of about 4 to 7 percent) generally retain viability considerably longer than seeds stored at room temperature and high relative humidity. Seeds of certain plants, however, soon become desiccated if stored under dry conditions, and the embryos die. Examples are citrus, maple, oak, hickory, and walnut.

It is often advisable before planting seeds, especially those of woody perennials and those which may have been stored for several years, to test the viability of a representative sample of the seed lot to be planted. There are several **seed viability tests.**

One easy means of determining the possible germinability of a seed lot is a **cut test.** Seeds of a representative sample are simply cut in half to see whether there is an embryo inside. Often the embryo has aborted or has been eaten by insects and, of course, the seed would not germinate. The mere presence of an embryo, however, does not mean it is alive.

Another simple test is to float the seeds in water. Quite often the "floaters" are empty seeds and can be skimmed off. The sound, full seeds sink and are the ones to be planted.

X-ray photographs of seeds do essentially the same thing as a cut test and are used in some seed laboratories to determine if the seed is empty or the embryo is shrunken. X-ray tests can also be used to determine the optimum time to harvest seeds by observing when the embryos have completely filled the seed.

These tests are not, strictly speaking, viability tests but are useful to rule out seeds that have no possibility of germinating. They still do not give the viability status of seeds with full-sized, apparently sound embryos.

GERMINATION TEST

The germination test is useful for flower, vegetable, and grain seeds that have no dormancy problems. The seeds can be tested for germinability by several methods, such as rolling them in several layers of moist paper toweling, or actually planting the seeds in flats of soil or sand in a greenhouse. Seed-testing laboratories have elaborate seed germination boxes with controlled lighting and temperature. After several days or weeks, viability is calculated as the percentage of seedlings developing from the number of seeds planted.

TETRAZOLIUM TEST

The chemical 2,3,5-triphenyl tetrazolium chloride, which is colorless when dissolved in water, changes to the red-colored chemical triphenyl formazan whenever it contacts living, respiring tissue. In living tissues, enzymes change the tetrazolium salt to formazan. In dead, nonrespiring tissues, these enzymes are not active. In this test, the seeds are usually soaked in water to allow them to become completely hydrated, then cut in half lengthwise to expose the embryo. They are then placed in a 0.1 to 0.5 percent tetrazolium solution and held at room temperature or somewhat higher for several hours or several days, the exact time depending upon the species of seed. The parts of the seed that are living (and respiring) will become red; the nonliving parts remain white. If the embryo turns red, the seeds are viable; if the embryo remains white, the seeds are nonviable. Sometimes only a portion of the embryo becomes red, making it difficult to interpret the results of the test. This difficulty in interpretation is the principal weakness of this test, which, nevertheless, is widely used.

EXCISED EMBRYO TEST

The embryos in the seeds of many woody plant species have profound dormancy conditions (see below) and do not respond in a direct germination test. However, if the embryos are carefully excised from the remainder of the seed and placed on moist paper in a covered dish, viable embryos will show some activity— possibly a greening and separation of the cotyledons with definite indications of life. Nonviable embryos remain white and succumb quickly to fungus and bacterial attacks. Although this method takes time and requires skill in removing the embryo, it is routinely used by some seed laboratories with good results.

Seed Dormancy

Seeds of many plant species, especially woody perennials, do not germinate when extracted from the mature fruit and planted, even though all temperature, light, and moisture conditions favor germination. This is an important survival mechanism for the species and a result of evolutionary development. These species have survived because their seeds have not germinated just before adverse weather conditions that would kill the young, tender seedlings. Thus, in nature, these dormancy factors prevent seed germination in the autumn, allowing the embryonic plant within the seed to overwinter in a very cold resistant form. Any plant species whose seeds did germinate in the fall in an area with severe winters would likely not survive in that region. Often, the causes for dormancy can persist indefinitely in the seed and require specific treatments to overcome them before germination will take place. This poses problems for the propagator and requires a knowledge of seed dormancy and how to overcome it. Seed dormancy can result from structural or physiological conditions in the seed coverings, particularly the seed coats, or in the embryo itself, or both.

SEED COAT DORMANCY

Seed coats or other tissues covering the embryo may be impermeable to water and gases, particularly oxygen, which therefore cannot penetrate to the embryo and initiate the physiological processes of germination. This situation usually occurs in species whose seeds have hard seed coats, such as alfalfa, clover, and other legumes as well as in some pine, birch, and ash species. In nature, continued weathering, the action of microorganisms, or passage through the digestive tract of animals can soften the seed coverings sufficiently so that they do become permeable and germination can proceed. In some species, the seed coats are apparently permeable to water and gases but have such high mechanical resistance to embryo expansion that germination does not occur unless the seed coats are softened in some manner.

Various artificial methods of softening seed coats are widely used to enhance germination. Three principal procedures are:

Scarification The surface of the seed is mechanically scratched or ruptured. This is often done by rubbing the seed between sheets of sandpaper or by blowing some small seeds, as alfalfa or clover, under pressure against abrasive carborundum boards, or by rotating and tumbling the seeds in drums that are lined with emery cloth. Studies of seeds of the different species determine how long the scarification must last until the seed coats are sufficiently scratched and abraded to result in good germination. Insufficient scarification will not improve germination, whereas excessive scarification will injure the embryo and other inner tissues.

Heat treatment In many kinds of seed, exposure to heat for a short time will disrupt the seed coat sufficiently to permit passage of water and gases. A convenient method is to pour the seeds into a container of boiling water; the volume of the water should equal three times the volume of the seeds. The heat under the water is turned off immediately after the seeds are added, then the seeds are allowed to remain in the gradually cooling water for 24 hours. After this they can be planted. It has been observed many times that after soaking rains have followed a brush or forest fire, many new seedlings develop in the areas that have been burned over. This does not occur in the unburned land. The heat from the fire has so disrupted the seed coats of seeds lying on or just under the soil that water penetrated and caused germination.

Acid scarification Soaking seeds with impervious coverings in concentrated sulfuric acid for the proper length of time will etch their coats enough for germination. Again, preliminary trials are necessary to determine the exact time the treatment should continue without damaging the inner tissues. The optimum time varies considerably—from 15 minutes to 3 hours or more depending on species. Occasional stirring is necessary since the seeds tend to cake together. After the seeds are removed from the acid, they must be washed for 10 or 15 minutes in clear water to remove all traces of the acid. This method, while useful for small seed lots, is not popular in treating large amounts of seed owing to the hazards of working with sulfuric acid.

> Sulfuric acid spilled onto body tissues or clothing can be very damaging and must be washed off immediately with large amounts of water.

EMBRYO DORMANCY

Embryo dormancy is very common in seeds of woody perennial plants. It is due to physiological conditions or germination blocks in the embryo itself that prevent it from resuming active growth even though all environmental conditions (temperature, water, oxygen, light) are favorable.

It has been known for hundreds of years that dormant seeds, if allowed to winter outdoors in regions with cold climates so that they received some chilling while being kept moist, will germinate readily in the spring. From this arose the practice known as **stratification,** in which boxes are filled with alternate layers of moist sand and seed and set outdoors in a protected shady place to overwinter. The following spring the seeds are removed from the box and planted. The critical conditions in seed stratification are:

1. *Chilling temperatures*—from about 1°C to 7°C (35°F to 45°F).
2. *Moisture.* The seeds should be soaked in water to start, then kept moist.
3. *Adequate oxygen.* The seeds should have adequate air and not be kept in an airtight container.
4. *Period of time.* The optimum stratification time varies considerably among species. Seeds of the American plum *(Prunus americana),* for example, require at least three months chilling while, at the other extreme, apricot seeds *(Prunus armeniaca)* need only 20 to 30 days.

More precise stratification treatments can be given if controlled refrigeration is used rather than natural outdoor winter cold, which can fluctuate considerably. Polyethylene plastic bags are suitable containers for stratifying seeds. The seeds are mixed with a slightly moist medium—sand, vermiculite, or peat moss—and placed in the bag. Polyethylene allows sufficient oxygen to pass through for the seeds' requirements but slows water loss. It is advisable to soak seeds in water for 24 hours to thoroughly saturate the tissues before the chilling treatment begins. Seeds of some species will germinate better if they are given a warm (24°C; 75°F) moist stratification period for several weeks just before the cold stratification period.

Many propagators plant seeds having embryo dormancy in an outdoor nursery in the fall, allowing the natural winter chilling to satisfy the embryo's chilling requirement.

There is evidence that during the stratification treatment, growth-promoting hormones (e.g., gibberellins and cytokinins) in the seeds increase while the level of growth-inhibiting hormones (e.g., abscisic acid) decreases, thus permitting germination (see Ch. 6).

The term **afterripening** is often used to describe the physiological changes in the seed that allow germination to take place.

DOUBLE DORMANCY

Seeds of some species have both seed coat and embryo dormancy. An example is redbud *(Cercis occidentalis).* To obtain good germination of such seeds, they first should be treated in some manner as described above to soften the seed coats, then given a cold stratification treatment to overcome the embryo dormancy.

RUDIMENTARY EMBRYOS

Some plants shed their fruits before the embryo within the seed has matured enough to germinate. Planting seeds when such fruits are mature will not result in immediate germination. A period of time—several weeks to several months—after harvest is required for the embryo to develop to the point where it can continue growth. This process can take place either while the seed is in storage or after planting. Seed dormancy due to rudimentary embryos occurs in such genera as *Fraxinus, Ilex, Pinus, Ranunculus,* and *Viburnum.*

CHEMICAL INHIBITORS

In many species, the seeds contain one or more chemicals that can block essential steps in the germination process. Sometimes, for example, in iris seeds—the inhibitor is not in the embryo but in the endosperm tissue. If the embryo is excised from the seed, it will start to grow readily in a sterile nutrient culture. Chemical inhibitors can also occur in seed coats or in the pericarp (ovary wall). Often, leaching such seeds in running water for several hours removes the inhibitors and permits germination.

Some of these germination inhibitors are well-known chemicals such as coumarin and caffeic acid. Seeds of certain fleshy fruits—tomatoes, lemons, strawberries—do not germinate while still attached to the fruit because of certain of these germination inhibitors in the fruits.

Seeds of some desert plants contain chemical germination inhibitors that are leached out by heavy soaking rains (but not by light showers). The heavy rains soak the soil sufficiently so that the seedlings can become established before the soil dries out. This interesting evolutionary phenomenon permits the continuation of these species by allowing survival of the seedling offspring in a difficult environment.

SECONDARY DORMANCY

Seeds that are ready to germinate after all germination blocks are removed often become dormant again because of exposure to some environmental condition. For example, seeds of some woody perennial plants, after undergoing stratification to overcome embryo dormancy, become dormant again if the germination temperatures reach 26°C to 32°C (80°F to 90°F).

Exposing winter barley or spring wheat seeds to certain unfavorable conditions, such as high temperatures or high moisture levels, can also induce a secondary dormancy.

Seed Germination

If the seeds have viable embryos, have all germination blocks removed, and are placed under proper environmental conditions of moisture, temperature, and (sometimes) light, the quiescent embryos in the seeds will resume their growth. The nutrients stored in the endosperm or cotyledons of the seed nourish the developing embryo until the new shoot rises above ground, develops leaves, and produces its own food by photosynthesis.

Germination can proceed in several ways, depending upon the species (see Figs. 5–2 and 5–3). Sometimes the cotyledons are pushed above ground (**epigeous germination**) and sometimes they remain below ground (**hypogeous germination**). The sequence of events during seed germination is:

1. *Imbibition of water by the seeds.* The colloidal properties of seed tissues give them great water-absorbing properties. Moist seeds may swell to a size much larger than the dry seeds. The cells become turgid and seed coverings soften and rupture, permitting easy passage of oxygen and carbon dioxide.

Fig. 5–2   Seed germination in a monocotyledonous plant, barley.

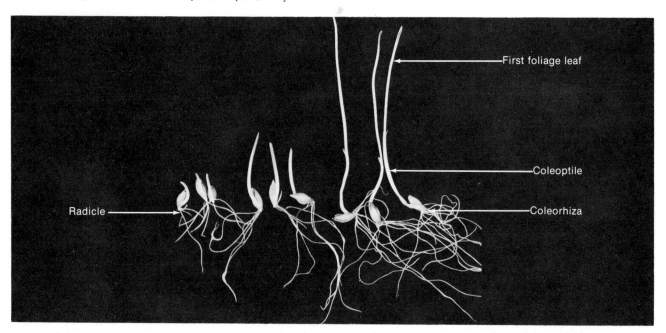

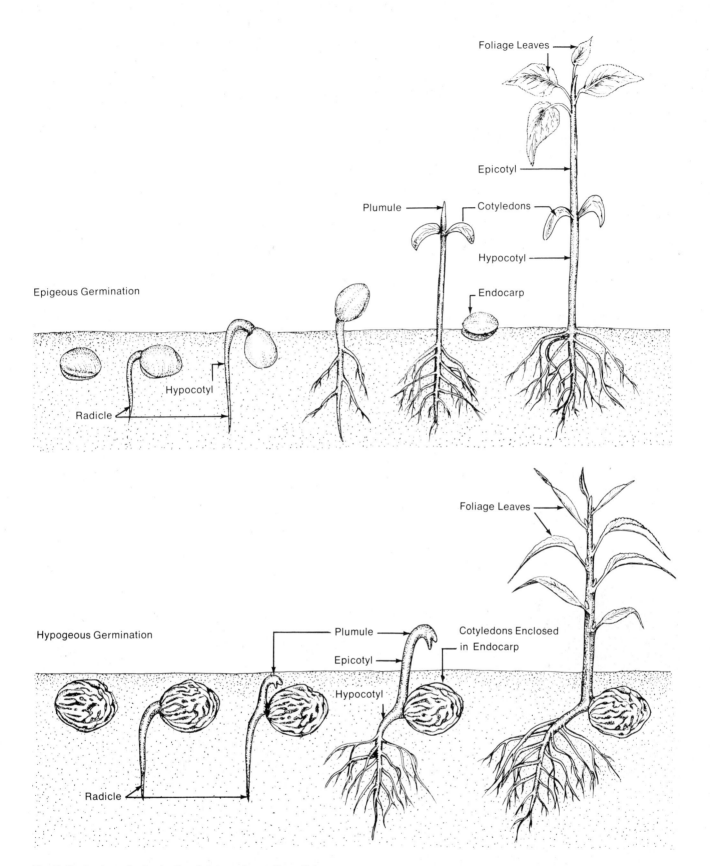

Foliage Leaves

Epicotyl

Plumule

Cotyledons

Hypocotyl

Endocarp

Epigeous Germination

Hypocotyl

Radicle

Foliage Leaves

Hypogeous Germination

Plumule

Epicotyl

Hypocotyl

Cotyledons Enclosed
in Endocarp

Radicle

Fig. 5–3 Seed germination in dicotyledonous plants. *Above:* Epigeous germination as shown in cherry. The cotyledons are above ground. *Below:* Hypogeous germination as shown in peach. The cotyledons remain below ground. *Source:* Hartmann, H. T., and D. E. Kester. 1975. *Plant propagation.* 3rd ed. Englewood Cliffs, N.J.: Prentice-Hall.

2. *Activation of hormones and enzymes.* After water is absorbed, various enzyme systems are activated, often as a result of stimulation by hormones (see Fig. 6–17). The enzymes convert complex food storage molecules into simpler chemicals that can be readily translocated and used for growth. Other enzymes are involved in the respiratory processes, which release energy for cell division and growth. Food materials are translocated to root and shoot growing points.

3. *Embryo growth and development.* The root-shoot axis (plumule, epicotyl, hypocotyl, and radicle) grows by cell division and enlargement. At the same time, food materials translocate to the growing points from the storage tissues, which gradually become depleted. The seed coat must have ruptured and photosynthetic tissue (green leaves and shoots) emerged into the light by this time if the seedling is to survive. In addition, the embryonic root (radicle) must have emerged and grown into moist soil to supply the newly developed leafy tissues with water, which will be lost through transpiration. By this time, if no unfavorable environmental influences interfere, the seedling has become established and can exist as an independent plant.

ENVIRONMENTAL FACTORS INFLUENCING SEED GERMINATION

For successful seed germination and seedling growth, certain environmental conditions are required. These are:

1. Adequate moisture
2. Proper temperature
3. Good aeration
4. Light (in some cases)
5. Freedom from pathogenic organisms
6. Freedom from toxic amounts of salts

MOISTURE   It is essential that water be available in adequate amounts to initiate the physiological and biochemical processes in the seed that result in reactivation of embryo growth. Germination usually takes place satisfactorily at moisture levels between field capacity and permanent wilting percentage (see p. 187), although seeds of some species (lettuce, peas, rice, beets, celery) germinate best at high soil-moisture levels, whereas those of others (spinach) do best with low moisture.

TEMPERATURE   The temperature can strongly influence the percentage and rate of seed germination, varying with the kind of seed. Seeds of the cool-season crops germinate best at relatively low temperatures of 0°C to 10°C (32°F to 50°F). Examples are peas, lettuce, and celery. Seeds of warm-season crops germinate best at temperatures ranging from 15°C to 26°C (60°F to 80°F); examples are soybeans, beans, squash, and cotton. Seeds of many other species will germinate over a wide temperature range (see Table 19–2). Many kinds of seeds, too, germinate much better when the temperature fluctuates daily about 10°C (18°F) between maximum and minimum.

AERATION   Respiration rates are high in germinating seeds, which thus require adequate oxygen. The usual amount in the air is 20 percent. If this concentration is decreased, germination rate and percentage germination of most kinds of seeds will be retarded, although in rice—a notable exception—germination will take place at oxygen levels lower than for most other kinds of seeds. Rice seeds have an anaerobic (without oxygen) respiration mechanism that permits germination under such conditions. Rice germination has been significantly improved, however, by treating seeds with calcium peroxide, which breaks down in the water to provide additional oxygen to the seeds.

In seedbeds that are overwatered and poorly drained, the soil pore spaces may be so filled with water that the amount of oxygen available to the seeds becomes limiting and germination of most kinds of seeds is retarded or prevented.

LIGHT   Light is essential to the germination of some kinds of seeds, such as lettuce, celery, most grasses, and many herbaceous garden flower plants. Such seeds should be planted very shallow for good germination. However, seeds of other plants—*Allium, Amaranthus, Nigelia,* and phlox—are inhibited by light and will not germinate unless planted deep enough to avoid light. The light requirement for seed germination is very complex, depending on the age of seed, degree of seed imbibition with water, temperature, day length, and certain germination-stimulating chemicals. A pigment in seeds—phytochrome—is involved in the controlling mechanism (see p. 126, Ch. 6).

PATHOGENIC ORGANISMS   **Damping off** describes the situation in which the seedlings die during or shortly after germination. Damping off is caused primarily by attacks of certain universally present and very destructive fungi—*Pythium ultimum* and *Rhizoctonia solani,* and to a lesser extent, *Botrytis cinera* and *Phytophthora* spp. Mycelia of these organisms and the spores of *Pythium* and *Phytophthora* are often found in the germination medium, on the seed surfaces, in the water, or on tools. The best control methods are fumigation or heat pasteurization of the germination medium (see Fig. 19–7), surface treatment of the seeds with fungicides before planting, and good sanitation procedures.

Both *Pythium* and *Rhizoctonia* develop best at temperatures between 20°C and 30°C (68°F and 86°F). If the seeds to be planted can be germinated above or below these temperatures, fungus damage will be minimized.

SALINITY PROBLEMS   If the germination medium is watered lightly but frequently after the seeds have been planted, evaporation of water from the surface leaves salt deposits. If this situation continues, the salinity can increase to such a level that it will injure or kill the seedlings as they germinate. This is a particular problem with small, shallow-planted seeds that may dry out quickly, and in areas having high salt concentrations in the water. Such salts may originate in the germination medium, the irrigation water, or added fertilizers. Salinity damage to seedlings often looks like damping-off injury. This problem can be prevented by using soil mixtures and water low in salts, withholding fertilizers, and by irrigating more copiously but less frequently so that excess salts are leached out (see p. 395, Ch. 18).

VEGETATIVE PROPAGATION

Vegetative or asexual propagation is accomplished entirely by mitosis, the cell division process by which the plant grows. Each daughter cell is an exact replica of its mother cell. Chromosome numbers and composition do not change during cell division. Mitotic cell division, as illustrated in Figure 5–4, produces the adventitious roots and shoots[4] as well as the callus[5] (parenchyma cells required for healing of a graft union) necessary for successful vegetative propagation (see Fig. 5–5).

Vegetative propagation is used primarily for woody perennial plants that are highly heterozygous; that is, ones that do not "breed true" from seed. In these plants, the mother plant's desirable characteristics will be lost if seed propagation is used. To maintain the genetic identity of the mother plant in such cases, it is necessary to avoid use of the flower and seed altogether in reproducing the plant. Vegetative tissues (stem, root, or leaf) are used to develop new plants by inducing the formation of adventitious shoots, roots, or both. If pieces of stem tissue will not produce adventitious roots, or if a particular kind of rootstock is required, it is necessary to graft or bud two pieces of tissue together, one to become the top part of the plant and one to become the root system (see p. 100).

As noted above, a cultivar that must be reproduced by asexual methods to maintain its characteristics is termed a clone, as distinguished from a line, which will maintain its characteristics without change by seed propagation (see Ch. 3). Almost all fruit and nut cultivars and many woody ornamental cultivars are clones. All plants that are members of the same clone have the same genetic makeup and are, in reality, exact descendants of the mother plant from which the clone originated, although the original mother plant may have died many years earlier. Some clones, such as the 'Thompson Seedless' grape, have been in existence since ancient times and consist of many millions of individual plants scattered all over the world.

Cultivated clones originate in two ways. The first, and usual way is as seedling plants that some person recognizes as having some superior qualities and proceeds to propagate vegetatively. For example, the world-famed 'Golden Delicious' apple originated as a seedling tree that A. H. Mullins found growing on his farm in Clay County, West Virginia. Mullins recognized this apple's value. Later it came to the attention of Stark Brothers Nurseries of Louisiana, Missouri, who in 1912 paid Mullins for the propagation rights to the tree. They named it 'Golden Delicious' and introduced nursery trees for orchard planting in 1916. Although the original tree died long ago, millions of 'Golden Delicious' apple trees are now growing throughout the world, all with the same genetic makeup as the one original tree and all producing the same kind of apples. Although many clones have originated as chance seedlings found growing in the wild they can also originate from controlled crosses made by plant breeders.

A second way clones originate is from mutations (bud sports). A single bud on a plant may have its genetic makeup altered during cell division so that, as the bud grows and develops into a branch, one or more of its characteristics differs from those of the rest of the plant. Many mutations are slight or inferior and go unnoticed. But occasionally some strikingly superior characteristic appears; someone notices it and propagates new plants taken from shoots on this mutated branch. This, then, becomes the start of a new clone. The popular dark red 'Delicious' apples, for example, originated as limb mutations found on the regular 'Delicious' apple trees. The pink-fleshed 'Ruby' grapefruit originated as a mutated branch on a tree producing white-fleshed fruits; this one branch became the start of a new clone.

---

[4]**Adventitious shoots** are those appearing any place on the plant other than from shoot terminals or in the axils of leaves. **Adventitious roots** rise any place on the plant other than from the radicle (root tip) of the seed or its branches.

[5]**Callus** is a mass of young, undifferentiated, and proliferating parenchyma cells.

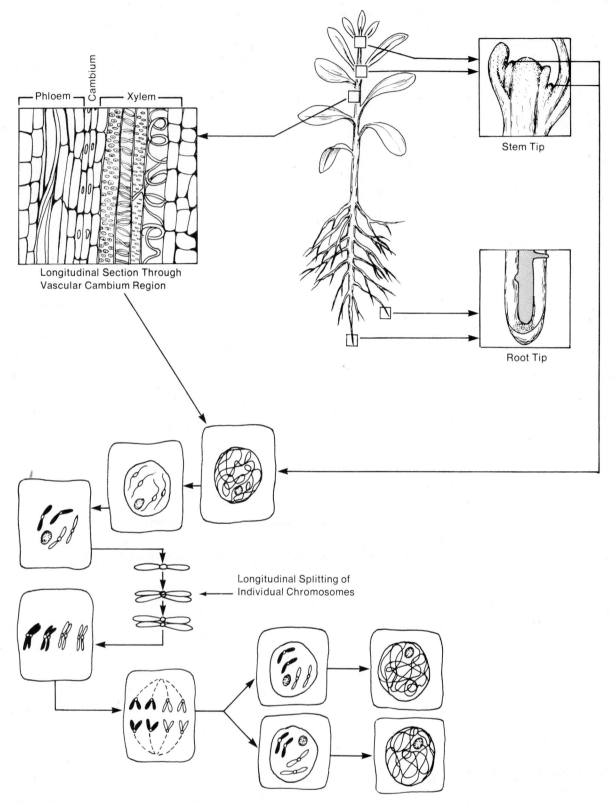

Phloem — Cambium — Xylem

Longitudinal Section Through
Vascular Cambium Region

Stem Tip

Root Tip

Longitudinal Splitting of
Individual Chromosomes

Fig. 5–4 The process of growth and asexual reproduction in a dicotyledonous plant. Mitosis occurs in three principal growing regions of the plant: the stem tip, the root tip of primary and secondary roots, and the cambium. A meristematic cell is shown dividing into two daughter cells whose chromosomes will (usually) be identical with those of the original cell. *Source:* Hartmann, H. T., and D. E. Kester. 1975. *Plant propagation.* 3rd ed. Englewood Cliffs, N.J.: Prentice-Hall.

Fig. 5–5   Regeneration in asexual propagation. *Left:* Adventitious shoots growing from a root cutting. *Center:* Adventitious roots developing from the base of a stem cutting. *Right:* Callus tissue produced to give healing of a graft union. *Source:* Hartmann, H. T., and D. E. Kester. 1975. *Plant propagation.* 3rd ed. Englewood Cliffs, N.J.: Prentice-Hall.

Fig. 5–6   A variegated pink 'Eureka' lemon, a type of chimera.

The primary advantage of clones is the uniformity of the member plants. All members have the same genetic makeup (genotype) and potentially they can all be exactly alike. However, environmental factors can so modify the appearance and behavior of the plant (phenotype) that individual plants can differ strikingly. For example, a vineyard of 'Concord' grapevines, pruned, irrigated, sprayed, and fertilized properly would appear totally different from an adjacent abandoned vineyard of the same cultivar, yet the vines in both would be genetically identical.

The mutation process can also cause undesirable genetic changes in clones. This happens frequently in citrus, for instance, and must be guarded against to prevent deterioration of the clone.

Some mutations, called **chimeras,** genetically change only a portion rather the entire shoot. Some of the variegated leaf patterns found in the foliage of certain plants such as *Pelargonium* or citrus are due to chimeras (Fig. 5–6).

91

Apomixis is an interesting phenomenon in which the genetic identity of the mother plant is transmitted to daughter plants that develop by seed formation and germination. Apomixis is a form of asexual propagation because there is no union of male and female gametes before seedling production. There are several types but a common one is that found in citrus seeds where, in addition to the sexual embryo formed through the usual pollination and fertilization processes, embryos also arise in the nucellar tissue (**nucellar budding**—see Fig. 6–13). The nucellar tissue enclosing the embryo sac has not undergone reduction division and has the same genetic makeup as the female parent. So the nucellar embryos, although developing in a seed, are exactly the same genetically as the mother plant and thus maintain the clone.

Such seeds can contain several nucellar embryos in addition to the sexual embryo. Thus several seedlings are obtained from one seed, a situation known as **polyembryony**.

Even though plants arising by apomixis from nucellar embryos maintain the clone, they go through the juvenile to mature transition stages (see p. 123) just as any woody plant seedling would, taking a number of years to flower and fruit.

DISEASE PROBLEMS IN CLONES

Propagating plants vegetatively with clonal material has one great disadvantage: clones can become infected with systemic viruses (see p. 250) and mycoplasma-like organisms (see p. 252) that are passed along to the daughter plants during asexual propagation procedures. In time, all clonal members may become infected with viruses. Some viruses are latent in particular nonsusceptible clonal material, but if this material is used in a graft combination where the virus can move through the graft union to the graft partner—which is susceptible—then the entire grafted plant will be killed by the virus. On the other hand, virus-free seedlings can be obtained in many species by seed propagation because the virus is not transmitted through the embryo.

Viruses can be removed from clonal material by **heat treatment.** The virus-infected plant material, perhaps a small nursery tree growing in a container, is held at 37°C to 38°C (98°F to 100°F) for two to four weeks or longer. This combination of time and temperature eliminates the virus. After treatment, cuttings can be taken for rooting, or buds may be taken for budding into virus-clean seedling rootstocks.

Another procedure to eliminate viruses from clones is **shoot-tip culture.** In virus-infected plants the terminal growing point is often free of the virus. By excising this shoot apex aseptically and growing it on a sterile medium, roots will often develop, producing a new plant free of the virus. Here again, a starting point becomes available for continued propagation of the clone but

without the virus. This method has succeeded with many herbaceous plants such as carnation, chrysanthemum, hops, garlic, rhubarb, orchid, and strawberry. Sometimes, in strawberry plants for example, both procedures are required—heat treatment of the plant, followed by excision and culture of the shoot tip—to free the plant of viruses.

In recent years certification programs have been established by government agencies in many states in the United States and in other countries to provide nurseries with sources of true-to-name, pathogen-free propagation material. Elaborate programs, for example, have been established for citrus in Florida and California and for deciduous tree fruits, grapes, strawberries, potatoes, and certain ornamentals in many states.

In such programs, mature flowering or fruiting plants known to be true to name and true to type are selected as mother plants. These are "indexed" by certain grafting procedures (see p. 100) to be sure no viruses or other diseases are present. If no pathogen-free source plants can be located, then procedures like those described above for eliminating viruses must be used to obtain pathogen-free plants. Once a "clean" source is obtained, it must then be maintained under isolated and sanitary conditions, with periodic inspection and testing to ensure that it does not again become infected. Sometimes it is necessary to grow the plants in insect-proof screenhouses or greenhouses or in isolated areas far from commercial production fields.

Distribution systems from these foundation plantings are necessary, sometimes requiring plots of land, "increase blocks," to grow a greater amount of propagating material that may be needed. This material can be termed "certified stock" if it is grown under the supervision of a legally designated agency with prescribed regulations designed to maintain certain standards of cleanliness and clonal identity.

Many of the major agricultural industries, based on crops that are susceptible to various pathogens, particularly viruses, could not exist without such certification programs. These crops include citrus, grapes, potatoes, roses, cherries, peaches, and strawberries.

Propagation by Cuttings

Propagation by cuttings is a vegetative method widely used for propagating herbaceous and woody ornamental plants and, to a much lesser extent, fruit species. A cutting is essentially a piece of vegetative tissue that, when placed under the proper environmental conditions, will regenerate the missing parts—roots, shoots, or both—and develop into a self-sustaining plant.

Cuttings can be classified according to the part of the plant from which they are obtained:

Stem cuttings
  Hardwood
    Deciduous
      Narrow-leaved
        evergreen
  Semihardwood
  Softwood
  Herbaceous
Leaf cuttings
Leaf-bud cuttings
Root cuttings

Stem cuttings, already have terminal or axillary buds (potentially a new shoot system), but new roots must develop at the base of the cutting before a new plant will be formed. Stem cuttings can be prepared to include the shoot tip, or cuttings can be made from the more basal parts of the shoot that have only axillary buds. **Leaf cuttings** have neither buds nor roots so both must form.

Leaf-bud cuttings have a bud at the base of the petiole—for the new shoot system—so only new roots must form. **Root cuttings** must produce a new adventitious shoot and continue growth of the existing root piece, or develop roots from the base of the new shoot. Figure 5–7 illustrates these types of cuttings.

Plant species and cultivars vary markedly in their ability to develop adventitious roots. Cuttings from some kinds of plants root easily even when the simplest procedures are used. Cuttings of others root only if the influencing rooting factors, as described starting on page 99, are carefully observed. Cuttings of still other kinds of plants have never been rooted, or rooted only rarely and in meager amounts, despite great efforts and much research. The basic reasons for such differences in rooting ability among different kinds of plants are not well understood.

STEM CUTTINGS

DECIDUOUS HARDWOOD STEM CUTTINGS Such cuttings are made in late winter or early spring, using leafless shoots that grew the previous summer. The shoots are cut into lengths of 15 to 30 cm (6 to 12 in)

Fig. 5–7 Types of cuttings. *A:* Hardwood stem cutting. *B:* Leafy stem cutting. *C:* Leaf cutting. *D:* Leaf-bud cutting. *E:* Root cutting.

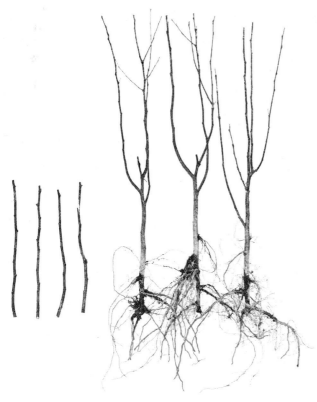

Fig. 5–8 *Left:* Hardwood cuttings of quince (*Cydonia oblonga*) prepared and ready for planting in early spring. *Right:* Rooted cuttings after one year in the nursery. *Source:* Univ. of Calif. Div. Agr. Sci. Leaflet 21103, p. 55. 1979.

Fig. 5–9 Propagation by narrow-leaved (conifer) hardwood cuttings. *Above:* Juniper cuttings ready for sticking in rooting medium. *Below:* Cuttings after rooting.

and grown outdoors in the nursery row, planted vertically with just the top bud showing. Figure 5–8 shows quince cuttings prepared for spring planting and the resulting plants after they rooted and grew through the summer. A porous, sandy loam soil is best for rooting hardwood cuttings. Many plants can be propagated in this manner, including some deciduous trees, such as willow and poplar; many deciduous shrubs, such as forsythia, weigela, privet, spiraea, honeysuckle, and roses; and several fruit species, such as grape, mulberry, currant, gooseberry, quince, olive, fig, and pomegranate.

NARROW-LEAVED EVERGREEN HARDWOOD STEM CUTTINGS Most conifers can be propagated by stem cuttings made in various lengths of about 7 to 15 cm (3 to 6 in). Cuttings are best made in early winter. Needles are removed from the lower half of the cutting but left on the upper, as shown in Figure 5–9. The cuttings are usually inserted into flats about 10 × 30 × 45 cm (4 × 12 × 18 in) in size filled with a rooting medium of sand or of equal parts perlite and peat moss. The flats of cuttings are set in a cool, humid greenhouse or cold frame, preferably with high light intensity, and kept lightly watered or misted until they root. Rooting may take several weeks or even months, depending upon the species.

SEMIHARDWOOD STEM CUTTINGS Most broad-leaved evergreen ornamentals—rhododendron, camellia, pittosporum, holly, evergreen azalea, escallonia, euonymus, and boxwood—as well as some fruit species—citrus and olive, for example—can be propagated by this type of cutting. Cuttings are best taken in midsummer, following the flush of spring growth. They are made about 10 to 15 cm (4 to 6 in) long. Four or five leaves should be retained on the upper portion of the cutting and all lower leaves removed, as shown in Figure 5–10.

The cuttings are inserted into flats containing a porous rooting medium of equal parts of perlite and peatmoss or of perlite and vermiculite. The flats are placed in a well-lighted, humid location to minimize water loss from the leaves. Closed rooting frames or flats covered with polyethylene plastic sheeting are suitable for keeping the humidity around the cuttings high.

Most commercial nurseries root this type of cutting in **mist propagating beds** (Figs. 5–11 and 5–12), where a fine mist is sprayed over the cuttings intermittently during the day. The mist is controlled by a time clock operating a magnetic solenoid valve that is set to turn the mist on long enough—three to five seconds—to wet the leaves. The mist then stays off until the leaves start to dry—from two to five minutes or longer—then turns

Fig. 5–10 Semihardwood leafy cuttings of escallonia showing typical method of preparing this type of cutting. Cuttings were treated with a rooting hormone—indolebutyric acid (see p. 135) at 0, 1000, 3000, and 8000 parts per million before they were stuck in the rooting bed.

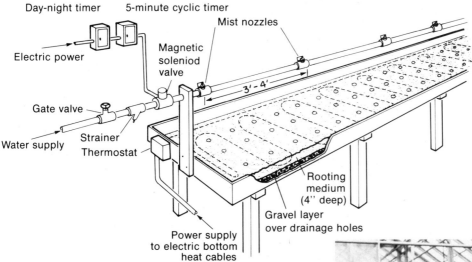

Fig. 5–11 Component parts of an intermittent mist propagating installation with electric bottom-heat cable. One timer turns the mist system on in the morning and off at night. The second is a short interval timer to provide the intermittent mist cycles. *Source:* Hartmann, H. T., and D. E. Kester. 1975. *Plant propagation.* 3rd ed. Englewood Cliffs, N.J.: Prentice-Hall.

Fig. 5–12 Mist propagation bed operating in a greenhouse. The mist is only on a few seconds—just long enough to wet the leaves—then turns off. When the leaves start to dry, the mist is again turned on. The operation is usually controlled by time clocks operating magnetic solenoid valves.

on again. The mist is off entirely at night. Mist propagating beds are very effective in keeping leafy cuttings cool and turgid, reducing transpiration from the leaves, and giving excellent rooting of cuttings.

SOFTWOOD STEM CUTTINGS   These are similar to semihardwood cuttings except they are prepared from young leafy shoots arising in the spring from deciduous trees or shrubs. Such plants as crepe myrtle, pyracantha, mock orange, forsythia, weigela, roses, pomegranates, and plums are easily propagated by this type of cutting. Cuttings are prepared in the spring in the same manner as semihardwood cuttings and are rooted under similar conditions. All leafy cuttings must be rooted under high humidity conditions to reduce water loss from the leaves.

HERBACEOUS STEM CUTTINGS   This type of cutting is used in propagating such plants as coleus, carnation, geranium, chrysanthemum, and many tropical house plants, all of which root easily. Commercial propagation of sugar cane would be classed as by herbaceous stem cuttings planted horizontally below ground (Fig. 5–13). As shown in Figure 5–14, the terminal cuttings are about 8 to 13 cm (3 to 5 in) long, with several leaves left at the top and all others removed. These succulent plants do not tolerate the high moisture levels of mist beds, so they are usually rooted in a closed frame constructed, for example, by draping a sheet of white polyethylene over a wire frame support in a greenhouse. Moisture is maintained by sprinkling the leaves daily by hand or by mist nozzles operating only once or twice a day. The cuttings are rooted in flats with the same type of rooting medium as for semihardwood cuttings.

Fig. 5–13   Propagation of sugar cane by a form of herbaceous stem cuttings. Stems of the mature plants are cut into sections and planted horizontally several inches deep. From each node shoots and adventitious roots develop, giving rise to new plants.

Fig. 5–14   Herbaceous stem cuttings of coleus. *Left:* Cuttings prepared and ready for rooting. *Right:* Rooted cuttings taken from propagating bed.

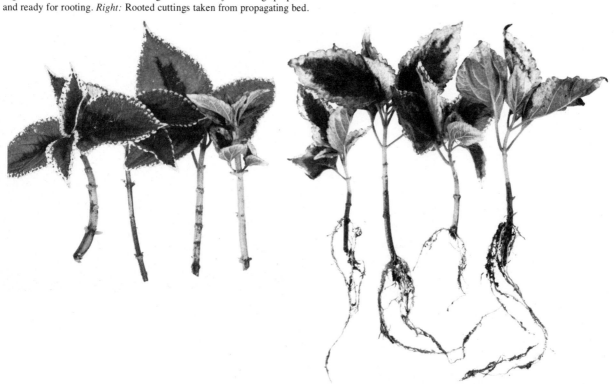

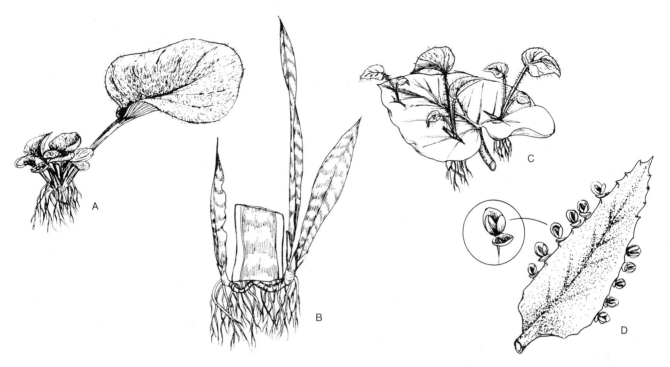

Fig. 5–15 Types of leaf cuttings. *A:* New plants arising from base of petiole in African violet (*Saintpaulia*). *B:* New plant arising from base of leaf blade in sansevieria. *C:* New plants arising from cuts in veins of a begonia leaf. *D:* New plants growing from notches of leaf in *Kalanchoe* (*Bryophyllum*).

LEAF CUTTINGS

There are various types of leaf cuttings, as shown in Figures 5–15 and 5–16. A common one consists of a single leaf blade and petiole, as might be taken from an African violet. The petiole is inserted into the rooting medium to a depth of about 2.5 cm (1 in). As with other types of leafy cuttings, the humidity must be kept very high, preferably by using a closed rooting frame, as for the herbaceous cuttings or by the use of a humid greenhouse. Roots and shoots generally develop from the same point at the base of the petiole and grow into a plant independent of the leaf blade, which functions to nourish the new plant. African violet, peperomia, begonia, and sansevieria are examples of plants commonly started by leaf cuttings.

LEAF-BUD CUTTINGS

Leaf cuttings of some species will form roots at the base of the petiole but do not develop a shoot, resulting only in a rooted leaf that may stay alive for months (or years). To avoid this, a leaf-bud cutting can be prepared. This cutting consists of a short piece of stem with an attached leaf and a bud in the axil of the leaf, as shown in Figure 5–17. Such cuttings are rooted under high humidity, as described for semihardwood or her-

Fig. 5–16 Rooted leaf cuttings of the piggy-back plant (*Tolmiea menziesi*). The new plants (see arrows) are arising from the junction of the leaf blade and leaf petiole.

Fig. 5–17 Leaf-bud cuttings of peperomia. Each cutting consists of leaf blade, petiole, axillary bud, and a piece of stem. Arrows show axillary buds starting to grow.

baceous cuttings. The axillary bud develops into the new shoot system. Leaf-bud cuttings are useful as substitutes for stem cuttings in obtaining as many plants as possible from scarce propagating material. Leaf-bud cuttings give one and perhaps two (if the plant has opposite leaves) new plants from each node, whereas each stem cutting generally requires a minimum of two nodes.

ROOT CUTTINGS

Many plant species can be propagated by cutting the small, young roots into pieces about 2.5 cm (1 in) long and planting them horizontally in soil about 1.3 cm (0.5 in) deep or vertically with the upper end (nearest the crown of the plant) just below the soil level. One or more new adventitious shoots form along the root piece, and either this shoot forms roots or the root piece itself develops new branch roots, thus producing a new plant (see Figs. 5–5 and 5–18). The best time to obtain the root pieces from the mother plant and to prepare and plant the root cuttings is late winter or early spring. The roots contain the highest quantity of stored foods at that time and the cuttings will start to grow at the beginning of the growing season. Cuttings can be planted in an outdoor nursery or in flats of soil in a greenhouse or cold frame.

ORIGIN OF ADVENTITIOUS ROOTS IN STEM CUTTINGS

In stem cuttings of herbaceous plants, adventitious roots generally originate laterally and adjacent to the vascular bundles, whereas in cuttings of woody perennials the roots originate in the region of the vascular cambium, often in young phloem parenchyma (Fig.

Fig. 5–18 Apple root cuttings. *Left:* Cuttings ready for planting. *Center:* Cuttings planted vertically with the end nearest the crown of the plant at the top. *Right:* Cuttings planted horizontally.

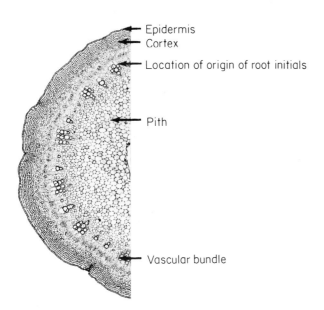

Epidermis
Cortex
Location of origin of root initials

Pith

Vascular bundle

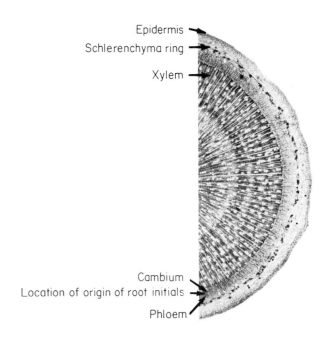

Epidermis
Schlerenchyma ring

Xylem

Cambium
Location of origin of root initials

Phloem

Fig. 5–19 Stem cross sections showing the usual location of origin of adventitious roots. *Left:* Young, herbaceous, dicotyledonous plant. *Right:* Young, woody plant. *Source:* Hartmann, H. T., and D. E. Kester. 1975. *Plant propagation.* 3rd ed. Englewood Cliffs, N.J.: Prentice-Hall.

5–19). In each case the new roots are in position to establish a vascular connection with the conducting tissues of the xylem and phloem in the cutting.

Much study has been given to the mechanisms that lead to the initiation of adventitious roots in cuttings. There is convincing evidence that auxin, one of the natural growth hormones, is essential (see Ch. 6). It has long been known that the leaves on cuttings strongly promote root initiation. Materials originating in the leaves, called rooting cofactors, are believed to be essential to rooting; they combine with auxin to form a complex that directs RNA to activate enzymes that cause root initials to form. The composition of these cofactors is not clear but some, at least, are likely to be phenolic compounds. Other natural hormones, such as gibberellins and abscisic acid (see Ch. 6), also influence adventitious root formation. Controlled studies under aseptic conditions have shown, too, that sugar, nitrogen, calcium, and other mineral nutrients must be present for roots to form.

FACTORS INFLUENCING THE ROOTING OF CUTTINGS

There is a large group of plants whose cuttings root only with considerable difficulty. It is necessary to carefully consider the factors described below in order to satisfactorily root cuttings in this group.

SELECTING THE CUTTING MATERIAL   Generally, the cuttings most likely to root come from stock plants that are growing in full sun at only a moderate rate and that have thus accumulated carbohydrates in their tissues. If the cutting material for woody plant species can be taken from young, nonflowering plants only a few years away from a germinated seed, rooting will be much better than when the cuttings are taken from old, mature flowering and fruiting plants. The **juvenility influence** in the young material can sometimes be retained by keeping the stock plants cut back heavily each year to force new shoot growth out from the lower part of the plants near the ground level (see Ch. 6, p. 123).

TIME OF YEAR THE CUTTING MATERIAL IS TAKEN   In woody perennial plants, cutting material can be taken at any time of the year. In some species the time the material is taken can dramatically influence rooting. Hardwood cuttings often root best if the material is gathered in late winter, while softwood cuttings usually root best if taken in the spring shortly after new shoot growth has attained a length of 10 to 15 cm (4 to 6 in). Semihardwood cuttings are best taken in midsummer after the spring flush of growth has matured somewhat. Herbaceous cuttings can be easily rooted any time of the year.

ETIOLATION It has long been known that stem tissue developing in complete darkness is more likely to initiate adventitious roots than tissue exposed to light. Thus if the basal part of shoots that are later to be made into cuttings can be kept in darkness, they are likely to form roots. Such techniques are used successfully in rooting cuttings of difficult species, such as the avocado. The mechanism for etiolation[6] in promotion of rooting is not clear, but the harmful effects of light on rooting may be due to photoinactivation of one or more natural rooting factors in the stem tissues.

TREATMENT OF CUTTINGS WITH AUXINS (See Ch. 6.) In the mid-1930s it was discovered that one of the natural plant hormones, auxin (indoleacetic acid, or IAA), stimulated the initiation of adventitious roots on stem cuttings. Synthetic IAA was just as effective as the natural material. But it was soon discovered that other closely related synthetic auxins—indolebutyric acid (IBA) and naphthaleneacetic acid (NAA)—were even more effective. This knowledge was quickly picked up by plant propagators, who now routinely treat the base of cuttings with one of these materials, particularly IBA, just before the cuttings are stuck in the rooting medium. Commercial preparations of IBA dispersed in talc are available; the lower end of the cutting is swirled around in the mixture to coat it with the powder. The propagator can also prepare solutions from the pure chemicals, then dip the base of the cuttings in the solution for about five seconds just before the cuttings are stuck in the rooting medium. The optimum concentration to promote rooting varies with the species but ranges from about 2000 to 10,000 parts per million (ppm).

To prepare 100 ml of a 4000-ppm solution of a root-promoting substance, weigh out 400 mg of the chemical and dissolve it in 100 ml of 50 percent alcohol (ethyl, methyl, or isopropyl).

An approximate 4000-ppm solution of indolebutyric acid can be prepared by dissolving a level quarter teaspoon of the pure crystals in 100 ml (3.3 fluid oz) of 50 percent alcohol.

BOTTOM HEAT IN THE CUTTING BEDS To secure rooting at the base of cuttings before shoot growth starts, it is advisable to maintain temperatures at the base of the cuttings at about 24°C (75°F)—or about 6°C (10°F) higher than that at the tops of the cuttings, 18.5°C (65°F). This is best done by providing bottom heat from

---

[6]Etiolation is the growth of shoots in the absence of light, causing them to be abnormally elongated and colored yellow or white due to the absence of chlorophyll.

thermostatically controlled electric heating cables or hot water pipes under the rooting frames (see Fig. 5–11). Bottom heat under the cuttings often greatly stimulates rooting.

Propagation by Grafting and Budding

Grafting and budding are vegetative methods used to propagate plants of a clone whose cuttings are difficult to root or to make use of a rootstock rather than having the plant on its own roots. Certain rootstocks are often utilized to obtain a dwarfed plant or resistance to soil-borne pests.

GRAFTING

Grafting can be defined as the art of joining parts of plants together so that they will unite and continue their growth as one plant. The **scion** is that part of the graft combination that is to become the upper or top portion of the plant. Usually the scion is a piece of stem tissue several inches long with two to four buds. If this piece is reduced in size so there is just one bud, with a thin layer of bark and wood under it, then the operation is termed **budding.** The **rootstock** (or **understock** or **stock**) is the lower part of the graft combination, the part that is to become the root system. **Root grafting** is a common method of propagation in which a scion is grafted directly onto a short piece of root and the combination is then planted. Sometimes grafting is used to change the fruiting cultivar in a fruit tree or grapevine to a different one (**top-grafting** or **top-working**). Grafting may be used to repair the damaged trunk of a tree (**bridge-grafting)** or to replace an injured root system (**inarching**). Grafting, or budding, is sometimes used to study the transmission of viral diseases (**indexing).** The indexing test involves inserting a bud from a plant suspected of carrying a virus into another indicator plant by T-budding (p. 104). A definite visual response results from the presence of a virus, such as gumming around the inserted bud.

Several standard methods of grafting and budding have been widely used over the world for a great many years.

WHIP GRAFTING The **whip graft** (Figs. 5–20 and 5–21) is useful in grafting together material about 0.6 to 1.3 cm (0.25 to 0.5 in) in diameter. It is often used to make **root grafts** in late winter. A small stem piece of the scion cultivar is grafted onto a root piece. The completed grafts are buried for two or three weeks in a moist material, such as wood shavings, at about 21°C (70°F) to encourage callusing or healing of the union. After the union has healed, the graft can be planted in the nursery.

PREPARING THE STOCK | PREPARING THE SCION

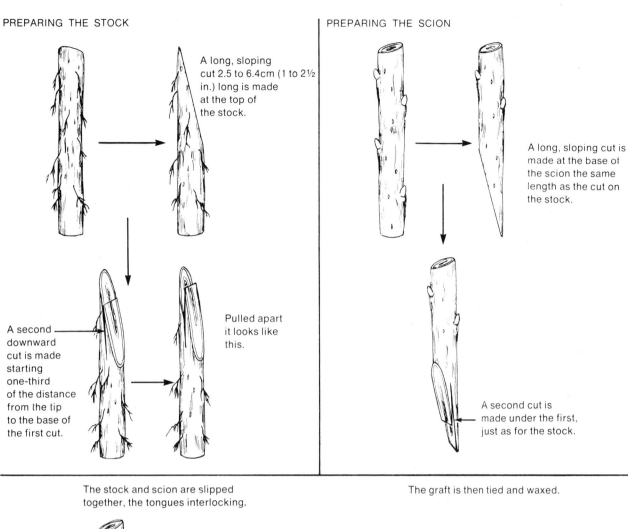

A long, sloping cut 2.5 to 6.4cm (1 to 2½ in.) long is made at the top of the stock.

A long, sloping cut is made at the base of the scion the same length as the cut on the stock.

A second downward cut is made starting one-third of the distance from the tip to the base of the first cut.

Pulled apart it looks like this.

A second cut is made under the first, just as for the stock.

The stock and scion are slipped together, the tongues interlocking.

The graft is then tied and waxed.

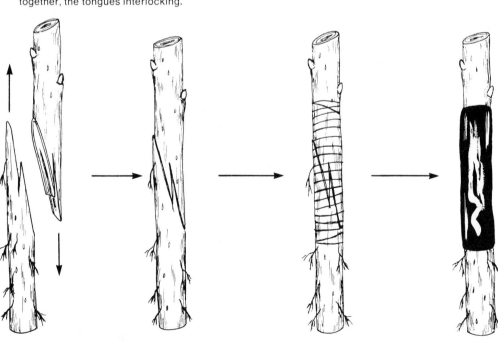

Fig. 5—20 The whip, or tongue, graft. This method is widely used in grafting small plant material and is especially valuable in making root grafts, as illustrated here. *Source:* Hartmann, H. T., and D. E. Kester. 1975. *Plant propagation.* 3rd ed. Englewood Cliffs, N.J.: Prentice-Hall.

Fig. 5–21 Longitudinal section of a whip graft showing healing at the graft union by callus production.

Fig. 5–22 Grafting machine *(above)* used to make apple root grafts *(below)*. *Source:* Univ. of Calif. Div. Agr. Sci. Leaflet 21103, pp. 27–28, 1979.

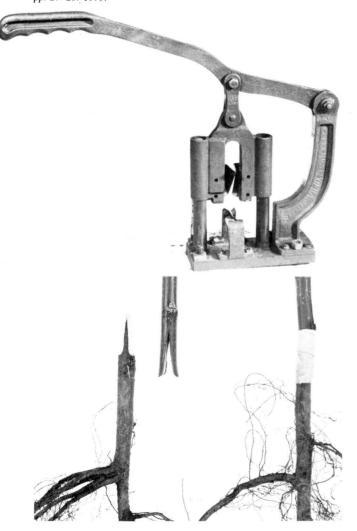

Various **grafting machines** can be used as a substitute for the whip graft and are considerably faster than hand grafting (see Fig. 5–22). Such machines have been used mostly in grape grafting but are also satisfactory for making fruit tree root grafts.

In all types of grafting and budding the two parts must be held together very tightly and securely by wedging, tying, nailing, or wrapping with string, rubber bands, or with plastic or cloth tape. The graft union must also be completely covered by grafting wax to prevent the cut surfaces from drying out. Polarity must be observed: the scions must be inserted so that the buds point upward.

CLEFT GRAFTING   The **cleft graft** (Fig. 5–23) is used mostly in top-grafting, where scions 0.6 to 1.3 cm (0.25 to 0.5 in) in diameter are inserted into stubs of older limbs that are 8 to 10 cm (3 to 4 in) in diameter after they have been cut off a foot or so out from the trunk of the tree. It is very important in cleft grafting to match the cambium layer of the scion as closely as possible with the cambium layer of the stock so that the two pieces will heal together. Cleft grafting is usually done in late winter or early spring.

BARK GRAFTING   The **bark graft** (Fig. 5–24) is also used for top-grafting. It can be done, however, only when the bark separates easily from the wood along the cambium layer. Thus bark grafting is usually done in early to mid spring after new growth is well underway. Bark grafting is easy to do and is widely used, especially for species considered somewhat difficult to graft successfully.

The proper selection of scionwood and budwood is very important in all types of grafting and budding. Scionwood and budwood should be taken from source trees true to type for the cultivar to be propagated. They should be free of known viruses and any other diseases. Some American states and some other countries have programs to supply propagating material of many fruit and woody ornamental species certified as produced under disease-free conditions.

For all types of grafting and budding, the buds on the scionwood and budwood must be dormant when the grafting or budding is done. For the whip and cleft graft, where the grafting is done during the dormant season, the scionwood can be collected from dormant source trees and used immediately in the grafting operation. For the bark graft, made later in the spring after vegetative growth has started, it is necessary to gather the scionwood earlier during the dormant season, wrap it in polyethylene bags with some slightly damp peatmoss, then hold it under refrigeration preferably at about 0°C (32°F) until grafting. For broad-leaved evergreens, such as citrus or olives, scionwood can be obtained from the tree at the time the bark grafting is to be done, using two-year-old shoots having dormant latent buds.

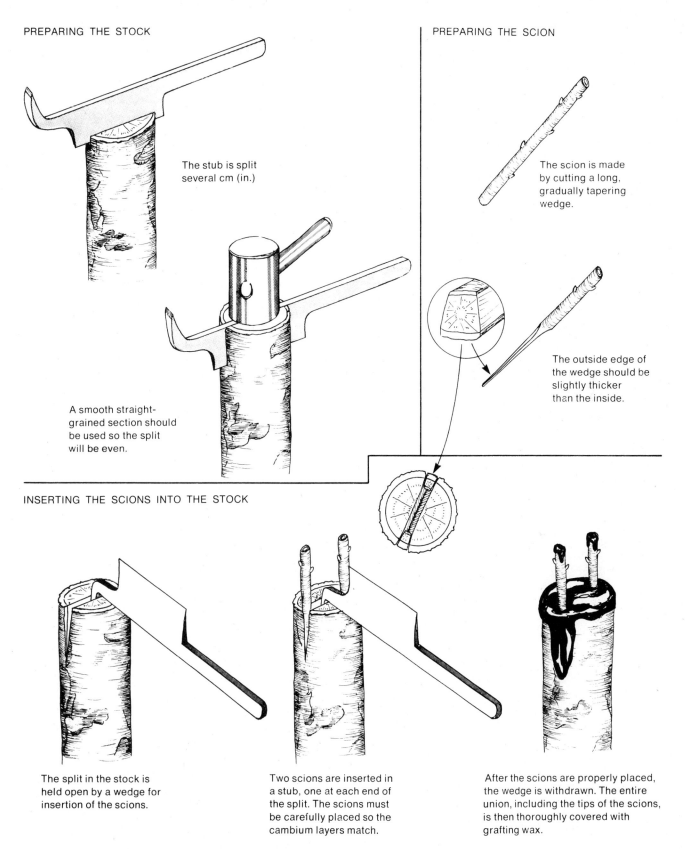

PREPARING THE STOCK

The stub is split several cm (in.)

A smooth straight-grained section should be used so the split will be even.

PREPARING THE SCION

The scion is made by cutting a long, gradually tapering wedge.

The outside edge of the wedge should be slightly thicker than the inside.

INSERTING THE SCIONS INTO THE STOCK

The split in the stock is held open by a wedge for insertion of the scions.

Two scions are inserted in a stub, one at each end of the split. The scions must be carefully placed so the cambium layers match.

After the scions are properly placed, the wedge is withdrawn. The entire union, including the tips of the scions, is then thoroughly covered with grafting wax.

Fig. 5–23 Steps in making the cleft graft. This method is very widely used and is quite successful if the scions are inserted so that the cambium layers of stock and scion match properly. *Source:* Hartmann, H. T., and D. E. Kester. 1975. *Plant propagation.* 3rd ed. Englewood Cliffs, N.J.: Prentice-Hall.

BUDDING

T-BUDDING This technique is widely used in propagating fruit trees and roses (Fig. 5–25). Buds taken from budsticks are inserted under the bark of small seedling rootstock plants a few inches above ground level. Buds are then inserted and tied into place with budding rubbers, but the tops of the seedling rootstocks are not cut off above the inserted cultivar bud until just before growth starts the next spring. For fruit trees, budding is usually done in late summer. Roses are usually budded in the spring, with the top of the rootstock broken over above the bud after about two weeks following budding. The break forces the bud to grow, and after the shoot has grown 10 to 20 cm (4 to 8 in) from the bud, the rootstock is completely cut off above the inserted bud. By fall, a sizable rose plant is ready to dig.

Fig. 5–24 Steps in making the bark graft. *Source:* Hartmann, H. T., and D. E. Kester. 1975. *Plant propagation.* 3rd ed. Englewood Cliffs, N. J.: Prentice-Hall.

PREPARING THE STOCK

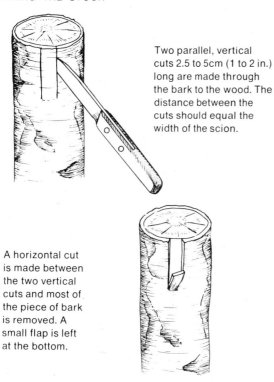

Two parallel, vertical cuts 2.5 to 5cm (1 to 2 in.) long are made through the bark to the wood. The distance between the cuts should equal the width of the scion.

A horizontal cut is made between the two vertical cuts and most of the piece of bark is removed. A small flap is left at the bottom.

PREPARING THE SCION

The scions are made with a long sloping cut on one side and a shorter cut on the opposite side.

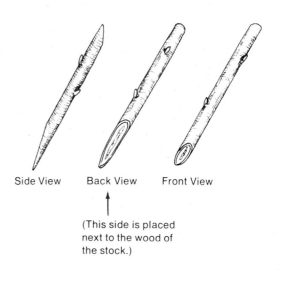

Side View   Back View   Front View

(This side is placed next to the wood of the stock.)

INSERTING THE SCION INTO THE STOCK

The scions are inserted into the slot made by the removal of the bark. The end of the scion is slipped under the raised flap of bark. Two nails are driven through the scion, one going through the flap.

The grafted stub is then thoroughly waxed.

PATCH-BUDDING Patch-budding, illustrated in Figure 5–26, is used mostly for such plants as walnuts, pecans, and other species that are difficult to T-bud because of their thick bark. Patch-budding must be done during the growing season when the bark on both the budstick and the rootstock is "slipping" easily (separating from the wood along the cambium layer). For propagating nursery trees, patch-budding is generally done in mid to late summer; the subsequent handling is the same as for T-budding.

HEALING OF THE GRAFT AND BUD UNION

In preparing a graft or bud combination, the two parts are joined by one of the methods just described

Fig. 5–25 T-budding. *A:* Cutting out bud from budstick. *B:* Three views of bud. *C:* T-cut made in seedling rootstock. *D:* Bud being inserted into T-cut. *E:* Bud in place and wrapped with budding rubber. *Source:* Univ. of Calif. Div. Agr. Sci. Leaflet 2990.

A

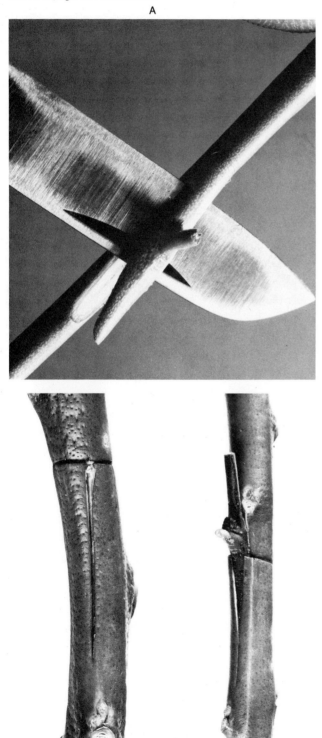

B

C   D   E

so that the cambial layers of stock and scion exposed by the grafting cuts are brought into intimate contact. They are held in place by wedging, nailing, or wrapping so that the parts cannot move about or become dislodged. Then the graft union is thoroughly covered with plastic or cloth tape or, better, by grafting wax to keep out air. The union heals by callus production from young tissues near the cambium layers of both stock and scion. Temperature levels must be conducive to cellular activity—generally from about 10° to 30°C (50° to 85°F)—and no

dry air must contact the cut surfaces because it would desiccate the tissues.

The steps in healing of a graft union are illustrated in Figure 5–27. Healing usually takes about two weeks and must be completed, with vascular connections made for translocation of water through the xylem, before the buds on the scion start to grow and develop leaves. The transpiring leaves would soon desiccate the scion unless the graft union has healed by this time.

LIMITS OF GRAFTING

There are certain limits to the combinations that can be successfully established by grafting or bud-

Fig. 5–26 Steps in making the patch bud. This method is widely used for propagating thick-barked plants. *Source:* Hartmann, H. T., and D. E. Kester. 1975. *Plant propagation.* 3rd ed. Englewood Cliffs, N. J.: Prentice-Hall.

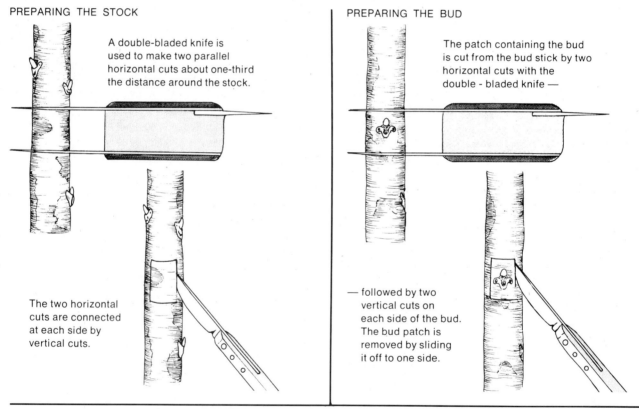

PREPARING THE STOCK

A double-bladed knife is used to make two parallel horizontal cuts about one-third the distance around the stock.

The two horizontal cuts are connected at each side by vertical cuts.

PREPARING THE BUD

The patch containing the bud is cut from the bud stick by two horizontal cuts with the double - bladed knife —

— followed by two vertical cuts on each side of the bud. The bud patch is removed by sliding it off to one side.

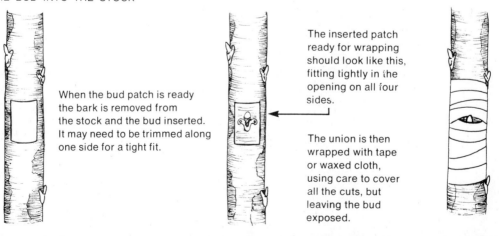

INSERTING THE BUD INTO THE STOCK

When the bud patch is ready the bark is removed from the stock and the bud inserted. It may need to be trimmed along one side for a tight fit.

The inserted patch ready for wrapping should look like this, fitting tightly in the opening on all four sides.

The union is then wrapped with tape or waxed cloth, using care to cover all the cuts, but leaving the bud exposed.

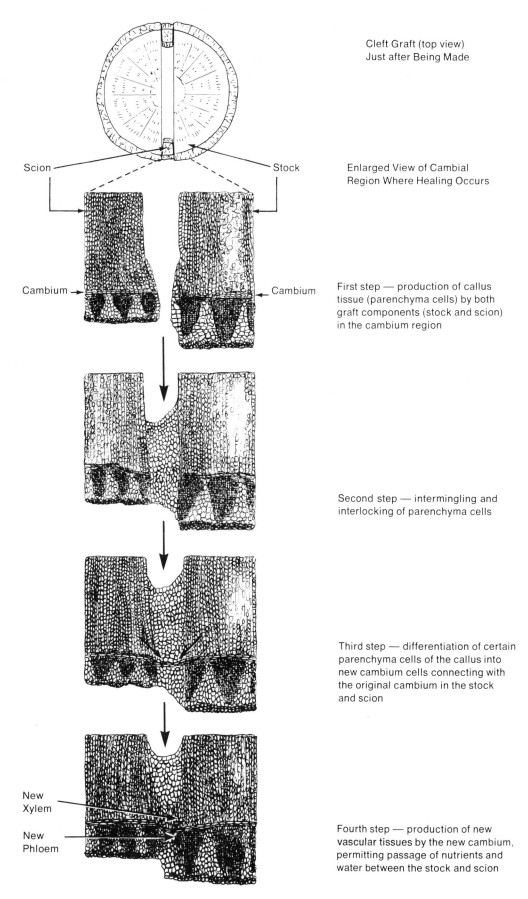

Cleft Graft (top view)
Just after Being Made

Scion   Stock

Enlarged View of Cambial
Region Where Healing Occurs

Cambium →   ← Cambium

First step — production of callus
tissue (parenchyma cells) by both
graft components (stock and scion)
in the cambium region

Second step — intermingling and
interlocking of parenchyma cells

Third step — differentiation of certain
parenchyma cells of the callus into
new cambium cells connecting with
the original cambium in the stock
and scion

New
Xylem

New
Phloem

Fourth step — production of new
vascular tissues by the new cambium,
permitting passage of nutrients and
water between the stock and scion

Fig. 5–27 Developmental sequence during the healing of a graft union
as illustrated by the cleft graft. *Source:* Hartmann, H. T., and D. E.
Kester. 1975. *Plant propagation.* 3rd ed. Englewood Cliffs, N. J.:
Prentice-Hall, Inc.

ding. The partners (stock and scion) in the combination must have some degree of botanical relationship—the closer the better. For instance, woody perennial plants in different botanical families have never, as far as is known, been successfully grafted together. For example, it is useless to attempt to graft a scion taken from a grapevine (VITACEAE) onto an apple tree (ROSACEAE).

In only a few cases have completely successful graft combinations been made between plants in the same family but different genera. For example, the thorny, deciduous large shrub trifoliate orange *(Poncirus trifoliata)* is widely used commercially as a rootstock for the common sweet orange *(Citrus sinensis)*, a large evergreen tree. Both are in the family RUTACEAE, but different genera—*Poncirus* and *Citrus.*

If the two graft partners are in the same genus but different species, then the chances of success are greatly improved. Still, many such graft combinations will not unite. Plant propagation books should be consulted for information that has been accumulated by trial and error over the years. For example, in the family ROSACEAE and the genus *Prunus,* it is well established that almonds *(P. dulcis),* apricots *(P. armeniaca),* European plums *(P. domestica),* and Japanese plums *(P. salicina)* can all be successfully grafted onto peach seedlings *(P. persica)* as a rootstock. But two other members of the genus *Prunus,* sweet cherry *(P. avium)* and sour cherry *(P. cerasus)* fail when grafted onto peach roots.

If the two partners are different cultivars (clones) within a species, the chances are almost 100 percent that the graft combination will succeed. For instance, if you have a 'Jonathan' apple tree *(Malus pumila),* you could successfully top-graft on it any other apple cultivar, for example, the 'Golden Delicious' *(Malus pumila).*

GRAFT INCOMPATIBILITY

There are many puzzling, unexplained situations among various graft combinations. Some pear cultivars are grafted commercially onto quince roots (an intergeneric combination), but scions of other pear cultivars grafted on quince roots soon die. The reverse, quince on pear roots, always fails. Plums can be successfully grafted on peach roots but peaches on plum roots are a failure. Japanese plums *(Prunus salicina)* can be grafted on European plum *(P. domestica)* roots, but in the reverse combination, the trees soon die.

There are many examples of incompatible graft combinations. **Compatibility** in grafting is the ability of two different plants, grafted together, to produce a successful union and to develop satisfactorily into one com-

posite plant. The causes for **graft incompatibility** are little understood in spite of many years of research into the problem. There is some evidence, however, that in certain graft combinations one partner (scion or stock) produces chemicals that are toxic to the other, killing the entire plant.

Effect of Rootstock on Growth and Development of the Scion Cultivar

Tree fruit growers often select a certain rootstock for a particular fruiting cultivar because it will dwarf the tree to some extent and thus make harvesting easier. This is particularly true in apples, where an entire series of clonal rootstocks (see p. 590) is available to produce apple trees with any desired degree of dwarfness. Quince roots will dwarf pear trees. Trifoliate orange roots will dwarf sweet orange trees.

These dwarfing influences extend to the tree only—not to the fruits produced by the trees. But in some species, particularly citrus, the kind of rootstock used can also strongly influence the quality of fruit produced by the scion cultivar. For instance, when sweet orange seedlings are used as the rootstock for orange trees, the fruits will be of much higher quality than when 'Rough' lemon is used as the rootstock.

What mechanisms are involved in such influences? Why are trees dwarfed by certain rootstocks? Considerable research has been conducted by plant physiologists and horticulturists over the years to try to explain these results, but convincing arguments are few. Probably the best hypothesis is that certain dwarfing rootstocks produce relatively large amounts of growth inhibitors, such as abscisic acid (see p. 139) that translocate through the graft union to the top fruiting cultivar and slow its growth. In addition, such dwarfing stocks produce low amounts of growth promoters, such as the gibberellins.

Layering

A simple and highly successful method of propagating plants is layering. Layering is similar to propagation by cuttings except that, instead of severing the part to be rooted from the mother plant, it is left attached and receives water and nutrients from the mother plant. After the stem piece (layer) has rooted—no matter how long it takes—it is cut from the mother plant and transplanted to grow independently. Various layering procedures can be used for many different kinds of plants (Fig. 5–28).

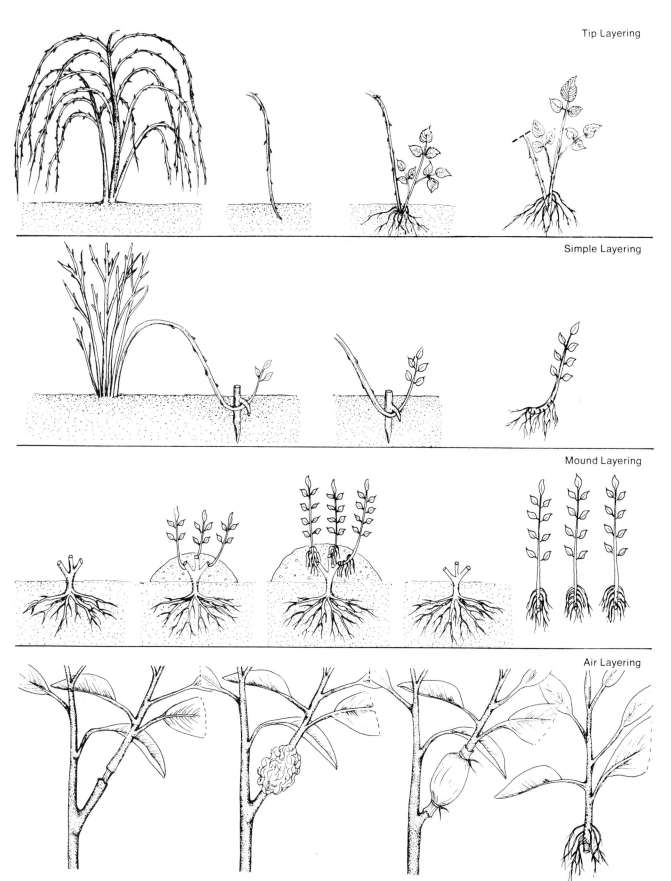

Tip Layering

Simple Layering

Mound Layering

Air Layering

Fig. 5–28 Steps in preparing four kinds of layers. See text for details.

TIP LAYERING

This is a natural means of vegetative propagation, shown by black raspberries and the trailing blackberries. The tips of the long canes, if buried a few inches deep in the soil toward the end of their first summer's growth, will root and produce a shoot that grows upward through the soil, forming a new plant. The cane can be cut from the parent bush and the new plant dug and replanted.

SIMPLE LAYERING

This method can be used with plants that produce long shoots arising from the plant at ground level. In early spring the ends of these shoots can be bent over, placed in a hole in the soil several inches deep, and recurved so that the shoot tip is exposed above ground. The curved section to be buried should be nicked or twisted slightly to retard translocation of food materials through the stem; this promotes rooting. The hole is then filled in with loose, moist soil tamped firmly in place. Sometimes it is necessary to drive a stake with a hook on it into the soil beside the layer to hold it in place. After the first summer's growth, the layer will usually have rooted and can be cut from the parent plant, dug, and transplanted. Simple layering is used to propagate filberts commercially.

MOUND LAYERING

This method, also called stooling, is widely used commercially to propagate apple and plum clonal rootstocks as well as currant and gooseberry cultivars. In late winter, the mother plants in the stool bed are cut back almost to the ground. As the new shoots start to grow in the spring, moist soil—or sometimes a mixture of soil and wood shavings or sawdust—is placed around the base of the shoots. As the shoots continue to grow, the mixture is mounded higher. The stool beds are kept continually moist, usually by overhead sprinklers. Roots develop from the base of these shoots, which by the end of the summer are well rooted. In early spring the soil is pulled away, and the rooted layers are cut off and transplanted to the nursery row for another season's growth. The stool bed is then handled again in the same manner during the next season.

AIR LAYERING

In this method the rooting medium is brought up to the stem to be rooted, rather than bringing the stem down to the soil. It is used for propagating the India "rubber" plant *(Ficus elastica)* or for *Dieffenbachia,* as well as many stiff-stemmed tropical plants, such as the

Fig. 5–29 Rooted litchi air layers. Polyethylene wrapping has been removed from layer on left to show the numerous white roots.

litchi *(Litchi chinensis)* and Jackfruit *(Artocarpus heterophyllus)*. The leaves of the branch to be air-layered are removed just below a good clump of foliage. The stem is girdled by cutting the bark away down to the wood for a width of 2.5 cm (1 in) and a root-promoting auxin powder (see p. 100) is rubbed into this cut. A ball (about two handfuls) of moist (not wet) sphagnum moss is wrapped around the girdling cut, then a sheet of polyethylene plastic or aluminum foil is wrapped snugly around the sphagnum moss and tied tightly above and below the ball. No further watering is needed because the moss absorbs moisture from the plant itself and the covering retards water loss. After several weeks, roots will start developing (Fig. 5–29). When a heavy root system has formed, the layer can be cut off just below the root ball, removed from the plastic, and, without disturbing the roots, planted in a large pot of soil. A few leaves should be removed to reduce water loss and the plant should be put in a cool, humid, and shady place until it becomes well established on its own new root system.

Fig. 5–30 Strawberry plant with new plants developing from nodes on the runners (stolons).

Other Plant Structures Providing Natural Propagation Methods

RUNNERS

Some plants, typically the strawberry (Fig. 5–30), grow as a rosette crown, with runners (stolons) arising from the crown. New plants arise from nodes at intervals along these runners. From these runner plants additional new runners arise, thus developing a natural clonal multiplication system. The runner plants must have favorable moist soil conditions to root. The strawberry produces runners in the summer in response to long days, and stops producing runners as the days shorten in the fall. Then the strawberry runner plants can be dug, packed in polyethylene-lined boxes, and placed in cold storage (−2°C; 28°F) for planting later, usually the following spring. Other plants with this natural asexual reproduction system are the ground cover *Duchesnea indica,* bugle *(Ajuga),* and the strawberry geranium *(Saxifraga stolonifera).*

SUCKERS

Some plants, such as the blackberry and red raspberry, produce adventitious shoots—or suckers—from their horizontal root system, which eventually spread to form a dense thicket of new plants. These individual shoots with a piece of the old root attached can be dug and replanted. This is a simple, highly successful asexual propagation method.

CROWNS

Many perennial plants exist as a single unit, becoming larger each year as new shoots arise from the crown (root-shoot junction) of the plant. Vegetative propagation of such plants consists of **crown division**—cutting the crown into pieces, each having roots and shoots, and transplanting to a new location (Fig. 5–31).

Fig. 5–31 Crown of an herbaceous perennial, the Shasta daisy. Lateral shoots develop from the underground portion of older stems and root. These rooted shoots can be cut from the mother plant and replanted. Underneath is a rooted shoot cut from the mother plant.

Propagation Using Specialized Stems and Roots

A number of herbaceous perennial plants have structures as **bulbs, corms, tubers, tuberous roots,** or **rhizomes** (see Ch. 20). These structures function as food storage organs during the plant's annual dormant period and also as vegetative propagation structures. In bulbs and corms, the newly formed plants break away from the mother plant naturally. This type of propagation is termed **separation.** The remaining structures—tubers, tuberous roots, and rhizomes—must be cut apart; this is termed propagation by **division.**

BULBS

These are short, underground organs having a basal plate of stem tissue with fleshy leaf scales surrounding a growing point or flower primordium (see Fig. 20–8). In the axils of some of these leaf scales, new miniature bulbs develop that eventually grow and split off from the parent bulb to form a new plant. There are two types of bulbs: (1) the **tunicate bulb** has a solid tight structure with fleshy scales arranged in concentric layers and covered by a dry membranous protective layer; examples are onion, daffodil, tulip, and hyacinth; (2) the **scaly bulb,** such as the lily, has loose, separate scales with no protective layer to prevent desiccation. The scales can be removed from the bulb; placing them under moist, humid conditions will promote the development of one or more new miniature bulbs at the base of each scale.

CORMS

A corm (Figs. 2–27 and 20–9) is the swollen underground base of a stem axis; it has nodes and internodes and is enclosed by dry scalelike leaves. The gladiolus, freesia, and crocus are examples of plants having a corm structure. Following bloom in gladiolus, one or more new corms develop just above the old corm, which disintegrates. In addition, several new small corms called cormels are produced just below each new corm. These may be detached and grown separately for one or two years to reach flowering stage.

STEM TUBERS

The edible Irish (white) potato (Fig. 2–26) is a good example of a plant having a tuber structure. The underground tuber consists of swollen stem tissue with nodes and internodes. When a potato tuber is cut into sections and planted, shoots arise from the buds (eyes) on the potato piece, which itself serves as a food supply for the developing shoot. From the lower portion of such shoots, adventitious roots develop, along with several underground horizontal shoots that are stem tissue. The terminal portions of these horizontal shoots enlarge greatly to form the fleshy potato tuber. Potato cultivars are clones and are propagated by dividing each tuber into several sections. The crop eventually developing from each section usually consists of three to six new tubers.

TUBEROUS ROOTS

These are root tissue. The dahlia, tuberous-rooted begonia, and the sweet potato (Fig. 5–32) are examples. Sweet potatoes are propagated vegetatively by placing the tuberous roots in beds so they are covered with about 5 cm (2 in) of soil. Adventitious shoots (slips) develop from these root tubers; from the base of the shoots adventitious roots form. These rooted slips are then pulled from the tuberous root and planted. As the sweet potato vines grow, some of their roots swell to form the familiar edible sweet potato.

Fig. 5–32 Sweet potato tuberous root, producing rooted adventitious shoots (*left*). *Right:* Two detached shoots (slips) ready for planting.

Certain plants, such as the German iris and bamboo (Fig. 5–33), have the main stem axis growing horizontally just at or slightly below the soil surface. This stem is a rhizome. Some plants have thick and fleshy rhizomes while others have thin, slender rhizomes. Like any stem, rhizomes have nodes and internodes. Leaves and flower stalks and adventitious roots develop from the nodes. Propagating plants with rhizomes is easy. At a time of year when the plant is not actively growing, the rhizome can be cut into pieces several inches in length and transplanted. Noxious weeds, such as Johnson grass, that have a rhizome structure cannot be controlled by cultivation because it merely breaks up the rhizomes and spreads the pieces about, each piece developing a new plant. Many important economic plants are propagated from rhizomes; examples are banana, ferns, ginger, and many grasses. Sometimes the above-ground horizontal stems are termed stolons particularly in such grasses as Bermuda grass.

Micropropagation

A major new advance in plant propagation involves the use of very small pieces of plant tissue grown on sterile nutrient media under aseptic conditions in small glass containers. These small pieces of tissue, called **explants,** will often regenerate many new root and shoot systems, which can be separated for growing into full-size plants. Some of the pieces of tissue are retained for further regeneration. The increase is geometrical, giving rise to fantastically large numbers of new individual plants in a short time. Micropropagation has been used mostly for herbaceous plants; regeneration with woody plants has been more difficult. Plants propagated commercially by these aseptic culture methods include ferns, orchids, ger-

beras, carnations, tobacco, chrysanthemum, asparagus, gladiolus, gloxinia, rhododendron, and strawberry.

Different parts of the plant can be taken as the explant. Entire seeds themselves can be used; for example, very tiny orchid seeds have been germinated commercially in sterile culture for many years. Embryos can be extracted from seeds and grown on a sterile nutrient medium. Shoot-tip culture involves excision of the growing point, which increases in size when kept in a nutrient medium and is divided over and over, greatly increasing plant numbers. This method has been successful with orchids, ferns, apples, and carnations. In other cases, tissue culture involves, for example, the excision of a piece of stem tissue and placing it on a nutrient medium. The explant then develops masses of callus by continuous cell division. From these callus clumps, roots and shoots may differentiate to form new plants. This method has been used with carrot, tobacco, asparagus, endive, aspen, Dutch iris, and citrus.

Single pollen grains of some plants, such as tobacco, have been germinated in sterile culture, when taken at just the right stage, to form haploid (1n) plants. Doubling the chromosome number with colchicine treatments yields diploid homozygous plants.

The nutrient media used for micropropagation are also favorable substrates for the growth of bacteria, fungi, and yeasts, so the prepared nutrient medium and its containers must be sterilized. The sealed containers are placed in an autoclave or pressure cooker for 20 to 30 minutes at 120°C (250°F). The plant tissue itself underneath the epidermis is sterile, but surface sterilization of the explants with a material such as a 10 percent Clorox solution is necessary, followed by rinsing with sterile water. Excision and insertion of the plant tissues onto the nutrient medium in the sterilized containers must be done with laboratory skill and procedures to prevent recontamination.

Fig. 5–33   Rhizome of bamboo with lateral buds and adventitious roots arising at nodes. Plants with rhizomes are propagated simply by cutting the rhizome into pieces and planting them.

Table 5–2 Components of the Murashige and Skoog Medium for Growing Tissue Explants Under Sterile Culture

NH_4NO_3	400 mg/l	indoleacetic acid	2.0 mg/l
$Ca(NO_3)_2 \cdot 4H_2O$	144	kinetin	0.04–0.2
KNO_3	80	thiamin	0.1
KH_2PO_4	12.5	nicotinic acid	0.5
$MgSO_4 \cdot 7H_2O$	72	pyridoxine	0.5
KCl	65	glycine	2.0
NaFe—EDTA	25	myo-inositol	100
H_3BO_3	1.6	casein hydro-lysate	1000
$MnSO_4 \cdot 4H_2O$	6.5	sucrose	2%
$ZnSO_4 \cdot 7H_2O$	2.7	powdered puri-fied agar	1%
KI	0.75		

Micronutrient elements may or may not be required but are usually added routinely. The following stock solution will provide the required materials. One milliliter of this solution is added per liter of culture medium.

$MnSO_4 \cdot 4H_2O$	1.81 g	$CuSO_4 \cdot 5H_2O$	0.08 g
H_3BO_3	2.86 g	$(NH_4)_2MoO_4$	0.09 g
$ZnSO_4 \cdot 7H_2O$	0.22 g	Distilled water	995 ml

Iron is usually essential and can be supplied in several ways: iron tartrate (1 ml of a 1 percent stock solution), inorganic iron ($FeCl_3 \cdot 6H_2O$, 1 mg/l) or $FeSO_4$, 2.5 mg/l; or chelated iron. Chelated iron can be supplied as NaFeEDTA, 25 mg/l, or by mixing, Na_2EDTA and $FeSO_4 \cdot 7H_2O$ in equimolar concentrations to give 0.1 mM Fe.

The nutrient media upon which the excised plant parts are grown include mineral salts, sugar, vitamins, growth regulators (auxins and cytokinins), and certain organic complexes such as coconut milk, yeast extract, or banana puree. The constituents of one widely used medium are given in Table 5–2. A mixture of micronutrient elements, including iron, is often added.

SUMMARY

Plants can be propagated either by seed (sexually) or by vegetative means (asexually), such as by cuttings, grafting, budding, or layering. Seeds are the product of pollination and fertilization in the flower, followed by fruit set and seed development. A seed contains a miniature plant (the embryo) and food storage tissue (endosperm or cotyledons) enclosed in the seed coats. Seeds of some plants become dormant and require various treatments, either to the seed coats or to the embryo, before they will germinate. For good germination seeds must have adequate moisture, proper temperature, good aeration to provide oxygen, light (in some cases), and an environment free of pathogenic organisms and toxic levels of salts. In asexual propagation various vegetative parts of the plant are excised and placed in an environment where they will regenerate the missing parts—stem cuttings must form roots, root cuttings must form shoots, leaf cuttings must develop both roots and shoots. Or grafting and budding may be done—a stem piece (with buds), which is to become the top part of the plant, is inserted properly into a root section of another plant. The union heals and the graft combination continues growth as one plant. Some knowledge is needed about which kinds of plants can be joined together by grafting. Other, less important kinds of vegetative propagation are suckering, in which shoots arise from root pieces and are cut off to include the root piece; layering, in which a stem piece is induced to form roots while it is still attached to the parent plant; and division, in which plants are cut into pieces to produce many new plants. Many herbaceous perennials propagate themselves naturally by such structures as bulbs, corms, root and stem tubers, and rhizomes. Finally, an entirely new technique of micropropagation is being developed by which plants can be propagated in vast quantities under aseptic conditions from miniature tissue explants.

REVIEW QUESTIONS

5–1. What are the two basic methods of propagating plants? In what fundamental respects do they differ?

5–2. For any propagation method to be successful it must accomplish two purposes. One is to attain a high degree of success in producing new plants. What is the other?

5–3. Most seeds must contain three basic structures for them to succeed as reproductive organs. What are they?

5–4. The seeds of most woody perennial plants become dormant by the end of the summer growing season and will not germinate at that time. What treatments are required to enable them to germinate?

5–5. Define the term *clone* and describe two ways by which new clones can originate.

5–6. In propagation by stem cuttings new adventitious roots must originate within the stem. What are the sites of origin in herbaceous plants as compared to woody perennial plants?

5–7. In clonal propagation, virus diseases can be perpetuated along with the newly propagated plants. Describe two methods for eliminating viruses from clones.

5–8. Some kinds of plants are much easier to propagate by rooting stem cuttings than others. What internal conditions in the plant itself could be responsible for this variability in root initiation?

5–9. Following a grafting operation, what changes must take place at the graft union to insure a successful graft combination?

5–10. What is meant by graft incompatibility?

5–11. Which grafting combination is more likely to be successful—plants in two different genera but in the same family, or plants in two different species but in the same genus?

5–12. Why is propagation by layering fundamentally more successful than propagation by cuttings?

5–13. Basically, what advantages does micropropagation have over conventional propagation methods?

5–14. Why do horticulturists propagate many kinds of woody plants by vegetative means, such as by cuttings or by grafting, rather than by sexual (seed) propagation?

5–15. If a scion from apple cultivar "A" is grafted onto apple cultivar "B," the fruit that is produced from the resulting tree will be (a) the same as cultivar "A," (b) the same as cultivar "B," or (c) intermediate between "A" and "B." Which is correct?

5–16. Which of these terms is incorrect to use: (1) an apomictic seed, or (2) an apomictic seedling? Explain your answer.

5–17. Give an example of a kind of plant propagated by each of the following structures.

Rhizome————
Stem tuber————
Tuberous root————
Stolon————
Corm————
Bulb————

5–18. What is meant by a "seed viability test"? Name three such tests and describe the procedures used in each.

5–19. For seeds of most species to germinate and produce vigorous seedlings five environmental factors must be correct. Name them.

5–20. Treatment of stem cuttings with an auxin, such as indolebutyric acid, is known to be helpful in propagation by this method. Basically, what is the beneficial mechanism involved in auxin treatments?

SUPPLEMENTARY READING

BAKER, K. F., ed. 1957. *The U.C. system for producing healthy container-grown plants*. Calif. Agr. Exp. Sta. Manual 23.

COPELAND, L. O. 1976. *Principles of seed science and technology*. Minneapolis: Burgess.

GARNER, R. J. 1979. *The grafter's handbook*. 4th ed. London: Faber & Faber.

GARNER, R. J., and S. A. CHAUDHRI. 1976. *The propagation of tropical fruit trees*. Hort. Rev. No. 4. East Malling, Kent, England: Commonwealth Bureau of Horticulture and Plantation Crops.

GENDERS, R. 1973. *Bulbs, a complete handbook*. Indianapolis: Bobbs-Merrill.

HARTMANN, H. T., and D. E. KESTER. 1975. *Plant propagation: principles and practices*. 3rd ed. Englewood Cliffs, N.J.: Prentice-Hall.

HINDS, H. V., ed. 1974. Special issue on vegetative propagation. *New Zealand Jour. Forest. Sci.* 4(2):120–458.

INTERNATIONAL PLANT PROPAGATORS' SOCIETY. *Proceedings of Annual Meetings*. Yearly.

KOSLOWSKI, T. T., ed. 1972. *Seed biology*, vols I–III. New York: Academic Press.

MAYER, A. M., and A. POLJAKOFF-MAYBER. 1975. *The germination of seeds*. 2nd ed. Oxford: Pergamon Press.

MOSSE, B. 1962. *Graft incompatibility in fruit trees*. Commonwealth Agr. Bur. Tech. Comm. No. 28.

MURASHIGE, T. 1974. Plant propagation through tissue culture. *Ann. Rev. Plant Physiol.* 25:135–66.

NYLAND, G., and A. C. GOHEEN, 1969. Heat therapy of virus diseases of perennial plants. *Ann. Rev. Phytopathol.* 7:331–54.

ROGERS, W. S., and A. B. BEAKBANE. 1957. Stock and scion relations. *Ann. Rev. Plant Physiol.* 8:217–36.

SCHOPMEYER, C. S., ed. 1974. *Seeds of woody plants in the United States*. USDA For. Serv. Agr. Handbook No. 450. Washington, D.C.: U.S. Government Printing Office.

STEFFERUD, A., ed. 1961. Seeds. USDA yearbook of agriculture. Washington, D.C.: U.S. Government Printing Office.

STREET, H. E. 1978. *Plant tissue and cell culture*. 2nd ed. Berkeley, Calif.: University of California Press.

Vegetative and Reproductive Growth and Development

VEGETATIVE GROWTH AND DEVELOPMENT

Shoot and Root Systems

In living plants we see primarily the shoot system, in all its diverse patterns—from the mosses to the magnificent towering redwoods, oaks, and pines. In many crop plants grown for livestock forage—alfalfa, corn for silage, and pasture grasses—the entire shoot system is harvested. A beautiful lawn results from the shoot and leaf growth of millions of small grass plants. A timber tree cut for lumber is the product of many years of shoot growth. The much-admired potted foliage plants in our homes are the shoot and leaf systems of particular kinds of plants brought into cultivation many years ago after their discovery by plant explorers in tropical lands.

In growing most plants—with the exceptions, perhaps, of bonsai[1] plants and container-grown ornamentals—we are interested in obtaining as much vigorous vegetative growth as we can as quickly as we can. This is particularly true for crop plants, where the difference between a profitable year and a loss for the farmer can be the amount of shoot growth harvested or the amount of leaf area produced to nourish the developing flowers, fruits, grains, or seeds.

The roots of plants are largely unseen and tend to be forgotten, but in the higher plants they are essential

[1]Bonsai is a Japanese term describing the art of dwarfing and shaping trees, shrubs, or vines grown in containers by careful pruning of roots and tops (see Fig. 15–16).

for growth. The structure of roots has been described in Chapter 2. The four principal functions of roots in higher plants are:

1. anchoring plants in the soil
2. absorbing water and mineral nutrients
3. conducting water and dissolved minerals, as well as organic foods
4. storing food materials, particularly in such plants as sweet potatoes, sugar beets, and carrots

The roots of some plants can also function in vegetative reproduction, as in root cuttings (9). This is explained in Chapter 5.

The root system and the shoot system tend to maintain a balance. As the top of the plant grows larger and larger, the leaf area increases and water loss through transpiration increases. This increased water loss is made up by water absorption from an increasing root system. The enlarging shoot system also requires greater amounts of minerals that are absorbed by the increasing root system (20, 21).

Definitions and Measurements

What is plant growth and how is it measured? We generally think of growth as an irreversible increase in volume or dry weight. The swelling of wood after it becomes wet is not growth because the wood will shrink upon drying.

116

Growth can be measured as increases in fresh weight or dry weight, or in volume, length, height, or surface area. As its gross size increases, a plant's form and shape change as directed by genetic factors. Plant growth is a product of living cells, with all their myriad metabolic processes. A definition of plant growth is: size increase by cell division and enlargement, including synthesis of new cellular material and organization of subcellular organelles.

Plant shoot growth can be classed as **determinate** or **indeterminate.** In determinate growth, after a certain period of vegetative growth, flower bud clusters form at the shoot terminals so that most shoot elongation stops. Many vegetable species and cultivars grow this way, remaining "dwarfed" bush plants; bush snap beans are an example of a determinate type. Indeterminate plants bear the flower clusters laterally along the stems in the axils of the leaves so that the shoot terminals remain vegetative and the shoot continues to grow until it is stopped by senescence (see p. 124) or some environmental influence. Trailing pole beans, grapevines, and forest trees are examples of plants with an indeterminate growth pattern. The determinate, bush-type plants produce much less vegetative growth than do the indeterminate type.

Fig. 6–1 Vegetative growth patterns of annual plants. *A:* Indeterminate, vine-type plants. *B:* Determinate, bush-type plants. *C:* Terminal-flowering plants, such as cereals and grasses. Arrows indicate times of flower initiation. *Source:* Adapted from Rappaport, L., and R. M. Sachs. 1976. *Physiology of cultivated plants.* Davis, Calif: UCD Bookstore.

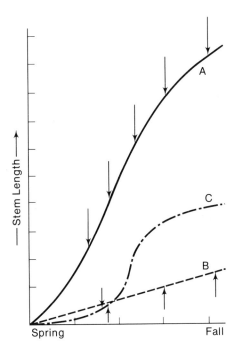

Annuals, which are herbaceous (non woody) plants, complete their life cycle (seed to seed) in one growing season. Shoot growth commences after seed germination and continues in a fairly uniform pattern—provided no environmental influences are limiting—until growth is stopped by frost or some senescence-inducing factor. Flowering, followed by fruit and seed production, occurs at intervals through the summer. General growth curves for the annuals are shown in Figure 6–1; a detailed growth curve for barley, an herbaceous annual, is shown in Figure 6–2.

Fig. 6–2 Growth curve of a field-grown barley plant from leaf emergence to grain maturity. ○ = plant height. ● = dry weight of plant minus grain weight. ▣ = dry weight of plant plus grain weight. *Source:* Adapted from Noggle, G. R., and G. J. Fritz. 1976. *Introductory plant physiology.* Englewood Cliffs, N.J.: Prentice-Hall.

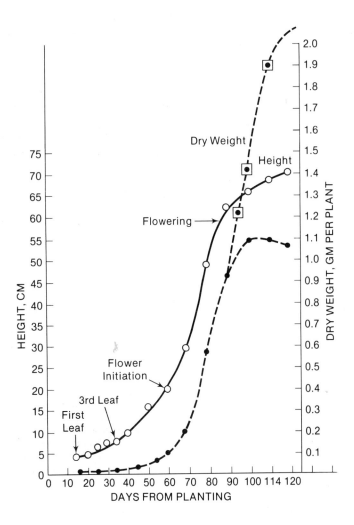

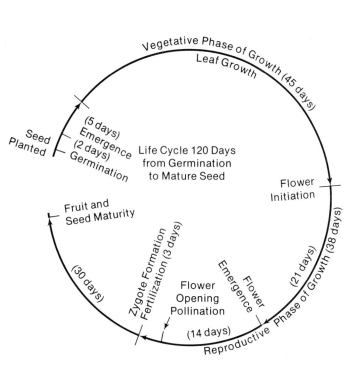

Fig. 6–3 Events in the life cycle of a typical annual plant—from seed planting to seed maturity—accomplished in four months. *Source:* Adapted from Noggle, G. R., and G. J. Fritz. 1976. *Introductory plant physiology.* Englewood Cliffs, N.J.: Prentice-Hall.

Fig. 6–4 Growth curves of biennial plants during the first growing season (vegetative growth only), a required winter chilling-period, and a second growing season (flowering, fruiting, and seed production). *Source:* Adapted from Rappaport, L., and R. M. Sachs. 1976. *Physiology of cultivated plants.* Davis, Calif.: UCD Bookstore.

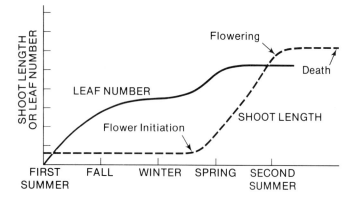

Fig. 6–5 Shoot growth patterns of herbaceous perennials over a two-year period. *A:* Plants such as garden (outdoor) chrysanthemums, peony, and phlox whose growth is stopped by cold weather in the fall. *B:* Bulbous plants such as tulips, narcissus, and hyacinths, whose growth is terminated after spring flowering. *Source:* Adapted from Rappaport, L., and R. M. Sachs. 1976. *Physiology of cultivated plants.* Davis, Calif.: UCD Bookstore.

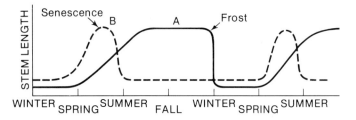

Figure 6–3 shows various events in the life cycle of a typical angiosperm annual plant. All these events occur during a single summer growing season.

The **biennials,** which are herbaceous plants, require two growing seasons (not necessarily two years) to complete their life cycle (seed to seed). As shown in Figure 6–4, stem growth is limited during the first growing season, the shoot system remaining mostly as a rosette. The plants remain alive but dormant through the winter. Exposure to chilling temperatures triggers hormonal changes leading to stem elongation, flowering, fruit formation, and seed set during the second growing season. Senescence and death of the plant follows shortly thereafter. Examples of herbaceous biennials are lettuce, beets, and such cole crops as cabbage and Brussels sprouts.

Most annual and biennial plants flower and fruit only once before dying. The production of the flowers and fruits or, perhaps, just the flowering stimulus itself, apparently causes the plants to senesce and die. In such plants, continued removal of flowers and fruits often delays senescence.

Perennials are either herbaceous or woody. In herbaceous perennials the roots and shoots can remain alive indefinitely but the shoot system may be killed by frosts in cold-winter regions or by senescence-inducing factors. Shoot growth resumes each spring from latent or adventitious buds at the crown of the plant. Figure 6–5 shows typical growth patterns for two types of herbaceous perennials.

In woody perennial plants both the shoot and root system remain alive indefinitely, each growing to the ultimate size for the particular plant as programmed by its gene complement (16, 34). Shoot growth of temperate zone plants takes place annually during the growing season, as indicated in Figure 6–6, adding to the growth accumulated in previous seasons. The magnitude of growth can vary considerably from season to season under the influence of several environmental factors, as described on page 120.

In the tropics some of the evergreen tree species grow vegetatively continually throughout the year but other species exhibit intermittent growth, sometimes correlated with changes in weather, especially rainfall. Vegetative growth of coffee trees, for example, is much greater in the wet season than in the dry.

In the temperate zones all trees show intermittent annual vegetative growth. These growth patterns can be placed into four categories:

1. A single flush of terminal shoot growth during the growing season followed by the formation of a

resting terminal bud; oaks, hickories, many conifers, and most fruit tree species are examples.

2. Recurrent flushes of terminal growth with terminal bud formation at the end of each flush; examples include the pines of the southeastern United States (*Pinus taeda* and *P. virginiana*) and certain subtropical evergreen and deciduous tree species such as citrus and Persian walnut.

3. A flush of growth followed by shoot tip abortion at the end of the season, with the shoot the following season starting up from a lateral bud. This gives rise to a zigzag pattern of shoot development, exemplified by the elm, birch, willow, beech, and honey locust.

4. A sustained growth flush for varying periods, producing new growing points that develop as late-season leaves, and ending the season with the formation of a distinct terminal bud; examples are the tulip tree (*Liriodendron tulipifera*) and sweet gum (*Liquidambar styraciflua*).

There is a pronounced diurnal variation in shoot growth of woody perennials. Shoots tend to grow more rapidly at night than in the day provided temperatures are favorable. This difference is probably due to a lower water stress at night than during the day. Some species show twice the growth at night compared with day growth.

Root Growth Patterns

Various studies of root growth patterns conclude that the roots of mature deciduous woody perennials start to grow in the spring before bud break and continue to grow after leaf drop in the autumn. Growth peaks in the spring and again in late summer or early autumn. The roots, however, continue to grow even during the winter months whenever soil temperatures and moisture are favorable. Not all roots of a tree may be growing at any one time. While some are actively growing, others may be quiescent. The spring flush of root growth results from the accumulated foods stored in the tree the previous year. When this source is depleted, root growth slows but, following gradual accumulation of carbohydrates from photosynthesis through the summer, root growth again increases in the autumn.

It does not appear that the growing points of the roots are under the same hormonal control as the shoot buds, which go into a resting period in late summer and require chilling through the winter to be reactivated (see p. 227).

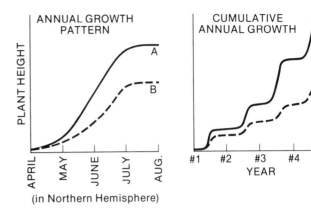

Fig. 6–6 Growth patterns for temperate zone woody perennials in the northern hemisphere during one growing season (*left*) and over a period of several years (*right*). A: Curve for a rapid-growing species such as poplar. B: Curve for a slow-growing species such as the oaks. *Source:* Adapted from Rappaport, L., and R. M. Sachs. 1976. *Physiology of cultivated plants.* Davis, Calif.: UCD Bookstore.

How the Plant Grows

The importance of meristems (see Ch. 2) in the growth of plants must be clearly understood. In dicotyledenous plants, vegetative buds at the shoot tips (apical meristems) and in the axils of leaves contain meristematic cells that are capable of dividing and redividing, by mitosis (Fig. 5–4) and cytokinesis,[2] producing millions of cells along a longitudinal axis. Cell division, together with cell elongation, causes the shoots to grow (22). A growing point at a shoot tip (see Fig. 2–6), with its meristematic region producing new cells year after year for many hundreds of years, can account for the towering height of the redwood, Douglas fir, and other forest trees. Similar meristematic cells are also located in the root tip, just behind the root cap.

The thickening of the trunks of growing trees and other woody perennials is due to secondary growth produced by another meristematic region, the vascular cambium (see Fig. 2–8), a cell layer that lies between the xylem and the phloem and encircles the tree from the roots to almost the top of the shoot (13). Cells of this vascular cambium also have the capability of dividing, producing both the permanent woody xylem tissues to-

[2]Cell division occurs in two parts: (1) *mitosis,* where one nucleus is divided into two nuclei and, (2) *cytokinesis,* which is the division of the resulting binucleate cell into two uninucleate cells. The latter is accomplished by the formation of the cell plate, a thin layer of polysaccharide materials that develops across the spindle between the daughter nuclei toward the end of mitosis, thus dividing the cytoplasmic constituents of the mother cell.

ward the inside that give the tree its girth and mechanical strength and the more fragile transitory phloem cells to the outside *(13)*. External to the vascular cambium is another meristematic region, the cork cambium (Fig. 2–8), which produces the cork in the bark layer.

GENETIC FACTORS AFFECTING PLANT GROWTH AND DEVELOPMENT[3]

One of the marvels of biology is the manner in which the offspring of plants and animals resemble, yet differ from, their parents. A chicken, not a turkey, hatches from a chicken egg. A peach tree, not a cherry tree, grows from a germinated peach seed. In a field planted with 'Marquis' wheat seed, 'Marquis' wheat plants develop, not oats or barley. The organism developing by cell division and elongation from the fertilized egg—the zygote—in every case is under the genetic control of the genes inherited from the parents at the time of fertilization. The genes, which direct the form and shape of the organism, are passed on to the daughter cells. Most of them are on the chromosomes in the nucleus of each cell of the organism.

As the plant enlarges from the fertilized egg (zygote) to its mature size many developmental processes take place. Certain segments of DNA (genes) direct the synthesis of enzymes that catalyze specific biochemical reactions required for growth and differentiation. The genes involved in protein synthesis are referred to as **structural genes**. Genes involved in regulating the activity of the structural genes are referred to as **regulatory** and **operator genes**. During a particular stage of development, not all the genetic information stored in the chromosomes is necessarily active. As development proceeds, some genes are activated—switched on—while other genes are inactivated—switched off. The regulatory genes are involved in activating or deactivating operator genes that, in turn, control the activity of structural genes.

What are the signals that trigger the action of the regulatory genes? Although not clearly understood, they are believed to include growth regulators (see p. 133), certain inorganic ions, coenzymes, and other metabolites. Environmental factors such as temperature or light can also function as signals during certain developmental stages. Thus, the particular combination of genes directs the form and size each plant is finally to assume, as altered by stresses from environmental influences, either beneficial or deleterious.

[3]For a discussion of some basic genetic concepts, see Chapter 4, page 69.

ENVIRONMENTAL FACTORS INFLUENCING PLANT GROWTH AND DEVELOPMENT

LIGHT   The sun is the source of energy for photosynthesis and other plant processes, as described in Chapter 7, but only a small amount of the sun's radiation reaches the earth's surface. The atmosphere is composed of several gases, water vapor, and dust that filter out much of the radiation. Ozone absorbs the long wavelengths, keeping the earth's surface from becoming too warm. Thus the atmosphere is a gaseous envelope that filters out many of the sun's rays but allows enough of the visible and some of the invisible rays (both long and short wavelengths) to pass to maintain the earth at the moderate temperature both plant and animal life needs. These rays of light strike the earth's surface, heating the soil and large bodies of water which, in turn, give off heat (reradiating long wavelengths) that is trapped by the atmosphere and warms it.

Light intensity is high where there are no clouds or where there is little moisture in the air, as in deserts. Light intensity is lower in humid or cloudy regions because the water vapor absorbs much of the radiation. Since the earth is tilted on its axis in relation to the sun (at an angle of 23½°), light intensity varies greatly with the season in the temperate zones. In the summer the sun's rays strike earth's surface more directly than in the winter. Day length varies greatly near the poles: 24 hours of light in summer and 24 hours of darkness in winter. These variations become less extreme toward the equator, where the day lengths range from 12 to 13 hours all year.

The narrow band of light that affects plant photoreaction processes ranges from about 300 nanometers (nm) to about 800 nm. The most important process, photosynthesis (see Ch. 7), is very efficient in the orange-red (650 nm) and in the blue range (440 nm) of the visible spectrum. The stomates, which have chlorophyll in their guard cells and allow carbon dioxide to enter, open in the light and are generally closed in the dark. They respond effectively to red light (660 nm) and blue light (440 nm); thus stomatal opening and closing is very closely correlated with photosynthesis. Stomates may close about midday, as the plants wilt slightly because of excessive transpiration.

Other plant processes strongly influenced by light are phototropism and photoperiodism. **Phototropism** is the movement or bending of stems, leaves, and flowers toward the light. This bending results from more cell growth on the side away from the light source than on the side toward it. It is believed that auxin, a natural hormone (p. 133), accumulates and is transported to the shaded side, promoting cell expansion there. Blue light is the most active in this process, but the exact pigment involved is unknown.

Photoperiodism refers to the physiological responses of plants to variations of light and darkness. Plants have many such responses. As the daylength gradually shortens in late summer and fall, a ''signal'' sent from the leaves starts certain processes that help the plant survive the winter. The onset of dormancy in some plants begins when days shorten in the fall, enabling the plant to survive the winter cold. Development of fall leaf color in certain trees is also attributed to the shortening day. Tubers of potatoes, dahlias, and tuberous-rooted begonias begin to form when the days start to shorten after midsummer; onions, on the other hand, form bulbs when the days begin to lengthen in late spring. Photoperiodism in flower induction is discussed later in this chapter (p. 125).

TEMPERATURE   The seasonal variation of light intensity is responsible for the temperature changes from summer to winter in the various temperature zones. Farmers depend on climatic records in their areas to predict the last day of frost in the spring and the number of available ''growing days'' before the first killing frost in the fall. The greater the distance from the equator, the fewer the number of available growing days to mature crops. It is possible to grow temperature-sensitive tomatoes in Alaska or northern Europe, but precautions must be taken to protect the seedlings from frost in early spring. But once summer arrives in these northern latitudes, the days are so long and the temperatures are warm enough that plants grow, flower, and set fruit rapidly. The growing season may be short but plants develop fast.

All plants have optimal temperatures for maximum vegetative growth and flowering, as noted for plants discussed as crops in subsequent chapters. Most temperate-region plants grow between temperatures of 4°C (40°F) and 50°C (122°F), but these generally are the limits of plant growth. The high temperatures destroy the protoplasm of most cells; however, some spores and seeds can withstand the temperature of boiling water for short periods. At the low temperatures, most plants just fail to grow owing to lack of cell activity. However, there are some arctic or mountain plants that function near freezing, but these are rare exceptions.

Plant parts are injured by very high temperatures, even if the exposure is short. Leaves may be **solarized** or sunburned when exposed to high light intensities. In the leaf, light energy converts to heat, which destroys the cells. Young trees in orchards are prone to sunscald, which kills the cambium layer just under the thin bark. Injury can be prevented by painting the bark white to reflect the heat. Occasionally, plants suffer heat damage when the relative humidity drops suddenly because of hot, desiccating winds. Heat damage in greenhouse grown plants can be prevented if the relative humidity is increased by misting in the immediate vicinity of the plant.

The most common low temperature injury is evident after the night of the first killing frost in the fall. The plant surfaces may be coated with frost depending on the dew-point temperature, but soon after the sun shines on the leaves, the damage is evident in blackened leaves. The contents of the cells are damaged by the ice and, upon thawing, the water in the protoplasm moves to the intercellular spaces, the protoplasm dehydrates, and death occurs (see Ch. 10). Frost damage to plants due to heat loss at night by radiation can be avoided to some extent by placing an opaque shield between the plant and the clear sky on a calm night. This shield prevents radiation from the leaves to the cold sky. Transparent polyethylene plastics allow heat from longwave radiation to escape at night so are useless as a radiation shield. Citrus and grape growers sometimes use smudge pots burning oil to create heat that radiates to the trees (Fig. 10–11). In locations where there are temperature inversions above the plants (slightly warmer temperatures in a layer some distance above the soil than at ground level), wind machines may be useful. These power-driven propellors mix the warm air above with the cool air below, thus preventing low temperature injury (see Fig. 10–12).

Some plants grown in locations with severe winters go into a rest period—brought on, in some cases, by shortening days in fall—and become resistant to low winter temperatures. A covering of snow helps the plants withstand the winter since it acts as a good insulator at extremely low temperatures.

Some plants of tropical origin may be injured at temperatures just above the freezing point. The leaves may wilt and never recover and developing fruits may not mature; some examples are avocado, banana, mango, okra, and tomato. Unripe tomatoes, which show pink color, will be injured and will not finish the ripening process if refrigerated at 4°C (40°F) or less. This is referred to as chilling injury (see Ch. 10).

WATER   Most growing plants contain about 90 percent water. It is stored in various plant tissues and is used as one of the raw materials for photosynthesis. A corn plant near harvest may contain as much as two liters (2.1 qt) of water, but during its growth from a seedling to a mature plant with ears, it may extract 100 times this amount from the soil. Some of this water is used in growth and development, but most of it is lost through the leaf stomates in the transpiration process. Therefore, in order to produce a mature crop of corn or tomatoes, the equivalent of 30 to 60 cm (12 to 24 in) of water must be applied to the soil surface as rain or irrigation. The quantity of water necessary depends on the crop (some plants use much more than others) as well as the available sunshine during the season. When the light from the sun is strong, the leaves tend to lose large quantities of water by transpiration and, additionally, the soil loses water by evaporation. Substantially more soil water is lost from transpiration by plants than by evaporation from the soil. The total soil water loss by both means is called **evapotranspiration.** The rate of evapotranspiration is known in many farming regions and is a guide to the farmer concerned with how much irrigation water must be applied to compensate for the soil water loss.

The plant obtains water from the soil by forces in the transpiration process. The mesophyll cells of the leaves, filled with water, are connected to the intercellular spaces that lead to the stomates; the stomates, when open, lose moisture to the air. Thus, water is "pulled" through the plant via the conducting tissue (xylem) (see Ch. 2, p. 21). If more water is lost through the stomates than the roots can supply, the plant wilts. Many plants wilt slightly at midday or later on a bright sunny day but usually recover during the night. Wilted plants eventually die if they cannot recover enough soil water to regain their turgidity. While the plant is wilted, the stomates are closed, cutting off the intake of CO_2 for photosynthesis thus reducing carbohydrate manufacture.

The quality of soil water, as determined by the quantity of minerals and salts dissolved in the water, is very important to the growth of plants. If there is too much dissolved salt, or if one salt, such as sodium chloride, predominates, the roots become damaged and the top of the plant suffers from lack of water. Some desert plants are resistant to high salts in water and manage to survive. In contrast, most greenhouse and garden plants require good quality water (see Chs. 17 and 18). Table 8–7 gives the tolerance of various plants to different levels of water quality.

Agricultural production is influenced by both the quality and quantity of water available in a region of favorable temperatures. The quality of water is no problem when there is adequate rainfall. However, if the rain must be stored as runoff water in reservoirs, poor quality may result if the water accumulates too much salt before it is collected and used in irrigation.

GASES The two gases most important to the growth of green plants are oxygen (O_2) and carbon dioxide (CO_2). Green land plants and the extensive phytoplankton of the oceans help keep a balance of O_2 and CO_2 throughout the world. Green plants use CO_2 for photosynthesis (Ch. 7) and return O_2 to the atmosphere. Plants and animals of all kinds use O_2 and give off CO_2 during respiration (Fig. 7–1). Ocean and fresh-water

algae account for about 90 percent of the photosynthesis in the world! These plants do most of the work to keep our atmosphere in a favorable balance. Of the land plants, the forests of the world account for most photosynthetic activity.

According to one theory, stomatal opening and closing is regulated by the CO_2 level. When the CO_2 concentration in the leaf cells below the stomata is lower than that found in the atmosphere—0.03 percent or 300 parts per million (ppm)—the stomata open. The use of CO_2 during photosynthesis keeps the concentration lower than 300 ppm and the stomata remain open if other conditions are favorable. (However, the whole process regulating stomatal opening and closing is more complex than just CO_2 level.)

Oxygen is important in the respiration of all plant parts. Soils saturated or waterlogged for long periods do not contain adequate O_2 for root respiration activity. Roots cannot absorb minerals from the soil if the soil is lacking O_2 due to low respiration rates. When plants are grown with their roots in water (hydroponics), air is bubbled through the water to supply O_2 in constant small quantities so that the roots can respire.

The plant shoots and leaves also respire and in complex processes use the raw materials of photosynthesis (sugars) plus minerals absorbed by roots to produce new plant tissue and allow for growth (see Ch. 7).

Atmospheric pollution is a byproduct of our civilized society *(5)*. We burn fossil fuels at an alarming rate for heat, transportation, and manufacturing. All this combustion releases pollutants into the air as harmful byproducts. The burning processes release CO_2, which is useful in photosynthesis, but there are other gases such as ozone, sulfur dioxide, fluorides, and ethylene, all of which can be harmful to both animals and plants.

Ozone is formed in a photooxidation process in the presence of strong sunlight. It is the major pollutant in smog and is usually found in large cities that have many automobiles. Exhausts from cars, in the presence of nitrogen oxide and abundant sunlight, produce ozone and peroxyacetyl nitrates (PAN), which harm both plants and animals. Plants affected by pollutants may have a leaf margin burn, as in some grasses, or the leaves—of petunias, lettuce, and beans—may lose chlorophyll in the center. This area of the leaf then becomes bleached or dies. Automobile exhausts also emit boron, lead (both used for better gas combustion), and ethylene into the air. Ethylene is a growth regulator (see p. 138) that can cause unusual plant growth patterns, such as leaf distortions. Sulfur dioxide results from the combustion of fossil fuels (except most natural gases) and is particularly evident in smelting processes using sulfide ores. Sulfur dioxide can cause pronounced areas of damage on leaves of sensitive plants. Fluorides can be emitted into the atmosphere by the manufacture of cement, glass, ceramics, bricks, aluminum, and phosphate fertilizers. Fluoride damage is usually seen along the margins or tips of leaves.

Phase Change:
Juvenility, Maturation, Senescence

Seedling plants undergo a phasic development throughout their lives that is essentially the same as in animals. They pass through embryonic growth, juvenility, a transition stage, maturity, senescence, and death *(32, 33, 35, 36).*

During maturation, seedlings of many woody perennial species differ strikingly in appearance at various stages of development. When eucalyptus trees are very young they have opposite, broad leaves with no petiole. As the tree gets older and taller, the leaves in the upper portion of the tree assume a different appearance: they become alternate, are narrower, and have a distinct petiole, and the leaf color changes from bluish-green to a deep green. Young citrus seedlings are very thorny but as they continue their growth to full-size trees, thorns are no longer produced on the shoots. Figure 6–7 shows the transition stages in leaf patterns of an *Acacia melanoxylon* seedling as the shoot elongates and ages.

The familiar English ivy *(Hedera helix)* in its juvenile stage has three- or five-lobed palmate alternate

Fig. 6–7 *Acacia melanoxylon* seedling showing phase change from juvenile to mature form. Lower, juvenile leaves have compound bipinnate structure. Upper, mature "leaves" are actually expanded petioles (phyllodia). Transition stages are evident in between. *Source:* Hartmann, H. T., and D. E. Kester. 1975. *Plant propagation.* 3rd ed. Englewood Cliffs, N.J.: Prentice-Hall.

leaves and hairy vinelike stems with no flowers. On the same plant can be found branches in the adult stage that have nonlobed ovate opposite leaves and smooth nonclimbing stems with prominent flower stalks and flowers.

The morphological changes of age are accompanied by important physiological changes. A primary criterion for judging that a plant is in the juvenile stage is its inability to form flowers and set fruit even though all environmental conditions are conducive to flowering. The onset of flowering and fruiting indicates the termination of the juvenile phase. Another important indication of phase change from juvenility to maturity is a loss or reduction in the ability of cuttings to form adventitious roots.

Seedlings of many woody perennial species, including conifers, undergo this juvenile-to-mature phase change. The juvenile stage in certain forest species can last as long as 30 to 40 years and during this time, flowering does not take place *(26).*

The phase changes are not genetic but result from little-understood biochemical and physiological alterations. These changes apparently originate in the apical meristem of the plant. Strangely, the lower part of many woody plants—the oldest in terms of calender days—remains physiologically the youngest, least likely to flower, and most likely to produce adventitious roots on its cuttings. On the other hand, the top of the plant—the youngest in time—develops into the oldest, most mature, most likely to flower, and the most unlikely to form roots when cuttings are taken.

Once the mature phase is attained, a plant is relatively stable and does not revert easily to the juvenile stage, although treatments with plant hormones such as gibberellins (see p. 135) or grafting tissues from mature plant parts back onto juvenile plants can cause the mature tissue to revert to the juvenile stage.

Breeders of fruit or nut crops are eager to bring the seedlings from their controlled crosses through the juvenile stage as rapidly as possible so that they will flower and fruit and the breeders can see the results of their work. Plant propagators, on the other hand, would like to maintain the juvenile stage in stock plants as long as possible so that cuttings from them will root rapidly and in high percentages.

Not every young woody perennial plant is necessarily in the juvenile growth stage. It may have been propagated vegetatively—perhaps as a rooted cutting taken from a plant in the adult phase—on the other hand, if it was propagated from a germinated seed it would be in a juvenile growth phase. Young nursery stock of all cultivars of fruit trees is propagated asexually from material taken from mature trees, and such stock is usually many generations from the original seedling mother tree for the cultivar—which itself did go through the transitory phases from a juvenile to an adult form.

AGING AND SENESCENCE *(1, 23, 25, 32, 33)*

The life spans of the different kinds of flowering plants differ greatly, ranging from a few months to thousands of years. Some of the coniferous evergreen forest trees are the earth's oldest living organisms. Living bristlecone pines, *(Pinus aristata)* said to be over 4000 years old are growing in California's Sierra Nevada Mountains (Fig. 6–8). Some of the giant California redwoods *(Sequoia sempervirens)* are known to be over 3000 years old. Olive trees with huge trunks found in the

Fig. 6–8 *Above:* Ancient olive tree *(Olea europaea)* growing on the Mount of Olives in Jerusalem. Trees of this species are known to live for several thousand years. *Below:* Bristlecone pine *(Pinus aristata),* which grows in the high mountains from California to Colorado. These trees are among the earth's oldest living plants, some reaching the age of 4000 years. *Source:* E. Memmler.

eastern Mediterranean area are believed to be several thousand years old (see Fig. 6–8).

There seems to be no reason why a clone[4] could not continue to exist indefinitely if it was protected from diseases (especially viruses) and other environmental stresses and repropagated frequently. Some clones are known to be very old—the 'Winter Pearmain' apple, cultivated in England, was being grown there about 1200 A.D. The 'Reine Claude' plum was also grown in England as long ago as 1500 A.D. The 'Black Corinth' grape has been grown in Greece for thousands of years. Other present-day clones of plants that are easily propagated by vegetative means, such as the fig, olive, and date, were being grown in Biblical times.

Senescence is considered to be a terminal, irreversible deteriorative change in living organisms, leading to cellular and tissue breakdown and death. It is a conspicuous period of physical decline, particularly evident toward the end of the life cycle of annual plants (population senescence) and of individual plants (whole plant senescence), but it can also occur in leaves, seeds, flowers, or fruits (organ senescence). Plants exhibit senescence in different ways. In annuals the entire plant dies at the end of one growing season, after and probably because of fruit and seed production. In herbaceous perennials, the tops of the plants die at the end of the growing season, perhaps killed by frost, but the shoot grows again in the spring and the roots can live for many years. In deciduous woody perennials, the leaves senesce, die, and fall off each year but the shoot and root systems remain alive for many years.

Senescence is usually considered to be due to inherent physiological changes in the plant, but it can also be caused by pathogenic attack or environmental stress. As individual trees age, for example, they are more and more vulnerable to lethal attacks by fungi, bacteria, and viruses. The long-lived trees mentioned above characteristically have very durable heartwood, containing high levels of resins and phenolic compounds that resist decay. As large trees get older, the ratio of foliage area to the surface area of roots, trunk, and limbs often diminishes progressively, thus lessening the amount of food the tree produces in relation to the amount it consumes in respiration. Eventually the leaves are unable to supply adequate amounts of food to nourish the tree. The reduced foliage cover for the trunk and large limbs as the trees age can also lead to sunburn damage and death of exposed tissues.

Considerable study has been given to senescence in

---

[4]A clone is genetically uniform material derived from a single individual and propagated exclusively by vegetative means, such as cuttings, divisions, or grafts.

plants, particularly in regard to leaves and their abscission. During leaf senescence DNA, RNA, proteins, chlorophyll, photosynthesis, starch, auxins, and gibberellins decrease, sometimes drastically. Senescence is not entirely degradation, however; particular mRNAs and proteins are synthesized only in senescing tissues.

Figure 6–9 shows the decline in photosynthetic activity of wheat plants following flowering; the decline in photosynthesis, of course, soon leads to senescence and death (27). Plant senescence is hastened, too, by the transfer of stored nutrients to the reproductive parts—the flowers, fruits, and seeds—as they develop and mature, at the expense of the root and shoot systems. As a result, senescence can be postponed in many plants by picking off the flowers before seeds start to form. In sweet peas, for example, removing the flowers once they start to wither and before seeds form prolongs the blooming period. Just as plant hormones (see p. 133) are involved in many plant functions they are involved, too, in senescence. For example, ethylene plays a role in fruit ripening and deterioration (see p. 138).

REPRODUCTIVE GROWTH AND DEVELOPMENT

Fruit and seed production involves several phases:

1. Flower induction and initiation
2. Flower differentiation and development
3. Pollination
4. Fertilization
5. Fruit set and seed formation
6. Growth and maturation of fruit and seed
7. Fruit senescence

Flower Induction and Initiation

Some annuals mature and can flower in only a few days or weeks after the seeds sprout; some forest and fruit trees require years before flowering. Once mature, the plant can be induced to flower by becoming sensitive to the conditions of its environment. What brings about the formation of flowers? In some species it is day length (photoperiodic effect) and/or low temperatures (vernalization), although in most trees neither day length nor cold temperatures induces flowering.

DAY LENGTH

The influence of day length on the flowering of several plant species was first studied in detail at the USDA in Beltsville, Maryland, and the results were published by W. W. Garner and H. A. Allard in 1920 (8).

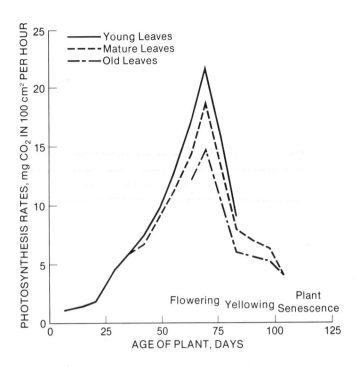

Fig. 6–9 | Photosynthetic rate in the wheat plant increases sharply as it matures, until flowering, when it decreases rapidly. Young, mature, and old leaves all exhibit the same behavior. *Source:* Leopold, A. C., and P. E. Kriedmann. *Plant growth and development.* 2nd ed. New York: McGraw-Hill. Originally appeared in Singh, B. N., and K. L. Lal. 1935. Investigations of the effect of age on assimilation of leaves. *Ann. Bot.* 49:291–307.

They grew plants in containers that could be wheeled into dark sheds at the end of the work day and returned to the sunlight in the morning. They found that 'Maryland Mammoth' tobacco and certain cultivars of soybeans and cosmos required short days for flower induction. A set number of successive short days was required to complete differentiation (change from vegetative to reproductive growing points or shoot terminals). Once induced by short days, the plants could be moved to a long day length without interfering with the flowering process. These plants were called **short-day plants.** Later studies by many other workers found that long days were necessary to induce flowering of some plants, such as spinach, sugar beets, and winter barley. These were classified as **long-day plants.** A third group of plants, including tomato, corn, fruit trees, and cucumber, were those in which flowering was not affected by day length and were called **day-neutral plants.** This phenomenon whereby day length controls certain plant processes, as noted above, was termed photoperiodism. Other workers in later experiments found that many plants did not fit into these three categories because of interactions of day length with temperatures. They discovered that the length of night rather than day was actually the critical factor, as in the cocklebur *(Xanthium),* for instance. However, the term *photoperiodism* still remains.

The short-day plant (SDP) is, of course, a long-night plant requiring a certain period of darkness not interruped by light. This is illustrated in Figure 6–10, which demonstrates how a flash of light (or night break) of sufficient intensity or duration will inhibit flowering of a short-day plant (long-night plant) but may induce flowering of a long-day plant (LDP). This information is useful to commercial chrysanthemum growers, who grow these short-day plants on a year-round schedule. When they want the young plants to reach a size adequate for flowering, the growers use incandescent lamps over the chrysanthemum plants (near midnight), each night for one to four hours, depending on time of year and latitude. This inhibits flowering until the plants reach the desired height. Conversely, when the natural daylight of summer is too long for chrysanthemum plants to flower, they cover the plants of proper size with black cloth or plastic each evening at 5 P.M. to 7 P.M. and remove it in the morning at about 8 A.M. This shortens the plant's day (lengthens the night) enough to induce and fully develop the flowers. These manipulations enable chrysanthemum plants to be flowered every day of the year in greenhouses—or outside if night temperatures do not fall below 15°C (60°F). There are hundreds of chrysanthemum cultivars, and they respond with flower induction to day lengths ranging from 12 to 15 hours. The flower grower must therefore choose the appropriate cultivar for the season and the location, or create the appropriate light or dark regime by artificial means.

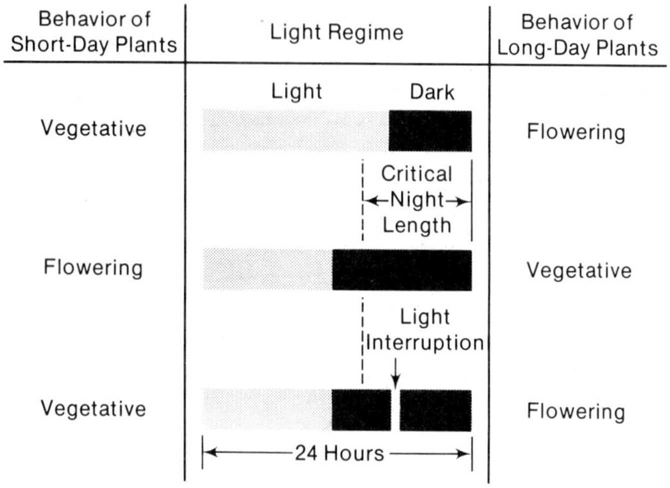

The flowering stimulus is formed in the leaves of the plants and transported to the apical meristem. This was discovered by partial leaf removal when plants were placed under an inductive photoperiod for flower formation, then failed to flower. The SDP *Xanthium* (cocklebur) exposed to long noninductive days would initiate flowers if light was blocked from a single leaf. Some experiments in which flowering plants (donor) were grafted to nonflowering plants (receptor) caused the latter group to flower. These and other experiments gave rise to the theory that a flowering hormone, florigen, which might be similar in all plants, was responsible for flower induction. However, florigen has yet to be isolated and transferred.

In the 1950s, USDA researchers *(12)* studied how interrupting the night with short lightbreaks affected cocklebur flowering. They found that red light, 660 nm, was the most effective part of the action spectrum for the inhibition of flowering. This could be nullified by subjecting the plants to a series of exposures of light at 730 nm. These wavelengths of light reacted with a natural pigment in the plant that the researchers called **phytochrome**. The pigment is present in two forms. The P_r form absorbs the red light (660 nm) and is converted to the P_{fr} form; the P_{fr} form, in turn, absorbs the far-red light (730 nm) and is thereby converted back to the P_r form. The P_{fr} form may also be converted to the P_r form slowly during the dark phase. The net transformation from the P_r (inactive) to the P_{fr} (active form) during the course of a changing day length affects the flowering mechanism, although that mechanism still is not completely understood.

in red light (660 nm)

$$\text{phytochrome}_{red} \longleftarrow \text{\hspace{3cm}} \longrightarrow \text{phytochrome}_{far\ red}$$

in far-red light (730 nm)

(instantaneous reaction)

in darkness

(slow reaction)

There has been considerable documentation to categorize plants as short-day, long-day, or day-neutral. Although not complete, one such list appears in Table 6–1 *(24)*. The critical day length of many of the species shown in the table may be changed by a slight shift in temperature above or below the optimum for that species. Table 19–3 shows the effects of day length on ornamental bedding plants.

Fig. 6–10 The effect of a light-flash interrupting the dark period on flowering in short-day and long-day plants. *Source:* Adapted from Galston, A. W., and P. J. Davis. 1970. *Control mechanisms in plant development.* Englewood Cliffs, N.J.: Prentice-Hall.

Behavior of Short-Day Plants	Light Regime	Behavior of Long-Day Plants
	Light Dark	
Vegetative		Flowering
	Critical ←Night→ Length	
Flowering		Vegetative
	Light Interruption ↓	
Vegetative		Flowering
	←——— 24 Hours ———→	

Table 6–1.   A Partial List of Long-Day, Short-Day and Day-Neutral Plants.

Long-Day Plants	Length of Daily Light Period Necessary for Flowering	Short-Day Plants	Length of Daily Light Period Necessary for Flowering
Althea *(Hibiscus syriacus)*	More than 12 hours	Bryophyllum *(Bryophyllum pinnatum)*	Less than 12 hours
Barley, winter *(Hordeum vulgare)*	More than 12 hours	Chrysanthemum *(Chrysanthemum*	
Bentgrass *(Agrostis palustris)*	More than 16 hours	*morifolium)*	Less than 15 hours
Bromegrass *(Bromus inermis)*	More than 12.5 hours	Cocklebur *(Xanthium strumarium)*	Less than 15.6 hours
Canary-grass *(Phalaris arundinacea)*	More than 12.5 hours	Cosmos, Klondyke *(Cosmus*	
Chrysanthemum maximum	More than 12 hours	*sulphureus)*	Less than 14 hours
Chrysanthemum frutescens	More than 12 hours	Kalanchoe *(Kalanchoe blossfeldiana)*	Less than 12 hours
Clover, red *(Trifolium pratense)*	More than 12 hours	Lespedeza *(Lespedeza stipulacea)*	Less than 13.5 hours
Coneflower *(Rudbeckia bicolor)*	More than 10 hours	Poinsettia *(Euphorbia pulcherrima)*	Less than 12.5 hours
Dill *(Anethum graveolens)*	More than 11 hours	Rice, winter *(Oryza sativa)*	Less than 12 hours
Fuchsia hybrida	More than 12 hours	Soybean *(Glycine max)*	Less than 12 hours
Henbane, annual *(Hyoscyamus niger)*	More than 10 hours	Strawberry *(Fragaria × Ananasia)*	Less than 10 hours
Oat *(Avena sativa)*	More than 9 hours	Tobacco, Maryland Mammoth	
Orchardgrass *(Dactylis glomerata)*	More than 12 hours	*(Nicotiana tabacum)*	Less than 14 hours
Ryegrass, early perennial *(Lolium*		Violet *(Viola papilionacea)*	Less than 11 hours
perenne)	More than 9 hours		
Ryegrass, Italian *(Lolium italicum)*	More than 11 hours		
Ryegrass, late perennial *(Lolium*			
perenne)	More than 13 hours		
Sedum *(Sedum spectabile)*	More than 13 hours		
Spinach *(Spinacia oleracea)*	More than 13 hours		
Timothy, hay *(Phleum pratensis)*	More than 12 hours		
Timothy, pasture *(Phleum nodosum)*	More than 14.5 hours		
Wheatgrass *(Agropyron smithii)*	More than 10 hours		
Wheat, winter *(Triticum aestivum)*	More than 12 hours		

Day-Neutral Plants
Artichoke, one cultivar *(Helianthus tuberosus)*
Balsam *(Impatiens balsamina)*
Bluegrass, annual *(Poa annua)*
Buckwheat *(Fagopyrum tataricum)*
Cape jasmine *(Gardenia jasminoides)*
Corn (maize) *(Zea mays)*
Cotton, one cultivar *(Gossypium hirsutum)*
Cucumber *(Cucumis sativus)*
English holly *(Ilex aquifolium)*
Euphorbia *(Euphorbia peplus)*
Fruit and nut tree species
Globe-amaranth *(Gomphrina globosa)*
Grapes
Honesty *(Lunaria annua)*
Lima bean, one cultivar *(Phaseolus lunatus)*
Potato, one cultivar *(Solanum tuberosum)*
Scrofularia *(Scrofularia peregrina)*
Senecio *(Senecio vulgaris)*
Strawberry, everbearing *(Fragaria × Ananasia)*
String bean, one cultivar *(Phaseolus vulgaris)*
Tobacco, one cultivar *(Nicotiana tabacum)*
Tomato *(Lycopersicon lycopersicum)*
Viburnum *(Viburnum spp.)*

Source: Based on F. B. Salisbury and C. Ross. 1969. *Plant physiology.* Belmont, Calif: Wadsworth.

Some plants, including many of the biennials, require low temperature for flower induction. The term for this is **vernalization**, which means "making ready for spring." It was first observed in winter wheat over a century ago. Vernalization is any temperature treatment that induces or promotes flowering. The temperatures required to vernalize a given plant and the length of the vernalization period vary among species and may even differ among cultivars of the same species. Broadly speaking, however, vernalization temperatures range between 0° and 10°C (32° and 50°F). Some of the biennials that require vernalization are beets, Brussels sprouts, carrots, celery, and some garden flowers such as Canterbury bells and foxglove. Winter annuals—such as the cereal crops, barley, oats, rye, and wheat—also respond to cold by flowering. Many plants, such as lettuce, peas, and spinach can be induced to flower earlier with vernalization, but vernalization is not an absolute requirement; they will eventually flower without it. Some species can be vernalized as seeds (beet and kohlrabi), but most plants must reach a minimum size or produce a certain number of leaves to be sensitized by the cold.

Garden perennials, plants with corms or tubers, and many flowering shrubs and fruit trees require low temperatures to overcome the rest period, but few require low temperatures for flower induction. The true bulb plants, such as the hyacinth, narcissus, and tulip, do not require a vernalization period to break rest, but low temperatures (see Ch. 20) are required to promote flower development once the flower has formed within the bulb. The olive tree *(Olea europaea)* does need vernalization for flower induction.

Experiments have shown that gibberellins (discussed later in this chapter) applied to the meristems of some long-day plants replace their low temperature requirement for flowering. The gibberellins stimulate cell division and activate the flowering stimulus.

It is important to note that many plants do not respond with flower induction to changed day length or low temperature. In fact, the majority of agricultural plants are self-inductive for flowering; that is, they initiate or form flowers at almost any photoperiod and without vernalization. Many of the garden annuals are good examples of plants that flower when they reach a certain morphological maturity. Most fruit trees, shrubs, woody plants, garden perennials (roses, carnations, gerbera) and vegetable crops (beans, peas, tomatoes, peppers, cucumbers) have self-induced flowering.

When a hormonal floral stimulus is transmitted from the leaves to the apical meristem, a change from a vegetative to a flowering state takes place (see Fig. 14–1). In the case of some short-day plants, such as *Xanthium,* only one inductive short day is required, whereas chrysanthemums, poinsettias, and kalanchoe require three to four consecutive short days for induction. Once the apex has changed to a flower primordium, the process is not reversible. The floral apex may abort, however, if the subsequent environmental conditions are not favorable for full flower development. In such a case the axillary buds below the aborted floral apex will usually grow vegetatively until day length or temperature conditions once again favor flower induction.

The number of days from flower initiation to anthesis (time of flower opening) depends on the species and the cultivar. The number of days required for complete flower maturation by some common ornamental plants is: chrysanthemum, 50 to 100; kalanchoe, 60; poinsettia, 75; fuchsia, 50; and greenhouse roses, 40. These periods of development can be modified somewhat by raising the temperatures slightly in the last third to half of the development phase. Very high temperatures in the early developmental stages, however, may cause flower abortion.

Pollination

In the production of most floral crops and flowering shrubs—for example, carnations, petunias, chrysanthemums, roses, and camellias—the flower itself is the desired product. There is little interest in any resulting fruits and seed, except in the case of the plant breeder working with such species. But in the food crops—the cereals, fruits, and many vegetable species—the postflowering structures are the desired products. It is the grains, fruits, and seeds that are harvested.

In angiosperms, **pollination** is defined as the transfer of pollen from an anther to a stigma. The anther and stigma may be in the same flower (self-pollination), in different flowers on the same plant (self-pollination), in different flowers on different plants of the same cultivar (self-pollination), or in different flowers on plants of different cultivars (cross-pollination).

Figure 6–11 shows the various parts of two typical, but simple kinds of flowers dependent upon pollination for fruit set.

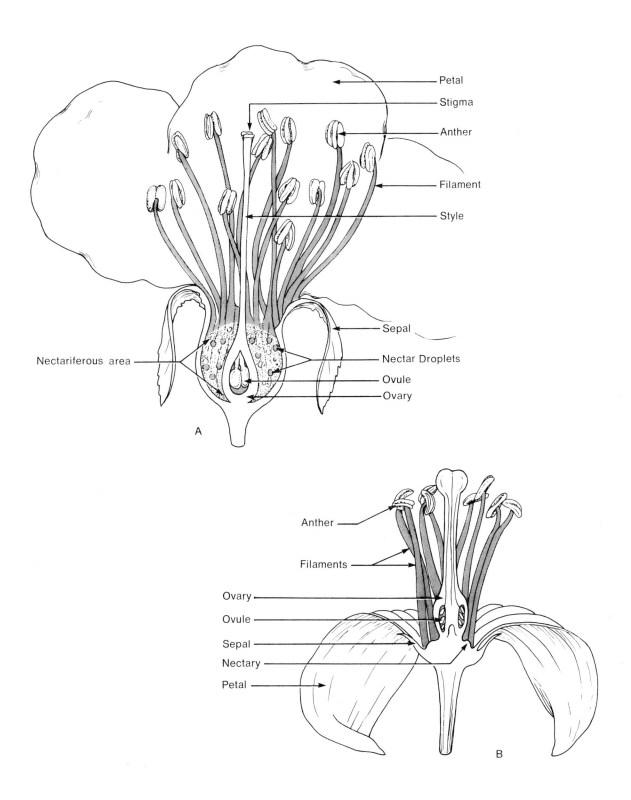

Petal

Stigma

Anther

Filament

Style

Sepal

Nectariferous area

Nectar Droplets

Ovule

Ovary

A

Anther

Filaments

Ovary

Ovule

Sepal

Nectary

Petal

B

Fig. 6–11 Longitudinal sections of flowers from two different kinds of
plants. *A:* Cherry. *B:* Grapefruit. *Source:* USDA.

If a plant is **self-fertile** it produces fruit and seed with its own pollen, without the transfer of pollen from another cultivar. If it is **self-sterile** it cannot set fruit and seed with its own pollen, but instead requires pollen from another cultivar. Often this is due to **incompatibility,** where a plant's own pollen will not grow through the style into its embryo sac (see Figs. 6–11 and 6–13). Sometimes, too, cross-pollination between two particular cultivars is ineffective because of incompatibility, which is believed to be due to factors that inhibit pollen tube germination or elongation.

Pollen transfer from the anthers to the stigmas is principally by:

1. insects, chiefly honeybees (Fig. 6–12). Insect pollination is common among cultivars with white or brightly colored flower parts and attractive nectar. Most fruit crops, many vegetables, and legume forage crops are pollinated by insects.
2. wind. This is the main pollinating agent for plants with inconspicuous flowers—the grasses, cereal grain crops, and forest tree species as well as some fruit and nut crops such as the olive, walnut, and pecan.

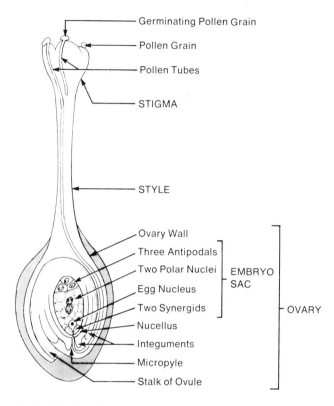

Fig. 6–13   A longitudinal section through the pistil of a flower following pollination and just before fertilization.

Fig. 6–12   Honeybees, collecting nectar from the flowers, also cause pollination by distributing pollen from the anthers to the stigma. Bees perform a great service in the culture of many crops by their pollination activities (19). *Source:* USDA.

Other minor pollinating agents are water, snails, slugs, birds, and bats.

Figure 6–13 shows a longitudinal section through the pistil of a flower following pollination. Note the elongated pollen tube. A pollen grain that germinated on the sticky surface of the stigma has grown down through the style carrying the male gametes to the embryo sac in the ovary.

PARTHENOCARPY

If pollination—and subsequent fertilization—does not occur, fruit and seed rarely develop. One important exception, however, is fruit that sets parthenocarpically. **Parthenocarpy** is the formation of fruit without the stimulation of pollination and fertilization. Without fertilization, no seeds are produced; therefore, parthenocarpic fruits are seedless. There are many examples of parthenocarpic fruits—the 'Washington Navel' orange, the 'Cavendish' banana, the oriental persimmon, and many fig cultivars. (Not all seedless fruits are parthenocarpic, however; sometimes, as in certain seedless grapes, pollination and fertilization occur and the fruit forms but the embryo aborts, thus no seed is produced).

In the angiosperms, as previously shown in Figure 5–17, the pollen tube grows through the micropyle opening in the ovule into the embryo sac and discharges two sperm nuclei (1N each). One unites with the egg (1N) to form the zygote (2N), which will eventually become the new plant. The other sperm nucleus unites with the two polar nuclei (1N each) in the embryo sac to form the endosperm (3N), which develops into food storage tissue. This process is termed **double fertilization.** The elapsed time between pollination and fertilization in most angiosperms is about 24 to 48 hours.

In the cone-bearing plants of the gymnosperms, the entire process of pollination and fertilization is different than in the angiosperms. Staminate, pollen-producing cones are produced on the tree separately from the ovulate cones. There is no wall enclosing the ovaries as in the angiosperms, thus producing "naked" seeds on the cone scales. The details of pollination and fertilization in gymnosperms are shown in Figure 4–5.

Following formation of the zygote—at which time the genetic makeup (the genotype) of the new seedling plant is determined—many significant changes occur, leading to the formation of the fruit and (usually) seeds within the fruit. Details on seed formation and development are given in Chapter 5.

Accessory tissues in the flower are often involved in fruit formation, such as the enlarged fleshy receptacle surrounding the ovary wall in the apple and pear (see Ch. 2 for the various types of fruits and the tissues involved). Botanically, however, the true fruit is the enlarged ovary.

Figure 6–14 shows various stages in the development of the different tissues in a lettuce fruit *(14)*.

In many plants only a small percentage of the flowers develop into fruits. This is particularly true in fruit crops where a tree could not possibly mature as many fruits as there are flowers. Many of the flowers drop without fertilization of the egg, and many of the flowers

Fig. 6–14 Developmental pattern of the tissues in a lettuce fruit, from the fertilized egg to the mature fruit. The ovary wall (the pericarp) is firmly attached to the seed coat (integument), so the structure is correctly considered a fruit and not a seed. P = pericarp; I = integument; N = nucellus; En = endosperm; Em = embryo. *Source:* Adapted by Hartmann, H. T., and D. E. Kester. 1975. *Plant propagation.* 3rd ed. Englewood Cliffs, N.J.: Prentice-Hall. From Jones, H. A. 1927. Pollination and life history studies of the lettuce (*Latuca sativa*). *Hilgardia* 2:425–79.

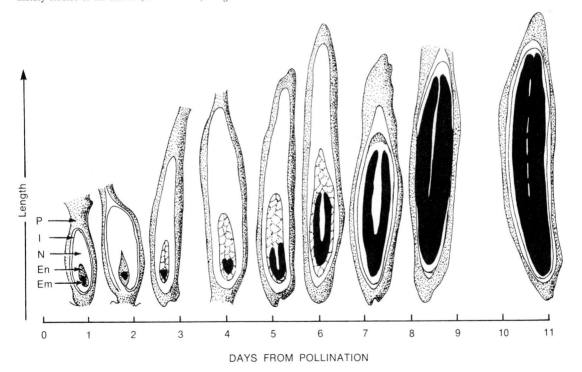

with a fertilized egg abort at the zygote stage or even later. When the zygote fails to develop and no seed forms, the immature fruit usually drops. In some seedless grapes, such as 'Thompson Seedless', the embryo starts to develop, then aborts; the seed fails to develop, but the fruit does not abscise but grows to full size.

Certain of the plant hormones (see p. 133) appear to be involved in fruit setting, but the actual physiological mechanisms are largely unknown *(3)*. In fruits of some species—tomatoes, peppers, eggplants, and figs—auxin can replace the stimulus of pollination and/or fertilization. Fruit set can also be induced in grapes, certain stone fruits—apricots, for example—and apples and pears by gibberellin sprays. Cytokinins also stimulate fruit set in grapes.

One of the chief problems in fruit production is obtaining the optimal level of fruit setting. Too low a fruit set gives a light, unprofitable crop. Too heavy a set leads to undesirably small, poor-quality fruits that mature late, possibly exhausting the tree's food supply and often resulting in little or no crop the following year. To overcome excessive fruit set, half—or more—of the fruits are removed at a very early stage, either by hand thinning, machine shaking, or chemical sprays (see Ch. 14).

As might be expected, temperature strongly influences fruit set. Temperatures that are too low or too high at this critical period are often responsible for crop failures. Low light intensity and lack of adequate soil moisture can also adversely affect fruit set.

*Fruit Growth
and Development*

Once fruit has set, the true fruit and, sometimes, various associated tissues begin to grow *(4)*. Food materials move from other parts of the plant into these developing tissues. Hormonal substances, such as the auxins, gibberellins, ethylene, and cytokinins (see p. 137), apparently are involved in some phases of fruit growth just as they are in fruit set. These materials originate in both the developing seeds and fruit, although it is significant to note that parthenocarpic fruits (without seeds) continue to grow to full size.

An interesting relationship between fruit growth and the presence of auxin has been observed in strawberry fruits. Removing some of the achenes ("seeds") from the surface of the strawberry at an early growth stage causes it to be lopsided; the strawberry fails to de-

velop under the section where the achenes were removed. The stimulatory effect of some mobile material originating in the achenes is lost. Presumably this material is an auxin, because application of auxin paste to the area where the achenes were removed allows the strawberry to develop normally.

Evidence of the participation of gibberellins in fruit growth has been shown in the grape. Application of gibberellin to 'Thompson Seedless' grape clusters at an early stage of berry development markedly increases ultimate fruit size. The size increase is so pronounced that virtually all table grapes of this cultivar grown in California are now treated with gibberellin. This effect on size also holds true for certain other grape cultivars (see Fig. 6–22).

While various plant hormones are undoubtedly involved in fruit growth, the basic mechanisms are still little understood. During flower development and in the early stages of fruit growth, there is considerable cell division. Following this period of intense cell division, most fruits increase in size because of cell enlargement.

Fruits have two basic patterns of growth, as shown in Figure 6–15. One is the simple sigmoid growth

Fig. 6–15 Growth curves of representative kinds of fruits showing the two characteristic types. *Top:* The sigmoid growth curve. *Bottom:* The double sigmoid growth curve.

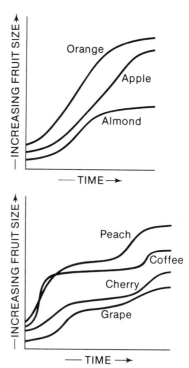

curve—typical of such fruits as the orange, apple, pear, pineapple, olive, almond, tomato, and strawberry—in which there is a slow start followed by a period of rapid size increase, then a decrease in growth rate near fruit maturity. The second pattern is a double sigmoid growth curve, in which the single sigmoid growth curve is repeated. Near the center of the growth period, the growth curve is flat; the fruit increases little, if at all, in size. The stone fruits—peach, apricot, plum, and cherry—as well as the grape and fig show a double sigmoid growth pattern. In the stone fruits, which have a hard endocarp or pit, the pit hardens during the second phase of fruit development. In addition, some important changes take place in seed development within the pit, as illustrated in Figure 6–16.

In Chapter 14, the maturation, ripening, and senescence of fruits are considered.

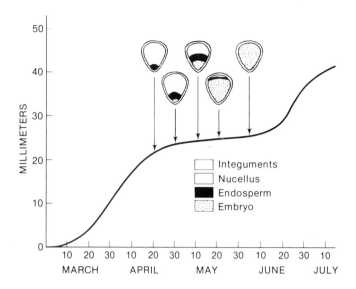

Fig. 6–16 Growth curve of an apricot fruit through the growing season. During the second growth period the pit (endocarp) hardens and the seed within the pit develops mostly from nutritive tissue (nucellus and endosperm) to finally consist entirely of the embryo. *Source:* Adapted from Crane, J. C., and P. Punsri. Comparative growth of the endosperm and the embryo in unsprayed and 2,4,5-trichlorophenoxyacetic acid sprayed Royal and Tilton apricots. *Proc. Amer. Soc. Hort. Sci.* 68:96–104. 1956.

PLANT GROWTH REGULATORS

In plants, as in animals, many of the behavioral patterns and functions are controlled by hormones. Hormones are produced in minute amounts at one site in the plant and translocated to other sites where they can alter growth and development. The natural hormones and other materials are essentially "chemical messengers," influencing the many patterns of plant development. (*7, 18, 29, 30, 31*)

A distinction must be made between the terms *plant hormone* and *plant growth regulator*. A **plant hormone** is a natural substance (produced by the plant itself) that acts to control plant activities. Plant hormones that are synthesized chemically can initiate reactions in the plant similar to those caused by the natural hormones. **Plant growth regulators,** on the other hand, include plant hormones—natural and synthetic—but also other, nonnutrient chemicals not found naturally in plants but that, when applied to plants, influence their growth and development.

There are five recognized groups of natural plant hormones: **auxins, gibberellins, cytokinins, ethylene,** and **abscisic acid** (Fig. 6–17). The discovery and subsequent study of these plant hormones is one of the most exciting and fascinating chapters in the history of plant physiology. Despite considerable study of hormones, however, their actions in the plant are still not well understood.

Auxins

Auxins were the first group of plant hormones to be discovered. The discovery came in the mid-1930s, and for many years thereafter auxins and their activities in plants were studied intensely throughout the world.

The auxins, both natural and synthetic, influence plant growth in many ways, including cell enlargement or elongation, photo- and geotropism, apical dominance (see below), abscission of plant parts, flower initiation and development, root initiation, fruit set and growth, tuber and bulb formation, and seed germination. Auxins operate at the cellular level, affecting such activities as protoplasmic streaming and enzyme activity. Auxins are related to many other chemical control mechanisms and are readily transported throughout the plant, principally in an apex-to-base direction.

The natural auxins originate in meristems and enlarging tissues, such as actively growing terminal and lateral buds, lengthening internodes, and developing embryos in the seed. Auxins are produced in relatively high amounts in the shoot tip or terminal growing point of the plant and move down the plant through the vascu-

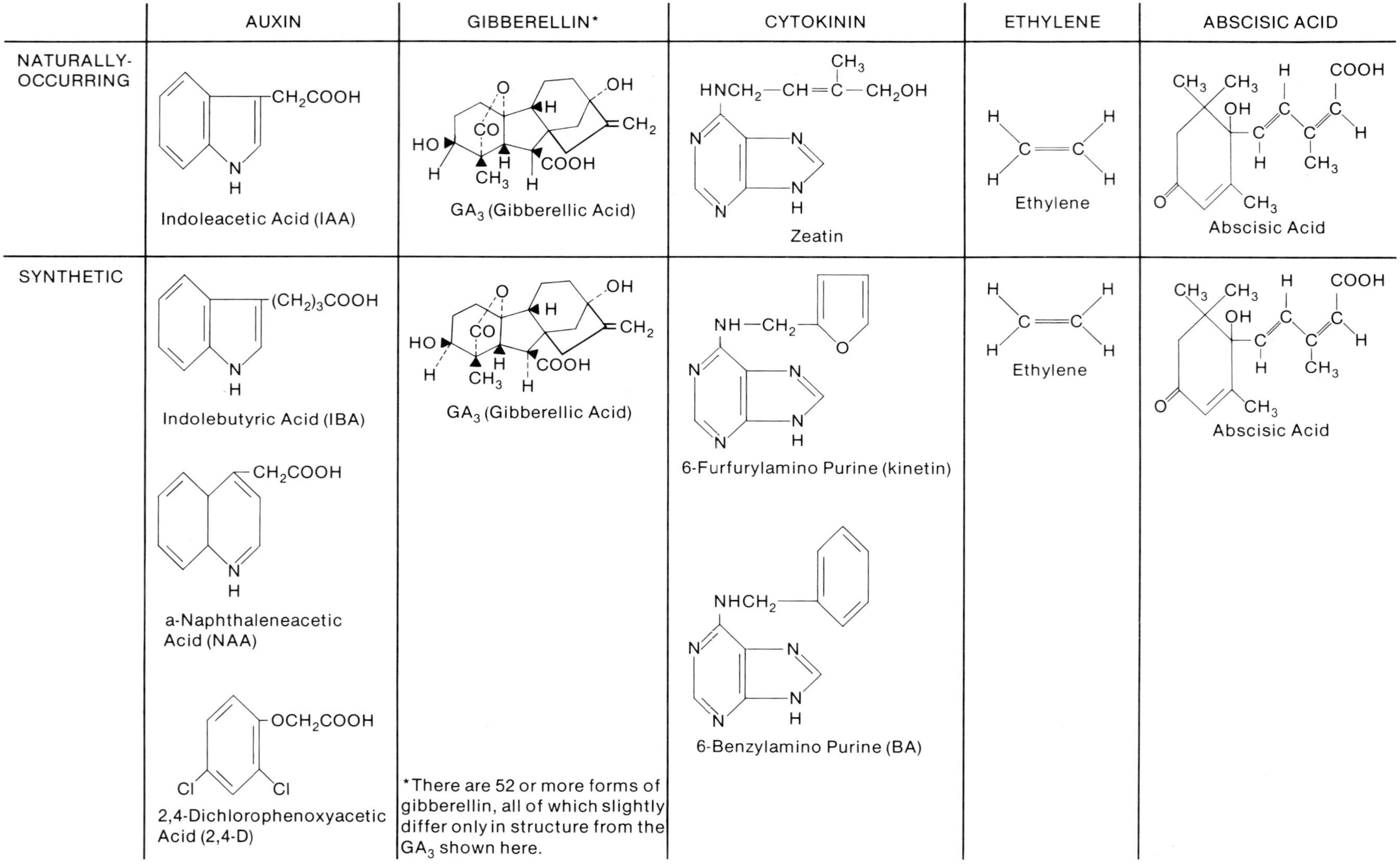

Fig. 6–17 Structural formulas of natural and some synthetic plant growth regulators.

lar tissues, causing the phenomenon known as **apical dominance** (blockage of growth of lateral buds by presence of terminal buds). High levels of auxin in the stem just above the lateral buds block their growth. If the shoot tip supplying this auxin is broken or cut off, the auxin level behind the lateral buds is reduced and the lateral buds begin to grow. This is part of the reason why, when a shoot tip is removed, many new shoots arise from buds down along the stem.

One of the most widespread auxins that occurs naturally in plants is indoleacetic acid (IAA) (see Fig. 6–17). Several other natural auxins have also been identified, and there are others whose chemical structure is yet unknown. There are also many synthetic auxins, which induce the same effects as natural auxin. Some of these are indolebutyric acid (IBA), naphthaleneacetic acid (NAA), and 2,4-dichlorophenoxyacetic acid (2,4-D). (See Fig. 6–17).

Some important commercial uses of these synthetic auxins are:

1. *Adventitious root initiation.* One of the first responses attributed to auxins was the stimulation of root formation in stem cuttings. Two synthetic auxins, indolebutyric acid and naphthaleneacetic acid, are now widely used commercially in treating the bases of stem cuttings to stimulate the initiation of adventitious roots (see Ch. 5).

2. *Weed control.* The synthetic auxin 2,4-dichlorophenoxyacetic acid is in widespread commercial use as a selective weedkiller that eliminates broad-leaved weeds growing in grass or cereal fields. The introduction of this material as a weedkiller in 1946 revolutionized weed control methods (see Ch. 11). Since 2,4-D is inexpensive and very potent—only 0.56 kg/ha (0.5 lb/ac) is needed—it provides a nontoxic means of removing broad-leaved weeds from the tremendous areas planted in cereal crops.

3. *Increasing fruit set.* Sprays of 4-chlorophenoxyacetic acid (4-CPA), a synthetic auxin very similar to 2,4-D, are used commercially to increase blossom and fruit set in tomatoes.

4. *Preventing preharvest fruit drop.* A problem in producing apple, pear, and citrus fruits is that they often drop to the ground shortly before they are ready to harvest. Sprays of the synthetic auxin naphthaleneacetic acid at about 20 ppm on apple trees and 10 ppm on pear trees applied before the fruits start dropping will keep them attached for several weeks until the fruit has matured suf-

ficiently for proper harvest. For oranges and grapefruit, sprays of the synthetic auxin 2,4-D at about 10 ppm effectively reduces premature fruit drop, mainly by delaying the development of an abscission zone in the fruit stem. Since this material has strong herbicidal action, it must be used carefully to avoid spray drifts, especially onto sensitive plants such as grapes and cotton.

5. *Spray thinning.* Sprays of the auxin naphthaleneacetic acid applied to young fruits shortly after bloom have been effective in thinning excessive fruit sets in apples and olives. It is remarkable that this material, which can cause abscission of very young apple fruits, can also prevent abscission when applied shortly before apple and pear harvest. Auxin apparently has different roles during the two physiological stages of fruit development. Beyond this, however, the mechanisms underlying the fruit thinning action of auxins are not well understood.

6. *Inhibition of stem sprouting.* Many kinds of woody ornamental trees produce masses of vigorous sprouts from the base of the trunk that, if not removed, would transform the tree into a bush. Continual removal of these sprouts by hand is costly and time consuming. It has been found that treatment of the tree trunks with the auxin naphthaleneacetic acid at about 10,000 ppm (1.0 percent) strongly inhibits the development of such sprouts.

7. *Tissue culture.* The initiation of roots and shoots on small pieces of plant tissue cultured under aseptic conditions has become a standard method of micropropagation of some plant species (see p. 113). Often an auxin, such as IAA or 2,4-D, has to be included in the culture medium for roots to initiate.

Gibberellins (GA)

The gibberellins *(15, 17)* are a group of natural plant hormones with many powerful regulatory functions. The most obvious is to stimulate stem growth dramatically, far more than auxins can. Gibberellins may stimulate cell division, cell elongation, or both and they can control enzyme secretion.

In some plants, GA is involved in flower initiation and sex expression (male or female flower parts). Fruit set as well as fruit growth, maturation, and ripening seem to be controlled by gibberellin in some species. Senescence of plant parts, particularly leaves, is also affected by GA. Certain dwarf cultivars of peas and corn,

Fig. 6–18 Overcoming dwarfness in corn by spraying with gibberellin. *Left:* Untreated, genetically dwarf corn plants. *Center:* Nondwarf corn sprayed with gibberellin. *Right:* Genetic dwarf corn sprayed with gibberellin. Photographs taken six weeks after spraying. *Source: From Plant Growth Substances in Agriculture* by Robert J. Weaver. W. H. Freeman and Company. Copyright © 1972.

if treated with GA, grow to a normal height, indicating that the dwarfed plants lack a normal level of gibberellin (Fig. 6–18).

Gibberellins are also involved in overcoming dormancy in seeds and in buds. Their role in the germination of barley seed has received much study (see Fig. 6–19).

Fig. 6–19 Longitudinal section of a barley seed. Germination commences with the addition of moisture if temperatures are favorable. The embryo secretes gibberellin, which flows to the living cells of the aleurone layer where enzymes are synthesized. The enzymes move into the endosperm, converting insoluble starches and proteins into usable sugars and amino acids to nourish the growing embryo.

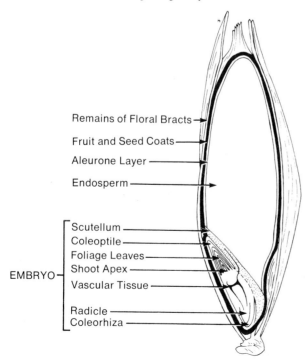

Remains of Floral Bracts
Fruit and Seed Coats
Aleurone Layer
Endosperm

EMBRYO
Scutellum
Coleoptile
Foliage Leaves
Shoot Apex
Vascular Tissue
Radicle
Coleorhiza

After the seed has been moistened and placed at room temperature, a natural gibberellin produced in the embryo translocates to the aleurone layer surrounding the endosperm. Triggered by the GA, cells in the aleurone layer synthesize such enzymes as amylases, proteases, and lipases. These enzymes then diffuse throughout the endosperm, hydrolyzing starches and proteins into sugars and amino acids that then become available to the embryo for its growth and development.

The molecular structure of the gibberellins is well known; a typical one is shown in Figure 6–17. By 1977 some 52 gibberellins had been discovered in tissues of various plants. Some common ones are GA_1, GA_3 (gibberellic acid), GA_4, and GA_7.

Gibberellins were first discovered in 1926 by Japanese researchers studying a disease of rice plants caused by the fungus *Gibberella fujikuroi*. Plants infected with the fungus grew excessively and abnormally. Extracts from this fungus applied to noninfected plants stimulated the same abnormal growth. By 1939 the active ingredient was extracted from the fungus, crystallized, and named gibberellin. This early work with gibberellin in Japan went unnoticed in the Western world until the early 1950s when a great surge of gibberellin research began, particularly in the United States and England. This research led to the isolation of many different forms of gibberellin extracted from the *Gibberella* fungus and from higher plants.

Gibberellins are synthesized in the shoot apex of the plant, particularly in new leaf primordia. They are also found in embryos and cotyledons of immature seeds and in fruit tissue. In addition, the root system synthesizes large quantities of gibberellin, which moves upward throughout the plant. GA translocates easily in the plant in both directions, unlike auxin, which moves largely in an apex-to-base direction.

Pharmaceutical companies produce crystalline GA_3 as the acid or the potassium salt for research studies and certain commercial applications. These preparations are all obtained from growth of the *Gibberella* fungus in a natural process similar to that used to produce antibiotics.

Even though it has been demonstrated that gibberellins occur naturally in many of the higher plants, little is known of the physiological mechanisms of gibberellin action or transport.

Although gibberellins are a powerful and important group of plant hormones involved in many of the plant functions, few agricultural uses have been found for them. Some are:

1. *Increasing fruit size of seedless grapes.* This is the principal commercial application of gibberellin. Practically all vines of the 'Thompson Seedless' grape grown for table use in California are sprayed each year. Treatments at 2.5 to 20 ppm at bloom are used for thinning clusters, and at 20 to 40 ppm at the fruit set stage for increasing berry size. Berry size of other grape cultivars, such as 'Black Corinth', is also increased by gibberellin sprays, as shown in Figure 6–20.

2. *Stimulating seed germination and seedling growth.* A number of cases have been reported where soaking seeds in solutions of gibberellic acid before germination greatly stimulates seedling emergence and growth. Such responses have been obtained with barley, rice, peas, beans, avocado, orange, grape, camellia, apple, peach, and cherry. Generally effective was a 24-hour soak at various concentrations from 20 to 10,000 ppm. Figure 6–21 shows the stimulation obtained with grape seedlings by gibberellin treatment.

3. *Promoting male flowers in cucumbers.* When pollen is wanted for hybrid seed production, a single application of GA_3 to the leaves stimulates maleness of cucumber. This has proved an important discovery for hybridizers.

4. *Overcoming the cold requirement for some plants.* Azalea plants require six weeks of cool temperatures (8°C or 46°F) to develop flower buds. Several leaf applications of 1000 ppm gibberellin will completely or partially replace this cold requirement for flower bud development. A single application of 25 ppm gibberellin is used on *Cyclamen periscum* to stimulate flower development. It has been shown experimentally that gibberellins applied to biennial plants that require a cold period before they flower causes early flowering. Most of these treatments, however, have limited commercial value.

Cytokinins (28)

This group of plant hormones primarily promote cell division but they also participate in a great many aspects of plant growth and development, such as cell enlargement, tissue differentiation, dormancy, different phases of flowering and fruiting, and in retardation of leaf senescence.

Cytokinins interact with auxins to influence differentiation of tissues. As shown in Figure 6–22 externally

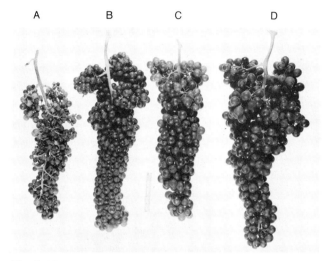

Fig. 6–20 Effect of gibberellin sprays on growth of 'Black Corinth' grapes. *A:* Untreated control. *B:* Stem girdling control. *C:* Plants sprayed at an early growth stage with gibberellin at 5 ppm. *D:* At 20 ppm. Photos taken 59 days after spraying. *Source:*
From *Plant Growth Substances in Agriculture* by Robert J. Weaver. W. H. Freeman and Company. Copyright © 1972.

Fig. 6–21 Effect of gibberellin on germination and growth of 'Tokay' grape seeds. Seeds soaked (before planting) at 0, 100, 1000, or 8000 ppm in potassium gibberellate solution for 20 hr. *Source:*
From *Plant Growth Substances in Agriculture* by Robert J. Weaver. W. H. Freeman and Company. Copyright © 1972.

Fig. 6–22 Effects of a cytokinin and an auxin on growth and organ formation in tobacco stem segments. *A:* Control, no treatment. *B:* Cytokinin—bud formation but no root formation. *C:* Auxin—root formation with prevention of bud development. *D:* Cytokinin plus auxin—stimulation of callus growth but no organ formation. *Source:* Adapted from Hartmann, H. T., and D. E. Kester. 1975. *Plant propagation.* 3rd ed. Englewood Cliffs, N.J.: Prentice-Hall. Originally in Skoog, F., and D. J. Armstrong. 1970. Cytokinins. *Ann. Rev. Plant Physiol.* 21:359–84.

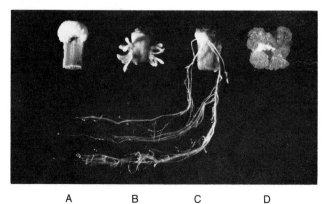

applied cytokinin alone stimulates bud formation in to-bacco stem segments; auxin applied alone causes roots to develop; but when cytokinin plus auxin are applied to-gether, there is a canceling effect—only masses of undif-ferentiated callus form.

There are both natural cytokinins, such as zeatin, and synthetic forms, such as kinetin and benzyladenine (BA) (see Fig. 6–17). There are probably over 100 known natural and synthetic cytokinins. Cytokinins occur in many plant tissues as both the free hormonal material and as a component of transfer RNA. They are found in abundance in embryos and germinating seeds and in young developing fruits—all tissues with consid-erable cell division. Roots supply cytokinins upward to the shoots.

The mechanism of cytokinin action in the plant is not clear. Cytokinins indirectly increase enzyme activity and increase the DNA produced in some tissues. Their regulatory effects seem to result from interactions with other hormones in the plant.

Cytokinins were discovered when scientists at the University of Wisconsin in 1955 used a synthetic ma-terial—kinetin, later named a "cytokinin"—to cause cell division of tobacco stem pith. After many interesting physiological activities of kinetin became apparent, plants were examined for possible natural similar mate-rials. In 1964 such a material was isolated from young corn seeds by researchers in New Zealand and was named zeatin. An active promoter of cell division known to exist in coconut milk was finally determined to be a zeatin-riboside.

Even though cytokinins are strongly involved in plant growth regulation, no important agricultural uses have been developed for them. In media for aseptic tis-sue culture, however (see p. 113), in many cases cytoki-nin has to be added to induce shoot development. Appli-cations of cytokinins to green tissue have been shown to delay senescence. These materials have also been used experimentally, and in limited commercial applications, on greenhouse roses and potted chrysanthemum plants to stimulate growth of axillary buds by overcoming natural bud inhibitors.

Ethylene

It has been well established for many years that ethylene gas (see Fig. 6–17) evokes many varied responses in plants. As long ago as 1924 it was found that ethylene could induce fruit ripening; in 1925, it was determined that ethylene could overcome bud dormancy in potato tubers; in 1931, that it could induce leaf abscission; in 1932, that it could induce flowering in pineapple plants;

in 1933, that it could cause roots to form on stem cut-tings. By the mid-1930s it was determined that ethylene was itself a plant product, and arguments arose among plant scientists about whether ethylene, a gas, should be considered a plant hormone.

Little further attention was paid to possible roles of ethylene as a natural growth regulator until the develop-ment in the 1960s of gas chromotographic techniques that permit the detection of ethylene in concentrations as low as one part per billion. Vast amounts of research on ethylene physiology in the 1960s and 1970s have estab-lished ethylene as a plant hormone.

Ethylene itself is a tiny molecule ($CH_2{=}CH_2$) com-pared with the other plant hormones. Plant biochem-ists are uncertain how plants manufacture ethylene in their tissues, but likely precursors are the amino acid methionine and the fatty acid linolenic acid. Ethylene, as a gas, diffuses readily throughout the plant, moving much like carbon dioxide, and it can exert its influ-ence in minute quantities. Its solubility in water also enhances its movement through the plant. The cuticular coatings on external cell surfaces tend to prevent losses from the plant. Ethylene apparently is produced in ac-tively growing meristems of the plant, in ripening and senescing fruits, in senescing flowers, in germinating seeds, and in certain plant tissues as a response to bend-ing, wounding, or bruising. Synthetic ethylene applied to plant tissues can cause a great burst of natural ethylene production—an autocatalytic effect.

Just how ethylene exerts its regulatory effects is no better known than the basic mechanisms involved in the action of the other plant hormones. One theory is that ethylene regulates some aspect of DNA transcription or RNA translation, thus changing RNA-directed protein synthesis and, consequently, enzyme patterns. But many other mechanisms are also likely to be in operation.

The possible commercial uses of ethylene were greatly increased with the development in the 1960s of ethylene-releasing compounds such as ethephon (2-chloroethyl phosphonic acid). This compound applied as an agricultural spray gradually releases ethylene into plant tissues. In contrast to some of the other plant hor-mones, ethylene and ethylene-releasing chemicals have several valuable commercial applications:

1. *Fruit ripening.* Ethylene gas, injected into airtight storage rooms, is used commercially to ripen bananas, honeydew melons, and tomatoes. The application of ethephon at 1000 ppm will ripen bananas in about the same time period as 100 ppm of ethylene gas. Ethephon will also ripen tomatoes that are green but horticulturally mature in 12 days

after they are dipped in a 5000 ppm solution for 30 seconds. Ethephon is also used as a preharvest spray to promote uniform ripening of apples, cherries, figs, blueberries, coffee, and pineapple. To harvest canning tomatoes and pickling cucumbers mechanically, where the entire crop is picked at one time, it is important that most of the fruits be ripe and fully colored at the time of harvest. Spraying the field with an ethylene-releasing material before harvest promotes uniform ripening of the green fruits.

2. *Flower initiation.* Ethylene gas released from ethephon has initiated flowers in several ornamental bromeliad species, including *Ananas* spp., *Aechmea fasciata*, *Neoregelia* spp., *Billbergia* spp., and *Vriesia splendens.* It is sprayed as a 2500 ppm solution on the foliage. The plants should be in the vegetative stage at the time of application but shortly afterwards should be subjected to short days to obtain proper conditions for flowering. Ethephon has also been used to promote uniform flowering in the cultivated banana.

3. *Changing sex expression.* Ethylene applications to certain plants, such as cucumbers and pumpkins, can dramatically increase the production of female flowers. Some cucumber cultivars produce both female and nonfruiting male flowers on the same plant. Spraying the vines with ethephon causes all flowers to be female, which develop into fruits and thus increase yields. This practice also hastens fruit maturity and permits harvesting in a single operation.

4. *Degreening oranges, lemons, and grapefruit.* Sometimes the rind of maturing oranges and grapefruits remains green owing to high chlorophyll levels, even though the eating quality, juice content, and ratios of soluble solids to acid are high enough to meet grade standards for harvest. Citrus packers can treat such fruits with ethylene at about 20 ppm for 12 to 72 hours. This breaks down the chlorophyll and allows the orange and yellow carotenoid pigments to show. During such treatments temperatures of 26°C to 30°C (80°F to 85°F) and 85 percent relative humidity are required. Dipping the fruits in a 1000 ppm ethephon solution has about the same degreening effect on citrus as the ethylene gas treatment.

5. *Harvest aids.* Certain fruit and nut crops, such as sour cherries and walnuts, are harvested by mechanical tree shakers that shake the trees until the crop falls into catching frames or onto the ground to be picked up later. Often this practice is not completely successful because the fruits or nuts are so tightly attached that the tree shakers do not remove them. However, by spraying the trees about a week before harvest with an ethylene-releasing compound—ethephon, for example—the abscission-inducing effects of the ethylene result in a much higher percentage of crop removed.

Ethylene can also harm plants. It can cause unwanted leaf abscission and can hasten senescence of most flowers. The introduction of a few parts per billion of ethylene into the surrounding air will cause carnation flowers to close, rose buds to expand prematurely, and orchid flower petals and sepals to develop a water-soaked appearance. The pollination of an orchid flower can generate sufficient ethylene to cause injury to the flower parts. Ethylene can cause flower bud abortion of bulbs during shipment. A few diseased tulip bulbs give off enough ethylene in a packing crate to stop further development of the flower buds within the bulbs.

Inhibitors

Some plant growth regulators inhibit rather than stimulate plant growth. One of these—abscisic acid—is a natural plant hormone. Other compounds found in plants, principally phenolic materials, inhibit growth but are not classed as plant hormones. A third group consists of synthetic chemicals, not found in plants, that have important and commercially useful growth-inhibiting or retarding properties.

ABSCISIC ACID (ABA)

Abscisic acid tends to interact with other hormones in the plant, counteracting the growth-promoting effects of auxins and gibberellins. ABA is involved in leaf and fruit abscission, as well as in the onset of dormancy in seeds and in the early stages of the rest period in vegetative and flower buds of woody perennial shrubs and trees. Dormancy induced by applications of synthetic ABA is overcome by gibberellin treatment—an example of the antagonistic effects of these two hormones. ABA is very effective in inducing closure of the stomata in leaves, indicating a possible role in the stress physiology in plants. Large increases in the ABA content of leaves have been noted following water stress in the plant.

Abscisic acid is widespread in the plant body and can be readily obtained by alcoholic extraction of many plant tissues. Chemically ABA is a sesquiterpene; its structural formula is shown in Fig. 6–17. Several bioassays are used to detect abscisic acid in plant material; one is based on the closure response of stomata mentioned above.

Studies conducted in California in 1964 on the development of maturing cotton fruits revealed an unknown inhibitory material whose concentration changed dramatically, reaching highest levels during fruit abscission. The material was isolated from cotton fruits, crystallized, and named abscisin II for its abscission activity. About the same time, in England, an inhibitory material was found in the leaves of sycamore trees, particularly in the autumn. This material, called dormin, was subsequently found to be identical to the abscisin II isolated from cotton. Then, by mutual consent, a decision was made to rename them both "abscisic acid." For many years before abscisic acid was identified, a widespread and powerful growth inhibitor or mixture of inhibitors in plants was known to exist and was referred to as the β inhibitor complex. Subsequently, one of the most important components was shown to be abscisic acid.

Abscisic acid moves readily through the plant. Fruits, especially rose fruits, are high in ABA. Also, ABA appears to be synthesized by leaves.

The mechanism of ABA action in plants is believed by some to involve an alteration in the nucleic acid and protein synthesis systems, although the rapid action of ABA when it is applied to plants implies a more direct effect.

Abscisic acid is difficult and expensive to synthesize, so it is usually used only in experimental studies that require small amounts. No commercial applications have been developed owing partly to the lack of adequate amounts of test material.

OTHER INHIBITORS

Plants accumulate a wide range of materials that seem to have no defined metabolic roles, although they can act as growth inhibitors and, in some cases, are toxic to feeding insects or animals. These inhibitors are largely phenolic compounds such as benzoic acid, cinnamic acid, caffeic acid, and coumarin (see Fig. 6–23). In some plants, they occur in very high concentrations, second only to carbohydrates.

SYNTHETIC GROWTH RETARDANTS (2)   A rather diverse group of growth retardants developed since about 1950 has several important commercial uses among ornamental plants, principally in obtaining compact, dwarf-type plants. These materials generally act by slowing, but not stopping, cell division and elongation in subapical meristems, usually without causing stem or leaf malformations. The primary effect of these materials is the opposite of gibberellin, often converting a tall-growing plant into a rosette. They may act by blocking gibberellin synthesis or action. Plants treated with these growth retardants have a compact scaled-down appearance, which is often more attractive than larger, untreated plants with a loose, open growth. The treated plants also often have darker, more attractive foliage and more flowers than untreated plants (see Fig. 6–24). Some of the better known synthetic growth retardants are described below.

SADH (succinic acid-2, 2-dimenthyl hydrazide, Alar, B-Nine). As shown in Figure 6–23, SADH is an organic acid. Tests have shown that it effectively retards growth and stimulates flowering of several kinds of herbaceous and woody ornamental plants. Species that re-

Fig. 6–23   Structural formulas of some natural inhibitors and some synthetic growth retardants.

SOME NATURALLY-OCCURRING INHIBITORS:

Benzoic Acid   Caffeic Acid   Cinnamic Acid   Coumarin

SYNTHETIC GROWTH RETARDANTS:

Succinic Acid-2,2-dimethylhydrazide (SADH; B-995; B-9; Alar)

(2-Chloroethyl) Trimethyl Ammonium Chloride (CCC; Cycocel®, Chlormequat)

α-Cyclopropyl, α-4-Methoxy-propyl, α-5-pyrmidine Methanol (Ancymidol, A-Rest®, EL531)

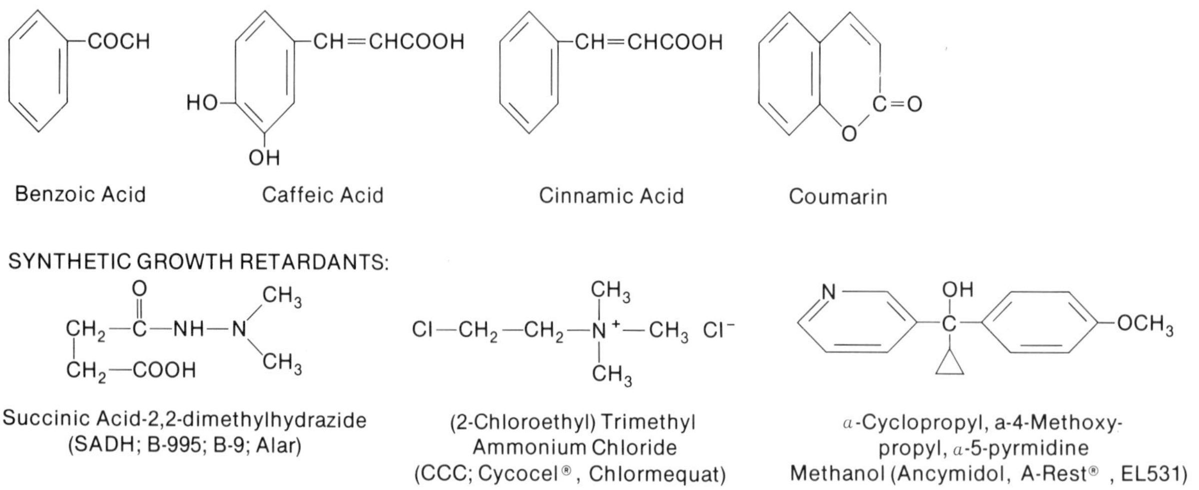

Fig. 6–24 Poinsettia 'Annette Hegg' treated with ancymidol to retard shoot growth. *Left:* Control, no ancymidol. *Center:* 0.25 milligram (mg) ancymidol per 15 cm pot. *Right:* 0.5 mg per 15 cm pot. Ancymidol was applied on October 19, and the photograph was taken on December 7. Note the very compact growth of the plant on the right because of an excessive treatment. The center plant is an ideal size.

spond well include chrysanthemums (2500 to 5000 ppm), various bedding plants (2500 to 5000 ppm), and azaleas (2500 ppm). Sometimes two applications two or three weeks apart are required to maintain the desired dwarf form.

Chlormequat [(2-chloroethyl) trimethylammonium chloride, Cycocel, CCC]. The structural formula of this material is shown in Figure 6–23. Chlormequat is effective in retarding the height of some ornamental plants. The height of red poinsettias may be controlled if chlormequat is applied as a drench to the soil (3000 to 6000 ppm) or as a spray to the foliage (1500 ppm) in the fall. Spraying azaleas or geraniums with about 2500 ppm will retard growth. Applications of chlormequat to the soil of geranium seedlings and bougainvillea (3500 and 200 ppm, respectively) hastens flower bud initiation. Another interesting use of CCC is in preventing lodging (falling over) of wheat plants. It is best applied between tillering[5] and rapid shoot growth, and retards internode elongation to give a shorter plant.

Ancymidol (A-Rest), α-cyclopropyl, α-4-methoxypropyl, α-5-pyrmidie methanol (6, 10, 11). This growth retardant is very effective for reducing the height of some bulbous potted plants (see Fig. 6–24). An-

cymidol is registered by the U.S. Environmental Protection Agency for height control of container-grown chrysanthemum, lilies, poinsettias, and tulips. It may be applied as a drench to the soil. Easter lilies *(Lillium longiflorum)* are treated when 7.5 to 15 cm (3 to 6 in) tall with 0.25 mg of ancymidol dissolved in 180 ml water (1.32 ppm) per 15 centimeter pot. Tulips in the same pot size may be drenched with 0.125 to 0.50 mg per 120 ml water one to four days after bringing the plants into a greenhouse from the cold room. Tulip cultivars vary in their response to ancymidol.

In the United States the application of chemicals to plants for commercial use is strictly controlled by Environmental Protection Agency (EPA) regulations. Before the chemicals can be used legally, an EPA registration must be obtained for each crop, starting the dosage allowable and the time of year application is permissible. Application for registration is usually made by the chemical company manufacturing the material after a patent has been obtained. Regulations for obtaining a registration for use of chemicals to be applied to food crop plants are much stricter than those for ornamentals, requiring residue data for the product and its metabolites from plant samples taken at intervals following application. Feeding tests on laboratory animals are also usually required to obtain information on a chemical's relative toxicity. (See p. 264, Ch. 11.)

[5]Tillering is the development of new shoots from the base of the original plant.

SUMMARY

The shoot system is the product desired in many kinds of plants; for example, in hay crops, pastures, lawns, foliage plants, forest and shade trees. The goal is to produce the shoot system as fast and as economically as possible. Plants may be annual, biennial, or perennial in their growth patterns. The annuals and biennials are herbaceous. The perennials can be either herbaceous or woody plants. The shoot system develops through the activities of meristems (dividing cells) found in terminal and lateral buds and in the cambial growth cylinder, surrounding the stem just under the bark. The growth patterns of all plants are controlled by genetic factors in the nucleus of the cells as modified by environmental stresses. The important environmental factors influencing plant growth are light, temperature, water, and the gases in the atmosphere.

As they grow from year to year, woody perennial plants undergo phase changes from the juvenile forms found in seedlings to intermediate stages and on to mature forms found in adult flowering stages. Morphological and biochemical (but not genetic) changes take place during this transition. Plants senesce with age but there are tremendous differences in the life span of different kinds of plants—some live only a few weeks or months while others survive for thousands of years.

Reproductive structures—flowers, fruits, and seeds—are the desired product in a great many kinds of plants, and cultural operations are geared to maximize the production of these plant parts. Flower formation is the goal in producing most ornamental, landscape, and house plants, but for edible crops, flower formation must lead on to fruit setting and fruit growth or, in many kinds of plants, to the development of seeds. Certain environmental factors, such as length of day (or length of night) and chilling temperatures, can trigger the onset of flowering in some kinds of plants. Other plants are self-inducing for flowering. Following flower formation, pollination and fertilization can lead to fruit setting, fruit growth, and seed development. Plant growth regulators, both natural hormones and synthetic regulators, play a critical role in growth and development of plants. Five plant hormones are now known: auxins, gibberellins, cytokinins, ethylene, and abscisic acid. Each of these has many functions in controlling plant growth and development.

REVIEW QUESTIONS

6–1. How do growth and flowering differ among annual, biennial, and perennial plants?

6–2. What tissues in plants are responsible for their increase in size?

6–3. What determines the form and size a given kind of plant ultimately reaches?

6–4. What are the four important environmental factors influencing plant growth and development?

6–5. What is meant by "phase change" in woody perennial plants grown from seeds?

6–6. What are the seven steps in the production of fruits and seeds starting with the planting of a seed and ending with seed harvest?

6–7. What two environmental factors can induce flowering in certain kinds of plants?

6–8. What is phytochrome and in what two forms can it exist?

6–9. What is the difference between pollination and fertilization?

6–10. The growth curves of developing fruits of certain kinds of plants, such as peaches and apricots, differ distinctly from those of other kinds, such as apples and pears. Draw growth curves of both types.

6–11. What are the five known natural plant hormones?

6–12. Growth is the irreversible increase in size, usually measured as an increase in dry weight. True or false?

6–13. Plants of most species grow better when temperature is constant during the day and night. True or false?

6–14. The temperature at which growth is most rapid is higher for tropical plants than for temperate zone plants. True or false?

6–15. Plants that develop in the light become etiolated. True or false?

6–16. Plants that bloom in greenhouses in the northern hemisphere at Christmas time without additional light are short-day plants. True or false?

6–17. Light is necessary for the normal development of plant roots and their tissues. (a) True, (b) False, (c) True and false. Explain.

6–18. Before light can be effective in any process, the light must be (a) assimilated, (b) absorbed, (c) diffused.

6–19. As far as is known, length of day has little or no effect on (a) the development of tubers or bulbs, (b) respiration, (c) photosynthesis, (d) flowering, (e) onset of dormancy.

6–20. Which of the following statements are false? (a)

Auxins are primarily formed in the apical buds and in young leaves. (b) Auxins are responsible for the control and promotion of cell elongation. (c) Auxins inhibit growth of axillary buds. (d) Auxin plays a role in the initiation and maintenance of cambium activity. (e) Auxins move upward in the plant, from roots to shoot tips.

REFERENCES

1. Addicott, F. T. 1969. Aging, senescence, and abscission in plants: phytogerontology. *HortScience* 4(2):114–16.

2. Cathey, H. M. 1964. Physiology of growth retarding chemicals. *Ann. Rev. Plant Physiol.* 15:271–302.

3. Crane, J. C. 1969. The role of hormones in fruit set and development. *HortScience* 4(2):108–11.

4. ———, and P. Punsri. 1956. Comparative growth of the endosperm and the embryo in unsprayed and 2, 4, 5-trichlorophenoxyacetic acid sprayed Royal and Tilton apricots. *Proc. Amer. Soc. Hort. Sci.* 68:96–104.

5. Dugger, M., ed. 1974. *Air pollution effects on plant growth.* Washington, D.C.: American Chemical Society.

6. Farnham, D. S., and R. F. Hasek. 1972. Tulip height control with EL-531—a progress report. *Flor. Rev.* 150(3889):21–23, 55–58.

7. Galston, A. W., and P. J. Davies. 1970. *Control mechanisms in plant development.* Englewood Cliffs, N.J.: Prentice-Hall.

8. Garner, W. W. and H. A. Allard. 1920. Effect of the relative length of day and night and other factors of the environment on growth and reproduction in plants. *Jour. Agr. Res.* 18:553–607.

9. Hartmann, H. T., and D. E. Kester. 1975. *Plant propagation: principles and practices.* 3rd ed. Englewood Cliffs, N.J.: Prentice-Hall.

10. Hasek, R. F., and R. H. Sciaroni. 1973. Height control of pot chrysanthemums with A-rest. *Flor. Rev.* 151(3924):53–54.

11. ———, ———, and D. S. Farnham. 1971. 1970–71 'Japanese Georgia' lily height control trials. *Flor. Rev.* 149(3849):22–24, 62–64.

12. Hendricks, S. B. 1956. Control of growth and reproduction by light and darkness. *Am. Scient.* 44:229–47.

13. Jensen, W. A., and F. B. Salisbury. 1972. *Botany: an ecological approach.* Belmont, Calif.: Wadsworth.

14. Jones, H. A. 1927. Pollination and life history studies of the lettuce (*Lactuca sativa* L.). *Hilgardia* 2:425–79.

15. Jones, R. L. 1973. Gibberellins: their physiological role. *Ann. Rev. Plant Physiol.* 24:571–98.

16. Koslowski, T. T. 1971. *Growth and development of trees,* vol. 1. New York: Academic Press.

17. Krishnamoorthy, H. N., ed. 1975. *Gibberellins and plant growth.* New York: John Wiley.

18. Leopold, A. C., and P. E. Kriedmann. 1975. *Plant growth and development.* 2nd ed. New York: McGraw-Hill.

19. McGregor, S. E. 1976. *Insect pollination of cultivated crop plants.* USDA/ARS Agr. Handbook No. 496. Washington, D.C.: U.S. Government Printing Office.

20. Noggle, G. R., and G. J. Fritz. 1976. *Introductory plant physiology.* Englewood Cliffs, N.J.: Prentice-Hall.

21. Rappaport, L., and R. M. Sachs. 1976. *Physiology of cultivated plants.* Davis, Calif.: UCD Bookstore.

22. Ray, P. M. 1972. *The living plant.* New York: Holt, Rinehart & Winston.

23. Sacher, J. A. 1973. Senescence and post-harvest physiology. *Ann. Rev. Plant Physiol.* 24:197–224.

24. Salisbury, F. B. and C. Ross. 1978. *Plant physiology.* 2nd ed. Belmont, Calif.: Wadsworth.

25. Sax, K. 1962. Aspects of aging in plants. *Ann. Rev. Plant Physiol.* 13:489–506.

26. Schopmeyer, C. S., ed. 1974. *Seeds of woody plants in the United States.* USDA Forest Service Handbook 450. Washington, D.C.: U.S. Government Printing Office.

27. Singh, B. N., and K. L. Lal. 1935. Investigation of the effect of age on assimilation of leaves. *Ann. Bot.* 49:291–307.

28. Skoog, F., and D. J. Armstrong. 1970. Cytokinins. *Ann. Rev. Plant Physiol.* 21:359–84.

29. Stutte, C. A. 1977. *Plant growth regulators: chemical activity, plant responses, and economic potential.* Washington, D.C.: American Chemical Society.

30. Weaver, R. J. 1972. *Plant growth substances in agriculture.* San Francisco: W. H. Freeman & Company Publishers.

31. Wellensiek, S. J., ed. 1972. Symposium on growth regulators in fruit production. *Acta Hort.* 34(1):1–507.

32. Woolhouse, H. W., ed. 1967. Aspects of the biology of aging. *Soc. Exp. Biol. Symp.* 21:1–634.

33. ———. 1978. Senescence processes in the life cycle of flowering plants. *BioScience* 28(1):25–31.

34. Zimmerman, M. H., and C. L. Brown. 1971. *Trees: structure and function.* New York: Springer-Verlag, N.Y.

35. Zimmerman, R. H. 1972. Juvenility and flowering in woody plants: a review. *HortScience* 7(5):447–55.

36. ———, ed. 1976. Symposium on juvenility in woody perennials. *Acta Hort.* No. 56.

BICKFORD, E. D., and S. DUNN. 1972. *Lighting for plant growth*. Kent, Ohio: Kent State University Press.

CHERRY, J. H. 1977. Hormone action. In *The molecular biology of plant cells*, ed. H. Smith. Berkeley, Calif.: University of California Press.

DOCHINGER, L. S. 1973. Trees for polluted air. Misc. Pub. 1230. USDA Forest Service.

DUGGER, W. M., and I. P. TING. 1970. Air pollution oxidants—their effects on metabolic processes in plants. *Ann. Rev. Plant Physiol.* 21:215–34.

EPSTEIN, E. 1977. The role of roots in the chemical economy of life on earth. *BioScience* 27(12):783–87.

EVANS, L. T. 1975. *Daylength and flowering plants*. Menlo Park, Calif.: Benjamin.

GALSTON, A. W., P. J. DAVIES, and R. L. SATTER. 1980. *The life of the green plant*. 3rd ed. Englewood Cliffs, N.J.: Prentice-Hall.

JACOBSEN, J. S., and A. C. HILL, eds. 1970. *Recognition of air pollution injury to vegetation—a pictorial atlas*. Air Pollution Control Assoc. Pittsburgh, Pa.: Herbick and Held.

KRAMER, P. J., and S. DUNN. 1979. *Physiology of woody plants*. New York: Academic Press.

LYONS, J. M. 1973. Chilling injury in plants. *Ann. Rev. Plant Physiol.* 24:445–66.

MOORE, T. C. 1979. *Biochemistry and physiology of plant hormones*. New York: Springer-Verlag, N.Y.

MUDD, J. B., and T. T. KOZLOWSKI. 1975. *Responses of plants to air pollution*. New York: Academic Press.

NAPP-ZINN, K. 1973. *Temperature and life*, pp. 171–94. Ed. H. Precht. New York: Springer.

NICKELL, L. G. 1978. Plant growth regulators: controlling biological behavior with chemicals. *Chem. Eng. News* 56(41):18–34.

ORMROD, D. P. 1978. *Pollution in horticulture*. Amsterdam: Elsevier.

SACHS, R. M., and W. P. HACKETT. 1972. Chemical inhibition of plant height. *HortScience* 7(5):440–47.

SALISBURY, F. B. 1963. *The flowering process*. New York: Macmillan.

THIMANN, K. V. 1977. *Hormone action in the whole life of plants*. Amherst: University of Massachusetts Press.

WENT, F. W. 1974. Reflections and speculations (air pollution). *Ann. Rev. Plant Physiol.* 25:1–26.

WITHROW, R. B., ed. 1959. *Photoperiodism and related phenomena in plants and animals*. Washington, D.C.: American Association for the Advancement of Science.

Photosynthesis, Respiration, and Translocation

PHOTOSYNTHESIS

It is principally through the plant kingdom that solar energy is converted to chemical energy and hence made available for use by the animal kingdom. The sun is the original source of all important fuels, including coal, oil, gas, wood, and alcohol. Plants are the source of all food, either directly as grains, fruits, vegetables, and nuts or indirectly through animals as meat, eggs, and dairy products. Medicine, flavoring, and clothing are examples of plant derivatives. The list goes on and on; even this page was a part of a plant at one time (see Ch. 1.).

This chapter describes how the sun's energy, in the form of light, is transformed by plants into usable chemical energy. The conversion of the sun's energy into chemical energy is the single most significant reaction on earth and could easily be called "the reaction of life." The conversion is the total of many reactions, which in a generalized form is called **photosynthesis.**

Total worldwide productive capacity, including steel mills, automobile factories, shipyards, oil production, mining, and so on is almost insignificant when compared to the quiet but continuing productive capacity of the earth's green plants. It has been estimated that about 1.4×10^{14} kg (3.1×10^{14} lb) of carbon from carbon dioxide in the air is converted to carbohydrates each year by the green plants that live on the land and in the oceans, seas, and lakes. A number of this magnitude is beyond our comprehension and meaningless to us. To put it another way, assume that the 1.4×10^{14} kg of

carbon[1] is converted entirely to an equivalent amount of coal, which would be 1.41×10^{11} MT (1.55×10^{11}t). Assume further that a standard-size railroad car holds 45.5 MT (50 t); then the carbon fixed annually by plants would yield enough coal to fill 97 cars every second of every hour of every day all year long.

The light energy from the sun is captured by chlorophyll in the green parts of plants, mainly the leaves, and is used to convert carbon dioxide from the air and water from the soil (plus some water vapor from the air) into carbohydrates, which are stored in the plant for future use. In some superficial ways, photosynthesis and respiration (p. 161) can be thought of as the same reaction, with respiration being the reverse of photosynthesis. Thus the products of photosynthesis are the raw materials for respiration, and the fuels for photosynthesis are the products of respiration (Equation [2]). Photosynthesis is a synthesizing (building up) reaction. In contrast, respiration is a degrading reaction in which carbohydrates are ultimately broken down to carbon dioxide and water with the release of the stored energy. Plants perform both reactions and are said to be autotrophic. Human beings and animals, on the other hand, are heterotrophic: they can carry on respiration only. Hence, all living organisms obtain their energy directly or indirectly from the photosynthetic process—the basis of our dependence on plants.

---

[1]Calculated from data given in Noggle and Fritz *(4)* and other sources.

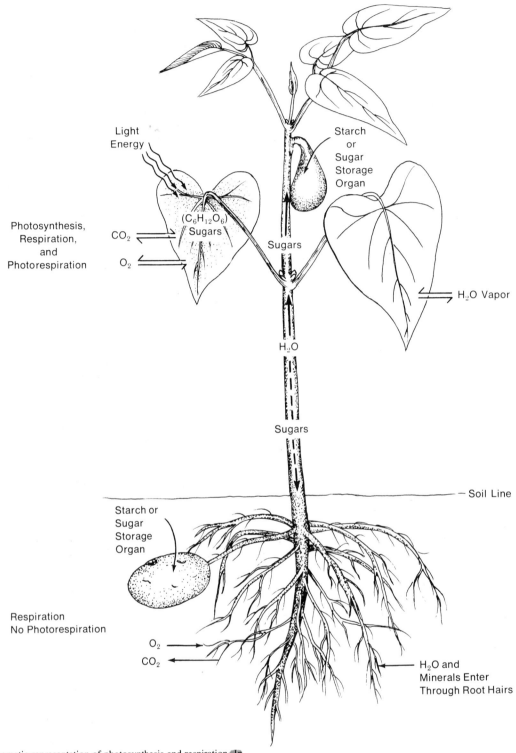

Light
Energy

Starch
or
Sugar
Storage
Organ

Photosynthesis,
Respiration,
and
Photorespiration

CO_2

$(C_6H_{12}O_6)$
Sugars

O_2

Sugars

H_2O Vapor

H_2O

Sugars

Soil Line

Starch or
Sugar
Storage
Organ

Respiration
No Photorespiration

O_2

CO_2

H_2O and
Minerals Enter
Through Root Hairs

Fig. 7–1 Schematic representation of photosynthesis and respiration. In the green leaves CO_2 from the air and water from the roots, plus light energy, interact through photosynthesis to produce sugars, with O_2 given off as a byproduct. The sugar is translocated throughout the plant and is often converted to starch in such storage organs as fruits or tubers. Respiration takes place in all living cells of the plant, both above and below ground. Stored carbohydrates react with O_2 to produce energy, releasing CO_2 as a byproduct. Minerals are absorbed also by the roots and are utilized in the formation of more complex compounds such as proteins and fats.

Requirements and Products

The requirements for photosynthesis are: (1) a living green plant in good health (generally green because of the presence of chlorophyll),[2] (2) an ample supply of carbon dioxide (normally present in the atmosphere, about 0.03 percent), (3) water (from the soil or water vapor in the air), and (4) light (at certain wavelengths).

The products of photosynthesis are: (1) carbohydrates (sugars and starches) and other complex compounds, (2) water (see generalized Equation [2]), and (3) oxygen (a waste product of photosynthesis but essential to all respiring plants and animals).

Photosynthesis occurs mainly in the leaves in most plants, but also to some extent in stems and green fruit. Many epiphytic (nonparasitic plants that grow on other plants) orchids (*Cattlyea, Phalaenopsis, Vanda, Aerides*) have chlorophyll in their root tips; thus, the roots of these plants also photosynthesize. Respiration occurs in all living plant tissues (Fig. 7-1).

All the photosynthetic reactions are summed up in a chemical equation:

$$n CO_2 + n H_2O \xrightarrow[\text{light}]{\text{green plant}} (CH_2O)_n + n O_2 \quad [1]$$

In a general way, the equation says that a green plant receives light, uses it in some way to join n number of carbon atoms together, and combines two oxygen atoms to form one molecule of oxygen gas (O_2). The new compound $(CH_2O)_n$, made up of carbon, hydrogen, and oxygen, is a carbohydrate. This general chemical formula represents any number of such compounds.

Energy Requirements for Photosynthesis

While Equation [1] indicates the raw ingredients and the final products, it neither shows the reaction quantitatively nor indicates the complexity of the mechanisms. It was recognized long ago that photosynthesis probably occurs in a series of numerous reactions, which can be summarized thus:

$$6\ CO_2 + 12\ H_2O \xrightarrow[\text{light energy}]{\text{green plant}}$$

$$C_6H_{12}O_6 + 6\ H_2O + 6\ O_2 \quad [2]$$

[2]Some bacteria (purple bacteria) have the ability to use hydrogen sulfide (H_2S) as green plants use H_2O to convert CO_2 into a bacterial protoplasm. They have a pigment similar to chlorophyll a. The overall reaction is

$$6\ CO_2 + 12\ H_2S \rightarrow (CH_2O)_n + 6\ H_2O + 12\ S.$$

Equation [2] shows that 6 molecules of carbon dioxide react with 12 molecules of water to produce one molecule of glucose, 6 molecules of water, and 6 molecules of oxygen. The reason that water appears on both sides of the equation is discussed on page 157.

The source of the released oxygen puzzled plant scientists for years. It was thought that carbon dioxide was the most likely source. The discovery and use of radioactive tracer elements made possible the study of the pathways of the atoms during the synthesis of compounds, which had been impossible. By using water enriched with the heavy isotope of oxygen (^{18}O),[3] scientists discovered that water was actually the source of the oxygen gas evolved in photosynthesis (Fig. 7-2). This discovery was one of the great breakthroughs in the study of photosynthesis. It also became evident that light provides the energy necessary to break apart the water molecules to produce hydrogen ions (with associated electrons) plus oxygen gas. The earth's primary renewable source of atmospheric oxygen is water. Oxygen is released from water by the photosynthetic activity of plants, again illustrating our dependence upon them.

During photosynthesis water is separated into hydrogen and oxygen ions. In addition, the oxygen in carbon dioxide is separated from carbon. The hydrogen atoms with their associated electrons from the water recombine with the carbon to form sugars (Fig. 7-3).

[3]The heavy isotope of oxygen is ^{18}O. The most abundant isotope found in the atmosphere is ^{16}O.

Fig. 7-2 C. B. Van Neil's work in the 1930s showed conclusively that water is the source of oxygen given off by green plants. The experiment used the heavy isotope of oxygen (^{18}O) as a radioactive tag to identify certain oxygen atoms.

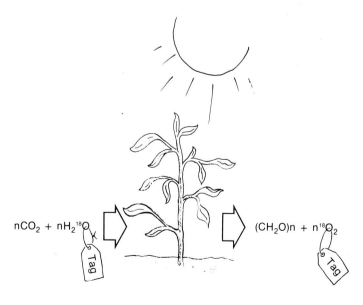

$$n CO_2 + n H_2{}^{18}O \qquad (CH_2O)n + n{}^{18}O_2$$

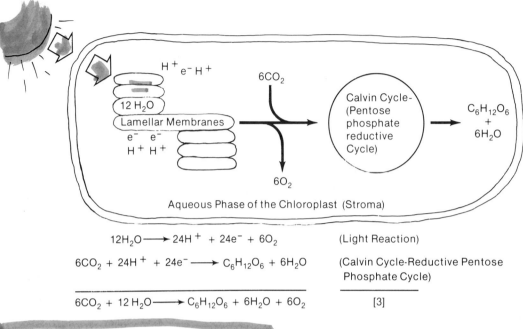

$$12H_2O \longrightarrow 24H^+ + 24e^- + 6O_2 \qquad \text{(Light Reaction)}$$

$$6CO_2 + 24H^+ + 24e^- \longrightarrow C_6H_{12}O_6 + 6H_2O \qquad \text{(Calvin Cycle-Reductive Pentose Phosphate Cycle)}$$

$$6CO_2 + 12H_2O \longrightarrow C_6H_{12}O_6 + 6H_2O + 6O_2 \qquad [3]$$

Fig. 7–3 Generalized view of photosynthetic processes in the chloroplast. In the lamellar membranes light is transformed to reducing equivalence (e⁻) and chemical energy (ATP), both of which are utilized in the Calvin reduction pentose phosphate cycle for the reduction of CO_2 to sugar.

In the photolysis of water,[4] 12 oxygen atoms ($O^{-2} \rightarrow O^0$) from water molecules donate 24 electrons; thus the oxygens in water are electron donors (reducing agents). When the 6 carbon atoms ($C^{+4} \rightarrow C^0$) in carbon dioxide accept the 24 electrons, they are the electron acceptors (Fig. 7–3).

The overall photosynthetic reaction is strongly endothermic,[5] requiring about 114,000 calories (114 Kcal) of energy for each 44 grams (1 mole) of carbon dioxide changed to carbohydrate. In nature, the light from the sun provides the necessary energy.

It is interesting to note that only a very small amount of the total energy received on earth from the sun is actually captured by plants. Efficiency of solar energy conversion has been calculated for a number of different crops and environmental conditions. The range of conversion of solar energy to chemical energy by plants varies from 0.1 percent for poor growing conditions on cloudy days and 3 percent for intensive cropping in good light to 25 percent for plants grown in controlled laboratory conditions. The average solar energy conversion efficiency for normal agricultural cropping systems is about 2.0 to 2.5 percent. The remaining 98 percent or so of the solar energy reaching the earth is lost by reflection and reradiation into the atmosphere; is used to evaporate water from oceans, lakes, and soil surfaces; and increases soil and plant temperatures. A later discussion (see p. 150) shows how plants absorb light only at certain wavelengths, thus further reducing their efficiency in the use of light energy.

Factors Affecting Rate of Photosynthesis

Environmental factors that affect the rate of photosynthesis are:

1. light quality (wavelength)
2. light intensity (brightness)
3. light duration (day length)
4. carbon dioxide concentration
5. temperature
6. water availability

[4]In photolysis, water breaks down into its primary constituents. Light supplies the energy needed for the breakdown; thus the *photo-* (meaning light) in photolysis. Photolysis is much the same as electrolysis in the breakdown of water except that, as the latter name indicates, electricity replaces light as the energy source.

[5]Endothermic reactions require energy in order to proceed. Exothermic reactions, by contrast, give off energy as they proceed.

The sun's energy is derived from thermonuclear reactions that convert hydrogen atoms to helium atoms with the release of tremendous amounts of energy. In the sun, four hydrogen atoms each weighing 1.008 units of atomic mass combine to form one helium atom weighing 4.003 units of atomic mass. Thus 4.032 atomic mass units of hydrogen are converted to 4.003 atomic mass units of helium with the conversion of 0.029 units of atomic mass to energy. The amount of energy is calculated from the equation $E = mc^2$ where the mass (m) is 0.029 amu times c^2—the speed of light (3×10^{10} cm/sec). The product of these equals 8.7×10^8 ergs. Researchers have estimated that the sun's mass is being converted to energy at the rate of 120 million tons per minute. This energy travels through space to the earth as electromagnetic radiation waves at the speed of light, about 300,000 km/sec (186,000 mi/sec). The wavelengths of this radiation vary from very long radio waves of more than one kilometer (0.62 mi) to very short cosmic rays of less than 10^{-4} nm (3.9×10^{-10} in). Visible light is that portion of the electromagnetic spectrum between 400 and 760 nm; however, plants respond to the somewhat wider spectrum of about 300 to 800 nm (Fig. 7–4). Light is transmitted to the earth in discreet bundles of energy waves called photons or quanta. The number of waves passing a given point in space per second is called its frequency. Light traveling in shorter wavelengths at higher frequencies is more energetic than light at longer wavelengths and lower frequencies. Figure 7–5 shows the relationship between wavelength and frequency.

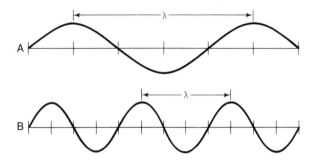

Fig. 7–5   The wave nature of light. The wavelength (λ) in A is twice that of B and the wave frequency in A is half that in B. The short wavelength and high frequency makes B more energetic than the long wavelength and low frequency of A.

Fig. 7–4   The electromagnetic spectrum of radiant energy.

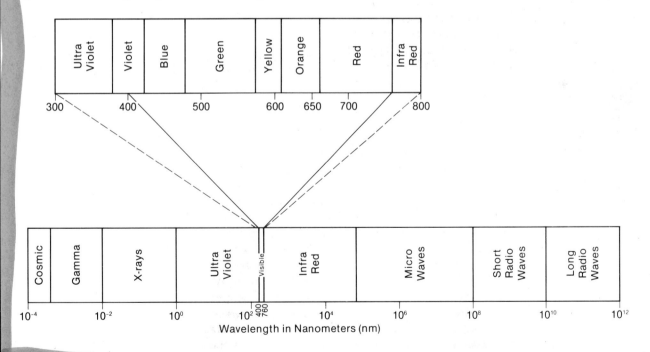

The color of visible light is a property of its wavelength; therefore, the energy level of different colors of light differs. Blue light with its shorter wavelength and higher frequency is about 1.8 times more energetic than the same number of photons of red light.

The plant must absorb light to keep the photosynthetic machinery running. Photosynthesis occurs in special structures, or organelles, called chloroplasts found within some plant cells. The chloroplasts contain pigments capable of intercepting light and converting electromagnetic energy into the chemical energy necessary to drive the photosynthetic processes. When these pigments (chlorophyll a, chlorophyll b, and some carotenoids) are irradiated with light containing all visible wavelengths, they absorb mostly from the red and blue portions of the spectrum and reflect the green portion. This can be demonstrated by growing groups of uniform plants at the same light intensity (brightness) but at different wavelengths, then measuring the photosynthetic activity ($CO_2 \rightarrow O_2$ gas exchange) of a leaf (see box) and plotting the activity against the different wavelengths. This kind of graph is called an action spectrum. The example given in Figure 7–6 shows peaks of activity in the blue and red wavelength range, indicating that these are the wavelengths of light most responsible for photosynthesis.

The rate of photosynthesis can be determined by measuring the rate at which carbon dioxide is absorbed by a leaf. A leaf is placed in a sealed glass chamber in the light, and the loss of carbon dioxide from inside the chamber is measured. But while carbon dioxide is being used by photosynthesis, some is also being evolved by the leaf in either light or darkness because of cell respiration. The above method of analysis measures **net photosynthesis** because some of the photosynthesis taking place is reusing the carbon dioxide evolved from respiration. **Total photosynthesis** is determined by measuring the carbon dioxide absorbed in photosynthesis and adding to this the carbon dioxide evolved during respiration in the light. The relationship is: rate of total photosynthesis = rate of net photosynthesis + rate of respiration in light.

Light quality is particularly important when plants are grown under artificial light. Ample radiation from the red and blue wavelengths must be assured for photosynthesis. When the action spectrum for photosynthesis is compared with a growth curve for plants, the similarity between the two curves is obvious. In one experiment, groups of green bean plants *(Phaseolus vulgaris)* were grown for six weeks under lights of similar intensities but different wavelengths—violet, blue, green, yellow, and red. The heights of the plants were measured and the averages plotted, as shown in Figure 7–7. The graph shows peaks of growth in the blue and red wavelength ranges similar to the action spectrum for photosynthesis in Figure 7–6.

Fig. 7–6 Action spectrum of a plant leaf, relating wavelength of light to photosynthetic activity.

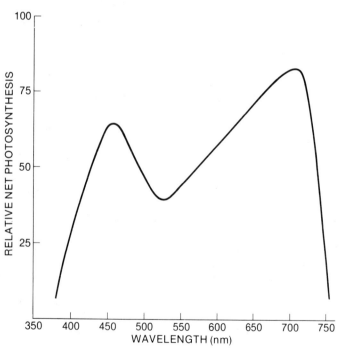

Fig. 7–7 The effect of light quality on growth of bean plants. Note the similarity of this curve to the action spectrum in Figure 7–6.

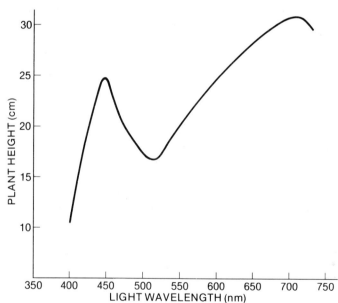

LIGHT INTENSITY

The intensity of light is the illuminance (brightness of light in the form of radiant energy) and is measured in luxes or footcandles.[6]

Light intensity affects plant growth, in part by influencing the rate of photosynthetic activity. The effect varies with different plants. Some species require high light intensities to grow well and are often termed ''sun-loving'' plants; examples are corn, potatoes, sugarcane, many turf grasses, and some fruit trees. On the other hand, plant species that do not grow well in high light intensities are sometimes referred to as ''shade-loving'' plants. Many such plants grow in the dense shade of the forest floor, and some of them are useful as house ornamentals. Other plant species are intermediate between the sun-loving and shade-loving types and grow well in moderately intense light.

Spermatophytic plants (plants bearing seeds) do some of their early growing in the total absence of light (zero intensity). This is easily demonstrated by germinating and growing bean *(Phaseolus vulgarus)* seedlings in total darkness for 15 to 20 days. Plants growing in darkness expend the energy stored in the endosperm or cotyledons of the seed in attempting to grow to light. Prolonged darkness eventually kills all plants regardless of seed size, but the large-seed plants live longer than small seed ones.

Light intensity distinctly affects the size and shape of leaves (Table 7–1). Generally, the leaves of a given plant species will grow longer and larger in area at the low light intensity of 10,000 lux (930 ft-c) than leaves grown at the high light intensity of 50,000 lux (4650 ft-c). Also, leaves of plants grown in high light intensities are thicker and broader than those grown in low light intensities.

[6]In the metric system, luxes are the number of lumens/m^2. Footcandles are the number of lumens/ft^2 in the English system (10.76 lux = 1 ft-c). The light intensity at noon on a cloud-free April day at Davis, California equals roughly 50,000 lux (4650 ft-c).

In a given plant, there is a light intensity at which photosynthesis and respiration rates are equal and net gas exchange is zero. This intensity is the **light compensation point** (Fig. 7–8). At the light compensation point, steady state equilibrium exists between respiration and photosynthesis but CO_2 is still exchanged. The gas is evolved in respiration at the same rate that it is used in photosynthesis. The plant is said to be **light saturated** when further increases in light intensity increase photosynthesis little or not at all. At very high light intensities, the rate at which CO_2 is available to the plant could limit the photosynthetic rate. The light intensity at which saturation occurs increases as the CO_2 concentration surrounding the plant rises (Fig. 7–9).

At equilibrium, the carbon dioxide concentration is such that the amount of carbon dioxide evolved in respiration exactly equals the amount fixed in photosynthesis. This CO_2 concentration is called the **carbon dioxide compensation point.** It is reached when a plant is growing at a constant light intensity higher than the light compensation point. At the CO_2 compensation point, photosynthesis reduces the CO_2 concentration in the ambient air to a level where no further assimilation (photosynthesis) occurs until an equal amount of CO_2 is evolved by respiration.

Fig. 7–8 The effect of light intensity on net photosynthetic activity.

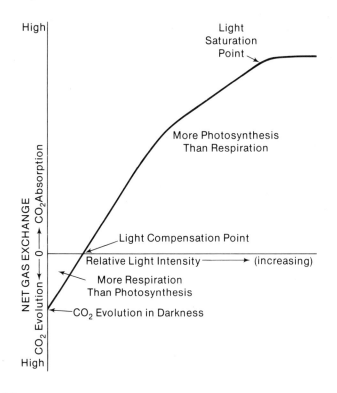

Table 7–1 Effects of Different Light Intensities on Bean *(Phaseolus vulgarus)* Seedlings

Total Darkness (etiolated)	High Light Intensity (50,000 lux)
No photosynthesis	High photosynthesis
Yellow to white in color	Green
Long internodes	Shorter internodes
None or tiny leaves	Large normal leaves
Spindly stem	Stout normal stem
Fine hairlike roots	Large normal roots

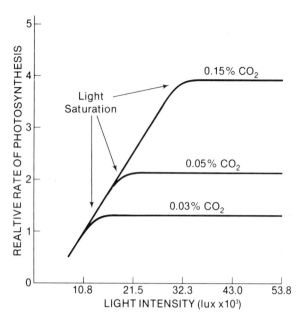

Fig. 7-9 Light saturation at different CO_2 concentrations, and at constant temperature of 25°C (77°F). Increasing CO_2 concentration increases photosynthetic activity. Note that the point of light saturation is also increased by increased CO_2 concentration.

LENGTH OF DAY

A plant's photosynthetic activity is directly proportional to the length of the day. Within limits, and other factors being equal, the longer the leaves receive light, the longer they photosynthesize and the faster the plant grows. People who use greenhouses for growing plants during the winter season often lengthen the light period with artificial light. However, it should be kept in mind that any significant effect on photosynthesis requires a fairly high intensity of artificial light (see p. 151).

CARBON DIOXIDE

The concentration of CO_2 in the air surrounding the leaves markedly affects photosynthesis. Normally the atmosphere contains an average of about 0.03 percent CO_2 and 21 percent O_2. Plant physiologists have found that increasing the CO_2 concentration in a closed system, such as a sealed greenhouse or an acrylic plastic chamber, to about 0.10 percent approximately doubles the photosynthetic rate of certain crops such as wheat, rice, soybeans, some vegetables, and fruits. Many greenhouse crops, such as carnations, orchids, and roses are grown commercially in a CO_2-rich atmosphere. Increasing the CO_2 concentration is feasible in the greenhouse or laboratory, but it is not possible to markedly increase the CO_2 concentration in the air above a corn or wheat field. Nevertheless, in view of the world food shortage and the need to increase crop production without additional drains on energy supplies for fertilizers and power, it would be desirable to find ways to improve yields by increasing the CO_2 availability to crop plants. The density of the crop and the height of the crop canopy are sometimes altered to increase the diffusion rate of CO_2 which, in turn, increases its concentration in the vicinity of the leaves. Applications of organic matter in the form of crop residues or green manure crops to the soil tends to increase CO_2 levels in the atmosphere above the soil. On a warm, sunny day after a rain and with no air movement, some plants grow so rapidly that CO_2 availability at the leaf surfaces becomes limiting. Under such conditions, wind machines can increase the available CO_2 by circulating and mixing the air.

TEMPERATURE

At low light intensities (20,000 lux, 1850 ft-c), temperature has little effect on the rate of photosynthesis because light is the limiting factor. However, as a general rule, if light is not limiting, the rate of photosynthetic activity approximately doubles for each 10°C (18°F) increase in temperature for many plant species in the temperate climates. The effect of temperature varies with species; plants adapted to tropical conditions require a higher temperature for maximum photosynthesis than those adapted to colder regions. However, excessively high temperatures will reduce the photosynthetic rate of some plants not accustomed to such high temperatures by causing the stomata of the leaves to close. A reduced rate of photosynthesis, together with the increased respiration rate at high temperatures, lowers the sugar content of some fruits (for example, the canteloupe) grown under these conditions.

WATER

Under conditions of water stress (low soil moisture and hot, drying winds), plants often lose water through transpiration faster than their roots can absorb it. The excessively rapid loss of water causes a sudden reduction of enzyme activity, which in turn causes the stomata to close and the leaves to wilt temporarily. When this occurs, the exchange of CO_2 and O_2 is restricted, resulting in a dramatic drop in photosynthesis. Water stress (high water deficit) thus reduces photosynthesis by limiting enzymatic activity.

Excessive soil moisture sometimes creates an anaerobic condition (lack of oxygen) around the roots, reducing root respiration and in turn limiting photosynthesis in the leaves.

As indicated at the opening of this chapter, not all reactions in the plant are synthesizing reactions. Some, as will be shown later, are destructive transformations that break carbohydrates and other substances down to simpler compounds. The constructive reactions (photosynthesis) and the destructive reactions (respiration) are collectively called **metabolism;** individually they are termed **anabolism** and **catabolism.** Anabolic processes occur in the plant only if energy is available. The atoms are joined together with chemical bonds that utilize and store the energy. In the catabolic processes, these chemical bonds are broken and the compounds degraded to simpler compounds, molecules, or atoms. These reactions release stored energy.

The role of enzymes should be emphasized in the story of photosynthesis. You can demonstrate to yourself the activity of enzymes by chewing a soda cracker for a short time without swallowing it. The change in taste from starchy to sweet is fairly easy to detect as the amylase enzyme in your mouth converts the starch to sugar.

Enzymes are proteins consisting of chains of amino acids[a] of varying length. These molecules are involved in one way or another in many photosynthetic or respiratory reactions and vary considerably in size, solubility, and function. It must be emphasized that while the enzymes are involved in these reactions, they themselves are not reactants and do not enter into the reactions as such. They are specific in the functions they perform. Some enzymes help reactions to proceed by acting alone, as in rearranging atoms to change fructose sugar to glucose. In some reactions, enzymes require the presence of a prosthetic group to carry out the reaction. A **prosthetic group,** or **enzyme cofactor,** is a nonprotein compound that is firmly associated with a protein and is essential for the protein's activity as an enzyme. Examples of prosthetic groups of this type are NAD^+ (NADH) and $NADP^+$ (NADPH). Consider the cofactor as a key that will operate a lock on the door. The key is the essential cofactor, the lock is the enzyme, and the opening of the door is the result of the reaction. The basis of selectivity of some herbicides (p. 240) is that an enzyme activity required for plant growth is blocked by applying a **cofactor analog**[b] to the plants that prevents the enzyme from performing the essential plant reaction, consequently causing the weed to die.

[a] Amino acids are fundamental building blocks of proteins. There are about 20 common amino acids in living organisms. All contain the elements carbon, hydrogen, oxygen, and nitrogen; some also contain sulfur.

[b] A cofactor analog is an enzyme cofactor that can associate itself with an enzyme but is not the proper cofactor for the particular reaction. The analog, therefore, blocks the proper cofactor from associating with the enzyme and thus prevents the essential reaction.

The overall process of photosynthesis is often stated rather simply in words or in brief generalized equations, but in reality, the total process is complex. Even today, all its parts are not clearly understood.

For convenience, the overall photosynthetic process is often separated into two parts. First, in the light reaction (Hill reaction), energy in the form of light is received by the plant and used to reduce nicotinamide adenine dinucleotide phosphate ($NADP^+$) to NADPH,[7] which can accept energy. Another compound called adenosine triphosphate (ATP)[8] is also important in the transfer of energy. Second, in the dark reaction (Calvin reaction), carbon taken into the plant as CO_2 from the air accepts the energy (by being reduced).

THE LIGHT REACTION

This occurs in the grana membranes within chloroplasts of green cells as the rays of white light fall upon a plant leaf. The chloroplasts contain molecules of chlorophyll a and chlorophyll b (pigments), both of which absorb red light (600 to 700 nm) and blue light (400 to 500 nm). Chloroplasts of higher plants also contain another group of pigments, the carotenoids, which absorb blue light but not red. A photon of light interacts with an electron in the pigment molecule. The electron accepts the light energy and becomes excited; that is, it is raised to a higher energy level. The electron returns to its ground (before excitement) state by different means, depending on the nature of the environment. It returns to its original state by heat emission, by chemical reaction with other molecules, by reemitting the energy as fluorescence, or by becoming involved in the photochemical reactions of photosynthesis. Assume that sufficient light strikes 24 molecules of chlorophyll with sufficient energy to raise 24 electrons (one in each molecule) to a higher energy level. Through a series of complex reactions in two photosystems, the energy is transferred to 12 molecules of water within the cell, causing the water to split.

[7]$NADP^+$ is a coenzyme hydrogen acceptor found in the chloroplasts and is involved in cytoplasmic reactions leading to and from the dark reaction (p. 154). NAD^+ is a coenzyme hydrogen acceptor found within the intramitochondrial reaction. $NADP^+$ is involved in photosynthesis and has three phosphate groups in its formula, while NAD^+ is involved in respiration (TCA cycle) and has only two phosphate groups. NADPH and NADH are the reduced forms of $NADP^+$ and NAD^+.

[8]ADP and ATP (adenosine di- and triphosphate) are nucleotides (nucleic acid) formed by joining adenine, ribose, and either two or three phosphate groups.

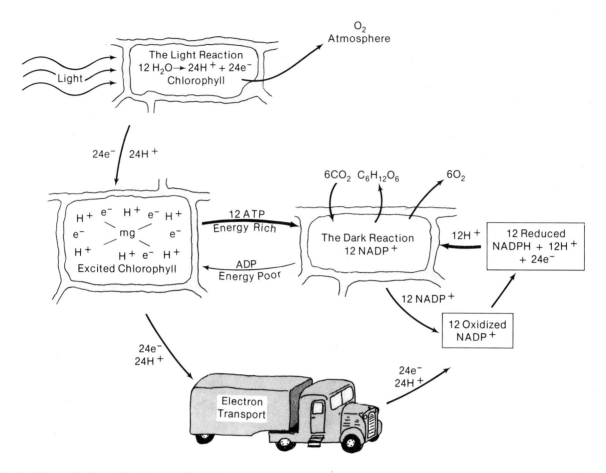

Fig. 7–10 Photosynthetic reactions that occur in the light.

$$12 \, H_2O \rightarrow 24 \, H^+ + 24 \, e^- + 6 \, O_2 \qquad [4]$$

The light reactions are schematically summarized in Figure 7–10.

THE DARK (CALVIN) REACTION

In the dark reaction, the energy captured in the light reaction is used to change carbon dioxide to carbohydrates and water. The overall reaction is

$$6CO_2 + 24 \, e^- + 24 \, H^+ \rightarrow C_6H_{12}O_6 + 6H_2O. \qquad [5]$$

The dark reaction is historically known as the Calvin cycle or the reductive pentose phosphate cycle. It is sometimes referred to as the Blackman or enzymatic reaction. It was first assumed that sugars were formed in the dark reaction from the stepwise synthesis of a number of intermediate products. Because of formaldehyde's formula CH_2O, early biochemists logically suspected formaldehyde as the first product of photosynthesis. These early attempts to discover the stepwise synthesis of sugars ended in failure because formaldehyde was never isolated. In fact, they showed that formaldehyde kills plant cells. Thus, the products and the steps involved in the dark reactions of photosynthesis remained a secret until radioisotopes became available. The classic experiment of Benson and Calvin *(2)* showed that after feeding plants radioactive carbon dioxide for five seconds, most of the radioactivity was located in a three-carbon compound, 3-phosphoglyceric acid. Following this discovery, many of the intermediate steps were then determined.

To illustrate the dark reactions, study Figure 7–11. In the first step, one molecule of CO_2 from the air enters the cycle. Bear in mind that there is no beginning or ending of the cycle; it is continuous. Also, it should be pointed out that while only one molecule of CO_2 enters at a time, six carbon atoms are required to synthesize the final glucose sugar ($C_6H_{12}O_6$); therefore, this cycle revolves six times to form one glucose molecule. The CO_2 molecule joins a five-carbon sugar (ribulose 1,5-diphosphate) that was synthesized earlier in the dark reaction. Some authors claim that an unstable six-carbon sugar is temporarily formed in the second step, which immediately enters the third step and splits into two three-carbon compounds (3-phosphoglyceric acid, or PGA). The plants that form these initial three-carbon compounds are called C_3 plants. As we will see later in this section (p. 156), some plants form four-carbon compounds first and are called C_4 plants. Each of the two 3-phosphoglyceric acid molecules contains one phosphate group. In the fourth step, a phosphate group from each of two ATP molecules from the light reaction joins the opposite end of each of the two 3-phosphoglyceric acid molecules, forming two molecules of 1,3-diphosphoglyceric acid and changing each ATP to ADP. The two ADP molecules return to the light reaction to be changed back to ATP by the addition of a phosphate group to each (rephosphorylated). In the fifth step, each of the two 1,3-diphosphoglyceric acid molecules loses one phosphate group by reacting with two NADPH molecules from the light reaction. This forms two molecules of a three-carbon phosphorylated sugar, called 3-phosphoglyceraldehyde and two $NADP^+$ molecules. In the sixth step, some of the glyceraldehyde 3-phosphate molecules join together to form a six-carbon diphosphosugar that is enzymatically transformed into glucose ($C_6H_{12}O_6$). In the seventh step, some of the 3-phosphoglyceraldehyde is recycled through a number of reactions, called the pentose phosphate shunt, to form more ribulose diphosphate by joining some two-carbon fragments with three-carbon (PGA) compounds, which is used to continue the cycle. Note that for every six molecules of carbon dioxide that enter the cycle and yield one glucose molecule, 18 molecules of ATP and 12 molecules of NADPH are used.

C_3, C_4, and CAM Type Plants

Three groups of plants can be distinguished by certain specific physiological, morphological, and biochemical characteristics—C_3, C_4, and CAM plants. One of the

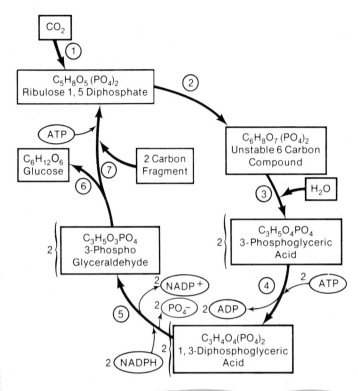

Fig. 7–11 A schematic representation of the dark (Calvin) reactions of photosynthesis.

characteristics is that a major pathway for photosynthetic carbon fixation is different for each group.

The C_3 plants fix carbon dioxide with ribulose 1,5-diphosphate to form two molecules of 3-phosphoglyceric acid (a three-carbon acid) via the Calvin-Benson pathway of photosynthesis. This reaction is catalyzed by the enzyme ribulose diphosphate carboxylase.

The C_4 plants fix carbon during photosynthesis by reacting CO_2 with phosphoenolpyruvic acid in the presence of the enzyme phosphoenolpyruvate carboxylase to produce oxaloacetic acid (a four-carbon acid) via the Hatch-Slack (3) pathway. The CAM-type plants often display a diurnal pattern of organic acid formation and fix CO_2 in a modified C_4 pathway called **crassulacean acid metabolism** (thus, CAM). Some of these plants have large succulent leaf cells, with stomata that open at night, allowing carboxylase enzymes to fix CO_2 into organic C_4 acids. Certain members of the cactus, orchid, and pineapple families are examples. The biochemistry of the different pathways of fixation all ultimately return to pathways that are parts of the Calvin cycle. The C_3 and C_4 pathways are compared in Figure 7–12.

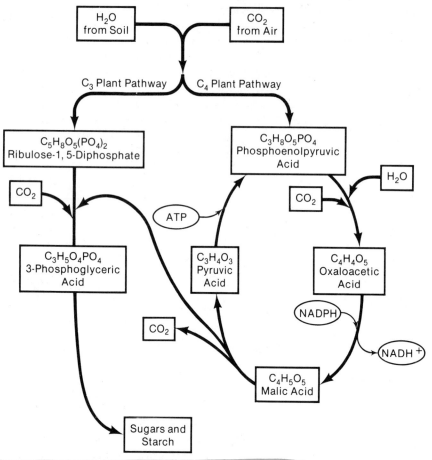

Fig. 7–12 Carbon dioxide fixation (photosynthesis) pathways for C_3 and C_4 plants. In the C_4 fixation of carbon, CO_2 and H_2O react in the presence of an enzyme to form a four-carbon compound oxaloacetic acid. This compound is transformed to malic acid, which is changed to pyruvic acid to regenerate more phosphoenolpyruvic acid. The CO_2 enters the Calvin (C_3) cycle via the pentose phosphate pathway.

Fig. 7–13 Effect of light intensity on net photosynthetic rates of a C_4 plant (corn) and a C_3 plant (barley). The C_4 plant is more efficient in using the sun's energy.

An important difference between C_3 and C_4 plants is their differential response in net photosynthesis to various light intensities (Fig. 7–13). C_3 plants have low net photosynthetic rates, high carbon dioxide compensation points (50 to 150 ppm CO_2), and high photorespiration rates (p. 162). Plants of this type include cereal grains (barley, oats, rice, rye, wheat), peanuts, soybeans, cottton, sugar beets, tobacco, and spinach, as well as some evergreen and deciduous trees. The C_4 plants, on the other hand, have high net photosynthetic rates, low carbon dioxide compensation points (0 to 10 ppm CO_2), and low photorespiration rates. This group includes about half of the species of the GRAMINEAE family (e.g., corn, sorghum, sugarcane, millet, crabgrass, bermuda grass) as well as many of the broad-leaf plants such as pigweed *(Amaranthus)* and *Atriplex*. The C_4 plants are the more efficient users of CO_2 (Fig. 7–13). C_4 plants have the additional advantage of greater water use efficiency than the C_3 plants, and the CAM plants are even more water efficient than the C_4 plants.

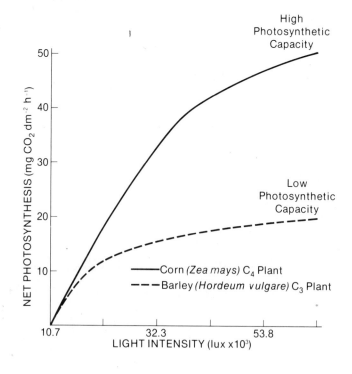

The CAM pathway occurs in at least two ferns (*Drymoglossum* and *Pyrrosia*). Some plants in several families contain all three photosynthetic pathways; for example AIZOACEAE, COMPOSITAE, EUPHORBIACEAE, and PORTULACACEAE.

Another characteristic difference between the C_3 and C_4 groups is that at the normal CO_2 concentration (0.03 percent), light saturation is difficult to attain for C_4 plants, but is easily reached at low light intensities for C_3 plants (11,000 to 43,000 lux or 1000 to 4000 ft-c).

PLANT RESPIRATION

The stepwise release of the energy captured and stored in photosynthesis is called **respiration.** Respiration reconverts the carbohydrates synthesized in photosynthesis to carbon dioxide, water, and energy. The biological processes responsible for these changes are of prime concern because the energy released by respiration is the source of the energy for life processes. Hexose (six-carbon) sugars such as glucose are commonly involved in respiration. The overall reaction is written:[9]

$$C_6H_{12}O_6 + 6\ H_2O + 6\ O_2 \rightarrow$$
$$6\ CO_2 + 12\ H_2O + energy\quad [6]$$

This generalized reaction proceeds in a series of subreactions, each of which is catalyzed by a specific enzyme and breaks down a complex molecule to a simpler one. From Equation [6], it is obvious that respiration resembles the burning of sugar. When sugar is ignited, the products are carbon dioxide, water, and heat. The principal difference between respiration and combustion is the rate of decomposition. Respiration is a stepwise process of degradation that releases a small amount of energy with each step; combustion releases the energy quickly.

Factors Affecting Rates of Respiration

TEMPERATURE

Temperature strongly affects respiration rates. Within the range of 0°C to 35°C (32° to 95°F), the rate increases about two to four times for each 10°C rise. The effect of temperature on respiration is an important factor in the storage of some crops. A harvested plant part that is stored or preserved is often living tissue and unless the product has been cooked or processed, the enzymes are active and vital processes continue. Since respiration is a degradation process, it should be retarded as quickly and completely as possible to prolong storage life. One way to retard respiration is to refrigerate the product. Temperatures must be carefully controlled, however. In some crops—apples, for instance—optimum storage temperature is 0°C (32°F); lower temperatures can severely damage the fruit. Some fruits such as bananas and tomatoes and certain flowers suffer tissue damage at storage temperatures below about 10°C (50°F) causing them to turn brown and soft (p. 274).

Most plants grow best when nighttime temperatures are about 5°C (9°F) lower than daytime temperatures. The higher daytime temperatures favor photosynthesis and thereby produce more sugars for storage and growth. Lower nighttime temperatures reduce the rate of respiration, again allowing more plant growth or storage of photosynthates produced during the daytime.

OXYGEN CONCENTRATION

Oxygen is an essential ingredient of respiration. With other factors being constant and not limiting, the rate of respiration decreases as oxygen concentration decreases. Lowering the oxygen concentration—accomplished by increasing the concentration of either carbon dioxide or nitrogen—is useful in storing certain fruit and vegetable crops. This modified storage atmosphere discourages rapid respiration (see p. 277).

SOIL CONDITIONS

Compacted or water-logged soils generally are poorly aerated. This condition reduces respiration in the roots, resulting in poor plant growth. Mineral nutrient deficiencies affect the respiratory enzymes, indirectly causing a reduction in respiration.

LIGHT

Plants grown in low light intensities exhibit lower respiration rates. Low light reduces photosynthesis, thus decreasing the amount of carbohydrates available for respiration.

Respiration Pathways

A sugar molecule is degraded during respiration by a series of reactions. The first series is commonly referred to as **glycolysis.** Glucose (a six-carbon sugar) is chemically split into two three-carbon pyruvic acid molecules in a series of stepwise reactions. The degradation of glu-

---

[9]The overall reaction for respiration is sometimes written with no water on the left side of the equation and only six molecules of water on the right side. This is algebraically correct but it cannot account for the net energy released, or the exchange of electrons (H^+ ions). Also, omitting water on the left side obscures the fact that oxygen does not react directly with glucose; it is the water molecules as intermediate products that do. The oxygen given off in photosynthesis came from the water. In respiration the hydrogen atoms from the breakdown of sugar are used to reduce the oxygen gas to water.

cose to pyruvic acid, catalyzed by cytoplasmic enzymes, proceeds either aerobically or anaerobically depending on the amount of oxygen in the cell's cytoplasm. The aerobic degradation of pyruvic acid to carbon dioxide and water is referred to as the Krebs cycle, citric acid cycle, or the tricarboxylic acid (TCA) cycle.

In this discussion glucose is cited as the substrate being respired, but other organic materials are also synthesized and respired by plants. Many different organic acids (e.g., malic acid and glycolic acid, starch, proteins, fats, and lipids) are consumed as substrate material in respiration.

GLYCOLYSIS

In glycolysis, glucose in the presence of the enzyme hexokinase accepts a phosphate group from adenosine triphosphate (ATP),[10] yielding glucose 6-

---

[10]In recent years there has been some debate over the long-standing theory that ATP stores chemical energy and releases it to other molecules upon conversion from ATP to ADP. See Noggle and Fritz (4).

phosphate (phosphorylated glucose) and converting the ATP to adenosine diphosphate (ADP). The stepwise degradation of glucose to pyruvic acid is schematically represented in Figure 7–14.

In glycolysis, each molecule of glucose yields two molecules of pyruvic acid. Two molecules of NAD[+] accept energy from four electrons and are changed to NADH. Two molecules of ATP are used to phosphorylate the sugar and four molecules of ATP are produced from four molecules of ADP, yielding a net gain of two molecules of ATP. It would be a mistake to consider the pathways of glycolysis as so many one-way streets. Most are reversible; that is, under certain conditions the plant cell is able to synthesize fructose 1,6-diphosphate from pyruvic acid or glucose from fructose 1,6-disphosphate that has been dephosphorylated. Thus, in some environments, plants not only consume carbohydrates during glycolysis but also are capable of synthesizing them with reverse glycolysis.

To summarize—glycolysis is often separated into two parts. In the first, ATP is changed to ADP; in the second, ADP is changed to ATP:

Fig. 7–14 Glycolysis. Numerals in front of the molecules indicate the number of molecules in the reaction.

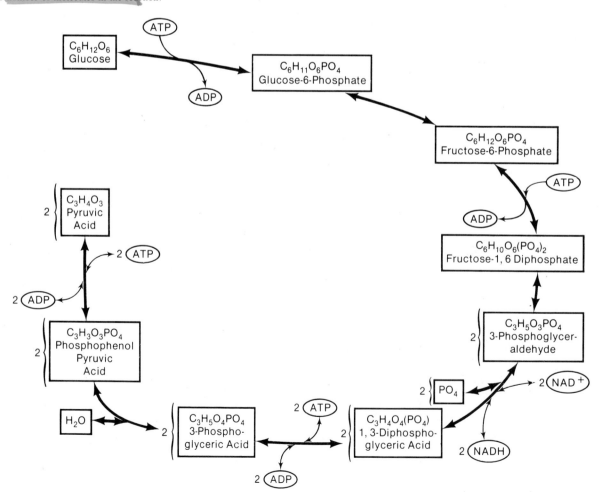

Glucose + 2 ATP→intermediate sugars→fructose
1,6-diphosphate + 2 ADP

Fructose 1,6-diphosphate + 2 NAD$^+$ + 4 ADP→
2 pyruvic acid + 4 ATP + 2 NADH

The formation of pyruvic acid is sometimes considered the crossroad in the respiration process. The intermediate products of glycolysis are the starting points for the formation of many important plant constituents.

The stepwise degradation of pyruvic acid begins the tricarboxylic acid or TCA cycle. These respiration reactions occur in the cell's mitochondria. Under normal aerobic conditions, the final products of the TCA cycle are CO_2 and H_2O. For simplicity we will consider only the main steps, omitting some of the intermediate products. There are specific enzymes that catalyze each reaction. The principal reactions are shown in Figure 7–15. Coenzyme A and NAD$^+$ (1 in Fig. 7–15) are

Fig. 7–15 The tricarboxylic acid (TCA) cycle represents the aerobic degradation of one molecule of pyruvic acid. Two molecules of pyruvic acid were produced from one glucose molecule; therefore, six molecules of CO_2 are released from one glucose molecule. Circled numbers and letters indicate places where NADH and CO_2 leave the cycle, respectively.

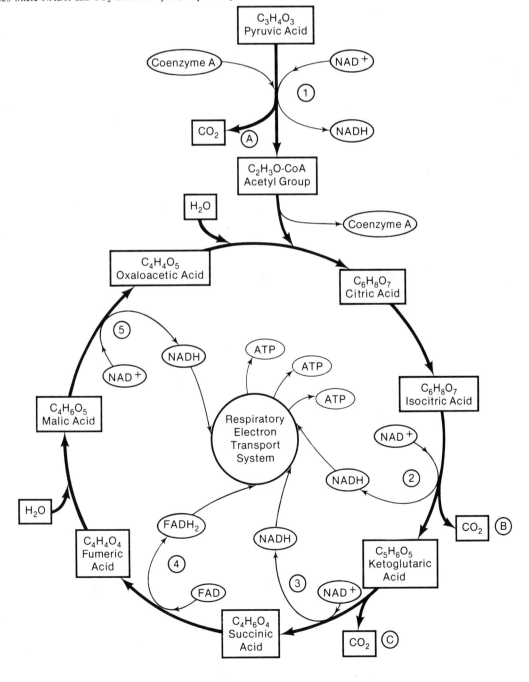

necessary for the removal of one carbon dioxide molecule (A in Fig. 7–15) from pyruvic acid, leaving a two-carbon fragment and one molecule of NADH. The two-carbon fragment joins with a four-carbon oxaloacetic acid (left over from the cycle) to form a six-carbon citric acid molecule. This molecule is enzymatically rearranged in two steps to form isocitric acid, which reacts with NAD^+ (2 in Fig. 7–15) to form αketoglutaric acid (a five-carbon) plus one carbon dioxide molecule (B in Fig. 7–15). NAD^+ is changed to NADH. In another series of reactions, catalyzed by several different enzymes, ketoglutaric acid is converted to succinic acid (four-carbon), and NAD^+ loses another carbon dioxide molecule (C and 3 in Fig. 7–15). Succinic acid is acted upon by FAD^{11} (4 in Fig. 7–15) and changed to fumaric acid, which is enzymatically converted to malic acid by the addition of a water molecule. Malic acid is finally changed by NAD^+ (5 in Fig. 7–15) to oxaloacetic acid, the four-carbon acid that started the cycle.

Anaerobic Respiration

Under anaerobic conditions, (i.e., where no molecular oxygen is available), pyruvic acid is also broken down to products such as acetaldehyde (a two-carbon compound) and ethyl alcohol. The latter is a product of fermentation used in the manufacture of wines and other alcoholic beverages (Fig. 7–16).

---

[11]Flavin-adenine dinucleotide (FAD), a hydrogen carrier, acts in a way similar to NAD^+ in biological oxidation reactions. $NAD^+ + 2\ e^- + H^+ \rightarrow NADH$, and $FAD + 2\ e^- + 2\ H^+ \rightarrow FADH_2$.

Fig. 7–16   Anaerobic respiration (fermentation). Plant tissue has much less anaerobic respiration than aerobic respiration.

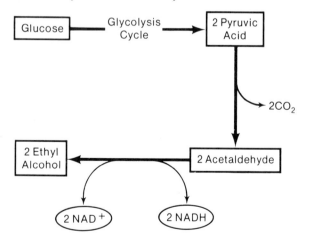

It has already been shown that many of the reactions of both photosynthesis and respiration require electron acceptors and donors. In the photosynthetic reactions, oxygen in water is the source of the electrons and their energy is increased by the sun's light energy. These electrons are transported from place to place in various electron transport systems along with such organic compounds as NADPH, NAD, and FAD. Arnon (1) found that chloroplasts placed in the light could generate ATP from ADP:

$$ADP + \text{inorganic phosphate } (P_i) \xrightarrow[\text{chlorophyll}]{\text{light}} ATP \quad [7]$$

There is considerable evidence that the formation of ATP and NADPH is linked to a flow of electrons from excited chlorophyll molecules in photosynthesis by a series of intermediate carriers:

$$12\ NADP^+ + 24\ e^- + 12\ H^+ + 12\ ADP + 12\ P_i$$
$$\xrightarrow[\text{chlorophyll}]{\text{light}} 12\ ATP + 12\ NADPH \quad [8]$$

In generalized Equation [6] for respiration, 12 molecules of water appear as products on the right side and 6 as ingredients on the left side. The opposite is true for photosynthesis. In the respiratory cycles, glucose molecules are stepwise stripped of hydrogen atoms and accompanying electrons as the carbon atoms release the stored energy and are oxidized to carbon dioxide:

$$C_6H_{12}O_6 + 6\ H_2O \rightarrow 6\ CO_2 + 24\ H^+ + 24\ e^-$$
$$\frac{6\ O_2 + 24\ H^+ + 24\ e^- \rightarrow 12\ H_2O}{C_6H_{12}O_6 + 6\ O_2 + 6\ H_2O \rightarrow 6\ CO_2 + 12\ H_2O} \quad [9]$$

As carbon in glucose loses hydrogen atoms, it also loses electrons; the electrons enter an electron transport system (Fig. 7–17) and are accepted by an electron acceptor:

$$12\ NAD^+ + 24\ e^- + 12\ H^+ \rightarrow 12\ NADH \quad [10]$$

In the electron transport system the electrons, with their associated hydrogen atoms, are carried by a group of dehydrogenase enzymes in a series of steps to finally combine with oxygen to form water. ATP and NADPH are a part of the electron transport system. They are es-

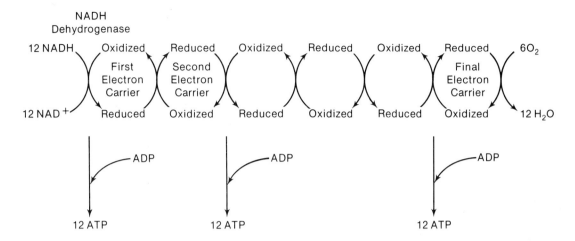

Fig. 7–17 The respiratory electron transport system. The light energy that is used to split water yields energized electrons. These electrons and their accompanying hydrogen ions are transported to sites where they are needed to drive the metabolic reactions within the cell. After a complex scheme of oxidative and reductive reactions, oxidized oxygen is finally reduced to water. *Source:* Noggle, G., and G. J. Fritz. 1976. *Introductory plant physiology.* Englewood Cliffs, N.J.: Prentice-Hall.

sential for the biosynthesis of sugar, starch, proteins, and fats as well as the respiration of these products to release their stored energy.

To summarize respiration—and to account for the ATP molecules produced—assume the complete degradation of glucose to carbon dioxide and water. As each glucose molecule is consumed in glycolysis, two molecules of ATP and two molecules of pyruvic acid form (Fig. 7–14). The two pyruvic acid molecules from the glycolysis of one glucose molecule enter the TCA cycle and yield six molecules of CO_2 (Fig. 7–15). Eight NAD^+ molecules accept energy from 16 electrons, and 2 FAD molecules accept energy from 4 electrons (a total of 20 electrons). Four electrons were accepted by two NAD^+ molecules during the glycolysis of glucose to pyruvic acid (Fig. 7–14). All 24 of the electrons involved in the photolysis of water are accounted for (Equation [3]). To complete the cycle, the 24 electrons and 12 hydrogen ions are carried by enzyme carriers and finally return to form 6 water molecules and 6 oxygen molecules (Equation [3] and Fig. 7–17). Each of the 8 NAD^+ molecules plus the 4 FAD molecules (total, 12) provide sufficient energy to convert 3 ADP molecules to ATP (Fig. 7–17). This makes a total of 36 molecules of ATP formed. Remember also that during the respiration of glucose to pyruvic acid, 2 molecules of ATP were formed. Thus, the grand total is 38 molecules of ATP. This completes

the transformation of the sun's light energy by the plant—from synthesis through storage as carbohydrates to degradation and utilization as chemical energy.

The principal characteristics of photosynthesis and respiration are summarized and compared in Table 7–2.

Table 7–2 Summarized Comparison of Photosynthesis and Respiration

Photosynthesis	Respiration
Requires CO_2 and water.	Requires O_2 and carbon compounds.
Produces O_2 and $C(H_2O)n$.	Evolves CO_2 and H_2O.
Light energy trapped by chlorophyll.	Energy released.
Occurs in light.	Occurs in both light and darkness.
Only cells with chlorophyll photosynthesize.	All living cells respire.
ATP produced (photophosphorylation).	ATP produced (oxidative phosphorylation).
Hydrogen from water used to reduce $NADP^+$ to NADPH.	Hydrogen from $C(H_2O)n$ used to oxidize NADPH to $NADP^+$ or reduce $NADH^+$ to NADPH.
ATP and NADP used mainly for synthesis of sugar.	ATP and NADP used for many reactions.

PHOTORESPIRATION

During the early studies of photosynthesis and respiration the rate of respiration was measured in the dark. Respiration was assumed to be independent of light intensity. Later this assumption was proven incorrect, and it was shown that for most higher plants respiration proceeds faster in the light than in the dark. Respiration rates stimulated by light have been termed **photorespiration.** Some respiration, termed **dark respiration,** is independent of light and proceeds at the same rate in both light and darkness. It has also been shown that dark respiration does not depend upon oxygen concentration but proceeds at about the same rate in low oxygen concentrations (2 percent) as in the concentration found in ambient air (20 percent). On the other hand, photorespiration rates increase as oxygen concentrations increase from 2 to 20 percent. The very small magnitude of photorespiration for an illuminated leaf, while difficult to measure, has been determined.

ABSORPTION, TRANSLOCATION, AND ASSIMILATION

The absorption and transport of raw materials used for photosynthesis in the green parts of the plant and the translocation of the products of photosynthesis to areas of storage or consumption are important to an understanding of plant growth and development.

Absorption and Conduction of Water

Water is absorbed by the roots from the soil and distributed throughout the plant even to its highest leaves— perhaps 60 m (200 ft) or more above the source. This formidable task requires considerable energy, estimated to equal about 16 kg/cm^2 (225 lbs/in^2) of pressure. Also, there must be a continuous water connection from the roots to the stems, leaves, flowers, and fruits. This link is the vascular system, principally the xylem (p. 21). To complicate the situation, water does not move alone; it carries with it essential mineral nutrients required for many plant functions. Examples are nitrates used in protein synthesis, phosphates used to make ATP during photosynthesis, and magnesium that becomes a part of the chlorophyll molecule. Another conducting system is the phloem, through which the manufactured sugars move from the leaves to storage organs and various tissues for utilization (p. 22).

Water absorption and translocation by the plant are of primary importance. Of all materials taken in by plants, water is absorbed in the largest quantities, but only a fraction of that taken in is used in metabolic processes. Most of the water is lost from the leaves by transpiration. Water loss in the plant is regulated to a certain extent by the opening and closing of stomata on the leaf surfaces (see p. 33).

The upward movement of water from the roots through the xylem in the stems to the uppermost leaves is sometimes called the **transpiration stream,** because transpiration is the primary cause of this movement. The upward transpiration pull in the leaves is started by the evaporation of water molecules from the outer surfaces of the mesophyll cells. As this water is lost, the mesophyll cells become water deficient and a potential difference is created between the dry mesophyll cells and the walls of adjacent moist cells. Because of water's cohesive properties (see p. 185), water from the wetter adjacent cell walls begins to diffuse into the less hydrated cells, thus relieving the pressure difference. Continued loss of water molecules at the leaf surface establishes a flow of water throughout the plant from cell to cell, from the roots to the leaves. In addition, a pressure difference exists between the outer cells of the root tips and the soil moisture, creating a driving force that moves water into the roots. Part of the water is absorbed into the roots by osmosis.[12] The proportion taken in by osmosis compared with the amount taken in by the transpiration stream depends upon the rate of transpiration. Normally, however, the amount entering by osmosis is relatively small.

Absorption and Transport of Mineral Nutrients

Like water, inorganic nutrients must be absorbed and transported within the plant. In higher plants, the minerals needed initially to start growth of a new plant are normally provided by the seed or stored in the propagating tissue. But as these are used, additional nutrients for the plant's continued growth must be absorbed from the soil.

---

[12]**Osmosis** is the flow or diffusion that takes place through a semipermeable membrane (as in a living cell) that typically separates either a solvent (water) and a solution, or a dilute solution and a concentrated solution. These concentration gradient differences create flow conditions through the semipermeable membrane until the concentrations of components on either side of the membrane are equal and equilibrium is established. At this equilibrium concentration osmosis ceases.

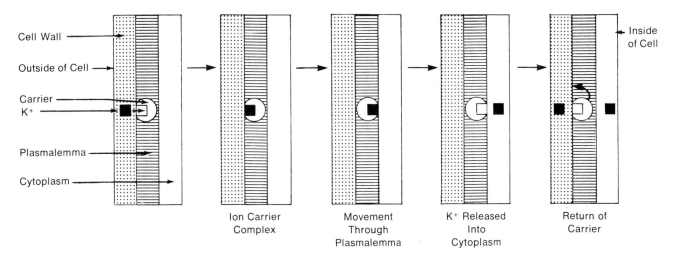

Cell Wall

Outside of Cell

Carrier
K+

Plasmalemma

Cytoplasm

Inside
of Cell

Ion Carrier
Complex

Movement
Through
Plasmalemma

K+ Released
Into
Cytoplasm

Return of
Carrier

Fig. 7–18 A schematic diagram of carrier ion transport. *Source: Adapted from Weier, T. E., C. R. Stocking, and M. G. Barbour. 1975. Botany: An introduction to plant biology.* 5th ed. New York: John Wiley.

Chemical analyses of the sap in root cells for various mineral nutrients reveal that these cells have concentrations 500 to 10,000 times higher than those of the same element in the soil solution. If simple diffusion was the only mechanism involved in taking up soil nutrients, the mineral nutrients could not move into the roots against such a high concentration gradient. However, this situation is prevented by the impermeability of the cell's membranes to the diffusive movement of the mineral ions. Energy is required to move ions against a concentration gradient. In the root cells, this energy is obtained from the respiration of starches and sugars that originated in the photosynthetic processes.

A plant absorbs mineral nutrients against a high concentration gradient by a process called **active transport** (see Epstein, 1977 in the supplementary reading at the end of the chapter). This transport process, sometimes called the "carrier hypothesis," has been proposed to explain how inorganic ions are transported across cell membranes. This hypothesis is one of many proposed to help explain active transport. An ion diffuses through the cell wall and comes in contact with the plasmalemma of the epidermal and cortical cells (p. 17). The ion combines with a complex carrier ion that has a particular attraction for the nutrient ion. The carrier ion then moves through the plasmalemma and releases the nutrient ion on the other side of the membrane into the cell cytoplasm. The carrier ion then returns to the outside of the root cell and is ready to transport another nutrient ion (Fig. 7–18).

Translocation of Sugars

Sugars which are synthesized during photosynthesis move throughout the plant, primarily in the phloem tissues. The movement is mostly downward from leaves to roots, but lateral or even upward movement from leaves to fruits or buds or other storage organs also occurs. Translocation takes place in the long sieve elements connected end to end to form sieve tubes. The mostly downward movement of photosynthates in the phloem is evidenced by the swelling of a girdled plant stem (Fig. 7–19). The

Fig. 7–19 Grape shoot girdled by removing the bark and the phloem and leaving the xylem intact causes sugars and other carbohydrates to concentrate above the girdle. Grape shoots are often girdled commercially to increase fruit size.

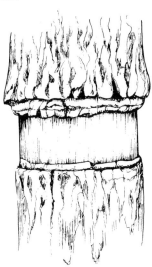

swelling results from the accumulation of sugars that cannot be transported downward because the phloem tissue has been removed (Fig. 7–19). A chemical analysis of the sap above the cut indicates a higher concentration of sugars than that in the sap below the cut.

The rate of translocation of sugars in the phloem is quite rapid, in some instances more than a thousand times faster than simple diffusion of sugar through water. The rate of translocation has been measured in many plants, and average values of 1 to 6 g/cm^2/hr have been found in developing fruits and tubers.

Much of the carbohydrate translocated within plants is sucrose. This disaccharide sugar, one of the major products of photosynthesis, is formed by the linkage of glucose and fructose and by the removal of a molecule of water.

Movement of materials in living plants has been observed to occur in different ways:

1. ordinary diffusion, which transports ions and molecules slowly
2. cytoplasmic streaming, which transports molecules and ions within the cytoplasm at a considerably faster rate than diffusion
3. downward mass flow translocation of amterial in the phloem
4. very rapid upward movement of water and mineral nutrients through the xylem
5. lateral transport of materials along the vascular rays radially from sieve tubes into the cambium tissue and xylem

SUMMARY

Photosynthesis uses solar energy to provide the only source of food and oxygen for animals, including humans. Thus, all animal life is dependent upon plants unless efficient alternate ways to reduce carbon dioxide could be found. It is through the stepwise reduction of oxidized carbon dioxide (a product of plant and animal respiration) that plant chlorophyll is able to use the sun's energy to convert energy-poor carbon dioxide into energy-rich carbohydrates.

Energy stored in plants as carbohydrates is made available to all forms of life (plant and animal) and is used to drive the mechanisms necessary to sustain life through a series of stepwise reactions called respiration. Thus, the reactions of photosynthesis are reductive and constructive, while those of respiration are oxidative and destructive.

The essential requirements for photosynthesis are carbon dioxide, water, light energy, and living green cells. The products are carbohydrates and oxygen. There are two types of reactions in photosynthesis: the light reactions, which require the presence of light, and the dark reactions, which proceed in either light or dark. Adenosine triphosphate (ATP) and reduced nicotinamide adenine dinucleotide phosphate (NADPH) are formed by photoreactions. These compounds are necessary for the transport of hydrogen ions and associated electrons formed by the photolysis of water. They are eventually used to reduce carbon dioxide to sugar. The oxygen derived from water is liberated as a gas. Phosphorus is essential to sustain life processes and is found in ATP and other intermediate products.

Most of the reactions of photosynthesis and respiration are enzymatically controlled with specific enzymes for each reaction. The rate of photosynthesis is influenced by such factors as light intensity, light quality, length of day, temperature, carbon dioxide concentration, relative humidity, and available soil moisture. The rate of respiration is influenced mainly by moisture, temperature, and oxygen concentration.

REVIEW QUESTIONS

7–1. The essential components for the chemical equation for photosynthesis are:
   a. _____   c. _____
   b. _____   d. _____

7–2. The source of carbon for photosynthesis is (a) sun, (b) water, (c) soil, (d) air, (e) sugars, (f) none of these, (g) all of these.

7–3. The source of carbon for respiration is (a) sun, (b) water, (c) soil, (d) air, (e) sugars, (f) none of these, (g) all of these.

7–4. Photosynthesis can occur in the dark as well as the light. True or false? Explain.

7–5. At the light compensation point, the rate of photosynthesis equals the rate of respiration. True or false? Explain.

7–6. If the rate of photosynthesis exceeds the rate of respiration, the excess photosynthate can be stored in the plant's (a) leaves, (b) roots, (c) stems, (d) tubers, (e) all of these, (f) none of these.

7–7. The energy from photosynthesis can be stored in the form of (a) sugars, (b) starches, (c) proteins, (d) all of these, (e) none of these.

7–8. If respiration exceeds photosynthesis (a) the plant is growing, (b) the plant is not growing. Explain.

7–9. When a plant is photosynthesizing, it gives off oxygen gas. The oxygen comes from (a) water, (b) air, (c) CO_2, (d) sugar, (e) starch, (f) all of these, (g) none of these.

7–10. Where does the hydrogen for the $NADP^+$ come from?

7–11. Carbon is (a) oxidized, (b) reduced during photosynthesis.

7–12. Carbon is (a) oxidized, (b) reduced during respiration.

7–13. The product of the anaerobic phase of glycolysis in plants is (a) sugar, (b) starch, (c) ethyl alcohol, (d) pyruvic acid, (e) ATP, (f) NADP.

7–14. The source of all energy on earth is the sun. True or false? Explain.

7–15. Relative to aerobic glycolysis there is (a) no, (b) some, (c) much energy produced during the anaerobic phase of glycolysis.

7–16. What is left when hydrogen is removed from the water molecule? What eventually happens to the remaining part of the water molecule?

7–17. What is the ultimate fate of hydrogen that is passed along the hydrogen transport system in respiration?

7–18. What percentage of the sun's energy is fixed by plants?

7–19. What does light-saturated mean in reference to photosynthesis?

7–20. What happens if respiration exceeds photosynthesis? Explain.

REFERENCES

1. Arnon, D. I. 1960. The role of light in photosynthesis. *Scient. Amer.* 302:105–18.

2. Benson, A. A., and M. Calvin. 1950. Carbon dioxide fixation by green plants. *Ann. Rev. Plant Physiol.* 1:25.

3. Hatch, M. D., C. R. Slack, and H. S. Johnson. 1967. Further studies on a new pathway of photosynthetic carbon dioxide fixation in sugarcane and its occurrence in other plant species. *Jour. Biochem.* 102:417–22.

4. Noggle, G., and G. F. Fritz. 1976. *Introductory plant physiology.* Englewood Cliffs, N.J.: Prentice-Hall.

SUPPLEMENTARY READING

AUGUSTINE, J. J., M. A. STEVENS, and R. W. BREIDENBACH. 1979. Physiological, morphological, and anatomical studies of tomato genotypes varying in carboxylation efficiency. *J. Am. Soc. Hort. Sci.* 104:338–41.

————, ————, ————, and D. F. PAIGE. 1976. Genotypic variation in carboxylation of tomatoes. *Plant Physiol.* 57:325–33.

BASSHAM, J. A., and M. CALVIN. 1957. *The path of carbon in photosynthesis.* Englewood Cliffs, N.J.: Prentice-Hall.

BLACK, C. C., JR. 1971. Ecological implications of dividing plants into groups with distinct photosynthetic production capacities. *Adv. Ecol. Res.* 7:87–114.

————. 1973. Photosynthetic carbon fixation in relation to net CO_2 uptake. *Ann. Rev. Plant Physiol.* 24:253–86.

BONNER, J. and A. W. GALSTON. 1952. *Principles of plant physiology.* San Francisco: W. H. Freeman & Company Publishers.

CONN, E. E., and P. K. STUMPF. 1976. *Outlines of biochemistry.* 4th ed. New York: John Wiley.

EPSTEIN, E. 1965. Salinity and the pattern of selective ion transport in plants. Res. Develop. Prog. Rep. No. 161. Washington, D.C.: Office of Saline Water, U.S. Dept. of Interior.

————. 1977. The role of roots in the chemical economy of life on earth. *BioScience* 27:783–87.

EHLERINGER, J. R. 1979. Photosynthesis and photorespiration: biochemistry, physiology, and ecological implications. *HortScience* 14:217–22.

GALSTON, A. W., P. J. DAVIES, and R. L. SATTER. 1980. *The life of the green plant.* Englewood Cliffs, N.J.: Prentice-Hall.

JOHNSON, C. R., J. K. KRANTZ, J. N. JOINER, and C. A. CONOVER. 1979. Light compensation point and leaf distribution of *Ficus benjamina* as affected by light intensity and nitrogen—potassium nutrition. *J. Am. Soc. Hort. Sci.* 104:335–38.

LOOMIS, R. S., and W. A. WILLIAMS. 1963. Maximum crop productivity, an estimate. *Crop Sci.* 3:67–72.

NEVINS, D. J., and R. S. LOOMIS. 1970. A method for determining net photosynthesis and transpiration of plant leaves. *Crop Sci.* 10:3–6.

QUEBEDEAUX, B., and R. F. W. HARDY, 1976. Oxygen concentration: regulation of crop growth and productivity. In *CO_2 metabolism and plant productivity,* ed. R. H. Burris and C. C. Black. Baltimore: University Park Press.

ROBINSON, J. M., and M. GIBBS. 1974. Photosynthetic intermediates, the Warberg effect, and glycolate synthesis in isolated spinach chloroplasts. *Plant Physiol.* 53:790–96.

ZELITCH, I. 1971. *Photosynthesis, photorespiration, and plant productivity.* New York: Academic Press.

————. 1976. The future of photosynthesis. *Horticulture* 60 (1):48–54.

Soil and Soil Water

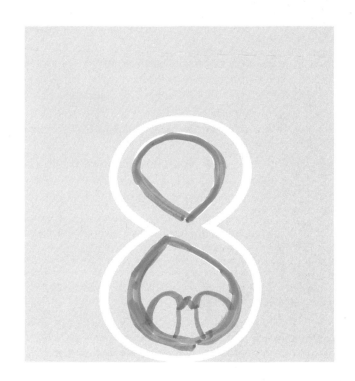

Plants need oxygen, carbon dioxide, water, and some mineral elements in order to grow and develop. As noted in Chapter 7, some of the oxygen and carbon dioxide are exchanged by the plant through the leaves and roots; oxygen and mineral elements are absorbed by their roots from the soil solution (Fig. 7–1 and p. 162). This chapter discusses the role of soil, soil water, and soil atmosphere in providing plants with anchorage, essential mineral nutrients, and water.

Consider the soil as a reservoir for providing storage and exchange sites for mineral nutrients, a system through which the soil air and soil water are transported to places where they are needed by plants, and a place in which plants are anchored. Two approaches have been suggested for studying soils *(4):* a pedological approach and an edaphological approach. **Pedology** is the science of naming, classifying, and describing the soil. **Edaphology** is the study of soil as it relates to crop plants. This discussion considers both approaches.

DEFINITION OF SOIL

The **soil** can be defined as the portion of the earth's crust that is formed by the decomposition of rocks and minerals by physical, chemical, and biotic forces. The soil is said to be mature if the decomposition occurred while the rocks and minerals were in place (not transported by wind or water) and with sufficient intensity that detectible layers were produced.

Soil can be divided into four major components:

1. the solid fraction; that is, rocks and minerals
2. the decayed and decaying organic matter, microorganisms, plant residues, and other living or dead organic constituents
3. the liquid fraction and its dissolved minerals
4. the soil atmosphere or soil air.

The voids found in the solid fraction are called **pore spaces.** Pore spaces vary in size and continuity and are an important physical property of soils.

The kind of soil and the capacity of a soil to grow plants are determined by the relative amounts of each of these four components. By volume, and disregarding soil texture, an "ideal" soil would contain about 25 percent air, 25 percent water, 40 percent mineral material, and 10 percent organic matter. Of course, these idealistic percentages seldom occur in reality, and they vary widely with moisture content at the time measurements are made.

The kind of soil therefore depends upon the ratio of the four components to each other. For example, a soil consisting of a high percentage of liquid relative to the other three components is likely to be a water-logged soil, requiring drainage before it can become productive. Water-logged soils are generally deficient in oxygen.

FACTORS INVOLVED IN SOIL FORMATION

Soil is derived from parent rocks, minerals, and decaying organic matter by indistinct steps. The two major processes in soil formation are: (1) accumulation and (2) differentiation of the parent material. **Parent material** accumulates from the breakdown of parent rocks by weathering. This process must occur before soil can begin to form. The parent material accumulates as an unconsolidated mass, which later differentiates into characteristic layers called **horizons.**[1] Differentiation occurs by mechanical separation and/or dissolution of the parent material. As the process continues, the horizons generally become more distinguishable and finally develop into a **soil profile.**[2]

The factors known *(14)* to be responsible for soil formation are: (1) parent material, (2) climate, (3) organic material (living and dead), (4) topography, and (5) length of time.

Parent Material

The formation and accumulation of material by chemical and physical weathering of parent rocks is the first step in the development of soil.

CHEMICAL WEATHERING

This entails four distinct processes.

(1) **Carbonation** is the reaction between carbonates or other minerals (such as feldspars) and carbonic acid (H_2CO_3) formed when carbon dioxide from the air dissolves in water. Carbonation reactions produce compounds that are less resistant to decomposition. For example, limestone ($CaCO_3$) reacts with water (H_2O) and carbon dioxide (CO_2) to form calcium bicarbonate [$Ca(HCO_3)_2$], a more soluble compound than the limestone:

$$CaCO_3 + H_2O + CO_2 \rightarrow Ca(HCO_3)_2$$

(2) **Hydration** adds molecular water to form a more hydrated material vulnerable to pulverization. An example is calcium sulfate ($CaSO_4$) absorbing water to form gypsum ($CaSO_4 \cdot 2\,H_2O$), a hydrated calcium sulfate:

$$CaSO_4 + 2\,H_2O \rightarrow CaSO_4 \cdot 2\,H_2O$$

(3) **Hydrolysis** is the reaction between the parent material and water to form a more soluble product. In the following hydrolysis reaction, for example, potassium ions (K^+) are made more available to plants by reacting the slowly soluble feldspar mineral ($KAlSi_3O_8$) with water (H_2O) to form the soluble potassium hydroxide (KOH) plus aluminum silicate (Al_2SiO_3):

$$KAlSi_3O_8 + H_2O \rightarrow HAlSi_3O_8 + KOH$$

$$2\,HAlSi_3O_8 + 8\,H_2O \rightarrow Al_2O_3 \cdot 3\,H_2O + 6\,H_2SiO_3$$

(4) **Oxidation** reactions form oxides of parent material by reacting with oxygen. For example, ferr*ous* oxide (FeO) reacts with oxygen (O_2) to yield ferr*ic* oxide (Fe_2O_3), a product more oxidized than the reactant:

$$4\,FeO + O_2 \rightarrow 2\,Fe_2O_3$$

PHYSICAL WEATHERING

Changes in temperature strongly affect the rate of physical weathering. Differential rates of contraction and expansion caused by temperature changes bring about cracking and peeling of the outer layers of rocks by a process called **exfoliation.** A second process is caused by the presence of different materials within a rock, each with its own characteristic coefficient of expansion. Because of these differences, sudden large temperature changes, causes uneven expansion or contraction, cracking the rocks. A third process is the cracking of rocks caused by the expansion of water as it freezes in rock fissures.

The mechanical action of glaciers causes rocks embedded in the ice to scrape against other rocks as the glacier moves. This action grinds the rocks into increasingly smaller rock fragments. This is a powerful physical process, which reached a tremendous magnitude during the Ice Ages (Pleistocene epoch). The product of glacial weathering is called **glacial till,** and it comprises rock particles ranging in size from clay to boulders. This material is deposited in various ways beneath, beside, and at the terminus of the melting glacier *(8)*.

Physical weathering is also caused by moving water, as stream erosion, sheet erosion, rill erosion, or wave action (Fig. 8–1). The action is similar to that of glaciers. Water from spring rains and melting snow moves rapidly down mountain streambeds, carrying par-

---

[1]Horizon—a distinct layer of soil resulting from soil-forming processes as seen in a vertical cross-section.

[2]Soil profile—a vertical section of soil through all its horizons extending from the surface to the parent material.

Fig. 8–1 Massive gullies formed by severe stream erosion during periods of heavy rainfall. These gullies are beyond reclamation by practicable methods. *Source:* USDA Soil Conservation Service.

ent rock fragments of varying sizes. As these fragments move along, they are gradually worn down to smaller and smaller particles, eventually forming parent material. In arid regions, wind action is similar to water. Coarse sand particles (parent material) are swept along the ground with sandblast action wearing away other larger parent rocks. The action of plant roots can sometimes physically break down parent rocks. For example, a tree root growing into a crack in a rock can ultimately fracture the rock. While this is not considered weathering, it is a physical soil-forming process. In this case, some chemical weathering must occur first to provide nutrients for the plants.

KINDS OF ROCKS

Parent rocks contain the nutrients that will be found in parent material, and later in the soil. Rocks are made up of consolidated material, unconsolidated material, or both (Fig. 8–2).

1. **Igneous** rocks—for example, granite formed ages ago or recently (as in Hawaii)—are consolidated, hard, and generally weathered in place. They are formed from the hardening of various kinds of molten rock material and are composed of the minerals quartz and feldspar, among others.

2. **Sedimentary** rocks are generally unconsolidated, composed of fragmental rock material that has been transported and deposited by wind, water, or glaciers. Limestone, sandstone, and shale are examples.

Fig. 8–2 Parent rocks from which soil can be formed. *A:* Igneous. *B:* Sedimentary. *C:* Metamorphic. *Source:* Rosa Maria Marquez.

3. **Metamorphic** rocks form from igneous or sedimentary rocks that have been subjected to sufficiently high pressures and temperatures to change their structure and composition *(13)*. Slate, gneiss, schist, and marble are examples of metamorphic rocks.

Climate

The climate affects soil formation. In areas of high rainfall, soils are highly leached and acid in reaction. Chemical weathering proceeds at a rapid rate, especially if high humidity is coupled with high temperature. The fertility level of soils formed under high rainfall is generally low because many of the plant nutrients are leached from the root zone. Many of these soils are red or yellow in color, indicating a relatively high percentage of iron oxide, which remains after other elements have been removed. These soils are classified as the Ultisols (red and reddish brown lateric soils) of the humid subtropic regions.

On the other hand, soils developed in arid climates are not highly leached. Calcium and magnesium carbonates tend to accumulate, and chemical weathering proceeds at a much slower rate. Soils formed under arid conditions often contain excessive quantities of other salts besides carbonates, and are not productive until the amounts of salts are reduced. Land can be desalinated by flooding with water and leaching the salts downward through the soil profile.

Organic Fraction

The organic components of the soil are organisms of any kind—living or dead, plant or animal. The amount and kind of organisms present are influenced by the climate. For example, the climate of an area determines whether grasses or trees predominate, which in turn influence the kind of soil-forming processes.

Vegetation aids soil formation by supplying organic matter in the form of dying and decomposing plants. Grasses decompose into a different kind of organic residue than do conifer trees. Also, the amount of organic matter varies according to the type of vegetation (Fig. 8–3). Peat soils form where reeds, sphagnum moss, and grasses grow. Soils in arid regions normally contain low amounts of organic matter because only desert grasses, shrubs, and cacti grow in these climates. Also, the total biomass of the flora is less in arid desert than in humid regions.

The amount of organic matter in soil is influenced to a large extent by the difference between the accumula-

Fig. 8–3 The organic matter produced from the decomposition of forest litter is different from that produced from prairie grasses. In this example, the forest is not so dense that it excludes grasses, and both types of vegetation are seen and produce both types of organic matter. *Source:* USDA Soil Conservation Service.

tion and decomposition of such material. In cases where decomposition rates are very high, it is not possible for the organic fraction to accumulate. Thus the amount of organic matter is always low. Consider the case where temperatures are high and rainfall or irrigation keeps the soil moist. Under these conditions the rate of decomposition exceeds the rate of accumulation, and organic matter "burns out" faster than it is added. On the other hand, in cold areas or sometimes under anaerobic conditions, decomposition is inhibited and the organic matter accumulates. Many factors affect the rates of accumulation or decomposition, all of which play a role in determining the amount of organic matter present in a given soil at a particular time and location.

The type of root system produced by the different plant species also influences soil formation. Dense fibrous root systems of grasses often lead to permeable soils, such as some of the Mollisols (prairie soils) formed in the central states of the United States and in some areas of the USSR.

Topography influences drainage and runoff. Steep slopes cause erosion because water flows faster downhill, leaving less to percolate into the soil. Erosion in turn affects the speed of the soil-forming processes. Leaching is also either speeded up or retarded by the topography. Soils developed in humid regions of high rainfall and flat topography are often highly leached or waterlogged, depending upon internal drainage. Gentle slopes heavily covered with vegetation slow the water flow and allow more time for water to percolate into the soil, creating a well-defined profile. Rapid surface runoff causes more erosion, and if the vegetation is removed, even deeper gullies are cut into the sloping land (Fig. 8–4).

Topography also affects soil temperature. On the average, temperature decreases 1°C for each 300 m (2°F/1000 ft) of elevation for the first 10 to 15 km (6 to 9 mi) of altitude. Thus an increase in elevation changes the kind and type of vegetation in the soil. Grasses and deciduous trees grow low on the slopes, with coniferous evergreens above them. Still higher, above timberline, little or no vegetation exists.

Hard-to-decompose rocks, such as granite, require millions of years before parent material can accumulate; softer rocks, such as limestone, require less time. Interactions between biological and chemical agents reacting with parent material over long periods of time differentiate the soil into horizons as aging takes place. Soils without well-developed horizons are classified as young soils even though the parent material may have been present for a great many centuries. For example, some desert soils, constantly shifted and transported by wind, are young soils because they lack profile development. Also, silt is often moved along in rivers and deposited, then moved again, leaving little chance for profile development. Such soils remain both pedologically and geologically young no matter how many years they may have been in existence.

As they develop, soils attain well-defined profiles consisting of three principal layers or zones (Fig. 8–5). The surface layer, the A horizon, is often referred to as the **zone of leaching.** It varies in depth and contains most of the plant roots. This leached zone often lacks some of

Fig. 8–4 Sloping topography accelerates rill erosion, which removes topsoil. Constant removal of topsoil exposes the parent material to weathering and more rapid soil formation. *Source:* USDA Soil Conservation Service.

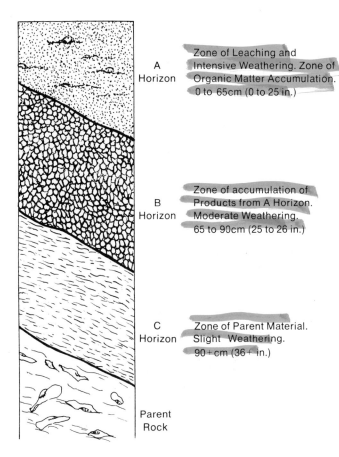

A Horizon	Zone of Leaching and Intensive Weathering. Zone of Organic Matter Accumulation. 0 to 65cm (0 to 25 in.)
B Horizon	Zone of accumulation of Products from A Horizon. Moderate Weathering. 65 to 90cm (25 to 26 in.)
C Horizon	Zone of Parent Material. Slight Weathering. 90+ cm (36+ in.)
Parent Rock	

Fig. 8–5   An idealized soil profile developed by weathering.

tors, the capacity of the soil to support plant life, which in turn influences the kind of vegetation. Topography interacts with vegetation and soil water, among other factors. Temperature interacts with organic matter. The amount of vegetation interacts with topography. Time interacts with parent material differently to yield different soil characteristics. Thus, each factor affects, and is affected by, all the others. It would be difficult to say that any one is more important than the other in soil formation.

PHYSICAL PROPERTIES OF SOIL

Soil Texture

An important physical property of soil is its texture. **Soil texture** is defined as the percentage of sand, silt, and clay of the fine-earth fraction (all mineral particles 2 mm or less in diameter). Soil particles vary in size from large rock fragments (2 mm) to those so small that an electron microscope is needed to observe them (Table 8–1). To measure soil texture, the soil particles are separated into their respective sizes and the percentage in each size category is calculated. One laboratory procedure is known as the Boyoucos method of mechanical analysis *(2, 6)*. When the percentage of any two of the separates is determined, a textural classification can be made with the aid of a soil textural triangle (Fig. 8–6).

the important mineral nutrients, but contains the largest amount of organic matter, both living and dead. The organic matter makes the A horizon permeable and dark-colored.

Below the A horizon is the B horizon, known as the **zone of accumulation** or **alteration.** Plant nutrients, silts, clays, and other materials from the upper layer are leached into and accumulate in this horizon. The color is generally lighter than that of the A horizon, and less organic matter is present (although the roots of deep-rooted plants do reach into the B horizon). The A and B horizons constitute what is known as the root zone, sometimes referred to as the **solium.**

The C horizon consists of unweathered to slightly weathered material, like or unlike that from which the A and B horizons are formed. It can also include accumulated calcium carbonates or other salts.

The factors affecting soil formation are obviously interrelated. Parent material affects, among other fac-

Table 8–1   Classification of Soil Texture According to Particle Size

Particle	Diameter Size (mm)	
	USDA SYSTEM	INTERNATIONAL SYSTEM
Gravel	>2.0	— —
---------------------fine earth---------------------		
Very coarse sand	2.0 –1.0	— —
Coarse sand	1.0 –0.5	2.0 –0.2
Medium sand	0.5 –0.25	— —
Fine sand	0.25–0.10	0.2 –0.02
Very fine sand	0.10–0.05	— —
Silt	0.05–0.002	0.02–0.002
Clay	<0.002	<0.002

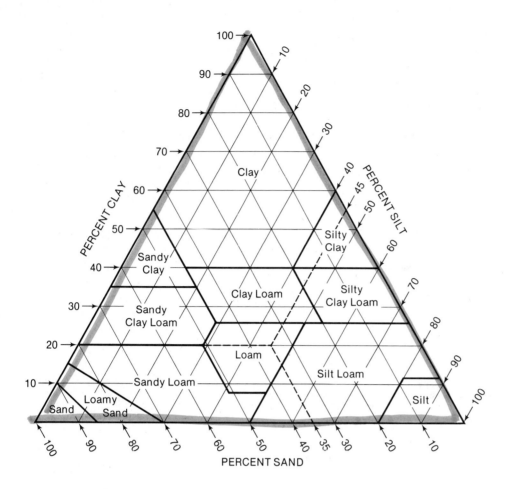

Fig. 8–6 A soil textural triangle. To illustrate how the triangle works, assume that a sample of soil has been analyzed and found to contain 35 percent sand, 20 percent clay, and 45 percent silt. On the triangle, locate the 35 percent value on the sand (bottom) axis and draw a line parallel to the lines in the direction indicated by the arrow. Next, locate either the 20 percent value for clay on the clay axis (left side of triangle) or the 45 percent silt on the silt axis (right side of triangle), and draw another parallel line along either of the two axes in the direction indicated by the respective arrows. The two lines intersect in the loam area of the triangle, thus this soil is classified as a loam. *Source:* USDA.

Soil texture influences many of the soil's properties pertaining to crop production (Table 8–2). The distribution and arrangement of particle sizes determine the ability of soils to hold and transmit water. Soil with a high percentage of sand loses water quickly, retaining little for plant use. Plants growing in these soils will suffer from water deficits sooner after irrigation than those grown in loam or clay soils. Texture also influences soil aeration. Plant roots need oxygen for respiration, and soils with low rates of gaseous diffusion restrict respiration and plant growth. Also, many beneficial soil microorganisms require well-aerated soils.

A soil consisting of a mixture of 40 percent sand, 40 percent silt, and 20 percent clay produces a loam soil

Table 8–2 Some Soil Properties Influenced by Soil Texture

Soil Property	Textural Class		
	SAND	SILT LOAM	CLAY
Aeration	excellent	good	poor
Cation Exchange	low	medium	high
Drainage	excellent	good	poor
Erodibility[a]	easy	moderate	difficult
Permeability[a]	fast	moderate	slow
Temperature (spring)	warms fast	warms moderately	warms slowly
Tillage	easy	moderate	difficult
Water-holding Capacity	low	moderate	high

[a] By water

172

that retains sufficient water for good plant growth and permits its movement without restricting aeration. From the point of view of its texture alone, such a soil would approach an ideal soil.

The soil's **specific heat capacity** is a significant property indirectly influenced by texture. Soil texture, structure, and organic matter content determine the soil's moisture-holding capacity which, in turn, influences its ability to absorb and transmit heat. Because sandy soils dry faster and have larger air spaces than clay soils, sandy soils are more resistant to heat transfer. Water is a better conductor of heat than air. Since sandy soils often contain less water, the surface layers of these soils tend to warm up earlier in the spring than clay soils, giving the farmer the advantage of an earlier crop.

Soil texture can affect soil fertility. A soil high in clay has a higher cation exchange capacity. This reduces leaching losses of positively charged nutrient cations (p. 178).

The ease of tillage (plowing, disking, cultivating) is influenced by soil texture. Sandy or loam soils, at the proper moisture content, are easier to till than clay soils and less energy is required. Root penetration is sometimes restricted in soils of high clay content. Other factors being equal, most crops grow better in loam soils than in either sandy or clay soils.

Soil structure is defined as the arrangement of primary soil particles into secondary units; that is, the manner in which individual primary particles clump and hold together. The kind of soil structure is determined not only by the relative amounts of each primary particle but also by the manner in which these particles are arranged into aggregates.

Descriptive words are used to classify soil structure, for example: prismatic, nutlike, subangular blocky, blocky, columnar, platy, crumb, and granular. These words are based upon the size, shape, character, and appearance of the aggregates (19) (Fig. 8–7).

Unlike soil texture, structure can be changed by mechanical operations. Tilling the soil when its moisture level is slightly lower than field capacity[3] can improve structure, but tillage at moisture contents higher than field capacity, can destroy good structure.

A soil with good structure has soil pores that are large enough to transmit water and air without restriction, yet small enough to retain some water against the

[3]Field capacity is that soil moisture content at which drainage by gravity from the soil profile has ceased for all practical purposes.

Fig. 8–7 Several kinds of soil structure. *A:* Platy. *B:* Prismatic. *C:* Columnar. *D:* Blocky. *E:* Subangular blocky. *F:* Crumb.

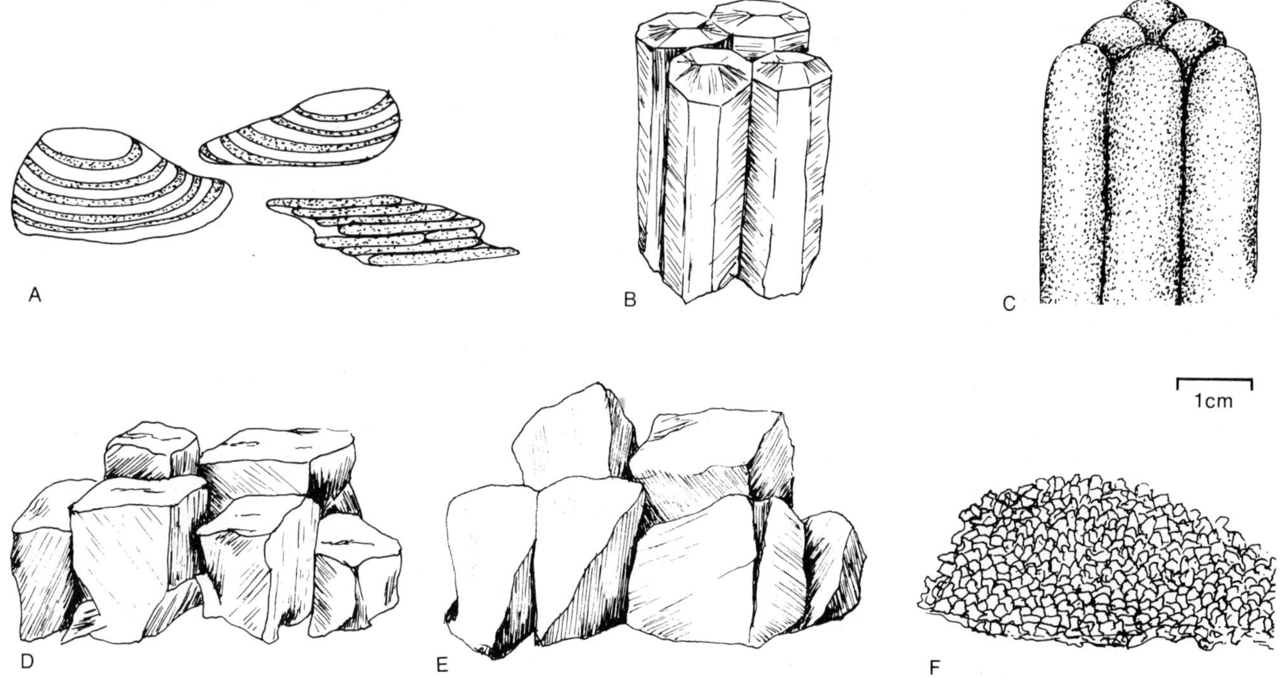

pull of gravity. To form pores of this size requires soil aggregates that are about 1.5 to 6 mm (0.06 to 0.24 in) in diameter *(3)*. Aggregates smaller than this form pores too small to permit adequate drainage, whereas larger aggregates form pores too large to hold much water, even though some is held within the aggregate itself. Good soil structure is necessary for good plant growth and can often be improved by additions of organic matter. Poor soil structure, sometimes brought about by the presence of silt in irrigation water which plugs the pore spaces, results in inadequate water penetration and storage. On the other hand, if excess water accumulates in the soil because of poor structure, plants will suffer from insufficient oxygen and cannot use the soil's mineral nutrients efficiently. Also, reduced soil microflora and microfauna populations resulting from inadequate soil oxygen could reduce soil nitrification and other biological activity (p. 180).

AERATION

Soil pore spaces serve as pathways for the transmission of oxygen (O_2) needed for respiration by plant roots and microorganisms and for the escape of waste carbon dioxide (CO_2). Soil aeration can become limiting when the soil water content is high (the soil pores are filled with water) or when the soil is so compacted that pores are few *(4)*. The relative amounts of oxygen (O_2), nitrogen (N_2), and carbon dioxide (CO_2) vary in the soil. Generally, soil air contains less O_2 but more CO_2 than the above-ground atmosphere. Concentrations of 5 percent CO_2 have been found in the soil air, whereas the atmosphere contains about 0.03 percent. Under flooded conditions, as in rice fields, O_2 contents in the soil are often low. Many plants suffer if O_2 concentrations in the soil atmosphere drop below 10 to 12 percent or if CO_2 concentrations rise above 5 percent *(20)*. Studies have shown that O_2 deficiency in soils causes poor plant growth more frequently than does CO_2 excess.

SOIL COMPACTION

The size of farm equipment has increased considerably in recent years, and it is not uncommon to see heavy tillage equipment make many trips back and forth across the fields. Also, trucks loaded with 10 to 20 MT (9 to 18 t) or more of harvested crops travel over the land. Any of these can seriously compact soil (Fig. 8–8).

Soil compaction is a serious problem, directly related to land preparation, tillage, and particularly to harvesting operations (Fig. 8–9). The term **soil compaction** is difficult to define precisely and often means different

Fig. 8–8 Heavy earthmoving equipment such as this can be a serious problem in creating soil compaction. This trailer when loaded can carry up to 20 MT (19.5 t). This equipment is used to level land for irrigation. *Source: The Daily Democrat.* Woodland–Davis, California.

Fig. 8–9 Seedbed prepared on soils having different degrees of compaction, using normal tillage operations such as plowing, double disking, and harrowing with spike-toothed harrow. Note excessive cloddiness on the moderately and severely compacted soils.

conditions to different people. To growers, a compacted soil is best described as one with abnormally high bulk density and too few or too small pore spaces. Soil is not compacted all at once. The problem develops slowly, worsening each time heavy equipment is used. Often years pass before the problem reveals itself in declining crop yield or quality *(10)*. Research has found no easy or simple solution to the problem, nor is it likely to. But the problem can be recognized and alleviated somewhat through proper soil management and organic matter additions. Soil compaction is especially serious for the fresh market vegetable farmer. To obtain top-quality fresh market produce, vegetables are often harvested when the soil is wet. Farmers in irrigated regions sometimes irrigate until time of harvest to keep plants fresh and turgid, then harvest the crop quickly with heavy equipment. Also, wholesale market prices for fresh vegetables frequently change dramatically from day to day. Thus, if prices are high, growers harvest the crop even though the soil moisture is high and the danger of soil compaction great (Fig. 8–10).

Whenever a soil becomes more compacted, the process is accompanied, among other changes, by an increase in **bulk density.** To measure bulk density, a known volume of soil is obtained in an undisturbed state, then dried in an oven at about 104°C (219°F) until the sample no longer loses weight. The bulk density is calculated by dividing the dried weight by the known volume. Bulk density is also known as the **apparent density.** In simple terms, an increase in bulk density means that the soil becomes more dense.

Compacting the soil causes the particles to be pressed tightly together, reducing pore space and therefore reducing the infiltration rate of water and gaseous diffusion (Figs. 8–11 and 8–12).

Soil compaction impedes root penetration and thereby limits the volume of soil from which plant roots can extract nutrients and water. Indirectly, this can result in nutrient deficiencies, particularly of phosphorus *(9)*.

Soil crusting, a form of soil compaction, appears as a dense, hard layer of varying thickness on the soil

Fig. 8–10 The upper portion of a soil profile showing a compacted layer about 25 to 30 cm (10 to 12 in) below the soil surface. This layer was caused by repeated traffic over the field when soil was wet. Photo was taken soon after a crop of tomatoes was harvested from the field. The previous fall and early winter, the field had been planted to spinach, which was harvested during the rainy season from excessively wet soil.

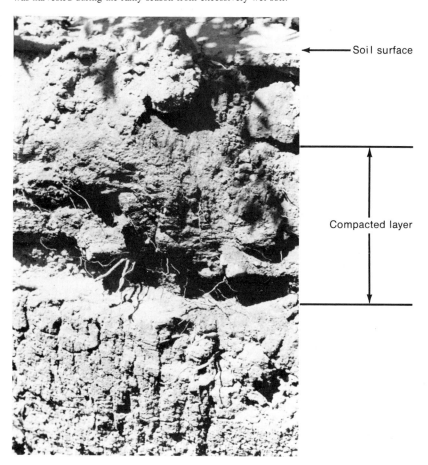

Soil surface

Compacted layer

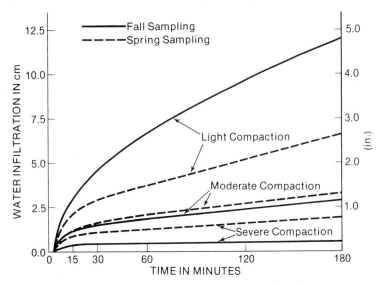

Fig. 8–11 Water infiltration rates were measured on each of three plots mechanically compacted to three densities. Tests were made in the fall after compaction and then repeated the following spring on the lightly, moderately, and severely compacted plots. Obviously, severe compaction decreases the water infiltration rate.

Fig. 8–12 Soil samples taken from the top 10 cm (4 in) of adjacent test plots of a compacted (*right*) and noncompacted (*left*) soil. The photographs are magnified 40 times. Note the greater porosity in noncompacted soil samples.

Fig. 8–13 This 25 percent stand of potato plants resulted from severe soil crusting that prevented and delayed shoot emergence. A loss of this magnitude necessitates redisking and replanting the field. *Source:* University of California Cooperative Extension.

Fig. 8–14 Soil samples from noncompacted and compacted fields were air-dried and screened to simulate tillage. Water was allowed to infiltrate into each for four hours. Note that much more water infiltrated into the noncompacted soil, showing that the ill effects of previous compaction still remained.

surface (Fig. 8–13). Soil crusts result from the action of raindrops or irrigation water, which disperse surface aggregates. Soil crusts restrict seedling emergence, gas exchange, and water infiltration.

In some instances a certain degree of soil compaction is beneficial. Some compaction after seeding assures intimate contact between soil and seeds, enhancing imbibition of soil water by the planted seeds and thus increasing chances of germination. Also, some soil fumigation procedures entail purposeful soil crusting. The crust slows the leaking of the injected toxic gases into the atmosphere and thus makes the fumigation more efficient.

Soil compaction is easier to prevent than to correct (Fig. 8–14). The risk of compaction can be reduced by good soil management. This includes using tillage implements of the lightest possible weight, avoiding unnecessary tillage, keeping equipment off the land when the soil is wet, and incorporating green manure crops or residues into the soil.

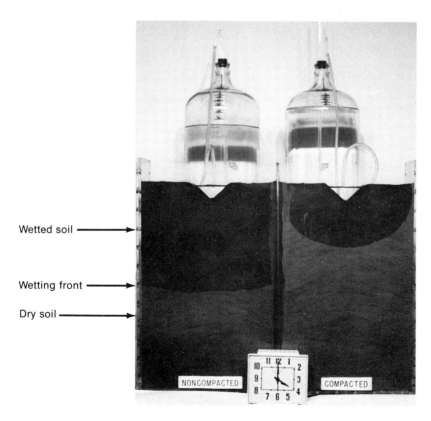

Wetted soil

Wetting front

Dry soil

Effect of Climate

The type of parent material predominately influences the chemical characteristics of young soils. As weathering proceeds, however, soils tend to show the effects of climate, and the resemblance to parent material lessens or disappears. The chemical properties of the soil are determined largely by the colloid-sized (not visible with an ordinary microscope) silicate and aluminosilicate clay minerals.

In the temperate zones, chemical weathering is less intense in arid than humid regions. Soluble salts released by weathering are not lost by leaching from soils in arid regions, and the soil becomes more alkaline—that is, it has higher pH.[4]

In tropical zones, with higher temperature and more rainfall than temperate regions, weathering and leaching is greater. The silicate and aluminosilicate minerals are more decomposed, resulting in soils known as Oxisols[5] (Laterites). These soils contain high concentrations of iron and aluminum, are generally red to reddish brown in color, and are low in cation exchange capacity, fertility, and organic matter. Even though large amounts of vegetation are produced, organic matter is low because dead plant matter is rapidly decomposed by high bacterial activity.

In the cold humid regions, forest vegetation, mainly conifer trees, combine with climatic factors to produce Spodosol (Podzol) soil groups. The silica content of these soils is high in the surface layer in contrast to the iron and aluminum content in the Oxisols. These soils are highly leached and inherently low in plant nutrients. Organic compounds produced by decaying conifer needles form acid solutions that dissolve iron and alumina oxides and basic compounds (Ca and Mg). The ions are leached to lower depths in the soil profile and redeposited there together with some aluminum and dissolved organic matter to produce a compacted layer 60 to 90 cm (2 to 3 ft) below the surface. These soils can be identified by an ashy, bleached white layer immediately above the compacted layer.

[4]$pH = -\log_{10} H_a^+$. In soils, only the active hydrogen ions—those dissociated from the colloids—determine soil pH; hydrogen ions on exchange sites do not. Therefore, it is more descriptive to refer to H_a^+ (hydrogen ion activity) than to $[H^+]$ (hydrogen ion concentration).

[5]Oxisols are true lateritic soils containing mainly oxides. Ultisols are lateritic soils that can be degraded further. They contain some silicates. Ultisols are found in Southeastern United States. Oxisols are found in Hawaii (see Table 8–6).

An important property of clay and of the organic humus fraction of the soil is their ability to attract and hold cations—positively charged ions, some of which are essential plant nutrients. The ability of one cation to replace or be replaced by another is called **cation exchange.** Clay colloids carry thousands of negative charges concentrated at the broken edges of the clay's alumina and silica layers. Thus, a clay colloid acts as a large, highly negatively charged particle (anion) (Fig. 8–15). A soil's capacity to hold cations is called its **cation exchange capacity** (CEC). The CEC is measured in terms of the number of meq[6] per 100 grams of soil. Not all cations are attracted or held with equal energy. The strength of attraction for some cations when present in equivalent amounts is:

$$hydrogen\,(H^+) > calcium\,(Ca^{++}) > magnesium\,(Mg^{++})$$
$$> potassium\,(K^+) > ammonium\,(NH_4^+)$$
$$> sodium\,(Na^+)$$

[6]meq = milliequivalent = 1/1000 of an equivalent. An equivalent is defined as 1 gm atomic weight of hydrogen or any other ion that will react with or replace this amount of hydrogen. When used with CEC, a more descriptive definition of meq is 6.023×10^{23} (Avogadro's number) charges in 1 gm atomic weight of a given cation.

Fig. 8–15 If a soil colloid made up of numerous negatively charged clay micelles is treated with fertilizer containing ammonium cations, the added ammonium cations will replace an equivalent amount of another cation such as calcium on the clay colloid and force Ca^{++} ions into the soil solution.

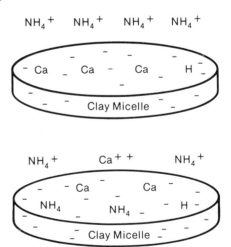

$$Ca\,clay + 4\,NH_4^+ \longrightarrow (NH_4)_2\,clay + Ca^{++} + 2\,NH_4^+$$

The cation exchange capacity depends somewhat on the soil's pH. Other things being equal, the cation exchange capacity is lower in acid soils and higher in alkaline soils.

Soil Acidity and Alkalinity

The acidity or alkalinity of the soil is defined by its pH. Unlike cation exchange capacity, pH is not a fixed characteristic of a soil and, depending on circumstances or conditions, varies over a period of time.

Values for pH vary considerably among soils, ranging from about 4.0 for an acid soil to 10.0 for an alkaline soil (Fig. 8–16).

Plant do not grow well in soils that are either highly acid or alkaline, but within these extremes plants differ in their pH tolerance. Some require an acid soil, while others grow better in an alkaline soil (Table 8–3). Some plants grow best in a neutral soil whereas others grow well over a wide pH range. The availability of some plant nutrients is regulated by the acidity or alkalinity of the soil. For example, in certain acid soils, aluminum solubility increases to toxic levels for some plants. Manganese can reach toxic levels at low pH values, but its availability decreases to deficient levels at high pH values. Iron and zinc become less available to plants as the pH increases, but molybdenum is more available at higher pH levels. Phosphorus is more available at a soil pH of about 6.5 to 7.0 than at either higher or lower values. Calcium, an essential plant nutrient, is also used as a soil amendment to raise the pH.

Soils in climates with high rainfall and humidity generally tend to be acid, while those found in arid climates tend to be alkaline. In wet climates the base elements (sodium, potassium, calcium, and magnesium) are removed from the soil by leaching as well as by the harvesting of crops that have absorbed them. As the base elements are lost, the exchange sites on the clay colloids become occupied with hydrogen ions, making the soil more acid.

Table 8–3 Soil pH Range for Optimum Growth of Selected Plants

4.5 to 5.5	5.5 to 6.5	6.5 to 7.5
azalea	barley	alfalfa
bent grass	bean (snap, lima)	apple
blueberry	Brussels sprout	asparagus
camellia	carrot	beets (sugar, table)
chicory	chrysanthemum	broccoli
cranberry	corn (field, sweet)	cabbage
dandelion	cucumber	cauliflower
endive	eggplant	celery
fennel	fescue	chard
fescue	garlic	hydrangea
gardenia	oats	(flowers become
hydrangea	peas	pink)
(flowers become	pepper	leek
blue)	poinsettia	lettuce (head, Cos)
potato	pumpkin	muskmelon
poverty grass	radish	onion
red top	rye	parsnip
rhododendron	squash	soybean
rhubarb	strawberry	spinach
shallot	timothy	sweet clover
sorrel	tobacco	
sweet potato	tomato	
watermelon	turnip	
	wheat	

Sudden or large changes in pH values do not occur; and relatively large amounts of either acid or alkaline materials and time are required to appreciably change the soil pH, and even more so for fine textured soils. This resistance to pH change is due to a phenomenon called **buffering.**

When necessary or desirable, soil pH can be altered by adding certain materials. The pH of an acid soil can be increased by adding basic amendments or fertilizers containing such elements as calcium, potassium, sodium, or magnesium (Ch. 9). Most often, calcium carbonate ($CaCO_3$), or agricultural lime as it is called, is used. This finely ground limestone is spread evenly over

Fig. 8–16 The pH for many mineral soils ranges from about 4 to 10. The pH range for most agricultural soils lies between 5 and 8.5.

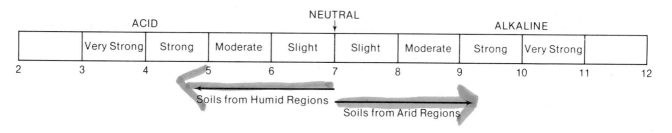

the surface and tilled into the soil (see Fig. 9–36). Estimating the amount of lime required involves several factors, including the soil pH, texture, organic matter content, structure, crops to be grown (Table 8–3), and the fineness of grind (mesh), cost, and method of application.

In arid regions, the soil pH is usually neutral or alkaline. Calcium is abundant, making liming undesirable. More likely, the pH has to be lowered to make iron, manganese, and zinc more available to the plants.

For high-value crops such as houseplants and container-grown ornamentals the soil pH can be lowered by mixing acid-forming organic materials—such as decomposing sawdust, pine needles, shredded tree bark, or peat moss—with the soil. These materials are too expensive and difficult to handle for large areas; therefore, the use of acid-forming chemicals is more feasible. Ferrous sulfate ($FeSO_4$), calcium sulfate ($CaSO_4$), and flowers of sulfur (S) produce sulfuric acid (H_2SO_4) through microbial oxidation and thus acidify the soil. To lower the soil pH in some irrigated areas, a saturated solution of calcium sulfate is allowed to drip into the irrigation water. Calcium sulfate can also be spread over the field in a dry powdered form and incorporated into the soil by tillage.

The prolonged use of chemical fertilizers that are residually acid tends to make the soil more acid: for example, ammonium sulfate [$(NH_4)_2SO_4$], ammonium nitrate (NH_4NO_3), and ferrous sulfate ($FeSO_4$).

Residually basic (alkaline) fertilizers make the soil reaction more alkaline; examples include sodium nitrate ($NaNO_3$), potassium nitrate (KNO_3), calcium nitrate [$Ca(NO_3)_2$], and calcium carbonate ($CaCO_3$).

Saline and Sodic Soils

Saline soils contain unusually large quantities of soluble salts. The soluble salts can be salts of any cation or combination of cations, for example, ammonium (NH_4^+), calcium (Ca^{++}), magnesium (Mg^{++}), iron (Fe^{+++}), potassium (K^+), and sodium (Na^+). Sodic soils differ from saline soils in that a large percentage (over 15 percent) of the total cation exchange sites of the soil are occupied specifically by sodium ions in sodic soils (Table 8–4). Agriculturally, saline and sodic soils are problem soils that require special handling for successful farming. Excessive amounts of soluble salts are harmful to plants and, when cations are predominantly monovalent (with single charge), they have adverse effects on soil structure. Soils can be classified on the basis of the kind and

Table 8–4 Characteristics of Saline and Sodic Soils

Soil	Electrical Conductivity	Exchangeable Sodium	pH
saline	>4 mmhos[a]	<15%	<8.5
saline-sodic	>4 mmhos	>15%	<8.5
nonsaline-sodic	<4 mmhos	>15%	>8.5

[a] mmhos = millimhos or 1/1000 mho, a practical unit of conductance. The mho is the reciprocal of ohm, a unit of resistance.

amount of salts present, as is done in Table 8–4. The salt content, or degree of soil salinity, of the soil is determined by measuring the electrical conductivity of a soil water extract (16).

SOIL ORGANISMS

A microscopic examination of a soil sample reveals a wide variety of animal and plant life, some beneficial and essential to human well-being, and some harmful, often causing problems for people or their livestock or crop plants. The animals include earthworms, gophers, insects, mice, millipedes, mites, moles, nematodes, slugs, snails, sowbugs, and spiders. Plant organisms in the soil include Actinomycetes, algae, bacteria, and fungi. Certain beneficial fungi live in symbiotic associations with plant roots; the fungus/root association is called **mycorrhiza.**

Soil organisms act both chemically and physically. They digest crop residues and other organic matter enzymatically by chemical action. They physically move the residues from one place to another, mixing it with the soil. Earthworms and burrowing animals, for example, mix large quantities of material with the soil mass. The kind and amount of soil organisms depend upon several factors, including climate, vegetation, soil pH, fertility level, temperature, and soil moisture.

Generally, soils in arid regions have different and fewer organisms than grassland soils, and the latter have different and fewer organisms than humid forests. Also, tilled soils usually have fewer organisms than virgin (untilled) land, but exceptions do occur. A well-managed and highly fertilized cultivated soil could contain more and a wider variety of organisms than a virgin soil.

Consider the ways that soil organisms increase crop productivity. Roots of higher plants are a good source of organic matter. Their decomposition produces humic (organic) acids and gluelike materials that bind soil particles together to form the aggregates necessary to good soil structure. Roots open channels in the soil, improving drainage and aeration. Organisms decompose stems, leaves, and other unwanted crop residues.

Nitrogen fixation, sulfur oxidation, and nitrification are processes carried on by soil bacteria essential to higher plants. It used to be common to grow legume crops inoculated with *Rhizobium,* a symbiotic nitrogen-fixing bacterium as a nitrogen source. As the legume crop grew, the bacteria converted unavailable atmospheric nitrogen (N_2) into nitrogenous compounds that the legumes could use and store in nodules on their roots; the plant furnished energy to the bacteria. Such a relationship between two dissimilar organisms living together for mutual benefit is called **symbiosis.** When the legume crop died or was plowed under and decomposed, the nitrogen compounds became the primary source of nitrogen for a succeeding crop.

With the passage of the Rural Electrification Administration Act in 1935 and establishment of the Tennessee Valley Authority (TVA), electric power and natural gas became sufficiently abundant to chemically fix nitrogen into synthetic fertilizers on a large scale. Now, most industrialized nations have synthetically manufactured fertilizers readily available, and they are used heavily as the principal nitrogen source. However, reductions in available energy and natural gas may reverse this trend in the future.

Elemental sulfur is not available to higher plants; it must first be oxidized to the sulfate form. Autotrophic *Thiobacillus* bacteria bring about this transformation through a complicated series of reactions. Under certain conditions, autotrophic bacteria oxidize iron and manganese to compounds that are less soluble and thus less available to plants. The action of these bacteria helps prevent toxic amounts of iron and manganese from being taken up by the plants.

Not all soil organisms are beneficial. Some of the most injurious plant pests are soil borne. For example, nematodes attack and destroy plants in a wide range of species (see Ch. 11). *Phylloxera,* a tiny eellike worm that attacks grape roots, devastated large vineyard areas until resistant rootstock cultivars were developed (see p. 598).

SOIL ORGANIC MATTER

The soil organic matter content has a profound effect on its biological, chemical, and physical properties. Through the decomposition of organic matter, chemical elements become available to crop plants. Organic matter provides food and energy for soil organisms, as they help build good soil structure. All organic matter, except for a small animal fraction, comes from plants. About 90 percent of it by weight is made up of carbon, hydrogen, and oxygen. The remaining 10 percent is sulfur, phosphorus, nitrogen, potassium, calcium, and magnesium plus a minute amount of microelements.

The speed of decomposition of organic matter varies according to the chemical composition, from rapid for simple carbohydrates to slow for fats and lignins. The decomposition reaction is essentially the oxidation of carbon compounds to carbon dioxide, water, and energy (see p. 157).

$$(CH_2O)_n + O_2 \rightarrow CO_2 + H_2O + energy$$

The proteins, fats, and other complex compounds decompose in a multitude of reactions to form amino acids, ammonia, nitrates, phosphates, carbon dioxide, and others. Some ultimately end up as plant nutrients for succeeding crops. After complete decomposition, a complex, amorphous, colloidal substance called **humus** remains that is resistant to further decomposition. This is the material that helps improve soil structure, imparts the dark color to the soil mineral fraction, and increases the soil's water-holding and cation exchange capabilities. For example, the cation exchange capacity of a mineral soil ranges from about 10 to 100 meq per 100 gm while the capacity of humus ranges from above 100 to 300 meq per 100 gm. Being colloidal in size, humus acts similarly to clay colloids in cation exchange reactions, but it is composed chiefly of carbon, hydrogen, and oxygen with small amounts of other elements, while clay colloids consist of aluminum, silicon, and oxygen.

Carbon:Nitrogen Ratio

A widely used practice for improving the physical condition of the soil is to incorporate crop residues, green manure crops, or other organic matter into it. This is a beneficial practice, but one must be aware of the resulting effect it has on the carbon:nitrogen (C:N) ratio. There is a close relationship between the amount of carbon and nitrogen in the soil. Under natural conditions, this ratio is nearly constant at about 12 parts carbon to one part nitrogen, in a given climatic region and on similarly managed soils. Variations seem to correlate with climate, especially temperature and rainfall. For instance, the C:N ratio tends to be smaller (less carbon, more nitrogen) in

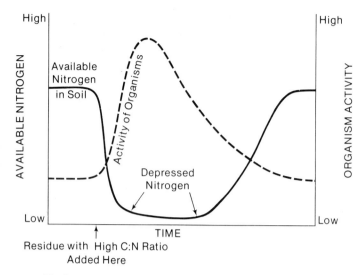

High ┤AVAILABLE NITROGEN

Available Nitrogen in Soil

Activity of Organisms

Depressed Nitrogen

ORGANISM ACTIVITY High

Low ┤ TIME ├ Low

↑ Residue with High C:N Ratio Added Here

Fig. 8–17 The relationship between the available nitrogen in a soil and the activity of soil microorganisms after a heavy application of organic matter with a high C:N ratio.

arid regions than in humid regions if temperatures are comparable. It appears to be smaller in warmer than cooler regions with about the same rainfall.

Suppose that a large quantity of organic residue with a high C:N ratio of 50:1 is incorporated into the soil (Fig. 8–17). For example, incorporating the straw residue from a high-yielding grain crop changes the soil's C:N ratio. Soil organisms, primarily fungi and bacteria, multiply rapidly because of the large source of new food. They also require large amounts of nitrogen (nitrates) for their own growth. These organisms tie up the soil nitrogen, causing a temporary nitrogen deficiency for the growing crop.

With time, the organic residues continue to decompose until the soil organisms exhaust their supply of food and themselves begin to die. The nitrogen from the decomposing organisms is then returned to the soil and made available to crops again at about the original nitrogen level.

Soil Classification

Soils, like plants, are systematically classified for study and identification. In the United States alone there are more than 10,500 soil series and 80,000 phases of the series. The first scientific system of soil classification was developed by the Russian scientist Dokuchaiev [7]. In 1935 C. F. Marbut of the USDA published his concept of soil classification. Marbut's system was modified in 1938, and extensively used until 1965 [5, 15, 17, 18]. The current system of soil classification was developed in a series of stages or approximations. The "seventh approximation" was adopted in 1965 and has since been officially named Soil Taxonomy—A Basic System of Soil Classification for Making and Interpreting Soil Surveys.

This system is constantly being revised as new information is developed and new techniques learned. As with plant classification, most of the names used derive from Latin or Greek. This classification system has six categories: order, suborder, great group, subgroup, family, and series. A phase is a subdivision of a series needed for practical purposes of soil management and mapping. Table 8–5 compares the classification systems for soils and plants.

The new system has two distinct advantages: it emphasizes the soil properties found in the field, and its names have precise, easily understood, and descriptive meanings. Any useful classification must identify, describe, and assign names so that the classification can be understood and have the same meaning for all who use it. Similar properties are assigned to characterize similar soils in the field where they are seen. To do this, the area being classified is sectioned into small, regular three-dimensioned volumes called pedons, from the Greek word meaning "ground." A **pedon** is

Table 8–5 Comparison Between the Botanical Classification of Sugarbeet and the Soil Classification of Yolo Loam

Plant Classification	Soil Classification
Phylum—Spermatophyta	Order—Entisol
Class—Angiospermae	Suborder—Orthents
Subclass—Dicotyledonae	Great Group—Xerorthents
Order—Caryophyllales	Subgroup—Typic Xerorthents
Family—CHENOPODIACEAE	Family—fine silty, mixed, nonacid, thermic
Genus—Beta	Series—Yolo (unit of classification)
Species—vulgaris	Phase[a]—loam

[a] The final official level of classification is the series. The phase is a subdivision used for the practical purposes of soil management and mapping.

the smallest volume of soil that can be practically recognized for the purpose of classification. It ranges from about 1 to 10 m² (0.9 to 11 yd²) on the surface, depending upon the variability of the horizons, and extends in depth to the parent rock or 2 m (1.8 yd), whichever is shallower. A group of contiguous pedons **(polypedon)** is an area of soil with similar characteristics in the landscape and becomes the unit classified by the system. A polypedon is limited in extent by adjoining unlike pedons or by any natural thing that is not soil, such as bodies of water (lakes) or rock formations (cliffs).

Names for the classified soil units are made up of syllables and are often roots of words in modern languages that relate in some way to diagnostic properties of the soil. When you learn the meanings of these formative elements, you can identify many of the soil characteristics from the classification name.

There are ten orders in the present system of soil taxonomy, and the soils are placed in an order based largely on their morphology and genetic formation. The names of all the orders end in the suffix *-sol,* meaning "soil" (Table 8–6). A handbook published by the USDA Soil Conservation Service describes the soil classification in detail *(18).*

Table 8–6   Soil Orders in the Soil Taxonomy System of Classification

Order	Formative Element	Derivation	Definition	Old System Equivalents[a]
Entisol	ent	none	recent	Alluvial, Azonal, some Humic Gley, lithosols
Vertisol	ert	L. *verto*	to turn	Grumusols
Inceptisol	ept	L. *inceptum*	beginning	Ando, Brown forest tundra, Humic Gley, some lithosols
Aridisol	id	L. *aridus*	dry	Desert, Red Desert, Sierozem, Solonchak, some Brown and Reddish Brown Solonetz
Mollisol	ell	L. *mollis*	soft	Chestnut, chernozem, prairie, Rendzinos, Brown forest
Spodosol	od	Gr. *spodos*	wood ash	Podzols, Brown Podzolic, ground water podzols
Alfisol	alf	none		Gray-Brown Podzolic, Non-Calcic Brown, Degraded Chernozems, some Half-bogs
Ultisol	ult	L. *ultimus*	ultimate	Red-yellow Podzols, Reddish-Brown Laterites, some Planosols, and Half-bog soils
Oxisol	ox	Fr. *oxide*	oxide	Laterite soils, Latosols
Histosol	ist	Gr. *histos*	organic	Bogs and some Half-bog soils

[a] Names used in soil classification before adoption of new system in 1965.

SOIL WATER

Characteristics of Water

Water is the universal solvent; it dissolves more substances than any other liquid. It is one of our renewable natural resources, the world's supply of which has not changed but is constantly being recycled. It exists in nature in the solid, liquid, and gaseous states.

The characteristics of water arise from its unique structure. Unlike other liquids, water becomes less dense upon changing from a liquid to solid—ice floats. Were this not true, all lakes, rivers, and oceans would have become frozen long ago and remained so. If water, upon changing from liquid to solid (ice), behaved as other liquids, the ice would not float, but would sink to the bottom of liquid water and remain frozen. Eventually all liquid water would become ice and the summers would not be long enough to melt it.

Water's physical structure also accounts for its remarkable stability. Water is one of nature's most stable compounds, so much so that for centuries it was considered a single element, not the compound it is. The water molecule in fact comprises two hydrogen atoms attached to an oxygen. The water molecule is not symmetrical. This lack of symmetry causes one end of the molecule to have a more positive electrical charge and the opposite end a more negative charge (Fig. 8–18). This phenomenon of polarity creates an attraction between water molecules: the positive end of one molecule attracts the

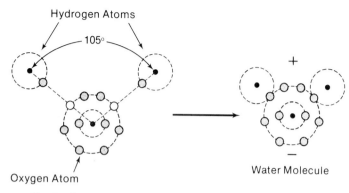

Hydrogen Atoms

105°

Oxygen Atom

+

−

Water Molecule

Fig. 8–18 Two hydrogen atoms join one oxygen atom at an angle of 105°, giving the water molecule an asymmetrical configuration that accounts for many of its unique properties. Note the electrical polarity of the molecule.

negative end of an adjacent molecule. Water molecules can also attract or be attracted by cations, such as Na^+, K^+, and Ca^{++}, or by anions or clay colloids in the soil.

Surface tension is that physical property of water in the liquid state that exists at the surface film due to the intermolecular attraction (hydrogen bonding) between the water molecules. The molecules in the surface film in water are inwardly attracted resulting in a strong surface tension. Were the water's surface tension not so strong, the soil would hold little water, water could not reach the top of a tall tree, and blood would not flow through our bodies. This strength of attraction between water molecules is illustrated by the fact that a steel needle can be floated on the surface of water. In the liquid state, the attraction is chaotic and random but as the liquid freezes, a rigid symmetrical lattice with an open porous structure forms. This arrangement accounts for the reduction in density as the water solidifies. Water also has an unusually high **specific heat**[7].

Uses of Water in the Plant

Water must be absorbed by seeds to initiate the enzyme activity necessary for germination. In addition, water is used in photosynthesis and all other metabolic processes associated with plant growth and development. Plants absorb more water than any other material, most of it entering the plant via the roots from the soil. Much of the water absorbed is not retained, however, but is released to the air as vapor by transpiration. Water transpired through leaf openings (stomata) requires heat to evaporate. Some of the heat comes from the plant's leaf, which tends to lower the temperature around the leaves.

Before nutrient elements can enter the plant roots,

[7]Specific heat is the ratio of the quantity of heat required to raise a body one degree to that required to raise an equal mass of water one degree.

they need to be dissolved in water. Water also functions as a transport system within the plant, moving nutrient materials to the sites where they are converted into products of photosynthesis. It then transports the synthesized materials to sites of storage or use in the plant.

The Energy Concept of Soil Water

Even though water is present in the soil, it sometimes is not available to the plant for reasons that will be discussed later in this chapter (p. 187). Water held by and moving within the soil supplies the plant with mineral nutrients and oxygen, as well as water. It moves through the soil pore spaces in the liquid or vapor state. The pore spaces are always filled with water, air, or a mixture of both. When the pore spaces are filled with water, the soil is said to be **saturated.** Saturation is an unhealthy condition for plants if it lasts long because the oxygen needed for respiration is missing. On the other hand, when the pore spaces are filled mostly with air, the soil is too dry for good plant growth. The number and size of the soil pores vary with the soil's texture and structure. Clay soils have smaller but more numerous pores than sandy soils. Thus, an equal volume of clay soil holds more water than a sandy soil when the pores are filled (Fig. 8–19). The ability of the soil to retain water is called its

Fig. 8–19 Fifty ml of water were added to each column. After one hour, water has drained to the bottom and some dripped out of the sandy soil (*left*), while the water remained in the top half of the clay soil (*right*). Obviously clay soil can hold more water.

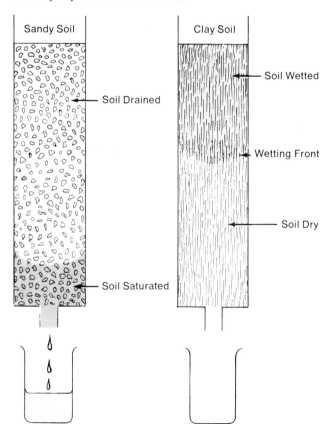

Sandy Soil

Soil Drained

Soil Saturated

Clay Soil

Soil Wetted

Wetting Front

Soil Dry

water-holding capacity. The capacities of different textured soils to hold water are plotted in Figure 8–20.

Three forces—gravity, adhesion, and cohesion—are responsible for water movement within the soil. **Gravity** causes water to move downward under no tension, and is the principal force when a soil is saturated. **Adhesion** is the force of attraction between unlike molecules (soil particles and water). **Cohesion** is the force of attraction between like molecules (water and water). The latter two forces can cause water to move by capillarity in any direction—upward, downward, or laterally—and are the principal forces that move water in an unsaturated soil.

The upward movement of water, called **capillary rise,** is responsible for the loss of water from the soil surface by evaporation. Capillary rise can be demonstrated with one end of a strip of blotting paper inserted partway into water or with capillary tubes (Fig. 8–21).

As soil dries, the water film surrounding each soil particle thins. Consequently, the adhesive and cohesive forces of attraction increase rapidly, making it more difficult for the plant to extract water.

There are two particularly important aspects to consider regarding soil moisture: (1) the quantity of water in the soil in terms of volume or weight—the quantity concept; and (2) the water's availability in terms of **free energy,** the force of attraction between soil particles and water—the energy concept (Fig. 8–22).

The movement and retention of water in the soil, its uptake and movement within the plant, and its transpiration into the atmosphere are responses to changes in energy levels *(11, 12)*. The total free energy comes from three sources: (1) **gravitation,** due to the earth's gravity; (2) **matric,** from the adhesion and cohesion between soil particles and water, resulting in adsorbed water and capillary water; and (3) **osmotic,** caused by dissolved salts in the soil water.

Consider a box with one transparent side, filled with dry soil. A small V-shaped channel simulates an irrigation canal in the soil surface. Water is applied at a constant rate to the soil. The water immediately begins to wet the soil by moving downward through the profile by free energy, the origin of which is the earth's gravity. Directly beneath the channel, all of the air in the pore spaces is displaced by water and the soil becomes saturated. Water movement under these conditions is called **saturated flow.** As water is added to the channel, it also moves slowly laterally as well as moving downward. Gravity does not move water laterally, so a different energy source must be responsible. The lateral movement of water is under the influence of matric energy resulting from the attraction between soil particles and water molecules (cohesive forces). Water moving up-

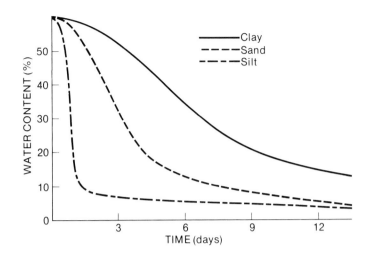

Fig. 8–20 The speed with which soil water moves into or out of a soil is determined by the soil's texture. For example, if a sandy soil (coarse texture), a silt soil (medium texture), and a clay soil (fine texture) are saturated at the same time (t = 0) and if the moisture contents of the three soils are determined and plotted with time, the graph shows that the sandy soil loses moisture very quickly, the silt loses water moderately, and the clay soil loses it slowly. As this indicates, sandy soils have to be irrigated more frequently than silt or clay soils.

Fig. 8–21 Capillary rise. Water ascends in capillaries, reaching higher levels in smaller tubes. Doubling the diameter of the tube doubles the area for the water molecules to adhere to—but it also quadruples the weight of the water to be pulled up. Therefore, water does not rise as high in the columns with larger diameters.

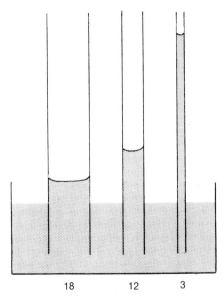

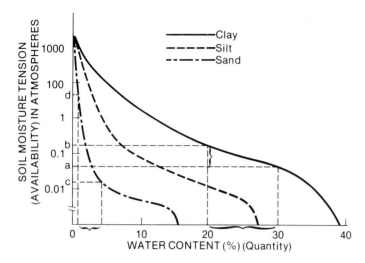

Fig. 8–22 Soil moisture release curves showing relationship between water content (quantity) and soil moisture tension (energy) with three different soil textures. For example, compare the 10 percent loss of water from the clay soil (30 percent–20 percent) and the accompanying slight increase in soil moisture tension (from *a* to *b*), with the 3 percent loss of water from the sandy soil (3 percent–1 percent) and the accompanying large increase in soil moisture tension (from *c* to *d*). A similar analysis can be made on this graph with the same textured soil in different soil moisture ranges. In the wet range (high soil moisture percentage) a large loss of water produces a small increase in soil moisture tension, but in the dry soil moisture range, a small loss of water produces an increase in soil moisture tension that could easily go from wet enough to sustain plant growth to the PWP very quickly.

Fig. 8–23 Effect of osmotic energy. Even though the plants in both beakers started with the same quantity of water, it was not equally available. In beaker *A* salt was added, creating an osmotic pressure too great for the plant to overcome. Since water was limited in its availability, the plant wilted. Beaker *B* contained pure water, which was readily available to the plant.

ward or laterally is doing so under **unsaturated flow** conditions, and the soil pores are filled with some air in addition to water. Salts are present in soil water. The salts create osmotic energy, and if the salts are present in a sufficiently high concentration, the osmotic energy prevents water movement into the plant (Fig. 8–23).

The energy concept is a more realistic approach than the quantity concept. Instruments called tensiometers are used to measure the tension in the soil, providing information useful in determining when to apply irrigation water to a crop. Tensiometers in theory can operate between 0.0 and 1.0 atm, but practically they operate between 0.0 and about 0.8 atm of soil moisture tension (Fig. 8–24).

The free energy is called **tension, suction,** or **negative pressure,** and it is measured in either bars or atmospheres.

After a prolonged rain or irrigation, the air in the soil pores is displaced with water. In this condition the soil is saturated, the soil moisture tension or suction is zero, and no energy is required to remove water from the soil particles (Fig. 8–25). This state will prevail as long as water is applied at a rate equal to the rate of water loss by drainage, by plant use, and evaporation. When no more water is added, losses continue, first from the larger macropores and then from the smaller micropores. Loss of water continues until the adhesive and cohesive

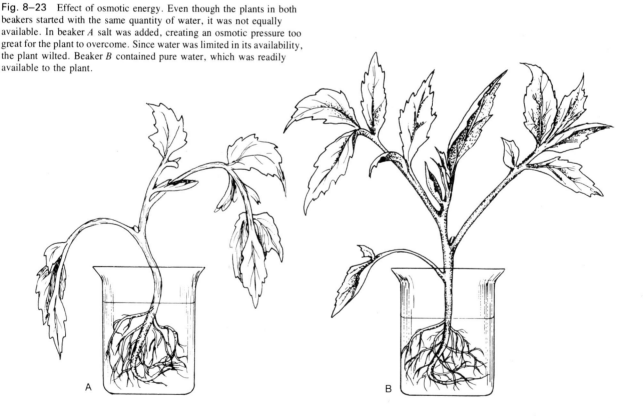

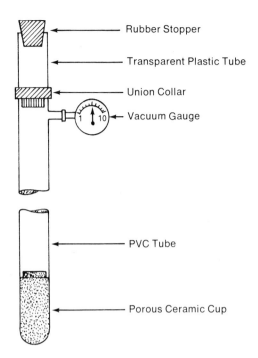

Fig. 8-24 Principal parts of a tensiometer. Before the tensiometer is placed in service, it is completely filled with water. As the soil dries, water is pulled out of the porous cup by the adhesive forces acting between the soil particles and water molecules. This creates a measurable partial vacuum inside the instrument indicated on the vacuum gauge. As the soil is wetted by irrigation, water moves into the instrument and relieves the partial vacuum.

— Rubber Stopper

— Transparent Plastic Tube

— Union Collar

— Vacuum Gauge

— PVC Tube

— Porous Ceramic Cup

Fig. 8-25 *A:* In a saturated soil, all the void spaces are filled with water, indicated by the vertical lines, and the tension (negative pressure) needed to remove it from the soil particles is zero. *B:* As the soil drains, the air:water ratio becomes larger and air occupies some of the void spaces. The tension at field capacity (i.e., when drainage ceases) is about 0.33 atm. *C:* If the soil continues to dry, then the water film becomes so thin that extracting the water requires a tension of 15 atm (15.2 bars). This is more than most plants can exert. Therefore, the plants wilt permanently.

forces equal gravity. This usually takes two to three days in a loam soil. At this moisture content, the soil is said to be at **field capacity.** The water has drained from the macropores but the micropores still contain water, and the soil moisture tension varies from 0.2 to 0.35 atm depending on the soil type. (For most loam soils field capacity is defined as the moisture content at 0.33 atm.) If plants are growing in the soil, water loss continues, and if no water is added, eventually the soil will reach a moisture content that does not sustain plant life and the plants will permanently wilt. The soil moisture content at which a plant wilts (the sunflower is often used as a reference) and cannot recover when placed in an environment of 100 percent relative humidity is termed the **permanent wilting percentage** (Fig. 8-25).

For an average loam soil, the soil moisture tension is about 15 atm, and all macropores and all but the smallest micropores are emptied of water. If the soil moisture depletes further, the soil becomes air dry. In this condition, all liquid water is gone except that held as a thin, tightly bound layer around the soil particles. This adsorbed water is called **hygroscopic water** and the soil moisture tension is far beyond the availability range for plant use. Another form of water, even less available to plants and called the **crystal lattice water,** is held in the soil's crystalline structure. This water can be removed only by applying sufficient heat to destroy the crystalline structure (Fig. 8-26).

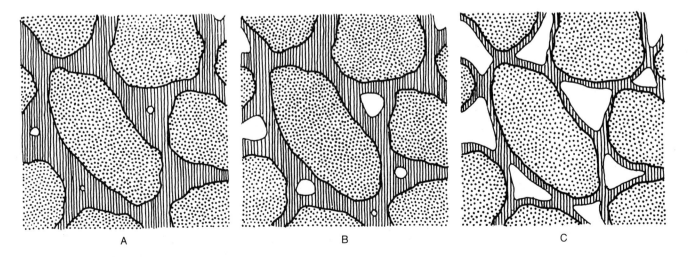

A   B   C

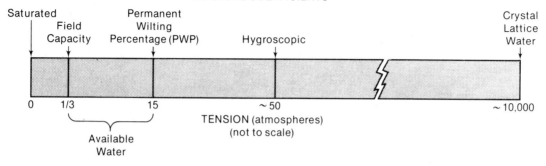

MOISTURE COEFFICIENTS

Fig. 8—26   Relationship between soil moisture tension and the moisture coefficients. Water available to plants is defined as the water between field capacity and PWP.

Farmers are interested mainly in the water available for plant growth. **Available water** (AW) is defined as the soil moisture between field capacity (FC) and the permanent wilting percentage (PWP).

$$AW = FC - PWP$$

Water between FC and saturation is not considered available because it is lost through drainage. Water at tensions greater than PWP (15 atm) is held too tightly by the soil for plants to remove. The definition of AW could imply that the water between FC and PWP is equally available to all plants, but this is not necessarily true. Water near PWP is not as available to most plants as that near field capacity. Also, the PWP is not the same for all plant species. For most irrigated crop plants, a soil moisture tension of between 0.2 and 2 atm in the root zone is best, although some deep-rooted crops grow well at higher tensions (1 to 7 atm).

WATER QUALITY

In evaluating the suitability of land for irrigated agriculture, both the availability and quality of water must be considered. Water used for irrigation always contains measurable quantities of dissolved substances which, in general, are soluble salts. These include small but important amounts of dissolved salts originating from the weathering of parent rocks. The value of water for irrigating crops is determined by the amount and kind of salts present. Problems will arise if the water is of poor quality; then special soil management practices are required to maintain crop growth (1).

Saline Water and Salinity

If irrigation water contains soluble salts in sufficient quantities to accumulate within the root zone and interfere with crop yields, a salinity problem arises. The concentration of salts in the water can increase soil salinity to the point where the osmotic pressure leaves plants unable to extract sufficient water for growth. The plants show much the same symptoms they would in a drought—wilting, reduced growth, and in some plants a color change from bright green to bluish green. The wide range of salt tolerance among agricultural crops permits the use of some saline water for irrigation: water too saline for one crop can be used for a more salt-tolerant crop (1). Table 8–7 gives the salinity tolerances for many crop plants.

Permeability

The presence of specific salts or the absence of any salts in irrigation water can reduce water infiltration rates in the soil enough to affect crop yields. Poor soil permeability adds to cropping difficulties by increasing soil crust formations, which interfere with seedling emergence. Water-logging of surface soil can also occur, increasing diseases, limiting gaseous diffusion, and causing nutritional problems.

The first step in evaluating soil permeability problems is to determine the total amount and kind of soluble salts in the water. Water with low salt content can result in poor soil permeability, just like water with an excessive salt content, because of the high capacity of pure water to dissolve (bring into solution) precipitated calcium and other soluble salts in the soil. The second step is to consider the ratio of the sodium to calcium plus

188

Table 8–7   Percent Yield Decrease of Selected Crops Due to Soil Salinity.
The Higher the Number, the More Resistant the Crop to Soil Salinity.

Crop	Percent Yield Decrease		
	10%	25%	50%
	Soil Salinity (ECe)[a]		
AGRONOMIC CROPS			
Barley[b] *Hordeum vulgare*	10.0 mmhos	13.0 mmhos	18.0 mmhos
Cotton, Upland *Gossypium hirsutum*	9.6	13.0	17.0
Sugarbeet[c] *Beta vulgaris* (Crass Group)	8.7	11.0	15.0
Wheat, common[bd] *Triticum aestivum* (Aestivum Group)	7.4	9.5	13.0
Safflower *Carthamus tinctorius*	6.2	7.6	9.9
Soybean *Glycine max*	5.5	6.2	7.5
Sorghum *Sorghum bicolor*	5.1	7.2	11.0
Groundnut (peanut) *Arachis hypogaea*	3.5	4.1	4.9
Rice (paddy) *Oryza sativa*	3.8	5.1	7.2
Corn, dent *Zea mays* var. *identata*	2.5	3.8	5.9
Flax *Linum usitatissimum*	2.5	3.8	5.9
Beans *Phaseolus vulgaris*	1.5	2.3	3.6
FORAGE CROPS			
Wheat grass, fairway crested *Agropyron cristatum*	9.9	11.0	15.0
Bermuda grass *Cynodon dactylon*	8.5	10.8	14.7
Crested wheat grass *Agropyron cristatum*	6.0	9.8	16.0
Trefoil, birdsfoot *Lotus corniculatus*	6.0	7.5	10.0
Harding grass *Phalaris tuberosa* var. *stenoptera*	5.9	7.9	11.1
Tall fescue *Festuca elatior*	5.8	8.6	13.3
Sudan grass *Sorghum sudanense*	5.1	8.6	14.4
Wildrye, beardless *Elymus triticoides*	4.4	6.9	11.0
Vetch, spring *Vicia sativa*	3.9	5.3	7.6
Trefoil, big *Lotus pedunculatus*	2.8	3.6	4.9
Alfalfa *Medicago sativa*	3.4	5.4	8.8
Lovegrass *Eragrostis* spp.	3.2	5.0	8.0
Clover, berseem *Trifolium alexandrinum*	3.2	5.9	10.3
Orchard grass *Dactylis glomerata*	3.1	5.5	9.6
Meadow foxtail *Alopecurus pratensis*	2.5	4.1	6.7
Clover, alsike, ladino, red, strawberry *Trifolium* spp.	2.3	3.6	5.7

Stock, common *Matthiola incana*	4.0	7.0	—
Rose, hybrid tea *Rosa odorata*	3.5	5.0	7.0
Poinsettia *Euphorbia pulcherrima*	2.5	6.5	12.0
Chrysanthemum *Chrysanthemum × morifolium*	2.0	2.5	8.0
China aster *Callistephus chinensis*	2.0	3.0	5.0
Carnation *Dianthus caryophyllus*	1.5	3.0	10.0
Gladiolus, garden *Gladiolus × hortulanus*	1.5	3.5	7.0
Lily, Easter *Lilium longiflorum*	1.5	2.5	5.0
Geranium, bedding *Pelargonium × hortorum*	1.5	2.5	5.0
African violet, common *Saintpaulia ionantha*	1.5	—	—
Gardenia, common *Gardenia jasminoides*	1.0	1.5	2.5
Azalea *Rhododendron* spp.	1.0	1.5	2.0

FRUIT CROPS

Date palm *Phoenix dactylifera*	6.8	10.9	17.9
Fig *Ficus carica*	3.8	5.5	8.4
Olive *Olea europaea*	3.8	5.5	8.4
Pomegranate *Puncia granatum*	3.8	5.5	8.4
Grape *Vitis spp.*	2.5	4.1	6.7
Grapefruit *Citrus × paradisi*	2.4	3.4	4.9
Orange *Citrus sinensis*	2.3	3.2	4.8
Lemon *Citrus limon*	2.3	3.3	4.8
Apple *Malus pumila*	2.3	3.3	4.8
Pear *Pyrus communis*	2.3	3.3	4.8
Walnut, Persian *Juglans regia*	2.3	3.3	4.8
Peach *Prunus persica*	2.2	2.9	4.1
Apricot *Prunus armeniaca*	2.0	2.6	3.7
Almond *Prunus dulcis [P. amygdalus]*	2.0	2.8	4.1
Plum, common *Prunus domestica*	2.1	2.9	4.3
Blackberry *Rubus* spp.	2.0	2.6	3.8
Boysenberry *Rubus* spp.	2.0	2.6	3.8
Avocado *Persea americana*	1.8	2.5	3.7
Raspberry, European *Rubus idaeus*	1.4	2.1	3.2
Strawberry *Fragaria* spp.	1.3	1.8	2.5

TURFGRASSES			
Sunturf bermuda *Cynodon mogennisii*	7.5	12.5	17.5
Tifway bermuda *Cynodon* hybrid	7.0	11.0	15.5
Ormond bermuda *Cynodon dactylon*	5.0	7.0	13.0
Fescue, meadow *Festuca elatior*	4.0	5.5	7.5
Seaside bent *Agrostis stolonifera* var. *palustris*	3.5	6.0	9.0
Tifgreen bermuda *Cynodon* hybrid	2.5	4.5	17.0
U-3 bermuda *Cynodon dactylon*	2.5	5.0	13.0
Kentucky bluegrass *Poa pratensis*	1.5	4.0	7.5
Bentgrass, colonial *Agrostis tenuis*	1.5	2.5	5.0
VEGETABLE CROPS			
Beets[c] *Beta vulgaris*	5.1	6.8	9.6
Broccoli *Brassica oleraceae* (Italica Group)	3.9	5.5	8.2
Tomato *Lycopersicon lycopersicum*	3.5	5.0	7.6
Cucumber *Cucumis sativus*	3.3	4.4	6.3
Muskmelon *Cucumis melo* (Reticulatus Group)	3.6	5.7	9.1
Spinach *Spinacia oleracea*	3.3	5.3	8.6
Cabbage *Brassica oleracea* (Capitata Group)	2.8	4.4	7.0
Potato, Irish *Solanum tuberosum*	2.5	3.8	5.9
Sweet corn *Zea mays* var. *saccharata*	2.5	3.8	5.9
Sweet potato *Ipomoea batatas*	2.4	3.8	6.0
Pepper, bell *Capsicum annuum* (Grossum Group)	2.2	3.3	5.1
Lettuce, garden *Lactuca sativa*	2.1	3.2	5.2
Radish *Raphanus sativus*	2.0	3.1	5.0
Onion *Allium cepa*	1.8	2.8	4.3
Carrot *Daucus carota*	1.7	2.8	4.6
Beans *Phaseolus vulgaris*	1.5	2.3	3.6

[a] ECe means electrical conductivity of the saturation extract of the soil reported in mmhos/cm at 25 °C. It measures degree of soil salinity. The higher the value, the more saline the soil.

[b] Barley and wheat are less tolerant during germination and seedling stage. ECe should not exceed 4 or 5 mmhos/cm.

[c] Sensitive during germination. ECe should not exceed 3 mmhos/cm for garden beets and sugar beets.

[d] Tolerance data may not apply to new semidwarf cultivars of wheat.

Source: Courtesy of the Food and Agriculture Organization of United Nations, Rome, Italy.

magnesium content [Na:(Ca + Mg)] in the water. Third, the carbonates and bicarbonates are evaluated because they too contribute to soil permeability.

Toxicity

High concentrations of some salts in water are toxic to some plants. The problem occurs when certain specific ions such as boron, chloride, or sodium are taken up by plants from the soil solution in sufficient quantities to reduce yield or stop growth.

Other Related Problems

Various other situations related to salt concentrations in water can arise. For example, excess nitrogen in irrigation water can cause lodging in grain, delay maturity of some fruit and vegetable crops, and increase vegetative growth at the expense of root or tuber growth. Sometimes, calcium, magnesium carbonates, or bicarbonates deposit on the leaves and fruits of orchard crops, grapes, and vegetable crops after sprinkle irrigation. These white deposits, while not particularly harmful, do tend to lower quality by creating an unsightly product.

SUMMARY

Soil is the portion of the earth's crust formed by the chemical and physical weathering of parent rocks. It is a complex and ever-changing body in which water, air, and mineral nutrients are stored. Soil's productive ca-

pacity is determined in part by the interrelationships among the five factors that influence its formation: parent rocks, organic material, topography, climate, and time. The component parts of a soil include the solid mineral, the liquid, the gaseous, and the organic (living and dead) fractions. The soil's characteristics are determined by the ratios of these four components.

The soil acts as a reservoir for the storage and exchange of mineral nutrient elements, a transport system for soil air and soil water, and as a support system to anchor plants. The ability of the soil to perform these functions depends upon its physical properties, one of which is texture. Soil texture is defined as the percentage of sand, silt, and clay in a soil as determined from a sample. Texture is a physical property that cannot be altered by agricultural operations. Structure and porosity, however, can be improved or impaired by tillage operations.

Soil water makes up the liquid fraction of soil and consists of water, dissolved salts, and humic acids. Plants take in more water than any other substance. Cohesive and adhesive forces of attraction between soil particles and water molecules and osmotic tension determine the amount of energy required by the plant to be able to absorb water. Thus soil texture and salt concentration affect the availability of water. The moisture content of a soil after being saturated with water either by rain or irrigation, then completely drained is field capacity. The moisture content of a soil, in which plants wilt and do not recover when placed in an environment of 100 percent relative humidity, is at the permanent wilting point. The soil moisture between field capacity and the permanent wilting point is called available water.

REVIEW QUESTIONS

8–1. A dark soil usually (a) is rich in organic matter, (b) has many fine rock particles, (c) has large rock particles, (d) is rich in air and water, (e) is well aerated.

8–2. The four components of the soil are:
a. _____
b. _____
c. _____
d. _____

8–3. In the A horizon, (a) minerals and clay particles are leached, (b) the leached material accumulates, (c) microbial activity is low, (d) the soil is lighter in color than the C horizon.

8–4. An alkaline soil (a) is high in exchangeable sodium, (b) is high in soluble salts, (c) has a pH greater than 7.0, (d) has a pH less than 7.0.

8–5. The soil acts as a storehouse for materials needed for plant growth. These materials are:
a. _____
b. _____
c. _____

8–6. Soil formation proceeds in two steps or stages. What are they?
a. _____
b. _____

8–7. The five factors influencing soil formation are:
a. _____ b. _____
c. _____ d. _____
e. _____

8–8. Growers of plants expect the soil to perform certain functions to grow good crops. Which of these are the required functions? (a) Store and exchange plant nutrients, (b) act as a reservoir and transport system for air and water, (2) provide anchorage for the plants, (d) all of the above.

8–9. The percentage of sand, silt, and clay in a soil is called its (a) structure, (b) water-holding capacity, (c) texture, (d) nutrient potential, (e) fertility level.

8–10. A silt loam is finer in texture than a clay loam. True or false?

8–11. Clay particles will attract and hold certain ions to their surfaces. These are (a) NO_3^-, (b) NH_4^+, (c) $H_2PO_4^-$, (d) Ca^{++}, (e) K^+, (f) only b, d, and e, (g) none of these, (h) only a and c, (i) a different combination.

8–12. A physical property that can be changed by tillage is (a) structure, (b) texture, (c) exchange capacity, (d) all of these, (e) none of these.

8–13. Irrigation has been practiced for about (a) 100 years, (b) 500 years, (c) 5000 years, (d) 50,000 years.

8–14. Water performs all of the following functions in the plant except (a) providing H^+ for photosyn-

thesis, (b) transporting nutrients, (c) cooling the leaves on hot days, (d) diluting salt concentrations, (e) providing OH^- ions in respiration, (f) initiating enzyme activity in germinating seeds.

8–15. Of all the materials used by plants, water is used in the largest amount. True or false?

8–16. The primary force moving water downward through a soil profile is (a) gravity, (b) pressure differential, (c) osmosis, (d) none of these, (e) all of these.

8–17. The pores of a soil at field capacity are full of water and lack air. True or false?

8–18. Water moving laterally in a soil profile is (a) saturated flow, (b) unsaturated flow, (c) neither of these.

8–19. For a given soil the drier the soil, the higher the tension. True or false?

8–20. To obtain the percent moisture on a dry weight basis, subtract dry weight from wet weight and divide the difference by the dry weight, then multiply the result by 100. True or false?

REFERENCES

1. Ayers, R. S., and D. W. Westcot, eds. 1976. Water quality for agriculture. Irrigation and Drainage Paper 29, pp. 1–96. Rome: FAO.
2. Bouyoucos, G. J. 1928. The hydrometer method for making a very detailed mechanical analysis of soils. *Soil Sci.* 26:233–38.
3. Brady, N. C. 1974. *The nature and properties of soils,* 8th ed. New York: Macmillan.
4. Buckman, H. D., and N. C. Brady. 1960. *The nature and properties of soils.* 6th ed. New York: Macmillan.
5. Cline, M. G. 1949. Basic principles of soil classification. *Soil Sci.* 67:81–91.
6. Day, P. R. 1953. Experimental confirmation of hydrometer theory. *Soil Sci.* 74:181–86.
7. *Encyclopaedia Britannica.* 1965. Soil classification. 20:927–28.
8. Flint, R. F. 1957. *Glacial and pleistocene geology.* New York: John Wiley.
9. Flocker, W. J., J. C. Lingle, and J. A. Vomocil. 1959. Influence of soil compaction on phosphorus absorption by tomato plants from an applied fertilizer. *Soil Sci.* 88:247–50.
10. Flocker, W. J. 1964. Soil compaction—sneaky, progressive, and accumulative. *Crops and Soils* 17(2):14–15.
11. Gardner, W. H. 1962. How water moves in the soil, part I—The basic concept. *Crops and Soils* 15(1):7–9.
12. ———. 1962. How water moves in the soil, part II—In the field. *Crops and Soils* 15(2):9–11.
13. Hambridge, G., ed. 1938. Soils and men. USDA Yearbook. Washington, D.C. U.S. Government Printing Office.
14. Jenny, H. 1941. *Factors of soil formation.* New York: McGraw-Hill.
15. Kellogg, C. E. 1949. Soil classification. *Soil Sci.* 67:77–80.
16. Richards, L. A., ed. 1954. Diagnosis and improvement of saline and alkali soils. USDA Handbook 60. Washington, D.C.: USDA.
17. Soil Survey Staff. 1951. Bureau plant industry, soils, and agricultural engineering. Soil Survey Manual, USDA Handbook 18. Washington, D.C.: USDA.
18. ———. 1975. Soil conservation service. USDA Soil Taxonomy Agr. Handbook 436. Washington, D.C.: USDA.
19. Wildman, W. E., and K. D. Gowans. 1975. Soil physical environment and how it affects plant growth. Univ. of Calif. Div. Agr. Sci. Leaflet 2280.
20. Yamaguchi, M., W. J. Flocker, and F. D. Howard. 1967. Soil atmosphere as influenced by temperature and moisture. *Soil Sci. Soc. Amer. Proc.* 31:164–67.

SUPPLEMENTARY READING

BAVER, L. D., W. H. GARDNER, and W. R. GARDNER. 197 *Soil physics.* 4th ed. New York: John Wiley.

BEAR, F. E. 1965. *Soils in relation to crop growth.* New York: Reinhold.

BLACK, C. A. 1957. *Soil-plant relationships*. New York: John Wiley.

BUCKINGHAM, F. 1975. Controlled traffic can stop compaction of agricultural soils. *Crops and Soils* 27:13–15.

DONAHUE, R. L., R. W. MILLER, and J. C. SHICKLUNA. 1977. *Soils: an introduction to soils and plant growth*. 4th ed. Englewood Cliffs, N.J.: Prentice-Hall.

KELLOGG, C. E. 1941. *The soils that support us*. New York: Macmillan.

———. 1950. *Soil. Plant Agriculture*. Readings from *Scientific American,* selected by Jules Janick, Robert W. Schery, Frank W. Woods, and Vernon W. Ruttan, San Francisco: W. H. Freeman & Company Publishers.

REVELLE, R. 1963. *Water. Plant Agriculture*. Readings from *Scientific American,* selected by Jules Janick, Robert W. Schery, Frank W. Woods, and Vernon W. Ruttan, San Francisco: W. H. Freeman & Company Publishers.

STRANDBERG, J. O., and J. M. WHITE. 1979. Effect of soil compaction on carrot roots. *J. Am. Soc. Hort Sci.* 104:344–49.

THOMPSON, L. M. 1952. *Soils and soil fertility*. New York: McGraw-Hill.

VOORHEES, W. B. 1977. Soil compaction—our newest natural resource. *Crops and Soils* 29:13–15.

Soil and Water Management and Mineral Nutrition

To a large extent, crop productivity is determined by the way the soil is managed. Soil management is the combination of tillage, cropping systems, and soil treatments that either complement or compete with each other. Desirable combinations minimize the objectionable effects of crop production, while poor management leads to low productivity and degrades the soil.

LAND PREPARATION

The purposes of land preparation are to: (1) level the land where needed; (2) incorporate crop residues, green manure, and cover crops; (3) prepare and maintain a seedbed in good **tilth**;[1] (4) help control weeds, diseases, and insects; (5) improve the physical condition of the soil; and (6) to help control erosion where needed.

One of the most striking features of agricultural progress has been the development of tillage procedures and tools. Within one generation, we have gone from hand and horse to machine and tractor. Tillage operations, however, remain a costly item of crop production.

In general, **tillage** is defined as the mechanical manipulation of soil to provide a favorable environment

for crop growth. Tillage is done any time soil conditions permit, with a wide variety of machines and many objectives.

The seedbed should provide seeds with an environment conducive to rapid germination and growth. For most crop plants, such a seedbed is one in which the surface soil is soft, mellow, and free of clods and trashy crop residues (Fig. 9–1). The subsoil is permeable to air and water and has adequate drainage and aeration. It should not be water-logged nor anaerobic (without oxygen).

Plowing

Generally, the first step in seedbed preparation is to plow the land. When large amounts of crop residues are left on the field from a preceding crop, they are often chopped with a disk or a rotary stalk cutter before plowing. Plows invert the soil and cover the trash, but they often leave the soil in large linear lumps that must be reduced in size.

A farmer has the choice between two plow types, the moldboard or the disk plow, each adapted to certain soil characteristics. Moldboard plows, of which there are many variations, range in size from a single moldboard, or bottom, to a gang of plows that turns 12 furrows (12 bottoms) simultaneously. Each moldboard shears and inverts a slice of soil 15 to 20 cm (6 to 8 in) deep and 30 to 45 cm (12 to 18 in) wide as it moves along, leaving the

---

[1]Tilth is the physical condition of the soil in respect to its capability to grow a specific crop. It is the "feel" of the soil—a soil in good tilth "feels good to touch," while one in poor tilth "feels harsh."

195

Fig. 9–1 A well-prepared seedbed for small-seeded crops such as lettuce, carrots, and sorghum (*left*). It should be free from trashiness from last season's crop residues or excess cloddiness (*right*).

Fig. 9–2 A four-bottom moldboard plow turning under a green manure legume crop before planting a grain crop. Note how well the green manure crop is buried. *Source:* Allis-Chalmers.

Fig. 9–3 A five-bottom two-way moldboard plow. This type of moldboard plow is used in irrigated areas to help maintain the soil level. Five moldboards are in the soil turning over a furrow, traveling from left to right, as in this photo. At the end of the field, the plow is rotated so that the moldboards now in the air turn the furrows on the return trip from right to left. This plow turns all furrows in the same direction, eliminating "dead" furrows in the middle of the field. *Source:* Allis-Chalmers.

top of the slice at the bottom of the furrow (Fig. 9–2). Moldboard plows are used when the soil is sufficiently moist to allow the plow to pass through easily but not so wet as to cause the furrow slice to stick to the face of the moldboard. If the soil is either too dry or too wet, excessive power is required and poor plowing results. The ideal moisture content for plowing loam soils is about 2 or 3 percent below field capacity.

Two-way reversible plows (flip-over plows) are used to eliminate "dead" furrows (unfilled furrows). They are also used in hilly areas for contour plowing (p. 218), in irrigated areas where dead furrows hinder irrigation, and in irregularly shaped fields. These plows have right- and lefthand moldboards mounted so that one series plows in one direction, then at the end of the row, the moldboards are mechanically rotated into position so that the second series can plow the return trip (Fig. 9–3). These two-way plows always throw the furrow slice in the same direction irrespective of the direction the plow travels.

Moldboard plows are used on bare fields, small grain stubble, corn stubble, sod pastures, and hay crop fields. The operation can be done in spring, summer, or fall if soil moisture content is satisfactory.

Many farmers prefer to plow in late summer or early fall, especially on small grain stubble fields. Fall plowing allows the clods to "slake" (crumble) because of alternate freezing and thawing in the winter. It also distributes the labor load by moving the plowing from the busier spring season to the fall.

The disk plow (do not confuse with the disk harrow) consists of a series of large disks 60 to 75 cm (24 to

30 in) in diameter that cut into the soil by rotating as the plow moves forward. There can be 3 to 10 or more disks on a plow. These plows are best adapted to dry, hard soils or ones too sticky for a moldboard plow (Fig. 9–4). In other respects, the two types of plow serve the same purpose and accomplish the same results, except that the disk plow generally does not cover crop residues as completely.

Disking

Disk harrows are used to reduce the size of larger soil clods by fracturing them with cleavage and pressure. Disking generally follows plowing, but under some conditions disking can eliminate the need for plowing. If the soil is in good tilth a satisfactory seedbed can be prepared by disking alone.

Disk harrows are general-purpose tillage implements consisting of gangs of concave disks. Most disks have two gangs, one behind the other. In operation, the front gang breaks in the middle into a V-shaped configuration so that the sideway forces will balance each other when half of the gang throws the soil to the right and the other half throws it to the left. The rear gang breaks into a Λ-shaped configuration and throws the soil in the opposite direction (Fig. 9–5). Many larger disks break into operating position by allowing one side of the front gang to break forward while the same side of the rear gang breaks back. This forms a <-shaped configuration (Fig. 9–6).

The depth of penetration is regulated by adjusting the angle of the gangs. The size of the implement varies considerably. Some small tractor-mounted disks cut swaths of 180 cm (6 ft), whereas other units cut swaths up to 12 m (40 ft) wide. A special purpose disk, called a stubble disk, has semicircular notches cut around the periphery of the disk blade (Fig. 9–6). The notches help cut crop residues more effectively.

Harrowing

The function of the harrow is to further reduce the size of soil clods left after disking, to smooth the soil surface, and to do small-scale leveling. Harrowing also kills any small weeds. This operation generally follows disking. In fact, farmers often attach a harrow behind the disk and do both operations simultaneously. This is the final touch to seedbed preparation unless beds are to be formed for irrigated row crops.

Fig. 9–4 The disk plow accomplishes essentially the same objective as the moldboard plow in that it turns over a furrow slice of soil in the preparation of a seedbed. However, the disk plow can operate when soil conditions are either too wet or too dry for the moldboard plow. The disks rotate as the plow moves forward, rolling the furrow slice over. Under soil conditions unfavorable for the moldboard plow, pulling the disk plow requires less energy.

Fig. 9–5 A disk harrow cutting and covering a crop residue for seedbed preparation. *Source:* Allis-Chalmers.

Fig. 9–6 A stubble disk is similar to a disk harrow except that the stubble disk has half-circle notches around the periphery of the disks to help cut dry stubble residues.

Fig. 9–7 A spring-tooth harrow is sometimes used in seedbed preparation. This type is effective in breaking up soil crusts, reducing clod sizes, and killing small weeds. *Source:* Allis-Chalmers.

Fig. 9–8 The shank spacing depth makes considerable difference when loosening compacted soil. These shanks were spaced about 50 cm (20 in) apart, and run about 40 cm (15 in) deep. In this case, however, the shanks were set too shallow. They did not get under the compacted soil layer to break it up. This can create more compaction. Generally, the closer the spacing and sufficient depth, the more effective the soil loosening. *Source:* William E. Wildman.

Fig. 9–9 A row-crop cultivator equipped with shovels to loosen soil and destroy weeds in 12 rows of soybeans simultaneously. The driver cabs in modern-day tractors are often air conditioned and have two-way radio-telephones and stereo tape decks or radios. *Source:* International Harvester.

A wide variety of harrows are used. The principal types are: (1) spike-tooth; (2) spring-tooth (Fig. 9–7); (3) chain or drag; and (4) cultipackers, packers, mulchers, and corrugated rollers. The fourth group crushes clods by applying pressure and tends to break up hard, dry clods better than drag-type harrows. They also pack the soil slightly, reducing large air spaces.

Listing

In some areas, row crops are planted on ridges formed by listers. A lister is a plow equipped with two moldboards that cuts a furrow slice two ways—half to the right and half to the left. This forms a ridge about 20 to 25 cm (8 to 10 in) high and 30 to 40 cm (12 to 14 in) wide at the base. Listers can be equipped with attachments to list, plant, and fertilize in one operation. Some farmers flatten the tops of the ridges with a roller, drag, or bed shaper before planting.

Cultivation

Cultivation is the tillage between seedling emergence and crop harvest. The main reason for cultivating is to control weeds, but other benefits are improved water infiltration, improved soil aeration, the conservation of soil moisture, loosening compacted soils (Fig. 9–8), and in some cases help with insect control. Some farmers claim that cultivation is neither necessary nor beneficial. Certainly, some row crops are cultivated much more frequently and deeper than necessary—a waste of both time and energy.

Cultivating equipment can be divided into three main classes: (1) row-crop cultivators; (2) field cultivators; and (3) rotary hoes.

Row-crop cultivators have variously shaped steel shovels that manipulate the soil (Fig. 9–9). The shovels on most equipment are short, narrow, curved, or pointed. For shallow cultivation, wide, thin, horizontal, knifelike blades are used. In fields where vine weeds appear, disks replace the shovels.

Field cultivators are not designed for row crops. They penetrate deeper than row-crop cultivators and are used on fallow ground or stubble fields to control weeds. These cultivators have longer and stronger shovels or sweeps. Some have spring teeth (Fig. 9–10).

Rotary hoes can be used on crops that are drilled or broadcast planted as well as for row crops. They are especially useful on young crops that are too small for other types of cultivators. Also, they are more efficient when operated at higher speeds than other types. Rotary hoes are made up of gangs of rimless wheels whose

198

Fig. 9-10 A field cultivator (ripper) is used to break up plowsoles or hardpans formed by plowing at the same depth many times. This type of cultivator is particularly useful in semiarid regions where, because of drought and high winds, it is best to leave the soil protected with a covering of plant residue to reduce wind erosion. *Source:* Deere and Company.

Fig. 9-11 A slip plow with the blade beginning to penetrate the soil. After penetration only the frame and the wheels remain visible on the surface, while the blade slips along horizontally well below the soil surface. *Source:* USDA Soil Conservation Service.

Fig. 9-12 A deep-tillage moldboard plow used to bury salts below the root zone. *Source:* USDA Soil Conservation Service.

spokes resemble slightly curved fingers mounted on a horizontal axle. Generally the equipment is made and used in tandem gangs.

Rototillers or rotary plows are used on small plots. Such implements, powered by gasoline engines, have an assembly of rotating knives or tines mounted on a horizontal axle. The small machines cut a swath of from 30 to 75 cm (12 to 30 in) wide, whereas some large models can till a swath 180 cm (6 ft). The knives rotate vertically and cut into the soil on the downward stroke to a depth of about 15 cm (6 in). Rototillers are used for seedbed preparation as well as for cultivation.

Deep Tillage

Some farmers, especially those in the western part of the United States where irrigation is prevalent, use deep tillage to improve problem soils. Extraheavy equipment is used for deep tillage when the soil is dry and before seedbed preparation. One type of implement called a slip plow uses a V-shaped blade that slips along horizontally from 120 to 180 cm (4 to 6 ft) below the soil surface and lifts the soil mass about 15 cm (6 in) as it passes through. This shatters the soil profile and breaks any deep, hard, cemented layers (Fig. 9-11).

Another deep-tillage tool is the deep moldboard plow used to turn a furrow slice 150 cm (5 ft) or more deep. The tool serves to bury surface salts *(25)* (Fig. 9-12).

Another deep-tillage tool is the ripper or deep chisel (Fig. 9-13). This implement consists of one to

Fig. 9-13 One type of deep chisel (ripper) used to break deep, compacted hardpans. This operation is used only when necessary because the power required makes it expensive. *Source:* USDA Soil Conservation Service.

three shanks that penetrate the soil from 60 to 120 cm (2 to 4 ft). It breaks up hardpans best when the soil is dry *(12)*. Unfortunately, some soils become recompacted and the operation needs to be repeated every three to seven years, depending on the nature of the compacted layer.

Deep tillage is expensive, and sometimes it does not materially increase crop yields. In established orchards, it can damage trees by severely cutting the roots.

Minimum Tillage

In many ways, modern tillage methods are similar to those used when horses were the source of power. In those days seedbeds were prepared by plowing, then by disking and harrowing until the clods were broken up, and finally the crop was planted. This procedure required many trips over the land, often causing undesirable soil compaction. Now, the farmer uses large machines powered by heavy tractors that compact the soil at an even faster rate. Much experimentation with less tillage has been done in the Great Plains and in the Corn Belt states of Ohio, Indiana, Illinois, and Wisconsin *(13)*. Several different methods of minimum tillage have been used. For example, increased yields of corn have been attained by planting seeds directly in plowed ground after a single pass with a rotary hoe *(28)*. In another trial, corn seeds were planted in tractor wheel tracks made in plowed ground. In other experiments, no tillage was performed and herbicides were used to kill sod and other undesirable vegetation. In recent years no tillage (Fig. 9–14) has been tried with several test crops and the results compared with crops tilled by usual methods. Reports indicate various degrees of success and failure to improve yields or limit soil compaction *(6, 27, 29)*.

A minimum tillage technique has been successfully used on severely compacted soils in some Australian orchards. The soil was mechanically tilled once, then covered with a thick layer of legume mulch. Angleworms were introduced and their growth encouraged by the decomposition of the mulch. No further traffic was permitted within 10 m (33 ft) of the tree trunks. After two years the angleworms numbered as many as 2000 per m³ (1.3 yds³) of soil. The soil had a network of worm paths, water penetration was high, and soil compaction was much alleviated.

Some researchers have proposed and experimented with setting aside permanent paths within the fields for equipment traffic, leaving crop strips that never receive any traffic. One researcher *(18)* has suggested that two zones are needed for best crop growth—the row zone (area around seed) and the interrow zone (area between rows). He believes that each should be tilled differently and, for some soils, the interrow zone need not be tilled at all if herbicides are used.

In a 1978 no-till test trial at Purdue University, researchers incorporated anhydrous ammonia into the soil in the spring, using an applicator with cutting wheels (colters) adjusted to cut through the residue. Plots receiving anhydrous ammonia plus a nitrification inhibitor yielded 22 percent more corn than those plots not receiving the inhibitor. The inhibitor prevented some nitrogen losses.

Not all minimum tillage results have been favorable. In some cases, yields of corn have been reduced and in others, little or no difference was observed *(5, 17)*. Even though the yield differences may be small between normal and minimum tillage, the saving in reduced fuel and machinery costs could be appreciable. An added benefit could also be the improved physical condition of the soil.

Land Leveling

Irrigated land generally needs to be leveled, especially if row crops are grown. Exceptions do occur; for example, some vineyards, orchards, and some high-value vegetables are grown on rolling land in contoured rows² (Fig. 9–15) with sprinkler or drip irrigation.

Land is leveled to permit water to flow and spread evenly over the soil surface without causing erosion. In considering the land's suitability for leveling, the land's productive capacity and the method of irrigation to be

Fig. 9–14 A 12-row planter planting corn directly into an alfalfa field with no previous land preparation (No-Til). *Source:* Allis-Chalmers.

---

²Contoured rows put each plant in the row at the same elevation as other plants in the same row.

Fig. 9–15 A field of rice ready to be planted. The levees follow contour lines to allow equal water depth over each paddy. *Source:* USDA Soil Conservation Service.

used are evaluated. Features that render a site unsuitable include: (1) excessively permeable soil, (2) soil that is very shallow, (3) rough topography (excessive grading will be needed), and (4) poor drainage.

If leveling the land is feasible, three alternatives are possible: (1) a civil engineer can be chosen to survey and calculate the grade while a contractor actually moves the earth; (2) a contractor can do the entire job; or (3) the farmer can do it all. In any case, heavy equipment will be needed (Fig. 9–16). Timing is important. Land should not be leveled in the rainy season because leveling is injurious to wet soil *(14, 19)*.

Fig. 9–16 A land plane is used to plane the land and make the final precision land leveling to the desired grade, in some cases 10 cm fall per 100 m run (0.1 ft/100 ft). *Source: The Daily Democrat.* Woodland–Davis, California.

To grow some crops, the soil has to be fumigated before seedbed preparation. These are high-value crops with a potential for pest damage severe enough to justify the cost of treatment. Fumigation normally is much too expensive to use extensively on most row or field crops. Certain chemicals are used to fumigate soil and destroy harmful bacteria, fungi, and nematodes as well as many weed seeds. The most widely used soil fumigant is methyl bromide (CH_3Br), a colorless, odorless, and potently toxic gas, which is usually mixed with chloropicrin (tear gas). Chloropicrin can be used to indicate the presence of the toxic CH_3Br because it is nontoxic in small amounts but it causes great discomfort to the eyes of people and animals.

Nurserymen often prefer to use steam instead of chemicals to ''partially sterilize,'' or pasteurize, their soil *(1)*. A closed container with some means of admitting live steam is used. The temperature at the center of the soil mass is brought to about 71°C (160°F) for 30 minutes to destroy disease-causing organisms. Some nurseries use aerated steam at about 60°C (140°F) for 30 minutes to do the same job. An easy test for the proper temperature is to cook a medium-size potato in the center of the soil (see p. 580). When the potato is properly cooked, the soil is properly pasteurized.

IRRIGATION

Farmers have irrigated crops for over 4000 years; thus, it was as old an art to the farmers in Christ's time as the practices of 2000 years ago seem to us today. Records indicate that crops were irrigated along the Nile, Ganges, Tigris, and Euphrates rivers as early as 2600 B.C. It has been suggested that crop irrigation contributed to the founding of the great civilizations in these areas *(9)*. It is interesting to note that early civilizations began along the rivers in arid or semiarid regions. Irrigation canals over 1000 years old have been found along the Gila River in Arizona. But, even more amazing, while irrigation has been practiced so long, modern practices date back less than 200 years, and even today farmers in many parts of the world lift water by treadmills or water screws.

The importance of irrigation is evident when precipitation patterns over the earth's total land area are considered. Seventy-five percent of the total land is semiarid to arid and receives, on the average, less than 50 cm (20 in) of rainfall annually; 20 percent receives less than 25 cm (10 in).

By the end of the twentieth century, the total irrigated area in the world will have more than tripled since 1900. Most of the increases have occurred in China, India, Pakistan, United States, and the Soviet Union. The expansion of water management and irrigation is illustrated by the increased number of plans and proposals executed since the 1950s. China has built no fewer than 46 dams, and India has almost doubled its irrigated acreage. Ambitious programs are in progress in many parts of the world, including Africa, Pakistan, Spain, Australia, Italy, and the United States *(11)*.

After completion of the Aswan High Dam in Egypt in 1967, the Nile River was no longer permitted to flood its banks. While this project permitted reclamation of large areas of desert, the settling of fertile silt in Lake Nasser removes plant nutrients that formerly were responsible for the creation of the fertile Nile Delta. Also, with irrigation water being available to Egyptian farmers upon demand at any time now instead of annually as before the High Dam, double and triple cropping is the common practice. This is causing a multitude of soil problems such as salinity and high water tables.

In 1957 a California water plan was adopted to better control, conserve, and utilize the state's water supplies. The plan provides for storage and transportation of water from water-rich northern California to water-deficient areas to the south through a system of aqueducts on both sides of the Central Valley (Fig. 9–17). That state is planning ahead to the distribution and management of its water resources through the year 2000 *(31)*.

Amount and Measurement

Water requirements vary widely among different crops, climates, seasons, soil conditions, and methods of applications. In areas where 30 cm (12 in) of rain falls during the growing season, an average of about 40 cm (16 in) of supplemental irrigation water is needed. If rainfall is less than 25 cm (10 in), then 100 to 175 cm (40 to 70 in) could be needed. Best results are obtained when the water requirements of the crop grown in a given area and climate are determined first, then the soil moisture content monitored so that the proper amount of water can be applied to insure an adequate supply of available water *(15, 22)*.

Methods of Application

Selection of the proper water distribution system can save expensive labor and assure better crop yields as well as saving water.

The method of application is important, especially if the cost of water is high. Some factors that determine the method and type of system used are: (1) climate, (2) type of crop, (3) cost of water, (4) slope of field, (5) physical properties of soil, (6) water quality, (7) water availability, (8) drainage capability, and (9) salinity or other problems *(25)*.

BORDER OR FLOOD METHOD

Flood irrigation is used where the topography is flat and level. This method is often used for drilled or broadcast crops, such as hay, pasture, and small cereal grains. Orchards and vineyards are also sometimes flood irrigated (Fig. 9–18).

The land must be graded and leveled for flood irrigation. The amount of grading needed depends upon the

Fig. 9–17 The Tehama-Colusa Canal is a part of the water transport system through which water from northern California flows down the west side of the Central Valley to southern California.

Fig. 9–18 An orchard irrigated by flooding. The levees are contoured, causing the water between the levees to be the same depth over the entire field. This provides even water distribution and uniform water penetration into the root zone. In an older orchard the root zone could be 2 or more m (6 or more ft) in depth. *Source:* USDA Soil Conservation Service.

topography, cropping system, and cost of grading. A uniform downslope of 0.1 to 0.4 percent[3] is used for most soils and crops, with little or no cross-field slope. Permanent or temporary levees are constructed running downslope, with a border disk forming ridges that divide the field into strips or checks, preferably not over 10 to 20 meters (33 to 66 ft) wide and 90 to 300 meters (295 to 990 ft) long.

Water from an irrigation pump or canal is turned into the supply, or head, ditch at the higher end of the field. It is released or siphoned into one or more checks and allowed to flow slowly downslope, spreading evenly and uniformly over each entire check as it advances toward the lower end. Ponding, excessive percolation, and inadequate wetting of the soil in different areas in the field should be avoided. Designing and operating such a system efficiently requires considerable experience, skill, and knowledge *(20)*.

FURROW IRRIGATION

Furrow irrigation is a modification of flooding—water is confined to furrows rather than wide checks. Water is used more efficiently with furrows than with flooding because the entire surface is not wetted, thus reducing evaporation losses.

Furrow irrigation is frequently used for row crops, orchards, and vineyards. The length of furrow varies from 30 m (100 ft) for small gardens to 450 m (1500 ft) for field crops, but lengths of 90 to 180 m (300 to 600 ft) are more common. Long furrows cause greater loss of water because of deep percolation and excessive soil erosion at the head of the field.

Furrow spacing is determined by the plant row spacing. One irrigation furrow is generally provided for each crop row (Figs. 9–19, 9–20). The furrow spacing can be 60 to 180 cm (2 to 6 ft), depending upon the type of crop and wetting characteristics of the soil *(20)*.

The depth of the furrow should be such that the water can be controlled. Water should flow in the furrow for sufficient time to allow it to percolate across the bed, wetting the surface but not leaving the plant standing in water. For most row crops and orchards, furrows from 20 to 30 cm (8 to 12 in) deep provide the necessary control. Furrows from 10 to 15 cm (4 to 6 in) in depth are better for small-seed crops.

Uniform crop maturity, necessary for mechanical harvesting, is easier to achieve with furrow than with flood irrigation (Fig. 9–21).

---

[3]A 0.1 percent downslope drops 0.1 meter in elevation for each 100 m of field length (0.1 ft/100 ft).

Fig. 9–19   Strawberries grown on beds covered with transparent polyethylene are furrow irrigated with water brought to the field through aluminum pipe.

Fig. 9–20   Newly seeded canning tomatoes being furrow irrigated. Two rows of plants about 40 to 45 cm (15 to 18 in) apart are grown on a single bed. The beds are 150 cm (5 ft) apart. To keep water close to the young seedlings, two irrigation furrows (*A*) are placed between each bed and close to the seeded rows. Later, as the plants get larger, a single irrigation furrow is formed at *B* between each bed by plowing the soil in the center toward the sides, filling up furrows at *A*. This technique of two-row planting per bed instead of the former single row has nearly doubled tomato yields. *Source:* William L. Sims.

Fig. 9–21   A field of tomatoes almost ready for harvest is being furrow irrigated with water brought to the field in an open ditch, then siphoned over the levee bank into the field with aluminum siphons. The water level in the ditch must be higher than that in the field. *Source: The Daily Democrat.* Woodland–Davis, California.

SPRINKLER IRRIGATION

Sprinklers are often used when flood or furrow irrigation is impractical. Sprinklers are selected over other irrigation methods because of: (1) excessively high or low soil permeability; (2) germination rate of small-seed crops; (3) the crop's need for cultivation; (4) soil topography; and (5) water costs. Sprinklers are sometimes used for frost control also.

Less labor is needed with sprinklers than either flood or furrow irrigation but the equipment and energy costs are higher. A line pressure of 3 to 4 kg per cm^2 (40 to 60 lbs/in^2) is needed to operate them.

Sprinkling requires less skill on the part of the irrigator. A properly engineered system offers the surest method of applying water. It can be used on sloping land with grades up to 3 percent.

There are several different types of sprinklers, each with certain advantages.

The **permanent set** type has all lines buried below the surface. Because of the high investment cost, this type of system is usually restricted to orchards, vineyards, high-value crops, or recreational facilities *(21)* (Fig. 9–22).

The **hand set** was the first type of sprinkler system developed. The main lines are either buried or portable. This system is used on many crops but is particularly useful for germinating small-seed crops, especially if the seedbed is rough. One disadvantage of the hand set system is the added labor required to move the lateral lines as each set is completed. The main line is located at the edge of the field and the laterals can be set either parallel or perpendicular to the furrows.

Fig. 9–23 A wheel line system of sprinkler irrigation is being used on this field of alfalfa. *Source: The Daily Democrat.* Woodland–Davis, California.

The **wheel line** system was designed to reduce labor by moving pipe across the field with a small gasoline engine instead of by hand. The lateral that carries the water is mounted on wheels spaced about 6 m (20 ft) apart. The lateral pipe, which also acts as the axle, can be up to 300 meters (985 ft) in length. The sprinklers are mounted in the lateral and another set is often dragged behind the line. To move to the next position, the gasoline engine turns the axle and propels the entire line across the field, saving labor and time (Fig. 9–23).

The **center pivot** system is another labor-saving variation of sprinkler irrigation. It is used extensively on the sandy soils in Nebraska, Kansas, Texas, Georgia, and the Columbia River Basin. The system is used more often in areas where land values are low or the availability of labor low. The line, mounted on wheels driven by water pressure or electric motors, pivots around a fixed point at one end of a circular path (Fig. 9–24). One disadvantage of the system is that the circular irrigation pattern leaves the corners in rectangular fields unirrigated (Fig. 9–25). In some areas where land and crop values justify the added costs, the system is

Fig. 9–22 It would be impractical to use methods other than sprinkling for irrigating this permanent pasture because of the uneven topography. This is a permanent set type of sprinkler system similar to those used for golf courses and athletic fields. *Source:* USDA Soil Conservation Service.

Fig. 9–24 A field sprinkle irrigated with the center pivot system. The sprinklers are rotated in a circular path around a central focal point, either by water pressure or gasoline engines. *Source:* Valmont Industries.

Fig. 9–25 Aerial view of grain fields in Nebraska being sprinkled by a center pivot system. The white radius liners are the sprinklers. By modifying this equipment, the corners of rectangular fields can be irrigated. *Source:* Valmont Industries.

modified by adding sprinklers that fold out as the corners of the field are approached, then close back as the line moves past the corner. Sometimes the corners are irrigated with a permanently buried auxiliary line of sprinklers, again increasing equipment costs.

The **hose drag** system is another variation for moving the sprinkler line mechanically. A tractor attached to one end of the flexible line drags it from place to place. This system is used mainly in orchards (Fig. 9–26).

Fig. 9–26 A citrus orchard sprinkle irrigated with a drag line system. The line is mounted on small wheels so that a tractor can be attached at one end to pull the entire line to a new location. This is a labor-saving arrangement. *Source:* University of California Cooperative Extension.

DRIP IRRIGATION

Drip or trickle irrigation is the latest development in irrigation systems. Small amounts of water are allowed to trickle slowly into the soil through mechanical devices called emitters, wetting the soil without runoff (Fig. 9–27). The emission rate of water ranges from about 2 to 8 l per hr (0.5 to 2 gal/hr).

Emitters are connected to a small plastic lateral tube, laid either on the soil surface or buried just beneath it for protection. The lateral lines are connected to a buried main line that receives water from a head source. The head source is the control station for the system. Here the water is filtered, treated with fertilizers, and regulated for pressure and timing of application. Some advantages of drip irrigation are: (1) smaller lines than for spinkler or furrow irrigation, (2) little interference with orchard cultural operations because much of the soil surface is not wetted, (3) less fluctuation of soil moisture because of the constant and slow drip application of water, and (4) less water needed to grow a crop. The area of wetted soil can be as little as 10 percent of the total area of newly planted tree crops or up to 60 percent of the area of a mature crop. The amount of soil wetted depends on the soil's physical properties, the time of application, and the number of emitters used. Some objections are: (1) the expensive filtration equipment needed because emitters clog frequently; (2) uneven water distribution on hilly land—more water from lower emitters, less from higher ones; (3) salts tend to concentrate on the soil surface because little water is moving downward to keep them washed from the root zone; and (4) the foraging ability of roots is restricted to the small volume of wetted soil *(3, 4, 23)*.

Fig. 9–27 One type of water emitter used in drip irrigation. The tiny plastic tubing is attached to a larger plastic tube from which the emitter receives the water. The number of emitters depends on the type and size of crop irrigated.

Fig. 9–28 A five-year-old peach orchard is drip-irrigated with emitters placed around each tree. Only the soil around the root area receives water. As the trees grow and enlarge their root systems, more emitters are added to wet a larger volume of soil.

Drip irrigation does not fit the needs of every crop or situation, but it is being used more each year—by orchardists, strawberry growers, ornamental nurseries, and some growers of high-value field crops (Fig. 9–28).

MINERAL NUTRITION

Fertilizers have probably increased crop yields and reduced hunger more than any other single agricultural practice. From 1940 to 1970, the use of commercial fertilizers increased eightfold in the United States. In other developed countries the increase has been about sixfold. Fertilizers, both natural and synthetic, are said to be the safeguard against starvation. In those areas where fertilizers are not used, famines are commonplace.

In addition to supplying nutrients to crops to increase yields, fertilizers can also cause marked changes in soil characteristics, some beneficial, some not. These secondary influences play an important role in the choice of fertilizer.

Sixteen chemical elements are known to be essential for the growth of most plants, and a few others are used by some plants under certain conditions. The essen-

tial elements are carbon (C), hydrogen (H), oxygen (O), nitrogen (N), phosphorus (P), potassium (K), calcium (Ca), magnesium (Mg), sulfur (S), iron (Fe), manganese (Mn), molybdenum (Mo), copper (Cu), boron (B), zinc (Zn), and chlorine (Cl) (10). Some halophytes (plants that require salts) have been shown to need sodium (8), and some microorganisms that fix nitrogen symbiotically or nonsymbiotically need cobalt (16).

Mineral nutrients are divided into groups according to the quantity plants use. The primary **macronutrients**—mineral nutrients used in largest amounts—are nitrogen, phosphorus, and potassium; the **secondary** mineral nutrients—used in lesser amounts than primary—are calcium, magnesium, and sulfur; and the remaining used in the smallest amounts are the **micronutrients**. Carbon, hydrogen, and oxygen are not mineral nutrients but they are essential elements.

Mineral nutrients are supplied to the soil by applying crop residues, animal manures, synthetic chemical fertilizers, or natural minerals. Other sources are the atmosphere, irrigation water, rainfall, and the solution of soil minerals. The source is unimportant to the plant so long as the mineral nutrients are available in sufficient quantity and can be easily assimilated (24). Nutrients are removed when any part of a crop is taken. Putting the residue of the removed part back in the soil does not replace all of the removed nutrients. To maintain the original fertility, nutrients must be added in one form or another in amounts equal to those removed by crop harvest (Figs. 9–29, 9–30). Generally, commercial fertiliz-

Fig. 9–29 Increasing amounts of fertilizer are being applied by air. Large areas of range land not readily accessible by other equipment, water-covered rice paddies, and large areas of land seeded to cereal grains are particularly suitable for aerial application of fertilizers and other chemicals. *Source:* Fred Meyer, National Fertilizer Development Center, Tenn. Valley Auth.

Fig. 9–30 Broadcasting a dry fertilizer to a harvested grain field in preparation for plowing. This kind of application is referred to by some farmers as a ''plow-down'' application. It could contain the entire fertilizer application or a portion of it, the remainder to be applied as a side-dressing after the crop emerges. *Source:* Fred Meyer, National Fertilizer Development Center, Tenn. Valley Auth.

ers are easier to apply and more satisfactory than manures and crop residues, but the latter two should not be disregarded. They are especially beneficial in adding organic matter to help improve soil structure.

A complete fertilizer contains the three primary nutrients: nitrogen, phosphorus, and potassium. It may also contain some secondary or micronutrients. Each bag of commercial fertilizer carries a label stating the analysis of its contents. This analysis is represented by three figures; for example, 5–10–5. The first figure is the percentage nitrogen by weight; in this case, 5 kg of nitrogen per 100 kg (5 lbs/100 lbs) of fertilizer. The second figure represents phosphorus, specifically 10 percent phosphoric acid (P_2O_5); the third figure is potassium, specifically 5 percent potash (K_2O).[4] Thus one ton of a 5–10–5 fertilizer contains 50 kg (110 lbs) of nitrogen, 100 kg (220 lbs) of phosphoric acid (P_2O_5), and 50 kg (110 lbs) of potash (K_2O), a total of 200 kg (440 lbs) of nutrients. The remaining 800 kg (1764 lbs) consists of other chemicals in the formulation or of filler.

While the label on the bag states the percentage of each primary nutrient, it does not indicate the compounds used to make up the fertilizer. The formulation is important because it informs the user of what compounds are used and their chemical form. It indicates the fertilizer's nutrient availability, effect on soil pH, ease of incorporating into the soil, and freedom from caking.

[4] % P = % P_2O_5 × 0.43
% K = % K_2O × 0.83
% P_2O_5 = % P × 2.29
% K_2O = % K × 1.21

Elemental nitrogen (a gas) cannot be used to formulate a fertilizer; it must be combined with other chemical elements. These elements determine the value of the fertilizer to the grower for a particular use.

Assume that nitrogen in the form of ammonium sulfate ($(NH_4)_2SO_4$), phosphoric acid as monocalcium diphosphate [$Ca(H_2PO_4)_2$], and potash as potassium chloride (KCl) are used to formulate a complete fertilizer. Their atomic weights are used to calculate the weight of each ingredient needed to supply the proper amount of nutrients. We find that it requires 238, 165, and 79 kg/MT (476, 329, 158 lb/t) of ammonium sulfate, calcium dihydrogen phosphate, and potassium chloride, respectively, to obtain a fertilizer with 5–10–5 percent of N, P_2O_5, K_2O. The three constituents total 482 kg/MT (963 lb/t). The balance needed to make up the weight is ''filler.'' The filler most often used is dolomitic limestone or gypsum, but other materials can be used.

Fertilizer recommendations are often given as a ratio. A ratio differs from an analysis in that it expresses the amount of one nutrient in relation to the other. For example, the analysis of the fertilizer above was 5–10–5, but the ratio is 1:2:1; that is, for each part of nitrogen by weight there are two parts phosphoric acid and one part potash.

The fertilizer's physical properties are worthy of consideration because a lumpy or caked fertilizer is difficult to apply evenly (Fig. 9–31). Some constituents, such as ammonium nitrate (NH_4NO_3), calcium nitrate [$Ca(NO_3)_2$], sodium nitrate ($NaNO_3$), and urea [$CO(NH_2)_2$] absorb water from the air (i.e., they are hygroscopic) and thus must be protected from moisture. They are packaged in moisture-proof bags, and often a conditioning material is added to decrease moisture absorption and caking.

Fig. 9–31 It is a common practice to spray fertilizers directly onto the leaves of some crop plants. These foliar applications may contain primary, secondary, or micronutrients. *Source:* Fred Meyer, National Fertilizer Development Center, Tenn. Valley Auth.

NITROGEN

In the past, farmers "grew" most of their nitrogen fertilizer; that is, they plowed under legume crops that had been inoculated with bacteria *(Rhizobium)* to fix atmospheric nitrogen biologically. This is still done to some extent in many areas today. Electrolysis of atmospheric nitrogen by lightning during thunderstorms fixes nitrogen gas as oxides. Animal manures are also a nitrogen source, returning to the soil that amount taken out by plants used to feed the animals minus that used by the animal for its own growth. However, in modern agriculture, the most important source of nitrogen is the synthetic fixation of atmospheric nitrogen gas.

Plants absorb nitrogen only as inorganic nitrate ions (NO_3^-) and, in a few cases, as ammonium (NH_4^+) or amino (NH_2^+) ions. Most natural soil nitrogen is in the organic form—that is, combined in some manner with carbon. Organic nitrogen occurs in manures, decomposing organic matter, and urea [$CO(NH_2)_2$] and must be oxidized before most plants can use it.

The transformation of organic matter to the mineral or inorganic form—for example, organic nitrogen to NH_4^+, NO_2^-, NO_3^-—by microorganisms is called **mineralization.** The conversion of the mineral form to the organic form is called **immobilization** (Fig. 9–32). When organic material with a carbon:nitrogen (C:N) ratio greater than 30 is applied to a soil, the nitrogen is immobilized during initial decomposition, then it is mineralized as decomposition proceeds.

Irrespective of the form absorbed, the plant reduces nitrogen to N^{2-}, NH^-, or NH_2, which are then synthesized into more complex compounds and finally

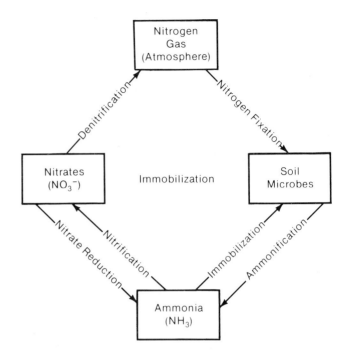

Fig. 9–32   The nitrogen cycle in soil.

into amino acids and proteins. Nitrogen is essential to all living organisms and is used in the synthesis of enzymes, nucleoproteins (proteins associated with nonamino nucleic acids), and chromosomes. In addition to its role in the formation of proteins, nitrogen is an important component of chlorophyll.

Continued use of nitrogen fertilizers can affect the pH of the soil (Table 9–1). Some fertilizers are residually acid forming, others residually basic, and some have

Table 9–1   Nitrogen Fertilizers, Their Composition, and Residual Effect on Soil pH.

Organic			*Inorganic*		
	%N	RESIDUAL EFFECT		%N	RESIDUAL EFFECT
Dried blood	12	acid	Anhydrous ammonia	82	acid
Guano, Peruvian	12	acid	Urea	46	acid
Fish meal, dried	10	acid	Ammonium nitrate	33	acid
Tankage	8	acid	Aqua ammonia	30	acid
Soybean meal	7	acid	Ammonium chloride	28	neutral
Peanut meal	7	acid	Nitrogen solutions	25–50	acid
Cottonseed meal	7	acid	Calcium cyanamide	22	basic
Activated sludge	6	acid	Ammonium sulfate	20	acid
Bone meal, raw	4	acid	Diammonium phosphate	20	acid
Garbage tankage	3	basic	Sodium nitrate	16	basic
			Calcium nitrate	16	basic
			Potassium nitrate	14	basic

little or no effect (see p. 208). Acid-forming fertilizers should be avoided on acid soils and basic fertilizers on alkaline soils. Fertilizers containing ammonium ions as the source of nitrogen are residually acid and should be used on alkaline soils. Fertilizers containing basic cations (Ca^{2+}, Na^+, or K^+) with nitrate (NO_3^-) anions as the source of nitrogen are residually basic and should be used on acid soils. In either case, the residual effect moves toward soil neutrality. Potassium sulfate (K_2SO_4) and potassium chloride (KCl) are residually neutral.

The kind of ion determines the mobility, solubility, and availability of nitrogen to the plant. For example, by ionic exchange, positively charged ammonia ions are held by negatively charged soil particles and are prevented from leaching out of the root zone. Under these conditions, the ammonium ion is considered to be immobile. The nitrate ions are negatively charged and are not attracted to the soil particles; therefore, they move freely in the soil solution. More of the ammonium ions are retained in fine-textured soils than in coarse-textured soils because the fine-textured soils have more exchange sites. Conversion of ammonium to nitrate ions (nitrification) speeds up nutrient losses by leaching.

Nitrogen fertilizers are applied as solids, liquids, or gases. They can be applied as preplant fertilizers, top-dressed after the crop has emerged (Fig. 9–33), broadcast evenly over the field and mixed with the soil by disking, drilled into the soil at desired depths (Fig.

Fig. 9–34   In potato production, anhydrous ammonia fertilizer is injected into the soil through tubing attached to the rear of a shank. The placement of the injection is regulated by the location and depth of the shank in relation to the plant. *Source:* William L. Sims.

9–34), dripped into irrigation water, or injected as a gas or liquid into the soil (Fig. 9–35). These methods can be combined, depending upon the crop, or fertilizing can be

Fig. 9–33   This farmer is applying a topdressing of a complete dry fertilizer to his cornfield. The material is visible as white pellets on the soil surface. It will dissolve and enter the soil with the first rain. *Source:* Fred Meyer, National Fertilizer Development Center, Tenn. Valley Auth.

Fig. 9–35   This farmer is injecting anhydrous ammonia (gaseous) directly into the soil. This method allows the fertilizer to be placed precisely at the desired depth and location within the row in relation to the plants, making for more efficient use of fertilizer. *Source:* Fred Meyer, National Fertilizer Development Center, Tenn. Valley Auth.

Fig. 9–36 Very often farmers drill a complete fertilizer (*A*) into the soil as they plant (*B*) the crop. The fertilizer is generally applied below and a little to one side of the seed to avoid salt damage. *Source:* International Harvester.

combined with planting (Fig. 9–36). Nitrogen fertilizers must not be placed in direct contact with the foliage because they burn the leaves. Ammonia is toxic to living tissue and is sometimes used to defoliate cotton before picking. Ammonium nitrate (NH_4NO_3) should be stored in a dry, well-ventilated place to reduce the danger of explosion.

Many plants deficient in nitrogen show pale green to yellow leaves, but each crop has its own characteristic symptoms. Nitrogen deficiency generally causes the plant to grow slowly and lowers crop yields (Table 9–2).

PHOSPHORUS

Phosphorus is needed by plants in smaller amounts than nitrogen or potassium, but this does not reflect its true importance in plant nutrition. Phosphorus is a key element in the formation of AMP, ADP, and ATP (adenosine mono-, di-, and triphosphate), which play essential roles in photosynthesis and respiration (Ch. 7). Phosphorus is a constituent of nucleic acid and phospholipids. It has been associated with early crop maturity, increased root proliferation, and seed forma-

tion. Deficiencies result in stunted growth, accumulation of anthocyanin pigment (purpling the leaves of some plants), and reduced yields of seeds and fruits.

Phosphorus is absorbed mainly as orthophosphate ions ($H_2PO_4^-$) and to a lesser extent as monohydrogen phosphate (HPO_4^{2-}). The quantity of either of these forms in the soil at any time is small, but the supply is constantly being renewed. The rate of renewal depends upon soil pH. Phosphorus is most available to the majority of crops in the pH range of 5.5 to 7.0. Iron and aluminum phosphates precipitate in acid soils, while calcium and magnesium phosphates precipitate in alkaline soils.

The primary source of phosphorus for fertilizers is mined apatite (rock phosphate), of which half the world's reserve is located in the United States. Apatite exists in several forms, all of which are more or less insoluble in water. To increase phosphorus availability to plants, apatite is treated with acids or heat when made into fertilizer. Rock phosphate treated with sulfuric acid yields superphosphate, the most abundant phosphorus source, containing 16 to 20 percent phosphoric acid

Table 9–2 Summary of Roles of Mineral Elements in Plant Nutrition

	Nutrient Element	Function in Plants	Deficiency Symptoms	Losses from Soil	Fertilizer
PRIMARY NUTRIENTS	Nitrogen (N)	Synthesis of amino acids, proteins, chlorophyll, nucleic acids, and coenzymes.	Stunted growth, delayed maturity, light green leaves; lower leaves turn yellow and die.	Erosion, leaching, crop removal.	Inorganic salts of ammonia, calcium, sodium, potassium, urea; organic fertilizers; legume crops; animal manures, crop residues, animal waste.
	Phosphorus (P)	Used in proteins, nucleo-proteins, metabolic transfer processes, ATP, ADP, photo-synthesis and respiration. Component of phospho-lipids.	Purplish leaves, stems, and branches; reduced yields of seeds and fruits, stunted growth.	Crop removal, fixation in soil. Reversion to unavailable form in soil.	Superphosphate, treble superphosphate, ammo-nium phosphate, animal manures.
	Potassium (K)	Sugar and starch formation, synthesis of proteins. Catalyst for enzyme reac-tions, neutralizes organic acids, growth of meri-stematic tissue.	Reduced yields; mottled, spotted or curled older leaves; marginal burning of leaves; weak root system, weak stalks.	Crop removal. Soil fixation leaching.	Potassium sulfate, potassium chloride.
SECONDARY NUTRIENTS	Calcium (Ca)	Cell walls, cell growth and division; nitrogen assimila-tion. Cofactor for some enzymes.	Deformed terminal leaves, reduced root growth. Some plants turn black, dead spots in midrib in some plants. Failure of terminal bud.	Leaching, crop removal.	Calcium sulfate, calcium nitrate, calcium carbonate.
	Magnesium (Mg)	Essential in chlorophyll, formation of amino acids and vitamins. Neutralizes organic acids. Essential in formation of fats and sugars. Aids in seed germination.	Plants usually chlorotic (interveinal yellowing of older leaves); leaves may droop.	Leaching, plant re-moval, and erosion. Some losses by fixa-tion to unavailable form in acid peaty soils.	Foliar sprays with magne-sium sulfate.
	Sulfur (S)	Essential ingredient in amino acids and vitamins. Flavors cruciferous plants and onions.	Light green leaves, reduced growth, yellowing of leaves. Weak stems. Similar to N deficiency.	Erosion, leaching, crop removal.	Ammonium sulfate, calcium sulfate, super phosphate, sulfuric acid, elemental sulfur.
MICRONUTRIENTS	Boron (B)	Affects flowering, pollen germination, fruiting, cell division, nitrogen metab-olism, water relations, hormone movement.	Terminal buds die, lateral branches begin to grow, then lateral buds die, branches form rosettes. Leaves thicken, curl, and become brittle.	Crop removal, leaching.	Sodium or calcium borate, animal manure, super-phosphate.
	Copper (Cu)	Constituent in enzymes, chlorophyll synthesis, catalyst for respiration, carbohydrate and protein metabolism.	Terminal leaf buds die. Chlorotic leaves. Stunted growth. Terminal leaves die.	Tie-up by highly organic soils and acid soils. Leaching.	Copper sulfate or other copper salts.
	Chlorine (Cl)	Not too much known except that it aids in root and shoot growth. Required for growth and development.	Plants wilt. Chlorotic leaves. Some leaf necrosis. Bronzing in leaves.	Never deficient under field conditions.	Chloride salts.
	Iron (Fe)	Catalyst in synthesis of chlorophyll. Involved in formation of many com-pounds. Components in many enzymes.	Paling or yellowing of leaves, chlorosis between veins at first. Grasses develop alternate rows of yellowing and green stripes in leaves.	Crop removal, leach-ing and erosion. Unavailable in alkaline soils.	Foliar applications of iron chelates, ferrous sulfate, or ferrous ammonium sulfate.
	Manganese (Mn)	Chlorophyll synthesis, acts as coenzyme.	Network of green veins on light green background of in-tervenous tissue. Leaves later become white and abscise.	May be unavailable in alkaline soil. Toxic in acid soils.	Manganese sulfate as a foliar spray or as a soil application.
	Molybdenum (Mo)	Essential in some enzyme systems that reduce nitro-gen. Protein synthesis.	Plants may become nitrogen deficient. Pale green, rolled or cupped leaves, with yellow spots. Leaves of crucifers become narrow, cereal glumes do not fill out.	May have been lack-ing when soil was formed or become unavailable.	Solution of sodium molybdate sprayed on plants or soil. Also dusted on seeds before planting.
	Zinc (Zn)	Used in formation of auxins, chloroplasts, and starch. Legumes need Zn for seed production.	Abnormal roots; mottled bronzed, or rosetted leaves. Intervenous chlorosis.	May not be available in alkaline soils; and toxic in acid soils. Crop removal.	Zinc sulfate as a foliar spray or added with other ferti-lizers.

Table 9–3 Approximate Composition of Some Common Phosphate Fertilizers

Source	Nitrogen (%N)	Phosphorus(%)		Potassium(%)	
		P	P_2O_5	K	K_2O
Ammonium phosphate (16–20–0)	16	7.0	16	—	
Superphosphate	—	7.0	16	—	
Triple superphosphate	—	18–23	42–50	—	
Dicalcium phosphate	—	23	52	—	
Phosphoric acid	—	24	54	—	
Potassium phosphate	—	18–22	42–50	30–45	36–54
Raw rock phosphate	—	10–17	25–30	—	
Calcium metaphosphate	—	27	62	—	

(P_2O_5). Other sources (Table 9–3) include basic slag, a byproduct of the steel industry and an important phosphorus source in many European countries. Liquid phosphoric acid (H_3PO_4) is made by treating apatite with sulfuric acid (a wet process that gives calcium sulfate as a precipitate). Ammonium phosphate results from treating phosphoric acid with ammonia. Superphosphate fertilizers do not appreciably affect soil pH, but phosphoric acid (H_3PO_4) is residually acidic.

POTASSIUM

Potassium is absorbed by plants in its ionic form (K^+). It plays roles in regulating the opening and closing of stomata and in water retention. It promotes the growth of meristematic tissue, activates some enzymatic reactions, aids in nitrogen metabolism and the synthesis of proteins, catalyzes activities of some mineral elements, and aids in carbohydrate metabolism and translocation (Table 9–2). Potassium does not appear to be an integral part of plant constituents—protoplasm, fats, or carbohydrates—as do other nutrient elements. Plants absorb macroquantities of potassium.

The first visible deficiency symptom appears in the leaves. Weak stems (lodging in grains), lower yield, lack of resistance to disease, and decreased crop quality have been associated with potassium deficiency.

Quantities of potassium salts are found in several areas of the world. Some lie below the earth's surface and some in dead lakes or seas. Potassium is found naturally in most soils. It comes from the decomposition of rocks and minerals, such as feldspars, muscovite, and biotite. West Germany, the Soviet Union, and Canada have the world's largest reserves, but the United States also has large deposits in New Mexico, Oklahoma, and Texas.

The most widely used potassium fertilizers are potassium chloride (KCl), potassium sulfate (K_2SO_4), and potassium nitrate (KNO_3), known commonly as muriate of potash, sulfate of potash, and saltpeter or niter. The nitrate form is the most expensive and is used mainly on orchards, vegetables, cotton, or other high-value crops.

Potassium is more mobile in the soil than phosphorus but less than nitrates, which can be readily leached from light sandy soils. Some soils can fix potassium (render it unavailable to plants), but unless the soils are very low in potassium, the fixing is not too important: since the reaction is reversible, the element is not fixed permanently.

Secondary Nutrients

CALCIUM

Calcium is absorbed by the plant in the ionic form (Ca^{2+}). It is essential to all higher plants. A deficiency kills terminal buds in shoots and apical tips in roots, reducing plant growth.

Calcium comes from dolomite, calcite, apatite, and some feldspars. Besides being an essential plant nutrient, calcium carbonate ($CaCO_3$, also called limestone or soil sugar) corrects soil acidity (Fig. 9–37). Calcium sulfate (gypsum) is used to help reclaim sodic soils and also to improve soil structure and aggregation in saline soils (Ch. 8). The best way to correct calcium deficiency in the soil is to add either limestone ($CaCO_3$) or gypsum ($CaSO_4$) (Fig. 9–38). The specific form depends upon the soil's pH.

Fig. 9–37 This truck is applying agricultural lime (CaCO₃), which is finely ground limestone, to counteract soil acidity. *Source:* Fred Meyer, National Fertilizer Development Center, Tenn. Valley Auth.

Fig. 9–38 Liquid lime (a suspension of CaCO₃) is being applied to an acid soil in Alabama. The wide tires are used to distribute the load and reduce soil compaction. *Source:* Fred Meyer, National Fertilizer Development Center, Tenn. Valley Auth.

MAGNESIUM

Like calcium, magnesium is absorbed by the plant as an ion (Mg^{2+}). It is an essential nutrient, the central atom in the structure of the chlorophyll molecule. Magnesium also appears to be necessary for the metabolism of the phosphorus and some enzymatic reactions. It is mobile and after translocation from the older to the younger leaves, its deficiency appears as an intervenous chlorosis (yellowing) in older leaves.

Magnesium is an exchangeable cation in the soil resulting from the decomposition of such minerals as biolite, dolomite, olivine, and serpentine. It also appears in the soil solution. In some arid areas of the world, magnesium occurs in such large quantities that it precipitates in the soil profile and, in rare instances, is so abundant that it is toxic.

A good source of magnesium (and calcium) for fertilizer is dolomitic limestone ($CaCO_3 \cdot MgCO_3$). Magnesium sulfate ($MgSO_4$) and potassium magnesium sulfate (K_2SO_4, $MgSO_4$) are also sources. Magnesium fertilizers are applied much the same as calcium.

SULFUR

Sulfur is absorbed by the plant as the sulfate ion (SO_4^{2-}). It is reduced to the disulfide (S—S) or sulfhydryl (SH) group before being metabolized in the plant. Sulfur plays a vital and varied role in plant nutrition. The plant uses it to metabolize several amino acids, to activate some enzymes, and to synthesize some vitamins. Sulfur also contributes to the characteristic flavors of some fruits and vegetables, such as cabbage, broccoli, and cauliflower.

The deficiency symptoms of sulfur can be confused with those of nitrogen, except that sulfur is not as readily translocated from older to younger leaves. Therefore, the younger leaves of a plant suffering from sulfur deficiency will appear yellow while the younger leaves of the same plant suffering nitrogen deficiency will appear greener. Reduced plant growth, uniform yellowing of younger leaves, and weak stems are characteristic symptoms of sulfur-deficient plants.

The primary source of sulfur is the decomposition of metal sulfides in igneous rocks. Appreciable quantities also come from the atmosphere and some from irrigation waters. Sulfur is present in the soil as sulfates and sulfides and in organic combinations in the soil humus.

Sources of sulfur for fertilizers are sulfate salts of aluminum, ammonium, calcium, iron (ferrous), magnesium, manganese, potassium, sodium, and zinc. Other sources are lime sulfur, sulfuric acid, and elemental sulfur.

Micronutrients

Micronutrients *(2)* are needed by plants in minute quantities, but this fact does not detract from their importance. Deficiency of a necessary micronutrient is as devastating to a plant as a deficient macronutrient. One characteristic common to all micronutrients is that while they are essential in small quantities, they are toxic in large quantities (Table 9–4).

Table 9–4   Approximate Range of Micronutrient Deficiency and
             Toxicity in Stems and Leaves (Dry wt.)

Microelement	Deficiency (ppm)	Normal (ppm)	Toxicity (ppm)
Boron	5–30	30–75	75
Copper	4	4–15	20
Manganese	15	15–100	depends on Fe:Mn ratio
Molybdenum	0.1	1–10	low toxicity
Zinc	8	15–50	200

BORON

Boron occurs in most soils in quantities of 20 to 200 ppm. In some arid areas it occurs in toxic amounts. In most humid regions, boron occurs as a borosilicate in the form of tourmaline *(7)*. This material is quite insoluble. Boron-deficient soils occur along the Atlantic coast from Maine to Florida, in the Gulf coast states, the North Central States, and along the Pacific coast from Washington to California. Borax ($Na_2B_4O_7 \cdot 10\ H_2O$) is water soluble, easily leached from sandy soils, and is a good source of boron.

COPPER

Many areas throughout the world have copper-deficient soils. In the United States, deficient soils are found in the Great Lakes area, the West Coast, and Florida. Copper deficiencies appear more frequently in highly organic soils but have been found in mineral soils in some countries. The amount of organic matter, soil pH, and the presence of other metallic ions influence the availability of copper. Large quantities of copper in the soil can cause iron deficiency in some plants, and there have been reports of copper toxicity. Copper deficiencies are corrected by applying copper salts to the soil or by foliar spraying with a solution of soluble copper salts. Copper sulfate ($CuSO_4 \cdot 5\ H_2O$) or copper ammonium phosphate ($CuNH_4PO_4$) are often used.

CHLORINE

Chlorine evaded detection as an essential nutrient for many years because it is so universally abundant in nature. Spray from ocean waves carrying huge amounts of sodium and potassium chloride are blown many miles inland by the wind. Large quantities are also deposited in the soil by precipitation. Larger amounts of this nutrient are used by crop plants than any other micronutrient except iron.

Most chlorine exists in the soil as simple chloride salts and is absorbed by the plant as chloride ions (Cl^-).

Because of their similarity, bromine can substitute for some chlorine in some plants. Chlorine deficiency is seldom seen in the field, but symptoms have been observed in tobacco, tomatoes, buckwheat, peas, cabbage, sugar beets, barley, corn, cotton, and potatoes. Deficiency symptoms of chlorine appear to be stunted root growth, leaf bronzing, and chlorotic leaves with some necrosis; often the plant wilts. Excess chlorine is toxic, especially to tobacco and potatoes.

IRON

Iron is more abundant in most soils than any other micronutrients, but often it is deficient because it is unavailable to plants for various reasons. Iron deficiency has been noted in crops grown on alkaline or calcareous soils and on acid soils with high phosphate levels. Citrus, deciduous fruits, soybeans, strawberries, vegetable crops, and many ornamentals have shown chlorosis caused by iron deficiency. The deficiency appears first in the younger leaves as an intervenous yellowing that later progresses over the entire leaf; in severe cases the leaves become almost white. Iron is essential in photosynthetic processes and also functions in several enzymatic reactions. The plant can absorb iron through its roots or leaves as either an ion (Fe^{2+}) or as a complex with organic salts (chelated) (see p. 215).

MANGANESE

Manganese is similar to iron in many ways. It is also a heavy metal and rather immobile in the plant. Manganese exists in the soil in several forms, depending upon the soil environment. It is most available to plants if in the manganous state (Mn^{2+}, MnO) as an exchangeable cation in the soil. In this state, however, it is more subject to oxidization by microorganisms to its trivalent state (Mn^{3+}, Mn_2O_3); in well-aerated soils it can be further oxidized to its least soluble, four-valent state (Mn^{4+}, MnO_2). High soil pH and good oxidizing conditions encourage MnO_2 formation. Poorly aerated or waterlogged soils favor the reduced manganous (Mn^{2+}) state. Manganese is absorbed by the plant in the manganous ionic form (Mn^{2+}), and is often applied to plants as manganese sulfate ($MnSO_4$) or chelated (complexed with some organic molecule). Manganese is applied as a foliar spray and absorbed through the leaves.

Like iron, the first deficiency symptoms show intervenous chlorosis in the younger leaves. This nutrient participates in photosynthesis, activation of enzymes, carbohydrate metabolism, and phosphorylation. Manganese toxicity from large amounts of the micronutrient has been observed in cotton (crinkle leaf) and tobacco on highly acid soils. Liming the soil corrects the malady.

MOLYBDENUM

Molybdenum is an essential nutrient in clovers, alfalfa, cereals, vegetables, soybeans, and forage grasses. A condition known as whiptail in cauliflower is caused by molybdenum deficiency. Soil environment affects the availability of this element to a large extent. It is unavailable to plants in strongly acid soil, where it reacts with iron and aluminum silicates to form insoluble compounds. Liming the soil usually increases the availability of molybdenum. In Australia about 0.7 kg molybdic oxide (H_2MoO_4) is mixed with one MT of superphosphate and applied to one hectare of soil (25 oz/t/ac).

Phosphates seem to aid plants in the absorption of molybdenum, but sulfates tend to hinder its uptake. Symptoms of deficiency vary among crops but intervenous chlorosis is often the first observable symptom. Legumes are stunted and the leaves turn yellow, as with nitrogen deficiency.

ZINC

Soil characteristics influence zinc availability. In calcareous alkaline soils deficiencies are expected, and in strongly acid soils toxicity is possible. Deficiencies occur in a wide range of soils but are most frequent in calcareous soils high in phosphorus. Zinc deficiencies have been observed in deciduous and citrus fruits, vegetables, and field crops such as corn, cotton, sorghum, and legumes. Zinc was one of the first micronutrients to be recognized as essential. Zinc attracted scientific interest early because of its importance in human nutrition, and considerable research was conducted in an endeavor to increase the concentration in plants. Zinc acts primarily as an enzyme activator in both plants and animals.

Zinc can be absorbed by the roots from the soil as the exchange cation (Zn^{2+}), or through the leaves when it is sprayed on the foliage as a $ZnSO_4$ solution or chelated (complexed as an organic compound). Deficiency symptoms first appear in the younger leaves as intervenous yellowing. Later, reduced shoot growth becomes evident. In many plants rosetting can be a symptom. The midrib and margins of corn leaves remain green while a broad band of bleached tissue appears from the base to the tip.

Chelating Agents (30)

Earlier in this section, the word *complex organic compounds* or *chelates* were used. The word **chelate** derives from a Greek word meaning claw. A chelate is a large organic molecule that attracts and tightly holds specific cations like a chemical claw, preventing them from taking part in inorganic reactions but at the same time allowing them to be absorbed and used by plants. Chelates combine with metallic cations—iron, manganese, zinc, and copper—to prevent the cations from reacting with inorganic anions that would render them insoluble and unavailable to plants. For example, chelated iron cannot react with hydroxyl anions (OH^-) to form insoluble ferric hydroxide [$Fe_2(OH)_3$]. Chelated cations are more soluble at higher pH than are inorganic ions. Chelates are also known as **sequestering agents.**

Several important agricultural chelates or sequestering agents are commercially available: (1) **e**thylene**d**iaminetetra**a**cetate, or EDTA, sequesters copper, iron, manganese, and zinc; (2) **e**thylene**d**iamine**d**i-o-**h**ydroxyphenylacetic acid, EDDHA, sequesters iron; (3) **d**iethylene**t**riamine**p**enta**a**cetic acid, or DTPA, sequesters iron; **n**itrito**t**riacetic acid, or NTA, sequesters zinc; and (4) **h**ydroxy**e**thyl**e**thylene**d**iaminetetra**a**cetic acid, or HEDTA, sequesters iron and zinc.

SOIL CONSERVATION

Soil degradation began long before people started farming, but the process was accelerated by permanent agriculture and land tillage. In America, erosion and soil depletion became problems as soon as settlers migrated from Europe. Their first task was to cut and remove trees for homes and fields. As population increased, more land was cleared, cropped, and depleted of nutrients. Much of the westward movement in the United States was a search for new, more fertile lands; Eastern soils had lost their productivity by continuous cropping. Under the Homestead Act, the United States government encouraged the movement by offering free land to those who would move west and settle.

George Washington and Patrick Henry were among the earliest American land conservationists. In his final message to Congress in 1796, Washington urged the creation of a board of agriculture. A half-century later Lincoln established the Department of Agriculture in 1862. Little interest in soil conservation was felt for the next 75 years because of the availability of new, western lands. During the 1920s a soil surveyor, H. H. Bennett,[5] called attention to the waste and depletion of America's greatest natural resource—land. Finally, in 1929, the Congress established ten soil conservation ex-

---

[5]H. H. Bennett was appointed chief of the first erosion control agency, which later became the Soil Conservation Service.

Fig. 9–39 Two consecutive years of drought, followed by high winds, blew immeasurable amounts of fertile topsoil from areas of Texas and Oklahoma into the Atlantic Ocean. This catastrophe created what came to be known as the "Dust Bowl" on Black Sunday, April 14, 1935. The late afternoon sun, a circular ball above the auto, is barely visible through the dust cloud. *Source:* Library of Congress.

periment stations, and assigned personnel to study and gather information on erosion control measures.

The Soil Conservation Service (SCS) was established in 1933 in the Department of Interior as one means of helping the United States recover from the Great Depression of 1929 to 1935. The need for immediate soil conservation became evident on Black Sunday, April 14, 1935 because that day the most severe dust storm in U.S. history completely blotted out the noonday sun (Fig. 9–39). During the summer and fall of 1935, the skies over Washington, D.C. and New York were darkened with topsoil blown from Texas, Oklahoma, and other prairie states. That same year the U.S. government created the first erosion control agency ever established by any nation. The first soil conservation act soon followed, charging the agency with the responsibility of cooperating with farmers to demonstrate good land management and erosion control practices (Fig. 9–40).

Fig. 9–40 Catastrophic soil erosion caused by drought and high winds occurred in the Texas panhandle during the early 1930s. Vast areas of previously productive farmland were devastated. *Source:* Library of Congress.

Soil conservation is the preservation and extension of the life of soil by using land wisely, keeping it in its most productive state for the present and future generations. Lands best suited for grazing of animals are planted to sod crops. Hilly or mountainous land is kept in trees, which are harvested as timber. Plowing up grassland prairie soils and planting them to row crops in semiarid regions without irrigation has proven to be disastrous. They should be left as grasslands. It does not take long for wind or water to erode and remove the fertile topsoil and form gullies (Figs. 9–41, 9–42). One of the complicating factors in soil conservation is our dependence upon the soil for food and fiber. The land must be used, but at the same time saved for future use. To do both takes wise land management. Land does not deteriorate unless it is used improperly.

Fig. 9–41 The beginning of a deep gully. Special care and treatment will be required to conserve this land. If it is left in grassland, however, further erosion can be prevented.

Fig. 9–42 Rill erosion has begun in this orchard, a forerunner of severe gully formation if not checked soon. *Source:* USDA Soil Conservation Service.

Extent of Erosion

Recent soil surveys in several countries show that vast areas of productive land have been damaged beyond recovery. Erosion continues to be critical in almost every agricultural region of the world except northwestern Europe and Britain. Erosion is particularly severe where intense torrential rains are frequent. Unfortunately, the need for food in some nations has overshadowed the danger of uncontrolled erosion. This is particularly true in East Africa, the Yellow River basin in China, Eastern Europe, Latin America, and parts of Australia, India, and the United States—all plagued with serious and widespread erosion. In this country erosion has damaged nearly 110 million hectares (272 million acres). At first glance, one might wonder why parts of Australia and the United States appear on the list of countries plagued with hunger and erosion while at the same time they are large grain exporters. The soil erosion problem in these nations is not over the entire nation, but it is severe in the semiarid regions and especially in those areas where irrigation is not used. Also, in times when the demand for food crops (at home and abroad) is high, economic pressure is put on the farmer to seed land to grain or other row crops when the soil should remain as grassland.

Fig. 9–43   Water does not erode level land. Leveling, as shown here, is one way of preventing erosion by water where irrigation is necessary. *Source:* USDA Soil Conservation Service.

FACTORS AFFECTING
EROSION

An important factor in erosion control is the amount of plant cover. Land covered with sod or trees loses little, if any, soil, while barren land can quickly lose considerable topsoil. The intensity, duration, and distribution of rainfall are also factors. A torrential rain of short duration on land with little plant cover causes severe soil losses while a gentle, evenly distributed rain causes less. Topography of the land is also a factor. Level land is less likely to erode than sloping land (Fig. 9–43). The soil's physical properties affect erosion. Deep permeable soils that absorb water are less likely to erode than shallow slowly permeable soils.

Gently sloping land can be cropped if proper erosion controls are used, but row crops that require tillage for weed control should never be planted in rows that run up and down steep hills. Row crops on gentle slopes require contoured rows. Sod crops or crops planted by broadcast methods should be used to reduce erosion losses.

*Methods
of Conservation*

The appropriate method of soil conservation depends upon the topography, soil type, cropping and livestock system, and climate. To help with these decisions, the U.S. farmer can call on the Soil Conservation Service (SCS). A professional conservationist will survey and classify the soil into one of eight broad land-capability classes according to its best use with least erosion (Table 9–5). The important consideration is that each parcel of land is managed according to its needs. This means that land not suitable for any type of agriculture, even though unaffected by erosion, should be left for wildlife and recreation; forest land should be used to produce trees, range and grassland, to produce forage for livestock, and crop land reserved for the production of crops.

Each kind of farming needs its own special conservation practices, but even with careful land management, additional measures are often necessary to improve land use.

Table 9–5 Land Capability Classes

Class	Use	Conservation Practices Needed
I	Few limitations. Suitable for wide range of plants. Can be used for row crops, pasture, range, woodland, and wildlife. Not subject to overflow.	Needs ordinary management practices—fertilizer, lime, cover, or green-manure crops, conservation of crop residue, animal manures, and crop rotations.
II	Some limitations. Choice of crop plants reduced. With proper land management, land can be used for cultivated crops, pasture, range, woodland, or wildlife.	Limitations few and easy to apply. Problems may include gentle slopes, moderate susceptibility to wind or water erosion, less than ideal soil depth, slight salinity. May require special conservation practices, water-control devices, or tillage methods, terraces, strip cropping, contour tillage, special crop rotations, and cover crops.
III	Severe limitations reduce choice of plants and/or require special conservation practices. May be used for cultivated crops, pasture, range, woodland, or wildlife.	May require drainage and cropping systems that improve soil structure. Organic matter additions might be needed. In irrigated areas, soils may have high water table, high salinity, or sodic accumulations. Soils may be slowly permeable.
IV	Severe limitations that reduce choice of plants. Requires very special management. Limited use for cultivated crops but can be used for pasture, range, woodland, and wildlife.	Limited cultivated crops because of steep slopes, susceptibility to wind or water erosion, effects of past erosion, shallow soils, overflows, poor drainage, salinity, adverse climate. May be suited for orchards and ornamental trees and shrubs. Special practices needed to prevent soil blowing and to conserve moisture.
V	Land limited in use—generally not suitable for cultivation. Little or no erosion hazard but has other limitations. Use limited to pasture, range, woodland, or wildlife.	May be nearly level but has excessive wetness, frequent overflow, rocks, or climate variations. Cultivation of common crop not feasible, but pastures can be improved and benefits from proper management can be expected.
VI	Severe limitations make the land unsuitable for cultivation. Restricted to pasture, range, woodland, or wildlife.	Pastures can be improved by seeding, liming, fertilizing, water control with contour furrows, drainage ditches, etc. Have severe limitations that cannot be corrected, thus not suited for cultivated crops. Some soils can be used for such crops as sodded orchards, berries, etc.
VII	Severe limitations make land unsuited for cultivation. Use limited to grazing, woodland, or wildlife.	Physical condition of soils prevents range or pasture improvement practices. Restrictions are more severe than those of Class VI. Can be used for grazing. May be possible to seed some areas.
VIII	Limitations preclude use for commercial plant production. Use restricted to recreation, wildlife, or water supply.	Cannot be expected to yield any significant return from crops, grasses, trees, but benefits from wildlife use and watershed protection or recreation are possible. Class VIII includes badlands, rock outcrops, sand beaches, river wash, mine tailings, etc.

Source: USDA Handbook 210, 1973.

GRASS WATERWAYS

These are strips of land of varying width permanently seeded to a grass sod. They conduct water to drainage outlets and control runoff from sloping land with cultivated crops. Waterways are used with contours or terraces that drain into them.

CONTOUR TILLAGE

One easy cropping practice that reduces losses of topsoil is to till the land on the contour (level) instead of up and down the hill. The land is plowed and the crop rows planted and cultivated around the slope, always at the same elevation from end to end. The rows are curved and sometimes come together in points. The ridges left by the tillage tools form small dikes to catch water, allowing more time for it to percolate into the soil instead of running down the hill.

CONTOUR STRIP-CROPPING

This effective practice is used to conserve both soil and water. Soil conservation is enhanced by alternating strips of solid-planted crops with row crops; for instance, strips of grain or hay crops can alternate with corn or sugar beets (Fig. 9–44). The strips always run on the contour. In some cases this practice cuts erosion 50 to 75 percent of what it is when either crop is planted alone.

Fig. 9–44 Contour strip cropping is useful for conserving water as well as reducing soil losses by wind erosion. In this case a cereal grain crop has been alternately planted with a hay crop. Sometimes if the area is subject to sudden but infrequent torrential rains, permanent flat, broad terraces are formed on the contour. *Source:* R. L. Haaland.

TERRACES

Terraces are used on long gentle slopes to decrease runoff and to increase water infiltration. On gently rolling land terraces are low, broad mounds that run on the contour and retain water that would otherwise run down the slope. The terraces are constructed with a slight grade so excess water will flow slowly to an outlet, often a grass waterway. Terraces are also used in some places on extremely steep slopes. They have been used for centuries in the Andes, Mesopotamia, and China. In Thailand, rice is grown on steep, terraced hillsides.

Wind Erosion

Wind erodes land by removing topsoil just as water does. As with water erosion, the best protection against wind erosion is to provide vegetative cover for the land during periods of high winds. Tillage methods such as stubble mulching have been helpful. Leaving the soil surface rough or cloddy reduces wind velocity at the soil surface, and windbreaks are helpful. These vary in size from tall trees to hedges planted close together perpendicular to the prevailing wind.

SUMMARY

Modern crop science is largely based upon the arts and skills developed by 200 generations of farmers. Many of the techniques used today, such as manuring, liming, and irrigation, were used in the same ways in ancient times and for the same reasons.

It is generally recognized that some land preparation is necessary for crop production. The principal reasons are (1) to prepare the land for irrigation (i.e., to level the land); (2) to incorporate crop residues, green manure, or cover crops into the soil; (3) to prepare and keep the seedbed in good tilth; (4) to help control crop pests; (5) to improve the physical condition of soil; and (6) to help control erosion. Tillage is the mechanical manipulation of the soil to provide conditions favorable for the growth of crops. Various implements have been developed to perform these operations, evolving from hand and horse to tractor.

Irrigation is the artificial application of water to the soil to provide essential water for crop growth. There are four basic methods of applying irrigation water: (1) border or flood, (2) sprinkling, (3) furrow, and (4) drip or trickle. The method to use depends upon the climate, crop, cost and availability of water, slope of field, soil properties, drainage, and salinity.

Sixteen chemical elements are known to be essential for the growth of most plants. Under certain conditions others may be used or needed. Nitrogen, phosphorus, and potassium are essential nutrients used in macroquantities, and they are called primary nutrients. Calcium, magnesium, and sulfur are secondary nutrients, and all the rest are classed as micronutrients, used by plants in minute amounts. The chemicals from which fertilizers are formulated determine the chemical and physical properties of the fertilizer. The lack of essential mineral nutrients produces identifiable symptoms within plants but for best crop yields the nutrients should be supplied to plants before deficiency symptoms appear. Fertilizers can be applied in the solid, liquid, or gaseous state.

Large areas of prairie grasslands in the Central Great Plains of the United States were plowed up and seeded to row crops by westward moving pioneers. Two successive years of drought accompanied with high winds caused devastating soil erosion, resulting in the abandonment of many farms. The recognition of such losses stimulated the establishment of the Soil Conservation Service and studies of methods for reducing topsoil losses. Today, effective procedures are used to reduce soil erosion.

9–1. The functions of land preparation are (a) to control weeds, (b) to help control insects, (c) to incorporate organic matter into the soil, (d) to level the land, (e) all of these.

9–2. Tillage is defined as any manipulation of the soil to provide conditions for favorable crop growth. True or false?

9–3. Tillage operations are a costly part of the total crop production. True or false?

9–4. A slip plow operates in the soil at depths up to 180 cm (6 ft). The purpose is to (a) break up hardpans, (b) incorporate organic matter, (c) level the land, (d) bury undesirable salts.

9–5. The basic cause of the U.S. Dust Bowl disaster in the 1930s was the result of (a) overcropping, (b) overgrazing, (c) overpopulation, (d) overplowing, (e) overwatering. Explain.

9–6. It is always beneficial to the succeeding crop to turn under organic matter. True or false? Explain.

9–7. The ill effects of weeds can be overcome by adding sufficient fertilizer and water for the weeds and crops. True or false?

9–8. Which of the following are not methods of irrigation? (a) Furrow, (b) border, (c) sprinkler, (d) subbing, (e) transection method.

9–9. Which is more important from the standpoint of the plant? (a) The availability of water, (b) the amount of water.

9–10. In general, it is better to plow the land in the (a) spring, (b) fall, (c) winter, (d) summer. Explain.

9–11. The primary mineral nutrient elements absorbed by plants and used in large quantities are _____, _____, _____.

9–12. A complete fertilizer contains the nutrient elements N, P, K, Ca, Mg, and S. True or false?

9–13. The chemical analysis given for a bag of fertilizer is the numbers 10–15–5. What does this mean?

9–14. In years past, farmers "grew" their own nitrogen fertilizer. Explain how this was done. Can you think of reasons why is it not done as extensively today?

9–15. _____ demands the preservation and extension of the soil's life by keeping it productive for present and future generations.

9–16. What is meant by a residually acid or residually basic fertilizer? Why does a farmer need to know what a fertilizer can do to soil pH?

9–17. Factors that determine the appropriate method of soil conservation are (a) _____, (b) _____, (c) _____, (d) _____.

9–18. Leaving the soil surface rough or cloddy over-winter reduces losses by wind erosion. True or false?

9–19. List four basic methods of irrigation.

9–20. Name one mineral nutrient that can be grown on the farm. How?

REFERENCES

1. Aldrich, R., P. J. West, and J. A. McCurdy. 1974. Treating soil, soil mixtures, or soil substitutes with aerated steam. Pa. Agr. Ext. Spec. Cir. 182.

2. Allaway, W. H. 1960. Agronomic controls over the environmental cycling of trace elements. *Adv. in Agron.* 20:235–74.

3. Anon. 1975. Try trickle for pickles. *Am. Veg. Grower* 23(2):16.

4. Anon. 1975. Drip irrigation acreage climbs. *Am. Veg. Grower.* 23(4):22.

5. Bateman, H. P., and W. Bowers. 1962. Planning a minimum tillage system for corn. Univ. of Ill. Ext. Cir. 846.

6. Blevins, R. L., L. W. Murdock, and G. W. Thomas. 1978. Effect of lime application on no-tillage and conventionally tilled corn. *Agron. Jour.* 70:322–26.

7. Bowen, J. 1977. Boron: the fine art of using enough, but not too much. *Crops and Soils* 29:12–14.

8. Brownell, P. F. 1968. Sodium as an essential micronutrient element for some higher plants. *Plants and Soil* 28:161–64.

9. *Encyclopaedia Britannica.* 1965. Irrigation 12:641.

10. Epstein, E. 1972. *Mineral nutrition of plants: principles and prospectives.* New York: John Wiley.

11. Fukuda, H. 1976. *Irrigation in the world.* Tokyo: University of Tokyo Press.

12. Gerard, C. J., and W. R. Cowley. 1964. Hidden hardpans steal profits. *Crops and Soils* 16:11–12.

13. Hanway, D. G. 1976. Improve production without irrigation—no-till in the Great Plains. *Crops and Soils* 29:11–12.

14. Hermsmeier, L. F. 1967. Land farming. A means of controlling surface water on level fields. USDA Leaflet 539.

15. Kasimatis, A. N. 1974. Vineyard irrigation. Univ. of Calif. Coop. Ext. AXT 199.

16. Kliewer, M., and H. J. Evans. 1963. Cobamide coenzyme contents of soybean nodules and nitrogen fixing bacteria in relation to physiological conditions. *Plant Physiol.* 38:99–104.

17. Larson, W. E. 1962. Tillage requirements for corn. *Jour. Soil Water Cons.* 17:3–7.

18. ———. 1967. Tillage: enough is enough. *Crops and Soils* 19:12–13.

19. Marr, J. C. 1957. Grading land for surface irrigation. Calif. Agr. Exp. Sta. Cir. 438.

20. ———. 1964. The border method of irrigation. Calif. Agr. Exp. Sta. Cir. 408.

21. Marsh, A. W. 1975. Irrigating at home. Do you know when to irrigate? Univ. of Calif. Div. Agr. Sci. Leaflet 2745.

22. ———, H. Johnson, L. J. Booher, N. McRae, K. Mayberry, P. Mobray, D. Ririe, and F. E. Robinson. 1969. Solid set sprinklers for starting vegetable crops. Univ. of Calif. Agr. Ext. AXT 294.

23. ———, R. L. Branson, S. Davis, C. D. Gustafson, and F. K. Aljibury. 1975. Drip irrigation. Univ. of Calif. Div. Agr. Sci. Leaflet 2740.

24. Noggle, G. R., and G. J. Fritz. 1976. *Introductory plant physiology*, pp. 289–91. Englewood Cliffs, N.J.: Prentice-Hall.

25. Rasmussen, W. W. 1965. Deep plowing for improving "slick spot" soils. *Crops and Soils* 17:10–11.

26. Reed, A. D., J. L. Meyer, and F. K. Aljibury. 1976. Irrigation costs. Univ. of Calif. Div. Agr. Sci. Leaflet 2875.

27. Swearingin, M. L. 1974. Double cropping winter wheat and soybeans in Indiana. Coop. Ext. Serv. Purdue Univ. ID 96:2–16.

28. Unger, P. W. 1977. Tillage effects on winter wheat production where the irrigated and dryland crops are alternated. *Agron. Jour.* 69:944–50.

29. Van Doren, D. M., Jr., and G. J. Ryder. 1962. Factors affecting use of minimum tillage for corn. *Agron. Jour.* 54:447–50.

30. Wallace, A. 1971. *Regulation of micronutrient status of plants by chelating agents and other factors.* Ann Arbor, Mich.: Edwards.

31. Welch, J. E. 1977. Water supply: policies and planning programs. *Calif. Agr.* 31:5–6.

SUPPLEMENTARY READING

BRADY, N. C. 1974. *The nature and properties of soils,* 8th ed. New York: Macmillan, Ch. 18.

BEATTY, M. T., G. W. PETERSON, and L. D. SWINDALE, eds. 1979. *Planning the uses and management of land.* Madison, Wisc.: Amer. Soc. Agron.

HUGHES, H. D., and D. S. METCALFE. 1972. *Crop production.* 3rd ed. New York: Macmillan.

ISRAELSEN, O. W., and V. E. HANSEN. 1962. *Irrigation principles and practices.* 3rd ed. New York: John Wiley.

JANICK, J., C. H. NOLLER, and C. L. RHYKERD. 1976. *The cycles of plant and animal nutrition, food and agriculture.* San Francisco: W. H. Freeman & Company Publishers.

NORDQUIST, P. and G. WICKS. 1976. A new way to fallow. *Crops and Soils* 28:16–18.

PETERSON, A. E., and J. B. SWAN, eds. 1979. *Universal soil loss equation: past, present, and future.* Madison, Wisc.: Amer. Soc. Agron.

PRATT, C. J. 1965. *Chemical fertilizers. Plant agriculture, selected readings from Sci. Amer.* San Francisco: W. H. Freeman & Company Publishers.

REVELLE, R. 1963. Water. *Plant agriculture, selected readings from Sci. Amer.* San Francisco: W. H. Freeman & Company Publishers.

SPLINTER, W. E. 1976. Center-pivot irrigation. *Sci. Amer.* 234:90–99.

THORNE, D. W., and M. D. THORNE. 1979. *Soil, water, and crop production.* Westport, Conn.: AVI.

TISDALE, S. R., and W. L. NELSON. 1975. *Soil fertility and fertilizers.* 3rd ed. New York: Macmillan.

TRIPLETT, G. B., JR., J. BEUERLEIN, and M. KROETZ. 1976. Relay cropping not reliable. *Crops and Soils* 29:8–10.

USDA Yearbook of Agriculture. 1955. Water. Washington, D.C.

USDA Yearbook of Agriculture. 1938. Soils and Men. Washington, D.C.

VAN DOREN, D. M., JR., G. B. TRIPLETT, JR., and J. E. HENRY. 1975. No-till is profitable on many soil types. *Crops and Soils* 27 (9):7–8.

VEIHMEYER, F. J., and A. H. HENDRICKSON. 1960. Essentials of irrigation and cultivation of orchards. Calif. Agr. Exp. Sta. Cir. 486.

Climatic
Influences
on Crop
Production

History shows that early people continually moved about, exploring and settling new areas that were often great distances apart. As they moved they took with them the seeds, cuttings, and nursery plants of familiar crops for planting in their new homeland. Many newly introduced plant species succeeded in their new environment; some, for various reasons, did not. Sometimes these new introductions formed the basis of new plant-growing enterprises. For example, coffee, bananas, macadamia nuts, papayas, and pineapples were introduced to the Hawaiian Islands from other tropical regions by voyagers during the 1800s.

The multitude of plant species and cultivars growing throughout the world are different genetically, each reacting to various environmental situations. To grow crops successfully the farmer must either: (1) grow those crop plants that are already known to be adapted to the climate, (2) grow plants altered genetically (new cultivars) for adaptation to a different climate, or (3) change the climatic environment by artificial means (greenhouses, hothouses, and other devices).

It has been a worldwide challenge for crop growers to correlate climatic environments with crops that grow best in those areas (Fig. 10–1). Farmers, agribusiness enterprises, and governments are continually looking for new crops that can be adapted profitably to their particular environment. For example, world citrus production increased from about 900,000 to 29 million MT (1 million to 32 million t) annually during the century ending in 1970. This increase was due primarily to the develop-

ment by governments and private enterprise of vast new citrus plantings in many parts of the world, especially in the Americas, Africa, and Australia, where favorable

Fig. 10–1 A meteorologist collecting weather data in an orchard. The instruments measure temperature, solar radiation, and wind velocity and direction. These data will be compiled with similar data from other stations in the area to predict local weather. *Source:* University of California Cooperative Extension.

222

climates were present. Safflower and sunflower are also examples of crops successfully introduced into new areas of production. Triticale (see p. 501) is an example of an entirely new, manmade plant being tried in certain arid regions primarily because of its climatic adaptability.

In the past, crop plantings were tried in new areas largely by trial and error. Recently, the climatic and growth requirements of the various plant species and cultivars have become better known, allowing predictions of the probable feasibility of certain crops for new areas.

Plant breeders have developed new cultivars that are productive in regions previously unsuited to the crop. For example, peaches are not generally suited to subtropical areas because they need considerable winter chilling to overcome the "rest" influence in the buds (p. 232). However, plant breeders have developed peach cultivars that do not require as much cold, thus extending peach culture to warmer-winter regions.

WEATHER AND CLIMATE

Weather is the immediate day-to-day, local (inplace) combination of such natural phenomena as temperature, precipitation, light intensity and duration, wind direction and velocity, and relative humidity. In any given location these weather factors assume a certain pattern, changing day by day, week by week, month by month, and season by season, and the same pattern repeats year by year. This pattern is the location's **climate.** If the area is small or near the ground surface, the pattern is called the **microclimate.** Thus, climate represents the summation of many decades of weather in a given area. Past climatic records allow one to predict with some accuracy the weather of a given area for a certain time of year.

An area's climate is determined by various factors. For example, climate will change with changes in altitude. This is demonstrated by the delayed flowering of about four days for some plant species for each 130 m (400 ft) increase in altitude; for each degree of latitude north or south of the equator, flowering of the same plant species is delayed about four days (Fig. 10–2). Also, there is a reduction of about 10°C (18°F) in the average dry-air temperature for each 1000 m (3280 ft) rise in elevation. The temperature reduction in moist air is less, about 6°C (11°F) for each 1000 m.

Large bodies of water close to land tend to moderate temperature extremes on the land in both winter and summer. Hills or mountains modify precipitation in some areas by increasing rainfall on the windward side and reducing it on the leeward side. Occasionally, the climate of long, narrow bands of 1 to 20 km (0.62 to 12 mi) wide across gently sloping hillsides is quite different from that in the bottom of the valley. Because cold air is more dense than warm air, the cold air drains to the valley floor, leaving the higher band of land warmer. Sometimes orchards are quite productive in these higher **thermal belts,** whereas fruit trees on the valley floor would be subjected to accumulations of cold air and subsequent blossom-killing frosts on spring mornings (Fig. 10–3).

Each plant species has certain climatic requirements for optimum growth, and the success or failure of the crop is based on how well the climatic requirements of that species or cultivar are met. A successful farmer makes a thorough study of the climate and weather for the area before planting any crop. This reduces the risk of disappointment and monetary loss.

Although the climate for a given region is established and well known, extreme variations in weather

Fig. 10–2   Vegetation types from equator to North or South Pole (*left*) are similar to those from the base to the top of a high mountain (*right*) in tropical regions. The principal factor involved in this comparison is temperature.

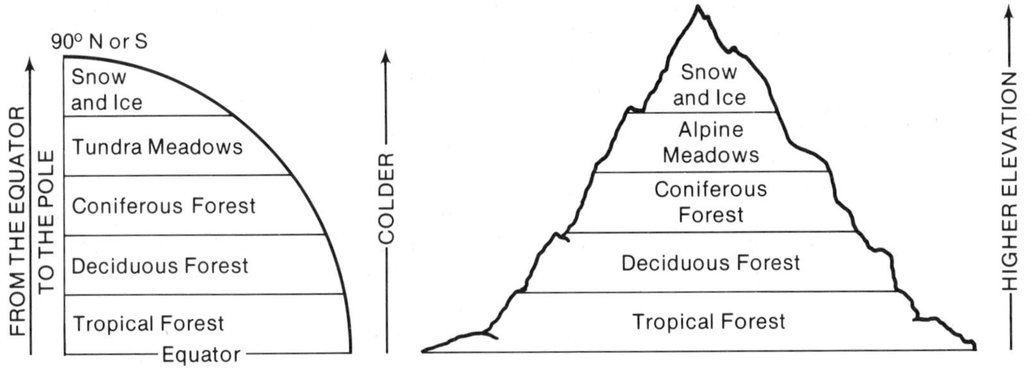

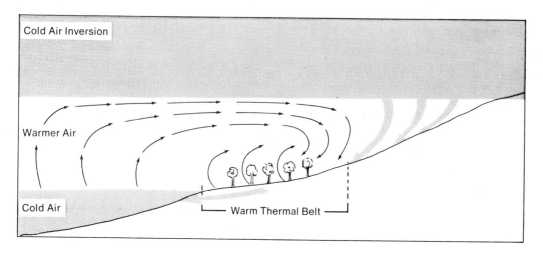

Cold Air Inversion

Warmer Air

Cold Air

Warm Thermal Belt

Fig. 10–3 Warm thermal belts can occur on slopes, permitting the culture of frost-susceptible crops in places otherwise too cold. Cold air, being more dense, drains down the slopes and sinks beneath the warmer air, pushing it upward. As the warmer air rises, it reaches a colder layer, then slides along the bottom of the cold layer until it reaches the hillside at the high altitude, creating a thermal belt.

patterns can eliminate a crop even though, on the average, such problems are unlikely. For example, a spring freeze during blossoming could eliminate the crop of an entire vineyard or orchard. This might not occur again for years but if it happened too frequently, such areas would become too risky for fruit growing and a more resistant crop would need to be substituted.

CLIMATIC FACTORS AFFECTING PLANT GROWTH

The world's distribution of crop plants is determined largely by climatic factors such as air movement, rainfall, temperature, and light.

Air Movement

Basically the air circulation patterns in the atmosphere result from the sun's radiation falling more directly on the earth's tropical regions than on the polar regions. The warmer air at the equatorial regions rises and flows toward the poles, cools, sinks as cold polar air, and then returns toward the equator as ground flow. The direction of the ground air flow is affected by several factors: (1) the earth's rotational spin from west to east, (2) the effects of seasons caused by the earth's inclination on its axis, (3) differences in heating and cooling between land and water masses, (4) differences in elevation, (5) effects

of mountain ranges, and (6) local storms resulting from interactions between warm and cold air masses. The final result of these interactions is the establishment of regions, some large and some small, each with a different climate. Sometimes areas with greatly different climatic patterns lie only short distances apart.

Crop yields can be severely impaired by strong winds at critical times in the crop's production cycle, such as the blooming period when bee activity is essential for pollination. Plant leaves or fruits are tender during the early stages of growth, and whipping winds can cause severe injury or desiccation. Continuous winds accompanied by high temperatures during the growing season markedly increase water losses by transpiration. Tall growing trees are often planted in rows perpendicular to the prevailing wind direction to reduce wind velocity and to make an otherwise satisfactory area suitable for growing crops. For example, in Hawaii tall Norfolk Island pines (*Araucaria heterophylla*) are planted in rows to protect macadamia nut plantings, and in California tall eucalyptus trees (*Eucalyptus* spp.) serve as windbreaks in the central coastal valleys.

Rainfall

Topography greatly influences the amount and distribution of rainfall. Air circulation patterns also affect the seasonal distribution of precipitation. It is common for certain valley areas to receive 100 cm (40 in) of rainfall while 50 km (31 mi) away only 15 cm (6 in) of precipitation falls. Mountain ranges present barriers to clouds, causing them to rise to higher elevations and generally colder temperatures. This causes the vapor to condense and water to fall on the windward sides as the clouds pass over, leaving the leeward side relatively dry. An area receiving adequate rainfall during two-thirds of the growing season may have enough water for many crops. Otherwise, some irrigation will be needed to supplement the rainfall. Areas receiving less than two-thirds of the required water supply during the growing season require irrigation. In such areas, dams, aqueducts, canals, or ground water wells are used.

Moisture influences the growth and distribution of plants because it is essential in every biological reaction within the plant, from seed germination to senescence. Water, of course, is the most abundant constituent in plants, ranging from about 75 to 95 percent of a plant's mass by weight. The role of water in plants includes: (1) involvement in all biological reactions, (2) a structural component in the proteins and nucleic acids in the plant cells, and (3) a regulator of plant temperature. In addition to its in-plant role, water also acts as an environmental regulator of the climate around the plant. Moisture is a major factor in determining climate.

Plants are divided into three categories based upon their need for moisture.

Desert plants, or **xerophytes,** have remarkable adaptation mechanisms enabling them to proliferate with very little water. These plants, such as the cacti, often have very shallow and fibrous root systems that can act as sponges and immediately absorb any slight amount of rainfall falling on the soil surface. Their leaves have been modified to reduce water loss by transpiration. Their stems are often covered with a thick, waxy, resinous material or they could be pubescent (stems and leaves covered with fine hairs) to reduce transpiration. The stems of some xerophytes can store tremendous quantities of water for long periods of time.

At the opposite end of the scale are the **hydrophytes,** the "fish" of the plant world. These plants thrive in or close to water. Water lilies, swamp and marsh plants, and many rice cultivars are examples of hydrophytes.

Between these two extremes are the **mesophytes,** most populous of the three groups. These include practically all of the economically important agricultural plants; they can adapt to quite diverse environments.

Humidity is a major force in regulating the earth's temperature. Moisture in the atmosphere intercepts and filters some of the solar radiation before it reaches the

earth's surface. It also blankets the earth and prevents heat losses by reradiation. Thus, atmospheric water both cools and warms the earth. The physical properties of water that make it useful for cooling harvested crops or reducing danger of frost damage (latent heat of vaporization and latent heat of fusion) also make it an excellent climatic insulator, thus giving more resistance to wide and extreme temperature variations.

Temperature

Every chemical, physiological, and biological process in plants is influenced by temperature. Plants of different species vary quite widely in their adaptability to temperature, but, within a species, they are restricted to rather narrow limits. Some algae survive temperatures of 90°C (195°F) in hot springs and certain arctic plants survive −65°C (−85°F), but such species are rare. Most plants live and grow in a temperature range of 0°C to 50°C (32°F to 120°F). Biological activities, in general, are limited at the lower temperature by the freezing point of water and at the upper range by the denaturation[1] of protein.

In some instances, small temperature differences can change the quality of the harvested product. For example, the sugar content of sugar beets is reduced if temperatures during the growing season are too low or the length of the growing season is shortened to the point where there are too few days when the daily mean temperature is high enough for sugar production.

MINIMUM WINTER TEMPERATURES

For each plant species there is a minimum temperature that kills the plants outright. From past experience and experimental freezing trials, this temperature is well known for most crops. Temperature sensitivity prevents the growing of certain species in many regions (Fig. 10–4). For example, oranges cannot be grown commercially in Canada because the trees would be killed the first winter by temperatures below about −7°C (19°F). In other regions winters with such killing temperatures are rare and the risk is worth taking. However, these winters can and do occur, as in southern Texas in 1951 when thousands of orange trees were killed, and again in Florida in 1977. Often growers take precautions against such calamities and use frost protection measures (p. 228).

[1]To modify or change a natural protein by heat, alkali, acid, or radiation so that it no longer performs its original function.

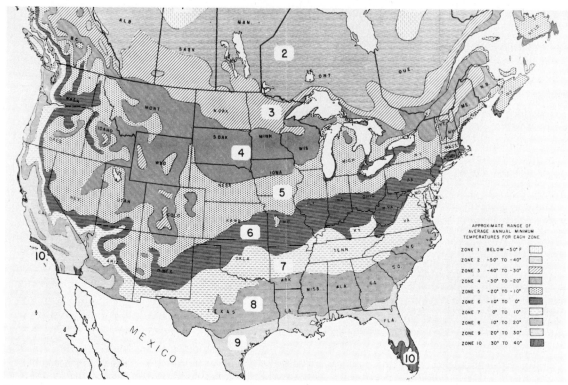

Fig. 10–4 Plant hardiness zones of the United States and southern Canada, showing average annual minimum temperatures. *Source:* USDA.

Low temperatures cause death to plants in different ways. They can kill the entire plant or, perhaps, only the tops but not the roots. Some trunk tissue of a dormant tree can be killed by plummeting temperatures. Sudden sharp freezes in the autumn can kill stem and leaf tissue that is actively growing and has not undergone the physiological change necessary to develop "hardiness." Unharvested fruits are often damaged by freezing in late autumn.

The plant's minimum lethal temperature can be modified by the length of exposure time. For example, a plant with a lethal minimum temperature of −2°C (28°F) can be exposed to that temperature for a few minutes without damage. However, four or five hours at the same temperature could cause severe injury.

Sometimes, plant tissues are exposed to temperatures several degrees below their freezing points very rapidly—they are supercooled—but if warmed gradually without disturbance, no injury results since no ice crystals form (p. 227). If, however, the plant is moved (by wind) or shaken while supercooled, ice crystals can form instantly, freezing and damaging the tissue.

SPRING FROSTS

Each year spring frosts or freezes cause concern to farmers in the world's temperate zones. One clear cold night can nullify a year's efforts and expenditures if freezing occurs at a critical time in the plant's development. Flower buds, from the time they start to open, are vulnerable to cold (Table 10–1).

Table 10–1 Relative Resistance of Fruit Buds to Cold. Temperatures Endured for 30 Minutes or Less Without Injury.

Fruit	Buds Closed but Showing Some Color		Full Bloom		Small Green Fruits	
	°C	°F	°C	°F	°C	°F
Apples *(Malus pumila)*	−4	25	−2	28	−2	28
Peaches *(Prunus persica)*	−4	25	−3	27	−1	30
Cherries *(P. avium)*	−4	25	−2	28	−1	30
Pears *(Pyrus communis)*	−4	25	−2	28	−1	30
Plums *(Prunus americana)*	−4	25	−2	28	−1	30
Apricots *(P. armeniaca)*	−4	25	−2	28	−1	31
English walnuts *(Juglans regia)*	−1	27	−3	27	−1	30
Oranges *(Citrus sinensis)*	−3	27	−3	27	−1	30

Source: Taken in part from N. W. Ross. 1974. Stanislaus orchard handbook. University of California Cooperative Extension.

Some seedlings are killed by spring frosts after they emerge from the soil; this is especially true of warm-season vegetable crops. A gentle wind or a cloud or fog cover reduces the danger of dropping temperatures by preventing radiant heat loss.

CHILLING TEMPERATURES

Low temperatures are sometimes required for satisfactory bud growth and development. For example, deciduous fruit trees develop a physiological "rest influence" by the end of the summer, after which they grow no further until they have been subjected to a certain amount of chilling through the winter (Ch. 14). This phenomenon limits the culture of some crops to the temperate zones, where ample cold temperatures occur. The cold temperature requirement is also the reason why some ornamental bulbs must be placed in cold storage during the winter before planting the following spring. Rhubarb roots and strawberry transplants require a low temperature treatment before they will grow in the spring. Some winter wheat cultivars require a cold treatment (vernalization; see Ch. 6) during seed germination and early seedling development in order to flower later and bear grain during the summer. Many biennial plants require a certain amount of winter chilling to flower.

FREEZING DAMAGE

Many plants can tolerate freezing temperatures. Metabolic responses to low temperatures change the physiology of the tolerant plants, a process known as **hardening.** These physiological responses to cold temperature are changes in the cell solute concentration, cell membrane permeability, or enzyme activity. Plants are hardened by placing them in increasingly severe environments—either warm or cold—until they can survive conditions that would kill them before hardening. This practice has been known and used by farmers for many years, but simple explanations for hardening physiology are rather difficult. Examples of easily hardened plants are tomatoes, cabbage, broccoli, cauliflower, onions, peppers, wheat, and many deciduous and evergreen trees. Sunflowers and beans are not easily hardened.

How Cells Freeze   An early explanation of frost damage was that, at temperatures below the freezing point of water, ice crystals formed in the cells and intercellular spaces causing the cells to expand and rupture. It has recently become apparent that this causes only minor damage in comparison to physical changes in cell contents caused by movement of water out of the cells during freezing.

At standard atmospheric pressure, the freezing point of pure water or melting point of ice is 0°C (32°F). Ice melts at this temperature but water seldom freezes. For ice to form there must be microscopic crystals of either ice or other biological materials in the water around which the ice crystals can grow. Ice crystal growth, called freezing, is preceded by microscopic ice crystal formation, a process called **nucleation.** Furthermore, the temperature at which water (a solvent) exists in equilibrium with ice (a solute) is its freezing point, and the addition of a substance being dissolved (solute) to a substance doing the dissolving (solvent) always causes a lowering of the freezing point. The higher the concentration of solutes in a solvent the more depressed the freezing point becomes. In nature, absolutely pure water does not exist, so varying degrees of supercooling occurs in all biological systems before ice crystals form. The degree of supercooling depends upon the concentration of solutes, colloids, and other material in the cell sap. Once ice crystal formation begins in the plant's cells and water changes from liquid to solid, the temperature in the plant part increases because of the release of the latent heat of fusion[2] as water changes to ice (Fig. 10–5).

[2]The latent heat of fusion for water is about 80 cal/g.

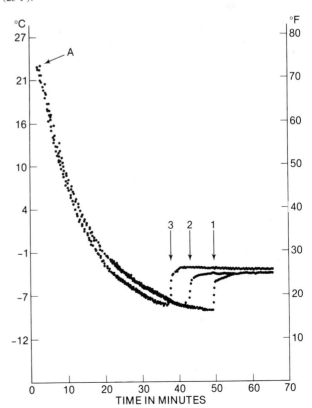

Fig. 10–5   Thermograph readings showing supercooling temperature patterns of fruits. Thermocouples were inserted into three separate raw olive fruits (1, 2, and 3) which, at point A, were placed in a cold box at a temperature of −12°C (10°F). Fruit temperatures dropped steadily for 35 to 50 minutes, supercooling to about −8.5°C (17°F). At this point the fruits started to freeze. As ice crystals formed, fruit temperatures rose abruptly to the freezing point for olives, as shown to be about −4°C (25°F).

After ice has formed in the intercellular spaces, water molecules move toward the regions of ice crystal formation because of a reduced water potential in intercellular regions. The removal of liquid water by freezing increases the solute concentration within the cells and lowers the freezing point even further. Under conditions of severe and quick freezing of unhardened plants, tissue is inevitably killed by intracellular ice formation within the cell protoplasts. Rapid thawing is harmful to plant tissue also because sudden changes in cell turgor redistribute the water.

In addition to below-freezing damage, some plants are injured by exposure to short periods of cold at above-freezing temperatures. The fruit tissue of tropical and subtropical fruits, such as pineapples, avocados, bananas, papayas, and tomatoes is injured during storage at temperatures of 0°C to 10°C (32°F to 50°F) (see p. 332).

AVOIDING CROP LOSSES DUE TO FROST

Each year frost causes considerable crop losses. Damage due to frost is most likely from unexpected cold periods in the spring, after young crop seedlings have emerged or flower buds opened. The risk is greatest during the hours just before sunrise on clear, still nights. The duration and magnitude of temperature drop is most critical at this time. If there is no cloud cover, soil radiates heat rapidly into the upper atmosphere during the night. Radiation losses are greater and more rapid from clean-tilled fields than from those covered with crops. Crop losses due to frost can be avoided by planting vegetable crops only when the danger of frost has passed. However, this is not always possible nor even desirable. For example, extra-early harvest can bring such a price advantage that it is worth risking damage by frost or bearing the added cost of frost protection. A price bonus generally is not available for earliness to fruit, grape, and nut growers. These farmers are forced to minimize their risks by protecting their crops against losses from freezing. Producers of ornamental potted plants prevent losses by using heated greenhouses, and some grain farmers avoid damage by planting frost-tolerant crops such as winter wheat.

Various techniques and equipment are used to minimize damage to crops when temperatures fall below freezing, as discussed below.

PLANTING DATES   Working with worldwide long-range weather patterns, meteorologists have determined the average last day for spring frosts in many areas (Fig. 10–6). Planting crops after this date decreases the likelihood of frost damage.

Fig. 10–6   Average dates over a 40-year period of last killing frost in spring. The risk of frost damage is minimized if susceptible crops are planted after the average date of the last killing frost. *Source:* USDA.

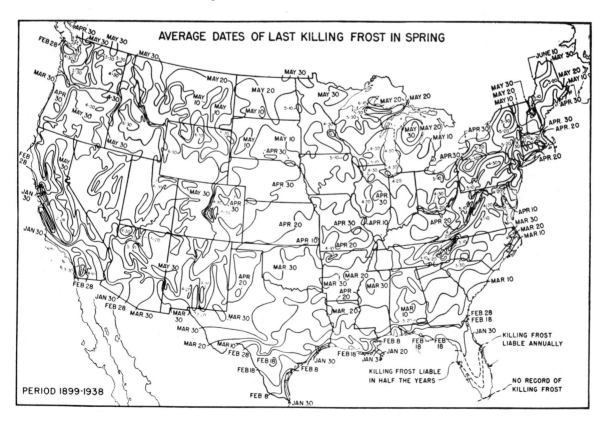

HOT CAPS   Vegetable growers sometimes grow crops at temperatures below the ideal in order to harvest an earlier crop in hopes of a higher price.

Hot caps are simple but effective devices to protect young plants from frost. These domelike structures are made of waxed paper supported with wire strands to retain their shape. They are about 30 cm (12 in) in diameter and 25 cm (10 in) high. The translucent domes are placed over the seedlings and held in place by covering their bases with soil. As the seedlings grow, the tops of the caps are torn open. The caps are removed after danger of frost has passed. Hot caps protect plants from freezing to temperatures as low as −3°C (27°F). This permits planting two to three weeks earlier than otherwise possible in some areas. Hot caps are inexpensive and disposable, but do require considerable labor to install. They are used with cucumbers, peppers, summer squashes, and tomatoes (Fig. 10–7).

Fig. 10–8   Bell peppers growing under heavy brown paper to protect the plants from prevailing cold winds. Paper traps the heat from the sun's rays, increasing air temperatures under the structure. This technique is called *brushing*.

Fig. 10–7   A field of young tomato plants to be grown for fresh market has been covered with waxed paper hot caps for protection against early morning frost.

BRUSHING   Brushing is sometimes used to protect young plants from cold winds and frost. Long ago, reeds harvested from along river banks and swamps were used. Today, stakes and heavy brown paper are used. The crop rows to be brushed are oriented east-west. A barricade slanting about 45° toward the south and standing about 45 cm (18 in) high is placed on the north side of each row. The slant and placement would be reversed in the southern hemisphere. The barricade is constructed by placing the sloping stakes in the soil about 60 cm (24 in) apart and weaving heavy brown paper about 45 cm (18 in) wide between the stakes. The plants are grown under the barricade, which protects them from the cold wind and which also traps and directs reflected sunlight, warming the soil. Air temperature under the paper during the day is as much as 3°C to 6°C (6°F to 11°F) warmer than outside. Brushing is used to protect tomato, pepper, squash, and cucumber plants (Fig. 10–8).

POLYETHYLENE TUNNELS   An innovative method of increasing the temperature of the microclimate and offering some frost protection is to grow plants in tunnels of transparent polyethylene sheeting (1.5 mil[3]). The tunnels are constructed by placing continuous polyethylene sheeting 100 cm (39 in) wide on each side of the row or bed and covering the bottom edge of the sheeting with soil to hold it in place. The top edges of the sheeting are brought above the row of plants and supported by two parallel wires running the length of the row. The two sheets are pulled together at the top and fastened to a third parallel wire about 60 cm (24 in) above the ground to form a tunnel. The top can be opened during the day if the temperature gets too warm inside (Fig. 10–9). Venti-

[3]A unit of length. 1 mil = 0.254 mm (1/1000 in).

Fig. 10–9   A field of fresh-market tomato plants protected from low temperatures by clear polyethylene tunnels. The tops of the tunnels are closed during the night and opened during the daytime.

Fig. 10–10 Cucumbers growing under clear polyethylene tunnels are protected from frost damage. The holes visible on one side provide ventilation when the tops are closed.

Fig. 10–11 This citrus orchard is equipped with large wind machines. The blades turn about 700 rpm and rotate a full 360° on a vertical axis. The machines mix the cold air at the soil surface with the warmer air above to increase tree temperatures and give some frost protection. If the temperature goes below about −1°C (30°F), oil-burning radiant heaters may also be used along with the wind machines. *Source:* University of California Cooperative Extension.

Fig. 10–12 Oil-burning heaters are sometimes used in orchards or vineyards to aid in frost protection. These heaters with a side return arm recycle the smoke. The result is an intense, practically smokeless heat. *Source:* University of California Cooperative Extension.

lation is provided by small holes prepunched in the sheeting (Fig. 10–10). The tunnels resemble miniature greenhouses.

WIND MACHINES AND HEATERS On clear, calm nights following warm sunny days the soil radiates heat into the atmosphere, leaving cold air to settle over the field. This condition is called an air inversion, with cold air underlying warmer air. Frosts developing under these conditions are called radiation frosts. When the warmer air or ceiling is not far above ground, the condition is called a strong inversion. In such cases wind machines, perhaps in conjunction with oil burning heaters or smudge pots, are used to reduce frost danger, most commonly in orchards and vineyards but for other crops as well. Wind machines are airplane propellers mounted on stands above the trees or vines and driven by gasoline engines or electric motors of various sizes (Fig. 10–11). The propellers turn in a vertical plane at a speed of 700 to 1000 rpm. Some propellers also rotate a full 360 degrees about every five minutes in a horizontal plane. It requires about 50 heaters per ha (20/ac) and one wind machine for four ha (1 per 10 ac) to raise the temperature 2°C to 3°C (4°F to 5°F).

When freezing temperatures are predicted, farmers are alerted by weather stations, and they prepare to operate frost protection equipment. As the temperature approaches 0°C (32°F), usually reaching freezing about an hour before sunrise, growers ignite the heaters and activate the wind machines, leaving them on until the temperature rises above freezing (Fig. 10–12).

SPRINKLERS Sprinkler-applied water can reduce frost damage to some crops because water releases its latent heat of fusion upon freezing (changing from liquid to ice). Additional heat is available for frost prevention if the applied water is warmer than 0°C (32°F) (1 cal/ degree/g water). Heat from these two sources (latent heat of fusion and heat lost upon cooling to freezing temperature) warms the developing buds on grapevines, fruit trees, or strawberry plants as ice forms. Moreover, the ice insulates the buds from air temperatures below freezing. This practice provides sufficient heat and insulation to reduce frost damage, but continuous sprinkling is needed during the danger period. If water is not applied, the temperature at the buds can drop to the danger point. On the other hand, excess water should be avoided to prevent a heavy ice build-up that can damage trees or vines by breaking the branches.

FURROW IRRIGATION Occasionally a crop is saved from frost damage by furrow irrigating the field. Applying warm water to soil warms it and the plants growing in it. The latent heat of fusion released by water changing from the liquid to the solid state yields further calories. Furrow irrigation can be used on row crops, but only once or twice before the field becomes excessively wet. Also, the freezing weather must be anticipated well in advance to allow time for the furrows to fill with water.

Light

Plants are generally spaced so maximum leaf area is exposed to light. Some plants do not require high light intensity and grow well in shaded areas. For example, coffee trees are often grown in the shade because they have a low light saturation point and grow better in less than full sunlight. Many ornamental house plants require subdued light to survive.

Some wavelengths of light are more effective than others in exerting some physiological plant responses (p. 150). Light quality, however, cannot be economically altered for field crops grown in full sunlight, and therefore it is not a factor in climate (see Ch. 7).

The length of day determines when many plant species will flower, thereby setting the time of crop maturity (see p. 125). Different cultivars of certain species, such as soybeans or onions, can differ in these requirements. The length of day changes daily throughout the year and cannot be directly controlled in field plantings. The farmer can modify its effect, however, by: (1) altering crop distribution (planting crops in areas where day lengths are desirable); (2) planting during seasons of favorable day lengths; (3) planting cultivars that have no daylength requirements (see Ch. 6).

Length of Growing Season

Plants require specific growing season lengths to complete their life cycles. These requirements vary widely with different species. For example, red raspberries (*Rubus strigosus*) are satisfactorily produced in Scotland's short, cool growing season while, at the other extreme, sugarcane (*Saccharum officinarum*) requires the long, hot, humid growing seasons of the tropical and subtropical regions. Other plant species can grow and produce well over a wide range of temperatures and length of season. Barley (*Hordeum vulgare*), for example, can be grown satisfactorily in temperature zones ranging from the subarctic to the subtropic.

CLIMATIC REQUIREMENTS OF SOME CROP PLANTS

Fruit and Nut Crops

Fruit and nut species are climatically adapted to the tropical, subtropical, or temperate zones (Ch. 29–31).

TROPICAL

Plants in the tropical group do not withstand freezing temperatures, and many do not grow well if temperatures drop below 10°C (50°F). This confines their growth to the equatorial belt, between about 20° north and 20° south latitudes, at low elevations where frosts never occur. These plants do not require cold temperature exposure for either vegetative growth or flower initiation.

SUBTROPICAL

Subtropical fruit plants tolerate some subfreezing temperatures; in fact, they generally require some cool weather for best growth and fruit development. But subtropical fruit plants are likely to be killed by temperatures below about −7°C (19°F). In completely tropical climates, subtropical fruits do not grow or produce well. Plants in the tropical and subtropical groups are mostly evergreen, except for some subtropicals, such as figs, almonds, and pistachios.

Subtropical fruits are grown at the lower elevations north and south of the tropics. The northern and southern latitudinal limits of these regions are ill defined, being greatly modified by other factors that influence climate such as ocean currents, large inland bodies of water, altitude, and mountain ranges. The subtropical belt includes both humid and semiarid regions.

Fruit plants of the temperate zone are winter hardy, some tolerating temperatures as low as $-34°C$ ($-29°F$) if properly hardened in the fall. Vegetative and flower buds of most temperate-zone plants enter a "resting" state in late summer or fall and require a substantial amount of winter cold before they can resume growth the following spring. This requirement rules out commercial growing of such fruits in tropical and many subtropical regions. The production areas for this group of plants lie in two belts around the world, at approximately 30° to 50° north and south latitudes, where the local climate is otherwise favorable.

Temperate-zone climatic environments can occur in the tropics at sufficiently high elevations. For example, grapevines normally grow in the temperature zones, but they can grow and fruit well in Bolivia, 16° south of the equator at an altitude of 2800 m (8500 ft), where typical temperate zone climates prevail. Likewise, in Kenya, 4° to 10° north of the equator, some temperate-zone fruits produce good crops at high altitudes.

Grain Crops

Most of the grain-producing areas lie in the temperate zones of the world where the annual precipitation is neither less than 38 cm (18 in) nor more than 100 cm (40 in), except in those areas where irrigation is used. In some places wheat and barley are grown with as little as 25 cm (10 in) of rainfall but irrigation or other cultural practices such as strip cropping (see p. 218) are used to supplement the water supply. In regions where rainfall exceeds 100 cm (40 in), grain crops do not thrive because of the prevalence of disease, leached soils, and lodging (falling over).

The growing season for grain crops should have at least 100 to 110 days of frost-free weather, but exceptions do exist. Some cultivars that mature in 90 days succeed in short growing seasons. Also, spring-seeded cereals are grown in short-season areas. Moving toward the north or south poles, summer days become longer. The long days cause earlier maturity in some cereals, helping to overcome the effects of the short season. Winter temperature is a factor in areas where winter grains are grown. Rye is grown farther north than other cereals because it is the most cold-tolerant. Some cereal grains are killed by cold temperatures that freeze the crowns of the small plants. Alternate freezing and thawing of the soil during the winter causes the plants to be pushed upward out of the soil, a process called "heaving." This also causes winter killing. Sometimes cereal plants suffer from lack of water during the winter if the ground remains frozen for long periods of time.

High temperatures cause excessive transpiration losses, which deplete the available soil moisture supply. High temperatures are especially harmful during seed grain formation and between grain formation and maturity of the grains. The fall weather pattern is important for fall-planted cereals. It is essential that these cereals grow as much as possible before cold weather sets in. Good growth before winter helps prevent heaving later on. Thus, cereal grain farmers hope for warm temperatures, ample rainfall, and good growing conditions during the fall.

Sugar Crops

Climate determines the choice between sugar beets (*Beta vulgaris*, Crass Group) and sugarcane (*Saccharum officinarum*). Sugar beets are cool-season crops grown in the north and south temperate zones. In the northern hemisphere, sugar beets are grown from about 35° to 60° north latitude. To prevent seed decay after planting, the soil should be no cooler than 7°C (45°F) at planting. Sugar beet seedlings are most sensitive to cold at emergence, but once out of the ground and hardened, the plants become quite cold resistant. During the summer months, mean daily temperatures of 21°C (70°F) or slightly higher promote rapid growth, but extremely high mean temperatures tend to retard growth. Temperatures in some sugar beet areas often reach 40°C (104°F).

Soil moisture affects the production of good-quality beets more than temperature. With warm temperatures and ample soil moisture, the vegetative growth of sugar beets during the summer and early fall months is rapid and luxurious. In irrigated areas, water is withheld about midfall, and farmers plan their fertilization program so that the plants exhaust the available nitrogen by this time. This practice, coupled with cool nights, retards the rate of vegetative growth. Warm fall days with bright sunlight augment photosynthesis; thus by late fall the sugar content in the roots should increase to between 18 and 20 percent. In some parts of California, sugar beets are cultured differently—planted in the late fall or early winter and harvested in July, when temperatures are highest. This practice is an apparent contradiction, but in reality it is not. Instead of allowing cool weather to retard plant growth, California growers halt vegetative growth of mature sugar beets by withholding irrigation water during the dry summer. The high light intensity of summer causes photosynthesis to proceed at a rapid rate, thus producing a high percentage of sugar.

Sugarcane requires the kind of climate found in the tropical and subtropical belts around the world. The tropical belts are found between the Tropic of Cancer and the Tropic of Capricorn, while the subtropical areas border these. Much of the area has a tropical rainforest climate. However, sugarcane is also produced commercially in arid tropics under irrigation (Peru) or even in temperate zones (Louisiana and parts of India). Sugarcane requires a continuous frost-free growing season, an ample water supply, and full sunlight. Short days and low temperatures are not conducive to good cane growth.

The wide climatic variation of the areas where sugarcane is produced must be reconciled with the climatic requirements of the plant. A part of the explanation is that no sexual cycles are involved; that is, the marketed product is sap from the vegetative cells; thus, neither fruit nor seed need be produced. As a result, day length imposes no limit on sugarcane production. As long as the total hours of daylight are available for maximum growth, sugarcane can succeed. For this crop there must be an ample supply of soil moisture when the temperature is sufficiently warm for good growth, and during the long growing season there must be at least one rest period during which growth is interrupted either by reduced temperature or rainfall.

Forage Crops

In all climates, irrespective of latitude or altitude, various forage crops are grown for livestock feed. Many species are used, each adapted to a particular environment (see Ch. 25).

LEGUMES

Alfalfa (*Medicago sativa*), widely distributed in the temperate zone, is remarkably adaptable to climate, provided its soil and water requirements are met. The crop requires considerable amounts of water but it produces best in relatively warm, arid climates with supplemental irrigation. Alfalfa is an important forage crop in the humid Northeast and North Central states. However, it grows better in the arid West and Southwest. Diseases are more prevalent in humid areas, and soils in high-rainfall areas are less favorable to alfalfa because of their high acidity. The combination of high humidity, high soil moisture, and high temperature is particularly unde-

sirable. During periods of drought, the deep alfalfa tap root—often 4.5 to 6 m (15 to 20 ft) long—can extract sufficient water from the subsoil to survive, if not enough to produce a profitable crop. However, alfalfa plants can be winter-killed because lack of water the previous summer so weakens the plant that it cannot stand the severe winter.

Alfalfa is more tolerant to high and low temperature extremes than most perennials. In the United States, alfalfa cultivars are classified on the basis of temperature tolerance as hardy, medium hardy, or nonhardy.

Another legume, commonly called sweet clover or melilot (*Melilotus*) even though it is not a true clover, includes about 20 species adapted to a wide range of climates. Sweet clover can be grown without irrigation in any part of the United States where the annual rainfall is at least 45 to 50 cm (18 to 20 in) and the soil reaction is neutral or slightly alkaline. Sour or bitter clovers (*M. inclica*)—also not true clovers—are adapted to the climates of the Gulf coast, southern California, New Mexico, and Arizona. If rainfall is lacking, irrigation is used. Cultivars differ widely in their adaptation to temperature, moisture, light, and day length.

Sometimes stands of red clover (*Trifolium pratense*) are winter-killed by low temperature, low soil moisture, alternating cold and warm temperatures, or heaving. Biennial sweet clover is more tolerant to freezing than red clover, but it is also more susceptible to heaving. Low winter temperatures definitely limit adaptation of the winter annual clover species. Sour or bitter clover (*M. inclica*) and berseem clover (*T. alexandrinum*) are among the least tolerant to low temperatures of all the clover species. The plant can better stand low temperature if it enters the cold season with good vegetative growth. Clover plants tolerate high summer temperatures if adequate soil moisture is available, but high summer temperatures inhibit germination of winter annual clover seeds.

Soil moisture is the most critical single climatic factor for the clovers. They all require a moist soil from time of seed germination to the end of their life cycle. If rainfall is not sufficient, supplemental irrigation must be used. Deep-rooted sweet clovers, if well established, are more drought-resistant than the others. Clovers are long-day plants, but the different species and cultivars vary in their response to day lengths. Clover is often grown with a grain crop for weed control, and the growth of the clover plants is sometimes stunted when they are shaded too much by the taller grain plants. Even when the clover stand is well established, growth might be slow. Then, when the grain is cut for harvest, sudden exposure of the clover plants to the hot summer sun could be fatal.

GRASSES

Over 1000 species of grasses grow in the United States, and about 100 of them are economically important as forage crops. Temperature and soil moisture are the dominant factors determining their distribution. For example, the cold northern humid regions are more suited for the growth of bluegrasses (*Poa* spp.), orchard grass (*Dactylis glomerata*), redtop (*Agrostis gigantea*), and timothy (*Phleum alpinum*, syn. *P. pratense*). In the warm southern humid regions we find bermuda (*Cynodon dactylon*), carpet (*Axonopus affinis*), and Dallis grasses (*Paspalum dilatatum*). In the wet South, there is carpet (*A. affinis*), St. Augustine (*Stenotaphrum secundatum*), and certain reed grasses (*Phalaris* spp.) In the drier northern areas, there is Canada bluegrass (*Poa compressa*), and bromegrass (*Bromus* spp.), while in the drier southern regions, bermuda grass (*C. dactylon*) and Bahia grass (*Paspalum notatum*) grow well (see Ch. 21).

In the dry western regions of the United States, the different grass species are spread over a wide temperature range. Soil moisture is more important than temperature. The native bunch grasses, such as bluebunch wheatgrass (*Agropyron spicatum*) and crested wheatgrass (*A. desertorum*), are found in the northern half of the semiarid region, while blue grama (*Bouteloua gracills*) and buffalo grass (*Buchloe dactyloides*) do well in the drier southern regions. In general, it appears that grasses adapted to the humid regions are influenced primarily by temperature, while those growing in the dry areas are influenced principally by moisture levels.

Fiber Crops

Cotton (*Gossypium hirsutum*) and flax (*Linum usitatissimum*) are the two most important fiber crops. Cotton is grown around the world because of its usefulness and adaptability. The climatic requirements for optimum yields of fiber crops are rather exacting. Freedom from frost, ample soil moisture, and an abundance of sunlight are three climatic requirements (see Ch. 25).

Production areas extend from about 35° south to about 45° north latitudes, but over 90 percent of the total cotton crop is grown north of the equator. Mean annual temperatures in these areas are about 16°C (61°F). For best cotton production, the mean maximum summer temperature should be about 32°C (90°F) and the mean minimum about 25°C (77°F). The growing season

should have at least 180 to 200 frost-free days. Some new cultivars mature in fewer days and are adapted to areas with shorter growing seasons. The annual rainfall in the United States Cotton Belt ranges from about 50 cm (20 in) in western Oklahoma to 140 cm (55 in) in parts of Texas. Cotton grown in the arid Southwest must be irrigated. There must be at least 50 percent cloud-free days during the growing season.

Ideal weather for cotton production is a warm spring with frequent light rains after planting, followed by a moderately moist summer with both warm days and nights. Cold wet weather in the spring can cause the seeds to decay before they germinate. Strong winds blow sand or soil particles over the soil surface and damage the seedlings. Wet summers encourage excessive vegetative growth and increase disease and insect problems. High temperatures cause considerable moisture loss through transpiration and drought. Heavy rains interfere with fruiting and can cause the cotton bolls to drop off.

Vegetable Crops

The climatic range in which different vegetable crops grow is quite narrow. Farmers widen the range for some crops by establishing suitable microclimates. Plastic or glass greenhouses, hot beds, cold frames, hot caps, plastic mulches, and wind machines used with smudge pots (oil-burning heaters) are examples of equipment used to modify the climate. Certain cultural techniques, such as changing the shape of beds and brushing, are sometimes used to modify the climate sufficiently to permit successful culture of some vegetable crops (p. 229). Irrigation can be used to either cool or warm the soil. For example, an application of water before planting will cool the soil sufficiently to permit lettuce seed to germinate for an early fall planting of head lettuce in the hot Imperial Valley of California. Early in the spring, if frost has been predicted, furrow irrigation with warm water could provide enough heat to ward off frost damage (p. 231).

Sometimes a certain climate is not suitable for a given physiological plant function. For example, perhaps a crop could not flower and produce seed under certain day length conditions but could grow well and produce a good crop of leaf or stem parts. The seed for this crop could be produced in areas where climatic conditions permitted seed production while the vegetative crop is produced in other areas. Crops are sometimes grown to follow the seasons. For example, in the northern hemisphere short-season crops move northward in the spring and southward in the fall, and vice versa in the southern hemisphere. Also, plant breeders continually introduce new cultivars with altered climatic adaptability. Finally, vegetable growers generally can accept more risk with weather than other growers because their crops are short-term investments.

The important vegetable-growing regions of the world are located in those parts of the temperate zones where sudden and extreme temperature changes do not occur. In the United States these areas are: (1) the coastal valleys of the Pacific coast states, (2) along the Atlantic and Gulf coasts from Massachusetts to Texas, (3) around large inland bodies of water such as the Great Lakes from New York to Minnesota, and (4) in the Rio Grande Valley of Texas.

Vegetable crops are divided into two groups by their temperature tolerance—cool season and warm season (Chs. 26–28).

Cool-season crops grow best at temperatures from 15°C to 18°C (59°F to 64°F). Certain crops, such as Brussels sprouts, turnips, rutabagas, spinach, and beets, can tolerate some freezing, but others are injured by freezing. The latter include cauliflower, lettuce, carrots, potatoes, peas, and onions.

Warm-season crops thrive best at temperatures between 18°C to 27°C (64°F to 80°F). Plants in this group are intolerant of frost or prolonged exposure to near freezing. In this group are melons, cucumbers, squash, pumpkins, tomatoes, sweet corn, peppers, sweet potatoes, eggplant, and okra. However, even warm-season vegetables do not grow well if temperatures are extremely high. For example, several consecutive days of temperatures over 40°C (104°F) will destroy pollen in sweet corn and cause blossoms to drop from tomatoes. Hot weather unduly hastens fruit maturity, shortens the harvest period, and causes rapid deterioration of the product.

CLIMATIC INFLUENCES ON PLANT DISEASES

Since people first domesticated and cultivated plants for food, their efforts have been plagued by plant diseases (see Ch. 11). At times, plant diseases have profoundly affected history. Wars have been fought, countries destroyed, and people have migrated en masse to new lands because of famines caused by plant disease. A recent and noted example was the Irish potato famine of 1846 and 1847, which caused half the population of Ireland to either starve to death or to emigrate.

Modern knowledge has demonstrated a definite relationship between climate and plant diseases. Weather influences the incidence of disease by: (1) favoring the growth of the pathogen itself (e.g., high humidity favors fungus development), (2) affecting the incidence of an insect carrier (aphids, for example, transmit viral dis-

eases), and (3) increasing the plant's suceptibility to disease (unfavorable weather weakens the plant and lowers its resistance).

Plant disease epidemics caused by fungi have been numerous, even in modern times. Four conditions are necessary for an epidemic to start, two of them environmental: (1) temperature must favor rapid growth of the pathogen; (2) high humidity, or an abundance of rain or dew; (3) a large number of pathogenic organisms; and (4) a susceptible host plant. The first two conditions can be controlled somewhat by cultural practices and selecting crops well adapted to the climatic conditions of that particular area. The last one cannot be controlled except by breeding for resistant cultivars. Today, breeding for disease resistance receives more attention than any other breeding objective, and the outlook for better disease control from this standpoint is bright indeed.

CLIMATIC INFLUENCES ON INSECT PESTS

Insects living in a given region have adapted themselves to the average climatic conditions of that region. Only when severe departures from these climatic norms occur at a critical period in the insect's life does that population change materially. The various factors of climate such as temperature, moisture, and air movement affect insects in varying degrees and at different times. Many insects have short life spans, some as short as a few days, others up to several weeks. Those insects with short life spans usually produce numerous generations in a single year. Each of the many generations could evolve slightly, which permits adaptation to rather abrupt climatic changes. The ability of some insects to adapt to environment can be illustrated by the increased resistance of the common housefly (*Musca domestica*) to the insecticide DDT (**d**ichloro-**d**iphenyl-**t**richloro ethane). This material, introduced in the 1940s, was a powerful and effective insecticide against the common housefly, but after 20 years its effectiveness was reduced because a resistance to its toxicity developed through many generations of flies.

Insects, at each stage of development (egg, larva, pupa, and adult) have a definite temperature tolerance which can be different at other stages. An insect dies at temperatures below a certain minimum. Most insects can withstand the low temperatures that normally occur in the inhabited parts of the world, but severe cold is usually endured during periods of hibernation. The insect remains dormant between the minimum temperature at which its life can exist and the temperature at which development occurs. The optimum temperature is the range in which most activity and maximum development occurs most rapidly. This temperature range can be wide or narrow, depending on the insect species. Temperatures above the optimum retard growth and development. From the upper limit of the optimum temperature to the temperature that causes death, the insect lives in a state of suspended activity called **aestivation.** Some water beetles, water bugs, and mosquitoes live normally in hot springs with temperatures ranging from 38°C to 50°C (100°F to 122°F). The longer the optimum temperature is present, the more generations of insects are produced.

The effect of moisture on insects is similar to those of temperature—there is a point of excessive dryness at which the insect dies, a moisture condition for optimum development, and an excessive moisture condition that causes death.

There are specific examples of the manner in which insects respond to climate. For example, San Jose scale—caused by the insect *Aspidiotus perniciosus*—is restricted to the fruit trees growing in the warmer climates. It will not extend into the colder climates unless, through many generations of evolution, the insect develops a tolerance to lower temperatures.

Temperatures of −18°C (0°F) are fatal to the cotton boll weevil (*Anthonomus grandis*). This factor of climate restricts damage to cotton by this insect to the warmer regions of the Cotton Belt, where it is one of the major limiting factors. Dry conditions during the early spring are favorable for the development of the chinch bug (*Blissus leucopterus*). All of the recorded outbreaks of this insect have occurred during periods of less than normal rainfall.

Very often the effect of climate on insects is a complicated one—not directly affecting a certain insect, but affecting others that prey on it. For example, one insect population increases drastically in a cool wet spring when temperatures are decidedly below those for optimum development of a parasite of this insect. Under normal temperatures the parasite develops in numbers sufficient to keep the host under control.

Weather changes from day to day, but the climate of a given area is not likely to change within a century. Weather is the result of daily variations in temperature, rainfall, light, and air movement for any given season. The climate of a given region is the summation of daily, weekly, monthly, and seasonal changes of weather over a period of decades. Longtime weather records allow fairly accurate predictions of future weather.

The climatic factors influencing plant growth include air movement, precipitation, temperature, and light. Basically air circulation patterns arise from solar-heated air around the equator. The hot air rises and flows to either of the poles, cooling as it heads poleward. The cooled air sinks and returns along the earth's surface to the equator. The eastward spin of the earth, seasonal temperature variations, differences in heating and cooling between water and land masses, variations in topography, all affect the general direction of air movement. Air circulation patterns and topography influence climatic rainfall distribution. Climatic changes in temperature give rise to seasonal variations that determine the worldwide distribution of plants. Crop growers must either modify environmental temperatures or change the plant to adapt to given temperatures. Plants of different species vary widely in their adaptability to temperatures, but within a given species the adaptability range is quite narrow.

Crops producers have developed a wide variety of devices and techniques to modify the microclimate around the plant in order to produce crops where they otherwise would not grow well. In some cases the grower alters such climatic factors as the soil's moisture content, the light intensity, light quality, day length, and even wind velocity to produce better crops. Climate can also influence plant diseases and insect populations. Climatic conditions that favor the growth of fungi have been responsible for plant disease epidemics. Changes in weather conditions can be either helpful or harmful to insect populations.

REVIEW QUESTIONS

10–1. The crop distribution pattern of the world is basically the result of _____ .

10–2. Weather results from the summation of long range climatic variations. True or false?

10–3. Discuss three characteristics that allow the desert plants (xerophytes) to survive with little water.

10–4. Name five factors that determine or modify the direction of the air flow patterns of the earth.
(a) _____ (b) _____
(c) _____ (d) _____
(e) _____ .

10–5. By knowing only the climatic conditions of a given area and the growth requirements of a plant, one can predict the plant's adaptability to the area. True or false? Discuss the reasons for your answer.

10–6. Normally, as water-laden clouds cross a mountain range, they lose their water on the _____ side of the mountain. Explain why.

10–7. Biological activities are in general restricted to temperatures between 0°C and 50°C (32°F to 122°F). Explain why.

10–8. Sometimes, plant tissue can be quickly cooled to below the freezing point and, if warmed gradually without disturbance, will suffer no harm. True or false? Explain your answer.

10–9. Metabolic changes in a plant's physiology can bring about a tolerance to freezing in some plants. Such a response is called (a) supercooling, (b) cold accumulation, (c) hardening, (d) heat tolerance, (e) none of these.

10–10. Absolutely pure water freezes (a) above 0°C, (b) at 0°C, (c) below 0°C. Discuss your answer.

10–11. Radiation losses are higher from a vegetation-covered field than a clean-tilled field because plants reflect light better. True or false? Explain your answer.

10–12. Domelike structures made of waxed paper on wire frames and used for frost protection for young plants are called _____.

10–13. Which of these cannot be hardened easily? (a) broccoli, (b) cabbage, (c) sunflower, (d) tomatoes, (e) beans.

10–14. The latent heat of fusion is a property of water that can be exploited to reduce crop losses due to freezing for some crop plants. True or false? Explain.

10–15. List five practices or techniques used to alter the microclimate around plants to reduce losses due to freezing. (a) _____ (b) _____ (c) _____ (d) _____ (e) _____.

10–16. On a windless and cloudless night the minimum temperature early in the spring is likely to occur (a) one hour after sundown, (b) at midnight, (c) one hour before sunup.

10–17. Cool-season crops (can/cannot) be grown successfully in the tropics. Discuss the reasons for your answer.

10–18. List four conditions necessary for a plant disease epidemic. (a) _____ (b) _____ (c) _____ (d) _____.

10–19. Ice melts at 0°C (32°F) but seldom does water freeze at that temperature. True or false? Explain your answer.

10–20. What are thermal belts and how do they form?

SUPPLEMENTARY READING

CHANDLER, W. H. 1950. *Evergreen orchards.* Philadelphia: Lea & Febiger. Ch. 2, Evergreen orchard environments.

CHANDLER, W. H. 1957. *Deciduous orchards.* Philadelphia: Lea & Febiger. Ch. 8, Climate for deciduous orchards.

Encyclopaedia Britannica. 1967. Climate and climatology. 5:914.

HAMBIDGE, G. 1941. Climate and man. USDA Yearbook. Washington, D.C.: U.S. Government Printing Office.

HUGHES, H. D., and D. S. METCALFE. 1972. *Crop production.* New York: Macmillan.

LEOPOLD, A. C., and P. E. KRIEDEMANN. 1975. *Plant growth and development,* 2nd ed. New York: McGraw-Hill.

LEVITT, J. 1980. *Responses of plants to environmental stresses,* vol. 1. 2nd ed. New York: Academic Press.

MACGILLIVRAY, J. H. 1953. *Vegetable production.* Toronto: Blakeston.

NOGGLE, G. R., and G. J. FRITZ. 1976. *Introductory plant physiology.* Englewood Cliffs, N.J.: Prentice-Hall.

REUTHER, W., ed. 1973. *The citrus industry,* vol. III. Berkeley, Calif.: Univ. of Calif. Div. of Agr. Sci. Ch. 9, Climate and citrus behavior.

ROSS, N. W. 1974. Stanislaus orchard handbook. Modesto, Calif.: Univ. of Calif. Coop. Ext.

THOMPSON, P. D., and R. O'BRIEN. 1965. *Weather.* New York: Time-Life Books.

Biological
Competitors
of Useful
Plants

Since the beginnings of agriculture, farmers have had to wage war continuously against weeds, plant diseases, and insects. Even today, with all the scientific research on crop protection, it is estimated that insects, diseases, weeds, and animal pests eliminate half the food produced in the world during the growing, transporting, and storing of crops. In the tropics, where heat and high humidity favor many pathogens, two-thirds of some crops are lost. Of the world's population of 4.5 billion, it is estimated that 500 million persons are seriously underfed and 1.5 billion inadequately fed. Obviously, losses to plant pests greatly aggravate the world hunger problem.

All of the thousands of kinds of cultivated plants—the ornamentals, the vegetables, the fruits, the forage and grain crops, and the forest species—often have difficulty in growing and producing their products. In addition to contending with the uncertainties of weather and soil conditions, plants have many biological competitors—weeds, insects, mites, and disease-producing fungi and bacteria—that contend with them or attack both their tops and roots. In addition, other soil-borne organisms, such as nematodes, as well as systemic pathogens such as viruses and mycoplama-like organisms attack cultivated plants. Various plant parasites, such as mistletoe and dodder, attack some plants and often eventually kill them. Birds are generally considered to be among the world's desirable animals, but certain species can become major pests to agriculture by feeding on and destroying certain crops. Deer and rabbits sometimes severely damage plants such as young fruit trees, especially during the winter, unless protective

measures are taken. Rats and other rodents destroy a major part of harvested grain crops in some countries.

Many plants carry genetic resistance to many of the pathogenic or parasitic organisms. As a result, no plant species is attacked by all possible pests. The decision to grow a certain crop or a particular cultivar in a certain area is often based upon the genetic resistance of that plant to a common pathogenic organism or insect pest. The development, by plant breeding, of new plant types with genetic resistance to pathogens and predators is one of the most effective means of combating these problems.

In the last 100 years we have learned to control the ravages of insects, diseases, and weeds fairly well by applying various agricultural chemicals: insecticides, fungicides, and herbicides (14). However, the ideal, long-term solution for saving food, fiber, and ornamental plants from attack by pests is biological control. Biological control can be used in a number of ways, as detailed later. For example:

1. New plant types can be bred that are genetically resistant to attacks of insects, diseases, nematodes, and other parasites and predators (see p. 243).

2. Insect populations can be controlled by infesting them with parasites or predators, such as other insects, bacteria, or viruses (see p. 244).

3. Some insect populations can be almost eliminated by releasing massive numbers of radiation-sterilized male insects. After mating, the females fail to produce offspring (see p. 256).

4. Insects are lured by synthesized natural attractants (pheromones) into bait traps where they are killed (see p. 259).

5. Some insects are prevented from reproducing by juvenile hormones, which prevent them from reaching the adult stage, and thus prevent their reproduction. This procedure is in the experimental stage (see p. 259).

6. Some weed species are controlled by releasing into the fields certain insects that feed on the weed but not on the crop plant. (Pulling weeds by hand from our gardens is also, of course, a form of biological control.)

7. A few plant diseases caused by fungi or bacteria have also been controlled with antagonistic or competing fungi or bacteria that are not pathogenic to the crop plants.

While these types of biological control are helpful and offer considerable promise for the future, they cannot be relied upon entirely at present. For now and into the foreseeable future, pesticides and herbicides must be used to enable the crop producers and distributors to furnish the kind and amount of food products consumers demand. No food products that show the slightest evidence of insects are tolerated in the market—no wormy apples, no insect parts in canned or dried fruits or vegetables, no burrowing passages in fresh vegetables. To maintain such quality standards, for the present at least, we must continue to use pesticides despite the problems they cause.

The modern concept of **integrated pest management** (*36*) employs many approaches to control a pest permanently, rather than relying solely on a single procedure. Integrated pest management develops information on such facets of the problem as:

1. dynamics of the pest population, predictions of the occurrence, population levels, and potential economic damage of pests

2. biology of the pest organism, of its natural enemies, and of the host plant, and their interrelationships in a given environment

3. effects of weather patterns on pest activities

4. effects of cultural practices such as crop rotation, cover and companion crops, and harvesting methods on pest activities

5. effects of various control strategies on each other and on the environment.

Proper integrated pest management uses a range of cultural, biological, mechanical, and chemical measures to hold the pests below economically damaging levels, while at the same time avoiding disruption of the agroecosystem. In the United States, integrated pest management systems are being developed largely for cotton, rice, apples, alfalfa, corn, potatoes, pears, and wheat. So far, the concept has been applied primarily to insect pests and only in a limited way to pathogens and weeds.

WEEDS

Ever since people began cultivating plants, they have had to fight weeds competing with crops for space, water, mineral nutrients, and sunlight (*6, 12, 17, 19, 20*). A weed has been described as any plant out of place. Wheat plants in a field of oats would be considered weeds, as would oat plants in a field of wheat. Some of the biggest problems with weeds in fields of cultivated crops occur in areas where substantial rain falls all through the growing season. The high moisture level keeps the weed seeds germinating, and unless the weeds are controlled, they either choke out and eliminate the desired plants or reduce yields.

Until recently, weed control was entirely physical. The weeds were simply cut off or dug out after they started to grow. Most kinds of weeds are annuals, developing from germinating seeds, but others—more difficult to control—are perennials developing from shoots that continually sprout from underground roots or stems (rhizomes).

The primitive tools used for mechanical weed control were sharpened sticks or metal objects, culminating with the common hoe. Even today in small gardens and flower beds and in fields of such crops as sugar beets and lettuce the hoe is often the best means of eliminating weeds as they appear. Commercial crops were planted in rows to allow horse-drawn cultivators to dig out the weeds. Cultivation continued through the summer as the weed seeds kept germinating. The final stage in mechanical weed control in commercial row crops was the multirow, tractor-drawn cultivator. Mechanical weed control in large expanses of soil entails tractor-drawn disks, harrows, and other weeders. Tall weeds, particularly in open spaces such as orchards, can be effectively controlled by mowing. This keeps them from producing seeds and reduces their photosynthetic capacity, decreasing the accumulation of stored foods in the roots. Mowing is not effective, however, in controlling low-growing or perennial weeds. Pasturing animals such as sheep or geese along ditch banks or in orchards can sometimes be used as an alternative to mowing, provided the animals do not disturb the crop plants.

Mulching is another effective way to physically control weeds in small areas. The spaces in and around cultivated plants are covered with wood chips, sawdust, gravel, straw, rice hulls, or similarly inactive materials. If they are thick enough, such mulches shut out light from young weed seedlings, thus preventing their growth. Mulching is ineffective against perennial weeds with heavy root systems that send strong-growing shoots right up through the mulch. Plastic film is often used for this purpose in nurseries and in strawberry plantings (see Fig. 29–1).

Fire has been used to control weeds along roadsides, ditch banks, and other work areas, but high fuel costs will curtail this practice. Special, highly maneuverable flame throwers are built for this purpose. Such burning has limited value in controlling weeds in crop lands, however, although special burners have been developed to burn off very small annual weeds in row crops such as cotton. Controlled burning has been of considerable value in removing unwanted brush from forest areas and range lands.

The accumulated costs in equipment, labor, and energy to control weeds in the world's crops by physical methods are almost unbelievable, calculated to be about $3.75 billion annually in the United States (6). These costs are, of course, added to the selling price of crops and have increased tremendously the prices people have to pay for their food. Removing weeds from crops is still one of the world's greatest users of energy.

Modern Weed Control Methods

In the early 1940s agriculturalists in many countries realized the staggering costs of mechanical weed control. Intensive research efforts to develop cheaper and more effective methods of controlling weeds began. These efforts led to a new body of scientific study involving large groups of research and extension workers in various agricultural colleges plus many other scientifically trained persons employed by agricultural chemical companies. Four basic methods of weed control were developed: (1) preventive measures, (2) crop competition, (3) biological control, and (4) chemical control.

Preventive measures entail attempts to reduce all sources of weed seeds such as roadside or ditch stands of weeds, seeds in irrigation canals, seeds blowing in from nearby weedy fields, and weed seed mixed in with crop seeds.

In **crop competition** the cultivated crop plants are simply induced to grow so fast and so vigorously that they shade out and overcome the weeds. This method is most useful in agronomic crops like the cereals and forage crops that completely cover the ground. It is of less value in row crops, vineyards, or orchards, where much

of the soil surface is bare—although once such crop plants become large enough, they can shade so much of the soil surface that young weed seedlings have difficulty growing.

Biological control of weeds succeeds best where a fungus or an insect predator, a "natural enemy," is introduced into an area where the population of the weed it attacks is large. A natural biological balance is set up between the weed (the host) and its pathogen, the weed population being reduced in numbers but not completely eradicated. There is always the hazard that the introduced controlling organism can develop into as serious a pest as the weed being controlled. Therefore, considerable advance study precedes any such introductions. Government quarantine officials are extremely reluctant to allow any fungi or insects into areas where they do not already exist.

Interesting examples of biological control of noxious weeds by introduced insects are the control of St. Johnswort (Klamath weed), a poisonous range weed in the western United States, by the leaf-eating beetle (*Chrysolina* spp.) (*33*), and the control of the prickly pear cactus in Australia by a moth borer (*Cactoblastis cactorum*) introduced from Argentina (*20*). However, this type of control is effective only in large expanses of a weed. It is mainly useful for weed control in forage and pasture lands.

CHEMICAL WEED CONTROL

Sporadic research with chemicals as a way to control weeds started about 1910 in both Europe and America, but the real basis for chemical weed control was laid with the initial studies of auxins and plant hormone physiology in the 1930s (see Ch. 6). The introduction of the auxin-type synthetic plant growth regulator 2,4-dichlorophenoxyacetic acid (2,4-D) as an herbicide in 1944 gave the initial impetus to chemical weed control. Production of pesticides is now a multibillion dollar industry, with sales of herbicides far surpassing both insecticides and fungicides.

Weed-controlling chemicals can be classified as either **selective** or **nonselective.** For example, 2,4-D is a selective herbicide. Sprayed on a lawn, it will kill broad-leaved weeds, such as dandelions, but not harm the grass. Nonselective herbicides, such as the high aromatic weed oils, kill all vegetation they are applied to.

Herbicides can be further classified according to the timing of their application in relation to the growth cycle of weeds or crops.

PREPLANTING TREATMENTS The herbicide is incorporated into the soil before the crop is planted. The crop seeds or plants must be highly tolerant of the herbicide. The herbicidal action on the weeds can be due to a direct contact killing, or it can be absorbed by the weed's roots, then translocated throughout the plant, interfering with various plant processes.

PREEMERGENCE TREATMENTS Herbicides are applied to the soil surface after the crop is planted but before the emergence of the weed seedlings, the crop seedlings, or both. For clarity in any particular case, it should be stated whether *pre-emergence* refers to the weeds, the crop, or both.

POSTEMERGENCE TREATMENTS Herbicide treatment follows emergence of the seedlings of the crop plants, the weeds, or both. Application could be postemergence for the crop plants but preemergence for the weeds. In an orchard or vineyard, herbicide applications would always be postemergence for the crop plants but could be either preemergence or postemergence for the weeds.

Another basis for classification of herbicides is the method of application:

1. *Broadcast*. This method covers an entire area uniformly, either by spraying a liquid or disseminating a granular form of the herbicide.

2. *Band treatment*. A relatively narrow band just covering the crop row is treated with the herbicide. Weeds between rows are controlled some other way, perhaps by tillage equipment.

3. *Spot treatment*. Herbicide sprays are directed to the foliage of a clump of weeds arising in a relatively clean area, such as an orchard, that has previously been cleaned of weeds by other control measures; or the soil may be spot treated in a small area where a particularly difficult clump of perennial weeds has established itself.

HERBICIDE APPLICATION EQUIPMENT Since herbicidal chemicals are often toxic to plant tissue, it is inadvisable to use the application equipment for other purposes. Enough of the herbicide may remain in the equipment to damage crop plants in other spray applications.

1. *Sprayers*. Power or hand-operated sprayers (Fig. 11–1) are most commonly used to apply herbicides as liquid formulations either directly on the weeds or onto the soil. The sprayer is either low volume, applying a concentrated form of the herbicide in a small amount per unit area, or high volume, applying less concentrated solutions but in larger amounts per unit area.

Fig. 11–1 Preemergence herbicides are often applied as a spray. This destroys the earliest weeds and gives the crop an advantage throughout the entire season. *Source:* Fred Meyer, Tennessee Valley Authority.

The amount of the herbicide applied is generally calculated in liters per hectare (gallons per acre) of a given concentration as directed on the label.

2. *Granular applications.* Equipment is available to apply granular forms of herbicides as a pre-emergence application to the soil over the crop rows when the seeds are being drilled into the soil. At high application rates, the granules of the herbicide itself are applied; at lower rates, the granules are first mixed with a carrier such as sand or vermiculite to increase the bulk, thus permitting better distribution of the active herbicide particles. Granular application eliminates the need for hauling quantities of water, and the application equipment is much simpler and less expensive than spray machinery. Granular application, however, is not as uniform as water sprays. Winds can blow the granules and carrier from where it should be applied; in addition, heavy rains or irrigation can wash the granules away. Granular forms of herbicides are generally more costly than other types because of higher shipping costs.

3. *Mixing with soil.* Preemergence herbicides, applied either as a spray or granules, are worked—by disking into the upper few inches of the soil to bring them into contact with weed seeds. This application method is effective only if the seed bed is well prepared, lacks large soil clods, and has

the proper soil moisture—neither dry nor excessively wet.

4. *Aircraft applications.* Applications of herbicides by airplane or helicopter are particularly useful for large areas or in situations where ground equipment cannot be readily used. Weeds and brush along utility lines or in firebreaks in mountainous areas are easily controlled by air. Large areas of grain or forage crops are covered economically in this manner, such as flooded rice fields that cannot be easily treated with herbicides in any other manner (Fig. 11–2). However, air application of herbicides is not used in populated areas owing to drift hazards.

Types of Weeds

Weeds, like all plants, are classified into annuals, biennials, or perennials (see Ch. 6). Control measures differ for the three types.

ANNUALS

These can be summer or winter annuals, completing their life cycle in one year. Annual weeds generally are easy to control, but they produce many seeds and are persistent.

Seeds of summer annuals germinate in the spring. The plants grow all summer and produce seeds, then die in the fall or winter. The seeds lie dormant all winter, then germinate the following spring. Typical summer annual weeds are crabgrass, foxtail, lambsquarter, ragweed, and cocklebur. These are a particular problem in summer crops such as corn, soybeans, cotton, and most vegetables.

Seeds of the winter annuals germinate in the fall. The plants grow through the winter (in mild climates), and mature their seed in the spring. The seeds lie dormant in the soil through the hot summer, then germinate in the fall. Examples of such weeds are shepherd's purse, cornflower, hairy chess, and chickweed. These are often a problem in such winter crops as winter barley, winter oats, and winter wheat and in fall sown nursery plantings.

BIENNIALS

The seeds of biennial plants germinate in spring. The plants grow vegetatively through the first summer. The following spring, after a winter chilling period, the plants flower. Seeds develop and mature by the end of the second summer. This category includes a few troublesome weeds such as mullein, burdock, wild carrot, and bull thistle, which are a problem in both summer and winter crops.

Fig. 11–2 Application by aircraft of a postemergence herbicide to crop plants. *Source:* Cessna Aircraft Company.

PERENNIALS

Perennial plants can live indefinitely although the tops may die down in winter. Once started, perennial weeds remain until they are killed. They usually start from germinating seeds, but many types spread naturally by vegetative means such as root pieces, rhizomes, stolons, or tubers (see Ch. 2). Some perennial weeds—such as dandelion, plantain, and dock—live for many years as single, individual plants. Other perennial weeds, in addition to producing seed, also propagate by vegetative means, making them difficult to control. Examples are bermuda grass, bindweed, Johnson grass, quackgrass, nutgrass, and red sorrel. Cultivating creeping perennial weeds often just breaks them up and spreads them. However, repeated cultivation for several years prevents development of much leaf area and, together with herbicide applications, brings them under control.

Table 11–1 lists some of the hardest-to-control weeds.

Table 11–1 Ten of the World's Hardest-to-Control Weeds

Purple nutsedge (*Cyperus rotundus* L.)
Bermuda grass (*Cynodon dactylon* (L.) Pers.)
Barnyard grass (*Echinochloa crusgalli* (L.) Beauv.)
Jungle rice (*Echinochloa colonum* L.) Link
Goose grass (*Eleusine indica* (L.) Gaertn.)
Johnson grass (*Sorghum halepense* (L.) Pers.)
Guinea grass (*Panicum maximum* Jacq)
Water hyacinth (*Eichhornia crassipes* Mart.) Solms
Cogon grass (*Imperata cylindrica* (L.) Beauv.)
Lantana (*Lantana camara* L.)

Source: Crafts, A. S. 1975. *Modern weed control.* Berkeley, Calif.: University of California Press.

Herbicidal Control of Different Weed Types

The development and use of herbicides is a changing situation. Older chemicals are being discontinued and new ones are replacing them. Herbicides in current use number in the hundreds. When herbicides are being considered for controlling weeds in any area, from the backyard garden to large acreages of crops, expert advice should be obtained, preferably from the local agricultural extension agent, an agricultural chemical supply dealer, or garden center operator. There is usually a choice of herbicides for the task, and it is essential to read the label on the package carefully and follow the directions explicitly. For large agricultural operations, it is often advisable to employ specialized spray operators, whose business it is to know the available herbicides for each crop and to be familiar with all the regulations governing their use.

PLANT DISEASES AND INSECT PESTS

The Food and Agriculture Organization (FAO) of the United Nations estimates that 35 percent of the world's wheat crop is lost to diseases and insects, as are 40 percent of the potatoes, 24 percent of the sugar beets, 30 percent of the apples, and 60 percent of the cotton (*32*). In the United States alone, plant diseases and insects cause about $12 billion a year in damage to crops, fruits, and ornamentals. With the increasing world population, such losses translate into human misery from malnutrition and starvation. The world's governments and agricultural interests, of course, try to reduce these losses by every means possible. If they did not, agriculture and the world's present life style would not exist. Success in lowering crop losses varies with the country, the efficiency of crop production, and the degree of agricultural mechanization.

The methods for combatting plant diseases and insect pests fall into four groups: biological control, control by cultural practices, government agricultural quarantine and pest eradication programs, and application of pesticides.

Biological Control

RESISTANT PLANT SPECIES AND CULTIVARS

Genetically resistant types of plants are selected naturally. Plants susceptible to a prevalent disease or insect pest tend to disappear, while resistant types remain. The work of geneticists and plant breeders in purposely developing resistant cultivars of agricultural species has been one of their most useful pursuits, and the world's population owes much to them. In many instances cultivars have been developed that grow and produce heavy crops in the presence of certain diseases or insects that eliminated previous, susceptible cultivars. The development of rust-resistant wheat cultivars, for example, has added food for untold millions of people. The development of resistant plant types also reduces the need for costly and sometimes dangerous pesticides. Ideally, all pests and diseases would be overcome in this manner.

The development of plant types resistant to disease and insect pests is a very active field of research in various agricultural experiment stations, using the combined talents of plant breeders, entomologists, and plant pathologists. For example, geneticists have developed wheat strains with hairy leaves and stems that resist attacks of the cereal leaf beetle by inhibiting the egg-laying activities of the females, making the plants practically insect-free. Several approaches are open to plant breeders in developing plants that are resistant to pests. They change the plant's color, surface texture, taste, or odor so that it is no longer attractive to an insect pest. They even introduce characteristics into the plant that repel or poison insects.

ANTAGONISTIC ORGANISMS (3)

A balance usually develops in nature among organisms, both plant and animal. Certain organisms are antagonistic to others and retard their expansion. Environmental or human-induced changes that upset this balance by eliminating one of the organisms can lead to explosive proliferation of the others and to subsequent attacks on vulnerable crops. In a similar manner, if an organism is introduced into an environment but its antagonizing organism is left behind, the results can be devastating to a vulnerable crop plant. Biological control in such a situation would consist of introducing the antagonizing organism of the pest into the area, thus bringing it under control again. Olive parlatoria scale in California olive orchards threatened the existence of the industry, but two parasitic wasps introduced from Asia became well established and, for practical purposes, eliminated the scale.

Control by Cultural Practices

Crop rotation is a simple but often effective means of controlling certain insect and disease pests. If the same annual crop is grown year after year on the same plot of land, a particularly serious pest may keep increasing year after year, overwintering in crop residues, until it reaches such overwhelming populations that the crop cannot be produced on that piece of land. But by rotating the crop in a one to several year rotation with other nonsusceptible crops the insect or disease pest, lacking a crop host for a long period, practically dies out. Crop rotation alone may give adequate control, but no stray susceptible host plants must be allowed to grow on the land during the interim period, since they would maintain a population of the pest.

Government Agricultural Quarantine and Pest Eradication Programs (38)

Many serious plant disease and insect pests were not known to occur in certain countries until they were brought in by travelers or shipped in, usually unknowingly, on contaminated plant material. The early colonists from Europe brought into North American certain insects and diseases on seeds and plants carried from their homelands. German soldiers hired by the British during the Revolutionary War brought the Hessian fly to North America with them in their straw bedding. This pest later moved westward through the United States, devastating wheat fields and ultimately causing far more problems for the new country than the soldiers did.

Strict government inspection[1] and fumigation procedures, plus quarantine of imported plants, plant products, and soil, have kept such pests out of many countries and many areas. Modern jet travel, taking people and their belongings swiftly from country to country, greatly increases the possibility of introducing pests dangerous to both crops and farm animals into new areas. In some cases, certain plants or plant products are forbidden entry into the country, and agricultural inspectors check luggage for such outlawed products. For example, mangoes, guavas, and passion fruit from Hawaii are not permitted entry into the U.S. mainland since they may be carrying the Mediterranean fruit fly, which is widespread in Hawaii but absent on the mainland. If introduced into California, for example, the fly could devastate the state's huge fruit industry. However, such plant products can be imported commercially if they are properly fumigated to kill the pests before shipping. Certain kinds of living plant material can be imported into the United States under permit or if quarantined after entry for two growing seasons to reveal any diseases. Travelers coming into the United States should not attempt to bring or send in such agricultural materials as fruits, vegetables, plants, bulbs, seeds, or cuttings unless advance arrangements have been made and a permit obtained.[2] Any such plant materials being carried or imported through commercial channels must be reported to agricultural quarantine or customs officials upon arrival.

Government eradication programs are conducted when a serious insect or disease pest breaks out. Often the trouble is eliminated before it has a chance to spread. Such programs require highly trained personnel who know the potential insect and disease problems and are able to recognize the pathogens and the symptoms of their activities. The dangerous Mediterranean fruit fly has been accidentally introduced into Florida on several occasions. Each time it has been eradicated, but always at considerable expense.

Application of Pesticides

The potential dangers of pesticide chemicals to humans, food products, farm and domestic animals, wildlife, beneficial insects, and the atmosphere makes them the least

[1]In the United States inspection is done by the USDA's Animal and Plant Health Inspection Service (APHIS), Plant Protection Quarantine Programs.
[2]Arrange for a permit in advance of the trip from Plant Protection Quarantine Programs, APHIS, USDA, Hyattsville, MD 20782.

desirable method of controlling harmful insects and plant diseases (*36*) (Fig. 11–3). However, pesticides are often the only method of control and without them the world would not be able to feed its ever-expanding population. Some of our most valuable crops are so suspectible to devastating diseases and insects that without chemical control measures such crops would simply disappear (Figs. 11–4, 11–5).

PLANT DISEASES

Cultivated plants are subject to a wide array of plant diseases induced by such infectious parasitic pathogens as bacteria, fungi, viruses, and mycoplasma-like organisms. Most plants are immune to most pathogens, but the majority of cultivated plants are susceptible to attacks by at least one pathogen in each of these groups and some crops are susceptible to many. The potato, bean, and cotton, for example, are each a host for at least 30 fungus species. The world's forest tree species, too, are vulnerable to many diseases that can cause immense timber losses (*4, 14, 26, 28, 32, 34*).

For an infectious disease to develop there must be a susceptible host, a causal agent, and a favorable environment for the pathogen. Infectious plant diseases are caused by pathogenic agents that are transmitted in some manner from a diseased plant—or in some instances, from plant debris or soil—to a healthy plant.

A **plant disease** is a harmful alteration of the normal physiological and biochemical development of a plant. The harmful change is exerted over time, rather than suddenly as in the case of a wound. This definition of plant disease is broad, and includes nonpathogenic abnormalities such as nutrient deficiencies or excesses or even lack of adequate soil moisture.

The appearance of an infectious disease requires a source of primary inoculum, which is a portion of the pathogen capable of being disseminated and causing infection. This inoculum may be bacteria, fungal spores or mycelia, or virus particles. To cause disease symptoms, the inoculum must penetrate the host plant and become established, causing infection and setting up a life cycle that includes the host plant. Sometimes the inoculum penetrates the tissues of the host plant but fails to become established because of high resistance of the host tissues or unfavorable environmental conditions. Host resistance may be a genetic characteristic or a reflection of the particular growth condition of the host plant—succulent or mature, vigorous or weak.

DISEASE SYMPTOMS

Symptoms of disease often change as the disease progresses. The initial symptoms may be quite

Fig. 11–3 When spraying pesticides to control insects and diseases in enclosed areas like greenhouses, workers should wear protective masks and clothing.

Fig. 11–4 Certain insect and disease pests are controlled in commercial orchards by insecticides and fungicides applied by power air blast sprayers. *Source:* USDA.

Fig. 11–5 Dusting grapes with sulfur dust to control powdery mildew caused by the fungus *Uncinula necator. Source:* Blue Anchor, Inc.

different than those in the final stages. These symptoms can generally be placed in the following categories:

1. *Abnormal tissue coloration*. Leaf appearance commonly changes. Leaves may become chlorotic (yellowish); mosaic or mottling patterns may appear, especially with virus diseases.

2. *Wilting*. If the infectious agent interferes with the necessary uptake of water by the host plant, a part or the whole of the plant may die. Verticillium wilt, which blocks the water-conducting tissues (xylem), is one disease that causes this symptom.

3. *Tissue death*. Necrotic (dead) tissue can appear in leaves, stems, or roots, either as spots or as entire organs. Decay of soft succulent tissue, as in damping off in young seedlings, is common. Cankers caused by death of the underlying tissue sometimes appear as sunken, dead tissue on the trunks or limbs of woody plants.

4. *Defoliation*. As the infectious disease progresses, the plant may lose all its leaves and sometimes drop its fruit.

5. *Abnormal increase in tissue size*. Some diseases increase cell numbers or cell size in the plant tissues, twisting and curling the leaves or forming galls on stems or roots (Figs. 11–6 and 11–7).

6. *Dwarfing*. In some cases the pathogenic organism will reduce cell number or size, stunting parts or the whole of the host plant.

7. *Replacement of host plant tissue by tissue of the infectious organism*. This occurs commonly where floral parts or fruits are involved; an example is corn smut, where the ears and tassels become infected and proliferation of the infectious pathogen takes place.

CLASSIFICATION OF INFECTIOUS PLANT DISEASES

The pathogens responsible for causing most plant diseases are (1) bacteria, (2) fungi, (3) viruses, (4) mycoplasma-like organisms, (5) parasitic seed plants, and (6) nematodes.

BACTERIA Bacteria are one-celled organisms with a cell wall. They occur singly or in colonies of cells—in pairs, chains, or clusters. Bacteria are found almost everywhere on earth in vast numbers. There are both beneficial and pathogenic bacteria. The beneficial bacteria are involved in such diverse processes as digestion in animals, nitrogen fixation in the roots of certain plants (see p. 208), breaking down animal and plant remains, and sewage disposal systems. Pathogenic bacteria, on the other hand, cause severe, often fatal,

Fig. 11–6 Peach leaves distorted by peach leaf curl, a disease caused by the fungus *Taphrina deformans*. The disease can be controlled by fungicidal sprays applied before the buds open in the spring.

Fig. 11–7 Galls on a young fruit tree infected by crown gall bacteria (*Agrobacterium tumefasciens*).

Table 11-2 Some Important Plant Diseases Caused by Bacteria

Common Name of Disease	Pathogen	Hosts Attacked	Control Measures
Crown gall	*Agrobacterium tumefasciens*	Woody ornamentals and tree fruits	Produce nursery stock free of bacteria, chemotherapy of galls.
Bacterial wilt of cucumbers	*Erwinia tracheiphila*	Cucumbers, muskmelons, squash, and pumpkins	Control insects (spotted and striped cucumber beetles) that carry the bacteria.
Bacterial wilt of corn	*Erwinia stewartii*	Corn (sweet and dent corn hybrids)	Resistant cultivars.
Common blight of beans	*Xanthomonas phaseoli*	Beans—field (dry), garden (snap), and lima	Disease-free seed; sanitation; disposal of crop residues; three-year crop rotations.
Fireblight	*Erwinia amylovora*	Pome fruits—apple, pear, quince —some ornamentals, such as pyracantha	Resistant cultivars; cut out diseased tissues; streptomycin sprays at bloom.
Bacterial canker	*Pseudomonas syringae*	Almonds, apricots, avocado, cherry, peach, plum	Resistant cultivars; cut out infected areas; spray with Bordeaux mixture.
Bacterial soft rot of vegetables	*Erwinia carotovora*	Vegetables with fleshy storage organs	Avoid bruising and mechanical damage during harvest. Use good ventilation during storage at 2°C to 4°C (36°F to 39°F).

diseases in both animals and plants. Plant pathogenic bacteria belong to six genera: *Agrobacterium, Corynebacterium, Erwinia, Pseudomonas, Streptomyces,* and *Xanthomonas.* Table 11-2 gives some examples of bacterial diseases.

Bacteria are classified into three groups: the spherical **cocci,** the rod-shaped **bacilli,** and the spiral-shaped **spirilli.** Only the bacilli are known to cause diseases in plants. Some types of bacilli and spirilli are motile— they have whiplike flagella that propel them through films of water. Bacteria multiply at alarming rates under suitable conditions by binary fission—splitting into two parts.

Bacterial diseases in plants are difficult to control. Measures include using resistant species or cultivars and bacteria-free seed, eliminating sources of bacterial contamination, preventing surface wounds that permit the entrance of bacteria into the inner tissues, and propagating only bacteria-free nursery stock. Prolonged exposure to dry air, heat, and sunlight will sometimes kill bacteria in plant material. They are also killed by antibiotic treatment.

Bacteria that cause plant diseases are spread in many ways—they can be splashed about by rains or moved on windblown dust, the feet of birds, or on insects. People can unwittingly spread bacterial diseases by, for instance, pruning infected orchard trees during the rainy season. Water facilitates the entrance of bacteria carried on pruning tools into the pruning cuts. Propagation with bacteria-infected plant material is a major way pathogenic bacteria are moved over great distances.

Most plant tissue under the protective bark layers is sterile. Bacteria may coat the bark surface, but they do not cause infection unless, with moisture present, they gain entry to inner tissues through stomata, or leaf, flower, or fruit scars, or wounds. Spraying with antibiotics is sometimes helpful; streptomycin is used, for example, to reduce fireblight *(Erwinia amylovora)* infection *(42)* in pears. But few chemicals are really effective in controlling bacterial plant diseases.

FUNGI   Fungi are classified into more than 50,000 species. Unlike the green plants, they do not contain chlorophyll, do not photosynthesize their own food, and must obtain their nutrients from some other source—a substrate of living or dead plant or animal tissue.

Fungi can be grouped into:

1. Obligate saprophytes, which live only on dead organic matter and inorganic materials.

2. Obligate parasites, which live and develop only on living tissues.

3. Facultative saprophytes, which are normally parasitic on living tissues but can live as saprophytes on dead tissue under certain conditions.

4. Facultative parasites, which are normally saprophytic but can live parasitically under certain conditions.

Some fungi are able to live on only one host species, while others develop on many different kinds.

Fungi, like bacteria, can be beneficial as well as pathogenic. Beneficial fungi participate in biological cycles, decaying dead animal and plant materials and thus converting them into plant nutrients that are absorbed by living plants. Some beneficial fungi grow in a symbiotic relationship with the root cells of higher green plants; this combination is termed a **mycorrhiza.** Roots of many cultivated plants—corn, soybeans, cotton, tobacco, peas, red clover, apples, citrus, pines, aspens, birches, and others—have mycorrhizal relationships with soil fungi. The mycorrhizae appear to be highly beneficial, often necessary, for optimum growth of many plants. Interest and research in such fungi-root symbiotic relations is considerable because establishing proper mycorrhizal fungi with cultivated plants offers a great potential for improved plant growth (*39*).

Certain fungi produce useful antibiotics and enzymes. *Pencillium* fungi produce the famous penicillin G, which has prevented countless deaths from bacterial infection, acting by inhibiting formation of the bacteria's cell wall. Many food-producing processes, such as the making of bread, wine, beer, and cheese, are based upon the activities of fungi. Mushrooms, which are fungi, are important as food.

Most plant diseases are caused by fungi, and the food loss to fungal diseases is staggering (Fig. 11–8). Some of the world's great famines can be blamed on pathogenic fungi. Wheat crops of the Middle Ages were ruined when the grains became infected with a dark, dusty powder now known to be the spores of the fungus called bunt or stinking smut (*Tilletia* spp.). The potato blight in Ireland and northern Europe, rampant during two successive seasons (1845–1846 and 1846–1847), was caused by the fungus *Phytophthora infestans*, resulted in the death of more than 1 million people by starvation. In the 1870s, an epidemic of downy mildew, caused by the fungus *Plasmopara viticola*, struck the grape vineyards of central Europe, causing great losses to the grape growers and wine makers. In the United States alone, hundreds of millions of bushels of wheat

Fig. 11–8   Fungal diseases can cause considerable damage to grain crops. Shown here is barley scald caused by the fungus *Rhynochosporium secalis*. The head on the left is only slightly affected while the one on the right is so severely damaged that the lack of photosynthesis has prevented the grains from filling. *Source:* University of California Cooperative Extension.

have been lost in epidemic years to stem rust (*Puccinia graminis tritici*).

Fungi are simple organisms. The vegetative body, or **mycelium** (pl., mycelia) of a typical fungus is made up of very small filaments or threads called **hyphae** that branch in all directions throughout the substrate. The hyphae are filled with protoplasm containing nuclei. The mycelia of pathogenic fungi absorb food from the cells of the host plant. Some fungi produce structures called **sclerotia,** which are dense, compact masses of hyphae. These species readily resist unfavorable environments, remaining alive until conditions are more favorable and then resume growth. Fungi reproduce by both sexual and asexual spores, which are similar to the seeds of higher plants except that they lack an embryo. The spores germinate under favorable conditions, producing hyphae and mycelia.

Fungal diseases of plants are generally easier to control than bacterial or viral diseases. The most satisfactory method of dealing with fungus diseases is strict sanitation to eliminate the pathogenic organisms, starting with the initial stages of propagation and growth of the potential host plants.

Control measures include:

1. Soil pasteurization (moist heat at 82°C [180°F] for 30 minutes.)
2. Soil fumigants and drenches containing fungicides
3. Planting only disease-free, certified seed
4. Seed treatments with fungicides
5. Foliage sprays with fungicides (protectants or eradicants)
6. Planting only resistant species and cultivars
7. Maintaining good soil drainage
8. Removing crop residues by burning or burying
9. Crop rotation
10. Growing crops in climates unsuitable for pathogenic fungi
11. Careful handling of the crop (vegetables and fruits) to prevent cuts and bruises during harvest and transit
12. Storage of crop products at the proper low temperatures
13. Postharvest treatment of fruits and vegetables with fungicides
14. Biological control by means of an organism, usually another fungus, that is antagonistic to the fungal pathogen

In many of the major crops, cultivars resistant to prevailing diseases are available and more are continually being developed by plant breeders. Obviously, growers should use such cultivars if they are available.

Several examples of cultivars genetically resistant to fungus disease are notable. Certain hybrid potato cultivars are resistant to late blight (*Phytophthora infestans*). Soybean cultivars resistant to downy mildew (*Peronospora manshurica*) have been developed. In the United States, apple cultivars have been developed at the Indiana and the New York agricultural experiment station that show high resistance or immunity to apple scab (*Venturia inaequalis*), a devastating disease of apples grown in cool humid climates with summer rainfall. In the cereal crops (oats, wheat, rye, barley), powdery mildew (*Erysiphe graminis*) can be controlled only by the use of resistant cultivars developed by plant breeders. Tomatoes can be grown in *Fusarium*-infested soils only if *Fusarium*-resistant cultivars are planted. Plant breeders are continuously breeding wheat cultivars resistant to stem rust *(Puccinia graminis tritici)*, but the fungus continuously mutates, attacking the formerly resistant cultivars. Still newer types then have to be developed. The importance of resistant cultivars in controlling fungus diseases is shown in Table 11–3.

Although complete eradication of the pathogen and the use of resistant cultivars are the most satisfactory ways of dealing with fungus disease, in many instances these measures are not possible. Often the disease appears and its development must be slowed or stopped by whatever means are available. Chemical sprays (fungicides) are an old and well-proven procedure for controlling many plant diseases, and they are relied upon heavily for certain fungus problems. It was only about a century ago that chemical weapons were first devised against plant diseases that had been destroying crops for countless centuries. There are now more than 100 useful fungicides, and new ones are continually being added and older ones dropped. It is best to seek advice from the local agricultural extension service, pest control consultant, or garden shop about which fungicides to use.

Agricultural fungicides are strictly controlled. In the United States, regulations of the federal Environmental Protection Agency (EPA) and of the States' agriculture departments specify on what crops and at what times and concentrations these chemicals can be applied. The regulations protect the applicator and the consuming public. Read package labels carefully and adhere strictly to their directions.

Table 11-3 Some Important Plant Diseases Caused by Fungi and Measures for Controlling Them

Common Name of Disease	Pathogen	Hosts Attacked	Control Measures[a]
Stem rust of wheat	*Puccinia graminis tritica*	Wheat	Eradicate barberry plants (an alternate host), and use resistant cultivars.
Corn smut	*Ustilago maydis*	Corn	Use resistant cultivars.
Fusarium wilt	*Fusarium oxysporum*	Tomato, pea, celery, banana, cotton, watermelon	Use resistant cultivars.
Powdery mildews	*Erysiphe polygoni*	Many hosts	Foliar fungicides except on cereals, where resistant cultivars should be used.
	Podosphaera leucotricha	Apples	
	Uncinula necator	Grape	
	Sphaerotheca pannosa	Rose	
	Erysiphe cichoraceaurum	Cucurbits	
	Erysiphe graminis	Cereals	
Rust	*Puccinia striiformis* and *P. graminis*	Turf grasses, especially bluegrass and ryegrass	Keep lawn growing rapidly by fertilization; use fungicides.
Brown patch	*Rhizoctonia solani*	Turf grasses, especially bent grass, bluegrass, Bermuda grass, fescues	Avoid nitrogen fertilization. Improve drainage. Use certain fungicides.
Brown rot	*Monilinia fructicola*	Stone fruits: peaches, apricots, plums, cherries, almonds, nectarines	Use resistant cultivars where available. Sanitation. Fungicide sprays. Prevent fruit injury during harvest. Refrigerate harvested fruit.
Apple scab	*Venturia inaequalis*	Apples	Protectant and eradicant sprays with fungicides. Use resistant cultivars where available.
Peach leaf curl	*Taphrina deformans*	Peaches and nectarines	Dormant spray of fungicide after leaf fall and before bud break.
Verticillium wilt	*Verticillium albo-atrum* and *V. dahliae*	A wide range of woody fruit and ornamental species; many kinds of herbaceous plants	Plant only resistant species and cultivars. Remove infected limbs or plants and burn. There is no chemical control.
Downy mildew of grape	*Plasmopara viticola*	Grape	Foliar sprays with a fungicide.
Late blight of potato	*Phytophthora infestans*	Potato and tomato	Use resistant cultivars. Destroy all cull potatoes in field. Spray with fungicides during growing season. Store potatoes at 2° to 4°C (36° to 40°F).
Damping off	*Pythium* and *Rhizoctonia* spp.	Seedlings of species	Fungicidal seed treatments. Soil fumigation or pasteurization. Improve soil drainage. Germinate seedlings at temperatures unfavorable for pathogen growth.
Dutch elm disease	*Ceratocystis ulmi*	Elm trees	Remove sources of infection and control European elm bark beetle, which spreads the fungus.

[a] Detailed directions on control of plant diseases can be obtained from local offices of the agriculture extension service or from commercial garden centers.

VIRUSES *(23, 28, 31, 34, 40)* Viruses are pathogenic particles that infect most higher plants and animals. Virus particles are extremely small (about 20 to 250 millimicrons) and can be seen only with an electron microscope. They consist of an outer sheath of protein and an inner core of nucleic acid that is usually, but not always, ribonucleic acid (RNA). Viruses do not carry on the usual functions of living organisms such as respiration and digestion. They are obligate parasites; that is, they cannot multiply and grow except within the host or insect vector cell. They can be removed from the host, however, and still cause infections. They force the host cell to transform its own components into virus substances that are then translocated throughout the plant, injuring or killing it. The virus carries the genetic information for its replication by the host. Many kinds of plants carry virus particles and show no symptoms. Some viruses, such as cowpea mosaic virus, occur as a complex of two component particles, each containing different nucleic acid cores. Both components have to be present in a plant for infection and replication to take place.

Whether viruses are "living" entities or not depends upon the definition of *living*. Viruses are certainly not independent living systems. They are unable to develop their own energy for multiplication, having to depend upon the enzyme systems of other living cells. Yet they do exhibit the three interrelated characteristics of living things: reproduction, variation, and selective survival.

Viroids

Some plant diseases—for example, potato spindle tuber, citrus exocortis, chrysanthemum chlorotic mottle, and chrysanthemum stunt—are caused by free low-molecular-weight RNA molecules (similar to the inner core of some virus particles but without the outer protein sheath). These infectious, free RNA molecules, which are about one-tenth the size of the smallest virus particles, have been called **viroids** or **infectious RNA** *(8)*.

To move from one plant to another, virus particles must have some transmitting carrier (vector). The vectors can be insects—aphids, leafhoppers, or, most commonly, thrips—or mites, certain primitive soil-borne fungi, nematodes, pollen grains, or infected seeds (carrying the virus from one generation to another). The activities of humans in propagating plants by budding and grafting or by cuttings is one of the chief ways viral diseases spread. In fact, virus investigators use grafting and budding procedures to transmit and detect viruses in their studies. The seedling offspring of a virus-infected plant is usually, but not always, free of the virus, depending upon the plant species and the kind of virus.

Viruses are difficult to classify and, for want of anything better, they are given descriptive names based upon a disease they cause—for example, tobacco ringspot, tobacco mosaic, citrus psorosis, citrus tristeza, sugar beet curly top, lettuce mosaic, maize dwarf mosaic, peach yellow bud mosaic, *Prunus* necrotic ringspot, carnation streak, and tomato spotted wilt. Many of these viruses also infect plants of other species. For example, tobacco ringspot virus causes a bud blight in

soybeans; maize dwarf mosaic infects sorghum, Sudan grass, sugarcane, and Johnson grass in addition to corn, but it still retains its original name.

Once whole plants are infected, little can be done to free them from the virus. No chemical sprays eradicate viruses although insecticides can be used to control insect vectors. Since different cultivars and species show different degrees of resistance to some viruses, resistant types should be planted whenever they are available. For orchard species, the best control measure is planting of nursery trees that have been propagated from known virus-clean sources. The citrus industries in both Florida and California, for example, have set up certification and registration programs to assure that citrus nursery stock is propagated from the most pathogen-free propagative materials available.

All plants of many vegetatively propagated cultivars (clones—see p. 89) are infected with viruses, either latent or active. Virus particles, occurring systemically throughout the plants, are readily moved along during the vegetative propagation procedures from the mother plants to all daughter plants (see Ch. 5).

Fortunately, some viruses are permanently inactivated by prolonged exposure of infected tissue to relatively high temperatures—for example, 20 to 30 days at 38°C (100°F). This procedure, called **heat therapy** *(23)*, frees individual plants or cuttings of the viruses. The clean tissue is then used as a propagative source, allowing large-scale production of new plants of the clone without the virus infection. This has been done with many cultivars of fruit and ornamental species. If insect vectors are kept out of the new virus-clean plantings, subsequent reinfection is unlikely, particularly if the planting is at a distance from virus-infected plantings.

Another successful way to eliminate viruses, particularly from herbaceous plants, is to excise the minute shoot tip of vigorously growing plants under aseptic conditions (see p. 92), then allow the tip to develop into a new plant on a nutrient medium. The new plant will usually be free of the virus and will provide a starting point for a clone minus the virus. This procedure is based on the fact, still not well understood by plant virologists, that the virus usually is not present in the actively growing shoot tip of an infected plant. This procedure has been used to clear many herbaceous cultivars of viruses.

Viruses in an infected mother plant usually (but not always) fail to appear in the daughter seedlings. However, if the clone is heterozygous (see p. 71), the new seedlings lack the characteristics of the clone. If, however, the parent plant is a type, such as citrus, that produces apomictic seedlings (i.e., the embryo in the seed arises from the nucellus rather than from a zygote, so that the seedling has the same genetic makeup as the mother plant; see p. 92), then the clonal characteristics are retained in the seedling plant. This procedure is the basis for the development of many vigorous nucellar cultivars of citrus species.

MYCOPLASMA-LIKE ORGANISMS *(13)* The mycoplasmas in animals and the mycoplasma-like organisms in plants are small parasitic organisms intermediate in size between viruses and bacteria. (It is uncertain whether the plant parasites are true mycoplasmas.)

The cells of mycoplasmas have a three-layered membrane enclosing the living protoplasm; they lack constant shape. In plants mycoplasmas occur in the phloem and multiply rapidly, disrupting translocation of food materials and usually causing symptoms of yellowing, wilting, distortion, reduced leaf size, and stunting.

Mycoplasmas have long been known to infect animals, including humans, but it has only been since about 1967 that organisms of this type have been recognized as a cause of plant diseases *(9)*. Many plant diseases formerly attributed to viruses are now known to be caused by mycoplasma-like organisms. Some of the diseases they cause are aster yellows, western-X of peaches, cherry bucksin, pear decline, mulberry dwarf disease, corn stunt, and stubborn disease of citrus. As with viruses, a disease caused by mycoplasma-like organism is named after the plant on which it was first studied, but it can also occur on many other plants. For example, aster yellows also affects other ornamentals—gladiolus and phlox, for example—and tomato, spinach, onion, lettuce, celery, carrots, strawberry, and many weeds.

Mycoplasmas, in contrast to viruses, have some characteristics of living matter. They can reproduce themselves, they have energy and enzyme systems, and their genetic information, like viruses, is stored as DNA and RNA. Their lack of a cell wall and their smaller size differentiate them from bacteria.

Species and cultivars vary distinctly in their resistance to mycoplasmas. For example, the common pear (*Pyrus communis*) is highly resistant to the pear decline organism, whereas the oriental pear (*Pyrus pyrifolia*) is very susceptible.

Like viral diseases, the infective bodies in diseases caused by mycoplasma-like organisms are moved about by sucking insects such as leafhoppers, aphids, and psylla. Studies of corn stunt provide evidence that once the insect vectors establish the infective particles in their bodies, the insects retain the ability to transmit them the rest of their lives.

One obvious method of controlling the spread of these diseases is an effective spray program that elimi-

nates the insect vectors. It has been established, too, that mycoplasma-like organisms are susceptible to certain antibiotics, particularly tetracycline, which has been used to treat pear trees with the pear decline disease. Trunk injections of solutions of tetracycline remit disease symptoms for at least one to two years. This procedure has been widely used in California pear orchards *(24)*.

PARASITIC SEED PLANTS

Some higher plant forms parasitize other plants and cause harmful reactions in their hosts. These parasites can be placed in three groups: the epiphytes, the hemiparasites, and the true parasites *(16)*:

The **epiphytes** do little or no harm to their host plants, using them merely for physical support and protection. Examples are Spanish moss and orchids, which in their native habitat commonly grow on tree limbs (Fig. 11–9).

Fig. 11–9 The epiphytic plant, Spanish moss (*Tillandsia usneoides*), a member of the pineapple family, is commonly found attached to trees throughout the southern United States. The tree shown here was near Baton Rouge, Louisiana. Spanish moss absorbs most of its nutrients and water directly from the atmosphere and only uses its host plant as a place to obtain support and light for photosynthesis. It gets no food or water from the host plant as do the parasitic plants. Similar appearing plants, which are called lichens (an algae and a fungus living in an intimate symbiotic relationship as a composite plant), are members of the *Usnea* genus and are sometimes called "old man's beard."

The **hemiparasites,** sometimes called water parasites, do injure their host plants, absorbing water and mineral nutrients from them. However, they possess chlorophyll and can manufacture their own carbohydrates by photosynthesis.

Witchweed (*Striga asiatica*) is a hemiparasitic seed plant that severely damages sugarcane, corn, sorghum, many other grasses, and some broad-leaved plants. It attaches itself to the host's roots and utilizes most of the host's water and mineral nutrients, causing it to wilt, yellow, stunt, and die. The best control is to plant a crop, such as Sudan grass, that stimulates the witchweed seed to germinate, then plow under the entire field. Crops should be rotated and susceptible crops should not be planted.

Mistletoe (*Phoradendron* spp.), another member of the hemiparasitic group, attacks many broad-leaved trees such as Modesto ash, silver maple, honeylocust, hackberry (see Fig. 11–10), cottonwood, walnut, oak, birch, and some conifers. The seeds germinate on limbs of susceptible hosts, forming an attachment disk on the bark. The sticky berries are disseminated throughout the tree and from tree to tree by birds and wind. The usual control, although not very effective, is to cut out the mistletoe branches deep into the tree under the point of attachment. No good herbicidal control has been developed. The best control is to plant only tree species resistant to mistletoe attacks.

True parasites lack chlorophyll and depend upon their hosts for all nourishment—carbohydrates, minerals, and water. Examples of this group are the dwarf mistletoe (*Arceuthobium* spp.) and dodder (*Cuscuta* spp.). Broomrape, (*Orobanche* spp.) is a serious parasitic pest in Europe and in recent years has caused extensive damage to tomatoes in California.

Dwarf mistletoe attacks many coniferous species in the western United States, reducing tree vigor and lowering lumber quality. The sticky seeds (not the fruits) are forcibly ejected and can travel up to about 19 m (60 ft). This is the principal means of dissemination. Birds are known to carry the sticky seeds on their feathers, but wind plays a very minor role in dissemination. The best control is removal of infected trees.

Dodder has many species but about six cause the major damage, attacking such crops as alfalfa, lespedeza, clover, flax, sugar beets, and some vegetable crops as well as some woody perennials (see Fig. 11–11). Dodder seriously reduces yields and quality of agronomic crops. Strict regulations prohibit the sale of crop seed contaminated by dodder seed. Great effort should be taken to avoid planting seed that has dodder seed mixed with it. Patches of dodder in field crops or along fences or ditch banks should be eradicated by burning or by herbicides.

Fig. 11–11 Olive branches attacked by dodder.

Fig. 11–10 Branch of a hackberry (*Celtis sinensis*) tree being killed by growth of mistletoe.

NEMATODES

Plant parasitic nematodes (*18, 37*) are microscopic, eel-like worms that attack the roots, stems, foliage, and inflorescenses of plants. They range in length from 0.5 mm to 3 mm (0.02 to 0.125 in). Nematodes are not closely related to earthworms, wireworms, or flatworms.

A number of genera and species of nematodes are highly damaging to a great range of hosts, including foliage plants, vegetable crops, fruit and nut trees, and forest trees. Some of the most damaging nematode species are:

Root knot (*Meloidogyne* spp.)

Cyst (*Heterodera* spp.)

Root lesion (*Pratylenchus* spp.)

Spiral (*Helicotylenchus* spp.)

Burrowing (*Radopholus similis*)

Bulb and stem (*Ditylenchus dipsaci*)

Reniform (*Rotylenchulus reniformis*)

Dagger (*Xiphinema* spp.)

Bud and leaf (*Aphelenchoides* spp.)

Typical root symptoms indicating nematode attack are root knots or galls (Fig. 11–12), root lesions (Fig. 11–13), excessive root branching, injured root tips, and stunted root systems. Symptoms on the above-ground plant parts indicating root infection are a slow decline of the entire plant, wilting even with ample soil moisture, foliage yellowing, and fewer and smaller leaves. These are, in fact, the symptoms that would appear in plants deprived of a properly functioning root system. Bulb and stem nematodes produce stem swellings and shortened internodes. Bud and leaf nematodes distort and kill bud and leaf tissue.

Parasitic nematodes are readily spread by any physical means that can move soil particles about—equipment, tools, shoes, birds, insects, dust, wind, and water. In addition, the movement of nematode-infected plants or plant parts will spread the parasites.

Various methods are available to reduce crop losses from nematodes:

Fig. 11–12 Galls on tomato roots caused by root-knot nematodes.

Fig. 11–13 Nematodes can severely damage white potato tubers. These microscopic roundworms drill into the tubers, damaging the skin, disfiguring the potatoes, and making them unmarketable. *Source:* University of California Cooperative Extension.

1. **Plant only resistant species and cultivars.** For example, in an area with soil heavily infested with the root-knot nematode, plant apricots, cherries, apples, pears, or plums, which are resistant, rather than peaches or nectarines, which are highly susceptible. (A root-knot nematode-resistant peach rootstock called 'Nemaguard' developed by USDA plant breeders is available, thus permitting peach production even on infested soils.) Certain vegetable crops—sweet corn, asparagus, and cabbage—are resistant to root-knot nematodes whereas radishes are susceptible. Resistant ornamentals include the African marigold, azalea, camellia, and oleander. In Long Island, New York, where the golden nematode is a serious problem for potato production, resistant cultivars are available.

2. **Use only nematode-free nursery stock for planting.** In most countries government nursery inspectors will condemn and destroy any nursery stock showing evidence of nematode infestation.

3. **Avoid importing soil (or plants with soil on their roots) from areas that could be loaded with a dangerous nematode species new to the area.** United States plant importation regulations forbid the introduction of plants with soil on their roots from other countries.

4. **Treat the soil area with a fumigant before planting.** Methyl bromide is often used to reduce the nematode population to levels not harmful to plants. Soil mixes for container-grown plants can either be treated with a fumigant or steam-pasteurized at 82°C (180°F) for about 30 minutes. This method is too expensive to use for field crops.

5. **In nursery operations, use benches raised off the ground and pot plants only into pasteurized soil mixes.** Keep containers, bins, benches, and flats clean. Fumigate outdoor growing fields where nursery stock will be grown.

6. **Use nematicides in certain cases.** All nematicides are poisonous and must be used carefully, following the directions on the containers exactly. Most such materials will injure or kill plants if applied too close to their root zone.

7. **Rotate crops to control certain nematodes.** Rotation is useful for types that have a narrow host range, such as sugar beets attacked by the cyst nematode. Where the crop value is too low to justify large-scale soil fumigation, crop rotation is the only practical method of nematode control.

Plants and plant products are one of the chief sources of food for insects. The result is a fierce competition between humans and insects for plants. A never-ending battle has gone on since early humans started cultivating agricultural crops (Fig. 11–14). The battle is likely to intensify in the future as the world's population increases and food supplies become more desperately needed. Insects also pose a secondary hazard in that they spread diseases among plants and animals (*1, 4, 15, 32, 33*).

Some insects, however, favor agriculture. Certain harmless insect species prey on other insect species that destroy plants or crops. The praying mantis and lady-bird beetle feed on aphids. The honeybee and other insects do a tremendous service in pollinating fruit trees and other crops, such as alfalfa. Some insects produce useful products, like honey and beeswax from the honeybee and silk from the silkworm. Certain insects are relished as food in some parts of the world. The *Drosophila* fly, because of its short life cycle, ease of handling, and the giant chromosomes of its salivary gland, has been of inestimable value to geneticists in their studies.

Fig. 11–14 Insect swarms can devastate crops, as in this stand of corn ruined by grasshoppers. Grasshoppers can be controlled biologically by dropping into infested areas wheat bran sprayed with spores of *Nosema locustae*, which causes a deadly disease of grasshoppers and crickets. This disease does not harm people, plants or other animals, affecting only grasshoppers and Mormon crickets. *Source:* USDA.

To tell the difference between insects, mites, spiders, and ticks:

INSECTS

The adults are characterized by:
1. three definite body regions: head, thorax, and abdomen
2. three pairs of jointed legs
3. one pair of feelers or antennae
4. eyes that are usually compound
5. one or two pairs of wings

MITES, SPIDERS, AND TICKS

These are characterized by:
1. two main body regions—the cephalothorax (head and thorax fused together) and the abdomen
2. four pairs of jointed legs
3. a lack of antennae and wings
4. simple eyes

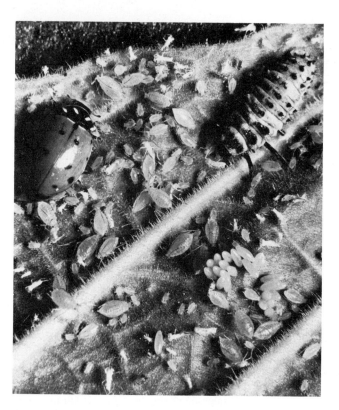

Fig. 11–15 Biological control of destructive insects: the lady-bird beetle adult *(left)* and larvae *(right)* feeding on aphids in various growth stages. *Source:* USDA.

Fig. 11–16 Natural biological control of a destructive insect: a hymenopterous parasite injects eggs into the body of a much larger larval insect (the large, hairy form with its head on the right). *Source:* USDA.

Nevertheless, there are innumerable kinds of insects and mites that, if left uncontrolled, would soon reduce the world's food supply to a shambles. Control methods for harmful insects are of four types:

1. Biological control systems (Figs. 11–15 and 11–16). Other biological entities—insects, viruses, fungal and bacterial pathogens—may be introduced as parasites into harmful insect populations. For example, there is a virus strain that attacks only the cotton boll weevil. Other viruses attack the gypsy moth, tussock moth, and codling moth.

2. Rearing and sterilizing by radiation massive numbers of male insects. Released by the millions, the sterile males mate with wild fertile females, but produce no offspring. This technique is being used to prevent the establishment of pink bollworm populations in California's cotton-growing areas and has long been a standard control measure against the screwworm in cattle, hogs, and sheep.

3. Genetic strains of plants resistant to insect attacks *(25)*. For example, plant breeders and entomologists have developed wheat cultivars resistant to the Hessian fly, practically eliminating this problem for the wheat farmer. Shortly after the discovery of the spotted alfalfa aphid in the United States, four resistant alfalfa cultivars were developed.

4. Pesticides. While probably the least desirable method of controlling insects and mites, for the present at least, pesticides constitute the chief weapon for protecting plants and conserving plant products.

CLASSIFICATION OF INSECTS

Just to classify insects is a monumental task. They dominate the land fauna with 850,000 species representing about 80 percent of the world's known animal life. If biological success is judged by numbers of species, numbers of individuals, wide distribution and adaptability, and persistence, the insects are perhaps the most successful animals.

The insect orders with the most species are:

Coleoptera (beetles)
Lepidoptera (butterflies and moths)
Hymenoptera (ants, bees, wasps)
Diptera (true flies)

Insects can be further classified by tbe type of metamorphosis they exhibit. The four types and some examples are shown in Figure 11–17. This classification is of considerable value in identification.

Fig. 11–17 Four types of insect metamorphosis from egg to adult.

	ORDERS	
Insects *without metamorphosis* emerge from the egg looking just as they will when grown, except they are much smaller.	Thysanura Collembola Mallophaga Anoplura	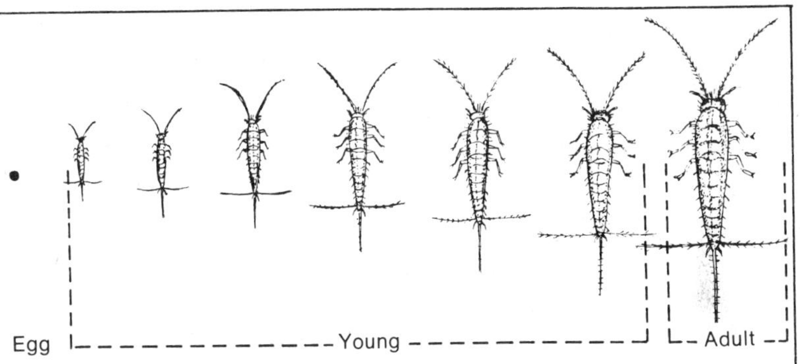 Egg — Young — Adult
Insects with *gradual metamorphosis* change shape gradually. Wings develop and, as growth takes place, the nymphs look like the adults.	Orthoptera Isoptera Corrodentia Thysanoptera Hemiptera Homoptera Dermaptera	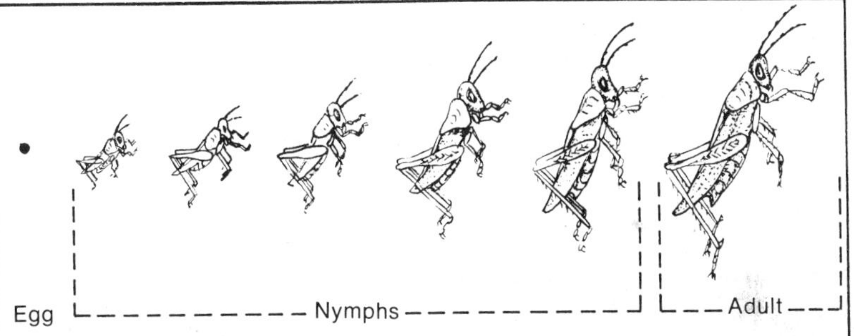 Egg — Nymphs — Adult
Insects with *incomplete metamorphosis* change shape gradually. They do not look like adults until shedding their last skin, when there is a quick change.	Ephemerida Odonata Plecoptera	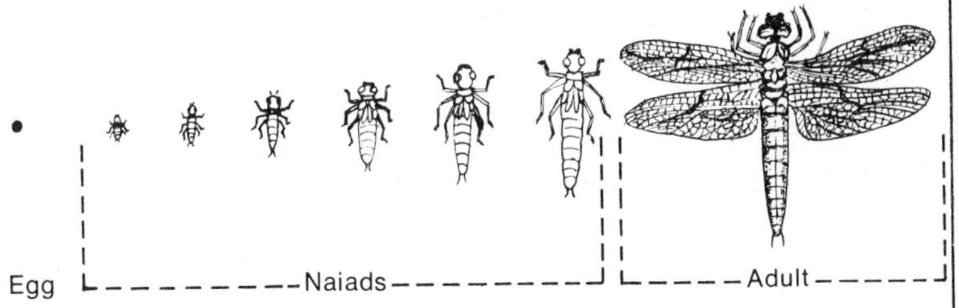 Egg — Naiads — Adult
Insects with *complete metamorphosis* go through four stages of growth. None of the young looks like the adult, but there is a great change in shape when the adult emerges from the pupal stage.	Neuroptera Coleoptera Strepsiptera Mecoptera Trichoptera Lepidoptera Diptera Siphonaptera Hymenoptera	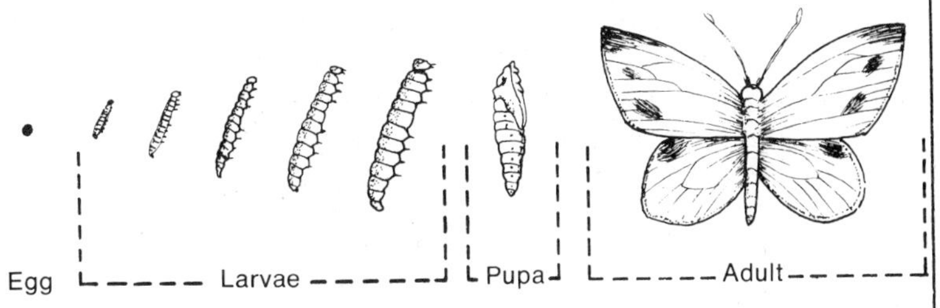 Egg — Larvae — Pupa — Adult

Fig. 11–18 The cabbage looper, an insect with chewing mouth parts, feeds on soybean leaves. Stomach poison insecticides sprayed on the leaves control such pests. *Source:* USDA.

Fig. 11–19 A sucking insect, the green peach aphid. *Source:* Robert O. Schuster.

Another distinction, important in planning control measures for insects attacking plants, is made between the chewing insects and sucking insects. The **chewing insects,** such as caterpillars and larvae and adults of other orders, feed on foliage, shoots, flowers, and fruit (Fig. 11–18). Poisonous sprays or dusts applied to the entire plant are consumed by the insect, causing its

death. **Sucking insects,** such as aphids, leafhoppers, and mites, consume little, if any, of the foliage or surface plant parts. Their mouth parts probe into the interior of the plant and suck out plant fluids (Figs. 11–19, 11–20, and 11–21). Insecticides applied to plant surfaces do little to control them. The effective insecticides are those that kill by direct contact with the insects' bodies.

Fig. 11–20 Cottony cushion scale (*Icerya purchasi*) feeding by sucking on a branch of an orange tree. *Source:* University of California Cooperative Extension.

Fig. 11–21 Olive fruits damaged by parlatoria scale.

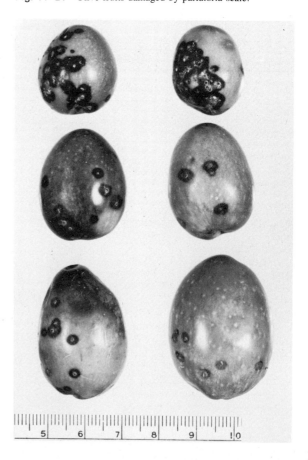

ACTION OF PESTICIDES USED TO CONTROL INSECTS AND MITES

STOMACH POISON ACTION   These materials enter the insect by mouth and kill by absorption into the body through the digestive tract. Formerly, such poisons were applied only to plant surfaces, but in recent years **systemic insecticides** have also become available. These penetrate all plant parts, exterior and interior, and will kill chewing or sucking insects. Systemic materials can be applied as foliar sprays or to the soil where they are absorbed by the roots and translocated throughout the plant.

CONTACT ACTION   These materials are applied so as to contact the body of the insect and act by affecting its nervous or respiratory centers.

FUMIGATION   Certain toxic volatile chemicals enter the insect's body in a gaseous form through the respiratory system. Fumigants are generally used in enclosed spaces but can also be used in the soil if the surface is sealed with water or covered tightly.

SUFFOCATION   Insects require oxygen to sustain life. Any material that coats their bodies and seals out air will cause death. Spray oils are commonly used on fruits and ornamentals, either as dormant or summer foliage sprays, to control certain scale insects and mites. Oil coatings plug the spiracles (breathing holes) on the sides of their bodies, thus killing by suffocation.

DESICCATION   The outer body wall of insects and mites is covered with an oily or waxy protective layer, which prevents loss of body moisture. Any material that will absorb this oily coating can cause excessive water loss and lead to desiccation and death. Such materials have not been used much on agricultural crops but have been effective in controlling household pests such as termites, cockroaches, ants, and crickets. The most effective materials are silica aerogels prepared as extremely lightweight powders that are blown into areas infested with such pests.

REPELLENT ACTION   Some materials applied to plants repel certain insects and prevent them from feeding or laying eggs. For example, Bordeaux mixture, a common fungicide, can act as a repellent against the potato flea beetle, psyllid, and leafhopper. Certain insecticides also have some repellent properties.

ATTRACTANT ACTION   Studies of insect physiology have shown that the female of many species—the codling moth, pink bollworm moth, and the cabbage looper, for example—secrete a material that even in extremely minute quantities strongly attracts the male and induces mating. Some of these materials, called **pheromones,** have been analyzed chemically and synthesized. They are now widely used in bait traps to detect the presence of certain insects in the vicinity so that eradicant spray chemicals can be applied at the proper times. The use of pheromone attractants will, no doubt, be extended in the future as a control measure for many insect pests.

HORMONE ACTION   Hormones control activity in insects, just as in other animals. Studies have discovered a juvenile hormone involved in minute amounts during the normal maturation of the insect. As long as the juvenile hormone is present, the insect remains in an immature stage and cannot advance to the adult, reproductive stage. Some of these juvenile hormones have been identified chemically and subsequently synthesized. Research efforts are underway to use synthetic juvenile hormones (or analogs) to prevent insect reproduction and thus reduce their populations.

INSECTICIDES

A great many chemicals have been used over the years in controlling insects. Some have been found to be so potentially harmful to human and other animal life, including beneficial insects, and on the environment that their use is no longer permitted. Use of all insecticides is tightly controlled in most countries. In the United States insecticides must be approved and registered by the Environmental Protection Agency (EPA), and usually by state agencies also, before they can be used. Even then there usually are heavy restrictions to confine use to certain plants at certain times and at certain concentrations. Residues on crop products exceeding fixed tolerances subject the product to seizure and destruction. More tolerance is generally allowed on ornamental plants than on crops since no food products are involved.

Insecticides can be classified as follows:

1. *Inorganic compounds.* These include arsenic, fluorine, phosphorus, and sulfur compounds. These insecticides have been used little in recent times.
2. *Organic compounds*
   a. *Plant derivatives.* These include such materials as **pyrethrum** (from the dried and powdered flowers of *Chrysanthemum cinerariaefolium*), which is a safe and effective insecticide; **rotenone** (from the roots of several plants in the pea family); and **nicotine** from *Nicotiana* spp. Many others could possibly be developed for commercial use if there were sufficient demand *(11).*
   b. *Synthetic organic chemicals.* After World War II an entirely new concept in insect control emerged with the development of organic insecticides.
      i. *Chlorinated hydrocarbons.* DDT, first developed in Germany in 1874, was widely and successfully used during and after World War II to control mosquitos,

flies, fleas, and many other insects. However, the build-up of DDT in the world's ecosystems to levels many scientists consider dangerous has led to banning its use in a number of countries, including the United States. Other chlorinated hydrocarbons, closely related to DDT, have also been very effective in insect control. They are not easily biodegraded, however, tending to build up in plants and in the soil and to be transmitted into fish, fish eating birds, meat, and milk products. Insects tend to become resistant to chlorinated hydrocarbons after their prolonged use as insecticides so that increased dosages or new formulations must be used.

  ii. *Organic phosphates.* Some of the compounds in this group were developed in Germany near the end of World War II and were found to have good insecticidal properties. They decompose more rapidly than the chlorinated hydrocarbons, but some of the materials are very toxic to mammals and must be used with great care.

  iii. *Carbamates.* Carbaryl was the first chemical in this group to be widely used. It has low mammalian toxicity and its residual action is short-lived. It is effective against a wide range of both sucking and chewing insects, acting as a contact insecticide.

c. *Spray oils.* Long used to control scale insects and mites on fruit trees and ornamentals, spray oils are prepared by the distillation and chemical refining of crude oils. A distillation range is chosen to give an oil fraction that is relatively nontoxic to plant tissue, yet lethal to scale insects. Spray oils are treated with hot sulfuric acid to remove many of the unsaturated molecules in the oil that cause plant injury.

d. *Fumigants.* Fumigant materials vaporize readily into toxic gases that kill insects on contact. They are used in enclosed spaces or injected into the soil. Some fumigants, such as methyl bromide, are extremely toxic to humans and must be applied only by trained and licensed operators using the proper equipment *(2)*. Methyl bromide is colorless and odorless, so its presence is difficult to detect. Methyl bromide is often used in combination with chloropicrin to extend the range of organisms killed. Methyl bromide is the common fumigant for stored grains, fruits and vegetables, seeds, bulbs, and nursery stock, and nursery soil mixes. Carbon bisulfide, ethylene dibromide, and ethylene dichloride are all used for fumigation of stored grains, but must be applied by trained operators using the proper equipment. Some fumigants, including carbon bisulfide, are extremely explosive when mixed with air, so that they cannot be used around flames or sparks.

e. *Microbial insecticides.* Some kinds of insects are susceptible to certain bacteria, fungi, and viruses. Often these pathogens cause the spectacular disappearance of insects. Such natural biological control of insects has been encouraged and used commercially. For example *Heliothis* virus is used commercially to kill the tobacco budworm and the cotton bollworm. It infects only these two insect species. Several species of caterpillars can be controlled by the toxins produced by the bacterium *Bacillus thuringiensis*. The toxins are applied in dust suspensions or sprays to foliage, which is then ingested by the caterpillars. These bacteria do not sustain themselves naturally and must be reapplied each time caterpillar control is needed.

IMPORTANT INSECT PESTS OF AGRICULTURAL CROPS AND PLANT PRODUCTS

There are innumerable insect pests of food crops, but certain ones are outstanding for the havoc they have wreaked over the years. A number of these species are listed below. When infestations of these or other pests occur, it is best to consult a local agricultural extension agent, pest control consultant, or garden supply center. Insecticide recommendations are continually changing. In more and more cases resistant cultivars are being developed, and they should be used wherever possible.

CORN EAR WORM (*Heliothis zea*) This insect, with three to five generations per year, occurs all over the world wherever corn is grown. Caterpillars feed on the corn silks and kernels, making the ears wormy. The worm also feeds on other crops—beans, cotton, lettuce, tomato, alfalfa, clover, peanuts, and tobacco. It is best controlled by insecticides.

CODLING MOTH (*Laspeyresia pomonella*) This insect, with two to three generations per year, attacks apples and pears wherever they are grown throughout the world. It is also a pest on walnuts. The larvae tunnel into the fruits, making them wormy. Unless insecticides are used, up to 90 percent of the fruits can become affected.

PEACH TWIG BORER (*Anarsia lineatella*) This species occurs all through the peach-producing areas of the United States. It also attacks most other stone fruits. Overwintering larvae bore into buds and shoots as they start to grow in the spring. There are two to three broods a year, the later ones feeding on the fruit.

LYGUS BUGS (*Lygus hesperus* and *L. elisus*) These insects principally attack alfalfa, Ladino clover, sugarbeets, safflower, beans, cotton, and carrots. The sucking mouth parts are inserted into buds, flowers, and young fruits, so damaging the crops that they may be unmarketable. In some seed crops, such as alfalfa, no seeds may develop owing to "blasting" of the flower buds by the lygus bugs.

SAN JOSE SCALE (*Quadraspidiotus perniciosus*) This scale insect is well established throughout North America, Europe, and Asia, attacking most fruit crops and many ornamental trees and shrubs. Heavy infestations of scale can reduce tree vigor and cause death unless they are controlled. Scale spots on fruits reduce their market quality.

GREEN PEACH APHID (*Myzus persicae*) This insect is found throughout the world. It is a sucking pest on many vegetable crops, all stone fruits, and many ornamentals. While its feeding reduces plant vigor, the chief source of damage is its transmission of viral diseases. Viral particles in its salivary fluid are injected into the host plant. Viruses known to be transmitted by the green peach aphid are sugar beet yellows, potato leaf roll, bean mosaic, lettuce mosaic, and cucumber mosaic.

EGYPTIAN ALFALFA WEEVIL *(Hypera brunneipennis)* This is a very destructive pest on alfalfa. Principal damage is done by the larvae, which feed on shoot tips, buds, and leaves.

SPIDER MITES (*Bryobia praetiosa, Panonychus ulmi,* and *Tetranychus telarius*) These pests (which are not true insects) are widely distributed and feed on many species of host plants, including a wide array of vegetable and field crops, greenhouse and nursery plants, fruits, nuts, and ornamentals (see Fig. 11–22). A typical webbing appears as the mite population increases, with a yellow stippling on leaf surfaces as defoliation begins, resulting from removal of plant fluids by the mites' piercing and sucking mouth parts. Six to ten generations per year can occur. Since spider mites have developed resistance to many miticides, there are no adequate control measures.

CEREAL WIREWORMS (*Agriotes* spp.) These are the main insect pests of such cereals as wheat, barley, oats, and rye, especially in the northern growing regions. They are the larval stage of so-called click beetles, which themselves do no harm. Their life cycle spans five years, most of which is spent in the larval wireworm stage.

COLORADO POTATO BEETLE (*Leptinotarsa decemlineata*) This well-known insect, with chewing mouth parts, occurs from Colorado to the eastern United States in all potato-growing areas. It is established on the European continent but has been eradicated from the British Isles. Both adult and larval stages feed on the foliage of the potato plant, completely denuding it. It seldom feeds on other plants. In both stages the insect is large and easily seen. It can be controlled without difficulty by spraying with stomach-poison insecticides.

COTTON BOLL WEEVIL (*Anthonomus grandis*) This insect attacks cotton plants in the United States, Mexico (where it originated), and Central America. Probably no insect, other than perhaps the codling moth, has had such an impact on agriculture and probably no other insect has received more study. The larvae develop inside the flower or boll, arising from eggs deposited by the female. They feed on the developing floral parts and fibers. Many generations occur in a single season. Losses are heavy unless insecticides are used.

Fig. 11–22 Spider mites can be very damaging to many plants. The lily plant on the left has a heavy infestation of mites. The plant on the right is free of mites. *Source:* University of California Cooperative Extension.

SUGAR CANE SHOOT BORER *(Diatraea saccharalis)* This is the most important insect pest of sugar cane in the Caribbean. Caterpillars feed on the leaves, then enter the stalk and bore into the center, killing the central growing shoot. Later generations bore into side shoots. Such mechanical injury causes the stalks to break and fall over. Yield and quality of extracted juice drops. Control attempts include resistant cultivars, insecticides, and the release of parasites of the borer; none is very effective.

MEDITERRANEAN FRUIT FLY *(Ceratitis capitata)* This notorious insect is of the greatest importance on all fruit species in the Mediterranean countries, south and central Africa (where it originated), western Australia, the west coast of South America, and throughout Central America. It has been kept out of the United States (except for Hawaii) by strict government inspection, and quarantine and eradication measures. The fly attacks peaches most heavily, but it will also infest pears, apricots, apples, citrus, and bananas. The fly is slightly smaller than the common housefly and is mostly yellow and brown in color, with black markings. It is controlled mainly by poisonous bait traps containing attractants and by the release of sterile male flies. Both the Oriental *(Dacus dorsalis)* and Mexican *(Anastrepha ludens)* fruit flies (see Fig. 11–23) can be devastating to fruit crops.

Fig. 11–23 Fruit flies, such as the Oriental, Mediterranean, and Mexican, attack many fruit crops and must be kept out of major fruit growing regions if at all possible. The insects in this photograph are adult Mexican fruit flies on an orange fruit. *Source:* USDA.

GRAPE BERRY MOTH *(Polychrosis riteana)* This is the principal insect pest on grapes in Europe, North Africa, and Japan. The caterpillar feeds on developing fruit. Two or three generations can occur during the season. Insecticide spray is the only control measure.

INSECTS ATTACKING DRIED FRUITS

A number of fruits are preserved by drying, either outdoors on trays in the sun or in forced hot-air dehydrators. Important dried fruits are raisins, prunes, dates, figs, apples, peaches, apricots, and pears. All these dried fruits are food for various insects, which are best controlled by fumigation treatments *(30)*. Several types of insects feed on dried fruits:

Beetles: dried fruit beetle, saw-toothed grain beetle, small darkling beetle, hairy fungus beetle, corn sap beetle, pineapple beetle, and date stone beetle

Moths: raisin moth, Indian meal moth, almond moth, dried fruit moth, navel orange worm, dried prune moth, and dusky raisin moth

Flies: vinegar fly *(Drosophila)*, soldier fly, blowfly, housefly

INSECTS ATTACKING STORED GRAINS

It is estimated that insects destroy at least 5 percent of the world's production of cereal grains, amounting to about 15 million tons annually *(5, 10)*. Important insects that feed on stored grains are the saw-toothed grain beetle, lesser grain beetle, flat grain beetle, red flour beetle, foreign grain beetle, larger black flour beetle, Angoumis grain moth, hairy fungus beetle, granary weevil, and the rice weevil.

Control measures include prompt harvesting, drying the grain with heated air to a low moisture content (11 to 13 percent), and storage in tight, insect-free bins raised above ground. After two to six weeks the grain is fumigated with such materials as carbon tetrachloride (alone or mixed with carbon disulfide), ethylene dichloride, or ethylene dibromide in various proportions. (Fumigation should be done only by professionals trained in the proper use of these materials, which are highly toxic to humans).

RODENTS AND VERTEBRATE WILDLIFE

Rodents, particularly Norway rats, roof rats, and house mice, cause great losses to food crops. Such losses occur mainly in stored grains and other food products in open storage, although rats also feed on unharvested fruits and vegetables. Sugar cane fields in Hawaii, for example, are often invaded by rats (*29, 35*). From about 110 million total MT of food produced in India in 1968, it is estimated that 1 million MT of grain were consumed by rats. The World Health Organization estimates that, worldwide, rats destroy about 33 million tons of stored grain annually.

The strategy in rodent control is, first, to remove all food and water available to them from the areas they inhabit, and, second, to place bait traps containing an anticoagulant rodenticide such as Warfarin in their runways. Control should be done around granaries just before harvest begins (*29*). Some rat species, however, show increasing resistance to rodenticides, and in the future the chemicals may not be effective. Chemical sterilants are under development to reduce rodent populations by acting as oral contraceptives.

Young fruit trees and fall-planted seeds in nurseries are often damaged by meadow, pine, and white-footed deer, and by mice, gophers, squirrels, and rabbits. Effective repellents of rodents and birds have been developed as coatings of forest seeds sown in logged and burned over areas (*27*).

Fig. 11–24 A nondestructive method of keeping birds from eating the grapes in a vineyard. Amplified bird distress calls are played at intervals during the day at harvest time. *Source:* Blue Anchor, Inc.

Certain birds—particularly starlings, blackbirds, scrub jays, and crows—are a major menace to some fruit and nut crops, such as cherries, grapes, prunes, plums, strawberries, almonds, pecans, walnuts, and pistachios. Blackbirds, in particular, can decimate grain crops just ready for harvest. They can also cause considerable losses in peanut crops. The use of nonlethal chemical repellents is one type of bird control. Scare devices—carbide explosives, shell crackers, and amplified recordings of bird distress calls (Fig. 11–24) are also used with varying degrees of success. Research on chemical reproduction inhibitors may eventually provide the best method of controlling depredating bird populations (*42*).

THE SAFE USE OF AGRICULTURAL CHEMICALS— HERBICIDES, INSECTICIDES, FUNGICIDES, MITICIDES, AND NEMATICIDES

The application of agricultural chemicals to food-producing plants must not create a health hazard. Many countries have elaborate procedures for determining whether agricultural chemicals are reasonably safe before they can be registered for sale to growers of agricultural crops. In the United States, the Environmental Protection Agency (EPA)[3] is responsible for determining the safety of agricultural chemicals; state and local government agencies can also add their own safety requirements (*2, 4, 21*).

Before the EPA grants approval for the sale of agricultural chemicals, exhaustive tests are conducted to show:

1. That the product will effectively do what the label claims
2. That the product, at the recommended application rate, has low toxicity levels (both acute and chronic) as determined by experiments with test animals
3. An absence of residues in food or feed crops—or, if there is a detectable residue, that it is no more than the tolerance level established as safe

[3]"The Environmental Protection Agency is charged by the United States Congress to protect the nation's land, air, and water systems. Under a mandate of national environmental laws focused on air and water quality, solid waste management, and the control of toxic substances, pesticides, noise and radiation, the Agency strives to formulate and implement actions which lead to a compatible balance between human activities and the ability of natural systems to support and nurture life." From the *EPA Journal.*

4. The fate of residues and breakdown products in the environment—in the soil, runoff water, ground water, or wildlife
5. Whether the product affects the environment by inducing changes in the natural populations of higher plants and animals or of microorganisms

It is estimated that an agricultural chemical company developing, for example, a new herbicide spends between $6 million and $12 million and that six to ten years of research are required to develop information sufficient to satisfy EPA standards.

When the EPA registers a pesticide for use, the label lists very specific restrictions on the product. It is registered for use on a certain crop or crops, to be applied at specific times and at specific concentrations. While a certain herbicide, for example, may be known to control a given weed species, it may not be permissible to use the herbicide to control such weeds if they are growing in a crop for which the herbicide is not registered.

In using pesticides, including herbicides, the warnings given below should be carefully read and followed.

The term *LD*$_{50}$ is seen on labels of agricultural chemicals. LD means "lethal dose" and refers to the chemical's toxicity. LD$_{50}$ is the dose that will kill 50 percent of test animals ingesting the chemical by mouth. LD$_{50}$ is expressed in milligrams of the chemical per kilogram of body weight of the test animal. The higher the LD$_{50}$ value, the safer the chemical. According to EPA toxicology guidelines, a chemical with an oral LD$_{50}$ of 50 or less must be labeled "DANGER-POISON (FATAL)"; one with an LD$_{50}$ between 50 and 500 is labeled "WARNING (MAY BE FATAL)"; an LD$_{50}$ from 500 to 5000, "CAUTION": and one with an LD$_{50}$ over 5000 is also labeled "CAUTION." All labels must also state "KEEP OUT OF REACH OF CHILDREN."

Warnings on the Use of Pesticide Chemicals and Suggestions for Their Proper Use

Pesticides are poisonous and should always be used with caution. The following suggestions for using and handling pesticides will help minimize the likelihood of injury from exposure to such chemicals to humans, animals, and crops other than the pest species to be destroyed.

1. Always read and exactly follow all precautionary directions on container labels before using sprays or dusts. Read all warnings and cautions before opening the container. Repeat this process every time you use the pesticide regardless of how often you use it or how familiar you think you are with the directions. Apply materials only in amounts and at times specified.

2. Keep sprays and dusts out of reach of children, unauthorized persons, pets, and livestock. Store all pesticides outside the house in a locked cabinet or shed and away from food and feed.

3. Always store sprays and dusts in their original labeled containers and keep them tightly closed. Never store them in anything but the original container.

4. Never smoke, eat, or chew anything while spraying or dusting.

5. Avoid inhaling sprays or dusts. When directed on label, wear protective clothing and a proper mask.

6. Remove contaminated clothing immediately and wash the contaminated skin thoroughly if liquid concentrates are accidentally spilled on the skin or clothing.

7. Always bathe and change to clean clothing after spraying or dusting. If this is not possible, wash hands and face thoroughly and change clothes. Wash clothing after applying pesticides; never reuse before laundering. Launder this clothing separately from the family wash.

8. Cover food and water sources when treating around livestock or pet areas. Do not contaminate fishponds, streams, or lakes.

9. Always dispose of empty containers so that they pose no hazard to humans, animals, valuable plants or wildlife. Never burn pesticide containers, especially aerosol cans.

10. Read label directions and follow recommendations to keep residues on edible portions of plants within the limits permitted by law.

11. Call a physician or get the patient to a hospital immediately if symptoms of illness occur during or shortly after dusting or spraying. Be sure to take the container or the label of the pesticide used to the physician.

12. Do not use the mouth to siphon liquids from containers or to blow out clogged lines, nozzles, etc.

13. Do not spray with leaking hoses or connections.

14. Do not work in the drift of a spray or dust.

15. Confine chemicals to the property being treated and avoid drift by stopping treatment if the weather conditions are not favorable.

16. Protect nearby evergreen trees and shrubs from the dormant sprays used on fruit trees.

17. Do not use household preparations of pesticides on plants because they contain solvents that can injure plants.

Source: Division of Agricultural Sciences, University of California.

PESTICIDE IMPACTS ON THE ENVIRONMENT

Insecticides, miticides, fungicides, nematicides, and herbicides can be thought of as necessary evils. Without these chemicals, large-scale agriculture and our standard of living would not exist. Too little food would be produced to feed the world's 4 billion people, and mass starvation would result.

Unfortunately, however, chemical applications in agriculture do not always do just what they are supposed to do and nothing else. This problem is recognized more and more now, and greater and greater precautions are being taken to avoid unwanted side effects from these chemicals. Government regulations on pesticides have become steadily tighter. Pesticides that are chemically stable and persist in ecosystems are the ones largely responsible for environmental contamination. The law has ordered the replacement of such persistent chemicals as the chlorinated hydrocarbons (DDT, DDD, dieldrin, aldrin, chlordane, BHC, and heptaclor) with the low-persistence organophosphates (malathion, diazinon, and parathion) and the carbamates (carbaryl and methomyl), which break down rapidly and are not taken up in food chains.

It was pointed out earlier in this chapter that many insect pests are held in check very well by their own natural enemies—often other insect predators. Reducing populations of one serious primary insect pest with insecticides may, at the same time, so reduce the numbers of insect predators feeding on a secondary insect that the secondary pest increases explosively. For example, insecticidal control of codling moth, pear thrips, and pear psylla in pear orchards is generally followed by large increases in spider mite populations because the spray applications have reduced other predaceous mites that feed on the spider mite.

Production of a number of major food crops relies on pollination of the flowers by honeybees and bumblebees. Many fruit tree species—almonds, apples, plums, and sweet cherries—as well as certain vegetables, such as muskmelons and honeydew melons, and such forage crops as seed alfalfa and seed clover require thorough working of the flowers by bees during bloom. Elimination of bees by haphazard insecticidal applications and drift cannot be tolerated. Some states impose strict legal requirements wherever honeybees could be involved.

Insecticides should not be applied in areas where bees are working, particularly with chemicals highly toxic to bees—the arsenicals, aldrin, BHC, diazinon, dieldrin, guthion, malathion, parathion, and carbaryl. Some insecticides are relatively nontoxic to honeybees:

Aramite, ethion, methoxychlor, nicotine sulfate, Omite, pyrethrin, rotenone, and tetradifon (Tedion).

The state of California requires that beekeepers post their names and telephone numbers on all hives. Anyone planning to apply pesticides in the vicinity must inform the beekeepers of upcoming spray applications. If potentially hazardous insecticides are to be used, spray applicators must notify all beekeepers within a one-mile radius and allow them 48 hours to move their hives.

Effects on Wildlife

There is no doubt that pesticides have harmed wildlife, even though such effects may be difficult to document. Some reported losses of fish and fish-eating birds have resulted from the improper or illegal use of pesticides, a fact that underscores the need to read and follow label directions implicitly. Certain of the pesticides most lethal to wildlife, such as DDT, have been withdrawn from general use in the United States.

Some of the adverse effects of pesticides on wildlife have been indirect. For example, in some areas the pheasant population has declined when the weed cover, which had offered protection and nesting places, was cleared out along ditch banks, fence rows, and fallow lands by herbicides.

SUMMARY

Growers of the world's crops have had to compete with weeds, plant diseases, insects, plant parasites, birds, and rodents since the earliest days of agriculture. The energy and labor used for such purposes throughout history would stagger the imagination. The losses of food to these competitors, in the face of world hunger and mass starvation in some areas, is a disaster. Traditional methods practiced in earlier days for controlling pests are generally unacceptable in modern times, especially in countries with advanced technology and with enlightened concepts for protecting the people's health and the environment. Eliminating weeds in crop lands with the hoe, killing insects with arsenical poisons, and controlling diseases with mercurial fungicides are not economically feasible and are no longer acceptable. Instead, among other advances, plant breeders now continually strive to develop new types of crop plants resistant to insects and diseases, while plant physiologists have developed selective synthetic plant hormones that in minute concentrations kill many noxious weeds without harming crop plants. The modern concept of integrated pest management, now being developed for use with many crops, brings into play information on the culture and growth of the crop, development and reproduction of the pests, natural factors that may control them, artificial means for their control, and the consequences of all these factors in terms of economics to the grower and the consumers, to the public health, and to the environment.

REVIEW QUESTIONS

11–1. What classes of pathogenic microorganisms cause diseases in plants?

11–2. For an infectious disease to appear in plants what two conditions, in addition to the presence of a pathogenic microorganism, must occur?

11–3. Name six basic methods for biologically controlling insect and disease pests attacking plants.

11–4. What is meant by integrated pest management?

11–5. Give five basic methods for controlling weeds in crop areas.

11–6. Weeds can be annual, biennial, or perennial plants. Which are the most difficult to control? Why?

11–7. Although many microorganisms cause diseases in plants, some are beneficial. Name three instances where microorganism activity benefits plant growth.

11–8. What do virus particles consist of? How do they differ from viroids?

11–9. Name two ways to eliminate viruses from infected plants.

11–10. Insects that destroy plants can be placed into two groups according to their mode of attack. What are these two groups? How do control methods for each differ?

11–11. List in proper order the four stages of the complete metamorphosis of an insect.

11–12. Weeds reduce crop yields due to competition for what four essentials?

11–13. Which of the following are not true insects? (a) Potato beetle, (b) peach aphid, (c) corn ear worm, (d) cabbage moth, (e) dog tick, (f) honeybee, (g) spider mite.

11–14. Pesticides are agents that kill (a) bacteria, (b) fungi, (c) viruses, (d) weeds, (e) none of these, (f) all of these, (g) all except _____.

11–15. Give two examples of parasitic plants.

11–16. Fungi are plants which contain chlorophyll. True of false?

11–17. Bacteria can enter the plant through the epidermal cells and cause disease. True or false?

11–18. The most effective way to eliminate nematodes is by _____ fumigation.

11–19. Discuss the difference between pest eradication and pest control. Which do you consider to be most practical for large scale crop production?

11–20. List four broad categories of plant pests.

REFERENCES

1. Anon. The bugs are coming. July 12, 1976. *Time*.

2. Bailey, J. B., and J. E. Swift. 1968. Pesticide information and safety manual. Univ. of Calif. Agr. Ext. Serv.

3. Baker, K. F., and R. J. Cook. 1974. *Biological control of plant pathogens*. San Francisco: W. H. Freeman & Company Publishers.

4. Burton, V. E., W. R. Brown, C. S. Davis, A. S. Deal, J. E. Dibble, E. C. Loomis, and W. Stanger. 1972. *Study guide for agricultural pest control advisers on insects, mites, and other invertebrates and their control in California*. Univ. of Calif. Div. Agr. Sci.

5. Cotton, R. T., and W. Ashby. 1952. Insect pests of stored grains. In USDA Yearbook of Agriculture. Insects. Washington, D.C.: Superintendent of Documents.

6. Crafts, A. S. 1975. *Modern weed control*. Berkeley, Calif.: University of California Press.

7. Crosby, D. G. 1973. The fate of pesticides in the environment. *Ann. Rev. Plant Physiol.* 24:467–92.

8. Diener, T. O. 1974. Viroids: the smallest known agents of infectious diseases. *Ann. Rev. Microbiol.* 28:23–39.

9. Doi, Y., M. Teranaka, K. Yora, and H. Asuyama. 1967. Mycoplasma or PLT group-like microorganisms found in the phloem elements of plants infected with mulberry dwarf, potato witches' broom, aster yellows, or paulownia witches' broom. *Ann. Phytopath. Soc. Jap.* 33:259–66.

10. Ebeling, W. 1975. *Urban entomology*. Univ. of Calif. Div. Agr. Sci.

11. Feinstein, L. 1952. Insecticides from plants. In USDA Yearbook of Agriculture. Insects. Washington, D.C.: Superintendent of Documents.

12. Fischer, W., and A. Lange. *Growers' weed identification handbook*. Univ. of Calif. Div. Agr. Sci. Handbook.

13. Hampton, R. O. 1972. Mycoplasmas as plant pathogens: perspectives and principles. *Ann. Rev. Plant Physiol.* 23:389–418.

14. Hayes, J., ed. 1966. Protecting our food. Yearbook of agriculture. Washington, D.C.: U.S. Government Printing Office.

15. Johnson, W. T., and H. H. Lyon. 1976. *Insects that feed on trees and shrubs.* Ithaca, N.Y.: Cornell University Press.

16. Kenaga, C. B. 1975. *Principles of phytopathology.* 2nd ed. Lafayette, Ind.: Balt.

17. Klingman, G. C., and F. M. Ashton. 1975. *Weed science: principles and practices.* New York: John Wiley.

18. Lear, B., and D. E. Johnson. 1975. Controlling nematodes in the home garden. Univ. of Calif. Div. Agr. Sci. Leaflet 2112.

19. McGourty, F., Jr. 1975. Weed control in the home garden. *Plants & Gardens* 31(2):1–65.

20. McHenry, W. B., and R. F. Norris. 1972. *Study guide for agricultural pest control advisers on weed control.* Univ. of Calif. Div. Agr. Sci.

21. Moller, W. J., D. H. Hall, A. H. McCain, and A. O. Paulus. 1972. *Study guide for agricultural pest control advisers on plant diseases.* Univ. of Calif. Div. Agr. Sci.

22. National Academy of Science. 1968. Weed control. U.S. Publ. No. 1597.

23. Nyland, G., and A. C. Goheen. 1969. Heat therapy of virus diseases of perennial plants. *Ann. Rev. Phytopath.* 7:331–54.

24. ———. and W. J. Moller. 1973. Control of pear decline with a tetracycline. *Plant Disease Reporter* 57:634–37.

25. Painter, R. H. 1951. *Insect resistance in crop plants.* Lawrence, Kansas: University Press of Kansas.

26. Peterson, G. W., and R. S. Smith, Jr., eds. 1975. Forest nursery diseases in the United States. USDA Forest Service Handbook 470.

27. Radranyi, A. 1972. Protecting coniferous seeds from rodents. Proc. Fifth Vertebrate Pest Conference, Fresno, Calif. ed. R. E. Marsh.

28. Roberts, D. A., and C. W. Boothroyd. 1972. *Fundamentals of plant pathology.* San Francisco: W. H. Freeman & Company Publishers.

29. Rowe, F. P., J. H. Greaves, R. Redfern, and A. D. Martin. 1970. Rodenticides—problems and current research. Proc. Fourth Vertebrate Pest Conference, Fresno, Calif., ed. R. H. Dana.

30. Simmons, P., and H. D. Nelson. 1975. Insects on dried fruits. USDA Agr. Handbook 464.

31. Smith, K. M. 1972. *A textbook of plant virus diseases.* 3rd ed. London: Longmans.

32. Stapley, J. H., and F. C. H. Gaynor. 1969. *World crop protection,* vol. 1. Pests and diseases. London: Iliffe.

33. Stefferud, A., ed. 1952. Insects. Yearbook of agriculture. Washington, D. C.: U.S. Government Printing Office.

34. ———, ed. 1953. Plant diseases. Yearbook of agriculture. Washington, D.C.: U.S. Government Printing Office.

35. Teshima, A. H. 1970. Rodent control in the Hawaii sugar industry. Proc. Fourth Vertebrate Pest Conference, Fresno, Calif., ed. R. H. Dana.

36. Thomason, I. J., and R. M. Boardman, eds. 1978. Integrated pest management. *Calif. Agr.* 32(2).

37. Thorne, G. 1961. *Principles of nematology.* New York: McGraw-Hill.

38. USDA, ARS. 1970. *A reference guide to federal plant quarantine and regulations.* Plant Quarantine Division. Washington, D.C.: Superintendent of Documents.

39. USDA Forest Service. 1971. Mycorrhizae: proceedings of the first North American conference on mycorrhizae. USDA Misc. Publ. No. 1189.

40. USDA/ARS. 1976. Virus diseases and noninfectious disorders of stone fruits in North America. Agricultural Handbook No. 437.

41. van der Zwet, T., and H. L. Keil. 1979. *Fire blight: a bacterial disease of rosaceous plants.* Washington, D.C.: U.S. Government Printing Office.

42. Woulfe, M. R. 1970. Reproductive inhibitors for bird control. Proc. Fourth Vertebrate Pest Conference, Fresno, Calif., ed. R. H. Dana.

SUPPLEMENTARY READING

AUDUS, L. D., ed. 1976. *Herbicides: physiology, biochemistry, ecology,* vols. 1 and 2. New York: Academic Press.

BOETHEL, D. J., and R. D. EIKENBARY, 1979. *Pest management programs for deciduous tree fruits and nuts.* New York: Plenum.

BORAIKO, A. A. 1980. The pesticide dilemma. *Nat. Geog.* 157(2):145–83.

CRAVENS, R. H. 1977. *Pests and diseases.* Alexandria, Va.: Time-Life.

NEW YORK STATE COLLEGE OF AGRICULTURE AND LIFE SCIENCES. 1979. Integrated pest management—a new strategy in an old war. Ithaca, N.Y.: *New York Food and Life Sciences Quarterly* 12(2):1–24.

SASSER, J. N. 1980. Root-knot nematodes: a global menace to crop production. *Plant Disease* 64(1):36–41.

TATTAR, T. A. 1978. *Diseases of shade trees.* New York: Academic Press.

WEBSTER, J. M., ed. 1972. *Economic nematology.* New York: Academic Press.

WEED SCIENCE SOCIETY OF AMERICA, HERBICIDE HANDBOOK COMMITTEE. 1979. *Herbicide handbook.* 4th ed. Champaign, Ill.: Weed Science Society of America.

Harvest, Preservation, Transportation, Storage, and Marketing

People and their domestic animals consume plants to obtain energy to live. Every part of the plant serves these food needs—roots, stems, leaves, flowers, fruits, and seeds. We have developed efficient methods and machines for harvesting, storing, and preserving the various plant parts for consumption.

HARVESTING

The growth and development of agriculture has been greatly stimulated by mechanization of all operations, from preparing land to processing produce. Agricultural practices are constantly changing to accommodate machines; plant breeders remodel plants to adapt them to machine harvest. Since the beginning of organized agriculture, crops have been selected for better quality, for easier production, and for better use. In fact, the greatest effort in recent years has been toward the development of labor-saving harvesting machines.

Mechanization of harvesting crops began with the cereal grains. The forerunner of the grain combine was the hand sickle and flail, which were used as far back as 5000 years ago. From the sickle came the longer-handled scythe, followed by the cradle, then the reaper or binder, the threshing machine, and finally the giant combine. Two other early and greatly appreciated machines were

the cotton picker and the cotton gin. The picker can relieve people of the backbreaking job of hand-harvesting cotton, and the cotton gin separated the fibers from the seed. Harvest mechanization of grains, sugar beets, and other field crops has relieved farmers of much hard labor. More recently in the United States there has been a great impetus to develop harvesters and labor-saving devices for vegetables, fruits, berries, grapes, nuts, and forage crops.

Crops grown for processing were harvested mechanically long before those grown for sale on the fresh market. For example, practically all processed tomatoes and sour cherries are machine-harvested. Fresh-market fruits are still mostly hand-harvested. Plant breeders and agricultural engineers cooperated to modify the growth characteristics of the tomato plant to adapt it to the harvesting machine. The fruits of processing tomato cultivars tend to ripen uniformly, their skins are tough, and they are oblong—characteristics that make machine harvesting possible (Fig. 12–1). Some wine grapes are harvested by machines. It is difficult to adapt some crops, such as strawberries and bushberries, to mechanization, but breeders and engineers are working on the problem.

Ever-increasing labor costs put pressure on farmers to mechanize harvesting wherever possible. It is becoming obvious that the harvest of fruits and vegetables for the fresh market will have to be mechanized or these

Fig. 12–1 This tomato harvester is equipped with an electronic device that automatically sorts the tomato fruits by color, discarding the excessively green ones while retaining those at peak ripeness. *Source: The Daily Democrat,* Woodland–Davis, Calif.

crops will be in danger of being dropped from large-scale production because they will not compete economically with crops grown for processing and harvested mechanically.

Function of Harvesting Machines

A machine must perform certain functions to harvest a crop. Functions required of harvesting machines are: (1) removing the plant by cutting or digging, (2) gathering or concentrating plant parts, (3) separating desired from undesired parts, (4) eliminating unused parts, (5) cleaning, and (6) loading crop for transport. These functions depend upon such factors as: (1) kind of crop (mature grain or fresh fruit), (2) crop use (corn for silage or grain), (3) part of plant harvested (roots or fruit), (4) stage of maturity (immature flowers or seeds), and (5) crop value (high-profit or low-profit crops).

Mechanically Harvested Crops

COTTON

Machine harvest of open-bolled cotton became common by 1940. Most commercial cotton grown in the United States is mechanically harvested either by pickers (Fig. 25–13) or strippers. Open-boll cotton is harvested by a machine that guides the plant into vertical rotating rollers equipped with moistened spindles that remove the fibers from the plant (Fig. 25–14). The fibers are removed from the spindles by counter-rotating doffing wheels and blown or conveyed into a large bas-

ket, from which they are loaded onto trucks for transport to the gin. Some growers defoliate cotton plants before harvest by spraying with ammonia (NH_3) (Fig. 25–15). The nitrogen is recovered as a plant nutrient by the succeeding crop when the cotton leaves are plowed under. Stormproof cotton (closed boll) is grown on the high plains of Texas and Oklahoma. The entire boll is removed by harvest machines called strippers, which were developed about 1880. The plant passes between counter-rotating rollers that strip the bolls from the plants.

GRAIN CROPS

The cereal grains—barley, corn, oats, rice, rye, sorghum, and wheat are all mechanically harvested similarly (Fig. 12–2). Grains are harvested as mature seeds. They are allowed to dry to a safe-storage moisture content in the field before harvest, or they are dried artificially after harvest and before storage.

The grain combine was developed in Michigan about 1800; later, as people moved west, its use spread to the grain fields of the Pacific coast states (Fig. 12–3). The modern self-propelled combine puts one person in complete control of the entire harvest operation. The harvester cuts the grain heads from the plant. The heads pass through rotating cylinders that beat the kernels from the hulls. The kernels, hulls, chaff, and stems move along "walkers" (shakers) that separate the kernels by sifting them through sieves, retaining the stems (straw) and chaff. The straw passes out of the harvester. The grain and chaff pass a blower that blows away the lighter-than-grain chaff. The grain is collected in the bottom of the machine and conveyed to a storage bin mounted on top, from which it is unloaded into a truck for transport to storage or market.

Fig. 12–2 Corn is mass-harvested with four-row self-propelled combines. The ears are removed from the stalk and the kernels separated from the cob in one operation. *Source:* Allis-Chalmers.

A

B

Fig. 12–3 (*A*): Mechanical harvest of wheat on a hillside in the western United States. Wheat is grown in these fields without irrigation (dry land); the only source of water is winter rainfall stored in the soil. The combine operator must keep the machine level during harvesting. *Source:* Allis-Chalmers. (*B*): While the principle of separating grain from straw has not changed over the years, the power source has. Here farm-grown grain and hay-fed horses provide the energy that now comes from petroleum fuels. *Source:* University of California Cooperative Extension.

HAY CROPS

Some hay is cut by tractor-mounted mowing machines, then placed in windrows by tractor-mounted rakes for curing and drying. After drying, the hay is picked up by self-propelled or tractor-drawn balers and compressed into compact bales (Fig. 12–4). Some balers have loading attachments that convey the bales directly from the baler to a trailer, allowing one person to do the entire operation (Fig. 12–5). In some areas, hay is cut by large self-propelled mower-swathers that cut and windrow the hay (Fig. 12–6). In other areas, hay is cut, and after curing, it is rolled into large loose rolls and stored in the fields. To facilitate handling, cured hay can be picked up mechanically from windrows and compressed into cubes about 4 cm (1.5 in) square (Fig. 12–7). Animals waste less hay because the cubes are bite-sized and there is no loose hay for them to pull from the feed trough and spoil by trampling. Cubes can be loaded and moved by conveyer belts, and their high density requires less storage space. Cubes are preferred for transport to distant and overseas markets (Fig. 12–8).

Some hay crops are cut and chopped immediately by a hay chopper without curing. The green chopped hay is blown into a truck or trailer, transported to a dehydrator to be dried, and processed into a meal or compressed into pellets. This method yields a high-quality animal feed and avoids the loss of leaves and nutrients by field-drying in the sun.

Fig. 12–4 Hay is cut, raked into windrows, and allowed to cure in the field for a few days. The time required depends on the relative humidity and temperature of the air. After drying, the hay is compressed into compact bales for storage. *Source:* John Dobie.

Fig. 12–5 Baled hay is often picked up in the field with automatic loaders or stackers and transported to the storage area for stacking. This machine eliminates the hand labor of lifting and loading bales, then unloading and stacking them. *Source:* John Dobie.

Fig. 12–6   This mower-swather cuts the hay and then places it in windrows for curing, thus combining two operations into one. After the hay is cured, it is baled or cubed. *Source:* Deere and Company.

Fig. 12–7   These machines are picking up cured alfalfa hay and compressing it into cubes about 4 cm² (1.5 in²). This hay is destined for transport to Japan via ship. *Source:* John Dobie.

Fig. 12–8   Hay cubing from cutting to storage. Note the degree of mechanization. *Source:* John Dobie.

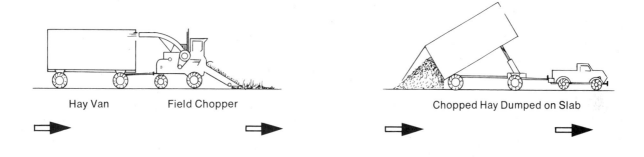

Hay Van   Field Chopper   Chopped Hay Dumped on Slab

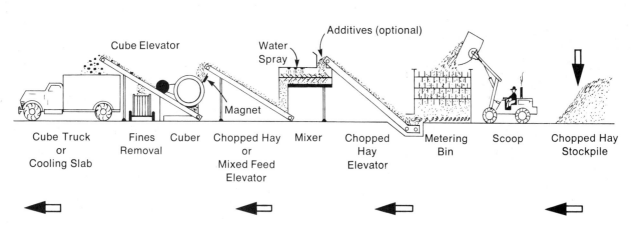

Cube Elevator   Water   Additives (optional)
                                 Spray

                                 Magnet

Cube Truck   Fines   Cuber   Chopped Hay   Mixer   Chopped   Metering   Scoop   Chopped Hay
   or   Removal   or   Hay   Bin   Stockpile
Cooling Slab   Mixed Feed   Elevator
                                 Elevator

ROOT AND TUBER CROPS

The mechanical harvesting of all root crops involves essentially identical operations. The roots are removed from the soil by digging, plowing, or pulling. They are then separated from the upper portion of the plant and conveyed to a truck or trailer for transport to a packing or processing plant. Almost all large plantings of white (Irish) potatoes, sugar beets, and carrots grown for processing are harvested mechanically (Fig. 12–9). Radishes, turnips, table beets, and sweet potatoes are harvested mechanically to a lesser extent. The machines used for root crops harvest one, two, or more rows simultaneously and are either tractor-drawn or self-propelled. Most sugar beets are topped before harvesting; that is, a machine (either separate or mounted on the harvester) cuts the tops from the beets before they are removed from the soil. Some harvesters pull beets from the soil by their tops, then cut the tops from the roots. Beet tops can be recovered and used for livestock feed.

Most Irish potatoes are harvested when their tops begin to die. Drying is hastened and harvesting facilitated if the plants are rolled to flatten them and the beds. The potato tubers are removed and separated from soil, then conveyed to trucks for transport. Several kinds of mechanisms are used to remove the tubers from the soil. One kind is a plow equipped with steel rods attached and spaced so that as the plow moves forward and lifts the tubers out of the soil the rods allow the loosened soil to pass through. The tubers then fall on a rod-chain shaker where soil clods are broken and more soil is separated from the tubers. Another type uses a middle buster (a right and left plow fastened together back to back) with rods to lift the tubers. A potato combine harvesting six to eight rows at a time has broad blades that run under the

Fig. 12–10 Grading potato tubers according to size. The removal of defective tubers insures good quality for packaging and storage or market. *Source:* University of California Cooperative Extension.

rows to loosen the soil. Behind the blades, a series of agitating rods attached to chains lift the tubers gently and shake the soil free. The soil drops through the shaking rods and the tubers are conveyed to trucks. Some machines carry a small crew to remove rocks, vines, and other trash. Tubers not cleaned in the field are delivered to a packing shed and emptied into vats of chlorinated water, scrubbed, dried, brushed, waxed, graded, and packaged for market (Fig. 12–10).

FRUIT AND NUT CROPS

Fruits vary considerably in the manner and the rate at which they mature; each species has its own characteristic pattern. Also, some fruits tend to drop during the maturation period. Thus, mechanical harvesting of fruit is difficult; in fact, fruit for fresh market is almost always hand-harvested. Often some mechanical aids are used; for example, hydraulic platforms that lift the pickers and move them around and about the tree can replace ladders, and conveyer belts can be used to transport fruits to bulk bins.

Fruits grown for processing are often harvested mechanically, as are most of the commercially grown nut crops (walnuts, almonds, pecans) (Fig. 12–11). The fruits or nuts are removed from the tree by vigorously shaking the main branches or trunk with a self-propelled, hydraulic shaker. Canvas catching frames held above the ground or rollout canvases catch the fruit and move it onto a conveyer belt. Foam-rubber padding on metal frame supports reduces bruising.

Mechanically harvested fruits include cling peaches, canning cherries, prunes for processing, and some raisin and wine grapes. Mechanical aids are used for harvesting some citrus crops. New machines are

Fig. 12–9 The harvest of white potatoes is completely mechanized. Tubers are removed from the ground, separated from vines and soil, then conveyed to trucks alongside the harvester. *Source:* University of California Cooperative Extension.

Fig. 12–11 Harvesting sour cherries in Michigan for canning. Fruits are shaken from the tree onto catching frames, then conveyed into a bin containing brine. *Source:* USDA.

Fig. 12–12 Harvesting blueberries mechanically in Michigan. This machine was developed and manufactured commercially, but the basic harvesting research was done by the U.S. Department of Agriculture and Michigan State University in cooperation with growers, packers, processors, and manufacturers. Harvesting equipment such as this tends to revitalize production of crops that have very high hand-picking costs. *Source:* USDA–Science and Education Administration/Agr. Research, and Michigan State University Agricultural Experiment Station.

being developed to harvest other fruits crops, such as blueberries, cranberries, and strawberries, and plant breeders are developing cultivars of some species, strawberries for example, with the idea of adapting them to mechanical harvesting (Figs. 12–12, 12–13).

Nuts are generally shaken onto clean, smooth ground, then swept into windrows with a mechanical sweeper (Fig. 12–14). They are picked up by a mechanical sweeper or vacuum and placed into bins for transport to a dehuller.

Fig. 12–13 Mechanical aids are used to make hand harvesting of some crops easier. In this case strawberry baskets are carried on a small cart mounted on wheels. The cart is easily pushed down the row. *Source:* University of California Cooperative Extension.

Fig. 12–14 Almond nuts have been shaken from trees onto smoothed, rolled ground and swept into windrows. They will be vacuumed into bins for transport to the processing plant.

Fig. 12–15 This pull-type bean harvester is specially designed to gently thresh green peas, lima beans, broad beans, or southern peas. The vines are cut from their roots and passed through a vining system that gently separates the fruits from the pods as the vines progress through the machine. *Source:* Food Machinery Corporation.

VEGETABLE CROPS

Several vegetable crops grown for processing are harvested mechanically (Fig. 12–15). A tomato cultivar suitable for processing and the tomato harvester were developed simultaneously, each being ready for use at about the same time. The tomato harvester cuts the vine at the soil surface and elevates the vine to a shaking bed where the fruit is shaken free by horizontal agitating bars. The bars are spaced so that the fruit falls between them while the vines stay behind. The vines are passed to the rear and dropped to the ground. The fruit is caught on a belt and divided; one-half moves along each side of the machine, where five or more workers stand on platforms to remove cull fruit and clods of soil. The selected fruit passes to another belt and is transported into trucks and trailers moving alongside the harvester. As Figure 12–1 shows, some harvesters are equipped with electronic sorters that separate the fruit by color.

POSTHARVEST PRESERVATION

The objective of crop preservation is to retard or arrest senescence of plant tissue and to present a finished product in an attractive or usable form.[1] The postharvest storage or handling of fresh commodities such as fresh fruit,

[1]For information on ways to preserve foods at home, write your state Cooperative Extension Service.

vegetables, meat, and dairy products must reduce the reactions that tend to break down the product. These degradation reactions are essentially those of respiration; the carbohydrates synthesized during photosynthesis are broken down to carbon dioxide and water. To prolong the life of the product it is desirable to reduce the rate of respiration and to prevent water loss by transpiration.

The preservation method used depends upon the nature of the product. Botanically, fruits are the mature structures of flowers that bear seeds. This classification covers a wide assortment of plant tissue. Some fruits are soft and fleshy, others are hard, and thus will require different methods of preservation. Some seeds are enclosed in hulls or shells and are harvested mature and dry; for example, the cereal grains, nuts, and spices. These need no preservation if stored dry. Fleshy dessert fruits (apples, pears, peaches) have much in common with some vegetable fruits (tomatoes, green beans, peas). These can be preserved similarly by canning or freezing. By common usage, fleshy dessert fruits are distinguished from fleshy vegetable fruits in that vegetable fruits are more often cooked and eaten with meat, while fleshy dessert fruits are often eaten fresh as a dessert and either are sweet by themselves or are sweetened before eating. Fruits and vegetables can also be distinguished on the basis of their respiration characteristics.

Preservation by Cooling

An important factor to consider in reducing the rate of respiration reactions is temperature. As a general rule, lowering temperature reduces enzyme activity and consequently respiration rate. Fruits differ in the lowest temperature they can tolerate without damage. Tropical fruits (bananas, tomatoes) suffer a malady known as chilling injury when stored at temperatures below 10°C to 13°C (50°F to 56°F), while onions, pears, and some apple cultivars tolerate 0°C (32°F) or lower. Storage at the lowest temperature a product can tolerate without chilling injury or freezing damage preserves that product longest. The temperature range for living plant tissue is about 0°C to 35°C (32°F to 95°F). The rate of respiration reactions increases with the temperature, then declines toward the upper limit. Generally for each 10°C reduction in temperature, the rate of respiration decreases by half, or conversely, for each 10°C increase in temperature the respiration rate doubles. This is important in the storage of fresh-market fruits and vegetables. Obviously, though, chilling injury temperatures should be avoided with susceptible warm-season crops (*12*). For best results cooling should follow harvest as soon as possible. Harvesting induces the climacteric (rapid rise in rate of respiration), in some fruits (see Fig. 14–4).

Fig. 12–16 Mechanically refrigerated dry-cold storage rooms are widely used to store many fruits and vegetables, such as the muskmelons shown here. The refrigeration units that cool these large rooms operate on the same principle as a home refrigerator. *Source:* Western Grower and Shipper.

REFRIGERATION

The most common method of cooling is the mechanical refrigerator, which can vary in size from a large warehouse to a small home model (Fig. 12–16). The mechanical refrigerator allows control of relative humidity as well as of temperature. Some crops require cool storage at high relative humidity while others store better in a cool, dry atmosphere. Practically all long-distance shipments of fresh fruits and vegetables are made in mechanically refrigerated trucks or railcars.

HYDROCOOLING

Produce packed in slatted wooden crates or boxes is placed on a slow-moving conveyer belt that moves the crates through a tunnellike construction about 9 m (30 ft) long. Water cooled with crushed ice is sprayed over the crates as they move forward on the conveyer. The degree of cooling is regulated by adjusting travel time through the cooler. As the product emerges, it is removed from the conveyer and either transported to refrigerated railcars or trucks or stored in a refrigerated room. Hydrocooling and vacuum cooling (see below) are sometimes combined for some crops (Fig. 12–17).

FORCED AIR (PRESSURE) COOLING

Some products, such as strawberries, do not store well if their skins are wet. These crops are often cooled by forced cold air. Strawberries are harvested into corrugated cardboard crates with ventilation holes and placed as soon as possible in the cooler. Air cooled by ice to 2°C (35°F) or below is drawn through vents into the cooler by fans on one side. The cold air flows through the containers and around the fruit, then exhausts from the opposite side of the cooler (Fig. 12–18).

Fig. 12–17 Hydro-vac cooling combines hydrocooling and vacuum cooling. It is used for vegetable crops that are difficult to cool by the vacuum cooler alone or that require lower storage temperature than hydrocooling can achieve. The hydro-vac cooler maintains the high moisture content of celery (generally hydrocooled) by spraying it with water while it is vacuum-cooled. *Source:* Western Grower and Shipper.

Fig. 12–18 Air which has been cooled by ice is drawn into this forced-air cooler through circular vents (upper right of photo) in the wall. After the cold air flows in and around the produce, it exhausts through holes in the opposite wall. This type of cooler is used extensively for strawberries, but in this case, cauliflower is being cooled. Cut flowers are also cooled by this method. *Source:* Western Grower and Shipper.

PACKAGE ICING

In this old method of cooling fresh-market crops, crushed ice is placed into the crates and around the produce. The disadvantages are: (1) extra weight; (2) the ice needs to be renewed; (3) the produce is not cooled evenly; (4) cooling the product takes time; and (5) it is messy. The product must be placed in a cold room after icing. This method is used on difficult-to-cool crops such as cauliflower, broccoli, and melons.

VACUUM COOLING

Fresh-market leafy crops are cooled by a vacuum cooler because it is efficient and rapid. Vacuum-cooled crops are packed directly in the field, eliminating central packing sheds. The tube-shaped cooler has doors at each end, permitting entry of the packed crop at one end and exit at the other (Fig. 12–19). Pallets of crated produce (one-quarter of a railcar) are pushed into the cooler, the airtight doors are closed, and a vacuum pump evacuates air until the internal atmospheric pressure is about 4 to 6 mm (0.16 to 0.23 in) of mercury [normal atmospheric pressure is 760 mm (30 in) of mercury]. At low atmospheric pressure, water changes from liquid to vapor. This change of phase absorbs heat from the only source available—the crop being cooled. This heat is called the **latent heat of vaporization** and amounts to about 580 cal/gm of water at 20°C. The amount of water lost by the crop on cooling from 25° to 0°C (77°F to 32°F) is negligible, estimated at about 0.5 percent. Still, produce is often wetted before cooling to help compensate for water loss.

Fig. 12–19 This very efficient vacuum cooler can cool one-fourth of a railcar of lettuce from 30°C to 1°C (86°F to 34°F) in about 30 minutes. While the cooler was originally designed for lettuce, other crops, such as the cauliflower shown here, are now cooled in this manner. *Source:* Western Grower and Shipper.

The drying of meats, vegetables, fruits, and berries by solar radiation was probably our first attempt at food preservation, and the popularity of dehydrated foods is increasing. Dates and figs were grown and sundried by early civilizations in the eastern Mediterranean area. Preservation by drying is successful because the organisms that cause decay cannot grow at moisture contents below 10 to 15 percent.

Some advantages of dehydration over other methods are a lighter and less bulky final product, no refrigeration requirement, and reduced transportation and storage costs.

The unique climate of California's Central Valley—long, rainless summers with low humidity—is ideal for dehydrating fruits in the sun (Fig. 12–20). Other areas with similar climates are found around the Mediterranean Sea, the Middle East, and parts of Australia. Crops now preserved by solar dehydration include apples, apricots, currents, grapes, peaches, figs, dates, pears, and plums.

Fig. 12–20 The brilliant cloudless summer days in the San Joaquin Valley in California are ideal for drying grapes to make raisins. The berries are picked by hand and (*A*) laid on heavy brown paper to dry. After drying they are rolled in the paper (*B*) for transport to the packing house for processing. A rain during this period is a catastrophe to raisin growers.

A

B

DEHYDRATION BY HOT FORCED AIR

The increased popularity of dehydrated fruits, such as peaches, pears, apricots, prunes, and raisins, stimulated the development of efficient methods of forced hot-air dehydration.

In general, the fruits are spread thinly on trays and passed through one or more tunnel dryers. Blanching (heating with steam for a short time) is sometimes done before drying to stop enzyme activity that causes the flesh to turn brown. Air heated to 60°C to 77°C (140°F to 170°F) is forced through the tunnels. The time needed for complete dehydration varies from 5 hours to as much as 36 hours depending on the kind and size of fruit.

Until recently, dehydrated vegetables were less readily accepted in the United States than dehydrated fruits, but onions, potatoes, and mushrooms are now commercially dehydrated in large quantities. The use of ready-mixed vegetables for soups and salads has increased the popularity of dehydrated celery, carrots, peppers, tomatoes, peas, Brussels sprouts, green beans, parsley, and chives.

DEHYDRATION BY FREEZING

Freeze drying is not used extensively but is a promising procedure. The process involves removing water by sublimation[2] of ice at temperatures below the freezing point. Upon rehydration, the quality of the products equals that of food preserved by freezing. Freeze-dried products are expensive but are particularly valuable when reduced weight is desirable, for instance for backpacking, biking, or space travel.

Preservation by Modified Atmospheres

Modified atmosphere[3] storage has been known for over 100 years (5). The first scientific study was made by Jacques Berard, a Frenchman, in 1819 and 1820 (2), but the idea was never applied. The idea was rekindled in the United States in the 1860s, but again, it was not accepted and died for lack of enthusiasm. Since World War I research on modified or controlled atmospheres has been profuse (10).

Temperature management is important in the storage of fresh products. In addition, the oxygen concentration must be lowered since oxygen is essential for aerobic respiration of both the food product and the live microorganisms that produce decay. Thus, lowering the oxygen concentration as well as the temperature around the products prolongs their storage life. A large percentage of Washington and Oregon grown apples are held in controlled atmosphere storage. Otherwise fresh eating apples would be available only a few weeks after harvest in the fall. With controlled atmosphere storage, fresh apples are available and economically priced throughout the year.

Three methods are used to lower the oxygen concentration: (1) increasing the carbon dioxide concentration; (2) injecting nitrogen into the storage chambers (increasing the nitrogen percentage lowers the percentage of oxygen); (3) evacuating air from the chamber. The concentration of CO_2 needed in the modified atmosphere varies considerably with each crop. For example, the 20 percent CO_2 concentration used to retard decay in strawberries injures head lettuce.

VACUUM STORAGE

This method—called hypobaric, subatmospheric, low pressure (LPS), or vacuum storage—is gaining in popularity (4). After the produce is placed in storage and the temperature lowered to the proper degree, air is pumped out and a partial vacuum maintained. As the air is evacuated from the chamber, some water-saturated air is allowed to enter. Vacuum storage prevents water loss from the product, reduces risk of CO_2 damage, lowers the oxygen supply, and sweeps ethylene[4] from the chamber. Removal of this plant hormone delays ripening. Hypobaric storage extends the storage of apples, apricots, avocados, bananas, cucumbers, green onions, green peppers, peaches, pears, sweet cherries, sweet corn, and tomatoes. Cut flowers, potted plants, and nonrooted and rooted cuttings have also been stored by this method (6).

RELATIVE HUMIDITY

Controlling relative humidity can help prolong storage. High humidity lowers water loss from plant tissue, thereby reducing desiccation and wilting. However, high humidity can promote the microorganisms that cause mold or decay in susceptible products. Most fleshy fruits store best at relative humidities of about 90 to 95 percent. These include apples, apricots, avocados, bananas, berries, figs, mangoes, papaya, pears, and pineapples. Easily wilted leafy vegetables should be

---

[2] Sublimation is the process by which a solid (ice) passes directly to a vapor without going through the liquid phase. Heat is absorbed in this process.

[3] Modified atmosphere (MA): atmosphere in which the concentrations of N_2, O_2, or CO_2 are changed but not necessarily precisely; temperature and relative humidity may be regulated. Controlled atmosphere (CA): atmosphere in which temperature, relative humidity, and concentrations of N_2, O_2, or CO_2 are precisely regulated within limits.

[4] Ethylene (C_2H_4), a natural plant hormone produced by some plants, promotes ripening (see p. 138).

stored at relative humidities of 95 to 100 percent. This group includes artichokes, broccoli, Brussels sprouts, carrots, celery, endive, lettuce, radishes, spinach, and turnips. Some vegetables store better at a lower relative humidity of 75 to 85 percent; for example, garlic, dry onions, pumpkins, some squashes, and sweet potatoes. Ventilation is needed in all storage facilities to keep undesirable gases from accumulating.

FUMIGATION

Some fruits and vegetables are treated with sulfur dioxide (SO_2), biphenyl ($C_6H_5C_6H_5$), methylbromide (CH_3BR), or other fumigants to kill decay-causing microorganisms on their surfaces. Sulfur dioxide is used to reduce decay in grapes, and biphenyl in citrus. Carbon monoxide or carbon dioxide can be used on crops that tolerate high concentrations of these gases.

Preservation by Processing

The preservation of foods by processing is relatively new. Because of a food shortage in France in 1795 and Napoleon's need for preserved food for his armies, a reward was offered for a safe method for preserving food. Appert, a Parisian, won the prize in 1809 by preserving

Fig. 12–21 Some tomatoes are canned whole with their peels removed. These are called whole or solid-pack tomatoes by the industry. Here a peel remover is removing the peels before canning. The tomatoes are first treated either by a caustic lye solution (NaOH) or by steam to loosen the peels so they can be removed by the disc peeler. A high-pressure water rinse removes peeling tags and any traces of lye solution. *Source:* Food Machinery Corporation.

certain foods in glass bottles that were sterilized by boiling. He could never explain how it worked, but his procedure was the beginning of the processing industry. The method came from England to Boston where America's first food-processing plant was established.

CANNING

The purpose of canning is to destroy spoilage organisms by heat, but complete sterilization is seldom necessary in commercial canning. The product is placed in a gas-tight container that can be hermetically sealed quickly and efficiently and can withstand considerable internal pressure (Fig. 12–21). The most popular containers are cans made from tin-plated sheet steel or glass bottles. The can interiors are painted with acid-resistant lacquers to reduce corrosion and discoloration when high-acid products are canned. Peas and sweet corn, while not strongly acid themselves, are canned in lacquered cans because they contain sulfur compounds that are converted to hydrogen sulfide (H_2S). Hydrogen sulfide causes the tin to turn black if not lacquered. After sterilization, the cans are quickly cooled in cold water or air, labeled, boxed, and stored in cool, dry warehouses until needed.

QUICK FREEZING

Many foods are successfully preserved by quick freezing and storage (7). Quick freezing is effective because microorganisms may survive but cannot grow or multiply at temperatures below about −10°C (14°F).

Freezing is not a new method of food preservation. Eskimos have used it for centuries to preserve their fish and game. A patent was granted to an Englishman in 1842 to freeze meat by immersion in a brine and ice water mixture. Freezing was not used extensively, however, until mechanical refrigeration was developed. Freezing was first developed to transport and store meats long distances. It was not until the early part of the twentieth century that fruits and vegetables were frozen. These early attempts showed that frozen plant products could be stored for long periods of time but upon thawing, cell tissue structure broke down and the food became even more susceptible to spoilage. Because of this structural change, fresh fruits and vegetables must be kept frozen until they are needed for consumption. Properly frozen fruits and vegetables can be stored for long periods of time, yet appear much like the fresh product. Most fruit juices (except citrus) can be stored safely for 12 months and most fruits and vegetables for 10 to 12 months if kept at −18°C (0°F).

PROCESSING WITH SUGAR

Some fruits are processed with high concentrations of sugar to become jams, jellies, marmalades, preserves, crystallized fruits, or candied peels. Sugar increases the osmotic pressure to levels where water is unavailable for microbial activity, thereby reducing spoilage. Sugar does not prevent yeast and fungus spoilage, however; sealing the product in airtight containers reduces these losses.

PROCESSING WITH SALT

The processing of vegetables with brine has changed little over the years. This process preserves cucumbers and gherkins as pickles, cabbage as sauerkraut, and onions, beets, beans, peppers, and olives. Fresh cucumbers or cabbage are allowed to ferment anaerobically in a salt solution concentrated enough to prevent the activity of spoilage organisms, but not high enough to destroy the bacteria producing lactic acid. Lactic acid lowers the pH, thus helping to prevent growth of organisms. Olives in California are often pretreated before salt storage with a 1 to 2 percent solution of sodium hydroxide (NaOH) to neutralize the bitter glucoside found in the fresh fruit.

PROCESSING BY MILLING

Milling is probably the oldest processing technique. It began simply with grinding cereal grains between two stones to give a coarse flour. Today cereal grain crops are processed into flours, breakfast foods, grains, and many other products. Milling processes comprise two parts: cleaning and preparing the grain, and extracting and grinding the endosperm tissue. Cleaning techniques are based on the differences in physical properties of the grain seeds and the contaminants, such as weed seeds, soil, stones, chaff, and other grain seeds. These differing physical properties (density, size, shape, magnetic properties, etc.) permit a high degree of separation, resulting in a product essentially free of contamination. The objective of milling is to obtain endosperm in a pure state by separating it from the bran and germ. Flours used mainly for baking are made from pure endosperm; they are white, with many of the nutrients removed (*11*).

Rice, an important human food grain crop, is processed by milling away successive layers of the grain coatings until ultimately only the endosperm remains. Grain rice from the thresher, known as **paddy rice,** includes the kernel and the hulls. Special machines (dehullers) remove the hulls (about 20 percent by weight), yielding brown rice. Brown rice contains more thiamine, protein, and nutrients than polished rice because it still has the bran layers. The next milling step is the successive removal of the bran layers, leaving polished rice. The byproducts are used in various ways. Broken kernels go into the manufacture of beer, starch, baby food (Fig. 12–22). The hulls are used for bedding, litter, and soil amendments.

Fig. 12–22 The milling of paddy rice yields about 20 percent hulls, 48 percent unbroken kernels of white rice (head rice), 21 percent broken kernels, 8 percent bran, and 3 percent polish. *Source:* John Dobie.

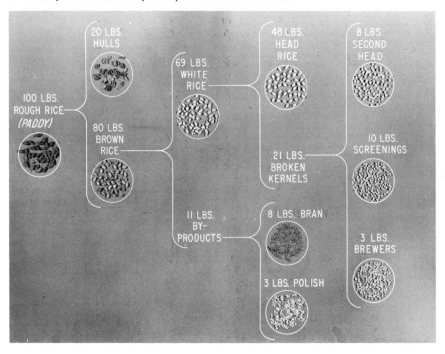

STORAGE OF RAW PRODUCTS

Proper storage prolongs the life of unprocessed plant products. Storage also moderates price by regulating the supply available to the market. Storage time varies widely depending upon the kind of crop stored, its condition and quality, and the conditions of storage.

Fruits and Vegetables

Fresh fruits and vegetables are stored for relatively short periods, compared with dried forage crops or cereal grains (8). Products of low quality should never be stored, because they are seldom worth the added storage costs, and storage never improves quality.

Factors to consider when storing fresh products are: (1) length of storage time, (2) temperature, (3) relative humidity, and (4) light.

In general, cool-season crops are stored at cool temperatures, 0°C to 1°C (32°F to 34°F), while warm-season crops are stored at relatively warm temperatures of 10°C to 12°C (50°F to 54°F) to avoid chilling injury. There are some exceptions. For example, sweet corn (warm season) should be stored at cool temperatures immediately after harvest to retard the conversion of sugar to starch, which lowers quality and taste. Potatoes destined to be made into potato chips should be stored at temperatures of 2°C to 4°C (36°F to 40°F). After storage, but three to seven days before being processed into chips they are removed from the cold and stored in warm rooms at 20°C (68°F) to encourage the conversion of sugar to starch. This prevents darkened chips, which result from the caramelization of sugar during cooking.

Commodities with high water content should be stored in wet rooms, which are cooled to 0°C to 1°C (32°F to 34°F) and have a relative humidity of 90 to 95 percent. Apples, apricots, artichokes, lettuce, radishes, spinach, celery, and endive are stored in these rooms. Carrots and cranberries are generally stored at humidities of 85 to 95 percent. Beans, melons, cabbage, cauliflower, and Irish (white) potatoes are stored in dryer rooms at 85 to 90 percent humidity. Garlic, onions, pumpkins, and winter squash are stored at humidities as low as 70 to 75 percent.

Light should be either subdued or absent during storage. Light must be kept away from stored Irish potatoes because light prompts the formation of the toxic alkaloid solanine, which appears green under the skin of the tubers.

Fig. 12–23 Baled alfalfa hay is often stored unprotected in the field in arid to semiarid regions to reduce the cost of storage. *Source:* John Dobie.

Hay

Forage crops harvested to feed livestock may be stored in outdoor stacks on the farm, in overhead lofts in barns, or in ground-level roofed areas (Fig. 12–23). Loose hay is stored unchopped and air-dried, but most hay is chopped, baled, or pressed into small cubes (see p. 271). These procedures reduce storage space, lower shipping costs, and facilitate bulk handling. Stored hay needs to be air dry and the storage facility must have adequate ventilation. Many barns have been destroyed by fires caused by the spontaneous combustion of hay stored too wet and inadequately ventilated.

Seeds

Dry seed crops—barley, beans, corn (shelled), oats, rice, rye, sorghum (grain), soybeans, and wheat—are relatively easy to store for long periods of time. For safe, prolonged storage the moisture content must be no more than about 12 to 14 percent. Seed crops can be sufficiently dry to store when harvested, but often it is desirable or necessary to harvest when moisture content is higher. Then artificial drying, an expensive operation, is used to reduce the moisture content.

Silage

Silage (ensilage) is an anaerobically fermented livestock feed made from any green forage. Grasses, grain, or legume crops are commonly used. Corn silage is made from the entire plant: leaves, stalks, and immature ears.

A silo, used for the storage of silage, is usually a tall, cylindrical building made from concrete or other materials into which the chopped, green forage is blown and tightly packed. A silo can also be a horizontal trench dug into the side of a hill perhaps 3 to 4 m (10 to 13 ft) or more wide and long enough to store the required amount of silage. The forage is loaded into the silo and packed tightly, and the top of the trench is sealed with boards and soil. After fermentation, the end of the trench can be opened and the cattle allowed to eat directly from the silo (Ch. 25).

MARKETING OF AGRICULTURAL PRODUCTS

Primitive societies had little marketing. Each family gathered or produced its own food and other necessities. This system has limitations, though. To widen the variety of products, a barter system and later money developed. Hunters could barter their game with growers of fruits and grains, enabling each to partake of new foods. Also, marketing permitted the development of specialty professions. Tribal chiefs, governors, and soldiers who produced no food could obtain or extract food from the producers. As civilization progressed, specialization developed to include tradesmen, doctors, lawyers, and teachers. Today, specialization has progressed to the point where some farmers have no gardens, produce no livestock, and grow only the crops best adapted to their particular area, soil, climate, preference, or proximity to markets.

Early in the development of marketing, the producer sold a diverse array of products (eggs, live poultry, fruit, vegetables, milk, honey, etc.) to the final consumer. There were few or no middlemen. To make the exchange of commodities easy, the farmers brought their produce to a central place (farmers' market) where they and the customer haggled prices. Farmers' markets are not widely used in the United States, but they are quite common in other parts of the world.

Today most marketing involves a series of middlemen. Some buy the raw product and process it, others transport the raw or processed commodity, still others distribute the commodity as wholesale jobbers. Finally, retailers subdivide, package, and retail the product for consumers. Middlemen are prevalent in the highly industrialized countries of Western Europe, Japan, Australia, New Zealand, the United States, and Canada. The middlemen are often looked upon as unnecessary, yet they are essential in the modern distribution process of all agricultural commodities.

The Importance of Marketing

In societies where production is highly specialized, marketing plays a key role in the distribution of the product. Neither the modern farmer nor the urban consumer can do without it; both depend upon the market for their food and other necessities of life. A breakdown in the marketing system would cause starvation, and in some areas of the world such breakdown is the primary cause of much hunger.

The Process of Marketing

Economists divide marketing into six areas.

ASSEMBLY

Assembly is the concentration of small quantities of any commodity into a central place for processing or other procedures before transport to market (Fig. 12–24). Concentration at convenient locations gives prospective buyers the opportunity to examine the product. Not all agricultural products need to be assembled; some are sold directly to processor, wholesaler, or retailer.

Fig. 12–24 Much produce is transported long distances. Before the journey to market begins, the produce is assembled and prepared for the trip by palletizing. Mechanical fork lifts are used for rapid loading and unloading of large trucks or cars. This machine is strapping produce to pallets for easy handling. *Source:* Western Grower and Shipper.

Fig. 12–25 Supermarkets have revolutionized the methods of marketing during the last decade to the point where the U.S. customer can buy practically any type of fresh fruit or vegetable any time of the year and at comparatively low prices.

DISTRIBUTION

Systems have been developed to distribute products from places of assembly to places of consumption. The extensiveness of the distribution system is the very foundation of marketing in the industrialized countries (Fig. 12–25). The system must be able to adjust the supply of commodities to market demand quickly and easily as either supply or demand changes.

In recent years food chains and fast-food restaurants have taken over a large share of the distribution of foods in the developed nations. In North America and Western Europe management of the retail distribution of food has concentrated into fewer and fewer hands. In the United States alone, three large food chains retail food through more than 10,000 stores with a total sales well over $10 billion each year. Three of the fast-food restaurant corporations prepare and serve more meals per day than do all households in the United States. Five food chains sell half of the food consumed in Canada. The same sort of food retailing occurs to some degree in Europe and England.

TRANSPORTATION

An essential part of marketing is transportation. Fast, dependable transport must be available (Fig.

Fig. 12–26 Fast, reliable transportation by air, sea, truck, or rail is an essential element in the distribution and marketing of food. Mechanically refrigerated railcars are used to ship large quantities of fresh fruits and vegetables from California to New York within a few days. Before the use of these self-contained refrigerated cars, the entire train was required to make about seven stops across the United States to refill the ice bunker in each car, adding several days to transit time. *Source:* Southern Pacific Co.

12–26). Raw materials are generally transported to railheads, ports, or processing plants by the producer or perhaps the first buyer. Interstate or transoceanic shipments are generally made by specialized transport firms and may constitute a part of the wholesale service. Transport from the wholesaler or processor can be done by the retailer, but transport from the retailer to the consumer is almost invariably the responsibility of the consumer.

STORAGE

Storage can be considered a part of the marketing system. Certainly, storage is needed at various stages in the marketing sequence. Buyers (wholesalers, brokers, processors, or retailers) can own and operate storage facilities in order to better control the time of resale of the commodity. Processing plants must operate storage facilities to hold surplus stocks to keep the plant operating when supplies are low.

EXCHANGE

Before any buying or selling can occur, the buyer and seller must meet, either in person or by communication. The exchange process involves two phases: contacting possible buyers and sellers, and negotiating an agreeable price. In many countries, the town square acts as the marketplace. Merchants—hundreds of them in some places—erect makeshift shelters to market their produce. Buyer and seller meet and negotiate. After they reach agreement, a sale is consummated. In larger markets, sales are negotiated for a fee (generally a percentage of the selling price) by professionals called auctioneers or brokers, who do not take possession of the goods. Often the buyers and sellers are several hundred miles apart and never meet. In the United States the Department of Agriculture grade standards are helpful in that they allow the buyer to know the quality of the product without actually seeing it. Advertising, news, and other specialized market information carried by the press, radio, and television provide information helpful to exchange.

FINANCING

Financing is essential in all marketing processes. Farmers, wholesalers, processors, and merchants must either have the capital or the credit to produce or hold a commodity until it is sold and they receive payment.

Market financing entails a certain amount of risk. One major risk is a falling market. Another is price fluctuation. Prices for agricultural commodities generally vary more than do those for manufactured products. Deterioration of quality is another financial risk. A buyer

must be aware that the quality of many commodities depreciates rapidly.

Commodity Markets and Exchanges

Commodity markets transfer products from producers to processors, manufacturers, or consumers, and determine the price for the exchange. The commodities generally handled by this type of market are foodstuffs or raw materials such as cereal grains, tea, coffee, rubber, and tobacco, as well as some metals. The commodity market is concerned with trading a given amount of a certain grade of commodity for present delivery. The goods need not be on hand at the time but can be in transit or stored in a warehouse. Prices can be arranged by telephone, telegraph, or bid. Payment is made by check, and title is transferred by warehouse receipt or bill of lading.

A **commodity exchange,** or **futures market,** differs from a commodity market in that the exchange involves the purchase or sale of a contract to deliver a certain amount of a given grade of commodity on an agreed date in the future. In actual practice, the seller of the contract does not intend to actually deliver the commodity, nor does the buyer intend to receive it. Each will buy or sell the respective contract before the transfer date, hoping to realize a profit by the transaction. The Chicago Board of Trade is an example of a commodity exchange handling mainly agricultural commodities—grains, oil seeds, and other such products.

Governmental Marketing Services

Most governments regulate marketing to some degree. Some go the extreme of setting prices, regulating production, and distributing products. For example, California regulates the price of milk, Egypt regulates the price of bread, and Uganda regulates many food prices. The United States regulates production of sugar beets, tobacco, and cotton. The United States government has tended to avoid price setting except in time of war. The principal services provided by the federal government are protecting public health, establishing standards and grades, and enforcing weights and measures. Federal and state governments cooperate to supply statistics on acreages planted to various crops, their condition, and other characteristics important to marketers. They also supply daily information on shipments and market prices and forecast production.

Grade standards are degrees of quality each established by definition. The standards define the color, size, and freedom from undesirable characteristics or any other attributes that pertain to quality. These standards are published and maintained by the USDA. Some states also establish grade standards used within the states. The departments provide the necessary inspection services and determine the grade standards for many agricultural products. These official grade standards permit marketing over long distances without the buyer's actual inspection of the commodity. For example, a buyer in Japan can buy a quantity of rice from a broker in California. The buyer specifies the quality grade (USDA No. 1) of rice desired and knows that the grade ordered will have those quality standards on the basis of an inspection made and a certificate of inspection issued at the seller's location. Fresh head lettuce from California or oranges from Florida are sold to buyers in New York who order these commodities by well defined grade standards, knowing before arrival that the desired quality has been guaranteed for delivery.

Agricultural Cooperatives

Farmers sometimes join together to form businesses known as co-ops. Co-ops differ from other businesses in that the farmers are the owners as well as the customers. The co-op members provide the capital, elect officers, and generally employ a professional manager. Farmers form and use the cooperatives to market their products (grain, animals, dairy), procure supplies (fuel, fertilizers, etc.), and services such as insurance, irrigation, credit, or electric power. They generally do not operate the business to make a profit but to lower costs through collective marketing or buying.

Marketing Boards

Marketing boards were originally developed in England and some of the Commonwealth nations to help recovery from the depression of 1930. Their primary objective is stabilizing producer prices. Examples of marketing boards that have been established in some countries are the National Coffee Board of Ethiopia, the Sri Lanka (Ceylon) Tea Propaganda Board, and the Australian Federal Marketing Board.

In the United States a similar program, called a marketing order, was established. Used originally for fruits and vegetables in California and later for milk in many milk-producing states, marketing orders are agreements among a group of farmers to solve a specific problem or to arrive at a given goal for the common good of all members. Under the authority of a marketing order, either state or federal, an elected administrative board can levy assessments to collect money to support

advisory services, promotional campaigns such as advertising, research, or control over sales of specific products.

TRANSPORTING COMMODITIES

The first movers of goods were probably women. Today in some primitive societies women play the same role. With progress, animals were used to help move materials. Dogs, oxen, horses, camels, and elephants all played a role as transporters. Carrying was the first method of transport. When it was found that one could pull more than one could carry, dragging replaced carrying. The wheel is a relatively recent invention, whose discovery created the need for roads.

Transportation has not been limited to land. Almost as soon as people walked on land, they began to travel on water. Now air, too, is a medium of transport.

Rail Transport

In the United States, the railroads transported most of the heavy goods during the period from the Civil War to World War I. Almost all long-distance shipments of grain and dry products were made by rail. Early refrigerated railcars were boxcars with ice bunkers at each end. Sometimes, if these cars were loaded with perishables, they would be attached to a passenger train for fast hauling to distant markets.

After World War II, most U.S. railroad companies replaced their ice bunker cars with mechanically operated refrigerator cars (Fig. 12–27). Because the trains were not required to stop for icing, the conversion reduced considerably the time required for transport.

The cooling system in the mechanically refrigerated cars is operated by a diesel motor located in one end of the car and it runs during the entire trip. If the shipper desires, the car arrives at the dock precooled with the unit running; heating or cooling is available as needed. Temperature is regulated by thermostats with sensors generally located in the return air ducts. Air is distributed throughout the load by blowers.

Another adaptation is truck-train transportation called the piggy back, which is a refrigerated truck-trailer carried long distances on a railroad flatcar. At the destination the truck-trailers are unloaded and attached to a tractor for transport to their final destination. Most of these units are owned by the railroads and are said to combine the truck's flexibility of delivery and the train's reduced cost of transport (Fig. 12–28).

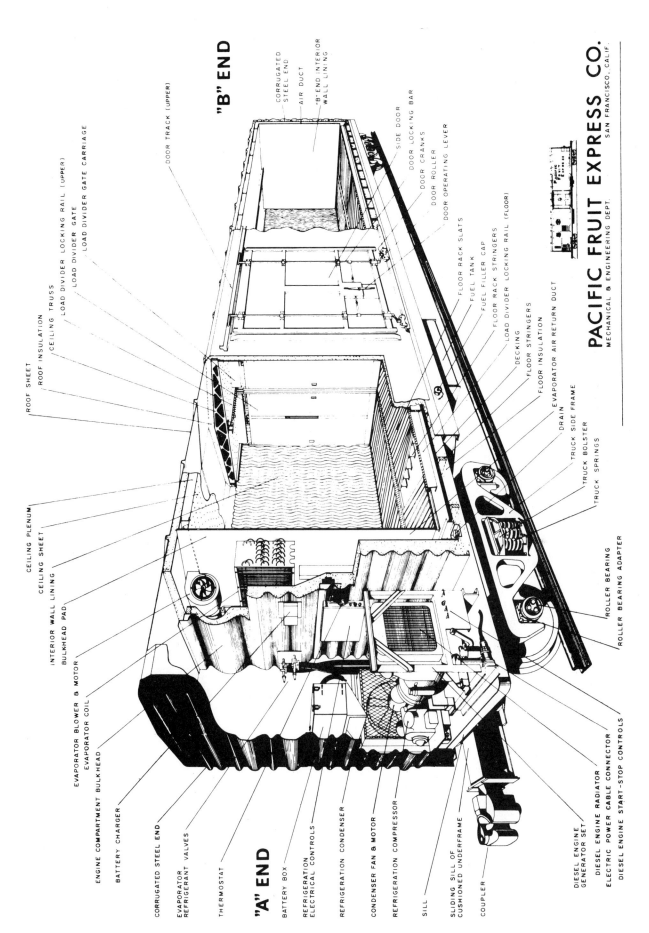

"B" END

CORRUGATED STEEL END
AIR DUCT
"B" END INTERIOR WALL LINING

DOOR TRACK (UPPER)

SIDE DOOR
DOOR LOCKING BAR
DOOR CRANKS
DOOR ROLLER
DOOR OPERATING LEVER

LOAD DIVIDER LOCKING RAIL (UPPER)
LOAD DIVIDER GATE
LOAD DIVIDER GATE CARRIAGE
CEILING TRUSS
ROOF INSULATION
ROOF SHEET

FLOOR RACK SLATS
FUEL TANK
FUEL FILLER CAP
FLOOR RACK STRINGERS
LOAD DIVIDER LOCKING RAIL (FLOOR)
DECKING
FLOOR STRINGERS
FLOOR INSULATION
EVAPORATOR AIR RETURN DUCT
DRAIN
TRUCK SIDE FRAME
TRUCK BOLSTER
TRUCK SPRINGS

ROLLER BEARING
ROLLER BEARING ADAPTER

CEILING PLENUM
CEILING SHEET
INTERIOR WALL LINING
BULKHEAD PAD
EVAPORATOR BLOWER & MOTOR
EVAPORATOR COIL
ENGINE COMPARTMENT BULKHEAD
BATTERY CHARGER

CORRUGATED STEEL END
EVAPORATOR REFRIGERANT VALVES
THERMOSTAT

"A" END

BATTERY BOX
REFRIGERATION ELECTRICAL CONTROLS
REFRIGERATION CONDENSER
CONDENSER FAN & MOTOR
REFRIGERATION COMPRESSOR
SILL
SLIDING SILL OF CUSHIONED UNDERFRAME
COUPLER

DIESEL ENGINE GENERATOR SET
DIESEL ENGINE RADIATOR
ELECTRIC POWER CABLE CONNECTOR
DIESEL ENGINE START-STOP CONTROLS

PACIFIC FRUIT EXPRESS CO.
MECHANICAL & ENGINEERING DEPT.
SAN FRANCISCO, CALIF.

Fig. 12–27 Cutaway drawing of a modern refrigerated railcar.
Source: Pacific Fruit Express Company.

Fig. 12–28 A Santa Fe Railroad marshaling yard used for handling piggy-back trucks. Large Travelift cranes (lower right foreground and upper left background) load piggy-back vans on and off. Vans to be loaded are parked at an angle next to the railroad flatcars they will be lifted onto. *Source:* Santa Fe Railroad.

Truck Transport

Transport by truck and truck-trailer combinations grew rapidly after World War II. Many shippers, experiencing problems with rail shipment, turned to the newer, larger trucks for shipping. The improved highway system and expansion of metropolitan areas gave the trucks some advantages over the railroads (*3*). The truck was as fast and in some cases faster than the railroad, offered dock to dock service, and often cost less. Today trucks haul over 60 percent of all perishable goods in the United States.

Most modern trucks have mechanically operated refrigeration systems similar to those already discussed, although some ice-cooled trucks are still used for short runs (*1*).

Sea Transport

Water transport requires less energy than either air or land. The Egyptians were among the earliest sea traders, sailing their *fuluccas* up and down the Nile and out into the Mediterranean Sea about 2000 B.C.. The Phoenicians may have been the first to navigate the oceans, followed by the Greeks and Romans. After the dark ages and before the Industrial Revolution, England and Spain entered into competition for world trade, and shipping rapidly grew to include the world, including the newly discovered Americas.

Since World War II there has been a gradual shift toward containerized transport (Fig. 12–29), a trend stimulated by increased labor and marketing costs. At first the containers were designed only for dry, unrefrigerated cargo, but the apparent advantages of containerization inspired the testing and development of refrigerated containers for all kinds of fresh freight (Figs. 12–30, 12–31). Containers for container ships are similar to refrigerated trailer vans for trucks. The units are refrigerated in a variety of ways, depending on the type of carrier (*16, 17*). Some ships with refrigerated holds still transport bananas and other commodities but their limitations are numerous (*17*). One serious disadvantage of the refrigerated-hold ship is that it cannot be mechanically loaded. Except for hoists and pallets to raise and lower cartons into the hold, the rest of loading and unloading is done by hand. Grains, wood chips, cubed alfalfa hay, and a few other dry commodities are transported in unrefrigerated ship holds.

Fig. 12–29 The containership M. S. Maui transports more than 1000 sealed containers between California and Honolulu on a regular schedule. Some of the containers are individually refrigerated. *Source:* Matson Navigation Company.

Fig. 12–30 Land-sea containers are moved overland to or from the dock by rail or pulled by tractors over highways. This refrigerated container is being readied for overland transport by truck. *Source:* Matson Navigation Company.

Fig. 12–31 A train load of containers has arrived via railroad flatcars in Oakland, California, and will soon be mechanically loaded aboard a ship bound for Hawaii. These containers can be sealed and refrigerated. *Source:* Matson Navigation Company.

Air Transport

The first notable shipments of cargo by air were made in the Graf Zeppelin, a lighter-than-air dirigible, in the early 1900s. But transportation by air, except for small packages and mail, was not important until after World War II. From about 1950 to the mid-1960s some parcel post and agricultural commodities were shipped via air freight. The cost was so high that it could be justified only for high-value commodities.

Two developments in the late 1960s made air shipment of agricultural products feasible and desirable. The first was the advent of the jet engine and the jumbo jet plane. The reduced operating cost per unit weight of cargo made it possible to use planes for cargo alone and not merely in combination with passengers. The second was the development of containerized cargo carriers (15). These giant cargo carriers are now in daily service over regularly scheduled and chartered routes throughout the United States and overseas (Fig. 12–32). Highly perishable cut flowers (roses, carnations, orchids, etc). leave California greenhouses in the afternoon and are in the florists' shops in New York the next morning (14).

Fig. 12–32   Large quantities of fresh fruits and cut flowers are carried in specialized containers by air cargo planes on regular schedule throughout the world. *Source:* United Airlines.

Pineapples, papayas, and orchids from Hawaii arrive fresh in California the day after harvest on planes that carried tourists to Hawaii the day before. The California strawberry market depends largely on reliable fast air transport (9). Some other crops shipped by air include apricots, avocados, berries, cherries, citrus fruits, figs, grapes, peaches, pears, and plums (13).

Air transport has opened up previously inaccessible markets. Also, less capital is involved for the farmer or broker because of faster turnover of payments. But a fast air schedule means little if handling at either terminal is slow. All air shipments of plant material (flowers, fruits, vegetables) must be precooled and brought to the starting terminal in refrigerated trucks. If the product is held at the terminal, it must be kept refrigerated. At the destination terminal, it must be unloaded quickly, placed in refrigerated trucks, and sent to its destination. Any delay by ground crews can negate the speed of the flight.

SUMMARY

The mechanization of agricultural operations, especially crop harvesting, has stimulated the growth of the agricultural industry considerably during the past half-century. The mechanization of harvesting equipment began with the flail and sickle, and has progressed to the point where practically all important crops except some fruits and vegetable crops for the fresh market can be mechanically harvested.

Preservation becomes the target of concern after harvest. The choice of preservation method depends upon the nature of the product, its future use, the length of time of preservation, and the conditions at time of preservation. The underlying principle is to retard as much as possible the respiration reactions that degrade the commodity by changing carbohydrates, fats, and proteins to carbon dioxide, water, and heat. One method of preserving some products is by controlling the temperature. Products are preserved either by lowering or by raising the temperatures depending on the nature of the product. Other commodities are preserved by moisture control, either by dehydrating them or by increasing relative humidity, again depending upon their nature. Some commodities are best preserved by modifying the storage atmosphere.

Storage of the commodity after it is preserved depends on the kind of crop, its condition, and its quality. Fresh commodity storage is quite different from dehydrated commodity storage.

Marketing plays an important role in the modern distribution of agricultural commodities. The marketing system is divided into: (1) assembling and concentrating, (2) transporting, (3) distributing, (4) storing, (5) exchanging, and (6) financing.

Commodity exchanges buy and sell commodities but generally do not physically handle them. They do help establish prices. To some degree marketing is regulated by governments, more in other countries and less in the United States, except during wartime. Often farmers join together and form cooperatives through which they buy some of their necessities and market their products. Cooperatives generally are not operated to make a profit; they serve only to lower the farmer's cost of production.

Transportation is an essential part of the business of agriculture. A breakdown in the transportation system would put a halt to the distribution of commodities. Modern transport systems use motor trucks and railroads for overland shipment, ships for overseas, and airplanes for fast overland and overseas shipments.

REVIEW QUESTIONS

12–1. Some factors to consider in determining when to harvest a crop include (a) the use of the crop, (b) crop quality, (c) market demand, (d) temperature, (e) all of these except _____.

12–2. Some factors that determine crop quality are: (a) maturity, (b) size, (c) color, (d) firmness, (e) cultivar, (f) freedom from injury, (g) all of these except _____.

12–3. Probably the first mechanical aid to help harvest crops was the (a) combine, (b) binder, (c) scythe, (d) sickle.

12–4. Almost all cereal grains are now harvested mechanically with a combine. True or false?

12–5. Most head lettuce is now cooled by (a) hydrocooling, (b) forced-air cooling, (c) crushed ice pack, (d) vacuum cooling, (e) liquid ice cooling.

12–6. The storage and preservation of a crop is as important as raising it. True or false?

12–7. Respiration is a degradation process that can be retarded by lowering the temperature. True or false?

12–8. Which of the following is not a factor affecting the storage of fresh produce? (a) Temperature, (b) light, (c) aeration, (d) moisture content (e) percentage of organic matter.

12–9. List two factors that developed during the 1960s that made air transport of commodities practical.

12–10. In general, for biological reactions a 10°C reduction in temperature (reduces/increases) the rate of respiration by (one-half/one/two/four) times. (Underline the correct answer.)

12–11. Explain how the latent heat of vaporization of water is used to cool fresh produce.

12–12. List three methods for lowering the concentration of oxygen in storage rooms.

12–13. Successful processing of a product by canning requires complete sterilization to destroy spoilage organisms. True or false?

12–14. The process of marketing is divided into six areas by some economists. What are they?

12–15. Describe a commodity market, what it sells, and what function it serves.

12–16. The principal services the federal government provides for the marketing process are (a) protecting health, (b) regulating prices, (c) establishing standards and grades, (d) controlling supply, (e) enforcing weights and measures.

12–17. Agricultural cooperatives help farmers increase their profits by lowering operating costs. True or false? Discuss your answer.

12–18. Marketing orders are used to permit marketing of commodities over long distances without actual inspection of the commodity. True or false?

12–19. Discuss the effect of mechanical refrigeration on land, sea, and air transportation of agricultural commodities.

12–20. List five plant commodities regularly shipped by air.

REFERENCES

1. Ashby, B. H. 1970. Protecting perishable food during transport by motortruck. USDA Handbook 105.

2. Berard, J. E. 1821. Memoire sur la maturation des fruits. *Ann. Chim. Phys.* 16:225–51.

3. Blevins, M. W. 1973. Trucks offer speed and flexibility. *The Packer* 90:7.

4. Burg, S. P., and E. A. Burg. 1966. Fruit storage at subatmospheric pressures. *Science* 153:314–15.

5. Dalrymple, D. G. 1967. *The development of controlled atmosphere storage of fruits.* Div. of Marketing and Utilization Sciences, Federal Extension Service, USDA.

6. Dilley, D. R. 1972. Hypobaric storage—a new concept for preservation of perishables. *Ann. Rept. Mich. State Hort. Soc.,* pp. 82–89.

7. Doremus, M., and R. Klippstein. 1967. Handbook for freezing foods. Cornell Ext. Bul. 1179. Ithaca, N.Y.: New York State College of Home Economics, Cornell University.

8. Duckworth, R. B. 1966. *Fruit and vegetables.* London: Pergamon. Ch. 7.

9. Harvey, J. M. 1973. Temperature and atmospheric effects on California strawberries transported by air to domestic and foreign markets. *Proc. Thirteenth Int. Cong. Refrig.* 3:161–66.

10. Kidd, F., C. West, and N. A. Kidd. 1927. Gas storage of fruit. Dept. of Scientific and Industrial Research, Food. Invest. Spec. Rept. 30.

11. Lockwood, J. F. 1960. *Flour milling.* 4th ed. Stockport, England: Henry Simon.

12. Pantastio, E. B. 1975. *Postharvest physiology, handling and utilization of tropical and subtropical fruits and vegetables.* Westport, Conn.: AVI Publishing, Ch. 10, Part I, II, III.

13. Ryall, A. L., and W. T. Pentzer. 1974. *Handling, transportation, and storage of fruits and vegetables.* Westport, Conn.: AVI Publishing. Ch. 15.

14. Stark. D. U. 1967. Developments in air transportation of perishables. Proc. Fruit and Veg. Perishables Handling Conf. Davis, Calif.: University of California, pp. 60–64.

15. Tyree, L., Jr. 1973. Refrigerated, containerized transport for jumbo jets. Proc. Thirteenth Int. Cong. Refrig. 4:515–25.

16. Westling, L. L. 1968. *Marine transport of frozen foods, freezing preservation of foods.* Westport, Conn.: AVI Publishing.

17. Westling, L. L. 1973. A critique on the development of refrigerated transport. Proc. Thirteenth Int. Cong. Refrig. 4:623–28.

UNIT

II

AN
OVERVIEW
OF
THE FRUIT
CROPS
AND
ORNAMENTAL
PLANTS

Cultural Practices in Orchards and Vineyards

The first essential step in the successful establishment of a fruit planting is to be certain that the crop to be planted is adapted to the climate of the region (Ch. 10). After this has been determined, a number of major critical decisions remain to be made, and there is only one chance to make many of them. All available pertinent information should be sought out before final commitments are made.

Since the production of most fruit crops is a long-term undertaking, poor initial decisions can be costly and impossible to correct later. Factors that should be carefully considered before any planting is done are:

1. Site selection
2. Selection of fruiting cultivars and rootstocks
3. Allowance for pollination requirements (see Chs. 6 and 14)
4. Planting distances and tree arrangements

SITE SELECTION

A thorough study should be made of the following aspects of the proposed site. Any one of them could affect the success or failure of the enterprise.

Climate

It is extremely important to learn as much as possible about the weather patterns of the proposed planting site. Such information can often be obtained from neighbors who have lived in the area for many years or, if recording instruments are located in the vicinity, from government weather services. Local cooperative extension or agriculture department agents usually can furnish much valuable information concerning weather patterns in their localities. Several weather conditions are of particular importance in fruit growing.

TEMPERATURE

Temperature patterns in the spring and fall are very significant. Avoid sites in low-lying areas, such as river bottoms or low spots in rolling hills, where cold air settles during frosty nights. This can be particularly dangerous when frosts occur during blooming periods in the spring or for cultivars with late-maturing fruits, which could be damaged by early fall freezes. It is much safer to select an orchard site on the upper portions or slopes of rolling terrain. Orchard heating, wind machines, or sprinkler systems can often overcome low-temperature injury problems in frosty sites (see Ch. 10), but this additional expense can make the enterprise noncompetitive with those that do not have such problems.

In regions with hot summers, site location can influence the temperature; a northern or eastern slope may be a few degrees cooler than southern and western slopes (in the northern hemisphere). For growing crops that cannot tolerate high summer heat, such as sweet cherries, the site location is of considerable importance.

The location of the proposed planting site in relation to large bodies of water should be considered. A planting site on the leeward side of a large lake is likely to have a microclimate modified considerably both in summer and winter, with the temperature lower in summer and higher in winter than similar sites at a distance from such bodies of water.

WIND

Avoid sites that have a history of strong winds. Wind can be detrimental from several aspects. Reduced bee activity during windy days in the pollination season can seriously reduce fruit set and yields. Wind can damage young, tender shoots in the spring and can scar and bruise young fruits. Windbreaks can help reduce this problem (see Ch. 10).

RAIN

Fruit plants require adequate soil moisture throughout the growing season. If no supplemental irrigation is possible, attention must be paid to the rainfall history of the proposed site to determine whether the total and summer rainfall is likely to be adequate and consistent. A better situation exists where water supplies for irrigation are available during times of drought. Some of the best fruit-growing areas in the world are located in areas where no rainfall normally occurs during the growing season. These regions depend entirely on irrigation.

A pattern of continual rains during the pollination period in the spring could result in poor crops by interfering with bee activity. Continual rains during the fruit harvesting period leads to problems, not only in getting the fruit picked but also in promoting various fungal diseases on the maturing fruits.

The proposed site should not be subject to periodic flooding from nearby rivers or streams. Most fruit plants will not tolerate water around their roots for any length of time, as the water stops air penetration to the roots. Areas with a high water table are usually unsuitable for fruit growing as only the soil mass above the water table is available for root development, and this is usually quite limited.

HAIL

Hailstorms during the summer when soft fruits such as strawberries, peaches, apricots, plums, and cherries are developing can so damage the fruits that they have little marketable value. The frequency of hailstorms at the proposed site should be determined in advance.

Soil Characteristics

The ideal orchard soil should be a deep—at least 1.8 m (6 ft)—well-drained, nonsaline, fertile silty loam to a fine sandy loam (see Ch. 8). The surface should slope gently, allowing good runoff from heavy rains and permitting good infiltration of irrigation water. There should be no impervious hardpans or claypans under the surface. Fine-textured clay soils or loamy sands generally make poor orchard soils and should be avoided.

Planting orchard trees on unsuitable soil handicaps the orchard's productivity for the life of the planting and can make the enterprise marginal or unprofitable. If a less than ideal soil type is used, such as a clay loam, it is best to consider planting a fruit species that does relatively well on fine-textured soils, such as plums, pears, or apples, and avoid planting peaches or almonds, which will not tolerate such soils. If the available soil is a loamy sand or sandy loam, plant peaches or almonds (if the climate is suitable). Some species, however, such as grapes, oranges, and olives do well on a wide range of soil types (see Chs. 29, 30, and 31).

It is essential that all available information be obtained about the soil in the proposed site before planting. A soil map of the area should be consulted at the library of the nearest agricultural college or the office of the cooperative extension or the Soil Conservation Service. The soil of the area to be planted should be systematically sampled with a backhoe and enough pits opened to inspect the soil profile to a depth of about 1.8 m (6 ft). The sample will divulge any hardpan or rock layers or sandy pockets and will show whether the soil is deep enough to support fruit trees. A shallow soil may support smaller fruit plants such as strawberries or bushberries.

A study of the history of the site, including information of other crops previously grown, can be useful in analyzing soil problems. If cotton or tomatoes have been grown there, expect trouble from verticillium wilt. If an old orchard has been pulled out, the soil could be infected with *Phytophthora* fungus (see Ch. 11). Often it is necessary to fumigate the soil before planting a new orchard in order to obtain good, vigorous tree growth.

Resistant rootstocks can often solve problems with soil pests. For example, many sandy loam soils, well suited for growing peaches, are infested with root-knot nematodes and large-scale fumigation may not be practical. But, by planting peach trees propagated on a nematode-resistant rootstock, such as 'Nemaguard' (see p. 600), good tree growth and productivity can be obtained in spite of the nematodes in the soil.

Irrigation Water—Availability and Quality

In low rainfall areas, assurance should be obtained that there is a potential source of ample high-quality irrigation water. The water should not contain total soluble salts in excess of 1400 ppm. Water containing high levels of chlorides or a high proportion of sodium ions in relation to calcium and magnesium should not be used for irrigation (Ch. 9). Water containing boron salts higher than 1 ppm will damage plant tissue and should not be used for irrigation. Water samples can be analyzed by commercial laboratories and unsuitable water sources detected before the planting is made. It is difficult, if not impossible, to correct poor-quality water.

Availability of Markets for the Crop

Utilization of the crop is generally assured for fruit plantings in the home garden—by the family, friends, and neighbors, plus canning, drying, or freezing and, perhaps, sales of surplus fruits and nuts. In a commercial planting, however, it is essential to know that a market will be available for the crop by the time production begins. The choices for marketing the crop should be thoroughly considered in advance. Are there marketing cooperatives or private packers and shippers available who will take the crop, or will the grower need to transport the fruit to city fruit markets? Or, perhaps, in locations with considerable highway traffic, particularly close to large cities, on-the-farm roadside or ''pick-your-own'' sales may utilize most or part of the crop. Sometimes mail-order enterprises can be developed with proper advertising.

The marketing situation for most fruit crops is often quite fluid and should be thoroughly studied before heavy planting commitments are made. New plantings of a particular fruit crop in a certain area would be questionable when experienced growers in that area are either not planting or are pulling out trees. Perhaps the influx of an insect or disease problem has added control costs that eliminated the profit margin for that crop. Heavy plantings of a crop in a given area because of enticingly high returns at the moment may lead to market gluts when the plants come into production.

Availability of Labor

In establishing a large, commercial fruit-growing enterprise the availability of reliable workers to do the extra labor required should be assessed. Extra labor is often needed to harvest the crop, to prune the trees, and for fruit thinning. Other operations, such as weed control, fertilization, and irrigation, can usually be handled with a minimum crew and are often done by the owner and manager.

In a fruit-growing enterprise, harvest labor is usually the most costly production expense and may deter-

State agricultural experiment stations and state departments of agriculture and soil conservation offices are located in all states in the United States. Equivalent institutions are found in many other countries as well. Generally these institutions have one or more experts for each major crop grown in the state who are available for consultation free of charge on all phases of crop production and utilization. There are agricultural economists, too, who can give valuable advice on the economic outlook for particular crops. All states in the United States, as well as in most other countries, have local county agents or farm advisors who are employed by the state-supported cooperative extension service. Their services are generally available at no charge for consultations in planning and operating agricultural enterprises. Most of these people have expert knowledge of the local soils and climate and the requirements of the various crops and, in addition, are well informed of the economic picture. They usually have publications available dealing with the production and utilization of all fruit crops grown in the locality.

In addition to these publicly supported sources of information, private agricultural management services in many areas are prepared to give assistance, for a fee, at different levels—from completely operating the enterprise to consulting. They generally specialize in certain crops or types of crops.

mine the profit (or loss) margin. Harvest labor costs and even the availability of harvest labor can fluctuate widely and may remain unknown until harvest is actually under way.

The harvest of some fruit and nut crops such as sour cherries, prunes, almonds, walnuts, pecans, canning peaches, and pineapples has been wholly or partly mechanized, and efforts are being made to mechanize the harvest of other fruit and nut crops. Mechanization will greatly stabilize fruit-growing production costs (see Ch. 12).

Costs in Establishing a Fruit Planting

There are certain costs to be considered in establishing an orchard, vineyard, or berry planting. The actual amounts vary considerably with the country, locality, and year. The first- or second-year costs are listed below, although not all of them may be required.

1. Land purchase, plus taxes
2. Preparing land for planting (leveling, disking, and fumigating) (see Ch. 9).
3. Installation of irrigation system (drilling one or more wells, installing pumps and electric motors or diesel engines—or connecting to existing irrigation district pipe lines; installing distribution pipes and outlets)

4. Purchasing nursery trees, vines, or bushes

5. Surveying, staking, and planting

6. Installing trellis or stakes for vines (and some dwarf trees)

7. Staking, tying, sunburn protection, and pruning and training of trees and vines

8. Irrigation by hauling water in tank trucks to newly planted trees

9. Weed control by cultivation or herbicides

10. Insect and disease control (materials plus application costs)

11. Depreciation and repairs (irrigation system, tractor, and other equipment)

12. Interest on investment

SELECTING FRUITING CULTIVARS AND ROOTSTOCKS[1]

There comes a time in the establishment of a large, commercial fruit-growing enterprise—or in the planting of a single, backyard fruit tree—or a vineyard, or a bushberry, or strawberry planting when one must decide which cultivar (and rootstock, if needed) to order from the nursery. Once the kind of crop to be grown has been decided, the cultivar will have to be selected, a decision that can determine the success or failure of the enterprise. This decision should not be taken lightly. It should not be left to the local nurseryman, and it should not be based upon what nursery stock happens to be on hand at the time. Sometimes this decision must be made and an order placed a year in advance so that the propagating wholesale nursery will have time to propagate the desired cultivar on the desired rootstock.

Information concerning the various fruiting cultivars can be obtained from the sources listed on page 295, directly from other fruit growers in the vicinity, and from neighbors. It is risky to accept the glowing testimonials often made in advertisements concerning the performance of new, untried cultivars.

Most fruit and nut trees and some grapevines consist of two parts—the top (fruiting) part and a lower part, which becomes the root system. These two parts are joined together by budding or grafting when the plants are propagated in the nursery (see Ch. 5). Other fruit plants, however, are propagated "on their own roots," with no graft union. The plants are started as rooted cuttings, suckers, layers, or by runners (see Ch. 5). Some examples are fig, mulberry, olive, quince, pomegranate,

currant, gooseberry, and some grape cultivars, as well as the bushberries and strawberries.

In fruit plants with two parts, it is very important that the prospective fruit grower decide not only what the top fruiting cultivar is to be but also what rootstock the trees will be on. Some fruit species offer a wide range of choices for the rootstock; with others, there is little choice. For example, there are about a dozen possible rootstock choices each for apples and oranges, but sweet cherries have only two or three rootstock possibilities (see Chs. 29 and 30). Commercial growers of oranges or apples are as concerned about the selection of rootstock for a new planting as they are about the fruiting cultivar.

Many nurseries attach a label to each nursery fruit tree that identifies the fruiting cultivar and the rootstock. Ideally the prospective fruit grower would be knowledgeable enough to specify to the nursery the desired fruiting cultivar and the desired rootstock. For almost every tree fruit or nut species certain rootstocks could be used but may result in poor tree performance as the trees get older. A well-informed fruit grower will know of these situations and avoid them (see Chs. 29, 30, and 31).

Rootstocks are generally selected on the basis of several factors:

1. *Tree size.* The ultimate tree size (dwarfed or large) of some fruit species, such as apple, pear, cherry, and citrus, can be determined by the kind of rootstock selected.

2. *Resistance to soil-borne organisms.* Certain rootstocks permit plants to be grown in soil that otherwise would be unsuitable for them. For example, the European-type grapes (*Vitis vinifera*) on their own roots are killed by phylloxera, the grape root louse (*Dactylosphaera vitifoliae*), if planted in soil infested with this pest. But if the plants are grafted onto native American grape rootstocks resistant to this pest—such as *Vitis riparia, Vitis rupestris,* or hybrids between them—the plants thrive and produce well in infested soil. Rootstocks resistant to other pests such as nematodes, verticillium wilt, and armellaria root rot are available for certain tree fruit species and should be used where these problems occur (see Ch. 29).

3. *Resistance to unfavorable soil conditions.* Rootstocks that will tolerate poorly-drained, heavy, or saline soils are available for some fruit species. Such rootstocks should be specified for plantings where these problems could exist.

4. *Resistance to low winter temperatures.* Certain tree fruit species, particularly apples and citrus, survive

cold winters better on some rootstocks than on others.

PLANTING AND CULTURE

Major decisions must be made when the time comes to plant a new orchard, vineyard, or berry planting (*14*). Planting distances and patterns must be determined. The distance between plants depends on several factors.

The ultimate tree size of the species and cultivar at maturity is an important consideration. It is obvious, for example, that mature walnut or pecan trees growing to a height of 12 to 15 m (40 to 50 ft) and a breadth of almost the same amount need to be planted much farther apart than plum trees growing only 4.5 m (15 ft) tall. Even within the same species, cultivars differ in size. Naturally dwarfed spur-type apple trees (such as the patented 'MacSpur') will not get nearly as large as those of the strong-growing, vigorous 'Northern Spy' apple and can, therefore, be planted much closer together.

The rootstock is a second factor determining planting distance. Are dwarfing or invigorating rootstocks going to be used? In apples, for example, the trees to be planted could have been propagated on the very dwarfing 'M. 9' rootstock, or they could have been propagated on an invigorating clonal rootstock, such as 'M.M. 104' (or an invigorating apple seedling rootstock) or on a clonal rootstock giving intermediate vigor and tree size. Apple trees on the most invigorating rootstocks would need to be planted about six times farther apart than those on the most dwarfing rootstocks.

Soil fertility is a third factor determining planting distance. Is the planting site a sandy, shallow, infertile soil—where the trees would be slow-growing and never get very large—or is it a deep, highly fertile clay loam, where the trees are likely to reach their maximum size?

The planned tree density is a fourth factor, one under the grower's control. In recent years, the so-called high-density orchard plantings, particularly with apples and to a lesser extent with citrus and pears, have become popular (*8*). Trees are planted close together, even as hedgerows, or tree walls. Dwarfing rootstocks are used to keep the trees small. The land can be utilized to the maximum by high-density plantings, especially when the trees are young. High-density plantings of the stone fruits—peaches, plums, apricots—have not been very successful for one reason or another; in particular, no completely satisfactory dwarfing rootstock is available for these species.

The different categories of planting densities and management systems in use today, particularly for apples, are:

1. *Low density*. Trees are widely spaced (fewer than 250 trees/ha; 100 trees/ac) so that after maturity each tree has ample space and light contact around it. Pruning is kept to a minimum to allow rapid development of maximum tree size. Dwarfing rootstocks are not used. Maintenance labor is minimal, but the yields and gross returns per unit area are also likely to be minimal, particularly for the first 15 to 20 years of orchard life, compared to higher-density plantings (of apples and pears). Fifteen to 20 years may be needed to reach full production.

   For the stone fruits, tree nuts, and citrus, low-density plantings may be the most profitable although there is considerable interest and experimentation in developing high-density management systems with these crops.

2. *Medium density*. Tree spacing (250 to 500 trees/ha; 100 to 200 trees/ac) is at least 1.2m (4 ft) closer than for low-density plantings, and pruning is heavier. Moderately dwarfing rootstocks are used, such as 'M.M. 106' (see p. 590) for apples. More labor is required in pruning and training the trees—30 percent more than for low-density trees, particularly during the early developing years. More care and supervision are required, and the investment per hectare—in nursery stock and, perhaps, irrigation equipment—is greater than for low-density plantings. However, the yield (for apples) per unit area is likely to be double that of low density plantings.

3. *High density*. Trees are planted very close together (500 to 1235 trees/ha; 200 to 500/ac) and specific training systems are used, such as the hedgerow (double or triple) or trellis supported. Training and pruning is very important, requiring at least twice as much time as in low-density plantings. Reduced tree size must be maintained by very dwarfing rootstocks, such as 'M. 9' and 'M. 26' (see p. 590) for apples. High-density systems are feasible only on fertile soils.

   The grower must be committed to the system and determined to make it work. Neglect of the planting can result in considerable financial loss. The investment per hectare is likely to be considerably more than for a low-density planting. However, the yield per hectare during the first 15 years of orchard life can be as much as five times greater than for the low-density planting.

Table 13–1 integrates the various factors that must be considered in determining the proper tree spacing for

Table 13–1 The Integration of Cultivar, Rootstock, Soil Type, and Management System in Determining the Tree Spacing for Apple Trees

Cultivar	A VF — CULTIVAR FACTOR	B Rootstock — EM 9	M. 26	EM 7	M.M. 106	M.M. 111 & EM II	M.M. 104 & SEEDLING	C Soil Type — LOW PRODUCTIVITY	MED. PRODUCTIVITY	HIGH PRODUCTIVITY	D Management Syst. — LOW DENSITY	MED. DENSITY	MED. HIGH DENSITY	HIGH DENSITY	TREE WALLS	E Tree Spacing
Sundale SturdeeSpur	2	2	4	6	8	10	12	2	4	6	0	−4	−6	−8	−10	
Red Chief Gallia Beauty Idared Miller SturdeeSpur SpureeRome MacSpur	4	2	4	6	8	10	12	2	4	6	0	−4	−6	−8	−10	
Golden Del. C449 Jonnee Dbl. Red Jonathan Quinte Macoun Imperial Red Delicious Paulared	6	2	4	6	8	10	12	2	4	6	0	−4	−6	−8	−10	
Beacon Cortland Red Prince Lodi Red Queen Spartan Tydeman's Red Turley Red Winesap	8	2	4	6	8	10	12	2	4	6	0	−4	−6	−8	−10	
Empire R.I. Greening Mutsu Northern Spy Spigold Red Stayman Red York	10	2	4	6	8	10	12	2	4	6	0	−4	−6	−8	−10	

Directions: Add the cultivar factor (column A), rootstock factor (one of the columns under B), and the soil type factor (one of the columns under C), then subtract the management system number (found in one of D columns). This will give a suggested distance to plant trees in the row. Next, add 8 ft to this figure for the distance needed between the rows. On steep slopes it is better to add 10 ft to get the distance between rows. For tree wall plantings, use 14 ft between rows. If E, the total of A + B + C − D, = 0 or less, the combination is unprofitable.

Formula: A + B + C − D = E (planting distance between trees in the row). This number plus 8 ft equals planting distance between rows.

Example:

A. Cultivar	Red Prince	Factor of 8
B. Rootstock	M.M. 106	Factor of 8
C. Soil Type	Medium Productiveness	Factor of 4
D. Type of Management	Medium High Density	Factor of −6
8 + 8 + 4 − 6 = 14 ft between trees in row		14 ft + 8 = 22 ft between rows.

Source: Hilltop Orchards and Nurseries, Inc., Hartford, Michigan 49057.

apples. Recommended planting distances for other fruit species are given in Table 13–2. It must be emphasized for these crops, too, that several factors can modify these recommended distances. Greater spacing would be used with conditions of high soil fertility, long growing seasons, vigorous, large-size cultivars, invigorating rootstocks, ample rainfall or irrigation, and heavy use of fertilizers; spacing would be closer in the opposite situations.

Table 13–2 Planting Distances for the Common Fruit and Nut Crops (for Apples, see Table 13–1)

Species	Planting Distances
Almond	7.5 × 7.5 to 9 × 9 m (25 × 25 to 30 × 30 ft)
Apricot	6.6 × 6.6 m (22 × 22 ft) (on plum roots)
	7.5 × 7.5 m (25 × 25 ft) (on apricot roots)
Avocado	12 × 12 m (40 × 40 ft)
Blueberry	1.2 m (4 ft) apart in rows
	3 m (10 ft) apart
Cherry, sour	6 × 6 m (20 × 20 ft)
Cherry, sweet	7.5 × 7.5 to 9 × 9 m (25 × 25 to 30 × 30 ft)
Date palm	9 × 9 m (30 × 30 ft)
Filbert (hazelnut)	4.5 × 4.5 m (15 × 15 ft)
Kiwi fruit	
(Chinese	5.4 to 6 m (18 to 20 ft) apart in rows
gooseberry)	4.5 m (15 ft) apart
Lemon	6.6 × 6.6 to 9 × 9 m (22 × 22 to 30 × 30 ft.)
Olive	9 × 9 m (30 × 30 ft)
Orange	6 × 6 to 7.5 × 7.5 m (20 × 20 to 25 × 25 ft)
Papaya	2.4 × 2.4 to 3 × 3 m (8 × 8 to 10 × 10 ft)
Peach	6 × 6 or 5.4 × 7.2 m (20 × 20 or 18 × 24 ft)
Pear	6.6 × 6.6 m (22 × 22 ft)
Pecan	9 × 9 to 15 × 15 m (30 × 30 to 50 × 50 ft)
Pineapple	30 × 81 cm (12 × 32 in)
Pistachio	7.2 × 7.2 m (24 × 24 ft)
Prune	6 × 6 m (20 × 20 ft)
Raspberry, black	0.6 to 1.2 m (2 to 4 ft) apart in rows 2.1 to 3 m (7 to 10 ft) apart
Raspberry, red	0.75 m (2.5 ft) apart in rows 1.8 m (6 ft) apart
Strawberry (matted-row system)	61 to 71 cm (24 to 28 in) apart, permitting a matted row, 38 to 61 cm (15 to 24 in) wide to develop from runners
Strawberry (double-row bed system)	beds 96 to 112 cm (38 to 44 in) apart, center to center; two rows in each bed 20 to 30 cm (8 to 12 in) apart. Plants in each row 23 to 36 cm (9 to 14 in) apart
Strawberry (single-row bed system)	beds 100 to 107 cm (39 to 42 in) apart, center to center; plants 20 to 25 cm (8 to 10 in) apart in rows
Walnut (Persian)	6 × 6 m (20 × 20 ft) to 10.5 × 10.5 m (35 × 35 ft) (Payne type)
	10.5 × 10.5 m (35 × 35 ft) to 12 × 12 m (40 × 40 ft) (Hartley type)

Five planting arrangements are used for orchard trees: the square, the quincunx, the hexagonal, and to a much lesser extent, the hedgerow, and the contour. Table 13–3 gives the number of trees per hectare and acre for the first three of these systems, and Table 13–4 gives the number for trees planted by the hedgerow system.

The **square system** is the most common (Fig. 13–1). It is easy to lay out and orchard operations (cultivation, irrigation, harvesting—hand or mechanical) can be conducted in either direction.

Fig. 13–1 Orchard planting layout on the square system.

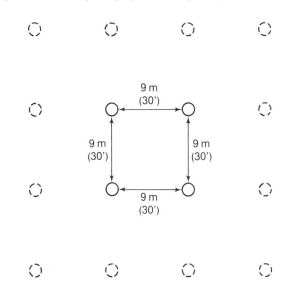

A variation of the square system is the **quincunx system** (Fig. 13–2). An extra tree, often a temporary one (see below), is set in the center of each square. This doubles the number of trees per unit area. The quincunx is useful for those species where the trees—for example walnuts, pecans, grapefruit, or olives—are long-lived and ultimately grow to a considerable size but only over a number of years. The quincunx system increases returns per hectare considerably over the square system in the early years of the planting while the trees are still small. It is even more profitable if the center, temporary, interplant trees are an early-bearer cultivar so that they produce for as many years as possible before they need to be pulled out. With the quincunx system the center tree must be pulled out to give the full space to the permanent trees if tree crowding starts. Failure or delay in removing the temporary trees on time is the weakness of this plant-

Table 13–3   Number of Trees per Hectare and Acre at Different Planting Distances by the Three Principal Planting Systems

Distance Between Permanent Trees		Number of Trees					
		Square		Quincunx		Hexagonal	
METERS	FEET	HECTARE	ACRE	HECTARE	ACRE	HECTARE	ACRE
4.8	16	420	170	840	340	482	195
5.4	18	331	134	662	268	380	154
5.7	19	299	121	598	242	343	139
6.0	20	267	108	538	218	309	125
6.3	21	245	99	489	198	304	123
6.6	22	222	90	445	180	264	104
7.2	24	188	76	375	152	215	87
7.5	25	173	70	346	140	198	80
7.8	26	158	64	316	128	185	75
8.1	27	148	60	296	120	173	70
8.4	28	136	55	271	110	161	65
9.0	30	119	48	237	96	138	56
10.5	35	86	35	173	70	101	41
12.0	40	67	27	133	54	79	32
13.2	44	54	22	109	44	62	25
14.4	48	47	19	94	38	54	22
15.0	50	42	17	84	34	49	20
18.0	60	30	12	59	24	35	14

ing system and can lead to overcrowded conditions, shading the lower fruiting wood and drastically reducing yield and fruit quality.

The **hexagonal** (or **triangular**) **system** has the advantage of equal spacing between trees in all directions (Fig. 13–3). This makes better use of the available land and light for each tree, relating better to the natural round configuration of trees. Hexagonal planting permits operation of orchard equipment in any of three directions. It will also allow the planting of 15 percent more trees in a given area than in a square system with the same tree spacing.

Table 13–4   The Number of Trees per Hectare and Acre at Different Planting Distances by the Hedgerow System

Hedgerow Planting Distances		Number of Trees	
METERS	FEET	PER HECTARE	PER ACRE
1.2 × 3.6	4 × 12	2240	907
2.4 × 3.6	8 × 12	1119	453
2.4 × 4.8	8 × 16	837	339
2.4 × 6.0	8 × 20	672	272
3.0 × 4.8	10 × 16	672	272
3.0 × 5.4	10 × 18	598	242
3.0 × 6.0	10 × 20	538	218
3.3 × 6.6	11 × 22	445	180
3.6 × 5.4	12 × 18	496	201
3.6 × 7.2	12 × 24	373	151

With the development of high-density planting systems a new tree layout—**hedgerows** or **tree-walls**—has appeared. Trees are set, for example, 1.8 to 2.4 m (6 to 8 ft) apart in rows 4.2 to 4.8 m (14 to 16 ft) apart. Solid walls of fruit-bearing surfaces develop with sufficient space between the rows to get implements and harvest trucks through the orchard. Tree-walls should be north-

Fig. 13–2   Orchard planting layout on the quincunx system. 0 = permanent trees; X = trees which may be temporary, to be removed when overcrowding begins.

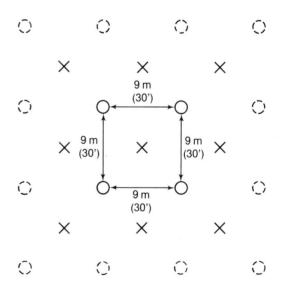

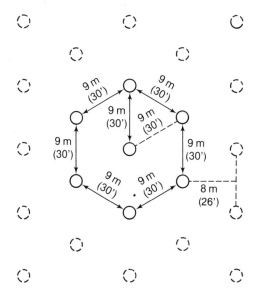

Fig. 13–3 Orchard planting layout on the hexagonal system.

When the time comes to plant the trees, all preparatory steps must have been completed. If the orchard is to be irrigated, all land leveling must be finished and irrigation pipelines installed. If a claypan is present, it should have been broken by ripping. If pathogenic soil organisms, such as nematodes, *Phytophthora,* or *Verticillium* (see Ch. 11) were found, soil fumigation must have been completed with ample time allowed for the dissipation of fumes. Weed control of the area by thorough disking must be completed. If perennial weeds like Johnson grass, were present, the proper herbicides (see Ch. 11) should have been used to bring them under control. Once the trees are planted, many options to perform these operations are closed.

When the young trees are due to arrive from the nursery, the spot where each tree is to be planted throughout the block of land must be marked in readiness for digging the holes for the actual planting. It is important that the trees in the rows be lined up properly. This will facilitate many future orchard operations. A tree out of line can be a target for cultivating disks and other equipment moving down the rows.

Planting the Trees

The best time to plant the nursery trees—or grapevines, or bushberries—is late winter in mild climates or early to late spring in severe-winter areas. The roots will be well-established by the time hot weather arrives and the plants will have a full growing season before they are faced by cold weather.

Deciduous plants should have dormant buds and no leaves when they arrive from the nursery. The roots must be protected from drying out by some moist packing material such as wood shavings. Roots must be continually protected up to the time the trees are planted. Broad-leaved evergreen fruit nursery trees, such as citrus or avocados, should arrive with their roots undisturbed in a soil ball in a container or covered with burlap or heavy plastic.

High-quality nursery stock has a strong, vigorous straight trunk with an abundance of roots well distributed around the trunk. No part of the trunk or root system should show evidence of damage from careless handling. A small shallow slice into the trunk should show bright green tissue below the bark with no evidence of brown areas from winter damage or sunburn. A slice into the roots should reveal a moist whitish color. No root tissue should be shriveled or look brown, gray, or black below the bark. In budded or grafted plants the union should be

south so that light is equally available on both sides of the wall.

The **contour planting system** is sometimes used on rolling slopes or hillsides where some terracing may be needed (see Ch. 9). This planting arrangement, while subject to problems, permits production from land that otherwise could not be utilized. Considerable care must be taken to stop erosion by heavy rains or by irrigation by diverting the water to run along the tree rows rather than straight downslope.

Certain fruit crops, other than tree fruits, are planted close together in long rows—for example, grapes, raspberries, blueberries, blackberries, strawberries, passion fruit, and kiwi fruit—at the planting distances given in Table 13–2. Some, such as grapes, passion fruit, and kiwi fruit are trellised because their long fruiting canes must be supported; some grapes, though, such as the 'Tokay,' can be free-standing, without a trellis. Other fruits, such as the pineapple, whose culture is highly mechanized, are grown about like an agronomic field crop, the plants being set close together and completely covering the area.

In planting fruit trees of a species requiring cross-pollination to set good commercial crops, it is of the utmost importance that trees of the pollinizing cultivar be appropriately spaced among trees of the principal fruiting cultivar (see Ch. 14).

well-healed and strong, with no more than a slight bend at the union. The union should be at least 10 cm (4 in) above the previous soil level so that scion rooting[2] is unlikely after planting. In deciduous nursery stock the dormant buds should be plump and well-developed and should look bright green when cut into. Dead buds may indicate low temperature or herbicide injury or lack of water during the growing season. Broad-leaved evergreen nursery stock should have normal-size leaves of a healthy deep green color and should show no nutrient deficiency symptoms or herbicide damage. Nursery stock should not be infected with any pathogens, insects, or mites. Each nursery plant or lot should be clearly labeled with the cultivar and species name and the rootstock species (and cultivar, if applicable). The size grade should also be stated on the label.

In planting the tree or vine it is important that the planting hole be dug to the proper depth. The base of the main supporting roots, which usually have been trimmed back, or the soil ball, in the case of evergreen plants, should rest on solid, undisturbed soil. If the hole has been dug too deep, necessitating some back-filling before planting, then the plant is apt to sink after watering and settling, putting the graft union below the soil level and leading to attacks of crown rot fungi, principally of the *Phytophthora* species.

The planting hole should be wide enough to easily accommodate the roots without bending and twisting. Tractor-operated soil augers are used for digging holes for large-scale plantings (Fig. 13–4). These have the advantage of working fast and saving labor, but unless operated properly the holes can be dug too deep, leading to crown rot. Also if the soil is too wet when the auger is used, the sides of the hole become severely compacted, making air and water permeability and root penetration difficult. A shovel should be used to break up the compacted sides of the holes when the trees are planted.

When evergreen nursery trees like citrus or avocados are planted, the bud union should be several inches above the soil level. Any burlap or other material around the soil ball should be loosened and split open around the top and sides. Metal containers should be removed before planting.

Filling loose soil around the roots once the plant has been set in the hole is an important operation. The soil should be worked around the roots as the hole is filled to ensure good soil-root contact, with the soil pressed firmly about the roots. If there are persistent summer winds from one direction, the tree can be leaned slightly into the wind at planting.

A shallow basin should be left at the top for filling with water. For those plants with a soil ball around their roots, the top of the soil ball should be slightly exposed at the surface of the basin so that added water can enter directly into and through the root ball. Often the nursery soil found in such root balls is light and porous and if, after planting, they are covered by the heavier clays of native soils, irrigation water will remain in the clays because of their smaller pores and high capillarity, leaving the lighter soil with the roots completely dry. A few days of hot desiccating winds can increase transpiration and severely injure trees planted too deep even though the basins have been filled with water.

The soil basins should be filled with water within a few hours of planting. This prevents dehydration of the roots and also settles the soil around the roots. Watering by filling the basins should continue until vigorous shoot growth is well underway, when the regular irrigation system or rainfall can be used. In heavy soils with drainage problems care must be taken to avoid overwatering, which can prevent good root aeration and lead to attacks by *Phytophthora* and other soil pathogens.

The trunks of the young trees must be protected from sunburn by wrapping them with paper or cardboard during the summer or painting with whitewash or water base paint (one part interior white latex paint and one part water). Inspect for bark damage at intervals during winter by rabbits, mice, or gophers at the soil level and take the necessary preventive measures (see Ch. 11).

It is best not to fertilize the trees at planting time. The developing roots could be injured by excessive salts. Generally the young trees obtain enough mineral nutrients from the soil for their initial growth.

---

[2]Roots developing above the graft union.

Fig. 13–4 Preparing holes for orchard tree planting by tractor-mounted soil auger.

THE DEVELOPING FRUIT PLANTING

Once the young trees or vines have become established and started to grow, they will need watchful care to avoid nutritional, disease, or insect problems. Weeds must be controlled by cultivation or herbicides (see Chs. 9 and 11). Irrigation and fertilization must be routinely and properly done (see Ch. 9).

Every effort should be made to bring the fruit planting into bearing in the fewest possible years. Delayed production is often a result of heavy pruning (see p. 307) and overfertilization with nitrogen, both of which keep the plants excessively vegetative.

PRUNING AND TRAINING

Terminology

Pruning and training has its own vocabulary. Here are some important terms and their meanings.

Heading back. Shoots or limbs are not removed entirely, but the terminal portions are cut off at varying distances from the end. This procedure forces out new shoots from buds below the cut and retards terminal growth of the branch (see Fig. 13–5).

Fig. 13–5 In pruning by heading back (*left*), scaffold branches are cut off to one-half or more of their length. In pruning by thinning out (*right*), certain scaffold branches are completely removed. Sometimes a combination of the two is used, thinning out, followed by heading back. *Source:* Gerdts, M., A. Hewitt, J. Beutel, J. Clark, and F. Cress. 1977. Pruning home deciduous fruit and nut trees. Univ. of Calif. Div. Agr. Sci. Leaflet 21003.

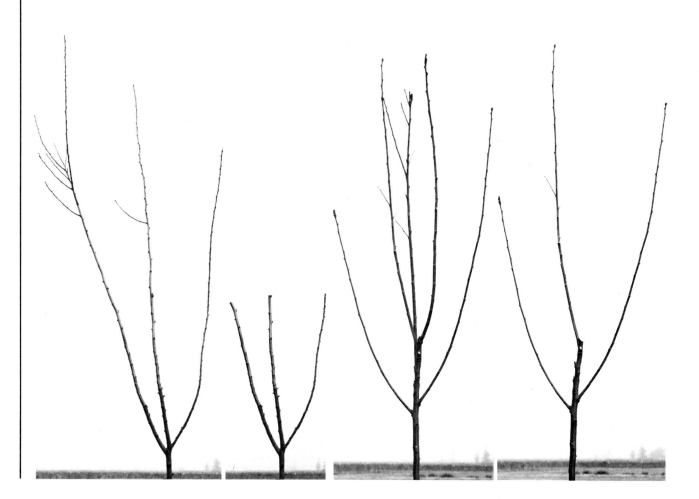

Fig. 13–6 *Left:* Young, unpruned apple tree. *Right:* After dormant pruning. Tree is being trained to a central leader system, retaining a dominant central trunk with several primary scaffold branches, well spaced around the tree and along the trunk. *Source:* Gerdts, M., A. Hewitt, J. Beutel, J. Clark, and F. Cress. 1977. Pruning home deciduous fruit and nut trees. Univ. of Calif. Div. Agr. Sci. Leaflet 21003.

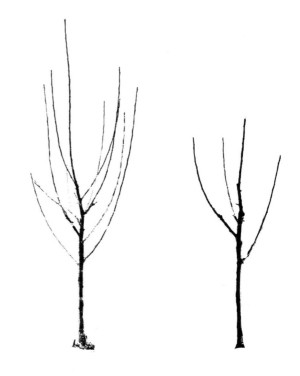

Thinning out. Shoots or limbs are completely removed at the point where they attach to the next larger (and older) limb. Thinning out corrects an overly dense area or removes interfering or unneeded branches (see Fig. 13–5).

Trunk. That portion of the tree up to the first main scaffold branch.

Primary scaffold branches. The main branches arising from the trunk of the tree.

Secondary scaffold branches. Supporting branches arising from the primary scaffold branches.

Central leader training system. A training system for fruit trees where one main vertical trunk remains dominant with all scaffold branches arising from it in an almost horizontal direction (see Fig. 13–6).

Modified leader training system. A central leader continues upward from the trunk, but its identity is lost as it becomes one of the primary or secondary scaffold branches.

Open center or vase training system. A trunk is developed, then at the top of the trunk (0.6 to 0.9 m; 2 to 3 ft from ground level) several primary scaffolds develop outward and upward at a 30° to 45° angle to form a vase configuration (see Fig. 13–7).

Fig. 13–7 *Below left:* Young, unpruned peach tree. *Right:* After dormant (winter) pruning to the open vase system. Three primary scaffold limbs were retained, spaced about 120° apart around the trunk and 5 to 7.5 cm (2 to 3 in) apart vertically. Heading back the scaffold limbs slightly promotes secondary branching. *Source:* Gerdts, M., A. Hewitt, J. Beutel, J. Clark, and F. Cress. 1977. Pruning home deciduous fruit and nut trees. Univ. of Calif. Div. Agr. Sci. Leaflet 21003.

Fig. 13–8 Development of fruiting buds laterally on one-year-old shoots (*top*) and laterally and terminally on fruiting spurs (*bottom*). *Top* (left to right): peach, almond, apricot, plum. *Bottom* (left to right): apple, sweet cherry, apricot, plum.

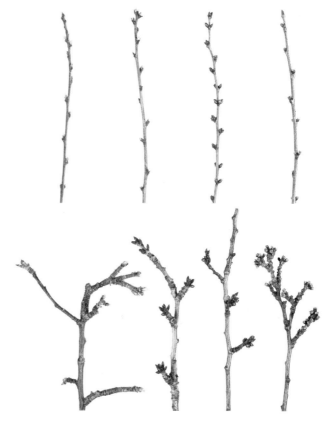

Weak crotch. A situation that can develop when two equal-size branches with a narrow angle between them grow for some years at the same rate. Eventually a considerable amount of bark inclusion develops between the two branches at their junction, with no connecting wood. With heavy loads of fruit—and strong winds—the limbs are almost certain to split apart. This problem can be prevented by completely removing one of the branches when they are young or heading one of them back heavily so the other becomes the main limb and the headed-back branch a lateral.

Fruiting wood. One-year-old shoots of certain species, such as peaches, arising from larger branches of the tree, on which flowers and fruits are produced. They often hang downward and are termed hangers (see Fig. 13–8).

Fruiting spurs. Trees of such species as apples, pears, plums, cherries, apricots, and almonds bear some or most of their crop on these short, thick shoots (see Fig. 13–8), which usually live many years. Care should be taken in pruning and harvesting not to cut or break off these spurs.

Stub. Pruning cuts of the thinning-out type must be properly done. Figure 13–9 shows one correctly made and one incorrectly made, with the protruding stub showing.

Fig. 13–9 *Above:* Proper method of sawing off branch during tree pruning. The branch is removed (*left*) very closely to the parent branch, leaving a smooth cut with no stub (*right*—see arrow) which will heal over quickly. *Below:* Wrong method of removing branch. Saw is too far out on branch (*left*) so that the cut will leave a stub (*right*—see arrow). This stub will prevent rapid healing and may permit decay organisms to become established leading to rotting of the limb.

Cutting off the branch leaves a wound, which must heal over by callus growth proliferating from the surrounding live tissue or else decay organisms can become established in the wound. If the cut is not made close to the adjacent limb and a stub is left, the wound cannot heal properly.

Watersprouts. Vigorous shoots usually arising from latent buds in the trunk or older limbs in the lower parts of the tree, growing upright through the center of the tree (see Fig. 13–10).

Suckers. Shoots arising from the underground parts of the plant, usually coming from adventitious buds on roots. In grafted trees they generally arise from the rootstock below the graft union. They should be removed as soon as they are noticed (see Fig. 13–10).

Fig. 13–10 The difference between suckers and watersprouts as shown here with pear trees. Suckers (*left*) arise from the roots around the base of the tree. Watersprouts (*right*) are vigorous shoots growing from the trunk and older branches up through the center of the tree.

Pruning of fruit plants is an integral part of the procedures used for high production of quality fruits (*23*). These procedures vary with the kind of plant being pruned. Grapes (*16, 19, 22*) are pruned in a certain manner, evergreen fruit species (citrus, avocados, olives, etc.) (*3, 6, 11, 13, 21*) in another, and deciduous fruit trees (*1, 2, 4, 15, 17, 18, 21*) in still another. Different species in these groups are pruned differently; for example, apple trees and peach trees are pruned in quite a different manner because of basic differences in their fruit-bearing habits (see Table 13–4).

Fruit plants, as they mature from planting through the early years of rapid growth to the stable growth of full maturity, require different pruning procedures. In successful fruit production it is essential that the fruit grower know the correct pruning procedures as well as to understand the reasons why pruning is done as it is.

REASONS FOR PRUNING

Fruit and Nut Trees

1. To develop a strong trunk and scaffold system of branches, well distributed around the tree, which are able to support heavy loads of fruit without limb breakage.
2. To control fruit production. Proper pruning encourages development of the type of shoot system that produces the fruit. In older trees with little vegetative growth rejuvenation pruning can force the development of productive fruiting shoots. Pruning can also be used to limit excess numbers of fruit by removing some fruit-bearing branches, giving a thinning effect that can improve fruit size and quality.
3. To remove dead, broken, or interfering branches.
4. To improve light penetration to the inside and lower parts of the tree.
5. To facilitate insect and disease control by opening the tree, thus increasing penetration of spray materials to the interior branches.
6. To limit tree size to the space allocated to it and to limit tree height to that from which fruit can be conveniently harvested.

Grape Vines

1. To aid in the establishment and maintenance of the vines in a form that facilitates vineyard cultural operations.
2. To distribute the fruiting wood to obtain maximum production of high-quality fruit.
3. To maintain vigor and production of fruiting canes.
4. To aid in control of crop size and increase berry size by reducing the number of fruiting clusters.
5. To remove old, nonproductive canes.

Bushberries (Raspberries, Blackberries, Blueberries, Currants, and Gooseberries)

1. To remove dead, weak, or diseased canes and old shoots that die following fruiting.
2. To thin out weak canes to give adequate light and space to the remaining canes, resulting in larger, better-quality fruit.
3. To develop lateral fruiting branches by summer topping (of black and purple raspberries and upright blackberries, but not red raspberries).

PHYSIOLOGICAL RESPONSES TO PRUNING

All plants, if not pruned, tend to develop a balance between growth of the shoot and the root systems. Cutting away part of the top, including the plant's photosynthetic apparatus and food storage tissues, together with reducing the number of vegetative growing points and flower buds while leaving the root system intact leads to some interesting physiological reactions. The fruit grower should be aware of these reactions in order to understand how to prune the plants properly.

1. *There is a reduction in total vegetative growth.* Removing a portion of the top reduces the total amount of growth, compared to an unpruned plant. The total number of growing points is reduced, resulting in fewer developing shoots, fewer leaves, reduced photosynthesis, reduced amounts of carbohydrates translocated to the roots, reduced root growth, followed by a reduction in mineral and water absorption, which, in turn, further decreases shoot growth. These effects dwarf the entire plant. Generally, the more severe the pruning, the greater the dwarfing.

   The remaining growing points following pruning, which utilize all the stored foods in the plant, usually show strong shoot growth. The increased vigor of these shoots may lead one to believe that the pruning has caused increased total growth, but numerous experiments have shown that this is not so. (If invigoration of the total plant is necessary, the judicious use of added fertilizers with ample soil moisture, together with moderate pruning, should be practiced.)
2. *Continual heavy pruning each year of young fruit trees can delay the onset of bearing.* This is particularly true for the broad-leaved evergreens (which store their foods mainly in the leaves, twigs, and branches rather than in the larger branches, trunk, and roots, as do the deciduous fruit trees).
3. *Pruning effects from removal of smaller shoots and branches tend to be localized.* Heading back of shoots during the dormant season, reducing the length of a shoot by 50 percent, for example, results in the development of one or more new shoots from buds just below the pruning cut. The total growth by the end of the summer will not be nearly equal to the total growth of an adjacent shoot that was not dormant pruned. This response is often used in pruning to retard the growth of one of two equal-growing shoots and thus prevent the development of a weak crotch.

4. *Severe pruning in early summer is more likely to weaken the tree and reduce total growth than dormant (winter) pruning, especially with young trees.* Much of the energy for new spring shoot growth comes from stored foods in the roots, trunk, and branches of the tree. These stored foods are not replaced until an appreciable number of new leaves have formed and photosynthesized enough to reverse carbohydrate movement into the larger branches, trunk, and roots. If summer pruning is done, partially removing these new shoots and reducing photosynthesis and the replenishment of foods already utilized, the tree can be intensely debilitated. However, a moderate pinching back of only the tips of the shoots in the spring to direct growth is not likely to be harmful.

5. *Dormant pruning of bearing deciduous fruit trees can be invigorating.* Although vegetative growing points are removed, flower buds are also removed, thus reducing the crop, consequently reducing the demand on the plant's stored foods. The surplus is then utilized for new vegetative growth.

6. *Moderate dormant pruning of bearing deciduous fruit plants can increase production.* Flowers are produced either laterally or terminally on one-year-old shoots and/or laterally or terminally on fruiting spurs (see Fig. 13–8 and Table 13–4). Such fruit-producing growth (shoots and spurs) must be stimulated to obtain continual crops. Moderate pruning, plus fertilizers and ample soil moisture, result in such growth stimulation. Mature broadleaved evergreen fruit species, such as citrus, olives, and avocados, should be pruned lighter than deciduous species. Experiments have shown that the yield of the evergreen species generally decreases in proportion to the severity of pruning (*6, 11*).

7. *Removing shoot terminals causes lateral branching.* Newly planted, one-year-old trees of some fruit species—for example, apples, cherries, pecans, pears, walnuts, quince, European plums, and figs—show strong apical dominance (see p. 310). If the terminal bud is not pruned, the tree will grow mostly as a straight, sparsely-branched trunk. If the terminal bud is removed (plus several inches of shoot below it for convenience) at planting time, however, the lateral buds remaining below the cut will develop, producing lateral scaffold branches. To cause further branching of these scaffolds the next year, the terminals of the scaf-

fold shoots must again be headed back by several inches.

Other tree species, such as apricots, peaches, almonds, and nectarines, do not show such strong apical dominance. Lateral buds develop into scaffold branches without heading back of the main shoot terminal growth (see p. 310).

PRUNING AND TRAINING
YOUNG DECIDUOUS
FRUIT TREES

After a young nursery tree has been planted in an orchard, the immediate goal is to develop a tree that has a strong straight trunk with three or four primary scaffold branches well spaced around the tree and vertically on the trunk. Scaffold branches having wide angles with the trunk should be retained so that the branch attachment will be strong. Those with narrow angles should be removed. Remember that the height of attachment of the scaffold branches from the ground will always remain the same, but the trunk and each scaffold branch will increase in diameter each year throughout the life of the tree because of cell division in the lateral cambium layers. There must be space for each of the scaffolds as they grow. All branches should not originate at the same height on the trunk.

If the species is one that is adaptable to mechanical harvesting by trunk shakers (almonds, prunes, cling peaches, olives, sour cherries, citrus), the main trunk should be high enough (before the attachment of the lowest primary scaffold branch) for the shaker clamp to attach.

At planting nursery trees are usually straight trunks 0.9 to 1.5 m (3 to 5 ft) tall. Some nurseries do not cut back the tops when they are dug; however, the top must be reduced in size to compensate for the root system lost when the tree was dug (see Fig. 13–11). The terminal end of the trunk should be headed back to 76 to 90 cm (30 to 36 in) from the ground to force shoots out from the lateral buds. Some of these shoots will later be selected for the primary scaffold branches. If the nursery trees already have short lateral shoots, they can be retained and used as starting points for the primary scaffold branches.

As the young trees start to grow in the spring, most of the lateral buds along the trunk are likely to develop. If none of these are removed, the tree may look like a bush by the end of the growing season, with shoots developing all along the trunk, and most of them will

Fig. 13–11 *Above:* Pruning of unbranched nursery fruit trees (*far left*) after planting consists only of cutting back a portion of the top to 50 to 60 cm (20 to 24 in) above the ground to force out lateral branches, as shown in the second photograph. If the nursery tree is well branched (*right*), pruning after planting consists of heading back the top, removing most laterals, and cutting the remainder back to stubs, from which new scaffold branches can develop (*far right*). *Source:* Gerdts, M., A. Hewitt, J. Beutel, J. Clark, and F. Cress. 1977. Pruning home deciduous fruit and nut trees. Univ. of Calif. Div. Agr. Sci. Leaflet 21003.

have to be removed during the following winter dormant pruning. Much can be done to direct this growth into permanent scaffold branches by judiciously removing or tipping back certain of these succulent lateral shoots as they start to develop in the spring. As soon as the shoots are 5 or 7.5 cm (2 or 3 in) long, each tree should be carefully inspected. Shoots arising around the base and lower half of the trunk should be removed. Toward the upper half of the trunk three or four of the new shoots that are well placed up and down and around the trunk can be retained to develop into the primary scaffold branches. There should be 15 to 30 cm (6 to 12 in) vertically between any two scaffolds. One should never be allowed to develop directly above another. All other shoots should have their tips pinched out to retard growth or, if there are many shoots, some could be removed. It

is not wise to remove too much leaf area since this can seriously retard growth of the young tree. Close inspection of each tree during the first summer can be most useful—to remove any suckers or strong-growing watersprouts arising from the base of the tree, and to remove or head back shoots not destined to be the primary scaffolds.

If the orchard site is windy, the trunks may be staked and tied to keep the trees from being whipped about. A strong stake should be driven in the ground on the windward side of the tree about 0.3 m (1 ft) from it. Then loose, soft cords should be used for tying the trunk at about three places. The trunk should be permitted to sway somewhat since a swaying trunk develops much stronger than does one immobilized by tight tying (5).

PRUNING AND TRAINING DURING THE FIRST DORMANT SEASON

Pruning can be done at any time after the leaves drop and before buds start to develop in the spring. In areas with severe winters it is best to wait until the coldest part of the winter is over. Pruned trees are more susceptible to cold damage than unpruned trees. In addition, any killing of tree parts by winter cold will obviously be a factor in deciding what to retain and what to remove during pruning. Early and mid-winter pruning can aggravate bacterial canker problems in young trees, as well as peach silver leaf and apricot limb die-back, which are associated with rainy weather. The peach tree short-life problem in North and South Carolina is worse with early winter pruning than with late winter or early spring pruning.

If the trees have been lightly shaped by pinching back or removing unwanted shoots the previous summer, the first dormant pruning is much simplified. Basically, the primary scaffolds already selected should be retained and all other shoots headed back or thinned out. Pruning should be light, however; heavy pruning on young trees has a dwarfing influence.

If no summer training has been done, the first dormant pruning is more involved. All branches arising from around the base of the tree should be removed. Then the strongest three or four shoots in the upper portion of the tree, well spaced around and up and down— 15 to 30 cm (6 to 12 in) apart vertically—should be retained. All others should be thinned out.

In species with strong apical dominance, such as apples, pears, cherries, figs, European plums, and prunes, lateral scaffold branches left during the first dormant pruning should have their terminal 7.5 or 10 cm (3 or 4 in) headed back to force out shoots, which will later develop into the secondary scaffold branches. The trunk terminal in central leader training should also be headed back. In species showing strong apical dominance, the uppermost scaffolds tend to grow more vigorously than the lower ones and may dominate the tree. In pruning, therefore, these upper scaffolds should be headed back more than the lower ones.

Other species, like almonds, apricots, and Japanese plums, do not show strong apical dominance and develop lateral branches readily without heading back. In these species the lower scaffolds tend to grow more vigorously than the upper ones and may dominate the tree. To overcome this, head back the lower scaffolds lightly and the upper ones not at all.

Peaches should be headed back to force out lateral branches to form the primary scaffold system. Side branches developing on current season's growth do not make satisfactory scaffold branches.

In all cases try to keep the pruning as light as possible and still accomplish the desired effects. Lightly pruned trees are apt to come into bearing one to three years earlier than those heavily pruned.

PRUNING AND TRAINING DURING THE SECOND SEASON

During the second growing season the secondary scaffold branches develop from the primary scaffolds. Some judicious pinching out of unwanted shoots arising from the primary scaffolds can be done during early summer, permitting two well-placed shoots on each primary scaffold to develop into the permanent secondary scaffolds. Through the summer, too, any vigorous watersprouts or suckers growing up through the center of the tree should be removed.

In the second dormant season, training to develop the secondary scaffold system can be continued. Two strong, well-placed branches arising from each primary scaffold, which will constitute the secondary scaffold system, can go unpruned except for those species (apples, pears, cherries, figs, European plums, and prunes) that do not develop lateral branches readily. Secondary scaffolds of these species should be headed back several inches to force out laterals. All other branches arising from the primary scaffolds should either be removed or headed back heavily. Peaches and apricot trees growing vigorously need to be headed back (0.6 to 0.7 cm; 24 to 30 in) at this time; otherwise the weight of the fruit may bend them out of shape even with rope or stake bracing.

In cool-weather areas with short growing seasons, or under poor soil and water conditions, three, or perhaps four, growing seasons may be required to complete this basic framework of the tree.

Training on into the third and fourth years is essentially the production of future fruiting wood from branching and rebranching arising from the secondary scaffolds. Pruning consists of thinning out where the branching becomes too heavy, removing limbs that cross over and rub against each other, and removing strong-growing watersprouts and suckers. Heading back is usually not advisable as the trees get into production. An exception is sweet cherries, which tend to continue to produce long, unbranched polelike branches unless they are headed back (see Figs. 13–12, 13–13, and 13–14).

310

Fig. 13–12 Central-leader apple tree after several years' growth. *Left:* Before dormant pruning. *Right:* After pruning. Some lateral branches were removed. In those retained, forked tips were cut to one outward growing branch. Spreader boards have been used with some laterals to develop a wider growth habit. *Source:* Gerdts, M., A. Hewitt, J. Beutel, J. Clark, and F. Cress. 1977. Pruning home deciduous fruit and nut trees. Univ. of Calif. Div. Agr. Sci. Leaflet 21003.

Fig. 13–13 Some fruit trees, such as pears, tend to develop an upright, narrow shape, as shown in the unpruned tree at left. Often, this cannot be corrected by pruning alone. With notched, spreader boards, as shown in the pruned tree at right, the primary scaffold branches can be trained to give a wider tree shape. Inner limbs should be removed and those retained pruned to outward facing branches or buds. *Source:* Gerdts, M., A. Hewitt, J. Beutel, J. Clark, and F. Cress. 1977. Pruning home deciduous fruit and nut trees. Univ. of Calif. Div. Agr. Sci. Leaflet 21003.

Fig. 13–14 Young, vigorous peach tree before (*left*) and after (*right*) pruning. Peaches require rather severe pruning. Many scaffold limbs have been removed, particularly those that grow low and horizontal. The stronger, moderately upright limbs were selected for the permanent primary scaffolds and were headed back to force out additional branching. *Source:* Gerdts, M., A. Hewitt, J. Beutel, J. Clark, and F. Cress. 1977. Pruning home deciduous fruit and nut trees. Univ. of Calif. Div. Agr. Sci. Leaflet 21003.

Pruning Bearing Deciduous Fruit Trees

As properly trained trees reach an age where they begin to form flowers and produce fruit, they have a strong trunk, three or four well-placed primary scaffold limbs, and nine to twelve secondary scaffolds, distributing the fruiting wood uniformly around the tree. Removal of any large limbs at this stage should not be necessary (see Figs. 13–15 and 13–16).

Bearing deciduous fruit trees require moderate annual pruning to:

1. Stimulate production of new fruiting wood
2. Allow light penetration into the tree and prevent the development of dense pockets of vegetative growth
3. Reduce excessive amounts of fruiting wood and lessen the need for expensive hand-thinning of fruits
4. Remove broken, diseased, dead, or interfering branches
5. Keep the trees from growing so tall that harvesting becomes difficult
6. Confine the trees to the space available to them

A light annual pruning of bearing trees is better than a heavy pruning every three or four years, giving more regular cropping.

FRUITING HABITS

To prune bearing fruit plants intelligently, one must know, for the various fruit species, the locations of the fruit buds on the plant and be able to identify them. Figure 13–17 shows the difference in appearance of fruit buds and vegetative buds, and Figure 13–8 shows the two basic positions of fruiting buds. Apples,

312

Fig. 13–15   A mature peach tree before (*left*) and after (*right*) dormant pruning. Many of the weaker branches were removed, retaining young fruiting shoots selectively spaced along the stronger scaffold limbs. Relatively severe pruning of peach trees forces growth of new shoots, which produce fruits the following year. *Source:* Gerdts, M., A. Hewitt, J. Beutel, J. Clark, and F. Cress. 1977. Pruning home deciduous fruit and nut trees. Univ. of Calif. Div. Agr. Sci. Leaflet 21003.

Fig. 13–16   Old fruit trees (*left*), if not pruned for several years, become dense and brushy, producing excessive numbers of small fruits, whose weight often breaks limbs. To correct such a situation, many of the limbs should be removed (*right*) during the dormant season to open the center of the tree, retaining strong, well-spaced limbs. If many limbs need to be removed, it may be best to spread the pruning over two years. *Source:* Gerdts, M., A. Hewitt, J. Beutel, J. Clark, and F. Cress. 1977. Pruning home deciduous fruit and nut trees. Univ. of Calif. Div.Agr. Sci. Leaflet 21003.

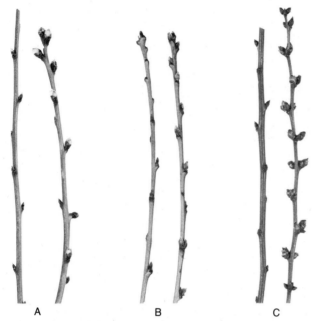

Fig. 13–17 The different appearance of vegetative and fruit buds in the almond (*A*), peach (*B*), and apricot (*C*). In each pair, the shoot with vegetative buds is on the left and that with fruit buds is on the right. Vegetative buds are small and pointed, whereas fruit buds are large and plump.

pears, apricots, cherries, and plums produce the fruits on spurs. Others produce the fruits laterally (or more rarely terminally) on shoots that grew the previous season. Peaches, nectarines, grapes, and olives produce most of their fruits laterally on shoots, while citrus, young pecan trees, some young walnut trees, and loquats bear fruits terminally on shoots (see Table 13–5).

Care must be taken not to prune or break off fruiting spurs, although in trees that consistently overbear to the detriment of fruit size and quality there may be some benefit in partial spur removal. Spurs do not live indefinitely and some renewal is constantly taking place. Annual pruning tends to stimulate new spur formation.

Fruit species producing fruiting buds laterally or terminally on shoots that developed the previous growing season should be pruned to encourage the growth of such shoots. This entails a moderate annual dormant pruning, together with moderate nitrogen fertilization and ample soil moisture. Excessive pruning plus heavy applications of nitrogen can cause excessive rank vegetative growth, which will not form flowers.

The severity of pruning needed by bearing trees to keep them in a state of optimum fruitfulness can be judged to some extent by the length of annual shoot

Table 13–5 Location of Fruit-Producing Buds on Various Kinds of Fruit Plants. Major Indicates Dominant Location. Minor Indicates Secondary Location.

Species	Lateral on Shoots	Terminal on Shoots	Lateral on Spurs	Terminal on Spurs
Almond	Minor	——	Major	——
Apple	Minor	Very minor	——	Major
Apricot	Minor	——	Major	——
Black raspberry	Major	——	——	——
Blueberry	Major	——	——	——
Cherry, sour	Major or minor	——	Minor or major	——
Cherry, sweet	Minor	——	Major	——
Citrus	——	Major	——	——
Cranberries	Major	——	——	——
Fig	Major	——	——	——
Grapes	Major	——	——	——
Loquat	——	Major	——	——
Olive	Major	Very minor	——	——
Peach and nectarine	Major	——	Minor	——
Pear	Minor	Very minor	——	Major
Pecan	Minor on young trees	Major on young trees	Minor on mature trees	Major on mature trees
Persimmon	Major	Minor	——	——
Plum, European	Very minor	——	Major	——
Plum, Japanese	Minor	——	Major	——
Quince	Major	Minor	——	——
Walnut				
(Payne type, many lateral buds fruitful)	Major on young trees	Minor on young trees	Minor or equal on mature trees	Equal or major on mature trees
(Franquette type, few lateral buds fruitful)	Minor on young trees	Major on young trees	Minor on mature trees	Major on mature trees

Source: W. P. Tufts and R. W. Harris. 1955. Pruning deciduous fruit trees. Calif. State Agr. Exp. Sta. Ext. Ser. Cir. 444.

Table 13–6 Desirable Amounts of Average Shoot Growth for Bearing Trees to Give Maximum Fruit Production

Species	Young Trees—Under 10 Years of Age		Older Trees—Over 10 Years of Age	
	CENTIMETERS	INCHES	CENTIMETERS	INCHES
Freestone peaches and nectarines	50 to 100	20 to 40	30 to 76	12 to 30
Clingstone peaches	76 to 100	30 to 40	30 to 76	12 to 30
Apricots	30 to 76	12 to 30	25 to 60	10 to 24
Plums (except prunes) and quinces	25 to 60	10 to 24	23 to 46	9 to 18
Almonds, prunes, apples, pears, and cherries	23 to 46	9 to 18	15 to 25	6 to 10
Olives	30 to 60	12 to 24	25 to 38	10 to 15
Figs	20 to 30	8 to 12	15 to 20	6 to 8

growth. Table 13–6 gives the amount of growth associated with good fruiting. If the annual growth of the average shoot exceeds these amounts, the severity of annual pruning should be reduced. If shoot growth is much below these amounts, severity of pruning should be increased as well as, perhaps, the amount of fertilizer applied annually.

Deciduous fruit trees are sometimes topped mechanically (mowing), giving a flat-top appearance to the orchard. There is evidence that summer topping of peaches and plums increases the development of fruit buds throughout the tree, especially in vigorous, young bearing trees. Such top mowing also reduces the amount of dormant pruning labor required and holds the tree heights to levels where pickers can reach the fruit.

Pruning and Training
Young Broad-Leaf Evergreen Fruit Trees

Trees of this type (citrus, avocados, olives, etc.) usually come from the nursery in full leaf with their roots in soil in a container of some sort. When the trees are planted, the container must be removed or opened so the roots can spread out. If the roots have spiraled and thickened in the container, the trees should be rejected and returned to the nursery. Such roots will not grow out sufficiently to prevent the trees from toppling over in strong winds.

Evergreen fruit trees must be pruned considerably lighter than the deciduous fruit trees. Heavy pruning of young evergreen trees causes dwarfing and delays the onset of bearing for years. Many avocado and citrus growers do little or no pruning with quite successful results. Olive trees during the early years require somewhat more pruning and training, but the pruning still should be very light.

The purpose of pruning young trees of this type is essentially the same as for the deciduous trees; that is, to develop a strong trunk and to form primary and second-

ary scaffolds to support the fruit-bearing surface. Removing broken or interfering branches is important. If rank growth in some branches in the young trees produces an unbalanced tree, the branches should be cut back to better shape the tree. Lemons, in particular, tend to develop a scraggly growth habit and must be pruned more heavily than trees of other citrus. Watersprouts or suckers growing up through the center of the tree should be removed.

Pruning Bearing Broad-Leaved Evergreen Fruit Trees

Bearing trees of these species are pruned much lighter than deciduous trees of comparable age.

Avocados need very little pruning, although height suppression of trees of particularly tall-growing cultivars by an annual light topping of upright growing limbs facilitates harvesting. All dead, broken, or low-hanging branches that would interfere with cultivation or irrigation should be taken out.

Bearing orange and grapefruit trees growing on fertile, well-drained soils and under good fertilization, irrigation, and pest control programs generally maintain vigorous growth and good yields with little or no pruning. Watersprouts and suckers growing up through the center of the tree should be removed, as well as any dead or broken limbs.

Lemons may develop masses of excessively dense vegetative growth, which need some thinning out to improve light penetration. A small amount of pruning of lemons is advisable. Lemon trees are vigorous growers and, as they grow larger, pruning back is necessary to keep them in the space available and permit passage of equipment through the orchard.

Mechanical pruning (hedging) and topping (mowing) of citrus orchards is an accepted practice in some localities. It seems to be satisfactory and saves considerable labor costs. The sides of the tree rows are cut back vertically, sometimes on a slant inward toward the top, increasing sunlight on the fruit-bearing surfaces. Small amounts of hedging and topping do not appreciably reduce yields and may increase yields if light penetrates better.

Bearing olive trees, if grown under good irrigation and fertilization practices, also yield best if pruned only moderately each year and the fruiting wood is allowed to reach almost to the ground, making hand picking of the fruit easier. Heavy pruning of mature olive trees reduces yields in proportion to the severity of pruning (6). It induces strong vegetative growth, which tends to keep the trees unfruitful. As the trees grow larger and taller, more pruning is needed to keep them within space allocations. Some moderate annual pruning of olives is required to force the development of new shoot growth on which the fruits are borne laterally the following year.

Mechanically harvested olive trees are pruned so as to expose the trunk and primary scaffold limbs for attachment of the shaker clamp. In addition, enough of the lower branches are removed to permit operation of the shaker arm and catching frame. Such mechanically harvested trees are allowed to grow much taller than would be advisable for hand harvest.

Mango trees are pruned very little except for training when the trees are young to form a strong trunk and primary scaffold system. Tall, upright-growing young trees may need to be cut back to force lower branching, and any dead or interfering branches are removed. Mango wood is very tough. Thus limbs in older trees rarely break.

Macadamia trees are trained to a central leader formation with four or five whorls of lateral branches 0.3 to 0.6 m (1 to 2 ft) apart up the trunk for 2.4 to 3 m (8 to 10 ft). Once this initial branching is established, little further pruning is needed except to remove dead or obviously interfering lateral branches.

Papayas are fast-growing, short-lived, almost herbaceous plants that grow and fruit as single stems. They require no pruning although overly tall old trees can be cut back to the ground, forcing out new shoots, the strongest of which is retained to form a new trunk.

Coffee trees are pruned lightly except for removing dead wood and reducing the trees' height if they become too tall. Some shoot removal annually can give more uniform crops of larger berries. Different training systems are practiced. One is to develop a central leader with a series of lateral scaffold branches. Another method is to allow multiple primary scaffolds to develop in low positions from the main trunk.

Pruning and Training Grapevines (16, 19, 22)

Grapes are pruned more heavily than fruit trees. The three main objectives in grape pruning and training are:

1. Establishing and maintaining the vines in a form that facilitates the various vineyard operations, such as cultivation, irrigation, spraying, dusting, and harvesting
2. Distributing the fruiting wood throughout the vine and between vines so as to give high production of good quality fruit over the years
3. Regulating the size of the crop, by reducing or eliminating the need for fruit or cluster thinning.

Grapevines produce their flower and fruit clusters mostly on new shoots arising from buds on canes that grew the previous summer. Thus in dormant pruning of grapevines it is essential that enough buds, but not too many, be retained to obtain a satisfactory crop the following summer.

Grapes adapt to a wide array of training systems. Since they are vines, they assume the shape of the supports used to hold them in place.

In California the principal training systems for the *Vitis vinifera* cultivars are:

1. The head-trained, spur-pruned system
2. The cordon-trained, spur-pruned system also used for muscadine grapes in the southeastern United States
3. The head-trained, cane-pruned system

These are shown in Figure 13–18. In the eastern United States, several training systems are used for the labrusca type grapes grown there, but the most popular is the four-arm Kniffin system, as illustrated in Fig. 13–18.

In the **head-trained, spur-pruned** system, a vertical trunk 0.3 to 0.9 m (1 to 3 ft) is developed with support arms uniformly positioned in a circular head. On these arms, short spurs of last year's growth with two buds are left during the winter pruning to produce the shoots that will bear the next year's crop and to furnish canes for the next year's spurs. This system is used in California for the Tokay, Ribier, and Emperor table grape and for most large-clustered wine grape cultivars. The trunk has to be supported by a short stake until it becomes strong enough to stand alone, usually in 10 years. No wire trellis is needed.

In the **cordon-trained, spur-pruned** system, a vertical trunk is developed to a height of 90 to 120 cm

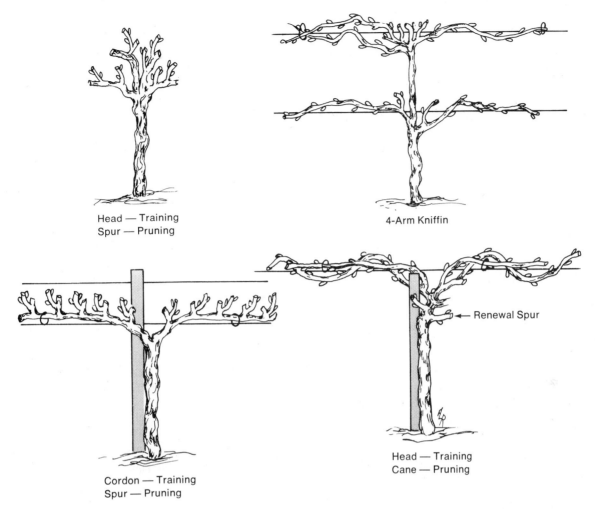

Head — Training
Spur — Pruning

4-Arm Kniffin

Cordon — Training
Spur — Pruning

← Renewal Spur

Head — Training
Cane — Pruning

Fig. 13–18 Four commonly used methods of training grapevines. The four-arm Kniffin system is used primarily with the labrusca-type grapes grown in the eastern United States. The others are used in training the vinifera-type grapes grown in California. *Source:* Adapted from Weaver, R. J. 1976. *Grape growing.* New York: John Wiley.

Fig. 13–19 A vineyard using the head-training, cane-pruning system as it appears in winter after leaf fall but before pruning. *Source:* Blue Anchor, Inc.

(36 to 48 in). From the top of the trunk the bilateral arms (cordons) extend in opposite directions for several feet along the lower wire of the trellis. From the upper side of these horizontal arms short spurs of the previous summer's growth are positioned during winter pruning to provide the shoots that will bear the grape clusters and that in turn, can be used for the following year's spurs. All other canes are removed. This system is widely used for large-clustered wine grapes and many table grape cultivars.

In the **head-trained, cane-pruned** system a vertical trunk is developed (Fig. 13–19) reaching to the top wire of the trellis. During the dormant season pruning, two to six canes of the previous summer's growth having 8 to 15 buds each are retained to produce shoots that will bear the fruit clusters the following summer. Often three or four renewal spurs with two buds each are left in the head trunk. From these will grow the canes to be retained for the following year's fruiting. All other canes are removed. This system is especially useful for 'Thompson Seedless,' which does not produce fruitful buds near the base of the canes, and for small-clustered wine cultivars.

The **four-arm Kniffin** system used in the eastern United States for the native American grapes and American-French hybrids is very similar to the head-trained, cane-pruned system. A two-wire trellis is required, with the lower wire about 0.9 m (3 ft) and the upper wire 1.8 m (6 ft) from the ground. The four canes retained during the winter pruning—two in each direction extending horizontally on each wire—may have from 8 to 12 buds each, depending upon the cultivar and the vigor of the vine, and vine spacing. Two-budded renewal spurs are retained near the base of each fruiting cane to provide canes for the following year.

GRAPE ARBORS

In pruning grapevines to cover an arbor with horizontal supports as high as 2.1 or 2.4 m (7 or 8 ft), the main trunk of the vines should be trained up to the top of the supporting posts, then bent horizontally to go along the top of the supporting wires or slats. Then either spur pruning or cane pruning can be done from this horizontal main stem, depending upon the species and cultivar being grown.

FRUIT THINNING

To obtain better yields of high-quality grape berries, one extra bud on half or more of the fruiting spurs (spur pruning) and an extra cane or two per vine (cane pruning) can be retained. Clusters or fruits should be thinned[3] to reduce the crop to the amount it would have been had the extra fruiting canes not been left. The increased leaf area produced by retaining the extra spurs or canes to support the same number of fruits per vine raises the yield and the quality of the berries.

Chapter 29 details pruning procedures for the various bushberry crops: blueberries, black and red raspberries, and blackberries.

---

[3]Thinning can be done as flower thinning—removal of part of the fruiting clusters before bloom—or cluster thinning—removal of clusters after the berries have set.

WEED CONTROL IN FRUIT PLANTINGS

A heavy growth of weeds utilizes soil moisture and mineral elements, particularly nitrogen, better used for the fruit plants. In addition, weeds interfere with orchard or vineyard operations—pruning, fertilization, thinning, irrigation, and harvesting. In winter as the weeds die they constitute a serious fire hazard and can harbor rodents that will damage tree trunks when food is scarce. In well-managed fruit plantings where irrigation water is scarce or expensive weeds are meticuously controlled. The various methods of weed control are considered in Chapter 11.

Some orchards are managed as a sod culture system in which low growing grasses cover the orchard floor. Sod culture is useful mainly for plantings on sloping hillsides where soil erosion is a problem and for areas where the water supply is plentiful and cheap enough to support both grasses and trees. If rainfall is abundant, water use by the grasses is not a problem. Extra nitrogen and, perhaps, potassium must be added, however, to compensate for what is used by the grasses. Thus sod culture entails increased fertilizer costs, the added cost of mowing the grasses, and possibly added irrigation costs. Sod orchards, due to shading of the soil surface, are particularly cold during bloom and, therefore, subject to crop losses from frost damage.

CULTIVATION AND IRRIGATION

Cultivation and irrigation are discussed in Chapter 9.

FERTILIZATION

The general principles of soil fertility and the procedures for fertilizing crop plants are discussed in Chapters 8 and 9.

It should be emphasized that for fruit plants—orchard trees, grapes, bushberries, and strawberries—nitrogen is the mineral element most likely to be deficient and to need replenishment. In some areas, such as the western United States, zinc and perhaps potassium deficiency are likely to occur and to need correcting. More rarely, deficiencies of phosphorus, boron, iron, calcium, magnesium, manganese, copper, or sulfur affect fruit plantings. However, unless leaf analyses and field trials show that the fruit plants will respond to applications of these elements, it is generally best not to apply them because of the additional cost.

In some instances potassium is deficient in orchard soils and must be added. For example, in some Michigan peach and apricot orchards (*9, 10*), New York apple orchards (*12*), and California olive orchards (*7*) potassium is deficient and the trees respond to added fertilizers.

Iron deficiency symptoms can sometimes be found in orchard trees, particularly in water-logged soils, soils with high levels of copper, or soils low in organic matter. Iron deficiency symptoms also occur in alkaline, high-lime soils where the problem is termed **lime-induced chlorosis.** Iron deficiency has been difficult to correct in citrus.

Some Florida soils on which citrus is grown are very low in magnesium, and the addition of this element in fertilizers has been essential for good yields. Florida citrus also requires the addition of copper to eliminate a shoot die-back problem, although corrective measures with added copper can cause an iron deficiency problem (*23*).

Zinc deficiency, widespread in many orchard soils, causes shoot die-back and reduces internode length and leaf size ("little-leaf"), consequently decreasing photosynthetic capacity. Annual sprays of zinc sulfate (1.2 kg of 36 percent material/100 l water; 10 lb./100 gal. water) applied in the fall at about normal leaf drop time can correct this problem.

REFERENCES

1. Banta, E. S., F. S. Howlett, and R. G. Hill, Jr. Pruning and training fruit trees. Ohio Coop. Ext. Serv. (unnumbered, undated).

2. Chandler, W. H. 1957. *Deciduous orchards.* 3rd ed. Philadelphia: Lea & Febiger. Ch. 15, Responses of deciduous orchards to pruning.

3. ———. 1958. *Evergreen orchards.* 2nd ed. Philadelphia: Lea & Febiger. Ch. 1, Growing and training dicotyledenous evergreen orchard trees.

4. Gerdts, M., A. Hewitt, J. Beutel, J. Clark, and F. Cress. 1977. Pruning home deciduous fruit and nut trees. Univ. of Calif. Div. Agr. Sci. Leaflet 21003.

5. Harris, R. W., A. T. Leiser, P. L. Neel, D. Long, N. W. Stice, and R. Maire. 1971. Tree trunk development: influence of spacing and movement. *Proc. Inter. Plant Prop. Soc.* 21:149–59.

6. Hartmann, H. T. and K. Opitz. 1966. Pruning olive trees in California. Calif. Agr. Exp. Sta. Cir. 537.

7. ———. 1977. Olive production in California. Univ. of Calif. Div. Agr. Sci. Leaflet 2474.

8. Heinicke, D. R. 1975. High density apple orchards: planning, training, pruning. USDA Agr. Handbook No. 458.

9. Johnston, S., J. E. Moulton, R. F. Carlson, and R. P. Larsen. 1966. Growing apricots in Michigan. Mich. Coop. Ext. Ser. Bul. 533.

10. Johnston, S., and R. P. Larsen. 1971. Peach culture in Michigan, Mich. Coop. Ext. Ser. Bul. 509.

11. McCarty, C. D., S. B. Boswell, R. M. Burns, R. G. Platt, K. W. Opitz, and L. N. Lewis. 1974. Pruning citrus trees. Calif. Agr. Exp. Sta. Ext. Ser. Cir. 565.

12. Oberly, G. H., and C. G. Forshey 1974. Cultural practices in the bearing apple orchard. New York Agr.Ext. Bul. 1212.

13. Platt, R. G. 1962. Prune avocado trees cautiously. Calif. Agr. Exp. Sta. Ext. Ser. Leaflet 140.

14. Platt, R. G. 1973. Planning and planting the orchard. In *The citrus industry,* vol. 3, ed. W. Reuther, Berkeley: University of California Division of Agricultural Sciences.

15. Ross., N. W. 1974. *Stanislaus orchard handbook.* Modesto, Calif.: University of California Cooperative Extension.

16. Shaulis, N. J., T. D. Jordan, and J. P. Tomkins. 1973. Cultural practices for New York vineyards. N.Y. State Coll. Agr. and Life Sciences Ext. Bul. 805.

17. Teskey, B. J. E., O. A. Brodt, R. Wilcox, and A. Hutchinson. 1965. Pruning and training fruit trees. Ontario (Can.) Dept. of Agr. Pub. No. 392.

18. Tufts, W. P., and R. W. Harris. 1955. Pruning deciduous fruit trees. Calif. Agr. Exp. Sta. Ext. Ser. Cir. 444.

19. Weaver, R. J. 1976. *Grape growing.* New York: John Wiley.

20. Westwood, M. N. 1978. *Temperate zone pomology.* San Francisco: W. H. Freeman & Company Publishers.

21. Williamson, J. F., ed. 1974. *Sunset pruning handbook.* Menlo Park, Calif.: Lane.

22. Winkler, A. J., J. A. Cook, W. M. Kliewer, and L. A. Lider. 1974. *General viticulture,* 2nd. ed. Berkeley: University of California Press, Chs. 12 and 13.

23. Ziegler, L. W., and H. S. Wolfe. 1975. *Citrus growing in Florida.* Gainesville: University of Florida Press.

Flowering and Fruiting in Fruit Crops

In any fruit planting, whether a commercial orchard or a single tree in the garden, the goal is to produce each year a large crop of high-quality fruits. After the trees (or bushes or vines) have reached an age where they are large enough to be productive, the grower expects the plants to bloom and the flowers to set fruits, which grow to a normal size, and develop the flavor and appearance characteristic of that fruit.

There are several steps that are critical to the production of large quantities of high-quality fruits. Briefly, these are:

1. The initiation of flower buds in the summer, followed (in most deciduous fruits) by the development of a physiological resting condition. This is overcome by chilling winter temperatures, and the flower buds continue development early the following spring.
2. Flower opening and pollination in the spring.
3. Fertilization of the egg in the flower, fruit setting, and beginning of fruit development.
4. Removal (thinning)—in some cases—of excessive numbers of fruits that have set.
5. Growth and development of the fruits through the summer.
6. Development of fruit to maturity, ripening, and harvest.

INITIATION OF FLOWER BUDS

Initiation (also called differentiation) involves the change of a vegetative growing point deep inside a bud in the axil of a leaf on a shoot (as in peaches) or on a fruiting spur (as in apples) into miniature flower parts. Initiation does not occur in fruit trees until they have reached a certain size or age (3 years or so for some peaches, and up to 10 or 12 years for some apples) and have accumulated a certain amount of stored nutrients—carbohydrates, nitrogen, and so forth. In some fruit plants this change from a vegetative to a reproductive state is triggered by certain environmental cues—such as the onset of short days in the fall, in the case of strawberries (see Ch. 6) or, in the case of olive trees, exposure to a series of days with diurnally fluctuating warm and chilling temperatures (6). With most deciduous and evergreen fruit species, however, no definite environmental factor is known that triggers the change in a bud from a vegetative to a reproductive (flowering) growing point.

Since fruit species differ in their developmental pattern of flower part formation, it is best to consider these different types separately.

Deciduous Fruit Species

Studies (19) many years ago showed that initiation of flower parts in the buds of apples, pears, peaches, cher-

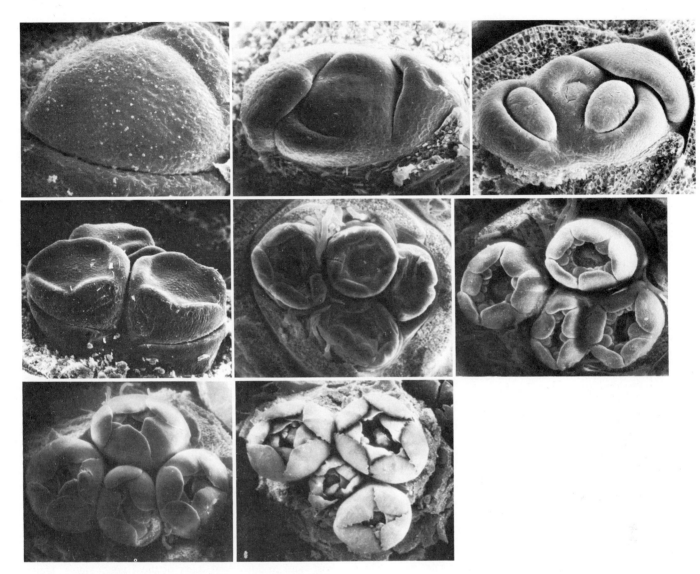

Fig. 14–1 Early stages in the development of flower parts in the buds of sour cherry (*Prunus cerasus*), sampled in Hart, Michigan, as shown by scanning electron micrographs. Sampling dates and magnification are:

Top row (left to right): June 10 (× 266); June 16 (× 293); July 3 (× 233).

Center row (left to right): July 30 (× 213); August 15 (× 120); September 29 (× 110).

Bottom row (left to right): November 4 (× 55); March 27 (× 40).

This shows that the cherry flowers that open in the spring have developed slowly in the buds during the preceding summer and fall. *Source:* D. H. Diaz.

ries, plums, raspberries, blueberries, and so forth begins between late spring and late summer during the year preceding bloom. Flower initiation starts after the new shoots have attained a certain diameter and length and a portion of their leaves have matured. Figure 14–1 shows various stages in flower bud initiation and development in the sour cherry.

The size of the subsequent fruit crop depends upon the number of buds changing from a vegetative to a reproductive state. This, in turn, depends upon the general health and nutritive condition of the fruit plant. A weakly growing fruit tree that has bloomed heavily in the spring and has set a large number of young fruits may be taxing its carbohydrate storage and photosynthetic capacity beyond its limits. Such a tree will not have available nutrients to also form, at the same time, new flower buds for the next year. This situation often occurs, particularly with some plums and apples, and results in alternate bearing—a heavy crop, no crop, a heavy crop, no crop, and so forth.

Trees that were pruned and fertilized heavily the winter before with nitrogen, then copiously irrigated are likely to become strongly vegetative, producing long, succulent shoots. Buds on such shoots are not likely to form flower buds for the next year. At the other extreme, weakly growing, slender shoots, especially on older trees that are low in vigor are not likely to form flower buds, particularly if the leaf area has been reduced by insect or disease attacks, which can also reduce the tree's photosynthetic capacity.

Severe and prolonged drought during the critical period of flower bud initiation in early summer can create water deficits in the trees that interfere with flower-bud formation. Slight water deficits are not likely to be harmful and can even stimulate flower initiation by reducing shoot elongation and causing carbohydrate accumulation from photosynthesis. It is evident that the care and management fruit plants receive strongly influences their productivity.

Once the flower parts are fully formed in the flower buds of deciduous fruit plants, the buds enter a physiological "resting" state in which they will not open even if the plants are subjected to favorable temperature, moisture, and light conditions. The same is true for vegetative buds (those that did not differentiate into flower buds) on the same tree. However, some trees, particularly almonds and plums, will often bloom in late summer or fall if partly defoliated by mites or drought and then wetted by rain or irrigation.

The beginning of this "resting influence" depends upon the species and the general vigor of the plant. The rest influence develops slowly, reaches a peak, then diminishes; the onset of the resting condition can range from midsummer to late fall. In shorter, slow-growing shoots it starts earlier than in the buds of longer, more vigorously growing shoots.

There is some evidence that the physiological resting condition develops because the buds accumulate certain natural growth inhibitors, such as abscisic acid (see p. 139), and lose native growth promoters, such as the gibberellins (20) (see Ch. 6).

The physiological build-up of such growth blockages in buds of deciduous fruit trees—which also oc-

curs in temperate-zone ornamental deciduous trees and shrubs—is an evolutionary development that increases the plants' chances of survival through the winter. Without this self-blocking mechanism for bud growth in the autumn, tender, succulent shoots and tender newly formed flowers developing from the buds would start to grow during the winter and would be killed by subfreezing temperatures. This physiological internal inhibition of growth occurs only in the buds—not in the roots.

Interestingly enough, chilling of the buds (both vegetative and flower) through the winter is needed to reverse the rest influence (4). If the chilling is long enough, the influences blocking bud growth disappear. Then, with the beginning of warm spring temperatures, plus adequate soil moisture, both vegetative and flower buds grow rapidly and vigorously. It is believed that the chilling temperatures may act on the buds to lower the levels of growth inhibitors—such as abscisic acid—and increase the amounts of growth promoters, such as the gibberellins (20, 21).

If the amount of chilling through the winter is marginal, as it can be in regions with normally mild winters, such as the fruit-growing areas of South Africa and the Central Valley of California, bud growth in the spring is erratic. Some flower buds may drop before opening, thus reducing the crop potential, or bud opening and the blooming period may be late and prolonged. **Delayed foliation** refers to this slow development of vegetative buds due to lack of sufficient winter chilling. A marginal winter chilling may not always be a disadvantage as it can lengthen the blooming period, giving bees more time to pollinate the flowers. It can also cause the flower buds to open later and avoid being killed by late spring frosts. In areas with long, cold winters, such as the East, Northeast, and Middle West parts of the United States, the buds always receive sufficient chilling and this problem does not exist.

Much study has gone into determining the amount of chilling required by buds of the different fruit species to overcome the rest influence (4). Table 14–1 summarizes much of this information, which is expressed as the number of hours below 7°C (45°F) required by the various species to overcome the rest influence (4). This is an arbitrary value selected to separate effective and ineffective chilling temperatures. Leaf buds require slightly more chilling than flower buds. Subfreezing temperatures are not necessary. High winter daytime temperatures can be detrimental for deciduous fruits, however, as they tend to counteract chilling night temperatures. Fog or overcast weather during the winter days can be beneficial in obtaining good bud chilling by keeping direct sun rays from the buds, which would raise their temperature higher than the air temperature.

Table 14–1 Amount of Winter Chilling Required to Overcome the Rest Influence in Buds of Various Deciduous Fruit Species

Species	Approximate Number of Hours Below 7°C (45°F)	Equivalent Time if Trees Are Continuously Exposed to Temperatures Below 7°C (45°F) (Approximately)
American plums (*Prunus americana*)	3600 hrs.	22 weeks
European plums (*Prunus domestica*)	800 to 1100	5 to 6½
Japanese plums (*Prunus salicina*)	700 to 1000	4 to 6½
Apple (*Malus pumila*)	1200 to 1500	7 to 9
Pear (*Pyrus communis*)	1000 to 1400	6½ to 9
Sour cherry (*Prunus cerasus*)	1200	7
Sweet cherry (*Prunus avium*)	1100 to 1300	6½ to 8
Peaches and nectarines (*Prunus persica*)	1100 to 1200	6½ to 7
Persian walnuts (*Juglans regia*)	700 ('Payne') 1500 ('Franquette')	4 to 9
Apricots (*Prunus armeniaca*)	700 to 1000	4 to 6½
Blueberries (*Vaccinium corymbosum*)	650 to 850	3 to 5
Almonds (*Prunus amygdalus*)	200 to 300	8 to 13 days
Oriental persimmons (*Diospyros kaki*)	less than 100	4 days
Figs (*Ficus carica*)	none	0

Note: Grapes, both *Vitis vinifera* (Old World) and *Vitis labrusca* (American), require some chilling to overcome the rest influence in the buds, but it is rather light, probably an amount similar to the almond.

There is confusion in the use of the word *dormancy* in relation to buds, and different authorities give it different meanings, some using it to refer to what has been termed here as the rest influence. Dormancy in relation to buds, as used by most horticulturists, refers to the state in which all internal blocks to bud growth have been removed and the only reason the buds are not growing is that environmental conditions, particularly low temperatures, do not permit growth. But with the onset of higher temperatures in the spring, the shoots grow and the flowers open.

Subtropical Fruit Species

Subtropical fruit species (e.g., citrus, avocados, olives) differ in regard to flower bud initiation and development.

The olive tree (*Olea europaea*) grows in parts of the world with a long growing season and minimum winter temperatures higher than about −9.4°C (15°F) (7).

Lower temperatures kill the trees. To produce flowers and fruits, most olive cultivars require chilling temperatures during the winter—but not to overcome the rest influence of previously formed flower buds. A certain amount of chilling days through the winter directly causes the vegetative growing points in the buds along the shoots to change, in late winter, into flower buds. With no winter chilling, all the buds remain vegetative. Olives, for this reason, are not grown for fruit production in such areas as Florida, Hawaii, or Central America, where the winter days are continually warm (7).

In citrus (*Citrus* species)—oranges, lemons, grapefruits, and so forth—chilling weather is not involved either in bud initiation or in overcoming flower bud dormancy. Some of the world's largest citrus plantings are in regions such as central Florida, which have no prolonged cold weather periods. Flower buds on citrus trees grown in subtropical climates are initiated in midwinter, with the first microscopic evidence of flower parts appearing about one month later. In areas with very mild winters and cool summers, certain lemon cultivars tend to bloom throughout the year but most heavily in the spring. In hot, tropical regions near the equator, citrus flower buds form and bloom all during the year unless they are influenced by drought (13).

Tropical Fruit Species

In coffee trees (*Coffee arabica*), flower induction apparently occurs a short time before flower initials appear microscopically in the bud. The flowers open about one month later. The time of flowering depends upon the climate. Following a prolonged dry period, flowers tend to appear about one month after the rains begin. With continuous adequate soil moisture and good growing temperatures, flowering and fruiting occur irregularly throughout the year.

Flower initiation in the mango (*Mangifera indica*) seems to follow an environmental event that slows growth, such as a prolonged cool or dry period. There is some evidence that a hormone originating in the leaves is translocated to the shoot to induce flowering at the site of actively dividing cells in the buds. This occurs, in Florida, in the fall, winter, or early spring (12). It has been shown experimentally that spraying mango trees with a solution of potassium nitrate will cause profuse flowering one to two weeks later, although the mechanisms involved are unknown (2).

Strawberries

The strawberry is an example of a fruit species whose flowering is triggered by a definite, easily defined, environmental factor. Most of the important strawberry cultivars are short-day plants. That is, with the onset of short days (and long nights) in the fall, vegetative growing points in the crown of the plant begin changing to reproductive growing points—or flowers. Such plants then bear a single crop the following spring. When the day length increases during the summer, flowering stops and the plants become vegetative and start producing runners (see p. 111). However, such cultivars also respond to temperature. These short-day plants grown under long days still produce flowers if the temperature is reduced from 21°C (70°F) to 15°C (60°F). This is the situation in the cool, coastal strawberry districts of central California, where very high yields are obtained, since short-day plants grown there produce fruit all summer long, even with long days. Certain strawberry cultivars, however, are not responsive to changing day length. They do not produce runners but continuously form flowers through the long days of summer. These cultivars are termed everbearers.

When the previously formed flower parts start to develop and the flowers open, a new critical stage begins in the production of the crop. The flowers must be adequately pollinated before fruit can set and develop.

Pollination occurs when pollen produced by the anthers, the male parts of the flower, is transferred to the stigma, a female part of the flower (see Fig. 6–15). In fruit species, development of flower parts into a fruit requires a complex series of events. Growth of the seed generally stimulates adjacent parts of the flower to develop into a fruit. (Chapter 6 describes pollination, fertilization, and fruit setting.)

Some fruit species have definite pollination requirements. Successful fruit growers know the needs of their fruit crops and provide for adequate pollination. For example, in both almonds and sweet cherries, the flowers of any given cultivar must be pollinated by those of a particular different cultivar. This means that pollen must originate in the anther of the flower of the pollenizer cultivar and be carried by bees (or other insects or wind) and deposited on the stigma of the flower of the cultivar that is to produce the main crop. In this example, all almond and sweet cherry cultivars would be **self-unfruitful** and certain cultivars would be **inter-unfruitful.**

Some fruit species, such as most apple cultivars, must be cross-pollinated, but the pollen can originate in flowers from any other cultivar of that species. Other fruit species, such as sour cherries, apricots, and oranges, are **self-fruitful.** The pollen can originate in any flower of the same cultivar, either on another tree, another flower on the same tree, or even from the anther of the same flower. These species would be self-pollinated, but pollen coming from flowers of different cultivars in the same species would also cause fruit to set.

Cultivars selected for cross-pollination must have overlapping blooming periods. The pollination requirements of the various fruit species are given in Table 14–2 (5).

Generally, fruit tree flowers are receptive to pollination for only about five days after they open. For fruit to set after pollination takes place, the pollen tube must grow through the style into the egg in the embryo sac (see Figure 6–15).

Temperature is an important factor during all the stages of pollination, pollen tube growth, fertilization, and fruit setting (see p. 128). A temperature range of 15.5°C to 26.5°C (60°F to 80°F) is considered optimum for deciduous fruits. Temperatures much above or below

Table 14–2   Pollination Requirements of Fruit Species

Group 1.   Species Usually Self-Fruitful. Cross-Pollination Not Required.

Apricot (except for a few cultivars; e.g., Perfection, Reeves, and Riland)
Cherry, sour
Citrus—oranges, lemons, mandarins
Coffee
Fig, except for the cultivar Calimyrna; other fig cultivars parthenocarpic (see p. 327)
Currant (most cultivars)
Gooseberry (most cultivars)
Grapes, *Vitis vinifera* (Old World) and *Vitis labrusca* (American) cultivars
Macadamia
Peach (except a few cultivars; e.g., J.H. Hale, which has defective pollen)
Pecan
Persimmon (fruits of Oriental persimmons are parthenocarpic)
Strawberry
Walnut (but requires pollen shedding when stigmas are receptive)

Group 2.   Species Usually Self-Unfruitful. Cross-Pollination Required.

Apple
Almond (certain cultivars are cross-incompatible)
Blueberry
Cherry, sweet (certain cultivars are cross-incompatible)
Kiwifruit (requires both male and female plants in a planting)
Feijoa (except for the cultivar Coolidge)
Filbert
Grape, Muscadine *(Vitis rotundifolia)*
Pistachio (requires both male and female trees in a planting)

Group 3.   Species Whose Cultivars Have Varying Pollination Requirements.

---

a. Cultivars that set a commercial crop without cross-pollination
b. Cultivars that set part of a crop without cross-pollination but whose crop is increased by cross-pollination
c. Cultivars that must be cross-pollinated to set a commercial crop.
Fruit species in this group are pear, European plum, Japanese plum, olive, and chestnut.

An example of the situation found in Group 3 is the pear. The Comice and Hardy cultivars are self-fruitful (class a) and trees can be planted in solid blocks. Yields of Bartlett[a] and Seckle pear (which are in class b) are improved by planting trees of other pollenizing cultivars in the orchard. LeConte and Winter Nelis pears (class c), which are self-unfruitful, must have trees of other pollenizing cultivars in the orchard to set satisfactory commercial crops.

---

[a]In California, however, Bartlett is usually self-fruitful due to parthenocarpy (see p. 327) (6).

---

this range impair good fruit setting. Temperatures much above 26.5°C (80°F) inhibit pollen germination. Pollen grains themselves are quite stable at low temperatures—even far below −18°C (0°F)—but temperatures dropping to −3°C or −2°C (27°F or 28°F) can kill the ovules in the open flowers of most fruit species.

Pollination Terms

Pollination   Transfer of pollen from an anther to a stigma of a flower.

Self-pollination   Transfer of pollen from anther to stigma of the same flower or to the stigma of another flower of the same cultivar.

Cross-pollination   Transfer of pollen from an anther in the flower of one cultivar to the stigma of a flower in a different cultivar.

Self-fruitful cultivar   One that sets and matures a commercial crop of fruit with its own pollen or as a result of parthenocarpy (see p. 327).

Self-unfruitful cultivar   One that is unable to set and mature a commercial crop of fruit with its own pollen or as a result of parthenocarpy.

Cross-compatible cultivar   One cultivar can pollinate another cultivar so that a commercial crop of fruit is set and matured. The reverse may not be true, however.

Cross-incompatible cultivar   One cultivar is unable to pollinate another particular cultivar so that a commercial crop of fruit is set and matured. (It may be able to pollinate other cultivars, however.)

Intercompatible cultivars   Two cultivars can pollinate each other so that commercial crops of fruit are set and matured.

Interincompatible cultivars   Two cultivars are unfruitful when pollinated by each other, although either one may effectively pollinate other cultivars.

Before the nursery trees are purchased for a planting of the fruit species listed in Groups 2 or 3, the grower must determine the pollination requirements of his proposed cultivars (5). Where cross-pollination is required, the planting should consist of the main fruiting cultivar, interspersed with trees of the pollinating cultivar. Quite often the latter trees are set in some arrangement such as every third tree in every third row, or if the main cultivar is one that tends to set fruit heavily, every fourth tree in every fourth row. Where two fruiting cultivars of equal value can be used, harvesting is easier if blocks of four rows of each of the two cultivars alternate. Or, alternate rows of two cultivars may be planted, or two rows of one, alternating with one row of another.

Flower Types (see Ch. 2)

Most fruit species produce perfect flowers; that is, each flower has both the male and female flower parts (see p. 36). Some fruit species, however, are unisexual—male plants have staminate flowers that produce only pollen; female plants have pistillate flowers that develop into the fruit. These species are termed **dioecious.** Examples of dioecious fruit plants are the kiwi fruit (*Actinidia chinensis*), the date palm (*Phoenix dactylifera*), and the pistachio (*Pistachia vera*). Dates are artificially pollinated, with one male tree planted for 40 or 50 female trees. For the kiwi, one male vine is planted for every 9 or 10 females, and in the pistachio, one male is required for every 6 female trees.

Some fruit species such as the papaya (*Carica papaya*) are **bisexual.** That is, there is a dioecious type (separate male and female trees) as well as hermaphroditic trees, which have both male and female flowers. In papaya hermaphroditic flowers have one pistil and about 10 stamens. Yields from these trees can average nearly as much as those from female plants pollinated by nearby male plants. For papaya one male tree for every 10 to 15 female trees is advisable.

A fourth group of species have male flowers and female flowers produced separately on the same tree. These are termed **monoecious.** Examples are the walnut (*Juglans* spp.), filbert (*Corylus avellana*) and chestnut (*Castanea* spp.). The problem with fruit set in such species is that the male flowers may not be shedding pollen at a time when the female flowers are receptive, and vice versa. This is a factor to consider when selecting cultivars because a second cultivar is needed to provide pollen when the pistils are receptive.

A fifth group has yet another type of flower development. In the coconut (*Cocos nucifera*), as an example, the inflorescences produce a globular female flower near the base of the inflorescence branch, with the small pollen-producing male flowers above it.

Insects and Pollination

Fruit species with large, showy flowers generally depend upon insects to transfer pollen. Bees, particularly honeybees, are the most important type of insect involved in pollination. (Some fruit plants, especially those with nonshowy flowers, as the walnut, olive, pecan, and filbert, are wind-pollinated. They generally produce large amounts of very light pollen that is carried considerable distances in the wind onto the stigmas of other flowers.)

Fig. 14–2 To obtain good crops of many fruit species (e.g. sweet cherries, almonds, plums, and apples) cross-pollination between cultivars is necessary. Fruit growers often set hives of bees in their orchards during bloom, as shown here. The bees, working the flowers for nectar, also transport pollen from tree to tree. *Source:* USDA.

In fruit orchards that require cross-pollination, even when the proper mixture of pollenizing cultivars is present, bees must be in the orchard during the blooming period to carry pollen from the flowers of one cultivar to the flowers of the other (Fig. 14–2). For one or two trees in a home garden enough bees are generally present for successful pollination, but an orchardist with a large number of trees that absolutely require cross-pollination will need to have bees brought in. Beekeepers, for a rental fee, will provide the necessary bees during the blooming season.

Honeybees work the flowers to collect pollen and nectar, which they use as food. Since the bees generally stay within about a 100-yard radius of their hives, hives are placed in an orchard no more than 150 to 180 m (500 to 600 ft) apart. Weather conditions affect bee activity. Below about 13°C (55°F) they are inactive; the optimum is from about 18° to 27°C (65°F to 80°F). Winds much above 15 miles per hour keep bees from flying. Continuous rains interfere with bee activity, but intermittent showers do not.

FERTILIZATION AND FRUIT SETTING

Following pollination, the pollen tube grows downward through the style and discharges two sperm cells into the embryo sac (see Ch. 6 for a full discussion of these events). One sperm cell unites with the egg (in the embryo sac) to eventually form the new embryo in the seed. The other sperm cell unites with the two polar nuclei to form the endosperm, a nutritive tissue in the seed. The two integuments and all tissues inside become the seed. Outside tissues, including the ovary and sometimes adjacent accessory structures, become the fruit.

When fertilization (the union of egg and sperm) has taken place, the seed and fruit start to grow. A hormone — an auxin — (see p. 133) produced by the developing seed stimulates the surrounding tissues to continue growth and become a fruit (*11*). However, many of the young fruits, even those containing a fertilized egg (a zygote), soon drop. This abscission period of young fruits may last as long as a month and is sometimes called the June drop. Often so many fruits drop that not enough are left on the tree to produce an acceptable crop. Quite often, though, too few fruits drop, and the tree is so overloaded that expensive fruit thinning procedures are required.

Parthenocarpic fruits are those that develop without fertilization of the egg. In such fruits the fleshy parts are stimulated to grow but they contain no seeds. Examples of parthenocarpic fruits are the navel orange, most fig cultivars, the Oriental persimmon, some bananas, pineapple, and some seedless grapes.

FRUIT THINNING

Very often peach, nectarine, apricot, plum, pear, apple, and olive trees set such heavy crops that the fruits do not grow to a satisfactory size (Fig. 14–3). Limbs may break because of an overload of fruit, and the drain on the nutrients in the tree as the fruit matures may be so great that no flower buds develop for the following year, thus forcing the tree to produce in an alternate-bearing pattern. Even if alternate bearing does not occur, several consecutive years of overcropping can so greatly weaken the trees through depletion of carbohydrate reserves that they may die. Some vines of certain wine grape cultivars die from overcropping. Fruit thinning to remove excessive numbers of fruits is one of the most important cultural procedures for an orchardist or a home gardener.

Sweet and sour cherries, prunes, almonds, walnuts, pistachio, filberts, citrus, avocados, strawberries, and the bushberries normally do not require fruit thinning. The fruit quality of grapes can often be markedly improved by thinning flower clusters, or immature fruit clusters, or parts of clusters (see p. 318).

Fig. 14–3 *Left:* Plum fruits on branch that was properly thinned. Spacing the fruits in this manner allows them to develop properly for fruit size, quality, and early maturity. *Right:* Unthinned fruits. Without thinning the fruits are small, late maturing, and poor quality. In addition, limbs often break.

Thinning should be done as early as practical during the period of fruit growth. Later thinning, while not as effective, is still better than none at all. Actually thinning begins at pruning time when excess fruiting wood is removed.

When the excess fruits are removed, the tree may then utilize all available nutrients to develop the remaining fruits to larger size, as well as to increase root and shoot growth. These, in turn, can absorb more nutrients from the soil to manufacture more carbohydrates through photosynthesis in this and succeeding years.

Amount of Thinning

It may be obvious that a fruit tree is overloaded with young fruits and needs thinning—but how much? It is difficult to give exact figures since a number of factors are involved, such as the cultivar, time of fruit maturity, general vigor and age of the tree, as well as growing conditions. Some general guidelines for fruit thinning can be given, however. Peaches are often thinned to about one fruit every 15 to 20 cm (6 or 8 in) of shoot. Another rule is 20 to 40 leaves per fruit for apples and about 50 leaves per fruit for peaches.

Final fruit size more or less depends upon the leaf-fruit ratio on a branch. The more leaves per fruit, the larger the final fruit size. The total yield at harvest is less for a thinned tree than for an unthinned one. In other words, fruit size is increased at the expense of total yield. This increased size can be highly profitable, however, where a premium is paid for larger-sized fruits.

Thinning to control yields and fruit size is so important in crops such as peaches and apricots that thinning tables have been developed to determine the optimum number of fruits to remain on the tree (15). These consider the distances between trees, fruit size desired (number per pound), and number of tons of fruit desired per acre. For example, with apricots where a 22.4 MT/ha (10 t/ac) harvest is needed and the trees are set on a 7.2 × 7.2 m (24 × 24 ft) planting distance, no more than about 3200 fruits should be left on each tree to attain a fruit size of at least 5 fruits/kg (12/lb). The fruits are actually counted on random sample trees throughout the orchard to determine if the fruit set is uniform.

Fruit thinning is the best way to increase the size of the unthinned fruits remaining on the tree, although flower thinning and bud thinning (by pruning out fruiting shoots) is also effective. Overirrigation or excessive nitrogen fertilization will not increase fruit size; in fact, they can stimulate new shoot growth, using up carbohydrates that could increase fruit size.

Chemical Thinning

The idea of using chemical sprays applied to trees to remove some of the fruits is definitely appealing, and much research has been given to develop thinning sprays. For such fruit species as apples and olives thinning sprays are available and are used commercially. For most stone fruits (peaches, plums, apricots), a completely satisfactory chemical fruit thinner is not available even though considerable research has been done to try to develop one.

Mechanical Thinning

As an improvement over slow and expensive hand thinning, long poles with rubber hose pieces at the end are used to hit fruiting branches and knock off some of the fruit. Hand thinning to remove missed fruiting clusters may follow. Mechanical tree shakers, used in harvesting

operations (see Fig. 12–11), are sometimes used to shake the trees when the fruits are very small to remove a portion of them. Shaking can be satisfactory, but is not very precise and the desirable larger fruits tend to be removed. A light machine shaking, followed by hand thinning or pole knocking, works well in some cases. Hand thinning gives the best results, however, and should be used whenever possible.

FRUIT GROWTH

Initial fruit growth results from the production of new cells (cell division) for about the first 30 days. From then until maturity, fruit growth consists of enlargement of the existing cells. In all of the many types of fruits (see Ch. 2), growth involves the enlargement of fleshy tissues in the flowers plus (sometimes) associated structures. Growth patterns of the fruits of the various fruit species have been given much study, and growth curves through the growing season have been developed, as shown in Figure 6–16 for several typical fruits. Such growth curves are determined by measuring representative tagged fruits on the plant at intervals through the growing period. Usually the diameter is measured. Sometimes representative fruits are detached, and volume or weight measurements taken. The latter method, however, can have a thinning effect and thus give distorted results.

The pome fruits—apples and pears—steadily increase in size throughout the season. The stone fruits—peaches, apricots, plums, and olives—show a period of rapid growth at first, followed by a period of reduced growth, in which the "pit" (or endocarp; see p. 133) hardens. Then there is a final period of rapid growth (the final swell) by cell enlargement. As both types of fruits mature, sugars, water, and substances responsible for the characteristic flavors and aroma move into the cells.

The fruits of different cultivars within a species—peaches, for example—mature at different times during the summer, generally because of different lengths of the second (pit-hardening) period. The first and third periods tend to be about the same length in all cultivars.

Citrus fruits show a growth pattern similar to the pome fruits (see curve for Valencia oranges in Fig. 6–16), starting with a period of rapid growth, then gradually decreasing until the fruit reaches full maturity (13).

Grapes (22) show a growth pattern similar to the stone fruits—an initial period of rapid growth, a second period with a reduced growth rate, then a final period of accelerated growth.

As the fruits grow and enlarge during the summer season, they depend upon carbohydrate, protein, and mineral storage within the tree, plus the absorbing ability of the roots for water and additional mineral nutrients. In addition, the photosynthetic capacity of the tree's leaf area must not only supply carbohydrates for the developing fruits but also replenish the food storage depleted in the very early stages of fruit growth when, in deciduous fruits, photosynthetic capacity is limited. During the summer, with deciduous fruits, while the fruit is growing new flower buds are being differentiated on the shoots or fruiting spurs. This also constitutes a drain on the photosynthetic capacity of the tree. In the evergreen fruit species, such as citrus, avocados, and olives, where food storage in the tree may be less than in deciduous fruits, carbohydrate supplies for the growing fruit depend more upon current photosynthesis.

FRUIT MATURATION, RIPENING, AND SENESCENCE

As fruits near the end of their seasonal growing period, significant changes lead to the end product—a fruit with an attractive color, soft enough to be palatable, sweet and juicy, with an accumulation of the other components that give it its own distinctive flavor and aroma.

The increase in sugars—or soluble solids—can be measured by a refractometer or hydrometer. Decreasing hardness can be measured by various kinds of pressure testers. Changing color, as the masking chlorophyll disappears, can be measured by color charts or color meters. Changing acids can be determined by chemical means or pH meters. All these procedures are used to determine quantitatively when the fruit is ready for harvest. In some states in the United States legal maturity standards demand such measurements to determine when fruit can be harvested. For example, the basis for legal maturity of oranges in California is a ratio of 8:1 for total soluble solids to titratable acidity.

The optimum stage of harvest maturity depends upon the intended use of the fruit. For example, pineapples in Hawaii to be crushed immediately for juice would be allowed to reach maximum maturity and ripeness, with the greatest juice content before picking, but they would not keep long after harvest. But if the pineapples were to be shipped to the U.S. mainland for sale in supermarkets, they would be harvested at a somewhat earlier, firmer stage and ripened on the way to the market.

The home gardener has an advantage over the commercial grower in that he can allow his fruit to reach optimum maturity right on the tree, and be eaten at the optimum degree of ripeness. For commercial production, however, involving perhaps, shipments in containers to great distances, the fruits must be picked firm enough to endure shipping stress and arrive at their destination in an acceptable condition.

All fruits on a tree do not mature at the same time. Those on the top and outside usually are ready to pick before the inside fruit. For the home gardener this is an advantage, as it prolongs the harvest period, but in a commercial operation where often only one picking is possible, some of the fruits are harvested at a less than ideal time.

The various kinds of fruits have different ripening patterns and require different storage procedures. It is essential to understand these in order to know how to harvest and handle the fruits properly. Most fruits reach maturation and ripen on the tree, vine, or bush, at which time they should be picked. If not picked, they enter a stage of senescence and deterioration. However, other fruits are best harvested when they reach maturity on the tree and are ripened to eating condition off the tree.

It must be emphasized that maturing and ripening fruits are living organisms. Their cells are respiring, and many other complex chemical and physical changes are occurring. Some types of fruits are said to be climacteric, and others are nonclimacteric (Fig. 14–4). In the climacteric fruits, the respiration rate of the cells slowly decreases as maturation proceeds. Then there is a rather abrupt reversal with the respiration rate rising as the fruit ripens and finally reaching a peak, the climacteric point. After that, respiration rates decline and a deterioration

process commences, leading to senescence and eventual death of all the fruit cells. In nonclimacteric fruits the respiration rate declines steadily and gradually during ripening, with no particular peak.

Apples, pears, peaches, apricots, plums, mango, banana, papaya, and avocado are examples of climacteric fruits. Most climacteric fruits show the same respiration pattern whether ripening on or off the tree. Avocado, however, shows the typical climacteric respiration pattern only after the fruit has been detached from the tree. Cherries, figs, oranges, lemons, strawberries, pineapples, grapes, and olives are examples of nonclimacteric fruits (*17*).

Refrigeration prolongs fruit life chiefly because the lowered temperatures reduce respiration rates. Controlled atmospheric storage (CA storage)—lowering the oxygen levels from 21 percent (the amount in air) to 1 percent to 3 percent as well as increasing the carbon dioxide to 1 percent to 8 percent instead of the usual 0.03 percent in air—can further lower respiration rates and greatly extend the storage life of fruits (see p. 277). The levels of O_2 and CO_2 that can be tolerated vary with species and cultivar. CA storage procedures have come into widespread use in recent years, especially for apples and to a lesser extent for pears. Apples, although harvested mainly in autumn, are now available in the markets the year round because of CA storage facilities.

Ethylene (C_2H_4) (see Ch. 6), which is given off by fruit tissues, can stimulate fruit ripening. An ancient Chinese custom was to ripen fruit in rooms where incense was being burned. In the earlier days of this century, kerosene stoves were widely used in California to stimulate color development in lemons. Ethylene, plus other gases, is given off by such combustion. Ripe fruits, like bananas and apples, give off ethylene and stimulate the climacteric ripening of other fruits confined in the same containers with them. Experiments in the 1960s (*3*) showed that ethylene is much involved in fruit ripening and is considered a ripening hormone (see p. 138). Applied ethylene is effective in stimulating the ripening of most climacteric and nonclimacteric fruits, although strawberry ripening seems impervious to ethylene stimulation. Gibberellin (see p. 135), a natural plant hormone, is known to counteract ethylene effects in promoting fruit ripening (*18*).

The biochemistry and physiology of fruit maturation, ripening, and senescence have received considerable study, and various theories have been proposed to explain the ripening mechanisms involved. One theory is that, during fruit ripening, new enzymes appear that cause the characteristic changes in the fruit. Energy from respiration provides for the synthesis of the enzyme systems and for their ripening actions. It is believed, too,

Fig. 14–4   Different fruits have different ripening rates as shown in the intensity of the respiratory climacteric. The avocado, which ripens rapidly, shows the most intense climacteric peak, followed by the banana, pear, and apple. *Source:* Adapted from Biale, J. B. 1950. Postharvest physiology and biochemistry of fruits. *Ann. Rev. Plant Physiol.* 1: 183–206.

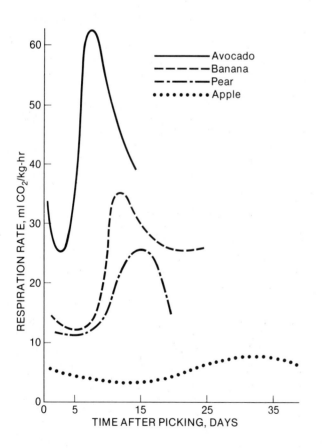

that in addition to the ripening process itself, hormonal (ethylene, gibberellin, and perhaps others) changes may make the fruits responsive to ripening signals.

The various kinds of fruits develop differently to the point where they are ready for harvesting and ripen-

ing. Some examples will show the variability among fruit species and will point out the necessity for understanding these patterns for proper harvesting and fruit ripening (Fig. 14–5).

Table grapes mature and ripen on the vine; the

Fig. 14–5 Steps in commercial harvesting and packing of 'Williams' ('Bartlett') pears. *Upper left:* The fruit is picked in late summer at a certain stage of maturity—when the firmness of the flesh, as measured by a plunger type pressure tester, drops to 7.7 to 10 kg (17 to 23 lb.) *Upper right:* The fruits are run over sorting belts and defective ones removed.
Lower left: Fruits are graded for size and packed into wooden boxes.
Lower right: Boxed fruits are loaded into refrigerated trucks for shipment to market. *Source:* Blue Anchor, Inc.

peak of fruit quality is reached and, ideally, the clusters are picked and consumed at that time. Once the clusters are removed from the vine, deterioration sets in. This can be slowed by placing the clusters in cold storage—0°C (32°F) at 95 percent relative humidity. Such stored grapes can remain edible from one to six months, depending upon the cultivar. In addition, the Old World (but not American) grapes require sulfur dioxide fumigation treatments (initially 1.0 percent SO_2 for 20 minutes followed by 0.25 percent at 7 to 10 day intervals throughout storage) to adequately control decay pathogens.

Apples also develop optimum maturity and ripeness while on the tree, and senescence begins with harvest. This can be delayed by cooling the fruits to 0°C (32°F) within two to three days after harvest and holding them in storage at a relative humidity of 90 to 95 percent. CA storage enables fruits of some apple cultivars to remain in good eating condition for as long as nine months by retarding the respiration rate (see Ch. 12).

Pears ripen differently. On the tree the fruits accumulate the maximum of stored foods and the firmness of the flesh decreases, and they should be picked. But for ideal eating characteristics, the pears should be ripened after harvest in a cool place (15.5°C to 22°C; 60°F to 72°F) at 80 to 85 percent relative humidity. Or, they can be placed directly into cold storage (−0.5°C; 31°F) at 90 percent relative humidity, where they will keep for several months, the length of time depending upon the cultivar. The fruits can be taken from cold storage at any time and moved to ripening rooms held at higher temperatures. Some pear cultivars, like d'Anjou, do not ripen properly unless held previously in cold storage for a time or treated with ethylene gas.

Oranges, grapefruits, and other types of sweet citrus fruits are edible and can be picked from the tree weeks, or even months, before full maturity is reached. This slow maturity contrasts markedly with rapid maturity changes noted in most other fruits. Citrus fruits "store" well on the tree and, in the home garden can be picked when needed, even after optimum maturity. After a time, however, senescence commences and the fruits generally deteriorate (14). Cold storage after harvest can be used for oranges but not at temperatures below 3.5°C to 9°C (38°F to 48°F), depending upon cultivar and growing area.

Avocados, too, can be stored on the tree after full maturity. They are firm when picked but soften and ripen rapidly once the fruits are removed from the tree. Avocados are not adapted to long-term cold storage.

Plums, when harvested for commercial shipments, are too firm for eating. They continue softening and ripening after harvest, however, to an optimum point for eating, after which deterioration commences. Plums are often stored under refrigeration at 0°C (32°F) just after picking to prolong the life of the fruits for two to four weeks.

Papayas, a tropical fruit, are considered mature enough for picking when they start showing a tinge of yellow at the apical end, but they can be left on the tree longer to develop more color and a stronger flavor. If left on the tree too long—till they are more than one-third yellow—they deteriorate faster after harvest. Storage at 10°C (50°F) slows ripening and prolongs edibility.

Fruits at maturity have the approximate chemical composition as shown in the table in the appendix. Note that most fruits are about 80 to 90 percent water, except dates, which are 20 percent. Fruits are low in proteins and fats, except for the avocado, which is 20 percent fat. Fruits are relatively low in carbohydrates, except for dates, and are low in acids, except for lemons, which are 5.5 percent acid. The strawberry and the subtropical fruits (except the avocado) are good sources of calcium. Several of the fruits—strawberry, grapefruit, orange, lemon, mango, and papaya—are particularly good sources of vitamin C. None of the fruits are high in B_1 and B_2 vitamins.

LOW TEMPERATURE FRUIT STORAGE AND CHILLING INJURY

Many fruits, once harvested, can be maintained in a satisfactory condition for long periods of time by placing them in cold storage at a temperature somewhat above the freezing point (0°C; 32°F). Such temperatures are effective because they reduce respiration and ethylene production by the fruits, thereby delaying ripening and senescence. Relative humidity must be kept high, however—80 to 90 percent—during cold storage, or water will be lost and the fruit will shrivel. Water loss is sometimes prevented by packaging fruit in polyethylene-lined containers or by using double-walled, jacketed cold storage rooms.

Fruits of many species, if held for lengthy periods below certain temperatures but above the freezing point, will develop typical damage symptoms, such as internal browning, pitting, scald, dull skin color, or a soggy breakdown. Such fruits become worthless. The lowest safe storage temperatures for a number of fruits are (9, 10):

Apple −0.5°C to 0°C (31°F to 32°F)

Avocado 4.5°C to 7°C (40°F to 45°F)

Banana 11.5°C to 13.5°C (53°F to 56°F)

Cranberry 2°C (36°F)

Grapes −1°C to 0°C (30°F to 32°F)

Grapefruit 10°C (50°F)

Lemon 11°C to 13°C (52°F to 55°F)

Olive 7°C (45°F)

Orange 3.5°C (38°F)

Papaya 7°C (45°F)

Pineapple 7°C to 10°C (45°F to 50°F)

REFERENCES

1. Biale, J. B. 1950. Postharvest physiology and biochemistry of fruits. *Ann. Rev. Plant Physiol.* 1:183–206.

2. Bondad, N. D., and E. Linsangan. 1979. Flowering in mango induced with potassium nitrate. *HortScience* 14(4): 527–28.

3. Burg, S. P., and E. A. Burg. 1962. Role of ethylene in fruit ripening. *Plant Physiol.* 37:179–89.

4. Chandler, W. H., M. H. Kimball, G. L. Philp, W. P. Tufts, and G. P. Weldon. 1937. Chilling requirements for opening of buds on deciduous orchard trees and some other plants in California. Calif. Agr. Exp. Sta. Bul. 611.

5. Griggs, W. H. 1953. Pollination requirements of fruits and nuts. Calif. Agr. Exp. Sta. Ext. Ser. Cir. 424.

6. Griggs, W. H., and B. T. Iwakiri. 1954. Pollination and parthenocarpy in the production of Bartlett pears in California. *Hilgardia* 22(19): 643–78.

7. Hartmann, H. T., and J. E. Whisler. 1975. Flower production in olive as influenced by various chilling temperature regimes. *J. Am. Soc. Hort. Sci.* 100(6):670–74.

8. Leopold, A. C., and P. E. Kriedmann. 1975. *Plant growth and development.* 2nd ed. New York: McGraw-Hill. Ch. 13.

9. Lutz, J. M., and R. E. Hardenburg. 1968. The commercial storage of fruits, vegetables, and florist and nursery stocks. USDA Handbook No. 66.

10. Lyons, J. M. 1973. Chilling injury in plants. *Ann. Rev. Plant Physiol.* 24:445–66.

11. Nitsch, J. P. 1953. The physiology of fruit growth. *Ann. Rev. Plant Physiol.* 4:199.

12. Reece, P. C. 1949. Flower induction in the mango. *Amer. Jour. Bot.* 36:734.

13. Reuther, W., Batchelor, L. D., and H. J. Webber. 1968. *The citrus industry,* vol. 2. Berkeley: University of California Division of Agricultural Sciences.

14. Reuther, W. 1973. Climate and citrus behavior. In *The citrus industry,* vol. 3, ed. W. Reuther. Berkeley: University of California Division of Agricultural Sciences.

15. Ross, N. W. 1974. *Stanislaus orchard book.* Modesto, Calif.: Cooperative Extension, Stanislaus County.

16. Ryall, A. L., and W. T. Pentzer. 1974. *Handling, transportation, and storage of fruits and vegetables, vol. 2, Fruits and tree nuts.* Westport, Conn.: AVI.

17. Sacher, J. A. 1973. Senescence and post harvest physiology. *Ann. Rev. Plant Physiol.* 24:197–224.

18. Scott, P. C., and A. C. Leopold. 1967. Opposing effects of gibberellin and ethylene. *Plant Physiol.* 42:1021–22.

19. Tufts, W. P., and E. B. Morrow. 1925. Fruit bud differentiation in deciduous fruits. *Hilgardia* 1:1–14.

20. Walker, D. R. 1970. Growth substances in dormant fruit buds and seeds. *HortScience* 5(5):414–17.

21. Wareing, P. F., and P. F. Saunders. 1971. Hormones and dormancy. *Ann. Rev. Plant Physiol.* 22:261–88.

22. Winkler, A. J., J. A. Cook, W. M. Kliewer, L. A. Lider. 1974. *General viticulture.* 2nd ed. Berkeley: University of California Press.

Landscape Trees: Deciduous, Broad- & Narrow-Leaved Evergreens

One day you will want to plant a tree. You should choose a species that will grow in the climatic conditions where you live. Undoubtedly you will have the exact site in mind, so the main decisions you have to make are to select the proper species and decide on what function the tree is to fulfill. Trees have many varied shapes and sizes. They have seasonal characteristics such as spring flowers, fall color, persistent leaves (evergreen), or dense foliage that provides shade. Some even have more than one desirable characteristic; for example, providing both shade and edible fruits, as do the English walnut and the pecan. Unfortunately these two lovely trees cannot be grown in all temperate-zone regions because they are hardy only in mild-winter areas (Table 15–1). If you live in the northernmost regions of the United States, you may have to settle for a hardy tree such as the Siberian crabapple to have a garden tree that also bears fruit. You must first choose a species that will survive the conditions of the region; perhaps the most important climatic condition is the severity of the winters.

A partial tree selection is given in Tables 15–1, 15–2, and 15–3, which list the deciduous, broad-leaved, and narrow-leaved evergreens. It is obvious that the selections based on the hardiness zones are more numerous in the southern states of the United States than in the north. Compare these tables with the hardiness zone map (p. 226) to make your choice.

Once you know the possible species, you have to choose the shape and ultimate size of the tree you wish to plant. Size is an important consideration because of the possible harm a tree can cause as it grows in the space that is allotted to it. It can branch out in such a way that it will interfere with your neighbor's or your own garden space or view or cut off light penetration to your garden. Maples, which generally grow very slowly, cast a dense shade under which very few plants can grow. The eucalyptus, poplar, mulberry, or plane tree all grow rapidly and can cause damage to sewers, overhead electrical wires, gutters, and roof tops. It is important to choose a species that will stay within the bounds available to the homeowner.

The tree's size and shape characteristics can be maintained or altered by pruning the tops or the roots. Pruning requires more effort than allowing the trees to grow naturally. Perhaps the personal satisfaction of training a tree to grow as you desire may be worth the added effort.

Some trees cast a slight shade without shading out certain grass species; red fescue grass will dominate in a lawn under such conditions (Ch. 21). You can have both shade and a lawn with the proper selection of tree and grass. Other trees sprawl and grow so large that they can only be used if there is a woodlot near the house in which they can develop fully. The best garden trees do not grow too rapidly or too large and fulfill a certain function in the garden over a long period. Some species rarely require pruning. Certain cities require a permit to plant a street tree in front of your own home and require that certain kinds be planted. Street trees are chosen primarily for the lowest maintenance cost to the municipality while still fulfilling the function of beauty or shade. Some trees are useful for producing a screen or windbreak; examples are

Table 15-1 Some Common Deciduous Trees of the United States and Southern Canada with Temperature Tolerances Indicated by Zones of Plant Hardiness Together with Some Characteristics and Possible Landscape Uses

Common and Latin Names	Plant Hardiness Zones[a]	Approximate Mature Height, Meters (Feet)	Shape of Crown	Growth Rate	Distinct Feature	Possible Landscape Uses
Alder, gray *Alnus incana* (L.) Moench.	3–8	15+ (50+)	Oval	Fast	Hardy	Screen
Alder, white *Alnus rhombifolia* Nutt.	5–9	15+ (50+)	Oval	Fast	Winter fruit	Along creek
Ash, Arizona *Fraxinus velutina* Torr.	8–10	12+ (40+)	Pyramidal	Fast	Withstands stress	Shade
Ash, white *Fraxinus americana* L.	4–9	15+ (50+)	Rounded	Fast	Fall color	Shade
Aspen, quaking *Populus tremuloides* Michx.	3–8	12 (40)	Rounded	Fast	Rustling leaves	Woodlot, shade
Beech, European *Fagus sylvatica* L.	5–10	15+ (50+)	Oval	Slow	Shiny	Shade, woodlot
Birch, canoe *Betula papyrifera* Marsh.	3–8	15+ (50+)	Oval	Fast	White bark	Woodlot, garden
Birch, European white *Betula pendula* Roth. (B. verrucosa)	3–9	12 (40)	Pyramidal (see photo)	Medium	Graceful	Groups in lawn
Boxelder *Acer Negundo* L.	3–9	12 (40)	Rounded	Fast	Hardy	Screen, shade
Carolina silver bell *Halesia carolina* L.	5–9	9 (30)	Oval (Fig. 15–13)	Medium	Flowers	Garden
Chestnut, Chinese *Castanea mollisima* Blume.	5–9	15+ (50+)	Rounded	Fast	Fruit	Shade, garden
Crabapple, Siberian *Malus baccata* (L.) Borkh.	3–8	12 (40)	Rounded	Medium	Flowers, fruit	Garden
Crape myrtle *Lagerstroemia indica* L.	7–9	9 (30)	Oval	Slow	Summer flowering	Garden, street tree
Cucumber tree *Magnolia acuminata* L.	5–10	15+ (50+)	Pyramidal	Fast	Flowers	Garden, shade
Dawn redwood *Metasequoia glystostroboides* H.H. Hu and Cheng.	6–10	15+ (50+)	Pyramidal	Fast	Foliage	Woodlot
Dogwood, flowering *Cornus florida* L.	5–9	12 (40)	Oval (see photo)	Medium	Flowers fall color	Garden, woodlot
Dogwood, Pacific *Cornus nuttallii* Audub.	7–9	12 (40+)	Oval	Medium	Flowers, fall color	Garden, woodlot
Elm, American *Ulmus americana* L.	3–9	15+ (50+)	Oval	Fast	Shape	Street tree
Elm, Chinese *Ulmus parvifolia* Jacq.	6–10	15+ (50+)	Rounded	Fast	Shape	Shade, street tree
Fig, common *Ficus carica* L.	7–10	12 (40)	Rounded	Fast	Fruit	Garden
Hackberry, common *Celtis occidentalis* L.	3–9	15+ (50+)	Rounded (see photo)	Slow	Fall color	Street tree
Hawthorne, downy *Crataegus mollis* (Torr. & A. Gray) Scheele	5–9	9 (30)	Rounded	Medium	Fruit	Garden, woodlot
Hawthorne, Lavalle *Crataegus × lavallei* Herincq.	5–9	6 (20)	Oval	Medium	Fruit	Garden
Honeylocust, thornless *Gleditsia triacanthos* var. *inermis* Willd.	5–9	15+ (50+)	Rounded	Fast	Fall color	Street tree, garden (see photo)
Horsechestnut *Aesculus Hippocastanum* L.	5–7	15+ (50+)	Rounded	Medium	Foliage	Shade, woodlot

[a]See hardiness zone map on page 226. Plants can be grown in the zones indicated (e.g., 3–8).

Table 15–1 (continued)

Common and Latin Names	Plant Hardiness Zones[a]	Approximate Mature Height, Meters (Feet)	Shape of Crown	Growth Rate	Distinct Feature	Possible Landscape Uses
Jacaranda *Jacaranda acutifolia* Humb and Bonpl.	9–10	12 (40)	Rounded	Medium	Graceful, flowers	Garden, street tree
Jerusalem Thorn *Parksonia aculeata* L.	8–10	9 (30)	Oval	Fast	Withstands stress	Shade, patio
Larch, European *Larix decidua* Mill.	3–8	15+ (50+)	Pyramidal	Variable	Foliage	Garden
Larch, Japanese *Larix kaempferi* (Lamb.) Carriere *(L. leptolepis)*	5–8	15+ (50+)	Pyramidal	Fast	Foliage	Garden
Little-leaved linden *Tilia cordata* Mill.	3–9	15 (50)	Pyramidal	Medium	Shape	Shade, street tree
Magnolia, saucer *Magnolia × soulangiana* Soul-Bod.	5–10	8 (25)	Rounded	Slow	Spring flowers	Garden, shade, street tree
Maidenhair tree *Gingko biloba* L.	5–9	15+ (50+)	Pyramidal	Variable	Fall color	Street tree, garden
Maple, Japanese *Acer palmatum* Thunb.	6–9	6 (20)	Rounded	Slow	Leaf color, size	Garden, patio
Maple, Norway *Acer platinoides* L.	4–9	15+ (50+)	Rounded (see photo)	Fast	Shape	Shade, street type
Maple, silver *Acer saccharinum* L.	4–9	15+ (50+)	Rounded	Fast	Fall color	Shade
Maple, sugar *Acer saccharum* Marsh.	4–9	15+ (50+)	Oval	Medium	Fall color, sugar	Shade, woodlot
Mountain ash *Sorbus americana* Marsh.	3–6	9 (30)	Rounded	Medium	Fall color, fruit	Garden, street tree
Mulberry, fruitless *Morus alba* L.	4–10	11 (35)	Rounded	Fast	Fall color	Shade, street tree
Oak, red *Quercus rubra* L.	4–9	15+ (50+)	Rounded	Fast	Fall color, shape	Shade, woodlot
Oak, white *Quercus alba* L.	4–9	15+ (50+)	Rounded	Medium	Shape	Shade, woodlot
Pear, Bradford *Pyrus Calleryana* 'Bradford' Decne.	5–9	9 (30)	Pyramidal	Slow	Flowers, fruit	Garden, street tree
Pecan *Carya illinoinensis* (Wangenh.) C. Koch.	6–9	12 (40)	Rounded	Slow	Fruit	Shade, woodlot

Dogwood (*Cornus florida*)

Honeylocust (*Gleditisia triacanthos* var. *inermis*)

Table 15–1 (continued)

Common and Latin Names	Plant Hardiness Zones[a]	Approximate Mature Height, Meters (Feet)	Shape of Crown	Growth Rate	Distinct Feature	Possible Landscape Uses
Persimmon *Diospyros virginiana* L.	5–9	12+ (40+)	Pyramidal	Medium	Fruit, fall color	Garden, woodlot
Pistache, Chinese *Pistacia chinensis* Bunge.	6–10	15+ (50+)	Rounded (see photo)	Fast	Fall color	Shade, street tree
Plane tree (sycamore) *Platanus × acerifolia* (Ait.) Willd.	5–10	15+ (50+)	Rounded	Fast	Bark, fruit	Shade, street tree
Plum, purple leaf *Prunus cerasifera* 'Atropurpurea' J.F. Ehrh.	4–9	9 (30)	Rounded	Fast	Leaf color, shape	Garden, street tree
Poplar, Lombardy *Populus nigra* 'Italica' Muenchh.	2–10	15+ (50+)	Columnar (see photo)	Fast	Fall color, shape	Windbreak, garden
Redbud, California *Cercis occidentalis* Torr.	6–9	6 (20)	Rounded	Medium	Flowers	Garden, woodlot
Redbud, eastern *Cercis canadensis* L.	5–9	12 (40)	Rounded	Medium	Withstands stress	Windbreak
Russian olive *Elaeagnus angustifolia* L.	3–9	6 (20)	Rounded	Medium	Withstands stress	Windbreak
Service berry, downy *Amelanchier canadensis* (L.) Medic.	4–8	15+ (50+)	Oval	Fast	Flowers, fruit	Garden, woodlot
Silk tree *Albizia Julibrissin* Durazz.	7–10	12 (40)	Spreading (see photo)	Fast	Graceful, flowers	Garden
Sumac, staghorn *Rhus typhina* L.	3–9	12 (40)	Rounded	Fast	Fall color	Garden, woodlot
Sweet gum, American *Liquidambar styraciflua* L.	6–10	15+ (50+)	Pyramidal	Fast	Fall color	Garden, street tree
Tulip tree *Liriodendron Tulipifera* L.	5–9	15+ (50+)	Pyramidal	Fast	Flowers	Garden, street tree
Walnut, English or Persian *Juglans regia* L.	8–9	15+ (50+)	Rounded	Fast	Fruit	Large garden, woodlot
Willow, weeping (golden) *Salix alba* var. *trista* (Ser.) Gaudin	3–10	15+ (50+)	Weeping	Fast	Leaf color, graceful	Garden, along creek
Willow, weeping (Wisconsin) *Salix × blanda* Anderss.	5–10	12 (40)	Weeping (see photo)	Fast	Shape, graceful	Garden, along creek
Zelkova, Japanese *Zelkova serrata* (Thunb.) Mak.	6–9	15+ (50+)	Rounded	Medium	Shape	Shade, street tree

Chinese pistache (*Pistacia chinensis*)

Weeping willow (*Salix alba var. trista*)

Table 15–2 Selected Broad-Leaved Evergreen Trees of the United States and Southern Canada with Temperature Tolerances Indicated by Plant Hardiness Zones Together with Some Characteristics and Possible Landscape Uses

Common and Latin Names	Plant Hardiness Zones[a]	Approximate Mature Height, Meters (Feet)	Shape of Crown	Growth Rate	Distinct Feature	Possible Landscape Uses
Acacia, Bailey *Acacia Baileyana* F.J. Muell.	9–10	9 (30)	Rounded	Fast	Flowers	Garden, tolerates poor soils
Ash, evergreen *Fraxinus Uhdei* (Wenz) Lingelsh.	9–10	15+ (50+)	Rounded	Fast	Glossy leaves	Street tree, garden
Avocado *Persea gratissima* C.F. Gaertn. (*P. americana*)	9–10	9 (30)	Rounded	Medium	Fruit	Garden, grove
Bottlebrush, lemon *Callistomen citrinus* (Curtis) Stapf.	10	6 (25)	Rounded	Fast	Flowers	Garden, street tree
Buckthorn, Italian *Rhamnus Alaternus* L.	7–10	8 (20)	Rounded	Fast	Shape	Hedge, windbreak
California bay (laurel) *Umbellularia californica* (Hook and Arn) Nutt.	7–10	15+ (50+)	Rounded	Slow	Leaves	Garden, woodlot
California pepper tree *Schinus Molle* L.	9–10	12 (40)	Weeping	Fast	Shape	Garden, street tree
Camphor tree *Cinnamomum camphora* L.	9–10	15+ (50+)	Rounded (see photo)	Variable	Shiny leaves	Garden, shade
Eucalyptus, silver dollar *Eucalyptus polyanthemos* Schauer.	9–10	15+ (50+)	Columnar	Fast	Gray foliage	Garden, woodlot
Gum, red-flowered *Eucalyptus ficifolia* F.J. Muell.	10	11 (35)	Rounded	Medium	Flowers	Street tree
Holly, American *Ilex opaca* Ait.	6–9	12 (40)	Pyramidal	Slow	Fruit	Garden
Holly, English *Ilex Aquifolium* L.	6–9	12 (40)	Oval	Slow	Foliage, fruit	Garden, patio
Iron bark, pink *Eucalyptus sideroxylon* A. Cunn. ex Woolls.	9–10	15+ (50+)	Weeping	Fast	Shape	Woodlot, windbreak
Laurel, English *Prunus Laurocerasus* L.	7–10	9 (30)	Rounded	Fast	Shiny leaves	Garden, hedge
Laurel (sweet bay) *Laurus nobilis* L.	8–10	9 (30)	Oval	Slow	Foliage	Garden, street tree, hedge
Madrone *Arbutus menziesii* Pursh.	6–9	15+ (50+)	Oval	Variable	Bark	Woodlot, garden
Magnolia, southern *Magnolia grandiflora* L.	7–10	15+ (50+)	Oval	Medium	Foliage, flowers	Garden, street tree
Melaleuca, pink *Melaleuca nesophylla* F.J. Muell.	9–10	6 (20)	Irregular	Fast	Bark	Garden
Oak, Cork *Quercus Suber* L.	8–10	15+ (50+)	Rounded	Medium	Bark	Street tree
Oak, southern live *Quercus virginiana* Mill.	8–10	15+ (50+)	Spreading	Slow	Shape	Woodlot
Olive *Olea europaea* L.	9–10	8 (25)	Rounded	Slow	Gray foliage	Garden, patio
Orange *Citrus sinensis* (L.) Osbeck.	9–10	8 (25)	Rounded	Medium	Fruit, foliage	Garden, grove
Palm, Canary Island *Phoenix canariensis* Hort. ex. Chabaud.	9–10	15+ (50+)	Rounded	Variable	Leaves	Street tree

[a]See hardiness zone map on page 226. Plants can be grown in zones indicated (e.g., 9–10).

Table 15–2 (continued)

Common and Latin Names	Plant Hardiness Zones[a]	Approximate Mature Height, Meters (Feet)	Shape of Crown	Growth Rate	Distinct Feature	Possible Landscape Uses
Palm, Coconut *Cocos nucifera* L.	10	15+ (50+)	Rounded	Variable	Leaves, fruit	Garden, street tree
Palm, Washington *Washingtonia filifera* (L. Linden) H. Wendl.	9–10	15+ (50+)	Rounded	Variable	Leaves	Street tree
Pear, evergreen *Pyrus kawakamii* Hayata	8–10	9 (30)	Rounded	Medium	Shape	Garden
Photinia, Chinese *Photinia serrulata* Lindl.	7–10	11 (35)	Rounded	Medium	Shiny leaves	Garden, windbreak
She-oak, drooping *Casurina stricta* Ait.	9–10	9 (30)	Oval	Fast	Drooping foliage	Woodlot, street tree
Weeping fig *Ficus benjamina* L.	10	6 (20)	Weeping	Medium	Graceful	Garden, patio

Norway maple (*Acer platinoides*)

Hackberry (*Celtis occidentalis*)

Camphor tree (*Cinnamomum camphora*)

Silk tree (*Albizia Julibrissin*)

Table 15-3   Selected Narrow-Leaved Evergreen Trees of the United States and Southern Canada with Temperature Tolerances Indicated by Plant Hardiness Zones Together with Some Characteristics and Possible Landscape Uses

Common and Latin Names	Plant Hardiness Zones[a]	Approximate Mature Height, Meters (Feet)	Shape of Crown	Growth Rate	Distinct Feature	Possible Landscape Uses
Arborvitae, oriental *Platycladus orientalis* (L.) Franco *(Thuja orientalis)*	7–10	12 (40)	Pyramidal	Medium	Shape	Garden, hedge
Cedar, Deodar *Cedrus deodara* (D. Don) G. Don.	7–10	15+ (50+)	Pyramidal (see photo)	Fast	Shape	Garden
Cedar, eastern red *Juniperus virginiana* L.	3–9	15 (50)	Pyramidal	Slow	Shape	Garden, woodlot
Cypress, Italian *Cupressus sempervirens* L.	8–10	15+ (50+)	Columnar	Medium	Shape	Garden, windbreak
Cypress, Monterey *Cupressus macrocarpa* Hartweg.	8–10	15+ (50+)	Spreading	Medium	Shape	Garden, windbreak
Cypress, smooth Arizona *Cupressus glabra* Sudw.	7–10	12 (40)	Pyramidal	Fast	Shape	Garden, windbreak
Fir, Douglas *Pseudotsuga menziesii* (Mirb.) Franco	4–9	15+ (50+)	Pyramidal	Fast	Shape	Woodlot
Fir, Veitch *Abies veitchii* Lindl.	4–7	15+ (50+)	Pyramidal	Fast	Shape	Garden, woodlot
Fir, white *Abies concolor* (Gord.) Lindl.	4–8	15+ (50+)	Pyramidal	Medium	Shape	Garden, woodlot
Pine, eastern white *Pinus Strobus* L.	4–8	15+ (50+)	Irregular	Fast	Shape	Woodlot
Pine, Canary Island *Pinus canariensis* Sweet ex K. Spreng.	9–10	15+ (50+)	Pyramidal	Fast	Shape	Windbreak, shade
Pine, umbrella *Pinus pinea* L.	8	15+ (50+)	Rounded (see photo)	Medium	Shape	Street tree

[a] See hardiness zone map on page 226. Plants can grow in zones indicated (e.g., 7–10).

Deodar cedar (*Cedrus deodara*)

Umbrella pine (*Pinus pinea*)

Table 15-3 (continued)

Common and Latin Names	Plant Hardiness Zones[a]	Approximate Mature Height, Meters (Feet)	Shape of Crown	Growth Rate	Distinct Feature	Possible Landscape Uses
Pine, Japanese black *Pinus thunbergiana* Franco	5–9	15+ (50+)	Irregular	Medium	Shape	Garden
Pine, Norfolk Island *Araucaria heterophylla* (Salisb) Franco	10	15+ (50+)	Pyramidal	Medium	Shape	Garden
Pine, Scots *Pinus sylvestris* L.	3–8	15+ (50+)	Pyramidal	Medium	Shape	Garden
Pine, Swiss stone *Pinus cembra* L.	4–8	15 (50)	Rounded	Slow	Shape	Garden
Pine, yew *Podocarpus macrophylla* (Thunb.) D. Don.	7–10	15 (50)	Irregular	Slow	Graceful	Garden
Redwood, coast *Sequoia sempervirens* (D. Don.) Endl.	8–10	15+ (50+)	Pyramidal	Fast	Shape	Woodlot, large garden, shade
Spruce, Colorado *Picea pungens* Engelm.	3–8	15+ (50+)	Pyramidal	Slow	Shape, color	Garden
Spruce, Norway *Picea abies* (L.) Karst.	3–8	15+ (50+)	Pyramidal	Fast	Shape	Garden, woodlot
Yew, Irish *Taxus baccata* L. 'Fastigiata'	6–8	8 (25)	Columnar	Medium	Shape, fruit	Garden, hedge
Yew, Japanese *Taxus cuspidata* Siebold. and Zucc.	4–7	8 (25)	Columnar	Slow	Shape	Garden, hedge

Lombardy poplar (*Populus nigra*)

Birch (*Betula pendula*)

boxelder, Russian olive, *Eucalyptus* spp. and Monterey cypress.

Trees are usually planted for the pleasure they give to the gardener or homeowner. One such pleasure is spring flowering. The experience of seeing a flowering dogwood, flowering crabapple, 'Bradford' pear, magnolia, or redbud at its prime is exciting. Flowering comes early or late in the spring season depending on the location, but one can almost count on it every year as the appearance of the first robin or crocus in the garden. Some of the flowers develop into fruit, which may also attract birds in the winter.

Some trees produce edible fruits and nuts, which may be harvested for home consumption. The pecan, walnut, orange, and crabapple are excellent garden trees with the bonus of fruit. The possibility of planting shade trees that produce fruits for canning or eating at their peak of ripeness (e.g., peaches, apricots, plums, cherries, apples, etc.) should also be considered. These are candidates for the garden in certain zones, and most are discussed in Chapters 29, 30, and 31. Some trees such as the mulberry, maidenhair (*Gingko*), and the olive, produce undesirable fruits, that drop and cover the ground. Male gingko trees that bear no fruit can be purchased at the nursery. Olive fruits can be discouraged from setting by spraying the trees at bloom with naphthaleneacetic acid (Ch. 6) to prevent flower settings. Also, a fruitless olive cultivar, Swan Hill, is available. Fruitless mulberry trees are also widely planted.

As the summer draws to a close, certain trees produce fall colors beyond imagination. The maples, oaks, ashes, poplars, dogwoods, pistachios, liquidambars, aspens, and the maidenhair tree are splendid examples. People travel long distances to New England and the Rockies in the United States to enjoy fall coloration. Trees with these characteristics are easily incorporated into the home landscape with the proper selection (Table 15–1). Some kinds of trees form excellent silhouettes against the snow in the winter; examples are the alder, beech, birch, plane tree, mountain ash, and many conifers.

ENVIRONMENTAL FACTORS TO BE CONSIDERED IN SELECTING SUITABLE TREE SPECIES

Temperature

The hardiness map (p. 226) and the zones of tree hardiness given in Tables 15–1, 15–2, and 15–3 are guides to selecting a tree for a given region. Small climatic pockets

or islands within these broad zones protected by hills or large bodies of water permit the planting of trees less hardy than could be used otherwise (see Ch. 10). On the other hand, one should consult the closest botanical garden, the local nursery dealer, knowledgeable neighbors, or the local weather bureau to find out the lowest temperatures recorded in that area. This additional information will help determine whether the chosen species can survive an extremely cold winter. Will the species you have chosen survive an unusually severe winter? If the odds are not good that it will, it is better to select a hardier species. Look at what is planted in the neighborhood and see which large trees have survived. However, this is not always a true test of hardiness because a severe winter may only occur once in 20 or 30 years.

Spring frosts are also a problem. Almond, apricot, and some peach cultivars bloom early and the flowers may be injured in spring, eliminating the fruit crop. These late frosts prohibit growing such fruits commercially (Ch. 10). Again, the local nursery dealer usually knows which fruits are susceptible to spring frost damage.

Certain locations in the country have winters that are too warm for proper chilling of some fruit species, preventing them from blooming or leafing out properly in the spring (see Chs. 14 and 29).

Light

Most trees require full sunlight to establish themselves and grow well, although the maples and beeches may tolerate semishady locations. The light intensity on a sunny day is much greater than needed for growth, but in a dense crown or tree canopy, the light diminishes quickly toward the center. In general, a sunny location should be chosen for most tree sites. Young trees receiving inadequate light usually become spindly and weak and cannot compete with larger trees.

Some trees are affected by dim light from street lamps. Light shining all night, even though it is of low intensity, stimulates vegetative growth if the temperature is adequate. This stimulation delays the onset of fall dormancy and the branches affected by the light can be subject to winter killing. Some maples, birches, elms, dogwoods, and sycamores are affected by street lighting.

Moisture

The amount of rainfall is an important consideration in tree selection. In locations that lack summer rainfall, one should select a species that can adapt to moisture stress. Where rainfall is not plentiful, one should be prepared to irrigate as needed to supplement rainfall. Native plants from regions of low rainfall are excellent candidates for dry-summer situations.

Wind

Wind affects the transpiration of leaves, and therefore more water is required to sustain growth. A gentle breeze up to about 6 km (4 mi) per hour helps replenish CO_2 around the leaves, but a prolonged and higher velocity can deform the tree. Recent experimental work at the University of California has shown that excess movement of tree tops reduces shoot growth up to 25 percent. Some protection from high winds is required to establish the trees.

CATEGORIES OF NURSERY TREES AVAILABLE FOR PLANTING

The available choices of nursery trees for landscape planting are a bare-root tree, a balled and burlapped tree (B&B), or a container-grown tree.

Bare-Root Trees

Most bare-root nursery trees are deciduous species with trunks less than 5 cm (2 in) in diameter and with the soil removed. Conifer seedlings up to three years old are also often sold as bare-root trees. Both kinds are grown in the field at a wholesale nursery, and are dug in late fall or early winter, when they become dormant and the leaves fall (for deciduous trees). After digging, the roots are pruned back and the trees may be packed in bundles with their roots in a plastic bag containing moist sawdust. Some trees are sold in bulk lots and the roots are kept moist by plunging the roots in sawdust at the local nursery. Good examples of bare-root plants are budded fruit trees (Ch. 29), which are sold for winter or early spring transplanting. Many deciduous landscape trees are also sold this way in winter. Be sure that the buds are alive and the root system has not dried out.

Balled and Burlapped Trees

B&B trees are evergreen, both narrow- and broad-leaved, grown in the nursery field until they reach a size suitable for sale. The soil is cut away from the base of the plant at a prescribed distance from the trunk and a ball is formed (Fig. 15–1). The soil ball is wrapped securely in burlap so that it can be removed from the ground and transplanted in another location. A plastic bag is often used to overwrap the burlap to avoid desiccation. B&B trees are available throughout the year. This common method of digging and transplanting evergreen trees, is being replaced by container-grown trees. Deciduous trees with a trunk diameter greater than 5 cm (2 in) are usually balled and burlapped. See that the root ball is not broken and the top is not dried out or dying.

Fig. 15–1   Balled and burlapped trees, showing how the root ball is tied to keep it intact. The ball and the tree should be handled carefully through the final stages of transplanting. If the ball is dropped, the soil will break away from the roots. The tree should be protected from the wind and direct sun to prevent desiccation (*left*). The soil ball should be kept moist.

Some trees are grown to a suitable size in plastic or metal containers from small cuttings or seedlings. They may remain in the nursery for a year or more, depending on the rapidity of growth. This method of growing is best suited to locations with mild winters because the roots in containers must be kept from freezing. In severe-winter areas the plants are usually protected by placing them inside small quonset-type polyethylene-covered greenhouses, which may or may not be heated.

Container-grown nursery stock offers several advantages:

1. There is a wide selection of plant material.
2. The nursery stock is available throughout the year.
3. The plants are remarkably uniform.
4. The plants are economically grown and can be transported long distances at reasonable prices.

Container-grown plants do have some disadvantages, though. A well-grown plant with a large top may wilt severely in a small container if not irrigated frequently at the retail nursery. If the plant is grown too long in the container, the root system becomes deformed and there may be difficulty in establishing the plant in the soil without proper root pruning (see Ch. 13).

WHAT TO LOOK FOR WHEN PURCHASING CONTAINER-GROWN TREES

1. *Avoid plants with circling or kinking roots* (Fig. 15–2). These roots are sometimes seen near the top of the soil. Such roots can be troublesome in later years if they are not pruned properly before planting, because they may continue to circle and eventually girdle the trunk (Fig. 15–3) or the tree can be blown over in winds (Fig. 15–4). If such a plant is purchased (which is not recommended), portions of the root system can be cut to discourage the circling habit of the roots. As much as 50 percent of the roots can be removed without affecting tree growth in some species. Root pruning stimulates new roots to form after transplanting. Care should be taken after root pruning and planting to keep the soil moist until the plant is well established with an abundance of new roots (Fig. 15–5).

2. *Look at the size of the top.* The largest tree top is not always the best because of the small and confined root system. A large top may indicate that the tree has been in the nursery too long or that it should have been shifted to a larger container. A large top to root ratio is not good because the large leaf area usually transpires

Fig. 15–2 Roots that have circled in the container continue to enlarge after planting, as has happened with this *Camellia japonica*. The roots are nearly the size of the trunk, which is 4 cm (2 in) in diameter near the base. This problem is avoided by cutting the roots to discourage circling at the time the tree is planted.

Fig. 15–3 Nursery trees held in containers too long will develop an undesirable circling root system. *Source:* Hartmann, H. T., and D. E. Kester. 1975. *Plant propagation: principles and practices.* 3rd ed. Englewood Cliffs, N.J.: Prentice-Hall.

Fig. 15–4 This tree with a weak root system was toppled in a wind storm. It was planted directly from the container without pruning or disturbing the roots. Before a tree is planted from a container, the circling roots should be cut to stimulate branching outward from the root ball.

Fig. 15–5 Correct way to plant a container-grown tree. *Source:* Univ. of Calif. Coop. Ext. Ser.

water faster than the roots can supply it, making top pruning necessary.

3. *Look at the taper of the trunk.* It should be larger at the soil level than it is a few feet above the base. A good taper indicates a strong trunk whereas a tree with a trunk with little or no taper may not be able to stand upright after the stake is removed (Fig. 15–6). Untapered trunks are usually seen on trees that are tightly staked. This staked trunk is unable to develop reaction wood (xylem), which is formed by continual gentle trunk movements in the breeze.

4. *Look for a good branching habit.* The branches should be well distributed, and some small branches should still be attached low on the trunk (Fig. 15–7). The lower branches shade the trunk after transplanting and also supply food to the lower trunk area. The crown (top branches) should be open to reduce wind resistance after transplanting. However, a large top can be pruned to a suitable size after transplanting.

5. *Look for a vigorous tree, free of disease, insect damage, or trunk injury.* Vigor is probably the most difficult factor to assess, requiring considerable experience.

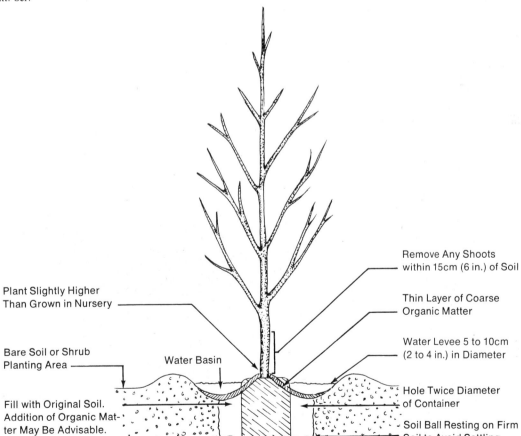

Plant Slightly Higher Than Grown in Nursery

Bare Soil or Shrub Planting Area

Fill with Original Soil. Addition of Organic Matter May Be Advisable.

Water Basin

Remove Any Shoots within 15cm (6 in.) of Soil

Thin Layer of Coarse Organic Matter

Water Levee 5 to 10cm (2 to 4 in.) in Diameter

Hole Twice Diameter of Container

Soil Ball Resting on Firm Soil to Avoid Settling

345

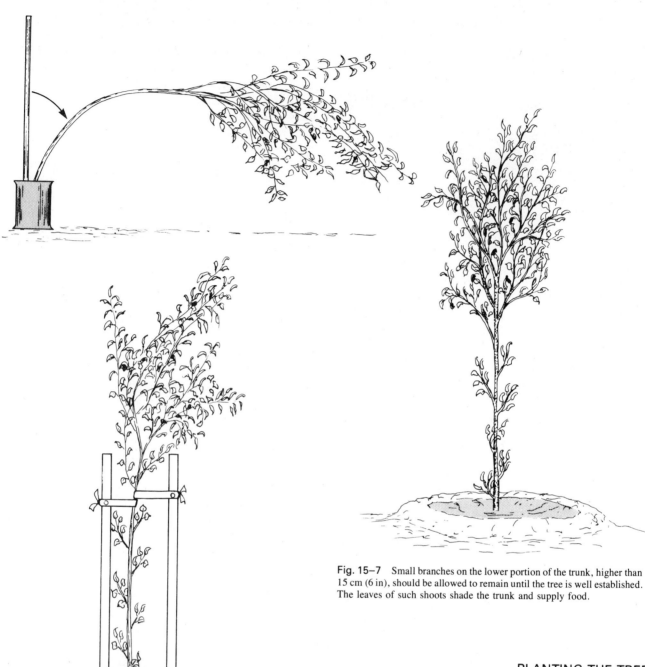

Fig. 15–6   A tree that has been tied to a rigid stake (*above*) may be very weak when the tie is removed. Such a tree should be staked after planting to allow the trunk to be somewhat free to move and develop strengthening tissue (*below*).

Fig. 15–7   Small branches on the lower portion of the trunk, higher than 15 cm (6 in), should be allowed to remain until the tree is well established. The leaves of such shoots shade the trunk and supply food.

PLANTING THE TREE

Soil

The site chosen for a landscape tree usually determines how it will eventually grow. If the soil is undesirable for the tree, the soil will need modification in order to sustain good root growth. A clay soil with poor structure and drainage needs organic matter added to make it more porous. A sandy soil needs organic matter to improve its waterholding and cation exchange capacity (nutrient retention; see Ch. 8). These amendments can be added over a large area or merely in the hole in which the tree is to be planted.

Sometimes soils are compacted by trucks during the building of the house. Such soil should be tilled with a rototiller or a spade. To this loosened soil incorporate 10 cm (4 in) of organic matter into the top 20 to 30 cm (8 to 12 in) of soil or beyond the limits of compaction. It is best then to irrigate the soil and allow it to settle and dry out before planting the tree.

The soil should be probed to 1 m (3 ft) deep to find any natural impervious layer (hardpan), which prevents root penetration resulting in a shallow root system. Similarly, the impervious subsoil does not provide adequate drainage and the roots will lack adequate oxygen. Layers such as these are often caused by an accumulation of cemented minerals (calcium, iron, or aluminum compounds) and can be penetrated if they are thin. A power soil auger (see Fig. 13–4) or a hand-operated posthole digger will penetrate layers up to 10 cm (4 in) thick. These holes can be filled with amended soil or plant residues so that the roots can enter the open soil layers under the hardpan. Layers thicker than 10 cm (4 in) are very difficult to penetrate without heavy equipment. Perhaps it would be wise to abandon the idea of planting a tall-growing tree in such a location, where it could be toppled in a wind storm because of its shallow root system.

Care of the Tree

After purchasing the tree one should take good care of it before planting. Bare-root trees should be placed in the shade to keep the tops cool, and the roots should always be kept covered and moist. If the trees are not planted at once, the roots should be plunged (heeled in) in moist sawdust, moist soil, or peatmoss. B&B trees should not be allowed to dry out; it is not easy to retain water in the ball unless the burlap is overwrapped with plastic which acts as a container. Extreme care should be taken not to break the ball when transporting it because the small roots are broken and lose contact with the soil.

Container-grown plants are perhaps the easiest to maintain temporarily. Still the plants should be kept in a shady, wind-protected area to reduce evapotranspiration. The containers should be well watered and should be protected from direct sun by covering them with aluminum foil or by plunging them in sawdust. Either method of covering prevents excessive heat build-up on the periphery of the container which is apt to kill the roots.

A young bare-root tree should be planted slightly higher than it was in the nursery to compensate for possi-

ble settling of the soil in the prepared hole. A tree planted too deeply or one that settles is subject to crown rot diseases. The soil ball of container-grown or B&B trees should rest on firm soil to avoid settling (Figs. 15–5, 15–8). The top of the soil ball should be slightly above

Fig. 15–8 The ball of the tree should be placed on firm soil in the hole so that the ball will not settle lower than the intended planting depth. If the crown of the tree is below the final soil level, the trunk is subjected to decay organisms. To plant a balled and burlapped tree, *A:* Place ball in hole carefully, taking care that it is oriented properly. Remove ropes and cut the burlap in many places or remove it if it has been treated to prevent decay. *B:* If the burlap is decomposable, as most are, cut away the top portion so that no burlap remains above the final soil level. *C:* Fill in the hole and tamp the soil firmly until the desired soil level is attained. Water the soil ball and replace soil.

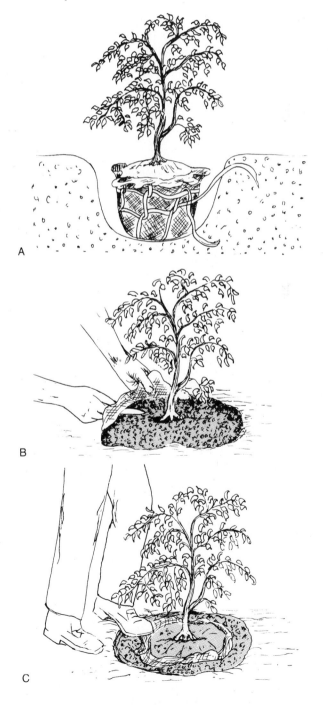

the original ground line (see p. 347). The hole should be about twice the diameter of the soil ball for a container-grown or a B&B tree to provide an adequate transition zone between the soil ball and the undisturbed soil. If the soil is a clay or sandy type, it should be removed from the hole, mixed with about 25 percent organic matter by volume, and packed firmly around the ball. Sphagnum peatmoss decomposes slowly, making it good organic matter for this purpose.

For bare-root trees, make the hole large enough to accommodate the roots so that there is room to spread them out (Fig. 15–9). Broken or very long roots are pruned before planting. The soil is gradually filled in, tamped in with a stick, and firmed down with the foot. Finally, irrigate to settle the soil around the roots. Use the excess soil to make a dike (saucer) around the tree to contain water in a basin. Note that the crown of the tree is always planted higher than the surrounding soil to ensure that water does not accumulate around the trunk. Avoid overwatering newly planted trees until the roots become established in the undisturbed soil. The reduced oxygen in a saturated soil discourages growth of new roots.

When a bare-root tree is planted in a lawn area with an amended soil, a basin should be constructed around the tree. The turfgrass should be kept away from the crown for at least two years to allow the young tree to become established. A bare soil area about 75 cm (30 in) across helps keep lawn mowers away from the trunk. Three sturdy stakes about 20 cm (8 in) high, spaced equidistant from the tree trunk, will prevent bark damage from lawn mowers.

The newly planted tree can be staked but it is not always necessary. The purpose of staking is threefold: to

Fig. 15–9 Plant bare-root trees in a hole large enough to accommodate the roots. Prune very long roots for ease in planting. Amend the soil taken from the hole with some organic matter before replacing it. Firm the amended soil well around the roots by tamping it as it is replaced. After the first irrigation soil that is not firmed will settle, and this should be avoided.

protect the trunk from mechanical damage by mowers or other equipment, to anchor the root system, and to support the tree in an upright position.

With large leafy B&B trees, the trees are usually anchored with guy wires. The top of the tree offers so much wind resistance that the small root ball cannot prevent the tree from toppling. Three well-placed guy wires usually maintain stability and also keep machinery from running into the tree. When the roots have grown into the native soil, the supports are removed, usually after one year's growth.

Many newly planted trees require trunk support because they have been staked or grown too close together in the nursery. These trees usually have tops that are too heavy for the trunk. The tree supports are placed as low as possible but still maintain the top in an upright position. This point is found with the method shown in Figure 15–10. The tie is flexible enough to allow some trunk movement. The best material is an elastic webbing that allows movement without abrading the trunk. If the top is leafy and offers much wind resistance, it should be pruned to reduce the wind load.

If the tree lacks small shading branches on the lower trunk, the trunk should be painted with white indoor latex paint (diluted with water) or wrapped with strips of burlap. Painting or burlapping prevents sun

scald of the trunk on bright days. If small branches are still growing along the entire length of the trunk (Fig. 15–7), those up to 15 cm (6 in) above the soil should be removed, but the others should be left. The lower branches shade and supply food to the trunk. A wire mesh encircling the tree to about 45 cm (18 in) above the ground protects the bark against rabbits and mice.

The support system should be checked occasionally. The ties can be removed after one full growing season, but the trunk should again be checked for strength as shown in Figure 15–10.

Planting Time

Trees are best planted in spring when the soil is warming, but the air is still cool and the transpiration rate low. Under these conditions the roots will grow into the soil rapidly and provide ample water to the tops. In warm areas (zones 8 to 10) fall planting of many hardy trees is recommended to allow the root system to grow during the mild winters.

Fertilizing Trees After Planting

Since the chances of applying too much fertilizer at transplanting time and burning the roots are great, trees

Fig. 15–10 To determine the point at which a tree should be staked, grip the trunk at various heights (*left*) and bend the top to determine at which point the trunk will spring back. *Right:* Tie the trunk a few cm above the point where the tree trunk returns to an upright position as shown in Figure 15–6.

are seldom fertilized when planted. However, some nitrate–nitrogen fertilizer can be applied on the soil surface and watered in after planting because the nitrate forms are soluble and move readily into the soil. Sandy soils should be fertilized more frequently but with lesser amounts than clay soils (p. 172), since sandy soils lack the mineral retention properties of clay soils. Trees planted in turf must be fertilized more often than those growing in bare soil without weeds. Turfgrass strongly competes for mineral nutrients added to the soil, leaving little for the tree roots.

Mulching the Soil Surface

All newly planted narrow- and broad-leaved evergreens benefit from organic mulches of wood chips, fir bark, pine needles, or sphagnum moss. A mulch layer 5 to 10 cm (2 to 4 in) thick may be placed at the base of the tree, extending out to the edges of the longest branches. Bricks or redwood boards, which resist rotting, can be used to keep the mulch in place. The mulch eliminates most weeds, prevents the soil from caking in the hot sun, and moderates soil temperature and water loss near the surface. Water usually penetrates the soil more easily below a mulch.

Irrigation After Planting

It is important to irrigate recently planted trees deeply to encourage the roots to grow downward. In dry, hot climates careful irrigation is necessary for the survival of the tree during the first summer. Watering with a soaker hose, which provides low volume over many hours, allows the water to penetrate deeply in many soil types.

Tree Care During the First Year— A Summary

The first year is the most difficult period in the life of the tree. New roots must develop to anchor the tree and develop feeder roots to supply the tree with water and mineral nutrients. Staking to keep the plant upright is necessary for trees with weak trunks and for those planted in windy areas. Deep irrigation encourages deep rooting if the subsoil drainage is adequate. Feeding the tree during the first year is usually unnecessary, since nutrients are obtained from the native soil. Overfertilizing young trees the first growing season can damage and seriously hinder root growth. Some top pruning is necessary to reduce the wind load on the top or to balance the root-top ratio. The trunks of some trees need protection from sun scald or rodents.

After the first full year, the strength of the trunk should be checked to determine if the support stakes are still necessary (Fig. 15–10). Usually stakes are not required after one year.

After the first year trees usually have to be fertilized to produce both good roots and branches. The best time to fertilize is shortly before the new burst of growth in the spring. As the soil warms, the roots absorb nutrients and make them available for the flush of growth. In all climates the fertilizer can be applied in late winter or early spring during the rainy season. A fertilizer containing only nitrogen is necessary for most kinds of trees. It can be applied to the soil surface and if it is in a readily soluble form (nitrate) it will leach into the root zone. The nitrogen fertilizer can also be placed in holes 25 to 30 cm (10 to 12 in) deep, bored into the ground, spaced at regular intervals of 60 to 90 cm (22 to 35 in) around the tree. The holes are best made with a soil sampling tube, which removes the soil, rather than by poking the soil with a stick and possibly compacting it, particularly in clay soils. The amount of nitrogen to apply is about 1.5 to 2.5 kg/100 m² (3 to 6 lb/1000 ft²). The fertilizer can be mixed with equal volumes of dry sand to dilute it for safer distribution. Place a little in each hole around the tree so that it is distributed fairly well about the tree. Cover the holes with soil or sand and irrigate the area slowly with a large volume of water. The nitrogen will leach into the root zone. In regions of heavy rainfall, the amounts given above can be divided equally and applied in halves at one-month intervals.

Liquid fertilizers can be injected into the root zone, but special equipment is necessary (Fig. 15–11). Devices are available that attach to the garden hose. Liquid fertilizers may have to be applied twice in a season because they are very soluble and leach away easily.

Fertilizer pills of various sizes can be placed in holes made around the tree. The pills have limited solubility and gradually release the nutrients as they slowly dissolve. The pills generally are complete fertilizers (containing nitrogen, phosphorus, and potassium) and since most landscape trees respond to nitrogen only, they are relatively ineffective for their high cost.

Trees growing in lawns are fertilized by the two methods described or by lightly spreading nitrogen fertilizers over the grass surface. Rains and melting snows will leach much of the nitrogen into the root zone. Once the grasses become active and start growing, fertilizers applied will be taken up by grass roots and little, if any, will benefit the tree roots. An area at least 75 cm (30 in)

Fig. 15–11 Liquid fertilizers can be injected below the soil surface with water pressure. The probe must be inserted in several places to ensure that the soil mass is fertilized equally. *Source:* Univ. of Calif. Coop. Ext. Ser.

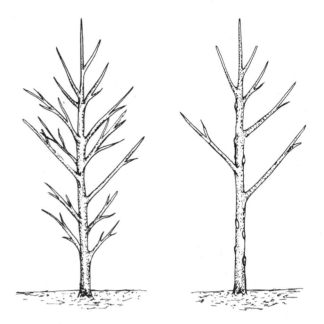

Fig. 15–12 *Left:* A young established shade tree before pruning. *Right:* the same tree with those branches retained that will produce the scaffold branches of the tree.

Fig. 15–13 The crape myrtle is chosen as a landscape tree because of its smooth bark and its profuse summer flowers. Very often it is grown not as a single trunk but a multiple branched tree as shown here on the right.

across around the trunk of young trees should be kept free of turfgrass so that the tree can be occasionally fertilized in this bare surface.

Young deciduous or broad-leaved evergreens may have to be pruned after the first year. The purpose of tree pruning is to control the shape or the size, stimulate vigor or, in the case of fruit trees, to affect the flowering and consequently the fruits which develop later (see Ch. 13).

The shape of the tree is directed early by selecting or choosing certain branches or buds to grow in a desired direction. The pruner can select one good leader branch and thin out badly placed branches so that a desirable, less-cluttered scaffold system remains (Fig. 15–12). An irregular tree form is sometimes desired, and no one single leader is then chosen. It is possible to prune certain trees so that there are multiple trunks and no single leader (Fig. 15–13). The crape myrtle is an excellent candidate for training in this fashion. A complicated form of pruning that requires much care is the espalier, in

Fig. 15–14 Pruning and maintaining a fruit or an ornamental tree so that it grows in a single plane is called espalier. Shown here are pear trees trained in two different forms. Very often trees are trained on a wall having adequate light. The pruning is done mainly in the winter when the branches are bare, but vigorous troublesome shoots may be removed any time to maintain the shape of the plant. Photographed at Wisley Gardens, Great Britain.

which fruit trees are trained against a fence or wall (Fig. 15–14).

The size and foliage density of shade trees is controlled by pruning at least once a year, but more frequent pruning is required for vigorous trees. Examples of such pruning control are creating a hedge out of closely planted trees to produce a screen, or pollarding trees (i.e., cutting them back severely each winter to let in more light in the winter but still have shade in the summer). Sycamore and fruitless mulberry trees lend themselves to this severe pruning (Fig. 15–15). Because of their vigorous growth, the pruned trees still produce long leafy branches by midsummer. The ultimate in controlling tree size is the Japanese treatment of bonsai (Fig. 15–16). These trees are maintained and kept in small containers for many years. Annual pruning of both roots and tops is necessary. Fruit tree pruning is discussed in Chapter 13.

Even though pruning controls growth, it also invigorates plants by thinning out branches and opening the center to more light. This thinning operation pro-

Fig. 15–15 Cutting a tree back severely each year during the dormant season (pollarding) is a way of keeping potentially large trees small. This fruitless mulberry tree is one of the many on Nob Hill in San Francisco, which are pollarded to keep their size down. The gnarled branches result from this severe pruning.

Fig. 15–16 Normally large trees such as black pine and junipers can be grown in small containers and pruned to reduce their size. These containers average 30 cm (12 in) long, and the trees are 10 to 20 years old. They are known as bonsai trees.

Fig. 15-17 Branches which have acute angles (*left*) may split when the branch matures and becomes heavy (*center*). Narrow angled branches should be removed and wide angled branches (*right*) should be encouraged.

duces a better top to root ratio so that water and nutrients are distributed more efficiently. The remaining shoots have less competition for light, water, and nutrients. In hot dry climates, less leaf surface remains after pruning thus limiting water loss by transpiration. The branch structure is strengthened by eliminating branches which produce narrow angles (Fig. 15-17).

PRUNING METHODS

The two basic pruning methods of heading back and thinning out are discussed in Chapter 13.

Before pruning any tree, one should ask three basic questions.

1. *What do I want to accomplish by pruning this tree?* Shall I head back the plant to keep it small? Shall I head it back to invigorate and strengthen it? Shall I reduce the flowering or fruiting potential? Just what is my goal?

2. *How will the tree respond to pruning?* Will it greatly alter the growth habit? Will severe pruning markedly reduce growth? Will many latent or adventitious buds be stimulated to sprout? Based on the normal habit of growth, is the method I am choosing for this tree suitable?

3. *How is it actually done?* Some basic pruning tools are necessary to make pruning easy. Bark splitting and ragged cuts should be avoided to allow for rapid healing.
    a. First remove any dead or dying branches or twigs. They usually have a gray lifeless (shriveled) appearance. Scratching through thin bark on small branches will show green tissue on live branches.
    b. Thin out the cross-over branches or those that are growing toward the center of the crown.
    c. Remove narrow angle branches that weaken the tree (Fig. 15-17).
    d. Assess what you have done so far, then thin out the crown to give it the desired size and shape.
    e. If not enough material is pruned this year, you can prune correctively next year after observing the resultant growth of this year's pruning operation.

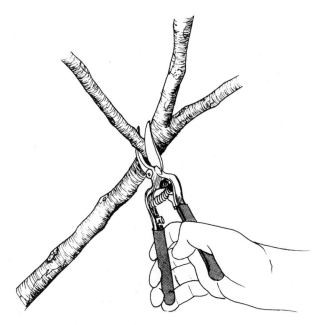

Fig. 15-18 When small branches are removed, they should be cut with pruning shears to obtain clean-cut surfaces. The cutting blade is held close to the main branch so that a stub will not remain.

Pruning can be done almost anytime of year except for such trees as the maples and the elms, which should be pruned in the late fall or early winter when the tree is not actively growing and the sap is not flowing. In areas with severe winters prune after the cold weather has passed.

Typical methods of cutting twigs or large branches with shears and saw are illustrated in Figures 15-18 and 15-19.

Narrow-leaved evergreens, or conifers, are shaped or kept within certain size limits by root pruning or top pruning. Root pruning (Fig. 15-20) is used occasionally to limit top growth. The lower branches are tied to make cutting the roots convenient. A nursery spade, which has

Fig. 15-19 The method of cutting large branches to avoid splitting the trunk below the cut. *Left:* Make a cut on the under side at A. *Center:* Remove the branch at B, leaving a stub. *Right:* Remove the stub at C.

Fig. 15–20 Roots of established conifer plants can be pruned to keep the trees small. Cuts are made in the soil to prune half of the roots one year and the remaining roots the next year.

Fig. 15–21 Pine trees can be held to a reasonable size by pruning one-half to two-thirds of the new growth (candles) each year in the late spring, thus reducing the height or width of the tree by shortening the distances between whorls.

a square cutting edge and a long blade, is used. Slices are made around the tree one season and alternate sections sliced the next year. The best time to root-prune conifers is in the spring when the soil begins to warm and just before the buds become active. Because more than one-half of the root system stays intact, the tree recovers before the onset of winter.

Pine tops can be reduced in size by nipping the "candles" of the current year's growth to about half size with the thumb and forefinger (Fig. 15–21). The remaining portion develops a group of short needles. The best time to prune the "candles" is in late spring when they have elongated but the needles are just beginning to grow.

If the leader on a conifer is broken, generally a branch below begins to bend upright. However, one of the adjacent laterals can be encouraged to take over by splinting it upright (Fig. 15–22) until it can remain erect without the aid of the splint. One full growing season is ample for this corrective procedure.

Some species of conifers are grown in large wooden tubs as living Christmas trees. Some spruces, firs, and the black pine are suitable for this type of culture. The trees must be irrigated properly to keep them

from drying out and to keep salts from accumulating in the container. In irrigating any container-grown plants, it is better to irrigate very heavily at one time so that leaching (dripping) is thorough rather than irrigating frequently with small amounts, which do not allow for leaching (p. 395). Thoroughly watered plants should be irrigated only when the soil surface becomes slightly dry. Some pruning of the candles of pines may be necessary to keep the top-root ratio reasonable. The root growth will be limited by the container so that the top should also be limited by pruning.

Growing bonsai plants (see p. 352) provides an excellent hobby (Fig. 15–16). City dwellers who have balconies or large windows with a south or an east exposure might attempt growing them. During the winter they must be taken indoors and protected. Because the roots are grown in shallow and small containers, watering can be a delicate operation. Care must be taken not to allow the soil to become too dry by infrequent irrigation.

Many insect and spider mite pests attack both deciduous and evergreen trees. Johnson and Lyon (1976) illustrate many of these for identification. Once the pest is known, the local county agent may be able to prescribe a control. Diseases are not easy to identify unless one can describe the exact symptoms to a plant pathologist knowledgeable in ornamental tree diseases.

Fig. 15–22 If the leader of a conifer is broken, a new one can be selected and encouraged to become the new leader with the aid of a splint (arrow) for one season. The splint may be removed as soon as it can be determined that the newly selected leader has become the dominant one.

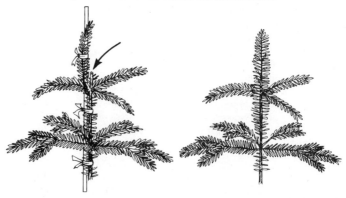

ANON. 1973. Trees for polluted air. USDA Misc. Pub. 1230.

CONOVER, C. A., and E. W. McELWEE. 1971. Selected trees for Florida homes. Univ. of Fla. Bul. 182.

CLARK, D. E., ed. 1975. *Garden trees*. Menlo Park, Calif.: Lane.

CROCKETT, J. U. 1971. *Evergreens*. New York: Time-Life.

————.1972. *Trees*. New York: Time-Life.

DAVIS, W. B. 1963. Landscape trees for the Great Central Valley of California. Univ. of Calif. Coop. Ext. AXT 93.

HARRIS, R. W., J. L. PAUL, and A. T. LEISER. 1977. Fertilizing woody plants. Univ. of Calif., Davis Leaflet 2958.

HARRIS, R. W., W. D. HAMILTON, W. B. DAVIS, and A. T. LEISER. 1975. Pruning landscape trees. Univ. of Calif., Davis Div. Agr. Sci. Leaflet 2574.

HARRIS, R. W., A. T. LEISER, and W. B. DAVIS. 1975. Staking landscape trees. Univ. of Calif., Davis Div. Agr. Sci. Leaflet 2576.

JOHNSON, W. T., and H. H. LYON. 1976. *Insects that feed on trees and shrubs—an illustrated practical guide*. Ithaca, N.Y.: Cornell University Press.

McCLINTOCK, E., and A. T. LEISER. 1979. An annotated checklist of woody ornamental plants of California, Oregon, and Washington. Univ. of Calif. Div. Agr. Sci. Publ. No. 4091.

PERKINS, H. O. 1975. *Handbook on flowering trees*. Brooklyn, N.Y.: Brooklyn Botanical Gardens.

TEUSCHER, H., ed. 1975. *Handbook on conifers*. Brooklyn, N.Y.: Brooklyn Botanical Gardens.

WALDHEIM, L. 1977. *The world of trees*. San Francisco: Ortho Book Division, Chevron Chemical Co.

WYMAN, DONALD. 1965. *Trees for American gardens*. 2nd ed. New York: Macmillan.

Ornamental Shrubs: Deciduous, Broad- & Narrow- Leaved Evergreens

Shrubs are low-growing (3 m; 10 ft) woody plants with multiple stems arising from a low crown (Fig. 16–1). Trees, by contrast, have a single trunk. Some plants may be grown as either trees or shrubs depending on how they are trained when the plants are young. The crape myrtle, the oleander, and the Russian olive are examples. Each shrub species has distinct characteristics that are useful in

Fig. 16–1 A large specimen of *Philadelphus coronarius* in bloom. This plant is about 2.5 m (8 ft) tall. *Source:* Robert A. H. Legro.

the garden. Shrubs can be used to accentuate a landscape, to hold soil on a bank from washing away, to act as a screen or windbreak, or to provide colorful blooms or berries. There are many species to choose from.

Because common names of shrubs vary more with location than do the names of trees or other crops, the Latin species names are given preference here. With the Latin name it is possible to communicate the identity of a shrub to the local nursery dealer or horticulturist. Horticultural and nursery catalogs usually carry both the Latin name and the common name used in the local region. Often the common name of a shrub can also be the name of the genus of that shrub. For example, one of the forsythias is *Forsythia × intermedia* and the slender deutzia is *Deutzia gracilis*. Many flowering shrubs in Table 16–1 have similar Latin and common names.

When choosing a shrub species, one must first consider whether the plant is hardy in the region. The term *hardiness* refers mainly to the ability of the plant to withstand the lowest temperature of that region. The amount of rainfall in a region may also be important, particularly in drought-ridden areas like the arid southwestern United States. Intolerance to drought, however, can be easily overcome by irrigation. Thus the primary factor in hardiness is the minimum temperatures a shrub can withstand.

A partial list of the best flowering shrubs for seven sections in the United States appears in Table 16–1. The climatic sections were determined by their lowest hardiness temperatures. At the borders between regions plants from either section could succeed. Flowering shrubs may be chosen from this table which fulfill certain require-

Table 16–1 A Selected Group of Flowering Shrubs for Seven Sections of the United States. These Were Chosen by Experienced Horticulturists for Dependability, Adaptability and Attractiveness in the Landscape for Their Region

Latin and Common Names	Approx. Mature Height, Meters (Feet)	Flowers	Other Features	Cultural Requirements	Possible Uses
NORTHEAST STATES					
Deutzia gracilis Siebold & Zucc., Deutzia, slender	2 (6)	White	Slender branches	Sunny location	Border, specimen[a]
Forsythia × intermedia Zab. Forsythia	3 (10)	Yellow	Pest free	Prune after flowering	Border, specimen
Kalmia latifolia L. Laurel, mountain	3 (10)	Pink to white	Glossy leaves (Fig. 16–6)	Acid soil	Natural grouping
Philadelphus coronarius L. Mock orange	3 (10)	White, fragrant	Vigorous (Fig. 16–1)	Prune after flowering	Specimen, screen
Rhododendron catawbiense Michx. Catawaba rhododendron	2 (6)	Lilac, purple	Evergreen	Acid soil, some shade	Specimen
Rhododendron pericylymenoides (*R. nudiform*) (Michx.) Shinn. Pinxterbloom	2 (6)	Pink, fragrant	Blue-green leaves	Acid soil	Border
Spiraea × Vanhouttei (C. Briot.) Zab., Spiraea, Bridal-wreath	2 (6)	White	Arching branches	Sunny location	Specimen
Syringa vulgaris L. Lilac, common	6 (20)	White to purple	Fragrant	Prune every other year	In groups
Viburnum carlesii Hemsl. Viburnum, Korean spice	2 (6)	White, fragrant	Black fruit	Remove suckers	Entrance plant
SOUTHEAST STATES					
Abelia × grandiflora (André) Rehd. Abelia, glossy	2 (6)	Pale pink, fragrant	Evergreen	Shady location	Border
Camellia japonica L. Camellia, common	3 (10)	White to red	Glossy leaves	Acid soil, some shade	Specimen, border
Chaenomeles speciosa Nakai (*C. lagenaria*) Quince, flowering	2 (6)	Deep pink	Flowers on bare twigs	Easy culture	Specimen
Gardenia jasminoides Ellis. Gardenia, Crape jasmine	2 (6)	White	Glossy leaves	Acid soil	Border
Hydrangea quercifolia Bartr. Hydrangea, oak leaf	2 (6)	White to purplish	Fall color	Easy culture	Specimen
Jasminum floridum Bunge. Jasmine, flowering	1 (3)	Yellow, fragrant	Arching branches	Sunny location	Border
Kalmia latifolia L. Laurel, mountain	3 (10)	Pink to white	Glossy leaves (Fig. 16–6)	Acid soil	Natural grouping
Lagerstroemia indica L. Crape myrtle	3 (10)	White to pink	Unique stems and bark	Prune in winter	Specimen
Osmanthus fragrans (Thunb.) Lour. Tea olive	3 (10)	White, fragrant	Evergreen; flowers add scent to tea	Easy culture	Specimen
Rhododendron obtusum (Lindl.) Planch., Azalea, Kurume	1 (3)	White to pink	Evergreen	Acid soil	Border
MIDWEST STATES					
Chaemomaeles japonica var. *Alpina* Maxim., Alpine Japanese, Quince	0.3 (1)	Orange	Dwarf	Easy culture	Border
Cornus alba 'Sibirica' Loud. Dogwood, Siberian	2 (6)	White	Blue fruits, red twigs	Easy culture	Border, woodlot
Cornus mas L., Cherry, Cornelian	5 (15)	Yellow	Edible fruit (Fig. 16–13)	Easy culture	Specimen, woodlot

[a] *Specimen* refers to the use of a single plant in an open area as an accent point.

Table 16–1 (continued)

Latin and Common Names	Approx. Mature Height, Meters (Feet)	Flowers	Other Features	Cultural Requirements	Possible Uses
Cotoneaster multiflorus Bunge. Cotoneaster	2 (6)	White clusters	Berries	Easy culture	Specimen
Forsythia ovata Nakai Forsythia, early	2 (6)	Yellow	Compact	Some pruning necessary	Border
Potentilla fruticosa L. Cinquefoil, shrubby	1 (4)	Yellow	Dwarf	Easy culture	Specimen or border
Rosa setigera Michx., Rose, prairie	1 (4)	Pink	Arching branches	Easy culture	Specimen or natural grouping
Syringa × persica L. Lilac, Persian	2 (6)	Lilac, fragrant	Glossy leaves	Easy culture	Specimen or border
Viburnum dentatum L. Arrow wood	5 (15)	White clusters	Fall color	Easy culture	Specimen or natural grouping
Viburnum Lantana L. Wayfaring tree	5 (15)	White clusters	Fruit	Easy culture	Border

ROCKY MOUNTAIN STATES

Latin and Common Names	Approx. Mature Height, Meters (Feet)	Flowers	Other Features	Cultural Requirements	Possible Uses
Caragana aurantiaca Koehne Dwarf pea shrub	1 (3)	Orange-yellow	Drought hardy	Sunny location	Border
Holodiscus dumosus (Nutt.) A. Heller. Spiraea, bush rock	2 (6)	White	Drought hardy	Sunny location	Natural grouping
Jamesia americana Torr & A. Gray. Jamesia, cliff	2 (6)	Waxy, white	Fall color	Sunny location	Rocky crevices
Kolkwitzia amabilis Graebn. Beauty bush	2 (6)	Pink	Arching branches	Open location	Specimen, or border
Potentilla fruticosa L. Cinquefoil, shrubby	1 (4)	Yellow	Dwarf	Easy culture	Specimen or border
Prunus tomentosa Thunb. Cherry, Nanking	3 (9)	White, pink	Edible fruit	Easy culture	Natural, specimen
Rhodotypos scandens (Thunb) Mak. Jet bead	2 (6)	White	Fruit	Sheltered location	Border
Ribes aureum Pursh. Currant, golden	2 (6)	Yellow	Edible fruit	Easy culture	Natural grouping
Rubus deliciosus Torr. Raspberry, Boulder	2 (6)	White	Hardy, thornless	Sunny location	Natural grouping
Spiraea trichocarpa Nakai. Spiraea, Korean	2 (6)	White	Hardy	Easy culture	Specimen

SOUTHWEST STATES

Latin and Common Names	Approx. Mature Height, Meters (Feet)	Flowers	Other Features	Cultural Requirements	Possible Uses
Acacia Farnesiana, (L) Willd. Acacia, scented	3 (10)	Yellow, fragrant	Minute leaves	Sunny location	Specimen
Caesalpinia gilliesi (Wallich ex Hook) Benth. Bird of Paradise shrub	2 (6)	Large, yellow	Compound leaves	Sunny location	Border
Cassia artemisioides, Gaud-Beaup. Cassia, silver	2 (6)	Yellow	Distinct in all seasons	Adequate space	Specimen
Justicia Ghiesbreghtiana Lemm. Jacobinia	1 (3)	Bright orange	Dwarf plant	Slight shade	Possible ground cover
Lagerstroemia indica L. Crape myrtle	3 (9)	White to pink	Unique stem bark	Prune to train	Specimen
Lantana camara 'Nivea' L. Lantana	1 (3)	White to bluish	Long blooming season	Sunny location	Hedge or ground cover
Leucophyllum frutescens (Berland) J.M. Johnst., *(L. texanum)* Sage, Texas silver	1 (4)	Pink	Drought hardy	Sunny location	Border

Table 16–1   (continued)

Latin and Common Names	Approx. Mature Height, Meters (Feet)	Flowers	Other Features	Cultural Requirements	Possible Uses
Melaleuca hypericifolia Sm. Bottlebrush	3 (10)	Red, large	Weeping	Sunny location	Specimen, hedge
Pyracantha coccinea M.J. Roem. Firethorn	2 (6)	White	Berries	Easy culture	Border
Tecoma stans var. *angustata* Redh. Trumpet bush	1 (4)	Yellow, large	Spreading	Easy culture	Specimen
Viburnum suspensum Lindl. Viburnum, sandankwa	2 (6)	White to pink	Evergreen	Easy culture	Specimen

PACIFIC COAST, SOUTH

Latin and Common Names	Approx. Mature Height, Meters (Feet)	Flowers	Other Features	Cultural Requirements	Possible Uses
Callistemon citrunus (Curtis), Staph. Bottlebrush, lemon	5 (15)	Red	Evergreen	Requires some pruning	Hedge, specimen
Carissa grandiflora, (E.H. Mey) A.DC. Plum, Natal	2 (6)	White	Fruit	Easy culture	Hedge, border
Cassia artemisioides, Gacid-Beaup. Wormwood senna	2 (6)	Yellow	Distinct in all seasons	Requires adequate space	Specimen
Cestrum nocturnum L. Jasmine, night blooming	3 (10)	Greenish, fragrant	Climbing	Easy culture	Against walls
Choisya ternata HBK. Orange, Mexican	3 (10)	White	Fragrance	Easy culture	Specimen, border
Hibiscus Rosa-sinensis L. Hibiscus, Chinese	3 (10)	Rose-red, large	Dark green leaves	Sunny location	Specimen
Leptospermum scoparium J.R. Frost and G. Frost Tea tree, Manuka	2 (6)	White to red	Evergreen	Sunny location	Specimen
Nerium oleander L. Oleander	5 (15)	White, pink	Drought resistant	Easy culture	Hedge, border
Osmanthus fragrans (Thunb.) Lour. Olive, sweet	3 (10)	Inconspicuous, fragrant	Flowers add scent to tea	Easy culture	Specimen
Pittosporum tobira (Thunb.) Act. Pittosporum, Japanese	3 (10)	White, fragrant	Evergreen	Easy culture	Border

PACIFIC COAST, NORTH

Latin and Common Names	Approx. Mature Height, Meters (Feet)	Flowers	Other Features	Cultural Requirements	Possible Uses
Arctostaphylos columbiana Piper Manzanita, Columbia	3 (10)	Pink, urn-shaped	Mahogany stems	Acid soil	Natural growing, specimen
Camellia × *williamsii* W.W. Sm. Camellia 'Donation'	3 (10)	Pink to rose	Evergreen	Acid soil	Specimen
Ceanothus impressus Trel. California lilac, 'Puget blue'	3 (10)	Gentian blue	Evergreen	Sunny location	Border, natural grouping
Cytisus battandieri Maire. Broom, atlas	2 (6)	Yellow, fragrant	Silvery gray foliage	Dry conditions	Border
Eucryphia glutinosa Baill. Eucryphia	6 (20)	White, large	Glossy leaves	Acid soil	Specimen, border
Hamamelis mollis D. Oliver. Witch hazel, Chinese	5 (15)	Orange-yellow	Fall color	Sun or some shade	Specimen, grouping
Mahonia aquifolium (Pursh) Nutt. Grape, Oregon	2 (6)	Yellow clusters	Foliage color	Fairly easy culture	Border
Penstemon fruticosus (Pursh) Greene Penstemon, shrubby	0.3 (1)	Pink to lavender	Evergreen	Requires winter rains	Rock garden, mass
Rhododendron × 'Bow Bells' Rhododendron	1 (4)	Pink, large	Evergreen	Acid soil, some shade	Specimen, natural grouping
Rhododendron luteum Sweet, Azalea, Pontic	2 (7)	Yellow, fragrant	Fall color	Acid soil, some shade	Specimen, natural grouping

Source: Harkness, B. ed. 1975. *Handbook of flowering shrubs.* Brooklyn, N.Y.: Brooklyn Botanical Garden.

ments in the landscape for mature height, flower color or other traits. In addition, a specific use may be chosen such as a single specimen for accent or for use in a border or as screen and hedge plants.

The partial list of shrubs in Table 16–2 aids the choice of a shrub based on such characteristics as fragrant flowers or fall color. This list also indicates some shrubs that tolerate particular environmental conditions such as wet or dry soils, acid soils, or heavy shade. The functional use of some shrubs includes some best suited for banks or slopes, for windbreaks or hedges, or simply for attracting birds because they produce edible fruits. A shrub, if it is to be valued in the landscape, should have one or more aesthetic or functional characteristics. These favorable traits become evident by observation in given landscape situations throughout the year. Certain shrubs may be in fashion for several years but, after being used too often, they may become too commonplace and fall from favor.

Table 16–2 A List of Shrubs by Ornamental Characteristics, Environmental Tolerance, and Landscape Use

Latin Name	U.S. Hardiness Zone (see p. 226)

SHRUBS FOR AUTUMN COLOR
RED LEAVES

Acer ginnala	2
Aronia arbutifolia	5
Berberis thunbergii	5
Cornus mas	4
Cotoneaster divaricata	5
Euonymus alata	3
Mahonia aquifolium	5
Nandina domestica	7
Nemopanthus mucronatus	7
Rhododendron calendulaceum	5
Rhus typhina	3
Ribes odoratum	4
Viburnum dentatum	4

YELLOW LEAVES

Amelanchier spp.	5
Celastrus scandens	5
Hamamelis mollis	5
Magnolia stellata	5

SHRUBS WITH FRAGRANT LEAVES

Artemisia spp.	2–5
Juniperus spp.	2–5
Laurus nobilis	6
Lavandula officinalis	5
Myrica spp.	2–7
Myrtus communis	9
Rhus aromatica	3
Santolina chamaecyparissus	7

SHRUBS WITH FRAGRANT FLOWERS

Abelia grandiflora	5
Carpenteria californica	8
Choisya ternata	7
Daphne odora	7
Gardenia jasminoides	9
Jasminum officinale	7
Lonicera spp.	3–7
Osmanthus illicifolius	6
Philadelphus coronarius	4
Philadelphus cymosus 'Conquete'	5
Philadelphus lemoinei 'Avalanche'	5
Rosa, most spp.	4–8
Rubus odoratus	3
Syringa vulgaris	3
Viburnum burkwoodi	5
Viburnum carlesii	4
Viburnum fragrans	5
Viburnum odoratissimum	9

SHRUBS WITH BIRD-ATTRACTING FRUIT

Amelanchier grandiflora	4
Cornus alba 'Sibirica'	2
Cornus sericea (C. stolonifera)	2
Cotoneaster spp.	4–7
Feijoa sellowiana	8
Heteromeles arbutifolia	9
Ilex verticillata	3
Lonicera maackii	2
Lonicera tatarica	3
Mahonia aquifolium	5
Malus sargentii	5
Myrica californica	7
Myrica pennsylvanica	2
Ochna serrulata	8
Pyracantha coccinea	6
Rhus aromatica	3
Rhus glabra	2
Rosa multiflora	5
Sambucus coerulea	5
Sambucus canadensis	3
Symphoricarpus chenaultii	5
Vaccinium corymbosum	3
Viburnum dentatum	2
Viburnum lentago	2
Viburnum prunifolium	3
Viburnum rufidulum	5

DWARF SHRUBS (1 m OR LESS)

Arctostaphylos uva-ursi	2
Andromeda polifolia	2
Berberis buxifolia nana	5
Buxus microphylla 'Koreana'	4
Buxus sempervirens suffruticosa	5
Calluna vulgaris	4
Cotoneaster horizontalis	4
Daphne cneorum	4
Daphne giraldii	3
Erica spp.	3–6
Euonymus alata 'Compacta'	3
Forsythia 'Arnold Dwarf'	5

Gaultheria procumbens 5
Hypericum calycinum 5
Ilex crenata 'Helleri' 6
Juniperus chinensis 'Sargenti' 4
Juniperus horizontalis 2
Kalmia angustifolia 4
Mahonia aquifolium 'Compacta' 5
Picea abies cultivars 2
Pinus mugho 2
Rhododendron obtusum 6
Rhododendron racemosum 5
Rosa wichuraiana 5
Ruscus aculeatus 7
Salix tristis 2

SHRUBS TOLERANT OF SOME SHADE

Abelia grandiflora 5
Alnus spp. 2
Amelanchier spp. 4
Berberis thunbergii 5
Camellia japonica 7
Cornus mas 4
Hydrangea arborescens 4
Kalmia spp. 5
Laurus nobilis 6
Mahonia spp. 5
Nandina domestica 7
Pachysandra terminalis 5
Philadelphus coronarius 4
Pittosporum tobira 8
Rubus odoratus 3
Viburnum dentatum 2
Viburnum tinus 7
Vinca minor 4

SHRUBS TOLERANT OF MOIST TO WET SOILS

Alnus spp. 2
Clethra alnifolia 3
Cornus sericea (C. stolonifera) 2
Cornus alba 2
Rubus odoratus 3
Salix caprea 4
Salix purpurea 4
Sambucus canadensis 3
Thuja occidentalis cultivars 2
Viburnum dentatum 2

SHRUBS TOLERANT OF DRY SOILS

Arctostaphylos uva-ursi 2
Artemisia spp. 2–5
Callistemon lanceolatus 9
Ceanothus americanus 4
Ceanothus thyrsiflorus 8
Cytisus spp. 5
Elaeagnus angustifolia 2
Euonymus japonica 8
Heteromeles arbutifolia 9
Hypericum calycinum 5
Juniperus communis 2
Juniperus horizontalis 2
Kolkwitzia amabilis 4
Nerium oleander 8

Rhus aromatica 3
Rosa rugosa 2
Rosmarinus officinalis 6
Santolina chamaecyparissus 7
Tamarix pentandra 2
Viburnum lentago 2

SHRUBS TOLERATING OR REQUIRING ACID SOILS

Amelanchier spp. 4
Calluna spp. 4
Camellia japonica 7
Cytisus spp. 5–6
Erica spp. 5–7
Ilex spp. 3–6
Juniperus communis 2
Kalmia spp. 4
Magnolia virginiana 5
Myrica pennsylvanica 2
Rhododendron spp. 2–6
Vaccinium spp. 2–3

SHRUBS FOR BANKS OR SLOPES

Arctostaphylos uva-ursi 2
Berberis thunbergii 5
Ceanothus americanus 4
Cornus sericea (C. stolonifera) 2
Cotoneaster horizontalis 4
Hypericum calycinum 5
Juniperus chinensis 'Sargenti' 4
Juniperus horizontalis 2
Pachysandra terminalis 5
Rhus aromatica 3
Salix tristis 2
Vinca minor 4

SCREEN AND WINDBREAK SHRUBS

Acer campestre 4
Acer ginnala 2
Cornus mas 4
Elaeagnus angustifolia 2
Kolkwitzia amabilis 4
Laurus nobilis 6
Ligustrum spp. 3–7
Philadelphus coronarius 4
Photinia spp. 7
Prunus laurocerasus 6
Syringa vulgaris 3
Thuja occidentalis 2
Viburnum dentatum 4
Viburnum lentago 2

Certain shrubs can give pleasure throughout most of the year by, for example, flowering in the spring, turning an attractive color in the fall, and displaying brightly colored berries on the bare twigs in the fall and winter. Many of the *Cornus* and *Viburnum* species as well as *Nandina domestica* have these unique characteristics.

Shrubs may have a functional use as a hedge or screen to eliminate an undesirable view or to reduce the force of the wind. Hedges or screens are usually comprised of a single species. They can be pruned formally to give a boxy appearance or may be allowed to grow freely. In the latter case, the shrubs may have to be pruned occasionally to hold them to a given size and to increase their vigor. In choosing a species for a hedge or screen, the ultimate size should be strongly considered. Indeed, in choosing any plant, the mature size is one of the most important considerations. If growth is slow for any reason, extra plants should be set close together to temporarily fill in the spaces. When crowding of the individual plants begins to hinder their vigor, alternate plants can be removed to reduce competition unless a screen or hedge is wanted. Then a crowded condition is desirable.

Hedges can be planted in trenches, which makes working the soil much easier than digging individual holes. The plants can be planted in a single row or in double rows in a staggered zigzag fashion. The spacing between plants depends upon how vigorous the species is and how soon the hedge is required.

A border in the garden can be both beautiful and functional. The shrub border can be used as a screen, and various species within the border can be mixed to create interest. A border can also vary in height, with the tallest plants in the back or along the boundary line. The border can be a foreground for large trees or a background for bedding plants or bulbs. The group of shrubs should not exceed a height of 2.5 m (8 ft) in most gardens. This height is usually ample to provide a background or screen for privacy unless a tall structure on the adjacent property requires additional screening.

The border may follow an irregular curved pattern to create interest. A flowering border can be staged in such a manner to create color much of the spring and summer by choosing species of varying sizes and flowering dates.

THE AVAILABILITY OF SHRUBS

Most nurseries carry the common hardy shrubs of the region, and usually the widest choice is available in the spring of the year. Shrubs are available for purchase as bare-root plants, balled and burlapped plants, and container-grown stock (see p. 343). The planting methods described for trees of each of these types also pertain to shrubs of the same type. However, because the growth habit of a shrub is different from that of a tree, i.e., multiple vs. a single trunk, the method of pruning both at the time of planting and subsequent maintenance is different for the two plant forms.

Since shrubs grow differently from trees, they are pruned differently. Shrubs are best pruned just before planting. In the case of bare-root stock, broken roots should be removed and extralong roots should be shortened to facilitate planting. If the top appears too large for the root system, the branches should be cut back to give the plant the right proportion.

Container-grown plants often have roots that are circling in the container (see Fig. 15–3). Such plants should be rejected but, if used, the roots should be cut in several places to break the circling pattern and to stimulate new growth. The tops of broad-leaved evergreens often need to be pruned to reduce the wind load and to reduce the transpiration surface. Remove about one-quarter of the leaf area by pruning immediately after planting. The tops of balled and burlapped shrubs should also be pruned for the same reasons, but the roots should not be disturbed other than loosening the burlap.

Once the shrubs are established in the landscape, maintenance pruning serves to control their size and shape by removing some stems from the multiple-stemmed crown (Fig. 16–2) to improve the shrubs' health, and to affect flowering. Some shrub species require more pruning than others because of differences in vigor and flowering habit.

Plant size is reduced by thinning out some of the branches. The tips of the branches may be headed back to increase peripheral branching if a hedge or formal effect is desired. Thinning will help maintain the natural form and shape of the shrub. In thinning shoots, the

Fig. 16–2 Two ways to prune a shrub to create different effects. The cuts are indicated by the black bars. *Source:* Adapted from USDA Home and Garden Bulletin 165.

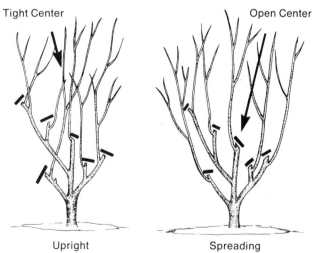

Tight Center   Open Center

Upright   Spreading

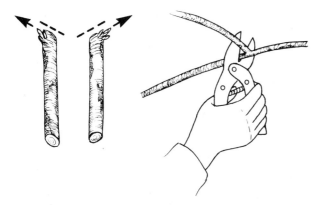

Fig. 16-3 Pruning cuts at certain buds directs the growth in a desired direction. The new shoot growth will follow the direction of the dotted line. *Source:* Adapted from USDA Home and Garden Bulletin 165.

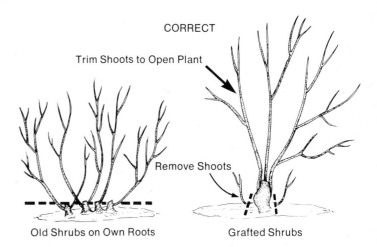

CORRECT

Trim Shoots to Open Plant

Remove Shoots

Old Shrubs on Own Roots   Grafted Shrubs

INCORRECT

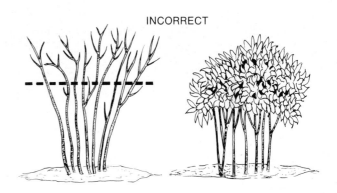

Fig. 16-4 Rejuvenating old shrubs. *Upper left:* In some cases it is best to cut back heavily and develop a new top. *Upper right:* With grafted shrubs, do not cut back below the graft union. Remove suckers from the rootstock (broken lines) or thin shoots to open up the plant. *Below:* Cutting or trimming the tops of old shrubs, as indicated by the broken line (*left*), produces an unsightly leggy plant with a bushy top (*right*). *Source:* Adapted from USDA Home and Garden Bulletin 165.

wood should be cut above a bud that will grow in the desired direction (Fig. 16–3). Selecting the buds to remain allows partial control of growth even in an informal and natural growth habit.

Shrubs may be thinned heavily by cutting some of the old branches back to the crown near ground level. The taller and older branches (i.e., those of greater diameter) should be cut out first but not more than one-third of the branches should be cut out in any one year unless complete rejuvenation is desired. Old shrubs can be rejuvenated as shown in Figure 16–4, by cutting back the entire plant. After many new shoots appear, weak ones are pruned out to leave the strongest and most desirable.

Young hedges are pruned gradually by cutting about six to eight inches above the previous cut. Mature hedges that have attained the desired size require frequent trimming to maintain their shape. The shape of the hedge should be slightly tapered, with the base wider than the top as shown in Figure 16–5. This method of pruning allows light to reach the lower leaves and keep them alive. Keeping a hedge in a formal shape once it has attained the desired size may require as many as four clippings during the growing season. Pruning frequency of a hedge depends on plant vigor, light, temperature, and the water available to sustain vigorous growth.

Diseased wood is pruned out to keep the plant healthy. Diseased branches are cut back to nondiseased wood so that a healthy sprout will grow. This type of pruning should be done when the disease is first noticed, especially in the case of fire blight of pyracantha, cotoneaster, quince, and other members of the rose family.

One of the best reasons for pruning is to affect flowering. Some shrubs initiate their flower buds the

summer before flowering (one-year-old wood) and thus should be pruned at different times than those that flower on current year's wood.

Fig. 16-5 A formal hedge should be pruned with a taper in the direction of the top (*left*). The light is able to reach the bottom leaves and keep them active. *Source:* Adapted from USDA Home and Garden Bulletin 165.

HEDGE PRUNING

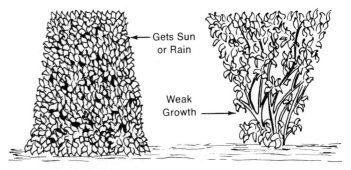

Gets Sun or Rain

Weak Growth

CORRECT   INCORRECT

Flowering on One-Year-Old Wood

Many fruit trees and shrubs initiate their flowers in summer, and the flower buds bloom the following spring when the weather becomes favorable (see Ch. 14). These species are called spring-flowering shrubs. Examples are *Cercis*, dogwood (*Cornus*), *Kalmia* (Fig. 16–6), lilac (*Syringa*), *Pyracantha*, *Rhododendron* (azalea), *Spiraea*, and *Viburnum*. Severely heading back the branches with the flower buds in winter or early spring cuts away the potential flowers. One should prune such spring-flowering shrubs soon after they have flowered (Fig. 16–7). Removing the old flowers and shoots stimulates the plant to branch and produce additional flowering wood for next year. This type of flowering is usually identified by the flowers developing on previous year's growth before the leaves come out, such as in flowering quince and peach, or *Chimonanthus praecox* (Fig. 16–8). Some species like the lilac produce large flower clusters (inflorescences) instead of single blooms, but these too are borne on the previous year's shoots.

Fig. 16–6 *Kalmia latifolia* flowers are prized spring blooms. *Source:* Robert A. H. Legro.

Fig. 16–7 Spring-flowering shrubs should be pruned after they have flowered and as vegetative growth begins. Unfortunately, many gardeners and homeowners prune these plants in the winter when the twigs are bare, and consequently they cut away the flower buds. Before pruning, study the growth habit of the shrub.

FIRST SPRING

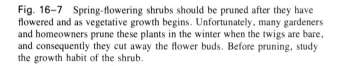
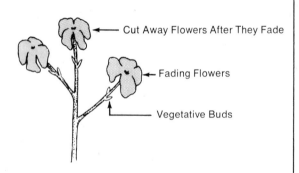

Cut Away Flowers After They Fade

Fading Flowers

Vegetative Buds

FIRST SUMMER

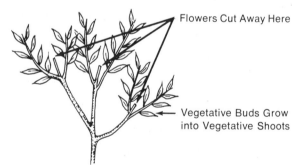

Flowers Cut Away Here

Vegetative Buds Grow into Vegetative Shoots

FIRST FALL

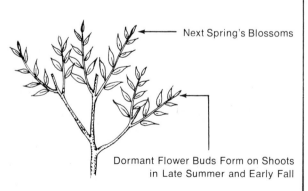

Next Spring's Blossoms

Dormant Flower Buds Form on Shoots in Late Summer and Early Fall

SECOND SPRING

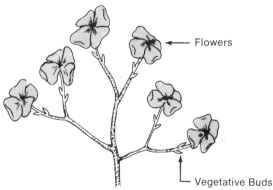

Flowers

Vegetative Buds

Fig. 16–8 *Chimonanthus praecox* flowers in the spring before the leaves appear. The flowers were initiated the summer before, and they received their necessary chilling during the winter. *Source:* Robert A. H. Legro.

Fig. 16–9 Summer-flowering shrubs can be pruned either in the fall after they have flowered or in the winter when the twigs are bare. The flowers form and develop on current second growth that originates from vegetative buds on the previous season's branches.

The branches of shrubs that flower on the current year's growth (sometimes called summer-flowering shrubs) should be pruned back in late winter or early spring before the buds have sprouted (Fig. 16–9). The resulting shoots have the capability of producing flower buds on the new growth. Some examples of summer-flowering species are *Abelia, Clethra,* crape myrtle, *Hibiscus, Nerium* (oleander), roses (floribunda and hybrid tea), and *Vitex.* This type of flowering is identified in some species by shoots that have light green leaves below the flower stalks. Flowers may also appear in several flushes or cycles during the growing season.

Shrubs not grown for flowers or fruits are pruned almost anytime of year except late summer. Late pruning often stimulates buds to sprout. Such shoots do not have adequate time to mature or "harden" before the onset of winter, leaving them susceptible to winter injury.

Shrubs, especially those grown as specimen plants, should be given ample space to develop properly. Most shrubs usually spread out as they grow taller. It is tempting to plant small shrubs close together to get the desired effect hurriedly. However, it usually becomes necessary to remove alternate plants when they begin to touch.

FIRST SPRING

Vegetative Buds

No Flower Buds Present

FIRST SUMMER, EARLY

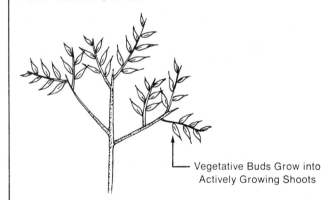

Vegetative Buds Grow into Actively Growing Shoots

FIRST SUMMER, LATE

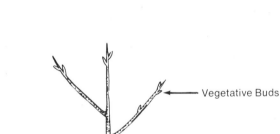

Shoots Form and Develop Flowers During Summer Months

FIRST FALL

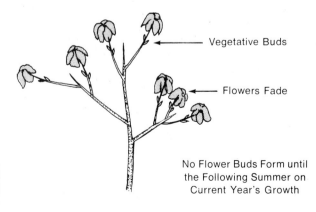

Vegetative Buds

Flowers Fade

No Flower Buds Form until the Following Summer on Current Year's Growth

Crowded plants do not develop the grace and beauty of those grown at recommended distances. Shrubs planted next to the house should be set far enough away to keep them from crowding into the building as they mature.

PRUNING ROSE PLANTS

Hybrid Tea Roses

Most roses are planted bare root in late winter or early spring depending on the hardiness zone. Generally these bare-root plants need no top pruning at the time of planting, but any broken roots should be pruned back behind the break. Roses are planted "high" like bare-root trees (Ch. 15). Low planting results in the development of crown rot diseases.

When the roots begin to grow and the weather warms, new shoots develop from the dormant canes. All leafy shoots are allowed to develop. In the very early stages (when the shoot and leaves are reddish), new growth primarily depends on stored food in the canes for energy. After the leaves turn green, they produce photosynthates that are translocated to the roots.

Hybrid tea roses flower on current year's growth and, therefore, can be pruned anytime. The only pruning before the first flush of flowers should be to remove all lateral flower buds, leaving the terminal bud on each shoot. Remove the lateral buds as soon as possible so that the carbohydrates concentrate in the terminal buds. The remaining buds will produce larger flowers than if the lateral buds were not removed. Allow all the terminal buds to bloom and develop fully in the first spring flush. Do not remove them until they start to drop their petals. This allows the rose bush to translocate most of the food from the mature green leaves to the roots on each flowering shoot. After this, prune away the fading flowers to just above a good bud located about midway from the original source of the cane and the flower. Cut back to a bud that is growing outward from the center of the bush. This allows the rose to spread out more than if inwardly growing buds are chosen. The rule in pruning away old flowers is to leave at least three or more compound leaves (and buds, which are in the axils of these leaves) on the cane. The leaves that remain produce the food for the new flush of shoot growth that originates from at least one of the buds. During the second or third flush of growth (usually by mid- or late summer) some flower buds can be removed for cut flowers in the home. By then the bush is well established and flowers plus valuable leaves can be removed. Buds that have just begun to unfurl one or two petals should be cut to the desired stem length, but always leave at least three leaves on the plant below the cut. The cut flower buds have enough sugars in the stems and leaves to permit them to develop into full-sized blooms. A flower preservative solution[1] keeps the flowers fresh longer than plain water alone.

In cold-winter areas where rose bushes must be covered for protection, late pruning reduces the size of the bush, making it easier to cover and protect than a large plant. After the leaves have dropped in the fall and the plant appears dormant, the tops are cut back to two-thirds or one-half of their length. Do not prune back into large-diameter wood (larger than 1.5 cm) at this time unless it is old and requires removal. Directly after pruning, the bushes are covered and wrapped with protective material such as straw, plastic sheeting, or building paper. Remove the protection in the spring and examine the canes to determine if any have been winter-killed. Remove the injured canes and cut back to healthy wood. In addition, remove small and weak canes.

In mild climates, fall pruning to reduce plant size is unnecessary. All pruning is best done in winter after the plants have lost their leaves and are dormant. Remove diseased and weak wood and cut to buds that will direct the plant in the desired shape. Some thinning is required (about one-half of the wood) to maintain an open center and reduce cane competition. Old woody canes should be removed as younger, more vigorous, shoots are clearly ready to take their place (Fig. 16–10).

[1]Sucrose, 1.5 to 2.0 percent, plus citric acid, 500 mg per liter. There are also many proprietary materials available at florist's shops.

Fig. 16–10 Some of the important operations in pruning a hybrid tea rose in the garden. *1:* Cut out all weak and dead wood. *2:* Prune and cut out all but three to six vigorous canes. *3:* Cut back those selected canes to vigorous buds as shown at places marked "3."

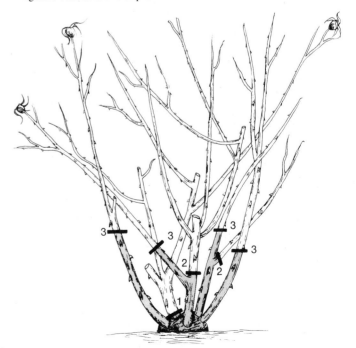

Floribunda and Polyantha Roses

These ever-blooming roses are pruned similarly to hybrid tea roses with two exceptions.

First, floribundas and polyanthas produce multiple flower heads, thus only the central flower bud in each cluster should be removed. This allows the remaining buds to bloom more evenly than if the central bud is left to develop. After flowering, the faded flower cluster is removed to stimulate the potential buds to sprout and produce another flush of flowers.

Second, only one-quarter of last year's growth should be cut out instead of up to one-half as with hybrid teas. If growth in the previous year was vigorous, then up to one-half of the wood is pruned. Canes over two or three years old near the base may not approach the girth of the vigorous hybrid teas. Therefore, it may be necessary to allow canes of 0.5 cm (0.25 in) or less diameter to remain to produce next year's shoots. Thinning out some canes to remove competition, however, invigorates the bushes.

Climbing Roses

Climbing or rambling roses flower best on canes that are two or three years old. Flowers originate from laterals on these canes. Care is taken to cut out canes only four or more years old. During the first few years after planting, the canes are trained on a trellis, fence, or wall with an adequate support system to prevent whipping and wind damage. Canes often attain a length of 2.5 to 3 m (8 to 10 ft) and should be trained horizontally or in an arch. Trained canes produce flowers at each node (Fig. 16–11) because the apical dominance of the growing tip is reduced, leaving all nodes in the horizontal plane and thus capable of flowering. After the plant has become established, "renewal" pruning should be done to maintain the vigor of the plant by removing back to the base large canes over three years old that have completed flowering. Such pruning will remove about one-third of the canes each year (Fig. 16–12). Retain the newer canes that will flower this or the following year. Ends of long canes are pruned back any time to keep them within desired bounds. Climbing roses are best pruned in early spring unless the plants must be taken down and covered for winter protection, in which case some fall pruning is necessary to reduce plant size.

Fig. 16–11 A climbing or rambling rose with canes that lie in a horizontal position often produce flower stalks at each node. Properly trained canes such as this respond with an abundance of flowers.

Fig. 16–12 The proper method of pruning climbing roses. Canes that are four or more years old should be removed. This thinning allows more space and light for the younger, more vigorous shoots that will flower in later years. If canes become too long, the ends can be removed to maintain the desired size. The darkened canes are retained and those shown in white are to be cut away.

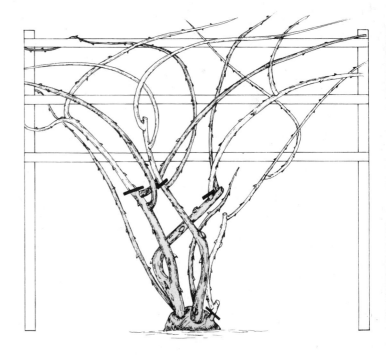

Fig. 16–13 The fruits of the cornelian cherry (*Cornus mas*) are a delight to see and can be made into a delicious jam. *Source:* Robert A. H. Legro.

SUPPLEMENTARY READING

AYRES, S., JR. 1966. *Flowering shrubs for year round color in southern California*. Arcadia, Calif.: California Arboretum Foundation.

BROWN, E. L., ed. 1966. *Trained and sculptured plants*. Brooklyn, N.Y.: Brooklyn Botanical Gardens.

CROCKETT, J. U. 1972. *Flowering shrubs*. New York: Time-Life.

FREESE, P., F., ed. 1974. *Pruning handbook*. Brooklyn, N.Y.: Brooklyn Botanical Gardens.

HARKNESS, B., ed. 1975. *Handbook of flowering shrubs*. Brooklyn, N.Y.: Brooklyn Botanical Gardens.

HARRIS, R. W. 1979. Arboriculture 133. A course in arboriculture at the University of California, Davis. Syllabus.

McGOURTY, F., JR., ed. 1973. *1200 trees and shrubs—where to buy them*. Brooklyn, N.Y.: Brooklyn Botanical Gardens.

McMINN, E. G., and H. E. McMINN. 1941. *Ornamental shrubs and woody vines of the Pacific coast*. Berkeley, Calif.: Gillick Press.

TAYLOR, N. 1965. *The guide to garden shrubs and trees*. New York: Identity and Culture Bonanza Books.

WILLIAMSON, J. F., ed. 1979. *New western garden book*. Menlo Park, Calif.: Lane.

WYMAN, D. 1969. *Shrubs and vines for American gardens*. 2nd ed. New York: Macmillan.

Floriculture: Greenhouse Flowering Plants

THE GREENHOUSE

Greenhouses (or glasshouses) date back to Roman times when wealthy people grew plants in small enclosures. The French developed the art of growing early vegetables and flowering annuals under small cloches, which protected the plants from early spring frosts. During the day when the sun shone brightly, the glass was lifted slightly to allow the trapped hot air to escape. Similar structures were called cold frames by the English. To add heat and make it a hot frame, decaying manure was buried about 0.5 m (18 in) under the structure. Both the cold and hot frames (Fig. 17–1) were constructed to allow a person to reach in and tend to the plants. Later

these units developed into pit houses (Fig. 17–2) and then into the modern greenhouse with its high sides and glass roof. The greenhouse was constructed to allow the rays of the sun to enter the roof perpendicularly in the winter but partially reflect them when the sun is high during the summer. Heat was supplied with circulating hot water and, at a much later date, with steam. The sash bars were usually made of thick wood, especially in areas with great snowfalls, to stand up to the stress of a snowpack. Lumber resistant to rot, such as cypress and

Fig. 17–2 A sash house with the walkway excavated below the ground level. Hot water heating pipes can be placed along the walls or the house can be used without heat simply for frost protection during early spring. The end door is opened for ventilation during the day. *Source:* Cornell University.

Fig. 17–1 A hotbed warmed by decaying manure. The glass sash is lifted during the day to allow excess warm air to escape. *Source:* Cornell University.

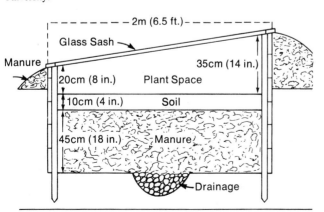

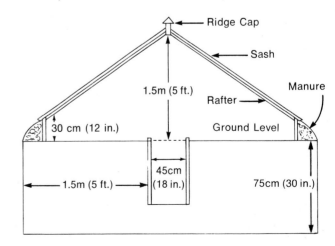

Fig. 17–3 Construction of a corrugated fiberglass structure. A crew of four can cover more than an acre per day. This type of commercial greenhouse is common because it is less expensive than conventional aluminum structured glasshouses (Fig. 17–4).

redwood, was found to be ideal, but because these woods are not particularly strong, the girth of the sash bars had to be large.

For decades greenhouses did not vary much in design except that the width of the glass increased as the technology of making better glass developed. With improvements in techniques for extruding aluminum, the wide wooden sash bars were replaced with narrow aluminum bars, which were very strong (6, 7, 17). Narrow sash bars and wide glass allow more light to enter during the winter when it is needed most. Corrugated fiberglass or polyethylene is often used as a substitute for glass (17, 34) (Fig. 17–3).

Greenhouses are heat traps that are cooled by applying white shading compound to the glass, by convection ventilation (by allowing the hot air to rise through the overhead ventilator), or by forced air removal with exhaust fans (Fig. 17–4). The greatest heat load in the

greenhouse occurs when the air is heated by the sun's rays and trapped by the enclosure of glass or plastic (27). Some form of heat must be added at night during the cold parts of the year because too little daytime heat is retained for that purpose. In extremely cold climates, supplementary heat is necessary even in daylight hours. In the future, perhaps, greenhouses will be partially heated by solar collectors that store heat from the sun's rays of the previous day. The technology for solar collectors now available indicates that the units are not efficient enough to store all the heat necessary to maintain temperatures throughout the night.

Modern greenhouses have sophisticated controls that maintain accurate daytime temperatures by exhausting hot air with fans and controlling night temperature with forced air unit heaters or with hot water or steam passed through radiating pipes (1, 6, 17, 27).

Night temperatures are very important for flower crop production. Flower crops can be classified into high, medium, or low temperature crops for optimum growth (27, 31). Green foliage plants and some orchids require night temperatures as high as 21°C (70°F) or higher. Roses, chrysanthemums, and azaleas do best at temperatures in the 16°C (61°F) range, whereas carnations, snapdragons, cinerarias, and calceolarias grow well at 10°C (50°F) (2, 8, 21, 22). A general rule for greenhouse culture is that daytime temperatures be from 2°C to 8°C (5°F to 15°F) higher than night temperature for most of these crops. Maintaining these temperature differences is easy on overcast days but difficult on bright days because of an extreme heat build-up from the sun. Proper day temperatures may not always be maintained, but growers use their knowledge of the plant requirements and can compensate for these high daytime temperatures. When bright conditions prevail, plants may have to be: (a) shaded more than usual (Fig. 17–5); (b) watered more often to compensate for excessive

Fig. 17–4 A glasshouse with aluminum sash bars. The glass is 61 cm (24 in) wide and is sprayed with a calcium-based shading compound (whitewash). The large boxes on the ends are exhaust fans for removing the hot air during the heat of the day. Louvers on the fan housings prevent heat from escaping during the night. The small fans near the top are used to bring cool air into the house during the early morning before the heat becomes intense from the sun's radiation. The whitewash shade is removed in the fall to allow more light to enter as the days become short.

Fig. 17–5 Cheesecloth shade over standard chrysanthemums within the greenhouse. This type of temporary shade prevents the flowers from becoming excessively hot from direct radiation from the sun. Flowers without the shade overheat and are sunscalded. Note the black plastic along the side posts to cover the plants and create a short day length. The black plastic is drawn manually by greenhouse workers at about 4 P.M., and removed at 7 A.M. to coincide with the working day or is drawn automatically with motors at 7 P.M. and removed at 7 A.M.

transpiration; or (c) sprinkled with an overhead mist to increase the humidity. All three of these procedures will compensate for the high light intensity conditions that can cause sunscald damage to leaves or flowers.

CONTROL OF FLOWERING

Some plants, such as azaleas, chrysanthemums, poinsettias, and some orchids, require short days (or long nights) to flower. To cause the plants to flower during the long days of summer, they are covered with a light-tight black cloth from 5 P.M. to 8 A.M. each day to shorten the day (Fig. 17–6). If delayed flowering of these same plants is desired late in the season (i.e., after their normal blooming season), this is accomplished by lighting the plants each night for about four hours with incandescent or fluorescent lamps (Fig. 17–7) to maintain long days. The lights are turned off about six to twelve weeks before the flowers are desired depending on the species being grown. This practice is used mostly in greenhouses but can also be done outdoors in warm climates (17, 22, 27, 30, 31) (Fig. 17–8).

Flowering in the greenhouse of some of the summer blooming annuals, such as China asters, Shasta daisies, and Marguerite daisies, is enhanced by supplementary lighting during the winter months (10). These plants are lighted for about four hours each night to encourage flower buds to initiate (form) and develop. Carnations, which are considered perpetual bloomers, are induced to bloom more heavily at certain times by exposure to low light intensities (11 to 22 lux; 1 to 2 ft-C) from incandescent lamps from dusk to dawn.

CONTROL OF PLANT HEIGHT

Potted plants grown in warm greenhouses often become tall or rank. It is now possible, with the aid of chemical retardants, to prevent excessive internodal growth (2, 22, 27, 30). Treating many plants (by spraying leaves or using a soil drench) with B-nine®, (SADH), Cycocel® (chlormequat), or A-rest® (ancymidol) during the phase of rapid vegetative growth or just after the flowers have been initiated limits plant height (p. 140). Potted chrysanthemums, poinsettias, lilies, and tulips are examples of plants that respond to such treatment. These growth retardants are also used as soil drenches to hasten flower initiation of potted azaleas (19), geraniums from seed (Table 17–1), and bougainvillea.

Fig. 17–6 A crop of potted chrysanthemums in a glasshouse with wooden sash bars. Note the black cloth along the posts for shortening the day length. The wide aisle enables the grower to use battery-operated carts for moving plants. *Source:* Carl Pearlstein.

Fig. 17–7 A simple method of providing supplementary incandescent lighting. The bulb sockets are connected by means of conduit and are spaced about 1 m (3 ft) apart and 1 m above the bench. The man is holding a reflector made of an aluminum pie plate that directs the light downward. A 40-watt bulb used with a reflector equals a 75-watt bulb without a reflector at this spacing, representing a considerable energy saving over a four-hour period each night. The lights are conveniently held above the bench with the chains shown at the top of the picture. A time switch is shown behind the aluminum reflector. This system is feasible for home greenhouses or school garden classes since it is portable.

Fig. 17–8 A commercial installation of incandescent lighting in a field of chrysanthemums in southern California. The lights are hung above every sixth row of plants to delay flowering from fall to winter. In this case 100-watt bulbs were hung about 2 m (6.5 ft) above the soil and 5.2 m (17 ft) apart, providing a minimum of 22 lux (2 ft-c), which is adequate to delay flowering outdoors.

Table 17–1 Propagation, Preforcing, and Forcing Requirements for Selected Florists' Flowering Plants

Latin and Common Name	Requirements for Propagation (See Ch. 5)			Growth and Flowering Requirements after Propagation		
	Plant Part Commonly Used	Environmental Conditions	Approximate Time Required	Preforcing (Established Plants)	Forcing (Flowering Conditions)	Approx. Forcing Time (Weeks)
Chrysanthemum × morifolium Ramat. Florists' chrysanthemum	Terminal cuttings	Mist, BH, LD, MinNT 17°C (63°F)	10–14 days	MinNT 17°C (63°F) + LD; Med–Hi light	15–16°C (60–61°F) + SD; Med-Hi light Figs. 17–13, 17–14	9–11
Cyclamen persicum Mill Florists' cyclamen	Seeds	MinNT 20°C (68°F) in dark	30 days	MinNT 16°C (61°F), Hi light	MinNT 16–17°C (61–63°F); ca. 25 ppm GA₃; Med Light	6–10
Euphorbia pulcherrima Willd. ex. Klotzsch. Poinsettia	Terminal cuttings	Mist, BH, LD, MinNT 21°C (70°F)	10–21 days	MinNT 21°C (70°F) + LD; Med light	MinNT 16–20°C (61–68°F) + SD; Med light (Fig. 17–19)	8–12
Fuchsia × hybrida Hort. ex. Vilm. Fuchsia	Terminal cuttings	Mist, BH, SD MinNT 15°C (60°F)	10–14 days	MinNT 17°C (63°F) + SD (Fig. 17–20)	MinNT 17°C (63°F) + 21 LD then SD to flower; Hi light	7–9
Hydrangea macrophylla Ser. Hydrangea.	Stem or terminal cuttings	Mist, BH, MinNT 15°C (60°F)	21–35 days	Refrigerated, dark storage, 2–7°C (35–45°F) for 6 weeks; remove leaves before storage. Plant in pots.	Greenhouse NT 17°C (62°F), Hi light.	11–14
Lilium longiflorum Thunb. Easter Lily	Scales, stem bulblets, yearlings (Fig. 17–22)	Cool field conditions in summer	Scales ca. 3 yrs.; bulblets ca. 2 yr.; yearlings, 1 yr.	Soil temp. below 10°C (50°F) for 6 wks. in dark	Ambient temp between 14–17°C (57–63°F) depending on bud stage; Hi light	12–14
Pelargonium × hortorum L.H. Bailey. Geranium	Terminal cuttings, seeds	Cuttings, mist, BH, MinNT 17°C (63°F); seeds, 21°C (70°F)	Cuttings, 14 days; seeds, 21–35 days (Fig. 17–25)	MinNT 15°C (60°F); Hi light; Cycocel, 3500 ppm drench for seedlings	NT between 12–15°C (54–60°F); Hi light	6–15
Rhododendron obtusum (Lindl.) Planch. Kurume azalea	Terminal cuttings	Mist, BH MinNT 15°C (60°F)	42–56 days	6–8 wks. above 18°C (64°F) NT + SD; Med light; followed by cool temps. (6–8 wks) or refrig. 4–9°C (40–48°F) with lights (1100 lux) for 12 hrs./day	MinNT 14–16°C (57–62°F); Med light (Fig. 17–26)	6–8
Saintpaulia ionantha Wendl. African violet	Leaf cuttings (Fig. 17–31)	BH (22°C, 73°F), MinNT 21°C (70°F), Lo light	28–42 days	MinNT 21°C (70°F); Lo light (<16,000 lux or ca. 1500 ft-c)	MinNT 22°C (72°F); Lo light (<14,000 lux or ca. 1200 ft-c)	26–30
Senecio × hybridus D.C. *(S. Cruentus)* Florist's cineraria	Seeds	MinNT 21°C (70°F)	10–14 days	NT between 12–15°C (54–60°F); Med light (Fig. 17–32)	NT near 10°C (50°F) for quality; Med light.	20–26

Symbols: BH = Bottom heat; ca. = circa (about); Mist = Mist propagation
LD = Long days; SD = Short days; Lo light = <22,000 lux; Med = 22,000 to 43,000 lux; Hi = >44,000 lux
MinNT = Minimum night temperature, C (F)   NT = Night temperature   < = Less than   > = Greater than
Source: Adapted from R. M. Sachs, A. M. Kofranek, and W. P. Hackett. 1976. Evaluating new pot plant species. *Flor. Rev.* 159(4116): 35–36.

Occasionally some flower growers add carbon dioxide (CO_2) to the greenhouse atmosphere produced from methane or propane burned in well-ventilated gas burners (*2, 17, 22, 27, 30*). During the winter when greenhouse ventilators are closed tightly and when ventilation is reduced to conserve heat, the CO_2 available to the plants may become deficient. The added CO_2 replaces the CO_2 absorbed by the plants for photosynthesis during the daylight hours (Ch. 7). Concentrations from 500 to 1500 ppm improve growth under such poorly ventilated conditions. The CO_2 concentration of outside air is about 300 ppm, and normal ventilation replenishes the CO_2 supply; therefore, little benefit is derived by burning these gases where there are about one to two air changes per hour in the greenhouse by either normal or forced ventilation.

Mineral Fertilization

Greenhouse plants are usually grown in containers such as pots, cans, benches, or wooden boxes. Roots are confined to a small soil volume and therefore must be irrigated and fertilized often to sustain maximum growth (*2, 17, 22, 27*). Mineral nutrients are usually supplied, often in the irrigation water, by frequent application of liquid fertilizers containing the macronutrient elements (Chs. 8, 18). Fertilizers that are relatively insoluble and immobile in the soil, such as phosphorus and calcium, are frequently incorporated into the soil mix before planting. Mineral deficiencies in greenhouse plants are seldom seen, because of the frequent application of fertilizers. Excesses of salts sometimes result from heavy use of these fertilizers. When salts build up in the soil, the containers must be supplied with an excess of water or liquid fertilizer at each irrigation (an excess of the capacity of the container) to avoid accumulation of excessive salts in the root zone (Ch. 18). A knowledge of the plant's requirements for mineral nutrients is useful in trying to achieve maximum growth in the shortest period. However, supplying plants with a well-balanced, complete liquid fertilizer solution every time they are irrigated can supplant the need for this specialized knowledge.

These greenhouse practices are referred to as **forcing**. Forcing means the manipulation of light (intensity and day length), temperature (mostly during the night), CO_2, time of propagation (Ch. 5), mineral nutrition, and application of chemicals to produce the highest-quality plants out of season.

The following pages discuss some common florists' plants. Some of their temperature and photoperiod (day length) requirements for propagation, growing and flowering are included in the text and in Table 17–1. Important or unique mineral requirements for rapid growth are also mentioned.

Antirrhinum majus L. Snapdragon. SCROPHULARIACEAE. (*2, 15, 21, 22, 27, 29*)[1]

Native to the Mediterranean region. This annual, grown for cut flowers, is best propagated by seeds germinating at 21°C (70°F). Supplementary lighting is used to hasten the growth of seedlings. After the seedlings are transplanted, the night temperature is maintained at 15°C (59°F) until they attain about 10 to 12 leaves or a reasonable height (15 cm or 6 in) for flower induction. Long days and high temperatures (15°C or 59°F) favor flower initiation. Temperatures then should be lowered to 10°C (50°F) for flower development for the winter flowering group, but maintained at 15°C (59°F) for the fall or spring groups.

Snapdragons can be grown either as a single- or a multiple-stem plant. Pinching or removing the growing points to induce branching delays the crop by three to four weeks. Single-stem crops can be flowered all year long by selecting the proper cultivar to flower in the season desired. In the Northern Hemisphere seeds of the winter flowering group are sown in August, the early spring flowering group in September to November, late spring group in December to February, and the summer group in April to June. Commercial flower seed companies categorize the colors, heights, flowering seasons, and sowing dates of the various cultivars.

Snapdragons do not require liberal fertilization and are subject to root damage from excessive soluble salts. Care should be taken to plant seedlings in soil relatively low in fertilizers and soluble salts. Superphosphate (p. 396) is added before planting. Young plants respond well to frequent applications of dilute liquid fertilizers.

A recently introduced snapdragon, for the garden, is the Madam Butterfly cultivar, which has open florets more like a pentstemon flower than a snapdragon (Fig. 17–9). Stem lengths vary from 30 to 75 cm (12 to 30 in) and the taller ones are suitable for cut flowers.

[1]Numbers refer to references listed at the end of the chapters.

Fig. 17–9 *Left:* 'Madame Butterfly' snapdragons resemble a penstemon flower which can be used as cut flowers or perhaps as a potted plant. *Right:* The common snapdragon, used both as a garden plant and as a cut flower.

Two cultural problems are "skips" (no flowers in certain positions on the spike) or hollow stems. Both problems have been attributed to low light intensity in the winter. Skips may also be caused by very low temperatures just as the flowers are being initiated on the spike. Some diseases are rust, mildew, and botrytis. Common pests are aphids, white flies, cabbage looper, and spider mites.

Calceolaria crenatiflora Cav. Calceolaria (pocket book plant). SCROPHULARIACEAE. (*2, 27, 29, 31, 32*)

Native to the high elevations of Peru and Chile. Calceolarias are grown as potted plants during the cool season (Fig. 17–10). Plants are propagated from seed at 21°C (70°F) from July to September for late winter production. Seedlings are spaced early and shaded from

Fig. 17–10 *Calceolaria crenatiflora* grown in a 10 cm (4 in) pot from seed. One of the common names is pocket book plant, because the flower resembles the shape of a woman's purse.

bright light. It is possible to overwater in the seedling stage and damage roots. In shifting to a larger pot, take care not to set the plants too deeply as the stems rot easily. Growth and flowering is best at a 10°C (50°F) night temperature after the seedling stage. Calceolarias also flower at high temperatures if the days are short and the light intensity is high. The plants are usually grown for Easter but if held for Mother's Day, they must be maintained in a well-shaded house to lower the temperature and to avoid heat damage.

Light-colored leaves from poor roots or too much light is a problem. The most troublesome pest is white fly. Aphids, thrips, and occasionally mealy bugs are also damaging.

Chrysanthemum × morifolium Ramat. Chrysanthemum. COMPOSITAE. (*2, 16, 21, 22, 25, 27, 28, 29, 31, 33, 35*)

Native to China. Chrysanthemums are grown commercially in greenhouses year round and outdoors during the mild seasons of the year. This perennial is propagated from terminal cuttings taken from pathogen-free stock plants grown under long days at 17°C (63°F). Garden plants are increased by division or offshoots in the spring as well as by terminal cuttings.

Flowering is induced by the onset of short days (long nights), which normally occurs as early as mid-July and as late as September in the northern temperate zone depending on the latitude and the cultivar grown. Usually three to four weeks of continuous short days at night temperatures of about 15°C to 16°C (59°F to 61°F) are necessary to complete flower initiation and early development. Full bloom is reached within 7 to 14 weeks after the first inductive short day, depending on the cultivar. Some cultivars are early blooming and others are midseason to late blooming. Flowering is accomplished on a year round program in the greenhouses or outdoors in subtropical climates where low night temperatures (below 10°C) do not limit the initiation of flower buds. When flower induction is desired, plants are covered with black cloth each evening to create short day conditions (Fig. 17–11) during the long days of summer. During the naturally short days of fall, winter, and early spring, black cloth is not necessary for flower induction. Flowering can be delayed by lighting the plants in the middle of the night (nightbreak) during the fall and winter, with either incandescent or fluorescent lamps (Figs. 17–7 and 17–12). The light intensity should be 55 to 110 lux (5 to 10 ft-c). Plants are grown in pots as short-stemmed flowering plants (Table 17–1, Figs. 17–13, and 17–14) or in ground beds for long-stem cut

Fig. 17–11   A convenient method of covering plants with black cloth to shorten the day length. The black cloth must drape below the bench to avoid light leaks. The black cloth or black plastic is folded above one end of the bench during the day to create the least shade. It is possible for one person to draw the black cloth if it is hung low enough to be reached almost halfway across the bench. The cloth slides on smooth heavy-gauge wire. Note the light sockets below the center of the black cloth. These fuchsias were being grown under short day conditions to prevent flowering, but a week later the black cloth was removed and light was added to create long days to induce flowering. The black cloth should be a black sateen with a minimum thread count of 64 × 104 to the inch. Black plastic can also be used but more care must be exercised to prevent tearing. This entire procedure is usually mechanized in large commercial installations.

Fig. 17–13   'Nob Hill' chrysanthemum grown in a 12 cm (5 in) pot. Single terminal cuttings were planted on January 6 under short-day conditions; plants were thoroughly sprayed on January 13 with 2500 ppm B-nine®. The single shoots were disbudded to one flower bud each (the terminal one) between February 17 and 24. This photograph was taken on March 17.

Fig. 17–14   The chrysanthemum cultivar Princess Anne grown as a potted plant. Five cuttings were planted in a 15 cm (6 in) pot and placed under supplementary incandescent light for two weeks before they were subjected to short days to form flower buds. Each plant was pinched (its apical tip removed) one week after planting to induce branching. All but three shoots on each plant were removed about three weeks after planting, leaving a total of 15 shoots for blooming. The plants were then sprayed to runoff with a solution of 2500 ppm B-nine®; a similar spray was applied again one week later (fourth week). B-nine® is a growth retardant used to reduce the length of the shoots. On the sixth and seventh weeks, each shoot was disbudded of all flower buds except the terminal one. This procedure is usually done over a two-week period if all shoots are not ready for disbudding at the same time. The resulting flowers are large since all the photosynthates of each shoot are directed to the one remaining terminal flower. This plant flowered 11 weeks after planting. It is important to shade the flowers with cheesecloth (Fig. 17–5) just after the color begins to develop to prevent sun scald.

Fig. 17–12   Fluorescent lamps can be used to prevent premature flowering of chrysanthemums (short day plants). One row of 120 cm (4 ft), 40-watt lamps placed 2.5 m (8 ft) above the soil provides an ample light intensity. Fluorescent tubes are spaced 120 cm apart within the row and the greenhouse is 7.3 m (24 ft) wide.

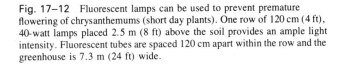

Fig. 17-15 Large standard chrysanthemums are packed in boxes for shipment to market. Most large long-stemmed chrysanthemums are grown in greenhouses or plastic houses (Fig. 17-5) in California. They are shipped by air freight or by refrigerated truck to eastern markets.

Fig. 17-16 To grow a specimen cyclamen to a large size requires about 18 months at 10°C (50°F) night temperature. *Source:* Carl Pearlstein.

Cyclamen persicum Mill. Cyclamen.
PRIMULACEAE. *(2, 22, 27, 28, 29, 31, 32)*

flowers (Fig. 17-5). A pot chrysanthemum requires less time after planting until short days are given for flowering than does a chrysanthemum grown as a tall cut flower. The time elapsed may be only one week for the pot plant but as long as five weeks for the cut flower. Potted chrysanthemums are generally sprayed with 2500 ppm B-nine® once or twice to retard growth (p. 140), particularly for naturally tall-growing cultivars (Fig. 17-13). Potted plants have about 20 blooms per 15 cm pot and are sold when three-quarters of the blooms are mature.

Flowers are cut fully open for market. Large flowers are sold in one-dozen lots and are carefully packed in boxes (Fig. 17-15). Pompom chrysanthemums are sold in small bunches containing a set amount of stems for a particular cultivar. Flowers may be cut in the bud stage and opened in a solution containing about 2 to 5 percent sucrose plus citric acid at 500 ppm and a biocide. Stems cut 60 to 80 cm with buds of 5 cm diameter open fully (15 cm diameter) in one week at 21°C *(12)*.

Chrysanthemums grow well in slightly acid soil and require large amounts of nitrogen and potassium fertilizers early in their life to ensure high-quality foliage and flowers. Fertilization is often suspended when the plants have flower buds 1 cm in diameter. They tolerate moderately high levels of soluble salts (Ch. 8). They are subject to pathogens carried in the soil *(Rhizoctonia* and *Verticillium)* and in the air *(Botrytis)*. The most common pests are aphids, leaf miners, thrips, and spider mites.

Native to Asia Minor. If you ever tour the eastern Mediterranean region between February and May, you will never forget these lovely wild plants blooming in profusion. They flower best during the cool months of the year.

More cyclamens are grown in Europe than in America, but nevertheless these potted plants are popular in the United States during late winter and early spring. Cyclamen is propagated by seeds sown in late summer to midfall for an 18-month crop (Fig. 17-16), but they are also sown in the spring to produce a smaller 9-month crop (Fig. 17-17) *(36)*. Seeds are large and are planted about 5 cm apart just under the soil surface. Germination is best at a constant temperature of 20°C (68°F) in the dark (Table 17-1). The best temperatures for seedling growth are 20°C (68°F) at night and 2°C to 5°C (5°F to 10°F) higher during the day. Plants develop rapidly at these temperatures but it is necessary to lower the night temperature to 16°C (61°F) about two and a half months before flowers are desired (Table 17-1). Plants require constant fertilization with a liquid fertilizer to ensure rapid growth, starting about two months after seed germination. The light intensity should be kept high during most of the year, however, shading is necessary in the summer to reduce heat when cyclamens are grown in the greenhouse. Carbon dioxide (CO_2) fertilization in the greenhouse aids growth during the winter months when greenhouse ventilation may be impossible. No apparent advantage has been noticed from CO_2 injection in the

Fig. 17–17 A cyclamen grown in a 10-cm pot for small-pot sales. This plant was produced in only nine months by first growing the seedling at a warm night temperature (20°C; 68°F) and then in a cooler night temperature (16°C; 61°F) for about two to three months before flowering is desired.

summer when ventilation is adequate. Plants do very well outdoors under partial shade in cool, moist climates.

The most common pests are aphids and spider mites. Occasionally the tubers develop a crown rot caused by *Botrytis* and bacterial soft rot caused by *Erwinia*.

Dianthus caryophyllus L. Carnation.
CARYOPHYLLACEAE. (*2, 8, 22, 27, 28, 29*)

Native to Europe. Carnations are best grown where nights are cool and light is intense, as in California, Colorado, western North Carolina, Colombia (South America), and in the Mediterranean area in winter.

Carnations are ever-blooming in warm winter climates or in heated greenhouses. Flowering is most profuse during periods of high light intensity (about 44,000 lux or 4000 ft-c) and long days. Flower quality is optimal when plants grow in high light and at cool night temperatures of 11°C (52°F).

This herbaceous perennial is propagated from terminal cuttings. Rooted cuttings are usually planted in late spring spaced about 20 × 20 cm (8 by 8 in) apart in benches or ground beds. The young plants are pinched

(the central growing point is removed) to induce branching or to delay flowering. Shoots pinched in the Northern Hemisphere in July and August flower about four months later, and those pinched in November and December flower in about six to eight months depending on the light in the spring. The time difference is attributed to the light intensity that hastens or delays flower development during these two periods (*8, 27*).

Carnations grow in almost any soil if it is properly irrigated and fertilized (*24*). A slightly acid soil (pH 6.5) is preferred. Phosphorus and calcium are mixed into the soil before planting. Nitrogen and potassium are applied frequently as liquid fertilizers.

Lateral flower buds below the terminal bloom are disbudded (removed) as early as possible, leaving only a single flower per stem to develop. Cultivars of miniature carnations are not disbudded and are grown as branched flowering stems. These are referred to as spray carnations. Flowers of disbudded types are usually cut when fully open, but are sometimes cut in the tight bud stage (with 2 cm of petals above the calyx showing, Fig. 17–18) and stored at 1°C (33°F). After storage, for up to six weeks, they must be opened in a 10 percent sucrose solution containing a biocide (*13*). Fully opened flowers with stems of about 50 cm (20 in) are graded, packed, and sold in bunches of 25. The important holidays for sale are Christmas, Easter, and Mother's Day.

Commercial plantings are replaced at least every two years because foliar (*Fusarium roseum*) and root pathogens (*Fusarium oxysporum* and *Rhizoctonia solani*) increase over time. Common pests are thrips and spider mites.

Fig. 17–18 Carnation buds in various stages of development. Flower buds on 25 to 50 cm (10 to 20 in) cut stems are ideal sizes (stages 2 and 3) to open in 10 percent sucrose plus a biocide such as 200 ppm Physan-20®, which is commonly used in swimming pools. Buds in stage 2 open in six days and those in stage 3 in four days at temperatures of 21°C (70°F) in a lighted room (110 lux).

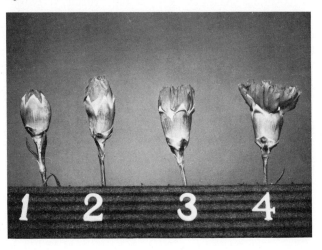

Fig. 17–19 A multiple-branched 'Annette Hegg' poinsettia in a 15 cm (6 in) pot for the Christmas season. Terminal cuttings were propagated in mid-August; rooted cuttings were planted about September 1 and pinched about September 15. Plants usually flower in early December if night temperatures are maintained at 17°C (65°F) and if extraneous light from other projects does not reach the poinsettia plants. Low intensities of light (22 lux or 2 ft-c) for several hours each night delay or prevent poinsettias from flowering. Plants should be covered each night with black cloth (Fig. 17–11) from October 1 to November 1 if extraneous light is suspected. The plant shown here was grown entirely under naturally shortened day lengths. *Source:* Carl Pearlstein.

Euphorbia pulcherrima Willd. ex Klotzsch. Poinsettia. EUPHORBIACEAE. (*2, 5, 20, 21, 22, 28, 29*)

Native to Mexico. Poinsettias are propagated from terminal cuttings (Table 17–1). Red cultivars are grown in pots for Christmas (Fig. 17–19). White and pink forms are available, but they are in less demand than the red colors. The free-branching cultivar, Annette Hegg, with its various shades of red is the most popular in Europe and the United States because of its relatively easy culture.

Poinsettias are short-day plants, which initiate flower buds in early October in the Northern Hemisphere. Light intensity should be 33,000 lux (3000 ft-c) to ensure proper bud initiation (Table 17–1). The plants flower in about 8 to 10 weeks. Thus flower initiation in early October gives flowering in early December. Flowering can be forced during all seasons with 17°C (65°F) night temperature and a short photoperiod (see Ch. 6), but there is no public demand for this plant out of season because of its traditional association with Christmas.

A slightly acid soil (pH 6 to 6.5), fertilized with moderate quantities of acid-forming fertilizers to prevent leaf chlorosis, is best. Troublesome pathogens are mostly soil-borne (*Rhizoctonia, Pythium,* and *Thielaviopsis*) and are prevented by soil pasteurization. Common pests are white flies and spider mites.

Fuchsia × hybrida Hort. ex Vilm. Fuchsia. ONAGRACEAE. (*2, 22, 32*)

Native to tropical America. Plants are propagated mostly from terminal cuttings but occasionally from seed. Stock plants are ideally kept under short-day conditions and 15°C (59°F) so they remain vegetative and produce many terminal cuttings. After the cuttings are rooted, they can be potted into 12 cm (5 in) pots in a porous soil mixture. When the shoots have about six to seven nodes, the growing tip can be removed (pinched) to leave four nodes on the plant to induce lateral shoots (Fig. 17–20). Four weeks after the growing tip is removed, the plants are given a four-hour night break lighting of 55 to 77 lux (5 to 7 ft-c.) for a minimum of three weeks to induce flowering (Table 17–1). The plants become rank and top-heavy if given too many successive long days (more than 21). Thereafter they can be grown under short-day conditions, similar to flowering chrysanthemums, to avoid undue stem elongation promoted by the lighting. The plants flower about 50 days from the first inductive

Fig. 17–20 A fuchsia grown in a 12 cm (5 in) pot is at the proper stage of growth to receive the long-day treatment for 21 consecutive days (Table 17–1). The area pointed out shows where the single stem plant was pinched (at the fourth node). Note the four shoots resulting from the pinch. Such plants should be returned to short day length conditions after receiving the 21 long days to prevent excessive shoot elongation. Plants can be expected to flower about 30 days after the shift back to short days.

378

long day under lights. The night temperatures best for growth and flowering are between 15° to 18°C (59° to 64°F). Plants can be flowered on a year-round schedule with this system, but flowering is most profuse in the spring and summer (*11*). Fuchsias do not thrive, however, in hot summer conditions. Since growth retardants are not too effective, this plant is best grown in a hanging basket. Common pests are white flies, aphids, thrips, and scale on older stock plants.

Hydrangea macrophylla Ser. Hydrangea.
SAXIFRAGACEAE. (*2, 21, 22, 28, 29, 31*)

Native to Japan. The hydrangea is usually grown as a florist potted plant (Fig. 17–21), but it can grow to 4m (12 ft) if planted outdoors in its native habitat or in a Mediterranean climate (with supplementary irrigation).

The inflorescence is a panicle (see p. 35) of flowers. The flowers are rather small and inconspicuous, but the sepals are large and showy. They develop rose, pink, white, or blue colors. The white ones have no pigment, but the red sepals contain anthocyanin. Accumulation of aluminum from the soil can change red to various shades of blue depending on the quantity of aluminum in the sepal cells and the cultivar. Growers may change the

Fig. 17–21 A hydrangea with two large inflorescences growing in a 15 cm (6 in) pot. This woody plant requires about 8 to 12 months to grow to this size from a terminal cutting. However, dormant plants (that have been cooled for six weeks) can be obtained from commercial flower growers in January and forced into flowers for early spring.

naturally red color of certain cultivars to blue by adding alum or aluminum sulfate to the soil before the inflorescences initiate and develop. Adding aluminum early ensures amounts necessary in the plant to cause the color change. In certain soils with large quantities of native aluminum, the soil acidity need only be lowered to about pH 5 by adding iron sulfate or elemental sulfur for the aluminum to become available to the plant in the soil solution. If only small amounts of aluminum are absorbed because the mineral is not readily available, bract color is intermediate between red and blue (magenta), which is considered undesirable for sale. To ensure that the clear reds and pinks develop, the soil should be made alkaline by adding sufficient limestone. In summation, plants grown for red and pink sepals should have a soil pH of 6.5 to 7.0, and those grown for blue should have a soil pH of 5.5 or lower.

Inflorescences are initiated in late September or early October outdoors at night temperatures near 15°C to 17°C (59°F to 63°F) with high light intensity and a shortening day length. The inflorescences develop best at lower temperatures of between 4°C to 7°C (40°F and 45°F). Flowers are visible microscopically on early-blooming cultivars about September 25 (in the Northern Hemisphere) and up to a month later for the later-flowering types. Once the inflorescences are initiated, the leaves are removed, and the potted plants moved to cold rooms at 4°C to 7°C (40°F to 45°F) for up to six weeks in the dark. Following this necessary cold period, plants are moved to greenhouses (usually in early January) to force them in to bloom. Usually 80 to 100 days at about 17°C (63°F) are required to force the plants for sale (Table 17–1). The largest market for hydrangeas is in the spring for Easter or Mother's Day.

To obtain dwarfs, plants are treated with SADH (B-nine) (see Ch. 6) to reduce the internodal length. Applications may be made the summer before forcing or during the spring forcing period (*2*).

Plants are propagated from terminal or one-node leaf-bud cuttings taken in midspring. After they root, they are potted into 10 cm (4 in) pots.

A serious problem is iron chlorosis, usually caused by poor roots or by alkaline soil (pH 7 or greater). Chlorosis can be overcome by spraying the foliage with iron sulfate or chelated iron. The prominent fungal pathogen is *Botrytis* of the inflorescence, which develops during cold storage. Leaf debris, which is a source of infection for this disease, must be removed from the storage rooms. A fungicide specific for *Botrytis*, such as benomyl, helps control the disease. Aphids and spider mites are pests during forcing.

Fig. 17–22 The relative size of bulblets (*left*), yearlings (*center*), and "commercial" size bulbs (*right*) of the Easter lily (*Lilium longiflorum*). The bulblets and yearlings will be planted in the field to increase in size, and the "commercial" will be sold to greenhouse operators who will force them for the Easter market. This photograph was taken in early October when Easter lily bulbs are dug from the field in the Pacific Northwest.

Lilium longiflorum Thunb. Easter lily.
LILIACEAE. (*2, 9, 21, 22, 27, 28, 29, 30, 31*)

Native to Japan. This white lily has long been associated with the Easter season. Bulbs (Fig. 17–22) are grown in fields in coastal California, Oregon, and in Japan because the cool climate during a long growing season allows the bulbs to grow large (Table 17–1). They are dug in September and October in California and Oregon and shipped to greenhouse growers for immediate planting into pots. In mild climates, such as California and the southern states, the bulbs are placed outdoors under straw after potting to prevent frost damage and to maintain good moisture. From October to December, roots develop and the bulbs begin to sprout. In cold parts of the country, the pots are placed in controlled temperature coolers for root development and vernalization (Ch. 6).

Immediately after Christmas, the lily pots are brought in from the outside or from the coolers and placed in 16°C (61°F) greenhouses (Table 17–1). They are forced into bloom in approximately 120 days, but the desired forcing time depends on the date of Easter in that particular year. The flowers are initiated just at the time the bulbs sprout. A high light intensity is required during the winter months to prevent abortion of the flower buds. The growing temperature has an important effect on the rate of growth during forcing. If some flower buds are developing too rapidly, the grower segregates all those that are equally advanced and moves them into a cool greenhouse, and moves the plants with the least ma-

ture buds into a warm house. When lily flowers are delayed in maturity for the Easter holidays, the greenhouse temperature is raised but, because of the high temperatures, the plants can become too tall (elongated) for sale. Until recently there was no absolute way of keeping the plants' height desirable, but now lily growers apply chemical growth retardants to the soil to reduce plant height. These chemicals are taken up systemically (through the roots and translocated) as the plant grows. This treatment is used most frequently for an early Easter (when heat is used to help accelerate flowering) rather than for a late Easter, when the plants are "grown cool." The registered growth retardant used is ancymidol (p. 141).

The most troublesome insects are aphids, which if not controlled on the flower buds, distort buds and flowers seriously. Spider mites (Fig. 11–22) can also cause plant distortion. There are several bulb rots caused by fungi. Viruses are controlled in the bulb field by constantly removing infected plants when they show virus symptoms.

Matthiola incana L. Column stocks.
CRUCIFERAE. (*2, 27, 31, 32*)

Native to southern Europe. This annual is grown for cut flowers. It is propagated by seeds sown in the spring for winter flowering and late winter for late spring flowering. After the seedlings are transplanted, the night temperature should be lowered to 16°C (61°F) whenever feasible. Flowers do not initiate if the temperature exceeds 17°C (65°F) for more than six hours per day. If the temperatures are unfavorable, the seedlings continue to produce leaves until conditions are correct for flower initiation (*31*).

A given sample of commercial seed produces both single (fertile) and double (sterile) flowers (Fig. 17–23).

Fig. 17–23 *Left:* A spike with infertile double flowers of stock (*Matthiola incana*). *Right:* The single flowers, which are fertile. At the bottom of the spike with single flowers are long upright fruits (siliques), which bear the seeds.

The proportion of each depends on the seed source and viability at germination. The "doubles" are more desirable as cut flowers than "singles." Since the "doubles" are more vigorous than the "singles," there is a net increase of "doubles" over "singles" in any planting. There are special trisomic strains that produce greater quantities of "doubles" than "singles."

Although stocks are grown successfully in cool greenhouses, most commercial flowers are grown outdoors in Arizona and California. Flowering is most abundant between late winter and midspring during the cool weather.

Stocks have a high requirement for nitrogen and potassium. Yellow leaves indicate nitrogen deficiency and marginal burning indicates a potassium deficiency.

Common diseases are bacterial stem rot and *Botrytis* rot of flowers. Insect pests are aphids and thrips, which spread viruses.

Pelargonium × *hortorum* L. H. Bailey. Geranium. GERANIACEAE. (*2, 22, 26, 27, 28, 29*)

Native to South Africa. This perennial (Fig. 17–24) is propagated from terminal and stem cuttings or seeds (Table 17–1). It is grown as a potted plant mainly in 10-cm pots for spring sales. Flowering is hastened under long

Fig. 17–24 A 'Carefree' geranium with two inflorescences fully developed and many more immature and developing rapidly. Seeds were sown in October and the photograph was taken in March.

Fig. 17–25 A 'Sprinter' geranium seedling in a 10 cm (4 in) pot. Seeds were sown on November 8, transplanted to a flat on November 17, potted on December 15, and the photograph was taken on January 11. Up to this stage seedlings were grown at night temperatures of 21°C (70°F). A plant of this size or slightly smaller is at the stage for shifting to a 15.5°C (60°F) night temperature and treating with Cycocel®. Thirty ml (1 fluid oz) of 3000 ppm Cycocel® is put into this size pot. Cycocel® enhances flower formation and aids in reducing the ultimate size of the plant. Treatment of this particular plant produced flowers in mid-March in California. Since the amount (duration and intensity) of daylight controls the time geranium plants flower, results can vary in different parts of the country.

days and high light intensities *(4)*, but plants flower sparsely during the winter under warm 15°C (59°F) greenhouse conditions (Table 17–1). Cycocel® enhances flowering of plants grown from seed (Fig. 17–25). The geranium is a popular summer bedding plant prized for its profusion of red, white, or pink flowers. Plants survive the winter in subtropical climates but are usually killed or severely damaged by frosts.

Geraniums tolerate neglect in the greenhouse although foliage quantity (color and size) or flower numbers will be reduced. They grow well in most soil mixtures and will respond with increased growth to a frequent application of liquid fertilizer (once or twice per week). Bacterial and fungal root pathogens are infectious in all climates, and foliar and floral pathogens (bacterial leaf spot and *Botrytis*) may be a problem in humid climates.

Primula malacoides Franch. Primrose. PRIMULACEAE. (*2, 3, 22, 31, 32*)

Native to China. Plants are propagated from seeds at 21°C (70°F) in late spring for midwinter flowering. Sowing seeds after midfall should be avoided; late plantings do not flower because of warm weather in late spring. Seedlings are transplanted to a 3 cm by 3 cm spacing in flats as soon as possible, and they should be kept cool by shading the greenhouse in the summer. The plants are transferred to pots when they are large enough for transplanting. As weather permits, the greenhouse night temperatures should be reduced to 10°C (50°F). Flowering normally takes place at this temperature, but at 16°C (61°F) or above, the days must be shortened with black cloth (as described for chrysanthemums) for 10 weeks before flowers are desired (*31*).

P. malacoides is grown more widely than *P. obconica* Hance. *P. obconica* commonly causes a skin rash on contact in some persons, whereas *P. malacoides* does not.

Poor roots can cause marginal leaf burn and yellowing of the foliage. The former is due to desiccation at the leaf edges and the latter due to poor iron uptake. Common pests are thrips, aphids, white flies, and spider mites.

Fig. 17–26   A 'Red Wing' azalea ready for sale. Most buds are open but others will open in the home. Azaleas require about two years to grow from a terminal cutting to a plant large enough for sale. Plants in bud and ready for forcing can, however, be purchased most any time of the year. After these plants are moved to a greenhouse with a 15°C (59°F) night temperature, flowering can be expected within five to seven weeks depending on the light intensity available. *Source:* Carl Pearlstein.

Rhododendron obtusum (Lindl.) Planch. Kurume azalea. ERICACEAE. (*2, 14, 21, 27, 28, 29*)

Native to Japan. Azaleas (Fig. 17–26) are broad-leaf evergreen perennials propagated by terminal cuttings (Table 17–1) or by grafting. They bloom in the garden in mild climates each spring, but can be forced into bloom during any season in the greenhouse when the proper photoperiod and temperature techniques are used (*19*). Flower buds initiate freely at night temperatures of 18°C (65°F). Short-day conditions hasten initiation but are not essential for all cultivars (Table 17–1). B-nine foliage sprays (2500 ppm) are also used to hasten flower initiation (*19*). After flower initiation and limited bud development, the developing flower buds eventually cease further development and enter a "resting" state. This resting state is overcome by a period of low temperature, after which the bud continues to develop and bloom at higher "forcing" temperatures. Commercially the plants are subjected to temperatures of 4°C to 9°C (40°F to 48°F) for six weeks in a refrigerator, with lights (1100 lux or 100 ft-c.) for 12 hours each day (Table 17–1). The final blooming (forcing) in the greenhouse works best at 15°C (60°F) under reduced light intensity (Table 17–1). All these processes occur naturally at slow rates during the summer, fall, and winter but are greatly hastened under the optimal conditions stated above.

The azalea of commerce is complex in its genealogy (*23*) and only one species of many is discussed here.

The many hybrids still retain the characteristics of plants classified as "acid-lovers." The rhododendron group generally grows on impoverished acid soils. Azaleas require an acid soil reaction to absorb iron from the soil. They also tolerate the large quantities of aluminum and manganese often found in acid soils which are toxic to many plants. This does not mean that rhododendrons are calciphobic (literally, "calcium-fearing"), as some literature sources suggest. Experiments have shown that calcium is required in small amounts for optimum growth. Azaleas, however, do not tolerate high soil salinity (Chs. 8, 18) and do best when small amounts of organic nitrogen fertilizers are added to the soil surface. Organic nitrogen, such as blood or cottonseed meal, requires up to six weeks during the summer for the nitrogen to become available to the roots, but there is little likelihood of injuring the roots with these materials.

Azaleas are grown in pots and are available all year round but are most popular for sale from Christmas to Mother's Day. From 14 to 36 months are required to provide a flowering plant from a terminal cutting depending on growing location and the size of the plant desired.

Common soil pathogens are *Phytophthora* and *Cylindrocladium*. Leaf gall and petal blight often occur on the upper portions of the plant under moist conditions. Common pests are nematodes, thrips, black vine weevils, and spider mites.

Fig. 17–28 Two rose shoots resulting from cuts (arrows) that removed flowering shoots from the plant. The shoots are about one month old and can be expected to flower in about two to three weeks. Both shoots are vigorous, indicating that the plant is healthy and that the light conditions are ideal for growth.

Fig. 17–27 One method of cutting rose flowers in the greenhouse. The shears are about to cut above the second five-leaflet leaf. Two or three leaves above the previous cut (arrow) are left on the shoot. These remaining leaves provide photosynthates for subsequent shoot growth. A new flower can be expected to result from removing the shoot about 45 days from the time the cut is made depending on the light intensity in the greenhouse.

Rosa hybrida. Hybrid tea rose. ROSACEAE.
(*18, 27, 28, 29, 31*)

Native to the northern temperate zone. These woody shrubs are propagated from cuttings or by grafting onto a suitable rootstock. The hybrid tea rose flowers perpetually in summer, in winter if the climate is warm, or in heated greenhouses, but it flowers most profusely during the long, warm bright days of summer.

Greenhouse temperatures are best maintained at about 14°C to 16°C (57°F to 62°F) at night. Cutting roses properly (Fig. 17–27) is an important factor in maintaining continuous production and good flower quality. Blooms can be timed to flower by pinching (removing the growing point of terminal shoots). In 35 to 54 days flowers are ready to harvest on the forced new shoots. The rapidity with which they flower depends on light intensity. A shorter time is required for blooming in spring and summer than in late fall and winter. Flowers form on all new shoots (Fig. 17–28) after the removal of a flower from the bush. Some flowers do not mature, aborting because of improper environmental conditions such as low light intensity that are not conducive to full flower development (*37*). Plants grow tall after one season and should be pruned during the winter in the garden (Ch. 16) or during the summer in the greenhouse. Greenhouse plants, if properly cut for flowers and pruned annually, may not have to be replanted for five to eight years de-

Fig. 17–29 A 'Cara Mia' rose flower ready for cutting. Most roses should have at least two sepals (see Ch. 2) turned downward when the cut is made. This indicates that the flower bud is mature enough to cut and the xylem in the neck just below the flower hypanthium is developed enough to withstand water stresses after cutting. Flower stems should be placed in water with a pH of about 3.5 (acid reaction) as soon as possible. Flowers should be placed in a shady location that is as cool as possible (down to 2°C or 35°F) to help prevent wilting. Rose flowers kept in water in a refrigerator overnight (16 to 24 hours) are said to be "hardened" and withstand the harsh conditions in the home better than flowers freshly cut and placed at once in the home. A commercial flower preservative — a combination of sugar, an acidifier (e.g., citric acid), and a biocide — will enhance opening and longevity of cut flowers.

The most common disease, powdery mildew, limits both outdoor and greenhouse culture. Aphids and red spider mites are difficult pests to control, especially during warm weather.

Saintpaulia ionantha Wendl. African violet.
GESNARIACEAE. *(2, 22, 27, 28, 29, 31)*

Native to Africa. These are propagated by mature leaf cuttings during any season (Table 17–1) (Fig. 17–30). The propagation mix should be porous (Fig. 17–31) and maintained at about 21°C (70°F) in high relative humidity. The light intensity for both plantlets and maturing plants (about to flower) should be between 10,000 and 16,000 lux (900 to 1500 ft-c). Direct or high light intensity damages foliage. Flowering ceases or greatly decreases below 8800 lux (800 ft-c) in the greenhouse except in the summer, when the long days compensate for the low light intensity. An optimum growing temperature is 21°C (70°F). Between 8 and 10 months' growing time is required for a leaf cutting to grow to flowering size in a 10 cm (4 in) pot.

Plants can be propagated, grown, and flowered entirely under fluorescent (cool white) lamps. At a light intensity of 6,600 lux (700 ft-c)[2] for about 16 hours per

[2] Two 120 cm (48 in), 40-watt tubes with a reflector placed 30 cm (12 in) above the plant tops.

Fig. 17–30 African violet (*Saintpaulia ionantha*) 'Julianne' about six months after propagation from a leaf cutting.

pending on the health of the plants and the structural quality of the soil mixture (permeability to water). Occasionally crown canker (a bacterial disease near the soil surface) will hasten the need for replanting.

Plants should be fertilized continuously with small quantities of nitrogen and potassium. Phosphorous and calcium are mixed into the soil before planting and should be applied on the soil surface annually. The soil should be slightly acid (pH 6.5).

Flowers are cut in the late-bud stage usually when one or two sepals (Fig. 17–29) have turned downward or just as one or two petals have unfurled. They are sorted and graded into uniform stem lengths that also have similar flower head (bud) sizes and quality. Long-stem roses, which have large flower buds of superior quality, command a premium price. Flowers are packaged in bunches of 10 in Europe and 25 in the United States. The most important U.S. holidays for rose sales are Christmas, St. Valentine's Day, Easter, and Mother's Day.

Fig. 17-31 The leaf cuttings of African violet on the right were just placed in vermiculite rooting medium. The rooted leaf cutting on the left is three and a half months old and shows the original leaf cutting (arrow) and the plantlet formed at the base of the short petiole. In transplanting the plantlet, the original leaf should be removed. Many of the roots may also be removed to make planting in the soil easy. Leaf cuttings of African violets should be propagated at night temperatures about 21°C (70°F).

Fig. 17-32 A mature cineraria (*Senecio × hybridus*) grown in a 15 cm (6 in) pot. New European hybrids have more dwarf characteristics than the plant shown.

day, a 21°C (70°F) minimum temperature is ideal for all stages. The low light intensity in combination with the 16-hour day is adequate for flowering. Growth is usually rapid because of uniform light and temperature conditions.

The most common free-flowering groups are Ballet®, Diane®, Melodie®, and Rhapsodie®. All retain their blooms even under adverse conditions.

A common trouble is ring spot in the leaves caused by application of cold water. Leaves are also injured if they are too close to the window glass in the winter. Light-colored leaves develop from overly intense light or inadequate nitrogen. Nematodes, cyclamen mites, and mealy bugs are common pests.

Senecio × hybridus (*S. cruentus*) DC. Florists' cineraria. COMPOSITAE. (*2, 22, 27, 28, 29, 32*)

Native to the Canary Islands. Seeds are sown at 21°C (70°F) during the late summer months for winter to spring flowering (Table 17-1). Seedlings are transplanted in small pots or in flats spaced about 6 cm by 6 cm as soon as possible. After the transplants are well established at temperatures of 12°C to 15°C (54°F to 60°F), the night temperatures can be reduced to 10°C (50°F) to encourage the production of robust plants (Fig. 17-32). Seedlings should be transplanted to the final 15

cm (6 in) pot when the temperature is lowered; this avoids crowding of tops or binding of roots in the flat. Growth is slow at 10°C (50°F); at least six weeks at these night temperatures are required for flowers to initiate. Care is taken to avoid crowding of the plants on the bench, which causes undesirable elongation. This plant generally has low mineral nutrient requirements.

Diseases are verticillium wilt and phytophthora root rot, which causes sudden wilting. Pests are spider mites, cyclamen mites, aphids, white flies, and thrips.

Sinningia speciosa (Lodd.) Hiern. Gloxinia. GESNARIACEAE. (*2, 22, 29, 31, 32*)

Native to Brazil. This summer flowering plant is most commonly propagated from seed at 20°C (68°F) in December and January for June flowering (Fig. 17-33). It can be propagated from tubers or leaf cuttings if a specific clone is desired. Seedlings are transplanted from the seeding pot and spaced 5 cm by 5 cm in flats or in peat pots as soon as possible to avoid stunting. The final planting is made to 12 or 15 cm (5 or 6 in) pots as soon as leaves begin to overlap in the flat. Night temperatures should be between 18°C to 21°C (64°F to 70°F); growth may cease at 15°C (59°F). The ideal light intensity at noon is about 22,000 lux (2000 ft-c) and plants should never be placed in direct sun. Seedlings grow rapidly with supplementary lighting from incandescent lamps for

Fig. 17–33 A gloxinia (*Sinningia speciosa*) grown in a 15 cm (6 in) pot. For commercial sale at least two flowers should be in full bloom and many other buds should be ready to develop in the home. This type has a long flower scape (stem) but some cultivars have short scapes. When ordering seed, specify the preference for long or short scapes.

about five hours during the night. Gloxinias, like African violets, can be grown entirely under fluorescent lamps and at the same light intensity (p. 384).

Disease problems are flower bud rot caused by *Botrytis* and root rot caused by *Rhizoctonia*. Pests are cyclamen mites, thrips, and mealy bugs.

All the crops mentioned in this section can be grown in small greenhouses with night temperatures of 10°C (50°F), 16°C (61°F), and 21°C (70°F). It is difficult, however, to grow roses and carnations because they require so much space as they grow older. All plants other than roses and carnations are grown in small containers and grow during the normal school year. Many popular foliage plants also grow in the 21°C (70°F) greenhouse. Their culture is discussed in Chapter 18.

REFERENCES

1. Augsberger, N. D., H. R. Bohanon, and J. L. Calhoun. 1978. *The greenhouse climate control handbook*. Muskogee, Okla.: Acme Engineering and Manufacturing.

2. Ball, V., ed. 1976. *The Ball red book*. 13th ed. West Chicago, Ill.: G. J. Ball.

3. Blasdale, W. C. 1948. *The cultivated species of Primula*. Berkeley: University of California Press.

4. Craig, R., and D. E. Walker. 1963. The flowering of *Pelargonium hortorum*, Bailey, seedlings as affected by cumulative solar energy. *Proc. Am. Soc. Hort. Sci.* 83:772–76.

5. Ecke, P., Jr., ed. 1976. *The poinsettia manual*. 2nd ed. Encinitas Calif.: Paul Ecke Inc.

6. Hanan, J. J., W. D. Holley, and K. L. Goldsberry. 1978. *Greenhouse management*. Berlin: Springer-Verlag.

7. Hix, J. 1974. *The glasshouse*. Cambridge, Mass.: MIT Press.

8. Holley, W. D., and R. Baker. 1963. *Carnation production*. Dubuque, Iowa.: Wm. C. Brown.

9. Kiplinger, D. C., and R. W. Langhans, ed. 1967. *Easter lilies. The culture, disease, insects and economics of Easter lilies*. Columbus, Ohio: Ohio State University.

10. Kofranek, A. M. 1959. Artificial light for controlling the flowering of asters and daisies. *Trans. Am. Soc. Agr. Engr.* 2(1):106–8.

11. ——, R. M. Sachs, and J. Kubota. 1970. The culture of fuchsia as a pot plant. *Flor. Rev.* 146(3791):18–21, 61–63.

12. ——, and H. A. Halevy. 1972. Conditions for opening cut chrysanthemum flower buds. *J. Am. Soc. Hort. Sci.* 97(5):578–84.

13. ——, D. S. Farnham, E. C. Maxie, and J. Kubota. 1972. Long term storage of carnation buds. *Flor. Rev.* 151(3906):29–30.

14. ——, and R. A. Larson, ed. 1975. Growing azaleas commercially. Div. Agr. Sci., Univ. of Calif. Sale Publication 4058.

15. Langhans, R. W., ed. 1962. *Snapdragons. A manual of the culture, insects, diseases and economics of snapdragons*. Ithaca, N.Y.: Cornell University.

16. ——, ed. 1964. *Chrysanthemums. A manual of the culture, disease, insects and economics of chrysanthemums*. Ithaca, N.Y.: Cornell University.

17. ——. 1980. *Greenhouse management*. Ithaca, N.Y.: Halcyon Press.

18. ——, and J. W. Mastalerz, ed. 1969. *Roses. A manual on the culture, management, diseases, insects, economics and breeding of greenhouse roses*. Ithaca, N.Y.: Cornell University.

19. Larson, R. A. 1975. Continuous production of flowering azaleas. In *Growing azaleas commercially*, eds. A. M. Kofranek and R. A. Larson. Div. Agr. Sci., Univ. of Calif. Sale publication 4058.

20. Larson, R. A., J. W. Love, D. L. Strider, R. K. Jones, J. R. Baker, and K. F. Horn. 1978. Commercial poinsettia production. *North Carolina Agr. Ext. Ser. Publ.* Ag 108.

21. Larson, Roy A., ed. 1980. *Introduction to floriculture*. New York: Academic Press.

22. Laurie, A., D. C. Kiplinger, and K. S. Nelson. 1979. *Commercial flower forcing*. 8th ed. New York: McGraw-Hill.

23. Leiser, A. T. 1975. Taxonomy and origin of azaleas used for forcing. In *Growing azaleas commercially*, eds. A. M. Kofranek and R. A. Larson. Div. Agr. Sci., Univ. of Calif. Sale Publication 4058.

24. Lunt, O. R., and H. C. Kohl. 1957. Influence of soil physical properties on production and quality of bench grown carnations. *Proc. Am. Soc. Hort. Sci.* 69:535–42.

25. Machin, B., and N. Scopes. 1978. *Chrysanthemums: year-round growing*. Poole, Dorset, U. K.: Blandford Press.

26. Mastalerz, J. W., ed. 1971. *Geraniums. A manual on the culture, diseases, insects, economics, taxonomy and breeding of geraniums*. University Park, Pa.: Pennsylvania Flower Growers.

27. ——. 1977. *The greenhouse environment. The effect of environmental factors on flower crops*. New York: John Wiley.

28. Nelson, Kenneth S. 1967. *Flower and plant production in the greenhouse.* Danville, Ill.: Interstate Printers and Publishers.

29. ———. 1977. *The greenhouse grower—a career in floriculture.* Danville, Ill.: Interstate Printers and Publishers.

30. Nelson, Paul V. 1978. *Greenhouse operation and management.* Reston, Va.: Reston Publ. Co.

31. Post, K. 1949. *Florist crop production and marketing.* New York: Orange Judd.

32. Preston, F. G. 1958. *The greenhouse.* New York: Abelard-Schuman.

33. Searles, S. A., and B. J. Machin. 1968. *Chrysanthemums the year round.* London: Blanford Press.

34. Thompson, J. F. 1976. Small plastic greenhouses. Univ. of Calif. Div. Agr. Sci. Leaflet 2387.

35. Waters, W. E., and C. A. Conover. 1969. Chrysanthemum production in Florida. Univ. of Fla. Bul. 730.

36. Widmer, R. E., R. J. Platteter, and J. Gembis. 1976. Minnesota fast crop cyclamen. Minn. State Florist Bul., April 1.

37. Zieslin, N., and A. H. Halevy. 1975. Flower bud atrophy in Baccara roses I. *Scientia Hort.* 3:209–16.

Floriculture: Houseplants

The houseplants considered in this chapter are primarily ornamental foliage plants. This chapter first considers the production of houseplants in a commercial *(3)* or school greenhouse and then their care and maintenance in the home. Those concerned only with home care should still study the first section to better appreciate the procedures for growing these plants before they are taken to the home or office.

GREENHOUSE PRODUCTION

Every houseplant species has an optimum environment under which it grows rapidly and luxuriantly. Because there are usually so many species grown in a single greenhouse, the grower must compromise on the light, temperature conditions, watering practices, and pest control. A large botanical greenhouse full of orchids, ferns, foliage and flowering plants is a compromise of these environmental conditions to produce one relatively suitable to most of the warm-house species grown there. Most plants tolerate some adversity, some species more than others, but under less than optimum conditions rapid or luxuriant growth cannot be expected. The best one can expect with a compromise is reduced growth or simple maintenance.

You may read that a certain species has an optimum temperature; however, if the light is reduced substantially, as from summer to winter, the prescribed temperature may also have to be lowered to compensate for the lower prevailing light. There are, of course, temperature limits to which one must adhere. Such things become quite obvious in time to some people growing houseplants in the greenhouse or the home. Those who learn quickly about the requirements of plants and implement them soon become known as people with a "green thumb." Some never put this knowledge of the plant's requirements to proper use at the proper time and the plants in their care show it! It is essential to have some basic knowledge of the requirements of houseplants, but it is also necessary to use common sense when implementing that knowledge.

All houseplant species require certain conditions for optimal growth. It is not possible to say which of these optimal environmental conditions is most important. When one condition such as temperature or light is too high or too low, the plant ceases to grow properly. Plant physiologists refer to this condition as a **limiting factor** for growth. It is difficult to attribute any greater importance to one limiting factor than to any other. They are all important. When one condition is not suitable for growth, the plant "responds" in predictable ways. For example, frequent wilting may indicate: (a) that the plant is not obtaining enough water from the soil because the pot is too small for that size plant; (b) the salt concentration is too high in the soil; (c) a disease or insect has destroyed the roots; or (d) the light or temperature is too high. Therefore, all of the requirements listed below are equally important.

Light Intensity

Most foliage plants of tropical origin grow well between 11,000 and 33,000 lux (1000 and 3000 ft-c), but some, such as *Aglaonema, Fittonia,* and *Maranta,* do best between 7700 and 13,000 lux (700 and 1200 ft-c). Since 33,000 lux (3000 ft-c) is about one-third summer outdoor light intensity at 40° N or S latitude, it is obvious that the greenhouse glass must be moderately shaded for 33,000 lux and heavily shaded for 11,000 lux. Some compromise of shading density is necessary when a wide variety of plants is grown in the same greenhouse. As the light diminishes toward fall and winter, some shade must be removed to keep light conditions near the optimum. It is not feasible to grow cacti and succulents at these low intensities, so these plants require another house where the light should be maintained between 44,000 and 66,000 lux (4000 to 6000 ft-c). Table 18–1 gives species requirements.

If flowering potted plants are included in the category of houseplants, then a light intensity above 33,000 lux is essential to provide the conditions for proper flower bud initiation and development. Chrysanthemums, poinsettias, hydrangeas, geraniums, and azaleas (Ch. 17) are such flowering plants. The African violet (*Saintpaulia*) on the other hand, requires only 10,000 to 13,000 lux (900 to 1200 ft-c) for optimal flowering conditions. Light intensity thus plays a limiting role as to whether this plant flowers or not, assuming the temperature is near 21°C (70°F).

Tropical foliage plants are less sensitive to low light, and the light can be compromised over a relatively wide range. If the light intensity is very low (5000 to 10,000 lux), growth is slower than at optimum light but the leaves become very dark green (assuming the nitro-

gen level is adequate). If the light intensity is high (44,000 lux), growth can be rapid (assuming no water stress), but the new leaves may be smaller and lighter green. The chloroplasts orient themselves differently (Fig. 18–1) as the light increases or diminishes. Cultivars of plants with variegated leaves, such as *Hedera helix,* do not varigate further but develop dark green foliage under light conditions lower than optimum. Extremely high light intensities burn the foliage unless the relative humidity is high or the leaves are cooled with frequent misting. Therefore it is possible to grow a large array of foliage species of reasonable quality in a single house with a light intensity range between 6000 and 35,000 lux (550 and 3000 ft-c.).

When plants are moved from the relatively high light of the greenhouse to the low light intensity of the home, the plant has to adjust to an abrupt light change. One of the first symptoms is the loss of chlorophyll from the leaves followed by leaf abscission. The severity of leaf drop depends on how drastically the light is reduced. The leaf loss continues until the plant adjusts to the lower light and produces enough photosynthates to make up for the sugars lost in respiration. This is called the compensation point for light (Ch. 7). The plant eventually stabilizes but, of course, the plant cannot be expected to grow during this period of adjustment. Moderate growth is possible after the plant becomes fully acclimatized to the lower light condition (5, 6, 7). The new leaves are longer and thinner than those grown under high-light conditions. In addition, the plant may become etiolated and the stems or petioles, or both, stretch.

All plants do not abscise their leaves as cleanly as *Ficus benjamina, Asparagus densiflorus* and *Pelargonium × hortorum,* which respond to changes of low light conditions by shedding leaves. Some plants do not have a definite abscission zone on the leaf petiole. These plants, which include the palms, dieffenbachias, and lilies, do not abscise their leaves. Instead, the leaves turn yellow, wither, and die, still clinging to the stem. The way the leaves die and then slough off, in either case, is a similar phenomenon and both are definite responses to the low light condition.

It is possible to acclimatize the plants to low light before removing them from the greenhouse. The light should be gradually reduced in three increments of about 5500 to 11,000 lux (500 to 1000 ft-c) for about two weeks at each level. This can be easily done by moving the plants to a shadier condition in three steps. Perhaps the last level can be very dense shade such as under a growing bench or a northern exposure with skylight only. Plants can be maintained in 60 to 80 percent shade for two months or more. If plants are placed under the

Fig. 18–1 Chloroplasts of many plants orient themselves to provide less surface exposure in full sun than in shade. *Left:* Chloroplasts in cells in sun. *Right:* Chloroplasts in shade cells.

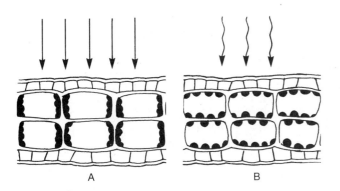

A   B

Table 18–1 Propagation Procedures and Subsequent Growing Conditions for Selected Groups, Genera, or Species of Foliage Plants in Controlled Temperature Greenhouses. Possible Growing Media for Reasonable Root and Top Growth Are Also Given.

Group, Genera or Species	Criteria for Propagation					Subsequent Growing Conditions			Soils or Media[d]
	Plant Part Commonly Used[a]	Mist[b]	Bench Bottom Heat Temp °C (°F)	Min Night Temp °C (°F)	Light Intensity Range[c]	Minimum Night Temp °C (°F)	Light Intensity Range[c]	Most Frequent, Cultural, Environmental, or Pest Problem	Best Possible Ratio
Adiantum spp. L. Maidenhair fern	Divisions, spores	–	–	21 (70)	Low	21 (70)	Low-med	Salts, low relative humidity (RH)	Org
Aeschynanthus pulcher (Blume) G. Don. Lipstick plant	Cuttings	+	22 (72)	21 (70)	Med	21 (70)	Low-med	Poor flowering	1:1, org
Aglaonema spp. Schott. Chinese evergreen	Terminals, cane, seeds	+	22 (72)	21 (70)	Med	18 (65)	Low-med	Mealy bugs, root rot	1:1
Anthurium Scherzeranum Schott. Flamingo flower	Seeds	–	23 (75)	23 (75)	Low	21 (70)	Med	Root rot, salts	Org
Aphelandra squarrosa Nees. Zebra plant	Terminals	+	22 (72)	21 (70)	Low	18 (65)	Med	Excessive light, salts	1:1, org
Araucaria heterophylla (Salisb.) Franco. Norfolk Island pine	Terminals, seeds	+	22 (72)	21 (70)	Med	15 (60)	High	Spider mites	1:1
Asparagus densiflorus, 'Sprengeri' (Knuth.) Jessop. Sprenger fern	Seeds, divisions	–	–	15 (60)	Med	15 (60)	High	Deficient light, salts	Tol
Aspidistra elator Blume. Iron plant	Divisions	+	–	18 (65)	Low	18 (65)	Low	Leaf burn	Tol
Asplenium nidus L. Bird's nest fern	Spores	–	23 (75)	23 (75)	Low	21 (70)	Low-med	Mealy bugs, salts	Org
Brassaia actinophylla Endl. (*Schefflera actinophylla*) Australian umbrella tree	Seeds, terminals	–	18 (65)	18 (65)	Low	18 (65)	Med-high	Excessive light, root rot, spider mites	1:1
Bromeliads (general)	Offshoots or "suckers"	–	–	18 (65)	Med	15 (60)	Med-high	Poor flowering	1:1, 2:1
Cacti (general)	Seeds, grafting (Fig. 18–12)	–	–	18 (65)	Med	18 (65)	High	Root rot	2:1
Calathea spp. G.F. Mey. Peacock plant	Cuttings, divisions	+	21 (70)	21 (70)	Low	21 (70)	Low	Root rot, salts, spider mites	1:1, org
Chamaedorea elegans Mart. Parlor palm	Seeds	–	27 (81)	23 (75)	Low	21 (70)	Low	Poor seed germination, salts, spider mites	1:1, org
Chlorophytum comosum (Thunb.) Jacques. Spider plant	Plantlets, divisions	–	–	21 (70)	Low	21 (70)	Med	Salts, fluorides	1:1, org

Plant	Propagation[a]	Mist[b]	°C (°F)	°C (°F)		°C (°F)	Light[c]	Problems	Mix[d]
Cissus spp. L. Grape ivy	Cuttings, seeds	+	22 (72)	21 (70)	Med	21 (70)	Med	Spider mites	Tol
Citrus reticulata var. *austera?* × *Fortunella* sp.? Calamondin	Terminals	+	22 (72)	21 (70)	Med	12 (55)	High	Scale, spider mites, root rot	Tol
Codiaeum spp. A. Juss. Croton	Terminals	+	22 (72)	21 (70)	Med	21 (70)	High	Deficient light, mealy bugs, spider mites	1:1
Coffea arabica L. Arabian coffee plant	Seeds	–	23 (75)	26 (80)	Low	18 (65)	Low-med	High light, salts	1:1, org
Coleus hybridus Voss Painted nettle, Coleus	Terminals	+	22 (72)	21 (70)	Med	15 (60)	High	Mealy bugs	1:1
Cordyline terminalis (L.) Kunth. Good luck plant, Baby doll	Terminals, cane	+	27 (81)	23 (75)	Med	18 (65)	Med	Root rot, salts, fluorides	1:1, org
Crassula L. (general)	Cuttings	–	–	21 (70)	Med	15 (60)	High	Deficient light, root rot	2:1
Cycas revoluta Thunb. Sago palm	Divisions, offsets	–	–	18 (65)	Med	15 (60)	High	Mealy bugs	2:1
Dieffenbachia spp. Schott. Dumbcane	Terminals, cane	+	22 (72)	21 (70)	Med	21 (70)	Med-high	Root rot, salts, spider mites	1:1, org
Dizygotheca elegantissima (Hort. Veitch.) R. Vig and Guililaum. (*Aralia elegantissima*) False aralia	Seeds, terminals	+	22 (72)	21 (70)	Low	18 (65)	Med	Red spiders	1:1
Dracaena spp. L.	Terminals, cane (Fig. 18–13)	+	22 (72)	21 (70)	Med	21 (70)	Med	Salts, fluorides, spider mites	1:1, org
Echeveria spp. DC. Hen-and-chickens	Leaf cuttings, offsets	–	–	21 (70)	Med	21 (70)	High	Deficient light	2:1
Fatsia japonica (Thunb.) Decne & Planch. (*Aralia japonica*) Japanese fatsia	Seeds, terminals	+	22 (72)	21 (70)	Med	21 (70)	Med-high	Spider mites, scale	1:1
Ficus benjamina L. Weeping fig	Terminals, air layers	+	22 (72)	21 (70)	Med	21 (70)	Med-high	Deficient light, salts, scale	1:1
Ficus elastica Roxb. ex Hornem. India rubber tree	Terminals air layers	+	22 (72)	21 (70)	Med	21 (70)	Med-high	Mealy bugs, scale	1:1

[a]Terminals = shoot tip cuttings; cuttings = all stem portions including terminals; leaf cuttings = leaves without buds; divisions = dividing plant at crown; cane = stems with buds but no leaves. See Ch. 5 for details.

[b]Intermittent mist during daylight hours in conjunction with a medium light intensity; + = OK to use; – = not necessary to use.

[c]Natural light conditions in the greenhouse. Low = less than 22,000 lux (2000 ft-c); Med = 22,000 to 44,000 lux (2000 to 4000 ft-c); High = greater than 44,000 lux (4000 ft-c); Low-Med = high range of low or low range of med, etc.

[d]Org = highly organic mix which could mean 1:2:sand:peat or possibly all sphagnum peatmoss or all fir bark; 1:1 = sand:peat or perlite:peat proportions; 2:1 = sand:peat proportions; Tol = tolerant to most soil mixtures, including those with clay and silt textures, if correctly managed. All mixes are proportioned by volume.

Table 18–1 (continued)

Group, Genera or Species	Criteria for Propagation					Subsequent Growing Conditions			Soils or Media[d]
	Plant Part Commonly Used[a]	Mist[b]	Bench Bottom Heat Temp °C (°F)	Min Night Temp °C (°F)	Light Intensity Range[c]	Minimum Night Temp °C (°F)	Light Intensity Range[c]	Most Frequent, Cultural, Environmental, or Pest Problem	Best Possible Ratio
Ficus lyrata Warb. (F. pandurata) Fiddle-leaf fig	Terminals, air layers	+	22 (72)	21 (70)	Med	21 (70)	Med-high	Excessive light, salts, scale, mealy bugs	1:1
Ficus pumila L. Creeping fig	Cuttings	−	22 (72)	21 (70)	Low	21 (70)	Med-high	Mealy bugs, scale	Tol
Fittonia verschaffeltii (Lem.) Coem. Nerve plant	Cuttings	+	22 (72)	21 (70)	Med	21 (70)	Low	Root rot	1:1, org
Gynura aurantiaca (Blume) DC. Velvet plant	Terminals	+	22 (72)	21 (70)	Low-med	18 (65)	Med	Mealy bugs	1:1
Hedera helix L. English ivy	Cuttings	+	—	18 (65)	Med	18 (65)	Med-high	Red spider, cyclamen mite	Tol
(Helxine soleirolli) Soleirolia soleirolli (Req.) Dandy. Baby's tears	Divisions	−	—	18 (65)	Low	18 (65)	Low-med	Dry conditions	Tol
Hemigraphis alternata (Burm f.) T. Anderson. Red flame	Terminals	+	22 (72)	21 (70)	Med	18 (65)	Med	Deficient light, mealy bugs	1:1
Howeia spp. Becc. Sentry palm	Seeds	−	27 (81)	27 (81)	Low	21 (70)	Med	Mealy bugs, scale, salts	Tol
Hypoestes sanguionolenta (Van Houtte) Hook. Polka-dot plant	Terminals	+	22 (72)	21 (70)	Med	18 (65)	Med	Aphids, mealy bugs	1:1
Iresine herbstii Hook. Beefsteak plant	Terminals	+	22 (72)	21 (70)	Med	15 (60)	High	Root rot	1:1
Maranta spp. L.	Cuttings, division	+	22 (72)	21 (70)	Low	21 (70)	Low	Root rot, salts nematodes	1:1, org
Monstera deliciosa Liebm. Cut-leaf philodendron	Terminals, air layers	+	23 (75)	22 (72)	Low	21 (70)	Med	Root rot, salts, scale	1:1, org
Nephrolepis exaltata (L) Schott. Sword fern	Division, spores	−	—	21 (70)	Low	21 (70)	Med	Scale, salts	Org
Pellionia Daveauana (Godefr) N.E. Br. Trailing watermelon begonia	Terminals	+	22 (72)	21 (70)	Med	18 (65)	Med	Root rot	1:1
Peperomia spp. Ruiz. & Pav.	Cuttings (Fig. 5–17)	+	22 (72)	21 (70)	Med	21 (70)	Med	Cyclamen mites, root rot	1:1

Plant	Propagation						Light	Problems	Soil
Philodendron scandens C. Koch & H. Sello. (*P. oxycardium*) Heart-leaf philodendron	Cuttings	+	22 (72)	21 (70)	Med	21 (70)	Med-high	Root rot	1:1
Philodendron spp. Schott. (Large leaf species)	Terminals, air layers	+	23 (75)	22 (72)	Low	21 (70)	Med	Root rot, salts, bacterial leaf spot	1:1, org
Pilea cadierei Gagnep. & Guillaum. Aluminum plant	Terminals	+	22 (72)	21 (70)	Med	15 (60)	Med	Root rot	1:1
Pittosporum tobira (Thunb.) Ait. Mock orange	Terminals	+	22 (72)	21 (70)	Med	18 (65)	High	Aphids	Tol
Platycerium spp. Desv. Staghorn fern	Spores, divisions	–	–	23 (75)	Low	18 (65)	Low-med	Salts, scale	Org
Plectranthus spp. L'Her. Swedish ivy	Terminals	+	22 (72)	21 (70)	Med	21 (70)	Med	Deficient light	1:1
Podocarpus macrophyllus (Thunb.) D. Don. Southern yew	Terminals	+	22 (72)	21 (70)	Med	18 (65)	Med	Deficient light, mealy bugs	Tol
Sansevieria spp. Thunb. Bowstring hemp or snake plant	Divisions, leaf cuttings	+	22 (72)	21 (70)	Med	18 (65)	Med-high	Planting cuttings too deep	Tol
(*Scindapsus aureus*) *Epipremnum aureum* (Linden and Andre) Bunt. Pothos	Cuttings	+	22 (72)	21 (70)	Med	21 (70)	Low-med	Root rot	1:1
Syngonium podophyllum Schott. Nephthytis	Cuttings, seeds	+	22 (72)	21 (70)	Med	21 (70)	Med	Salts, root rot	1:1
Tolmiea menziesii (Purch) Torr. & A. Gray. Piggyback plant	Leaf cuttings (Fig. 5–16)	–	–	15 (60)	Low	12 (55)	Med	Excessive heat, salts	1:1
Tradescantia spp. L. Spiderwort	Cuttings	+	–	21 (70)	Med	21 (70)	Med-high	Deficient light, salts	1:1
Zebrina pendula Schnizl. Wandering Jew	Cuttings	+	–	21 (70)	Med	21 (70)	Med-high	Deficient light, salts	1:1, org

bench, care should be taken to avoid splashing water on the foliage from above and to keep the plants off the ground soil. Both precautions prevent contamination from root pathogens. The entire process of acclimatization should take about six weeks, but it is well worth the effort to avoid leaf yellowing and abscission. Withholding fertilizer and watering moderately also aid in the acclimatizing plants.

The growing or maintenance of tropical foliage plants entirely under flourescent lamps is covered later in this chapter.

Temperature

If a single night temperature must be selected for growing a majority of the foliage species or houseplants, it should be about 21°C (70°F). Table 18–1 gives ideal growing temperature conditions for groups and species. A large number of the popular foliage plants can be maintained at 15°C (59°F), but they grow little or not at all. Very high night temperatures generally result in etiolated growth and leaf quality suffers when the plants are moved to a lower temperature in the home. Many foliage plants are grown outdoors in such areas as southern Florida and Puerto Rico, where night temperatures seldom go below 15°C (59°F). These conditions are suitable for low cost commercial growing of foliage plants.

Flowering potted plants have relatively narrow and specific night temperatures for flowering. However, many of these flower best at about 15°C (59°F) except for the African violet and a few others (Ch. 17).

Relative Humidity

Relative humidity (RH) between 70 and 80 percent is adequate for most tropical foliage plants, including the temperate zone ferns. It is not necessary to increase relative humidity by misting. The relative humidity reaches equilibrium at a high level in a tight, shaded greenhouse when the floor is kept moist. Very often the desire to maintain a high relative humidity is overemphasized by growers. Plants grow well in the absence of a high RH if they are not water-stressed and have the proper light and temperature conditions. However, air movement from improper ventilation can replace the desirable moist air within the house with dry air from outside. Such improper ventilation should be avoided to prevent relative humidity below 40 percent. Never allow the greenhouse doors to remain open for extended periods.

A high RH is not necessary for such plants as peperomias and sansevierias, as well as most other succulents, such as the cacti and bromeliads. High relative humidity conditions favor mildew and other detrimental leaf diseases. Wherever leaf diseases, such as bacterial leaf spot of philodendron, are present, misting or overhead watering should be avoided.

Carbon Dioxide (CO_2)

On occasion, CO_2 may be deficient in tightly closed greenhouses. Since foliage plants are generally grown in low light intensity houses and since it is necessary to maintain the day temperature higher than the night (see Ch. 17), little or no ventilation is employed. During winter months when greenhouses are tightly shut, CO_2 can become deficient. As the plants photosynthesize, they soon use up much of the available CO_2 built up during the night. Unless the house is ventilated to bring in CO_2 from outside, the air can become CO_2 deficient. Decaying organic matter in the pots and on the floor supplies some CO_2 but not enough to sustain rapid plant growth. It may be desirable to inject CO_2 into the greenhouse under such conditions (Ch. 17), but it should be determined whether the treatment is economically feasible. A CO_2 concentration up to 1000 ppm (0.1 percent) during the daylight hours when the temperature is between 21°C (70°F) and 31°C (90°F) is ideal for most plants although the natural CO_2 level of outside air is only 300 ppm (0.03 percent). Since a foliage plant house is freely ventilated only during hot periods, it is difficult to take advantage of the readily available CO_2 of outside air.

Water Quality

Water quality alone can make the difference between success and failure in growing high-quality plants. Water with a high salt concentration, if improperly used, can cause a burning injury along the leaf margins. Water with high sodium or boron can cause similar leaf damage. A source of low-salt water should be found or the means provided to remove the harmful salts or ions by a process called deionization. Table 18–2 gives the criteria for water quality used for irrigation purposes (*1*). The water can be analyzed by private consulting firms or the companies that service deionizers or water softeners. If the water comes from a municipal water district, that agency should be able to provide data on the quality of its water.

If the water analysis indicates an electrical conductivity (EC_ω) of 0.175 mmho or less, and the sodium (Na) below 60 percent of the total cations, and boron (B) content less than 0.5 (ppm), then that water quality would be considered excellent for tropical foliage plants. Any

Table 18–2   Selected Quality Guidelines for Irrigation Water.

Problem or Related Constituent	Water Quality Guidelines		
	No Problem	Increasing Problem	Severe Problem
Salinity[a], EC_ω, of water (mmhos/cm)	< 0.75	0.75–3.0	> 3.0
Specific ion toxicity, boron (mg/l or ppm)	< 0.5	0.5 –2.0	2.0–10.0

Symbol	Name
EC_ω	Electrical conductivity of water
mmho/cm	Millimhos per centimeter
<	Less than
>	Greater than
mg/l	Milligrams per liter
ppm	Parts per million

[a] This figure assumes that water for the crop plus water needed for leaching requirement is applied.

Source: Adapted from R. S. Ayres. 1976. Quality of irrigation water. Soil and plant-tissue testing in California. Univ. of Calif. Div. Agr. Sci. Bul. 1879.

combination of numbers higher than these are marginal, and the water quality would be classed as poor or substandard. If the Na percentage is lower than 60 percent of the cations and B content is low but the total salt content is above 0.75 mmho, there is a good chance that the water can be used for delicate foliage plants (including ferns). The water, however, must be used in large quantities to provide adequate leaching at every irrigation. The general rule for proper watering of container grown plants is: "the higher the salt concentrations in the water, the greater the amount of water that must be applied at every irrigation to prevent salt accumulations in the potting soil." Large quantities of water leach (wash) the salts out, and there is less likelihood of salts accumulating than if small quantities of water are used. Should the Na percentage be greater than 60 percent of the cations, it would be necessary to deionize the water to remove the sodium. B content above 0.5 ppm is difficult to correct since it is not removed from water by deionization. A high B content in the water results in accumulation of B in the leaf margins, which manifests itself as a marginal leaf necrosis or burning of leaf edges. If the water is high in boron a different water source should be used.

Whenever containers are irrigated with good quality water (<0.75 mmho), a general rule is to supply enough water to the top of the soil to allow for leaching from the bottom of the pot. This means that about one-third of the total water applied should run out the drain holes. If the total salt concentration of the water is very high (EC_ω 1.5 to 2.0 mmho), the quantity of water applied at any one time should be two to three times greater, so that large quantities of water drip from the drain holes.

Irrigation

Irrigation should be frequent enough to prevent any peat moss in the soil mixture from drying out. As the soil mix dries out, the effective salt or fertilizer concentration in the soil solution increases to a point where it can become toxic to the roots. One of the most important jobs in the greenhouse is the proper watering of plants. It is better to irrigate less frequently with large volumes of water to ensure some leaching than it is to apply small amounts frequently. Automatic drip irrigation that supplies water through an individual hose to each pot (Fig. 18–2) is an excellent labor saver, but care must be taken to keep it operative by correcting faulty (slow-dripping) or plugged outlets. A wilted plant indicates a faulty hose. No watering system is truly automatic and trouble-free. Even with drip irrigation, it is necessary to wash out some of the accumulated salts with a thorough manual irrigation with a garden hose.

Fig. 18–2 A method of irrigating similar-sized pots. The water comes from large polyethylene pipe (arrow) and is distributed to equal-length, small-diameter tubes. The lead weights on the ends keep the tubes in the pots. The water is turned on manually for a given time to wet the soil thoroughly and provide some leaching. It is not wise to mix pots of varied sizes containing different species unless the quantity of water is applied for the largest pot.

Tropical foliage plants require large quantities of nitrogen in comparison to the other mineral elements. It is generally recommended that a liquid fertilizer be applied in the irrigation water with every watering. The liquid fertilizer ratio of NPK should be in the ratio of about 3:1:1 or a 3:1:2. (Ch. 9). One possible recommendation is a mixture of 500 gr (1.1 lb) of 30-10-10 fertilizer in 400 l (106 gal) of water. If the water quality is good (Table 18–2), this amount is safe to use with every irrigation. However, some growers leach with plain water at every third or fourth irrigation to ensure that no salts accumulate from the liquid fertilizer solution. The rule of applying enough liquid fertilizer to leach a little at every irrigation lowers the likelihood of an excess of salts.

The soil should have adequate quantities of relatively low-solubility fertilizers or amendments incorporated into it before planting. Mixing before planting allows for uniform nutrient distribution to the root system. Dolomitic limestone at the rate of 2 to 3 kg/m³ (equivalent to 3 to 5 lb/yd³) is an adequate amount to mix in the soil prior to planting. (See page 419 for preparing small quantities of a soil mixture.) Superphosphate should not be used because it contains fluorides, which will injure some foliage plants such as dracaena, wandering Jew, and chlorophytum. Use bone meal or treble superphosphate as a phosphorus source for these.

Soil Mixtures

Adequate water retention and soil aeration are two important characteristics of the potting medium. The small volumes and shallowness of pot containers create different physical properties than if the growing medium was a garden soil of indefinite depth (9). On the bottom of a shallow pot, a water-saturated zone forms directly after a thorough irrigation, creating a water table that cannot drain away even though there is a free drainage hole at the bottom of the pot. The water content of the soil decreases (less than saturation) from the bottom to the top of the pot. Therefore the soil mass can be saturated at the bottom and relatively dry at the top directly after an irrigation depending on the pore size of the mixture. As Figure 18–3 shows, the difference in water content from top to bottom over a depth of 25 cm (10 in) in a coarse sand (A) is extreme, but in the case of silty clay loam (C), the entire soil mass is temporarily saturated just after irrigation. As one can see, the coarse sand provides excellent aeration, but near the top it would have hardly enough water for the plant. The silty clay loam (C) has

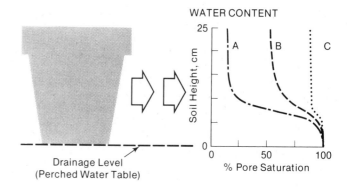

Fig. 18–3 The water retention in three soil textures following a thorough irrigation and after the clay pot has drained. **A** is coarse sand, **C** is a silty clay loam, and **B** is a combination of **A** and **C** in the ratio of four parts **A** and one part **C** by volume. A saturated condition exists at the bottom of the pot (at about 7 to 9 cm) for **A** and starts at about 12 cm for **B**. The horizontal axis of the graph represents the percentage of pores saturated with moisture. **A** near the top of the pot is only 10 percent saturated, **B** near the top is over 50 percent saturated, and **C** is almost totally saturated from top to bottom. *Source:* Spomer, L. A. 1976. Container soils are different. Ill. State Flor. Assoc. Bul. 363.

poor aeration, but provides a high water content (almost saturated) throughout the soil mass. The disadvantages of both these extremes can be partially overcome by creating a mixture with the correct ingredients so as to provide the proper particle size, proper pore space for adequate aeration, and good water retention. Mixing organic matter together with a sand of uniform particle size can create such a condition. One such mixture is listed on page 419. Mixtures often used for growing foliage plants combine peat and perlite (3:1 ratio) or peat and vermiculite (2:1 or 1:1 ratio) (p. 418). These mixtures are essentially pathogen-free at the onset and can be reproduced with consistency because the ingredients are easily duplicated and readily available. The pH (Ch. 8) of these mixtures is acid, which is suitable for many foliage plants. The chief disadvantage of these mixtures is their extremely light weight. The pots may topple over when the mixture becomes relatively dry; however, the water content should never be allowed to get that low. Sawdust and leaf mold can be used instead of sphagnum peat moss, but these materials can vary extremely in composition, depending on their source.

A suitable soil mixture for potted plants should allow water to pass through relatively easily. Proper leaching reduces the risk that harmful salts accumulate in the soil mixture. Sand, perlite, vermiculite, and sphag-

Fig. 18-4 These cactus plants were grown from seed and transplanted into flats for continued growth.

Fig. 18-5 A good way of holding spiny cactus plants. Taping the thumb and forefinger with electrician's tape eliminates the need to wear rubber or plastic gloves.

num peat moss (Ch. 19) leach well, but clay soil allows water to pass through only very slowly. Therefore a clay must be amended with organic matter to improve its permeability. An organic amendment, such as sphagnum peat moss, is best because it is relatively resistant to decay.

Most commercial soil mixtures sold in plastic bags or in bulk have a large percentage of organic material and, therefore, have pore sizes that allow them to drain easily. Their high organic content also aids in retaining water. Thus, they are excellent mixes for tropical house or flowering plants normally grown in pots. It is also possible to grow many of the tropical houseplants in pure sphagnum peat moss or fir bark (medium grade) if adequate ground or dolomitic limestone is sprinkled on the surface about once a month. The limestone counteracts the acidity (low pH) of these materials. Both of these would be examples of the organic media mentioned in Table 18-1.

Cacti, succulents, and bromeliads can be grown in soil mixtures with a higher sand content and less peat moss (Figs. 18-4 and 18-5). An ideal mixture might be sand and peat at 2:1 or 3:1 by volume. Ground limestone should also be added once a month.

Table 18-1 gives the recommended soil mixtures for other groups or species.

Sanitation

In growing houseplants of any type, care must be exercised to start with a clean growing medium, sterile containers, a sanitized bench, and, most important of all, pathogen-free plant material. Baker *(2)* gives most of the steps for growing healthy container plants. If all sanitary precautions are taken at the outset, later troubles will be few and relatively easy to manage. Soil pathogens occasionally contaminate the mix even when all precautions are taken, but small disease outbreaks here and there can be overcome with the appropriate soil fungicide. Some examples of these are Truban ®, Benlate®, Dexon®, and Ban Rot®. It is almost impossible to use these fungicides for complete disease control when the entire crop is infected with a soil-borne pathogen, but they are effective against minor outbreaks if the pathogen can be identified.

Some soil mixtures can be easily pasteurized by heat (electric or steam) or by chemicals (2). The method used depends upon equipment or budget and also on the training of the personnel who are to pasteurize the mixture (Fig. 18-6). Clay soil mixtures with organic amendments may temporarily become toxic after steaming and must be allowed to stand for several weeks before using. Therefore peat-sand or peat-vermiculite or perlite mixtures are encouraged.

Fig. 18–6 Small amounts of soil can be pasteurized in a steel trailer (*above*). The pipe on the far end (arrow) is connected to a three-prong fork (grid) made of pipe with holes drilled in it (similar to the one being held, *below*). The grid lies on the bottom of the trailer. The trailer is hauled to a steam plant where the forked grid is connected by a hose to a steam outlet. The perforated thongs on the fork which allow the steam to escape through the soil and the plastic tarp retains much of the heat generated. When the coldest part of the soil mass reaches 82°C (180°F), the steam is cut off and the heat is allowed to permeate the soil for an additional half hour. Loose soil mixtures containing large quantities of sand and peat can be used for potting as soon as it cools. The conveyer behind the man (*below*) can transport the soil into a bin that unloads through a trap door onto a potting bench.

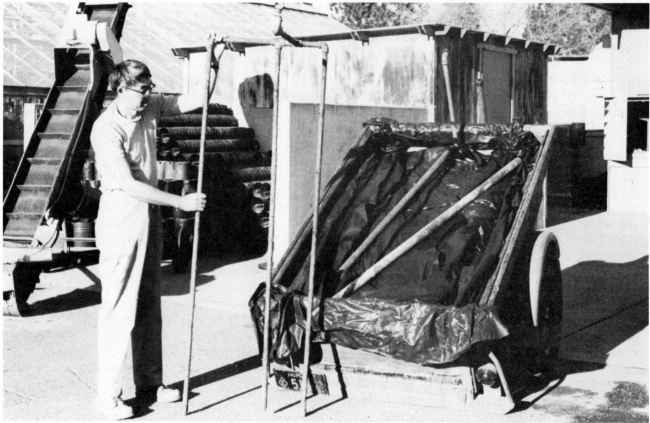

The biggest problem is recognizing the pest that is causing plant damage. Once the pest is identified, its control can be effected. No attempt will be made here to recommend controls because controls often change owing to EPA, state, and county regulations. Page 410 lists troublesome insects and other pests commonly associated with houseplants.

Plant nematodes are microscopic unsegmented worms that attack roots or foliage (Ch. 11). They are controlled by steaming or chemically treating the soil before planting. The soil media can become contaminated again by infected plant material (most common source), by the irrigation water (hardly possible when the water is treated with chlorine), or from contaminated tools. Nematodes are perhaps the source of trouble least understood by foliage plant growers. Many departments of nematology in state universities produce publications on plant symptoms and the nematode control procedures although there may be less information on ornamental plants than for field crops.

Propagation

Successful culture of houseplants demands proper propagation procedures. Details on nomenclature and general methods are described in Chapter 5. Table 18–1 lists the specific plant parts commonly used for vegetative propagation and the optimal environmental conditions required. It is assumed that cuttings will be treated with a rooting hormone (IBA or NAA; see Ch. 5) to ensure rapid root regeneration. In general, if intermittent mist is used, the light intensity during propagation can be higher than if mist is not used. Mist is a cooling process and, therefore, the plants tolerate more light during the daylight hours. For foliage plants that normally require low light for growth, such as *Calathea* and *Maranta,* the cuttings should be given only low to medium light, even under intermittent mist. Certain foliage plant species root better without mist (Table 18–1). When mist is not used, however, some provision must be made to provide shading and keep the relative humidity high.

Bottom heat (p. 100) provided by electric heating cables can be beneficial in the rapid rooting of cuttings. The temperature of the cables should be slightly higher than the night time air temperature in the greenhouse.

The light intensity must be adjusted to the proper level for each species to prevent desiccation and burning of the leaves during rooting. The cuttings cannot absorb water to compensate for the water loss by transpiration under high light intensity; hence mist is valuable to cool the leaves and to provide water.

A person may attempt to grow plants in the home or simply try to maintain their vigor and appearance with only a moderate amount of new growth. Growing plants in most homes is difficult, mainly because of inadequate light. Maintaining the quality of the plants is easier than growing them because most foliage plants will acclimate to and tolerate low-light conditions. Under these low light environments the plants adjust; if a new leaf develops, one of the old leaves may be sloughed off. If the light is too low, few new leaves are produced and the original and older leaves gradually die. Light is most often the limiting factor for good plant growth in the home unless the plants are kept on a sun porch with adjustable and controllable light.

Temperature is seldom a problem in an American home since most families prefer temperatures of 20°C (68°F) and above during the active hours. During the night, temperatures may be allowed to drop to 15.5°C (60°F). This lower temperature slows down growth but is noninjurious to most plants. Excessively high temperatures cause the plants to elongate especially when light is low (Table 18–3).

Proper watering or irrigating is probably the cultural practice least understood by houseplant enthusiasts. Some of these points were discussed in the previous section but they bear repeating. Houseplants are always grown in containers such as pots, tubs, or metal cans. All have a small volume, and are shallow and therein lies the potential problems of improper watering. After shallow containers are given a thorough watering and the water ceases to drip, the bottom of the container is completely saturated even if adequate drainage is provided. The soil surface may look dry but the soil is still very moist near the bottom (p. 409). This is especially true if the soil is largely clay, and the pore sizes are small (see Fig. 18–3). When one sees that the soil surface is dry, it may seem apparent that the pot should be watered again, but the soil may not really require any more water. If the pot is irrigated too often, the soil has no chance to aerate properly. The overmoist soil condition can also be an ideal environment in which water mold pathogens proliferate. So the hobbiest with a "green thumb" who says, "Let the pot dry out between waterings, but when you do water, be sure you add enough water to cause the bottom to drip thoroughly," knows from experience the irrigation method best for most houseplants.

After the pot stops draining, the remaining water can dissipate from the container in three ways: through the sides (if it is a porous clay pot), from the soil surface by evaporation, and by transpiration from the leaves (especially if the light is good and other conditions for

Table 18–3   Environmental Conditions and Soil Moisture Necessary to Sustain Reasonable Growth of Selected Houseplants in the Home. Only Maintenance of Plants Can Be Expected with Light Intensities and Temperatures Lower Than Those Recommended.

Groups, Genera, or Species and Common Names	Environmental Conditions — Light Conditions: Natural Window Exposure[a]	Environmental Conditions — Light Conditions: Under Fluorescent Lamps for 16 Hrs/Day[b]	Temp for Growth[c]	Chances of Success in the Home	Soil Moisture Status to Sustain Growth[d]	Possible Cultural and Environmental Problems Which May Be Encountered in the Home
Adiantum spp. L. Maidenhair fern	E-N	Low, M; High, G	Warm	Poor-fair	Moist-wet	Scorch, salts
Aeschynanthus pulchera (Blume) G. Don. Lipstick plant	E	Low, M; Med, G	Med	Fair	Moist	Poor flowering
Aglaonema commutatum Schott. Chinese evergreen	E-N	Low, M; Med, G	Warm	Excellent	Moist-wet	Relatively trouble free
Aphelandra squarrosa Nees. Zebra plant	E	Med, M	Warm	Fair	Moist-wet	Scorch, salts, stretches, poor flowering
Araucaria heterophylla (Salisb.) Franco. Norfolk Island Pine	S	High, G; Med, M	Cool-med	Fair	Dry-moist	Stretches, yellow leaves, deficient light
Asparagus densiflorus 'Sprengeri' (Kunth.) Jessop. Sprenger fern	E-S-W	Med, M; High, G	Med	Fair	Dry-moist	Leaf yellowing and abscission
Aspidistra elatior Blume. Iron plant	E-N	Low, M; Med, G	Warm	Good	Moist	Marginal crinkle, scorch and salts
Asplenium nidus L. Bird's nest fern	E-S	High, G; Med, M	Med	Fair	Moist	Stretches, yellow leaves, leaf scorch
Brassaia actinophylla Endl. Schefflera or Australian umbrella tree	E-S-W	Med, M; High, G	Warm	Fair	Moist	Leaf spotting and abscission
Bromeliads (general)	E-S-W	High, M	Med-cool	Fair	Dry	Poor flowering, scorch
Cacti (general)	S-W	High ?, M	Warm	Fair	Dry	Root rot
Calathea spp. G.F. Mey. Peacock plant	E-N	Low, M; Med, G	Warm	Fair	Moist	Scorch, salts, stretches
Chamaedorea elegans Mart. Parlor palm	E-N	Low, M; Med, G	Med	Excellent	Moist	Spider mites
Chlorophytum comosum (Thunb.) Jacques. Spider plant	E-N	Med, M; High, G	Med	Good	Moist	Scorch, few aerial plantlets, fluorides
Chrysanthemum × *morifolium* Ramat. Florist's chrysanthemum	S	High ++, M	Med	Good	Moist	Flowering ceases[e]
Cissus spp. L. Grape ivy	E-N	Med, M; High, G	Med	Good	Moist	Scorch, stretches
Citrus reticulata var. *austera*? × *Fortunella* sp.? Calamondin	S-W	High ++, G; High, M	Cool	Poor	Moist	Leaf abscission, poor flowering and fruiting
Codiaeum spp. A. Juss. Croton	S	High ++ G?; High, M	Warm	Poor	Moist	Loss of foliage color, stretches
Coleus × *hybridus* Voss Painted nettle, coleus	E-S	High ++ G,; High, M	Med	Excellent	Moist	Loss of foliage color, stretches

Plant	Exposure	Light, Growth	Temp.	Maintenance	Moisture	Problems
Cordyline terminalis (L.) Kunth. Good luck plant, baby doll	E-S	Med, G	Warm	Fair	Moist	Scorch, leaf loss, salts
Crassula arborescens (Mill.) Willd. Chinese jade plant	S-W	High ++ G, High, M	Med	Excellent	Moist-dry	Relatively trouble-free
Crocus vernus (L.) J. Hill. Dutch crocus	S	High, M	Cool	Good	Moist	Flowering ceases[e]
Cycas revoluta Thunb. Sago palm	E-N	High +, G High, M	Cool	Good	Dry	Leaf renewal slow, scorch
Cyclamen persicum Mill. Florist's cyclamen	S	High ++ ?, M	Cool	Fair	Dry-moist	Flowering ceases,[e] yellow leaves
Dieffenbachia spp. Schott. Dumbcane	E-N S	Med, M High, G	Warm	Excellent	Moist	Scorch, leaf loss, salts, spider mites
Dizygotheca elegantissima (Hort. Veitch) R. Vig and Guilliaum (*Aralia*) False aralia	E-N	Med, M High, G	Warm	Excellent	Moist	Some stretch, spider mites
Dracaena deremensis 'Warneckii' Engl.	N-E	Med +, G High +, G	Warm	Good	Moist	Scorch, salts, fluorides
D. fragrans 'Massangeana' (L.) Ker-Gowl. Corn plant	N-E	Med +, M High, G	Warm	Good	Moist	Scorch, salts, fluorides
D. Sanderana Hort. Sander ex. M.T. Mast. Belgian evergreen dracaena	E	Med +, M High, G	Warm	Good	Moist	Scorch, salts, fluorides
D. surculosa Lindl. (*D. godseffiana*) Gold-dust plant	E	Med +, M High, G	Warm	Good	Moist	Scorch, salts, fluorides
Euphorbia pulcherrima Willd. ex. Klotzsch. Poinsettia	S	High ++ ?, M	Med	Fair-Good	Dry-moist	Flowering ceases,[e] stretches, scorch
Fatsia japonica (Thunb.) Decne & Planch. (*Aralia japonica*) Japanese false aralia	E-S	High, G Med, M	Med	Good	Moist	Stretches
Ficus benjamina L. Weeping fig	E	Med, M High, G	Warm	Fair	Moist	Leaf abscission, small leaves
F. elastica Roxb. ex Hornem. India rubber tree	E	Med, M High, G	Warm	Excellent	Moist	Older leaves yellow then abscise
F. lyrata Warb. (*F. pandurata*) Fiddle-leaf fig	E	Med +, M High, G	Warm	Good	Moist	Scorch, leaf abscission
F. pumila L. Creeping fig	E	Med +, M	Warm	Good	Moist	Yellow leaves, stretches
Fittonia verschaffeltii (Lem.) Colm. Nerve plant	E-N	Med, M High G	Warm	Fair	Moist	Scorch, salts, stretches, root rot

[a]Natural light entering unobstructed windows within 1 m (3 ft) of the plants: N = North, skylight only; E = East, direct morning light usually for a short period; S = South, light can be direct for a long period (depending on the overhanging eave and time of year); W = West, light plus heat radiation from hot objects makes this exposure difficult for many plants to tolerate. Boldface exposure is the best possible choice.

[b]Light intensity from cool white lamps: Low = 275–800 lux (25–75 ft-c); Med = 800–2150 lux (75–200 ft-c); High = 2150–4300 lux (200–400 ft-c); High + = 4400–6600 lux (400–600 ft-c); and High ++ = 6600–14,400 lux (600–1200 ft-c); M = the maintenance of the plant can be expected for 4 to 12 months; G = the plant will grow but normal greenhouse growth cannot be expected. A question mark indicates no data available.

[c]Night temperatures: Cool = 10–15°C (50–60°F); Med = 15–18°C (60–65°F); Warm = 18–23°C (65–75°F).

[d]Dry = withstands dry conditions before irrigating again; Moist = irrigate soil mix shortly after the surface appears dry; Wet = never allow the soil mix to become dry. In all cases, irrigate the soil mixture sufficiently for excess water to drip from drain hole of containers.

[e]These plants are usually brought into the home with flowers which last only a short while. Repeat flowering in the home cannot be expected. In some locations, plants may bloom again if planted out of doors.

Table 18–3 (continued)

Groups, Genera, or Species and Common Names	Environmental Conditions			Chances of Success in the Home	Soil Moisture Status to Sustain Growth[d]	Possible Cultural and Environmental Problems Which May Be Encountered in the Home
	Light Conditions		Temp for Growth[c]			
	Natural Window Exposure[a]	Under Fluorescent Lamps for 16 Hrs/Day[b]				
Fuchsia × *hybrida* Hort. ex Vilm.	E	High ?, M	Cool	Poor	Moist	Leaf abscission
Gardenia jasminoides Ellis. Cape jasmine	E-S	High, M	Med	Poor	Moist	Leaf yellowing, abscission of leaves and flower buds
Gynura aurantiaca (Blume) DC. Velvet plant	E-**S**	High, G / Med, M	Med	Fair	Moist	Stretches
Hedera helix L. 'California' English ivy	E-**S**	Med, M / High, G	Cool	Good	Dry-moist	Leaf spot, stretches
(*Helxine soleirolii*) *Soleirolia soleirolii* (Req.) Dandy. Baby's tears	E	High, G / Med, M	Cool	Fair	Moist-wet	Petioles stretch, small leaves
Howea spp. Becc. Sentry palm	E-**N**	Med, M / High, G	Cool	Good	Dry-moist	Scorch, petioles stretch
Hoya carnosa (L.f.) R. Br. Wax plant	E-S	Med, M	Med	Good	Dry-moist	Relatively trouble-free
Hyacinthus orientalis L. Dutch hyacinth	S	High +, M	Cool	Fair	Moist	Flowering short-lived[e]
Lilium longiflorum Thunb. Easter lily	S-**W**	High +, M	Cool	Fair	Moist	Flowering short-lived[e]
Maranta leuconeura E. Morr. Prayer plant	N-E	Med, M / High, G	Warm	Fair	Moist	Scorch, stretches
Monstera deliciosa Liebm. Split-leaf philodendron	E-S	High, M	Med	Good	Moist	With deficient light, leaves will not "split"
Narcissus spp. L. Jonquils or daffodils	S-**W**	High +, M	Cool	Fair	Moist	Flowering short-lived[e]
Nephrolepis exaltata (L.) Schott. Sword fern	E-**N**	Low, M / Med, G	Warm	Excellent	Moist-wet	Scorch, salts
Pelargonium × *hortorum* L.H. Bailey House geranium	S-**W**	High+ ?, M	Cool	Fair	Moist	Yellow leaves, flowering ceases[e]
Peperomia argyreia E. Morr. (*P. sandersii*) Watermelon peperomia	E-N	Low, M / Med, G	Med	Good	Dry-moist	Stretches
Philodendron scandens C. Koch & H. Sello (*P. oxycardium*) Heart philodendron	E-**N**	Low, M / Med, G	Warm	Excellent	Moist	Relatively trouble-free but stretches
Philodendron spp. Schott. (Large-leaf species)	E-S	High, M	Warm	Fair	Moist	Leaf scorch, stretches
Pittosporum tobira (Thunb.) Ait. Tobira or mock orange	S-E	High, M / High +, G	Cool	Good	Dry-moist	Relatively trouble-free
Platycerium spp. Desv. Staghorn fern	E-**N**	Low, M / Med, G	Warm	Fair-poor	Moist-wet	Scorch, salts

Plant	Exposure	Light	Temperature	Quality	Moisture	Remarks
Plectranthus spp. L'Her. Swedish ivy	S	High, G; Med, M	Med	Excellent	Moist	With deficient light, leaf color changes
Podocarpus macrophylla (Thunb.) D. Don. Southern yew	S	Med, M; High +, G	Cool	Good	Moist	Scorch, salts, deficient light
Rhododendron simsii Planch. Azalea	S	High, M	Cool	Fair	Moist-wet	Flowering ceases,[e] leaf loss
Saintpaulia ionantha H. Wendl. African violet	E	High, M; High +, G	Warm	Excellent	Moist	Leaf spot, petioles collapse, poor flowering
Sansevieria trifasciata Prain. Bowstring hemp or snake plant	E-N	Low, M; High, G	Warm	Excellent	Dry-moist	Relatively trouble-free
Schulmbergia Bridgesii (Lem.) Lofgr. Christmas cactus	S	Med, M; High, G	Cool	Fair	Dry	Flowers poorly with deficient light
Epipremnum aureum Linden and Andre. Pothos (*Scindapsus aureus*)	E-N	Low, M; Med, G	Warm	Excellent	Dry-moist	Relatively trouble-free. Loses variegation under low light
Senecio mikanioides Otto. German ivy	S-E	High, M	Cool	Good	Dry-moist	Stretches
Sinningia speciosa (Lodd.) Hiern. Gloxinia	E	High +, M	Warm	Good	Moist	Flowering ceases,[e] scorch
Syngonium podophyllum Schott. Nephthytis or arrowhead	E-N	Low, M; Med, G	Warm	Excellent	Moist-wet	Relatively trouble-free
Tolmiea menziesii (Purch.) Torr. and A. Gray. Piggyback plant	E-N	Low, M; Med, G	Cool	Fair	Moist-wet	Leaf spot, plant dries out easily
Tradescantia fluminensis Vell. Wandering Jew	E-N	Low, M; Med, G	Warm	Excellent	Moist	Stretches, leaf scorch, fluorides
Tulipa hybrida L. Garden tulip	S	High, M	Cool	Fair	Moist	Flowering short-lived[e]
Zebrina pendula Schnizl. Wandering Jew	E-N	Low, M	Warm	Excellent	Moist	Stretches, leaf scorch, fluorides

transpiration are favorable). Transpiration is influenced most by light since light influences stomatal opening and the vapor pressure of water when the light heats the leaf. If light is low, the transpiration rate is also low. If the air in the room has a low relative humidity, the transpiration rate does not necessarily increase, since the stomates may already be closed, but the evaporation from porous pot walls or soil surface is enhanced. One cannot expect a container to dry out rapidly under low light conditions. Experience shows the proper timing for irrigating houseplants under a given set of environmental conditions.

Having mentioned the two most common causes of failure in growing or maintaining houseplants (poor light and improper watering), let us continue to discuss in more detail the home environmental conditions, various growing media, and the key points to remember when watering the plants.

Natural Light Intensity in the Home

The different light requirements of the various foliage and flowering plants are summarized in Table 18-3. In the home environment it is possible to maintain a plant's acceptable appearance for many months, but it is often difficult to obtain much new growth unless the plant has a naturally low light requirement. Any natural light exposure in the home usually has two disadvantages: first, the light is usually unidirectional and, second, the light that enters a particular window is only effective for a few hours at best. Unidirectional light can result in distorted growth. Plants receiving only a few hours of light may have difficulty retaining their leaves. If the light is marginal or submarginal for that plant, enough leaves abscise to allow the plant to acclimatize to the available light (p. 389). Some plants do not have the ability to adapt to low light and either become etiolated (stretched) or soon die under such conditions. Most of the commercial foliage plants have been selected for their ability to adapt to low-light conditions in the home, yet some knowledge is required to choose the best exposure for a given species.

The light for plants can come from four possible exposures. In the Northern Hemisphere, the southern exposure has the strongest light and the longest duration at any time of year. In the winter, when the sun is low in the sky, direct light may enter the south windows but the rays are not as strong as in the summer. Overhanging eaves may also keep out much of the direct sun in the summer, which is beneficial in preventing too much light

from entering. The light duration in the summer can be 50 percent greater than in the winter because of the long day length. Light entering a south window can be effective up to about 3 m (10 ft) back from the glass when there are no obstructions. The most effective light is within 1 m (39 in) of the glass. Plants requiring a high light intensity do fairly well under such light exposure.

The western exposure is the next strongest light. It is considered stronger than the eastern exposure because of the additional radiation that enters the glass from objects that are heated throughout the day. Indeed, the additional radiation can even be detrimental to high-light-tolerant plants. Excess transpiration and consequent drying of the soil can be a serious problem for plants in a western exposure. Slight shade from a curtain drawn over the window can often help.

The eastern exposure is considered moderate light for plants because the light is good, but excessive heat radiation has not had a chance to develop before the sunlight moves away from that window. Perhaps this exposure is best for most foliage plants. Most plants can withstand direct sun in this exposure. The light duration is not too long and therefore the sun does not usually damage the leaves.

The northern exposure is indirect for most of the year except for a few weeks in the summer in northern latitudes when the sun rises north of east and sets north of west. The sunlight at either of these times is usually weak because the sun is low in the sky. Many species maintain their quality and even grow slowly in this exposure. The effective distance at this exposure is within 1 m of the glass.

The information in Table 18–3 on best window exposure is for the maintenance and perhaps for slight growth of the plant. In all cases the plant would have to acclimatize to the light intensity at the particular exposure. It is assumed that the light entering any of these exposures is unobstructed light. Obstruction can change an exposure. For example, trees shading an eastern exposure may make it equivalent to a shadeless northern exposure.

Reflected light within the home is useful for plant growth. A white surface or a mirror can reflect up to 90 percent of the light that enters a window; a dark green or light brown surface reflects only up to 50 percent of the light. Reflective walls outside the windows can redirect light and, in essence, extend the period of light duration. Reflected light into north windows is very beneficial. There is an excellent reference (8) on the subject of exposures and how to modify them for plants.

It is possible to grow excellent plants entirely under artificial illumination with the proper lamps. Incandescent lamps emit much red light, including infrared. These wavelengths increase heat that can damage leaves if they are too close to the source. The blue portion of the light spectrum is low in these lamps. As a result, incandescent lamps alone are unsuitable for growing high-quality plants. Fluorescent lamps, on the other hand, emit light across a broad spectrum (Fig. 18–7) and are suitable for growing many houseplants. The following discussion on lamps for plant growth is directed to fluorescent lamps only.

The advantage of fluorescent lamps is their high output of light and uniform illumination. The lamps can be programmed to illuminate the plants for any desired time. Sixteen hours per day, in many cases, provide more total light than any natural light that enters from windows. The light intensity multiplied by the duration of light is important to the plant. The light intensity under fluorescent lamps can be adjusted somewhat by regulating the distance of the plants from the lamps. One more important consideration is the spectral distribution of light from the lamp. Several fluorescent lamps have been designed to emit much light in the red and blue portions of the spectrum, that portion used in photosynthesis. However, recent research *(4)* has shown that the

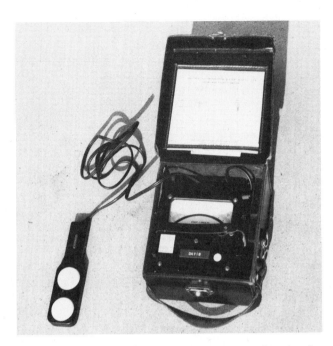

Fig. 18–8   A light meter commonly used for measuring intensity of natural and artificial light. This light meter has its limitations, however, since it is most sensitive to the yellow portion of the spectrum, which coincides with the sensitivity of the human eye. Plants, however, are very responsive in the blue and red portions of the spectrum.

most effective lamps for foliage plant growth are sold as "cool white." This type of lamp comes in many lengths, since it is often used in offices, schools, and so forth. It is easy on the eyes and is inexpensive.

The light intensities from "cool white" fluorescent lamps necessary to maintain or grow various house plants appear in Table 18–3. These figures are based on data gathered by various research workers. If a question mark appears, no experimental evidence is available, but the range indicated is likely to maintain plant quality. Note that some of the plants requiring high light intensity are those that are questionable (Table 18–3).

Light intensity is measured with a special light meter, which is not the same as a photographer's light meter and which registers in lux or foot candles (Fig. 18–8). This light meter is sensitive mainly in the yellow and green portion of the spectrum, the same portion to which the human eye is most sensitive. Footcandles and lux are not the best ways to express the light sensitivity of plants, but these units are the most common way of expressing the intensity of light (see Ch. 7).

On the next page are the light intensities of some common situations. All figures are in lux with footcandles in parentheses.

Fig. 18–7   Comparison of three action spectra: (A) photosynthesis curve (natural light), (B) cool white fluorescent lamp, and (C) incandescent lamp. *Source:* GTE Sylvania, Inc.

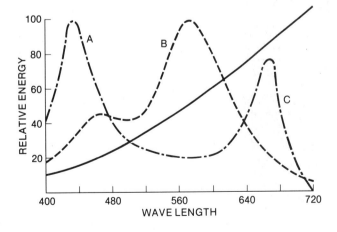

Home

General illumination, 55 (5)
Reading or writing, 220 (20)
Ironing or sewing, 440 (40)
Work bench, 440 (40)

Libraries or Offices

Reading, 330 (30)
Typing, 550 (50)
Conference rooms, 330 (30)

Stores

Circulating areas, 220 (20)
Merchandising area, 550 (50)
Displays or show windows, 1100–5500 (100–500)

Outdoors

Bright summer days, 110,000 (10,000)
Cloudy winter days, 5500–22,000 (500–2000)

Figures 18–9 and 18–10 illustrate the light intensity of two types of flourescent lamps at various distances from the source. The 1500 MA lamps are very high output (VHO) lamps, whereas the standard 40-watt fluorescents are the very common, 120 cm (4 ft) tubes. Fluorescent ballasts give off heat, and excessive heat may accumulate if they are confined in a small room or enclosure. The heat should be removed by ventilation if it exceeds the ranges given in Table 18–3. High temperatures combined with low or marginal light intensity results in weak growth and spindly plants.

Fig. 18–9 The light intensity at different distances from two very high output (VHO) fluorescent lamps. *Source:* USDA.

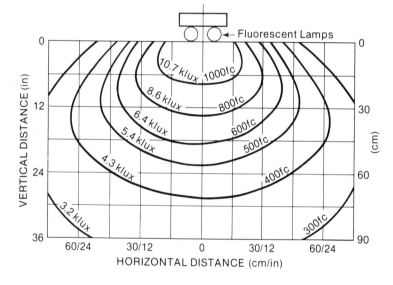

Fig. 18–10 The light intensity at different distances from two ordinary fluorescent lamps. *Source:* USDA.

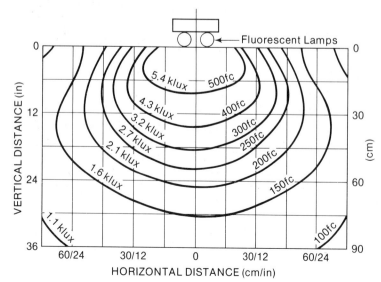

Tropical houseplants generally grow best at temperatures between 18°C and 25°C (65°F and 77°F) if other conditions are optimal. These are the temperatures designated as "warm" in Table 18-3. All those temperature ranges listed are for growth of the plant. Weak spindly growth can be expected above the suggested temperatures and no growth at slightly lower temperatures. If the temperature is lowered by a few degrees, the plants can only be maintained. When the temperature is lowered to 2°C to 4°C (35°F to 40°F) for 2 to 24 hours, foliar and root damage can occur to tropical foliage plants. This is called **chilling injury** and may happen when tropical plants are transported during cold weather in an unheated vehicle. Plants should be kept warm during moving from one location to another.

Most houseplants, other than the succulents and bromeliads, grow best at high RHs. Most homes have a low RH, especially during the winter months, but the RH around the plants can be partially raised by a dish of moist pebbles placed under the pot or by a box constructed as shown in Figure 18-11. As mentioned earlier, low RH has no great effect on transpiration but does affect evaporation from the soil surface and the sides of porous container surfaces. If a higher RH is desired, it is necessary to minimize air movement. This means avoiding drafty locations. Misting with an atomizer temporarily raises the RH only in the immediate vicinity of the misting and is of little practical value.

Fig. 18–11 A cut-away view of a box that raises the humidity around houseplants. The box is watertight, and it is lined with sphagnum moss on the sides and gravel on the bottom. The sphagnum moss must be watered periodically to provide moisture from its large evaporation surface. *Source:* USDA.

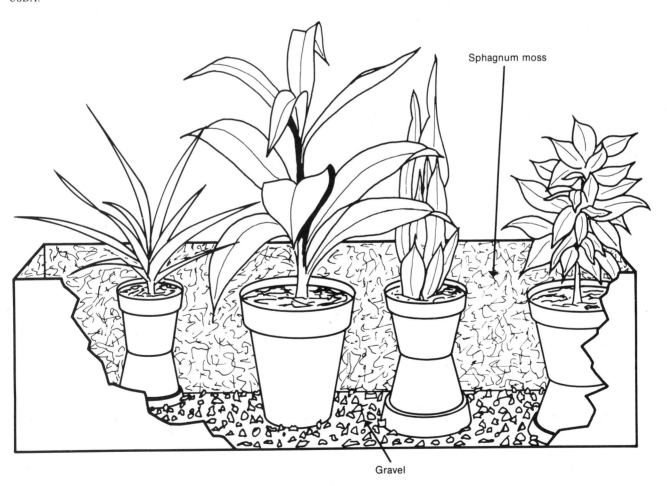

Sphagnum moss

Gravel

Table 18–4 A Guide to Common Problems of Foliage and Flowering Plants Grown or Maintained in the Home.

Symptoms	Possible Causes	Possible Remedies
1. Leaf edges or tips scorched or brown; gradual progression.	a. Soil too dry for an extended period. b. Too much fertilizer. c. Salts too high in soil.	a. Irrigate more b. Fertilize less and irrigate with greater volume. c. Irrigate more frequently with greater volume than previously.
2. Leaves become yellow especially older (lower) ones; leaves may later abscise or cling to stem, depending on the species.	a. Light intensity too low; probably the period of light adjustment is too brief. b. Soil saturated for an extended period. c. Poor drainage, therefore poor aeration. d. A combination of a. and b. above; i.e., soil too moist for the light available. e. Nitrogen deficiency.	a. Increase light (better location) or gradually acclimatize plant before moving it to a low-light condition. b. Irrigate less frequently but do apply a large volume when irrigating! c. See b. above but also remedy the inadequate drainage situation. d. Remedy one situation at a time or use care if changing both. e. Increase nitrogen fertilization.
3. Leaf abscission or leaves cling to stem; leaves may or may not become yellow.	a. Light intensity reduced too quickly. b. Sudden change to low temperatures; may happen when transporting plants. c. Saturated soil which favors root rot organisms or causes root injury. d. Lack of nutrients (extreme cases). e. Gas fumes.	a. See 2a. b. Avoid any chilling temperature; use adequate protection. c. See 2b. and 2c. d. Fertilize with a complete fertilizer. e. Check gas heater, stove, and other gas appliances for gas leaks.

4. Leaf damage
   a. Large necrotic spots in center.
 	
   b. Small spots; halo around spot.
   c. Small spots on African violets.
	a. Light intensity suddenly too high.
	
	b. Bacterial or fungal infection.
	c. Collapsed palisade cells in fleshy leaves.
		a. Avoid bright light on plants that have been acclimatized to low light.
		b. Do not mist or spray foliage; lower RH.
		c. Do not irrigate overhead with cold water.

5. Pale yellow leaves over entire plant; new leaves may be small.	a. Lack of nitrogen. b. Saturated soil. c. Temperature too high. d. Spider mites.	a. Supply a nitrogenous fertilizer. b. See 2b. c. Lower temperature. d. Wash with mild detergent.
6. Etiolated growth (leggy or stretched stems); new leaves small.	a. Light intensity too low. b. Temperature too high. c. Too much incandescent light.	a. Move to higher light. b. Lower the temperature. c. Decrease exposure to incandescent light.
7. Stunted growth; small leaves.	a. Saturated soil. b. Soil too dry for an extended period. c. Lack of fertilizer. d. High soluble salts. e. Virus infection.	a. See 2b. b. Irrigate more frequently. c. Use a complete fertilizer in modest quantities at start. d. Leach soil, see 1c. e. Discard plants.
8. Terminal growing point inactive, dead or dying.	a. Saturated soil. b. Poor drainage. c. High soluble salts. d. Light intensity suddenly too high. e. Cyclamen mites.	a. See 2b. b. Remedy drainage problem. c. See 1c. d. See 4a. e. Use proper miticide or discard plant; very infectious to other plants.
9. Entire plant wilts; Problem aggravated with successive irrigations. Recovers from wilting after irrigation.	a. Saturated soil. b. Poor drainage. c. Root or stem rot. d. Soil too dry for an extended period. e. Root-bound plant.	a. See 2b. b. See 2c. c. Modify watering practices or use proper fungicides. d. Irrigate more frequently. e. Shift plant to a larger pot.
10. Poor flowering of a normally good flowering plant.	a. Light intensity too low. b. Temperature too high. c. Saturated soil. d. Poor drainage. e. Root rot problems.	a. Move to higher light. b. Lower temperature. c. See 2b. d. See 2c. e. See 9c.

The Growing Medium

When a houseplant is purchased, one has no choice but to accept the growing medium in the pot. If the medium is a heavy clay mixture (p. 418), it may be worthwhile to repot the plant into a coarse organic mixture of the sort suggested in Table 18–1. A medium with large pores and with abundant organic matter provides both good water retention and aeration if properly irrigated.

It is better to know how to water one or two media well than to try to attempt to become acquainted with many unknown formulations. It is possible to grow houseplants in almost any medium, but care must be exercised to become acquainted with the physical characteristics of the particular medium. A medium with a high clay content may not allow for good water infiltration and once wet, the medium will stay moist much too long. Such conditions kill the roots or encourage root pathogens, which, in turn, result in yellowing and dropping of leaves (Table 18–4). A coarse porous medium, made up largely of sphagnum peat moss, can be irrigated thoroughly to leach out excess salts and still provide excellent aeration in the top two-thirds of the container. Once a coarse medium is chosen, it is then only a matter of determining how often to irrigate it for good plant growth.

*Irrigation Frequency
to Sustain Growth*

In determining the watering schedule for a porous growing medium, keep these few fundamentals in mind:

1. It is important to consider the species being grown because some species or genera are prone to infection by various soil-borne pathogens that kill the young feeder roots. Watering should be done only as the soil becomes dry (at least on the surface). This group of plants is indicated as "moist" in Table 18–3. Some plants cannot thrive in dry soils and the medium must be kept moist always; this group is indicated as "wet." Of course, some groups, such as succulents, cacti, and bromeliads, can withstand dry soil conditions because of their xerophytic leaves; this group is listed as "dry" in Table 18–3, under "Soil Moisture Status."
2. The size of the plant for the pot size often indicates how often the medium must be irrigated. A large plant in a small pot soon uses all the available water and therefore must be irrigated frequently. Shifting the root ball to a larger pot to provide a greater soil volume for more available water rem-

edies the problem. You can also prune the plant to reduce the number of leaves without shifting the plant to a larger pot. Sometimes a small plant is "overpotted"; i.e., it is planted in too large a pot. Since leaf transpiration is the major factor in removing the soil water, the plant may not be able to transpire enough water to overcome the saturated condition near the bottom of the container. Since most people tend to irrigate the soil when the surface appears dry, the medium never dries out. The roots of the small plant will not enter the saturated zone, which may also become a place for soil pathogens to become established. It is, therefore, best to transplant plants into a container of the appropriate size. Good judgment or experience helps make the correct choice.

3. The transpiration conditions under which the plant is growing largely determine the irrigation frequency. If the plant is growing under low light intensity, the transpiration rate is low, but high light (to a point) has the greatest influence on the rate of transpiration.
4. The water quality determines not only the irrigation frequenty but the quantity of water that should be applied at any irrigation (see p. 394). If a water has an electrical conductivity (EC_ω) below 0.75 mmho/cm (Table 18–2), less leaching is required through the soil than if the irrigation water has an EC_ω above 1.5 mmho/cm. If poor water is used for irrigation, more water must be applied to avoid an accumulation of salts in the medium. Likewise, with a poor irrigation water, one should irrigate more frequently than with good water to prevent a rise in salt concentration as the medium becomes dry or nearly dry. Many root and leaf damage problems can be attributed to high levels of soluble salts in the growing medium. Many of these troubles can be overcome by using large quantities of water to leach the salts and by irrigating more frequently than normal to avoid drying out of the medium. There is no substitute for good experience and for knowing the quality of the water.

Cultural Problems

Each plant species has its own problems under home environmental conditions. The most important ones are listed in Table 18–3; a guide to common problems of houseplants appears in Table 18–4. Seven species are listed in Table 18–3 as relatively trouble-free; that is, under the environmental conditions listed, no major problems should be expected.

Some Common Pests of Houseplants

Aphids of almost any color and about 2 mm (1/16 inch) long, congregate near the growing points in clusters and suck the plant juices. The shoots become sticky from a secretion exuded by the colonies. *Control:* Wash with a mild detergent (1:10 parts of water) or use a proper insecticide in severe cases.

Mealy bugs are small white insects, with cottonlike protective coatings, that cover the underside of leaves along the midribs. *Control:* Touch the insect directly with a cotton-tipped swab soaked in rubbing alcohol; do not touch the plant with the alcohol. Wash the leaves with a mild detergent. If the infestation is severe, use an appropriate insecticide.

Spider mites are not easily seen because of their minute size but their webbing is easily detected if they become abundant. Under a 10× hand lens they appear sand-colored. Their damage is easier to see than they are. The leaves look whitish or silvery, especially between the veins, where the pests suck out the juices from the leaves. Spider mites are a problem particularly with low RH. *Control:* Wash the mites off with a mild detergent or use a suitable miticide if the infestation becomes severe. Repeat treatment as directed on the label.

White flies are minute white insects that fly when disturbed. The larvae feed and the adults lay eggs on the underside of the leaves. A new generation appears in less than a week under ideal conditions. The young flies (nymphs) do not move much and suck out the plant juices from the leaves. They give off a honeydew secretion. Many foliage plants are ideal hosts for this insect. *Control:* Wash leaves with a mild detergent or use a suitable insecticide if the infestation is great. Repeat the treatment as directed on the label.

Thrips are small rod-like insects that vary in color. They move rapidly when disturbed on the underside of leaves. The insect scrapes the leaf surface and then sucks out the juices. Small irregular patches are formed by this rasping. *Control:* Washing is difficult because of the thrips' ability to hide. Use the proper insecticide.

Scale insects are small-bodied yellow crawling insects that eventually become covered with a hard oval shell-like structure (about 2 to 4 mm in diameter). They are found on the undersides of leaves and along the midribs and on the stems, resembling rows of brownish and blackish oval-shaped bumps. These insects suck the plant juices from under their protective hiding place on the underside of the leaf. The top portion of the leaf becomes pale. They secrete a honeydew substance. *Control:* It is possible to scrape the scale off the leaves if only a few appear. Wash the leaves with a mild detergent when the insects are in the crawling stage (moving to a new location). Dip the infected leaf and stem portions in a suitable insecticide.

Cyclamen mites are one of the most difficult pests to detect and control. They feed in the plant's growing points and only after they become well established is their presence evident. The growing points stop growing and may look grayish, as is the case with African violet. Common hosts of this infectious pest are African violet, gloxinia, English ivy, begonia, geranium, and, of course, cyclamen. *Control:* Use the proper miticide. Discard seriously infected plants before the mites can infest other plants.

Fungus gnats live on organic matter in the soil but can also injure plant roots. The larvae are the dangerous stage but are not as easily detected as the small black adults (flies) that scurry about the soil surface when disturbed. *Control:* A soil drench of the proper insecticide controls the larvae.

REFERENCES

1. Ayres, R. S. 1976. Quality of irrigation water. Soil and plant-tissue testing in California. Univ. of Calif. Div. Agr. Sci. Bul. 1879.

2. Baker, K. F., 1957. The U.C. system for producing healthy container-grown plants. Univ. of Calif. Manual 23.

3. Ball, V., ed. 1976. *The Ball red book.* 13th ed. West Chicago, Ill. G. J. Ball.

4. Biran, I., and A. M. Kofranek. 1976. Evaluation of fluorescent lamps as an energy source for plant growth. *Jour. Am. Soc. Hort. Sci.* 101(6):625–28.

5. Boodley, J. 1973. Plant acclimatization. New York State Flr. Ind. Bul. 40.

6. Conover, C. A. 1975. Acclimatization of tropical foliage plants. *Am. Nurseryman* 142(5):64.

7. Larson, R. A., ed. 1980. *Introduction to floriculture.* New York: Academic Press.

8. Ray, R. M., ed. 1975. *The facts of light about indoor gardening.* San Francisco: Ortho Books.

9. Spomer, L. A. 1976. Container soils are different. Ill. State Flor. Assoc. Bul. 363.

ANON. 1976. *How to detect and solve plant problems*. Lansing, Mich.: John Henry.

CARPENTER, W. J., and G. H. SULLIVAN. 1966. Interior decoration with living plants. Kansas State Univ. of Agri. Bul. 494.

CROCKETT, J. U. 1972. *Foliage house plants*. New York: Time-Life.

GRAF, A. B. 1976. *Exotic plant manual*. 4th ed. East Rutherford, N.J.: Roehrs.

HULL, H. S., ed. 1974. *Handbook on ferns*. Brooklyn, N.Y.: Brooklyn Botanical Gardens.

PERKINS, H. O., ed. 1975. *House plants, a handbook*. Brooklyn, N.Y.: Brooklyn Botanical Gardens.

RAY, R. M., ed. 1974. *House plants, indoors/outdoors*. San Francisco: Ortho Books.

SPOMER, L. A. 1974. Two classroom exercises demonstrating the pattern of container soil water distribution. *HortScience* 9(2):152–53.

Herbaceous Ornamentals: Bedding Plants

The desire to create an environment of beauty in public places for the enjoyment of oneself or others has resulted in phenomenal growth for the American bedding plant industry. In 1970 the United States wholesale sales of the industry was over $60 million; by 1980 it was conservatively estimated to be over $225 million. There are three reasons for this dramatic increase. One is the improved marketing of the plants in lots of half and whole dozens in small plastic containers (Fig. 19–1). This innovation

has enabled the wholesale grower to virtually mass-produce and mass-market these plants at a low price, which benefits the home gardener, the ultimate consumer. Second, people have more success transplanting small plants from these individual containers than they do with transplants that have had to be cut out of a flat (Fig. 19–2) like pieces of sheet cake. The soil ball would break before the plants were brought home from the nursery. The increased transplanting success from small plastic containers has given the gardener an added incentive to use flowering annuals more frequently for spring and fall plantings. Third, the growth and flowering characteristics of annuals have improved considerably

Fig. 19–1 A tray of empty plastic cell packs that will contain six seedlings each. The packs are filled with soil mixture with an automatic soil filler (Fig. 19–9) and brought into the greenhouse, where seedlings are planted directly into each cell. The depressed notch between each cell allows for water to disperse easily even if the cell packs are not exactly level.

Fig. 19–2 A wooden flat of marigold seedlings without partitions. These seedlings must be cut out of the flat with a putty knife or spatula. Since the root system is small at the time of sale, much of the soil mixture separates from the roots. Seedlings transplanted without soil adhering to the roots often wilt and die because of moisture stress. For these reasons this method of growing is not as satisfactory as that shown in Figure 19-1.

Fig. 19–3   The effective use of pansies (*Viola tricolor*) at entrance to a home.

Fig. 19–4 *Above:* A large bedding plant area in front of the greenhouse of a horticultural school in Wooster, Ohio. All plants were grown and planted in three concentric rings by the students. *Below:* A close-up of the two inner rings showing dusty miller (lower left) and petunias in the large middle circle. The high containers have trailing ivy geraniums which are surrounded by the inner ring of annual impatiens. The entire area is planned and planted differently each year by the students, certainly a worthy project to contemplate during the long winter.

because of the development of improved hybrids (see p. 76).

What are bedding plants? The term was originally used by gardeners who wanted to use annual or perennial plants in a permanent border or in a specially designed flower bed (see p. 425). In recent years the term has been expanded to include flowering ornamental plants, vegetables, and herbs, mostly annuals (Ch. 6). Bedding plants are used in large or small containers, on patios, in window boxes, in hanging baskets, in small gardens and, of course, in beds and borders. People have begun to use species seasonally adapted for their location in various ways. Figures 19–3 and 19–4 illustrate some of these adaptations.

Some small vegetable plants that are better transplanted into the garden from containers than started from seeds are also classified as bedding plants. Examples are tomatoes, eggplants, peppers, and squashes for spring plantings and cabbage, Brussels sprouts, and cauliflower for fall plantings in some locations. All of these species are now available seasonally in many cultivars at garden centers throughout the world. An apartment dweller can have a vegetable garden of sorts with chives, parsley, or low-growing herbs on the windowsill or container-grown tomatoes or peppers on the balcony. The bedding plant industry has responded to the needs of a range of "gardeners" from the sophisticated to the novice, by offering a variety of plants in large, medium, or small containers (Fig. 19–5) and a variety of species from which to choose.

This chapter examines how bedding plants are produced by wholesale growers and how bedding plants can be used to beautify the garden with variety and seasonal color.

Fig. 19–5   Bedding plants are available in large (*left*) and small plastic containers (*right*). The containers are generally labeled with a plastic tag giving the plant's name and some cultural instructions for the homeowner.

Fig. 19–6 Well-ventilated fiberboard containers for shipping flats of bedding plants long distances by air freight.

Fig. 19–7 Soil mixtures are usually pasteurized before use in the greenhouse. One method is to allow steam to flow through the mixture in metal boxes that are used for potting or filling flats when the mixture cools. The sides drop down to make a work surface. This method discourages contamination of the soil mixture because it is not moved from the steam treatment chamber to the potting bench.

In temperate climates, bedding plants are produced in protective shelters such as plastic or glasshouses. The temperature is maintained at a desired level for uniform seed germination and seedling growth.

Producers of bedding plants select species and hybrids that will sell well in their sales area. For small growers, this area extends a few miles from the greenhouse. But large California, Florida, and Michigan growers ship bedding plants long distances by air (Fig. 19–6) or by truck. Distant air or truck transport adds much to the final cost of the product, so as a rule bedding plants are generally sold within a 300-mile radius of where they are produced.

Seed Germination

After the proper kinds of plants are selected, producers of bedding plants determine the best seed germination conditions. Most kinds of seeds have certain optimum germination temperatures (Table 19–1). This table also includes the number of seeds per ounce, a figure growers must know to determine how many seeds have to be purchased from the seed supplier. Often seed packets state the percentage of germination to allow calculation of extra seeds required to cover germination losses. Since most kinds of seeds lose their viability with age, it is best to use fresh seed at the beginning of each season. Purchasing seed annually allows producers to keep up with the latest award-winning hybrids the seed companies are offering. This is important for retail sales

Fig. 19–8 Soil mixes are best pasteurized to kill harmful microorganisms by heating to temperatures of about 60°C (140°F) for 30 minutes. This treatment does not kill beneficial organisms or cause a breakdown of minerals in the mix that can release harmful amounts of manganese or ammonia, as does heating to higher temperatures (82°C). Aerated steam can be used economically to produce a temperature of 60°C. In this portable aerated-steam soil pasteurizer the soil mix is placed in the heavy metal box with a thick marine plywood cover. The lower 9 in of the metal box is an open plenum with a heavy perforated metal cover. The steam-air mixture is blown into this plenum and is forced by the blower up through the soil mix. Steam is introduced into the air stream from the blower. When the temperature of the soil mix reaches 60°C as measured by a recording thermograph, it is maintained for 30 minutes, and then the steam is shut off. The air continuing to blow through the mix cools it rapidly so that it can be used within an hour.

Plywood lid

Discharge tray

Stainless steel box

Steam air injection into plenum

Electric outlet

Steam outlet

Blower, with air control

Steam injection with valve

Portable battery-powered thermograph

Table 19-1 Some Seed Germination Characteristics for Selected Ornamental Annuals.

Name		Seeds per ounce[a] (thousands)	Days to Germinate at Optimum Temperature	Germination Temperature (Degrees)		Seed Viability (Years)
Common or Genus	Latin			°C	°F	
Ageratum	A. Houstonianum (A. mexicanum)	200	8	21–26	70–80	2–3
African daisy	Dimorphetheca sinuata (D. auranthiaca)	9.5	10	21	70	1–2
Alyssum, sweet	Lobularia maritima	90	8	21	70	2–3
Asparagus	A. densiflorus 'Sprengeri'	0.65	42	21	70	1
Aster, China	Callistephus chinensis	12	8–10	21	70	1
Bachelor button	Centaurea cyanus	7	10	18	65	1–2
Balsam	Impatiens balsamina	3.3	8	21–23	70–75	3–4
Begonia	B. × semperflorens-cultorum	2000	14–21	21	70	2–3
Cactus	Various genera	12	35	21	70	
Calendula	C. officinalis	3	10	21	70	3–4
Candytuft	Iberis amara (I. coronaria)	9.5	8–10	21	70	2–3
Carnation, annual	Dianthus caryophyllus	14	14–21	21	70	3–4
Cineraria	Senecio × hybridus (S. cruentus)	150	10	21–23	70–75	2–3
Cockscomb	Celosia argentea 'Cristata'	28	8–10	21	70	2–3
Coleus	C. blumei	100	10	18–23	65–75	2–3
Dusty miller	Centaurea gymnocarpa	7.3	10–15	15–18	60–65	1–2
Dusty miller	Centaurea cineraria	10	10–15	15–18	60–65	1–2
Gazania	G. regins (G. splendens)	12	10	15	60	
Geranium	Pelargonium × hortorum	6	21	21–23	70–75	1–2
Globe amaranth	Gomphrena globosa	5.5	14	18–21	65–70	2–3
Impatiens	I. Wallerana (I. holsti or sultanii)	50	18	21	70	2–3
Larkspur	Consolida orientalis (Delphinium ajacis)	8	2	12	55	1
Lobelia, edging	L. Erinus	700	20	21–23	70–75	2–3
Marigold, French	Tagetes patula	9	7	21–23	70–75	2–3
Nasturtium, garden	Tropaeolum majus	0.0175	10	18	65	4–5
Nemesia	N. strumosa 'Suttonii'	90	10	12	55	2–3
Pansy	Viola tricolor	20	10	18–23	65–75	1–2
Petunia	P. × hybrida	285	10–12	21–26	70–80	1–2
Periwinkle, rose	Catharanthus roseus (Vinca rosea)	21	15	21–23	70–75	1
Phlox	P. Drummondii	14	10	18	65	1
Portulaca	P. grandiflora	280	10	21	70	2–3
Salvia	S. splendens	7.5	12–15	21	70	1
Sea Lavender	Limonium spp.	13	15–20	21	70	2–3
Sensitive plant	Mimosa pudica	4.5	12–15	26	80	2–3
Snapdragon	Antirrhinum majus	180	7–14	18–21	65–70	3–4
Stock	Matthiola incana	18	14	18–23	65–75	3–4
Strawflower	Helichrysum bracteatum 'Monstrosum'	36	7	21	70	2–3
Tobacco, flowering	Nicotiana alata (N. affinis)	300	15	21	70	2–3
Verbena	V. × hybrida (V. × hortensis)	10	20	18	65	2–3
Wishbone flower	Torenia Fournieri	375	15	21	70	1–2
Zinnia	Z. elegens	2.5–6.5	7	21	70	4–5

[a]Convert ounces (Avdp) to grams (approximately) by multiplying ounces by 28.
Source: Adapted from V. Ball, ed. 1976. The Ball red book. 13th ed. West Chicago, Ill.: G. J. Ball.

since garden magazines publicize these new cultivars in their late winter or early spring issues as newsworthy items. Customers remember these articles and often demand the latest offerings. Many bedding plant breeding programs have created vigorous F_1 hybrids (Ch. 4) and many new introductions.

Seeds are sown on a prepared medium that is usually light in weight, but retains water well and is easily separated from the seedling at transplanting time. Many mixes fit these specifications (see p. 418 for a discussion of soil mixes). The mix is pasteurized to kill organisms that cause damping off of the seedlings at the time of germination. Soil mixes are pasteurized by the industry in several ways depending on the quantity of material used at any one time (see p. 398 and Figs. 19–7, 19–8, 19–9).

Fig. 19–9 A semiautomatic flat or cell pack filler. The empty units are placed on the rollers in the rear of the revolving drum. The soil mixture is placed in the hopper with the skip loader shown behind the drum. The filled cell packs or flats are removed by hand onto a battery driven cart that moves them into the greenhouse.

Fig. 19–10 Trays of newly planted cell packs covered with empty trays to reduce the light intensity. When the newly transplanted seedlings become established within a day or two, the empty trays are removed permanently. The seedlings are watered with the plastic "water stakes" in the center of the bench. The water comes out in a fine spray and is usually turned on manually many times each day.

Fig. 19–11 A method of moving flats or pots on a bench with a portable table. The wheels are grooved to fit on a plastic pipe track. The cheesecloth shade along the posts on the right is drawn on wires over the seedlings to cast a shadow. This portable shade helps prevent wilting when the seedlings are newly transplanted.

After the seeds are sown in flats, the mix is thoroughly watered and misted occasionally (Fig. 19–10) or kept under automatic mist of periodic duration (Fig. 5–12). If mist is not used, natural light intensity must be reduced somehow (Figs. 19–11 and 19–12). As soon as the cotyledons appear (Ch. 5), the portable shade may be removed. The seedlings should then be transplanted as soon as the seedling can be conveniently held for transplanting (Fig. 19–13). Occasionally they remain in the germination flat too long. Their roots permeate the mix and grow too long for easy transplanting. Seedlings remaining in flats too long become crowded and "hard" (no longer succulent). Such seedlings will be retarded in their growth and remain stunted after transplanting. Commercial bedding plant producers use efficient transplanting crews, and must time their germination schedule (Table 19–1) so that seedlings in flats do not accumulate and become hard.

No fertilizer is applied to the medium directly after the seeds are sown since excess salts can build up in the medium (Ch. 18) and impair germination. Because there are no mineral nutrients in the germination mix, the seedlings have to be transplanted as soon as possible in the final soil mix, which contains many of the nutrients necessary for rapid growth. Growing mixes should only contain relatively low amounts of soluble mineral nutrients, which should be applied as liquid fertilizer (Ch. 17). The plants must be kept growing at a uniform rate without setbacks (allowing the seedlings to become hard) from any of the following stresses:

Fig. 19–12 Rows of seedlings in flats. When the seedlings are large enough (Fig. 19–13), they are transplanted into cell packs (Fig. 19–1). The sheet of glass reduces the light and increases the relative humidity. The empty tray is used over the glass for additional shade. Each flat is labeled to identify the species of seed sown.

Fig. 19–13 A marigold seedling ready for transplanting. Seedlings with a simple root system as shown here are easy to transplant. A root system that has branched because it remained in the germination medium too long is difficult to transplant. Seedlings large enough to hold between the thumb and forefinger are usually ready to be transplanted. This seedling came from seed sown six days earlier.

1. Lack of mineral nutrients (especially nitrogen) soon after germination stunts growth.

2. Too high a mineral nutrient level, which results in an accumulation of soluble salts, causes stunting or death depending on the quantity of salts.

3. Too little water just after seed germination causes water stress and stunting.

4. Too much light causes excessive transpiration and therefore creates water stress.

5. Too little light causes plants to etiolate (stretch). Such plants topple when transplanted.

6. Sowing seeds too thickly overcrowds the seedlings in the germination flat. Etiolation is the first result, but seedlings can also become hard if left too long before transplanting.

7. Delayed transplanting causes roots to become too large (well established) and the tops become hard.

Transplanting Seedlings

After germination, the young seedlings are transplanted to a final spacing of approximately 2.5 to 5 cm (1 to 2 in) apart. At transplanting they have a limited and often injured root system, and initially it is difficult for seedlings to obtain water from the medium. To limit transpiration the plants should be covered with some kind of portable shade on sunny days. Frequent watering or misting, par-

ticularly with a nutrient mist, is beneficial. The plants get both water and nutrients; however, there is a possibility of not applying enough mist to leach the medium thoroughly. Misting without thorough leaching causes a build-up of soluble salts, which severely stunts or kills the seedlings. The containers must be irrigated thoroughly to avoid this possible salt damage.

Fertilizers must be added as soon as the little seedlings can stand upright. The most important mineral nutrient is nitrogen, which is generally added to the irrigation water. Potassium, like nitrogen, is soluble and is needed constantly. Both nitrogen and potassium are added in the liquid fertilizer program. Phosphorus and calcium, which are less soluble, are incorporated into the soil mix before planting. An example of one satisfactory mix including additions of phosphorus and calcium before planting is given on page 419. Other possible mixtures are mentioned in Table 18–1.

Once the plants have established a good root system, usually in a week, the shade may be removed for most of the species that thrive in full sun in the garden. However, the seedlings of some species that require shade in the garden should be kept in subdued light of approximately 22,000 to 33,000 lux (2000 to 3000 ft-c) in the greenhouse (see p. 389).

Hardening off Seedlings

In the greenhouse plants are very succulent and tender because of the high temperatures and relative humidities plus the frequent watering and fertilizing. About a week or two before the seedlings are to be sold to the commercial retail outlet, growers allow the seedlings to harden (lose succulence) by gradually lowering the greenhouse temperature or by moving them to a greenhouse with a lower night temperature. They also reduce the frequency of irrigation and fertilization. The cell walls become more rigid and the cells accumulate sugars and other solutes, enabling the seedlings to withstand greater stresses that come from transplanting into the garden.

Many gardeners transplant bedding plants which they have purchased only to find they wilt and die. The four most common causes of transplanting failures in the garden are:

1. The plants are not irrigated frequently enough after transplanting (water stress).

2. The plants are not shaded properly (often only a single layer of newspaper in sunny locations is enough shade) and they lose water faster than they can absorb it (water stress).

3. The plants may not be protected properly from the wind and become desiccated (water stress).

4. Because the small soil ball of the seedling is usually a porous mix (see below) and the garden soil is less porous, the two media lack continuity. Water is, therefore, transmitted poorly or not at all from the garden soil to the transplant ball, even though the garden soil may be very moist or wet (again, water stress).

Obviously, lack of water is the major cause of death from transplanting. If the plants are properly hardened before transplanting, they have a much better chance of survival than if they are transplanted in a succulent condition.

Growing Mixes

The media used for planting transplants into the small plastic containers usually contain little or no true soil as defined in Chapter 8. Bedding plant growers synthesize mixtures having many of the following characteristics:

1. Such mixtures are easily reproduced year after year for uniformity.
2. They are easily pasteurized with steam without causing chemical changes in the ingredients, which can have harmful after effects on the seedlings.
3. They do not break down, or decompose, readily.
4. They have a low nutrient or soluble salt content initially, but nutrients may be subsequently added in the desired proportions.
5. They have good porosity, but still have high water-holding capacities.
6. They have high cation exchange capacity (nutrient-holding) which is not absolutely essential but desirable.
7. They are weed- and pest-free.
8. They must be reasonably priced.

Several single components are mixed or blended in various porportions to give the desired mixture characteristics. Below are some of the ingredients which are commonly used. Some desirable and undesirable qualities of each are mentioned.

Sphagnum peat moss is perhaps the most desirable component available. It is low in salts, does not decompose readily, has both high water- and nutrient-holding characteristics, is uniform and relatively disease free. It can be pasteurized without harmful effects. It is expensive, but its other attributes usually outweigh the price.

Vermiculite is a sterile expanded mica, which holds water and nutrients well and does not decompose *per se* (although the granules separate). It is uniform and reasonably priced if purchased in bulk. It is conveniently stored in bags.

Perlite is a heat-expanded (about 1100°C or 2000°F) aluminum silicate rock that becomes porous and lightweight when expanded. By itself, it does not hold large quantities of water, but it is an excellent amendment when mixed with peat moss or vermiculite. After processing, it is sterile, but is easily contaminated if left out in the open. It can be pasteurized, is reasonably priced, and can be purchased in bags for easy storage.

Sand is easily obtained and reasonably priced. It should be relatively free of silt and uniform in particle size to provide rapid water infiltration. It is easily pasteurized, drains freely, but does not add water- or nutrient-holding qualities to the mix. Its heavy weight is a disadvantage.

Wood products, such as ground bark, sawdust, or shavings, are often excellent soil amendments depending on the tree species. California and Oregon growers use redwood products but the material must first be leached with large amounts of water. Some batches may have large quantities of manganese, which is toxic to young seedlings. Leaching removes manganese. Pine bark is used fresh or composted. The decomposition of these wood products requires nitrogen, thus reducing the nitrogen available for the roots of the young growing seedlings (see p. 181). Supplementary nitrogen should be added when these wood products are used.

Clay loam soil is sometimes used by some growers in the United Kingdom as a mix component, but only after it is properly composted for over a year from pasture-grass sod. As one might gather, the area of pasture sod necessary to prepare large quantities of mix is difficult to maintain. Clay loam is heavy, but if properly amended with organic matter (other than that from the sod), it develops good drainage as well as excellent water- and nutrient-holding characteristics. When pasteurized with steam at temperatures above 82°C (180°F), however, the clay can release quantities of mineral elements harmful to plants, such as aluminum or manganese. Clay loam soils can be highly variable in their ratios of clay, silt, and sand (Ch. 8), depending on where they are found.

Because of the great variability of bulk density (weight per volume) of these components, they are always mixed by volume rather than weight. A common mixture used is equal volumes of peat moss and vermiculite or equal volumes of peat moss, sand, and ground bark. To each cubic meter or cubic yard of these mixtures, measured amounts of superphosphate and limestone are added (see p. 396). A source of organic or slow-release nitrogen can also be added, especially if wood products are used.

Commercial mixtures are usually steam pasteurized or chemically treated to control the pathogens that might be harmful to seedlings (Figs. 19–7 and 19–8). If the mixes are not pasteurized, various damping off fungi are likely to kill the seedlings as they germi-

---

Preparing a Small Quantity of Soil Mix for Home Use

Many possible mixtures can be prepared but many of the ingredients are not always readily available. The following "mix" is suggested because of the availability of the ingredients and the ease of preparation.

The mix consists of equal volumes of mortar sand and sphagnum peat moss. Moisten the sand, remove excess water, and place in an oven set at 84°C (180°F). Spread the sand out in a shallow layer for effective heat penetration. Allow the sand to remain for about an hour at that temperature.

Remove sphagnum peat moss from the plastic bag, crush the large lumps to small marble size granules and place in a pail of water. The peat moss is sufficiently sterile to use as is. Soak the peat moss thoroughly by mixing with your hands occasionally. You will note that it is difficult to wet. Once wet, drain off the water through a fine screen or gather the peat moss from the water by squeezing the water from it. Squeeze as much water as you can from the peat moss before using in the mix.

Obtain a clean container such as a clay flower pot for measuring the volume of both materials. Clay pots can be placed in the oven along with the sand to sterilize them before using. Do not place plastic pots in the oven.

The peat and sand should be mixed on a clean plastic sheet or any surface that can be disinfected with a solution of 10 parts water and one part household bleach. Allow the diluted bleach to evaporate before mixing on the surface. The bleach solution is also used to sterilize plastic pots.

Add equal volumes of the materials and mix thoroughly. A good measuring unit is a 12 cm (5 in) clay pot, which holds about a liter when full. To each 2 l of mix add one level teaspoon of ground limestone or oyster shell limestone and also one level teaspoon of single superphosphate. Sprinkle each over the pile and blend it to get a homogeneous mixture. This mix can be used at once or stored for a long period in clean polyethylene bags until ready for use.

This mixture is useful for starting seeds (although the oven-treated sand alone is adequate) and growing seedlings or most houseplants. Certain dracaenas, wandering Jews, and chlorophytum are sensitive to fluoride, which is often in single superphosphate. Eliminate single superphosphate from mix for these houseplants. Nitrogen and potassium must be used eventually, but these can be supplied later in a liquid fertilizer applied as frequently as desired or as suggested on the label. The liquid fertilizer should be used in large enough quantities to cause dripping through the bottom of the flat or pot to prevent a build-up of soluble salts.

---

nate. However, it may not be possible to use steam or chemicals for pasteurization for various reasons. In such cases, seeds may be sown on fine-grade vermiculite that is sterile in the bag. Plastic pots or flats may be sterilized with one part household bleach in 10 parts water. They should be free of chlorine fumes before use.

After steam pasteurization all synthetic mixtures, except those containing clay loams, can be used as soon as they are cool enough for planting. This is a distinct advantage for growers who use large amounts of mix during the peak seasons.

Steer or cow manure has many disadvantages and is not recommended for use in these mixes. It can vary extremely because of the source of supply and degree of decomposition. Manure may contain quantities of excess soluble salts unless it is composted and leached for about six months before use. Once in a mix, it can further decompose. Manure becomes a source of trouble because batches are dissimilar from each other and these mixes are seldom reproducible.

Mechanization of Operation

Many labor-saving devices have been employed in the bedding plant industry to keep costs from rising. Small individual containers have made mechanization possible (Fig. 19–1). Flats and containers are filled with the mix by semiautomatic fillers and moved by conveyers to workers who transplant the seedlings into them. Other operators may fill the plastic packs and move them to the greenhouse benches where they are transplanted in place (Fig. 19–9).

Flats and containers are very seldom carried by hand any distance in the modern greenhouse. They are usually stacked in racks and are moved by battery-operated carts from flat fillers to the benches and from the benches to the loading platform for shipment.

Each container has one plastic label to identify the plant (Fig. 19–5). Some labels may have planting instructions or mention the conditions under which the species does best in the garden, (e.g., full sun, semishade, or dense shade). These labels are valuable sales aids for retailers and in self-service nurseries.

Growth Regulators for Ornamentals

Some commercial growers spray seedlings of ornamental plants (not food crops) with chemical growth regulators. These result in stocky, compact plants, which have a good appearance in the retail nursery for a long time. Several chemicals can be used (see Ch. 6), but the best one for bedding plants is B-Nine (SADH) because it controls the growth of a wide spectrum of ornamental plants. A foliar application is made with a liquid formulation (about 2500 to 5000 ppm) before the seedlings begin to elongate (about two to four weeks after transplanting). Several applications (early and later on in growth) may be necessary to control growth, depending on the species, the season, and the temperature when the application is made. SADH-treated petunias have been reported to be less susceptible to air pollution damage and to withstand greater moisture stress upon transplanting than untreated plants.

Seedling Growth
Under Controlled Light Conditions

All seeds have an optimum temperature for germination (Tables 19–1 and 19–2). Once the seeds have germinated, the subsequent growth depends on temperature, light, moisture, and nutrients. It is possible to germinate and grow seedlings to the transplanting stage entirely under artificial light in a room where the temperature can be properly maintained. Experimental work has shown that 7700 to 11,000 lux (700 to 1000 ft-c) from cool white fluorescent tubes for 16 hours each day is ample

light to grow seedlings properly for a short period after germination. This light intensity can be obtained by spacing eight 40-watt fluorescent tubes (120 cm or 48 in long) to cover a width of 75 cm (30 in); that is, 120 cm by 75 cm in size and 20 cm (8 in) above the soil surface. These lamps also provide some heat, and adequate forced ventilation should be provided when the lamps are in operation.

Seedlings grown under these light conditions can reach or exceed the quality of those grown in a greenhouse under proper germination and growing conditions. The "lighted" plants are usually dark green and stocky (not etiolated). Growing plants in controlled rooms can be a distinct advantage during periods of low natural light intensity in the winter months. "Lighted" plants are uniform because the growing conditions are uniform regardless of the season.

Some seeds require a small amount of light (photoperiodic), such as 55 lux (5 ft-c) for 10 minutes per day to induce germination. The seeds of certain lettuce and petunias cultivars, for example, require light to germinate; therefore they should not be covered with soil. However, seeds of the majority of plants germinate in the dark.

Table 19–2 Seed Germination Data for Selected Vegetables Used to Produce Transplants for the Garden or Field

Name of Vegetable (Common)	Name of Vegetable (Latin)	Seeds per ounce[a] (thousands)	Days to Germinate at Optimum Temperature	Germination Temp °C	Germination Temp °F
Broccoli	Brassica oleracea, Italica Group	6–9	10	21	70
Brussels sprouts	Brassica oleracea, Gemmifera Group	7	10	21	70
Cabbage	Brassica oleracea, Capita Group	7	10	21	70
Cauliflower	Brassica oleracea, Botrytis Group	7	10	21	70
Celery	Apium graveloens var. dulce	71	10–21	21	70
Chives	Allium schoenoprasum	33	14	21	70
Cucumber	Cucumis sativus	1	7	26	80
Eggplant	Solanum melongena	6	14	26	80
Lettuce	Lactuca sativa	15	7	21	70
Melon	Cucumis melo (several groups)	0.8	10	26	80
Onions	Allium cepa	9	10	21	70
Parsley	Petroselinum crispum	18	15–20	26	80
Pepper	Capsicum annuum	4	10	26	80
Pumpkin, autumn	Cucurbita pepo	0.2	7	26	80
Squash, winter	Cucurbita maxima	0.4	7	26	80
Tomato	Lycopersicon lycopersicum [L. esculentum]	8–11	7–14	26	80
Watermelon	Citrullus lantanus (C. vulgaris)	0.8	10	26	80

[a] Convert ounces (oz Avdp) to grams by multiplying ounces by 28.
Source: Adapted from V. Ball, ed. 1976. *The Ball red book.* West Chicago, Ill.: G. J. Ball.

Photoperiodic Control of Growth and Flowering

The vegetative growth and the flowering of certain garden annuals are partially controlled by day length. The temperature, of course, must be in an optimum range for day length to be effective. Plants can be grown in the greenhouse out of season and given a photoperiodic treatment by either increasing the day length with supplementary lighting or by reducing the day length with a black cloth (Ch. 6). Incandescent light from 60-watt bulbs spaced 120 cm (4 ft) apart and 90 cm (3 ft) above the plants (Fig. 17–7). provides a minimum of 77 to 110 lux (7 to 10 ft-c). For increasing the day length, supplementary lighting is most effective when given in the middle of the night, 10 P.M. to 2 A.M. as for chrysanthemums, as it is the length of the dark period that affects flowering (Ch. 17). To produce a short photoperiod, sateen or black cloth or black plastic should be drawn over the plants at about 5 P.M. and removed as early as possible in the morning to avoid heat build-up from the sun. Usually a 14-hour period of darkness is adequate (Fig. 17–11).

The influence of long and short days on some common annual flowering plants is given in Table 19–3. This table is only general. For example, all cultivars of marigolds, salvias, and zinnias may not respond specifically as indicated in the table. One should not expect abrupt changes from the vegetative stage to the flowering stage by merely changing the photoperiod. The plants usually react gradually after a photoperiod treatment. Some of these long or short day treatments make excellent demonstrations for class (Fig. 19–14).

Fig. 19–14 A demonstration to show how petunia seedlings ('Pink Cascade') respond to supplementary light and to high night temperatures. The seedlings were transplanted to 10-cm pots and transferred to the four environmental conditions 12 days after planting. The photographs were taken in midwinter when the light intensity is normally very poor. The plants are in full flower under the condition of high greenhouse temperatures (21°C, 70°F during the night) and with 16 additional hours of fluorescent light (ca. 3000 lux). *Upper left:* Normal daylength; 21°C (70°F) nights. *Upper right:* Normal daylength + 16 hrs fluorescent light; 21°C (70°F) nights. *Lower left:* Normal daylength; 15°C (59°F) nights. *Lower right:* Normal daylength + 16 hrs fluorescent light; 15°C (59°F) nights.

Table 19–3 Growth and Flowering Responses of Some Bedding Plants Affected by Day Length

Common Name or Genus	Effect of Day Length	
	Long Days	*Short Days*
Alyssum	None	None
Centaurea	Induces buds, stem elongation	Delays flowering, causes rosetting
China aster	Induces stem elongation	Delays flowering in rosette; hastens flowering after stem elongation
Coleus	Promotes vegetative growth	Hastens flowering
Dahlia	Promotes vegetative growth	Induces flowering
Feverfew	Induces flowering	Promotes vegetative growth
Gaillardia	Induces flowering	Promotes vegetative growth
Impatiens	None	None
Marigold	Promotes vegetative growth, delays flowering	Hastens flowering
Pansy	Increases flower number	Strengthens stems
Perilla	Promotes vegetative growth	Induces flowering
Periwinkle	None	None
Petunia	Induces flowering	Promotes vegetative growth
Phlox (annual)	Induces flowering	Promotes vegetative growth
Rudbeckia	Promotes vegetative growth	Induces flowering
Salvia	Promotes vegetative growth	Induces flowering
Verbena	Induces flowering	Promotes vegetative growth
Zinnia	Delays bud development	Hastens bud development

Source: Adapted from J. Mastalerz, ed. 1976. *Bedding plants.* 2nd ed. University Park, Pa.: Pennsylvania Flower Growers.

It should not be inferred that all bedding plants require a precise day length to flower. Most of the annual bedding plants are self-inductive (Ch. 6) and flower when they reach a certain size or morphological age and the environmental conditions in the garden are suitable.

Scheduling

The greatest demand for bedding plants comes in the spring. Since spring arrives in different regions at different times, bedding plant producers must schedule the proper species for the most desirable date. For example, tomatoes, peppers, and petunias can be planted in the garden in southern California or Florida as early as March 15, in northern California or southern Texas by April 1, northern Illinois and New York by May 1 to 15, and in Minnesota not until after June 1 (see Fig. 10–6). There is no advantage in setting out warm-temperature plants too early. The plants will not grow and flowers will not form properly and, if fruit is desired, as in the case of tomatoes, peppers, eggplants, or squash, the flowers will not be properly pollinated during low temperatures. Therefore, bedding plant growers must know their market area so that they do not schedule the desired species too early for retail sales.

The most common greenhouse temperature for bedding plants is about 15°C (59°F) during the night. Temperatures are raised 2°C to 8°C (4°F to 15°F) higher during the day depending on the sunlight available. Seed may be germinated in separate houses where proper temperatures can be maintained for a specific crop. After seedlings are transplanted, they are moved to 15°C (59°F) greenhouses until almost ready for sale. They are then moved to a lower night temperature (7°C to 10°C; 45°F to 50°F) for several weeks to harden them and produce stockier plants. This entire sequence from sowing to sales takes two and a half to three months for sales in April, but takes only one and a half to two months for June sales, because the days are longer, the sun is higher in the sky (light intensity is higher for a longer period), and day temperatures become higher, contributing to faster growth than in the late winter or early spring.

Seed is sown from mid-December to mid-April, depending on the species and the time when plants are required for sale. Some bedding plant growers grow three crops on the same bench area in the greenhouse by scheduling the various species and by using outside area that is partially shaded and protected from frost to harden the plants before sale.

USE OF ANNUAL BEDDING PLANTS BY THE HOME GARDENER

The garden soil should be properly amended with organic matter to give it the proper tilth before planting. Since water stress causes most transplant failure, much attention must be paid to preventing water loss or to supplying enough water at intervals to assure survival. The transplants should be spaced as recommended by garden books or directions on the label to obtain a desirable yield (in the case of vegetables) or to have flowers cover the designated area in the shortest possible time.

A permanent shrub border or rock garden can be accented with color by using the proper flowering annuals. The choice of colors is wide and the plant sizes and shapes are numerous. Annuals can be used for other accents or to fulfill a desired garden function. Some of these possible uses are listed in Table 19–4.

Summer flowering annuals in the eastern United States are frequently planted in the bulb garden. Since many bulbs grow, bloom, and maintain themselves year after year, they "naturalize" in a given location (Ch. 20). The bulb plants are usually at their peak of flowering in late March, April, and May. After they begin to fade, it is then time to transplant annuals. Summer flowering annuals such as petunias, marigolds, zinnias, and ageratum can be interspersed in the bulb garden for summer color. When frost comes in October and November, all summer annuals should be removed to allow space for the late winter and early spring growth of the bulbs.

On the West Coast and in the South, it is possible to plant summer annuals as early as February while some winter annuals, such as calendulas, snapdragons, stocks, and pansies, are still blooming profusely. A decision must be made whether to remove the winter annuals or allow them to finish in April. As the warm weather of spring approaches, the leaves of winter annuals turn yellow from the heat and the flowers begin to fade. The plants can then be removed to make way for the summer annuals. The process is then reversed in October. When the summer annuals begin to fade, it is time to transplant the winter annuals or other cool-season plants. In many cool foggy areas, such as coastal areas of the Pacific coast states, winter annuals can be grown even during the summer.

The design of a bed devoted to annuals depends on the gardener. Conventionally, most beds along a fence have the tallest plants in the back and the shortest (procumbent) on the border of the walk or turf. If the bed is an island, the central plants are usually the tallest unless

Table 19–4 Garden Uses and Ultimate Sizes of Some Selected Ornamental Annuals

LOW PLANTS, 10 to 30 cm (4 to 12 in)

Ageratum, 15–30 cm (6–12 in)	Dianthus, 30 cm (12 in)	Myosotis, 30 cm (12 in)
Alyssum, 10–15 cm (4–6 in)	Dusty Miller such as *Centaurea Cineraria*	Nemesia, 20 cm (8 in)
Begonia, 10–30 cm (4–12 in)	and *C. maritima* 'Diamond' 15–25 cm	Nierembergia, 15 cm (6 in)
Calendula, 30 cm (12 in)	(6–10 in)	Phlox, 20–37 cm (8–15 in)
Candytuft, 20 cm (8 in)	Gazania, 20 cm (8 in)	Pansy, 15–20 cm (6–8 in)
Centaurea (dwarf bachelor buttons)	Gomphrena, 20 cm (8 in)	Petunia, 20–37 cm (12–15 in)
25–30 cm (10–12 in)	Heliotrope, 30–37 cm (12–15 in)	Portulaca, 10–15 cm (4–6 in)
Celosia (dwarf, such as 'Firey Feather' or	Impatiens, 15–20 cm (6–8 in)	Snapdragon 'Floral Carpet' 15–20 cm
'Jewel Box', 10–30 cm (4–12 in)	Lobelia, 20 cm (8 in)	(6–8 in)
Coleus, 30–37 cm (12–15 in)	Marigold-dwarf, 10–20 cm (4–8 in)	Torenia, 20–30 cm (8–12 in)
	Carpobrotus (Mesembryanthemum)	Verbena, 20–30 cm (8–12 in)
	15 cm (6 in)	Vinca, 25 cm (10 in)
		Zinnia-dwarf 15–30 cm (6–12 in)

MEDIUM PLANTS, 36 to 75 cm (15 to 30 in)

Balsam, 37 cm (15 in)	Dusty miller *(Centaurea gymnocarpa),*	Petunia, 30–37 cm (12–15 in)
Basil, 37 cm (15 in)	60 cm (24 in)	Rudbeckia, 40–45 cm (16–18 in)
Bells of Ireland, 60 cm (24 in)	Gaillardia, 60–75 cm (24–30 in)	Salpiglossis, 50–75 cm (20–30 in)
Blue lace flower, 45–60 cm (18–24 in)	Geranium ('Carefree' strain) 45–60 cm	Salvia, 45–75 cm (18–30 in)
California poppy, 30–45 cm (12–24 in)	(18–24 in)	Schizanthus, 45 cm (18 in)
Carnation, 36–50 cm (15–20 in)	Gomphrena, 45 cm (18 in)	Snapdragon, 37–60 cm (15–24 in)
Celosia (medium *'Cristata'* types, such as	Helichrysum, 60–75 cm (24–30 in)	'Vacationland', 'Hit Parade', 'Sprites',
'Fireglow'), 50–60 cm (20–24 in)	Impatiens, 37–45 cm (15–18 in)	'Kneehigh', 30–37 cm (12–15 in)
Cynoglossum, 45 cm (18 in)	Marigold, 37–60 cm (15–24 in)	Verbena, 30–60 cm (12–24 in)
Dahlia (such as Unwin's Dwarf Mix),	Nicotiana, 37–60 cm (15–24 in)	Zinnia, 40–75 cm (18–30 in)
50–60 cm (20–24 in)		

TALL PLANTS, 75 to 150 cm (30 to 60 in)

Amaranthus, 90–120 cm (36–45 in)	Cleome, 90–120 cm (36–48 in)	Larkspur, 60–90 cm, (24–36 in)
Celosia (tall Plumosa sorts such as 'Forest	Cosmos, 90 cm (36 in)	Marigold, 75–90 cm (30–36 in)
Fire'), 75–120 cm (30–48 in)	Dahlia (such as cactus and giant-flowered	Scabiosa, 60–90 cm (24–36 in)
Centaurea cyanus (bachelor buttons,	types), 75–120 cm (30–48 in)	Statice, 75 cm (30 in)
75 cm (30 in)	Hollyhock, 120–150 cm (48–60 in)	Snapdragon (rockets), 75–90 cm
China Asters, 90 cm (36 in)		(30–36 in)
		Zinnia, 75–90 cm (30–36 in)

FOR THE MIXED BORDER

Ageratum	Petunia	Cynoglossum
Alyssum	*Salvia farinacea* and *S. splendens*	Larkspur
Balsam	Centaurea	Snapdragon
Bells of Ireland	Cleome	Statice
Marigold	Cosmos	Zinnia
Nicotiana		

FOR GROUND COVERS (spreading or trailing)

Cobaea	Morning glory	Sweet pea
Creeping zinnia *(Sanvitalia procumbens)*	Myosotis	Thunbergia
Lobelia	Nasturtium	Verbena
Carpobrotus (Mesembryanthemum)	Nierembergia	Periwinkle
	Portulaca	
	Sweet alyssum	

FOR FOLIAGE

Amaranthus	Castor bean	Grasses, ornamental
Basil	Coleus	Kochia
Canna	Dusty Miller	Perilla

Table 19.4 (continued)

FOR POOR SOIL		
Alyssum	California poppy	*Carpobrotus (Mesembryanthemum)*
Calendula	*Centaurea cyanus* (bachelor button)	Nasturtium
		Portulaca

FOR PARTIAL SHADE		
Alyssum	Calendula	Nicotiana
Balsam	Coleus	Pansy
Begonia	Impatiens	Salvia
Browallia	Lobelia	Torenia
	Myosotis	

FOR WINDOW BOXES		
Ageratum	Geranium, 'Carefree'	Pansies
Alyssum	Lobelia	Cascade petunias
Begonia semperflorens	Marigolds	Salvia, dwarf
Coleus	Nierembergia	Thunbergia
		Verbena

FOR THE SEASIDE		
Alyssum	Gazania	*Carpobrotus (Mesembryanthemum)*
California poppy	Hollyhock	Petunia
Dusty miller	Lupine	Statice

FOR THE ROCK GARDEN		
Ageratum	China pink	Pansies
Alyssum	Gazania	Portulaca
Candytuft	*Carpobrotus (Mesembryanthemum)*	Verbena

FOR CUT FLOWERS		
Annual chrysanthemum	Gaillardia	Salpiglossis
Bells of Ireland	Gerbera	Salvia
Carnation	Gomphrena	Scabiosa
Celosia	Larkspur	Snapdragon
Centaurea cyanus (bachelor buttons)	Marigold	Statice
China asters	Nasturtium	Tahoka daisy *(Machaeranthera tanacetifolia)*
Cosmos	Pansies	
Cynoglossum	Petunia	Verbena
Dahlia	Rudbeckia	Zinnia

Source: Adapted and modified from *Ball bedding book. A guide for growing bedding plants.* 1977. West Chicago, Ill: G. J. Ball Co.

the bed is designed with a single cultivar to provide an even height. Some examples are shown in Figure 19–15.

The most popular annuals, based on sales of bedding plants for direct planting, are marigolds, petunias, zinnias, impatiens, alyssum, geraniums, nasturtiums, calendulas, snapdragons, pansies, stocks, and sweet peas. The final five species do well in cool areas in summer, but all the others require warm summer temperatures for optimum flowering. This group allows a gardener to select the height and color range. The marigolds, zinnias, and salvia offer a wide range of height to choose from (Fig. 19–16). The label that accompanies the container plant or the 6-pack of annuals usually states the ultimate growing height of the cultivar.

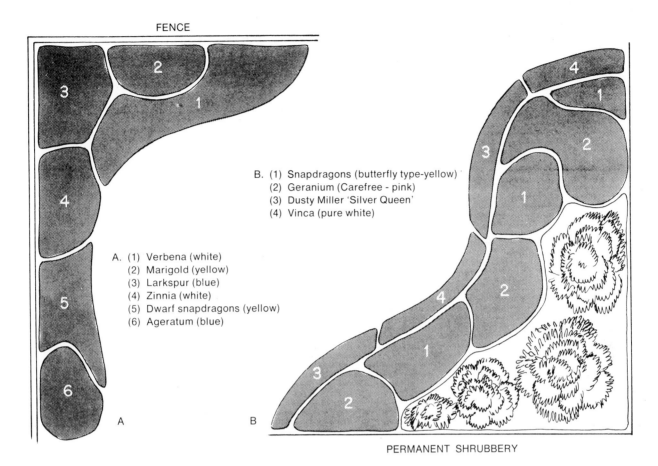

FENCE

B. (1) Snapdragons (butterfly type-yellow)
   (2) Geranium (Carefree - pink)
   (3) Dusty Miller 'Silver Queen'
   (4) Vinca (pure white)

A. (1) Verbena (white)
   (2) Marigold (yellow)
   (3) Larkspur (blue)
   (4) Zinnia (white)
   (5) Dwarf snapdragons (yellow)
   (6) Ageratum (blue)

PERMANENT SHRUBBERY

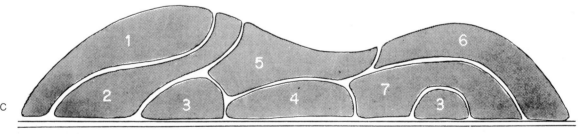

FENCE OR WALL

C. (1) Dwarf French Marigold   (4) Amaranthus (tricolor)
       (e.g. King Tut)   (5) Petunia (multi-flora - red)
   (2) Zinnias (yellow)   (6) Verbena (white)
   (3) Snapdragons (tall white)   (7) Celosia (yellow)

Fig. 19–15 Three possible garden designs with appropriate ornamental annuals based on height, habit, and color coordination. See Table 19–4 for height classification.

425

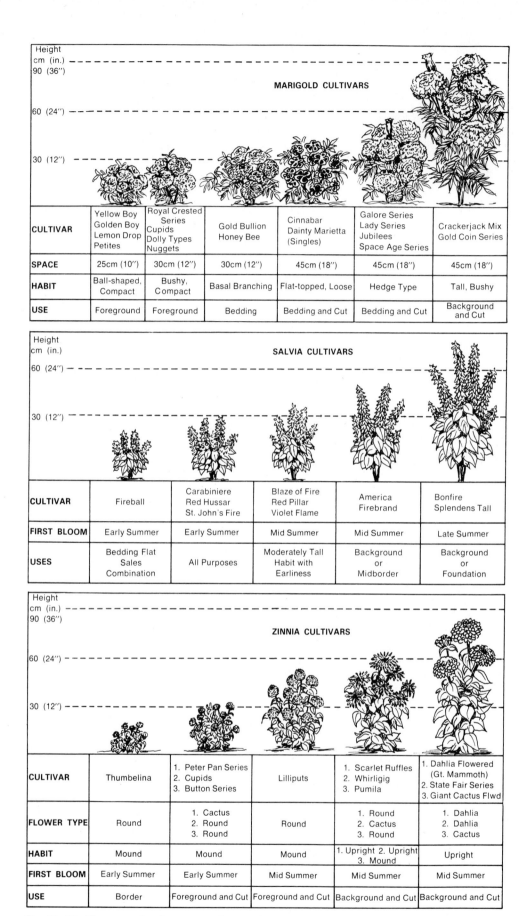

MARIGOLD CULTIVARS					
CULTIVAR	Yellow Boy Golden Boy Lemon Drop Petites	Royal Crested Series Cupids Dolly Types Nuggets	Gold Bullion Honey Bee	Cinnabar Dainty Marietta (Singles)	Galore Series Lady Series Jubilees Space Age Series	Crackerjack Mix Gold Coin Series
SPACE	25cm (10")	30cm (12")	30cm (12")	45cm (18")	45cm (18")	45cm (18")
HABIT	Ball-shaped, Compact	Bushy, Compact	Basal Branching	Flat-topped, Loose	Hedge Type	Tall, Bushy
USE	Foreground	Foreground	Bedding	Bedding and Cut	Bedding and Cut	Background and Cut

SALVIA CULTIVARS					
CULTIVAR	Fireball	Carabiniere Red Hussar St. John's Fire	Blaze of Fire Red Pillar Violet Flame	America Firebrand	Bonfire Splendens Tall
FIRST BLOOM	Early Summer	Early Summer	Mid Summer	Mid Summer	Late Summer
USES	Bedding Flat Sales Combination	All Purposes	Moderately Tall Habit with Earliness	Background or Midborder	Background or Foundation

ZINNIA CULTIVARS					
CULTIVAR	Thumbelina	1. Peter Pan Series 2. Cupids 3. Button Series	Lilliputs	1. Scarlet Ruffles 2. Whirligig 3. Pumila	1. Dahlia Flowered (Gt. Mammoth) 2. State Fair Series 3. Giant Cactus Flwd
FLOWER TYPE	Round	1. Cactus 2. Round 3. Round	Round	1. Round 2. Cactus 3. Round	1. Dahlia 2. Dahlia 3. Cactus
HABIT	Mound	Mound	Mound	1. Upright 2. Upright 3. Mound	Upright
FIRST BLOOM	Early Summer	Early Summer	Mid Summer	Mid Summer	Mid Summer
USE	Border	Foreground and Cut	Foreground and Cut	Background and Cut	Background and Cut

Fig. 19–16 Three examples of summer garden annuals showing sizes, habits, blooming dates in the Chicago area, and their possible uses. Seed packets usually describe all these plant characteristics. *Source:* George J. Ball Company.

Bedding plants sometimes have their problems. Since most of the commercial bedding plant producers generally use hygienic methods to grow the plants, they are usually not infected with pathogens and do not carry insects when they are purchased. However, some garden soils may be infested with root diseases that can, under certain climatic conditions, become epidemic and may kill most of the transplants. Also, if conditions are optimum for foliage diseases, insects, spider mites, or snails, these may also pose a serious hazard. One must constantly be aware of the possibility of these troubles and be prepared to take measures to control them.

Direct Seeding of Bedding Plants into the Garden

Most annuals grow best in full sunlight, but there are some exceptions (Table 19–4). After a sunny location is selected, the soil should be prepared by incorporating large quantities of organic matter into it. Possible materials are peat moss, compost, leaf molds, ground bark, sawdust (redwood, pine or other types), or well-decomposed manure. From 5 to 10 cm (2 to 4 in) of organic material can be spread over the surface and spaded or rototilled into the soil to 15 to 25 cm (6 to 10 in) deep. About 1 kg (about 2.2 lb) of a complete N-P-K fertilizer (5-10-5) per 10 sq. m (about 110 sq. ft.) should also be incorporated into the soil prior to sowing the seeds. The seedbed should be leveled with a rake to ensure uniform moisture distribution.

Seeds of most species should usually be sown after the soil warms above 15°C (60°F). However, with some of the cool-season plants such as cornflower, phlox, poppy, stocks, and sweet alyssum, seeds may be sown in cool soil. The times and conditions for sowing seeds directly into the garden soil are usually given on the seed packet. The seeds are sown in a row. Scratch out the row on the surface with a pointed object. The row should be as deep as the packet recommends. After the seeds are spread out in the row, they should be covered with a layer of sand or vermiculite to prevent crusting above the seeds. This is especially important if the soil is a heavy clay. Covering seeds with clay or silt soils may result in crusting after the first irrigation; seedlings penetrate this crusted layer only with difficulty. The rows should be irrigated or sprinkled after planting to provide sufficient moisture for germination. Covering the rows with newspaper or white opaque plastic prevents the soil from drying out between sprinklings. Protection with a wire mesh may be necessary to prevent damage by birds.

After the seedlings have developed at least one true leaf (not just the cotyledons), they should be thinned to the spacing suggested on the seed packet. Thinning reduces excessive competition among seedlings for water, nutrients, and later for light. Of course, weed seedlings should be pulled out as soon as they are spotted. When the annual has developed about three to four mature leaves, the very top of the seedling can be tipped back to induce branching. In the case of marigolds and zinnias, the first bloom can be removed to induce branching. **Pinching**, as this is known, creates a shorter and stockier plant than one allowed to grow as a single-stem plant.

Many flowering annuals are monocarpic plants (i.e., they die after the fruit matures)and respond to removal of the senescent or faded flowers. Flower removal prevents the seeds from maturing which may cause the plant to senesce and take carbohydrates and nutrients that should be available for vegetative growth and flowering of other portions of the plant. The removal of old or faded flowers on a weekly basis encourages lateral flowers to develop and reduces potential disease problems.

This chapter has primarily considered annual bedding plants since these are better adapted to college or high school horticulture classes and garden projects than are perennial bedding plants. In mild climates seeds of winter flowering annual bedding plants can be sown in the fall. Later plantings of the spring flowering annuals can be started in the greenhouse and then flowered outdoors before classes terminate. Perennial bedding plants, on the other hand, remain in the garden from year to year and may only flower in specific seasons depending on the location and species. These perennial beds, therefore, require maintenance throughout the year to keep them in prime condition. Careful planning is also essential to have a group of species growing in the same bed flower in a particular season. This is a task for well trained gardeners. Many perennials require close attention during the summer months. In cold climates many perennials may winter-kill if not given proper preparation for winter.

In chapter 20 bulbs and bulbous-like plants are discussed. For the most part these are perennial plants but in many climates they are treated as annuals, i.e., they are purchased and planted each year or removed from the soil and stored in cellars or refrigerators before the onset of winter. Many of the summer flowering bulbous species which are planted in the spring require little attention during the summer and are usually still in bloom when classes start in the fall. Therefore both annual and perennial bulbous plants lend themselves well to both fall and spring horticulture class projects.

BALL, V., ed. 1976. *The Ball red book.* 13th ed. West Chicago, Ill.: G. J. Ball.

———. 1977. *Ball bedding book. A guide for growing bedding plants.* West Chicago, Ill.: G. J. Ball.

GOLDSMITH, G. A. 1968. Current developments in the breeding of F_1 hybrid annuals. *HortScience* 3(4): 269–71.

HANAN, J. J., W. D. HOLLEY, and K. L. GOLDSBERRY. 1978. *Greenhouse management.* Berlin: Springer Verlag.

LARSON, R. A., ed. 1980. *Introduction to floriculture.* New York: Academic Press.

LAURIE, A., D. C. KIPLINGER, and K. S. NELSON. 1979. *Commercial flower forcing.* 8th ed. New York: McGraw-Hill.

MASTALERZ, JOHN, ed. 1976. *Bedding plants.* 2nd ed. University Park, Pa.: Pennsylvania Flower Growers.

———. 1977. *The greenhouse environment.* New York: John Wiley.

NELSON, P. V. 1978. *Greenhouse operation and management.* Reston, Va.: Reston Publishing.

Ornamentals Grown from Bulbs, Corms, Tubers, and Rhizomes

Many species of plants have a fleshy underground storage organ capable of carrying the plants through seasonal cold/warm or dry/wet periods. Such structures are popularly called bulbs, but they are defined more accurately as bulbs, tuberous roots, tubers, corms, or rhizomes[1] (Fig. 20–1). They all have one or more buds for flower production or renewed vegetative growth. The true **bulb**, such as the lily, hyacinth, muscari, narcissus, tulip, and onion, has numerous fleshy scales or leaf bases attached to a distinct basal plate (stem), that gives rise to roots and shoots distinct from aerial or above-ground leaves. They may or may not have one or more impervious covering layers. **Tubers** are enlarged fleshy stems with adventitious buds (eyes) near the upper surface, as in the tuberous begonia, *Eranthis* or *Caladium*, or in a systematic pattern or arrangement, as in the Irish potato. Some organs are enlarged roots and are classified as **tuberous roots,** such as *Agapanthus, Dahlia,* and *Hemerocallis.* **Corms** have solid shortened stems with buds systematically arranged under a paper-thin, protective covering of leaf base or scale. *Crocus, Gladiolus, Freesia,* and *Ixia* are examples. The **rhizome** is a fleshy, horizontal underground stem that grows laterally; examples are the rhizomatous iris, calla lily, and the gingers.

[1]The terms *bulb* and *bulb-like structure* are often used in this chapter for ease of reading although technically the underground structure may be something else, such as a corm, stem tuber, tuberous root, or rhizome.

Roots originating from the base plates or lower portion on all of these structures are adventitious. Some lilies also have adventitious roots arising from the underground portion of the stem above the main bulb. The shoots that originate either inside the bulb or on the surface, as in the corm or tuber, give rise to stems that bear the foliage and the flowers. Flowers can be initiated within the bulb during the previous growing season *(Narcissus)* or just after the new shoots begin to emerge from the soil (bulbous iris, lilies, gladiolus). All these types of plants have storage tissues that can produce a flowering stem after going through the seasonal dormant period. The dormancy period ranges from a few months to almost a year under certain environmental conditions.

This group of flowering plants is admired by temperate zone gardeners because of their many qualities. They are easy to grow and colorful, and they bear fragrant flowers in a large array of shapes, sizes, and colors. There is a wide choice of seasonal flowering habits among this group of plants. Some flower in late winter *(Galanthus* and *Chionodoxa).* Flowering begins early in spring with the *Crocus* and tulips. Begonias, cannas, and gladioli flower during the summer. Fall is the flowering season for *Colchicum* (Table 20–1). In addition, many bulbs can be grown out of season in the home, greenhouse, or protective shelters by controlling the rate of development of shoots and roots, which is called forcing (Table 20–1) *(3, 4).*

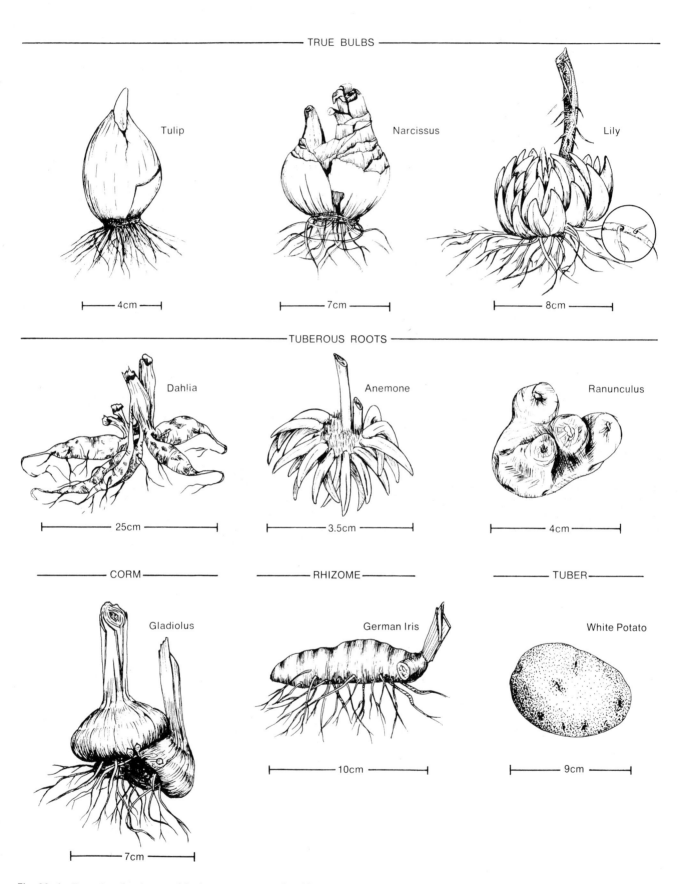

TRUE BULBS

Tulip |—— 4cm ——|

Narcissus |—— 7cm ——|

Lily |—— 8cm ——|

TUBEROUS ROOTS

Dahlia |—— 25cm ——|

Anemone |—— 3.5cm ——|

Ranunculus |—— 4cm ——|

CORM

Gladiolus |—— 7cm ——|

RHIZOME

German Iris |—— 10cm ——|

TUBER

White Potato |—— 9cm ——|

Fig. 20–1   Examples of underground food storage structures found in some herbaceous plants. Sizes given are approximate.

Table 20–1 Information on Selected Groups, Genera, and Species of Bulbous and Bulb-like Plants for Garden Culture and the Suitability for Winter Forcing in Heated Greenhouses

Group, Genus, or Species	Type of Storage Organ	Garden Hardiness in Zones 5 and 6 (H = hardy, SH = semihardy, T = tender)	Season (Sp = Spring, Su = Summer, F = Fall and W = Winter)		Approx. Month Dormancy Begins in Zones 5 and 6
			Planting Time and Depth (cm)	Flowering Time in Zones 5 & 6 or in Mild Climate (M)	
Agapanthus africanus (L.) Lily of the Nile	Tuberous rooted	SH	Sp (3)	Sp	Oct.
Allium giganteum Regel. Giant allium	Bulb	H, SH	F (15)	Sp	Aug.
Amaryllis belladonna L. Belladonna lily	Bulb	SH	Su, F (0)	Sp	Oct.
Anemone coronaria L. Windflower	Tuber	H, SH	Sp (5)	Sp	June
Begonia × tuberhybrida Voss. Tuberous begonia	Tuber	T	Sp (0)	Su	Oct.
Caladium bicolor Ait. Venten. Elephant ear	Tuber	T	Su (5)	Su	Oct.
Canna × generalis L.H. Bailey Common garden canna	Tuberous root	SH	S (12)	Su	Oct.
Chinodoxa spp. Boiss. Glory-of-the-snow	Bulb	H	F (10)	W, Sp	Aug.
Colchicum autumnale L. Autumn crocus	Corm	H	Su (8)	F	May
Crocus spp. L. Crocus	Corm	H	F (8)	W (M), Sp	June
Cyclamen persicum Mill. Florist's cyclamen	Tuber	T, SH	Sp (8)	W (M), Sp	May
Dahlia spp. Cav. Garden dahlia	Tuberous root	T	Sp (10)	Su	Oct.
Freesia × hybrida L.H. Bailey Freesia	Corm	T, SH	Sp (8)	Su	Aug.
Fritillaria imperialis L. Crown-imperial	Bulb	H, SH	F (10)	Sp	July
Galanthus nivalis L. Common snowdrop	Bulb	H	F (10)	W, Sp	May
Gladiolus hortulanus L.H. Bailey Garden gladiolus	Corm	T	Sp (10)	Su	Sept.
Gloriosa Rothschildiana O'Brien. Gloriosa lily	Tuber	T	Sp (10)	Su	Sept.
Hemerocallis fulva L. Orange daylily	Tuberous root	H	Sp (3)	Su	Oct.
Hippeastrum × hybridum Amaryllis, Barbados Lily	Bulb	T	Sp (0) (pots)	Su	Oct.
Hyacinthus orientalis L. Dutch hyacinth	Bulb	H	F (15)	Sp	July
Hymenocallis narcissiflora (Jacq.) Macbr. Peruvian daffodil	Bulb	T, SH	Sp (12)	Su	Aug.
Iris xiphium L. Spanish iris	Bulb	H, SH	F (10)	Sp (M), Su	Aug.
Iris × germanica L. Flag iris	Rhizome	H	Su (0)	Sp	Oct.
Ixia maculata L. Corn lily	Corm	T, SH	F (8)	Sp	Aug.
Leucojum aestivum L. Summer snowflake	Bulb	H	F (10)	Sp	Aug.

Table 20–1 (continued)

Group, Genus, or Species	Type of Storage Organ	Garden Hardiness in Zones 5 and 6 (H = hardy, SH = semihardy, T = tender)	Season (Sp = Spring, Su = Summer, F = Fall and W = Winter)		Approx. Month Dormancy Begins in Zones 5 and 6
			Planting Time and Depth (cm)	Flowering Time in Zones 5 & 6 or in Mild Climate (M)	
Lilium spp. L. Lily	Bulb	H	F (15)	Sp	Sept.
Muscari botryoides (L.) Mill. Common grape hyacinth	Bulb	H	F (5)	Sp	July
Narcissus pseudonarcissus L. Trumpet narcissus	Bulb	H	F (18)	Sp	Aug.
Nerine bowdenii W. Wats. Nerine	Bulb	T	Su, F (0)	Su	Aug.
Polianthes tuberosa L. Tuberose	Tuber	T	Sp (5)	Su	Nov.
Ranunculus asiaticus L. Persian buttercup	Tuber	SH	Sp (5)	Sp	Aug.
Scilla siberica Andr. Siberian squill	Bulb	H	F (8)	Sp	July
Tigridia Pavonia (L.f.) DC. Tiger flower	Bulb	T	Sp (10)	Su	Oct.
Tritonia crocata (L.) Kerr-Gowl. *(Montbretia)* Saffron tritonia	Corm	SH	Sp (10)	Su	Sept.
Tulip × hybrida L. Garden tulip	Bulb	H	F (18)	Sp	Aug.
Watsonia Beatricis Mathews and L. Bolus Bugle lily	Corm	T, SH	Su, F (8)	Su	Oct.
Zantedeschia aethiopica (L.) K. Spreng. *(Richardia aethiopica)* Calla lily	Rhizome	T, SH	Sp (5)	Su	Oct.
Zephyranthes candida (Lindl.) Herb. Zephyr lily	Bulb	SH	Su (5)	Su, F	Aug.

Table 20–1 (continued)

Group, Genus, or Species	Necessary Treatment After Dormancy Begins Climate = Cold, Mild or All[a]	Approx. Months of Storage Time and Temp °C(°F)	Winter Forcing in the Greenhouse		
			Suitability for Forcing	Month to Plant	Literature Citation for Cultural Details
Agapanthus africanus (L.) Lily of the Nile	Dig (cold), naturalize (mild, 6)	Ca 7 4 (40)	—	—	—
Allium giganteum Regel. Giant allium	Naturalize	—	No	—	—
Amaryllis belladonna L. Belladonna lily	Dig (cold), naturalize (mild, 10)	Ca 8 8 (45)	Yes	Aug.	6
Anemone coronaria L. Windflower	Replant every year (all)	—	Yes	Aug.[b] (seed)	9, 12
Begonia × *tuberhybrida* Voss. Tuberous begonia	Mainly pot culture (all), dig (all)	Ca 6 10 (50)	Spring only	Dec.[b] (seed)	1
Caladium bicolor Ait. Venten. Elephant ear	Dig (all)	Ca 7 10 (50)	Yes	Dec.	1, 9
Canna × *generalis* L.H. Bailey Common garden canna	Dig (cold), naturalize (mild)	Ca 7 4 (40)	—	—	—
Chinodoxa spp. Boiss. Glory-of-the-snow	Naturalize (all, 4)	—	Yes	Sept.	10
Colchicum autumnale L. Autumn crocus	Naturalize (all, 3)	—	Yes	July	10
Crocus spp. L. Crocus	Naturalize (all, 3)	—	Yes	Sept.	1, 3
Cyclamen persicum Mill. Florist's cyclamen	Dig (cold), naturalize (mild)	Ca 6 4 (40)	Yes	July	Ch. 17
Dahlia spp. Cav. Garden dahlia	Dig (all)	Ca 7 8 (45)	Yes	March	—
Freesia × *hybrida* L.H. Bailey Freesia	Dig (cold), naturalize (mild)	Ca 6 2 (35)	Yes	Aug.[b] (seed)	1, 6, 10
Fritillaria imperialis L. Crown-imperial	Dig (cold), naturalize (mild)	Ca 3 4 (40)	No	—	—
Galanthus nivalis L. Common snowdrop	Naturalize (all)	—	Yes	Sept.	10
Gladiolus hortulanus L.H. Bailey Garden gladiolus	Dig (cold), naturalize (mild, 2)	Ca 6 2 (35)	Yes	Sept.	6
Gloriosa Rothschildiana O'Brien. Gloriosa lily	Dig (all)	Ca 6 8 (45)	Yes	Jan.	10
Hemerocallis fulva L. Orange daylily	Naturalize (all)	—	No	—	—
Hippeastrum × *hybridum* Amaryllis, Barbados Lily	Pot culture (all), naturalize (mild)	Ca 6 21 (70)	Yes	Nov. to Apr.	6, 11
Hyacinthus orientalis L. Dutch hyacinth	Naturalize (all, 3)	—	Yes	Sept.	1, 3, 4, 11
Hymenocallis narcissiflora (Jacq.) Macbr. Peruvian daffodil	Dig (all)	Ca 7 15 (60)	Yes	Sept.	10
Iris xiphium L. Spanish iris	Dig (cold), naturalize (mild, 4)	Ca 6 26 (79)	Yes	Sept.	1, 4, 6, 11
Iris × *germanica* L. Flag iris	Naturalize (all, 5)	—	No	—	—
Ixia maculata L. Corn lily	Replant every year (all)	—	Yes	Aug.	10
Leucojum aestivum L. Summer snowflake	Naturalize (all)	—	Yes	Sept.	5, 10
Lilium spp. L. Lily	Naturalize (all, 2)	—	Yes	Oct.	1, 4, 11

[a] If the bulbs naturalize in the landscape, the number represents the maximum number of years that may elapse before necessary digging, respacing, and replanting. All = pertains to all climates; cold = cold climates only (zones 3–6); mild = mild climates only (zones 7–10) (see p. 226).

[b] Seeds may be used as well as the tuber or corm.

Table 20–1 (continued)

Group, Genus, or Species	Necessary Treatment After Dormancy Begins Climate = Cold, Mild or All[a]	Approx. Months of Storage Time and Temp °C(°F)	Winter Forcing in the Greenhouse		
			Suitability for Forcing	Month to Plant	Literature Citation for Cultural Details
Muscari botryoides (L.) Mill. Common grape hyacinth	Naturalize (all)	—	Yes	Oct.	3, 9
Narcissus pseudonarcissus L. Trumpet narcissus	Dig (cold), naturalize (mild, 5)	—	Yes	Aug.	1, 3, 4
Nerine bowdenii W. Wats. Nerine	Pot culture (cold), naturalize (mild, 3)	Ca 6 8 (45)	Yes	March	6, 13
Polianthes tuberosa L. Tuberose	Dig (all), pot culture	Ca 6 13 (55)	Yes	Jan.	9, 10
Ranunculus asiaticus L. Persian buttercup	Replant every year (all)	Ca 6 4 (40)	Yes	Aug.[b] (seed)	9, 12
Scilla siberica Andr. Siberian squill	Naturalize (all)	Ca 7 4 (40)	Yes	Sept.	9, 10
Tigridia Pavonia (L.f.) DC. Tiger flower	Dig (cold), naturalize (mild, 4)	Ca 7 10 (50)	Yes	Apr.	10
Tritonia crocata (L.) Kerr-Gowl. *(Montbretia)* Saffron tritonia	Dig (cold), naturalize (mild)	Ca 6 4 (40)	Yes	Apr.	10
Tulip ×*hybrida* L. Garden tulip	Naturalize (all), replant (mild)	—	Yes	Sept.	1, 3, 4
Watsonia Beatricis Mathews and L. Bolus Bugle lily	Dig (cold), naturalize (mild, 3)	Ca 8 2 (35)	No	—	—
Zantedeschia aethiopica (L.) K. Spreng. *(Richardia aethiopica)* Calla lily	Dig (cold), naturalize (mild, 5)	Ca 6 10 (50)	Yes	Oct.	9, 10
Zephyranthes candida (Lindl.) Herb. Zephyr lily	Dig (cold), naturalize (mild)	Ca 8 8 (45)	Yes	Aug.	6, 10

Bulbous and tuberous plants are used principally in the garden or as pot plants and cut flowers. Table 20–1 provides three hardiness categories of some of the common bulbs. The hardy ones (H) withstand the winters of zones 4, 5, and 6 in the United States (see p. 226). During severe winters like those in zones 3 and 4, some plants of this group perish unless they are well protected. The semihardy types (SH) survive mild winters (zones 7–10), but they must be dug and stored in a protected place before the onset of winter in cold locations (zones 4–6). The tender types (T)—caladiums, cannas, dahlias, and tuberoses—cannot withstand soil temperature below freezing for even short periods. They should be removed from the soil after the foliage dies or certainly after the first frost. Digging and preparing for storage should commence at the beginning of the rest period. The specific month varies with location. Table 20–1 gives the normal time for zones 5 and 6. In mild areas (zones 7–10) dormancy may be delayed by one or two months over zones 5 and 6. In the cold areas, bulbs requiring **lifting** (removal from the soil) and must be harvested before killing temperatures reach the bulb level.

Many bulbs—for example, the daffodils and crocus—do not require annual harvest or storage. On the other hand many species do require such handling. Harvesting or digging is usually done after the leaves have died, but the plants with very tender storage organs (tuberous begonia or *Hymenocallis*) require digging after the foliage begins to turn yellow in early fall. Care must be taken not to injure the storage structures during removal. Dig far enough from the clump to avoid injuring the fleshy storage organs. Remove loose soil immediately, then allow the soil to dry out a few days so that it will fall away easily by gentle cleaning. Before storage, the bulbs can be separated. Cut surfaces should be relatively dry to avoid mold growth. In addition, dusting with an approved fungicide is a desirable measure.

After cleaning, the bulbs should be cured at moderate temperatures of 15°C to 21°C (59°F to 70°F) in a well-ventilated room. Moving air over the bulbs should be avoided. Curing allows the portions recently separated from the mother structure, e.g. gladiolus corm, to suberize (form a corky layer) over the wound area. Some bulblike structures require only two to three days for curing; examples are *Caladium*, calla, *Canna, Dahlia*, and tuberous begonia. An extended period of curing causes shriveling. Other groups require curing for about three weeks, for example, *Freesia, Gladiolus, Tigrida, Tritonia*, and *Watsonia*.

For long-term storage, bulbs or bulblike structures that require annual lifting, usually those in the tender and semi-hardy groups, should be placed in shallow layers and covered with dry sphagnum peat moss or vermiculite (Fig. 20–2) and then placed in a cellar or a refrigerator at

Fig. 20–2   The annual cycle of a tuberous begonia (*Begonia* × *tuberhybrida*) when it is planted in a pot or directly into the garden. Because these tubers are very sensitive to cold, they must be protected from chilling temperatures below 4°C (40°F). They should be lifted from the soil and stored in moist peatmoss at a temperature of about 10°C (50°F). Flowers form under long-day conditions. *Source:* Adapted from Rockwell, F. F., and E. C. Grayson. 1953. *The complete book of bulbs.* Garden City, N.Y.: American Garden Guild and Doubleday.

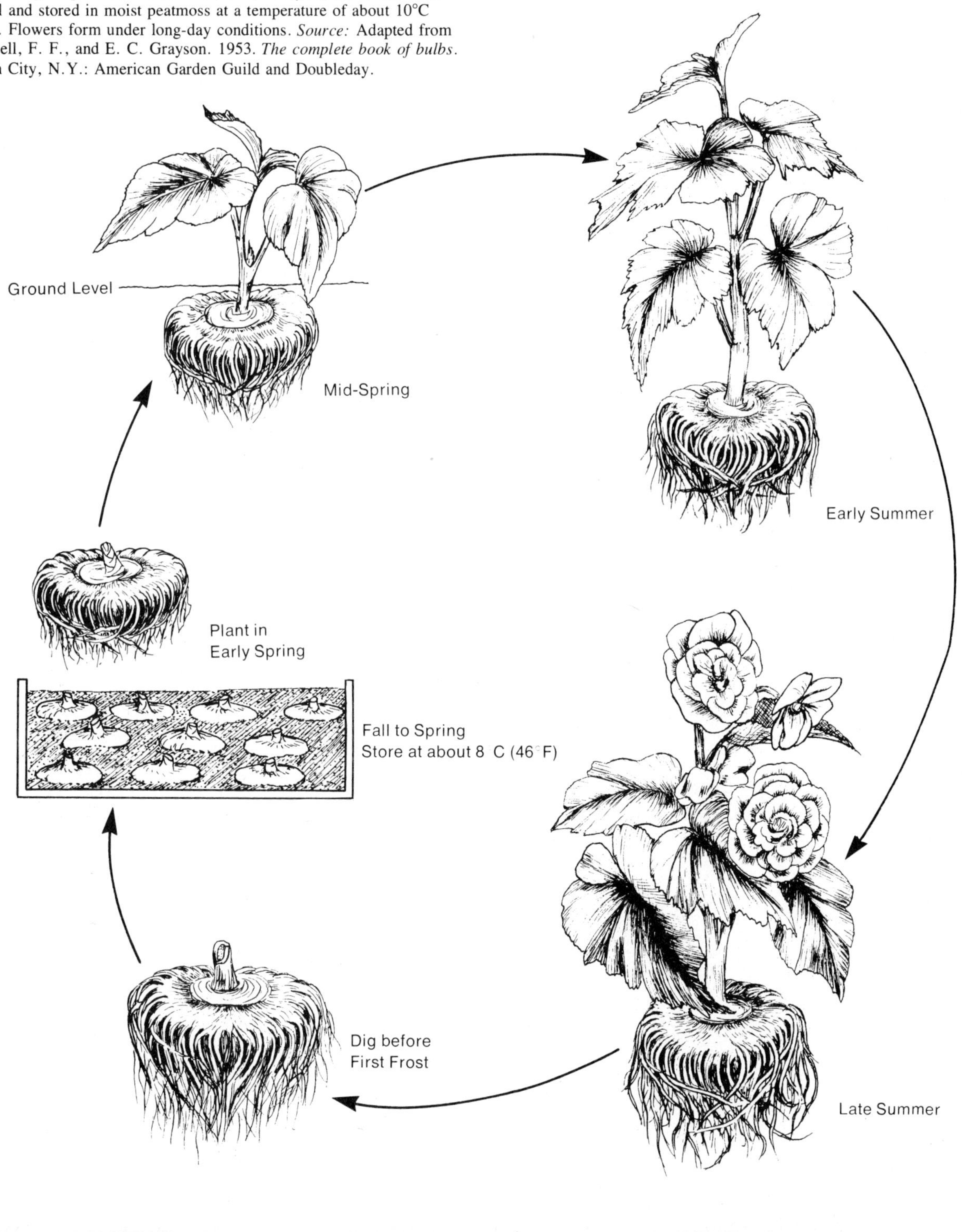

Ground Level

Mid-Spring

Early Summer

Plant in
Early Spring

Fall to Spring
Store at about 8 C (46°F)

Dig before
First Frost

Late Summer

the uniform temperature indicated in Table 20–1. Some of the SH group, such as *Gladiolus* and *Freesia,* may be stored at temperatures as low as 2°C (35°F), but others are very sensitive to these low temperatures even during the dormant storage period. Examples are calla lily, *Canna,* tuberose, and tuberous begonia.

STRUCTURE, MORPHOLOGY, AND DEVELOPMENT

The structure and some characteristics of many bulbs and tuberous plants are illustrated in Figure 20–1 and listed in Table 20–1. To help you understand more clearly how these structures develop, produce flowers, and eventually increase in numbers (reproduce vegetatively), we will discuss the life cycles of five genera, namely: *Hippeastrum, Tulipa, Narcissus, Gladiolus,* and *Dahlia.*

Hippeastrum

The *Hippeastrum* bulb is made up of leaf bases and no scales. The genus is indigenous to tropical and subtropical South America. The commercial hybrids were developed from these species by plant breeders. In the temperate zone, bulbs are grown in pots in greenhouses or homes and are stored at 20°C to 23°C (68°F to 73°F)

Fig. 20–3   The *Hippeastrum* bulb. The immature inflorescence for the next cycle is within the bulb when the plant is in full bloom, but the primordium requires almost another year for development. *Source:* Adapted from Rees, A. R. 1972. With permission from *The growth of bulbs, applied aspects of the physiology of ornamental bulbous crop plants.* Copyright by Academic Press Inc. (London) Ltd.

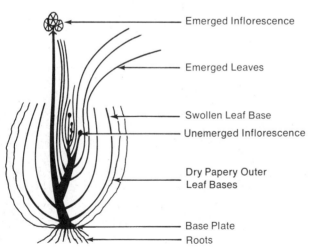

during the dormant period in fall and winter. Depending on the cultivar and its handling, the flower stalk elongates in December to April, usually before leaf growth. The flower stalk should be removed after the flower fades, but the leaves are retained to produce food for next year's growth and flowering. During the summer, leaves emerge from the center of the bulb, reaching a peak in June and July, and these leaf bases add to the bulb girth. The leaf bases do not thicken like those of some other bulbs. New growing points are initiated near the center of the bulb during spring and summer with as many as 8 to 12 new leaves and 2 to 3 inflorescences. A large bulb (26 to 30 cm in circumference) may have as many as six leaf and inflorescence units in various stages of development (Fig. 20–3). The estimated time between initiation and emergence is 3 to 8 months for a leaf and 11 to 14 months for an inflorescence. An inflorescence persists for about three to four weeks from emergence to final wilting.

New bulbs, called **offset bulblets,** develop in the axils of the older leaf bases near the outer edges. When the outer parts of the old bulb (the mother bulb) die, the new bulbs (daughter bulbs) are released. The *Hippeastrum* daughter bulb produces only leaves (Fig. 20–4) until the girth is sufficient for an inflorescence to initiate and develop. New bulbs may be propagated by scoring or wounding the basal plate or by cutting the bulb longitudinally and placing the segments into a moist rooting medium at about 23°C (73°F). New bulblets form at the junction of the scale and basal plate (Fig. 20–3).

Tulipa

The tulip is made up principally of concentric fleshy scales adjoined to the compressed stem or bulb basal plate. A stem in the center of the bulb emerges in the spring with the true leaves and single terminal flower (Fig. 20–5). After the flower senesces, the leaves continue to photosynthesize and nourish the daughter bulbs adjacent to the stem base and just above the basal plate (Fig. 20–6). The mother bulb dies in late spring, but one to three daughter bulbs grow to maturity (Fig. 20–5). However, not all daughter bulbs reach the minimum flowering size of 6 to 7 cm in circumference. When the soil temperature becomes warm and favorable, a flower bud is initiated in the large bulbs for the next season's flowering. In commerce the bulbs are usually lifted from the soil before flower formation begins. The flower buds continue to form in controlled temperature rooms.

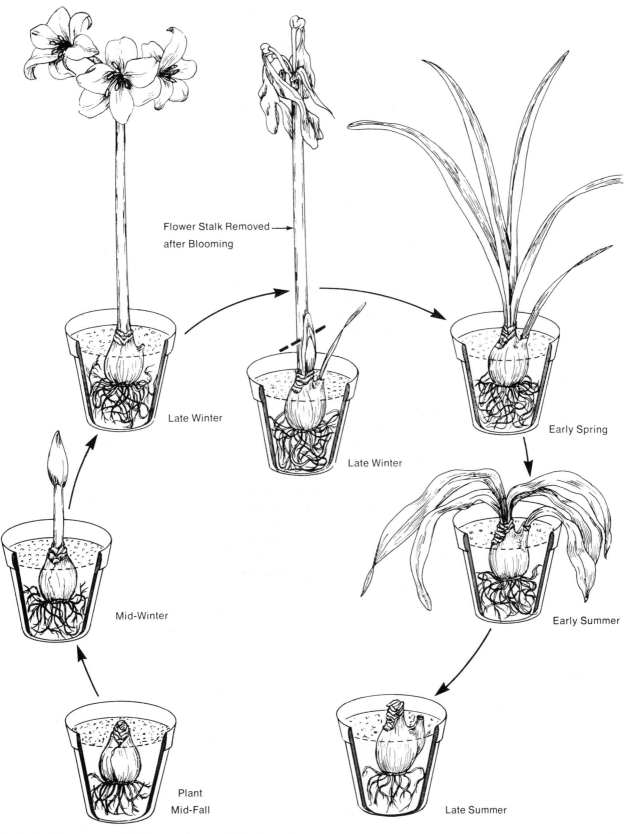

Flower Stalk Removed → after Blooming

Late Winter

Late Winter

Early Spring

Mid-Winter

Early Summer

Plant
Mid-Fall

Late Summer

Fig. 20–4 *Hippeastrum × hybridum*, a tender perennial bulb, must be grown in pots in protected locations in most parts of the country. This figure illustrates the annual cycle, including the growth of a daughter bulb (offset) emerging in winter at the side of the main bulb. *Source:* Adapted from Rockwell, F. F., and E. C. Grayson. 1953. *The complete book of bulbs.* Garden City, N.Y.: American Garden Guild and Doubleday.

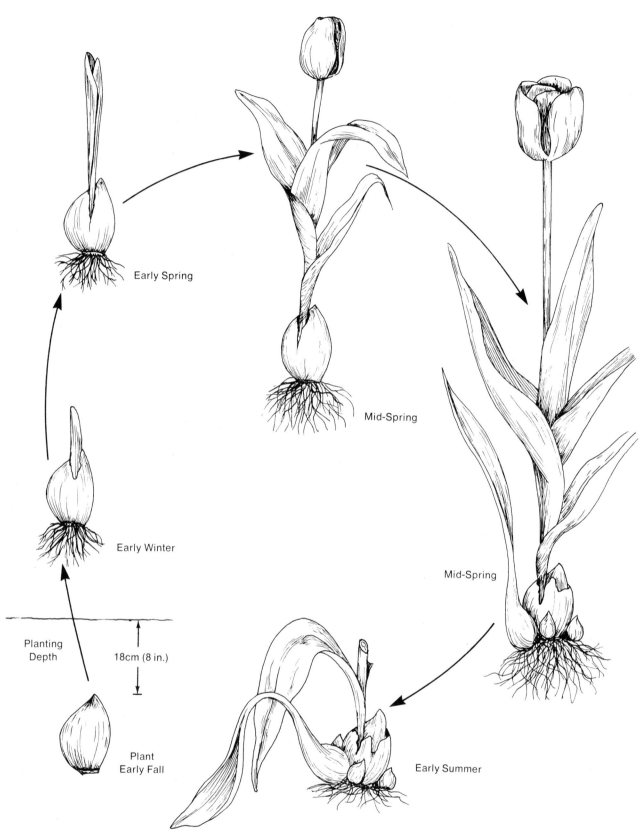

Fig. 20–5 The life cycle of a tulip in the garden. In the garden the bulb is planted about 18 cm deep to protect it from freezing in the soil. In contrast to the planting dates shown above, in warm climates of the northern hemisphere garden tulips can be planted in August and they flower in late February. When planted in pots or flats, the ''noses'' can be placed above the soil line (Fig. 20–20). *Source:* Adapted from Rockwell, F. F., and E. C. Grayson. 1953. *The complete book of bulbs.* Garden City, N.Y.: American Garden Guild and Doubleday.

Early Spring

Mid-Spring

Mid-Spring

Early Winter

Planting
Depth

18cm (8 in.)

Plant
Early Fall

Early Summer

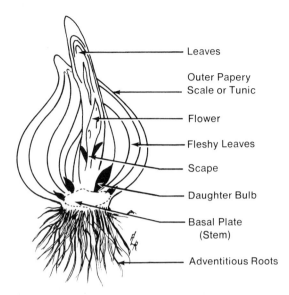

Leaves

Outer Papery
Scale or Tunic

Flower

Fleshy Leaves

Scape

Daughter Bulb

Basal Plate
(Stem)

Adventitious Roots

Fig. 20–6 A longitudinal section of a tulip bulb. All the flower parts are complete at planting time and require only proper root development, and temperature treatments to cause the scape (stem) to elongate and the flowers to develop. The lowest leaf, the first to emerge, is always placed next to the flat side of the bulb. The tulip is an annual bulb and is propagated naturally by the initiation and subsequent development of the daughter bulbs.

In its natural habitat of Asia Minor, the tulip bulb's rhythm of growth is influenced by hot summers and cold winters. Daughter bulbs and flower initials continue to grow even when the bulbs are in the so-called resting state. During the winter the bulb receives the low temperatures it requires for flower development and for stem (scape) elongation within the bulb (Fig. 20–6). In the spring when the soil air temperature increases, the scape elongates and the flower completes its development. Subsequently the leaves continue to grow and produce food for the enlarging daughter bulbs until the weather becomes too hot and the leaves wither. The commercial culture of tulips is based on this natural rhythm. The bulbs are harvested in the fall after the leaves wither and are graded into flowering and nonflowering sizes. Large bulbs are temperature treated at 17°C to 23°C (63°F to 73°F) to fulfill the flower initiation process, which ensures flowering in the greenhouse or garden. The small daughter bulbs (6 to 10 cm) incapable of flowering are replanted in the field to increase in size and add to the population.

Narcissus

The *Narcissus* or daffodil bulb is composed of both storage scales and foliage leaf bases. A mature bulb is a

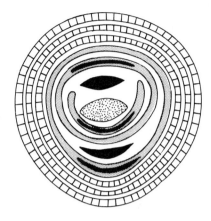

Fig. 20–7 A cross-section of a *Narcissus* bulb showing the three scales (cross-hatched) enclosing the three foliage leaves (stippled) and the innermost leaves adjacent to the inflorescence (dotted). The future terminal bud (black) is next to the present inflorescence. The lower black crescent is a lateral bud. *Source:* Adapted from Rees, A. R. 1972. With permission from *The growth of bulbs, applied aspects of the physiology of ornamental bulbous crop plants.* Copyright by Academic Press Inc. (London) Ltd.

branched system comprising individual units of scales, leaf bases, and inflorescences. Each growing point produces one terminal unit each year and each unit is made up of about three scales, two or three foliage leaves, and the inflorescence (Fig. 20–7). In addition, lateral units of leaves, scales, and inflorescence are initiated in some one-year-old units. The combination of several of these units of leaves and scales total 22 or 24 depending on the cultivar *(11)*. A ''double nose'' bulb (one with two major growing points) is capable of producing at least two flowers. The original bulb is surrounded by offsets (Fig. 20–8). If allowed to remain undisturbed for several years, the offsets give rise to more units and become a persistent branched system *(11)*. This leads to crowding in a garden situation.

The large bulbs begin initiating an inflorescence in May (in the Northern Hemisphere) while the leaves are still green and are actively producing food. The flower stem also contributes photosynthates to the bulb, and the food reserves are reduced if it is removed *(11)*. When the bulb is lifted in July, it contains all parts of the inflorescence except the center part of the flower, the trumpet or the paracorolla *(6)*. After harvest, the bulb must not be subjected to high temperature conditions or the flower within will be injured. Temperatures between 17°C and 20°C (63°F and 68°F) are ideal. Later the bulbs are placed in cool storage (9°C; 48°F) where the flower buds continue to develop for early forcing (p. 446). Garden bulbs are replanted in September and October (Fig. 20–8).

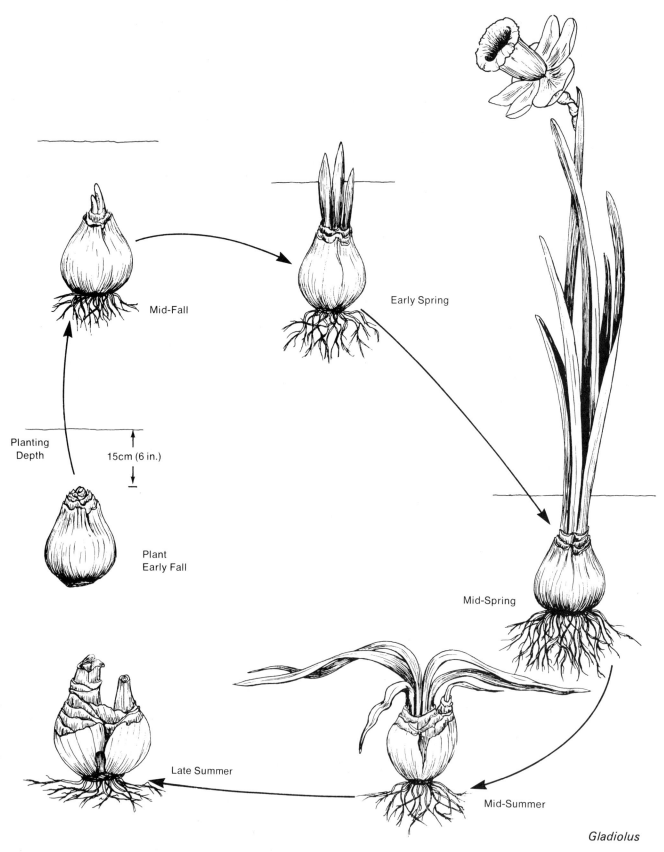

Planting
Depth

15cm (6 in.)

Mid-Fall

Plant
Early Fall

Early Spring

Mid-Spring

Late Summer

Mid-Summer

Gladiolus

Fig. 20–8 The annual cycle of the perennial daffodil (*Narcissus pseudonarcissus*) grown in a cold climate illustrating planting the bulbs in the garden to digging them in late summer. In mild climates (zones 6–9) the bulbs may remain in the soil all winter to naturalize. In such cases the bulbs multiply and can be dug about every five years to reduce and thin out their population. *Source:* Adapted from Rockwell, F. F., and E. C. Grayson. 1953. *The complete book of bulbs.* Garden City, N.Y.: American Garden Guild and Doubleday.

Gladiolus is classified as a corm. Its solid storage organ is a shortened stem, with many buds spaced in a definite order around its upper half. It is not made up of scales as *Tulipa* and *Narcissus*.

Usually one bud sprouts near the top of the corm when planted (Fig. 20–9), but some cultivars having

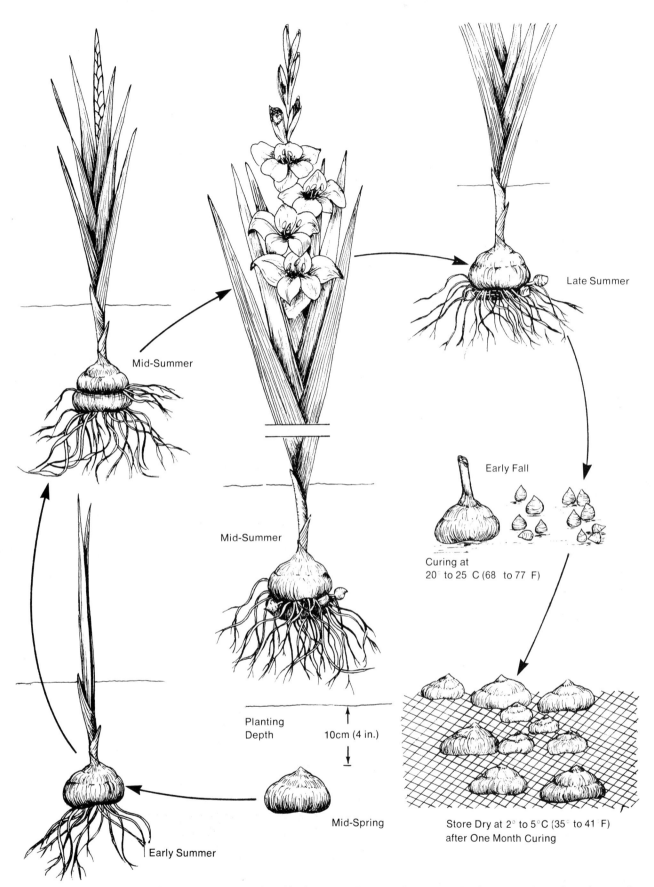

Fig. 20-9 The annual cycle of the gladiolus. Corms are planted in the spring about 10 cm (4 in) deep when the soil becomes warm. The basal roots are the first to emerge, followed by one or two shoots from buds near the top of the corm. When the flower spike is visible, the base of the shoot begins to swell, which eventually develops into the daughter corm. Contractile roots between the mother and daughter corm emerge. These roots are very active in supplying water and mineral nutrients. After the spike is in full bloom, cormels (i.e., immature corms incapable of flowering) are produced on extended rootlike structures in the same region as the contractile roots. The daughter corm and cormels continue to enlarge rapidly after flowering when photosynthates are directed downward. The leaves continue to supply food to the corms and cormels until the leaves wither about two months after flowering. The daughter corm may be pulled into the soil deeper by the contractile roots if the mother corm was originally planted very shallow. The daughter corms enter a dormancy if the soil is warm at the time of digging. *Source:* Adapted from Rockwell, F. F., and E. C. Grayson. 1953. *The complete book of bulbs.* Garden City, N.Y.: American Garden Guild and Doubleday.

Labels within figure: Mid-Summer; Mid-Summer; Late Summer; Early Fall; Curing at 20° to 25°C (68° to 77°F); Planting Depth 10cm (4 in.); Mid-Spring; Store Dry at 2° to 5°C (35° to 41°F) after One Month Curing; Early Summer

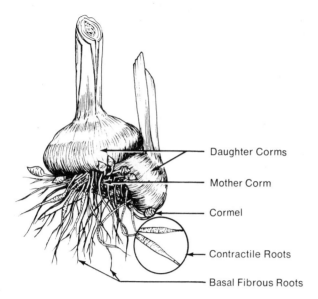

Daughter Corms

Mother Corm

Cormel

Contractile Roots

Basal Fibrous Roots

Fig. 20–10 When gladiolus daughter corms are dug in the fall, they are connected to the withered mother corm. The mass of cormels and some soil should be lifted and then air-dried (cured) in a shady location to prevent overheating in the sun. After about one month of curing, the soil, daughter corms, and cormels can be easily separated from the mother corm, which is then discarded. The daughter corms are placed in ventilated trays and stored in a refrigerator or a bulb cellar at about 2°C (35°F) until spring. Cormels can be planted to increase the population, but flowering does not occur for about two to three years, depending on the growing conditions and the vigor, size, and spacing of the cormels. Corms and cormels with vascular diseases lack vigor and do not grow properly because they are under constant water stress.

large corms develop two shoots. Roots emerge from the basal plate and provide the moisture for the sprouting bud. After the shoot has emerged about 10 cm (4 in) above the soil, it is capable of flower initiation. The flower develops fully from 50 to 75 days after planting of the corm. Just before flowering (when the first floret begins to show color), the base of the new flowering shoot begins to swell and eventually becomes a new daughter corm. In the region between the mother and the daughter corm, **contractile roots** form (Figs. 20–9 and 20–10). The function of these roots is twofold: to supply moisture and nutrients and also to pull the newly formed daughter corm downward into the soil. After flowering, the mother corm begins to wither, but the green leaves continue to translocate food to the daughter corm. About two months after flowering, the enlarged daughter corm is mature and by early autumn becomes dormant in the warm soil.

In mild climates (zones 8–10), the cold requirement to break dormancy may be fulfilled if the corms are allowed to remain in the soil throughout the winter.

Sprouting then occurs as the soil warms sufficiently in the spring. In climates with severe winters (zones 2–6), the new corms must be removed from the soil in the fall before the first frost, separated from the shriveled mother corm and stored at low temperatures of 2°C (35°F) for a minimum of eight weeks to satisfy their chilling requirement. The daughter corms are planted again in spring (Fig. 20–9). Smaller corms (cormels) can also be planted but they only increase in size and do not flower.

Dahlia

The *Dahlia* storage organ is an enlarged storage tuberous root with several adventitious buds on the attached stem near the ground level (Fig. 20–11). When the root is planted in the spring, the bud sprouts to form a shoot that flowers in about 10 weeks in midsummer (6) (Fig. 20–11). With the onset of shorter days in late summer, the present year's *Dahlia* roots enlarge and form a clump of tubers connected at the central stem (crown). These roots are under photoperiodic control and can be induced to enlarge prematurely during the long days of summer by subjecting the plants to short-day conditions or by constantly pruning the growing tips of new shoots as they appear. Pruning the tips diverts the photosynthates to the tubers instead of to the shoots and causes the tuberous roots to enlarge.

The tuber clumps are harvested after the first frost and should be divided in the spring before planting. Each individual tuberous root is cut to provide an attached apical bud (Fig. 20–11). The tubers should be stored in a slightly moist medium at about 8°C (45°F) over the winter.

FLOWER INITIATION AND DEVELOPMENT

In the Netherlands the initiation and development of flowers have been the focus of much research over the years with emphasis on the commercial handling of bulbs and bulb-like structures. The periodicity of vegetative growth and flowering has been described for many species. Hartsema (6) categorizes these plants into seven groups by the pattern of flower formation. What follows is a modification of her classification.

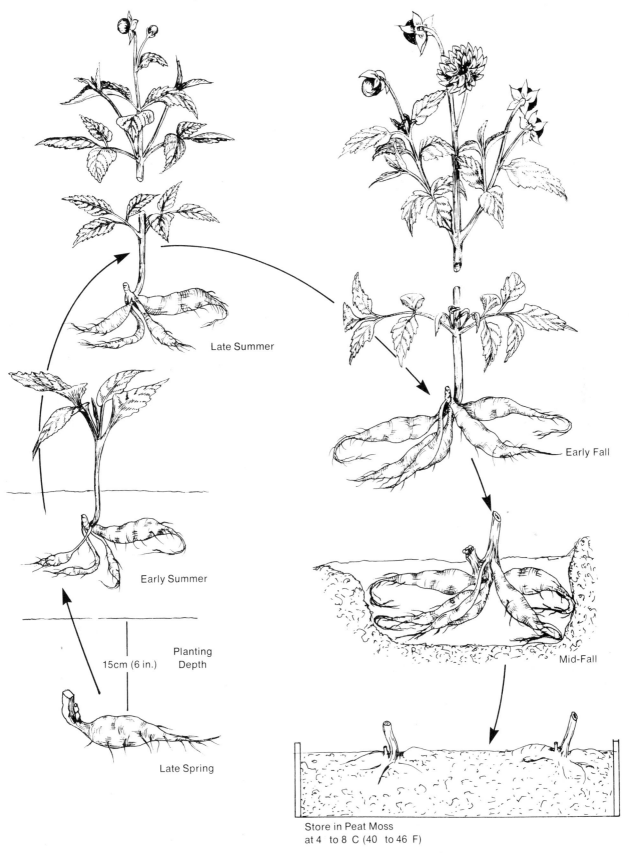

Late Summer

Early Summer

Planting
Depth

15cm (6 in.)

Late Spring

Early Fall

Mid-Fall

Store in Peat Moss
at 4 to 8 C (40 to 46 F)

Fig. 20–11 The growth cycle of the tuberous-rooted *Dahlia*. At least one bud must be on each tuber planted. The bud sprouts and develops roots, which enlarge to form tuberous roots after flowering. The roots enlarge when the days shorten in late summer and when most of the photosynthates are redirected downward. The clumps are usually dug after the first frost and stored in moist material to prevent desiccation over the winter. *Source:* Adapted from Rockwell, F. F., and E. C. Grayson. 1953. *The complete book of bulbs.* Garden City, N.Y.: American Garden Guild and Doubleday.

1. The flower buds form during the spring and summer of the previous year, usually when flowering in the field is nearly over but just before the bulbs are dug from the soil (*Narcissus, Galanthus,* and *Leucojum*).

2. Flowers form at the end of the previous growing period or, perhaps, after they have been harvested and placed in storage. Bulbs of this group have flower buds when they are replanted in the fall (*Hyacinthus, Tulipa,* and *Iris reticulata*).

3. Flowers are initiated some time after replanting and after some low temperatures in winter and early spring. This group is somewhat like group 1 and 2 (plants requiring quick replanting), but also resembles group 4, where the flowers form during the winter months (bulbous irises except *Iris reticulata*).

4. Flowers are initiated towards the end of the storage period but development continues after the bulbs have been planted (*Allium cepa, A. escalonicum, Galtonia, Solanum tuberosum,* and some lilies).

5. Flowers are initiated after replanting (*Freesia, Gladiolus,* and *Anemone*).

6. Flowers are initiated more than a year before flowering (*Amaryllis belladonna, Nerine sarniensis*).

7. Flower initiation occurs throughout the entire growing season but alternately with leaf formation. Undeveloped or newly initiated flower buds may be present when the plants are in full bloom (*Hippeastrum* and *Zephyranthes*).

Bulbs and bulb-like plants initiate flowers under varied environmental conditions, but it appears that high temperatures favor flower formation more than low temperatures do. Hartsema *(6)* lists the optimum temperature for flower initiation for some species: *Hyacinthus,* 25.5°C (78°F); *Tulipa,* 17°C to 20°C (63°F to 68°F); *Lilium* and *Amaryllis,* 23°C (73°F). Some bulbous iris require lower temperatures (9°C to 13°C; 48°F to 55°F), but flower initiation is accelerated if the bulbs are subjected to 32°C (90°F) for about 10 days directly after harvesting and before placing them at the lower temperatures. On the other hand, flowering in bulbous iris can be retarded for up to a full year if the bulbs are held at 25.5°C (78°F). Flowers form after this retardation period when the bulbs are transferred to a lower temperature *(2)*.

Some examples of the early classic research conducted in the Netherlands are illustrated in Figures 20–12 and 20–13, which show how temperatures for tulip or hyacinth bulbs should be controlled to promote the best flowering. The modified system *(6)* of describing the developmental stages in many bulb species originally used by Blaauw and his coworkers appears below. These terms are used by scientists, growers, horticulturists, and sales people to describe the stage of flower development within ornamental bulbs.

Fig. 20–12 The temperature sequence to produce early flowering of *Tulipa gesnerana* 'William Copland'. Flower formation starts in the soil during the warm weather before digging. Flower organ formation (Fig. 20–16) can be completed within several weeks of lifting in storage at 20°C (68°F). Temperatures are then lowered to 8°C (45°F) and the bulbs are planted later. After proper root formation and shoot emergence, the temperatures are gradually raised and the plants placed in the greenhouse where they receive ample light. *Source:* Adapted from Hartsema, A. M., I. Luyten, and A. H. Blaauw. 1930. The optimal temperatures from flower formation to flowering of Darwin tulips II (Dutch). *Verk. Kon. Ned. Akad. Wet. Natuurk.* Sect. II. 27(1):1–47.

Fig. 20–13 Manipulation of temperatures to bring about early flowering of *Hyacinthus orientalis* 'L'Innocence'. High temperatures (34°C; 93°F) are required for flower organ formation compared to 20°C (68°F) for tulips. The stem also extends at higher temperatures than in tulips. When shoots are 4 cm above the soil, the plants are moved to higher forcing temperatures. The soil should be kept slightly cooler than the plant tops. *Source:* Adapted from Luyten, I., M. C. Versluys, and A. H. Blaauw. 1932. The optimal temperatures from flower formation to flowering for *Hyacinthus orientalis* (Dutch). *Verk. Kon. Ned. Akad. Wet. Natuurk.* Sect. II. 29(5): 1–64.

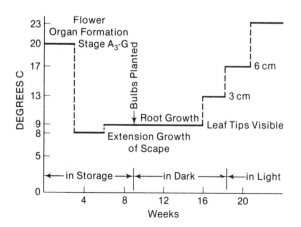

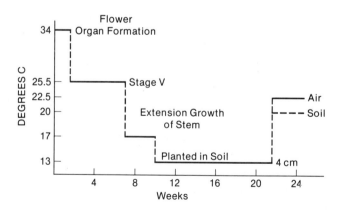

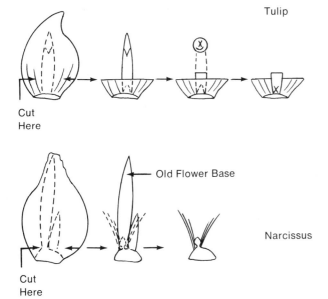

Tulip

Cut
Here

Old Flower Base

Narcissus

Cut
Here

Fig. 20–14 A diagram showing one method by which tulips and narcissus bulbs can be dissected to study the flower organ formation. *Source:* Adapted from Rees, A. R. 1972. With permission from *The growth of bulbs, applied aspects of the physiology of ornamental bulbous crop plants.* Copyright by Academic Press Inc. (London) Ltd.

Developmental Flower Stages:

apex vegetative, flat

apex vegetative, dome-shaped

Sp, spathe initiated *(Narcissus)*

P_1, three outer perianth primordia distinguishable

P_2, three inner perianth primordia distinguishable

A_1, three outer anther primordia distinguishable

A_2, three inner anther primordia distinguishable

G, three carpel primordia distinguishable (critical for tulips)

Pc, paracorolla (trumpet) apparent (in *Narcissus*)

Fig. 20–15 A slightly different tulip dissection technique from that shown in Figure 20–14 for studying the stage of the flower organs. *Source:* Netherlands Flower Bulb Institute.

A method of determining the later flowering bud stages of tulip is illustrated in Figures 20–14 and 20–15. A sharp knife and a hand lens are the only tools needed to make the dissection and determine the flower bud stage. In tulips stage G is desired (Fig. 20–16). A representative sample of each cultivar of tulips is commonly dissected to determine whether flower buds are present and whether they may have been injured by heat or disease. This simple procedure prevents the waste of treating and storing bulbs that have no embryonic flowers or have only unhealthy ones.

Fig. 20–16 The A_2 stage (*above*) and the G stage (*below*) in tulip (see p. 447). Note the tepals (sepals and petals) on the outside, the six anthers and the carpel primordia in the center. Bulbs in the G stage are ready for storage at 8°C (Fig. 20–12). *Source:* Netherlands Flower Bulb Institute.

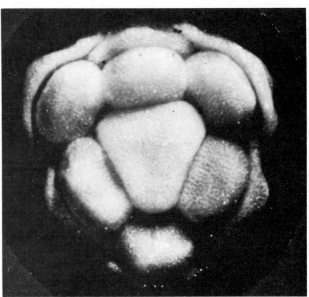

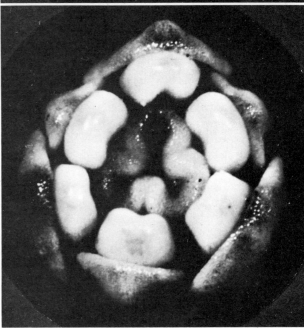

STORAGE AND FORCING TREATMENTS FOR GREENHOUSE FLOWERING

Generalizations regarding the flowering of bulbs, tubers, or corms under protective cultivation cannot be made. Upon arrival at the greenhouse, bulbs vary in their stage of flower development (see pp. 442 and 444). Some bulbs such as the daffodil, already have an immature flower and may have already been precooled and are ready to be planted and forced into bloom. Others must first be given the proper low temperature treatment (precooling). Then the bulbs must be planted in containers and moved to low temperature rooms to establish a good root system before they are brought into a moderate temperature greenhouse (13°C to 17°C; 55°F to 65°F) or a cool room. Temperatures are critical for each species and cultivar. Proper cooling prevents later flowering problems and also ensures good flower quality.

Many bulbous crops can be grown for greenhouse forcing during winter and spring, but only three of the most important and readily available species will be discussed here. The actual operations concerning specific cultivars and for early or late season forcing should be studied in detail in the articles by DeHertogh *(1, 3, 4)*. Specific cultural details should be followed in order to ensure success.

Daffodils (Narcissus)

Daffodils are available in the late summer and have a complete set of flower parts (stage Pc) within the bulb when they are received. However, a sample of the bulbs should be examined to determine if the flowers have been injured and the basal region should be examined for pathogens before purchase. The early forcing bulbs should be precooled at 9°C (48°F) at the end of August and planted in early October. At this time one must decide whether cut flowers or potted plants are desired. The subsequent cold temperature treatments may vary as much as four weeks with the same cultivar depending on the desired stem length. After planting in flats (for cut flowers) or in pots, the containers are first placed in a rooting room at 9°C (48°F) until fully rooted; the temperature is then lowered to 5°C (41°F). A temperature of 1°C (33°F) is used if the sprouts start to become too long. This holds the plants until they are ready to move to the greenhouse. This treatment is especially necessary in the spring. The earliest flowering date is midwinter and the latest is midspring. The bulbs used for the late and very late forcing should not be precooled at 9°C (48°F), but should be held at 13°C to 15°C (55°F to 59°F) until they are planted and placed in the rooting room in early

to late fall. These late-forcing bulbs receive chilling in the rooting room to ensure proper flower development.

The best night temperature for forcing daffodil pot plants is 15°C to 16°C (59°F to 62°F), but 10°C to 13°C (50°F to 55°F) is best for cut daffodils to ensure slow development to produce the long stems often in demand.

Hyacinths (Hyacinthus)

The principal source of bulbs is the Netherlands, and they arrive in the United States in early fall. Two types are available: the ''prepared,'' which already have complete flower buds (stage G) for early forcing, and the regular bulbs (incomplete flower initials) for later forcing. The subsequent cold requirements differ based on whether they are ''prepared'' or not and the desired time of flowering. Hyacinths are primarily grown in pots and are planted with almost half of the bulb above the soil level (Fig. 20–17). Early forcing ''prepared'' bulbs should be stored at 9°C to 13°C (48°F to 55°F) upon arrival and the regular bulbs at 15°C to 17°C (59°F to 63°F) until planting. The temperature sequence in the rooting room is essentially the same as with potted daffodils.

Fig. 20–17 Five hyacinth bulbs forced in a single pot. The shallow planting depth of the bulbs provides ample root space. *Source:* Netherlands Flower Bulb Institute.

Greenhouse temperatures for early crops (Christmas) should be as high as 23°C (73°F) for the first 10 to 14 days, followed by 17°C (63°F) until flowering. The night temperature for forcing the late hyacinths (spring) is 15°C (59°F). Only a few of the many cultivars can be used for both early and late forcing (Table 20–2). Some cultivars have a problem called loose-bud, which is a separation of the inflorescence from the base of the bulb *(11)*. This problem is caused partially by overwatering or by a rooting temperature over 9°C (48°F) at a critical period of flower development. Loose-bud occurs after planting and cannot be attributed to any treatment in growing the bulbs in the field.

Most of these bulbs available in the United States come from the Netherlands, but some also come from Japan and the state of Washington. A sample bulb of each cultivar should be dissected to determine whether they are in stage G (Fig. 20–16) and whether there has been any flower abortion, indicated by brownish flower primordia, due to heat injury. Precooling should not be attempted before stage G. Dry storage of the bulbs in trays at temperatures between 17°C and 20°C (63°F and 68°F) enhances development of the flower to stage G.

For the earliest flowering, bulbs should be given a precooling temperature of 7°C (45°F) before planting. Those for later flowering should receive 9°C (48°F) starting a few days after the first group. Later-forcing bulbs need not be precooled but should be planted directly into pots or flats and placed in the rooting room. For forcing early tulips, the rooting room (Fig. 20–18) temperature sequence differs slightly from that for daffodils and hyacinths.

Dry bulbs can be precooled by subjecting them to 5°C (41°F) for 9 to 12 weeks just before planting directly into the greenhouse *(11)*. This system has also been employed to precool tulips for planting outdoors in warm climates where soil temperatures are too high for natural precooling.

Table 20–2 Tulip, Hyacinth, Daffodil, and Crocus Cultivars Suitable for Forcing

Type of Bulbs	Time of Flowering	
	Mid to Late Winter	Early Spring
Tulip	Red—Cassini, Paul Richter, Prominence, Christmas Marvel, Topscore, Trance, Charles, Bing Crosby, Olaf	Red—Couleur Cardinal, Red Queen, Utopia, Robinea
	Yellow—Levant, Bellona	Yellow—Makasar, Ornament
	White—Snow Star, Pax	White—Blizzard
	Salmon—Apricot Beauty	Orange—Orange Sun
	Variegated—Madame Spoor, Merry Widow, Roland	Variegated—Carl M. Bellman, Golden Eddy, United Europe, Edith Eddy, Paris
	Pink—Preludium	Pink—Pink Supreme, Pearless Pink, Rose Beauty
Hyacinth	Red—Jan Bos	
	Pink—Anna Marie, Eros, Lady Derby	Pink—Lady Derby, Pink Pearl, Marconi
	Blue—Ostara, Bismarck	Blue—Ostara, Blue Giant, Perle Brillante
	White—Carnegie, L'Innocence	White—Carnegie
Daffodil	King Alfred, Golden Harvest, Carlton	Gold Medal, Rembrandt, Van Sion, Geranium, Cheerfulness
Crocus	Remembrance, Pickwick, Joan of Arc, Grand Maitre, Peter Pan	Pickwick, Peter Pan, Joan of Arc, Remembrance, Grand Maitre

Source: Extension Bulletin 593, Michigan State University.

Fig. 20–18 Tulip bulbs forced for cut flowers are grown in wooden flats and stored on shelves in the rooting room. When the shoots are about 10 cm tall, they are moved to a warm greenhouse for forcing. The tall ones flower in three weeks or less.

Fig. 20–19 Planting tulip bulbs in clay pots. The flat side of the bulb should be placed against the pot because the first leaf emerges from the flat side. *Source:* Netherlands Flower Bulb Institute.

In potting tulips, the flat side of the bulbs should always be adjacent to the rim of the pot (Fig. 20–19). The lowermost large leaf always emerges from the flat side, and leaves facing outward produce a more desirable looking pot. About one-fourth of the bulb can be above the soil to provide adequate rooting space (Fig. 20–20).

Fig. 20–20 After the tulip bulbs are firmly placed on top of a layer of soil (Fig. 20–19), they may be partially covered with sand, as shown, or with potting soil. The bulbs are planted with their "noses" out of the soil. *Source:* Netherlands Flower Bulb Institute.

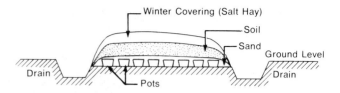

Fig. 20–21 A method of storing tulip bulbs in pots outdoors in cold winter climates (zones 1–4). When the weather warms (early spring) the pots are uncovered and brought into a warm greenhouse for forcing. *Source:* Netherlands Flower Bulb Institute.

It is also possible to store the pots outdoors under soil covered with hay or straw (25 cm or 10 in) where the outdoor climate is appropriate and a rooting room or cold cellar is not available (Fig. 20–21). The temperatures must be close to those recommended for the rooting room (see p. 447). The soil temperature may start at 13°C (55°F) and drop to 9°C to 10°C (48°F to 50°F) by late fall and then gradually drop to 2°C to 5°C (35°F to 41°F), but it should never go below 0°C (32°F). A period of approximately 15 weeks is necessary at these temperatures to enhance flowering. A recording thermograph can be placed permanently in the soil at the pot level to make periodic temperature checks.

Many tulip cultivars can be chosen for early and late forcing *(1, 3)*. The correct ones must be selected (Table 20–2).

FORCING SELECTED BULBS IN THE HOME

Narcissus 'Paper white', sometimes called 'Chinese sacred lilies' and 'Soleil d'Or', can be forced at moderate home temperatures on a bed of gravel no deeper than 6 cm (2.5 in). The gravel is kept constantly moist and the container is placed in an exposure with ample light (south window). Single-nose bulbs (one growing point) placed very close to one another give a pleasing mass-flower effect (Fig. 20–22).

Hyacinths can be grown in special containers as shown in Figure 20–23. The bottom part of the container is kept full of water. The water should be changed several times a week. Prepared bulbs are essential for this procedure because the flower parts are already formed within the bulb. The bulbs should be started in a dark, cool location to establish the root system completely to the bottom of the container. Then transfer them to a low light location with a 10°C (50°F) temperature to encourage the top to grow. When the sprout is about 5 to 8 cm (2 to 3 in) tall, the pot can be moved to a sunny location at normal home temperatures. Normally this process should take 10 to 13 weeks.

Fig. 20–23 Two methods of growing hyacinths in the home. *Left:* Common culture in a pot of soil. *Right:* The bulb grown in a Dutch hyacinth glass. The bulb in the glass is placed near the water line and the entire container is placed in the dark since the roots grow better in the dark. If a dark place is not available, cover the glass with aluminum foil to darken the roots. The bulbs can be brought to a bright window (sunny if possible) after the shoots are about 6 cm tall and the roots are about 10 cm long. Check the root growth periodically.

Crocuses may be planted in large containers or in ordinary 15 cm (6 in) clay or plastic pots. Place the bulbs slightly below the soil surface and very close together for a good flowering effect (Fig. 20–24). The bulbs should be planted in early fall when they first become available, placing them outdoors in a protected shady location to receive the chilling required for sprouting. Occasional

Fig. 20–24 A method of placing crocus corms in small and large containers. The distance between the corms is about 1 cm. After the corms are placed on a firm level soil, additional soil is heaped over the corms and firmed. Allow at least 1 cm between the top of the soil and the pot rim for watering. *Left:* About seven to nine corms can be planted in a 15 cm pot. *Right:* A small piece of broken pot (shard) is used to cover the pot hole to prevent sandy soils from washing out.

Fig. 20–22 *Narcissus tazetta* 'Paper white' can be grown in the home without the requirement of low temperatures for rooting as with other *Narcissus*. Bulbs are planted in a shallow bowl and covered with pea gravel in September for December flowering. After the bulb is planted high as shown, the water level is kept just below the bottom of the bulb so that the emerging roots do not dry out. The bowl is stored in a cool (10°C; 50°F) dark place until shoots are about 10 cm tall, and then it is moved to a sunny location. Bulbs can be planted every two weeks and forced periodically to give a sequence of blooms from December to March. *N. tazetta* is a polyanthus type of narcissus (several flowers per stalk). Double-nose bulbs produce two or more stalks per bulb and produce many flowers in a container. Besides the 'Paper whites', the polyanthus group also includes 'Chinese sacred lilies' and 'Soleil d'or' (yellow), which have a similar culture.

Fig. 20–25   The common grape hyacinth can be planted in a 15 cm pot as crocus corms are (Fig. 20–24). Pots should be placed outdoors in warm climates or in a bulb cellar in harsh climates to provide the necessary chilling before they are brought into the home for forcing. Sunny locations are necessary for forcing.

The Hardy Bulbs

The H group (Table 20–1) has many possible uses in temperate zone climates (zones 4–6). The most common garden use is informal borders that also have annuals during the summer months. Public parks and institutions use bulbs such as hyacinths and tulips in formal beds, but great care must be exercised in planting these at an even depth to ensure uniform flowering. In all cases, the soil should be worked up well with organic matter before planting to create a friable and loose soil. Some form of phosphorus fertilizer (bone meal or single superphosphate) should be incorporated into the soil as it is prepared. No other fertilizer is generally required for bulbs unless they naturalize and remain in the same location for many years; then a complete fertilizer should be given. If summer flowering annuals follow the naturalized spring bulbs, usually enough nutrients are left over from the annuals to fertilize the bulbs.

Bulbs should be planted at the proper depth for the species (Table 20–1). Failure to do so causes poor sprouting, uneven flowering, or the loss of the bulbs after one season. Bulbs planted too close to the surface in cold climates may heave from the soil or freeze. If the bulbs are allowed to become established or naturalized in the landscape, they should be dug up after a given number of years (Table 20–1); the clumps are divided and spaced at the proper distance again at replanting. Digging and respacing invigorates the bulb population by reducing the competition within the clumps for space and moisture (Fig. 20–26).

It is possible to plant the small and very early flowering bulbs in a lawn area for purposes of being naturalized. These usually flower during the late winter or early spring while the lawn is dormant and before it must be mowed. The bulbs are dormant during the summer and fall and the beauty of the summer lawn is not affected. Excellent candidates for this category of planting in the landscape are *Crocus, Chionodoxa, Galanthus,* and *Leucojum.* These naturalize in the lawn and remain established for many years (Figs. 20–27 and 20–28).

All bulbs have an optimum planting time. Bulbous or tuberous plants are usually available to gardeners when their buds are dormant.

The hardy bulbs (H) usually flower in spring or early summer, increase their bulb size during the summer, and become dormant in the fall. During this dor-

watering ensures a good root system. When the sprouts begin to show, bring the plants in the house and place in a sunny location. It is best not to mix crocus cultivars because they may flower at different times. Grape hyacinths *(Muscari)* may be handled in a similar manner (Fig. 20–25).

Tulips and daffodils (large trumpet) may also be grown in pots outdoors in zones 6, 7, and 8 where they receive sufficient cold temperature for rooting but do not freeze in the pots. In zones 3, 4, and 5, the potted bulbs must be placed in a cool dark cellar or buried (Fig. 20–21). The soil must be moist to encourage root growth. After the sprouts are about 5 cm (2 in) long, they may be moved to a very sunny location in the home for forcing. This process requires between 13 and 15 weeks.

Fig. 20-26 *Narcissus pseudonarcissus* planted in the garden directly from the pots in which they flowered. After flowering in pots, the plants are placed outdoors if night temperatures stay above freezing. They are watered regularly until the tops wither and die back. The entire soil ball is removed from the pot, and bulbs and soil are placed in a hole deep enough that the soil ball can be covered with at least 10 cm (4 in) of garden soil. Some bulbs of the clump will flower the next spring if the conditions (soil and climate) are suitable for such culture. Bulbs so treated naturalize in zones 5 to 8.

Fig. 20-27 *Crocus vernus*, the so-called Dutch crocus, is one of the first ''bulbous'' (actually a corm) plants to bloom in the spring. This makes it a candidate for planting in the lawn because it can flower before the lawn requires mowing. The leaves should be allowed to die back naturally so that photosynthates move downward into the corm after flowering. *Source: Robert A. H. Legro.*

Fig. 20-28 The common snow drop (*Galanthus nivalis*) is an early flowering bulb (sometimes in the snow) and can be used as a lawn bulb or for a bulb in the border. Can spring be far behind when one sees a snow drop? *Source:* Robert A. H. Legro.

mant period the bulb producer digs, cleans, and packages them for sale at retail outlets. The hardy bulbs, such as tulips, narcissus, hyacinths, muscaris (Table 20-1), are offered for sale in late summer and fall. They should be planted as soon as possible so that root action begins before the onset of very cold weather (zones 4-6). In mild winter climates (zones 7-10) it is best to delay planting these hardy genera until after cool weather begins in the fall. The bulbs should be planted at the proper depth (Table 20-1) for best flowering and survival. In zones, 2, 3, and possibly 4, it may be necessary to cover the bulb bed with a layer of hay or reeds to a depth of 6 to 10 in after the soil freezes. Do not cover before the soil has a crust of frost or the hay will act as an insulator, allowing the roots to stay warm and continue to grow, possibly resulting in root injury with the onset of very low temperatures. As the weather warms in the spring, the cover should be gradually removed.

Semihardy Bulbs and Bulb-like Structures

The SH group of bulbs must be dug in the fall in zones 3, 4, 5 and possibly 6, but may be allowed to naturalize in the mild locations of zones 7 to 10. *Amaryllis, Freesia,*

451

Canna, and calla lilies are good examples of types that become well established in mild areas (Table 20–1). Once established in the landscape they, too, must be lifted, divided, and replanted at intervals of a few years to reduce root competition.

In cold climates the semihardy bulbs must be lifted each fall or summer, then cleaned and stored in unheated cellars (5°C to 10°C; 41°F to 50°F) until planting in spring. Some bulbs in this group require planting every year in both cold and mild climates. Viruses, fungus diseases, or even unfavorable summer conditions may reduce bulb vigor for the following season. *Anemone, Ixia,* and *Ranunculus* usually require annual planting.

Tender Bulbs

Tender bulbs (T) must be lifted, cleaned, and stored each year soon after they become dormant. This is true for all the zones except 10, where *Hippeastrum* and *Tigridia* can be naturalized. In most areas almost all the species in this group are cultured in pots because they are susceptible to frost damage and may require some protection early in the fall. It is easy to move the pots from one environmental condition to another as the season progresses. Tuberous begonia seeds may be sown in winter and the seedlings transplanted into pots in spring. The tubers enlarge as the days shorten in late summer. The newly formed tubers can be removed from the pots and stored in slightly moist peat moss (Fig. 20–2) at a relatively high storage temperature for bulbous crops (10°C; 50°F). The tubers may then be planted into pots in the spring for summer flowering. *Hippeastrum* can also be cultured in pots, but the bulb is seldom removed from year to year except to shift the plant to a larger pot. Actually the *Hippeastrum* is never really dormant but is simply quiescent during the fall.

PESTS AND DISEASES

The many fungal diseases of bulbs are difficult to identify specifically without plating them on sterile media in the laboratory for positive identification. However, *Botrytis* spp., or "fire" disease of tulips, is easy to spot even for the amateur gardener. During wet weather both leaves and flowers become infested (appear water-soaked) with a disease from spores carried on a few bulbs. After the moisture dries off the foliage and flowers, the flower bed appears as if a fire had passed through it. When conditions are ideal during the moist period, the diseased portions sporulate, producing gray fuzzy masses of spores. This disease carries to other genera, such as *Narcissus,* lilies, and *Gladiolus.* The pathogen can overwinter in the soil or may be carried on bulbs. Fortunately there are fungicides that can control the disease.

The diseases difficult to identify are the ones affecting the vascular tissues within the bulb. These are usually referred to as **basal** or **bulb rot** and may be found in tulips, daffodils, and hyacinths. It is not possible to cure or control the disease of seriously infected bulbs; they should be discarded.

Viral diseases are usually distinguishable by patterns of streaks or blotches in the leaves and flowers. In tulip flowers, this so-called color breaking may even be desired. During the sixteenth century in the Netherlands color break in tulips was highly prized and not thought to be a disease. A virus usually weakens the plants, however, and in bulb-growing areas these days, bulbs with virus are eliminated from the fields when they can be identified at full bloom. These viruses are usually transmitted by sucking insects, such as aphids, but they can also be spread by contaminated tools during propagation and digging operations.

Bothersome insects are the *Narcissus* bulb fly (the grub damages the bulb) and wireworms, which live in the soil and feed on the bulbs. Thrips and aphids can be carried over during bulb storage but they can also migrate to the bulb bed when the plants are in full bloom. Thrips streak the flowers by rasping the flower surfaces as they feed.

Plant nematodes (small eel-worms) (see p. 254) cause bulb damage similar to bulb rot. The wholesale bulb producer usually controls nematodes by hot-water treatment of the bulbs before they are planted in his propagating field. Most nematodes thrive better in sandy soils than in clay soils.

Slugs and snails destroy flowers and foliage and should be controlled with poisonous baits specific for these pests.

In some gardens, deer, gophers, ground squirrels, and mice can be very troublesome to tulip and crocus beds. The bulbs should be covered with a wire mesh large enough for the shoots to emerge. The daffodil is not molested by these animals and therefore is suitable for naturalization in home gardens.

REFERENCES

1. Ball, V., ed. 1976. *The Ball red book.* 13th ed. West Chicago, Ill.: G. J. Ball. (See chapters on crocuses, daffodils, hyacinths and tulips by A. DeHertogh.)

2. Beijer, J. J. 1952. Experiments on the retardation of Dutch Irises. *Acta. Bot. Neerl.* 1:268–86.

3. DeHertogh, A. 1973. *Holland bulb forcer's guide*. New York: Netherlands Flower Bulb Institute.

4. ———. 1974. Principles for forcing tulips, hyacinths, daffodils, garden lilies, and Dutch iris. *Scientia Hort*. 2(4):313–56.

5. Hartsema, A. M., I. Luyten, and A. H. Blaauw. 1930. The optimal temperatures from flower formation to flowering of Darwin tulips II (Dutch). *Verk. Kon. Ned. Akad. Wet. Natuurk*. Sect. II. 27(1): 1–47.

6. Hartsema, A. M. 1961. Influence of temperature on flower formation of bulbous and tuberous plants. In *Encyclopedia of plant physiology*, ed. W. Ruhland. Berlin: Springer-Verlag. Vol. 16, pp. 123–61.

7. Luyten, I., M. C. Versluys, and A. H. Blaauw. 1932. The optimal temperatures from flower formation to flowering for *Hyacinthus orientalis* (Dutch). *Verk. Kon. Ned. Akad. Wet. Natuurk*. Sect. II 29(5):1–64.

8. Mulder, R., and I. Luyten. 1928. On the periodicity of the Darwin tulip (Dutch). *Verk. Kon. Ned. Akad. Wet. Natuurk*. Sect. II 26(3):1–64.

9. Post, K. 1949. *Florist crop production and marketing*. New York: Orange Judd. (See specific species.)

10. Preston, F. G., ed. 1958. *The greenhouse*. New York: Abelard-Shuman.

11. Rees, A. R. 1972. *The growth of bulbs: applied aspects of the physiology of ornamental bulbous crop plants*. New York: Academic Press.

12. Rockwell, F. F., and E. C. Grayson. 1953. *The complete book of bulbs*. Garden City, N.Y.: American Garden Guild and Doubleday.

13. Sytsema, W. 1971. Effect of storage and date of planting on flowering and bulb growth of *Nerine bowdenii*. *Acta Hort*. 23(1):99–105.

SUPPLEMENTARY READING

ANON. 1976. *Forcing flower bulbs*. English ed. Parklaan 5, Hillegom, The Netherlands. Netherlands Flower Bulb Institute, Bulb Information Center.

CROCKETT, J. U. 1971. *Bulbs*. New York: Time-Life.

GENDERS, R. 1973. *Bulbs, a complete handbook*. Indianapolis: Bobbs-Merrill.

GOULD, C. J., ed. 1957. *Handbook of bulb growing and forcing*. Northwest Bulb Growers' Assoc. (Available from R. L. Nowadnick, Skagit Valley Junior College, Mt. Vernon, Wash.)

GREY, CHARLES, H. 1938. *Hardy bulbs*. 3 vols. London: Williams and Norgate Ltd.

OLIVER, R. W., ed. 1959. *Handbook on bulbs*. Brooklyn, N.Y.: Brooklyn Botanical Gardens.

MCFARLAND, J. H., R. M. HATTON, and D. J. FOLEY. 1941. *Garden bulbs in color*. New York: Macmillan.

WENTZELL, G. K., ed. 1975. *How to grow bulbs*. Menlo Park, Calif.: Lane.

Lawns and Turfgrasses

WRITTEN BY
JOHN H. MADISON

Growing turf is a multimillion dollar industry. The replacement value of turf in the United States has been estimated to exceed $8 to 12 billion, and annual maintenance costs have been estimated at over $4 billion. Much of the turf is public grass growing in schoolyards, parks, cemeteries, and golf courses, along highways, on military installations, and on other public lands.

Turf is a unique crop in that the product is not what is harvested but what remains. The crop is grown densely as an entire population instead of individual plants spaced apart so that each grows vigorously. An appreciation of these differences is basic to being a good turf horticulturist.

There are three principal reasons for growing a lawn: (1) as a carpet, to protect the home from mud and dust, and to soften glare and heat; (2) for recreation; and (3) for beauty and pleasure. Studies have shown that lawns so please us that many of our earliest memories are of grass and trees.

Turf culture differs from other horticultural pursuits in one important way. In nature, plant growth is often limited by competition with many other plants for water, nutrients, and light. Thousands of seeds germinate and die for every one that lives and grows. Successful horticulture comes from spacing plants and eliminating weeds so that each plant has soil, water, and space

John H. Madison is professor of environmental horticulture, University of California, Davis. He is the author of many publications on turfgrass culture and management.

allotted to it alone. Grass is the exception. In growing a lawn, even more plants are crowded into a given space than would grow there naturally. We strive to grow dense lawns similar to a fine carpet. The more we succeed in growing a dense lawn, the more stress each individual plant gets through competition from its crowding neighbors.

On an infertile dry soil, lack of nutrients and water limits plant growth, and results in a poor lawn. We can grow a better, denser lawn by fertilizing and irrigating. But as the number of plants (shoots) increase, there is a point where plants shade each other and compete for sunlight. Beyond that point individual plants are smaller, have fewer roots, and use nutrients and water less effectively. Thus cultural practices that result in a dense, tight lawn can also result in individual plants of reduced quality and vigor.

STRESS

Turf differs from other horticultural plantings in that, instead of relieving the stress that results from competition, we increase it. The goal in growing lawns is not to grow individual plants of high quality but a plant population of fine appearance. In addition to suffering stress from competition, most lawn plants also suffer climatic stress at some season of the year. In managing a lawn, we can fertilize, mow, and use other practices to either increase or decrease stress. There is a limit, however, to the stress a plant can withstand before weakening to the point of dying.

The stress concept gives us a tool for evaluating the effects of cultural practices on grass. In a figurative way, there is a stress budget for turfgrass. If plant competition is high and midsummer weather imposes a heat stress, little more allowable stress is left in the stress budget. Cultural practices that reduce stress, such as watering, should then be followed. On the other hand, early fall temperatures are often ideal for growth of turfgrass. Then certain stressful management practices—for example, power raking to thin out plants—that would have damaged a bluegress lawn in summer's heat can be used. Throughout this chapter different management practices are evaluated in terms of the stress they cause. The practices that increase stress are not necessarily bad, but care should be exercised to select and use these practices in appropriate seasons, and not to use several high-stress operations at inappropriate times.

The word **lawn** originally referred to a natural area of grass without trees. Today it refers to any expanse of ground on which grass is growing. **Turf** originally meant a layer of matted earth formed by soil and thickly growing grass plants. This meaning has gradually changed over the years, so that the word *turf* is used by horticulturists to refer to grass that is mowed and cared for. **Turfgrass** refers to the grass used in growing a horticultural turf.

Turf culture can be divided into two procedures: (1) establishment, and (2) maintenance for decorative or family use with modest traffic, or for heavy traffic by the public, or for athletic competition. Maintenance for athletic competition requires more detailed information than can be covered in this chapter, so the interested student is referred to advanced turfgrass books such as Beard (1973) and Madison (1971) listed at the end of this chapter.

ESTABLISHING A TURF

A first step in growing a turf is to learn something about the species of plants used and their requirements. Turfgrasses are divided into two groups: (1) cool-season or temperate grasses, such as bluegrass and bent grass adapted to cool climates of the northern United States; and (2) subtropical grasses, such as bermuda grass and St. Augustine grass, adapted to the warmer areas of the southern United States.

Between these regions is a transition zone where neither cool-season nor subtropical grasses perform at their best. Cool-season grasses grow well during cooler parts of the year, but during hot summer weather they become dormant or suffer heat injury and disease. Subtropical grasses in the transition zone do well in the hot summer but become dormant and turn brown in winter (Fig. 21–1, p. 456).

In the western, arid portion of the U.S. plains states, where water is not available for irrigation, native drought-tolerant grasses such as buffalo grass or grama grass are sometimes grown. While their season of growth is limited, they do cover and protect the soil during the dry period.

Commonly used turfgrasses are described in Table 21–1 (pp. 458–59).

TURFGRASS STRUCTURE

Turfgrass anatomy is illustrated in Figure 21–2 (p. 457). Table 21–2 (p. 460) gives a key for identifying common turfgrasses. The key is limited since it distinguishes only among the common cultivated turfgrasses.

Turfgrasses are well adapted to their role as a carpet. As with most monocots, growth of an individual shoot is **determinate** (ends in a flower), and the plants have fibrous roots without tap roots. Each shoot dies after a time, but is replaced by new shoots growing from axillary buds. These new shoots produce adventitious roots at the nodes. In this way turf continually rejuvenates itself. In many grass species, axillary buds produce horizontal creeping stems. If these grow over the surface of the ground they are called **stolons;** below ground, they are termed **rhizomes**. Both structures enable grass plants to invade open areas and to spread. Other species of turfgrasses grow only new erect shoots or **tillers,** arising from axillary buds. Tillering grasses do spread but slowly.

Turfgrass flowers develop on elongated stems at certain seasons. The rest of the year the tiller shoots are condensed with the vegetative growing point nestling among the leaves. The growing point produces **intercalary meristems;** that is, regions of cell initiation that lie across a stem or leaf and that by dividing interpose—or intercalate—new tissue between existing older tissues. The division and elongation of the intercalary meristems "extrudes" leaves and leaf sheaths. Internodes of the stem of grass plants do not elongate except to produce stolons, rhizomes, or flower stalks.

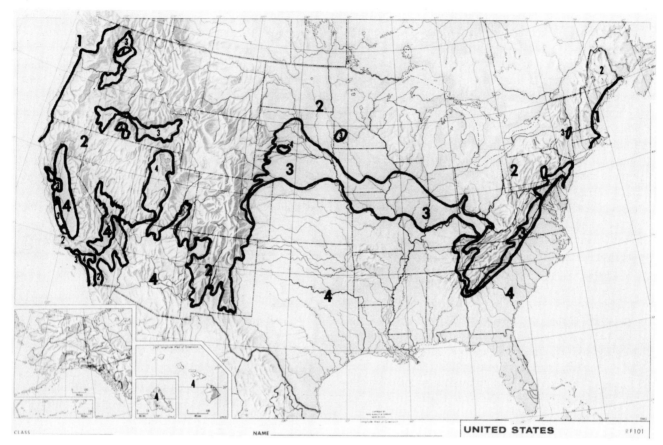

Fig. 21–1   Areas of turfgrass adaptation. 1: Areas adapted to temperate grasses, particularly bentgrasses (*Agrostis*). 2: Areas of general adaptation of temperate grasses. 3: Transition zone where subtropical grasses suffer winter cold and temperate grasses are stressed by summer's heat. 4: Area of adaptation for subtropical bermuda and zoysia grasses. The more tender subtropical grasses are limited to hardiness zones 8, 9, and 10 (see Fig. 10–4). This map is based upon mean July temperatures, not the low winter temperatures of the hardiness zone map. The boundaries are not sharp and are greatly influenced by local microclimates, especially in the mountain states, where elevation and exposure affect adaptation. Alaska is too cold for all but one or two cultivars of turfgrasses, which survive in milder areas of the state. Hawaii is subtropical-tropical.
ⓒ Rand McNally & Co. RL 80-Y-99

456

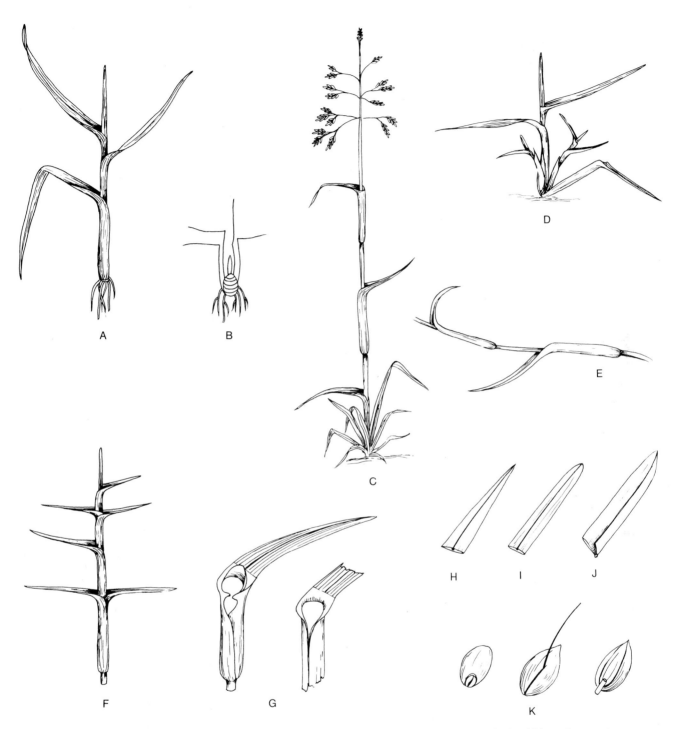

Fig. 21–2 *A:* The vegetative turfgrass plant usually has a small stem with short internodes and bears one leaf and several adventitious roots at each node. *B:* Enlargement of lower portion of *A. C:* The stem elongates prior to flowering. *D:* Buds at the nodes produce tillers. *E:* Elongated spreading horizontal stem (stolon). *F:* Stolons of some grasses produce occasional short internodes alternating with longer ones so that some of the leaves appear opposite. *G:* The leaf consists of a blade and a sheath (sheathing the stem). The region where the blade joins the sheath is called the *collar.*

An outgrowth of the collar is the *ligule,* which may be a membrane or a fringe of hairs. The collar may develop clasping *auricles.* Leaf blades may be pointed (*H*), rounded (*I*), or boat shaped (*J*), and edges may be parallel (*I, J*) or tapered (*H*). *K:* The grass "seed" is properly a fruit— a caryopsis—and may be naked or enclosed in a hull. The hull may have one or more awns and may have a small piece of stem attached.

Table 21–1 Characteristics, Regions, Improved Cultivars, and Uses of the Common Turfgrass Species. The First Nine Species are

Turfgrass Species	Turf Characteristics	U.S. Regions Where Used	Desirable Characteristics
Agrostis stolonifera L. Creeping bent grass	Able to produce a dense turf of good color and fine texture under extremely close mowing (0.25 in and less).	North, through the transition zone and with care into parts of the South.	Ability to stand low mowing. Withstands salinity.
Agrostis tenuis Sibth. Colonial bent grass	Variable grass adapted to northern coastal climates. Spreads. Color fair. Coarse-textured mowed high; fine textured mowed low.	Well adapted to north coast, useable throughout the north.	Adaptable. Withstands acid soils of low fertility and wet soils.
Agrostis spp. 'Highland' bent grass	In a mixture it forms dense patches of blue-green grass of puffy character unless mowed under one inch. Tolerates more heat and less water than other bents.	Better adapted to transition zone heat and dryness than above.	Performs well in irrigated Mediterranean climate.
Festuca elator L. (*F. arundinaceae*) Tall fescuegrass	A coarse-textured bunch grass suited only for growing in pure stands.	Adapted to transition zone. Not fully cold hardy.	Deeprooted. Tolerates wear, drought and neglect.
Festuca pratensis Huds. Meadow fescuegrass	Much like perennial ryegrass when young but becoming coarse with age. Less aggressive than other turfgrasses.	North into the transition zone.	Low cost, fast germination.
Festuca rubra L. var. *rubra* Creeping red fescue	Fine-leaved, drought-tolerant grass tolerant of some shade. Spreads by rhizomes. Favored by high mowing. Competitive under low fertility.	North. Does poorly in the transition zone.	Fine texture, spreading. Tolerates some drought, shade, infertility.
Festuca rubra L. var. *commutata* Chewing's red fescue	Fine-leaved, drought-tolerant grass. Tolerates some shade. Spreads slowly. Tolerates lower mowing than above.	North.	Tolerates closer mowing than above.
Lolium perenne L. Improved perennial ryegrass	Turf cultivars have good color and fine texture like bluegrass. A patchy hard-to-mow clump grass unless well fertilized and watered.	Transition zone north. Not fully hardy. Winter grass in South.	Good color and texture. Tolerates traffic.
Poa pratensis L. Kentucky bluegrass	A dense, fine-textured, beautifully colored grass spreading by rhizomes. Seeds produce uniform apomictic seedlings. The aristocrat of lawn grasses.	Best with cool nights and days under 84°F. Fair in transition zone.	Best color. Sod repairs itself from stolons. Heat and dry dormancy.
Cynodon dactylon (L) Pers. Bermuda grass	A dense vigorous grass creeping by stolons and rhizomes. Withstands neglect but a handsome turf when well cared for. Brown in winter.	South and valleys of Southwest.	Vigorous. Withstands drought, wear, and salinity.
Eremochloa ophiouroides (Munro) Hack Centipedegrass	A dense vigorous grass creeping by large stolons. Adapted to low maintenance lawns on acid or infertile soils.	Florida, Gulf states, coastal plains, parts of California.	Withstands low fertility and acidity. Low maintenance.
Lolium multiflorum Lam. Wintergrass, annual ryegrass	A coarse short-lived grass used only for overseeding winter dormant grasses for winter color in the South and transition zone.	Wintergrass in South.	Grows at low temperatures near freezing.
Paspalum notatum Fliigge Bahia grass	Forms an open coarse turf.	Gulf states and coastal plains of South.	Heat tolerant. Low water need.
Stenotaphrum secondatum (Walt.) O. Kuntze St. Augustine grass	Strong, dense, coarse grass creeping by large stolons. Adapted to shade.	Florida, Gulf states, and parts of California.	Vigorous. Withstands drought, some shade.
Zoysia japonica Steud. Koreangrass, *Z. matrella* (L.) Merrill Manilla grass	Extremely dense grower of good color. Spreads by rhizomes and stolons.	*Z. japonica* hardy through zones 6–10, *Z. matrella*, 8–10.	Very dense—crowd out weeds. Good color and texture.

Northern U.S. Grasses; the Last Six are Southern.

Undesirable Characteristics	Improved Cultivars	Special Care Requirements	Uses
Subject to disease and insect pests. Invasive.	Pencross, Emerald, Seaside	Regular day to day maintenance, mow short, control pests.	Fine turf for putting and bowling greens
Coarse if neglected. Some disease and insect problems.	Astoria, Exeter, Holfior	Mow 1 in or less; use low fertility for low maintenance.	Decorative lawns and utility turf
Does not mix well with other grasses.	Highland	Mow 1 in or less, dethatch in fall.	Decorative lawns and utility turf
Coarse. Weedy in a mixture.	K-31, Alta, Fawn	Mow regularly 1.5 in plus, use infrequent deep irrigation.	Decorative lawns and utility turf; sports turf
Tendency to coarseness and clumpiness.	None	Use in mixes. Give care for other grasses.	To dilute mixtures to reduce cost
Intolerant of heat, salinity, close mowing.	Fortress, Pennlawn, Rainier, Ruby	Mow 2 in plus, light fertilizer. Unmowed for erosion control.	Decorative lawns and utility turf; overseeding subtropical grasses for winter color; unmowed for erosion control; sports turf
Intolerant of heat, salinity.	Cascade, Dawson, Highlight, Jamestown, Wintergreen	Mow 2 in or less, fertilize lightly.	Decorative lawns and utility turf; overseeding subtropical grasses for winter color; sports turf
Limited cold tolerance. Difficult to mow clean. Clumpy if unfertile.	Citation, Derby, Manhattan, Pennfine, NK-200, Yorktown, and others	Mow 1.5 in plus with sharp mower. Fertilize and irrigate to keep dense.	Decorative lawns and utility turf; sports turf
Disease susceptible.	Too many to name: Adelphi, Baron, Flyking, Merion, Pennstar, Sodco, Sydsport, Touchdown, among many good ones	Mow 1.5 in plus, keep up lime level, main fertilizing in fall.	Decorative lawns and utility turf; sports turf
Invasive. Severe thatch builder. Disease susceptible in humid climate.	Common, Ormond, Santa Ana, Sunturf, and Tifway are among many good cultivars. Only common from seed.	Close frequent mowing, dethatch, overseed for winter color.	Decorative lawns and utility turf; sports turf; fine turf for putting and bowling greens
Coarse. A thatch builder.	Common, Oaklawn	Keep fertilizer low, no lime, dethatch if needed.	Decorative lawns and utility turf
Coarse. Disease susceptible.	Gulf, Tifton 1	Open turf so seed touches soil. Mow as needed.	Overseeding subtropical grasses for winter color
Not cold hardy. Openness favors weed invasion.	Argentine, Pensacola, Tifhi 1, Wilmington	Mow 1.5 in plus, low fertility. Reduced water need.	Decorative lawns and utility turf; sports turf
Coarse, invasive, disease and insect prone. Vegetative planting.	Bitter blue, Floratam, Floratine	Mow closely and dethatch. Control pests.	Decorative lawns and utility turf
Vegetative planting. Slow recovery of injury. Too dense to overseed.	Meyer, Midwest (Z. japonica); Flawn (Z. matrella); Emerald (hybrid)	Low fertility and water need. Mow closely, or neglect for erosion control.	Decorative lawns and utility turf

Table 21–2   A Dichotomous Key to Common Turfgrasses

Both couplets (same numbers) should be read before deciding where to proceed. Continue to succeeding couplets, eliminating those choices not appropriate until the species in question is determined based on the information given. Weedy grasses are not included in this key (see Fig. 21–2).

1—Ligule is a membrane. Leaves are alternate and more or less evenly spaced. Proceed to 2.

1—Ligule is a ciliate membrane or a fringe of hairs. Mixed long and short internodes may result in the appearance of occasional pairs of opposite leaves alternating with single leaves. Proceed to 10.

2—Leaves folded in the bud and opening by unfolding. Proceed to 3.

2—Leaves rolled in the bud and opening by unfurling. Proceed to 5.

3—Leaves of many plants with auricles at the collar. Back side of blades shiny. Red pigment usually present at base of leaf sheath. Perennial ryegrass (*Lolium perenne*)

3—Distinct auricles not present. Proceed to 4.

4—Tips of leaves boat-shaped. Blades flat with a slight constriction near the tip. Kentucky bluegrass (*Poa pratensis*).

4—Blades often narrow and needle-like with the margins rolled in. Very fine leaved. Red fescuegrass (*Festuca rubra*).

5—Auricles present though often little developed. Red pigmentation is usually found at the base of newer leaf sheaths. Blades smooth on the lower surface. Proceed to 6.

5—Not as above. Proceed to 8.

6—Auricles prominent. Margins of the leaf smooth. Annual ryegrass, wintergrass (*Lolium multiflorum*)

6—Auricles not well developed, margins of leaf rough. Ligule a short truncate membrane. Proceed to 7.

7—A few ciliate hairs are usually found at the margins of the leaf collar. Tall fescuegrass (*Festuca arundinacea*).

7—No ciliate hairs on the collar. Meadow fescue (*Festuca pratensis*).

8—Plants spreading by stolons with a well developed leaf at each node. Ligule elongate to a point. Creeping bentgrass (*Agrostis stolonifera*).

8—Plant spreading by fine rhizomes or short determinate stolons. Rhizome leaves appear as brown scales. Proceed to 9.

9—Ligule evenly truncate, grass more or less mixing with other grasses. Colonial bentgrass (*Agrostis tenuis*)

9—Ligule tends to form three peaks of uneven height. Grass forms segregated patches in a mixed turf. Grass has a cast on the bluish side of green. 'Highland' bentgrass (*Agrostis* spp.)

10—Leaves folded in the bud and opening by unfolding. Proceed to 11.

10—Leaves rolled in the bud and opening by unfurling. Proceed to 14.

11—Leaf sheaths are greatly flattened. Collar is compressed to form a short stalk for the leaf blade. Spreads by stolons. Proceed to 12.

11—Leaf sheaths round or slightly flattened. The collar does not form a petiole. Spreads by both stolons and rhizomes. Proceed to 13.

12—Ligule a fringe of very short hairs. Sheaths have a few hairs at the margins and at the summit of the keeled sheath. The collar is smooth. Saint Augustine grass (*Stenotaphrum secondatum*)

12—Ligule is a ciliate membrane. The collar is pubescent and the blades are ciliate. Centipedegrass (*Eremochloa ophiuroides*)

13—Stolons and rhizomes long and slender (2–4 mm). Bermuda grass, devilgrass (*Cynodon dactylon*)

13—Stolons and rhizomes short and thick. Bahiagrass (*Paspalum notatum*)

14—Stolons and rhizomes absent to well developed but slender. Forms a dense turf of fine texture. Manilla grass, mascarenegrass (*Zoysia*)

14—Stolons and rhizomes short and thick. Forms a somewhat open turf of coarse texture. Bahiagrass (*Papalum notatum*)

CHOOSING TURFGRASSES

Of the turfgrasses, Kentucky bluegrass is unique in producing a large percentage of seedlings by apomixis.[1] Superior plants are tested for turf characteristics such as low growth, disease resistance, cold tolerance, drought tolerance, and so forth. If they are indeed superior, they can be increased and released as a cultivar (see p. 47).

---

[1]In this type of apomixis, the embryo resulting from sexual fusion of an egg and pollen nucleus aborts, but an embryo is produced from somatic cells of the embryo sac (female tissue). In this way it is possible to get seedlings which are genetically identical to each other and to the female parent.

As a result, there are many clonal cultivars of bluegrass but few or none of the other turf species.

Named clones of other grasses can be vegetatively propagated with sod or stolons, or named cultivars are sexually propagated as a genetic mixture of seed from parents carefully selected to a standard of excellence.

Named cultivars of bluegrasses are excellent, but have the disadvantage of complete genetic uniformity so that a turf is totally subject to any weaknesses. For example, a pure stand of 'Merion' bluegrass appears orange at times because of spores of a species of stem rust disease to which it is particularly susceptible. Consequently, bluegrass seed is often prepared as a blend.

Seeds of four or five cultivars are mixed to take advantage of the good qualities of each while avoiding the extensive damage that could occur when a pure stand of a single cultivar develops a weakness.

When selecting a grass to grow on bare soil—and to grow in intense competition—choose an aggressive grass that can dominate the area. This is sometimes described as a colonizing species. Many such colonizing species can be considered as weeds. In fact, some of the worst weeds in turf of a desired species are other turfgrass species with a different color, habit, or texture.

Colonial bent grass *(Agrostis tenuis)* is a native of northern Europe. Introduced by colonists to the New World, it quickly took over the coastal regions from Rhode Island to Nova Scotia and from Oregon to British Columbia. It also became widespread along the coasts of New Zealand. Kentucky bluegrass *(Poa pratensis)* is thought to have been introduced at Vincennes, Indiana, by the French about 1720. By the end of the Civil War it was established throughout the Middle West, and the westward settlers thought it was a native grass. Similarly, bermuda grass *(Cynodon dactylon)* was introduced into New Mexico in 1750 and within 50 years has spread throughout Southwest.

In any location in the United States, several turfgrasses can be grown and, with good management, all can look good. In a few locations one certain grass is particularly well adapted to the climate. It will gradually invade and dominate lawns in that area. It might be difficult to choose among several grasses when all grow well in an area or to see any reason why one cultivar or another should be preferred. Among good grasses, differences appear only under conditions of stress such as cold, heat, drought, wet soil, shade, low mowing, or disease; each of these take a toll at one time or another. The best species or cultivar for a given location is most likely to be determined, not by appearance or growth habit, but by its ability to survive the few days or weeks in the year when growing conditions are unfavorable. Such characteristics are given in Table 21–1.

Heredity endows certain grasses with the ability to grow and survive stress. Culture determines how well a grass achieves its potential.

SOIL PREPARATION

Soil preparation is a first step in planting a turf, and it includes grading and tilling. Grading should result in a convex swell of the soil surface, free from dips, swales, or pockets where surface runoff water can puddle or pond. Tilling breaks up soil to form a seedbed with good porosity and aeration. In time, tilled soil settles back to its original density, but initial root growth of new turf is aided by the loosened soil.

During tillage, fertilizers and chemical or physical soil amendments should be incorporated in the soil. Chemical amendments include materials such as lime or gypsum used to improve the chemical and physical properties of the soil. Physical amendments are mineral or organic and are generally used to improve the physical properties of a heavy soil or to add organic matter to a biologically impoverished one. Since physical amendments must be used at very high rates to have beneficial effects (often 70 to 90 percent amendment), their use is questionable unless the particular soil problem has been thoroughly analyzed.

Organic amendments serve as food for soil organisms and usually improve soil structure. Peat or manure incorporated into the top 1 to 2 cm (0.4 to 0.8 in) of the seedbed helps seedlings emerge from crusting soils. Incorporation of other organic wastes improves the root zone environment, but some materials can be toxic (e.g., fresh cedar sawdust). Many organic wastes result in severe temporary nitrogen deficiencies in the soil unless the carbon to nitrogen ratio in the waste is less than 20:1 (see p. 181). Composting organic wastes for a time before application usually corrects such imbalances and toxicities.

When the seedbed is a sterile subsoil, added organic matter and nitrogen fertilizer enhances biological activity. Where the soil is shallow, a few centimeters of additional soil are often added. A sterile soil may be a fill soil, or it may result from leveling or from spreading out soil from a basement excavation. Sometimes, developers remove topsoil for sale to boost their earnings from a project.

Competing weeds are a major problem in raising a new turf. They shade and suppress the grass, and removing them requires time and effort. It is good practice to irrigate the seedbed to germinate weed seeds before sowing grass seed. Weed seedlings are then removed or killed with herbicides. The seedbed should then not be disturbed to the extent that new weed seeds are brought to the surface where they could germinate.

Grass seed is available either in mixtures or pure lots. Most mixtures are designed to be sold to home gardeners rather than to professional turf growers. These seed mixtures represent compromises by the seed companies and the mixtures will produce an acceptable lawn irrespective of the management given. The label names the species or cultivar of each grass, the percentage of crop and weed seeds, and the percentage of inert matter (Fig. 21–3).

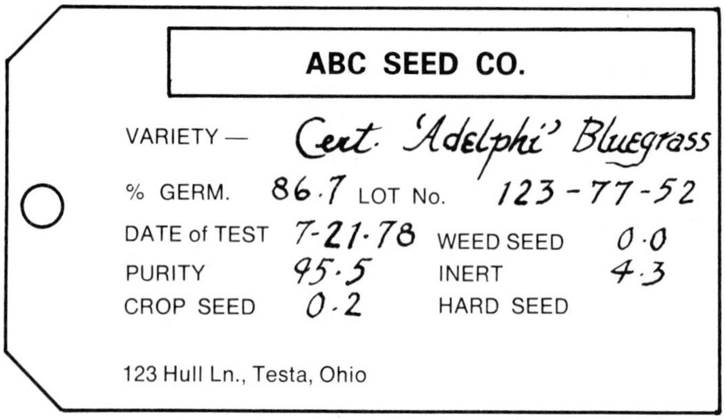

```
┌─────────────────────────────────────┐
│  ┌───────────────────────────────┐   │
│  │        ABC SEED CO.           │   │
│  └───────────────────────────────┘   │
│                                       │
│   VARIETY —  Cert. 'Adelphi' Bluegrass│
│                                       │
│   % GERM.  86.7  LOT No.  123-77-52   │
│                                       │
│   DATE of TEST 7-21-78  WEED SEED  0.0│
│   PURITY       95.5     INERT      4.3│
│   CROP SEED    0.2      HARD SEED     │
│                                       │
│   123 Hull Ln., Testa, Ohio           │
└─────────────────────────────────────┘
```

Fig. 21–3 Example of a seed tag or label showing the information required by law in the United States.

Germination varies from 75 percent for bluegrass seed produced in a poor crop year to over 95 percent for ryegrass seed produced in a good crop year. In general, seed germination should be over 85 percent. Inert matter represents an inevitable amount of chaff or other material. Noxious weed seeds are of small concern in turf as most such weeds are subsequently destroyed by mowing. Turfgrass seed sometimes include pasture grasses of no concern in a meadow or pasture, but they form coarse undesirable persistent weeds in a fine lawn. To avoid contamination by such grasses, seed of sod quality, which is free of such contaminants, is often purchased at a premium price.

When named cultivars of grass are used, certified seed carries a certification statement that the plants were inspected while growing in the seed field and found to be pure and true to type.

In the northern two-thirds of the United States, a typical packaged mixture of high quality seed is likely to contain a large percentage of several cultivars of Kentucky bluegrass. This blend forms the basic grass. To this will be added a blend of red fescue grasses. Red fescue mixes well with bluegrass and grows better in the dry, shady, and less fertile areas. Where winters are not severe, seed of fine-leaved cultivars of perennial ryegrass are also blended with the bluegrass to help the mixture resist seasonal disease problems. A low percentage of a bent grass is usually added. Bent grass finally predominates if the resulting lawn is mowed too short for survival of the blue, rye, and fescue grasses. In addition, bent grass often survives better than the others in areas with wet soils.

Such seed mixtures can be diluted, more or less, with seeds of a filler grass to adjust the price of the mixture. A good filler is meadow fescue (*Festuca pratensis*), which looks like bluegrass during its first few months.

Later it becomes coarse, but tends not to persist in a well-tended turf. Red top (*Agrostis alba*) is often used as a filler but is not desirable because it is coarse and persistent. Some mixtures are blended solely for low price and often contain large amounts of pasture grasses or the less desirable turfgrasses.

A high-quality seed mixture selected by a knowledgeable horticulturist might consist of a blend of the first three grasses mentioned, but not include bent or filler grasses. Bent grass tends to be a weed in bluegrass (and vice versa). Along the coasts of New England, Oregon, Washington, and southern Canada, one might choose a colonial bent grass alone. Bent grasses are well adapted in those regions.

In the southern United States a bermuda grass, centipede grass, bahia grass, or carpet grass lawn might be started from pure seed. St Augustine grass or hybrid bermuda grass could be started from stolons or sod.

SEEDING RATES

Once the kind of grass is chosen, the rate at which to sow the seed is considered. Seedlings become crowded and are unable to develop properly when seed is sown too heavily; it takes a long time to get a mature usable lawn. Sown too thinly, the plants are far apart, with space left for weeds to start. An initial stand of about one plant per 1 to 5 cm^2 (0.4 to 2 in^2) will develop rapidly into a strong turf. If the soil is free of weeds and if seed is sown in season (best, six to eight weeks before autumn frost; second best, early spring), 0.25 to 0.5 kg per are[2] (0.5 to 1 lb per 1000 ft^2) is a good rate to sow seed. In weedy soil, double the rate. If one sows off season (e.g., late fall or early winter) when seed germination is slow, one should increase the rate. For sowing into weedy soil under favorable conditions one should use as much as 1 to 2 kg of seed per are (2 to 4 lbs of seed per 1000 ft^2). The 2 kg rate is high except for tall fescue and perennial ryegrasses. Seed of these grasses is coarse and a still higher rate can be used.

Special machines are available for sowing seed, covering it, firming the soil, and even mulching it. For hand operations, however, either box or cyclone fertilizer spreaders sow seed satisfactorily. The opening is reduced to a size appropriate to the seed. Hand sowing tends to scatter seed unevenly since few persons are skilled seed sowers. When hand sowing is necessary, seed should be vigorously thrown forward in a sweeping arc. The falling seed is more apt to drift into a random

[2] 1 are = 100 m^2. 100 are = 1 hectare.

462

pattern than when seeds are dribbled out close to the ground.

When both large and small seeds are used, they are best sown separately in two operations. On small areas, rather than calibrate the spreader, the operator may prefer to reduce the seeder opening to a low rate, then cover the area two or three times in different directions to insure even coverage. Small amounts of seed are often diluted with sand to adapt the volume of seed to the area covered.

SEEDING DEPTH

Another determination is the depth to cover the seed. Turfgrass seeds are small, varying from about 1 million per kilogram for rye and fescue grasses to over 4 million for bluegrasses and over 10 to 17 million for bent grasses. Relatively few seedlings emerge from depths over 1 cm (0.4 in), and seedling emergence for the smaller seeds is best when they are covered to less than 1 to 5 mm. Uniform coverage is not generally possible. A light raking or dragging of the soil surface after seeds are sown covers seeds at depths from 0 to 5 or 10 mm. Some seedlings on the surface die of desiccation, and some deeper ones fail to grow to the surface, but seeding rates allow for such losses.

TIME TO SOW

At any given geographical location there is a best week in the year in which to sow grass seed. In the southern parts of the United States subtropical grasses are best sown in early summer after annual weeds are removed following their principal flush of seed germination. Seeds of temperate zone grasses are best sown in late summer or early fall so that there is time for the seedlings to become well established and to cover the ground before freezing weather arrives. Fine, vigorous grass stands are easiest to obtain with fall-sown seed. Fall weed problems are less, and shorter days and cooler temperatures reduce evaporation and the need for frequent irrigation. The next best time to sow grass seed in the temperate zones is as early in the spring as the soil can be prepared. Grass seed will germinate and the seedlings grow in cool soil; if a dense stand can be obtained before summer weed seeds germinate, the weed problem is reduced.

After the seed is sown, the seedbed should be rolled, unless one is relying on rainfall to germinate the seed. Rolling firms the soil around the seed and thus encourages capillary movement of available moisture. If there is insufficient moisture for good seed germination, a mulch should be used. A light cover (2 to 5 mm) of clean, weed-free sand or organic waste slows moisture loss from the soil surface. However, light mulching materials such as peat moss tend to wash or blow or to gather in pockets. Such materials are best worked into the top inch of soil before seeding.

SEED GERMINATION AND SEEDLING ESTABLISHMENT

Water is the most critical factor during seed germination, whereas nitrogen fertilizer is more critical during seedling establishment. In warm weather most turf seeds begin to germinate five to seven days after sowing and continue for another week. Bluegrass seed, however, is slower and continues to germinate for a month. Germination is slower in cold weather. During germination, soil moisture is necessary in the surface layer at all times. Differences in available water in the root zone soon appear as differences in color and stand of the grass seedlings. At the same time, excess surface water encourages damping-off pathogens, a complex of *Rhizoctonia, Phytophthora, Pythium, Fusarium,* and other species of fungi. Ideally the top soil layer should remain moist, but if the soil surface is allowed to dry at least once a day mycelia of damping-off organisms shrivel and die.

Once germination has occurred, seedling roots begin to explore the soil. The period between irrigations is gradually extended so there is regular drying of the soil surface between irrigations. Irrigations should wet the soil deeper than the roots extend.

As grass seedlings grow, they may deplete the soil of nitrogen. Growth slows, and the seedlings' color becomes pale green to yellowish. Regular feedings of nitrogen fertilizer to provide about 0.25 kg of N per are (0.5 lb/1000 ft^2) keep the grass growing vigorously and help it suppress weeds. If seedling growth slows and the blade color is dark green, with some red anthocyanin pigment present, the seedbed probably contains insufficient phosphorus for initial seedling establishment.

As the turf grows and becomes thick and tall enough for the first mowing, the most suitable height for mowing must be decided. The mower should be sharp and set for the correct height (see p. 465). A dull mower pulls up seedling plants or tears leaves instead of shearing them. When the new grass is 2.5 to 5 cm (1 to 2 in) higher than the desired mowing height, the soil should be allowed to dry for a day or two before the grass is mowed. If the clippings are scattered and the weather is dry, clippings will shrivel and fall from sight. But if the clippings form heavy clumps and the weather is moist, they should be removed to prevent smothering and disease.

In the United States it may take 5 months in southern states to 12 months in northern states after seed germination for the turf to form a vigorous mature lawn rugged enough for play.

SODDING

Sod is used as a quick alternative to growing turf from seed. Sod is pregrown turf cut to include the adhering top 1 to 2 cm (0.4 to 0.8 in) of soil. A high-quality sod provides a mature weed-free turf of desirable grasses and establishes itself during the first month after planting to give an "instant" lawn. Sod has the same requirements as seed except that the seedbed grade must be lowered next to walks, drives, and buildings to accommodate the thickness of the sod, and some soil must be stockpiled for topdressing the sod to level it and smooth the surface. Thinly cut sod produces roots more rapidly, but dries out faster, than thick sod. Sod cut with 1 to 2 cm (0.4 to 0.8 in) of soil usually has an adequate reserve of moisture to sustain it during transport and a short period of storage and readily produces new roots. Best results from sod come when it is carefully laid in the fall or spring on moist, well-tilled, weed-free soil to which nitrogen and phosphorus fertilizers have been added. Newly laid sod should be watered within an hour. Sod of subtropical grasses establishes itself most vigorously in the summer.

MAINTENANCE GOALS

Maintenance begins once the grass is up. Maintenance consists primarily of mowing, fertilizing, irrigating, and controlling weeds, insects, and diseases. These procedures should be programmed to produce a beautiful dense turf and vigorous healthy plants. As noted earlier, these goals are not completely compatible. There must be some compromise area appropriate to the climate, to the equipment available, and to the level of maintenance one is prepared to pursue.

Not only must the chosen program compromise between beauty and vigor, but there is the added possibility that a goal can be achieved equally well with different management programs. If the desired result is achieved with reasonable economy of effort and resources, no program is more right or more wrong than another. The lack of positive answers makes turf management com-

paratively difficult or confusing for some and challenging to others. For this reason turf culture is best considered in terms of principles rather than applications.

PRINCIPAL TURF MANAGEMENT PRACTICES

There are three principal turf management practices and many secondary practices. The principal ones are mowing, fertilization, and irrigation. Each of these has a large effect on grass growth, and the manager manipulates them to change grass vigor and appearance.

Mowing

Mowing is a regular chore. There are a number of choices to make in mowing; for example, the kind of equipment to use, the mowing height, frequency of mowing, and whether to remove clippings or leave them.

MOWING EQUIPMENT

There are four kinds of modern mowing machines for lawns. Two kinds of power mowers—flail and sicklebar—are used only for large scale and heavy work.

The **flail mower** is used on roadsides and in rough park areas. It has a rapidly rotating horizontal axle that swings a number of vertical knives inside a housing. The mower requires high energy, mows tall grasses and weeds, and reduces them to a mulch.

The **sickle bar mower** resembles a hair clipper with a 2 m (6 ft) horizontal blade. It uses low energy; mows grass, weeds, and woody seedlings; and lays them in a swath with the stems parallel, convenient for raking. This mower is the same type used to mow forage hay.

The **rotary mower** rotates a horizontal blade on a vertical axle at high speeds. It used high energy, cuts by impact, handles tall grass, and may or may not recut leaves to reduce them to a mulch. The rotary mower is available from a 40 cm (16 in) diameter blade home mower to a large industrial size that cuts a swath 1 m (3.3 ft) or more wide.

The **reel mower** uses a series of helical blades that gather the grass and shear it off against a stationary blade known as the bed knife. It is a low-energy mower. It does not cut tall grass well, but it produces the highest quality cut of all kinds of mowers.

Reel and sickle bar mowers cut by a clean cut shearing action with low energy input. Rotary and flail mowers cut by impact. Since the blade must move at a high velocity, they require more energy. Impact cuts are often ragged and the high velocity increases the potential danger of accident.

Mowers should be sharp. Grass recovers from a clean cut from a sharp blade more readily than from a bruising cut made with a dull blade.

Mowing Stress

Mowing places a stress on the grass and reduces its vigor. Root growth is slowed for a few hours to several days depending on the severity of mowing. The total leaf production for the season is reduced by each mowing. Mowing opens the grass canopy to allow more light to enter so more plants can grow in the same area, thus increasing competition. The greatest stress is added to the stress budget when grass is mowed very short. High populations of weak plants result. With exceptionally vigorous and invasive grasses, such as bermuda grass or kikuyu grass, frequent short mowing can be used to deliberately weaken them.

MOWING FREQUENCY

Increased mowing frequency increases stress, but less than does mowing grass short. Stress is greatest when a high percentage of the leaf surface is removed in one mowing. The high stress results from the combination of a short cut with a long interval between mowings. In general, it is not desirable to mow more often than every fifth day during the growing season. An interval of more than about 10 days between mowings is undesirable for a neat, formal appearance.

MOWING HEIGHT

Decreasing mowing height gives the turf a carpetlike appearance, but greatly increases stress. There are upper limits for mowing height. Bent grasses mowed higher than 2 to 3 cm (0.8 to 1.1 in) tend to become puffy and somewhat coarse-textured. When mowed above about 8 cm (3 in), bluegrasses, fescues, and ryegrasses tend to appear open and stemmy. Where an informal or neglected ground cover is wanted on a steep bank or around a vacation cabin, red fescue or zoysia grasses can be left unmowed except for yearly removal of flower stalks. Some zoysia and other subtropical grasses can be mowed less than 2 cm (0.8 in) to control their natural vigor and encourage a renewed, finer-textured growth.

CLIPPINGS

When clippings are left, nutrients are recycled in balanced amounts. Turf appears consistently better fertilized if clippings are allowed to remain and fertilizer added once or twice a year than if clippings are removed and fertilizer applied every few weeks throughout the growing season. There is no particular virtue in removing clippings. A thatch of dead plant materials builds up above the soil layer on many lawns, but thatch results primarily from increased use of fertilizers, water, and pesticides rather than from fallen clippings. If grass is managed so short pieces of mowed leaves fall out of sight between grass blades, turf nutrition benefits from leaving the clippings. But if long clippings fall on a short, tight turf, they appear unsightly and should be removed, but at the cost of greater stress. Grass growth varies throughout the season and mowing should be adjusted to seasonal changes in growth.

Fertilizer

The response of lawns to fertilizer use can be placed in three categories.

NITROGEN

A turf does not become thick and dense without adequate nitrogen from repeated fertilizations. On a new turf, fertilizer applications should add 3 to 5 kg of N per are (6 to 11 lbs N/1000 ft^2) before dense turf is achieved.

Once turf is thick and dense, nutrients can be recycled by leaving the clippings. As some nitrogen is lost through leaching, one or two applications of 0.5 kg of N per are (1 lb N/1000 ft^2) should be applied to a turf early in the fall. But if clippings are removed, nitrogen has to be supplied throughout the year. Other nutrients can be added on a yearly basis.

Nitrogen fertilizers produce a deep green grass of high density but with a shortened root system. Fall color holds later and spring greenup comes sooner with higher levels of N. If N fertilization is overdone, however, susceptibility to disease and stress tends to increase.

PHOSPHORUS AND POTASSIUM

Phosphoric acid (P_2O_5) and potash (K_2O) are mineral nutrients used in macro amounts by turfgrasses. In many parts of the world, soil P_2O_5 and K_2O are adequate and need not be added, although a light application of P_2O_5 in the soil hastens seedling or sod establishment. The local county agricultural agent knows whether local soils are deficient in P_2O_5 and K_2O. If clippings are removed, added phosphorus and potassium will undoubtedly be needed for good grass growth. The frequency and amount of application varies considerably with local conditions. Some turfgrass fertilizers are especially formulated for gardeners who remove lawn clippings. These contain mineral nutrients in about the proportion in which they are removed in clippings (i.e., 5 N:2 P_2O_5: 3 K_2O).

CALCIUM, MAGNESIUM, AND MICRONUTRIENTS

Soils become acid when calcium or magnesium are deficient. Acid soils are generally low in fertility and, in addition, the availability of some nutrients is reduced (see p. 209). Calcium or magnesium fertilizers are seldom used on turfgrasses unless they are required to correct soil (pH) reaction.

In much of the western United States, soils are alkaline (pH over 7.0). This can decrease the availability of phosphorus and certain micronutrients to turfgrasses. Except for using acid residue fertilizers, nothing is usually done to alleviate high pH. As excess sodium adversely affects both soil and plants, calcium as gypsum (calcium sulfate) is applied to counteract the sodium problem (see p. 212).

Micronutrient problems are uncommon in turf if the soil pH is between 5.6 and 6.8. Any micronutrient deficiencies must be diagnosed and dealt with as local problems.

Irrigation

Almost everywhere in the United States rain is deficient at some time during the year; however, in the eastern one-third of the country rain is often excessive. The prin-

cipal value of irrigation is to prevent severe drought stress, but in arid and semiarid areas irrigation is required to make turf culture possible. The management of water can affect weediness of turf, as either overirrigation or underirrigation favors growth of certain weed species.

Proficiency in turf irrigation is attained when knowledge of the soil, climate, exposure, and grass is integrated into a seasonally changing program. Figure 21–4 shows relative amounts of water needed to wet soils of various texture to various depths. Turfgrasses have most of their roots in the top 5 to 10 cm (2 to 4 in) of soil. If keeping grasses in active growth under bright summer skies is desired, this soil depth should be wetted with about two irrigations per week (or three where the weather is windy or hot). Some subtropical grasses are deep-rooted. If the soil is soaked deeply about once a month, these grasses continue to produce some replacement growth. Both growth and water use by the plants are less than when water is applied more frequently. Rooting depth and water use of turfgrasses are affected by many variables, and exceptions are common and many.

Even when severe drought dries turf, some individual plants of all species recover following rain or irrigation. Bermuda grass recovers well in the South and Southwest, and in the north fescues and 'Highland' bent grass recover best. Turfgrass breeding could provide more drought-tolerant selections of most turf species.

Fig. 21–4 Water applied to the soil completely wets it to about the depths shown.

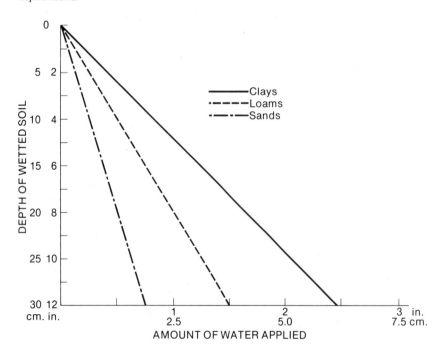

SECONDARY
MANAGEMENT PRACTICES

Pest Control

Problems of pest control are universal (see Ch. 11). Weeds, diseases, insects, nematodes, and other pests all afflict turfgrasses. Since such organisms tend to occupy the enviroment to the full extent of its capacity to support them, turf always has insects feeding on grass leaves and roots, fungi consuming dead grass clippings, and weeds filling in any bare spots of soil.

INSECTS

Insects attacking turf include various caterpillars, beetle grubs, bill bugs, wireworms, flea beetles, chinch bugs, frit flies, leafhoppers, scales, and aphids. In the spider group, mites attack certain species of grass. Of all these, caterpillars and beetle grubs are likely to affect all lawns.

Caterpillars, the larvae of various species of moths, build silk-lined burrows among the grass crowns and feed nocturnally on the leaves. Caterpillars stay close to their burrows, and each thins out a small area of grass around its burrow, about 2 or 3 cm (0.8 to 1.2 in) in diameter. Damage is inconsequential until populations build up to several dozens per square meter. At that point, turfgrass is rapidly thinned out as caterpillars mature and their appetites increase. To treat this problem, grass is mowed to reduce leaf area. Leaves are then sprayed with a stomach poison or contact insecticide (see p. 259). Irrigation water is withheld for a day or two so the insecticide is not washed from the leaves.

Grubs that live in the soil and feed on roots are a different problem since it is difficult to get insecticide into the soil at control levels. In their early growth stages grubs are small and seldom a problem. But in the fall or the spring following their emergence, they are large and hungry and they eat so many roots that patches of grass die. The grubs will be found 2.5 to 5 cm (1 to 2 in) deep in the soil at the edges of the brown dead patches.

WEEDS

A weedy turf is symptomatic of poor management and often indicates that not enough attention has been given to practices that produce a vigorous turf. Weeds are frequent when turf is undernourished, overwatered, or mowed too short. Soils compacted by heavy traffic tend to grow poor turf but do support a large population of certain weed species.

Unwanted perennial grasses are the most difficult weeds to control in turf; broad-leaved annuals are the easiest.

The first step in weed control is to improve management to encourage the grass to grow vigorously. Then weeds can be dug, pulled, or treated with an herbicide. With the grass growing vigorously, space formerly occupied by a weed fills with grass. Control is then successful. If the space is recolonized by other weeds, management practices should be reexamined as the first step in further control efforts.

HERBICIDES

Herbicides (see p. 240) used to control turf weeds should be used cautiously and with restraint. They are plant poisons that, at recommended rates are more toxic to weeds than to the turfgrasses. Herbicides recommended for weed control on turf also injure and cause stress to the turfgrass plants, though the turf outgrows the injury in time. If herbicides are used repeatedly or at times when the grass is under stress or not growing well, the grass might be so retarded that weed problems worsen.

Contact herbicides kill plants they touch and are sometimes used as spot sprays to kill a few individual difficult weeds in a turf. The results, however, are unsightly spots that the grass slowly recolonizes.

Preemergence herbicides control annual weeds by soil application before weed seeds germinate. The herbicide kills seedlings as they push through the treated surface soil layer.

Postemergence selective herbicides are used to remove broad-leaved weeds from grass. Such herbicides are most effective on weeds in the seedling stage. As weeds become older, they become more resistant. Many species of weeds are killed by routine mowing, which continually defoliates them. Weeds that persist tend to be low-growing species that spread out below the mower blades.

If a lawn has only scattered weeds, it is more prudent to dig them out than to mix chemicals and wash spray tanks and thus avoid the risk of spray drift onto garden flowers. The county agricultural agent or local garden center can recommend suitable herbicides to use on lawns.

DISEASES

Three important turf diseases are mildew, rust, and smut. Mildew forms a white dust on grass leaves in the shade and can be controlled only by opening up the area to provide the grass with better light and ventilation. Rust is sometimes prominent in the fall when the orange fruiting bodies discolor grass. Fertilizing with nitrogen usually controls rust. Smut occurs in the late spring or summer as a grass disease that produces a line of black greasy spores along the leaf blade.

Soils contain many saprophytic fungi, which live on dead leaves and other soil organic matter. Some of these are facultative parasites (see p. 247) which cause turfgrass diseases if predisposing factors are present. These diseases are often most common on the best cared for lawns. For example, a *Pythium* water mold destroys turf when fertility, moisture, and temperature are all at high levels. Excess water soaks the soil, causing stress because of poor soil aeration. Add the stress of high temperatures favorable for growth of *Pythium,* and the pathogen rapidly kills the nitrogen-rich grass.

Among diseases that commonly appear on the ordinary lawn are *Fusarium* and *Rhizoctonia* brown patch, both of which form rings of dying turf in the summer. These diseases are predisposed by heat stress on the grass. When snow covers turf for a long time, the melting snow reveals patches of dead grass killed by winter-active organisms, such as *Fusarium* and *Typhula* species. Cold and darkness encourage these organisms to cause turf disease. Long periods of wet overcast weather in the spring or fall favor growth of the *Helminthosporium* ''melting out'' pathogen. Growth of *Sclerotina*, or dollar spot, is favored by nitrogen-deficient grass. Organisms causing all of these diseases are generally present but do not infect the grass until a particular factor or combination of factors develops, such as dark overcast days, winter snow cover, high summer temperatures, or excessively wet or compacted soils.

When fungal lawn diseases are a problem, observation shows that grass areas most affected are those predisposed to fungal attack by such factors as compacted soil, reflected heat onto a lawn by buildings or fences, or excessively short mowing. In the South, hot spots are not a problem for the subtropical grasses; instead, shaded or wet spots lead to diseased turf.

SALT DAMAGE

Salt used to remove snow and ice damages turf bordering sidewalks and roads. The excess salt causes turf injury and often death. The treatment for this problem is to apply lime on acid soils and gypsum on alkaline soils so that calcium replaces the sodium used in the snow-melting mixture.

Scald, a nonpathogenic problem, occurs on turf when puddles of water overheat in the sun, causing heat injury to the grass plants.

COMPACTION

Soil compaction is a stress factor on lawns. On expensive turf, such as a golf putting green, the compaction problem can be solved by removing the loam soil and substituting a sand, which remains porous and well aerated even when compacted. Most lawns soils cannot be easily changed, though, and are treated by cultivation practices. For small isolated areas, the soil can be loosened by inserting a garden fork in the turf and prying up gently to crack and fracture the soil without disturbing the turf. A hollow tined spading fork, built specially for hand cultivating, can be used to loosen and aerate the turf.

TURF CULTIVATION

Cultivation is done mechanically by coring machines or by machines that slice the soil. Coring is desirable for compacted soils. It improves aeration, allows the soil to dry faster, and aids entry of water. The general effect of coring or slicing is to relieve compaction in the surface by moving the compacted layer down to 5 to 7 cm (2 to 3 in) below the surface.

OVERSEEDING

A common practice in the southern United States is to overseed dormant subtropical grasses whose leaves become brown during the winter. To keep the lawn green, seeds of a cool-season species are sown in the dormant turf in the fall. This provides winter color until the warming soil and vigorous spring growth of the subtropical grasses crowds and suppresses the ''winter grass.'' The traditional grass for such overseeding is annual ryegrass *(Lolium multiflorum),* but red fescue or perennial ryegrasses are also suitable and are finer-textured. Other cool-season grasses are also used.

Timing is important in overseeding. There should be enough warm weather yet to come for germination and seedling growth, but if overseeding is done too early, hot weather is likely to encourage growth of damping-off pathogens.

RENOVATION

An old, thin, or weedy lawn can be renovated by introducing new seed with improved management practices. To germinate and become established, the new seed must contact soil. A seedbed for either overseeding or renovation is prepared in the existing turf by raking vigorously, by power raking, or by using a coring, thatching, or vertical mowing machine to tear out a dense dead thatch and weak plants and to expose soil between the grass plants. Seed is sown, then kept moist during germination by sprinkling. Sown seed should also be lightly topdressed with compost or sand. As soon as germination begins, a fertilizer should be applied to provide both nitrogen and a small amount of phosphorus. In renovating, an herbicide can be used in advance to kill undesirable grasses in portions of the lawn.

THATCH CONTROL

Stolons of stoloniferous grasses, such as bent and bermuda grasses, are stems that creep along the surface of the ground and, dying, build up a thatch layer of organic matter resistant to decay. Dried thatch often sheds water, creating areas of dry soil. When thatch is wetted by frequent rains, grass plants tend to produce growing roots in the shallow thatch, but few or no roots in the soil. Such plants do not withstand drought. A deep thatch layer is puffy and attracts offensive insects such as earwigs. Thatch is removed by hand or power raking or by a special thatching machine. Thatching and raking machines have a rotating horizontal shaft. Fingers of spring steel wire are attached to the shaft of the rake. A series of coarse-toothed rotary blades on the shaft of the thatching machine cut or tear out the thatch. Thatching can be done annually as preparation for overseeding. If overseeding is not done, thatching is best done at a season when vigorous growth favors grass recovery.

WATERING IN

When soluble fertilizers or other concentrated chemicals are applied to turf, they can burn the tissues by plasmolyzing the cells. Such chemicals should be thoroughly watered in. Sufficient water is applied to dissolve the chemicals and wash them from the plant and into the soil as a dilute solution.

MISCELLANEOUS MANAGEMENT PRACTICES

When frost heaving has raised grass crowns out of the ground in cold-winter areas, they can be pressed back into the soil by rolling.

Dyes are available for coloring brown or off-colored areas of turf. Such cosmetic practices are considered important when visible turf is a part of television presentations, movies, or public spectacles.

Plugs removed from sod, can be planted into another turf to introduce a new grass species. Plugs are also used to repair small damaged areas. Devices are available to cut and remove plugs of various sizes and to cut similar holes in the soil to receive the plugs.

If grass reaches a stage of incipient wilt, it takes on a recognizable gray cast. Spraying the grass with water will relieve such water stress for a few hours. This can preserve grass from desiccation when thorough irrigation must be delayed because of sports or other activities.

Soil, compost, sand, or other such materials can be applied to turf as a topdressing. Topdressing is used to level an uneven surface, to fill a hollow, or worked into thatch to firm the loose organic surface.

Turf growth is often retarded by competition with tree roots. Judicious pruning of the tree's roots often greatly improves a turf.

Golf, tennis, and bowling greens are precise playing surfaces with grass under severe stress. Special management practices are used to maintain optimum playability of these critical surfaces. These are discussed in detail in some of the cited references.

SEASONAL GROWTH

The seasonality of grass growth is illustrated in Figure 21–5. The dotted curve in Figure 21–5 can be applied either to subtropical grasses growing in southern United States or to temperate grasses growing in northern states or at high elevations. Low temperatures limit winter growth. As the season warms in the spring, growth increases, peaking in the summer months, provided drought is not limiting. After late summer growth declines until it is again stopped by low winter temperatures. Growth of temperate grasses over most of the urban United States is illustrated by the solid line in Fig. 21–5. Depending on winter temperatures, growth can either cease, or slow down in the transition zone. The solid curve is similar to the dotted curve except that during the summer months, temperature optima are exceeded and growth slows. If high temperatures are accompanied by drought, grass can become semidormant, with little growth in summer. As temperatures cool in late summer, active growth resumes. Fall growth of Kentucky bluegrass differs from spring growth. Fall growth

Fig. 21–5 Seasonal growth of grasses. The solid line represents a seasonal growth pattern for Kentucky bluegrass, a typical temperate grass. The start of spring growth occurs earlier or later depending on local climate. Summer dormancy is more or less severe depending on the degree of heat and water stress. The dotted curve represents growth of the subtropical grasses such as bermuda grass. Most of these make their greatest growth during the hottest weather, provided water is adequate. In the southernmost areas of the United States growth continues through the winter at a low rate.

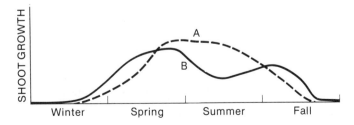

spreads and does not produce as many clippings. Growth comprises mostly new tillers and emerging rhizomes. The spreading form of growth decreases with dropping fall temperatures.

An awareness of the annual growth cycle in local regions can help in planning the best time for various operations. Coring, raking, thatching are operations that should be done when growth is vigorous so recovery will be rapid. Herbicides are best applied during the rising growth curve in spring, when injury to the grass would be low because of cool temperatures, and when rapid growth leads to rapid recovery.

Fertilizing Kentucky bluegrass during the rising growth curve in spring leads to excessive leaf growth. The same fertilizer applied during the rise of the growth curve in late summer results in more tillers and a more spreading growth. New leaves promoted by the fertilizer photosynthesize extra carbohydrate for winter storage.

The falling curve in summer represents a period of stress. This is an appropriate time to apply preventive fungicides—at the time predisposing factors develop. Reduced summer growth results from climatic stress, so the manager is careful not to add extra stress at this time. One would not reduce mowing height nor increase mowing frequency at this time; instead, mow higher and less often.

It is best not to apply nitrogen fertilizer during summer stress. Heat stress results in part from depletion of carbohydrates through higher respiration rates accompanying higher temperatures. Mowing also reduces carbohydrate reserves by reducing the leaf surface available for photosynthesis. Nitrogen fertilizer also depletes carbohydrate reserves, diverting them to protein synthesis. Nitrogen fertilizer at this time puts an extra demand on the plant that can weaken its resistance to disease. Thus,

during summer, it is best to withhold fertilizer or, if necessary, apply it only in small amounts of 0.125 kg/are (0.25 lb/1000 ft²) or in forms that are slowly available to the plant.

When the growth curve rises in the fall, plants can take extra stress. The low spreading growth pattern and the favorable weather enables the turf to recover from all sorts of abuse.

Summary of Management

The principal items of management can be summarized as follows: A fine turf resembling a beautiful carpet costs money and effort. Otherwise, settle for something less. Some effort still can result in an adequate turf. Overmanagement can also result in failure from trying too hard.

A turf consists of a population of many individual plants in competition. Competition creates stress for the individual. For beauty, it is necessary to mow and edge a lawn. Mowing creates another stress on the grass plants. Over much of the United States, summer temperatures are sometimes too high or periods of overcast are too long, resulting in a weather stress on the grasses. Other uncontrolled stresses occur from drought. When all these stresses are summed, they predispose a turf to disease and threaten its survival. To enable a turf to survive those stresses which are beyond control, stressful operations are avoided at certain times of the year. When weather stresses are high, herbicides, fertilizers, too short or too frequent mowing, power raking, and thatching operations are avoided. Stress from compaction on trafficked soils is reduced by coring. Poor aeration or overwet soil is avoided with improved irrigation management. Success is aided by growing those grasses suited to the region.

SUPPLEMENTARY READING

BEARD, J. B. 1973. *Turfgrass, science and culture.* Englewood Cliffs, N. J.: Prentice-Hall.

———. 1975. *How to have a beautiful lawn.* Kansas City, Mo.: Intertec Publishing Corp.

COUCH, H. B. 1972. *Diseases of turfgrass.* Huntington, N.Y.: Robert E. Krieger Publishing Co.

CROCKETT, J. U. 1971. *Lawns and ground covers.* New York: Time-Life Books.

HANSON, A. A., and F. V. JUSKA, eds. 1969. *Turfgrass science.* Madison, Wi.: American Society of Agronomy.

HITCHCOCK, A. S. Rev. by A. Chase. 1960. *A manual of the grasses of the United States.* Agricultural Research Administration. Reprinted by Dover Publications, New York.

MADISON, J. H. 1971. *Practical turfgrass management.* New York: Van Nostrand Reinhold.

———. 1971. *Principles of turfgrass culture.* New York: Van Nostrand Reinhold.

POHL, R. W. 1954. *How to know the grasses.* Dubuque, Iowa: Wm. C. Brown.

ROBERTS, E. C., ed. 1976. *Proceedings of the second interna-*

tional turfgrass research conference. Madison, Wi.: American Society of Agronomy.

SCHERY, R. W. 1976. *Lawn keeping*. Englewood Cliffs, N.J.: Prentice-Hall.

SPORTS TURF RESEARCH INSTITUTE, ed. 1970. *Proceedings of the first international turfgrass research conference*. Bradford, England: Alf Smith and Co.

VOYKIN, P. N. 1959. *A perfect lawn the easy way*. New York: Rand McNally.

WILLIAMSON, J. T., ed. 1960. *Sunset lawn and ground cover book*. Menlo Park, Calif.: Lane Book Co.

YOUNGNER, V. B., and C. M. McKELL, eds. 1972. *The biology and utilization of grasses*. New York: Academic Press.

Landscaping for the Home and Community

History tells us of the hanging gardens of Babylon and the gardens of the Egyptian pharaohs where many plant species were cultivated. Ramses III was responsible for the development of 514 sacred gardens alone. The Romans created gardens with shrubs clipped to resemble objects, grew plants in large containers, created ponds and fountains. They planted groves of pines, maples, oaks, palms, and various shrubs, which were developed into intricate mazes for their amusement. The ancient walled Arabian gardens contained ponds, fountains, fruit trees, and shrubs with fragrant flowers—oases walled off from the harsh desert. An example of such gardens can still be seen in the famous Alhambra at Granada, Spain (Fig. 22–1). These magnificent Arabian gardens were the forerunners of the patios of Spain, which have been copied in the mild southern California and Arizona climates.

During the Italian Renaissance, artists were inspired to create architectural gardens with walls, steps, ponds, and flowing water, but plants did not play an important role in these gardens. This mode of landscaping was carried on into France and Austria where the ultimate formal gardens of the Baroque period were developed. The palace of Louis XIV at Versailles is perhaps the best present day example of this type of formal landscaping. During this era, trees, shrubs, and other plants began to be used in the landscape.

The cottage gardens of England and of early New England contained a great variety of plants, such as vegetables, fruit trees, berry bushes, and small herb plantings. Flowering garden plants such as sweet peas, hollyhock, delphinium, pansies, asters, and chrysanthemums were common. Vines of various species covered walls and trellises. These useful gardens were far different than the formal gardens of continental Europe.

The Eastern gardens of China and Japan had their beginnings long before the Christian era. These gardens showed the people's love of nature. Most gardens were designed around the theme of water and mountains, but were constructed on a small scale in a small area (Fig. 22–2). Both of these cultures designed pictorial gardens that were used for privacy, contemplation, and occasional family ceremonies. The oriental tradition of withdrawal to the privacy of the garden for thought or ceremony may have developed as a form of escape during feudal periods. Many similar gardens with an accent on simplicity and privacy have been developed on the West Coast of the United States by Asian-Americans.

Landscaping means different things to different people. On the simplest level it means some vegetable gardening and the maintenance of the plants established around the home. It may mean a simple landscape design of a small property or home setting. On the other hand, it may mean planning and developing the aesthetic, recreational, and functional uses of a large city park. It may mean landscape engineering or landscape architecture, a profession that encompasses the design, planning engineering, and selection of plant material to fulfill func-

Fig. 22–1   A garden in the Alhambra at Granada, Spain created before the time of Columbus and still maintained today as a tourist attraction. The fountains are supplied with water from the surrounding mountains to create a feeling of coolness. High walls surround the small gardens, which contain small fruit trees, closely clipped shrubs, and plants grown in containers.

Fig. 22–2   *Left:* A pine tree in a Japanese garden kept small by continuous pruning. All proportions must remain the same for the desired effect. Natural rocks and stones play an important part in Japanese gardens. *Right:* Different textures created by gravel, stones, and blocks. *Source:* Landscape Architect Richard Mayer.

Fig. 22–3 During urban renewal, large trees can be spared and new buildings built close to or around them, as shown here. The tree is a *Cedrus deodora* perhaps 50 to 70 years old. Low-growing shrubs and ground covers were planted after the construction.

Fig. 22–4 A rustic landscape plan created for a hotel near Seattle, Washington. A forest feeling is produced by pools, logs, rocks, and conifers. The maintenance is low compared to having lawns and pruned shrubs. This type of landscaping is feasible in western Washington where the rainfall is adequate the year round.

tional and aesthetic qualities. Typically, the landscape architect draws on and coordinates the work of a large staff. Examples of modern concepts in landscape architecture are shown in Figures 22–3, 22–4, and 22–5.

Fig. 22–5 *Top:* A typical, well-maintained highway rest stop providing picnic facilities and pleasant surroundings for automobile travelers. The trees, from left to right, are pines, birches, and purple-leaved plums. *Middle:* One tiny corner of Golden Gate Park in San Francisco, a huge park designed originally in 1877 by John McLaren to keep a three-mile stretch of beach sand from shifting. The park has landscaped facilities for everyone, from playgrounds for children to polo grounds for adults. *Bottom:* The University of California, Davis is a campus of bicycles. Because Davis has a flat terrain, the landscape architect created visual interest by designing two hills and a bikeway with a bridge leading to the library. This effective landscape design was created by first excavating a bike path and then using the soil to make two mounds.

THE HOME LANDSCAPE

Most homeowners design their own landscaping plan and plant hardy plants recommended for their locality. Such a landscape plan usually entails three basic design considerations: the aesthetic qualities, the utility or practical functions of the plan, and the personal preferences of the family. The relative value of these three considerations vary with the homeowner's background or objectives.

Some persons desire beauty in the garden landscape, which may be viewed and enjoyed by the family from a picture window in the living room. The landscape plan can produce splendor in all four seasons with spring flowering shrubs and bulbs, summer annuals or late flowering shrubs, a show of fall color, and finally bare but perhaps colorful twigs laden with fruit for birds in winter. Such an arrangement takes some planning but it can be accomplished by proper plant selection (Chs. 15, 16).

Other persons might want a functional garden with a large expanse of lawn for games, a barbeque area for summer evenings, a vegetable garden, and a small fruit orchard. If there are children, some play area should be provided for them.

Gardening is a popular hobby. Gardening requires intensive maintenance because of weeding, spraying, pruning, and irrigating. It is, however, very gratifying, and it is often combined with an aesthetically beautiful garden by setting off the utilitarian section in the corner. Many kinds of fruit trees are very picturesque and can often be used instead of ornamental trees, thus providing both shade and fruit. Most fruit trees produce spectacular flowers in early spring. However, it must be remembered that both the vegetable garden and the home orchard require full sun for most of the day for maximum productivity.

In any planned garden, privacy from the adjoining property may be strongly desired. Planting high shrubs, not necessarily trimmed to a formal hedge, can accomplish this goal. Both trees and shrubs can also be used to reduce road noise if they are properly selected and placed. A large deciduous shade tree placed on the south side of the home provides good shade in summer, but also allows needed light to penetrate through the bare branches in winter (Fig. 22–20).

Designing the landscaping for the front yard or entry also follows the personal preferences of the planner. One factor should seriously be considered: how much effort is one willing to expend on the public side of the home? Most persons like to have a neat, good-looking landscape because of community pride. However, it should not require so much maintenance that it becomes a burden.

In planning any landscape project, one must consider not only personal preference but budget as well. The cost of shaping the land, building fences, and buying plants could be too great. Many persons do their own maintenance on weekends, but this could also be burdensome. Hiring someone to mow a large lawn area may not be too expensive, but the continued costs of an adequate total maintenance program may be excessive.

Some Problems of Designing a Landscape Plan

The climate of the region dictates the plants to choose for your plan. It is folly to select plants that are not hardy in your area. Chapters 15 and 16 list selected trees and shrubs for the various hardiness zones in the United States. Selections should be based first on the hardiness zone and then on the other characteristics of the plant. Rainfall in the area is also an important consideration in selecting the plants for drought hardiness. If you do not intend to irrigate the landscape plants during the summer in an arid region, it is wise to choose native trees and shrubs of the locality well adapted to local climatic conditions.

Consider the microclimate you live in. There may be an unusual condition for your area; for example, high winds in a canyon. Planting a windbreak can partially solve this problem. Or you may be located in a valley where plants and blooms are apt to be damaged by frosts and freezes because of cold air draining into the area (p. 223). Such a low spot may also be susceptible to water accumulating during the rainy season and leading to soggy soil or flooding. A hillside location may be free from frost and water accumulation, but it could have problems of a shallow soil and erosion. Special plants can be planted to hold the soil.

Soils vary greatly from location to location. The soil may drain slowly, a problem that should be remedied before planting trees and shrubs. The slope of the land should be able to carry away excess water. Soils can be improved by adding organic amendments before planting (p. 181). This partially improves the porosity of clay soils and adds water-holding properties to sandy soils.

The topography or the slope of the land sometimes causes landscaping problems but can also provide opportunities for attractive results. A slope of up to 5 feet in 100 feet (5 percent grade) offers no difficulty for mowing a lawn, but a grade of 12 percent or greater does present problems in placing plants or holding recently disturbed soil. The views from a hillside location should be accented without creating unnecessary maintenance problems. Planting shrubs that require frequent watering or pruning should be avoided on inaccessible sites.

The natural surrounding landscape should be considered in developing a plan. A forest or rural location offers many more possibilities than a small city lot confined by fences or other homes. Plants in the natural surroundings can be blended by selecting native plant material or accent plants that compliment those already established.

In an urban or suburban location homes and lots usually offer a garden of only limited size. It can be a challenge to design an aesthetic plan with privacy that provides a place for meditation, much like the Japanese gardens. Small gardens with ample sun can include a small vegetable plot and flowering annuals in raised beds. Dwarf fruit trees and shrubs should be used instead of the large forms. The size and shape of the garden area help determine what to plant.

The style of home associated with the garden often influences the landscape design. A Spanish style with a patio suggests potted geraniums, hanging baskets, and flowering shrubs. A Cape Cod home goes well with cottage gardens that have a few vegetable plants, herbs, and summer annuals. This design is usually very informal but has great utility. The landscape plan chosen should compliment the home style. Picture windows facing the gardens offer a challenge to provide a continuity between the outdoors and the living room. A deck overlooking the garden could have large container-grown plants and perhaps a window box with annuals for continuity to the garden area.

Planning the Home Landscape

In planning the landscape, both the indoors and outdoors should be considered as one unit. This provides for greater usefulness of the total space. The private home and garden has four functional areas: (1) the public area or entry, (2) the public living area, (3) the private living area, and (4) the work area.

The public entry area includes the front yard or garden area, perhaps a driveway, a walkway to the porch, and the entry. This area may be landscaped to compliment the style of the home or to conform to neighborhood landscaping patterns. Shrubs selected for different heights may offer some privacy but are usually used as foundation plantings to allow the house to blend into the landscape (Fig. 22–6). There usually are front lawn areas of various sizes and perhaps, small hedges along walkways or driveways.

The living area of a home includes the living, dining, family rooms, and study. One of these rooms may extend out into the garden by way of a patio or deck. The patio may be used for year-round outdoor living in mild climates or only during the summer months in cold-winter areas. Some shade trees or a patio cover can be

Fig. 22–6   Three Italian cypress trees only 20 years old have grown too large for the effect once intended by the homeowner. Annual pruning of the leader and the peripheral branches once the trees reached their desired height would have kept them at the desired height and breadth.

provided to make the area more comfortable. A surrounding lawn area reduces both heat and glare. Spring bulbs, flowering shrubs, or flowering annuals can provide the garden, patio, and living room with color.

The private living area includes the bedrooms and baths and, perhaps, a sun porch. Shrubs outside the windows should be selected for showy flowers as well as to give privacy and reduce street noise.

The work area consists of the workshop, laundry, garage, and storage. Shrubs can hide unsightly storage and work areas.

The indoor area can be landscaped, so to speak, with houseplants in selected locations depending on their light requirements (Ch. 18). The entry way to the house could have a potted palm or vine, or it can be an ideal location for an atrium with a grouping of many foliage and flowering plants. A brightly lit kitchen is ideal for plants that require high light. The living or family room should be the location for the family's favorite plants since much time is spent in these two rooms. Plants in containers can be grown under fluorescent lamps if natural light is inadequate. In all cases, care should be taken to provide the foliage plants with adequate natural or artificial light to ensure maintenance of leaf size and color.

Functional Uses of Plants in the Landscape

Plants are used in the landscape for many functional purposes: to reduce glare, to aid in air purification, to settle dust, to diminish noise by absorbing sound, to direct

Fig. 22–7 Plants can be strategically placed in the landscape to reduce glare, to purify the atmosphere, to control noise, or to direct pedestrian traffic. *Source:* Adapted from Robinette, G. O. 1972. Plants, people, and environmental quality. Washington, D.C.: U.S. Government Printing Office.

pedestrian traffic, and to screen certain areas from public view and provide privacy (Figs. 22–7, and 22–8). Plants must reach their mature effective size before they become fully functional.

Glare Reduction

Acoustical Control

Atmospheric Purification

Traffic Control

Glare Reduction

Fig. 22–8 Plants can solve certain environmental problems such as screening an undesirable view, directing a person's attention to interesting views, or providing privacy. *Source:* Adapted from Robinette, G. O. 1972. Plants, people, and environmental quality. Washington, D.C.: U.S. Government Printing Office.

Screening Objectional Views

Progressive Realization

Privacy Control

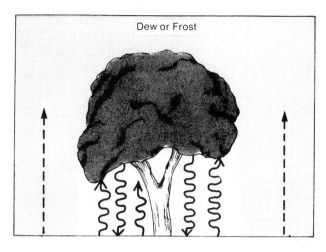

Dew or Frost

Fig. 22–9 Plants grown under trees with leaves are protected from **radiation** frosts. Plants are likewise protected from frosts under eaves or patio covers. *Source:* Adapted from Robinette, G. O. 1972. Plants, people, and environmental quality. Washington, D.C.: U.S. Government Printing Office.

Plants can partially moderate climate by reducing radiation frosts (Fig. 22–9) or acting as wind or snow barriers (Fig. 22–10). In hot, dry, clear climates, radiation from the sun makes for hot days and radiation to the clear sky during the night causes cold nights. Plants, particularly shade trees, can be used as radiation barriers to modify such patterns, shading the soil during the day and preventing excess radiation at night (Fig. 22–11). Shade trees lead to a more even soil temperature as compared to the bare soil. The soil thermometers in Figure 22–11 indicate an equitable temperature under the trees. Soil under tree cover has a more even temperature from season to season than does bare soil exposed to the sun (Fig. 22–12). A concrete wall shaded by ivy or other climbing plants has a much lower temperature than a bare wall open to the full sun. A group of closely planted ever-

Fig. 22–10 Evergreen conifers act as snow barriers if planted properly in relation to the prevailing winds. *Source:* Adapted from Robinette, G. O. 1972. Plants, people, and environmental quality. Washington, D.C.: U.S. Government Printing Office.

Snow

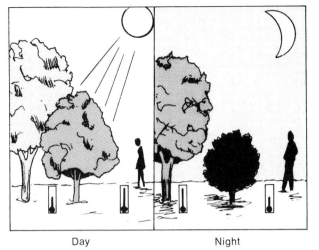

Fig. 22–11 Trees and shrubs moderate wide diurnal variation in ground temperatures. They reduce radiation from the sun and prevent excess radiation from the soil to the sky on a clear, cloudless night. *Source:* Adapted from Robinette, G. O. 1972. Plants, people, and environmental quality. Washington, D.C.: U.S. Government Printing Office.

Fig. 22–12 Broadleaf evergreen trees and shrubs reduce wide seasonal temperature variations by modifying radiation at the soil surface. *Source:* Adapted from Robinette, G. O. 1972. Plants, people, and environmental quality. Washington, D.C.: U.S. Government Printing Office.

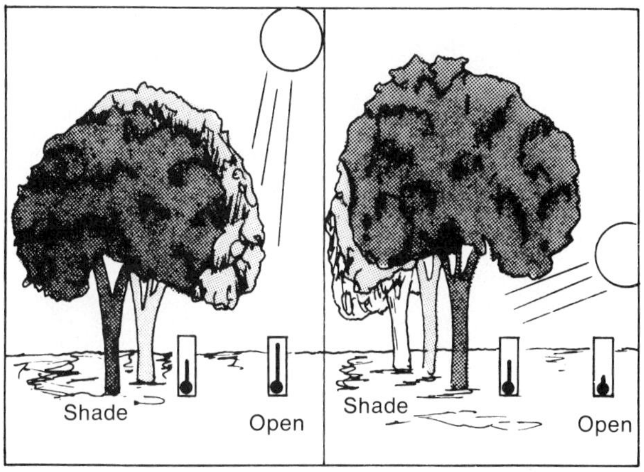

Fig. 22–13 An evergreen tree or shrub planted near a wall facing south or west creates a dead air space that becomes "insulation" to maintain even summer temperatures. *Source:* Adapted from Robinette, G. O. 1972. Plants, people, and environmental quality. Washington, D.C.: U.S. Government Printing Office.

green trees next to a wall can create a dead air space (Fig. 22–13) much like the dead air space in the walls of the house. This tends to maintain an even temperature between the plants and the wall.

Plant materials that can be used for these various functions are available in many forms, shapes, and sizes. A few of these are depicted in Figure 22–14. Landscape architects must be aware of the hardiness of plants that can be functionally used in their plans. In addition, they must supply specifications for soil mixes, drainage requirements, and maintenance care. The ultimate size of these plants must be known if they are to be used to their best advantage. Figure 22–15 shows growth habits of some specimen plants often used in the landscape. These tree and shrub characteristics must be known for choos-

Fig. 22–14 Plants of all shapes and sizes can be chosen to create effects or fulfill functions to beautify the environment. *Source:* Adapted from Robinette, G. O. 1972. Plants, people, and environmental quality. Washington, D.C.: U.S. Government Printing Office.

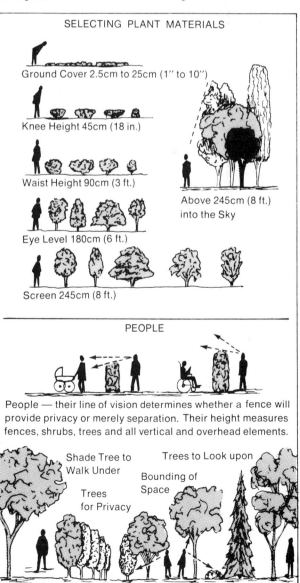

Plant Arrangements in Space
The individual plant is a specimen in which, through spacing, it becomes fenestration,* hedges, baffles, tracery, clumps, canopy.

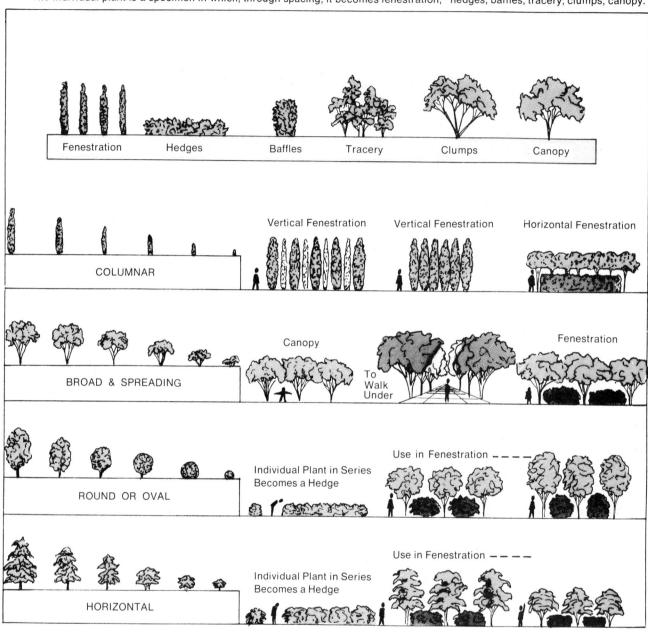

*Arrangement and proportioning of openings.

Fig. 22–15 Groups of trees or shrubs can produce desired effects if chosen wisely. These groups are based on trees of various shapes (see Tables 15–1, 15–2, 15–3, and 16–1). *Source:* Adapted from Robinette, G. O. 1972. Plants, people, and environmental quality. Washington, D.C.: U.S. Government Printing Office.

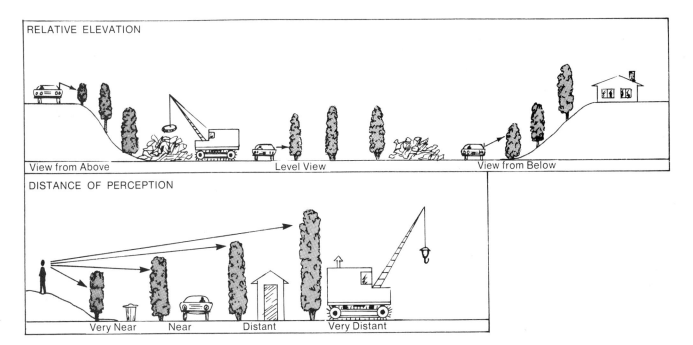

Fig. 22–16 Examples of how trees and shrubs can be used to hide undesirable views. *Source:* Adapted from Robinette, G. O. Plants, people, and environmental quality. Washington, D.C.: U.S. Government Printing Office.

Fig. 22–17 Formal hedges used on a small scale as screening or privacy control. *Source:* Adapted from Robinette, G. O. 1972. Plants, people, and environmental quality. Washington, D.C.: U.S. Government Printing Office.

Privacy Control Planting

Screen Planting

ing the most desirable plant for the plan. Some of these characteristics are listed in Tables 15–1, 15–2, 15–3 and 16–1.

Plants are often used to screen undesirable activities or unsightly surroundings (Fig. 22–16). People are becoming more aware of their surroundings, and city, county, and state governments now request certain industries to screen ugly scenes from public view. In the 1960s a highway beautification act was initiated in the United States to encourage attractive landscaping of federally funded highways.

Hedge plants are used for privacy in many small and large gardens (Fig. 22–17), a practice of ancient origin. These same hedges also act as windbreaks and sound barriers.

Areas of high air pollution are usually plagued by unpleasant odors. Plants are useful in ridding the air of such odors (Fig. 22–18) by absorbing them and thus purifying the air. Plants also help remove dust from the air. Dust particles attach to the leaves, and the next rainfall washes the dust away (Fig. 22–19). Carbon dioxide (CO_2) is a waste gas exhaled by humans and animals but absorbed by plants. The plants convert the CO_2 to sugars by photosynthesis and give off pure oxygen in the process. This is a part of the balancing cycle between plant and animal life.

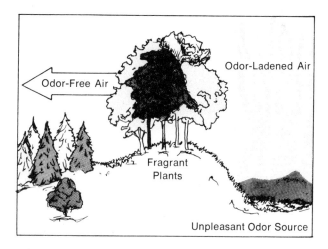

Fig. 22–18 Plants can help reduce some unpleasant odors in the atmosphere. *Source:* Adapted from Robinette, G. O. 1972. Plants, people, and environmental quality. Washington, D.C.: U.S. Government Printing Office.

Fig. 22–19 Plants together with rain can help clean the air. *Source:* Adapted from Robinette, G. O. Plants, people, and environmental quality. Washington, D.C.: U.S. Government Printing Office.

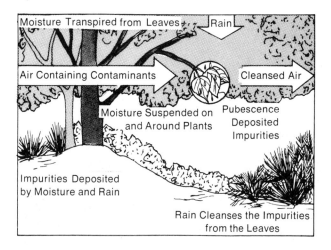

Fig. 22–20 Trees and shrubs placed in the proper way can reduce the sun's radiation and glare throughout the day. *Source:* Adapted from Robinette, G. O. 1972. Plants, people, and environmental quality. Washington, D.C.: U.S. Printing Office.

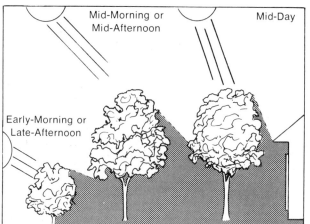

Glare can be controlled by shading created by trees during different hours in the day (Fig. 22–20). The mature plant size necessary to be effective can be calculated from the angle of the sun during the four seasons. Shade is usually desired in summer but not in winter, making deciduous trees and vines most effective (Fig. 22–21). Species of trees vary in the shadow patterns they cast (Fig. 22–22). Density of shade can change with the leaf canopy and species. Plants also vary in the amount of solar radiation they reflect. In general, green plants reflect only about 10 to 25 percent of the radiation (Fig. 22–23), whereas a white building reflects about 90 percent and unpainted concrete about 35 percent.

Glare from street lamps may be blocked by planting trees as illustrated in Figure 22–24. People who live at the end of a dead-end road or a cul-de-sac find hedges or tall shrubs a necessity to reduce glaring lights from oncoming cars.

Windbreaks of various sorts have been used for centuries to slow or divert strong winds. Studies have been made on the effect of solid versus incomplete barriers on the velocity and pattern of the wind (Figs. 22–25 and 22–26). Tall shrubs and hedges used as windbreaks reduce wind speed by increasing the resistance to the wind flow. Coniferous trees, as shown in Figure 22–26, that have thick dense branches clear to the ground are the best all-year plants for windbreaks.

Plant Selection

The landscape plan is only partially complete until the particular plant species have been chosen to fulfill the functions intended in the plan, but a knowledge of plants and their behavior is essential in making landscaping selections. Certain kinds of shrubs can be trained to become formal hedges because they become dense after pruning. Tree selection is based on their ultimate size, shape, shade, and other desirable characteristics. Dense shade trees, like the maples or beeches, discourage or eliminate most plant species under them. However, many kinds of trees produce filtered shade so that certain shade-requiring shrubs or flowering annuals flourish beneath them. Plant selection, of course, must be based on hardiness zone (Fig. 10–4), but the particular environmental conditions of the planting site must also be considered. Finally, choices need to be made on growth habit necessary to enhance the landscape plan. Partial lists of annual bedding plants, bulbs, common trees and shrubs available for making such selections are given in Chapters 15, 16, 19, and 20. There are, of course, many

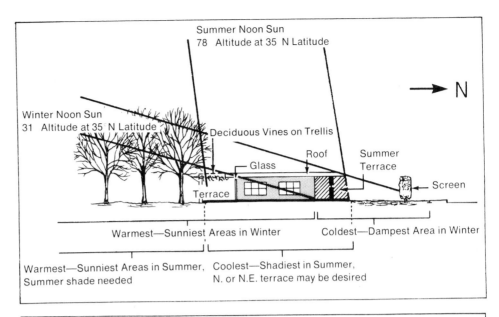

Fig. 22–21 For maximum comfort, the design of the house and the placement of trees, shrubs, and vines must be considered. The plan shown here gives good protection from the sun in summer and allows penetration through the deciduous trees of the sun's rays in winter. *Source:* University of California Cooperative Extension.

Summer Noon Sun
78° Altitude at 35° N Latitude

Winter Noon Sun
31° Altitude at 35° N Latitude

Deciduous Vines on Trellis

Roof

Summer Terrace

Glass

Screen

Terrace

N

Warmest—Sunniest Areas in Winter

Coldest—Dampest Area in Winter

Warmest—Sunniest Areas in Summer, Summer shade needed

Coolest—Shadiest in Summer, N. or N.E. terrace may be desired

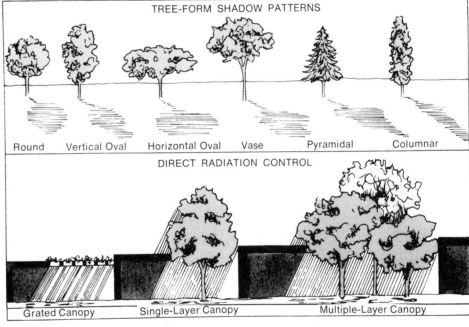

Fig. 22–22 Each tree species has a unique shadow pattern. Trees also vary in the density of shade they give. Knowledge of these shade characteristics is valuable in developing a landscape. *Source:* Adapted from Robinette, G. O. 1972. Plants, people, and environmental quality. Washington, D.C.: U.S. Government Printing Office.

TREE-FORM SHADOW PATTERNS

Round   Vertical Oval   Horizontal Oval   Vase   Pyramidal   Columnar

DIRECT RADIATION CONTROL

Grated Canopy   Single-Layer Canopy   Multiple-Layer Canopy

Fig. 22–23 Plants can modify solar radiation by diffusion and shading. *Source:* Adapted from Robinette, G. O. Plants, people, and environmental quality. Washington, D.C.: U.S. Government Printing Office.

Fig. 22–24 The glare from street lights can be modified or completely controlled by planting trees in the proper location.

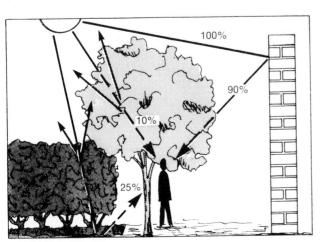

100%

90%

10%

25%

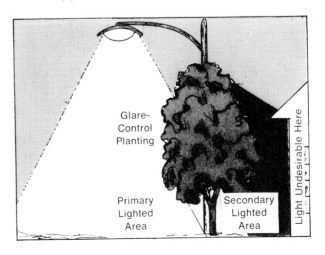

Glare-Control Planting

Primary Lighted Area

Secondary Lighted Area

Light Undesirable Here

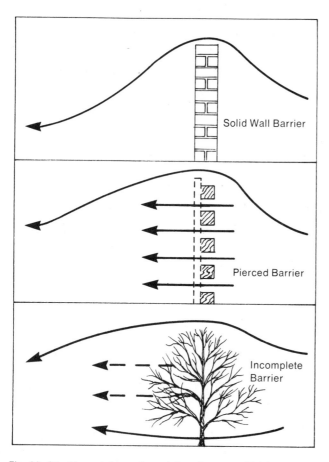

Fig. 22-25 How winds are directed through or around barriers.

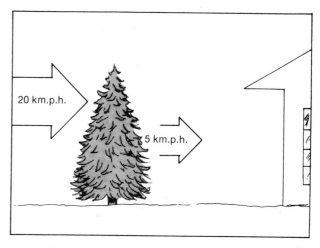

Fig. 22-26 Coniferous evergreen trees or shrubs effectively cut wind velocities next to structures when planted at a distance from the house which is at least twice the height of the barrier. *Source:* Adapted from Robinette, G. O. 1972. Plants, people, and environmental quality. Washington, D.C.: U.S. Government Printing Office.

more species and horticultural cultivars than those listed that can be used in the various climatic regions. It is very important that a careful, detailed study be made before finally selecting the specific landscape plants to be used for the various aesthetic and functional purposes discussed in this chapter.

SUPPLEMENTARY READING

CARPENTER, P. L., T. D. WALKER, and F. O. LANPHEAR. 1975. *Plants in the landscape.* San Francisco: W. H. Freeman & Company Publishers.

COFFIN, M. C. 1940. *Trees and shrubs for landscape effects.* New York: Scribner's.

CROCKETT, J. U. 1971. *Landscape gardening.* New York: Time-Life.

CROWE, S. 1959. *Garden design.* London: Country Life.

ECKBO, G. 1950. *Landscape for living.* New York: F. W. Dodge.

———. 1956. *The art of home landscaping.* New York: F. W. Dodge.

McDOWELL, J., ed. 1975. *Ideas for Japanese gardens.* Menlo Park, Calif.: Lane.

McELWEE, E. W. 1966. *Landscaping Florida homes.* Univ. of Fl. Bul. 179C.

ROBINETTE, G. O. 1972. Plants, people and environmental quality. Washington, D.C.: U.S. Government Printing Office.

VERITE, M. 1963. *Gardens through the ages.* London: Odham.

UNIT

III

MAJOR AGRONOMIC, VEGETABLE, AND FRUIT CROPS

Agronomic Crops Grown for Food or Feed

Worldwide food scarcity in the years ahead is a real possibility unless measures are taken to control population, increase food production, or both. The need for a more efficient agriculture is clear, and a likely area for success is increased grain production.

Increased food production must come primarily from crop plants with high caloric output per unit area of land. Generally these crops are high carbohydrate producers, such as cereal grains, bananas, potatoes, cassava, and sugar crops (see the table in the Appendix). World grain production in 1978 was estimated at 1.2 million MT or about 0.75 kg (1.7 lb) per person per day—three-fourths of which was corn, rice, and wheat. Cereal grains are a concentrated source of energy easily processed, stored, and distributed. They provide the world's population with over 80 percent of its total food calories. The word *cereal* comes from the name of the goddess Ceres, who is said to have given wheat to the early civilizations. All of the world's most important agronomic crops are discussed in this chapter in alphabetical order.

Barley (*Hordeum vulgare* L.) GRAMINEAE
(7, 8, 25, 48, 55, 56, 58, 59, 60, 63, 71)

Barley, a widely adapted small-grain cereal, is used for human food, livestock feed, malting (beer and other alcoholic products), and pearling.[1]

Barley and wheat are the most ancient of all cereal grains, both dating back 7000 years. Barley apparently was grown in Mesopotamia in prehistoric times (68). It is believed

[1]Whole kernels of grain from which the outer husk has been removed by polishing. Partially pearled grain is sold as "pot" barley, and kernels pearled to pure endosperm are called "pearled" barley.

to be native to southwestern Asia, but many wild species now grow in Ethiopia and southern Tibet. There are two main barley species: *H. vulgare*, the common six-rowed barley (six rows of kernels per spike) grown mainly for food; and the two-rowed barley, whose ancestor is probably *H. spontaneum*, used in many parts of the world for malting and pearling (8). The crop is classified according to its growth habit as spring or winter barley.

Barley is widely adapted because of its drought resistance, tolerance to alkaline and saline soils, and early maturity. Some cultivars grow in subarctic climates, some grow only in the temperate zones, and others grow in the subtropics. The crop may ripen in as few as 60 to 70 days but normally 90 to 120 days are required. The principal production areas are the United States, USSR, China, Europe, Canada, and India. In the United States barley is grown mostly in North and South Dakota, California, Montana, and Idaho. The area where barley is grown has increased considerably worldwide but declined somewhat in the United States over the past decade.

Over 100 cultivars of barley are grown in the United States and Canada. In selecting a cultivar, the yield, disease resistance, winter hardiness, straw stiffness, nonshattering characteristics, and ultimate use are considered.

Barley grows best on a well-drained, fertile loam soil. Its roots penetrate 90 to 180 cm (3 to 6 ft) in a permeable soil. The seedbed must be prepared thoroughly, with fall plowing preferred in some areas.

Seed is drilled or broadcast at the rate of 70 to 100 kg/ha (60 to 90 lb/ac) when the crop is to be irrigated. But on highly fertile, irrigated land, however, some farmers sow up to 160 kg/ha (145 lb/ac). The rate of seeding is reduced to 35 kg/ha (31 lb/ac) on unirrigated fields.

In most of the barley-growing areas of the United States, Europe, and Asia, the crop is seeded in the early or midspring months. In the western United States and Canada, Australia, and New Zealand, barley is seeded in the late fall months. In

Fig. 23–1 Lodging, as shown here, is the breaking of stems, causing the plant to fall over. This condition causes serious crop loss of grain in such grain crops as barley, rice, and wheat. It also makes harvesting difficult and expensive. Excessive nitrogen fertilization causes the heads to become too heavy with grain. Lodging is aggravated by strong winds.

California, spring barley cultivars are actually used but are seeded in the late fall because of the mild winters.

A complete fertilizer is often applied at seeding. In the western United States, additional nitrogen is used for irrigated crops. Excessive use of nitrogen is avoided to reduce lodging (Fig. 23–1) or to grow grain to be used for malting.

Barley is grown in California during the winter when most of the rain falls; therefore less irrigation is needed than for other California-grown crops. If rain has not fallen by planting time in late fall or early winter, 30 to 50 percent of the crop land is generally irrigated before planting.

Some tillage for weed control is done before planting, but most weeds are controlled by postemergence selective herbicides.

Diseases that cause serious losses include powdery mildew, stripe mosaic, yellow dwarf, leaf scald, stem and leaf rust, and Fusarium blight. The parasitic fungus *Helminthosporium* and a smut (*Ustilago*) also attack barley.

Barley has numerous insect pests. The principal ones are wireworms, chinch bugs, and green bugs. In some areas at various times grasshoppers, army worms, aphids, and thrips are also troublesome.

Barley is harvested with a combine in the late spring or early summer. In the northern Great Plains, Idaho, and Montana it is cut in August or September. In Europe or Asia it is sometimes harvested by hand. Yields vary widely from about 1000 to 5000 kg/ha (900 to 4500 lbs/ac). Some farmers like to burn the stubble after harvesting the grain to reduce trash in fields and help control some diseases.

Beans (*Phaseolus* spp. L., *Vigna* spp. Sari, *Vicia* spp. L.) LEGUMINOSAE (1, 8, 17, 25, 42, 54, 58, 59)

Several species of field beans and related field peas or cowpeas are grown as minor crops for food. These include broad beans (*Vicia Faba*), red beans, pink beans, and kidney beans (*P. vulgaris*), mung beans (*Vigna radiata*), black-eyed peas, and cowpeas or field peas (*Vigna unguiculate*). The black-eyed pea is one of the oldest crops. Native to Central Africa, it spread to Asia and the Mediterranean areas of Europe. The red kidney bean grown in the United States originated in Central and South America and was unknown in Europe before Columbus. Bean cultivars can be grown for dry seeds only where the climate is cool enough and the growing season is frost-free. Such areas are found in the temperate regions of North and South America, Europe, Asia, Africa, and Australia. In the United States most of the dry beans are grown in the western and northwestern states.

The soil requirements, culture, pests, and harvest of dried beans are similar to those of soybeans and green beans (see p. 511 and 534).

Corn (*Zea mays* L.) GRAMINEAE (3, 6, 8, 11, 14, 25, 34, 36, 50, 52, 58, 59, 61, 71)

The botanical origin of corn is vague (see p. 61), evidence coming mainly from specimens discovered in caves in the Tehuacan Valley of Mexico in 1961. The earliest samples appear to date to 5000 B.C. (36). The modern history of corn begins with the first voyage of Columbus, who discovered not only the Americas but also corn. Later explorers found Indians growing corn in all parts of the Americas from Canada to Chile. The first Indians to plant and cultivate the crop probably lived in Peru, Bolivia, and northern Chile.

Corn is a tall annual plant with strong erect stalks, a fibrous root system, long narrow leaves spaced alternately on opposite sides of the stem, and separate male and female flowers on the same plant (monoecious).

Several botanical varieties of *Zea mays* have economic importance (25):

1. Dent corn (*Z. mays* var. *indentata*) is the principal commercial feed type grown in the United States. The grain is normally yellow or white (hominy), hard and horny, with a starchy endosperm in the crown of the kernel. Endosperm does not cover the crown entirely, causing a dent to form when the mature kernel dries.
2. Flint corn (*Z. mays* var. *indurata*) kernels are not indented when dry. They contain little soft starch. The ears are long and slender with fewer rows of large broad kernels. There are some small-kernel types.
3. Flour corn (*Z. mays* var. *amylacea*) is also known as soft or squaw corn. It has little or no horny endosperm. This type is preferred by Indians because it is easily ground into flour or chewed; otherwise it has limited commercial value in the United States.
4. Sweet corn (*Z. mays* var. *saccharata*) has wrinkled, translucent seeds with much sugar.
5. Pod corn (*Z. mays* var. *tunicata*) kernels are enclosed in husks or pods and the ears are covered with husks.
6. Popcorn (*Z. mays* var. *praecox*) is an extreme type of flint corn with an excessive proportion of horny endosperm. The kernels and ears are smaller than dent corn.

Although corn originated in the Americas, it is now also grown in Canada, the USSR, Chile, Australia, and South Africa. It is grown from below sea level in the Caspian Plain to altitudes above 3000 m (9150 ft) in Peru. Limited amounts grow where seasons vary from 70 days, as in parts of Canada, to the continuous tropical climate of Colombia.

Optimal production of corn requires an ample and continuous supply of available soil moisture. The annual precipitation in the U.S. Corn Belt varies from 60 to 115 cm (24 to 45 in), with about one-fourth falling during the three summer months. Corn is a warm-season crop, requiring high temperatures during the day and night. Best summer daytime high temperatures range from 20°C to 47°C (68°F to 80°F), and with nighttime lows no less than 14°C (57°F). Seeds do not germinate well at temperatures lower than 10°C (50°F), and temperatures above 40°C (104°F) slows pollination.

The growing season varies according to cultivar, but on the average, about 130 to 140 frost-free days are usually needed. Some cultivars mature in 90 days. Corn requires abundant sunlight for optimum yields and does not grow well in shade. Day length markedly affects the rate of maturity. Cultivars adapted to short days ripen earlier near the equator (shorter day length), while those adapted to long days sometimes fail to mature before frost in the northern areas. It has been estimated that, in summer ears of a given cultivar ripen one day earlier for each 15 km (9 mi) north (south in Southern Hemisphere) of the equator.

In the United States, corn is best adapted to the Midwestern states, where the term *Corn Belt* appropriately applies to Iowa, Illinois, Indiana, Nebraska, Missouri, Ohio, North and South Dakota, and Minnesota. Some corn is also grown in eastern Kansas and Montana and in western Kansas under irrigation.

The development of hybrid corn by isolating inbred strains with desired characteristics (see p. 81) was a significant advance in our efforts to produce more food. Before 1930, hybrid seed was not available and farmers saved their own seed each year. Today, practically all corn seed is hybrid seed from cultivars developed for a certain location and a set of local environmental conditions. Before hybrid cultivars, yields of 1800 to 2800 kg/ha (1600 to 2500 lb/ac) of shelled corn were considered good. Today, 9000 to 11,000 kg/ha (8000 to 10,000 lb/ac) or more are not uncommon.

Corn grows best on well-drained, fertile loam soils, but if adequately fertilized it can do well on a wide variety of soils. The best soil is porous, friable, well supplied with organic matter, and not subject to waterlogging. Corn grows best at pH 5, slightly acid, but can do well in soils with higher pH. In the Corn Belt, corn is sometimes followed in a rotation by an inoculated[2] legume crop (*17*).

The seedbed is commonly prepared by plowing 15 to 20 cm (6 to 8 in) deep with a moldboard plow, followed by sufficient disking and harrowing to provide a firm clodfree seedbed (see Fig. 9–2). Interest in minimum tillage has stimulated many innovations in seedbed preparation to reduce tillage costs and minimize soil compaction. One method is to plant directly into freshly plowed soil. The tractor wheels are ad-

[2]Legume seed treated with nitrifying bacteria (*Rhizobia*) that are capable of oxidizing atmospheric nitrogen to nitrates for the plant's use (p. 208).

Fig. 23–2 Corn stalks are generally disked after the grain has been harvested. It is difficult to cover the stalks by plowing unless they have first been chopped and mixed with soil. *Source:* Allis-Chalmers.

justed to the desired row spacing so that the planter shoes run in the tire tracks (Ch. 9). Some farmers disk the stalks and plow them under in the fall, then use minimum tillage the following spring (Fig. 23–2). If fertilizer is added at planting time, one-half of it is drilled 5 cm (2 in) below and 5 cm (2 in) to the side of the seed. The other half is applied with the first cultivation.

Commercial corn fields are planted by drilling seed in rows 90 to 100 cm (36 to 40 in) apart. In some areas (the South and the eastern Great Plains) corn is planted in ridges with a lister (Ch. 9). Planting hybrid seed in rows as narrow as 50 cm (20 in) increases yields even further by increasing the plant population (*59*).

A crop of 2500 kg (5600 lb) of corn grain removes 70 to 80 kg (150 to 175 lb) of nitrogen, 25 to 30 kg (55 to 65 lb) of phosphoric acid (P_2O_5), and 32 to 36 kg (70 to 80 lb) of potash (K_2O) plus a small amount of secondary and micronutrients from one hectare (2.5 ac) of land. To maintain the original fertility level, more than this amount of nutrients must be added to the soil because leaching losses also must be resupplied. Solid fertilizers are usually incorporated into the soil, and nitrogen (liquid or gas) is often injected or sidedressed along the side of the plant row. Some farmers apply part of the fertilizer in the fall or spring before the corn is planted and the remainder at planting time.

More corn fields are being irrigated in the Corn Belt states of Kansas, Nebraska, and Minnesota. In other states, irrigation would sometimes be profitable. Some fields in New York receive supplemental irrigation during drought. In California and other arid states, it is essential to irrigate corn.

Cultivation for weed control is done only when weeds are small and easily killed. Excessive tillage or deep cultivation injures the corn roots. In areas where weeds are a serious problem, herbicides are also used.

Stalk rots are devastating diseases of corn. Diploida rot and northern leaf blight are serious diseases in the Corn Belt. Ear smuts are troublesome in some areas. Southern leaf blight has been serious in the South, and it reached epidemic proportions in the Corn Belt in 1972. Stewart's leaf blight is a serious bacterial disease, primarily affecting sweet corn.

Fig. 23–3 Corn is harvested mechanically with a combine that picks the ears from the stalks, then removes the kernels from the cob. *Source:* Allis-Chalmers.

Destructive insects include corn earworms, European corn borer, chinch bugs, corn rootworms, and grasshoppers.

Practically all U.S. corn is harvested as grain for livestock feed when the moisture content is about 20 to 30 percent, then artificially dried for storage. Most corn is harvested by picking and shelling in the field with a picker-sheller combine that separates the ears from the plant and shells the kernels from the cobs (Fig. 23–3). In parts of the Midwest, corn is harvested at a moisture content of 25 percent or more, shelled in the field, and tightly packed in specially lined, airtight silos. This procedure, known as high-moisture grain storage, produces a high-quality feed without the expense of drying. Propionic and acetic acids are popular preservatives for corn. Some farmers grind the high-moisture grain. Hogs or cattle are sometimes used to salvage corn that the harvest machinery missed. Some corn farmers feed their grain to hogs or cattle and market their crop through these animals, especially in those years when bad weather delays or prevents machine harvest.

In some areas, ear corn is stored in cribs with slotted sides to permit maximum ventilation for drying (the kernels are shelled from the cobs later), but this method has become less and less popular. Safe storage is possible in cribs when kernel moisture content is about 20 to 22 percent. Field-shelled corn almost always requires artificial drying to a moisture content of 14 to 16 percent before storage in metal bins. There is a price penalty for corn sold with excessive moisture. Also, corn stored at a high moisture content is subject to heat damage or spontaneous combustion.

A considerable amount of corn is made into silage. The entire plant—stalk, leaf, and ear—is chopped in the field while still green, transported to silos, and tightly packed for storage (p. 524). In the silo, it is allowed to ferment to ensure preservation before it is fed to cattle.

Oats (*Avena sativa* L.) GRAMINEAE
(8, 15, 25, 58, 59, 71)

Oats grew wild in Western Europe during the Bronze and Iron Ages. From there oat culture spread to other temperate zone regions *(15)*. Today, oats are grown principally for animal feed but some are processed for human food.

Oats grow 60 to 120 cm (2 to 4 ft) tall, with fibrous root systems. The flowers are borne on panicles, either nearly symmetrical or one-sided. The panicle is made up of numerous (20 to 120) small branches and spikelets composed of two glumes and usually two florets (except hull-less cultivars, which contain more).

Most oats are produced in the temperate zones. Important oat-producing countries are the United States, the USSR, Canada, Germany, France, and Poland. In terms of land area planted and harvested for grain and hay, the leading states in the United States are: South Dakota, Minnesota, Iowa, North Dakota, Wisconsin, and Texas.

Northwestern Europe, some northern sections of the United States, and southern Canada produce a few late-maturing common white oats. The Soviet Union grows the small-kerneled yellow cultivars. Red oats are grown in the Mediterranean area, California, and the warmer parts of the southern states. A hull-less oat (*A. nuda*) is grown in India and other parts of Asia.

Disease problems have stimulated the introduction of many resistant cultivars. Some recent oat cultivars include: Alamo, Beedee, and Radar; some older favorites are Garry, Rodney, and Suregrain.

Oats have less demanding soil requirements than most crops and do fairly well on highly acid, less fertile sandy soils. They also grow well on fertile soils.

Most oats grown in the United States are sown as early as possible in the spring, often being the first crop planted in the new season. There are many plantings of winter oats in the southern states.

Oats generally follow corn in a crop rotation in the Corn Belt. They are often sown with other grasses or legumes as a companion crop and are used later for forage. Oats are fairly easy to grow, and seedbed preparation is minimal—disking two or three times and harrowing once. Oats are planted by broadcasting the seed or by drilling. The seeding rate varies widely but an average is 90 kg/ha (80 lb/ac). Oats are also grown for fall or winter grazing by seeding in early fall at a rate of 100 to 150 kg/ha (90 to 135 lb/ac).

In most areas oats are fertilized as needed to obtain good crop yields. Nitrogen is especially needed if the crop is planted so early that excessively low soil temperatures retard or prevent soil nitrification. Applications of 45 to 55 kg/ha (40 to 50 lb/ac) of nitrogen plus the same amount of phosphoric acid (P_2O_5) and potash K_2O are often used. Excessive nitrogen tends to increase lodging.

Generally, the value of the oat crop does not justify expensive weed control but if a severe problem occurs, herbicides can be applied.

In most areas of the world oats are attacked by a multitude of viral and fungal diseases, with rusts and smuts being the most prevalent of the fungus offenders. Although smut is controlled by seed treatment, there is little protection against these hazards other than growing resistant cultivars. Other serious diseases include yellow dwarf, blast, and septoria leaf spot.

Insect pests include grasshoppers, cutworms, aphids, thrips, armyworms, and green bugs.

Practically all oats are harvested by combines at maturity. In some areas a fraction is harvested for hay or silage for livestock feed before the grain matures. In these cases the crop is mowed and windrowed for curing. Oat straw makes excellent bedding for livestock and the straw is sometimes harvested for that purpose.

Fig. 23–4   Young lowland rice plants growing through the water held by earth levees in a flooded rice paddy. *Source:* U.S. Soil Conservation Service.

Rice (*Oryza sativa* L.) GRAMINEAE (4, 5, 8, 13, 25, 28, 29, 30, 38, 39, 40, 41, 47, 64, 67, 70)

Knowledge of the origin of rice is ancient and cloudy (see p. 62). Some writings pertaining to rice found in the Orient and India date as far back as 2800 and 3000 B.C. The relative importance among corn, rice, and wheat as a food for humans has long been debated. Each has been prevalent in certain areas. The early natives in the Americas had corn, those in the Far East (China, Japan, India) had rice, and those of the Fertile Crescent (eastern Mediterranean) area had wheat.

The cultivated plant is a semiaquatic annual grass that grows erect. It has narrow parallel-veined leaves. Spikelets are borne on a loose panicle and each contains one flower enclosed by the lemma and palea. The flower has six stamens and one ovary.

Rice is classified several ways. Based on the chemical characteristics of the starch and grain aroma, rice can be classified into three groups: (1) waxy or glutinous types (starchy endosperm contains no amylose[3]); (2) common types, more or less translucent nonglutinous (endosperm contains one-fourth amylose and three-fourths amylopectin[4]); and (3) aromatic or scented types, grown in India and southeast asia. The glutinous types, consisting entirely of amylopectin, are not important in the United States but represent about 10 percent of the total production in China and 8.4 percent in Japan. Worldwide, the first two types comprise over 90 percent of the total rice grown.

Rice cultivars are classified as lowland rice (continuously or pond flooded) or upland rice (nonirrigated, or irrigated but not pond flooded continuously) (Fig. 23–4). Upland and lowland do not refer to elevation. More than 80 percent of the world's rice grown is the lowland type. Rice cultivars are also classified on the basis of kernel characteristics into short-, medium-, or long-grain types. The average length of unhulled kernels is 7.2, 8.4, and 9.9 mm respectively. Most Asian people who eat rice prefer the short-grain types (also known as pearl rice) because the kernels are sticky when cooked. Most Americans and Europeans prefer the nonsticking, long-grain types.

Another rice classification is based on maturity. The rate of maturity is genetically controlled and is measured by the number of days required for the plants to reach 50 percent heading. In California, very early maturing cultivars require less than 90 days, early cultivars require 90 to 105 days, and late-maturing cultivars require more than 105 days (*13*). In the southern United States, the same cultivars respectively may mature in somewhat fewer days.

Rice is also classified on the basis of its cultured adaptation as japonica or indica types. The japonica cultivars are usually short-grain and adapted to a temperate climate, while the indica types are long-grain and tropical. The so-called miracle rices, developed by the International Rice Research Institute (see p. 62), are of the indica type.

Rice is grown only where ample water is available. Important production areas lie along great rivers in northern Africa, China, India, Japan, Pakistan, Indonesia, Thailand, and Burma. Rice is also grown in Italy, Argentina, and Korea. About 95 percent of the total U.S. crop is produced in six areas (*4*): the Grand Prairie in east central Arkansas; northeastern Arkansas; the Mississippi River delta, covering 34 counties on both sides of the Mississippi River in Louisiana, Arkansas, and Mississippi; southwestern Louisiana near the Gulf of Mexico; the Coastal Prairie of Texas along the Gulf of Mexico; and the Sacramento Valley in the northern part of California's Central Valley.

The 1976 annual report of the U.S. Rice Milling Association reported that of a total of 1,030,468 ha (2,544,368 ac) planted in the United States more than 60 percent was the long-grain type, represented by Starbonnet, Labelle, and Lebonnett cultivars. Thirty-two percent was of the medium-grain type, represented by the cultivars Calrose, Nato, and Saturn. Colusa and Caloro were the two short-grain cultivars, (Table 23–1).

Rice grows well on light, medium, or clay soils. For best yields, the fields are flooded for most of the growing season. Clay, clay loam, or silty clay loam soils are most frequently used to conserve water by minimizing seepage losses. Even organic and light-textured soils are used provided they have an underlying hardpan or claypan that will prevent water seepage losses. The soil pH ranges between 5.0 and 7.5 for satisfactory plant nutrient availability. Upon flooding, acid or alkaline soils shift 0.5 to 2.0 pH units toward neutrality. Rice cultivars vary in their tolerance to salinity, but all are adversely affected by excessive salts.

In most Asian countries, the centuries of simple, nonmechanical methods of flooding, terracing, leveling, and other wetland rice cultural operations have produced soils with com-

---

[3]Amylose is a component of starch characterized by the lack of tendency of its aqueous solution to gel.

[4]Amylopectin is a component of starch characterized by the tendency of its aqueous solution to set to a stiff gel at room temperature.

Table 23-1 Rice Cultivars Harvested in the United States

Cultivar	Percentage of Total Crop Harvested
LONG-GRAIN	
Starbonnet	21.18
Bluebelle	3.30
Belle Patna	0.23
Dawn	0.44
Bonnet 73	0.85
Labelle	23.94
Lebonnet	10.96
Toro	0.17
Percentage of total harvest	61.07
MEDIUM-GRAIN	
Saturn	8.84
Nato	9.96
Calrose	10.13
Nova	1.26
Vista	0.90
Brazos	1.44
Percentage of total harvest	32.53
SHORT-GRAIN	
Pearl (Colusa and Caloro)	5.71
Nortai	0.69
Percentage of total harvest	6.40

Source: 1976 annual report of the United States Rice Milling Association. Published in *Rice Jour.* 79 (Nov.-Dec. 1976).

mon characteristics. The immediate soil surface is oxidative and the subsoil strongly reducing (oxygen deficient). These soil conditions create what is called a **rice paddy soil**.

Soil is usually worked wet or flooded to prepare land for rice production in the humid tropics. The wet fields are plowed with implements drawn by water buffalo (Fig. 23–5). The fields are harrowed crosswise and lengthwise until the soil is well puddled (a soft muddy mass). This helps create a hardpan that limits water percolation and facilitates the hand transplanting operation.

Fig. 23–5 Working the flooded field is the usual method of preparing land for rice in the humid tropics of southeast Asia. Most Asian farmers using simple equipment drawn by water buffaloes plow and harrow the flooded field until the soil is puddled. This helps control weeds, creates a plow pan which reduces water percolation losses, and makes hand transplanting easier. *Source:* R. L. Haaland.

Fig. 23–6 The seedbed for rice is prepared much the same as the seedbed for other small-grain crops in the United States. On the heavy soils of California or delta soils of the Mississippi River, seedbed activities are performed with offset disks or heavy tandem disks, as shown here. The usual sequence is two, three, or more times with tandem disks at varying time intervals. *Source:* Marlin Brandon, University of California Cooperative Extension.

In most developed countries, seedbed preparation is completely mechanized (Fig. 23–6). Disk plows are used when the soil is hard and dry, and moldboard plows are more satisfactory in moist soils.

The method of seeding determines whether the seedbed surface is left smooth or rough. If rice is to be seeded into water by airplane, the soil surface is left rough (Figs. 23–7 and 23–8). If the seed is to be drilled, the surface needs to be smooth and mellow. In the South, after the levees are constructed, a spiketooth harrow is passed over the seedbed to provide the desired preparation before the seed is drilled or broadcast.

Fig. 23–7 Several methods are used in the United States to seed rice. On dry or moist soils rice can be drilled or broadcast and disked to cover. Rice is also broadcast by plane into flooded paddies, as shown here. The pilot is using a flagman at each side of the field as a guide to where seeding has already been done. This is a typical biwinged airplane used for seeding crops, spreading fertilizers, and applying herbicides or insecticides. These planes are equipped with at least a 600 hp engine and have been structurally modified to enable them to carry a 450 to 675 kg (1000 to 1500 lb) load. In order to apply the seed accurately, pilots fly only 3 to 10 m (10 to 33 ft) above the field. *Source:* University of California Cooperative Extension.

Fig. 23-8 Trucks are equipped with special funnel-shaped buckets to load rice seed, fertilizer, herbicides, or insecticides into the bins on airplanes.

Fig. 23-9 Most of the world's rice, except in the United States, is transplanted by hand into flooded puddled fields as shown here. The seeds are started in seedling beds and then after 30 to 50 days the young plants are transplanted. *Source:* R. L. Haaland.

More and more rice farmers worldwide are recognizing and using the improved, high-yielding rice cultivars developed by the International Rice Research Institute in the Philippines. The choice of seed is an important consideration, and many rice-growing areas have seed certification programs designed to provide high-quality seed. Such seed is varietally pure, produces at least 80 percent germination, and is free of weed seeds and other impurities.

For years, California growers have soaked rice seed in water for 24 to 48 hours before planting by airplane. The seeds imbibe water and initiate germination. The imbibed water makes the seeds heavy, and they sink quickly through the water into the seedbed. Dry seeds flown onto flooded paddies would float and drift toward the levee walls if the wind were blowing. Some California growers now use dry seed that has been coated with a sticking agent to hold a mixture of talc (which adds weight so the seeds will sink in water), needed micronutrients, a fungicide, and a selective herbicide *(40)*. The dry coated seed eliminates many physical, biological, and ecological problems affecting soaked seed, yet permits rice growers to plant the flooded field by airplane. Some of the disadvantages of using presoaked seed are that they weigh significantly more than dry seed, therefore increasing the number of loads that must be flown onto the fields. Such seeds are more subject to physical damage, especially if they have started to germinate. Herbicides or fungicides are not glued to presoaked seeds—they must be sprayed from the air with the possibility of drifting to other fields. Paddies are seeded in the spring when the weather is warm enough for seed germination and seedling growth.

In the southern rice states, the rate of seeding is about 100 to 125 kg/ha (90 to 112 lb/ac) if drilled and about 130 to 170 kg/ha (115 to 150 lb/ac) when broadcast by plane. California growers, planting in water, seed from 140 to 225 kg/ha (125 to 200 lb/ac). Several methods of planting rice are available. The seed can be broadcast over water by plane, broadcast on dry land by plane or end-gate seeder and then covered by disking and harrowing, or drilled 4 to 5 cm (1.5 to 2 in) deep in the soil with a grain drill. Broadcasting by plane is most popular because it is fast and requires less machinery. Rice seedlings are not transplanted into muddy paddies in the United States, as in most of the other world rice producing areas (Fig. 23–9).

In addition to the 16 essential mineral nutrients (p. 206), rice needs silica. In Japan, rice yields increased 9 percent by addition of 1000 kg/ha (900 lb/ac) of calcium silicate ($CaSiO_3$). Tropical rice soils in the Far Eastern rice-growing countries of Burma and Thailand are often deficient in nitrogen and phosphorus. Even so, except in Japan, Korea, and Taiwan, little commercial fertilizer is used, resulting in low yields. Fertilizer tests sponsored by the United Nations' Food and Agriculture Organization in developing Asian countries have shown that in addition to nitrogen, phosphorus and potassium are needed, yet most of the developing Eastern areas do not use and cannot get adequate amounts. Although commercial fertilizers are not generally used in all rice-producing countries, most countries have established recommended rates of application *(28)*.

In the United States rates of fertilizer application vary widely with location, culture, and soil types. In some areas of Louisiana and Texas, proper use of fertilizers increases rice yields up to 50 percent. In fact, practically all commercial production areas in these states use fertilizers. In the Grand Prairie region of Arkansas, as much as 180 kg/ha (160 lb/ac) of nitrogen is applied, which is higher than in most other states. Phosphorus or potassium is best applied only when soil tests indicate their deficiency. In the delta area of Arkansas and Mississippi, nitrogen is applied at about 45 to 90 kg/ha (40 to 80 lb/ac). Rice growers in all areas generally agree that all of the phosphorus and potassium and a part of the nitrogen are best applied at seeding time. In general, the ammonia forms of nitrogen are preferred to the nitrate forms, but sometimes mixtures of ammonium nitrate and urea are used. In California, nitrogen applications vary from 40 to 180 kg/ha (36 to 160 lb/ac) generally applied as ammonium sulfate, urea, and anhydrous ammonia, or ammonium phosphate. Applications of 40 to 60 kg/ha (36 to 53 lb/ac) of phosphoric acid (P_2O_5) are about average in California, Louisiana, and Texas.

In areas with alkali spots (see Ch. 8), rice can suffer severe iron deficiency. This can be corrected by applications of 100 to 200 kg/ha (90 to 180 lb/ac) of ferrous sulfate ($FeSO_4$). Soils with high pH and zinc deficiency produce alkali disease. This can be corrected by applications of 10 to 20 kg/ha (9 to 18 lb/ac) of elemental zinc applied as zinc sulfate ($ZnSO_4$) or Zn EDTA chelates (see p. 215).

Fig. 23–10   Small hand driven tractors have contributed largely to the reduction of hand labor required to produce rice in southeast Asia. Compare the 2200 man hours of labor without tractors necessary to produce one hectare of rice (900 hr/ac), with 1790 hr/ha (725 hr/ac) with small hand driven tractors, to the mechanized methods used in the United States where 1000 liters of petroleum fuels plus 12 workhours can produce one hectare (400 gal + 4.75 hr/ac) of rice. *Source:* R. L. Haaland.

Fig. 23–11   Under mechanized rice culture, seedbed preparation usually begins shortly after harvest with disposal of the current year's rice straw and stubble. Some states permit the burning of rice straw in the field, as shown here. This procedure is sometimes used for other cereal grains, such as wheat and barley. To minimize air pollution, daily weather data determine the ''burn'' days, when certain designated areas can be burned. Farmers are assigned ''burn'' days and are notified a day in advance if they can burn. The straw is also burned to destroy certain diseases (stem rust in rice). *Source:* Marlin Brandon, University of California Cooperative Extension.

Fig. 23–12   Rice paddies are flooded before seeding by air. Levee (bund) construction is an important preparation procedure for growing rice because levees are a key device for regulating water depth in rice fields. They are constructed on the contour, high and compact enough to hold water at a depth of 8 to 15 cm (3 to 6 in). A levee gate is installed in each levee to allow water to flow gently without erosion from one paddy to the next. *Source:* Marlin Brandon, University of California Cooperative Extension.

Rice culture has always been a labor-intensive endeavor in Eastern countries. It was estimated that as late as 1948 in Japan 2223 hours of labor were required to produce one hectare of rice (900 hr/ac). Since then many small tractors have been introduced, but production still requires about 1790 hr/ha (725 hr/ac) (Fig. 23–10). In the United States and Australia, only 18.5 hours/ha (7.5 hr/ac) are needed because of mechanization. This reduction in back-breaking hand labor is possible because of the substitution of machines powered by petroleum fuels for human labor. It probably would not be feasible or even desirable, however, for all countries to mechanize rice production to the extent it is in the United States because many rice-growing countries are overpopulated and the people need jobs, farms are too small for efficient use of large machines.

Since continuous rice growing depletes the soil organic matter and causes the physical condition of the soil to deteriorate, rice is sometimes rotated with other crops. But because of the cost of seedbed and levee preparation, two, three, or more rice crops are sometimes grown before the land is rotated.

Most U.S. rice is grown on land that is relatively level and slopes slightly toward some drainage outlet. The exception is upland rice, which is sometimes grown on rolling land.

In some areas, rice stubble is disked immediately after the crop is harvested to give the straw more time to decompose, and thus aid in next year's seedbed preparation. Whether disking is done in fall or early spring, a well prepared seedbed is needed. Many rice growers burn the stubble after harvest to help control some rice diseases (Fig. 23–11).

It is important that levees be constructed to hold water on the land at an average uniform depth of 8 to 15 cm (3 to 6 in). The divisions created by the levees in the field are called paddies or bays (Fig. 23–12). Each levee follows a contour; that is, a line along which all points are of the same elevation. The difference in elevation between two adjacent contours is from 3 to 6 cm (1.1 to 2.3 in). Whenever winds cause sufficient wave action to wash out contour levees, other levees are constructed perpendicular to the direction of the prevailing winds. In the South, levees are built with gently sloping sides and can be crossed with tillage and harvesting eqiupment; in California, levees are high with steep sides, and each paddy is harvested as a single field. In the South, the base of the levee is made with a three-bottom plow, followed by a levee disk mounted on a large tractor. In California, a large V-shaped disker is pulled by two or more crawler-type tractors to construct levees. Freshly made levees are often 75 to 90 cm (30 to 36 in) high and settle to 40 to 50 cm (16 to 20 in) after compaction.

Levees made from plastic sheeting have been used experimentally and found to be feasible and economical *(30)*. Reports show that the plastic levees save considerable money over soil levees.

Water covers the soil from seeding to maturity on all rice grown in the United States, but good drainage is also essential. Since the water requirement of rice is high, a dependable supply of good-quality fresh water is essential. In the southern states 90 to 120 cm (3 to 4 ft) of water is needed during the growing season, and in California 2 to 5 m (6.5 to 16 ft) is used.

Weeds are one of the major causes of low rice yields. In most countries, weeds are partially controlled by regulating the depth of the water. When rice is planted in rows, several kinds of push-type weeders are used and a large amount of rice is hand-weeded. In Japan, as late as 1961 hand weeding accounted for 26 percent of the before-harvest labor. Since 1945 there have been remarkable developments in chemical weed control (p. 243). Today, rice farmers all over the world have a wide choice of chemicals available to control problem weeds. Since chemicals move easily with water, especially when paddies are being drained, extreme care is needed to avoid environmental pollution.

Rice farmers lose a part of their crop each year to diseases. It has been estimated that in the southern United States diseases reduce rice yields about 5 percent annually (5). The principal diseases are seedling blight and seed rot. Brown leaf spot is a serious disease in Texas and Louisiana. Blast is a fungal disease in the southern states that causes long, narrow necrotic spots on rice leaves. Stem rot, caused by a soil-borne fungus, is important in Arkansas, Louisiana, Texas, and frequently in California. Several root rot diseases are troublesome.

Insects and other animal pests are often serious problems to rice growers. Some of the serious insect pests are the rice leaf miners, rice water weevils, midges, rice leaf folders, armyworms, leafhoppers, thrips, and water scavenger beetles.

It is strongly recommended that the preventive use of insecticides be avoided and that the chemical control of insect pests be restricted only to registered compounds that are effective. Pesticides should be used only when the insects have increased to damaging numbers.

In some regions, mosquitoes are a byproduct pest of rice culture since the paddies provide a good breeding ground for them. They are somewhat controlled biologically with a tiny fish called the mosquito fish (Gambusia affinis).

Animal pests that attack rice include tadpoles, shrimp, crayfish, muskrats, and some waterfowl.

Practically all rice grown in the United States is harvested with large self-propelled combines. It is cut when the moisture content of the grain is about 20 to 22 percent; the rice is then artificially dried to about 12 to 14 percent before storage or milling.

The combines are equipped with large tanks from which the threshed rice is augered into self-propelled carts called bankouts (Fig. 23–13). These transport the grain from the field to large trucks waiting at the roadside to transport the grain to the dryer (for milling, see p. 279). Small amounts of rice for seed are sometimes cut, swathed, and threshed from windrows.

Fig. 23–13 In the United States, rice harvest is completely mechanized. When the accumulation tank on the combine is full, the grain is transfered quickly into a bankout carrier traveling alongside the combine and the harvesting continues nonstop. The bankout carries the grain to a waiting truck for transport to the grain elevator for drying and storage. *Source:* Marlin Brandon, University of California Cooperative Extension.

Wild Rice (*Zizania aquatica* L.) GRAMINEAE
(8, 16, 18, 43, 45)

Wild rice, a member of the grass family, is not closely related to common rice (*Oryza sativa* L.). Minnesota is the leading production state in the United States. Wild rice has been used there for food by American Indians for more than 300 years. The seeds sprout under water from grain that fell into the water the previous year, germinating in the spring and producing a single root and a thin submerged leaf. Later in the season the ribbonlike leaves float on the surface of the water. During the summer a flower stalk elongates and emerges from the water, bearing female flowers at the top of a spike with many drooping male flowers below them. This arrangement almost guarantees cross-pollination between plants. By late summer the plants are 90 to 120 cm (3 to 5 ft) tall and covered with leaves. The top grains ripen first and those below ripen subsequently over a period of about 10 days more. In Minnesota, mechanical harvesting of wild rice is prohibited by law; therefore harvesting is done by hand with flails. The heads are bent over boats in the water and the kernels beaten into the boats with flails. About 25 percent of the grain is harvested—the rest is lost into the water—but this lost portion does provide the seed for next year's crop. Wild rice yields roughly 112 kg/ha (100 lb/ac), which yields about 45 kg (40 lb) of processed rice suitable for food. The crop is considered a culinary delicacy and is relatively expensive. Because of the price, some farmers in Minnesota and California are attempting to cultivate wild rice (16). The cultural techniques used are similar to those for common rice, except harvesting, which must be done several times because of the uneven ripening and shattering. New shatter-resistant cultivars are being developed, but commercial production of wild rice remains limited and mostly experimental.

Rye (*Secale cereale* L.) GRAMINEAE
(8, 25, 58, 59, 62, 71)

Apparently, rye originated in southwestern Asia. There is evidence of early cultivation in western Asia, but rye is not mentioned in early Egyptian records. Several species have been found growing wild, but only one species is grown as a crop in the United States.

Until the early 1900s rye was grown principally in Europe and Asia to make bread. Because of its extreme hardiness, it is widely grown all over Europe, Asia, and North America. However, it is the least important of all the cereals and is often grown only where environmental conditions are unfavorable for other cereal crops.

Rye is used for human consumption, livestock feed, hay, pasture, silage, and a cover crop for soil improvement, and the manufacture of some distilled beverages.

There are both spring and winter cultivars, but since rye is very winter hardy, most of the rye grown in North America is fall seeded.

Rye is cross-pollinated and self-sterile; hence there are few true cultivars. Rosen, an old cultivar, was one of the first developed for the U.S. Corn Belt. 'Dakota' was selected for its winter hardiness for the Dakota areas, 'Emerald' was released in Minnesota, 'Pierre' in South Dakota, and 'Svalof Fourex,' a Swedish cultivar, was introduced into California. 'Wren's Abruzzi' is grown on large areas in the southern United States for forage.

The cultural practices for rye are similar to those for winter wheat (p. 502), but because of its winter hardiness rye is often seeded two weeks later than winter wheat. Rye is seldom fertilized except when grown on poor soil, in which case it responds well.

Ergot, a fungal disease, results in black bodies in the grain called sclerotia. The sclerotia are unpalatable and, if present in quantity, are poisonous to animals, including humans. They are, however, used in pharmaceuticals such as ergosteral, ergotoxine, and ergotamine for migraine headaches and various obstetrical practices. Other fungal diseases causing varying yield reductions are snow mold, leaf and stem rusts, stalk and head smuts, blotch, and some root rots.

Many of the same insects that attack barley, oats, and wheat attack rye.

Harvesting entails threshing with combines, as with other small-grain cereals.

Fig. 23–14 Because sorghums are grown for grain, silage, pasture, syrup, and straw for brooms, the sorghum breeder has a variety of objectives. These short-stemmed, dwarf grain cultivars have been bred for adaptation to mechanical harvesting, early maturity, and resistance to lodging and shattering. These mature heads of grain are ready for harvest.

Sorghum (*Sorghum bicolor* Moench) [*S. vulgare* Pers] GRAMINEAE (2, 8, 11, 20, 26, 50, 53, 58, 59, 66, 71, 72)

Sorghum is believed to have originated in Africa. Grain sorghums are known by several names, such as durra, Egyptian corn, great millet, or Indian millet. In India sorghum is known as jowar, cholum, or jonna. In the United States, different types of grain sorghum are known as milo, kafir, hegari, feterita, shallu, and kaoliang.

In both Africa and Asia, sorghum is one of the leading cereal grains. This important crop was introduced to the United States in the early part of seventeenth century from Africa. It is also grown in India, Pakistan, China, Manchuria, and to some extent in the USSR, the Middle East, Argentina, Australia, and southern Europe. Resistant to heat and drought, it is best adapted to warm areas. The principal U.S. production areas are Texas, Oklahoma, and Kansas, but significant acreages are grown in other states, including Nebraska, Colorado, New Mexico, Arizona, California, Missouri, and South Dakota.

There are hundreds of cultivars. Agronomically, sorghum is a common name applied to all plants of the genus *Sorghum*. However, the plants do have markedly different characteristics and uses. Thus some authors have grouped the cultivars into four types (71):

1. The **grain sorghums** (Caffrorum Group) are the nonsaccharine plants, including milo, kafir, feterita, hegari, and hybrid derivatives, among others. These plants are grown for grain used principally for poultry and livestock feed (Fig. 23–14). The grain is similar in composition to corn except it is somewhat higher in protein and lower in fat. Some grain is ground into meal and made into bread or porridge. Whole grains are sometimes popped or puffed for cereal. Grain sorghums are also used to make dextrose, starch, paste, and alcoholic beverages. The stalks have a dry pith and are not very juicy, except for milo and kafir, which are semijuicy, dual-purpose types of grain and forage.

2. **Sweet or forage sorghums** or sorgos (Saccharatum Group) are used mainly for forage and silage and to make a colored molasses. The stalks are juicy, sweet, and are chewed by many people in various countries. This type is grown principally in the United States and South Africa.

3. **Broom corn** (Technicum Group) is a sorghum grown for its brush, which is manufactured into brooms. This woody plant has dry pith, little foliage, and fibrous seed branches 30 to 90 cm (1 to 3 ft) long.

4. **Grass sorghum** (*S. sudanense*) or Sudangrass is grown for pasture, green chop, silage, or hay. Some of the new hybrid sorghum-Sudangrasses have up to 90 percent of the food value of corn silage for dairy or beef cattle (2). Sudangrass is usually ready to pasture in five to six weeks, but to avoid prussic (hydrocyanic) acid poisoning, it is at least 45 to 60 cm (18 to 24 in) tall when grazed. The acid in the form of glucosides occurs in young plants only a few cm tall, branches in the leaf axils on injured plants, and in new shoots. It is highly toxic because it inhibits cellular oxidative processes.

Plant breeders have developed numerous new grain sorghum hybrids and cultivars, each adapted to a local region or set of conditions, Many cultivars are designated by a number based on their rates of maturity. Often these numbers are preceded by initials of the state for which the cultivar is recommended; for example, NB-123, (Nebraska). Some have RS for "regional sorghum" like RS-610. Or a seed company release will bear the initials of the company; for example NK-125 (Northrup King). Cultivars are even named for a given location where they are particularly well adapted; for example, Meloland. The most important production factor in grain sorghum is selection of the correct cultivar for a given area.

496

Grain sorghum grows best on fertile sandy loam soils, but with adequate fertilizers it succeeds on a wide variety of soils. The best soils are porous, friable, well drained, and pH neutral. Sorghum is more tolerant to sodic (alkali) and saline soils than most field crops, but yields are reduced by about 50 percent on soils with high (more than 12 mmho/cm) soluble salts *(51)*.

Sorghum land is generally plowed either in the fall or spring with a moldboard or disk plow, then disked and harrowed until the seedbed is firm and mellow. If the previous crop was wheat or sorghum, the stubble is often disked before plowing.

Sorghum seeds need a warm soil to germinate, ideally 18°C (64°F) at planting depth. In the Great Plains, from northern Texas to South Dakota, and in the western Corn Belt area, planting begins in mid-May to early June. In the arid Southwest, sorghum is planted from midspring to midsummer, but late plantings sometimes do not mature.

Factors that result in poor stands are cold soil, poor-quality seed, poorly prepared seedbeds, soil crusting, or improper adjustment of planting machinery. Some farmers try to prevent poor stands by planting more seed than recommended. Assuming a fertile soil, good seedbed, and full irrigation, it is estimated that maximum yields are obtained with rows 25 to 50 cm (10 to 20 in) apart and seeds 5 to 10 cm (2 to 4 in) apart within the row. If the grain is to be harvested with a combine and herbicides are used for weed control, the closer row spacing is preferred.

Sorghum seed is best planted about 2.5 cm (1 in) deep in moist soil, but in dry soil 5 cm (2 in) gives better germination. Sorghum seedlings cannot emerge from soil when the seeds are planted too deep or if the soil is hard or crusted. Soil crusts can be broken with rotary hoes before the seedlings emerge. Row crop planters are used if sorghum is planted on beds that will be irrigated or in rows wide enough for tractor cultivation (Fig. 23-15). If rows are close, the seed is generally planted with a grain drill. Often, for high plant densities and irrigated sites, two rows 25 cm (10 in) apart are planted on beds 75 cm (30 in) apart. This gives the same plant density as rows 50 cm (20 in) apart.

Fig. 23–15 A young field of sorghum planted on beds to facilitate irrigation. *Source:* U.S. Soil Conservation Service.

Sorghum uses plant nutrients heavily and the crop must be fertilized for high yields. The rates vary considerably among locations and soil types, but 30 to 60 kg/ha (27 to 54 lb/ac) of nitrogen is commonly used in the Great Plains states. On better soils in irrigated regions the rates vary from 60 to 85 kg/ha (54 to 75 lb/ac). Some farmers apply from 110 to 170 kg/ha (98 to 150 lb/ac) of nitrogen if the sorghum is grown on sandy soils low in organic matter, especially if the crop follows wheat, cotton, corn, or sorghum. Nitrogen is applied before planting, at planting time, or as a side dressing with the last cultivation. If banding—i.e., placing the fertilizer in continuous narrow bands—is used at planting time, it is better to place the fertilizer about 5 to 8 cm (2 to 3 in) to the side and below the seed. Some farmers dissolve the fertilizer in the irrigation water.

Phosphorus and potassium are not needed and are often omitted from the fertilization program for sorghum on many soils. On low-phosphorus soils or under intensive cropping systems, sorghum responds well to applications of phosphorus. Soil or leaf tissue tests determine the need for phosphorus or potassium. In the Corn Belt and southern states, calcium is sometimes deficient and limestone is applied both to correct acidity and to make up the calcium deficiency. In many other areas the soils are calcareous and thus calcium is ample. Iron and zinc deficiencies have appeared in some areas: foliar applications of chelated iron or zinc are used to alleviate these symptoms.

Grain sorghum must be irrigated in the arid Southwest. In fact, more than one-fourth of all sorghum acreage grown in the United States is irrigated. Even though sorghum tolerates drought, it responds well to ample soil moisture. For high yields (7000 to 9000 kg/ha; 6200 to 8000 lb/ac) high plant populations, adequate nitrogen, and a plentiful supply of good quality water are essential. Normally, sorghum plants are shallow-rooted, and they extract about half of their water from the top 30 cm (1 ft) of soil. The amount of water needed varies, but on the average, high yields of sorghum are obtained with 50 to 65 cm (20 to 25 in) of water in the Great Plains and 65 to 75 cm (25 to 30 in) in the Southwest. In some areas a part of this is supplied by rainfall. For best results water is applied three times: the tillering stage, the boot stage,[5] and two weeks after heading. If only two applications can be made, apply them when the crop is in the boot stage and two weeks after heading. If only one application can be made, be sure that it is applied during the boot stage.

When the plants are small or under adverse conditions, sorghum does not compete well with weeds. Thus weeds must be controlled. A preplanting irrigation germinates a weed crop that is then destroyed by preplanting tillage. Mechanical tillage used as necessary keeps weeds under control. For drilled or closely spaced rows, rotary hoes are the only practical mechanical control. Selective herbicides are also effective.

Sorghum is attacked by a variety of fungi, bacteria, and viruses, which cause seed rots, seedling blights, foliar diseases, flower and head diseases, and root or stalk rots. Resistance to some diseases has been bred into several new hybrids and cultivars. Some of the more common diseases are loose kernel smut, covered kernel smut, head smut, Pythium root rot, bacterial spot, bacterial streak, crazy top, downy mildew, Fusarium stalk rot, leaf blight, milo disease, and Rhizoctonia stalk rot.

[5]The stage of maturity at which the inflorescence expands.

Several insects attack sorghum, often the same ones that attack other cereal grain crops. In some years, chinch bugs cause severe losses if not controlled. Other insects include the corn earworm, leaf aphid, corn borer, armyworm, sorghum webworm, southwestern corn borer, sorghum midge, and, recently, the green bug.

Most grain sorghum is harvested with combines. The heads are cut from the plant standing in the field and grain is removed and cleaned as it passes through the machine. In the northern part of the Great Plains, the crop sometimes is not mature enough for harvest until frost stops further growth and permits harvest, but in the other areas, it is harvested when the grain is mature. Sorghum threshes easily when the moisture content is 20 to 25 percent, but at this moisture content the grain is artificially dried for safe storage. In arid or semiarid areas, the grain is harvested safely at a moisture level of 12 to 14 percent.

Sugar Beets (*Beta vulgaris* L., Crassa Group J. Helm) CHENOPODACEAE (*8, 22, 23, 24, 31, 32, 33, 37, 46, 58, 59*)

Beets are native to the Mediterranean area. The cultivated kinds fall into two groups. The Crassa Group includes those grown chiefly for their roots or leaves. The roots are used as a vegetable or for sugar and are known as the garden beet, red beet, sugar beet, mangel, and mangold (Fig. 23–16).

The sugar beet is an annual or biennial plant with simple leaves arranged in a basal rosette or alternately on the stem *(8)*.

Fig. 23–16 The sugar from sugar beets and sugarcane is chemically the same. The sugar beet was used as a garden vegetable and fodder for cattle long before it was recognized as a source of sugar. The sugar beet is grown as an annual, and weeds must be strictly controlled by cultivation or herbicides. Beets are often stored in the soil (not dug) until the mill is ready to accept them. This weed-free field is almost ready for harvest. Many farmers use the tops for cattle feed that is almost as nutritious as alfalfa hay. *Source:* F. J. Hills.

Leaves are ovate to oblong-ovate. The flowers are borne in clusters in the axils of the leaves. As the ovaries mature the perianths fuse, resulting in a ''seed ball'' containing several ovaries or seeds.

Sugar beets are by far the most important beet grown commercially. The average sugar concentration is about 15 percent, but many farmers produce beets exceeding 20 percent. The roots are typically sharply tapered, white-skinned, and white-fleshed.

The principal growing areas are the USSR, United States, and Europe. Leading states are California, Idaho, Colorado, Minnesota, Michigan, Washington, North Dakota, Nebraska, Montana, and Wyoming.

During the past few years new hybrids have been developed that are resistant to bolting (development and growth of a seed stalk) and to many viral diseases. They also outyield older cultivars by 10 to 20 percent. The newer hybrids are mostly monogerm instead of multigerm; that is, the seed ball contains only one seed instead of many. Thinning sugar beets is an expensive cultural operation. In former years when multiple-germ seed was planted, one seed ball containing many seeds was planted, which produced many plants, making thinning necessary. The introduction of monogerm seeds helped reduce this cost by allowing the grower to plant one seed ball containing one seed and get one plant, each spaced so that the desired number of plants per unit area of land was obtained. Most new sugar beet cultivars are adapted to a specific area or set of environmental conditions. Thus hundreds of cultivars are grown in the United States. Some are referred to merely by number. For example, two cultivars released jointly by the USDA and the University of California were identified simply as US H9 and US H10.

Sugar beets grow well on a wide range of soils. Highly organic clay and clay loam soils produce high-yield crops if they have good drainage and deep profiles. In the later stages of growth, sugar beets are quite salt tolerant (up to 8 mmho/cm), but in the early stages of seed germination they are extremely sensitive. Special precautions need be taken *(24)* even on slightly saline soils during planting and irrigating to avoid concentrating salt in the seed rows (Fig. 23–17).

Fig. 23–17 Two methods of preventing damage to sugar beet seedlings from accumulating salts. *A:* When sugar beets are germinating in single rows, alternate rows are irrigated. This reduces salt damage because the salts accumulate on the side of the bed away from the seedlings. *B:* When double rows on a single bed are used, the excess salt tends to accumulate between the rows of seedlings, where it does less damage. *Source:* University of California Cooperative Extension.

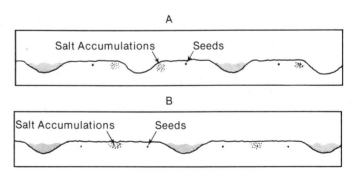

A fine, clod-free seedbed is essential to encourage fast seed germination and seedling growth. In many areas fall plowing is advisable but it is not necessary if soils are friable. Ripping, chiseling, or even subsoiling is necessary to break up compacted layers if they interfere with root or water penetration. On the other hand, some muck soils are so loose they need to be firmed before planting.

Planters capable of metering a single seed at a desired spacing are used. The stand of beets is much more even with monogerm seed that has been cleaned, processed, graded into uniform size, and properly treated with fungicides and insecticides. Some farmers prefer to use pelleted seed.[6] Good yields require proper spacing without crowding. Regardless of row spacing, sugar beet plants should be no closer than 13 to 15 cm (5 to 6 in) apart in the row, and 20 to 30 cm (8 to 12 in) is better. Young plants are thinned by hoes or by synchronous thinning machines. Row spacing can vary from 60 to 75 cm (24 to 30 in) for single rows planted on 10 to 15 cm (4 to 6 in) high beds; two rows are spaced 35 cm (14 in) apart on beds with 100 cm (40 in) centers. In flat areas of adequate rainfall or under sprinkler irrigation, rows 50 cm (20 in) apart can be planted (Figs. 23–18, and 23–19).

The amount of nitrogen used depends upon the soil type and many other factors, but profitable rates of application range from 55 to 170 kg/ha (50 to 150 lb/ac). Part of the nitrogen is applied at planting time, with care taken to avoid salt damage. The fertilizer is applied about 15 cm (6 in) below and 20 to 25 cm (8 to 10 in) to the side of the seed. The remainder of the nitrogen is applied as a sidedressing or in the irrigation water. Most farmers plan their fertilizer programs to exhaust the soil nitrogen supply about six to eight weeks before harvest and ensure maximum sugar production (p. 500) when, ideally, the plants show nitrogen deficiency symptoms. Profitable rates of phosphoric acid (P_2O_5) application range between 45 and 90 kg/ha (40 to 80 lb/ac) applied at planting time. Most soils on which sugar beets are grown are well supplied with potassium except for some muck soils. Some local areas of the United States show minor-element deficiencies. Boron and manganese deficiencies have been found in some mineral soils in the humid regions of Michigan and Wisconsin.

In the arid Southwest, irrigation is essential for best production. Beets can be sprinkle-irrigated but more commonly they are furrow irrigated (Fig. 23–20). It is a good practice to preirrigate the soil before planting, then in the first 10 weeks or so—the period of rapid plant growth when roots are sparse and shallow—several light, fast irrigations are applied. Heavier irrigations are required during midseason. Since the amount of water needed to produce the crop depends on several factors, it varies from 45 to 60 cm (18 to 24 in) in cooler areas to 90 to 150 cm (3 to 5 ft) in warm arid regions.

Weeds compete with beets for light, nutrients, space, and moisture, and provide shelter for insects that in some cases, act as hosts for viruses. Herbicides provide full-season weed control when properly applied. Mechanical cultivation, along with hand hoeing, also keeps weeds under control.

Diseases are a perennial problem for sugar beet farmers, and profitable production is threatened continually. In some

---

[6]Seed coated with a material primarily to increase its size and uniformity. The coating material sometimes contains nutrients, herbicides, insecticides, and fungicides.

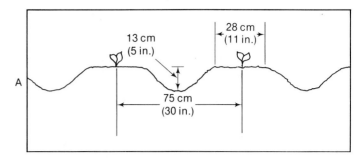

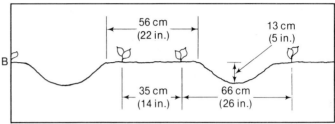

Fig. 23–18 Two examples of common sugar beet spacings. The total length of plant rows per unit of area provided by these spacings is 13,300 m/ha (17,000 ft/ac) in *A* and 19,600 m/ha (26,150 ft/ac) in *B*. *Source:* University of California Cooperative Extension.

Fig. 23–19 The yields of sugar beets produced from a three-year study of two plant spacings. By increasing the spacing between plants within the row from 5 to 15 cm (2 to 6 in) sugar beet root yields increased dramatically, but as spacings between plants within the row increased beyond 20 cm (8 in) yields were reduced. *Source:* University of California Cooperative Extension.

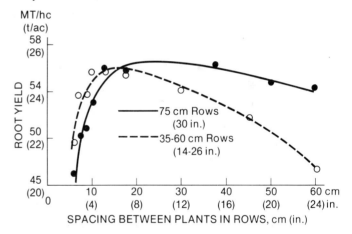

Fig. 23–20 This young stand of sugar beets planted in a single row per bed is being irrigated by the furrow method. This field was initially irrigated by the alternate-row method as shown in Figure 23–17A.

Fig. 23–21 The harvesting of sugar beets is entirely mechanized. Here the tops have been cut from the roots before digging. The roots are then removed from the soil with a lifting plow and elevated into trucks moving alongside. In some cases the roots are taken from the soil by pulling on the tops, then cut loose. The tops can be used for cattle feed. *Source:* F. J. Hills.

Fig. 23–22 Sugar beet roots are transported to assembly areas such as this one to await further transport to the sugar mill—in this case, by river barge. In many places, special sugar beet railcars carry the roots to the mill. *Source:* University of California Cooperative Extension.

western states beet yellows and western yellows have often practically destroyed the crop. Curly top, another prevalent viral disease, is often severe in Colorado and other Rocky Mountain areas and in the San Joaquin Valley of California. Two major fungal diseases are Cercospora leaf spot and powdery mildew. Downy mildew, rust, mosaic, and savoy are minor diseases that sometimes cause significant damage. *Rhizoctonia* and other fungi sometimes attack mature roots.

Some insects, notably aphids and leafhoppers, carry diseases to sugar beet plants. Others damage the plant directly. Some root-damaging insects are root maggots, wireworms, and white grubs. Insects that attack crowns, stems, and foliage include flea beetles, cutworms, sugar beet crown borers, beet webworms, armyworms, alfalfa loopers, and grasshoppers. Preventive practices include crop rotation and field sanitation.

There are also some beneficial insects that help control insect pests on sugar beets, such as green lacewings (aphid lions), lady beetles, assassin bugs, damsel bugs, flower bugs or pirate bugs, syrphid flies, ground beetles, and some wasps.

Sugar beet harvesting, formerly a difficult and tedious task, is now completely mechanized. Mechanical harvesters lift the beets from the soil and load them into trucks moving alongside (Fig. 23–21).

Beets are best harvested when the sugar content is highest, but often the harvest date becomes the date when the processor calls for the product to be brought to the mill. Sugar beets in California are stored over the winter in the soil for spring harvest. Many farmers prefer this practice because of the higher yields obtained by continued growth during the warm sunny California winter days, while others dislike it because it ties up valuable crop land, weeds accumulate, and often the sugar concentration decreases if the beets start flowering in the spring.

Sugar beets are usually grown on contract with a sugar manufacturing plant. The price, acreage, cultivar, harvest date, and other management arrangements are included in the contract. Often the seed is provided by the processor. Upon harvest

the beets are delivered to the processor, where they are unloaded and stored outside on concrete floors in huge piles until needed (Fig. 23–22).

Sugarcane (*Saccharum officinarum* L.)
GRAMINAEAE (*8, 9, 12, 25, 44*)

Sugarcane supplies two-thirds of the world's sugar and, in places where labor costs are low, at a lower cost than any other crop. Sugarcane is said to be the most efficient converter of solar energy and carbon dioxide to chemical energy. Indeed, sugarcane produces more calories per unit area than any other crop.

Sugarcane probably originated in New Guinea, where it has been grown since ancient times. Earliest mention is found in Indian writings about 1400 to 1000 B.C., but no references have been found in ancient Chinese or Egyptian writings (*9*). From India, sugarcane spread to China, then to Java and other tropical Pacific islands. It also spread westward from India to Iran, Egypt, and into Santo Domingo about 1510. Sugarcane was first planted in the United States in 1751 near New Orleans.

Sugarcane is a tropical plant that matures in one or two years (Fig. 23–23). It is a tall grass, often attaining a height of 2 to 4 m (6.5 to 13 ft). Sugarcane has essentially the same structure as other members of the grass family. During flowering, a slender flower-producing shoot appears at the uppermost part of the stalk. The plant produces flowers in the subtropical countries, but they often do not produce fertile pollen. The inflorescence is an open-branched panicle containing hundreds of tiny flowers.

Sugarcane is grown in tropical regions around the world. The main production areas are the warm, humid regions of North, Central, and South America and of Africa, Asia, and Oceania, including Australia. In the United States sugarcane is grown in Louisiana, Florida, Hawaii, and Puerto Rico.

Fig. 23–23 A field of mature sugarcane growing in the delta area of Louisiana. The canes grow to a height of 2 to 4 m (6.5 to 13 ft).

Sugarcane grows best on fertile, moist, tropical soils of a wide variety of types, ranging from sandy to heavy clays. Each soil type requires its own particular management and fertilization treatment.

The cultural methods vary widely and must be adapted to local conditions. In general, the amount of rainfall—which determines whether full irrigation, supplemental irrigation, or no irrigation is used—demands different cultural practices, costs, and yields. Heavy, rugged machinery is essential to sugarcane production. Soil is plowed when it is moist to a depth of 35 to 40 cm (14 to 16 in). The field is left to weather for a time; then, if necessary, compacted layers are broken up by deep tillage. Deep tillage is best done in dry soil and cannot be used in wet climates. In wet regions raised beds hasten drainage.

Sugarcane is propagated vegetatively by planting sections of the stems containing three or four nodes (Fig. 5–13). In Florida, canes are set in furrows 10 to 20 cm (4 to 8 in) deep and 120 cm (4 ft) apart. The stem sections are sometimes planted by hand but are now mostly planted mechanically. A tractor drawn two-row planter opens the furrow, plants the precut and treated seed stalk pieces, and applies fertilizer. In wet regions, rows 140 cm (4.5 ft) apart with about 20,000 plants/ha (8100 plants/ac) have been found suitable. Plantings are made anytime soil temperature and moisture are suitable.

The timing, method, and rates of application of fertilizers vary widely. Phosphorus fertilizers are generally applied at planting time, but nitrogen fertilizers are delayed since they tend to damage the developing buds and young roots on the stem pieces. Sugarcane uses large amounts of plant nutrients and heavy applications are needed to maintain high yields.

Maximum sugar yields depend upon an ample supply of soil moisture, which comes either from rainfall or irrigation. The crop transpires an enormous amount of water, with records indicating up to 625 cm/ha (100 in/ac) each year.

Weeds are controlled by hand weeding and hoeing, by mechanical tillage with various types of cultivators, by flaming,[7] or by chemical herbicides.

Sugarcane is attacked by a wide variety of diseases and insect pests, with each producing country facing its own special problems. To prevent entry of these pests into the continental United States, the USDA has an effective quarantine program headquartered in Beltsville, Maryland. Cane cuttings imported from other parts of the world are admitted, inspected, and treated by this office. Some of the important diseases are mosaic, gumming disease or gummosis, red rot, smut, and ratoon stunting disease.

Troublesome insect pests are corn aphid (a vector for mosaic), cane leafhopper, and moth borer.

Rats have been a problem on some plantations in Hawaii and Florida. They are controlled mostly with poison baits.

Before harvest, randomly selected canes are tested for maturity and the juice is assayed for sugar content with a hand refractometer. Testing generally starts four to six weeks before the proposed harvest date. As with sugar beets, the mill needs a steady supply of canes, which farmers provide by coordinating their harvest. Thus, the rate of harvest is governed by the crushing capacity of the mill. Sugarcane is harvested either by hand or mechanically. In the West Indies the canes are generally sent to the mills remarkably free from undesirable leaves and stems because they are removed when canes are harvested by hand. The cane is cut free at the bottom, topped, and stripped, leaving only the main stalk ready for milling. In other areas, especially where labor costs have hastened the adoption of mechanization, delivery of trashy canes to the mill has been a serious problem. To reduce trashiness and facilitate mechanical harvesting, firing the cane before cutting is a normal practice. Burning mature cane does not harm it unless the fire is exceptionally hot. The work of cutting and loading is greatly reduced by preharvest burning. The top of the plant and the attached young leaves need to be removed because they contain invert sugars,[8] nitrogen compounds, and starch—all of which interfere with the extraction of sucrose sugar.

There are essentially three types of cane harvesters: (1) tractor-drawn mechanical cutters that cut the canes and leave them on the ground (some harvesters remove the tops, some do not); (2) self-propelled harvesters that cut the tops and bottoms off the canes and strip them, leaving long, clean canes; and (3) tractor-mounted harvesters that cut the tops and bottoms, and then cut the canes into short pieces.

Triticale (× *Tritiosecale*) GRAMINEAE (*10, 19, 65*)

Triticale, a cross between wheat *(Triticum)* and rye *(Secale)*, is said to be the first man-made plant. The name *triticale* derives from the wheat genus *Triticum* and from the rye genus *Secale*. The first triticales were developed and released by the University of Manitoba in Canada. Since then, intensive research in plant breeding programs by various governments and private institutions has developed and released many improved triticale cultivars. All of the cultivars now being tested are hexaploid types obtained by hybridizing tetraploid wheat with diploid rye (p. 495).

[7]Several propane burners mounted on wheels are passed quickly over some crops to burn weeds. The practice is timed so that the weeds are young and tender but the crop is more mature and able to withstand the heat.

[8]Glucose and fructose are undesirable invert sugars produced upon the decomposition of sucrose.

As a newly introduced cereal grain, triticale must compete for land area with other cereal grains, mainly wheat and barley. If there is little difference between them in selling price, then triticale yields or quality characteristics must be significantly higher or production costs significantly lower. Tests conducted in California since 1968 have shown that neither yields nor costs are much different than for the other cereal grains. Triticale yields in northern California exceed 6720 kg/ha (6000 lb/ac) and approach yields of the highest-yielding wheat cultivars (19). Grain yields have improved considerably since 1968; however, no triticale cultivar consistantly produces more than wheat.

In dry areas, severe losses of mature grain result from shattering. Most current cultivars are tall and often lodge, but some short-stemmed cultivars have been released. Another characteristic of many triticales is that the crop requires more water to reach maturity than other cereals.

Further improvements are needed before triticale can compete with wheat, but it is remarkable that this crop performs well within only a few years of its development. Specific areas of needed improvement are: (1) shorter stems to reduce lodging; (2) elimination of wrinkled grain to improve test weight; (3) further improvement in spike fertility to improve yields; (4) improved resistance to shattering; and (5) increased resistance to barley yellow dwarf virus and other diseases.

At the present stage of development, little triticale is milled or used for flour; most of the crop is used for livestock feed. The protein content of triticale is somewhat higher than wheat, and no palatability problems with livestock have been encountered (10, 19).

Wheat (*Triticum* spp. L.) GRAMINEAE (*8, 21, 25, 27, 35, 49, 57, 58, 59, 69, 71*)

Wheat and barley are probably the most ancient crops. The Egyptians and Mesopotamians grew wheat as well as rye, barley, and oats. Today, about half of the world's cultivated land is used to produce cereal grains, and about two-fifths of that total grows wheat. Experts tend to disagree on the relative importance of wheat compared with rice, both in tonnage and number of people fed. Each is important, as are corn and sorghum.

Two wild species are still found growing in Syria and Asia Minor, where wheat probably originated. It is known that present-day species originated from the combination of several different species. The species are grouped according to the number of chromosomes (Table 23–2).

Wheat is classified into market classes by the color of the grain and the plant's growing habits; the latter also determines the production area of each class. The classes are: (1) hard red spring, (2) durum, (3) hard red winter, (4) soft red winter, and (5) white.

Wheat is grown in every state in the United States except in New England and parts of the South. The concentration is highest in the Great Plains. Some wheat is grown in the southeastern United States for grazing.

The severity of the winter determines whether winter or spring types are grown. If winters are severe, spring-type cultivars are planted in the spring. If winters are not extremely

Table 23–2 Some Domesticated Wheat Species (*Triticum*)

Group	Species	Common Name	Chromosome Number
Diploid	*T. monococcum*	Einkorn	7
Allotetraploid*	*T. turgidum*, Dicoccon Group	Emmer	14
	T. turgidum, Durum Group	Macaroni wheat	14
	T. turgidum	Poulard wheat	14
	T. turgidum, Polonicum Group	Polish wheat	14
Allohexaploid*	*T. aestivum*, Aestivum Group	Common winter and spring wheat	21
	T. aestivum, Spelta Group	Spelt	21
	T. aestivum, Compactum Group	Club wheat	21

*An organism with 4 (tetra) or 6 (hexa) sets of chromosomes, each set more or less dissimilar and derived from different ancestral species.

cold, winter cultivars are planted in the fall. If winters are mild, as in California, Texas, and Mexico, spring-type cultivars are planted in the fall. This difference creates what is known as the winter or spring wheat belts in the United States.

Hard red spring cultivars are grown principally in the northern Great Plains states of North and South Dakota, Montana, and Minnesota. These states produce a high-grade wheat used principally for bread flour. Durum wheat cultivars, used to make semolina flour for macaroni and similar pasta products, are also grown in these states. Hard red winter wheat, grown on more acreage than any other, is cultivated in Kansas, Nebraska, Oklahoma, Colorado, and northern Texas. This hard red winter wheat area ranges from Utah to north central Illinois. Hard red winter wheat is used to make bread flours. Soft red winter wheat production is concentrated in Ohio, Indiana, and southern Illinois but the belt ranges from eastern Texas to the Atlantic Ocean. The northern limit follows the northern boundaries of Indiana, Ohio, and Pennsylvania. This wheat is milled into flour for cakes and pastries.

Extensive wheat breeding programs have been undertaken in practically every wheat-growing country in the world. Breeders continually introduce new cultivars that are more resistant to disease, insects, drought, lodging, and shattering. Plant breeders have improved quality (size, texture, weight) and increased yields and winter hardiness. One of the most dramatic improvements in wheat cultivars came with the development of the semidwarfed cultivars or so-called Mexican wheats (see p. 61). Several selections resulting from hybridization have since been released by scientists working in the Centro Internacional De Majoramiento De Maiz Trigo located in Sonoro, Mexico. Semidwarf cultivars have been widely accepted in many of the world's wheat-producing areas. These cultivars are 13 to 25 cm (5 to 10 in) shorter than conventional cultivars. They resist lodging, respond to high fertilizer rates, and use high irrigation applications to their advantage. The particular cultivars used are those best adapted to the local environments. Plantings change as new and better cultivars are released.

Wheat is grown on a wide range of soils in temperate climates where annual rainfall ranges between 30 and 90 cm (12 to 36 in). Such areas constitute most of the grasslands of the world's temperate regions. Many of these soils are deep, well-drained, dark-colored, fertile, high in organic matter, and they represent some of the world's best soils. The prairie soils of the United States and Canada and the steppes of the Soviet Union are examples of such soils. Wheat does less well on sandy soils.

Production methods vary throughout the world. In areas of extensive acreages (North America, Australia, Argentina, and the Soviet Union) mechanization is high. In other areas, methods are still primitive, and even today one can see wheat harvested by hand with a sickle and threshed with a flail or by animals walking over the harvested heads to remove the grain kernels.

Seedbed preparation depends upon the method of growing. In areas with less than 38 cm (15 in) of average annual rainfall, an alternate crop and fallow system is used. Wheat—either the entire field or strips within a field—is planted one year and the ground left fallow in alternate years (Fig. 23–24). This practice stores and conserves water during the fallow year for the wheat crop the next. Soil is a good reservoir for water provided no vegetation is allowed to grow. The soil is often plowed after harvest and left rough, cloddy, and barren the following year. The rough surface traps and absorbs the scant rainfall and reduces wind erosion. If weeds appear during the spring, a light disking or herbicide application kills them.

The seedbed is prepared in late summer for an early fall planting of winter wheat or for early spring wheat. In semi-humid regions (more than 38 cm, or 15 in, of rain) plowing is often needed as the first step in seedbed preparation. Wheat is sometimes grown continuously in these areas; thus the soil is plowed after harvest, then disked and harrowed for fall planting. Supplemental irrigation is either applied at this time or the field is left arid until fall planting. In humid regions, fall-planted wheat often follows soybeans. In this case plowing

Fig. 23–25 A well-prepared seedbed ready for fall planting of wheat. Deep, well-drained, dark-colored, heavy soils well supplied with organic matter produce the best wheat crops. The prairie soils of the United States, Canada, and the U.S.S.R. are good examples of wheat soils.

is seldom needed because soybean culture often leaves well-structured soils friable. Disking and harrowing generally are sufficient to provide a good seedbed. In any case, the seedbed at time of planting needs to be firm, mellow, and clod-free (Fig. 23–25).

It is essential that seeds and seeding equipment of the best quality be used to insure good wheat stands. The added cost of certified seed is almost always worthwhile. Unreliable seeding equipment leaves skips in the field and uneven stands. The most popular seeding tool is the grain drill, of which there are many variations. The objective is to get the seed evenly distributed at a uniform depth. Often seed drills have attachments to inject fertilizer at the time of planting. The depth of seeding varies from 2.5 to 8 cm (1 to 3 in) and the rate from 25 to 170 kg/ha (22 to 150 lb/ac).

The date of planting also varies. In areas where the Hessian fly occurs, it is imperative that no wheat be planted before the announced "fly-free" date. In the winter wheat areas, planting begins in early fall in the northern regions and late fall in the southern. It is best to plant when soil moisture is adequate to germinate seed or to sprinkle irrigate after seeding if moisture is not available. In the Pacific Northwest, winter wheat is seeded in early fall. In the spring wheat areas, early seeding gives the best results. In the northern United States, wheat is seeded as soon as seedbeds are prepared in late spring; in the southern states, planting comes much earlier.

Wheat responds well to fertilizers, and the kind and rate of application vary with location and soil. The usual practice in the Corn Belt and western United States is to apply a complete fertilizer to winter wheat. In states east of the Corn Belt it sometimes is not necessary to use a complete fertilizer. All of the fertilizer is often drilled with the seed but sometimes a part is applied later, especially if the application is large. In most of the Great Plains, nitrogen is recommended and often applied. Nitrogen increases not only yields but also protein content of the grain, which improves the milling quality of the flour.

Wheat responds to irrigation in areas where rainfall is less than 45 cm (18 in). In dry-land farming[9] areas, a combina-

[9]Dry-land farming is the growing of the crops in areas of limited rainfall and without additional irrigation.

Fig. 23–24 Crop fallow strip farming is used in areas where insufficient rainfall occurs in one year to produce a crop. Alternate bands of soil are left fallow in alternate years allowing two years of rainfall to accumulate for a crop every other year. Strip farming also helps prevent wind erosion because all the land is covered either with a growing crop or harvested stubble. *Source:* R. L. Haaland.

tion of irrigation and fertilizers increases yields three to four times. This was vividly demonstrated in India with the new short-stem cultivars.

A crop that is drilled with closely spaced rows is seldom cultivated. If weeds become a problem, selective herbicides are used to control them without damaging the crop.

Three rust diseases caused by fungi seriously attack wheat: stem rust, leaf rust, and stripe rust. These are also called black, brown, and yellow rust, respectively. The smuts are another group of diseases that cause considerable damage to wheat. Bunt (stinking smut) and loose smut are examples. Stinking and loose smuts are controlled by seed treatment and resistant cultivars. Wheat scab is serious in humid areas. Often soil-borne and insect-transmitted viruses give problems and, at times, root rots or crown rots are troublesome.

Several insects damage wheat. In the eastern United States, the Hessian fly is notorious. In the northwestern states and Canada, the wheat stem sawfly is a serious pest. Wheat jointworms, strawworms, chinch bugs, aphids, and grasshop-

pers are other insects that cause varying degrees of damage in certain areas.

In the large wheat-growing areas of the world, the crop is harvested by combines. Some harvesting is done by contract harvesters who own and operate many combines. They start early in Texas and continue through fall in the Dakotas or Canada. Present-day wheat harvest is so well mechanized that only 1 to 1.5 manhours/ha (0.4 to 0.6 hr/ac) are required as compared to 20 to 24 hr/ha (8 to 10 hr/ac) with the neighborhood threshing ring, binders, and bundle wagons of years ago. Wheat grain stores satisfactorily if the moisture content is about 14 percent or less; if the moisture content is higher, artificial drying is required.

Wheat grain keeps indefinitely if it is properly stored in clean, cool, dry (12 to 14 percent) storage bins or warehouses, free from insects and rodents. Rodents are a real problem in some areas, notably India, where rats eat or destroy up to 50 percent of the stored grain each year.

REFERENCES

1. Allard, R. W. 1953. Production of dry edible lima beans in California. Univ. of Calif. Agr. Exp. Sta. Cir. 423.

2. Anon. 1969. Sudangrass and sorghum-Sudangrass hybrids for forage. USDA Farmers Bul. 2241.

3. Anon. 1971. Drying shelled corn and small grains. USDA Farmers Bul. 2214.

4. Anon. 1971. Resource use adjustments in major U.S. rice areas. Part III. Southern Cooperative Series Bul. 160. Agr. Exp. Sta. of Arkansas, California, Louisiana, Mississippi, and Texas cooperating with Farm Prod. Econ. Div., Econ. Res. Serv. USDA.

5. Atkins, J. G. 1972. Rice diseases. USDA Farmers Bul. 2120.

6. Bacon, O. G., T. Lyons, and R. S. Baskett. 1963. Control of spider mites in dent corn. *Calif. Agr.* 17(7):8–10.

7. Baghott, K. G., C. W. Schaller, and M. D. Miller. 1968. Response of six barley varieties to selected cultural practices. *Calif. Agr.* 22(7):10–12.

8. Bailey, L. H., and E. Z. Bailey and Bailey Hortorium staff. 1976. *Hortus third.* New York: Macmillan.

9. Barnes, A. C. 1964. *The sugar cane.* New York: Interstate Publishers.

10. Bishnoi, U. R., P. Chitapons, and J. Hughs, and J. Nishimuta. 1978. Quantity and quality of triticale and other small grain silages. *Agron. Jour.* 70:439–41.

11. Bowen, W. R., V. E. Burton, R. W. Bushing, H. T. Reynolds, V. M. Stern, J. E. Swift, and N. C. Toscano. 1976. Pest and disease control program for field corn and sorghum. Univ. of Calif. Div. Agr. Sci. Leaflet 2746.

12. Brandes, E. W. 1956. Origin, dispersal and use in breeding of the Melanesian garden sugarcanes and their derivatives. *Proc. Int. Soc. Sugar Cane Tech.,* 9th Congr., vol 2, pp. 709–50.

13. Brandon, D. M., K. E. Mueller, T. Prichard, G. J. St. Andre, C. M. Wick, J. M. Williams, and D. R. Woodruff. 1977. California rice varieties: description and performance. Paper presented at Univ. Calif. Coop. Ext. Winter Rice Meetings, Univ. of Calif., Davis.

14. Brunson, A. M., and D. L. Richardson. 1958. Popcorn. USDA Farmers Bul. 1679.

15. Coffman, F. A. 1961. Origin and history. Oats and oat improvement. Monograph 8. Amer. Soc. Agron.

16. Elliott, W. A., and E. A. Delke. 1977. New era for wild rice. *Crops and Soils* 29:8–11.

17. Erdman, L. W. 1967. Legume inoculation: what it is—what it does. USDA Farmers Bul. 2003.

18. Finrock, D. C., and M. D. Miller. 1959. Wild rice. Univ. of Calif. Exp. Sta. Leaflet 116.

19. Gustafson, J. P., C. O. Qualset, J. D. Prato, Y. P. Puri, W. H. Isom, and W. F. Lehman. 1976. Triticale in California. *Calif. Agr.* 26(2):3–5.

20. Halisky, P. M., and D. G. Smeltzer, 1961. Head smut. *Calif. Agr.* 15(1):10–12.

21. Heyne, E. G., and G. S. Smith. 1967. Wheat breeding. Wheat and wheat improvement. Monograph 13. Amer. Soc. Agron.

22. Hills, F. J., G. V. Ferry, A. Ulrick, and R. S. Loomis. 1963. Marginal nitrogen deficiency of sugar beets and the problem of diagnosis. *J. Am. Soc. Sugar Beet Tech.* 12(6):476–84.

23. ———, and S. S. Johnson, 1973. The sugar beet industry in California. Univ. of Calif. Agr. Exp. Sta. Cir. 562.

24. ———, R. L. Sailsbery, W. E. Bendixen, R. A. Brendler, D. W. Henderson, R. A. Ayers, R. G. Curley, D. R. Woodruff, and R. W. Hagemann. 1976. Sugar beets—establishing a stand. Univ. of Calif. Div. Agr. Sci. Bul. 1877.

25. Hughes, H. D., and D. S. Metcalfe. 1972. *Crop production.* New York: Macmillan.

26. Jensen, M. E., and J. T. Musick. 1962. Irrigating grain sorghums. USDA Leaflet 511.

27. Johnson, V. A., and J. W. Schmidt. 1968. Hybrid wheat. *Adv. in Agron.* 20:199–232. New York: Academic Press.

28. Kemmler, G. 1971. Proc. Int. Symp. Soil Fert. Evaluation. Indian Soc. of Soil Sci. Indian Agric. Res. Inst.

29. Lange, W. H., and M. D. Miller, eds. 1970. Insects and other animal pests of rice. Univ. of Calif. Agr. Exp. Sta. Cir. 555.

30. Lewis, D. C., V. H. Scott, K. E. Mueller, K. L. Viste, A. F. Babb, and D. R. Fox. 1962. New levee concepts. *Rice Jour.* 65(4):6–16.

31. Loomis, R. S., and D. J. Nevins. 1963. Interrupted nitrogen nutrition effects on growth, sucrose accumulation and foliar development of the sugar beet plant. *J. Am. Soc. Sugar Beet Tech.* 12(4):309–22.

32. ———, and C. W. Bennett. 1966. Competitive relationships in virus-infested sugar beet fields. *J. Am. Soc. Sugar Beet Tech.* 14(3):218–31.

33. ———, L. D. Doneen, and F. J. Hills. 1976. Sugar beet irrigation. Univ of Calif. Div. Agr. Sci. Leaflet 2396.

34. Mangelsdorf, P. C. 1950. The mystery of corn. *Sci. Amer.* 183:20–24.

35. ———. 1953. Wheat. *Sci. Amer.* 189:50–59.

36. ———, R. F. MacNeish, and W. C. Galinat. 1964. Domestication of corn. *Science* 14:538–48.

37. McFarlane, J. S., and F. J. Hills. 1964. Hybrid sugar beet varieties. Univ. of Calif. Agr. Ext. AXT-8.

38. Mikkelsen, D. S., and N. S. Evatt. 1966. Rice in the United States: varieties and production (soils and fertilizers). USDA/ARS Handbook 269.

39. ———, J. H. Lindt, Jr., and M. D. Miller. 1967. Rice fertilization. Univ. of Calif. Agr. Exp. Sta. Leaflet 96.

40. Miller, M. D. 1977. Personal communication. Univ. of Calif.

41. ———, ed. 1977. *Eighth annual report to the California rice growers.* Calif. Rice Research Board, Yuba City, Calif.

42. Morrison, K. 1955. Growing field beans in central Washington irrigated areas. State Coll. of Wash. Ext. Ser. Bul. 497.

43. Moyle, J. B., and P. Krueger. 1968. Wild rice in Minnesota. Univ. of Minn. Agr. Ext. Ser. Agron. Notes, pp. 18–23.

44. Nickell, L. G. 1977. Sugarcane. In *Ecophysiology of tropical crops,* eds. P. de T. Alvim and T. T. Koslowski. New York: Academic Press.

45. Oelke, E. A., and W. A. Brun, 1969. Paddy production of wild rice. Univ. of Minn. Agr. Ext. Ser. Agron. Notes, pp. 37–38.

46. Peay, W. E. 1966. Sugar beet insects: how to control them. USDA Farmers Bul. 2219.

47. Peterson, M. L., S. S. Lin, D. Jones, J. N. Rutger, 1974. Cool night temperatures cause sterility in rice. *Calif. Agr.* 28(7):12–14.

48. Puri, P. Y., and K. G. Baghott. 1973. Effects of nitrogen and irrigation on yield of feed barley. *Calif. Agr.* 27(4):5–6.

49. Qualset, C. O., J. D. Prato, J. A. Ruppert, H. E. Vogt, M. A. Khalif, W. F. Lehman, and W. H. Isom. 1973. Anza—A new high yielding, short-statured wheat variety. *Calif. Agr.* 27(2):14–15.

50. Rauschkolb, R. B., A. L. Brown, J. Quick, R. L. Sailsbery, J. D. Prato, R. E. Pelton, and F. R. Kegel. 1976. Field evaluation of nitrogen nutritional status for corn and sorghum. Univ. of Calif. Div. Agr. Sci. Leaflet 2257.

51. Richards, L. A. 1954. Diagnosis and improvement of saline soils. USDA Handbook 60.

52. Robins, J. S., and H. F. Rhoades. 1958. Irrigation of field corn in the west. USDA Leaflet 440.

53. Ross, W. M., and O. J. Webster. 1970. Culture and use of grain sorghum. USDA/ARS Handbook 385.

54. Sallee, W. R., and F. L. Smith. 1969. Commercial blackeye bean production in California. Univ. of Calif. Agr. Exp. Sta. Cir. 549.

55. Sarquis, A. F., B. B. Fischer, F. G. Parsons, and M. D. Miller. 1961. Geographic origin of barley seed produces no effect on yield. *Calif. Agr.* 15(4):3.

56. Schaller, C. W., and J. D. Prato. 1965. Briggs and Numar—two new barley varieties for California. *Calif. Agr.* 22(12):14–15.

57. Sears, E. R., and L. M. S. Sears, eds. 1973. International wheat genetics symposium. Proceedings of the 4th International Wheat Symposium. Columbia: University of Missouri.

58. Stefferud, A., ed. 1952. Insects. USDA Yearbook. Washington, D.C.: U.S. Government Printing Office.

59. ———. 1953. Plant diseases. USDA Yearbook. Washington, D.C.: U.S. Government Printing Office.

60. Stern, V. M., and W. R. Bowen. 1967. Control of aphids on barley. *Calif. Agr.* 21(3):14–15.

61. Stickler, F. C. 1964. Row width and plant population studies with corn. *Agron. Jour.* 56:438–41.

62. Suneson, C. A. 1959. New winter rye. *Calif. Agr.* 13(8):6.

63. ———, M. D. Miller, and J. D. Prato. 1963. Grande barley. *Calif. Agr.* 17(11):14–15.

64. Thysell, J. R., M. D. Miller, K. E. Mueller. 1963. California rice varieties and seed selection. Univ. of Calif. Exp. Sta. Leaflet 161.

65. Tsen, C. C. 1974. *Triticale: first man-made cereal.* St. Paul, Minn.: American Association of Cereal Chemists.

66. Walter, E. V. 1953. The sorghum smidge. USDA Farmers Bul. 1566.

67. Webster, R. K., D. H. Hall, J. Bolstad, C. M. Wick, D. M. Brandon, R. Baskett, and J. M. Williams. 1973. Chemical seed treatment for the control of seedling diseases of water-sown rice. *Hilgardia* 41(21):689–98.

68. Wiebe, G. A. 1968. Barley: origin, botany, culture, winter hardiness, genetics, pests. USDA Handbook 338.

69. Williams, J. C., J. D. Prato, and M. D. Miller. 1964. New wheat variety introductions reduce stripe rust losses. *Calif. Agr.* 18(5):8–10.

70. Williams, W. A., M. D. Morse, and J. E. Ruckman. 1972. Burning vs. incorporation of rice crop residues. *Agron. Jour.* 64:467–68.

71. Wilson, H. K. 1948. *Grain crops.* New York: McGraw-Hill.

72. Worker, G. F., W. E. Pendery, R. L. Sailsbery, and J. D. Prato. 1976. Univ. of Calif. Div. Agr. Sci. Leaflet 2873.

Oil Crops

24

Plants were used for oil long before petroleum. In fact, some of the earliest writings tell of the use of oil from plants for illumination, heat for cooking, and anointing the skin. Olive oil was widely used for these purposes by early Mediterranean civilizations. Linseed oil from flax was mixed with mineral or plant pigments and used for painting. Castor oil from the castor bean was used to lubricate the wheels of wagons and later in paint, varnish, and cosmetics and as a cathartic. After the discovery of petroleum as a fuel and the invention of the internal combustion engine, the primary source of oil was the earth's underground supply. But as these supplies become more limited, interest in vegetable oils will undoubtedly increase. Some of the important oil producing crops and their production methods are discussed in this chapter.

Oil is found in all living plants, even in the bacteria and fungi. Seeds of some plant species vary in oil content from 1 to over 50 percent. Vegetable and animal oils yield two to three times more calories per gram than carbohydrates.

Castor Bean (*Ricinus communis* L.) EUPHORBIACEAE

The castor bean plant is grown for the oil in its seed. The petal-less flowers are produced on panicles, from which brown spine-covered capsular fruits containing three large and variously marked seeds develop (Fig. 24–1). Besides the castor oil, the seeds contain the protein ricin, which is extremely poisonous. Commercially the oil has many uses. It is used in paints, plastics, printing inks, cosmetics, greases, and hydraulic fluids.

Fig. 24–1   The development of castor bean flowers to seed pods. *Source:* University of California Cooperative Extension.

Coconut (*Cocos nucifera* L.) PALMAE

The coconut, in addition to being an important nut crop, is an important oil crop. The culture of this crop is discussed in Chapter 31.

Corn (*Zea mays* L.) GRAMINEAE

Field corn is grown primarily as a grain crop for livestock feed. Some is cut green and made into silage. Sweet corn is grown mostly for human consumption. Corn grain is also processed into a polyunsaturated oil used for cooking and margarine. For a discussion of the culture of corn see Chapter 23.

Flax (*Linum usitatissimum* L.) LINACEAE

In the United States flax is grown for its oil but in other parts of the world it is also grown as a fiber crop to make linen. A discussion of flax culture is found in Chapter 24.

Olive (*Olea europaea* L.) OLEACEAE

Olives have produced fine oil for centuries but they are also grown for their fruits. For a discussion on the production of this crop see Chapter 30.

Palm Oil (*Elaeis guineensis* Jacq.) PALMAE (9, 10, 11)

This tree was called the prince of the plant kingdom by Linnaeus because of its majestic appearance. The oil palm is botanically related to the coconut palm. When mature, the oil palm tree may attain a height of nearly 30 m (100 ft) but generally it grows no taller than 10 m (32 ft). At the top it bears a crown of feathery leaves, each 3 to 4.5 m (10 to 15 ft) long, that are pinnately divided into 50 or more leaflets. The trees are monoecious (male and female flowers on the same tree). The flowers grow on a short spadix[1] that develops into a cluster containing more than 1000 drupes (fruits). The female flower normally has three ovaries but generally only one is fertilized. The fruit matures about six months after pollination.

The oil palm, native to tropical West Africa, is an important source of vegetable oil. It is grown most abundantly along the west coast of Africa from Gambia to Angola. Oil palms are also cultivated to some extent in the rain forest regions of the Congo, Kenya, Indonesia, and Malaysia. There are small plantings in some Central and South American countries.

There have been some breeding trials to obtain shorter trees and better flowering characteristics. Shorter trees aid in harvesting fruit, and improved flowering would produce a higher percentage of oil. Four common varieties, based on the ratio of kernel to pericarp, include: (1) *macrocarpa*, 50 percent kernel to 50 percent shell; (2) *dura*, 70 percent kernel; (3) *tenera*, 90 percent kernel; and (4) *pisifera*, no shell. The *dura* variety is the most common in West Africa, but it yields a higher percentage of oil in Malaysia than it does in Africa.

The oil palm grows well on a wide variety of soil types. The trees do best on deep, well-drained soils that are neutral to slightly alkaline in reaction, but they are grown successfully on acid soils in Malaysia. Loose alluvial soils are best; tight, heavy, poorly drained, black soils do not support good trees.

Oil palm trees must be propagated by seeds, since there are no suitable asexual methods. In Malaysia the oily pericarp is removed from the seeds before they are germinated in beds containing washed sand about 30 cm (1 ft) deep. The seeds are planted about 2.5 cm (1 in) deep and 8 cm (3 in) apart in the sand, with the germ pores pointed slightly downward. One can expect about 75 percent germination with good seed within 15 to 18 weeks. Germination is higher and more rapid if the beds are kept quite warm. The seedlings are transplanted into a nursery bed of friable soil when the first leaf appears above the sand. Seedlings remain here for one to two years until they become small trees. Trees left in the nursery for three years suffer severe shock when transplanted and take several years to recover. Trees are best transplanted from the nursery into the field during the rainy season. The trees are placed in holes large enough to admit the root system (60 cm, or 2 ft, in diameter) and refilled with a good friable topsoil. Care should be taken to avoid burying the crown. A 10 m (32 ft) grid is a desirable spacing for trees.

Trees growing in Malaysian soils generally respond to phosphorus applications and sometimes to potash. In South Africa, a bronze spotting of leaves seems to be caused by potassium deficiency. Magnesium has been found to be deficient in West Africa and causes a condition known as the orange frond disease.

Irrigation is not necessary for oil palms because they are grown only in tropical areas where rainfall is abundant and even.

A number of diseases have been reported in Malaysia but a fungus-caused stem rot is the most prevalent. The fungi enter the trunk of the tree when the leaves are cut off, and infected trees often die in two or three years. This fungus *(Marasmium palmivorus),* causes the acid content of the oil to increase in ripening fruit.

A red-striped weevil causes some damage to trees in Malaysia.

In Malaysia, the fruit is harvested throughout the year but the heaviest harvest takes place in late summer to early fall and the lightest in late winter to early spring. Both the shell (pericarp) and the kernel contain oil. Four-year-old trees yield about 2.2 MT/ha (1 t/ac) of fruit. Ten-year-old trees yield 7 to 9 MT/ha (3 to 4 t/ac) from which about 800 kg (1760 lb) of pericarp oil (palm oil) and 210 kg (460 lb) of kernels are obtained. The kernels in turn produce about 100 kg (225 lb) of kernel oil and 110 kg (240 lb) of kernel meal.

---

[1]A spadix is a spike with a succulent axis usually enclosed in a spathe. A spathe is the large sheathing bract (or pair of bracts) enclosing an inflorescence, especially a spadix on the same axis. For example, the Jack-in-the-Pulpit flower.

Harvesting is done by hand. A worker climbs the tree carrying an ax or a chisel and mallet to cut off the leaf fronds below the fruit stalks. The fruit stalks contain clusters of fruit that weigh from 10 to 45 kg (22 to 100 lb) each. After removing the lower fronds, the worker is able to reach the fruit stalk, cut it from the tree, with the ax or chisel, and lower it to the ground. About 60 stalks is considered a good day's work. Before going to the extraction plant, the fruit and bunches are treated with steam pressure of about 2.1 kg/cm² (30 lb/in²) for about an hour, depending on the degree of ripeness. A higher steam pressure darkens the oil. At the extraction plant, the fruits are first separated under steam from the bunches. Next the pericarp and seeds are separated and the oil is extracted by steam or by pressure. This crude oil is then refined. The pericarp mash is good feed for livestock and can also be used as fertilizer.

Palm oil is deep yellow to red-brown in color, and thick in consistency. It is used for making soap, candles, and lubricating greases. It is also used in processing tin plate and as a coating for iron plates. Kernel oil is light yellow in color and used principally in the manufacture of edible products such as margarine, chocolate candies, and pharmaceuticals.

Fig. 24–2 Peanut flowers are fertilized above the soil. Fertilization is followed by the development of a subterranean pod after gynophore (peg) has elongated and buried. Soil penetration provides the necessary moisture and darkness for fruit enlargement, which rarely occurs above ground. *Source:* USDA.

Peanut (*Arachis hypogaea* L.) LEGUMINOSAE (6, 12, 23, 24, 28)

The peanut is native to South America. It was introduced into Africa where, along with bananas, it forms a large part of the diet of the peoples of East Central Africa. From Africa the peanut was taken to India, China, and the United States during colonial times.

The peanut is an annual plant with sturdy, hairy branches that can grow nearly prostrate or upright. The leaves are pinnately compound with two pairs of leaflets. The flowers are axillary and sessile, and what appears to be a flower stalk is really the calyx tube, which is about 4 cm (1.5 in) long and rather slender. After pollination, the flower withers and drops off, leaving a unique stalklike plant part called a ''peg.'' The tip of the peg contains the fertilized ovules, which the growing peg carries down and pushes into the soil. The tip then develops into the peanut pod we all know (Fig. 24–2).

There are three distinct peanut growing regions in the United States: the Virginia-Carolina area, which primarily grows the large Virginia cultivars; the Georgia-Florida-Alabama area, which grows the Southeastern Runner and some Virginia and Spanish cultivars; and the Oklahoma-Texas district, which grows the Spanish cultivars. The three cultivars are separated on the basis of clearly identifiable agronomic characteristics. These characteristics include branch form, bunch habit, pod size and shape, number of seeds per pod, and color of seeds after storage. Typically the Virginia types have true runners, spreading branch forms, and two seeds per pod. The Spanish types have erect bunch forms and pods are mostly 2-seeded. The runner types have true runners, spreading branch forms, and 2 to 6 seeds per pod. In the southern states, peanuts are surpassed only by tobacco and cotton as a cash crop.

In the United States peanuts are produced mainly for grinding into peanut butter, for roasted and salted nuts, and for candy and bakery goods. Some are used for livestock feed in the South. In other parts of the world, peanuts are grown mainly for their edible oil. After the nuts are harvested, the stems and leaves are often used for hay. Sometimes fields are harvested for hogs that root the nuts from the ground for feed.

The USDA, state universities, and seed companies have cooperated to develop and release new cultivars. These hybrids were developed for adaptation to specific local climatic conditions, high yields, disease resistance, and improved nut quality. Some popular Spanish-type cultivars include Argentine, Starr, Spanhoma, Span Cross, and Tiftspan. Some of the runner types are Early Runner or Dixie Runner. A Virginia-type cultivar is Florigiant.

The soil, especially its texture and structure, is an important factor in peanut culture. The best soils are well-drained sandy loams with deep profiles. These soils allow the pegs to penetrate readily and the nuts to be harvested clean. Clay loam soils produce good crops provided the moisture content is optimal, but if the soil gets dry and hard, yields are reduced because the nuts break off and are lost during harvest. In addition, soil particles stick to the pods, dirtying the product and lowering its grade.

Peanuts are often rotated with other crops such as potatoes, corn, and clover. In preparing a good seedbed residue from the previous crop is shredded or disked before plowing to bury the debris. Disking also breaks up any hardpans or compacted layers. Disking and harrowing follow until the seedbed is firm, mellow, and clod-free.

Only the best certified seed is recommended for planting. Before the planting season, the seed is carefully shelled to avoid injury. Broken or split kernels are useless as seed. Poor stands reduce yields and often result from seeds with seed coats scratched or damaged by machine shelling. The seed coat contains a tanninlike chemical that retards the breakdown of the oil in the seed, preserving viability. This material also helps prevent bacteria and fungi from attacking the seeds. Most farmers treat peanut seeds with a fungicide or disinfectant to kill decay-causing organisms on the seed surface. Extreme care is taken to prevent treated seed from being consumed by humans or livestock or used for oil.

Planting dates vary with location. In Texas, peanuts are planted from early spring to midsummer; in the Southeast, most plantings are made during midspring; in Virginia, planting in late spring is most likely. The seed is planted 5 to 8 cm (2 to 3 in) deep in light-textured soils or more shallowly in heavy clay soils. Rows are 60 to 90 cm (2 to 3 ft) apart and seeds are spaced 5 to 10 cm (2 to 4 in) apart within the row. A growth regulator such as 2-chloroethyl phosphonic acid (CEPA) (see p. 138) is often used to reduce growth of stem internodes, giving short bushy plants with the usual number of leaves. This allows farmers to increase the plant population considerably by placing the rows 45 cm (18 in) apart instead of 90 cm (3 ft), thereby increasing yields up to 50 percent.

Peanuts are heavy feeders of plant nutrients, and they respond well to added fertilizers. Most farmers apply fertilizer by broadcasting it before planting. If the soil is more acid than pH 6.0 to 6.5, finely ground limestone is added. The kind and amount of fertilizer vary considerably with soils and location. In California, peanuts have responded profitably to 90 to 110 kg/ha (80 to 98 lb/ac) of nitrogen and 45 to 65 kg/ha (40 to 58 lb/ac) of phosphoric acid. Potassium is not recommended. In the peanut growing areas of the United States, only small amounts of nitrogen are needed if the seeds have been inoculated with nitrogen-fixing bacteria. If the soils are low in phosphorus and potassium, the usual applications are 45 to 110 kg/ha (40 to 98 lb/ac) of phosphoric acid and 90 to 225 kg/ha (80 to 200 lb/ac) of potash. Certain minor elements, particularly copper, boron, and sulfur, are lacking in some areas. Calcium has been found deficient in some parts of Georgia, and gypsum is used to correct the problem.

In semiarid regions, peanuts must be irrigated, requiring about 60 cm (24 in) of water. Many farmers irrigate the soil before planting, particularly if winter rains have been scarce and failed to wet the top 91 cm (3 ft) of the soil profile. Irrigation during the growing season is frequent enough to maintain a moist soil during the critical stages of blooming and seed development. Irrigation is discontinued when the plants cease rapid growth so that the ground will dry for harvest.

Some cultivation is necessary and important for weed control in peanuts but excessive cultivation is avoided (Fig. 24–3). Two periods of weed control are critical: when the seedlings are emerging, and when the plants are setting fruit. Cultivators must not be allowed close to the plant where they can interfere with the developing pegs. Selective herbicides are now used in many areas.

The most serious diseases of peanuts are leaf spot (caused by three fungi), southern blight (also known as white mold or southern stem rot), collar rot, peg rot, and black rot.

The most prevalent insect pests are cutworms, thrips, leafhoppers, corn earworms, armyworms, and lesser cornstalk borers. Several insects infect storage facilities and destroy the stored peanuts. Some of these are cadelle beetle, carpet beetle, confused flour beetle, flour and grain mites, and rice weevil.

Three nematodes (root-knot, meadow, and sting) damage peanuts.

Peanuts are ready for harvest when the plant no longer grows rapidly, the leaves begin to yellow, and the kernels are fully developed, as indicated by darkening of the veins inside the hull. Harvesting earlier results in shriveled nuts but harvesting too late can cause losses because of sprouting. The date of

Fig. 24–3 This farmer is carefully cultivating a field of peanuts. Cultivation is done primarily to control weeds. Note that the shovels behind the tractor are set very shallow thereby avoiding damage to nuts forming at this stage of growth. This probably will be the last cultivation for weed control. *Source:* R. L. Haaland

harvest is critical, and as that time approaches, the crop is inspected every day or two to estimate the best date.

If peanuts are grown for home consumption, they are hand harvested by digging the entire plant, then the vines are allowed to wilt. The pods are plucked from the vines, dried, and cured. For commercial production, peanuts are harvested mechanically. A blade is passed below the soil surface under the peanuts to cut the tap roots and to loosen the soil. The vines are pulled and placed in windrows mechanically. After drying a few days, the peanuts are removed from the vines by a combine, collected in trucks, and transported to warehouses for cleaning, curing, and storage.

Safflower (*Carthamus tinctorius* L.) COMPOSITAE (2, 8, 13, 17, 18, 22, 25, 27)

Safflower, a relatively new crop to the United States, is actually one of the world's oldest crops. The plant is thought to be native to the Middle East and southwest Asia, where it has been known for centuries. The flowers were first used as a source of red dye for cloth. Safflower is now grown principally for its seed oil, which is used in paint, varnish, edible cooking oils, margarine, salad oil, and mayonnaise.

Safflower is a spiny plant that produces a light-colored oil with a high percentage of polyunsaturated fatty acids. When used as a food, oils of this type are reported to be better for health than solid fats. Safflower is an annual plant belonging to the composite family. Cultivars have red, orange, yellow, or white composite flowers with green bracts (Fig. 24–4). The plant reaches a height of 90 to 150 cm (3 to 5 ft).

Safflower is grown commercially in India, Egypt, Spain, Australia, Israel, Turkey, Mexico, Canada, and the United States. The crop was introduced into the United States experimentally in 1925 but is still not an important crop. It is grown commercially in parts of the northern Great Plains, the dry

Fig. 24–4 Safflower is a relatively new commercial oil crop. Safflower plants are characterized by their brightly colored orange-red flowers and thorny leaves. *A:* A field of safflower in full bloom is a beautiful sight, but the thorny leaves make it a difficult crop to harvest. Commercial cultivars without spines have not been produced. The excellent oil obtained from the seed is used in paints, varnishes, cooking and salad oils, and margarine. *B:* The seeds in the teaspoon are about the same size as wheat but more angular in shape and white in color. *Source:* University of California Cooperative Extension.

areas of the northwestern states (eastern Montana and western North Dakota), Arizona, and since 1950 in California.

Many new and improved cultivars have been released, and the number is increasing rapidly as the popularity of the crop grows. Breeders are developing higher-yielding cultivars that have a higher oil content and greater disease resistance.

Some cultivars yield a monounsaturated oil similar to olive oil which is used for cooking. Spineless cultivars have not succeeded commercially because of lower yields and lower oil content.

Safflower grows well on a wide range of soils but does best on a soil neutral in reaction, with a deep, well-drained profile. It can grow in either heavy clay soils or light-textured sandy soils. The light-textured soils, however, require more frequent irrigation because of their low water-holding capacity. Safflower tolerates high salinity nearly as well as barley.

The seedbed is usually prepared by preirrigating the soil. If the soil is in good tilth with little or no previous-crop residue remaining, plowing is omitted and a satisfactory seedbed prepared by disking and harrowing. The seedbed should be similar to that for any small grain crop—firm, mellow, and clod-free. For furrow irrigation, raised beds are used.

Safflower can be seeded by drilling, broadcasting, or row planting. Seed is often drilled in nonirrigated farming areas but planted on raised beds in irrigated regions. If a grain drill is used, the seed is planted about 2.5 to 5 cm (1 to 2 in) deep, but never deeper than 10 cm (4 in), preferably into moist soil. Seeding rates vary from 17 to 45 kg/ha (15 to 40 lb/ac) in nonirrigated areas. For best yields there should be about 32 to 43 plants/m^2 (3 to 4 plants/ft^2). When the crop is planted in rows on irrigated land, the rate of seeding is 22 to 28 kg/ha (20 to 25 lb/ac) to get 50 to 100 plants/m^2 (5 to 10 plants/ft^2). From 35 to 70 kg/ha (31 to 62 lb/ac) of seed is used for broadcasting on irrigated land. Seed is sometimes broadcast by airplane in California.

If the soil is low in nitrogen, safflower yields usually increase with additional fertilizer. If safflower follows an inoculated legume crop, especially one that was plowed under, no nitrogen is needed. For an irrigated field of safflower, an application of 85 to 170 kg/ha (75 to 150 lb/ac) nitrogen is often profitable. In nonirrigated areas, 45 to 90 kg/ha (40 to 80 lb/ac) is adequate. Soil tests or plant tissue tests determine the need for phosphorus or potassium. In irrigated areas, 45 to 55 kg/ha (40 to 50 lb/ac) of phosphoric acid is often used.

Safflower responds well to ample soil moisture, and irrigation is essential in arid regions. If irrigation is used, it is best to pre-irrigate to a depth of 180 to 300 cm (6 to 10 ft). Later, as many as five irrigations are applied as needed. If the plants suffer water stress between irrigations, phytophthora root rot damage can be severe. Beds permit furrow irrigation and provide better drainage. Safflower develops root rots if over-irrigated.

Safflower does not compete well with weeds, especially when the plants are young and small. The best weed control is prevention, i.e., crop rotation and field sanitation. If the crop is planted in rows, some shallow cultivation is used to kill the young weeds. Harrowing or rotary hoeing on broadcast plantings kills weeds that emerge before the safflower. Preplant herbicides control some weeds, and selective postemergence chemicals have successfully controlled other weeds.

The most prevalent diseases are rust, phytophthora root rot, verticillium wilt, fusarium wilt, leaf spot, and bud rot. Rust is more troublesome in irrigated areas or areas of high humidity. Phytophthora root rot is caused by a fungus that occurs widely in the western United States, where the crop is irrigated. Leaf spot is a fungal disease aggravated by rainfall. It causes severe leaf damage and discoloration in areas of high humidity, such as along rice fields and rivers.

Insect damage has not been as severe in safflower as in some other crops. The major insect pests are flower thrips, lygus bugs, bean and peach aphids, wireworms, and loopers.

Safflower matures in about 120 days when sown in the late spring and it is harvested when the seeds are white, the leaves brown, and the stems dry. The plant does not lodge, nor do the seeds shatter unless they get excessively dry. If the seed is dry, harvesting is often done at night or early morning when humidity is high. Safflower is harvested with a grain combine of the same sort used for barley or wheat. The moisture content of the seed should be about 8 percent. The crop is sometimes cut and placed in swaths for drying when the moisture content of the seeds is as high as 25 percent. The swaths are picked up and threshed with a combine five to seven days later.

Soybean (*Glycine max* [L.] Merrill) LEGUMINOSAE (1, 3, 4, 5, 7, 14, 15, 16, 19, 21, 26)

The soybean, also known as the soja or soya bean, is native to eastern Asia. It was cultivated in China and Japan long before written history and was mentioned in Chinese literature as early as about 2800 B.C. Because of its great importance as a high-protein food source, the soybean became one of the five sacred crops of China, joining rice, wheat, common millet, and glutinous millet. Europeans first learned of the soybean about

Fig. 24–5 Soybeans are erect, branching plants that in their early growth closely resemble vegetable beans or navy beans. Most cultivars have deep root systems, which give them more resistance to drought than other bean cultivars. Nearly all cultivars are pubescent. Here an excellent stand of soybeans about 60 cm (2 ft) high is growing on rich prairie soil in the Illinois Corn Belt.

1700, but not until 1875 was there any great interest in the plant. The soybean in the U.S. was first mentioned about 1800 in Pennsylvania, where it was reported to grow well.

The soybean is an annual plant of the legume family. It is erect and bushy with many branches (Fig. 24–5). It varies in height from about 30 to 150 cm (1 to 5 ft) and its root system extends to 150 cm (5 ft) if the soil is permeable. The leaves are alternate and trifoliate except for a pair of opposite simple leaves at the first node above the cotyledons. Most cultivars are pubescent (hairy). Flowers are borne on racemes (clusters) of 3 to 15 flowers, and are white, purple, or combinations of these colors.

The annual production of soybeans worldwide has more than tripled since World War II. The United States is the leading producer, growing an estimated 70 percent of the world total. Since the different cultivars of soybean mature their fruits over a wide range of photoperiods, the soybean is adaptable to areas from southern Canada to southern United States.

The great increase in production was due to: (1) the development of more productive, disease-resistant cultivars; (2) the extension of soybean production from the U.S. Corn Belt to the southeastern states; (3) the utilization of research done by the USDA, first at Urbana, Illinois, and later at the Northern Regional Research Laboratory at Peoria, Illinois; and (4) the worldwide increase in demand for both the meal and the oil. Formerly China and Manchuria led in production. Other important growing areas are Brazil, Japan, Korea, and Indonesia; minor growing areas include south and east Africa, southern Europe, and Argentina. In the United States, the primary production states lie in the Mississippi River Valley and include southern Minnesota, Iowa, Missouri, Illinois, Tennessee, Arkansas, Mississippi, and Louisiana, Indiana, Ohio; states along the Atlantic coast are also important areas of production.

It is important to select cultivars adapted to local conditions. Because of their response to day length (photoperiod), soybean cultivars are grouped according to their rate of maturity in order to take full advantage of the seasons available. The United States has been divided into 10 bands running east to west approximately 160 to 240 km (100 to 150 mi) wide, from north to south. These growing areas extend from the northern border of the United States to the Gulf of Mexico, and are numbered north to south from 00 to VIII. Cultivars with maturity times corresponding with the zone's latitude have been developed; those requiring long photoperiods are in the northern latitudes; those requiring short photoperiods in the southern latitudes. Cultivars are classified as determinate (terminating vegetative development before flowering) or indeterminate (vegetative development continuing for several weeks after the beginning of flowering).

Besides optimum maturity, cultivars are selected for resistance to lodging, shattering, and disease. Breeders are incorporating these characteristics into their newest releases.

Soybeans do best on a fertile, well-drained soil of light texture but can grow better than many crops on poorly drained soils of low fertility.

Soybeans do not grow well on saline soils with soluble salt concentrations above 5 to 7 mmho/cm electrical conductivity. Boron is toxic to soybeans at concentrations exceeding 0.75 ppm. Soybeans are more tolerant to acid soils than most legumes, but if the pH is much below 6.5, they benefit from an application of limestone. On acid soils, molybdenum becomes limiting and the plant responds to applications of this nutrient.

Seedbed preparation is an important cultural operation. Fields are prepared for soybeans much as for other row crops. The ground is plowed either in the fall or spring, depending on workload and the farmer's preference. For heavier soils, fall plowing is generally preferred. Disking after plowing breaks up clods and kills weeds. Harrowing before planting yields a firm, mellow, clod-free seedbed.

Soybeans need inoculation with nitrogen-fixing bacteria unless it is known that the bacteria are already in the soil from a previous crop. Some farmers prefer not to take the chance and always inoculate the seed. Treating the seed with fungicides is sometimes recommended, especially if lower-quality seed is used, but fungicides generally reduce the effectiveness of inoculation.

Temperatures and day length determine the time of planting. Farmers in the northern Corn Belt states plant when the soil temperature is warm enough for fast germination and rapid growth. This generally occurs immediately after corn planting. Early-maturing cultivars are used if planting is delayed in the northern Corn Belt states. Full-season cultivars give the highest yields. Soybeans are seldom planted later than early to midsummer. In the southern states, they are not planted before early May, even if the soil is warm. Because of the short day length, early planting results in early flowering, which reduces yields because the beans form and mature too soon to take advantage of the full growing season.

In the northern areas, rows are normally 45 to 60 cm (18 to 24 in) apart on fertile soil; however, full-season cultivars yield almost as much with rows 91 to 100 cm (36 to 40 in) apart. In the southern areas, plants branch more prolifically and 90 to 100 cm (36 to 40 in) spacings are used. In California, because of irrigation, plantings have single rows 70 to 76 cm (28 to 30 in) apart or two rows 30 to 40 cm (12 to 16 in) apart on beds 100 cm (40 in) from center to center. Because of salt accumulation in the center of the bed in some areas, the rows are placed on the shoulders to avoid salt injury to the plants.

Seed within the row should be spaced no less than 2.5 cm (1 in) apart. The rate of seeding varies with the cultivar, seed size, row width, and seed viability.

In some areas an ordinary grain drill is used to plant soybeans. Row width can be widened to the desired distance by covering some of the holes in the seedbox of the grain drill. The seed is drilled to a depth of 2.5 to 5 cm (1 to 2 in) in moist soils. If the soil is dry, some farmers adjust the planter to push the dry soil aside and plant the seed in the moist soil at the bottom of the shallow furrow. If no moisture is present at 10 cm (4 in), it is best to wait for rain, since soybeans have difficulty penetrating this depth of soil.

If the seed was properly inoculated and the roots show good nodulation, the crop does not need additional nitrogen. The bacteria in the nodules fix the nitrogen the plant needs from the air. In fact, some trials have shown reduced yields with additional nitrogen. If there are no nodules on the roots and yellowing leaves show a deficiency in nitrogen, an application of 34 to 45 kg/ha (30 to 40 lb/ac) of nitrogen improves yields. Soil or plant tissue tests indicate any need for phosphorus or potassium.

Soybeans are not generally irrigated in the United States except in California and isolated areas where supplemental irrigation helps the crop through periods of drought. Need for water is identified in soybeans, as in cotton, by a change in leaf color from a light, brilliant green to a darker, dull green. Soybeans suffer greatest yield loss from insufficient water during pod formation. Sprinklers are the common method of applying irrigation water in the southern and midwestern states where supplemental irrigation is used. In western states both sprinkler and furrow irrigation methods are used.

Weeds drastically reduce soybean yields—sometimes by as much as 50 percent. Early cultivation and careful seedbed preparation help minimize these losses. Whether planted in rows or drilled, soybeans are easy to cultivate with a harrow, rotary hoe, or weeder. These tools destroy weeds before the beans emerge. They are even used after seedling emergence, but they should be avoided at the time of emergence. Cultivation should be no deeper than necessary to kill weeds. Selective herbicides are effective as preplant, pre-emergence, or post-emergence applications.

Soybeans have many diseases but few are serious since several disease-resistant cultivars have been developed. Pythium rot generally occurs early in the season because its development is favored by cold temperature. Rhizoctonia rot results in damping off or death of small seedlings. Fusarium rot is a seed-borne root rot disease most frequent on small seedlings. Anthracnose causes poor seed germination or death of seedlings. Soybean mosaic causes crinkly or ruffled leaves. Bacterial blight appears early as a small leaf spot on young plants. Downy mildew is a mildew growth appearing on the first leaves as they open. Stem canker kills the plant during the last half of the growing season. Phytophthora root rot attacks soybeans of all ages.

Several insects cause losses to soybean growers, but few are considered serious economic pests. These include seed corn maggots, seed corn beetles, wireworms, white grubs, thrips, southern corn rootworms, bean leaf beetles, Japanese beetles, grasshoppers, alfalfa hoppers, blister beetles, cabbage loopers, stink bugs, and velvet bean caterpillars.

The soybean cyst nematode, root-knot nematode, and the sting nematode cause problems for the soybean farmer.

Soybeans are physiologically mature when the leaves yellow and abscise (even without frost). The beans lose moisture quite rapidly, depending upon the weather and the relative humidity. Soybeans to be dried artificially are harvested with a combine when seed moisture is 15 percent or higher, but harvest efficiency is better at 12 to 14 percent.

Harvesting is more critical for soybeans than most crops because of shattering losses. A loss of 10 percent easily occurs under poor conditions and can represent the entire profit for the year's work. Harvest losses result from poor cultivar selection, bad weather, untimely harvest, or excessively high or low moisture content in the beans.

Delaying harvest until the moisture content is low enough for safe storage is risky because of shattering losses. A 10-day delay in harvest because of wet weather causes some cultivars to shatter as much as 20 percent. On the other hand, severe losses of beans that are too dry (6 or 7 percent) occur because of excessive shattering and breakage of beans in the harvester. For safe storage, the moisture content should be no more than 13 percent. The height of the cutter bar is important and the lower it is set, consistent with field conditions, the better. Excessive reel speed increases yield losses by shattering the beans before the cutter bar and header receive them. The difference between an average job of combining and an excellent job is often as much as 135 kg/ha (120 lb/ac). Too many green weeds in the field also cause harvest losses. The use of defoliants to remove leaves before harvest has not been successful.

Soybeans that are harvested with a moisture content greater than 14 percent require artificial drying. The maximum drying temperature is about 54°C to 60°C (130°F to 140°F).

A limited amount of soybeans are grown for hay. There are forage-type cultivars with fine stems used for this purpose. Most farmers prefer to cut soybean hay when the bean pods are about half filled. At this time the leaves are about maximum size and the stems are not yet excessively woody. The hay is cured in the swath for two to three days before it is raked into windrows. Good-quality soybean hay is about equal in feed value to other legume hays but is difficult to cure without loss of leaves, reducing quality. Soybean hay should be used as a supplement to or an emergency substitute for alfalfa hay, but not as a replacement.

The sunflower is a native of the Great Plains area of the United States. It is a tall (1 to 3 m; 40 to 120 in) annual plant with rough, hirsute stems. The flower heads are 8 to 15 cm (3 to 6 in) wide in wild specimens.

The cultivated plant is grown for its sweet, yellow, polyunsaturated oil similar to olive or corn oil. The oil cake is used for animal feed, the flowers yield a yellow dye, and the leaves are used for fodder. Seeds from large-seed cultivars are roasted like nuts, either with or without the hull and used for confection. The small seeds are pressed for oil.

Sunflowers are commercially important in the Soviet Union, Rumania and adjacent countries, Argentina, Spain, India, and the United States (Fig. 24–6). In the United States there has been a tremendous increase in sunflower plantings. For example, North Dakota and Minnesota doubled the area planted to sunflowers between 1977 and 1978. South Dakota, Texas, and California have been added to the list of producing states.

Through active plant-breeding programs, new cultivars have been developed with short stems (120 to 150 cm; 1 to 5 ft), a 50 percent increase in oil content, and early maturity (90 to 120 days). With these improvements, the plant is more adapted to mechanical methods of culture and harvest. Hybrids with disease and insect resistance are grown in the United States and many other countries. With the interest in low chloresterol foods, we can expect a rapid increase in production of crops such as sunflowers that produce high percentages of polyunsaturated fatty acids.

Under irrigation, sunflowers are grown on shallow beds with their centers 70 to 75 cm (28 to 30 in) apart. Usually a single row is planted on each bed with seeds spaced about 20 cm (8 in) apart within the row. In some areas, up to four rows are planted on wider-spaced beds. Irrigation is needed to produce sunflowers in semiarid regions, and bees must pollinate

Fig. 24–6 The land area devoted to production of sunflowers is rapidly increasing. The whole seed contains from 25 to 35 percent oil which is high in polyunsaturated fatty acids. The oil is used in margarine, salad oils, and other foods. The oil cake remaining after the oil is extracted contains about 32 percent high-quality protein and is used mostly for livestock feed. Some is used as fertilizer.

the plants. Hives should be located no farther than 400 m (440 yds or 0.25 mi) from the field.

Sunflowers, at least in desert areas, are troubled by diseases and insects, especially in the late plantings. Rust, downy mildew, head mold, and sclerotinia rot are major disease pests.

Salt marsh caterpillars, stalkborers, and sunflower moths are serious insect pests.

Sunflowers are harvested with combines in the same manner as the cereal grains.

REFERENCES

1. Anon. 1964. *Soybean blue book 1964.* Hudson, Ia.: American Soybean Association.

2. Anon. 1966. Growing safflower—an oilseed crop. USDA Farmers Bul. 2133.

3. Barber, S. A. 1978. Growth and nutrient uptake of soybean roots under field conditions. *Agron. Jour.* 70:457–61.

4. Barnhart, F. 1954. *Soybeans.* Caruthersville, Mo.: Floyd Barnhart.

5. Beard, B. H., and P. F. Knowles, eds. 1973. Soybean research in California. Calif. Agr. Exp. Sta. Bul. 862.

6. Beattie, J. H. 1954. Growing peanuts. USDA Farmers Bul. 2063.

7. Caldwell, B. E., ed. 1973. Soybeans: improvement, production, and uses. Monograph 16. Amer. Soc. Agron.

8. Carlson, E. C. 1969. Pesticides increase seed yields of late safflower. *Calif. Agr.* 23(12):4–5.

9. Chandler, W. H. 1958. *Evergreen orchards,* 2nd ed. Philadelphia, Pa.: Lea & Febiger. Ch. 15.

10. *Encyclopaedia Britannica.* 1965. 16:902–4.

11. Ferwerda, J. D. 1977. Oil palm. In *Ecophysiology of tropical crops,* eds. P. deT. Alvim and T. T. Kosloski. New York: Academic Press.

12. French, J. C. 1972. Peanut insect control. Univ. of Ga. Coop. Ext. Ser. Cir. 543.

13. Henderson, D. W. 1969. Safflower irrigation. Proc. 3rd Safflower Res. Conf. Univ. of Calif., Davis.

14. Hughes, H. D., and D. S. Metcalfe. 1972. *Crop production.* 3rd ed. New York: Macmillan.

15. Johnson, H. W., J. L. Cartter, and E. E. Hartwig. 1967. Growing soybeans. USDA Farmers Bul. 2129 (revised).

16. Knowles, P. F., G. H. Abel, R. T. Edwards, and Milton D. Miller. 1957. Soybean tips for California farmers. Calif. Agr. Exp. Sta. Leaflet 94.

17. ———, M. D. Miller, and W. H. Isom. 1963. Safflower—an established crop in California. Calif. Agr. Exp. Sta. Leaflet 162.

18. ———, and M. D. Miller. 1965. Safflower. Calif. Agr. Exp. Sta. Cir. 532.

19. ———. 1973. Morphology and development of the soybean plant. Calif. Agr. Exp. Sta. Bul. 862, pp. 7–10.

20. Lehman, W. F., F. E. Robinson, P. F. Knowles, and R. A. Flock. 1973. Sunflowers in the desert valley areas of southern California. *Calif. Agr.* 27(8):12–14.

21. Miller, R. J., and B. H. Beard. 1967. Effects of irrigation management on chemical composition of soybeans. *Calif. Agr.* 21(9):8–10.

22. Miller, M. D. 1969. Safflower competition. Proc. 3rd Safflower Res. Conf. Univ. of Calif., Davis.

23. Mnzava, N. A., and W. J. Flocker. 1978. Effect of morphactin on growth and geotropism of peanut gynophore explants. *J. Am. Soc. Hort. Sci.* 103:574–75.

24. Purseglove, J. W. 1968. *Tropical crops • Dicotyledons 1.* New York: John Wiley.

25. Rubis, D. D. 1969. Development of hybrid safflower. Proc. 3rd Safflower Res. Conf. Univ. of Calif., Davis.

26. Scott, W. O., and S. R. Aldrich. 1970. *Modern soybean production.* Champaign, Ill.: S and A Publications.

27. Smith, D. L. 1969. Breeding safflower varieties for international utilization. Proc. 3rd Safflower Res. Conf., Univ. of Calif., Davis.

28. Woodroff, J. G. 1973. *Peanuts: production, processing, products.* Westport, Conn.: AVI.

Forage and Fiber Crops

FORAGE CROPS

Forage crops are grass and legume plants grown primarily for their stems and leaves to be used as feed for ruminant animals—beef and dairy cattle, sheep, and goats (deer, camels, and giraffes are also ruminants).[1] Forage crops provide feed (1) directly, when the animals graze on pasture or rangeland; (2) as hay—loose, baled, or sometimes pelleted—after harvesting and curing; (3) as chopped green material for direct feeding; or (4) as silage, a fermented product, for later feeding.

The tremendous beef and dairy cattle industries, which are the backbone of agriculture in the United States, are based upon the production and utilization of forage crops. Cash receipts to American farmers from beef cattle, dairy cattle, sheep, poultry, and their products are about $25 billion annually, about one-third of all farm cash receipts. The value of the forage crops fed to these animals is about $12 billion annually, far greater than any other crop.

More land is devoted to forage crops than to all other crops combined—about five times more than to all grain crops, for example. Much of this land, however, is rocky, hilly, or too wet or too dry for growing other crops.

Either grain or forage crops can be used for feeding cattle, but usually it is a combination of both. The percentage of each depends upon economic conditions. For example, when strong export demand for American grain raises the price, less

grain and more forage crops are fed to livestock. In the United States, corn, barley, oats, sorghum, and rye are the grains generally fed to livestock, while wheat is used primarily for human food.

With the increasing worldwide shortage of food, it is sometimes suggested that it would be more efficient for people to consume plants and plant products directly than to feed them to animals and then consume the meat and dairy products. But the types of forage feeds consumed by the ruminant animals are largely high-cellulose vegetative materials that cannot be easily digested by humans. In addition, many of the grains fed to livestock—sorghum, rye, barley, and oats—are not particularly relished by most people. The natural grasses covering much of the land expanses of the earth can be converted to human food products economically only by the pasturing ruminant animals. Finally, many forage crops grow well in soils that are often unsuitable for growing other crops, making productive land areas that otherwise would be of little value (15).

If the increasing need for food should require the use of more and more concentrated-energy grain supplies for direct consumption, the ruminant animals could be maintained on forage crops alone. However, this would reduce the amounts of beef and dairy products unless researchers develop forage crops much higher in digestible energy than those now available. However, production of grass-fed beef is already practical to some extent and is economical in many areas. The lower-fat beef is a more healthful food.

The many forage crop species grown for ruminant animal feed belong to two large plant families—GRAMINEAE, the grasses (Fig. 25–1), and LEGUMINOSEAE, the legumes (Fig. 25–2). These two families also furnish many important human foods—wheat, corn, rice, sugarcane, oats, and barley in the grasses, and soybeans, peanuts, beans, and peas in the legumes (7).

---

[1] A ruminant animal has a multichambered stomach with a huge population of microorganisms that break down tough, fibrous materials (high in cellulose, hemicellulose, and lignins) to simpler, easily absorbed materials. The ruminants also digest concentrated foods, such as the cereal grains.

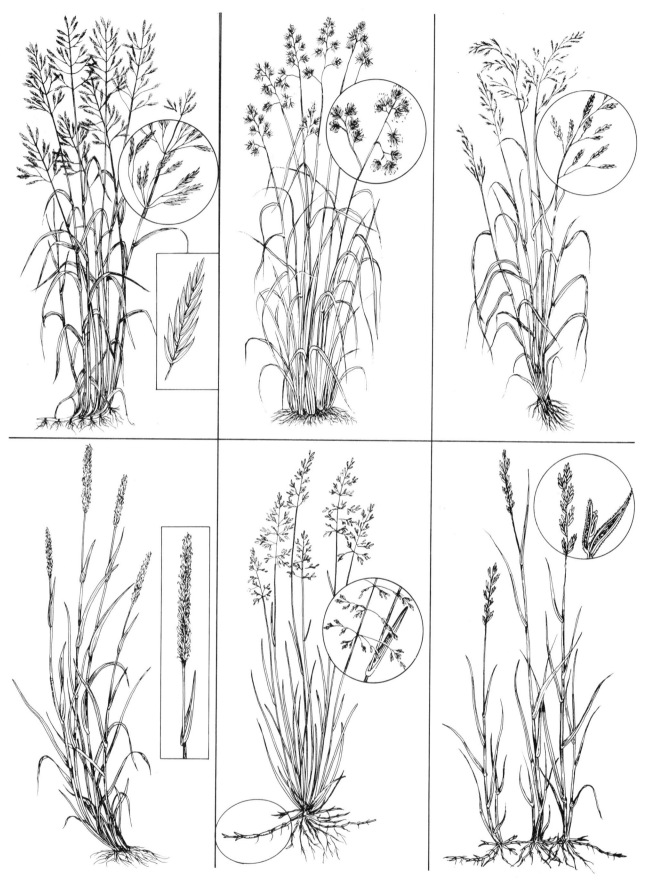

Fig. 25-1 Some of the leading grass species used as forage crops.
Above (left to right): Smooth bromegrass, Orchard grass, Tall fescue.
Below (left to right): Timothy, Bluegrass, Western wheatgrass.

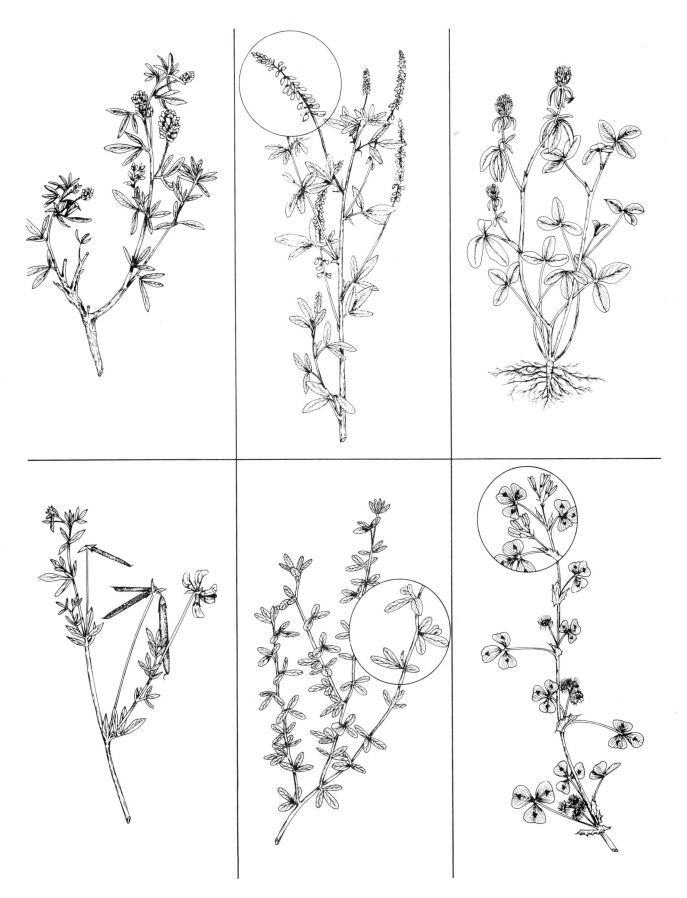

Fig. 25–2 Some of the principal legume species used as forage crops.
Above (left to right): Alfalfa, White clover, Red clover.
Below (left to right): Birdsfoot trefoil, Lespedeza, Bur clover.

Most forage crops are herbaceous perennials. Some are annuals requiring replanting each spring, but others reseed themselves.

The production of seed for the various types of forage crops is a large industry involving many commercial seed companies in various parts of the world. They produce the seed in areas with especially favorable climates. At present, much of this is sold as certified seed (see p. 82). Certified seed is relatively free of other crop and weed seeds and has a high germination percentage. Some American states have seed-certifying agencies that are legally responsible for arranging sources of reliable forage-crop seeds.

Forage Grasses

Plants in the grass family generally have a greatly branched, fibrous root system that grows several inches to several feet deep, depending upon the species (*11, 14, 25*). The initial root system develops from the germinated seed, but the permanent root system develops as adventitious roots from the stems above the seed roots. Several shoots, or tillers, of varying lengths develop from each plant. Plants of some grass species have horizontal stems—rhizomes, stolons, or both (see p. 113). The leaves are long and narrow with parallel veins, typical of the monocotyledons, to which the grasses belong. The inflorescence of the forage grasses may be either a spike (see p. 37), as in the wheat grasses, or a panicle (see p. 37), as in smooth bromegrass.

Forage grasses can be classified as bunch types, which maintain a distinct clump, or sod formers, which spread vegetatively by rhizomes or stolons to form a solid carpet. The forage grasses may also be classified as **cool season** or **warm season** types. Most of the cool-season grasses originated in northeastern Asia or northern Europe and require a cool climate with ample rainfall (or irrigation) for optimum growth.

IMPORTANT COOL SEASON PERENNIAL FORAGE GRASSES

Smooth Bromegrass (*Bromus inermis* Leyss.)

This grass is widely grown in the United States except along the Pacific coast and in the southern states. It was introduced from Europe about 1890. It has a panicle inflorescence and spreads by rhizomes. Smooth bromegrass is drought resistant, gives high yields, and is highly palatable for animals. It is very nutritious and can be used for pasture, hay, or silage. It requires a fertile, well-drained soil. Many cultivars have been developed including Southland, Carlton, Sac, Lincoln, and Saratoga.

Orchard Grass (*Dactylis glomerata* L.)

A native of Europe, this forage grass has been grown in the United States for over 200 years, mainly in the northeastern states but now also in the Rocky Mountain area, in most areas along the Pacific coast, and in the transition zone between warm and cool climates. It is a bunchgrass with many broad basal leaves and a tall panicle inflorescence. Orchard grass is high yielding if amply fertilized and can be used for pasture, hay, or silage. It loses palatability rapidly with the onset of seed maturity. It is not as winter hardy or drought resistant as some of the other cool-season grasses. A number of improved cultivars have been developed; popular ones are Pennmead, Pennlate, and Potomac. Most plantings, however, are still the common, domestic type.

Tall Fescue (*Festuca elatior* L.)

Tall fescue is grown in the transition zone between warm and cool climates. It is popular in the Ohio River Valley and elsewhere in the eastern United States except New England and Florida. It is also grown in scattered parts of the West and the Pacific Northwest. It is grown for pasture and for hay. There are other fescue species, but this one is the most important. The fescues are less palatable to animals than some other grasses because of their alkaloid content (perloline and perlolidine). Breeding of fescue grasses with lower alkaloid levels is being attempted. Fescues tolerate shade, flooding, and alkaline soils. 'Alta', 'Goar', and 'Fawn' fescue are grown in the western states and 'Kentucky 31', 'Kenmont', and 'Kenwell' in the eastern. 'Kentucky 31' is the most important cultivar.

Reed Canary Grass (*Phalaris arundinacea* L.)

This is grown in the northern part of the United States and in southern Canada. If properly managed, it produces a highly nutritious pasture, or it can be harvested for hay and silage. As with most grasses, it loses palatability upon reaching full maturity, and it also has a problem with high alkaloids. Reed canary grass has a strong root system that tolerates wet, poorly drained land and spreads by rhizomes to form a dense sod. It is useful for stabilizing gully areas in pastures. The cultivars Ioreed, Rise, and Vantage have been developed.

Timothy (*Phleum pratense* L.)

Timothy was first found growing wild about 1700 along the Piscataqua River near Portsmouth, New Hampshire and named after a Timothy Hanson. In the United States timothy is grown mainly in the northeastern states. It is a bunchgrass that attains a height of about 0.8 m (30 in). It is unusual among forage grasses in that it has an enlarged bulblike stem structure (haplocorm) at the base, which acts as a storage organ. Buds on the haplocorm produce new shoots each year, maintaining the plant's perennial growth habit. Individual shoots are biennial, growing vegetatively the first year and flowering the second. Timothy can be used as pasture, hay, or silage. It is highly palatable, especially to horses. It is often grown in association with legumes. Timothy is winter hardy but not drought resistant, and it does not tolerate close grazing because of its shallow root system. Many cultivars have been developed; some important ones are Climax, Clair, Champlain, Essex, Itasca, and Verdant.

Bluegrass (*Poa* spp.)

These grasses are widely distributed throughout the world in the cooler parts of the temperate zones. Kentucky bluegrass (*P. pratensis* L.) is extensively grown over many of the cool parts of the United States as a pasture grass and a lawn grass (see Ch. 21). Its rhizomatous growth habit produces a thick sod. It is a highly palatable pasture grass and withstands close grazing, but is less productive than some of the other grasses. Kentucky bluegrass does not tolerate heat and drought owing to its shallow root system. It tends to go dormant during the heat of late summer. Bluegrass seed must be planted very shallow, as freshly harvested seeds require light for germination. In addition to the common Kentucky bluegrass, several cultivars have been developed—primarily for lawns and turf rather than for pasture. Bluegrass seedlings are about 90 percent apomictic (forming vegetatively from female parent tissue).

IMPORTANT WARM SEASON PERENNIAL FORAGE GRASSES

Bermuda Grass (*Cynodon dactylon* [L.] Pers.)

This grass is grown extensively throughout all the tropical and subtropical areas of the world and the southern areas of the United States. It probably originated in Africa. Bermuda grass is an aggressive plant that can spread rapidly by seeds, rhizomes, and stolons. It is used for both pasture and hay crops. Bermuda grass grows best on fertile, clay soils in full sun. In winter it turns brown, making it undesirable for lawns. Improved cultivars are more productive, more frost tolerant, and more drought resistant than common bermuda grass. Some of these are Coastal, Suwanee, Midland, and Coastcross-1.

Dallis Grass (*Paspalum dilatatum* Poir.)

This is a clump grass native to northern Argentina, Uruguay, and southern Brazil. It grows to a height of 0.6 to 1.2 m (2 to 4 ft) and produces many basal leaves. It was introduced into the United States about 1842. It is best adapted to the warm southern areas of this country. It is a productive pasture grass, starting growth early in the spring and continuing on into late fall. Proper management and cutting is necessary to keep the plants growing vegetatively and to maintain palatability. It does not tolerate close grazing. In California, Dallis grass often becomes the dominant species in irrigated pastures during the hot summer months when the growth of other, more palatable grasses is markedly slowed. Dallis grass is often considered a serious weed pest along irrigation canals—the plant grows well in ditch bank habitats. Its abundant seeds are light, flat, and oily and are carried to all areas irrigated with water flowing from the contaminated ditches.

Bahia Grass (*Paspalum notatum* Flügge)

In the United States, this grass is best adapted to the Gulf coast and Florida, where it is used as a pasture grass. Bahia grass, native to South America, is a strong-growing, deep-rooted rhizomatous plant that forms a thick sod. Its deep root system adapts it well to sandy or dry soils. Some cultivars have been developed, such as Argentine, Paraguay, Penscola, and Tifhi 1.

SOME IMPORTANT PERENNIAL RANGE AND DRYLAND GRASSES

Many native and introduced forage grasses are used for pasture and hay in the rangelands of the western United States and in low-rainfall areas of the central Great Plains.

Crested Wheatgrass (*Agropyron sibiricum* [Willd.] Beauvois)

This is a vigorous tetraploid bunchgrass with a deep, spreading root system. It was introduced to the United States from Siberia about 1890 and has become a valuable forage crop. It is drought tolerant, cold hardy, and tolerant of close grazing. It starts to grow early in the spring, producing a palatable and nutritious pasture feed for livestock. Two cultivars are Nordan and Summit.

Intermediate wheatgrass (*Agropyron intermedium* [Host] Beauvois)

This was introduced into the United States from the Caspian region of Russia in the early 1900s. It is well adapted to the Pacific Northwest and the Great Plains range and dryland regions. It produces best when the weather is cool during spring, early summer, and fall. Intermediate wheatgrass is used for pasture and is often planted with alfalfa to form a high-producing hay crop. It spreads by rhizomes, forming a good sod with an extensive root system, but it is only moderately drought resistant. Some cultivars are Oahe, Chief, Greenar, Amur, and Tegmar.

OTHER SPECIES   A number of other native and introduced wheatgrass species are grown for forage under range and dryland conditions. Some of these are Western wheatgrass (*Agropyron Smithii* Rydb.), bluebunch wheatgrass [*A. spicatum* (Pursh) Scribn. & Smith], slender wheatgrass [*A. trachycaulum* (Link) Malte], pubescent wheatgrass [*A. trichophorum* (Link) Richt], and tall wheatgrass [*A. elongatum* (Host) Beauvois].

In addition to the wheatgrasses, there are several important range or pasture grasses in many areas of the central and western United States. Among these are grama grasses [*Bouteloua curtipendula* Michx.) and *B. gracilis* (HBK) Lag. ex Steud.], bluestems (*Andropogon* spp.), buffalo grass [*Buchloe dactyloides* (Nutt.) Engelm.], switchgrass (*Panicum virgatum* L), wild ryegrasses (*Elymus* spp.), and tall oatgrass (*Arrhenatherum elatius* L. Presl.).

SOME ANNUAL MONOCOTYLEDONOUS PLANTS USED AS FORAGE CROPS

Several annual plants, which must be reseeded each year, make substantial contributions as forage crops.

Corn (*Zea mays* L.)

Among its many uses, corn is made into silage for ruminant livestock. Corn is grown over most of the United States for this purpose. It is harvested by machines that finely chop the entire plant, including the ears, before storage in silos (see Fig. 25–8).

Sorghum (*Sorghum bicolor* [L.] Moench)

Sorghum was introduced into the United States from France about 1855. The sorgo type, which has a sweet juice, is grown over much of the United States as a silage crop. Sorghum is a drought-tolerant, warm-season crop that grows well at high temperatures. Sorghum does not withstand low temperatures.

Sudan Grass (*Sorghum sudanese* [Piper] Staph)

This type of sorghum is extensively cultivated over the United States as a forage crop for silage and for pasture. It has been replaced to a considerable extent in the northeastern states by sorghum-sudan grass hybrids, which are more productive.

Italian Ryegrass (*Lolium multiflorum* Lam.)

This forage crop is grown for pasture, hay, and silage in the southeastern United States and in the Pacific Northwest.

Forage legumes (7, 14)

Legumes are valuable forage crops because of their relatively high protein content—often 15 to 30 percent. Legumes have a symbiotic relationship with *Rhizobium* bacteria, which invade the plant through the root hairs and live in gall-like nodules on the roots. These bacteria in the nodules change atmospheric nitrogen primarily to ammonia. Energy for this reduction of free nitrogen gas (N_2) from the atmosphere to ammonia (NH_3) is supplied by the plant's carbohydrates (see Ch. 8).

For maximum yields from forage legumes, it is essential to inoculate the seed properly with fresh, pure cultures of the correct strain of *Rhizobium*. Legume seeds may be inoculated by the seed seller or processor, or by the grower just before planting. Soil pH must be above 5.5 for the bacteria to survive; often the soil must be limed.

Stems of the various legume species vary greatly in length, size, branching, and woodiness. The leaves are compound and arranged alternately along the stem. Most legumes have taproots. Flowers are in racemes (pea), in a spikelike

raceme (alfalfa), or in heads (clover). Some species, such as white clover, spread by stolons (above-ground horizontal stems). Generally rhizomes (below-ground, horizontal stems) do not occur in the legumes except for certain types of alfalfa. Most forage legume species are perennials but a few are annuals.

SOME IMPORTANT LEGUME FORAGE CROPS

Alfalfa (*Medicago sativa* L.) (12)

Called "lucerne" in many European countries and in Australia and New Zealand, alfalfa is believed to have originated in Persia. It has been a valuable forage crop since earliest recorded history. Alfalfa is sometimes called the queen of the forage crops since it is one of the most widely planted and useful forages in many parts of the world. It is a perennial plant grown in all parts of the United States except Hawaii, covering about 116 million ha (290 million ac). Alfalfa has been a mainstay in the development of U.S. agriculture, starting with its introduction into California about 1850 from Chile, where it had been planted by Europeans in the sixteenth century. Alfalfa requires a deep (usually more than 1 m) and well-drained soil for maximum production. It produces more protein per unit area than any other forage crop. The variegated type is very winter hardy and cultivars from this group are recommended for the northern United States and Canada. Other, non-hardy types are widely planted in mild-winter areas since they recover and grow rapidly after cutting, giving high yields.

Alfalfa and alfalfa-grass mixtures account for about half the hay produced in the United States. Alfalfa is also used for pasture and silage. Alfalfa outyields all other legumes and most grasses in comparative tests in the same environment. In irrigated areas with a long growing season, yields of about 27 MT/ha (11 t/ac) can be obtained from five to seven cuttings during the growing season. In the northern states, with a shorter growing season, yields are 7.5 to 15 MT/ha (3 to 6 t/ac) from two to four cuttings.

Alfalfa often is grown in combination with other legumes such as red clover, or with certain grasses such as smooth bromegrass. Alfalfa is a nutritious feed palatable to livestock, but it must be harvested properly to retain its nutritive properties. An optimum maturity stage has to be selected so that the crop retains the nutritive value and palatability of the early shoot and leaf growth, yet provides the higher yields of the more mature growth. Such a maturity stage is believed to occur when about one-tenth of the flowers have opened. In northern areas, where winter damage can be a problem, the last cutting should be at least four weeks before the first killing frost to permit the plants to store carbohydrates and develop cold resistance.

One of the disadvantages of alfalfa, as well as of some other legumes, is that it can cause bloat—accumulation of large amounts of gas in the animal's stomach—in pasturing cattle and sheep.[2] Bloat can be minimized, however, by certain prac-

---

[2]Estimates place the annual economic loss in the United States from bloat in cattle at well over $100 million. Death loss is calculated to exceed 5 percent of the cattle population.

tices such as chopping up the hay and mixing it with other rations before feeding.

Alfalfa is susceptible to bacterial wilt, but resistant cultivars such as Iroquois and Vernal are available. Leaf spot is a problem in the eastern United States, damaging leaves and reducing the feed value. The alfalfa weevil, which does considerable damage, is best controlled chemically. Lygus bug is a serious pest in some areas.

Certified seed of many alfalfa cultivars is available in the United States for planting. Some popular cultivars are Saranac, Iroquois, Team, WL305, and Vernal.

White Clover (*Trifolium repens* L.)

This is a widely grown legume, finding considerable use as a perennial pasture crop for livestock. It is believed to have originated in the eastern Mediterranean region.

There are three types of white clover—the small, intermediate, and large. Small or common white clover is found in lawns over much of the United States and Canada. The intermediate type is grown in the southern states in permanent pastures with bermuda grass, bahia grass, or dallis grass, but it requires frequent renovation. The large types—such as the cultivars Merit and Pilgrim—are grown mostly in northern regions and usually in association with the orchard grasses, the ryegrasses and the fescues. They yield much more than the smaller types, provided they are fertilized heavily.

'Ladino' clover has several characteristics that make it a valuable pasture legume: it is very productive if soil mositure is ample; it is highly palatable and high in protein—20 to 30 percent; it tolerates poor drainage; it is a strong-growing plant, spreading by stolons, that recovers easily after grazing; it competes well in grass mixtures; and it reseeds itself easily.

Like alfalfa, white clover can cause bloat in ruminant animals. It is a desirable feed crop for single-stomach animals such as hogs.

Red Clover (*Trifolium pratense* L.)

This species is native to southeastern Europe and Asia Minor. Although a perennial, red clover is widely grown in the northeastern United States and southern Canada as a biennial pasture, hay, and silage forage crop—disease and insect problems limit its longevity. Red clover has been losing popularity in recent years; other legumes are replacing it. However, red clover is well adapted to a wide range of climatic conditions. The cultivars are easy to establish, grow rapidly, and give good yields (but less than alfalfa). Cultivars include Kenland, Chesapeake, Lakeland, Ottawa, Tensas, and Kenstar.

Two main types of red clover are grown in the United States and Canada. Medium red clover is planted largely in the Pacific Northwest, along the Atlantic coast, and in the Midwest. It produces two hay crops a year. The planting is generally replaced after the second cutting of the second year. The second type is known as the American mammoth red clover. It grows slower than the medium red clovers, producing only one hay crop. Red clovers alone cause bloat in pasturing ruminant livestock, so grasses are usually also seeded in a pasture mixture.

Alsike Clover (*Trifolium hybridum* L.)

Alsike clover is grown for pasture, hay, and silage primarily in the New England and north central states as well as in the Pacific Northwest and eastern Canada. It is also an important forage crop in northern Europe, where it has been grown for centuries. Alsike clover is best adapted to cool climates and wet soils, and even tolerates flooding. It grows on a wide range of soil types. Alsike clover is often planted with grass, such as timothy, which aids in holding it erect. Aurora is a cultivar developed in Canada. 'Tetra' is a tetraploid type released in Sweden.

Bird's-foot Trefoil (*Lotus corniculatus* L.)

The broad-leaved bird's-foot trefoil is an excellent long-lived, highly nutritious pasture crop producing most heavily in mid to late summer. It is a native legume in Europe and parts of Asia, being brought into cultivation in Europe some time after 1900. It is a perennial plant grown in the northeastern and north central United States and in southeastern Canada. It is also grown along the Pacific Coast under irrigation. In the Pacific coast states, bird's-foot trefoil does not compete with 'Ladino' clover. It survives only where the soil is too dry or too infertile for 'Ladino'.

Bird's-foot trefoil is one of the most salt-tolerant forage legumes and, when planted with 'Goar' fescue as an irrigated pasture crop, is a most useful plant in alkali reclamation projects. It is used primarily as a pasture forage crop and does well mixed with grasses such as timothy or smooth bromegrass. It is not ordinarily used for hay. Most cultivars are winter hardy in northern United States and southern Canada. 'Dawn', 'Empire', and 'Viking' are recommended. Bird's-foot trefoil grows well on a wide range of soil types but is difficult to establish. The seeds of various cultivars require inoculation with special strains of *Rhizobium* bacteria specific for the species. Unlike most legumes, bird's-foot trefoil does not cause bloat in ruminant animals.

Crimson Clover (*Trifolium incarnatum* L.)

This is a winter annual legume pasture crop grown in the southeast United States (except peninsular Florida) and along the Pacific Coast. It does well under a wide range of soil and climatic conditions. Crimson clover was grown in Italy, France, and Hungary in the eighteenth century and was introduced into the United States in 1819 from Italy.

It tolerates some soil acidity and grows well on either sandy or clay soils but requires good drainage. It grows more at lower winter temperatures than most other clovers. For fall and winter grazing, seeds are sown from July to November in the northern hemisphere. Crimson clover can be used for winter pasture and then harvested for seed in the summer. It does well in mixtures of such grasses as bermuda grass or dallis grass. Good yields of high-quality hay may be obtained if it is harvested just before the half-bloom stage. Reseeding cultivars such as Dixie and Tibbee have been developed. The seeds germinate gradually over a long period in autumn.

Lespedeza (*Lespedeza* spp.)

Three species of lespedeza are grown in the United States—Korean (*L. stipulacea* Maxim.), striate [*L. striata* (Thunb.) H. & A.], and Sericea [*L. cuneata* (Dumont) G. Don.] The first two are annuals; the third, perennial. Lespedeza-producing areas in the United States run from southeastern Nebraska to southeastern Texas and extend eastward to the Atlantic Coast, excluding the Florida peninsula. The lespedezas are important warm-season legumes grown for summer pasture and for hay in the United States since the early 1930s. Some Korean type cultivars are Iowa 6, Rowan, Yadkin, and Summit. Kobe is a striate-type cultivar. Arlington and Serala are sericea-type cultivars. Lespedezas are best used in combination with other crops, such as small-grain cereals and grass sods.

OTHER FORAGE LEGUMES Winter-growing, reseeding annual legumes such as subterranean clover (*Trifolium subterraneum* L.) and the annual medics such as bur clover (*Medicago hispida* Gaertn.) are rapidly increasing as important introduced forage plants in the Mediterranean-type range areas of the Pacific coast. The many cultivars of these plants, when properly inoculated, not only are prolific forage producers but also fix large amounts of nitrogen for associated annual grasses that make up the bulk of the range cover.

Utilization of Forage Crops

Livestock grazing on rangelands and pastures are fed at the lowest cost since the animals themselves do the harvesting (Fig. 25–3). A distinction is made between rangeland and pasture. Rangeland refers to extensive grazing areas consisting largely of native vegetation, whereas most of the pasture lands in the United States are located in the eastern and central sections and are seeded with introduced forage species. Rangelands may or may not be fenced. Pasture land is always fenced.

Fig. 25–3 Beef cattle feeding on irrigated permanent pasture. *Source:* University of California Cooperative Extension.

RANGELANDS

In the United States there are about 283 million ha (700 million ac) of rangeland, mostly in the western states. In addition to livestock grazing, rangelands provide wildlife feed, recreation, and timber resources. Over half the rangelands in the western United States are owned by the federal government but permits for grazing can be obtained from the Forest Service's Bureau of Land Management or Bureau of Reclamation.

The proper management of rangelands gives maximum livestock production while conserving the land and its vegetative cover. Proper rangeland management can do much to upgrade the land's ability to feed livestock. Undesirable forage species can be eliminated by fire, chemical or mechanical means, or competition from more aggressive plants. Undesirable plant communities can often be replaced by seeding the area to species that are more productive and more nutritious and palatable for livestock. Proper grazing management also increases the percentage of desirable species.

PASTURES

Pastures are land areas seeded to various introduced forage species. In the eastern and midwestern United States, pasture lands are generally supported by rainfall but in arid and semiarid western areas, irrigation of the pastures is necessary.

Pastures may be classified as:

1. **Permanent pastures**, maintained indefinitely for grazing.
2. **Temporary pastures**, in use as pastures for less than one year.
3. **Cropland pastures**, rotated with other crops on the same land.

PERMANENT PASTURES Permanent pastures develop from a stand of natural grasses, by intentional seeding of one or more perennials or reseeding annuals, or from abandoned cultivated fields invaded spontaneously by one or more aggressive forage plants. Permanent pasture is often the only practical economic use of land that is too hilly or too wet for other agricultural activities.

For a permanent pasture to be productive and support an economic number of cattle, it must be given care. In the absence of legumes, fertilizers are likely to be needed, especially nitrogen. Leguminous pasture crops may require phosphorus, potassium, and sulfur. In high-rainfall areas, the soils become acid and require added lime for best growth of the pasture vegetation. More desirable species may be reseeded to upgrade the pasture's productivity or to extend the grazing period. A seedbed should be prepared and the seeding done in early spring or early fall, depending on the species.

The grazing periods and the number of animals on a given land area must be regulated to maintain a pasture in good condition. Poor grazing management can ruin a fine pasture. In regions with severe winters, late fall grazing should be avoided since it lowers nutrient reserves in the plants and decreases their winter survival rate. Legumes in pastures need at least four weeks without grazing before the average date of the first killing frost.

Rotational grazing—that is, using different sections of the pasture in sequence—permits the most flexible and efficient use of pasture areas. A series of fenced adjacent pastures allows the moving of animals from one section to the next, thus giving each section a time to recover. Some fields may not be pastured but allowed to grow for hay or silage.

Low-quality permanent pastures are often best improved by renovation. This consists of:

1. complete or partial elimination of the existing sod by chemical or mechanical means
2. growing of at least one annual crop, such as a small grain
3. preparation of a smooth, well-pulverized seedbed
4. soil tests to determine the need for fertilizers or lime, which should be applied before seeding
5. reseeding at the proper time of year with improved selected legume and/or grass cultivars

Renovated pastures should not be heavily grazed during the first year or until the plants become well established.

TEMPORARY PASTURES   Sometimes large amounts of pasture forage are needed on an emergency basis. This need can be met by utilizing such annual crops as Italian ryegrass, Sudan grass, wheat, oats, millet, or crimson clover, depending upon the climate of the area.

CROPLAND PASTURES   Some pastures are included in a rotation scheme with other crops. If the pasture is to serve for a single year, annuals such as Sudan grass, ryegrass, or annual sweet clover might be used. If the pasture is to occupy several years in the rotational cycle, perennials such as orchard grass, timothy, or bromegrass plus alfalfa or red clover could be used.

When pastures, especially those with legumes, are included in a crop rotation, the land benefits in several ways: the nitrogen level in the soil is increased, soil erosion is reduced, good soil structure is maintained, and the productivity of crops in the cycle is raised. A larger proportion of total U.S. pasture production comes from these cropland pastures than from the low-productivity rangelands and permanent pastures.

HAY

Hay is defined as the shoots and leaves—and in some cases, the flowers, fruits, and seeds—of forage plants that are harvested and dried for future feeding to livestock. Hay usually consists of grasses, legumes, or a combination of the two. The harvested material is dried to a moisture level of 15 to 20 percent or less. Hay is the most important type of stored forage and provides considerable flexibility in animal-feeding operations. Properly dried and stored, it can be kept for several years with little loss of nutritive qualities. In severe-winter regions, it permits feeding ruminant animals a nutritious bulk material when outside pastures are covered with snow or otherwise unavailable.

Hay is a cash commodity that can be bought and sold, whereas pasture forage can be converted into cash only by animal feeding.

In general, the best time to harvest hay for maximum yields and still maintain an acceptable degree of palatability is near heading, when the flowers first appear. Some forage crops, such as American mammoth red clover, give only one

cutting of hay during the growing season. Others, such as alfalfa, provide several.

Hay quality is determined by plant maturity leafiness, color, and amount of foreign material. During harvest and transportation, every effort should be made to retain as much of the leaf area as possible since most of the protein is in the leaves. High-quality hay has a fresh green color, a good aroma, and a pliable texture. It is nutritious and palatable. Detrimental foreign material includes weeds, poisonous or thorny plants, spiny seeds, and such objects as pieces of wire, nails, rocks, and dirt clods.

Hay may be stored loose, chopped, baled, or as cubes or wafers. Harvesting of hay is now highly mechanized. The older systems of cutting the hay—with the mowing machine, or still earlier, the hand scythe—and working it into windrows for drying, loading onto wagons and hauling to the barn, and storing it loose in barn lofts required considerable hand labor as well as storage space (see Ch. 12).

Today many kinds of machines are available for handling hay. Special stack wagons are used to pick hay up from the windrows and compress it into high-density stacks weighing 1 to 6 t with curved tops to shed rain and snow (Fig. 25–4). These stacks may be transported from the fields to feeding or storage areas.

Fig. 25–4 Hay, after cutting and curing in a windrow, can be collected into stack wagons, compressed into tight, dome-topped, weather-resistant stacks that are left in the field for storage and future feeding. *Above:* A 6-t stack wagon collecting hay from the windrow. *Below:* A smaller 1.5-t, 8ft high stack being unloaded in the field. *Source:* Deere and Company.

Fig. 25–5 Alfalfa hay curing in windrows after cutting and before baling.

Fig. 25–6 A hay baler being pulled by a tractor. This baler picks up the cured hay and compresses it into bales that are placed along the row for later hauling to storage sheds. *Source:* Deere and Company.

Fig. 25–7 Picking up baled hay for hauling to storage areas.

Hay baling by modern methods is shown in Figures 25–5, 25–6, and 25–7. The hay is cut, put into windrows, and baled by moving machinery. This saves considerable labor over earlier methods of hauling hay to stationary hay balers. Most hay in the United States is now stored as bales, an efficient use of space. Bales may be small-square, small-round, or large-round types. They are a commodity that can be bought, sold, and transported more easily than hay in loose form.

Machinery is now available to chop hay, green or dry, in the field into particles small enough to be blown in an airstream into trucks. The hay is then transported to feeding areas to be fed green to livestock or to dehydration equipment for storage and later feeding.

Hay is cubed, pelleted, or wafered in parts of the United States with rainless summers of low humidity, such as California, Arizona, New Mexico, and eastern Washington. In these areas hay can be field-cured down to a moisture level of about 12 percent. Field cubing has become very popular. This procedure permits almost complete mechanization of the harvesting, transporting, and feeding of hay. The initial investment in equipment is high, but the practice is considered economically successful owing to reduced labor costs. In cubing, the hay is gathered from windrows by machine, then cut and compressed into small chunks about $6 \times 6 \times 12$ cm ($1.25 \times 1.25 \times 2.5$ in). It is then loaded into trailers for hauling to feeding bunkers or to storage facilities. The cubes spoil if they are stored with a moisture level over about 15 percent (see Fig. 12–8).

SILAGE

The feeding of silage to livestock is an ancient practice in Europe dating back many hundreds of years but the first silo was not constructed in the United States until 1876, when the U.S. farmer no longer had unlimited rangeland.

Silage is green chopped forage, allowed to ferment under anaerobic conditions. Entire green corn plants are most often used for making silage, but many other green, moist forage crops can also be used, alone or mixed. Some of these are sorghum, Sudan grass, smooth bromegrass, orchard grass, Italian ryegrass, reed canary grass, timothy, alfalfa, alsike clover, and red clover.

In silage fermentation by the direct cut method, the green chopped forage material—at a moisture content of about 70 percent is blown into the silo. Silos are airtight structures, either vertical or horizontal. They may be made of wood, concrete, glass-coated steel plates, or they may be mere trenches in the ground. After the oxygen in the mass of chopped material is used up by enzymatic reactions and aerobic bacteria, anaerobic bacteria act on the carbohydrates in the plant tissue to form lactic acid, which essentially "pickles" the plant material. The pH drops to 4.2 or below, inhibiting spoilage bacteria and enzyme action and thus prevents deterioration. The fermentation process is completed in two to three weeks. Silage can be kept in good condition for several years if air is kept out, moisture stays high, and the pH remains below 4.2.

Modern silage preparation is highly mechanized. It starts with cutting the corn plants—or other forage material—by special harvesters that blow the ground-up material into trailers for hauling to the silo. Silos are filled at the top and the preserved feed withdrawn from the top or the bottom, depending upon the construction (Fig. 25–8).

Fig. 25–8 *Top:* Harvesting corn for silage. This machinery cuts the corn stalks, including the ears, grinds and blows them into wagons for hauling to the silos. *Source:* R. L. Haaland. *Bottom:* Typical silo which is filled with the ground material.

FIBER CROPS

Many kinds of plants are cultivated for their fibers, which are used to make yarn, fabrics, rope, paper, insulation, raw cellulose, and hundreds of other products.

Fiber-producing plants can be categorized as:

1. Those in which the fibers are produced on the surface of the plant parts in association with floral structures. The principal examples are cotton and kapok, where the fibers develop as outgrowths of the seed coat epidermal cells.
2. Those in which the fibers are located in the stems or, more precisely, in the outer phloem tissues of the bark. Botanically, these are phloem fibers, which are groups of very long, thick-walled cells just external to the conducting phloem sieve tubes. Plants producing such soft stem-fibers include flax, hemp, jute, kenaf, and ramie.

3. Those in which the fibers are located in the leaves. These are monocotyledenous plants with hard, stiff fibers extending longitudinally through the leaves to give them rigidity. The agave plant, which produces sisal fibers, is the most important example in this group.

Many of these fiber-producing crops have long been used. People in early days obtained many needed materials from these plants for their clothing, for ropes and sails for their ships, and cord for their fishing nets. In more recent times, innumerable other products have been made from such fibrous materials.

Various types of cotton plants were naturally dispersed throughout many of the warm parts of the world thousands of years before the Christian era, and their lint was spun and woven into cloth. The Egyptians made linen cloth from flax fibers, and ancient writings show that the hemp plant was being grown for its fiber in China north of the Himalaya mountains as long ago as 2800 B.C. Ramie was cultivated by early civilizations; the cloth made from it was used to wrap mummies in ancient Egypt. Chinese literature also mentions ramie as early as 2200 B.C.

In recent times these natural fibers have had to compete with man-made fibers; that is, fibers made by the alteration of natural fibers, such as rayon, made from cellulose in a technique developed about 1900. Some man-made fibers are completely synthesized, made from polymers (long-chain molecules of carbon, hydrogen, oxygen, and nitrogen). An example of a synthetic fiber is nylon, which is from such raw materials as water, air, coal, and natural gas. Blends of natural fibers like cotton with synthetics have helped maintain the market demand for the natural products.

Plants Producing Surface-Fibers in Association with Floral Parts

Cotton (*Gossypium* spp.) MALVACEAE (*1, 2, 3, 4, 5, 6, 7, 8, 10, 13, 16, 17, 21, 22, 23, 24*)

Cotton has been one of the world's most important crops since the beginning of civilization. It continues to make immense contributions to people's comfort. In spite of competition from synthetic fibers, cotton is still basic in the world's textile industry (26). Cotton is grown principally for its lint although the seed produces a valuable and widely used food oil. The seed residue, called cottonseed meal, is used as a livestock feed or processed into a high-protein flour.

The various cotton species originated in several warm regions of the world. There is evidence that cotton was grown and processed into cloth as long ago as 5000 B.C. in Mexico, 3000 B.C. in Pakistan, 2500 B.C. in Peru, and 2000 B.C. in India. Cotton fabrics found in Indian pueblo ruins in Arizona indicate its use there about 500 B.C. Alexander the Great is credited with bringing cotton to Europe from India about 325 B.C. Cotton was introduced into Florida in 1556 and was taken to Virginia in 1607, where it soon developed into a major crop and became a significant factor in the agricultural, political, and social development of the southern states.

Only 4 of the 20 or so cotton species are cultivated for their spinnable fibers. Two are diploid Old World species—*G. arboreum* L. and *G. herbaceum* L.—which are believed to have originated in southern Africa. These have a 2n chromosome number of 26 and produce a short—1 to 2 cm (0.4 to 0.8 in)—coarse lint. The other two are tetraploid New World species—*G. hirsutum* L. and *G. barbadense* L. They have a 2n chromosome number of 52. About two-thirds of the cotton grown in the world and almost all that is grown in the United States is known as American Upland cotton and belongs to the species *G. hirsutum*. This species originated in Central America and southern Mexico as a perennial shrub. Improvements through breeding and selection have altered it to an annual plant. American Upland cotton produces fibers varying from short to long—2.2 to 3 cm (0.9 to 1.1 in)—according to the cultivar. Seventy to 80 cultivars are now grown.[3] Some important ones in the United States are:

> Deltapine 45A
> Stoneville 213
> Lankart LX 571
> Acala SJ-2
> Acala SJ-4
> Coker 201
> Paymaster 111
> Stoneville 7A
> Stripper 31

G. barbadense L., originating in the Andean region of Peru, Ecuador, and Colombia, accounts for no more than 1 percent of the cotton grown in the United States, where it is known as American Pima. It is an extralong staple cotton with fibers up to 3.2 cm (1.25 in) long. There are two types of Pima cotton: Sea Island, grown very little now, and American-Egyptian, which is grown in irrigated regions of the Southwest such as the Salt River Valley of Arizona and the upper Rio Grande Valley. Pima S-1 is the principal American-Egyptian cultivar being grown; it brings a premium price because its lint has good spinning quality, although yields are lower than with Upland cotton.

The large cotton-producing countries and the approximate amount of lint produced, in millions of bales (1 bale = approx. 218 kg or 480 lb) are:

> USSR (10.8)
> United States (10.3)
> China (7.0)
> India (4.4)
> Pakistan (2.4)
> Brazil (2.3)
> Egypt (2.3)

The remainder of the world's cotton comes from almost all tropical and subtropical countries. In some countries such as Egypt, cotton is a major crop and a very important revenue

[3]In cotton, a cultivar is not a clone, pure line, or a primary mixture of pure lines (see p. 47). It is usually a progeny row selection, bulked and mass multiplied. Insect pollination may play an insignificant or a major role, depending upon the pollinator population during the blooming period.

source. Hand harvesting of cotton is laborious. Cotton production is therefore limited to those countries that have an abundant supply of cheap labor or, as in the United States, that grow the crop with almost complete mechanization. Texas, California, Mississippi, Arkansas, Alabama, and Louisiana are the leading cotton-producing states. The cotton plant grows well in subtropical climates and the warm parts of the temperate zones.

In planting, cotton acid-delinted certified seed that has been treated with a fungicide is used, spaced 8 to 20 cm (3 to 8 in) apart in rows 91 to 107 cm (36 to 42 in) apart. Planting is done with a 4- to 8-row mechanical drill planter that covers the seed 2.5 to 5 cm (1 to 2 in) deep. Some planters also apply fertilizers and pesticides in the row. Planting comes after all danger of frost has passed and soil temperatures have reached at least 20°C (68°F). In the United States this ranges from early March in southern Texas to early May in the northerly areas of the Cotton Belt.

Maximum productivity is achieved with high temperatures during the growing season, high light intensity, ample soil moisture, and good soil fertility. Cotton cannot tolerate frost and requires at least 200 frost-free days from planting to crop maturity.

Optimum day temperatures during the flowering period range from 32°C to 38°C (90°F to 100°F). Because of breeding and selection programs in the temperate regions, cotton is no longer subjected to major photoperiodic control, but high light intensity promotes maximum production of fiber and seeds.

Depending on the cultivar and environment, flowering branches in cotton originate at about the seventh node on the main stem. Floral buds, called squares, are visible on those branches about three weeks before flower opening, which occurs about two months after the seed is planted. The cotton plant initiates far more flower buds than develop into flowers, and far more flowers than mature into profitable bolls—the ovaries or fruits that contain the seeds (ovules) bearing the fibers.

The cotton flower is perfect (containing both male and female organs) and is open-pollinated (fertilization entails either self- or cross-pollination) (see Fig. 25–9). Although in-

Fig. 25–9 Cotton flowers ready for pollination. *Source:* National Cotton Council of America.

sects, principally honeybees, aid in pollination, most bolls set by self-pollination.

In most commercial cottons, petal color is cream to pale yellow on the day the flowers open. The notable exception is Pima cotton, whose flowers have a deep purple throat and bright yellow petals. Coincidental with flower opening is anther dehiscence and the release of pollen grains, which germinate about one-half hour after they are deposited on the stigma surface.

Varying slightly among cultivars and influenced by the environment, Upland cottons initiate development of the important lint fibers as protuberences of epidermal cells of the ovules. This happens the morning the flowers start to open. Fertilization occurs by the end of the first day after flower opening. According to current thinking, fertilization initiates processes that cause the formation of a plant hormone essential to seed formation—and thus fruit set—and continued fiber elongation (Fig. 25–10).

All commercial cultivars of Upland cotton produce two types of fibers: **lint** and **fuzz** (the latter called **linters**). As described, lint fibers and fuzz fibers originate as epidermal hairs, but while lint fibers initiate the morning of flower opening, fuzz fibers originate about 6 to 12 days later. Although variable, fuzz fibers are usually less than one-fifth as long as lint fibers. Lint fibers elongate for about 28 days, during which time they are bounded by a thin primary wall coated with a very thin cuticle. The cellulose content of the primary wall does not exceed about 20 percent. The lumen of the fiber cell consists of a large central vacuole and a thin peripheral layer of cytoplasm.

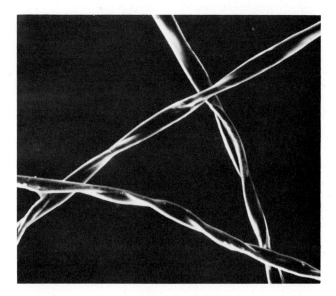

Fig. 25–11   Scanning electron micrograph of mature cotton lint fibers. Magnification is 225×. *Source:* C. A. Beasley.

About 14 days after flower opening, the cellulose content, the chief constituent of the secondary cell wall, rises dramatically. Secondary walls begin to be deposited well in advance of cessation of elongation.

At maturity, lint fibers (Fig. 25–11) have narrow and delicate shanks at their bases and thus are easily removed during ginning. Fuzz fibers thicken at their bases and are retained by the seed. After lint removal, seeds for certification and future planting are treated with acid to remove the linters and are coated with a fungicide. Removal of fuzz fibers from the seed is essential for the operation of precision planting equipment.

Cotton is classed as a C-3 plant (see p. 155), along with soybeans and peanuts, and, as such, is not as efficient a user of light energy as C-4 plants, such as corn, sugarcane, and sorghum.

Cotton is often grown in rotation with other crops, partly to control soil pests such as nematodes. It may be a two-year rotation with small-grain cereals (oats, barley, wheat) or a three-year rotation with small-grain cereals and corn.

Cotton plants are deep-rooted and are moderate to heavy water users, particularly after blooming. Many of the production areas, especially in the western United States, are irrigated, while in the southern and eastern states water is supplied only by rainfall. For maximum yields under irrigation, it is important to time water applications properly so that the plants grow steadily throughout the season. Irrigations given too late in the season can interfere with harvest operations.

Cotton grows on a wide range of soil types from moderately acid to moderately alkaline, but a pH from 6.0 to 6.5 is optimum. Very acid soils or those high in alkali or salts should be avoided. Like most other crops, young cotton plants have a high nitrogen requirement, but they also need potassium and phosphorus. For soils of moderate fertility about 41 to 68 kg (90 to 150 lb) of nitrogen, 23 kg (50 lb) of phosphoric acid, and 45.5 kg. (100 lb) of potash per acre annually are recommended. Fertilizers are best applied in concentrated bands in the root zone before, during, or after planting the seeds.

Fig. 25–10   Open and unopened cotton fruits (bolls). *Source:* National Cotton Council of America.

Readily available soil nitrogen should be mostly used up by the end of the season so that vegetative growth declines and fruit maturation is maximized.

Weed control in cotton plantings is necessary. This is best done by applications of preemergence or postemergence herbicides, (see Chap. 11)—plus mechanical cultivators and flame weeders, which throw jets of fire onto the weeds in the rows. Flame weeding can be safely done after the cotton stalks are about 1 cm (0.4 in) in diameter if the burners are adjusted and positioned carefully.

Although diseases in cotton are less devastating than insect pests, some can be serious. Damping-off fungi can kill the young seedlings, although the problem can be prevented by using fungicide-treated seed and delaying planting until the soil is warm enough to give rapid seed germination and seedling growth.

Cotton plants are susceptible to two soil-borne fungi that attack the roots, causing fusarium wilt and verticillium wilt. The best control is to plant only resistant cultivars.

Bacterial blight of cotton is best controlled by seed treatments and crop rotations with nonsusceptible plants. No serious viral diseases of cotton are now known.

Much cotton is lost to insect pests. In the United States it is estimated that one out of every five to six bales of the potential crop is lost to insects, mostly to the boll weevil. Various other insect pests—the pink bollworm, cotton bollworm (corn earworm), thrips, cotton leafworm, fleahopper, tobacco budworm, banded wing whitefly, lygus bug, cotton aphid, and spider mite—also contribute to these losses.

The cotton boll weevil (*Anthonomus grandis*) is believed to have originated in Mexico from which it entered the cotton-growing regions of Texas in 1892, spreading from there to the other cotton-producing states. The larvae attack only cotton but the adults have been known to feed on other related plants, such as okra, hollyhock, and hibiscus. The cotton boll weevil is found only on the North American continent. Boll weevil damage is due to the larvae feeding on the floral parts in the unopened buds or on the lint in developing seeds, causing the young bolls to dry up and fall off. The most effective control is application of insecticides by aircraft (Fig. 25–12) or by large tractor-mounted ground rigs to kill the adult females, which puncture the developing bolls and deposit their eggs inside. Few other insects have had such an impact on agriculture or received more study than the cotton boll weevil. It does not thrive in rainless, low-humidity climates so it has not been the problem in the semiarid western states that it has been in the eastern cotton-producing regions.

Fig. 25–12 Spraying insecticide on a cotton field. *Source:* National Cotton Council of America.

Fig. 25–13 Mechanical three-row cotton picker in operation. *Source:* International Harvester.

The pink bollworm (*Platyhedra gossypiella*) is widely distributed in most cotton-producing countries and has been a serious problem in Egypt and India. It also poses a major threat to the large California cotton plantings. Larvae of this insect enter developing buds, flowers, and bolls and consume both lint and seed. Since some larvae may exist in a resting stage for long periods of time, the pest may be disseminated when seed is transported.

Various species of nematodes attack cotton roots. Control is either costly soil fumigation or long-term crop rotation with nonsusceptible crops, such as the cereals.

Cotton is still harvested by hand in most countries other than the United States, where mechanical pickers were introduced in the 1940s. In the United States about 99 percent of the cotton crop is harvested by machines which can be either a "spindle-type" picker (Fig. 25–13) or a "stripper." The picker has vertical drums with many revolving steel spindles that engage and twist the cotton and the seeds from the open bolls as it passes along the rows of cotton plants (Fig. 25–14). Any unopened bolls are left for later pickings. A two-row spindle picker can harvest cotton at the rate of about 1000 kg (2,200 lb) per hour, yielding 227 kg (500 lb) of lint per acre. A worker picking by hand would harvest 9 to 11 kg (20 to 25 lb) per hour.

The stripper harvester—used mainly in eastern Texas and western Oklahoma—has roller or mechanical fingers that pull entire bolls, mature and immature, from the plant. This machine can be used effectively only with cultivars whose bolls mature at about the same time. Stripper harvesters remove only about 1000 lb of cotton per hour. Cotton harvesting can extend over a long time, from midautumn into midwinter if the weather is dry.

Before machine harvesting starts, chemical defoliants (for the spindle-type harvesters) or chemical desiccants (for the stripper-type harvesters) are sometimes applied. The defoliants accelerate leaf drop so that the spindles can remove the bolls easier and lessen contamination (Fig. 25–15). Desiccants

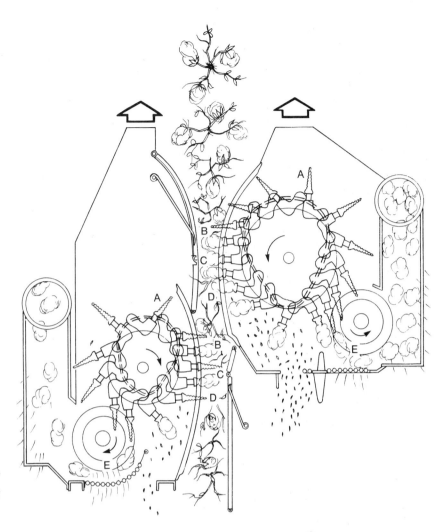

Fig. 25–14   How a mechanical cotton picker works. Overhead view of a one-row picker. *A:* Moistener pad for revolving spindle. *B, C, D:* Sprinkler removing lint plus seeds from cotton bolls. *E:* Doffer drums removing cotton lint plus seeds from spindles. *Source:* National Cotton Council of America.

Fig. 25–15   Mature cotton plants ready for harvest. *Left:* Before defoliation. *Right:* After spraying with harvest-aid defoliant chemical. *Source:* (left) USDA; (right) National Cotton Council of America.

Fig. 25–16 Harvested cotton in trailers ready for ginning, which separates lint from seeds. *Source:* National Cotton Council of America.

rapidly kill the leaves but they stay attached to the plant. Both types of chemicals are applied two to fourteen days before harvest by aircraft or by ground rig sprayers. In the United States chemical harvest aids are regulated by the Environmental Protection Agency and cannot be used unless approved and registered for this purpose. For example, ammonia can be used as a chemical harvest aid on cotton, acting both as a defoliant and a desiccant.

After the cotton has been picked from the plants by the harvesters, it is emptied into large wire-covered trailers for hauling to the cotton gins (Fig. 25–16). Upon reaching the gin, the loose cotton (plus seeds) is pulled by vacuum pumps into the building through tubes inserted into the trailers. Some cotton must first go through driers to lower its moisture content for easier processing. The cotton is then transferred to equipment that removes dirt, trash, and foreign material. From there it goes to gins (Fig. 25–17), where the lint is removed from the seed by circular saws mounted very close to each other on a

Fig. 25–17 Cotton gins separating cotton fibers from the seeds. *Source:* National Cotton Council of America.

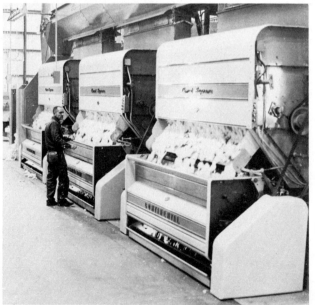

revolving shaft. These saws project through narrow slits called ribs in a grating. As the cotton lint passes against the saws, their teeth pull the lint off the seeds and bring it through the grating, which is too large for the seeds to pass through. The lint is removed from the teeth of the saws either by air blasts or by brushes mounted on a drum. The seed-free cotton lint is then baled and moved to the textile mills for processing into yarns and fabrics. The seeds that are left behind fall into a seed pan where they are collected and moved to seed-processing houses for fuzz removal. The seed coats are then cracked and the kernel is removed for oil extraction by pressing or chemical procedures.

Kapok (*Ceiba pentandra* [L.] Gaertn.) BOMBACACEAE (*3*)

Moisture resistant fibers called kapok are derived from the seeds in the pods of the kapok tree. These trees grow wild in tropical American forests and have been introduced to other tropical regions throughout the world. Almost all commercial kapok production—several thousand tons annually—now comes from the Orient, particularly Thailand, Indonesia, and Cambodia. Most kapok is sold to the United States where it is used as insulation in sleeping bags and as filling in life preservers. Synthetic fibers are rapidly replacing kapok for such purposes. The hollow kapok fibers are similar to those produced by the cotton plant. The fibers are too brittle to be spun into cloth but have a remarkable buoyancy and resiliency and are very impervious to water. The large kapok trees bear a great many of the football-shaped pods, up to 15 cm (6 in) long, which are filled with the fiber-producing seeds. The pods either fall to the ground or are cut off by knives attached to long poles. After drying, the fibers are extracted from the seeds by hand. An edible oil, similar to cottonseed oil, can be pressed from the seeds.

Plants Producing Soft Stem-Fibers

Flax (*Linum usitatissimum* L.) LINACEAE (*3, 4, 19*)

The flax plant is a slender, herbaceous annual grown in many subtropical and temperate zone countries for its oily seed and for its stem fibers. The fibers make linen cloth, book and cigarette papers, and paper currency.

In the United States, culture of flax for its fibers became unprofitable and ceased in the mid-1950s. Currently, all United States flax is produced for seed. Linseed oil is pressed from the seed for paint manufacture, and the residue, called linseed meal, is used as a livestock feed. North and South Dakota, Minnesota, and Texas are the leading flax-producing states.

The USSR is by far the leading producer of flax fibers. Poland, France, Czechoslovakia, Rumania, Belgium, and the Netherlands are also major producers.

Flax is a cool-season plant. In areas with mild winters, seeds are sown in the fall and the crop harvested early the following summer. In cold-winter regions, seeds are sown in early spring and, if used for fiber production, the stems are harvested 80 to 100 days later, when about half the seeds are mature and the leaves have dropped from the lower two-thirds of the stem. Different cultivars are planted for fibers than for seed production. Cultivars grown for their fiber require a cool growing season with ample soil moisture, but at harvest weather should be dry to "cure" the plants properly.

The fibers are obtained from the stems of the flax plant by a process called retting. Commonly, the retting involves spreading the flax straw evenly and thinly on grassy ground where it is exposed to weathering from the morning dew and to the action of soil-borne bacteria on the straw. This partial rotting for one to three weeks dissolves gums that hold the fibers to the woody xylem tissues and destroys soft tissues around the fibers. The stems then pass through machines that break up the woody parts but retain the flexible fibers largely intact. Other machines separate the short, woody sections from the fibers, which are then baled and shipped to spinning mills.

Hemp (*Cannabis sativa* L.) CANNABINACEAE (*3, 4, 27*)

The hemp plant is a seed-propagated herbaceous annual adapted to mild temperate zone climates. The stem fibers of certain hemp cultivars are used to prepare tough threads, twines, ropes, and in some countries, textile products. Most hemp produced for fiber is grown in such temperate countries as the USSR, Yugoslavia, China, Rumania, Hungary, Korea, Poland, Italy, and Turkey, but various hemp cultivars can be found cultivated or wild in almost all countries in the temperate and tropical zones.

For fiber production, the plants are seeded thickly and grown to a height of 1.5 to 3 m (5 to 10 ft). Hemp seed is planted early in the growing season, and the plants are uprooted or cut off for fiber harvest during the period from start of bloom until full maturity. The stems are hollow except near the base. The fibers are located in the phloem and pericycle tissues of the bark.

The straw is retted like flax to aid in separating the fibers from the other tissues in the stem. Machines are used to further separate the fibers.

Because certain low-growing types of *Cannabis sativa* are the source of the drugs marijuana and hashish, cultivation of such plants is outlawed or is strictly regulated in many countries.

Jute (*Corchorus capsularis* L. and *C. olitorius* L.) TILIACEAE (*3*)

Plants of these two jute species are herbaceous, seed-propagated annuals cultivated in hot, moist climates with at least 7.5 to 10 cm (3 to 4 in) of rain per month. The plants grow from 1.8 to 4.5 m (6 to 15 ft) high. The fiber strands are located in the stem just under the bark, some running the full length of the stem, and are embedded in nonfibrous tissue. The fibers are held together by natural plant gums.

As a fiber-producing crop, jute ranks next to cotton in importance. It is grown primarily on small farms in Bangladesh and in several districts in India. Jute is chiefly used in the manufacture of bulky, strong, nonstretching twines, ropes, and burlap (Hessian) fabrics, bags, and sacks for packaging many industrial and agricultural commodities. It has a great many other industrial uses—such as backings for carpets and linoleum coverings, webbings for upholstered furniture, packing in electric cables, and interlinings in tailored clothes.

Jute seeds are broadcast over the soil in the spring and the plants are later thinned to about $33/m^2$ ($3/ft^2$). The crop is harvested by cutting off the stems about the time the flowers start to fade. The bundles of stems are left in the fields for a time to shed their leaves.

To release the fibers from other tissues, the stems must be retted. To do this bundles of the stems are submerged under water in pools or streams for 10 to 30 days—long enough for bacterial action to break down the tissues surrounding the fibers, but without damaging the fibers themselves. At the proper time the fibers are loosened from the wet stems by beating the small bundles with paddles, then breaking the stems to expose the fibers, which are jerked off the remainder of the stems. The fibers are then washed in water and hung on poles or lines to dry. The dried fibers are taken to baling centers where they are sorted and graded according to strength, cleanliness, color, softness, luster, and uniformity, then pressed into bales. The bales are shipped to local spinning mills or exported.

Kenaf (*Hibiscus cannabinus* L.) MALVACEAE (*3, 9, 18, 22*)

Kenaf has been cultivated for centuries in many places throughout the world between about 45° N and 30° S latitudes. Thailand, India, Brazil, China, and the USSR are the major kenaf producers. Kenaf competes with jute as a stem fiber crop but has less exacting soil and climatic requirements. Kenaf produces an excellent fiber, tougher and stronger than jute but somewhat coarser and less supple. Kenaf fibers are used for making twines, ropes, and fishing nets and are also suitable for paper manufacture.

The kenaf plant is an herbaceous annual with a strong taproot and a long, unbranched stem reaching to a height of 1.5 to 4.5 m (5 to 15 ft). The plants require a growing season of 110 to 140 days with considerable moisture from either rainfall or irrigation. Harvesting, retting, and drying are done during drier weather. The stems are harvested just as flowering starts by uprooting the plants and tying them into bundles that are placed horizontally in water for retting, as described for jute. Retting may take 10 to 20 days. The fibers are then stripped off the stalks and dried.

Ramie (*Boehmeria nivea* [L.] Gaud.-Beaup.) URTICACEAE (*3*)

Ramie fibers are long strands in the inner bark of the ramie or China grass plant, a many-stemmed perennial shrub with slender shoots about 2.5 cm (1 in) thick and up to 2.4 m (8 ft) long and heart-shaped leaves along the upper third of the stem. New stems arise from the crown after the older ones are harvested. Three harvests can be obtained annually, and the plant can live for several years before it has to be replaced.

Ramie has been cultivated for thousands of years, and is mentioned in Chinese writings as early as 2200 B.C. It apparently is native to the Chinese area of eastern Asia. It was also cultivated by the ancient Egyptian civilizations. Present-day ramie production centers mostly in warm, humid regions of China, the Philippines, Japan, Indonesia, and Malaysia with fertile soils. Several attempts at ramie culture in England and the southern United States were not a great success, but the plant is grown in limited amounts in Florida, Louisiana, Texas, and California.

The cells making up ramie fibers are among the longest known—up to 0.3 m (1 ft). The fibers are eight times stronger than cotton and have a fine durable texture and a good color. Ramie fibers are superior in many ways to flax, hemp, and jute. However, the chief problem with ramie has been the difficulty in freeing the fiber bundles from the gummy tissues surrounding them, along with problems in mechanizing the processing of the fibers—the extraordinarily smooth surface of the fibers makes spinning difficult with machinery developed for other fibers.

As with other stem-fiber crops, retting is required to free the desirable fibers from the other stem tissues. This is done by bacterial action, which decomposes the thin-walled surrounding cells and leaves the thick-walled fibers intact. Ramie is more difficult to rett than flax and hemp. Just wetting the stems is insufficient to break down the cementing gums. Pounding and scraping is also required, followed by chemical treatments with acid or lye to remove the tenacious gums and resins to produce completely smooth fibers. After degumming, the fibers are washed, then softened with glycerine, soaps, or waxes. Ramie fibers are generally spun on the machinery designed for silk. Ramie fabrics are usually blends with other materials, such as cotton or wool.

Agave (*Agave sisalana* Perr.) AGAVACEAE (*3, 20, 22*)

The long hard sisal fibers used in making twines, cords, and ropes are obtained from the 0.6 to 1.2 m (2 to 4 ft) leaves of agave plants. Sisal is produced mainly in Tanzania, Brazil, Angola, Kenya, Mozambique, Madagascar, and Haiti. About 0.6 million ha (1.5 million ac) in Africa and 120,000 ha (300,000 ac) in Brazil are used to grow sisal. A related plant known as henequen (*A. fourcroydes* Lem.) is also grown for its fibers, which are much weaker than sisal. Plants of these two species are similar in appearance to the common century plant (*A. americana* L.).

The agave plant consists of a rosette of still, heavy, dark green leaves 10 to 20 cm (4 to 8 in) wide, 60 to 120 cm (2 to 4 ft) long, and 2.5 to 10 cm (1 to 4 in) thick, arising from a short trunk. The plant grows very slowly but after about four years, it reaches full size and harvesting of the lower leaves begins. About 185 leaves can be harvested for fiber extraction, then leaf growth ceases and a flower stalk grows upward rapidly to a height of 4.5 to 7.5 m (15 to 25 ft) and bears light yellow flowers. During the next six months, flowering and fruiting take place, followed by the death of the entire plant.

Agaves are vegetatively propagated by suckers arising around the trunk of the plant or by bulbils (small bulbs) that develop in the flower clusters after flowering, thus allowing growers to maintain improved forms.

In harvesting for fiber, the lower leaves are cut off and bundled after the spines are removed. Cleaning machines scrape the leaves, removing the pulp and waste material and leaving the fibers exposed. The fibers are then dried in the sun, or artificially, and are brushed, graded, and baled. The final product is yellow to yellow-white in color, flexible, and strong. Sisal is used mostly in making cords, such as binder twine; it has only limited use in fabric manufacture.

REFERENCES

1. Anon. 1961. Cotton production on blackland prairies of Texas. Tex. Agr. Ext. Ser. Exp. Sta. Bul. 984.

2. Anon. 1972. *Cotton from field to fabric*. Memphis, Tenn.: National Cotton Council of America.

3. Berger, J. 1969. The world's major fibre crops: their cultivation and manuring. Zurich: Centre d'Etude de l'Azote.

4. Brouk, B. 1975. *Plants consumed by man*. London: Academic Press.

5. Brown, H. B., and J. O. Ware. 1958. *Cotton*. 3rd ed. New York: McGraw-Hill.

6. Buxton, D. R., 1975. Cotton of the future, *Crops and Soils*, 28(1): 13–16.

7. Chapman, S. R., and L. P. Carter, 1976. *Crop production: principles and practices*. San Francisco: W. H. Freeman & Company Publishers.

8. CIBA-GEIGY. 1972. Cotton. Technical Monograph No. 3. Basel, Switzerland: CIBA-GEIGY.

9. Crane, J. C. 1947. Kenaf—fiber plant rival of jute. *Econ. Bot.* 1:334–50.

10. Eaton, F. M. 1955. The physiology of the cotton plant. *Ann. Rev. Plant Physiol.* 6:299–328.

11. Hanson, A. A., 1972. Grass varieties in the United States. USDA Handbook 170.

12. Hanson, C. H., ed. 1972. *Alfalfa science and technology*. Madison, Wis.: American Society of Agronomy.

13. Hawkins, B. S., and H. A. Peacock. 1972. Agronomic and fiber characteristics of upland cotton. Ga. Agr. Exp. Sta. Res. Bul. 101.

14. Heath, M. E., D. S. Metcalf, and R. E. Barnes, 1973. *Forages*. 3rd ed. Ames: Iowa State University Press.

15. Hodgson, H. J. 1976. Forage crops. *Sci. Am.* 234(2):60–75.

16. Hoover, M., D. W. Grimes, and H. B. Cooper. 1971. Cotton irrigation. Univ. of Calif. Agr. Ext. Ser. AXT 23.

17. ———, and V. T. Walhood. 1974. Chemical harvest aids for cotton. Univ. of Calif. Agr. Ext. Ser. AXT 208.

18. Killinger, G. B. 1969. Kenaf (*Hibiscus cannabinus* L.) a multi-use crop. *Agron. Jour.* 61:734–36.

19. Knowles, P. F., W. H. Isom, and G. F. Worker. 1959. Flax production in Imperial County. Calif. Agr. Exp. Sta. Ext. Ser. Cir. 480.

20. Lock, G. W. 1962. *Sisal.* London: Longmans.

21. McArthur, J. A., J. D. Hesketh, and D. N. Baker. 1975. Cotton. In *Crop physiology,* ed. L. T. Evans. London: Cambridge University Press.

22. McGregor, S. E. 1976. Insect pollination of cultivated crop plants. USDA/ARS Handbook 496.

23. Peacock, H. A., B. S. Hawkins, S. H. Baker, and J. B. Weaver, Jr. 1970. Performance of cotton varieties and strains in Georgia. Ga. Agr. Exp. Sta. Res. Rpt. 92.

24. Roland, C., H. Womack, J. Crawford, and G. Seigler, 1972. Cotton. Ga. Ext. Ser. Bul. 603.

25. Sprague, H. B. 1974. *Grasslands of the United States: their economic and ecological importance.* Ames: Iowa State University Press.

26. van Winkle, T. L., J. Edeleanu, E. A. Prosser, and C. A. Walker. 1978. Cotton versus polyester. *Amer. Sci.* 66(3):280–90.

27. Wright, A. H. 1942. What about growing hemp? Univ. Wis. Agr. Ext. Ser. Spec. Cir.

Vegetable Crops Grown for Fruits or Seeds

Vegetables are an important and substantial source of food. In addition, vegetables are significant for contributing to the quality of our diet. Vegetables enhance our lives by adding variability and nutrition to our eating. Without vegetables our daily diets would indeed be a humdrum mix of meat and cereals. A major nutritive contribution of vegetables to our diets is vitamins A and C. Carrots, sweet potatoes, spinach, tomatoes, and broccoli are good sources of vitamin A, and tomatoes, cabbage, melons, green leafy vegetables, potatoes, and sweet potatoes are rich in vitamin C. Of the almost $100 billion total U.S. farm income in 1975, $43 billion came from animal products including poultry, eggs, and dairy; $47.5 billion came from agronomic crops; $5 billion came from vegetables, including potatoes; $3 billion came from fruit and nut crops; and $0.5 billion from flowers and foliage plants. These values illustrate the relatively small amounts spent for the vegetables and fruits, which contribute so much to the palatibility of our food supply.

Beans, Snap or Green (*Phaseolus vulgaris* L.) and Lima Beans (*Phaseolus limensis* Macf.)
LEGUMINOSAE (*1, 2, 3, 4, 6, 8, 9, 10, 11, 14, 20*)

The edible parts vary from fleshy pods containing immature to fully mature dried beans. Beans are probably native to tropical America but had spread and were found growing over much of both continents by the time the early explorers arrived.

Snap beans, both climbing (pole beans) and bush type, have pods with thicker walls than do the dry field types (navy, pinto, kidney). Beans are annuals propagated by seed and the flowers are self-pollinated.

Snap beans are grown extensively in home gardens and for commercial production (Fig. 26–1). The leading states for fresh market production are Florida, California, New York, North Carolina, New Jersey, Virginia, South Carolina, Georgia, Michigan, and Tennessee (*1*). Leading states in dollar value of processed beans (frozen and canned) are Oregon, Wisconsin, New York, Tennessee, and California. Beans are grown to some extent in almost every state. They are also grown in southern Europe, northern Africa, and parts of Asia.

Snap and lima beans (Fig. 26–2) are a warm-season crop requiring a frost-free growing period, but they drop their blossoms or pods if the weather becomes excessively hot or humid. Since snap beans are harvested immature, they have a shorter growing season than dry beans. Seeds germinate best when soil temperature is 20°C to 25°C (68°F to 77°F).

There are a large number of snap bean cultivars, most of which have been developed for a particular region. Some good proven cultivars are listed in Table 26–1.

Fig. 26–1 'Tendercrop' snap beans are high yielding and mosaic resistant. They have tender, round, green pods and the plants have a wide range of adaptability. *Source:* USDA.

Table 26–1 Selected Bean Cultivars

Cultivar	Days to Maturity	Pod Color	Pod Shape	Seed Color	Remarks
GREEN POD (BUSH)					
Astro	53	Medium green	Straight, round	White	High yielder, for fresh market or processing
Bluecrop	55	Dark green	Round	White	Good for freezing and canning
Blue Lake 272	53	Medium green	Round	White	General purpose processing
Commodore Improved	58	Dark green	Near round	Reddish purple	Home gardens and local markets
Contender	49	Light green	Oval	Buff	High yielder, good shipper
Early Gallatin	52	Medium green	Round	White	Good for freezing and canning
Greencrop	55	Medium green	Broad, flattened	White	Food for home gardens, processing and market
Harvester	53	Dark green	Round	White	Good for home gardens, processing and market
Provider	50	Medium green	Smooth round	Purple	Resistant to bean mosaic and some rusts, fresh market
Sprite	54	Medium green	Near round	White	Good for home canning
Tendercrop	53	Medium green	Round	Purple with buff	High yielder, good freezer
Tendergreen	53	Dark green	Round	Purple with buff	Home canner and freezer
GREEN POD (POLE)					
Genuine Cornfield	72	Medium green	Round	Buff brown stripes	Home garden
Kentucky Wonder	67	Medium green	Round oval	Buff or brown	Home or market
Stringless Blue Lake	66	Dark green	Round	White	Home canning and freezing
Dade	55	Dark green	Flat oval	White	Home or market
WAX BEANS					
Goldcrop	53	Bright yellow	Straight	White	Processing and fresh market
Earliwax	54	Deep golden yellow	Round	White	Processing and freezing
Cherokee Wax	53	Bright yellow	Oval	Black	Home garden
Kinghorn Wax	53	Bright yellow	Round	White	Canning or freezing

Cultivar	Days to Maturity	Seed Color	Seed Shape	Seed Size	Remarks
LIMA BUSH					
Burpee's Improved	75	White	Broad flat	Large	Large flat pods
Fordhook 242	78	Cream with light green	Flat	Small	Green baby limas
Henderson's Bush	65	Creamy white	Broad flat	Small	Popular baby lima
LIMA POLE					
Florida Butter	85	Buff	Flat	Small	Home, market
Small Sieva	78	White	Flat	Small	Home
King of the Garden	88	Greenish white	Flat	Large	Good for freezing and canning
Thaxter	74	Pale green, white seedcoat	Flat	Small	Downy mildew resistant

Fig. 26–2 Climbing lima beans supported by strings in a home garden. *Source:* USDA.

The seedbed must be firm and free from clods for the seedlings to emerge without injury. Whether beans are planted on beds or flats, a row spacing of 75 cm (30 in) and 5 cm (2 in) between plants in the row is recommended. Seeds are planted about 2.5 cm (1 in) deep. If irrigation is used, it is best to plant in dry soil and irrigate immediately thereafter to get uniform seedling emergence.

Beans grow on a wide range of soils from sandy to clay loams, but silt or sand loams are best. Beans do not tolerate soil salinity, high soil boron concentration, or sodic soils. Acid soils (pH less than 5.5) should be limed.

Bush beans are not heavy feeders on mineral nutrients. Excess nitrogen should be avoided because it increases vine growth at the expense of pods.

Cultivate shallow for weed control to avoid damaging the roots. Soil thrown on the plants spreads the pathogenic fungus, *Anthracnose.*

Soil should always be kept moist. Serious blossom loss occurs if the soil dries during flowering. Since beans are shallow-rooted and sensitive to excess water, frequent, light irrigations are preferred to long heavy ones.

The bean leaf beetle feeds on the leaves and the larva feeds on the roots. Sometimes the seed-corn maggot causes damage by feeding on the seed before and during germination. *Rhizoctonia* and *Pythiaceae* fungi attack in cool weather below the soil surface and *Fusarium* attacks in warmer weather. Many cultivars are resistant to common bean mosaic and some of the rust diseases.

Snap beans reach harvest stage two weeks after bloom. High yield and quality are the primary consideration for determining the day of harvest. Most commercially produced snap beans are machine-harvested for processing when the pods are nearly fully developed but the seeds are still small. Snap beans harvested in hot weather lose quality if not cooled quickly to about 4°C (39°F).

Cucumber (*Cucumis sativus* L.) CUCURBITACEAE (*1, 2, 3, 4, 8, 9, 10, 11, 14, 20*)

The cucumber is a prostrate, branching vine native to Asia (probably northern India) and introduced to Africa and Europe before written history. Early explorers brought the plant to the Americas. The oblong, cylindrical fruit is used primarily for slicing, salads, or pickling (Fig. 26–3). The plant is an annual with hairy leaves and tendrils. The first flowers generally are staminate (male) and produce no fruit, followed by pistillate (female) flowers from which fruits are borne.

Soil, climate, markets, and transportation determine production areas. The United States leads in cucumber production, but the crop is also grown in Europe, India, the Far East, and Africa. Two-thirds of the cucumbers grown in the United States are processed into pickles, but in most other countries, they are consumed fresh. Intensive greenhouse production centers around large cities, both in America and Europe. The leading producers of fresh market cucumbers are Florida, California, Texas, North Carolina, Virginia, and South Carolina. The greatest dollar values of pickling cucumbers come from North Carolina, Michigan, Wisconsin, South Carolina, and Texas (*1*).

Cucumbers are a warm-season crop, intolerant of frost but, because of their short growing season, they are grown almost anywhere in the United States. They thrive best at temperatures ranging from 18°C to 25°C (64°F to 77°F). Pickling cucumbers are harvested smaller in size than fresh cucumbers and can be grown in areas where temperatures average lower. Cucumbers are insensitive to day length for flowering except for certain cultivars grown in greenhouses during the fall or winter.

Some recommended cultivars for slicing and pickling are listed in Table 26–2. Special cultivars have been developed for greenhouses, particularly the new gynomonoeious types (all flowers are female), which give higher yields than those with both male and female flowers.

Cucumbers are deep rooted and grow on any good soil as long as it is well drained, but they thrive best on sandy or sandy loam soils that are slightly acid (pH 6.0 to 6.5). Where irrigation is needed, raised beds flattened on top are used.

Fig. 26–3 'Palomar' cucumbers are dark green and downy-mildew resistant. They are excellent for slicing. *Source:* Ferry-Morse Seed Company.

Table 26–2 Selected Cucumber Cultivars

Cultivar	Days to Maturity	Length/ Diameter Ratio	Spine Color	Shape	Skin Color	Remarks
SLICING CUCUMBERS						
Ashley	70	4.0	White	Straight, taper	Dark green	Resistant to downy mildew and powdery mildew
Gemini	64	3.7	White	Blocky	Dark green	Multiple disease resistance
High Mark II	70	3.8	White	Blocky	Dark green	Multiple disease resistance
Marketer	70	4.0	White	Slight taper	Dark green	Good market and shipping
Marketmore	70	3.8	White	Tapered	Dark green	Adapted for northern areas
Palomar	64	3.8	White	Slight taper	Dark green	Downy-mildew resistant
Poinsett	70	3.8	White	Slight taper	Dark green	Rated better than Ashley
Straight Eight	62	3.6	White	Straight smooth	Medium green	Popular old cultivar
PICKLE CUCUMBERS						
Chipper	54	2.7	White	Straight	Medium green	Disease resistant, small seed cavity
Explorer	54	2.8	White	Blocky	Medium green	Desired for its disease resistance
Model	50	2.7	White	Blocky	Dark green	Widely used in South, attractive fruit
Pioneer	52	2.9	Black	Blunt cylindrical	Medium green	Developed for machine harvest
SMR 58	54	2.8	Black	Slight taper	Medium green	Resistant to cucumber mosaic and scab

Cucumbers are propagated by seed and planted when danger of frost has past, although some growers risk frost damage to plant earlier for an earlier maturing crop in hopes of a higher price. They often successfully avoid frost damage by growing the plants under hot caps or in clear polyethylene tunnels (Figs. 10–7, 10–9, 10–10).

Cucumbers respond well to fertilization. For poor soils or areas of high rainfall where leaching occurs, sidedressing the plants with nitrogen once during the growing season is recommended. If soil is low in fertility along the Atlantic coast, 75 to 100 kg/ha (67 to 90 lb/ac) of nitrogen, 175 to 225 kg/ha (155 to 200 lb/ac) of phosphoric acid, and the same amount of potash can be applied (10, 11). If the soil is fairly high in fertility, about one-half as much phosphoric acid and potash is used. In California and Texas about 100 kg/ha (90 lb/ac) of nitrogen is recommended for pickles.

Cultivate to destroy weeds when seedlings are visible but use care to avoid breaking the vines.

Good yields depend upon adequate soil moisture throughout the season either by irrigation or rainfall.

The striped cucumber beetle and the 12-spotted cucumber beetle chew the plant's leaves and serve as carriers for wilt and mosaic (20). Pickleworm larvae bore into the fruits and ruin them. Aphids are sometimes a severe problem. Bacterial wilt losses are reduced by controlling the beetles that spread the disease. Cucumber mosaic, spread by beetles and aphids, stunts the plant and fruits. Angular leaf spot, a bacterial disease, causes lesions on the leaves, stems, and fruits. *Anthracnose,* a fungus, causes brown or yellowish lesions on any part of the plant. Scab causes dark brown spots on fruit, and is particularly severe in hot, humid weather. Some cultivars are resistant to some or all of the following diseases: angular leaf spot, downy mildew, cucumber mosaic virus, anthracnose, powdery mildew, and cucumber scab.

Fresh market cucumbers, grown in greenhouses on trellises, are harvested by cutting the marketable fruit from the vines daily. Field-grown slicing cucumbers of market size are hand-harvested for fresh market every day or every other day. Fruit should be deep green in color and should never be allowed to ripen sufficiently to turn white or yellow.

Pickling cucumbers are machine-harvested smaller than slicing cucumbers in a once-over operation (Fig. 26–4).

Cucumbers can be stored for 10 to 14 days at 7°C to 10°C (45°F to 50°F) with 95 percent relative humidity. Temperatures below this cause chilling injury (soft spots) in the fruits, which become infected with molds. Higher storage temperatures ripen and turn the fruit yellow.

A whitish to yellow skin indicates a mature fruit with hard seeds. Slicing cucumbers should have soft immature seeds. Excessively large cucumbers are often overmature. Shriveled, withered, or puffy cucumbers indicate poor or long storage.

Fig. 26–4   A blunt cylindrical, black spined cucumber developed primarily for mechanical harvesting. The range in size for pickling cucumbers shown here varies from about 15 to 5 cm (6 to 2 in). *Source:* Ferry-Morse Seed Company.

Eggplant (*Solanum melongena* L.) SOLANACEAE
(1, 2, 3, 4, 8, 9, 10, 11, 14, 20)

The eggplant, known also as eggfruit, aubergine, or guinea squash, is probably native to south and eastern Asia, but it has also been grown in China for many centuries. As it was moved into Europe, much folklore developed about it. It has been called the "mad apple" by some and "love apple" by others. Its common name stems from resemblance of the fruit of the ancient cultivars (some still exist) in size, shape, and color to a white hen's egg.

Eggplants are produced commercially only in Florida, New Jersey, and Texas, but they are grown in home gardens and for local markets in many areas (*1*). They are grown in countries around the Mediterranean Sea, India, southeast Asia, and East Africa.

Eggplants are more sensitive to frost than most vegetable crops. They are a warm-season crop thriving best in areas where day temperatures are 27°C to 32°C (80°F to 90°F) and night are 21°C to 27°C (70°F to 80°F).

Black Beauty is the most important cultivar, but others include Early Long Purple, Florida Purple, and Special Hibush. Black Magic is a hybrid adapted to areas with short growing seasons.

Eggplants grow best in light, well-drained sandy or sandy loam soils, high in organic matter and neutral to slightly acid in reaction.

Seeds require up to 30 days to germinate and the plants grow slowly, requiring more care than most vegetable crops. Plants are best started in hot beds or in flats and grown for 8 to 10 weeks before transplanting into the field. Another procedure is to plant a seedling in a biodegradable pot when it is at the two-leaf stage of development, then later set the pot with the plant in it in the field without disturbing the roots. A rich potting soil is used and an occasional watering with a nitrate solution is needed. Plants are spaced in the field 60 to 90 cm (2 to 3 ft) between plants and rows 90 to 120 cm (3 to 4 ft) apart.

A complete fertilizer that supplies about 50 kg/ha (45 lb/ac) nitrogen, 100 kg/ha (90 lb/ac) phosphoric acid, and 50 kg/ha (45 lb/ac) potash is often recommended for highly productive soils in the western areas. The amount of nitrogen is doubled for soils of low productivity. In the eastern seaboard states 85 to 110 kg/ha (75 to 100 lb/ac) nitrogen, 140 kg/ha (125 lb/ac) phosphoric acid, and 140 kg/ha (125 lb/ac) potash are recommended for soils of low fertility. About one-third less phosphorus and potassium is recommended for highly productive soils. A sidedressing of 35 kg/ha (31 lb/ac) of nitrogen midway through the season is often wise (*10, 11*).

In arid regions, eggplants are always irrigated.

Flea beetles cause damage in hot beds and fields. The Colorado potato beetle is particularly damaging in areas where potatoes are grown. Red spider mites, which attack the undersides of leaves, are particularly destructive in dry weather. Aphids also attack eggplants. Fusarium and verticillium wilt are serious fungal diseases, for which no easy control except seedbed and field sanitation and crop rotation exists. Fruit rot, caused by the fungus *Phomopsis vexans,* attacks all parts of the plant.

Florida Market and Florida Beauty cultivars are resistant to phomopsis blight and fruit rot ("tip-over" phase of phomopsis).

Eggplants are harvested by cutting them from the vine, leaving the calyx and stem ("cap") on the fruit. Harvest can be done any time after the fruits are one-third to full-sized (Fig. 26–5). Care must be exercised in handling and packing to avoid bruising. The market prefers small, uniform, immature fruit. The maturity of a fruit can be estimated by pressing it slightly with the thumb; an indentation indicates advancing maturity.

Eggplants are consumed fresh, baked, fried, grilled, or stuffed. The best fruits are heavy for their size, firm, and deep purple. The skin is shiny and free of scars, cuts, bruises, disease, or insect damage. A wilted, shriveled, soft, or flabby fruit often tastes bitter. Eggplants are stored for short periods at 7°C to 10°C (45°F to 50°F) at about 85 percent relative humidity.

Fig. 26–5   'Black Beauty' eggplants ready for harvest. *Source:* USDA.

Muskmelon (Cucumis Melo L., Reticulatus Group)
CUCURBITACEAE (1, 2, 3, 4, 8, 9, 10, 11, 14, 20)

The muskmelon (commonly called cantaloupe) is believed to have originated in Asia, particularly Iran and India. The ancient Egyptians probably grew it, and the Greeks and Romans definitely did. The muskmelon was introduced to the Americas by Columbus.

Commercial muskmelon production in the United States centers mainly in California, Texas, and Arizona, although some acreage is harvested in Indiana, Georgia, Michigan, Colorado, and South Carolina (1). Muskmelons are also grown in the Middle East, southeast Asia, Europe, and Australia.

Muskmelons are warm-season plants, intolerant of frost (Fig. 26–6). Seeds are planted after all danger of frost has passed; they germinate best when soil temperatures are 18°C to 24°C (65°F to 75°F). The minimum seed germination temperature is 10°C (50°F). Long, hot, sunny days with low relative humidity are ideal, provided soil moisture is ample.

Many different cultivars are grown, with new ones introduced frequently (Fig. 26–7). The commercial grower is interested primarily in cultivars with good shipping qualities, but the home gardener selects those with high sugar content and flavor. Where diseases are prevalent, resistant cultivars are used. Some popular cultivars are listed in Table 26–3.

Seeds are usually drilled into the soil about 2.5 to 5 cm (1 to 2 in) deep in rows 150 to 180 cm (5 to 6 ft) apart, then thinned to in-row spacing of 75 to 120 cm (2.5 to 4 ft) apart. They can also be planted in hills at the same spacing.

Muskmelons grow on a wide variety of soils, but do best in well-drained sand to sandy loams that are neutral to slightly acid (pH 6.5 to 7.5). Saline or sodic soils are avoided.

This crop is a heavy feeder on mineral nutrients and generally responds well to fertilizers. Many farmers growing muskmelons on relatively infertile soils apply 85 to 110 kg/ha (75 to 98 lb/ac) of nitrogen, 170 to 225 kg/ha (150 to 200 lb/ac) of phosphorus, and 170 to 225 kg/ha (150 to 200 lb/ac) of

Fig. 26–6 In an attempt to obtain an extra-early crop of muskmelons, some farmers plant the seeds under hot caps, which give some frost protection to the tiny seedlings and permit earlier planting than otherwise. These plants were planted on the shoulder of a 150 cm (5 ft) bed with the irrigation furrow close to the seedlings. This method insures better wetting of soil for young seedlings. Vines are trained to grow toward the center of bed. Tomatoes, squash, peppers, and other crops are also grown under hot caps for early season market. *Source:* U.S. Soil Conservation Service.

Fig. 26–7 'Gold Cup 55' muskmelons have thick-walled fruits with good color. They ship well and are excellent melons for market. Cantaloupe is a muskmelon commonly grown in Europe. It has a hard ridged rind. The word *cantaloupe* is loosely applied to any muskmelon cultivar. *Source:* Ferry-Morse Seed Company.

Table 26–3   Selected Muskmelon Cultivars

Cultivar	Days to Maturity	Average Weight kg (lbs)	Rind, Rib	Net	Flesh Color	Remarks
Delicious 51	86	1.5 (3.3)	Hard, ribbed	Coarse	Salmon	Good for local market
Gulf Stream	90	1.0 (2.2)	Firm, ribbed	Heavy	Salmon	Powdery-mildew resistant
Hale's Best Jumbo	88	1.5 (3.3)	Firm, ribbed	Heavy	Orange	Good shipper
Harvest Queen	95	1.5 (3.3)	Tough, ribbed	Coarse	Orange	Fusarium resistant
No. 45	95	1.0 (2.2)	Hard, slightly ribbed	Heavy	Salmon	Powdery mildew resistant
Perlita	90	1.0 (2.2)	Firm, ribbed	Heavy	Salmon	Downy-mildew resistant
Persian (small)	110	2.5 (5.5)	Dark green	Fine	Orange	Western United States only
Top Mark	95	1.0 (2.2)	Firm, sl. ribbed	Heavy	Salmon	Suited for Ariz., Texas, Calif., and Mexico
OTHER MELON TYPES						
Casaba	102	3.5 (7.7)	Yellow, wrinkled	None	White	Western United States only
Crenshaw	110	4.0 (8.8)	Yellow, corrugated	None	Pink, Sweet, juicy	Western United States only
Honey Dew	110	3.0 (6.6)	Smooth, white	None	Light green	Sweet fruit

potash. On more fertile soils the phosphoric acid and potash are reduced to 85 to 110 kg/ha (75 to 98 lb/ac). A portion (one-fourth to one-half) of the fertilizer is sometimes applied at seeding time in bands about 10 cm (4 in) beside and below the seeds. In the eastern states, recommendations vary widely with soil type and previous cropping. Applications of 50 to 85 kg/ha (45 to 75 lb/ac) nitrogen, 45 to 170 kg/ha (40 to 150 lb/ac) phosphoric acid, and 45 to 170 kg/ha (40 to 150 lb/ac) potash are applied (10, 11). One-half of the total is often applied before planting and the balance at planting. In the southwestern states nitrogen alone is often used at about 90 kg/ha (80 lb/ac).

Muskmelons require abundant water during rapid vine growth and fruit setting, but excessive water should be avoided during fruit ripening. Roots penetrate deep in light-textured (sandy) soils. If high soil moisture has been maintained during early vine growth, a large reserve moisture supply is available for the plant during fruit ripening and harvest. If rainfall is insufficient, the crop needs irrigation. Enough water is applied to thoroughly wet the soil to ensure uniform seed germination, then irrigation is withheld after seedling emergence until flowering. Excess irrigation increases the number of melons culled because of growth cracks and oversize melons.

Powdery mildew and downy mildew attack muskmelons, as do bacterial wilt, fusarium wilt, and verticillium wilt. The latter three cause plants to wilt and collapse.

Wireworms, cutworms, seed-corn maggots, aphids, leaf hoppers, red spider mites, leaf miners, and cucumber beetles attack muskmelons. Regular spraying or dusting with insecticides is essential if good yields of high-quality melons are expected. Root knot nematodes are avoided by crop rotation. Soil fumigation is generally too expensive for melon production.

The harvest date of muskmelons is determined by the travel time to market, the cultivar, the method of shipment, and the field temperatures at harvest time. Fruit appearance alone is not a good guide. A common criterion of maturity is how easily the melon is removed from the vine. Muskmelons are mostly harvested by hand at the "full-slip" stage of maturity. At "full-slip" the stem slides easily from the melon and leaves a clean abscission with no pieces of stem attached (Fig. 26–8).

Fig. 26–8 Mechanical aids are used to facilitate the harvest of some muskmelon fields. The melons are removed from the vine by hand and placed on belts and conveyed to bins or trailers for transport from the field. In this example a different kind of aid is used. The melons are picked by hand and placed in three rows on the ground. This machine picks the melons up and conveys them to the truck. In the strictest sense these aids cannot be considered mechanical harvesters. True melon harvesters are in the experimental stage of development. *Source:* Michael O'Brien.

Fig. 26–9 Muskmelons are often sent to nearby markets in bulk bins and not boxed. For long distance shipment they are generally boxed in cardboard cartons or wooden crates. This is an experimental container, a two-thirds wrap-around crate made of wax impregnated fiber with particleboard ends. The large vents allow good circulation of cooling air. *Source:* Western Grower and Shipper.

Practically all muskmelons are consumed fresh, but one can find frozen melon balls at large supermarkets. Fresh fruits are available in the markets throughout the summer months depending on the location of growing areas (Fig. 26–9). Muskmelons cannot be stored for more than a few days after removal from the vine.

Okra (*Abelmoschus esculentus* L. Moench) [*Hibiscus esculentus* L.] MALVACEAE (1, 2, 3, 8, 9, 20)

Okra, also called gumbo, gobo, gombo, or lady's finger, is either Asian or African in origin. This vegetable is of minor importance in the United States except in the southern and southwestern states. However, production is increasing rapidly in other areas. It is easily grown in home gardens and gives good yields of pods. Okra is also a popular vegetable around the Mediterranean area and in parts of Africa and India.

This warm-season crop is intolerant of frost, and it requires a long growing season with hot days and warm nights. Slow seed germination is hastened by soaking the seeds for 24 hours in water before planting.

The cultivars of okra are classified as dwarf or tall, with short or long pods. Desirable cultivars have spineless pods that range in color from pale white to dark green. Some popular ones include Clemson Spineless, White Velvet, Perkins Spineless, Emerald, Louisiana Green Velvet, and Dwarf Long Pod (Fig. 26–10).

Okra is adapted to a wide variety of soils but grows best in deep fertile sandy loams with good drainage. A soil temperature of at least 10°C (50°F) is needed before seeds are planted.

Whether directly seeded or transplanted, plants do best when thinned to a spacing of about 30 cm (12 in) in the row for the dwarf cultivars and 60 cm (24 in) for the tall cultivars. Rows are 90 cm (3 ft) apart.

Well-rotted manure applied at the rate of 25 to 30 MT/ha (11 to 13 t/ac) helps soils of low fertility. In addition, an appli-

Fig. 26–10 Only the tender, young okra pods are eaten either pickled or prepared in soups or gumbos. Because the fruits contain large quantities of mucilage, they are commonly used to thicken broths and soups. In some countries the seeds are used as a substitute for coffee. This 'Red River' okra produces a deep green fruit. *Source:* Ferry-Morse Seed Company.

cation of 30 to 60 kg/ha (27 to 54 lb/ac) of nitrogen, 55 to 110 kg/ha (49 to 98 lb/ac) of phosphoric acid, and 30 to 60 kg/ha (27 to 54 lb/ac) of potash is often profitable.

Okra plantings are easily kept free of weeds by cultivation or by a recommended herbicide although some hand hoeing is also generally necessary.

In semiarid regions, irrigation is needed for good production. Foliage of some cultivars shows a slight bluish color and becomes darker when water is needed.

Cotton bollworms, aphids, corn ear worms, and stink bugs are serious insect pests of okra. Nematodes are also a common problem. Okra is extremely sensitive to verticillium wilt and is sometimes grown among other crops as an indicator plant to detect this soil-borne fungus. Fusarium wilt and some leaf spot diseases are troublesome but less so than verticillium.

Harvest generally begins about two months after planting, and continues for three to four months. About four to six days after the flower opens, the edible pods are at their prime at about 8 to 10 cm (3 to 4 in) long. Pods are snapped from the plant by hand and placed in a bag carried by the picker. Gloves are worn to avoid hand irritation and to prevent bruising of pods. Plants yield about 2 to 4 MT/ha (0.9 to 1.8 t/ac) on the average.

Part of the crop is processed by canning or by preserving the pods in brine. Freezing is also popular. A large portion of the crop is processed into soups and stews.

Good-quality pods deteriorate rapidly after harvest; to prevent this the pods are cooled quickly and maintained at 7°C (45°F) with 90 percent relative humidity. Lower temperatures cause chilling injury.

High-quality pods are tender, young, clean, and fresh with few or no fibers. Small to medium pods, 6 to 8 cm (2.5 to 3 in) in length, are more desirable than large ones. Tenderness is assured if pods snap easily when bent.

Peas (*Pisum sativum* L.) LEGUMINOSAE (*1, 2, 3, 4, 7, 8, 9, 10, 11, 14, 20*)

The garden pea (sometimes called the English, green, or common pea) is an annual, cool-season plant grown for the edible green seed, but some cultivars are grown for the edible pod. Peas are native to Europe and northern Asia, introduced later to India and Africa and then to North America about 1600.

Few peas are grown for fresh market except in local areas around large cities. They are principally grown for processing by freezing and secondarily for canning. Peas are grown in most areas of the United States, and the states producing the largest tonnage of peas for processing are Washington, Wisconsin, Minnesota, Oregon, California, Idaho, and Delaware (*1*). They are also grown in large quantities in Europe, Asia, the Middle East, and parts of Africa. Some cultivars (snow peas) form an important part of the diet in China, Japan, and Europe.

Peas grow best at temperatures of 13°C to 18°C (55°F to 64°F) but are damaged by frost. Temperatures of 27°C (81°F) lower the quality of processing peas (*7*).

Cultivars of peas are often classified into two groups according to color of the seed coat pigment. Cultivars with light green seed coats are preferred for commercial canning, but some dark green peas have been canned in the United States. The dark green cultivars are canned in Europe and some other areas. In the United States the dark green peas are frozen or sold fresh.

Pea cultivars are also classified as smooth or wrinkled. The smooth seeds have a more starchy flavor than the sweeter wrinkled cultivars. Some recommended cultivars are given in Table 26–4.

Peas are grown on most soil types. Fertile, sandy, well-drained soils favor early production and high yields. Peas are very sensitive to soil pH; they do best at pH 6.5 but fail at pH below 5.5.

Peas are planted as early in the spring as weather permits. Processing types are planted in rows about 20 cm (8 in) apart with grain drills, fresh market or home garden peas are planted in rows 60 to 90 cm (2 to 3 ft) apart, 5 cm (2 in) apart within the row, and about 2.5 cm (1 in) deep. Where irrigation is used, peas are planted in two rows 30 cm (12 in) apart on beds 100 cm (40 in) apart. Seeds are placed in moist soil even if this requires deeper planting. Seeds set in dry soil germinate unevenly.

Peas respond less to fertilizer than most vegetable crops and are sensitive to excess nitrogen and potassium, which injure the roots or cause excessive vegetative growth. On less fertile soils in the north central states, fertilizer is applied at the rate of 45 to 85 kg/ha (40 to 75 lb/ac) of nitrogen, 90 to 170 kg/ha (80 to 150 lb/ac) of phosphoric acid, and 90 to 170 kg/ha (80 to 150 lb/ac) of potash (*11*). Along the Atlantic Coast, 35 to 55 kg/ha (31 to 49 lb/ac) of nitrogen, 35 to 110 kg/ha (31 to 98 lb/ac) of phosphoric acid, and 35 to 110 kg/ha (31 to 98 lb/ac) of

Table 26-4 Selected Cultivars of Peas

Cultivar	Days to Maturity	Plant Height cm (in)	Length cm (in)	Pod Shape	Color (Green)	Peas/pod	Remarks
Alaska	58	75 (30)	6 (2.5)	Blunt	Pale	6–8	Fusarium wilt resistant
Alderman	74	150 (60)	10 (4)	Pointed	Dark	8–10	Fusarium wilt resistant, high quality and yield
Early Frosty	64	60 (24)	9 (3.5)	Blunt	Dark	7–8	Early, heavy yields
Freezonian	62	100 (40)	10 (4)	Blunt	Dark	7–8	Fusarium wilt resistant, early, good freezer
Little Marvel	64	60 (24)	8 (3)	Blunt	Dark	6–8	Excellent quality, high yields
Progress #9	60	50 (20)	10 (4)	Pointed	Dark	6–8	Early, large pods
Rondo	72	70 (28)	10 (4)	Pointed	Dark	8–10	Large, late, attractive
Thomas Laxton	65	85 (33)	9 (3.5)	Blunt	Dark	7–9	Fusarium wilt resistant, popular all purpose, early
Wando	69	75 (30)	7 (3)	Blunt	Dark	8–10	Small pods, midseason to late

potash are used (*10*). In most western states only nitrogen is applied at the rate of about 35 to 70 kg/ha (31 to 60 lb/ac). A part of the application is often made as a sidedressing when plants are 10 to 15 cm (4 to 6 in) tall.

In the semiarid western states of the United States irrigation is likely to be needed during the last one-third or one-half of the growing season.

Ascochyta blight, a seed-borne fungal disease, is best controlled with disease-free seed. Bacterial blight and downy mildew are favored by cold, damp weather. Fusarium wilt is controlled only by resistant cultivars. Powdery mildew, a fungal disease, is controlled by dusting with sulfur. Root rot quickly kills seedlings.

Lygus bugs, pea aphids, pea leaf miners, pea weevils, spider mites, and seed corn maggots cause damage to peas whose severity varies with the locality, season, and year. Nematodes attack peas, causing severe losses in some areas. Crop rotation is the only practical control since soil fumigation for this crop is too expensive.

Peas for processing are harvested mechanically when they give the highest yield of a top-quality product (Fig. 26–11). Maturity can be estimated by squeezing a pea between the thumb and forefinger. One that breaks into its two cotyledons (halves) when pinched is too mature; one that is crushed is tender and of prime quality. Local market and home garden peas are generally picked two, three, or more times by hand.

Peas are frozen or canned whole or processed into soups, baby foods, and fully prepared meals. The availability of frozen peas has greatly reduced the demand for fresh market peas, which are often difficult to find in markets. People do not like to shell them, and they are often more expensive and of lower quality than frozen peas with the exception of the locally grown fresh product.

Peppers (*Capsicum annuum* L.) SOLANACEAE (*1, 2, 3, 4, 5, 8, 9, 10, 11, 14, 16, 20*)

There are three basic types of peppers. Bell peppers (sweet types) are native to Central America, and were taken by Columbus to Europe, where they spread rapidly over most of the continent. This species bears a mild, large, sweet fruit with a distinctive flavor (Fig. 26–12). *Capiscum frutescens* (hot type),

Fig. 26–11 'Pacific Freezer' peas developed especially for western areas of the United States for quick freezing. *Source:* Ferry-Morse Seed Company.

Fig. 26–12 'California Wonder' is a popular general market sweet bell pepper. It yields well and has good color. *Source:* Ferry-Morse Seed Company.

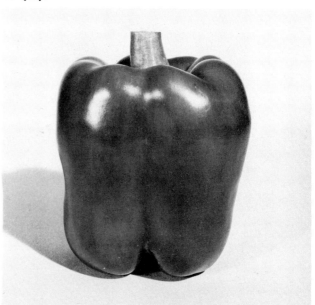

also in the SOLANACEAE family and a native of Central America, is the more pungent green or red pepper (Fig. 26–13). Common black pepper (*Piper nigrum*) is ground for seasoning. It belongs to a different botanical family and is not grown in the United States.

Commercial bell pepper production is concentrated in Florida, California, New Jersey, Texas, North Carolina, and Michigan (*1*). Some hot peppers are grown in California, New Mexico, and Arizona. Mexico produces large quantities of hot peppers for export to the United States and Canada. Bell peppers are grown in the Ukraine, the Caucasus, central and southeast Asia, and northern Africa (Egypt) for local use and export to Europe.

Excessively high temperatures result in poor fruit set. Yields are higher when temperature ranges from 20°C to 30°C (68°F to 86°F). Pepper plants do not tolerate frost.

There is a large selection of cultivars to choose from and most seed producers offer their own selections for sale. New cultivars are introduced frequently, many with disease resistance. Several sweet and hot cultivars are listed in Table 26–5.

Peppers grow best on light-textured sandy loam soils well supplied with organic matter. The pH should range from 5.5 to 7.0.

Fig. 26–13 'Floral Gem' is a yellow hot pepper. It is prolific and has good market qualities. *Source:* Ferry-Morse Seed Company.

Table 26–5 Selected Pepper Cultivars

Cultivar	Days to Maturity	Size cm (in)	Fruit Bearing	Fruit Walls	Flavor	Remarks
Aconcagua	70	15 × 6 (6 × 2.5)	Pendant	Medium	Sweet	Two or three lobes in fruit
Allbig	65	13 × 10 (5 × 4)	Pendant	Medium	Sweet	Good for short seasons
California Wonder	75	10 × 10 (4 × 4)	Upright	Thick	Sweet	Standard bell type
Early Calwonder	70	11 × 10 (4.3 × 4)	Upright	Medium thick	Sweet	Heavy yields
Canape Hybrid	62	9 × 6 (3.5 × 2.5)	Pendant	Thick	Sweet mild	Early market type
Keystone Giant	80	11 × 9 (4.3 × 3.5)	Pendant	Thick	Sweet	Good for shipping and home gardens
Sweet Banana	72	14 × 4 (5.5 × 1.5)	Pendant	Thin	Sweet	Good for frying, ornamental
Thick Wall	70	13 × 9 (5.5 × 3.5)	Pendant	Medium	Sweet	Long tapering fruit
Yolo Wonder	75	10 × 9 (4 × 3.5)	Pendant	Thick	Sweet	Blocky fruit
HOT TYPE						
Anaheim	80	18 × 4 (7 × 1.5)	Pendant	Thin	Medium pungent	Prolific, used for drying and canning
Hungarian Yellow	65	16 × 5 (6.3 × 2)	Pendant	Thin	Hot	Good for market and canning
WAX						
Jalapeno	75	6 × 2 (2.5 × 1)	Pendant	Medium thick	Very hot	Good market canner
Long Thin Cayenne	72	13 × 1 (5 × 0.5)	Pendant	Thin	Very hot	Good for canning and drying

Pepper plants are transplanted to the field from hot beds or cold frames or seeded directly. To reduce damping-off, the seeds are treated with a fungicide before planting. At planting time, soil temperature should be about 20°C (68°F) and all danger of frost past. The rows are about 90 cm (36 in) apart, with plants about 45 cm (18 in) apart (5).

Plowing under a green manure crop in the fall to provide organic matter is often recommended. High pepper yields from most soils require a complete fertilizer. For many vegetable soils of low fertility applications of 30 to 45 kg/ha (27 to 40 lb/ac) of nitrogen, 55 to 90 kg/ha (49 to 80 lb/ac) of phosphoric acid, and 55 to 90 kg/ha (49 to 80 lb/ac) of potash are recommended. On highly productive vegetable soils the phosphoric acid and potash can be reduced by 50 percent. In some Atlantic coast states, rates of applications are slightly higher. Applications of 55 to 85 kg/ha (49 to 75 lb/ac) of nitrogen, 55 to 110 kg/ha (49 to 98 lb/ac) of phosphoric acid, and a like amount of potash are used. In the West only nitrogen is generally used, applied at the rate of 60 to 110 kg/ha (54 to 98 lb/ac). Fifty percent of the application is often plowed under during seedbed preparation and the balance drilled in bands 8 to 10 cm (3 to 4 in) below and to the side of the seeds at planting time (16).

Weed control is started when weeds first become evident; shallow cultivation is best. Deep cultivation damages roots, reduces plant vigor, and lowers yields.

Peppers require an uninterrupted supply of water for high yields. Thus in semiarid regions irrigation is used to maintain a moist soil.

Blossom-end rot (a physiological disorder) causes light brown, sunken spots on the ends or sides of the fruits. Root rot (Phytophthora) comes from a fungus that attacks the stems and roots at the soil surface. Bacterial spot causes brown spots on the leaves and fruit. Southern blight is a serious disease in the southern states. Other diseases of peppers are fusarium wilt, downy mildew, spotted wilt, and anthracnose.

The spinach or green peach aphid severely damages peppers. Small white grubs of the pepper weevil cause the young fruit to drop prematurely. The pepper maggot lays its eggs through the wall of the fruit, and when they hatch, the larvae feed upon the inner core, causing the fruit to rot. Other insect pests include cutworms, flea beetles, leaf miners, and hornworms. Root-knot nematodes attack peppers in the west and southwest United States.

Sweet peppers are harvested when fully developed but mostly still green, although some are picked when they are partly or wholly red. The fruit is cut from the vine with a sharp knife.

Hot peppers are usually harvested when they become completely red. Some cultivars (Jalapeno) are harvested at all stages, ranging from small and green for eating fresh to mature and bright red for drying. Hot pepper fruits are sometimes dried and ground into powder for seasonings. Some are harvested green and pickled. Pimento peppers are mostly canned when they become completely red.

Fresh bell peppers are stored for three to four weeks at 5°C to 7°C (41°F to 45°F) with a relative humidity of 90 percent. Some dried hot types are stored for several months by hanging in a dry atmosphere.

Best quality in hot peppers is determined mainly by their deep brilliant red color. Good quality in bell peppers is indicated by fruits that are firm and fresh and bright green and whose walls are thick and fleshy.

Pumpkins and Squashes (*Curcurbita* spp. L.)
CUCURBITACEAE (*1, 2, 3, 4, 8, 9, 10, 11, 14, 20*)

Pumpkins and squashes are divided into three groups according to their use: summer squash (*C. pepo* L.), winter squash (*C. moschata* Poir. and *C. Maxima* Duchesne), and pumpkin (*C. mixta* Pang.) [*C. argyrosperma* Hort.]. Summer squashes are immature fruits that are eaten either raw or cooked. Winter squashes are generally eaten after baking.

Pumpkins are used to feed livestock or baked mostly for pies. The flesh of pumpkins is generally coarse and the flavor too strong to be used as a baked vegetable.

In the United States, summer squashes are grown commercially in Florida, California, Texas, Georgia, North and South Carolina; winter squashes in Florida, New York, New Jersey, Michigan, Texas, and Massachusetts; and pumpkins primarily in California, Illinois, Indiana, New York, New Jersey, Ohio, and Michigan. Some pumpkins and summer squashes are grown in Mexico, South America, Europe, and around the Mediterranean Sea.

Pumpkins and sqaushes are native to the Americas. They are warm-season crops, intolerant of frost, and grow best when the mean monthly temperature is 20°C to 25°C (68°F to 77°F) (Fig. 26-14).

Some selected squash and pumpkin cultivars are listed in Table 26-6, and others are shown in Figure 26-15. Many new hybrid releases are better for different localities.

Pumpkins and squashes grow best on well-drained, fertile soils amply supplied with organic matter. Light-textured, sandy loam soils are preferred for the summer types. Heavy loam soils are suitable for winter cultivars grown for late summer and fall harvest. Soils ranging in pH from slightly acid to slightly aklaline (pH 6.0 to 7.5) are best.

Direct seeding in the field is the most feasible method of propagating. Plant summer squash seeds about 15 cm (6 in) apart in rows about 150 cm (5 ft) apart. When plants reach the two to three true leaf stage, thin to about 30 cm (12 in) apart in the row. Winter squashes and pumpkins, which have long vines, are planted in hills 240 to 300 cm (8 to 10 ft) apart each way.

Fig. 26-14 In the San Diego, California area some summer squash is grown in the late winter and early spring under polyethylene plastic tunnels to increase the temperature of the microclimate around the plants. This method of culture produces fruits during the off-season when prices are high.

Table 26-6 Selected Pumpkin and Squash Cultivars

Cultivar	Days to Maturity	Size Length or Weight	Shape	Skin Color	Remarks
			PUMPKINS		
Big Max	120	huge 45 kg (100 lbs)	Round	Pinkish orange	Good for pies
Connecticut Field	115	medium 10 kg (22 lbs)	Fairly round	Orange	Standard field type, good for pies, good shipper
Jack-O'-Lantern	100	small 5 kg (11 lbs)	Round	Bright orange	Orange flesh, smooth skin
Small Sugar	100	small 3.5 kg (8 lbs)	Round, slightly ribbed	Bright orange	Best for pies and general use, rich orange flesh
			SUMMER SQUASH		
Seneca Bubberbar Hybrid	43	15–20 cm. (6–8 in)	Long cylinder	Bright yellow	High yielding, attractive
Seneca Prolific Hybrid	44	15–18 cm. (6–7 in)	Tapered cylinder	Bright yellow	Uniform, attractive
Caserta	40	13–18 cm. (5–7 in)	Tapered cylinder	Green mottled	Early, prolific
Cozini	42	15–20 cm. (6–8 in)	Cylinder	Dark green	Glossy skin, prolific, early
Early Prolific Straightneck	46	13–18 cm. (5–7 in)	Tapered cylinder	Lemon yellow	Popular standard, good market type
Early Yellow Crookneck	48	10–15 cm. (4–6 in)	Curved neck	Lemon yellow	Popular market type
White Bush Scollop	50	10 cm. diameter (4 in)	Pie shaped, scalloped	Pale green	"Patty pan" type
Zucchini	42	13–18 cm. (5–6 in)	Cylinder	Mottled green	Firm flesh, good flavor
			WINTER SQUASH		
Blue Hubbard	100	6.0 kg (13.2 lbs)	Pointed ends, oval	Gray	Good storage, fine quality
Boston Marrow	97	3.0 kg (6.6 lbs)	Near round	Orange	For market or processing
Buttercup	105	2.0 kg (4.5 lbs)	Turban shaped	Dark green	Keeps well, cooks dry and sweet, good flavor
Pink Banana	105	5.0 kg (11.0 lbs)	Cylinder pointed	Pink	For market or processing
Royal Acorn	90	2.0 kg (4.5 lbs)	Heart shaped	Dark green	Ribbed skin, large
Table King	80	0.5 kg (1.1 lbs)	Heart shaped	Dark green	Good storage, ribbed skin, good flavor
Table Queen	85	0.7 kg (1.5 lbs)	Heart shaped	Dark green	Ribbed skin, small baker, good market type
Waltham Butternut	85	2.0 kg (4.5 lbs)	Cylinder straight	Creamy tan	Excellent keeper, delicious flavor, superior cooker

Fig. 26–15 An assortment of winter squashes including banana (*A*), acorn (*B*), hubbard (*C*), and butternut (*D*), along with some pumpkins (*E*). *Source:* USDA.

Winter squashes and pumpkins are harvested when fully mature with hard rinds. The fruits are cut from the vines with a sharp knife.

Pie pumpkins and winter squashes are canned. The zucchini summer squash and some winter squashes are frozen. Only hard-rind pumpkin and squashes can be stored, and it is important that they remain dry during storage. Summer squashes are best consumed fresh but they are also stored for two to three weeks at about 10°C (50°F) and 95 percent relative humidity.

The entire fruit (skin, seeds, and pulp) of soft-skinned summer squashes is eaten. They are best when the fruits are young, tender, crisp, fresh, and fairly heavy. Tenderness is the prime factor in quality. Winter squashes and pumpkins, on the other hand, should have hard rinds and a color typical for the cultivar.

Sweet Corn (*Zea mays* L., var *rugosa*, Bonaf.)
GRAMINEAE (*1, 2, 3, 4, 8, 9, 10, 11, 12, 14, 17, 20*)

Corn, a native of Central or South America and grown by Indians throughout the Americas long before Columbus, was not popular as a vegetable until about the middle of the nineteenth century.

Sweet corn is grown in home gardens in almost every state and commercially in about 20 states (Fig. 26–16). It is grown for human consumption in Europe, Asia, Africa, and South America. Its culture is very similar to that of field corn (p. 488)

Corn is a warm-season crop that thrives best with warm, humid days and nights. Growth is most rapid at about 30°C (86°F), but some cultivars grow satisfactorily at lower temperatures. Freezing temperatures kill corn plants.

The fertilizer requirements of pumpkins and squashes are similar to those of muskmelons or cucumbers (p. 536) although less is required on fertile soil. On light, sandy soils additional nitrogen is needed to produce maximum yields. Like cucumbers, pumpkins and squashes have extensive root systems that are damaged by excessive or deep cultivation.

In irrigated areas, if the soil profile has been thoroughly wetted during the rainy season, 45 cm (18 in) of additional water from irrigation or rainfall produces a crop. Misshapened fruits result from lack of water.

Damping off, downy mildew, and powdery mildew are troublesome diseases causing stunted or weak plants. Fusarium root rot usually begins as a soft stem rot at the soil surface, causing the plant to wilt and die. Squash mosaic, prevalent in the western and southwestern United States, is spread by aphids.

The worst insect pests are the 12-spotted and the striped cucumber beetles. They cause damage by eating the leaves and by carrying bacterial wilt. The melon aphid is also very destructive to cucumbers. Squash bugs feed on the sap from the leaves, causing the plant to wilt. The root-knot nematode attacks squash and pumpkins.

Summer squashes are harvested at an immature stage when the rind is soft and easily cut by the thumbnail. Beyond this stage some cultivars become stringy and are not good.

Fig. 26–16 Sweet corn ears of good quality display well-developed kernels. The time of harvest for optimum quality is determined by change in color of silks from pale green to brown and exudation of "milky sap" when kernel is crushed by the thumbnail. *Source:* USDA.

Table 26–7   Selected Sweet Corn Cultivars

Cultivar	Days to Maturity	Plant Height cm (in)	Ear Height cm (in)	Ear Length cm (in)	Ear Shape	Wilt Resistance	Remarks
YELLOW HYBRIDS							
Bonanza	82	200 (80)	60 (24)	21 (8.5)	Slight taper	Good	Performs well in Florida and Calif.
Gold Crest	67	150 (60)	35 (14)	20 (8)	Slight taper	Good	Early, high quality
Golden Beauty	75	160 (63)	45 (18)	18 (7)	Cylinder	Good	High yields, vigorous plants
Golden Cross Bantam	84	200 (80)	56 (22)	20 (8)	Slight taper	Good	Favorite for home garden and market
Golden Fancy	87	215 (85)	65 (26)	22 (9)	Cylinder	Good	Exceptional tolerance for drought
Illini Xtra Sweet	85	190 (75)	65 (26)	20 (8)	Slight taper	Good	Extremely sweet and tender
Iochief	86	200 (80)	75 (30)	21 (8.5)	Much taper	Good	High yielding market type
Merit	84	215 (85)	75 (30)	20 (8)	Tapered tip	Good	Good for roadside and local market
Presto	75	150 (60)	45 (18)	16 (6.5)	Cylinder	None	Adapted for early planting
Stylepak	85	200 (80)	70 (28)	22 (8.5)	Slight taper	Good	Good for processing
WHITE HYBRIDS							
Evergreen Hybrid	90	215 (85)	90 (36)	22 (8.8)	Cylinder	Good	Good quality, large ears
Stowell's Evergreen	96	240 (95)	90 (36)	21 (8.5)	Medium taper	Good	Leading white hybrid for market and home
White Cross Bantam	85	215 (85)	80 (32)	20 (8)	Cylinder	Moderate	Early, attractive
OPEN POLLINATED, YELLOW							
Golden Bantam, Early	70	150 (60)	40 (16)	18 (7)	Slight taper	None	An old favorite now replaced by hybrids
OPEN POLLINATED, WHITE							
Country Gentleman	100	215 (85)	90 (36)	19 (7.5)	Medium taper	Some	Irregular rows
ROASTING EARS (A WHITE FLINT CORN, EATEN AT MILK STAGE)							
Truckers' Favorite	95	240 (95)	90 (36)	22 (8.5)	Medium taper	None	A favorite in the South

High-yielding, sweet-tasting, even-maturing, and fast-growing hybrids are continuously introduced. Some selected cultivars are given in Table 26–7.

Sweet corn grows better and usually matures earlier on well-fertilized sandy loam soils high in organic matter than on less-fertile clay or clay loam soils.

Best results are obtained when high-quality seeds, treated with insecticides and fungicides, are planted. To prolong the harvest, the home gardener often makes several small plantings at about two-week intervals through the early part of the growing season. Home gardeners usually plant seed in hills of three to four kernels each, 30 cm (12 in) apart in rows 90 cm (36 in) wide and about 2.5 to 4 cm (1 to 1.5 in) deep if the soil is moist; if dry, the seed is planted into moist soil. In commercial plantings, seeds are generally drilled into the soil with a corn planter. Since corn is wind pollinated, better pollination is obtained by planting in rectangular blocks rather than in long rows.

Sweet corn responds well to fertilizers in many areas. In western and southwestern United States, large quantities of nitrogen are used on irrigated soils. Nitrogen at 125 to 225 kg/ha (110 to 200 lb/ac) is often recommended. Farmers in the midwestern states use 55 to 80 kg/ha (49 to 70 lb/ac) of nitrogen and phosphoric acid applications range from none to 170 kg/ha (150 lbs/ac). In the eastern states a complete fertilizer is recommended at a rate of 100 kg/ha (90 lb/ac) of nitrogen, 200 kg/ha (175 lb/ac) of phosphoric acid, and 200 kg/ha (175 lb/ac) of potash. On fertile vegetable land the phosphoric acid and potash are reduced to 100 kg/ha (90 lb/ac) each.

Cultivation is shallow and done only to destroy weeds.

In most of the United States, sweet corn is grown with natural rainfall, but in the arid West and Southwest, it is grown with irrigation (Fig. 26–17). Corn indicates a need for water by "rolling" its leaves, but when this occurs, yields have already been reduced. A crop of sweet corn requires from 30 to 60 cm (12 to 24 in) of water.

The most common disease of corn is smut. Crop rotation and field sanitation are the best control measures. Bacterial wilt, or Stewart's disease, commonly occurs; planting resistant

cultivars is the best preventive measure. Ear mold and pink rot cause unmarketable ears.

Corn earworms are the most devastating pests of sweet corn. These voracious caterpillars destroy the ears by eating the kernels at the tip. Armyworms and cutworms kill the plants by boring inside the stalks. The Atlantic two-spotted spider mite also does severe damage.

The harvest period is critical for sweet corn because of the relatively short time the kernels are high in sugar. Experienced growers judge maturity by the firmness of the ear and the development of brown silks. Sweet corn is mostly harvested by hand but, for processing, some is machine harvested.

Sweet corn kernels are processed by canning or freezing. A small amount is frozen on the cob. Best quality is obtained by harvesting the ears at night or early in the day and processing quickly. If not cooled immediately after harvest, corn continues to respire, lowering its quality. Natural sugars are quickly converted to starch as soon as the ears are removed from the stalk, thus reducing their sweetness. If delays are foreseen, loss of sugars is reduced by spraying ice cold water over the ears and placing them in a refrigerated holding room. This also applies to home freezing or canning. Even with the best of care, unprocessed sweet corn does not store well. Storage temperature is maintained as close as possible to 0°C (32°F) without freezing, and the relative humidity is kept at 95 percent. Canned or frozen corn is stored without difficulty for long periods.

Fig. 26–17 In semiarid to arid regions most sweet corn is furrow-irrigated. This is the last irrigation for this field of corn since it is ready for harvest. In areas of adequate rainfall, sweet corn requires no supplemental irrigation. *Source:* University of California Cooperative Extension.

Tomatoes (*Lycopersicon Lycopersicum* (L.) Karst. ex. Farw.) [*L. esculentum* Mill.] SOLANACEAE (*1, 2, 3, 4, 8, 9, 10, 11, 14, 15, 19, 20*)

Tomatoes are the most popular crop for the home gardener. As recently as the nineteenth century, they were thought to be poisonous and were grown only as ornamentals. Tomatoes are native to South America and were grown by the Indians long before Columbus took plants to Europe. Cultivation of tomatoes spread from Italy and Spain to northern Europe and then back to North America.

Tomatoes are grown in almost every state in the United States, with California, Ohio, Florida, Indiana, New Jersey, and Pennsylvania leading in processed and fresh market production.[1] They are extensively grown in Mexico and Central and South America. Considerable area is planted to tomatoes in Europe, North Africa, the Middle East, and India.

Tomatoes are warm-season perennials grown as annuals. They are planted after danger of frost has passed and require at least four months to produce a crop (Fig. 26–18). Tomatoes thrive best when the weather is clear, dry, and warm. Optimum mean monthly temperatures are 21°C to 27°C (70°F to 80°F).

Many cultivars are available, and the choice varies with use and locality. Some recommended favorites are given in Table 26–8.

[1] Processed tomatoes are produced for canning as tomato fruits or processed into juice, catsup, puree, soup, paste, or sauce. Fresh market tomatoes are grown to be sold as fresh whole fruits for table use.

Table 26-8 Selected Tomato Cultivars

Cultivar	Use	Maturity	Resistance[a]	Grown	Fruit Size	Fruit Shape	Harvest Method
Ace	Home garden	Midseason	F, V	West	Medium	Globular	Hand
Earlypak 7	Market	Early		West	Medium	Globular	Hand
Heinz 1350	Market	Midseason	F, V	East	Medium	Globular	Hand
Jack Pot	Market	Early	F, V, N	Calif.	Medium	Globular	Hand
Jet Star (F$_1$)[b]	Market	Midseason	F, V	East	Medium	Globular	Hand
New Yorker	Market, process	Early	V	East	Medium	Globular	Hand
Nova	Process	Early	F, V	East	Medium	Plum	Hand
Redpack (F$_1$)	Market	Early	F, V	East	Large	Globular	Hand
Royal Flush (F$_1$)	Market	Midseason	F, V	All U.S.	Large	Globular	Hand
Spring Set (F$_1$)	Process	Early	F, V	East	Medium	Plum	Hand
Supersonic (F$_1$)	Market	Early	F, V	East	Medium	Globular	Hand
U. C. 82	Process	Midseason	F, V	All U.S.	Small	Plum	Mechanical
U. C. 134	Process	Midseason	F, V	All U.S.	Small	Plum	Mechanical
V F 145	Process	Early	F, V	West	Medium	Plum	Mechanical
Westover	Market	Midseason	F, V	East	Medium	Globular	Hand
6718	Market	Early	F, V	Calif.	Medium	Globular	Hand

[a] F = Fusarium wilt; V = Verticillium wilt; N = Root-knot nematode.
[b] F$_1$ = F$_1$ hybrid (see p. 74).

Fig. 26–18 Early fresh market tomatoes growing in southern California under clear polyethylene tunnels. These fruits will be harvested February, March, and April for the off-season market. This method of culture has been introduced to the mild-winter areas of southern Europe.

Fig. 26–19 Young emerging tomato seedlings often fail to break through the soil surface because of soil crusting. This farmer is using a "squirrel cage" cultivator to break up the crust. These canning tomatoes were planted with two rows on beds 150 cm (5 ft) apart. *Source:* William L. Sims.

Tomatoes produce highest yields of early maturing fruits on well-drained, fertile sandy loams. Neutral or slightly acid soils (pH 5.5 to 7.0) are best.

Almost all commercial plantings are directly seeded, but some are also set out as transplants. For commercial production of processing tomatoes in the eastern part of the United States, about 560 g/ha (0.5 lb/ac) of seeds are planted in single rows 90 to 120 cm (3 to 4 ft) apart or 150 cm (5 ft) apart with double rows (Fig. 26–19). Seeds are dropped at the rate of about 20 to 25 seeds per m (6 to 8 seeds/ft) and covered about 1 to 2.5 cm (0.5 to 1 in) deep. In the semiarid areas of the western United States, single rows about 150 cm (5 ft) are seeded at the same rate. Some farmers using the smaller-vined and more determinate cultivars plant twin rows 30 cm (1 ft) on beds 150 cm (5 ft) apart. Commercial plantings are made on beds, then irrigated.

Ideally growers of processing tomatoes try to get 25,000 to 50,000 plants/ha (30,000 to 60,000 plants/ac). Plants are thinned to this density if necessary.

Transplanting is restricted mostly to smaller fresh market production and to home gardens; greenhouse grown transplants should be "hardened off"[2] before they are planted in the field.

Some fresh market tomato farmers support the plants with stakes driven into the soil (Fig. 26–20). This conserves space and improves quality by keeping the fruit off the ground. The plants are tied loosely to the stakes as they grow. Stakes are spaced 25 to 50 cm (10 to 20 in) apart with rows 90 to 120 cm (3 to 4 ft) apart. Unstaked tomato plants are spaced 45 to 120 cm (1.5 to 4 ft) with rows 90 to 180 cm (3 to 6 ft) apart.

A well-fertilized soil is required to produce high yields of good-quality tomatoes. On land of low fertility in the eastern United States, 1000 kg/ha (900 lb/ac) of superphosphate is often broadcast before the direct-seeded crop is planted. If the crop is transplanted, however, an additional starter solution is used.

[2]Reducing the plants' rate of growth by subjecting them to lower temperatures or withholding nutrients, or withholding water. Such plants withstand the rigors of transplanting better.

Fig. 26–20 Many farmers growing tomatoes for fresh market tie the plants to stakes to make hand harvest easier and to keep the fruit off the ground. This is a commercial planting of staked fresh market tomatoes.

Fig. 26–21 The culture of tomatoes grown for processing is almost completely mechanized. However, in some cases weeds become a problem with mechanical harvesting. To reduce the volume of plant material passing through the harvester, field workers are moving through the tomato field cutting weeds just before harvest. *Source: The Daily Democrat,* Woodland–Davis, California.

Fig. 26–22 Most fields of tomatoes grown for processing are sprinkle-irrigated to ensure even seed germination. After seedlings are well established, sprinkling is discontinued and furrow irrigation is used. Two rows are planted on each bed. *Source:* William L. Sims.

Fig. 26–23 This farmer is preparing a field for furrow irrigation. Two rows of tomato seeds are planted on each bed and the farmer is using a lister to plow two irrigation furrows between each bed (*A*). This allows the water to flow closer to the seeded rows for better wetting. After the plants are well established, the furrow is moved to the center of the row (*B*) by plowing the ridge between the two irrigation furrows toward each bed, leaving one furrow in the center. *Source:* William L. Sims.

Generally, 50 to 100 kg/ha (45 to 90 lb/ac) of nitrogen, phosphoric acid, and potash is recommended. Excessive nitrogen delays fruit maturity, causes secondary growth that makes mechanical harvest more difficult, and causes uneven fruit maturity.

Cultivation is required to control weeds but it should be shallow to avoid damage to plant roots (Fig. 26–21).

In areas where rainfall is inadequate, irrigation must be used. In areas of marginal rainfall, supplemental irrigation is often profitable (Figs. 26–22 and 26–23).

Fusarium and verticillium wilt are serious diseases controlled by planting resistant cultivars. Tobacco mosaic, spotted wilt, and curly top are diseases spread by insects and cultural operations. Blossom-end rot is a physiological disorder that appears on green fruit.

Tomatoes are attacked by several insect pests, including tomato and tobacco hornworms, cutworms, flea beetles, and tomato russet mites.

Nematodes are severe pests of tomatoes controlled only by rotation or resistant cultivars. Damage by slugs and snails can be prevented with poisoned bait.

A   B   A   B   A

Fig. 26–24 Mechanical harvester for canning tomatoes. This machine is equipped with an electronic sorter to automatically separate any green tomatoes from red ones at optimum maturity. *Source: The Daily Democrat*, Woodland–Davis, California.

Fig. 26–25 Processing tomatoes, brought from the field in these fiberglass truck trailer beds, are being unloaded by water washing the fruits out of the truck and into a water-filled receiving tank. This technique reduces injury by bruising to a minimum and also helps lower the fruit temperature quickly. *Source:* Western Grower and Shipper.

Fig. 26–26 Tomato trucks pull into a grading and inspection station where a random sample of tomatoes is automatically taken and inspected for defects by state inspectors. *Source: The Daily Democrat,* Woodland–Davis, California.

In the United States most mechanical harvesting of process tomatoes begins when about 75 percent or more of the fruits are red ripe. About two to three days later up to 95% of the fruit will be red ripe (Figs. 26–24, 26–25, and 26–26).

Hand-harvested fruits are picked red ripe for local fresh market or pink in the "breaker"[3] stage for distant markets. Machine harvest of fruits for fresh market is rapidly gaining in Florida and California with about 30 percent of the crop harvested by machine in summer of 1979 (*15*). Fresh tomatoes are subject to chilling injury below 13°C (55°F) and thus are not successfully preserved by freezing.

Fresh tomatoes cannot be stored for long periods of time. If the fruits are harvested at the mature-green stage, they can be kept in storage for two to three weeks at 13°C (55°F) while those harvested pink can be stored for 7 to 10 days at 13°C (55°F). After storage they are ripened at between 15°C to 21°C (59°F to 70°F).

There are no well-established guides for the consumer to use to select tomatoes of good quality. Color cannot always be used as a criterion because some people prefer tomatoes with some green and others prefer red. Tomatoes picked at an immature green stage do become red but generally have less juice and a poor flavor.

Watermelon (*Citrullus lanatus* Thunb.) *C. vulgaris* Schrad. CUCURBITACEAE (*1, 2, 3, 4, 8, 9, 10, 11, 13, 14, 20*)

The watermelon is a warm-season annual. The vine grows prostrate with stems 300 to 450 cm (10 to 15 ft) in length. They are reported to be native to Africa. They were grown in Europe during the sixteenth century and the Americas as early as 1629.

Principal commercial producing states are Florida, Texas, Georgia, California, South Carolina, Alabama, Indiana, and Missouri. The Ukraine, the Caucasus, and Central Asia grow watermelons for export to northern European markets. Mexico, southern Europe, northern and central Africa, and the Middle East also produce watermelons in large quantities.

Watermelons require a four-month, frost-free growing season. They grow best when the mean monthly air temperature is above 20°C (68°F) with soil temperatures between 25°C to 30°C (77°F to 86°F).

Watermelon cultivars vary considerably in size, shape, and color. Some recommended cultivars are given in Table 26–9.

Watermelons grow best on fertile, well-drained sandy or sandy loam soils well supplied with humus and slightly acid (pH 6.5 to 7.0).

Five seeds are planted about 4 cm (1.5 in) deep in hills and are thinned later to two plants per hill. The hills are 200 to 300 cm (6.5 to 10 ft) apart. Each plant on the average requires about 3 m² (10 ft²). If irrigation is used, the melons are planted on beds.

For maximum yields, many farmers use a complete fertilizer. One-half is applied before planting and the remainder when the plants are 8 to 13 cm (3 to 5 in) tall. General recommendations are 45 to 100 kg/ha (40 to 90 lb/ac) nitrogen, 90 to

[3]Tomatoes at the breaker stage of maturity are mature-green, with the shoulders of the fruits just beginning to turn pink.

Table 26–9 Selected Watermelon Cultivars

Cultivar	Days to Maturity	Weight kg (lbs)	Shape	Rind	Flesh	Remarks
Charleston Gray	85	9 (20)	Oblong	Lt. green veins	Bright red	Fusarium wilt resistant
Congo	90	11 (24)	Semilong	Med. green, dk. stripes	Red, sweet	Good shipper, Southeast
Crimson Sweet	85	11 (24)	Blocky oval	Lt. green, dk. stripes	Deep red sweet	Fusarium wilt resistant
Dixie Queen	85	18 (40)	Oval	Lt. green	Deep red	Home garden
Florida Giant	90	14 (31)	Near round	Deep green	Red, firm	All purpose, popular
Jubilee	90	14 (31)	Oblong	Lt. green, dk. stripes	Bright red	Good shipper
Klondike Striped	90	9 (20)	Oblong	Lt. green, dk. stripes	Deep red sweet	Good market and shipper
Seedless Hybrid	80	5 (11)	Oval	Green stripes	Solid red	Small edible white seedcoats
Sugar Baby	75	3 (6.5)	Round	Very dark green	Med. red sweet	Good local market
Yellow Baby Hybrid	75	3 (6.5)	Round	Lt. green	Bright yellow	Few small seeds

200 kg/ha (80 to 180 lb/ac) phosphoric acid, and 45 to 100 kg/ha (40 to 90 lb/ac) potash.

Three or four shallow cultivations generally are necessary to control weeds, starting as soon as the weeds appear.

In areas where irrigation is needed, water is applied after planting to germinate the seeds. The crop requires 50 to 75 cm (20 to 30 in) of water, perhaps more on sandy soils.

Fusarium and verticillium wilts are serious diseases for which no control is known except resistant cultivars and crop rotation. These diseases seldom kill the plants, but they do lower yields. Watermelon mosaic prevents plants from producing fruits.

Insects that attack watermelons are wireworms, aphids, red spider mites, leafhoppers, and cutworms. Root-knot nematodes cause some damage to watermelons.

Watermelons are harvested at full maturity but not overripe; they do not develop further red color nor additional sugar after being removed from the vine. The ground spot (that portion of the melon resting on the soil) changes from a pale white to creamy yellow color as the fruit matures. At harvest the melons are cut from the vine with a sharp knife, leaving as long a stem as possible. Watermelons do not store well and are not held for any length of time.

REFERENCES

1. Anon. 1979. Vegetables. Annual summary, acreage, yield, production, and value. Statistical Reporting Board. USDA.

2. Bailey, L. H., and E. Z. Bailey and staff of L. H. Bailey Hortorium. 1976. *Hortus third*. New York: Macmillan.

3. Bauske, R. J. 1976. *Home horticulture*. St. Paul, Minn.: West.

4. Dunmire, J. R., ed. 1979. *Sunset new western garden book*. 4th ed. Menlo Park, Calif.: Lane.

5. Hall, H., S. Wada, and R. E. Voss. 1975. Growing peppers. Univ. of Calif. Div. Agr. Sci. Leaflet 2773.

6. ———. 1976. Growing beans. Univ. of Calif. Div. Agr. Sci. Leaflet 2912.

7. ———. 1976. Growing green peas. Univ. of Calif. Div. Agr. Sci. Leaflet 2913.

8. Hayes, J., ed. 1977. Gardening for food and fun. USDA Yearbook. Washington, D.C.: Government Printing Office.

9. Johnstone, D. B., and E. H. Brindle. 1976. *Vegetable gardening basics*. Minneapolis, Minn.: Burgess.

10. Maynard, D. N., and C. L. Thompson. 1970. Nutrition of vegetable crops in Massachusetts. Coop. Ext. Ser. Publ. 63.

11. Minges, P. A., A. A. Muka, and R. F. Sandsted, A. F. Sherf, and R. D. Sweet. 1976. *Commercial vegetable production recommendations*. Ithaca, N.Y.: New York State College of Agriculture and Life Sciences.

12. Otto, H. W. 1975. Growing sweet corn. Univ. of Calif. Leaflet 2728.

13. Schweers, V. H., and W. L. Sims. 1970. Watermelon production. Univ. of Calif. Agr. Ext. AXT 331.

14. Seelig, R. A. 1975. *Selection and care of fresh fruits and vegetables*. Washington, D.C.: United Fresh Fruits and Vegetable Association.

15. Sims, W. L., R. W. Scheuerman, and D. Ririe. 1979. Mechanized growing and harvesting of fresh market tomatoes. Rev. ed. Univ. of Calif. Div. Agr. Sci. Leaflet 2815.

16. ———, and P. G. Smith. 1976. Growing peppers in California. Univ. of Calif. Div. Agr. Sci. Leaflet 2676.

17. ———, R. F. Kasmire, and O. A. Lorenz. 1971. Quality sweet corn production. Univ. of Calif. Agr. Exp. Sta. Cir. 557.

18. ———, and V. Schweers. 1971. Growing summer squash. Univ. of Calif. Agr. Ext. AXT 291.

19. ———, V. H. Schweers, R. W. Scheuerman, and D. Ririe. 1971. Mechanized growing and harvesting of fresh market tomatoes. Univ. of Calif. Agr. Ext. AXT n4.

20. Ware, G. W., and V. P. McCollum. 1975. *Producing vegetable crops*. 2nd ed. Danville, Ill.: Interstate.

SUPPLEMENTARY READING

Lorenz, O. A., and D. N. Maynard. 1980. *Knott's handbook for vegetable growers*. Somerset, N.J.: Wiley-Interscience.

Vegetable Crops Grown for Flowers, Leaves, or Shoots

Immature flowers, leaves, or shoots are commonly eaten plant parts, often used to add flavor or eye appeal to an otherwise monotonous meal. Many meals are served with a sprig of parsley or some green leafy plant part to decorate the plate. Most of the crops are cool season and are either biennial or perennial. Some perennial crops grown for their immature flowers, leaves, or shoots are the globe artichoke, asparagus, rhubarb, sea kale, and sorrel. Among the vegetable crops (except for white potatoes) the cole crops (cabbage, cauliflower, broccoli) and the salad crops (lettuce, celery, endive) are consumed in the largest quantity.

The leafy vegetables are particularly high in vitamin A, and they also are a good source of iron and calcium.

This chapter discusses the important vegetable crops whose flowers, leaves, or shoots are grown for food.

Artichoke (*Cynara scolymus* L.) COMPOSITAE (2, 3, 4, 5, 6, 8, 9, 12, 14)

The globe artichoke, cultivated for over 2000 years, is a thistlelike herbaceous perennial plant native to North Africa and the western Mediterranean area. The part eaten is an immature bud, made up of numerous overlaid bracts, plus a fleshy receptacle (Fig. 27–1).

Artichokes require a frost-free climate with cool, foggy, summer days. Hot dry climates cause the buds to open, destroying their tenderness. Freezing temperatures blister the buds and make them scaly and poorly colored. Practically all of the artichokes grown commercially in the United States are produced along the Pacific coast of California (*12*). Some artichokes are produced in small amounts in the Gulf States and in the south Atlantic coast states.

Artichokes are propagated vegetatively from pieces of roots or from rooted offshoots from the base of old plants.

Fig. 27–1   The globe artichoke is an herbaceous thistlelike plant related to the noxious Canadian thistle weed. The edible parts are the fleshy bases of the immature flower heads together with the attached fleshy bases of the large bracts.

Plants grown from seeds do not reproduce true to cultivar (Fig. 27–2). For small scale plantings, plants are set 90 cm (3 ft) apart in rows 90 cm (3 ft) apart. Spacings of 240 cm (8 ft) between rows and 180 cm (6 ft) in rows are used for commercial plantings (Fig. 27–3).

Artichokes grow well on a wide variety of soils but produce best on ones that are deep, fertile, and well drained.

They respond well to fertilizers, especially nitrogen. Organic matter in the form of animal manure is helpful. In southeastern United States a complete fertilizer is often applied in the spring.

California farmers generally cut the top growth back to the soil surface between late spring and early summer. As a

Fig. 27-2 Each year after the artichoke buds are harvested and the flowers form, the aboveground parts are cut off below the soil surface. New shoots arise from buds on the underground crown for next season's growth. After six to ten years of production the clusters of rosettes from the crown become crowded. The fields are rejuvenated or entire new plantings are made by planting divisions of the crown or rooted offshoots, such as this, that arise from the crown.

Fig. 27-3 A field of artichoke plants in late winter growing along the mild central California coast. These plants are generally cut back to the soil surface in late spring and are dormant until late summer.

result the artichoke plant is dormant during the summer and out of production for a three- to four-month period. Fertilizer is applied during the late summer when new growth becomes vigorous. Nitrogen is applied at the rate of about 45 to 50 kg/ha (40 to 45 lb/ac) and about the same amount of phosphoric acid if needed. Potash is seldom used. If the plants lack vigor, the following spring another application of about 30 to 35 kg/ha (27 to 31 lb/ac) of nitrogen is added (*12*).

During the growing and producing season, artichokes require ample soil moisture from either rainfall or irrigation. A total of about 90 to 120 cm (3 to 4 ft) of water is needed each year. Water deficiency during bud formation produces loose buds of poor quality. For early fall production in California, irrigation is started in late spring or early fall after the old stalks are cut and continued on a ten-day to two-week interval for five to eight irrigations. Furrow irrigation is a common method of application on level land, and sprinklers are used on rolling land.

Curly dwarf virus curls the leaves, dwarfs the plant, and reduces the number of buds. Botrytis is a fungal disease that develops on injured tissue, especially during long periods of warm wet weather. There is no practical control.

The artichoke plume moth is the most serious insect pest. The female lays eggs on the stems below the buds. The larvae hatch and bore into the buds or stems, causing damage and lower bud quality.

Artichoke harvest begins in midsummer in the southeastern United States and in the fall in California continuing through the winter with peak harvest in the spring. Buds are harvested by cutting each from the stem by hand when the bud is 5 to 10 cm (2 to 4 in) in diameter and before the bracts begin to separate. Yields of 18 to 20 buds per plant are not uncommon. They are sorted, graded, and boxed in special wooden crates or cardboard boxes and precooled to about 4°C (39°F). Artichokes are stored for about a month at 0°C to 4°C (32°F to 39°F) with relative humidity at about 90 percent.

Best-quality buds are compact, heavy, and plump with tight, fleshy, bright green bracts.

Asparagus (*Asparagus officinalis* L.) LILIACEAE (*2, 3, 6, 8, 10, 11, 14*)

The edible portion of this perennial grows from fleshy, underground stems called crowns. The plants bear either staminate (male) or pistillate (female) flowers (Fig. 27-4). Asparagus, thought to be native to southern Russia, has been found growing wild in Europe, England, Poland, and around the Mediterranean Sea.

Asparagus is grown in almost every state of the United States, but California leads in production. Other states include New Jersey, Washington, Michigan, and Illinois. The crop is extensively grown in Europe, the Far East, the Philippines, and South America.

Better quality and higher yields of asparagus spears are produced when monthly temperatures during the growing season average about 15°C to 21°C (60°F to 70°F) with at least five-months of dormancy. In colder northern climates the growing season is too short for maximum shoot production. In warmer climates the shoots tend to grow rapidly into the inedible fern stage.

Fig. 27–4 A female asparagus plant. These plants bear only pistillate flowers. The flowers were fertilized by pollen from a nearby male plant. Note the seed berries. Asparagus is a good example of a dioecious plant (male and female flowers on separate plants).

Several new asparagus cultivars are available, but the most important by far is Mary Washington and strains developed from it.

Since a planting remains in the field for 10 to 15 years or longer, only fertile, light-textured or loamy soils are used although muck or peat soils also produce good asparagus crops. A deep, well-prepared seedbed is essential for the establishment of a good stand.

Asparagus is propagated by planting seeds directly in the field, by transplanting nursery grown plants, or by planting small sections of divided crowns. Seeds, transplants, or crown divisions are generally planted in the bottom of a furrow 20 to 30 cm (8 to 12 in) deep and covered with about 5 cm (2 in) of soil. The furrows are gradually filled as the young plants grow. The rows are 150 to 180 cm (60 to 72 in) apart with plants spaced 30 cm (12 in) apart within the row. Directly seeded fields require 2 to 3 kg/ha (1.75 to 2.5 lb/ac) of seed.

Fertilizer recommendations vary widely but, in general, 45 to 90 kg/ha (40 to 80 lb/ac) nitrogen, 90 to 180 kg/ha (80 to 160 lb/ac) phosphoric acid, and 90 to 180 kg/ha (80 to 100 lb/ac) potash are applied—half early in the spring before harvest begins, and half after harvest.

Weed control entails shallow disking early in the spring before shoots appear. Chemical herbicides generally give better results than mechanical cultivation in excessively weedy fields.

Fig. 27–5 A field of asparagus ready for harvest, with the spears appearing above ground on the bed. If weather conditions are ideal (warm), harvest occurs at least every other day. All fresh market asparagus is harvested by hand.

Asparagus is not irrigated except in arid or semiarid regions, but if these areas have some winter rainfall, large quantities of water are not needed. In western and southwestern United States, about 50 cm (20 in) of water is often applied in the late summer, between the end of harvest and seed formation.

The principal diseases are asparagus rust, phytophthora root rot, and fusarium.

The asparagus beetle is a serious insect pest.

In the cool spring, spears are harvested every two to four days but as the days get warmer, daily harvest is often needed (Fig. 27–5). The spears are cut by hand with a special knife with a flat blade and the end sharpened to a V-shaped notch. The blade is attached to a long shank. The knife is pushed into the soil at an angle of about 45° to cut the spear below the soil surface. The spears are stacked in piles on the ground to be picked up later and transported to a central packing shed, where they are washed, sorted, and graded by diameter. They are then crated in specially designed wooden crates and hydrocooled (see p. 275). Very little asparagus is mechanically harvested.

Good quality spears are straight, tender, and bright green with compact tips. Crooked or misshapened spears are graded as culls. After harvest, the spears are allowed to "go to fern," that is, the stems elongate into fernlike plants 90 to 150 cm (3 to 5 ft) tall (Fig. 27–6). The ferns die as the plants become dormant in the fall and should be removed by cutting and then either burned or disked into the soil.

Fig. 27–6 After six to eight weeks, it is necessary to cease harvesting asparagus spears and let the plants develop fine leaves ("go to fern"), as shown here. This allows the leaves to photosynthize and resupply the roots with nutrient material for another harvest season.

The flowers of the cole crops—broccoli, Brussels sprouts, cabbage, and cauliflower—have four sepals and four petals arranged in the form of a cross. This structure gives the family the name CRUCIFERAE, which in Latin means "cross bearers," and from which the English words *crucify* and *crucifix* are derived.

There are two types of broccoli; the little-grown heading type (Botrytis Group, similar to cauliflower) and the more popular sprouting type (Italica Group), which has green, branched and less compact heads. The word broccoli comes from the Latin word *bracchium*, meaning arm or branch. The plant is probably native to Asia and was introduced into the United States from Europe in the early 1920s. It soon became popular. Broccoli is highly nutritious and easily prepared, and has a characteristic flavor with favorite sauces. Most home gardeners find it is easy to grow. Most cole crops are biennials, but broccoli and cauliflower are annuals (*3*). Broccoli has thick, waxy leaves, is blue-green in color, and tolerates some frost.

Main production areas are Europe and the United States, especially California, Oregon, Texas, and Arizona.

Most American cultivars are of the Italian Calabrese type. Some popular U.S. cultivars are listed in Table 27–1.

Practically all commercial plantings of broccoli are seeded directly into a well-prepared seedbed in the field, although some home gardeners use six- to eight-week-old transplants for early planting. Rows are spaced about 90 to 106 cm (36 to 42 in) apart with about 45 cm (18 in) between plants. Early-maturing cultivars are spaced somewhat closer. For the home gardener six to eight plants per person will provide enough fresh broccoli for eating and canning or freezing.

This crop grows best on fertile, medium-textured soil high in organic matter. Broccoli needs to be fertilized, and generally 55 to 135 kg/ha (49 to 120 lb/ac) nitrogen, 55 to 180 kg/ha (49 to 160 lb/ac) phosphoric acid, and 55 to 180 kg/ha (49 to 160 lb/ac) potash are recommended. These amounts are adjusted to soil fertility and previous cropping systems. Half of the fertilizer is often broadcast before planting and the remainder drilled into bands 8 to 10 cm (3 to 4 in) below and to the side of the seed at planting time. Thirty-five kg/ha (31 lb/ac) of nitrogen is often applied two to three weeks after planting as a sidedressing. Sometimes a second sidedressing is needed before harvest.

Weeds are controlled by mechanical cultivation or by the use of pre- and postemergence herbicides. In particularly weedy areas some hand cultivation supplements the herbicides.

Fig. 27–7 An immature broccoli inflorescence ready for harvest. These so-called "flowers," as they are known in the trade, are removed from the stem by cutting with a knife. *Source:* USDA.

Black leg, root rot, downy mildew, and mosaic are the most serious diseases.

The most common insects include the cabbage looper, cabbage worm, cabbage maggots, corn earworm, cutworms, and aphids.

The immature flowers (which is the part eaten) are hand-harvested by cutting them from the stalk with a sharp knife, leaving about 20 to 25 cm (8 to 10 in) of the stem. The flowers are harvested while they are compact and tight, usually about 7.5 to 15 cm (3 to 6 in) in diameter (Fig. 27–7). During cool weather a second or third harvest is possible. These later heads are smaller but excellent for splitting in half for freezing.

Broccoli is very perishable and requires immediate cooling. Good quality is indicated by deep green, firm, and compact heads. Low quality is indicated by open stringy, overmature flowers.

Table 27–1 Selected Broccoli Cultivars

Cultivar	Planting Season	Location	Head Size	Remarks
De Cicco	spring, summer	East and South	Medium, large	Compact medium, tall
Green Comet	spring	East Coast	Large, compact	Heat and disease resistant
Medium Late 145	late fall	Central and southern California	Large, compact	Excellent producer
Spartan Early	very early	Michigan and Midwest	Heavy, large	For spring and summer
Topper 430	late fall	Coastal valleys of California	Medium	Shipping and processing

Brussels Sprouts (*Brassica oleraceae* L. Gemmifera Group) CRUCIFERAE (*2, 3, 6, 8, 9, 11, 14*)

This cabbage-flavored vegetable probably evolved from a Mediterranean cabbage. It received its name from Brussels, Belgium, where it was grown and became popular. The plant develops miniature cabbagelike heads about 2.5 to 5 cm. (1 to 2 in) in diameter along the main unbranched stalk (Fig. 27–8). The plant grows 60 to 90 cm (2 to 3 ft) tall, requires a cool climate, and withstands some slight freezing. It is grown extensively in northern Europe, in the coastal valleys of California, and in New York State.

The principal cultivars grown in the New York area are Long Island Improved and Jade Cross. In California, Half Dwarf and Fancymost 50-A are popular.

For commercial plantings, seeds are sown directly in the field, then thinned to about the same spacing as broccoli. Home gardeners often prefer to transplant plants started in a greenhouse or hotbed. The culture of Brussels sprouts is similar to that of cabbage, detailed below. These plants are extremely heavy feeders of plant nutrients and require a fertile, medium-textured soil with supplemental fertilization. Organic matter is often helpful.

Brussels sprouts require a constant supply of water for proper development; thus in arid or semiarid regions irrigation is always needed. Most plantings on medium-textured soils require a total of 38 to 50 cm (15 to 20 in) of water in addition to the fall and winter rains.

Brussels sprouts are troubled by the same insects and diseases that bother other members of the cabbage family, but aphids are particularly damaging to sprouts. Club root is the most prevalent disease.

The crop is normally harvested when the sprouts are 2.5 to 5 cm (1 to 2 in) in diameter. The lower leaves are first removed from the stalk to expose the buds, which are cut from the stalk with a sharp knife. The buds are brought to a central location for further trimming, packaging, and cooling.

Fig. 27–8 In the early stages of development, Brussels sprouts closely resemble cabbage, but as the plant matures, the main stem elongates 60 to 90 cm (2 to 3 ft) and the axillary buds along the stem develop into small cabbagelike heads about 2.5 to 5 cm (1 to 2 in) in diameter. *Source:* Ferry-Morse Seed Company.

Cabbage (*Brassica oleraceae* L., Capitata Group) CRUCIFERAE (*2, 3, 6, 8, 9, 11, 14*)

Cabbage grows best in cool climates. It is normally a cool-season biennial, tolerant of slight freezing. It does, however, tolerate somewhat warmer temperatures than most cool-season crops. The head is formed by numerous leaves overlapping a small terminal bud. Cabbage is believed to have developed from a wild type native to the chalk-cliff areas of the English east coast and the western European coasts. Evidence indicates that the early Egyptians used cabbage as a food and medicine.

Cabbage is a favorite vegetable worldwide because of its adaptability to a wide range of climates and soils, its ease of production and storage, and its value as a food. It is grown in Europe, Asia, Africa, North and South America, and Australia. Cabbage is produced commercially in 26 of the 50 states. The principal ones in order of production are Florida, New York, Texas, Wisconsin, California, North Carolina, New Jersey, Ohio, Michigan, and Pennsylvania.

The cultivar chosen depends largely on the earliness desired, the size and shape of the head, and the use of the crop. Some popular cabbage cultivars are noted in Table 27–2.

For good quality and large yields, cabbage is grown on a highly fertile, well drained soil. Light-textured soils produce earlier crops than heavier-textured soils.

Cabbage is grown from small plants started in greenhouses, cold frames, or hotbeds or seeded directly in the field. Transplants are planted mechanically or by hand. About 210 to 250 gm of seeds produce enough transplants to plant 1 ha (3 to 4 oz/ac). One kilogram of seeds directly seeds 1 ha (1 lb/ac). Transplants are started 8 to 10 weeks before planting and are hardened before planting in the field. Directly seeded plants do not suffer transplanting shock; thus the crop matures in about two weeks less time. Seeds planted directly are sown thinly in rows 60 to 90 cm (2 to 3 ft) apart. When the plants are about 15 cm (6 in) tall, they are thinned to about 45 to 60 cm (18 to 24 in) apart. Transplanted crops are set to the same final spacing although spacing varies somewhat with the size of the plant, cultivar, and method of irrigation.

Cabbage, a heavy feeder of plant nutrients, responds well to fertilizers. The most frequent recommendations are 55 to 135 kg/ha (50 to 120 lb/ac) nitrogen, 110 to 225 kg/ha (100 to 200 lb/ac) phosphoric acid, and 110 to 225 kg/ha (100 to 200 lb/ac) potash. Fifty-five to 70 kg/ha (50 to 60 lb/ac) of additional nitrogen is often sidedressed after the plants have recovered from transplanting and are growing rapidly.

Since cabbage is a shallow-rooted crop, deep tillage is avoided to prevent root damage. Except in very weedy conditions, two or three shallow cultivations should suffice. Cultivations after heads have formed should not be done. Chemical weed control is often recommended for commercial plantings.

Cabbage is grown on slightly raised beds in irrigated areas. In arid regions, 45 to 60 (18 to 24 in) of water is needed to raise a crop. Water application to cabbage suffering from drought can cause heads to burst.

Cabbage is susceptible to a host of diseases, insects, and physiological symptoms. Black leg, club root, downy mildew, and yellows are the most prevalent diseases. Only resistant cultivars should be grown in areas where yellows is a problem.

Table 27–2   Some Popular Cabbage Cultivars

Cultivar	Days[a]	Season[b]	Head Type	Size kg (lbs)	Remarks
Chieftain Savoy	90	Fall	Crumpled	2.3 (5)	Good for home gardens
Copenhagen Market	69	Spring, summer	Round	1.6 (3.5)	Grown in short seasoned areas
Early Glory	74	Spring, fall	Nearly round	2.3 (5)	Makes good kraut
Globe	80	Summer, fall	Round	2.7 (6)	Yellows resistant, kraut
Golden Acre	64	Spring	Round	1.4 (3)	Used for late spring market
Greenback	74	Spring to fall	Nearly round	2.3 (5)	Yellows resistant
Jersey Wakefield	65	Spring	Conical	1.8 (4)	Good for home gardens
Late Flat Dutch	100	Fall	Flattened	5.4 (12)	Used for storage and processing
Marion Market	79	Summer	Round	2.5 (5.5)	Red cabbage for home gardens
Red Acre	74	Spring to fall	Round	2.3 (5)	Red cabbage for home gardens
Red Rock	100	Fall	Flattened	3.2 (7)	Red heads for boiling and pickling
Round Dutch	71	Spring, fall	Round	1.8 (4)	Important in Southeast
Ruby Red Hybrid	68	Spring	Round	1.4 (3)	Dark red heads
Stein's Flat Dutch	90	Fall	Flat	4.5 (10)	

[a]From transplanting to market size.
[b]Season of maturity.

The cabbage aphid, cabbage worm, cabbage looper, cabbage maggot, and the harlequin cabbage bug are the most common and troublesome insect pests.

Cabbage is harvested when the heads have reached full size for the particular cultivar (Fig. 27–9). The head is bent over and the stalk severed with a sharp knife at the base. It is desirable to leave two to three wrapper leaves on the head to give new cabbage a green, fresh appearance. Fields of early-maturing cabbage for fresh market can be cut several times, but late cabbage fields are harvested only once. Care must be taken to avoid bruising.

High-quality cabbage is indicated by fresh, firm, white heads free of damage. Heads weighing from 1 to 1.5 kg(2 to 5 lbs) are most popular.

Fig. 27–9   A field of heading cabbage shortly before harvest. There are three common horticultural forms of *Brassica oleraceae:* (1) those with loose leaves (kale and collards) or with leaves rolled into heads (savoy cabbage and common cabbage, shown here) or in small axillary buds (Brussels sprouts); (2) immature flowers (sprouting broccoli or cauliflower); and (3) stems expanded into bulbous structures (kohlrabi). *Source:* USDA.

Cauliflower (*Brassica oleraceae* L., Botrytis Group)
CRUCIFERAE (*1, 2, 3, 6, 8, 9, 11, 13, 14*)

Cauliflower, sometimes mistaken for heading broccoli (*B. oleraceae* Botrytis Group), is closely related to sprouting broccoli (*B. oleraceae* Italica Group). Sprouting broccoli, described on page 557, has green heads made up of branching flowers, while heading broccoli has white, compact, short-stemmed flowers like cauliflower. Sprouting broccoli and cauliflower are easily distinguished, but even expert horticulturists sometimes confuse heading broccoli with late-maturing cauliflower.

The origin of cauliflower is obscure, but it is thought to have developed from sprouting broccoli in northwestern Europe; at least, the crop was grown there early in recorded history. Now it is widely grown throughout Europe and the United States. California leads the nation in production, by far, followed by Oregon, New York, Arizona, Michigan, and Texas.

Of all the CRUCIFERAE, cauliflower has the most exacting climatic requirements. It seldom grows well except in cool, moist climates. The cool, foggy coastal valleys of California are particularly well adapted to cauliflower production. It grows best when mean monthly temperatures are 15°C to 20°C (59°F to 69°F), but unlike cabbage, cauliflower is intolerant of frost or excess heat. High temperature leads to poor quality by producing "leafy or ricy" curds (loose, open flowers, sometimes with green leaflets).

The primary difference among the few cultivars of cauliflower is their rate of maturity. The Snowball type has medium to large, white, tight curds that mature early and ship well. Some early-maturing cultivars of the Snowball type are: Snowdrift, Early Snowball, Snowball X, and Snowball A.

Cultural procedures, fertilization, irrigation, and pest problems are the same as for cabbage (see p. 558). Cauliflower

559

production should be attempted only on fertile and well-drained soils.

Direct sunlight yellows the white curds, resulting in poor quality and off flavors. Leaves cover and protect the small curds when they form, but as the curds enlarge, the inner leaves are forced apart, exposing the curds to the sun's rays. To protect them and to insure blanching, the longest leaves are gathered together over each curd every two or three days and tied with string or tape. Some farmers estimate the number of days needed for the curd to reach harvest size, then as they tie the leaves, they use different colored twine to indicate the different numbers of days still needed. When harvest day arrives, the curds with the proper-colored strings are cut. Fully developed curds do not grow larger; they merely become overmature and lose quality. It is better to harvest early, before the curd is fully developed, and sacrifice some loss in weight than to harvest late and lose quality. The curds are severed from the stalk with a sharp knife, leaving one or more sets of leaves attached for protection. Curds are then transported to a central packing shed where they are further trimmed, graded, boxed, and cooled for shipment.

Good-quality cauliflower is indicated by fully developed, compact, clear, white curds. Discolored, yellow stained, open, "ricy" curds are of poor quality. Heads about 15 cm (6 in) in diameter are preferred.

Celery (*Apium graveolens* L., var. *dulce* [Mill.] Pers.) UMBELLIFERAE (*2, 3, 6, 8, 9, 11, 14*)

The UMBELLIFERAE family, named for the characteristic umbel form of the inflorescence (see p. 35), includes celery, carrots, parsnips, parsley, and others. Celery was first used as a medicine in the fifth century A.D. and as a cultivated food crop in the early 1600s. It is thought to be native over a wide area from Sweden to Egypt, Algeria, Abyssinia, and parts of Asia. Celery has been found growing wild in California and New Zealand. In the United States, California by far produces the largest crop in tonnage and dollar value. Other important producing states are Florida, Michigan, and New York.

Celery, a biennial plant, has rather exacting climatic requirements, needing relatively cool temperatures, especially at night. Best growth occurs when rain or irrigation is evenly distributed throughout the growing season. California and Florida produce most of the winter and early spring crop, while New York and Michigan produce the late summer and early fall crop.

The cultivars of celery are generally divided into two types: the yellow self-blanching type, and the Utah or green type. Blanched celery has lost its popularity and is seldom found in the market today. Cornell 19, 619, Burpee's Fordhook, Golden Self-Blanching, and Golden Detroit are cultivars of the yellow type. Cultivars of the Utah type are Giant Pascal, Tall Utah 52-75, Summer Pascal, Utah No. 52-70 R, Surepak, and Florida 683.

Celery often produces a larger biomass of plant material than most vegetable crops, sometimes up to 135 MT/ha (60 t/ac), thus, it consumes mineral nutrients heavily. In addition to its high nutrient demand, celery also requires large quantities of water. Soils most likely to fulfill these nutrient and water requirements are peat or fertile muck soils. Loose, friable sandy loam soils, high in organic matter with a high water-holding capacity, are also suitable.

Almost all celery is grown from transplants because celery seeds germinate slowly and require constant wetness. Seeds are germinated in hotbeds, cold frames, greenhouses, or in open outdoor beds. Seedlings are allowed to grow until they are about 10 cm (4 in) tall; this usually takes 6 to 10 weeks. The transplants are hardened by withholding water before planting in the field. Planting is done either by machine or by hand with the plants spaced 15 to 20 cm (6 to 8 in) apart in rows 45 to 90 cm (18 to 36 in) apart. If irrigated, water is allowed to flow in the furrows immediately after the seedlings are transplanted.

Of all vegetable crops, celery is probably the most heavily fertilized—in fact, some farmers tend to overfertilize. Green manure crops like rye are sometimes plowed under to maintain a high organic matter content. Florida growers cannot raise celery without additional fertilizer, and they often use from 70 to 170 kg/ha (60 to 150 lb/ac) of nitrogen, 90 to 225 kg/ha (80 to 200 lb/ac) of phosphoric acid, and 90 to 225 kg/ha (80 to 200 lb/ac) of potash. If large quantities of fertilizer are used, portions are applied in several applications as sidedressing. In California, fertilizer recommendations differ considerably because of variability of soil type and location. Most growers apply commercial mixes of 225 to 450 kg/ha (200 to 400 lb/ac) of nitrogen, 450 to 900 kg/ha (400 to 800 lb/ac) of phosphoric acid, and 450 to 900 kg/ha (400 to 800 lb/ac) of potash. Late season applications usually consist of nitrogen only.

Celery fields must be kept free of weeds. Celery grows slowly and the shallow roots explore a relatively small volume of soil; thus weeds can damage the crop considerably. Control usually entails shallow cultivation with small-toothed or small-bladed cultivators although weed oils or certain selective herbicides are used while the plants are young.

Most of the celery produced in the United States is irrigated. In California, the furrow method is most common, but many farmers are installing sprinkler systems and there is interest in the trickle or drip irrigation method (see p. 205). Florida celery is grown mostly with subirrigation,[1] a system that can be used for both irrigation and drainage.

Blackheart, in which the young leaves turn black and the affected tissue dies, is a physiological condition that renders the crop unmarketable. Fluctuating soil moisture, high salt content, and calcium deficiency in the soil have been reported as possible causes of this trouble. Boron deficiency in the soil gives rise to another physiological condition called cracked stem, which causes the petioles to crack.

Celery is also affected by several diseases that are best controlled by chemical methods or prevented by field sanitation or certain cultural practices. The most serious of these are early blight, late blight, and pink rot.

The tarnished plant bug, carrot rust fly, celery leaftier, celery looper, leaf hoppers, aphids, and cutworms are the most destructive insects attacking celery.

The large part of the cost in celery production is harvesting and packing, which are still done mostly by hand. Some celery is harvested with a tractor-mounted machine

---

[1]In some localities, water is allowed to percolate laterally and upward from ditches, or drains, located below the surface of the soil. In some soils these occur naturally or they are installed.

Fig. 27–10   There are several different practices used in the hand harvest of celery. In this field the cutters use a special knife. The blade is broad and sharpened on the blunt end so it can cut the plant's roots with a jabbing motion just below the soil surface. The edge of the blade is also sharp so that the plant is topped to the approximate height with a chopping motion. Some growers top the celery while it is standing in the field with a mowing machine adjusted to the desired height. The celery is further trimmed in a packing shed. *Source:* University of California Cooperative Extension.

Fig. 27–11   Chives, sometimes called elephant garlic, can be grown in a pot in the kitchen window and harvested as needed throughout the year. The upper portion of tubular leaves is chopped and used for flavoring in cheeses, sauces, soups, and so forth. *Source:* USDA.

equipped with knives that cut the plant off just below the crown. Most commercial fields are prepared for harvest by mowing the plant tops at a desired uniform height. The plants are cut and trimmed in the field with a special knife; they are then placed in large bins or small crates and trucked to a central packing shed for further trimming, washing, grading, and crating (Fig. 27–10). The crates are cooled by hydrocooling or vacuum cooling (see p. 275).

Chive (*Allium schoenoprasum* L.) AMARYLLIDACEAE (2, 3, 6, 8, 9, 11, 14)

Chives are small, bushy, onion-like perennials grown for their leaves, which are used in salads, soups, stews, omelets, cottage cheese, and cream cheese. Chives grow wild from Newfoundland to Alaska and in northern Europe and Asia. They are of minor economic importance but have been cultivated for centuries. In the United States chives are grown commercially in California and Texas.

Chives are cool-season crops with climatic requirements similar to onions and garlic. For home use they are often grown in small plots about 0.2 m² (2 ft²) or along flower borders (Fig. 27–11). Chives are propagated by seed, and the clumps of plants are divided every two to three years. The separated bulbs are planted in rows in the spring. Sometimes bulbs are available in the markets during the fall. These can be planted in pots and grown in the house as ornamentals during the winter. Cultural practices, fertilization, and pests are the same as for onions (see p. 577).

The leaves are cut from the plant as needed for seasoning. This practice seems to stimulate bulb formation.

Collards and Kale (*Brassica oleraceae* L., Acephala Group) CRUCIFERAE (2, 3, 6, 8, 9, 14)

Collards and kale are nonheading cabbage-like plants, very popular in southern United States for cooking greens. Both are closely related to wild cabbage and have been cultivated for several centuries (Fig. 27–12). They are used as food and sometimes as ornamentals because of their attractive, crinkled leaves. The plants are winter-hardy biennials and can withstand more heat than cabbage.

These crops are grown mostly from Virginia to Texas, but some are also grown in California, Europe, and North Africa. Recommended cultivars of collards are Georgia and Green Glaze. There are two types of kale: the Siberian type, with less crinkled leaves, and the Scotch type. Dwarf Blue Scotch or Tall

Fig. 27–12 Collards are closely related to cabbage but the leaves are nonheading. The leaves are broader than those of kale, and the lower ones are generally harvested first, progressing up the stalk to a rosette of leaves at the top. The leaves are popular as winter greens in the southern United States. *Source:* USDA.

Green Scotch are the important kale cultivars. Dwarf Siberian is a Siberian-type cultivar.

Propagation, soil requirements, cultural practices, fertilization, irrigation, and pests of collards and kale are similar to those of cabbage (see p. 558).

Kale and collards are harvested before the leaves get large, tough, and fibrous. Tender, high-quality leaves come from well-fertilized and quick-growing plants. The young plant is cut off with a sharp knife and placed in cartons or hampers for transport and storage. On older plants, only the young leaves are harvested. Some people claim the flavor of these crops is improved after the plant has been somewhat frosted.

Endive (*Cichorium endivia* L.) COMPOSITAE (2, 3, 6, 8, 9, 14)

Endive has been grown for centuries and was eaten by the early Egyptians. It probably originated in eastern India. It is a cool-season crop similar to lettuce in appearance, except that it does not form heads. The plant matures more slowly than lettuce and the leaves grow in a rosette. Endive is grown mostly in Florida during the winter and early spring but some is also grown in New Jersey and Ohio during the summer and early fall. The plant starts flowering after being subjected to a certain amount of cold weather followed by long days.

There are two types of endive. The curled or crinkled type is characterized by the Green Curled Ruffec and Salad King cultivars. The second type is a smooth, broad-leaved plant, commonly called escarole, represented by the cultivars Florida Deep Heart, Broad Leaved Batavian, and Full Heart. The broad-leaved type is often used as a potherb[2] as well as a salad.

It is essential for good yields, high quality, and sweet flavor that plants grow rapidly. Therefore, a fertile soil high in organic matter is best. Fertilizer and irrigation requirements are similar to those of head lettuce (see p. 567). A fertilizer that supplies 55 to 85 kg/ha (49 to 75 lb/ac) nitrogen, phosphoric acid, and potash (K_2O) has been found to be profitable on many soils.

The crop is planted on raised beds (see p. 565) much as lettuce is, either from transplants or direct seeded. Plants are spaced 25 to 30 cm (10 to 12 in) apart in rows 38 to 45 cm (15 to 18 in) apart. Blanching of leaves is often desirable because it tends to reduce bitterness. Blanching is accomplished by pulling the outer leaves together over the center leaves and tying them for two to three weeks. Closer spacing causes some blanching of the center leaves. To reduce premature flowering induced by cool temperatures, plants are not started in greenhouses nor directly in the field until temperatures remain above 15°C (59°F).

Aphids are the most serious pest of endive and need to be controlled.

This crop is harvested by cutting the plants at the soil surface. Discolored or undesirable outer leaves are trimmed off and the remaining leaves are pulled together and placed in a carton or box. The plants are cooled quickly by icing, hydro-cooling, or vacuum cooling.

Good quality is indicated by clean, fresh, tender, crisp leaves free from disease or insect damage.

Kohlrabi (*Brassica oleraceae* L., Gongylodes Group) CRUCIFERAE (2, 3, 4, 5, 9, 11, 14)

Kohlrabi is a cool-season biennial grown for its turnip-like, above-ground enlarged stem (Fig. 27–13). Compared to other vegetables, it has not been used long as food. This seems strange, because most people prefer the mild, more delicately flavored kohlrabi to the turnip.

The culture and climatic requirements of kohlrabi are similar to those of turnips (see p. 587). This crop is one of the easiest to grow and does well anywhere turnips grow. There are only two popular cultivars; White Vienna and Purple Vienna. A fertile sandy loam or loam soil is best and, if manure is available, it is always wise to apply it. The crop is generally seeded directly in rows about 45 cm (18 in) apart for hand cultivation or 60 to 75 cm (24 to 30 in) apart for machine cultivation. Plants are thinned to 10 to 15 cm (4 to 6 in) apart within the row. Cultivate shallow and early to prevent weed growth.

[2]An herb boiled and used as a vegetable. More commonly, a boiled vegetable.

Fig. 27–13 The enlarged stem of kohlrabi is the part that is used. Some people prefer kohlrabies to turnips and claim they are milder. The stem on the left is the green type, while the one on the right is the purple type. *Source:* USDA.

Fig. 27–14 Leek is a relatively large onionlike plant with a somewhat flattened stem. This plant does best in regions having cool to moderate temperatures. These plants are near harvest. *Source:* USDA.

Rapid and continuous growth produces tender, tasty kohlrabies. On most average soils 55 kg/ha (49 lb/ac) of nitrogen, 110 kg/ha (98 lb/ac) phosphoric acid, and 55 kg/ha (49 lb/ac) potash are applied.

Kohlrabies are harvested when the swollen stems reach about 5 cm (2 in) in diameter. Delayed harvest produces tough woody stems. They are pulled by hand, the roots cut off, and the stems tied in bunches or sold in bulk.

Leek (*Allium ampeloprasum* L., Porrum Group)
AMARYLLIDACEAE (*2, 3, 4, 6, 8, 9, 11, 14*)

Leek, a biennial closely related to onions, is grown for its blanched leaves. The leaves do not form bulbs as do onions but are flat, solid, and 2 or 3 cm thick. The leaves are delicious raw or in soups or other foods; their flavor is mild and delicate. Nero, the ancient Roman emperor who according to legend regularly ate considerable amounts of leek to improve his voice, was given the nickname Porroplegus, which means "leek-throated." Leek is believed to be a native for the Mediterranean area, where it has been grown for centuries. It has never been popular in the United States, and what little is produced is grown by small growers near large cities, mainly for consumers of foreign extraction.

The most popular cultivar is Large American Flag.

Leek grows best on fertile sandy loam to loam soils well supplied with organic matter. Seedbed preparation, culture, fertilizer requirements, disease and insect problems are similar to those for onions (see p. 577).

Leek is propagated mainly by direct seeding in the field or in flats in the greenhouse to produce plants for transplanting later in the field.

The leaves of leek are blanched to improve quality by pulling the soil up around the plant when it is over half-grown. It is easier to draw the soil around the plant if it has been planted in a trench 15 to 20 cm (6 to 8 in) deep, but cultivation for weed control is more difficult. The best length for the blanched portion of the leaves is 15 to 20 cm (6 to 8 in) and about 2.5 to 5 cm (1 to 2 in) in diameter.

Leek is harvested in the fall just before frost by pulling the plants from the soil (Fig. 27–14). The plants are cleaned, trimmed, bunched, and sold in the same manner as green onions. It is possible to store leek for several months in cold storage with the roots and old leaves trimmed.

Lettuce (*Lactuca sativa* L.) COMPOSITAE
(*2, 3, 6, 7, 8, 9, 11, 14*)

Lettuce is an annual or biennial plant that has been cultivated for centuries (*3*). It was served to Persian kings about 600 years before Christ. The Romans grew the romaine or cos type as early as the beginning of the Christian era. The Chinese have grown the crop since the fifth century A.D., and by the sixteenth century it had been taken to Central and South America.

Cultivated lettuce is closely related to the common wild or prickly lettuce (*L. Serriola*) weed. The many different kinds of lettuce are often grouped into three types. The most common is head lettuce, of which there are the crisphead (or iceberg) and butterhead cultivars. The romaine or cos type forms loose, upright heads. The leaf type is nonheading and loose-leaved (Fig. 27–15).

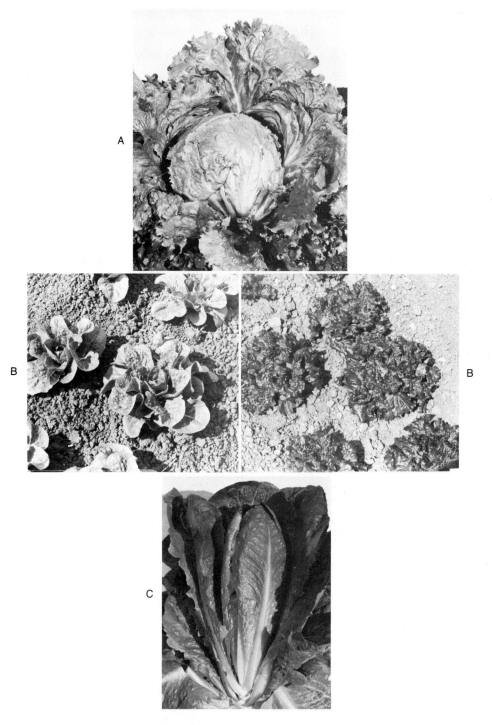

Fig. 27–15 Lettuce is a widely grown salad crop where climatic conditions are favorable. The heading type (*A*), represented by crisphead or iceberg, is the most popular in America. The leafy or curled leaf types (*B*) are represented by butterhead and red lettuce cultivars. While not so popular as the heading type in the United States, they are rapidly gaining in popularity because of their increased use in tossed green salads. The romaine or cos type lettuce (*C*) forms upright cylindrical heads that are not as tight as the heading types. This type of lettuce is more popular in Europe, Asia, and Africa than in the United States. *Source:* Ferry-Morse Seed Company.

Lettuce is, by far, the most important salad crop. It is grown commercially in about 15 states in the United States and in home gardens in most of the others. California produces by far the largest amount of crisphead lettuce in both area and dollar value. Other producing states, include Arizona, Florida, Colorado, Texas, New Mexico, New York, New Jersey, Washington, and Michigan. Lettuce is grown in Europe, Asia, and highlands of Kenya, Australia, and New Zealand. Production in leaf and romaine types has increased recently because of the increased popularity of tossed green salads.

Lettuce is a cool-season crop and grows best at a relatively cool temperature of about 12°C to 15°C (55°F to 60°F). It is grown during the summers in the northern states, at higher altitudes, or along the coast (e.g., Salinas Valley) in California, in Oregon, and in Washington. In Florida, Texas, Arizona, New Mexico, and the desert valleys of California (Imperial Valley), lettuce is grown during the winter months (Table 27–3). Heading is prevented by seed stalk formation when temperatures reach 21°C to 26°C (70°F to 79°F); also the leaves develop a bitter taste. Some slow-bolting cultivars have been developed to delay premature seed stalk formation (Table 27–4). Lettuce seedlings tolerate some slight freezing, but the larger, more mature leaves are injured. Seeds germinate best at soil temperatures from 5°C to 25°C (41°F to 77°F).

Plant-breeding programs conducted jointly by the USDA and some university experiment stations have been responsible for the release of lettuce cultivars adaptable to particular environmental conditions and locations or resistant to diseases and pests.

The more popular cultivars of lettuce and some of their characteristics are given in Table 27–4.

Lettuce grows well on a wide variety of soils provided the climatic requirements are met, especially temperature. Lettuce grows on muck soils in Florida, sandy loams in Texas, New Jersey, New Mexico, and Arizona, and on clay or clay loam soils in the Salinas Valley of California. Fertile soils high in organic matter are preferred by most farmers. If high temperature is a problem, remember that heavier soils are often cooler than light sandy soils. Soils with high water-holding capacity and good drainage are better for the lettuce root system.

Lettuce seeds are small; therefore, a well-prepared, fine seedbed is of paramount importance. Other conditions being equal, fall plowing is generally desirable for spring planting because it gives winter rains and freezing temperatures time to break hard clods. Disking, harrowing, and rolling reduce the size and number of clods to a minimum and facilitate easy planting and uniform germination. Compared to other crops, lettuce is expensive to grow, but money spent for good seed from a reliable seedhouse is a good investment.

Lettuce growers have realized the importance of uniform spacing to reduce the hours of labor needed to thin the crop. Spacing single seeds at 8 to 10 cm (3 to 4 in) intervals is desirable but difficult with the small, irregularly shaped seed. One common technique is to coat the seeds to make them larger, rounder, and more uniform in shape. The coating material is generally diatomaceous earth or montmorillinic clay. The process, called seed pelleting, has been so successful that about 75 percent of all head lettuce sown in the Salinas Valley of California is pelleted. Coated seeds have also been tried with other small-seeded crops such as carrots, celery, onions, and tomatoes.

Most commercial plantings and many home gardeners plant seeds directly in the soil, but for an earlier crop a few farmers and some home gardeners use transplants. Commercial fields are directly seeded with tractor-mounted mechanical seeders, some of which plant eight rows at a time. In areas where irrigation is needed, the crop is grown on raised beds spaced 100 cm (40 in) apart with two rows, 25 to 30 cm (10 to 12 in) apart on each bed (Fig. 27–16). Some growers prefer to plant seed 1 to 2.5 cm (0.5 to 1 in) deep in dry soil, then irrigate to cause germination; others prefer to plant seed in moist soil,

Table 27–3   Relation of Average Monthly Temperatures to Average Monthly Shipments of Lettuce from California

Month of Shipment	Salinas Valley			Imperial Valley		
	Average Temp. °C	(°F)[a]	Shipments (Carloads)[b]	Average Temp. °C	(°F)[c]	Shipments (Carloads)[b]
Jan.	9	49	0	12	53	5348
Feb.	10	51	0	13	56	6672
Mar.	12	53	0	17	63	2828
Apr.	13	56	1422	21	70	0
May	15	59	6646	25	77	0
June	16	61	6163	29	85	0
July	17	62	4325	33	91	0
Aug.	17	62	5287	33	91	0
Sep.	17	62	5137	29	85	0
Oct.	15	59	2338	25	77	0
Nov.	12	54	172	16	61	15
Dec.	10	50	0	12	54	2994

[a]Temperatures for Salinas Valley based on 69-year averages.
[b]Shipments based on the year 1975.
[c]Temperatures for the Imperial Valley district based on 33-year averages.

Fig. 27–16 In the Salinas and Imperial valleys of California, where irrigation is practiced, two rows of head lettuce are planted on each raised bed. Normally the beds are 100 cm (40 in) apart and the plants thinned to 25 to 30 cm (10 to 12 in) apart within the row. This field of lettuce is beginning to form heads.

Table 27-4 Selected Lettuce Cultivars

Cultivar	Location	Harvest Season	Head Size	Head Color	Core Size[a]	Resistance (Tolerance)	Remarks
CRISPHEAD TYPE							
Calmar	Calif. coastal	Spring, summer	Large	Medium	Large	Downy mildew, tipburn	Smooth, solid heads
Climax	Calif. Imperial	Winter	Large	Medium	Large	Tipburn, rib discolor	Solid heads
Empire	N.J., Calif.	Fall	Medium	Medium	Medium	Tipburn, rib color	Very slow bolting[b]
Great Lakes 659	Calif., Ariz.	Fall	Medium	Dark	Medium	Tipburn	Slow bolting[b]
Hanson	Midwest, N.Y.	Spring or fall	Medium	Light	Medium	Tipburn	Home gardens
Ithaca	N.Y.	Summer	Medium	Medium	Medium	Tipburn, brown rib	Very slow bolting[b]
Mesa 659	Calif., Ariz.	Fall	Large	Dark	Medium	Tipburn	Slow bolting[b]
Minetto	Midwest, Fla., N.Y.	Fall and winter	Small	Medium	Small	Tipburn	Small compact heads
Montemar	Calif. coastal	Summer	Large	Medium	Large	Downy mildew, tipburn	Serrated leaf margin
New York 515	N.Y.	Summer	Medium	Light	Medium	Tipburn	Home gardens
Vangard	Calif., Ariz.	Winter, spring	Large	Medium	Large	Tipburn	Used in desert areas

	Days	Size	Leaf	Color	
BUTTERHEAD TYPE					
Bibb	56	Very small	Smooth, thick	Deep green	Early, bolts in hot weather
Dark Green Boston	70	Small	Short, smooth	Medium dark	Most popular, excellent
White Boston	70	Medium	Smooth, wavy	Light green	Home gardens and market
COS OR ROMAINE TYPE					
Dark Green	70	Large	Slightly savoyed[c]	Dark green	Good for home gardens
Paris Island	70	Large	Slightly savoyed	Dark green	Slow bolting
Valmaine	68	Large	Slightly savoyed[b]	Dark green	Resistant to downy mildew
White Paris	70	Large	Slightly savoyed	Light green	Favorite old cultivar
LOOSE LEAF TYPE					
Black Seeded Simpson	45	Large	Broad, crumpled	Light green	Favorite old cultivar
Grand Rapids	45	Medium	Coarsely crumpled	Medium light	Resistant to tipburn
Prize Head	45	Large	Broad, frilled	Reddish	Home gardens
Salad Bowl	45	Large rosette	Long, deeply notched	Light green	Slow bolting, home gardens

[a] Core size refers to the core in the lettuce head, actually the stem to which the leaves are attached.
[b] Rapid growth of flower stalks after sufficient chilling or a favorable photoperiod.
[c] Savoyed = wrinkled around the edges of the leaves.

after a preplanting irrigation. Plants are always thinned if directly seeded. This costly and time-consuming task is done when the seedlings have emerged sufficiently to be identified. Excess plants are removed by chopping with a hand hoe (sometimes mechanical thinning machines are used), leaving clumps of lettuce seedlings spaced about 30 to 40 cm (12 to 16 in) apart. A few days later the seedlings reach the two-leaf stage, and the clumps are thinned to one plant by hand. It is important that only one plant per hill remain; otherwise heading is hindered. In areas where irrigation is not needed, lettuce is planted without raised beds in rows 40 to 60 cm (16 to 24 in) apart. Butterhead and romaine types are planted closer.

Lettuce is a moderately heavy consumer of nutrients. Rapid growth is desirable during the first part of the season to ensure crispness: thus a complete fertilizer with a high chemical analysis is often recommended. In general, the fertilizer is

Fig. 27–17 A small planting of red leaf lettuce being irrigated by furrows. Water is being syphoned from head ditch. A new dam has been installed below the one being used. After this section of field has been irrigated, the upper dam will be removed, allowing the water to move down to the next section. The syphons will then be repositioned for the new area to be irrigated.

Fig. 27–18 While many different machines and mechanical aids have been tried to harvest head lettuce, it remains essentially a hand harvest operation. Cardboard boxes are assembled and distributed in the field ahead of the cutters. The heads are cut at the soil surface by cutters (upper lefthand man) using a jabbing motion with a knife sharpened on the end. The cutters place the heads bottomside up in the middle of the row. A packer (center foreground) has placed a box on a wheelbarrow and after trimming off excessive wrapper leaves packs the designated number of heads, with butt ends down, on bottom layer and butt ends up on top layer. He leaves enough wrapper leaves to protect the heads. After the box is filled, he sets it on the ground and moves on. Another man (right foreground) equipped with a pressure sprayer sprays water over the heads to wash off the plant sap which turns an undesirable pink color if left on the head and to add a little water to the carton for vacuum cooling (see Ch. 12). The next worker (not shown) closes the carton and with a staple gun staples the carton closed. The cartons are gathered on a truck (background) and transported to a vacuum cooler for cooling. *Source:* University of California Cooperative Extension.

applied when the seedbed is prepared, and any additional nitrogen needed is sidedressed after the crop is thinned. In irrigated areas many growers apply about 225 kg/ha (200 lb/ac) nitrogen, 110 to 225 kg/ha (98 to 200 lb/ac) phosphoric acid, and 110 to 225 kg/ha (98 to 200 lb/ac) potash.

Shallow, precise cultivation keeps the crop free from weeds and provides a light soil mulch. Cultivation beyond this damages the roots and is avoided.

The frequency and amount of irrigation depends upon soil type, age of plant, and climatic conditions (Fig. 27–17). In the western United States, where most crisphead lettuce is grown, the amount of water applied varies from 30 to 38 cm (12 to 15 in) in the foggy California coastal valleys and from 45 to 60 cm (18 to 24 in) in the Imperial Valley during the winter. In the Salt River Valley of Arizona, irrigation is sometimes used to lower soil temperature to improve seed germination for crops planted in September for winter harvest.

Lettuce is troubled with a wide variety of plant pests. Diseases include tipburn, downy mildew, big vein, aster yellows, mosaic, bottom rot, and lettuce drop. Tipburn is a nonparasitic disease that causes the margins of inner younger leaves to turn brown. Some cultivars are more resistant to tipburn than others.

Aphids are the most troublesome of all insects. Other important insect pests are cutworms, cabbage loopers, sixspotted leaf hoppers, and wireworms.

Harvest of leaf or romaine lettuce begins when the leaves reach maximum size but before they become tough or bitter. Both types are harvested by cutting the plants at the soil surface and removing soiled or damaged leaves before packing. Most head lettuce is harvested in the same manner and field packed in cardboard cartons (Figs. 27–18 and 27–19). The cartons are moved from the field to a central vacuum cooler where they are cooled before shipment (see Fig. 12–19). There are several mechanical aids and modifications in commercial harvesting methods.

Fig. 27–19 Several types of machines are being developed for the complete mechanical harvesting of head lettuce. Some are equipped with mechanical or electronic devices to detect the density of the head to ensure selective cutting of heads ready for harvest, leaving immature heads in the field. This machine, being tried in the Salinas Valley, California, was developed by the USDA. This particular model is selectively harvesting only those heads that have been measured by pressure testing and found to be mature enough. *Source:* USDA Science and Education Administration.

Mustard (*Brassica juncea* L., *B. hirta* Moench., *B. nigra* W. D. J. Koch) CRUCIFERAE
(2, 3, 6, 8, 9, 11, 14)

Mustard is a cool-season annual. The leaves of *B. juncea* and *B. hirta* are used for greens or salads (Figs. 27–20 and 27–21), and the seeds of *B. nigra* are used to prepare the commercial mustard condiment. Some growers plow under mustard as a green manure crop to increase soil organic matter. Mustard has been grown in many parts of the world since Biblical times. Most of the U.S. crop used for greens is grown in the southern states, and the seed crop is grown in California. Mustard requires cool weather to grow well and produce good foliage. Long, warm days result in seed formation.

Popular cultivars for the production of large, tender leaves are suggested in Table 27–5.

The cultural and soil requirements for mustard are similar to those of spinach. The crop grows well on a fertile, moist soil, from sandy loams to adobe clays. Seed is sown early in the spring for a spring or an early summer crop, or it is planted in

Fig. 27–21 'Southern Giant' mustard produces a large plant with crinkled leaves. To many people mustard leaves add zest to any salad, and others like the leaves steeped in hot water. *Source:* Ferry-Morse Seed Company.

Fig. 27–20 Tenderleaf mustard is a smooth-leaved cultivar. It produces large tender leaves and is high yielding. *Source:* Ferry-Morse Seed Company.

late summer for fall or winter harvest. The seed is drilled in rows 30 to 60 cm (12 to 24 in) apart and thinned to 20 to 25 cm (8 to 10 in) when the plants become crowded. If irrigation is used, the seeds are planted in two rows 35 to 40 cm (14 to 16 in) apart on raised beds 100 cm (40 in) apart. The crop responds well to fertilizers. Applications of 55 to 110 kg/ha (49 to 98 lb/ac) nitrogen, especially in cool damp weather, are usually recommended. The plants are kept free of weeds by shallow cultivation or preemergence herbicides. In arid regions, irrigation is needed to start the late-summer crop. The early-spring crop should be harvested before hot, dry weather begins.

The young plants are ready to harvest about four to six weeks after seeding. The plant is harvested either by cutting the entire plant at the soil surface or by removing the larger leaves. Mustard often becomes a troublesome weed if allowed to go to seed.

Table 27–5   Selected Mustard Cultivars

Cultivar	Days	Plant Type	Leaf	Color	Remarks
Florida Broad Leaf	50	Large, spreading	Large, thick, broad oval, toothed edges	Bright green	Slow bolting[a]
Fordhook Fancy	40	Large, erect	Deeply curled	Dark green	Slow bolting
Green Wave	55	Large, upright	Large, wide, very curly	Dark green	Slow bolting
Southern Giant	45	Large, erect	Large, wide, curly edges	Bright green	Used in South for market
Tendergreen	35	Large rosette	Medium large, thick smooth, tender	Dark green	Widely adapted

[a] Rapid growth of flower stalks after sufficient chilling or a favorable photoperiod.

Parsley (*Petroselinum crispum* (Mill) Nyman ex A. W. Hill) UMBELLIFERAE (*2, 3, 6, 8, 9, 11, 14*)

Parsley, a biennial plant native to Europe, has been grown as a cultivated crop for over 2000 years. A close relative of celery, the crop is widely used as an herb, flavoring, and garnish. Three types are grown for foliage and one type grown for roots. The foliage types are the plain or single-leaf type (preferred for flavoring food), the double-leaf type, and the moss or triple-curled leaf type (used mostly for garnish) (Fig. 27–22). A rooted type is grown for its edible parsnip-like roots and is used mostly by Europeans. Some popular cultivars include Curled Dwarf, Extra Triple Curled, Plain Italian, Mass Curled, and Hamburg Rooted.

Parsley seed is small and slow to germinate, making the crop difficult to start but easy to grow once started. It takes about 75 days for the leaf types to mature, and 90 days for the rooted type. Often the seeds are soaked overnight before planting in hotbeds or cold frames. The crop resists cold and is often transplanted into the garden as early as cabbage. Large plantings are seeded directly in the field to avoid the cost of transplanting.

Parsley grows best on a fertile sandy loam soil well supplied with organic matter and with a high water-holding capacity. The fertility requirements are similar to those for carrots (see p. 574). Plants are spaced 10 to 20 cm (4 to 8 in) apart within rows that are 30 to 60 cm (12 to 24 in) apart. Weed control is important and generally accomplished with shallow

Fig. 27–22 Parsley is related to celery and is a delicious additive to stews and soups. It is, however, mostly used as a decorative garnish to add color to a plate and is often not eaten. This is the triple-curled leaf type used mostly as a garnish. *Source:* Ferry-Morse Seed Company.

tillage, weed oils, or both. If irrigation is used, the seeds are planted in two rows 30 to 35 cm (12 to 14 in) apart on raised beds 90 to 100 cm (36 to 40 in) apart.

Harvesting begins as soon as the leaves reach a desirable size, generally about two and one-half to three months after seeding. Home gardeners sometime cut the large outer leaves and retain the smaller inner ones to photosynthesize food for the plant's continued growth. Plants are sometimes potted and grown in the kitchen window to supply leaves during the winter. Some commercial growers cut the leaves above the ground by hand, leaving stems long enough to tie into bunches for market, but the largest percentage of the commercial crop is harvested by mowing the leaves, then conveying them into a truck for transport to the dehydrator for processing into dried seasonings. The crop can be harvested several times.

Rhubarb (*Rheum rhabarbarum* L.) POLYGONACEAE (*2, 3, 6, 8, 9, 11, 14*)

Rhubarb is a large-leafed plant grown for its thick leaf petioles, which are stewed and used for pie filling or sauces. The plant is a cool-season perennial, and often the first vegetable ready for consumption in the spring. It is dormant in the winter in regions where freezes occur; under these conditions it produces a crop in the early spring and summer. In regions having hot, arid summers, the plant is dormant and produces the crop in the fall and winter. The plant does not grow well at temperatures above 25°C (77°F).

Two popular cultivars grown in western United States are Cherry Red and Crimson Winter. Ruby, Sunrise, and Valentine are grown in the North and Northeast.

Rhubarb is grown on a wide variety of soils ranging from sandy loams to clays or peat soils, but it does best on fertile well-drained loams high in organic matter. The plant feeds heavily on mineral nutrients and often responds to fertilizer applications of 110 to 170 kg/ha (98 to 150 lb/ac) nitrogen. For an early crop or for sandy soils, the higher rate is recommended.

Commercial and home growers propagate rhubarb by dividing crowns from previous growth. Carefully selected, vigorous crowns are divided early in the spring where freezing winters occur or in the winter in milder climates. The crowns are cut into pieces, each of which needs at least two or three strong buds. Each piece is planted with the buds about 5 to 10 cm (2 to 4 in) below the soil surface and spaced 90 to 150 cm (3 to 5 ft) apart. Two to four plants normally provide enough rhubarb for a family of four. They are often placed along the edge of the garden with other perennials so as not to interfere with soil preparation for the annual crops. Some gardeners use them as ornamentals because they are quite attractive.

The rhubarb beds are normally maintained free of weeds by shallow cultivation.

The most serious disease of rhubarb is brown rot, caused by a fungus that induces rotting at the base of the petioles. The rusty snout beetle causes damage by boring into the petioles or crowns.

Rhubarb is harvested by pulling the petioles to one side and upward so that the stipules remain attached. The leaf blades, which are poisonous, are removed by cutting and then four or five petioles are tied in a bunch. In areas with long growing seasons, some light harvesting is done during the second year and full harvest begins the third year. In areas where growing season is short, full harvest does not usually begin until the third year.

Spinach (*Spinacia oleraceae* L.) CHENOPODIACEAE (2, 3, 6, 8, 9, 11, 14)

Spinach, table beets, and sugar beets are closely related members of the goosefoot family. Spinach is an annual and usually dioecious (male and female flowers on separate plants), but some plants are monoecious (male and female flowers on the same plant). Spinach, probably a native of Africa or Asia, was cultivated in Persia over 2000 years ago, being taken to Europe during the thirteenth century. In the United States, California, Texas, New Jersey, Maryland, Virginia, and Colorado lead in the production of spinach for the fresh market, while California, Arkansas, and Oklahoma lead for freezing and canning. Spinach is grown in many home gardens in the United States.

Spinach is a cool-season crop. It grows best when monthly temperatures average about 15°C to 18°C (59°F to 64°F). It tolerates some slight freezing, but temperatures of 20°C to 25°C (68°F to 77°F), especially with long days, cause the plant to flower and produce seed stalks (bolting).

The two main types of spinach are smooth-leaved and savory-leaved or wrinkled. The smooth-leaved type is further divided into smooth-seeded and prickly-seeded. Some of the more popular cultivars and their characteristics are shown in Table 27-6. Virginia Savoy and Viroflay are best suited for freezing and canning, while Dark Green Bloomsdale and Long Standing Bloomsdale are excellent for fresh market or home gardens.

Spinach grows well on a wide variety of soils, including sandy loams, clay loams, and muck soils. For the winter crop, the sandy loams are better because they are generally warmer and better drained.

Climate is important in deciding planting dates for spinach. In areas where the summers are cool, it can be planted in the spring for summer harvest. In areas with severe winters, it is planted as soon as the soil can be prepared in the spring for early summer harvest. In areas with mild winters, like Arizona, California, Florida and Texas, spinach is planted in the fall or early winter for winter or early spring harvest.

Spinach is seeded at the rate or 9 to 17 kg/ha (8 to 15 lb/ac). The larger amounts are needed for the prickly-seeded cultivars. Seeds are generally drilled into the soil 1 to 2.5 cm (0.5 to 1 in) deep in rows 35 to 50 cm (14 to 20 in) apart. Seeds should be treated with a fungicide. The necessity for thinning the plants is often avoided by using good-quality, viable seeds, and accurate seeding rates. Seed treatment with fungicides reduces plant loss due to fungal diseases giving a full crop stand.

It is difficult to generalize fertilizer recommendations since spinach is grown on such a wide variety of soils and in widely varying climates. In areas where the winters are mild and the temperatures cool, little soil nitrification occurs so that the crop often responds to applications of 335 to 670 kg/ha (300 to 600 lb/ac) ammonium sulfate $[(NH_4)_2 SO_4]$. In some of the western states under irrigation (California, Washington, Oregon) 55 to 110 kg/ha (49 to 98 lb/ac) nitrogen, 70 to 135 kg/ha (60 to 120 lb/ac) phosphoric acid, and 70 to 135 kg/ha (60 to 120 lb/ac) potash are often profitable. In some of the eastern areas of the United States, farmers apply 85 to 110 kg/ha (75 to 98 lb/ac) nitrogen, 85 to 110 kg/ha (75 to 98 lb/ac) phosphoric acid, and 85 to 170 kg/ha (75 to 150 lb/ac) potash. Higher amounts of potash are often recommended for peat or muck soils. Some Oregon soils are deficient in boron and applications of this element are needed. Dry fertilizers are applied by broadcasting the material uniformly and mixing it into the soil by disking before the crop is planted. Some growers prefer to split the application and apply half of it as a preplanting fertilizer

Table 27–6   Selected Cultivars of Spinach

Cultivar	Days	Plant Shape	Leaf Type	Leaf Color	Leaf Size	Season	Remarks
America	50	Spreading	Savoy	Dark	Small	Summer	Slow bolting[a]
Avon Hybrid	44	Large	Semisavoy	Dark	Large		Slow bolting
Bloomsdale Dark Green	40	Medium erect	Savoy	Medium	Medium	Fall, winter	Good shipper
Bloomsdale Long Standing	42	Medium erect	Savoy	Dark	Medium	Late spring	Slow bolting
Chesapeake	43	Medium erect	Semisavoy	Medium	Medium	Winter	Adapted to machine harvest
Dixie Market	37	Compact	Savoy	Medium	Medium	Fall, winter	Resistant to downy mildew
Hybrid No. 7	40	Large erect	Semisavoy	Medium	Large	Fall, winter	High yielding
Hybrid No. 424	38	Large erect	Smooth	Medium	Large	Fall to spring	For South and West
Savoy Supreme	48	Erect	Savoy	Dark	Large	Spring, summer	High yielding
Virginia Savoy	39	Medium erect	Savoy	Dark	Medium	Fall, winter	For Southeast
Viroflay	40	Spreading	Smooth	Dark	Large	Fall, winter	For processing

[a] Rapid growth of flower stalks after sufficient chilling or a favorable photoperiod.

and sidedress the second half later in the season when the crop is about half grown.

Weed growth is prevented in spinach for two reasons. Weeds drastically lower the market quality of the crop for processing, and spinach does not compete well with most weeds thus lowering yields. Shallow cultivation is often used, along with preplanting herbicides. Excessive cultivation is entirely avoided if weeds are not a problem.

Spinach requires a constant and uniform water supply to produce large, tender, crisp leaves. Since spinach is shallow rooted, the crop is likely to require irrigation wherever natural rainfall is inadequate. However, much of the crop is grown during the rainy season, and as little as 15 to 30 cm (6 to 12 in) additional water is needed even in the arid western and southwestern United States.

Spinach is susceptible to many diseases; downy mildew, mosaic, curly top, and damping off are the most serious. Aphids and spinach leaf miners are two important insect pests.

Spinach is grown for its leaves, which are harvested in the rosette stage (Fig. 27–23). The use of the crop determines the harvest method used. Spinach leaves grown for freezing or canning are generally cut with a mowing machine equipped with a rotating paddle wheel that lays the cut leaves on a moving canvas to be conveyed into a truck or trailer. Spinach harvested for fresh market or home use is cut by hand just below the soil surface so that the leaves remain attached in a bunch. Unsightly leaves are removed and two or three plants tied together. The market price has considerable effect on the time of harvest. Smaller plants are often harvested when prices are high, while growers tend to delay harvest if prices are low. The price does not have this effect on processed spinach since much of it is grown at a prearranged price.

Good quality is indicated by freedom from weeds, insects, disease, or mechanical damage. First-quality leaves are bright green and medium large to large in size.

Swiss Chard or Chard (*Beta vulgaris* L., Cicla Group) CHENOPODIACEAE (*2, 3, 4, 6, 8, 9, 11, 14*)

This plant, normally a biennial, is a beet that develops large, crisp, fleshy leaf stalks and large leaves rather than enlarged roots. It has been known and eaten for over 2000 years.

There are only a few cultivars of Swiss chard. The most important ones are Lucullus, Giant Perpetual, Rhubarb, and Large Ribbed White (Fig. 27–24). The Rhubarb cultivar has brilliant red petioles and midribs.

Swiss chard is a widely adapted, cool-season crop that tolerates hot weather better than spinach. It is one of the easiest crops to grow. Plants are either started in greenhouses and transplanted early in the spring or seeded directly in the field. In areas with mild winters the crop is planted in the late summer for fall or early winter harvest. The plants grow well on a wide variety of soils but, like spinach, a fertile, well-drained sandy loam produces the best crops. The rows are about 45 to 60 cm (18 to 24 in) apart. Weeds are controlled by preplanting herbicides, shallow cultivation, or both. On sandy soils the crop generally responds to fertilizers applied at the rate of 55 to 110 kg/ha (49 to 98 lb/ac) each of nitrogen, phosphoric acid, and potash.

Chard is susceptible to the same diseases and insects as beets.

The crop is harvested by cutting the petioles at the base of the plant with a sharp knife. Care is taken to avoid injury to the growing point, allowing new leaves to grow, thereby providing continuous harvest throughout the summer. For fresh market, six to eight petioles with leaf blades remaining intact are tied together to form a bunch of desired size. Two or three plants normally provides sufficient chard for a family of four.

Fig. 27–23 This field of spinach is ready to be harvested by mowing and then transported to the processing plant for freezing.

Fig. 27–24 'Fordhood Giant' Swiss chard has large, crisp, white petioles with large leaves. This crop is grown for its tender leaves and petioles; the leaves are cooked and served like spinach and the petioles can be cooked and served like asparagus. Swiss chard is popular because it can be cultivated easily and is productive and more heat tolerant than spinach, thus providing greens when weather is too warm for other crops. *Source:* USDA.

REFERENCES

1. Anon. 1975. Growing cauliflower and broccoli. USDA Farmers Bul. 2239.

2. Anon. 1979. Vegetables. Annual summary, acreage, yield, production, and value. Statistical Reporting Board. USDA.

3. Bailey, L. H., and E. Z. Bailey and staff of L. H. Bailey Hortorium. *Hortus third.* New York: Macmillan.

4. Bauske, R. J. 1976. *Home horticulture.* St. Paul, Minn.: West.

5. Dunmire, J. R., ed. 1979. *Sunset new western garden book.* 4th ed. Menlo Park, Calif.: Lane.

6. Hays, J., ed. 1977. Gardening for food and fun. USDA Yearbook. Washington, D. C.: U.S. Government Printing Office.

7. Lange, A., H. Agamalian, J. Lyons, and E. Stilwell. 1969. Weed control in lettuce. Univ. of Calif. Agr. Ext. Leaflet 202.

8. Maynard, D. N., and C. L. Thompson. 1970. Nutrition of vegetable crops in Massachusetts. Coop. Ext. Ser. Publ. 63.

9. Minges, P. A., A. A. Muka, R. F. Sandsted, A. F. Sherf, and R. D. Sweet. 1976. *Commercial vegetable production recommendations.* Ithaca, N.Y.: New York State College of Agriculture and Life Sciences.

10. Sims, W. L., F. Takatori, H. Johnson, and B. Bensen. 1971. Direct seeding of asparagus. Univ. of Calif. Agr. Ext. AXT 348.

11. ———, H. Johnson, Jr., R. F. Kasmire, V. E. Rubatzky, K. B. Tyler, R. E. Voss. 1977. Home vegetable gardening. Univ. of Calif. Div. Agr. Sci. Leaflet 2989.

12. ———, V. H. Rubatzky, R. H. Sciaroni, and W. H. Lang. 1977. Growing globe artichokes in California. Univ. of Calif. Div. Agr. Sci. Leaflet 2675.

13. Thompson, R. C. 1961. Cauliflower and broccoli varieties and culture. USDA Farmers Bul. 1957.

14. Ware, G. W., and J. P. McCollum. 1975. *Producing vegetable crops.* 2nd ed. Danville, Ill.: Interstate.

SUPPLEMENTARY READING

LORENZ, O. A., and D. N. MAYNARD. 1980. *Knott's handbook for vegetable growers.* Somerset, N.J.: Wiley-Interscience.

Vegetable Crops Grown for Underground Parts

Underground plant parts used for food consist of tuberous roots, bulbs, rhizomes, corms, and stem tubers. Some plants store excess food (photosynthate) not needed during the growing period in these organs. Rhizomes, corms, and tubers are stems that have buds and send forth roots, leaves, or more stems. Tubers are thickened stems with little internodal elongation (p. 31). The "eyes" of the potato tuber are leaf or stem buds. Under certain environmental conditions, potatoes produce aerial tubers. Bulbs, like the onion, are underground growing leafy scales attached to short compressed stems (p. 31). Food is stored in the onion leaves (not roots), causing them to enlarge into bulbs. The sweet potato, a tuberous-rooted plant, is a very important food crop.

Underground plant parts are an important source of food. The Irish potato plant, which stores excess starch in its underground tubers, is recognized as an efficient converter of solar energy to chemical energy, second only to sugarcane in calories and to soybeans in protein per unit area in the United States according to the National Potato Council.

This chapter discusses the important crop plants whose underground parts are used for food.

Beets (*Beta vulgaris* L., Crassa Group J. Helm) CHENOPODIACEAE (*1, 6, 7, 9, 12, 13, 15, 16, 17*)

Table beets, native to Europe and North Africa, are cool-season biennials grown mainly for their roots. However, the tender young tops are sometimes used as greens. Beets were first used for food about the third century A.D.

Beets are grown extensively in Germany and France and in lesser amounts in other European countries, Africa, Asia, and South America. In the United States, Wisconsin and New York lead as producers of beets for processing and Texas leads as the producer for the fresh market. Other states producing canning beets include California, Michigan, New Jersey, and Ohio. Beets are grown in home gardens in most states.

Beets are rather hardy and tolerate some freezing, but they also grow well in warm weather. Excessively hot weather, however causes zoning—the appearance of alternating light and dark red concentric circles in the root. Beet seeds germinate when soil temperature ranges from 5°C to 25°C (41°F to 77°F).

During the first growing season the plant normally produces a thickened root and a rosette of leaves. Following this, winter temperatures of 5°C to 10°C (41°F to 50°F) for at least 15 days cause flowering and seed stalk formation.

Some popular cultivars are listed in Table 28–1.

Good beets are produced on a wide variety of soils, but deep, well-drained loams or sandy soils are best. The best seedbeds are well prepared by plowing 15 to 20 cm (6 to 8 in) deep followed by sufficient disking and harrowing to pulverize the clods. Well-rotted manure or other organic matter added to the soil is always good.

Except for a few fields that are planted with beet transplants for extra early market, seeds are usually planted directly in the field by sowing "seedballs" that contain one or more seeds. The balls are planted at the rate of 7 to 9 kg/ha (6 to 8 lb/ac) in rows 45 to 60 cm (18 to 24 in) apart and are thinned later to an in-row spacing of 8 to 10 cm (3 to 4 in). Beets grown for processing are seldom thinned because of labor cost.

Best-quality beets are produced when environmental conditions encourage uninterrupted rapid growth. Beets generally respond to fertilizers. The kind and amount varies with soil type, inherent fertility, and previous fertility program. In general, commercial growers use mixed fertilizers and apply 112 to 225 kg/ha (100 to 200 lb/ac) of nitrogen, phosphoric acid, and potash. For soils low in phosphorus the 225 kg (200 lb) rate is recommended. Home gardeners use 220 to 245 g/m² (4.5 to 5 lbs/100 ft²). Some farmers prefer to sidedress half their fertilizer when the crop is about half grown. A physiological

573

Table 28–1   Popular Table Beet Cultivars

Cultivar	Days to Maturity	Root Shape	Top Length	Use
Crosby's Egyptian	55–60	Shallow globe	Medium tall	Fresh market, home
Detroit Dark Red	60–70	Full globe	Medium tall	Processing fresh market
Early Wonder	55–60	Shallow globe	Tall	Fresh market, home
Red Pack	70	Full globe	Short	Processing
Ruby Queen	55–60	Round, small tap root	Short	Processing

symptom known as internal black spot caused by boron deficiency is prevented with applications of borax ($Na_2B_4O_7 \cdot 10 H_2O$) applied at the rate of 10 to 45 kg/ha (9 to 40 lb/ac).

Weeds drastically decrease yields and should be controlled. Mechanical cultivation controls weeds between rows, but herbicides are needed within the rows. Deep cultivation is not recommended because many of the most difficult weed roots grow near the surface. Cultivation beyond that needed for weed control not only is costly but is harmful to the plants.

Leaf spot is the most widespread disease of beets, especially during the rainy seasons in the eastern and midwestern states of the United States.

The larva of the beet leaf miner is the most injurious insect pest.

Fresh market beets marketed with their tops left on and 4 to 5 cm (1.5 to 2 in) in diameter, are pulled by hand, graded according to size, waxed, and tied in bunches of four or five. However, large commercial fresh market plantings marketed with tops removed are dug mechanically. This latter method lengthens shelf life by reducing water loss from the beets. Processed beets are handled in a similar manner. They are topped and dug mechanically with a harvester, conveyed to a truck for transport to a packing shed, where they are washed and sent to the processor or into storage. Beets store well at a temperature of 0°C (32°F) and 90 percent relative humidity.

Carrots (*Daucus carota* L.) UMBELLIFERAE
(6, 7, 9, 11, 12, 15, 16, 17)

The carrot, a cool-season crop, is grown for its fleshy storage root. It is a native of Europe and parts of Asia. While the carrot is mentioned in some of the ancient Greek writings, it is likely that the crop, as we know it, is relatively new due to improvements by plant breeding. The carrot was introduced in North and South America in the early 1600s. The wild type is an annual, but the cultivated types are biennials (*11*). The root is slender and varies in length from 5 to 25 cm (2 to 10 in) when harvested.

Carrots are grown in Europe, parts of Asia, North and East Africa, North and South America, New Zealand, and Australia. Their worldwide consumption has increased over the years until they are now one of the most popular vegetable crops. The principal production areas in the United States for both fresh market and processing are California, Texas, Washington, Wisconsin, Michigan and Florida. Carrots are harvested somewhere in the United States every month of the year.

Carrots grow best at temperatures ranging from 15°C to 20°C (59°F to 68°F). In the seedling stage the plants are sensitive to both high and low temperatures, and mild freezes at harvest cause some leaf damage. Many young plants are injured or killed on hot, sunny days. Long periods of hot weather often cause a strong flavor and coarse root texture. Temperatures below 10°C (50°F) tend to cause longer, more slender, and paler roots. Color develops best at about 10°C to 15°C (50°F to 59°F).

Carrots are often divided into classes according to shape and length of root, with each class represented by several cultivars (Fig. 28–1). Some of the more popular cultivars reported in seed catalogs are given in Table 28–2.

Carrots grow best in deep, sandy loam soils, but some are grown in muck soil. Heavy clay soils tend to restrict root development and cause forked roots. Muck soils tend to produce rough-skinned roots.

Fig. 28–1   The 'Imperator' carrot is long and slightly tapered, a good carrot for home garden and commercial freezing. It has a bright orange color and is high yielding. *Source:* Ferry-Morse Seed Company.

Table 28–2 Selected Carrot Cultivars

Cultivar	Days to Maturity	Average Length cm (in)	Average Diameter cm (in)	Shape	Remarks
Chantenay Red Cored	72	15 (6)	5 (2)	Wide shoulders, blunt tip	Favorite with home gardeners
Danvers	75	19 (7.5)	5 (2)	Heavy shoulders, stumped	Bright orange flesh, tender
Gold Pak	80	23 (9)	4 (1.5)	Broad shoulders	Excellent fresh, frozen, or canned
Hi-Color	77	28 (11)	4 (1.5)	Slender tapered	Adapted for muck soils
Imperator	77	23 (9)	4 (1.5)	Long, slender, slight taper	Good for home garden and freezing
Nantes	70	16 (6.5)	4 (1.5)	Cylindrical, blunt	Good flavor raw, cooked, or frozen
Royal Chantenay	70	18 (7)	4 (1.5)	Broad shoulders, tapered roots	Grows well in heavy soils
Spartan Hybrid	75	21 (8.5)	4 (1.5)		Fine-grained, crisp, deep orange roots

Carrot seeds are small and germinate slowly, and the tiny seedlings require some time to become established. The seeds are planted in a firm, well-prepared seedbed free of clods. The best soils do not puddle or crust severely when irrigated or rained on.

Tillage is done primarily to control weeds, and the number of operations is kept to a minimum.

Mineral soils almost always benefit from plowing under of well-rotted manure or green manure. On mineral soils in humid regions, some farmers find 55 to 110 kg/ha (49 to 98 lb/ac) of nitrogen ample. If additional nitrogen is needed, it is added as a sidedressing at the rate of 35 to 50 kg/ha (31 to 45 lb/ac). On peat or muck soils, less nitrogen is needed. Soils low in phosphorus often require 55 to 110 kg/ha (49 to 98 lb/ac) phosphoric acid applied as a commercial mixture. Potash is applied at rates of 55 to 110 kg/ha (49 to 98 lb/ac) on soils where the need for potassium is indicated by either soil test or plant symptoms. This fertilizer is also included in some commercial mixtures. In the western and southwestern United States potassium is rarely needed.

A constant water supply, either in the form of rainfall or irrigation, is essential for seed germination and high yields of good-quality carrots. A deficiency of good-quality water decreases root size and increases skin roughness. In the semiarid United States about 45 to 60 cm (18 to 24 in) of irrigation water is needed. Even in humid regions, like New York, use of supplemental sprinkler irrigation increases yields.

Aster yellows, a viral disease transmitted by the six-spotted leaf hopper, is sometimes a serious pest. Cottony rot is also a serious disease caused by a fungus.

The carrot beetle and carrot rust fly are destructive insect pests.

Most fresh market and processed carrots are harvested mechanically. A blade is passed under the roots to loosen them from the soil. They are lifted and the tops removed. The roots are transported to the packing shed where they are washed, sorted according to size, packaged in polyethylene bags, and cooled. Some fresh market carrots are sold with their tops left on. Green tops attached to the roots do not ensure freshness, nor do they prolong shelf life. In fact, except for appearance the tops do more harm to the roots than good. Carrots with tops are generally tied in bunches and packed in crushed ice. Topped carrots for fresh market are often packed in cellophane bags. Processed carrots are dug and topped in the same manner.

Celeriac (*Apium graveolens* L., var. *rapaceum* Gaud-Beaup.) UMBELLIFERAE (*6, 7, 12, 13, 17*)

Celeriac and celery are closely related, both belonging to the same species. Celeriac is commonly known as turnip-root. The above-ground parts look similar to celery except that the foliage is often less dense, more dwarfed, and darker green. The edible part is the enlarged root, which is creamed, used to flavor soups, or tossed in fresh salads (Fig. 28–2). The crop is not grown extensively in the United States, and only two cultivars,

Fig. 28–2 The enlarged celeriac root (turnip-rooted celery) is a close relative of celery that has an edible root instead of an edible petiole. The finer roots were removed during harvest. This plant is not as popular in the United States as in other parts of the world. *Source:* Ferry-Morse Seed Company.

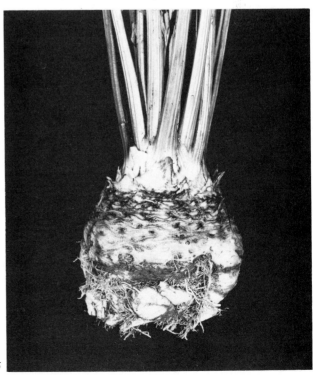

Large Smooth Prague and Alabaster, are usually grown. In Europe the crop is better known and more widely used.

The climatic requirements and cultural procedures for celeriac are similar to those for celery (see p. 560) except that the rows are generally spaced closer—45 to 60 cm (18 to 24 in) apart. Like celery, celeriac is either directly seeded or transplanted. The plants are harvested by pulling, cutting the branching roots at the base, and removing the tops when the roots are about 5 to 6 cm (2 to 2.5 in) in diameter. Sometimes they are tied in bunches of four to six roots. Like most root crops, celeriac stores well in a cool, dry environment.

Garlic (*Allium sativum* L.) AMARYLLIDACEAE (6, 7, 13, 14, 17)

This crop is grown especially for its strong characteristic flavor, of which a little goes a long, long way. The edible part is a compound bulb consisting of segments called cloves, each surrounded by a thin white or pink sheath. The leaves are solid and flattened rather than hollow and round as in onions.

Garlic has been grown for centuries, and at one time the bulbs were used as currency.

In the United States, garlic is principally grown in California, with a small amount grown in Texas and Louisiana. Some is also grown in South and Central America, Italy, and Egypt.

Garlic is a cool-season crop grown during the early fall in the coastal valleys of central California or during early spring in areas where freezing occurs. A few plants are sufficient for the average family and are easily grown in a home garden.

There are several cultivars of garlic, each adapted to certain areas and conditions. The most common are California Late, California Early, and Creole. California Late produces more cloves that are smoother and of better quality than the others, but the total yield is less because the cloves are smaller. California Early does not store well, but has the advantage of high yield with bulbs reaching maturity two or three weeks earlier than California Late. Creole is mostly grown in Mexico, South America, and California's Imperial Valley. It matures about a month earlier than California Early. The cloves are covered with a purple sheath.

Garlic grows well on a wide variety of soils but does best on light sandy loams. Weed control and harvesting are difficult with heavy clay soils. To prevent some diseases, garlic is best planted on land that has not grown garlic the previous year. The crop is propagated by planting cloves broken apart just before planting. The small center cloves are discarded. Seed is never used for propagation. If irrigation is used, the land is leveled and a loose, friable seedbed prepared. Garlic is usually planted on raised beds 100 cm (40 in) apart with two rows on a bed. The rows are about 30 cm (12 in) apart and the cloves about 5 cm (2 in) apart within the row.

Garlic generally responds to fertilizer but is not so demanding as other vegetable crops. If the previous crop was well fertilized, with some carryover, no additional fertilizer is needed. If not, best results are obtained by applying up to 90 kg/ha (80 lb/ac) of nitrogen. For the fall-planted crops, half is applied at planting time and the other half in the spring when the bulbs begin to enlarge.

Shallow cultivation controls weeds.

Excessive irrigation discolors the sheath covering the cloves and is best avoided. However, for high yields the upper 60 cm (2 ft) of the soil needs to be kept moist. Generally, winter rains are sufficient to start and grow the crop until spring.

Many of the diseases of onions also attack garlic. Onion thrips are the most destructive insect. Stem and bulb nematodes are troublesome in some areas.

Garlic cloves sent to dehydraters for processing are mechanically harvested; otherwise, the cloves are pulled by hand. A tractor-mounted blade, passed under the row when the tops become partially dry and bent over, permits easier hand-pulling of the cloves. Several rows are gathered together and placed in a windrow with tops up to protect the cloves from sun. These plants are allowed to dry and cure in the field for a week or two. The tops and roots are removed by shears, leaving about 1.3 cm (0.5 in) of the root and 2.5 cm (1 in) of top attached to each clove. They are again covered with the tops and left in the field for further drying.

Horseradish (*Armoracia rusticana* P. Gaertn., B. Mey. & Scherb.) CRUCIFERAE (2, 6, 7, 13, 15)

Horseradish is a hardy perennial, native to eastern Europe. The leaves and roots have been used as food or condiment since the Middle Ages and before that for medicinal purposes. The plant is grown for its pungent compound, allyl isothiocyanate (C_3H_5CNS).

The area around St. Louis, Missouri and East St. Louis, Illinois is considered the horseradish capital of the United States. Horseradish is also grown in Washington, Wisconsin, Pennsylvania, and northern California, but not as an important commercial crop.

There are two types of horseradish, with little choice of cultivar. The common type has broad, crinkled leaves and produces high-quality roots. The Bohemian type has narrow, smooth leaves, is more disease resistant, but produces lower quality roots. In selecting a cultivar, the main concern is to choose rootstock that is healthy, vigorous, and adapted to the area.

While horseradish grows in almost any soil, it does best in deep, fertile, well-drained loams or sandy loams. It also grows well on peat soils but no so well on shallow, compacted, or heavy clay soils with hard subsoils. Poor soils produce prong-shaped, poor-quality roots.

Horseradish is a perennial but is commercially grown as an annual to prevent it from becoming a weed pest. It is easily propagated from root cuttings and sometimes from crowns, but never from seed (see Ch. 5). The root pieces are planted as early as possible after frost in the spring and the plants occupy the land until fall. After the larger marketable roots are harvested and trimmed, the smaller slender roots are stored and saved to be used as root cuttings for planting next year's crop. It is necessary to use correct polarity and identify the upper and lower end of the pieces, commonly by making a square cut at the top (proximal) end of the root (closer to crown) and a diagonal cut at the bottom (distal) end (farther from crown). These root pieces are tied in bundles and stored in an outdoor pit or in moist sand in a cold cellar until spring.

Before planting the root cuttings, the soil is plowed as

deeply as possible. A firm, mellow seedbed is prepared by disking and harrowing until free of clods. Furrows are formed about 75 cm (30 in) apart and 13 to 23 cm (5 to 9 in) deep. The planting stock is placed, all slanting in one direction, about 30 to 38 cm (12 to 15 in) apart in the row. Care is taken to place the square cut end up in the furrow. Set the roots with a little soil as they are distributed down the row, then fill in the furrow later with cultivator.

Shallow cultivation early in the season prevents weeds. Late cultivation is avoided. Twice during the growing season, the plants are ''stripped'' to get good-quality roots for market. This involves carefully removing the soil from around the top of the main root and leaving the soil at the lower end undisturbed. The small lateral roots are then rubbed off by hand. This procedure produces marketable roots that are free of side roots.

If the soil is clay or clay loam, it is helpful to plow under a green manure crop or some well-rotted manure. Horseradish is considered a heavy feeder of plant nutrients, thus some commercial fertilizer is often recommended. For average soils not heavily fertilized from previous crops, an application of 55 kg/ha (49 lb/ac) of nitrogen, 110 kg/ha (98 lb/ac) of phosphoric acid, and 55 kg/ha (49 lb/ac) of potash is sufficient if manure is also used. If no manure is used, an application of 110 kg/ha (98 lb/ac) nitrogen, phosphoric acid, and potash is recommended.

The roots grow best late in the growing season; therefore harvest is delayed as long as possible in the fall. The roots are removed by plowing them out and cutting off the tops and side roots. The upper 25 to 35 cm (10 to 14 in) of the root is used for market, processing, or storage.

Onions (*Allium cepa* L.) AMARYLLIDACEAE (6, 7, 9, 12, 13, 14, 15, 16, 17)

Onions are one of the oldest vegetables, used as far back as history records. Two thousand years before Christ, the ancient Egyptians stated in the Giza pyramids the value of onions as a food and medicine. They are probably a native of the area from southwestern Asia eastward to India.

Onions are produced in almost every country in the temperate zone. The early-maturing bulb onions are produced in the southern and southwestern United States, while the late maturing come from the northern states. California is the largest producer of onions for bulbs and fresh market, followed by Texas, Oregon, New York, Idaho, Michigan, Colorado, and New Mexico. Onions are harvested somewhere in the United States each month from April through October.

Onions are cool-season plants that grow well at temperatures ranging from 10°C to 25°C (50°F to 77°F). Seeds can germinate from 7°C to 30°C (45°F to 86°F) but do best at about 18°C (64°F). During the early stages of growth (before bulbing) onions grow better at relatively cool temperatures, but during bulbing, harvesting, and curing, higher temperatures and low relative humidity are desirable. Bulbing is initiated primarily by day length and not by the age of the plant. Cultivars have very critical photoperiod requirements for bulb formation and do not bulb if the day length is too short. The optimum photoperiod varies from 12 hours for the short-day cultivars to 15 hours for the long-day types. Thus it is impossible to obtain bulbs with long-day cultivars in the southern latitudes because in the cool season the days are too short and when the photoperiod is sufficiently long the temperature is too high.

Onions vary considerably in size, shape, color, flavor, keeping quality, and maturity dates. New and better cultivars are continually appearing from breeding programs of universities, seed companies, and the USDA. Cultivars are often grouped according to the latitudes where they grow best. Group 1 cultivars require short days and are well adapted to areas between 24° and 28° latitude. These are best grown in the United States in southern Texas for fall planting and early spring harvest. Group 2 cultivars have medium-day requirements and are adapted to regions in latitudes between 32° and 40°. They are grown principally in the mild-winter areas of California, Texas, and the eastern coastal states, where they are planted in the fall for late spring or early summer harvest. Group 3 cultivars are adapted to areas north of 36° latitude. They are planted in early spring, when day lengths are increasing, for late summer or early fall harvest.

Popular cultivars and some of their characteristics are given in Table 28–3.

The most desirable soils for onion production are sandy loams, loams, peats, and mucks. Clays or coarse sandy soils are best avoided. Clay soils do not remain friable under cultivation and thus retard bulb enlargement. Coarse sandy soils do not retain sufficient water to keep the rather restricted root system of onions well supplied with moisture.

The seedbed is prepared by plowing deep, followed by sufficient tillage to break up clods and to provide a firm, mellow seedbed. In irrigated areas the land is often leveled and smoothed with a land-plane as a part of the seedbed preparation.

There are three common methods of propagating onions; the method chosen is determined by the location, maturity date, and the crop use. The methods are direct seeding, transplanting, and planting sets or small bulbs. The direct-seeding method is used for most crops grown commercially for market as bulbs or for processing by dehydration into onion powder, flakes, salt, and so forth. Seeding rates vary considerably, depending upon soil fertility, use, and row spacing. Normally, 7 to 11 kg/ha (6 to 10 lb/ac) of seed are planted in rows spaced 30 to 60 cm (12 to 24 in) apart for a crop grown for dry bulbs. If a wider row spacing is used, proportionally less seed is needed. A farmer producing small bulbs for sets increases the seeding rate to 85 kg/ha (76 lb/ac) or more, producing extremely crowded growing conditions to hasten maturity. This practice gives smaller and more desirable sets.

Dry sets produce higher yields and earlier bulbs than direct seeding. They also produce earlier green onions. Most home gardeners prefer to plant dry sets in their gardens. One liter (0.9 qt) of sets plants 20 to 30 m (65 to 100 ft) of row. They are planted in shallow furrows, in an upright position, 2.5 to 5 cm (1 to 2 in) apart for green onions or 8 to 10 cm (3 to 4 in) apart for bulbs. Machines are used for large field plantings. Transplants about the size of a pencil are sometimes planted by hand directly in the field, especially for early crops. This method eliminates thinning but is costly and time consuming and is seldom done commercially.

Early cultivation for weed control is especially important for onions because they are slow starters and serious losses in crop yields occur if control practices are delayed. Many farmers weed the crop by hand once during the season. Chemical weed control is used extensively in most commercial plantings.

Table 28–3   Selected Onion Cultivars

Name	Growing Season (Days)	Shape	Size	Color	Flesh	Storage	Remarks
GROUP 1 (PRODUCES BULBS UNDER SHORT DAY LENGTH)							
Crystal Wax	180	Flat	Medium	White	White, mild	———	Green onions
Eclipse	180	Flat	Medium	White	White, mild	———	Spring bulbs
Excel[a]	180	Flat	Medium	Yellow	White, mild	———	Spring bulbs
Grano, Texas	170	Top-shaped	Large	Yellow	White, mild	———	Resistant to bolting[c]
Granex, Yellow[a,b]	165	Flat	Large	Yellow	White, mild	———	Attractive bulbs
Granex, White[a,b]	170	Flat	Large	White	White, mild	———	Resistant to bolting[c]
GROUP 2 (PRODUCES BULBS UNDER MEDIUM DAY LENGTH)							
San Joaquin	220	Tapered globe	Large	Yellow	Mild	Little	Bulbs or bunching
Pronto S[a,b]	210	Globe	Large	Yellow	Mild	Little	
GROUP 3 (PRODUCES BULBS UNDER LONG DAY LENGTH)							
Abundance[a]	105	Globe	Large	Yellow	Firm, pungent	Fair	High-yielding bulbs
Autumn Spice[a]	95	Globe	Medium	Brown	Firm, pungent	Good	For short season
Ebenezer, Yellow	105	Flat	Small	Yellow	Firm	Fair	Sets or early bulbs
Fiesta[a]	110	Globe	Large	Yellow	Firm, pungent	Good	Relatively early maturing
Granada[a,b]	110	Globe	Medium large	Yellow	Firm, sweet	Limited	Resistant to bolting[c]
Ruby	105	Globe	Medium large	Red	Firm, pungent	Good	Earlier than Southport
Southport, Red	110	Globe	Medium	Red	Firm, pungent	Good	Standard for long days
Spartan Banner[a]	115	Globe	Medium large	Brown	Firm, pungent	Best	High yielding
Spartan Bounty[a]	105	Globe	Medium	Brown	Firm, pungent	Best	Attractive bulbs
Spartan Gem[a]	115	Globe	Medium	Brown	Firm, pungent	Best	For Midwest muck

[a] Hybrids.
[b] Tolerant to pink root.
[c] Rapid growth of flower stalks after sufficient chilling or a favorable photoperiod.

Onions do not grow well on acid soils (pH less than 6.0). Finely ground limestone or hydrated lime is applied to bring the soil to a neutral reaction. Mineral soils are often improved by applications of organic matter such as well-rotted manure. It is better to apply the manure to the crop preceding onions if there is danger of adding weed seeds with the manure. Plowing under green manure crops avoids this problem. Muck or peat soils do not require additional organic matter. Rates of application and kinds of commercial fertilizers differ widely in different areas. On mineral soils that have not received manure, 55 to 85 kg/ha (49 to 75 lb/ac) of nitrogen, 110 to 170 kg/ha (98 to 152 lb/ac) of phosphoric acid, and 110 to 170 kg/ha (98 to 152 lb/ac) of potash are often recommended. In the irrigated regions of California, Arizona, and New Mexico, potassium is seldom needed, but 85 to 110 kg/ha (75 to 98 lb/ac) of nitrogen and 170 to 225 kg/ha (152 to 200 lb/ac) of phosphoric acid should be applied. Applications of 560 to 675 kg/ha (500 to 600 lb/ac) of 16-20-0 fertilizer are often recommended. Later in the growing season, additional nitrogen at 35 kg/ha (31 lb/ac) can be supplied by sidedressing. On muck soils potassium is often the limiting nutrient, and applications of potassium sulfate or potassium chloride usually give good response. Phosphorus and occasionally nitrogen fertilizers are helpful. In New York applications of 55 to 85 kg/ha (49 to 75 lb/ac) of nitrogen, phosphoric acid, and potash are not unusual on the fertile muck soils.

In the absence of rainfall, onions require irrigation. The plants should not be allowed to suffer from a lack of water. Early onions require 5 to 7 irrigations, while a late crop needs 7 to 10. The amount of water needed varies between 38 and 75 cm (15 to 30 in) depending upon maturity date, soil type, and location. Irrigation is generally started immediately after seeding and is continued at required intervals until plants begin to mature. Irrigation is then stopped and the soil allowed to dry to prevent secondary root growth. Onions are irrigated by furrow or sprinkler methods or by flooding with raised borders (see p. 202).

Onion smut, pink root, neck rot, and downy mildew are the most serious onion diseases. Onion thrips and onion maggots are the most troublesome insect pests.

Most onions are harvested as dry bulbs either for market as such or for processors to dehydrate (Fig. 28–3). Onions are also harvested before they bulb, bunched, and sold as fresh green onions (Fig. 28–4). Some are harvested for their seeds or sets (Fig. 28–5). Harvesting for mature bulbs generally begins when the tops start to turn brown and fall over, but this varies with season and environmental conditions. In the southern and western parts of the United States harvest begins when about 20 to 25 percent of the tops are down, ideally while the weather is still warm. In the East and Midwest, where temperatures are cooler, harvest is delayed until over 60 percent of the tops are down. Most bulb onions are harvested mechanically. A small

Fig. 28–3 'Sweet Spanish' onions when grown under environmental conditions that encourage bulb formation form large, mild-flavored bulbs. *Source:* Ferry-Morse Seed Company.

Fig. 28–4 Some onions are not allowed to bulb but are harvested early as green onions, trimmed and tied in bunches, and sold fresh. *Source:* Ferry-Morse Seed Company.

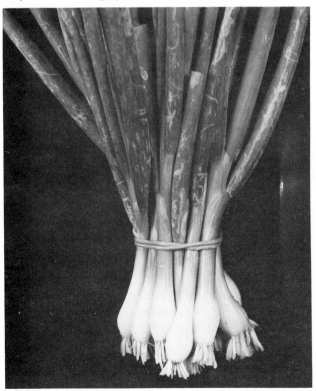

Fig. 28–5 Field workers hand-harvesting a crop of onion seeds in Idaho. Machine harvest has been tried but is not as successful as hand-harvesting. The heads are cut from the stalks and placed into bags. They are carried from the field, dried, and then threshed. *Source:* Ferry-Morse Seed Company.

onion plow is passed under the bulbs to loosen the soil (Fig. 28–6). They are then pulled and laid in windrows on top of the ground or placed in crates for further curing and drying. The curing time varies from a few days to two or three weeks depending upon temperature and relative humidity. Care is taken during harvest to avoid damage by bruising. After the tops have been removed, the onions are cleaned and graded according to size, shape, and color. Grade standards vary with each cultivar. Most bulbs are packaged in 23 kg (50 lb) open-mesh bags.

Fig. 28–6 A commercial onion planting being machine-harvested. This type of machine is also used on other root crops such as radishes, carrots, turnips, and sugar beets. A small plow or blade passes under the root or bulb to loosen the soil. Two belts moving close together and upward toward the rear of the machine grab the stems of the plants and pull them from the soil, depositing them in a gathering bin. From here they are elevated into trucks, bins, or as in this case, bags. *Source:* University of California Cooperative Extension.

Some onion cultivars have characteristics that permit relatively long storage, while others do not. The Bermuda type generally are not stored, but if they are stored for short periods, they are kept in a dry atmosphere at about 0°C (32°F). They must have been properly cured and not damaged by bruising or disease. Treatment with maleic hydrazide prevents sprouting in storage.

Green onions are mostly grown in small areas for local markets. The young plants are pulled by hand just as the bulb begins to swell. The outer skin or leaf scale is peeled off, leaving a clean, white stalk several centimeters long. The tops are trimmed evenly after they are tied in bunches. The bunches are packed in crates for transport to market.

Parsnips (*Pastinaca sativa* L.) UMBELLIFERAE (3, 6, 7, 9, 12, 13, 15, 16)

Parsnips are considered a native of Europe and Asia and have been used for food since the Greek and Roman eras. They were introduced into the United States in Virginia and Massachusetts in the early 1600s. The plants are cool-season biennials but are grown as annuals. They are not important commercially. Parsnips are slow growing and require a long season to form their white, fleshy edible roots. This crop occupies expensive vegetable land for longer periods of time than most farmers prefer.

Parsnips are extensively grown in the temperate zones of Europe and Asia. Most commercial production in the United States occurs in those states where cooler temperatures prevail, such as Pennsylvania, Illinois, parts of California, and New York. Good parsnip stands are difficult to obtain in the warmer southern states.

Parsnips grow best when they are planted and grown during a relatively cool summer and harvested in a cool fall. In California they are grown in the coastal valleys where summers are mild.

Few parsnip cultivars are listed in seed catalogs; the most common ones are All America, Harris Model, and Hollow Crown. All three cultivars produce roots with white flesh, small cores, and are relatively free from unsightly lenticel growth which lowers quality. Roots are tapered and grow 25 to 30 cm (10 to 12 in) long. All America is the earliest cultivar, requiring about 105 days to reach harvest maturity, while Harris Model and Hollow Crown need about 120 days.

Parsnips do best in a deep, fertile, well-drained, loam or sandy loam soil. Well-shaped, smooth roots are difficult to grow in heavy clay soils. Soil preparation and culture is much the same as for carrots (see p. 575). The seedbed should be carefully prepared by plowing to a depth of 15 to 20 cm (6 to 8 in) and working the soil until it is free of clods. Cloddy or stony soil causes rough, misshapened roots. Parsnip seed loses its vitality quickly, even when stored under good conditions; thus seed over a year old should not be used. Seed is planted into moist soil 1 to 2.5 cm (0.5 to 1 in) deep as soon as possible after the weather and soil have warmed. Parsnip seed germinates slowly; the optimum soil temperature for germination is about 20°C (68°F). Rows are placed 38 to 45 cm (15 to 18 in) apart for hand tillage and 60 to 75 cm (24 to 30 in) for tractor tillage. Fifteen grams (0.5 oz) of seed plants about 30 m (100 ft) of row. Nine to 15 m (30 to 50 ft) of row provides sufficient

parsnips for most home gardeners with a family of four. After plants are up, they are thinned to an in-row spacing of 8 to 10 cm (3 to 4 in).

Parsnips compete poorly with weeds; therefore, weeds must be controlled either by machine cultivation or hand hoeing throughout the growing season, which lasts up to the first frost.

Parsnips respond well to applications of rotted animal manure, but fresh manure is best avoided because it encourages branching of roots. Fertilizer recommendations are about the same as for table beets and perhaps a little less than for carrots (see p. 575). A general recommendation is 55 to 110 kg/ha (49 to 100 lb/ac) of nitrogen, 110 to 225 kg/ha (98 to 200 lb/ac) of phosphoric acid, and 55 to 110 kg/ha (49 to 100 lb/ac) of potash.

Where rain is lacking, soil moisture is maintained by either furrow or sprinkler irrigation. Water requirements are similar to those for carrots.

Parsnips have no serious disease or insect pests.

Parsnip roots withstand some freezing; thus the roots are often stored in the soil and harvested from late fall to early spring. In areas of severe winters, however, roots are best harvested during the fall because of the difficulty of digging them from frozen ground. Large plantings are harvested by loosening the roots with a plow and removing them by hand. The home gardener digs parsnips with a spading fork. At harvest time parsnips are high in starch, but after storage either in the soil or in a cool, moist pit or cellar at about 0°C to 1°C (32°F to 34°F), the starch is rapidly converted to sugar, markedly improving the flavor.

Potatoes (*Solanum tuberosum* L.) SOLANACEAE (6, 7, 9, 12, 13, 15, 16, 17)

Potatoes are closely related to eggplants, peppers, tobacco, and tomatoes, all belonging to the SOLANACEAE family. The potato plant is a bushy, herbaceous annual 60 to 90 cm (2 to 3 ft) in height. The edible tuber is a swollen underground stem. The "eyes" on the tuber are buds and are more numerous on the apical (distal) end (opposite the end of attachment) than the basal (proximal) end.

As a source for human food, the potato is the world's leading vegetable crop, ranking only behind wheat, rice, and corn. Corn, tomatoes, and potatoes are the only important food crops that the New World has contributed to our food supply. Potatoes are South American in origin and were cultivated in Chile and Peru by the Indians before the white man came (p. 63). Early Spanish explorers transported them to Europe about 1575, and from there they returned to North America with the colonists settling along the Atlantic coast. In those early days, however, potatoes were not a significant food source in North America, until the influx of Irish immigration which began in the early 1700s, and reached a maximum later, after the potato famine in Ireland in 1846. Potatoes then became America's favorite carbohydrate food because their cost was low and most people liked them (Fig. 28–7). Today potato culture encircles the globe; they are grown extensively on every continent in both temperate zones. European countries produce, by far, the largest percentage of the world's potatoes. Russia is the leading country followed by Germany, France, United States, England, and Spain. Potatoes are grown in every state in the

Fig. 28–7 Each year an increasing percentage of the total potato crop in the United States is processed into many new products. Here, Idaho russet potatoes are prepared for crinkle-cut potato chips. *Source:* University of California Cooperative Extension.

United States at some time during the year. Leading production states are Idaho, Washington, Maine, Oregon, California, North Dakota, Wisconsin, Minnesota, New York, Colorado, and Michigan.

Potatoes are a cool-season crop, slightly tolerant of frost, but damaged by freezing weather near harvest. Maximum yields of high-quality tubers are produced when the mean temperature is between 15°C and 18°C (59°F and 64°F) during the growing season. Tubers form best when the average temperature is about 18°C (64°F). Tuberization (tuber formation) is reduced at 20°C (68°F) and inhibited at 29°C (84°F).

Flowers are common but fruit rarely sets because the climate and day length requirements are precise. Fruiting requires a cool climate or a day length of 16 to 17 hours. The fruits are berries, similar to small tomatoes, within which seeds are produced. The true seeds are used in breeding programs but are never planted for commercial production.

New potato cultivars appear as a result of widespread breeding programs in the USDA and agricultural experiment stations (Fig. 28–8). Many of the older cultivars are being replaced by newer ones. Cultivars differ widely in maturity time, yield, appearance, cooking quality, storage, and resistance to pests. A cultivar developed for a particular growing condition or location might fail utterly in another. Certified "seed" tubers are used to propagate potatoes commercially; thus the amount of certified tubers produced indicates well the relative popularity of that cultivar. Some of the more popular cultivars are listed in Table 28–4.

Table 28–4 Selected Potato Cultivars

Cultivar	Maturity	Locality	Resistance to:	Tuber				
				Skin	Eyes	Size	Shape	Color
Bliss Triumph	Early	South, Midwest and Colo.	Resistant to few diseases	Smooth	Medium	Large to medium	Round	Red
Cherokee	Medium	North central	Late blight, scab, mild mosaic	Smooth	Medium	Medium	Round	Creamy white
Chippewa	Medium	Wide adaptation	Mild mosaic, net necrosis	Smooth	Shallow	Large	Oblong flat	White
Cobbler	Early	Wide adaptation	Mild mosaic, wart	Smooth	Medium to deep	Large to medium	Round blunt ends	White
Green Mountain	Late	North, East	Susceptible to net necrosis	Smooth or netted	Medium	Medium	Oblong flat	White
Katahdin	Late	Wide adaptation	Mild mosaic, yellow dwarf	Smooth	Shallow	Large	Elliptical	Creamy buff
Kennebec	Late	Wide adaptation	Late blight, mild mosaic	Smooth	Shallow	Large	Elliptical	Creamy buff
Pontiac	Late	North central and Florida	Yellow dwarf	Smooth	Shallow to medium	Large	Oblong, blunt ends	Red
Russet Burbank or Netted Gem	Late	Ia., Wash., Ore., Calif.	Scab	Russetted, netted	Many shallow	Large	Long, cylindrical	Russet
Russet Rural	Late	Northeastern states	Scab	Netted	Shallow	Large	Oblong, flat	Russet
Sebago	Late	Northeast, West, and Fla.	Yellow dwarf, mild mosaic	Smooth	Shallow	Large	Elliptical	Ivory
White Rose	Early to medium	Calif.	Scab	Smooth	Medium	Medium	Long, flat	White

Fig. 28-8 A potato breeding trial in which cultivars are being tested for resistance to a certain virus. *Source:* University of California Cooperative Extension.

High-yielding tubers of good quality are produced on a wide variety of soils, provided management is proper. The most popular soils are light-textured mineral soils and mucks. A fertile soil with good water drainage and aeration is important. Good quality potatoes do not come from water-logged soils because the excess water tends to enlarge lenticels. Heavy clay soils or stony soils produce irregular-shaped and rough-skinned tubers. Compacted soils not only reduce yield, but also often produce unmarketable, knobby potatoes (Fig. 28-9).

The seedbed is prepared by plowing 15 to 20 cm (6 to 8 in) deep followed by sufficient disking and harrowing to free the soil of clods.

Potatoes are propagated vegetatively by planting either small whole tubers or cut "seed" pieces. It is not worth the risk, even for the home gardener, to plant anything but certified disease-free seed pieces. Certified seed tubers are produced in the northern tier of states, as well as California and Colorado (under strict state inspection and regulation) by certain farmers who specialize in this production.

Immediately after harvest, the buds ("eyes") on potato tubers enter a rest period of five to six weeks, during which time they will not sprout naturally even if they are placed in a favorable environment. For planting, the tuber is cut into two to six pieces. The size or weight of the seed piece is important; the ideal is about 40 to 55 g (1.5 to 2 oz). Small (55 g) tubers are often planted whole. Each piece contains at least one healthy bud, preferably two.

The planting date depends upon the climate, location, and the desired harvest date. High soil temperature (30°C; 86°F) prevents tuber formation; thus planting dates are chosen to keep tubers from forming during hot weather. Potatoes are planted as soon as soil temperatures reach about 5°C (41°F). This is the best time for early potatoes in Idaho, Montana, Maine, New York, Minnesota, and Wisconsin. In the southern states and Texas, main planting comes in late fall or early winter. In California, planting dates vary from winter to spring to fall; in the Tule Lake area near the Oregon border, planting is done during late spring to early summer; in the Imperial Valley, in late fall to early winter; and in the southern San Joaquin Valley, early spring planting occurs.

Home gardeners often plant potato pieces by hand in hills 30 cm (12 in) apart with rows 45 to 50 cm (18 to 20 in) wide. Pieces are planted 8 to 10 cm (3 to 4 in) deep. Commercial producers using mechanical planters plant two to six rows at a time (Fig. 28-10). The rows vary from 75 to 120 cm (30 to 48 in) apart with in-row spacings between plants of 20 to 30 cm (8 to 12 in). In many areas, especially where furrow irrigation is needed, potatoes are planted in ridges. In other areas they are planted flat then, ridges are formed during cultivation.

Cultivation is done only deeply enough and often enough to control weeds. Deep cultivation damages surface roots and

Fig. 28-9 A research plot of potatoes growing in soils that have been compacted to three levels. Plants on plots in upper right hand of photo were growing on severely compacted plots. Compare this poor stand with those growing on noncompacted plots in upper left hand of photo. Those in center are growing on moderately compacted plots. In these studies the effects of the compaction treatments were evaluated by measuring plant growth characteristics, yield of tubers, and tuber quality.

Fig. 28-10 This four-row potato planter drops "seed" pieces (tuber sections or whole tubers) and applies a fertilizer at the same time. The two men riding the planter watch to see that a "seed" piece is in position to be dropped at each interval. *Source:* D. N. Wright, University of California Cooperative Extension.

excessive tillage compacts the soil. During the last cultivation, soil is thrown up close to the plant to form ridges that bury weeds and protects the tubers from light and sunburn. The best weed control is by applications of herbicides.

Potatoes are heavy users of mineral nutrients; thus they need ample fertilization. Recommendations for fertilizer applications vary widely with location, climate, and soil type. For example, potatoes growing on some mineral soils in the southern San Joaquin Valley of California respond well to applications of 110 kg/ha (98 lb/ac) of nitrogen, but little to phosphoric acid and not at all to potash. Peat soils respond well to all three primary nutrients, and many farmers prefer to use complete commercial mixes. Some mineral soils with little organic matter need applications of 70 to 200 kg/ha (60 to 180 lb/ac) of nitrogen, 225 to 280 kg/ha (200 to 250 lb/ac) of phosphoric acid, and 170 to 280 kg/ha (150 to 250 lb/ac) of potash. Heavily cropped soils in the northeastern United States respond well to somewhat larger applications. The time of application and the chemical form of the fertilizer are important. On the irrigated alkaline soils of the western United States the ammoniacal form of nitrogen is preferred; in the eastern and midwestern states best results have been obtained with nitrates.

Most potatoes are grown without irrigation east of the Mississippi River and depend entirely upon rainfall. But in some areas farmers have found it profitable to supplement rainfall with sprinkler irrigation. It is futile to attempt to grow potatoes without irrigation in the western and southwestern states. Furrow irrigation is the most popular method. Sprinkler irrigation is used to some extent in many areas where furrow irrigation is not practical. When irrigation is used, the soil is never allowed to dry. Alternating wet and dry soil conditions during tuber formation produce growth cracks and knobby or multiple tubers. Smooth tubers result from rapid continuous growth. In general, a crop of potatoes requires between 50 and 75 cm (20 to 30 in) of irrigation water.

Potatoes are subject to a host of disease and insect pests. To reduce losses, the use of disease-free seed pieces, seed piece treatment, crop rotation, and field sanitation are all essential practices. Chemical pest control, if necessary, is best when integrated into the total control program. The important potato diseases include early blight, late blight, scab, verticillium wilt, black leg, and ring rot. The most important insect pests are Colorado potato beetles, flea beetles, leafhoppers, aphids, white grubs, blister beetles, and wireworms. Nematodes are destructive potato pests (see Fig. 11–13).

Almost all commercial potato farmers harvest their crop mechanically, some with huge harvesters. The potatoes are lifted from the soil as gently as possible to avoid bruising. Bruising contributes to a physiological malady known as internal black spot, a blackening of the tissue inside the tuber. After the potatoes are removed from the soil, they are elevated into the harvester where shakers remove any adhering soil. They are then conveyed to trucks moving alongside the harvester. The tubers are transported to a central packing shed and emptied into a large vat of chlorinated water (Fig. 28–11). The water reduces bruising to a minimum, washes away any soil on the tubers, and disinfects them. They are removed from the water on belts and scrubbed mechanically with a soft brush, dried, graded and sometimes waxed (Fig. 28–12). Small commercial growers use smaller machines; hand digging and picking are seldom used except by the home gardener.

Fig. 28–11   Emptying a truckload of white potato tubers into a vat of chlorinated water. The water acts as a cushion to reduce bruising and the chlorine disinfects the skins.

Fig. 28–12   Often potato tubers are harvested before they are fully mature. This generally causes the skins to develop an unsightly condition known as feathering as shown here, although there is no damage to the tuber itself. *Source:* University of California Cooperative Extension.

Radish (*Raphanus sativus* L.) CRUCIFERAE (6, 7, 9, 12, 13, 15, 16, 17)

Of all vegetable crops, radishes are the easiest and quickest to grow. They produce a crop within four to six weeks of seeding. The radish, probably native to Europe or Asia and cultivated for centuries, was well known to the ancient Egyptian pharaohs.

Radishes are widely grown in Europe, Asia, Africa, South America, and the United States. Practically every home gardener plants radishes for an early spring vegetable. Commercial production centers mainly around large cities for ready markets.

Radishes are a cool-season crop tolerant of some slightly freezing weather. They grow best when the monthly temperature averages about 15°C to 18°C (59°F to 64°F). They are somewhat intolerant of temperatures exceeding 25°C to 27°C (77°F to 81°F).

Radish cultivars are grouped according to the time to harvest and the season of year they are grown. Quick-growing, early-spring radishes are popular with commercial growers and home gardeners. Later-maturing, summer radishes are less popular but are grown to fill in this harvest period. Slow-growing winter radishes require about twice as much time to reach market size as the early spring cultivars. Some of the more popular cultivars found in seed catalogs are shown in Table 28–5.

Radishes are grown on all types of soils from muck to sandy. Light-textured, fertile sandy loams produce roots of the highest yield and best quality; however, radishes are often grown on soils that would not produce other root crops successfully. Care is taken to obtain a seedbed that is clod free. The soil surface is generally smoothed by dragging a heavy plank to help in planting the seeds at a uniform depth.

Since radishes are hardy, they are planted early in the spring, and to lengthen the harvest season, several plantings at 10 to 12 day intervals are often made. Most cultivars used in the United States are intolerant of high temperature, so planting in midsummer is generally avoided. Radishes are planted in slightly raised beds where furrow irrigation is used, or on flat ground if sprinkled or not irrigated. Two rows, 25 to 30 cm (10 to 12 in) apart, are planted on beds that are 100 cm (40 in) apart. In fields planted without beds, rows are 38 cm (15 in) apart. The in-row spacing is about 6 to 8 seeds/5cm (3 to 4 seeds/in) of row and the depth of seeding is about 1 cm (0.5 in).

Fig. 28–13 Radishes are almost always included in every home garden and are generally the first crop harvested in the spring. Several plantings at regular intervals provide an ample supply of roots throughout the summer and into fall. They produce abundantly on a small amount of land. *Source: Ferry-Morse Seed Company.*

The crop is kept free of weeds by cultivating no deeper than 5 cm (2 in). Since radishes grow quickly, cultivation is often not required except on unusually weedy land.

Radishes grow better if well fertilized. To produce tender, crisp roots many farmers broadcast 45 to 55 kg/ha (40 to 50 lb/ac) of nitrogen, 90 to 110 kg/ha (80 to 100 lb/ac) of phosphoric acid, and 90 to 110 kg/ha (80 to 100 lb/ac) of potash in the spring if several plantings (up to 12 plantings a year in southern California) are made on the same land during the season. Less fertilizer is used if only one early crop is to be grown and if the previous crop was well fertilized.

Diseases are not a serious problem with radishes. The only disease of any consequence is fusarium wilt. Aphids, cabbage root maggots, and flea beetles are the most serious insect pests.

For the fast-maturing, early-spring radishes harvesting begins about 21 to 29 days after planting (Fig. 28–13). They

Table 28–5 Selected Radish Cultivars

Cultivar	Days to Maturity	Shape	Tops	Color	Remarks
Champion	28	Large globe	Large	Deep red	Excellent market type
Cherry Bell	23	Globe	Short	Bright red	Good for greenhouse or warm weather
Crimson Giant	29	Round	Medium	Deep crimson	Favorite for home and market
Early Scarlet Globe	24	Globe	Medium	Bright red	White, mild, crisp flesh
Icicle	27	Long, cylindrical	Short	Clear white	Good producer on muck soils
Red Devil	22	Oval globe	Medium	Deep red	Holds color well
Red Prince	23	Globe	Short	Scarlet	Fusarium wilt resistant
So. Market Globe	23	Globe	Medium	Deep scarlet	Excellent for shipping
Sparkler	26	Round	Medium	Scarlet with white tips	Popular with market growers

584

become bitter and pithy if harvest is delayed. Commercial growers use a single-row harvester that pulls the plants from the soil, cuts the roots from the tops, then places them in burlap bags for transport to a packing shed. Here the roots are washed, graded, and bagged in plastic bags for market. They are cooled immediately. For markets that prefer the radishes with their tops intact, they are generally pulled by hand and tied in bunches in the field. They are then transported to the packing shed, where they are washed and packed in crates and placed in cooling rooms.

Rutabaga (*Brassica Napus* L., Napobrassica Group) CRUCIFERAE (*4, 6, 7, 9, 12, 13, 15, 16, 17*)

Rutabagas are a cool-season root crop grown mainly in Canada, England, and Northern Europe. Limited amounts are grown in the United States for stock feed and human consumption. They are sometimes called Swedes, Swedish turnips, Russian turnips, Canadian turnips, or yellow turnips. The cultural practices for rutabagas are similar to those for turnips (see p. 587). The two differ in appearance; rutabagas have denser, more rounded roots than turnips, which are flattened (Fig. 28–14). The principal production area in the United States is the north central states and Washington. The only cultivar of any significance grown in the United States is the American Purple Top. Seeds are planted in late spring or early summer and the

Fig. 28–14 The rutabaga is a close relative of the turnip. In fact the roots sometimes look very similar, except that properly developed rutabaga roots tend to be round while turnip roots tend to be more flattened. Rutabaga leaves are hairless and bluish, while turnip leaves are hairy and greener. *Source:* Ferry-Morse Seed Company.

crop is harvested in midfall or early winter. The roots are pulled by hand and trimmed in the field. They are stored at low temperatures and high humidities. Those going to market are washed and waxed to increase shelf life by reducing water loss and shriveling.

Salsify (*Tragopogon porrifolius* L.) COMPOSITAE (*6, 7, 9, 10, 12, 13, 15*)

Salsify is a hardy biennial, sometimes called oyster plant or vegetable oyster. It has long, cylindrical roots, used mainly in soups for its delicate oysterlike flavor. The plant grows wild around the Mediterranean Sea, in southern England, and along roadsides in the United States and Canada. During its second season, it bears a purplish flower that looks like an enlarged dandelion head. Salsify is of little importance as a market vegetable crop, but is grown in many home and small truck gardens near large cities for local markets.

Salsify is a cool-season crop tolerant of some freezing weather. Seeds are planted about the time of the average date for the last frost in the spring.

The only cultivar listed in most U.S. seed catalogs is the Mammoth Sandwich Island. This slow-growing cultivar requires the entire season to develop, and like parsnips, its quality is improved after a heavy frost or cold storage for at least two weeks. The tapered roots are 20 to 23 cm (8 to 9 in) long, 2.5 to 4 cm (1 to 1.5 in) thick, with creamy white flesh.

The crop requires a deep, moist, fertile, loamy soil to produce good yields of high-quality roots. Rocky, shallow, or heavy clay soils tend to produce misshapened roots. Salsify grows best on calcareous soils because of its rather high lime requirement. Acid soils should be limed to increase pH (see p. 212).

The culture of salsify is practically identical to that of parsnips (see p. 580). The home gardener plants the seeds 1 cm (0.4 in) deep in rows 45 cm (18 in) apart. The plants are thinned to about 8 to 10 cm (3 to 4 in) apart. Like parsnips, the viability of salsify seed deteriorates rapidly with age, and seeds over a year old are not recommended for use. The home gardener usually plants about 1 gm of seed/m (1 oz/100 ft) of row. The commercial grower drills 9 to 11 kg/ha (8 to 10 lb/ac) of seeds in rows 60 cm (24 in) apart to ensure a good stand.

Machine cultivation or hand hoeing is necessary to eliminate weeds. Salsify seeds germinate slowly and the young plants do not compete well with weeds. Pre-emergence herbicides are used for partial weed control.

A fertile soil is needed to produce high yields. The crop responds well to high soil organic matter, also to applications of about 110 kg/ha (98 lb/ac) each of nitrogen, phosphoric acid, and potash.

In semiarid regions, salsify requires irrigation. The methods used and the water requirements are similar to those of parsnips or carrots (see p. 574).

There are no serious disease or insect pests of salsify, making it a relatively easy crop to grow.

Roots are ready for harvest in late fall. Except where the ground freezes hard, the roots are left in the soil until needed for use or market. They are harvested by digging, and if marketed, they are topped, washed, and tied in bunches of 10 to 12 roots. Salsify roots are stored in moist pits or cellars.

The moist, soft-textured sweet potato cultivars are often erroneously called yams to distinguish them from the dry-textured sweet potato cultivars. This is an unfortunate misnomer since true yams are different plants entirely, not even slightly related to sweet potatoes. True yams belong to the DIOSCOREACEAE family.

Sweet potatoes are native to tropical America, and were transported to the Pacific islands and on to Asia early in history. They were cultivated as food in the southern parts of the United States by the Indians and were later taken to Europe. There is no evidence that the ancient civilizations of Egypt, China, Persia, or Greece knew of sweet potatoes.

Sweet potatoes are perennial vines that grow prostrate on the ground. They belong to the morning-glory family and are grown for their tuberous roots. Sweet potatoes are of particular importance as a food crop in the tropical and subtropical regions of Africa, India, China, Indochina, South America, the South Pacific islands, and the southern United States. In the South, they are referred to only as "potatoes" (common white potatoes are called white or Irish potatoes).

The production of sweet potatoes has declined in recent years, but they are still an important crop in North Carolina, the largest producing state (by weight) in the United States, and Louisiana. Other important producing states include California, Virginia, Texas, Mississippi, Georgia, and Alabama.

Sweet potatoes are warm-season plants that do not tolerate frost nor grow well in cool weather. Temperatures below 10°C (50°F) cause chilling injury. They require a long, warm growing season and grow best when mean monthly temperature is above 20°C (68°F) for at least three months.

The crop is propagated vegetatively; therefore, seeds are not listed in U.S. seed catalogs. Cultivars are divided into moist-flesh and dry-flesh types. The moist-flesh types (mistakenly called yams) are softer and sweeter with red skins and golden flesh. The dry-flesh types have yellow skins with yellow flesh and are called sweet potatoes (Fig. 28–15).

The most important cultivar of the moist-type is the Porto Rico. Other new cultivars are Allgold, Goldrush, Georgia Red, Nemagold, Nancy Gold, and Nugget. Important dry-flesh cultivars are Yellow Jersey, Bigstem Jersey, Maryland Golden, and Centennial.

The ideal soil for sweet potatoes is well-drained sand or sandy loam with a clay subsoil. However, loams and clay loams grow good sweet potatoes if they are well drained.

The seedbed is carefully prepared by plowing 15 to 20 cm (6 to 8 in) deep followed by disking and then harrowing to eliminate all clods. Any residue of the previous year's crop is completely buried. Most farmers prefer to prepare their land three to four weeks in advance of planting. In most areas, the crop is planted on ridges whose height is determined by the soil type, drainage, and rainfall. The ridges are broad and flat rather than narrow and pointed.

Sweet potatoes are grown from plants or sprouts sometimes called slips (see Fig. 5–32). These plants are grown by embedding small- to medium-sized sweet potato tuberous roots in hotbeds filled with sand. The sand is kept moist and at a temperature of 20°C to 25°C (68°F to 77°F). After the sprouts appear above the sand, an additional sand layer about 10 to 13 cm (4 to 5 in) deep is added to encourage longer stems with

Fig. 28–15 The edible portion of a sweet potato is a tuberous root. The sweet potato makes up a large portion of the human diet in some African countries, India, China, South America, the South Pacific islands, and the southern United States. Sweet potatoes are tasty and nutritious. *Source:* University of California Cooperative Extension.

more roots. The slips are pulled when they are 20 to 25 cm (8 to 10 in) long with six to eight well-developed leaves and a good root system. Transplants are pulled from the parent tuberous root two or three times. An adequate number of slips are grown from 450 to 675 kg (400 to 600 lb) of bedded tuberous roots to plant one hectare. This method of vegetative propagation poses some danger of spreading diseases or nematodes that might be on the transplants.

The slips are planted either by hand or with a single or multirow transplanting machine. They are planted in rows 90 to 100 cm (36 to 40 in) apart and spaced 30 to 45 cm (12 to 18 in) within the row. Closer spacing tends to increase the yield of marketable tuberous roots.

Cultivation is necessary for adequate weed control, but excessive cultivation must be avoided because of added costs, root injury, and the possibility of unnecessary soil compaction. Hand hoeing may be necessary later when the vines interfere with the cultivator blades. Chemical herbicides are helpful.

As a general rule, high yields of good quality sweet potatoes require fertilizers on all soils. The recommendations are for moderate amounts of nitrogen with higher proportions of phosphorus and potassium. A reasonable application varies from 35 to 70 kg/ha (30 to 60 lb/ac) nitrogen, 45 to 90 kg/ha (40 to 80 lb/ac) phosphoric acid, and 70 to 145 kg/ha (60 to 130 lb/ac) of potash. Many farmers incorporate about half the application into the soil during seedbed preparation by banding the fertilizer slightly below and to each side of where the plant roots will be located in the ridge. The other half of the fertilizer is applied as a side- or topdressing two or three weeks after planting. Avoid placing the fertilizer so close to the plants as to cause salt damage to the roots.

Sweet potatoes are mainly grown in warm humid regions where the annual rainfall averages about 100 cm (40 in) and is fairly evenly distributed throughout the growing season. However, some farmers in the drier parts of the United States are realizing greater success with sweet potatoes by supplementing the rainfall with sprinkler irrigation when moisture is deficient.

In the arid Southwest, sweet potatoes are irrigated. Studies have indicated that four to eight irrigations supplying 45 to 60 cm (18 to 24 in) of water are needed to produce a crop.

Sweet potatoes are attacked by several bacterial and viral diseases. Stem rot, black rot, scurf, soil rot, soft rot, surface rot, Java black spot, and internal cork are the most troublesome.

Damage to sweet potatoes by insects is relatively minor, except for that caused by the sweet potato weevil. Other insects that sometimes cause problems include flea beetles, white flies, and cut worms. Termite damage has been observed in Florida. Nematodes severely reduce yield in badly infested fields.

Sweet potato roots attain highest yield and best quality when harvested mature (fully developed). However, some roots are harvested for an extra early market, despite reduced yield and lower quality, for a higher price. Farmers in northern areas often allow sweet potatoes to remain in the field until after the first frost to kill the vines and allow easier digging. The tuberous roots are dug as soon as possible to prevent vine decay accompanied by development of organisms in the vines that move down into the roots causing root decay. Also, soil temperatures below 10°C (50°F) cause chilling injury to the roots. Before digging, the general procedure is to remove the vines either by hand, by a vine-cutting machine, or by a sharp colter (a cutting wheel) attached to the plow used for digging. The sweet potatoes are then either spaded out by hand or plowed out with any one of various types of plows. The tuberous roots come out clean and easy if they are dug when the soil is dry. They are allowed to dry and then the stems are snapped off. The tuberous roots are placed in containers as soon as possible to avoid exposure to the bright sunlight. Sweet potatoes are susceptible to damage by bruising and are handled carefully. Cardboard boxes, baskets, or hampers serve as containers for storage and marketing. Successful storage depends upon proper curing at a temperature of about 30°C (86°F) and a relative humidity of 85 percent for a period of 10 to 15 days. After curing, the storage temperature is maintained at 13°C to 15°C (55°F to 59°F) and the relative humidity at 80 to 85 percent. The temperature is never allowed to drop to 10°C (50°F) because of chilling injury.

Turnip (*Brassica Rapa* L., Rapifera Group)
CRUCIFERAE (*4, 6, 7, 9, 12, 13, 15, 16*)

Turnips are one of the easiest vegetables to grow and the most widely adapted of the root crops. They are native to northern Asia and extensively grown in Europe, Asia, and almost every state in the United States. They are used as food for both animals and humans. The roots are eaten raw or cooked and the leaves make delicious greens. The plant is a cool-season biennial; temperature below 10°C (50°F) are likely to cause flowering. Seeds are sown either early in the spring (for a fall crop) or in the fall (for a spring crop) for the roots to mature during cool weather. The plants resist frost and mild freezing. In most areas spring and fall crops are grown since only 60 to 80 days are required for the roots to reach maturity.

As with all vegetable crops, a moderately deep, friable, fertile, well-drained soil is ideal for turnips. Extremely tight clay soils or very sandy soils are avoided if possible, but except for these extremes a satisfactory crop can be grown on most soils.

The most common cultivar is the Purple Top White Globe. It is probably the standard cultivar for home and market gardens. The root has white flesh, and its skin is white on the bottom and purple on top. Seven Top is another popular cultivar, especially for the South where it is used for greens. The roots are large, rough, and inedible for humans. Shogoin is a white flesh, quick growing, semiglobe-shaped Japanese cultivar used mainly for greens and salads. This cultivar is somewhat resistant to aphids.

Turnips are generally planted in rows 45 to 60 cm (18 to 24 in) apart and thinned to an in-row spacing of 8 to 10 cm (3 to 4 in). On very fertile soil the seed is sometimes broadcast, but only if weeds are no problem. Some home gardeners plant a row of turnips between rows of sweet corn to save space. Shade does not hinder the turnips' growth. Like any other root crop shallow cultivation is used for weed control.

Heavy application of expensive fertilizer is generally not profitable for turnips. For soil of average fertility, 17 to 35 kg/ha (15 to 30 lb/ac) nitrogen, 55 to 85 kg/ha (49 to 75 lb/ac) of phosphoric acid, and 17 to 35 kg/ha (15 to 30 lb/ac) of potash usually give satisfactory results. Turnips are seldom grown where irrigation is required, except for home gardens in arid regions.

Diseases are seldom a serious problem. The most troublesome ones include clubroot, leaf spot, white rust, scab, mosaic, and root rot. The turnip thrip is the most troublesome insect pest.

Turnip roots are harvested by pulling them from the soil. If the soil is dry and hard, the soil needs to be loosened with a spade or plow first, especially if the tops are to be left attached. Roots to be sold for early spring market are pulled when they are about 5 cm (2 in) in diameter, washed free of soil, then tied in bunches of five or six roots. The tops are usually left on but some are topped for bulk marketing.

REFERENCES

1. Anon. 1974. Growing table beets. USDA Leaflet 360.
2. Anon. 1968. Commercial growing of horseradish. USDA Leaflet 547.
3. Anon. 1967. Growing parsnips. USDA Leaflet 545.
4. Anon. 1966. Production of turnips and rutabagas. USDA Leaflet 142.
5. Anon. 1960. The sweet potato weevil. USDA Res. Ser. Leaflet 431.
6. Anon. 1979. Vegetables—Annual summary, acreage, yield, production, and value. Statistical Reporting Board. USDA.
7. Bailey, L. H., and E. Z. Bailey and staff of L. H. Bailey Hortorium. 1976. *Hortus third*. New York: Macmillan.
8. Barber, J. M., and P. Colditz. 1976. Growing sweet potatoes in Georgia. Univ. of Ga. Coop. Ext. Ser. Bul. 677.
9. Bauske, R. J. 1976. *Home horticulture*. St Paul, Minn.: West.
10. Beattie, W. R. 1946. Production of salsify or vegetable oyster. USDA Leaflet 135.

11. Boswell, V. R. 1963. Commercial growing of carrots. USDA Leaflet 353.

12. Dunmire, J. R., ed. 1979. *Sunset new western garden book*. 4th ed. Menlo Park, Calif.: Lane.

13. Hayes, J., ed. 1977. Gardening for food and fun. USDA Yearbook. Washington, D.C.: U.S. Government Printing Office.

14. Jones, H. A., and L. K. Mann. 1963. *Onions and their allies*. New York: Interscience.

15. Maynard, D. N., and C. L. Thompson. 1970. Nutrition of vegetable crops in Massachusetts. Coop. Ext. Ser. Publ. 63.

16. Minges, P. A., A. A. Muka, R. F. Sandsted, A. F. Sherf, and R. D. Sweet. 1976. *Commercial vegetable production recommendations*. Ithaca, N.Y.: New York State College of Agriculture and Life Sciences.

17. Sims, W. L., H. Johnson, R. F. Kasmire, V. E. Rubatzky, K. B. Tyler, and R. E. Voss. 1977. Home vegetable gardening. Univ. of Calif. Div. Agr. Sci. Leaflet 2989.

18. Steinbauer, C. E., and L. J. Kushman. 1971. Sweet-potato culture and diseases. USDA Handbook 388.

SUPPLEMENTARY READING

LORENZ, O. A., and D. N. MAYNARD. 1980. *Knott's handbook for vegetable growers*. Somerset, N.J.: Wiley-Interscience.

Temperate Zone Fruit and Nut Crops

This chapter considers the important fruit and nut crops grown in the temperate-zone regions of the Northern and Southern hemispheres. These plants withstand very cold winter temperatures and do, in fact, require winter chilling for good productivity. Most of the species are deciduous; that is, they drop their leaves in winter, and, except for the strawberry, all are woody perennials. All of these fruits are highly heterozygous. They do not reproduce true from seed and must be propagated by asexual methods (see Ch. 5).

Almond (*Prunus dulcis* [Mill] D. A. Webb) [*Prunus amygdalus* Batsch.] ROSACEAE (*26, 27, 38, 42, 50, 51, 54, 79*)

Almonds are one of the oldest nut crops, originating probably in southeast Asia and later moved to the Mediterranean region. Almond trees have exacting climatic requirements for growth and productivity. They resist moderate winter cold, but the small amount of winter chilling needed to overcome bud dormancy causes them to bloom very early in the spring. Almond culture is confined, therefore, to areas without late spring frosts. A temperature of −4°C (25°F) for 30 minutes at full bloom damages 20 to 100 percent of the flowers, depending upon the cultivar. In addition, almonds require a long, hot growing season to mature the nuts properly. Such conditions are found in countries around the Mediterranean Sea, in the Central Valley of California, and in iimited areas of Argentina, Chile, South Africa, Australia, and southeast and central Asia. California leads in almond production, with more than 120,000 ha (300,000 ac), followed by Italy and Spain. The requirement of almond trees for some winter chilling eliminates their culture from the tropical regions of the world.

The almond fruit is very similar to that of the peach. The "flesh" (mesocarp), however, becomes hard and dry, splitting open to reveal the thin "pit" or "shell" (endocarp), containing the almond "nut" (seed) inside. The part that is eaten is the seed.

Almond trees are relatively small—up to 9 m (30 ft) in height—propagated by budding (see Ch. 5) the named cultivars onto almond or peach seedling rootstocks. Certain plum and peach-almond hybrid rootstocks can also be used. The leading almond cultivars grown in California are Nonpareil, Ne Plus Ultra, IXL, Mission (Texas), Drake, Peerless, Merced, and Kapareil.

Young almond trees are trained to a vase shape, using three well-spaced primary scaffold limbs (see Ch. 13). Mature trees need little detailed pruning. The tree can be invigorated and shoots with new fruiting spurs produced by removing crowded limbs and upright watersprouts.

Almonds do not set fruit with their own pollen, so at least two cultivars must be planted together for cross-pollination. However, some, such as Nonpareil and IXL, do not pollinate each other, so proper cultivars must be selected taking care, too, to pick ones that bloom at the same time. Bees are required for adequate pollination—one to three colonies per acre.

As almonds are grown in regions where summer rainfall is light or nonexistent, irrigation is needed for good tree growth and yields. Almonds do not grow well on heavy, poorly drained soils. They require annual nitrogen fertilization and, in some areas, potassium and zinc.

Almonds are harvested in late summer after the hulls split open. In earlier days the limbs were beaten with padded mallets to cause the nuts to fall to the ground or onto canvases where they were picked up. In advanced growing areas the harvest is now completely mechanized. Mechanical tree shakers drop the fruit to smoothly prepared ground where mechanized pick-up machines gather the almonds into bins (see Fig. 12–14). After harvest the almonds are fumigated to control insects.

Some almond cultivars are subject to a genetic, noninfectious disorder (almond bud failure) intensified by high growing temperatures. The almond is relatively free of insect and disease pests but some, such as navel orange worm, mites, oak root fungus, *Ceratocytis* canker, and bacterial canker can become serious problems.

Apple (*Malus sylvestris* Mill., *M. pumila* Mill., *M. domestica* Borkh.). ROSACEAE (*9, 11, 13, 14, 50, 54, 59, 61, 72*)

Apple cultivars grown today apparently originated as hybrids of several wild species native to western Asia. Apples were grown in Greece about 600 B.C., and there is evidence that they were cultivated in the Nile Valley during the reign of Ramses III in the twelfth century B.C. The best seedling trees from natural crosses have been selected since early times, and in recent years plant breeders have used controlled hybridization. At one time there were about 7000 apple cultivars, but by 1970 in the United States only about 13 were important. Apple cultivars fall into two main groups—those eaten fresh, and those cooked. Some can be used both ways. At present the two best and most widely grown apple cultivars throughout the world are Delicious—plus its highly colored red sports (mutations—see p. 75)—and Golden Delicious. Both originated in the United States as chance seedlings. Other cultivars popular in this country are McIntosh, Rome Beauty, Jonathan, York Imperial, Winesap, Stayman, Yellow Newton, and Gravenstein. The development of the attractive red-skinned sports of the popular 'Delicious' apple (e.g., 'Topred', 'Red Prince', 'Sharp Red', 'Starking Full Red') was a major advance in apple production and has greatly stimulated fruit sales. Such highly colored sports have also been found for several other cultivars. Development of the so-called spur-type sports also stimulated apple production, particularly of the 'Red Delicious' and the 'Golden Delicious'. This occurred mostly during the 1950s and 1960s. These bud sports are similar to the parent cultivar except that the trees are more dwarfed and more productive. Starkrimson, Redspur, Red Chief, and Oregon Spur are cultivars of this type. The branches all over the trees, even the main limbs, are heavily covered with fruiting spurs. These trees can be planted close together, particularly if dwarfing rootstocks are used (see p. 108), and give very high yields.

The apple tree is adaptable to the environmental conditions found in the two temperate zones and is a major fruit crop in these areas. Leading apple producing countries are the United States, France, Italy, and West Germany. In the United States Washington is the leading apple producing state by far. Others are New York, Michigan, Indiana, Pennsylvania, and California. Canada also ranks high in apple production. The European countries together produce over twice as many apples as do the North American countries.

The apple produces highest yields of high-quality fruits in regions having long daylight hours with high light intensity during the growing season plus relatively warm days with cool nights and low relative humidity. In such areas irrigation is necessary. Trees of most modern cultivars are likely to be injured by winter temperatures lower than −26°C to −29°C (−15°F to −20°F).

Apple trees are generally trained to a central leader or a delayed open center form (see Ch. 13) to develop a strong trunk with several well-spaced lateral primary scaffold branches. As the trees grow older, the main pruning consists of removing crowded or crossing branches. Annual pruning of bearing apple trees is needed to stimulate production of new growth—about 20 to 30 cm (8 to 12 in) per year per shoot—and a continual renewal of the fruiting spurs. Large amounts of vegetative growth with light crops indicate excessive pruning (and, perhaps, overfertilization). Very little shoot growth and large numbers of small fruits indicate a need for heavier pruning.

Apple trees bloom later than cherries and most peach cultivars, but the flowers can be damaged by late spring frosts. A few cultivars are self-fruitful but most require cross-pollination with other cultivars to set heavy crops. Apples tend to set too much fruit in many years, leading to alternate bearing (a heavy crop of small fruits one year and little or no fruit the next). This is best overcome by fruit thinning in the "on" year (removing many of the small fruits shortly after they have set). A few trees can be thinned by hand, but for commercial orchards chemical spray thinning is necessary (see p. 328).

Apples are propagated by budding or grafting onto rootstock plants—either seedlings (from 'Delicious', 'Golden Delicious', 'McIntosh', or 'Rome Beauty' seeds) or plants propagated by such asexual methods as cuttings or layering (see Ch. 5). Great advances have been made with the apple in developing clonal dwarfing rootstocks. A range of such stocks is available, all producing smaller trees than seedling rootstocks.

Dwarfing rootstocks for apples (all the Malling and Malling-Merton stocks were developed in England)

Malling 27 . . . . .extremely dwarfing
Malling 9 . . . . .very dwarfing
Malling 26 . . . . .dwarfing
Malling 7 . . . . .semidwarfing
Malling-Merton 106 . . . . .semidwarfing
Malling-Merton 111 . . . . .invigorating
Malling 2 . . . . .invigorating
Apple seedlings . . . . .very invigorating

Apple trees grow best in deep, well-drained loam soils. If shoot growth averages less than about 15 cm (6 in) per year, the trees should be fertilized annually with nitrogen (e.g., 2.3 kg; 5lb, ammonium sulfate per tree per year), and in some soils with potassium. In arid or semiarid regions the trees must receive summer irrigation.

Apples are subject to many disease and insect pests. Diseases are scab, powdery mildew, and fire blight (see Ch. 11). These are less a problem in dry climates than in areas with summer rainfall. Insect pests are the codling moth, plum curculio, and wooly aphid. Mites can also be a problem. To produce high-quality apples, a series of sprays is required, depending upon the diseases and insects present and the prevailing climate. The series starts with a dormant spray before the blossom buds start to open and ends with three or more cover sprays applied while the fruit is developing. A total of 10 or more sprays may be required in humid growing regions. Apples are also susceptible to root lesion nematodes (see Ch. 11). These are best controlled by fumigating the soil before the trees are planted.

For highest-quality apples it is important that the fruit be picked at the proper stage of maturity. At harvest the best-quality fruits are firm, unbruised, crisp, and juicy, well-colored, and good-flavored. Apples picked too soon are sour, astringent, starchy, and poor-flavored. Those picked too late soon become soft and mealy and do not store well.

To maintain the quality of apples picked at optimum maturity, they should be refrigerated immediately at about 0°C (32°F) and stored at 90 percent relative humidity. Some cultivars, however, such as McIntosh and Yellow Newton, are best stored at higher temperatures—about 1°C (36°F). If held at room temperature, apples soon become overripe, soft, and mealy. Apples held under controlled atmospheres (CA), 1 to 8 percent CO_2 and 1 to 3 percent O_2 (see Ch. 12), to lower their respiration rate keep well under refrigeration for many months. This practice has permitted the year-round marketing of apples. Millions of kilograms of 'Delicious', 'Golden Delicious', 'McIntosh', 'Rome Beauty', 'Yellow Newton', and 'Jonathan', in particular, are stored each year.

In addition to fresh apples other important apple products include pasteurized apple juice, cider, canned applesauce and apple slices, jelly, apple butter, and dried and frozen apples.

Apricot (*Prunus armeniaca* L.) ROSACEAE (*26, 27, 34, 50, 54, 59*)

The apricot is believed to have originated in western China, where it has been cultivated since about 2000 B.C. It was introduced into the Mediterranean region about the beginning of the Christian era. Apricots were being grown in England in the thirteenth century and were brought to the United States in the early 1700s. The United States leads the world in apricot production, followed by Spain, Turkey, Italy, and France. California now produces about 40 percent of the world's apricot supply. Washington and Utah also produce commercial quantities.

Apricot trees are hardy to winter cold. Though the flower buds have a moderate chilling requirement to overcome their rest influence, they bloom early in spring. Subsequent frosts may kill the flowers and fruits. Apricots in full bloom require −5.5°C (22°F) to kill about 90 percent of the flowers. This early blooming habit rules out apricot production in regions with late spring frosts. In regions with mild winters apricot buds tend to drop without opening.

The apricot is one of the stone, or drupe, fruits; the edible portion is the enlarged mesocarp of the ovary wall. The endocarp is the pit or stone, and the exocarp is the skin of the fruit. The true seed is within the endocarp.

Apricot trees are propagated by T-budding (see Ch. 5) named cultivars onto apricot, peach, or plum seedling rootstocks. In California over half of all apricot trees are propagated on peach seedlings, but some cultivars in Michigan and Canada are incompatible with peach roots.

Commercial apricot cultivars are Tilton and Blenheim (Royal), Perfection, and Riland. 'Tilton' is a heavy producer but the fruits have a poorer color and flavor than those of 'Blenheim' ('Royal'). These cultivars are all self-pollinated except for Perfection and Riland, which require another cultivar for cross-pollination. New apricot cultivars with high-quality fruits are needed.

Apricot trees are generally trained to a vase-shaped form in their early years (see Ch. 13). As the trees mature, some of the older branches bend downward. These are cut back to upright growing laterals. Although apricots bear fruit on spurs, some heavy top-pruning may be required as the trees age to stimulate growth and production of new spurs. This is done by completely removing crowded limbs and cutting back those showing excessive horizontal growth.

If the trees grow poorly with yellowish foliage and produce small, early-ripening fruits, they will probably respond to nitrogen fertilizers. Add just enough to correct the problems. Excessive nitrogen can cause heavy vegetative growth, delayed fruit maturity, and uneven ripening. Apricot trees require ample soil moisture throughout the growing season either from rainfall or irrigation.

Apricots tend to set too much fruit and must be thinned so that the fruits are about 4 to 8 cm (1.5 to 3 in) apart by the time they are 2.5 cm (1 in) in diameter. Otherwise the fruit will be very small with, perhaps, no crop the following year. Proper thinning is very important in apricot production.

Apricots are one of the first fresh fruits on the market in the spring and early shipments often bring handsome prices. Depending on the growing region, they are shipped to markets on into late summer. Apricots can be used fresh, canned, or dried. Tree-ripened apricots are highest in quality but fresh fruits to be shipped to distant markets are picked somewhat earlier than optimum and allowed to ripen en route. Fresh apricots are very perishable but can be stored for one or two weeks at about 0°C (32°F) and 90 percent relative humidity. Best ripening temperature is about 21°C (70°F). For eating, apricots should be plump and a uniform golden color. Avoid dull-looking, soft fruits or those that are hard and greenish yellow in color. Fruit for commercial or home canning or for jams is picked at a riper stage than for fresh eating—fully ripe but firm. Apricot fruits dry well if they are left on the tree as long as possible to attain a high sugar content, but picked before they become too soft to handle.

The main disease is brown rot fungus, which attacks both blossoms and fruits, especially when the weather is rainy and humid. Several sprayings with a fungicide during the blooming period are necessary. Shot hole fungus causes defoliation and fruit damage but can be controlled by spraying with a fungicide in the fall just after the leaves drop. Insect pests generally are not serious on apricots.

Blackberry (*Rubus* spp.) ROSACEAE (*7, 8, 37, 50, 54, 55, 56*)

The two main centers of origin of the blackberries seem to be in eastern North America and the European continent. It is speculated that blackberries started their development with the retreat of glaciers during the Ice Age. Cultivation began early in the nineteenth century, chiefly on the North American continent.

Blackberries include many species in both upright and trailing types. The upright forms produce self-supporting arched canes and do not need trellising as the trailing types do. The upright types are more winter hardy than the trailing, but the fruits are less sweet.

Blackberries are best adapted to temperate zone climates, the erect types growing best in areas with cool, humid summers. The trailing types can be grown successfully in regions with hot, dry summers provided they are irrigated. Blackberries are not suitable where winter temperatures are severe—below −29°C (−20°F)—since the canes are killed. In the United States the most cold resistant types are not grown north of hardiness zone 5 (see p. 226), with many of the trailing types confined to zones 7 and 8.

Blackberries grow best on deep, fertile soils on sloping land that provides good air and water drainage. Ample soil moisture and protection from hot, drying winds are also needed. Avoid bottom land with frost pockets where the blossoms could be killed in the spring. Established plantings usually respond to nitrogen fertilizers.

Erect types are grown in hedge rows with the original plants set about 0.6 m (2 ft) apart in rows 2.4 to 2.7 m (8 to 9 ft) apart. The hedges fill in from suckers arising from the roots. Trailing types on trellises have wider spacing: 1.2 to 2.4 m (4 to 8 ft) apart in rows separated by 2.4 to 3.0 m (8 to 10 ft). A good herbicide treatment of the soil before planting to eliminate perennial weeds is advisable.

Some popular erect cultivars are Eldorado, Darrow, Ranger, and Hedrick. Semitrailing thornless types are Thornfree, Raven, Smoothstem, and Thornless Evergreen, none of which are hardy in northern climates. Suitable trailing types are Boysenberry, Loganberry, Nectarberry, Himalaya, and Youngberry. Blackberries generally are self-fruitful, but some cultivars benefit from cross-pollination. Bees are helpful in pollination, even with self-fruitful types, to obtain good fruit sets. Blackberry fruits consist of many individual druplet fruits aggregated over an elongated receptacle to which they are attached.

Blackberry plants have a distinctive growth habit, which must be known to obtain good fruit production. The roots are perennial, with new shoots arising each year from the crown of the plant. These shoots, or canes, which produce lateral branches, grow vegetatively during the first year and form flower buds. When the first-year shoots reach a height of 1.2 to 1.5 m (4 to 5 ft), they should be tipped back to induce more lateral shoot formation. The second year these shoots produce fruits, then die and must be cut out. At the beginning of the fruit-producing season cut the laterals back to about 30 cm (12 in) in length to obtain the best fruit quality. Excessive root suckers arising in the rows should be thinned out each year; otherwise, a dense thicket eventually develops. Suckers arising between rows must be removed. After fruiting is over in the summer, cut out all fruiting canes and dispose of them. Thin out the new vegetative shoots arising from the crowns. Canes of trailing types are not cut back but are thinned to 10 to 15 per hill with the long canes tied to a trellis system.

Upright types of blackberries are easily propagated by digging up suckers with a piece of the root attached. Trailing types are propagated by burying the tips of the canes a few inches below ground. They root and produce shoots to form a new plant that can be detached from the parent plant. Blackberries can also be propagated by root cuttings (see Ch. 5), but when this method is used with some types of thornless blackberries, the new plants revert to thorny forms.

Blackberry fruits should be picked when they turn from red to black and are fully ripe and sweet but still firm. Pick early in the morning every other day as the fruits ripen during the season. They keep in good condition for several days under refrigeration at about 7°C (45°F). Some commercial plantings

for fruit processing are harvested by machines that straddle the rows and shake the berries off.

Blackberries have few insect pests, which generally are not a serious problem. Nematodes can be brought in on the roots of nursery plants, so they should be carefully checked. Blackberries are susceptible to verticillium wilt, which can be especially severe if plantings are set out on land previously planted to such crops as tomatoes, potatoes, eggplant, peppers, or cotton. Soil fumigation before planting with chloropicrin plus methyl bromide kills the fungus. Orange rust is a systemic disease that kills the plants. A yellowish cast with orange pustules appears on the underside of the leaves. Dig and destroy all infested plants. A virus is prevalent among blackberry cultivars that interferes with fruit set or causes misshapen berries. Any plants showing this disease should be removed and destroyed. In starting a new planting it is best to plant only state-certified, virus-clean nursery stock from nurseries producing such material.

Blueberry (*Vaccinium* spp.) ERICACEAE (*20, 23, 33, 40, 50, 54, 64*)

The blueberry is the most recent major fruit crop to be brought under cultivation from native wild species. Selection and hybridization in the United States since the early 1900s has developed vastly improved cultivars that have formed the basis for an entirely new agricultural industry. Considerable interest in the blueberry has also developed in Europe and Canada.

Cultivated blueberries are mostly the highbush (*V. corymbosum* L.) and, to a much lesser extent, the rabbiteye (*V. ashei* Reade) species. There are about 24 cluster-fruited blueberry species native to the eastern part of the United States and Canada. About 12 other species in other *Vaccinium* subgenera exist in the Pacific coast states and western Canada. Large quantities of blueberry fruits were harvested from natural wild stands in the eastern United States and Canada for about 300 years after the Pilgrims landed and before any attempt was made to develop improved cultivars and grow them commercially. The important highbush cultivars now being grown resulted from hybridization among the native wild species. They produce berries three to four times larger than the wild types and have an excellent flavor. Crops of the lowbush blueberry (*V. angustifolium* Ait.) are today taken mostly from natural wild stands although breeding efforts are under way to develop improved cultivars. This type is a plant only 15 to 46 cm (6 to 18 in) tall.

Blueberries have rather exacting soil and climatic requirements for good growth and productivity. The soil must be acid (pH 4.0 to 5.5) and must be well drained and porous and have a high organic matter content. Blueberries are rather shallow-rooted and need ample soil moisture from either rainfall or irrigation. Blueberry roots are believed to have developed a symbiotic association with a mycorrhizal fungus that probably transforms organic soil nitrogen into available forms.

In the United States, highbush production is found along the Atlantic coast from eastern North Carolina into New England, in southern Michigan and northern Indiana, in western Oregon and Washington, and in Canada. New Jersey and Michigan are the top producing states, followed by North Carolina, Maine, Washington, and Oregon. Blueberries grow well in either warm or cool, moist summer climates with long sunny days and cool nights during the fruit-ripening period. Plants are killed by winter temperatures below about $-29°C$ $(-20°F)$. They require about as much winter chilling as the peach to overcome the rest period of the buds and permit normal growth and blossoming in the spring. This rules out their production in areas with mild winters, such as Georgia, Florida, and southern California, although low-chilling rabbiteye and hybrid cultivars grow well in mild-winter areas.

The best commercial highbush blueberry cultivars vary with the region. Bluecrop, Bluetta, Jersey, Rubel, Weymouth, Blueray, Collins, and Lateblue are used in the northern districts; Morrow, Wolcott, Croatan, Harrison, Murphy, and Berkeley are favored in the southern.

Cross-pollination is necessary for good crops of large fruits. Two cultivars should be planted together, as two rows of one, two of the second, and so forth. In addition, one to five colonies of bees per acre should be provided to disperse the pollen.

Plants are usually set 1.2 to 1.5 m (4 to 5 ft) apart in rows 2.7 to 3.0 m (9 to 10 ft) apart. Blueberries are often planted on the poorer soils, so a complete fertilizer is generally required for good growth.

The blueberry produces its fruit on shoots that grew the previous season, with the largest fruits on the most vigorous growth. Blueberries tend to overbear, producing small, late-maturing fruits unless pruned somewhat. Pruning consists of thinning out small, weak branches, cutting out some of the older stems in the center of the bush, and removing low drooping branches close to the ground. Pruning is best done in the winter after the coldest weather is past.

Blueberries are propagated by hardwood or softwood cuttings. Hardwood cuttings (see Ch. 5) 10 to 13 cm (4 to 5 in) long made from dormant shoots (without fruit buds) of the previous summer's growth, are usually used, planted in a peat moss-sand mixture under covered frames with automatic watering. Cuttings of some cultivars root much easier than those of others. Blueberries reproduce naturally by shoots arising from spreading below-ground stems (rhizomes). Most blueberries root well from softwood stem cuttings under intermittent mist.

Blueberry fruits are mostly hand-picked, but machine-harvesting is also used for processing fruits. In one type, electric-powered vibrators shake the berries off into a catching frame. Large, over-the-row, self-propelled machines are also used to shake the berries off (see Fig. 12–12). Lowbush blueberries are harvested by hand-held scoops with rake-type teeth passed through the low-growing bushes to separate the berries from the plants.

Blueberries are fully ripe and ready to harvest when they are light to dark blue or blue-black. Overripe fruits become watery and soft. Blueberries are truly a convenience food item with no pitting, peeling, or waste. They are ready to eat with just washing. Blueberries are marketed fresh, canned, or frozen. Fresh berries can be held in good condition for two to four weeks, depending on the cultivar, at $0°C$ $(32°F)$ at 90 percent relative humidity.

Blueberries are attacked by a number of viral, fungal, and bacterial diseases, as well as by nematodes and certain insect pests. Local agricultural extension service workers should be consulted for proper control measures. Blueberries are attractive to birds. The plants may have to be covered with plastic netting suspended on a framework for small plantings.

Cherry (*Prunus avium* L. and *P. cerasus* L.)
ROSACEAE (6, 16, 26, 27, 50, 52, 54, 59, 70)

The commercially important cherry cultivars belong to two species: the sweet cherries (*P. avium*) and the sour cherries (*P. cerasus*). The cherry apparently was domesticated from wild forms growing in south central Europe and Asia Minor and has been grown throughout Europe since ancient times. Cherries were introduced into North America from Europe by the earliest settlers shortly after Columbus' voyages. At present the USSR, West Germany, the United States, Italy, and France are the leading cherry-producing countries.

In the United States most sour cherries are produced east of the Rocky Mountains, particularly in Michigan and New York, while sweet cherries are grown mainly in Washington, Oregon, California, Michigan, and New York. Sour cherry trees are hardy to winter cold and are adaptable to a range of soil types if they are well drained. The fruits are generally used for processing in pies, jams, and jellies.

Sweet cherry trees are less tolerant of low winter temperatures than the sour cherry. They grow best where they obtain sufficient winter chilling to overcome bud dormancy and where the summers are mild—some but not excessive summer heat—and humidity is low. All commercial sweet cherry cultivars require cross-pollination to set fruit, along with bees to distribute the pollen. Not all cultivars are interfruitful, so care must be taken to plant sweet cherry trees of at least two cultivars that will bloom together and cross-pollinate each other. A temperature of $-4°C$ $(25°F)$ at full bloom will kill 90 percent of cherry flowers.

Some sweet cherry cultivars commonly planted are Bing, Lambert, Royal Anne (Napoleon), Black Tartarian, and Van (use Black Tartarian and Van as pollinizers for the other cultivars). The main sour cherry cultivars are Montmorency, Early Richmond, and English Morello. They are all self-fruitful and set heavy crops in solid block plantings provided enough bees are present. The Duke cherries, intermediate in types between the sweet and sour, are considered hybrids between these two groups.

Cherry trees are propagated by T-budding (see Ch. 5) on seedling rootstocks. Both *P. avium* (Mazzard) and *P. mahaleb* seedlings are used as rootstocks for sweet cherries whereas sour cherries are grown mainly on *P. mahaleb* roots. A clonal cherry rootstock—'Colt'—has been developed in England.

Young sweet cherry trees tend to grow upright with long, unbranched scaffolds. Dormant pruning for the first several years must include heading back these limbs to outward-growing buds to encourage branching and removing any crowded inside limbs. As the trees mature and develop fruiting spurs, little pruning is needed other than removal of interfering branches, thinning out dense growth, and thinning out vigorous, upright-growing shoots. Some pruning is needed to keep new growth developing upon which additional fruiting spurs form to replace older unproductive ones. Sour cherry trees are more spreading than sweet cherries and are usually pruned to a vase-shaped form. Mature trees are pruned to thin out dense growth and to invigorate shoots for production of fruiting spurs.

Cherry trees, especially sweet cherries, require a continuous supply of soil moisture during the growing season but do not tolerate wet, poorly drained soils. A deep, well-drained loam soil should be used. The trees respond to nitrogen fertilizer applications and in some areas to zinc. High nitrogen fertilization can cause excessive tree vigor, poor fruit quality, and delayed fruit maturation.

Cherries are stone fruits, the edible parts of the fruit being the outer layers of the mature ovary wall, the flesh (mesocarp) and the skin (exocarp). The pit (endocarp) encloses the seed.

Cherries are harvested in May and June in California and in mid-June through July in most other cherry-producing states.

Cherries for fresh shipment are very perishable and require careful handling. They can be held in cold storage for two weeks at 0°C (32°F) at 95 percent relative humidity if placed in storage immediately after harvest. Best-quality fresh fruits are firm, juicy, and well colored. Substantial amounts of cherries are brined and reach the consumer as bottled maraschino cherries, canned cherries, canned fruit cocktails, package glace cherries, pies, jellies, and ice cream toppings.

Cherries are subject to several fungal diseases, particularly brown rot and leaf spot. Bacterial gummosis, *Phytophthora* crown or root rots, and verticillium wilt can be problems. Several viruses (ring spot, yellows, X-disease) attack cherries, so it is important that only certified virus-free nursery trees can be planted. Insect pests are not particularly troublesome, but black cherry aphid and plum curculio infestation can be a problem.

Cranberry (*Vaccinium macrocarpon* Ait.) ERICACEAE (*19, 23, 32, 50, 54, 59*)

The cranberry is a native American fruit species from which commercial culture started about 1815 on Cape Cod, Massachusetts. It was found growing wild and used by the Indians when the Pilgrims landed on the New England coast. It is now an important crop in Massachusetts, Wisconsin, New Jersey, Washington, and Oregon. Canada (Nova Scotia, Quebec, and British Columbia) also has substantial production. Cranberries are little grown elsewhere in the world, although there is much interest in this crop in some European countries. Cranberry production is confined to temperate zone regions with cool moist climates and, in nature, to acid soils along the edge of streams and bogs.

The cranberry is a low-growing evergreen vine. In late summer upright shoots form flower buds that develop into flowers by midsummer the following year. Insect pollination is required for fruit set. The four leading cultivars, accounting for the bulk of commercial production, are Early Black and Howe (Massachusetts and New Jersey). Searles (Wisconsin), and McFarlin (Washington, Oregon, and British Columbia). These all originated as single vines selected in native bogs. Cranberry breeding programs have been activated in several of the producing states to develop improved cultivars, and a number of new cultivars have been introduced.

Cranberries are grown in bogs about 0.8 ha (2 ac) in size that can be flooded and drained at the appropriate times. Levees, pumps, and drainage ditches are required, which increase cost of production. The bogs are leveled, then covered with a layer of sand about 1.3 cm (0.5 in) deep. Vines are planted by cutting them up into 7.5 or 10 cm (3 or 4 in) pieces with a device such as a corn chopper. The pieces are broadcast over the bogs at about 1120 kg/ha (1000 lb/ac) and are then pressed into the soil with a heavy mechanized roller that has parallel ridges several inches apart. After about 2.7 m² (30 ft²) are planted, the area is sprinkled immediately and, after the entire bog is planted, it is thoroughly watered. The pieces root quickly and, with subsequent nitrogen fertilization, vigorous vine growth is encouraged to bring the planting into production as soon as possible. Herbicide sprays are used to control weeds. The bog is sanded again every three to four years.

Cranberry bogs in some areas are flooded in late autumn as soon as the soil freezes so that the plants winter over in or under a thin layer of ice. This prevents the plants from being killed from desiccation during the winter, and it helps eliminate some insect pests. Water is drained from the bogs in the spring after danger from severe freezes is over. Sprinkler irrigators in the bog are used for the plants during the summer growing season. Three to five years are required for the bog to develop full production.

To obtain large berries a good seed set is required; thus adequate pollination is necessary. Two to four hives of bees per hectare are necessary during the blooming period.

The harvest season extends from early fall through mid-winter. Harvesting is mechanical. The bogs are flooded to about 15 cm (6 in) deep, then small motor-operated harvest units beat the vines to knock the berries off. The harvester then scoops up the floating berries and drops them into boxes. Sometimes the berries are dried but, more often, they are cleaned and frozen directly. Cranberries for fresh market can be stored up to four months at 2°C to 4.5°C (36°F to 40°F) at 90 to 95 percent relative humidity. Good ventilation is required to provide the berries with oxygen.

Cranberries are processed into sauces for meats and poultry and blended into juice drinks.

Cranberries are subject to several fungal vine diseases and storage diseases of the harvested fruits. In setting out new plantings it is important to obtain vine cutting material from a disease-free source. It is estimated that storage rots beginning in the growing fields can cause a 25 percent crop loss.

There are a number of insect pests on cranberries. Flooding the bogs at appropriate times can control some of these. Other methods include application of insecticides by air or rotary sprinkler systems.

Currant (*Ribes* spp.) SAXIFRAGACEAE (*16, 41, 50*)

There are some 150 species in the genus *Ribes* distributed mostly in the temperate zone regions of the Northern Hemisphere. Currants were domesticated from wild plants within the last 400 years. Black currants (*R. nigrum*) were grown in England in the seventeenth century and brought to North America by the Pilgrims in the early 1600s. The red currant (*R. sativum*) derived from *R. petraeum* and *R. rubrum* is the principal type grown in the United States and is best adapted to climates with cool, humid summers. They do not grow well in hot arid regions. Red currants are very winter hardy. They are easy to grow and do well on medium- to heavy-textured soils that range from slightly acid or slightly alkaline. They are shallow rooted and need ample soil moisture from rain or irrigation. The roots do not tolerate standing water very long.

Red currants grow as bushes with upright shoots developing from the crown of the plant. Fruit is produced from buds at the base of one-year-old shoots and from spurs on older wood. Since the older shoots become less fruitful, they should be retained only for about three years, then removed to be replaced by new shoots. This pruning should be done annually in early spring. Currant bushes should be fertilized annually either with a well-rotted manure in the fall or a complete fertilizer in early spring.

Currants are easily propagated by hardwood cuttings (see Ch. 5) planted in late autumn to early spring before the buds develop.

Leading red currant cultivars are Red Lake, Perfection, and White Imperial (a white-fruited type). Comparatively few insect or disease pests affect currants.

Currant bushes are an alternate host to the white pine blister rust and have been eradicated in many parts of the United States.

Filbert (*Corylus avellana* L.) CORYLACEAE (*38, 43, 54, 58, 69*)

There are about 10 species of *Corylus*, all indigenous to North America, Europe, and Asia. Pollen records show that plants in this genus were the dominant vegetative form all over northern Europe following the retreating glaciers of the Ice Age. Filberts were being cultivated during the ancient Greek civilizations. The European filbert (*C. avellana*) is the species usually cultivated for the nuts. Nearly 70 percent of the world's filbert production comes from the Black Sea coast of Turkey. Smaller amounts are produced in Spain, southern Italy, and the United States, where 95 percent of the production is in the Willamette Valley of Oregon.

Filberts grow best in areas with mild climates and no temperature extremes, usually moderated by large bodies of water nearby. The buds require some winter chilling, however, to overcome their dormancy conditions. Filbert trees grow in a wide range of soil types. Fertilization is usually unnecessary unless shoot growth is weak, when they should receive 0.22 to 0.45 kg (0.5 to 1 lb) of actual nitrogen per tree per year.

In Europe filberts are trained as a multistemmed bush, but in Oregon and Washington they are trained as trees to facilitate mechanized orchard practices. Regardless of the training system, suckers should be removed to aid nut harvest. When trained as a tree, four to five main scaffold branches are selected. Pruning is done primarily to stimulate new growth and to remove any broken or interfering branches.

Filberts are monoecious plants; that is, the pollen-bearing male flowers (catkins) and the female (pistillate) flowers are produced separately on the same tree. In addition, most filberts are self-unfruitful; that is, two cultivars must be interplanted for cross pollination. Furthermore, the pollen must be shed on one cultivar at the time when the pistils are receptive on the other. If all these conditions are not met, poor crops of nuts result. Filbert pollen is spread by wind rather than by insects.

The shell of the filbert is the matured ovary wall of the flower and the nut meat inside is the matured embryo. The husk surrounding the shell is called the involucre.

The most important commercial cultivars of the European filbert grown in the United States are Barcelona and Daviana, the latter being the pollenizer. These grow well in western Oregon but not in the eastern United States because of a fungal disease called eastern filbert blight. The native American filbert (*C. americana*), usually called hazelnut, resists this disease. Breeding projects crossing these two species have developed some hybrid cultivars, like Reed and Potomac.

Filberts are harvested by picking the nuts up, either by hand or by mechanical pick-up machines, from a smooth, well-prepared soil surface after they drop. This should be done promptly to maintain quality. The nuts are washed and dried in forced warm (37.5°C; 100°F) air. Dried filberts can be stored in good condition for as long as 15 months at about 21°C (70°F) if their moisture content is kept below 10 percent.

Filbert cultivars are best propagated by simple layering (see Ch. 5) using young mother plants. Seedling trees are easily started by planting the seeds (nuts) in the spring after a three-month stratification period at 4.5°C (40°F).

There are relatively few insect and disease pests of filberts although filbert blight is a major problem for European filbert cultivars grown in the eastern United States.

Gooseberry (*Ribes* spp.) SAXIFRAGACEAE (*41*)

Gooseberry culture was not mentioned in the writings of the early Greek and Roman botanists. The crop was apparently grown in Britain and western Europe in the late thirteenth century. The European gooseberry (*R. uva-crispa* L.) did not thrive in America when it was brought over by the early settlers because of American gooseberry mildew and a generally unsuitable climate. Hybridization between the European and the native American gooseberry (*R. hirtellum*) produced Houghton and its seedling Downing, which were long the standard gooseberry cultivars grown in the United States. More recently developed cultivars are Poorman, Welcome, Pixwell, and Oregon Champion.

Climatic requirements and culture for the gooseberry are essentially the same as those for the red currant (see p. 594). The gooseberry is also an alternate host for white pine blister rust. Although gooseberries are popular in Europe, in the United States interest in them seems to be declining. They are grown mainly in home gardens and rarely produced commercially. Gooseberries are used primarily for jam, jelly, and pies.

Grape (*Vitis* spp.) VITACEAE (*1, 2, 3, 17, 21, 50, 54, 59, 68, 74, 78*)

Grapes are one of the world's major fruit crops and have been since earliest recorded history. World production exceeds that of any other fruit (see p. 5). The European grape (*Vitis vinifera* L.) is believed to have originated in the area between the Black and Caspian seas, where it still grows wild. From there it was introduced into the Mediterranean region and on throughout Europe and later by explorers to all the continents. There is evidence that the ancient Egyptians were cultivating grapes some 6000 years ago. *V. vinifera* is, by far, the most important species.

About 18 species of grapes important to viticulture as fruiting or rootstock types are native to North America. These include such species as *V. labrusca* L., which has several important fruiting cultivars, and *V. riparia* Michx., *V. rupestris* Scheele, and *V. Berlandieri* Planch. and *V. champini* Planch., from which a number of rootstocks resistant to phylloxera and to nematodes have been derived. In addition, the Muscadine grape (*V. rotundifolia* Michx.) has several fruiting cultivars.

Grapes are widely grown on every continent in the two temperate zones, but three countries—Spain, Italy, and France—dominate grape production, with over half the total world's supply. Other major grape-producing countries are the USSR, Turkey, Portugal, Rumania, Algeria, Argentina, Yugoslavia, Hungary, Greece, Germany, and the United States. In the United States, California leads, by far, in grape production with about 2 million MT produced annually. New York is second with about 100,000 MT, followed by Washington (65,000 MT) and Michigan (55,000 MT).

Although grapes are used mostly for wines and juices, considerable amounts are consumed as fresh table grapes, jams, and jellies and dried into raisins.

The important *V. vinifera* cultivars are not grown in areas with severe winters. Dormant vines are killed at temperatures ranging from −18°C to −12°C (0°F to 10°F). They are not grown nearer the equator than about 20° latitude (unless the elevation is high) since in the tropics the vines become evergreen and unfruitful. Grapevines require a period of inactive growth to overcome bud dormancy.

The native American species are much more winter hardy than *V. vinifera*, and their cultivars are grown in areas with severe winters. However, dormant vines of *V. labrusca* cultivars can be damaged by temperatures ranging from −22°C to −28°C (−8°F to −18°F).

V. vinifera cultivars have rather exacting climatic requirements during the growing season for heavy production of a high-quality product. A long, warm or hot and dry summer is best. High humidity and rains result in disease problems for the vine and fruit. *V. labrusca* and *V. rotundifolia* cultivars, on the other hand, do well in regions with summer rains and high humidity. For best-quality wines from *V. vinifera* cultivars, a long growing season is required to produce enough sugar in the grapes to ferment to alcohol. Relatively cool temperatures produce grapes with high acidity to contribute quality to the wine. Such climatic conditions are found in northern coastal California, the Burgundy and Bordeaux districts of France, northern Spain, central and northern Italy, and Yugoslavia.

Over 90 percent of the world grape production comes from *V. vinifera* cultivars and, in the United States, about 90 percent of the grapes harvested are from this species, which is grown almost entirely in California. About 60 percent of the California *V. vinifera* grape crop is used for wine, 28 percent for raisins, and 12 percent for fresh table grapes. Some of the best California wine-growing regions are in the interior and coastal valleys north and south of San Francisco Bay.

The important present-day grape cultivars are listed in Table 29–1. About 8000 cultivars worldwide have been named and described. In addition to these, some French hybrid cultivars are widely grown in the eastern United States, particularly for making wine. Examples are 'Aurora', 'Baco Noir', 'Foch', and 'Seyval Blanc'.

That grapes grow well over such a wide area of the world shows that they are adapted to a wide range of soil types. Generally, however, heavy clay, shallow, sodic, or poorly drained soils should be avoided. Traditionally, especially in Europe and the eastern United States, vineyards are heavily fertilized with manures or straw. Grapes respond to nitrogen fertilizers but apparently have a relatively low nitrogen requirement. They do not show pronounced visual deficiency symptoms. Potassium deficiency (black leaf areas, leaf margin chlorosis, and necrosis) in grapes is common, and the vines respond markedly to potassium fertilizers. There are no known responses of grapes to phosphorus. Zinc deficiency sometimes occurs (little leaf and foliar chlorosis). Grapes require ample soil moisture during the growing season either from rainfall or irrigation.

As in deciduous tree fruits, flower parts and clusters in the grape initiate in buds on new shoots shortly after bloom ends the preceding season, continuing on through the summer. Following the winter dormancy period, shoots then develop from buds produced the previous season. These shoots bear the buds that develop into the flower clusters.

V. vinifera and *V. labrusca* cultivars are usually self-pollinated but, in some instances, cross-pollination by wind or insects improves fruit set. *V. rotundifolia* cultivars are dioecious (separate male and female plants) and require pollen transfer from the male to female flowers. Fruits of most grape cultivars have seeds, but seedlessness in the important Thompson Seedless cultivar is due to early embryo abortion.

Grapes, except *V. rotundifolia* cultivars, generally are easily propagated by rooting cuttings, either hardwood or leafy softwood under mist (see Ch. 5). This is the usual propagation method unless certain resistant rootstocks are required to protect the roots of *V. vinifera* cultivars from attacks of the soilborne grape phylloxera (*Dactylasphaera vitifoliae*) or from root knot nematodes (*Meloidogyne* spp.). In these cases grafting or budding (see Ch. 5) is done using as rootstocks rooted or unrooted cuttings of certain hybrid rootstocks (e.g., 'AxR#1', 'Harmony', 'Dogridge', and 'St. George'). These have been developed for this purpose from resistant native American species, such as *V. champini*, *V. riparia*, *V. rupestris*, and *V. Berlandieri*, as one of the parents.

Grapes must be pruned heavily and in a certain manner, depending upon the fruit-bearing habit, in order to obtain maximum production. Pruning of grape vines is described in Chapter 13.

Table grapes are harvested when the berries attain their most attractive appearance and eating quality. They do not ripen further after harvest. Quality is highest just as the clusters are cut from the vine, and deterioration starts at that point. Quality loss can be slowed by immediate cooling of the clusters to about 0°C (32°F) with relative humidity at 85 to 95 percent. Fumigation of vinifera table grapes with sulfur dioxide (1 percent for 20 minutes) as soon as possible after harvest and before storage or shipment reduces decay and permits fruit storage of some cultivars, such as Emperor and Calmeria, for as long as six or seven months. Grapes held in prolonged cold storage are refumigated at about 10-day intervals. American grapes are injured by sulfur dioxide, so they are not fumigated.

Wine production from the fruit of the grape has intrigued people since Neolithic times. Many books have been written about all phases of wine production and utilization. A few are listed at the end of this chapter.

Wine production is based upon a rather complex alcoholic fermentation process, first explained by Pasteur in 1866, whereby the sugars (glucose and fructose) in grapes are converted to alcohol and carbon dioxide by the activity of the enzymes produced by wine yeast (*Saccharomyces cerevisiae* var. *ellipsoideus*).

$$1 \text{ glucose } (C_6H_{12}O_6) \xrightarrow{\text{yeast}} \begin{array}{l} 2 \text{ ethyl alcohol } (CH_3CH_2OH) + \\ 2 \text{ carbon dioxide } (CO_2) + \\ \text{about 56 kilocalories of energy} \end{array}$$

Other chemical constituents in the grape produce the characteristic flavor, color, and odor of wine.

Wine becomes vinegar if certain bacteria (*Acetobacter*) develop in the wine, changing the ethyl alcohol to acetic acid.

Table 29–1   Some Important Grape Cultivars of the World

Vitis vinifera *(European)*			Vitis labrusca *(American)*			Vitis rotundifolia *(American)* Table and
Wine	*Table*	*Raisins*	*Wine*	*Table*	*Juice*	*Wine*
RED						
Aleatico	Thompson Seedless	Thompson Seedless (Sultana, Sultanina, Oval Kishmish)	Concord	Concord	Concord	Scuppernong
Alicante Bouschat	Almeria		Niagara	Niagara		Hunt
Barbera	Calmeria	Muscat of Alexandria	Catawba	Catawba		Thomas
Cabernet Sauvignon	Cardinal	Black Corinth (Zante currant)	Delaware	Delaware		Burgaw
Carignane	Dattier (Rosaki, Waltham Cross)			Isabella		Topsail
Carnelian		Black Monukka		Worden		Dearing
Carmine	Emperor			Portland		Tarheel
Gamay	Malaga			Pierce		Willard
Gamay Beaujolais	Olivette blanche			Golden		
Grenache	Perlette			Muscat		
Grignola	Red Malaga					
Mataro	Ribier (Alphonse Lavalleé)					
Merlat	Rish Baba					
Mission	Flame Tokay					
Petit Sirah						
Pinot noir						
Rubired						
Ruby Cabernet						
Sangioveto						
Tinta Madeira						
Valdepenas						
Zinfandel						
WHITE						
Aligote						
Chardonnay						
Chenin blanc						
French Colombard						
Grey Riesling						
Muscat blanc						
Palomino						
Pinot blanc						
Sauvignon blanc						
Semillon						
Thompson Seedless						
White Riesling (Johannisberger Riesling)						

1 ethyl alcohol (CH_3CH_2OH) + oxygen (O_2)

$$\xrightarrow[\text{Acetobacter}]{} \text{1 acetic acid (}CH_3COOH\text{)} + \text{1 water (}H_2O\text{)}$$

Keeping equipment and containers clean and preventing the exposure of wine to air minimizes the acetic acid reaction.

Raisins are dried grapes of a cultivar with a high sugar content, like Thompson Seedless. The grapes are harvested for raisins when the total soluble solids (mostly sugars) reach about 20 percent. Grapes below 17 percent soluble solids give a poor product and should not be dried for raisins. About 194 kg (432 lb) of raisins can be obtained from a MT of harvested grapes. Raisin grapes are usually dried on paper sheets placed in the sun between the vine rows (see Fig. 12–20). The grapes are turned once during drying, then they are rolled in the paper for further "curing," finally being emptied into boxes for delivery to the packing plant. At this time the raisins should contain 10 to 15 percent moisture.

Grapes are subject to many diseases, and production may be eliminated from areas where they occur. High humidity promotes the development of certain fungus diseases, such as anthracnose, deadarm, botrytis, bunch rot, black rot, and downy mildew, which do not occur in dry, semiarid regions. Powdery mildew, however, develops easily in dry climates and is, by far, the most troublesome fungal disease on grapevines in California. It is controlled by repeated dusting of the vines with sulfur throughout the growing season (Fig. 11–5). Diseases caused by bacteria generally are not a major problem with grapevines. There are several viral diseases, such as fan leaf, yellow mosaic, vein banding, yellow vein, arabis mosaic, leaf roll, and corky bark, that cause stunting, deformity, chlorosis, delayed fruit maturity, poor color, and reduced fruitfulness. Best control of viral diseases is not to take propagating material from infected vines but to use certified planting stock. With the modern practice of heat therapy to eliminate viruses from plant material (see p. 251), it is now possible to obtain propagating material from vines free of these known viral diseases.

Insects and other pests harmful to grapevines and their fruit include the grape leafhopper, grape leaf folder, omnivorous leaf roller, spider mites, grape mealy bug, grape bud beetle, grasshoppers, nematodes, and phylloxera.

Phylloxera, a type of aphid attacking only the grape roots in California is native to the United States east of the Rocky Mountains where it feeds on vines of the native American species but does not kill them. It was identified in France about 1868, having been introduced earlier on the roots of some imported American vines. This pest spread rapidly throughout France and within 30 years 75 percent of the vinifera grape vines in France were destroyed. Phylloxera was also found in California grape-growing areas in 1873. The only method of growing vinifera grapes where phylloxera is present in the soil is by grafting onto roots of special resistant hybrid rootstocks that include some parentage of the native American *Vitis* species (see p. 596). In about 20 percent of the California vineyards the vines are grown in heavy soils where such resistant rootstocks must be used. In the sandy soils phylloxera is not a problem but often nematodes are. Nematode-resistant rootstocks must be used. Propagation by cuttings is the usual method, however, where these pests are not present.

Peach and Nectarine (*Prunus persica* L. Batsch.)
ROSACEAE (*15, 22, 24, 27, 35, 39, 44, 50, 54, 59, 62, 76*)

The peach and nectarine differ chiefly in the lack of the typical peach pubescence (fuzz) on nectarine fruits and in fruit flavor, sugar content, and aroma. Both have the same tree characteristics. Mutant limbs producing nectarines have been found on peach trees.

The peach originated as a wild form in China and apparently was cultivated there about 2000 B.C. It was taken westward to Persia and later to Greece about 350 B.C. The Romans were cultivating the peach about the time of Christ and spread it all through their empire in Europe, from which it later was disseminated over the world into all countries of the temperate zones. Nectarines have also been grown since ancient times, being mentioned in Pliny's writings about 50 A.D.

The peach is now one of the most popular commercial and home garden fruits. The United States leads in world peach production (about 1,426,000 MT annually), followed by Italy with about 1,128,000 MT, France with about 497,000 MT, and Japan with about 279,000 MT. In the United States, California produces annually about 11 million bushels of freestone peaches, followed by South Carolina with 6 million, Georgia with 4 million, and Michigan, Pennsylvania, and New Jersey with 2 million each. Almost the entire commercial canned peach production in the United States comes from California, with an annual production of about 750,000 MT (32 million bushels).

Areas that regularly have late spring frosts are unsuitable for peach production as the opened blossoms are easily killed. Low-lying frost-pocket planting sites must be avoided. Peaches attain their highest quality in regions with warm to hot summers and in areas with low summer humidity; fungal disease control is much easier there than where summer rains prevail.

Peach fruits can be canned, consumed fresh, dried, frozen, and preserved and jellied. There are two types of both peaches and nectarines—clingstone (flesh firmly attached to the pit) and freestone (flesh separating easily from pit). In both types there are yellow-fleshed and white-fleshed cultivars. Peaches are one of the stone or drupe fruits (see p. 38).

Commercial canned peach production in California is based mainly on such clingstone cultivars as Halford, Carolyn, and Loadel, and new cultivars are continually being introduced. Clingstones generally make a better-looking canned product than freestones because of their firmer textured flesh, which retains its shape during canning. Also the flesh is brighter and more uniform and the juice stays clearer. Freestone peaches are used to some extent for canning, but they are mainly eaten fresh.

There are many freestone peach cultivars in production, most of the important ones having originated from controlled crosses made by government-supported or private plant breeders. Fruits of peach cultivars ripen at different times so that fresh peaches are available in the markets from midspring to midautumn. Some of the leading freestone peach cultivars in the U.S. markets are Springcrest, Suncrest, Dixired, Redhaven, Redtop, Triogem, Redglobe, Sunhigh, Loring, Redskin, Elberta, Fay Elberta, and Rio Oso Gem. Prominent nectarine cultivars are Red June, Independence, Early Sun Grand, Sun Grand, Red Grand, LeGrand, Late LeGrand, Regal Grand, and September Grand. With these newer nectarine cultivars, far

How Fine Wines Are Made

After harvesting at the desired sugar and acid levels, the grapes (*Vitis vinifera* wine cultivars) are hauled to the winery in large steel tanks or gondola trailers holding from 1 to 5 MT (1.1 to 5.5 t). The grapes must be clean and in good condition. The grapes, either red or white, are dumped onto a conveyer that carries them to the crusher-stemmer. This can be two rollers set close together (crusher only), but usually consists of revolving paddles that slap the berries free of the stems and at the same time crack them open (crusher-stemmer). The crushed berries, free from the stems, collect in the bottom of the crusher-stemmer and are pumped out into the fermenter tanks. To counteract oxidation, growth of "wild" yeasts and other undesirable microorganisms, and development of "browning" enzymes, all of which would reduce wine quality, sulfur dioxide is introduced into the crushed grapes. For white wines the juice is pressed from the white grapes immediately after crushing to prevent extraction of bitter tannins and other undesirable materials from the skins. The juice is pumped to tanks for overnight settling and removal of any grape pulp or other semisolid materials. The next morning the clear juice is transferred into closed fermenting tanks where it is inoculated with an exact amount of specially cultured wine yeast to start a controlled fermentation in which the grape sugars are converted to alcohol and CO_2 (see p. 597). After fermentation starts, the temperature must be held between 7°C and 10°C (45°F and 50°F) for white wines. The fermentation process gives off heat that must be removed. If the temperature should exceed 32°C (90°F), the wine yeasts are destroyed and fermentation stops (this is called a "stuck wine"). Air is kept out since oxidation darkens the juice and eliminates the fresh, fruity grape flavors. In earlier days of wine making, temperature was controlled by placing fermentation tanks in cool, constant-temperature tunnels and caves dug into rocky hillsides. Modern wineries attain exact temperature control with large refrigeration rooms with jacketed stainless steel tanks individually controlled by refrigeration.

In making red wines the grape skins, pulp, and seeds, along with the juice, are included during the fermentation process to obtain the color, tannins, and flavors characteristic of the red wines. Fermentation is started in the crushed red grapes by inoculation with a pure yeast culture. About 665 liters (175 gal) of juice are obtained from each short ton of red grapes (with white grapes 57 to 76 l (15 to 20 gal) less of juice per ton are obtained).

Temperatures during red wine fermentation are much different than for white wines. The best temperature for the reds is between 21°C to 26.5°C (70°F and 80°F). These warmer temperatures are necessary to extract the tannins, color, and flavors from the skins.

Rosé or pink wines are made from red grapes but the color—coming from the skins—is controlled by the length of time the juice is in contact with the skins. After fermentation continues for a few hours and the juice becomes pink, it is drained and pressed free from the skins, with fermentation continuing in closed tanks at the same temperature, 7°C to 10°C (45°F to 50°F) used for the white wines.

After fermentation has proceeded to a certain point in making all types of wines, the still cloudy juice (wine) is transferred to closed storage tanks. Particles settle out and the clear wine is poured off (racked). This may be repeated several times to eliminate all sediment. Clarifying agents are added to help pull down particles staying in suspension. The wine is finally filtered to remove all suspended material and give it a brilliant clarity.

High-quality wine must be aged in oak casks or barrels, which are kept completely full to prevent oxidation and spoilage. Some wine evaporates through the pores of the wood, so the casks are continually topped to keep them full. Aging in the wood barrels varies with the type of wine. Reds take one or two years, most whites nine months, and the rosé wines less. Some wineries then stop the wood aging process by transferring the wine to large glass-lined tanks for further aging, perhaps up to 12 months, during which time the wine constituents change chemically, allowing flavor, color, and odor characteristics to develop more fully.

Bottling of the wines is the final critical process. Every effort is made to avoid introducing harmful oxygen into the wines. Inert nitrogen under gentle pressure is often used instead of pumps to move the wine from storage tanks to the bottling area. Empty bottles are freed of air by purging each one with nitrogen just before the wine enters. Bottles are stoppered by creating a vacuum just before the corks are inserted. Aging and maturing of the wines still continue after bottling. A peak of quality is reached, after which the quality starts to decrease. The rosé wines are the shortest lived. The white wines generally reach a peak of quality after two or three years. The red wines keep developing quality longer and are slower to decline. Cabernet Sauvignon, for instance, is likely to keep improving up to 20 years in the bottle.

In commercial wine-making enterprises all operations along every step of the way are carefully controlled. Laboratory examinations and analytical procedures are used to determine the microbiological processes, chemical composition, and sensory qualities.

Wine making from *V. labrusca* grapes, like 'Concord', which are low in sugar, differ somewhat from that described for *V. vinifera*. The crushed grapes are immediately transferred into a holding vat where enzymes are added to break down mucilagenous substances in and around the pulp. Heating is done during this process to develop the desired color, after which the juice is pressed out and cooled. It is then transferred to the first fermenting tank where sulfur dioxide, yeast, and extra sugar are added. Following this, the movement of the wine through settling vats and aging tanks is similar to that described above for the vinifera grapes.

Wines can be classed as either the dry table wines, which have no more than 14 percent alcohol, or the sweeter "aperitif" and "dessert" wines (sherry, port, muscatel), which have an alcohol content of about 20 percent because of the addition of brandy distilled from wine. Sparkling wines, like champagne from white wines and sparkling burgundy from reds, are prepared by a secondary fermentation of dry table wines in a closed container. This involves the addition of a certain amount of sugar and a pure yeast culture, and the wine undergoes a second fermentation and produces enough carbon dioxide to develop a pressure of 4 or 5 atm (4 to 5 kg/cm²).

superior to those grown in earlier days, more plantings are being made of this delectable fruit, which now competes with fresh peaches in the markets. Considerable work in breeding both peaches and nectarines by public and private agencies continues, and further improved cultivars are likely to be introduced.

Peaches and nectarines generally are self-fruitful, and trees can be planted in solid blocks without pollination problems. Exceptions are 'J.H. Hale', 'Hal-berta', 'June Elberta', and 'Alamar', which have defective pollen and require trees of a different cultivar in the planting to provide pollen plus a bee population to transfer it.

Peach trees in most years tend to set more fruit than they can properly mature. It is essential, therefore, that excess fruits be removed by hand from the tree by thinning to 13 to 25 cm (5 to 10 in) apart when the fruits are still small (see Ch. 14). Although a costly operation, thinning increases fruit size, improves fruit color and quality, and prevents limb breakage.

For best tree growth and production of peaches and nectarines, a deep, reasonably fertile, well-drained sandy loam soil is preferable. Heavy, poorly drained soils should be avoided.

Generally, peaches have a high nitrogen fertilizer requirement, and, in humid regions particularly, they respond to potassium fertilizers but little or not at all to phosphorus. Peaches grown in zinc-deficient soils develop a little-leaf or rosette condition that is corrected by dormant spray applications of zinc sulfate. Iron deficiency can be a problem in sodic soils. Peach trees must have continuous soil moisture during the growing season, from either rainfall or irrigation.

Nursery trees of peach cultivars are usually propagated by T-budding (see Ch. 5) onto peach seedling rootstocks, using seeds of such cultivars as Lovell or Elberta. Seeds must be planted to obtain a seedling on which to do T-budding. Since peach roots are susceptible to nematode attacks, it is advisable in areas where nematodes are a problem to use seedlings of a nematode-resistant rootstock, such as 'Nemaguard', developed by the USDA. This rootstock may not be winter hardy, however, in the colder peach-growing regions.

Young peach trees are generally pruned to an open-center or vase-shaped form, keeping the pruning to a minimum to avoid growth retardation and a delay in the onset of bearing (see Ch. 13). Peaches and nectarines bear fruits laterally on shoots that grew the previous summer so that relatively heavy pruning of mature trees is necessary to ensure a continuing supply of vigorous shoots. If the trees are not pruned, little shoot growth takes place and fruit production is minimal.

Peach fruits are mature and ready to pick when the skin background color becomes creamy yellow. They continue to ripen and soften after picking but the highest-quality fruits are those allowed to become fully ripe on the tree. Peach fruits, although not adapted to long storage, can be held from two to four weeks, depending upon the cultivar and harvest maturity, at about 0°C (32°F) at 90 percent relative humidity. Higher temperatures—2.2°C to 5°C (36°F to 41°F) and above—are not suitable for peach storage. Rapid cooling to 0°C (32°F) after harvest is desirable to retard ripening and to prevent development of decay organisms. In commercial operations, a hydrocooling apparatus is installed at the end of the fruit-packing line. The fruits are cooled by a swift-flowing shower of 0°C (32°F) water with a fungistat (see Ch. 12).

Peach and nectarine trees are subject to a number of disease and insect problems. Peach leaf curl, due to a fungus that distorts the leaves, is easily prevented by dormant fungicide sprays. Verticillium wilt and *Armillaria* root rot are caused by fungi attacking the roots. *Cytospora* canker is due to a fungus that invades wounds in limbs and shortens tree life. Bacterial canker is found mostly on young trees, causing lesions in the bark and death of branch and trunk tissues. Brown rot fungus causes fruit decay, especially in nectarines, and particularly when humid, rainy weather occurs, but this can be controlled by some of the newer organic fungicides. Several viral diseases affect peaches and nectarines—peach yellows, red suture, phony disease, peach rosette, peach mosaic, and yellow bud mosaic. Peach X-disease is believed to be caused by mycoplasma-like bodies (see Ch. 11). Virus problems are best avoided by planting only trees certified by a nursery to be free of such diseases.

Insects affecting peaches are plum curculio, peach tree borer, San Jose scale, and Oriental fruit moth.

Pear (*Pyrus* spp.) ROSACEAE (*10, 26, 27, 28, 29, 30, 46, 50, 54, 59, 61*)

There are two groups of pears based upon their origin—(1) those species originating in the western Asian region around the Caspian sea, the best known being *Pyrus communis* L., to which the present-day pear cultivars belong; and (2) the Oriental pears, originating in northern Asia, including *P. pyrifolia* (Burm. f.) Nakai, *P. ussuriensis* Maxim., *P. betulaefolia* Bunge, and *P. Calleryana* Decne. There are named cultivars of the second group, particularly *P. pyrifolia,* which are often called apple-pears for their apple-shaped fruits (*29, 30*). There are some hybrid cultivars of *P. pyrifolia* and *P. communis*, such as Kieffer, LeConte, and Garber.

Pears are an ancient fruit, cultivated during the early Egyptian, Greek, and Roman civilizations. Homer mentioned the pear in his writings about 800 B.C., and later Theophrastus, about 300 B.C., wrote of the wild and cultivated types, described methods of propagating pears by grafting, and mentioned the need for cross-pollination. Pears flourished in early France and were later introduced into England and Germany, from which they were taken to the other temperate zone countries over the world. Pears rank second to apples in world production of deciduous tree fruits. Italy has remained, by far, the world's leading pear-producing country, followed by the United States, Japan, Spain, France, West Germany, Turkey, and Australia. In the United States, California produces about 325,000 MT (357,500 t) of pears annually, followed by Washington with 210,000 MT (231,000 t), Oregon with 175,000 MT (192,500 t), New York with 13,500 MT (14,850 t), and Michigan with 9,800 MT (10,780 t).

Like apples, pears must be grown in regions with enough winter cold (about 1000 hr. under 7°C; 45°F) to overcome the rest influence in the vegetative and flower buds so they will develop in the spring. This requirement eliminates pear production from tropical and subtropical regions. Pear trees are not hardy below about −29°C (−20°F) so they are not grown in areas with very severe winters. The best pear cultivars are very susceptible to the disease fire blight caused by the bacterium *Erwinia amylovora*. This organism is native to the Western Hemisphere and flourishes in regions having warm, humid springs and summers with prolonged rainy spells. It has recently spread to England, northern Europe, and New Zealand. This disease confines large-scale commercial pear production to semiarid regions such as California (where blight attacks can still occur), or to regions where the fire blight bacteria do not exist. Pears, particularly the popular 'Bartlett', grow well in areas with hot summers.

Pear trees produce best on river bottom silt loam but tolerate wet, clay soils better than most other deciduous fruits. They must have continuous soil moisture through the growing season, from either rainfall or irrigation.

Pear trees require nitrogen fertilizers for adequate vegetative growth, but overfertilization can cause excessively rank, vigorous growth, making the trees more susceptible to attacks by fire blight bacteria. In humid rainy regions, where this is a major problem, it is difficult to maintain sufficient vegetative growth for good productivity without bringing on fire blight attacks. In most soils pears do not require other fertilizers, although there are a few instances where applications of potassium, phosphorus, or magnesium have helped.

The most important pear cultivar, by far, is the Bartlett, which is known outside North America by its original name, Williams Bon Chrétien, given when it was found in England in 1796. 'Bartlett' is considered a summer pear, ripening in California in July and August. Important later-ripening winter pear cultivars are Anjou, Bosc, and Comice. The 'Kieffer' pear is grown to a limited extent in the eastern United States, since it is resistant to fire blight.

Most pear cultivars require cross-pollination to set good crops. There are places, however, where certain cultivars set heavy crops parthenocarpically (see p. 327), without cross-pollination, and produce seedless fruits. An example is the 'Bartlett' in the Sacramento Valley of California. Temperatures during the blooming and fruit setting period are usually warm, and heavy crops are produced in solid block plantings without pollinizer trees. In most regions 'Bartlett' trees must be interplanted with those of other cultivars to obtain good fruit set. 'Anjou', 'Bosc', and 'Seckel' set some fruit when planted alone but produce more if cross-pollinated. Other cultivars, like Winter Nelis, are self-unfruitful and must be cross-pollinated to set any fruit.

Pears are not prone to alternate bearing, as are apples, and fruit thinning is generally unnecessary unless an obviously excessive crop has set. A temperature of $-4.5°C$ ($24°F$) at full bloom kills approximately 90 percent of Bartlett flowers.

Pear trees are propagated either by T-budding onto seedling rootstocks in the nursery or by winter bench grafting (see Ch. 5) onto short pear root pieces for planting in the nursery in the spring. *P. communis* seedlings are the best rootstock for pear cultivars, but the seed source is important to ensure that only *P. communis* trees are the parents. Where fire blight is a severe problem, rooted cuttings of a blight-resistant type like 'Old Home' can be allowed to grow to form the roots, trunk, and primary scaffold branches of the tree. When the scaffolds are one year old, they can be top-budded (see Ch. 5) to the desired fruiting cultivar. If fire blight attacks the top of the tree, it usually stops at the 'Old Home' tissue and does not kill the entire tree. Later, after all blight is cut out, the 'Old Home' branches can be rebudded to the fruiting cultivar.

Rooted quince cuttings can be used as the rootstock for partially dwarfed pear trees, but certain cultivars—Bartlett, Bosc, Winter Nelis, and Seckel—are not directly compatible

with quince. These require an interstock like 'Old Home' or 'Hardy' pear and two graft unions between the quince roots and the fruiting top cultivar.

Young pear trees are best trained in the United States to a modified leader system (see Ch. 13) with as little pruning as practicable. Young trees tend to grow very upright so pruning during the first several years should include complete removal of some of the upright shoots. Once the trees start to bear, the weight of the fruit aids in developing a spreading growth habit.

Pear fruits are produced on fruiting spurs and, to a lesser extent, laterally on shoots that grew the preceding year. Some moderate annual pruning by thinning out shoots stimulates renewal of both spurs and fruiting shoots. Light pruning should be used to obtain maximum yields and to avoid stimulation of vigorous shoot growth, which is very susceptible to fire blight.

Pears are utilized as fresh, canned, or dried fruit. A pear cider, perry, is made in some European countries.

Pear fruits must be picked from the tree when they are mature but still hard and ripened off the tree at a temperature of $20°C$ to $21°C$ ($68°F$ to $70°F$) for 10 to 12 days at a relative humidity of about 85 percent. Higher ripening temperatures detract from flavor and appearance. A characteristic yellow color develops during ripening, along with flesh softening and aroma and flavor changes.

Bartlett pears are considered to be mature and ready to pick when the fruits are full-sized (at least 6.0 cm; (2 3/8'' in diameter) and change color from a deep green to a yellowish green, or when the soluble solids, as measured by a refractometer, are not less than 10 percent, or when a pressure test made by a 0.79 cm (5/16'') plunger into the pared flesh is not over 9.9 kg (22 lb). Immature pears do not ripen properly and give a good product.

Mature but unripened pears can be kept for several months if they are stored immediately after harvest at about $-1°C$ ($30°F$) and 90 to 95 percent relative humidity. 'Bartlett' fruits keep as long as two and a half to three months; 'Bosc' and 'Comice', three to four months; and 'Anjou', four to eight months. Anytime during these periods the fruits can be removed from cold storage and placed at $20°C$ to $21°C$ ($68°F$ to $70°F$) for ripening, which then occurs rapidly—four or five days.

"Pear decline" has been a severe problem in Italy and in the U.S. West Coast pear districts, killing hundreds of thousands of pear trees grafted on certain Oriental pear rootstocks. Death is due to a mycoplasma-like organism spread from tree to tree by the insect, pear psylla. The 'Bartlett' (*P. communis*), for example, is itself resistant but the organism, moving down the phloem to the Oriental rootstock (e.g., *P. pyrifolia*), kills its phloem tissue and girdles the trunk, and the tree's roots die from lack of food materials from top. Best control is the use of nonsusceptible rootstocks, as *P. communis* and *P. Betulaefolia* seedlings. Remission of symptoms has been obtained by trunk injections with the antibiotic tetracycline.

Codling moth can cause wormy pear fruits, but it is easily controlled by properly timed insecticide sprays during the growing season. Several kinds of mites, as well as pear psylla, can become major pests.

Pecan (*Carya illinoinensis* Wangenh.)
JUGLANDACEAE (*38, 48, 49, 54, 60*)

The pecan is a large deciduous tree native to the south central United States. The early French and Spanish explorers and settlers in this area found the native Indians using the nuts as food. They were called "pacanes" by the Indians, meaning any nut so hard it had to be cracked with a rock. In the United States pecans are grown commercially in the southern states. Georgia leads in production, followed by Texas, Alabama, Louisiana, Oklahoma, and Mississippi.

Pecans require a long, frost-free growing season with hot days and warm nights to properly mature the nuts. The tree does, however, require some winter-chilling to overcome bud dormancy and permit proper vegetative growth in the spring. For this reason it is not adapted to tropical or subtropical regions. Pecan trees tolerate considerable winter cold without damage.

For good tree growth and heavy production, pecans require a deep, well-drained, and well-aerated soil free of hardpan layers. The trees do not do well on saline or highly alkaline soils. Pecans respond to nitrogen fertilizers by increased growth. Deficiency of nitrogen is shown by yellowish foliage. Added nitrogen to maintain vigor and productiveness is particularly useful as the trees mature. Pecans are very sensitive to zinc deficiency in the soil and may require several foliar spray applications of zinc sulfate per year to keep them growing properly. Continuous soil moisture, from either irrigation or rainfall, is necessary for good tree growth and production.

In the early days pecan groves consisted of native and planted seedling trees. From about 1850 to 1910 selections from the best trees were made and named for further vegetative propagation. From this came the cultivars Schley, Success, Stuart, Mahan, and Desirable, which today are the predominant ones being grown in the southeastern United States. Pecan hybridization began about 1914, culminating with the establishment in 1930 of a large pecan breeding program by the USDA and the Texas Department of Agriculture at Brownwood, Texas. USDA cultivar releases from Brownwood include Barton (1953), Comanche (1955), Wichita and Choctaw (1959), Apache and Sioux (1961), Mohawk (1965), Cado and Shawnee (1968), Cheyenne (1970), Cherokee (1971), Chickasaw and Shoshoni (1972), Tejas (1973), and Kiona (1976). Many of these have been heavily planted in recent years, particularly Wichita.

Pecans have both nut-producing pistillate (female) flowers and pollen-producing (male) catkins on the same tree. For a good crop to be set, the pollen must be shed at a time when the female flowers are receptive. Because some of the best pecan cultivars do not do this, often another cultivar is used in the planting to provide pollen at the proper time. In addition, self-pollination is not desirable.

Pecan cultivars can be propagated by patch budding or whip grafting (see Chap. 5) onto two-year-old pecan seedling rootstocks grown in the nursery row. For good germination the seeds are best soaked in water for 24 hours, then stored in damp vermiculite in polyethylene bags for three to four months at about 1°C to 3.5°C (34°F to 38°F) before planting. Pecan seeds dry out and lose viability, so they should be kept cool and damp from the time they are harvested until stratification begins (see p. 85).

Young pecan trees are best trained by light pruning to a modified central leader system (see Ch. 13), which can give strong, wide-angled scaffold branches. Narrow-angled scaffolds are weak and can easily break under heavy crop loads.

Pecans are ready to harvest when the hull loses its green color and starts to split. The trees are harvested commercially by mechanical tree shakers that shake the nuts off the branches onto cloth sheets or the ground, where they are picked up mechanically. The nuts are air-dried after harvest to remove 10 to 20 percent of the moisture. The whole nut keeps in good condition for several months in a cool, dry place. If too warm, the nut meats become rancid. Most of the pecan crop is handled through shelling equipment, with the nut meats used in baked goods, ice cream, and confections.

Pecans grown in the humid areas of the South with frequent rains develop a serious fungal disease called scab that attacks both the foliage and the nuts, although some cultivars show high scab resistance. Pecans are attacked by various insects such as pecan weevil, hickory shuck worm, pecan casebearer, and several kinds of pecan aphids.

Plum and Prune (*Prunus* spp.) ROSACEAE (*26, 27, 45, 50, 54, 59, 75*)

Native wild plums encircle the globe in the northern temperate zone region. There are groups indigenous to Europe, America, and Asia. Cultivated plums are grown throughout the two temperate zone regions of the world. Some types of plums require considerable winter cold (700 to 1100 hr. below 4°C; 45°F) to break bud dormancy and permit growth and flowering in the spring. This requirement prevents their culture in tropical and subtropical regions (except at higher altitudes). Plum trees generally are quite winter hardy.

The cultivated European firm-textured plums are in the species *Prunus domestica* L. and *P. insititia* L. The Japanese plums belong to *P. salicina* Lindl. The American plums include *P. americana* Marsh., *P. hortulana* Bailey, and *P. munsoniana* Wight and Hedr.

P. insititia is believed to have originated in southeastern Europe and parts of Asia. It is the plum mentioned in the writings of the early Greek poets during the sixth century B.C. The European plums (*P. domestica* and *P. insititia*) have been distributed throughout the world by seeds and scions for grafting and are the source of the best commercial cultivars. Prunes are firm-fleshed fruits of *P. domestica* cultivars that have a high enough sugar content that they can be dried whole, without fermenting around the pit, to produce a firm, tasteful product that can be stored for long periods. *P. cerasifera* Ehrh. cultivars are used as ornamentals and for plum rootstocks.

Certain cultivars of Japanese plums (*P. salicina*) were introduced into the United States about 1870 by Luther Burbank and others. It is likely that this species originated in China since there are Japanese reports that it was introduced there from China about 1720. There are many cultivars of *P. salicina*, some of which are the most popular market types.

The native American plums were found growing—and being used as food by the Indians—in the areas east of the Rocky Mountains by the early explorers and settlers. Many cultivars of American plums have been developed, but they do not compete well in the markets with fruits of the European and Japanese types.

Among the stone fruits, plums rank next to peaches in total production. Yugoslavia is the world's leading producer of plums and prunes with about 1 million MT (1.1 million t) annually. West Germany is second with about 600,000 MT (660,000 t) and the United States is third with about 500,000 MT (550,000 t). About 90 percent of Yugoslavia's fresh prune crop is processed into brandy. California is, by far, the leading producer of both plums and prunes in the United States, followed by Washington, Oregon, Michigan, and Idaho.

Japanese plums are early blooming and are well adapted to areas with mild winters and hot summers. European plums are late blooming and produce best under colder winters and moderate summer temperatures.

Plums grow well on many soil types but do best on deep, well-drained soils of medium texture. They tolerate heavier soils than most other stone fruits, unless grown on peach roots. Japanese plums respond to heavy applications of nitrogen fertilizers with increased growth and larger fruits. European plums seem to require less nitrogen but, unlike Japanese plums, respond well to potassium fertilizers in some soils. Some prune orchards in California have suffered heavily from potassium deficiency. Zinc deficiency has appeared in many California prune orchards, but it can be corrected with dormant sprays of zinc sulfate. For good vegetative growth and crop production plums require continuous soil moisture throughout the growing season from rainfall or irrigation.

Plum cultivars can be grouped into those used primarily for fresh consumption, canning, and jellies, and those used for drying (prunes). Fresh market plums are mainly cultivars of the Japanese types (or hybrids with Japanese parentage) like Santa Rosa, Duarte, Climax, Laroda, Wickson, Red Beaut, Nubiana, Queen Anne, Kelsy, and Eldorado. European fresh-eating plums include Tragedy, President, Green Gage, Stanley, and Yellow Egg. Cultivars used for prune production are such *P. domestica* types as French, Imperial, Sugar, Robe de Sergeant, and Italian.

Plums are one of the stone or drupe fruits (see p. 38).

Most Japanese plum cultivars are self-unfruitful and require pollinator trees of the same species for setting crops. Many of these cultivars are inter-unfruitful, so advice from the local agricultural extension service is necessary so that the proper combinations are used to satisfy the pollination requirements. Some of the European cultivars like Agen, French, Damson, Pershore, Stanley, Methley, French prune, and Sugar prune are self-fruitful and can be planted in solid blocks. Others, like Diamond, Grand Duke, President, Tragedy, and Italian prune are completely or partially self-unfruitful and require pollinizer trees of another cultivar. It is wise in planting plums to mix two or more cultivars. All European plum cultivars seem to cross-pollinate readily provided their bloom periods overlap. A good bee population in the orchard at bloom is essential to ensure proper pollination.

There has been considerable interest in the United States, Canada, and in Europe in plum breeding by crossing the various species. For example, Luther Burbank's Santa Rosa plum, the leading shipping cultivar grown in the United States, is a mixture of *P. salicina*, *P. americana*, and *P. simonii*.

Fruit thinning is often required with plums, especially the Japanese types, spacing the fruits 10 to 15 cm (4 to 6 in) apart. Unless properly thinned, fruit size is small and tree growth weak, with little or no crop the following year (see Fig. 14–3).

Plum trees are propagated by T-budding (see Ch. 5) onto seedling rootstock trees in the nursery. These may be seedlings of myrobalan plum (*P. cerasifera*) or peach (*P. persica*) especially 'Nemaguard', which is resistant to root knot nematodes. Rooted hardwood cuttings of such plum cultivars as Myrobalan 29C, Myrobalan B, Brompton, Pershore, St. Julian A, and Marianna 2624 make good rootstocks for plums and are widely used.

Plum trees are best trained to an open-center shape (see Ch. 13) with three or four primary scaffolds and seven to nine secondary scaffold branches. Shoots of Japanese plums form lateral branches readily, but those of European plums in the first two years should be headed back to force out lateral branching to develop the scaffolds. As plum trees come into bearing the fruits are borne mostly on fruiting spurs that live for five to eight years, developing laterally on the larger branches. Pruning bearing trees consists mainly of thinning out fruiting wood to reduce the crop load and to stimulate renewal shoots for future crops. Insufficient removal of fruiting wood leads to excessive fruit set and high thinning costs.

Fresh market plums should be left on the tree until they are well matured, but they will continue to ripen after picking. At optimal harvest time the fruit should soften to yield to gentle pressure, be juicy and aromatic, and have a final skin color typical of the cultivar. Although fresh plums do not adapt to long storage, they can be held for two to four weeks, depending on the cultivar, if they are placed at 0°C (32°F) and 90 percent relative humidity immediately after harvest.

To produce high-quality prunes the fruit must be harvested at the proper maturity stage. The flesh color (of French prunes) should change from green to full yellow or amber and the skin should become red; flesh firmness should sharply decrease and soluble solids of the extracted juice should be at least 22 percent. Prune harvest in large orchards is generally fully mechanized with mechanical tree shakers (see Fig. 12–11) removing the fruits, which fall onto mechanized canvas catching frames. In smaller operations the fruits are allowed to fall on the ground when ripe or hooked poles are used to shake the branches. The fruits are then picked up by hand.

Plum and prune trees are susceptible to bacterial canker, crown gall, oak root fungus, crown rot, *Cytospora* canker, and such viruses as ring spot and prune dwarf. Insect problems include San Jose scale, peach twig borer, and codling moth. Several species of mites also attack plums and prunes.

Quince (*Cydonia oblonga* Mill.) ROSACEAE (*31, 50*)

The quince is an ancient fruit believed to have originated in the region stretching from Iran eastward to northern India and Tibet. There is evidence that it was cultivated about 4000 B.C. by western Asian peoples. The quince was a popular fruit of the ancient Greeks and Romans. It is a small, slow-growing deciduous tree well-adapted to many areas of the temperate zones. It requires a slight amount of winter chilling for the buds to develop properly in the spring. Unlike most other deciduous fruit trees, quince fruit buds do not form the preceding summer but develop at the terminal ends of new shoots produced in the spring of the current year. The quince grows well and produces crops in either cool or hot summers.

Main production areas at present are Iran, Afghanistan, and southern Europe. The quince is not held in high esteem in present-day horticulture although its fruit can be used baked or made into a very tasty jelly or used to flavor cooked apples and pears. Rooted cuttings of the Angers Provence cultivar are used widely in pear culture as a rootstock that produces a dwarfed pear tree.

The quince is adapted to many soil types as long as they are well drained. Relatively little pruning is needed, just enough to stimulate new shoot production and to remove dead or interfering branches. Quince cultivars are propagated by T-budding (see Ch. 5) on rooted 'Angers' cuttings. Cuttings of some, but not all, cultivars root easily.

There are a number of quince cultivars—Orange, Pineapple, Champion, Van Deman (originating in the United States); Smyrna, Angers, Bourgeat, and Portugal (originating in Europe); and Tetoro and Beretzki (originating in the Balkans). In the United States, Pineapple is the most important cultivar. The quince is self-fruitful, so only one cultivar need be planted.

Quince fruits are ready to harvest when the skin loses its greenish color and a pronounced fragrance develops. Fruits keep well in cold storage.

Fire blight is the chief disease of the quince. Codling moth and Oriental fruit moth are major insect pests. Control requires three or four sprays per year.

Raspberry (*Rubus* spp.) ROSACEAE (*5, 47, 50, 54, 55, 59, 63*)

Although the genus *Rubus* contains 400 to 500 species, there are only three important raspberry species—often grouped together as the "brambles." These are the European red raspberry (*R. idaeus* L.), which is native to many areas in Europe; the American red raspberry, (*R. idaeus* var. *strigosus* Michx.), native to the eastern and northern United States and southern Canada; and the black raspberry (*R. occidentalis* L.), which is native to many areas in North America. Purple raspberries are hybrids between red raspberries and *R. occidentalis*. The red raspberry is the most important commercially.

Pliny, a Roman who wrote just before the beginning of the Christian era, mentioned that the raspberry was originally found growing wild on Mount Ida in Greece. Linnaeus commemorated the place of discovery when he named the raspberry *R. idaeus*.

Raspberries differ from blackberries in that the fruit itself separates readily from the receptacle on which it is produced. Blackberries do not separate readily.

The largest commercial raspberry plantings are found in Poland, Scotland, Yugoslavia, the United States (Washington and Oregon), and Canada (principally British Columbia). While world raspberry production has increased since 1900, production in the United States has decreased, probably because of virus problems and high hand-labor costs for harvesting the very tender fruits. Use of virus-free nursery stock and mechanical harvesting equipment may reverse this trend, however.

Although there are cultivar differences, the red raspberry is considered to be resistant to cold if the bushes are properly hardened before winter, but injury can occur from alternating warm and cold periods in late winter. Raspberries should be grown in areas with cool summers and on sloping sites that have good air drainage to avoid frost pockets.

Raspberries grow best in a deep, well-drained, medium-textured, slightly acid loam soil with large amounts of organic matter. Heavy fertilization with manure or inorganic fertilizers is required for strong vegetative growth and high yields. Irrigation is required in areas where rainfall is unreliable.

Raspberries are bush-type plants that fruit on biennial branched, upright canes. These canes grow vegetatively the first summer, initiating fruit buds in the fall. The following spring short lateral shoots develop from these buds, which flower and produce fruits in early summer. After this the entire cane dies to the ground and should be pruned out to leave space for newly developing vegetative canes for next year's fruit. In early spring, before growth starts on the fruiting canes, they should be pruned to a height of 1.2 to 1.5 m (4 to 5 ft) to limit the crop and give larger berries of better quality.

Red raspberries produce many upright canes from the crown of the plant. After fruiting and removal of the old fruiting canes, the newly formed vegetative canes for next year's crop should be thinned out, removing weak shoots and suckers from the red raspberry plants—and all canes under about 1.3 cm (0.5 in) in diameter from black and purple raspberries.

Some popular red raspberry cultivars are Latham, Willamette, Heritage, Newburgh, Fairview, Meeke, Taylor, and September. Black raspberry cultivars are Bristol, New Logan, Cumberland, Dundee, Allen, Jewel, Allegany, and Huron. Purple raspberries are Clyde, Sodus, Brandywine, Amethyst, and Marion.

Red raspberries are easily propagated by digging and transplanting in the fall suckers arising from the roots. Or it is possible to wait until spring to dig either the one-year suckers or new ones just starting. A piece of the old root should remain attached in either case. Red raspberries can also be propagated by root cuttings (see Ch. 5). Root pieces are cut into sections 5 or 7 cm (2 or 3 in) long in early spring and planted about 5 cm (2 in) deep in nursery rows.

Black and purple raspberries are propagated by tip layering (see Ch. 5). The tips of the new nonfruiting canes are pinched back when they are about 0.6 m (2 ft) tall. This causes many lateral branches to form, which arch over with their tips touching the ground. In late summer the tip of each of these laterals is buried 10 to 15 cm (4 to 6 in) deep. Roots and a new shoot develop from the tip. The following spring the cane is cut from the parent plant leaving about 15 cm (6 in) attached to the new plant. The plant can then be dug out and set in the nursery row to grow another year or directly in place in a new planting.

Raspberry fruits are highly perishable and should be carefully picked when the berries are beginning to soften and separate easily from the cap (torus). Overripe or decaying berries should be discarded. The fruits should be chilled to about 0°C (32°F) at 90 percent humidity immediately after harvest, and they can be kept for about a week. A planting should be picked twice a week. Some raspberries are eaten fresh but more are frozen.

Raspberries are susceptible to such viruses as raspberry mosaic, leaf curl, mild streak, and ringspot. Anthracnose, powdery mildew, cane blight, leaf spot, orange rust, and spur blight are fungal diseases that can be controlled by fungicides or cane removal and destruction. Raspberry roots are attacked by several nematode species. To avoid this problem only nematode-free nursery planting stock should be used, and the proposed planting site should be fumigated with a nematicide.

Several insect pests attack raspberries. Aphids are serious because they transmit viruses. Raspberry fruitworm feeds on buds and new foliage. Other pests are leaf rollers, thrips, and mites. Tarnished plant bugs feed on flower parts, causing fruit to be misshapen, crumbly, and small.

Strawberry (*Fragaria* × *Ananassa*) ROSACEAE (*18, 25, 36, 53, 65, 71, 73, 77*)

The strawberry is a small, herbaceous plant with a short central stem (the crown). From the crown grow the leaves and other structures including branch crowns, flower stalks, and runners, which are all branches originating from leaf axils of the main stem.

Various strawberry species grow wild all over the world, but the cultivated strawberry is based upon two species, *F. chiloensis* (L.) Duch., native to the west coast of North and South America, and *F. virginiana* Duch., native to the Atlantic seaboard and to the Sierra Nevada, Cascades, and Rocky Mountains of North America. Hybrids between these two species were the ancestors of all modern strawberry cultivars. A French intelligence officer, A.F. Frézier, carried *F. chiloensis* plants from near present-day Concepción, Chile back to France in 1714. The plants were set out in French gardens near those of *F. virginiana* previously brought to France from the Atlantic seaboard of North America. Natural hybridization between these two species provided the basis for the large-fruited garden strawberries we know today all over the world. Since then, private and government-supported plant breeders have introduced many hundreds of new cultivars. Those well adapted to one set of climatic conditions often do poorly under different conditions, so that plant breeders throughout the world have developed new cultivars for their own particular conditions. Strawberries are native to the temperate zones, but adapted cultivars are grown most successfully in subtropical areas such as southern California and Florida.

Leading strawberry producing countries are the United States, Mexico, Poland, Japan, and Italy. In the United States, California leads by far, producing over 70 percent of the nation's crop, followed by Oregon, Washington, Florida, and Michigan. In California average production is about 45 MT/ha (20 t/ac), with harvesting continuing from February to about mid-October. U.S. production outside California averages about 6 MT/ha (2.7 t/ac).

Strawberry cultivars can be classified arbitrarily into two types based upon their fruiting habits. First, the spring cropping type are facultative short-day plants, forming fruit buds with the onset of short days in the fall. Normally the plants then flower and fruit the next spring, after which vegetative runners develop in response to the long days of summer. Most strawberry cultivars are of this type. Examples of popular U.S. strawberries are 'Tioga', 'Fresno', 'Tufts', 'Toro', 'Heidi', 'Hood', 'Northwest', 'Puget Beauty', 'Olympus', 'Rainier', 'Tatem', 'Shuksan', 'Headliner', 'Midway', 'Surecrop', 'Raritan', and 'Guardian'.

The second type has been called "everbearing" because the plants fruit in recurrent cycles throughout the growing season, including the long days of summer. Many cultivars of this type runner very little and, because they fruit during the summer and fall months, they behave as if they were long-day plants. Cultivars of this type are Geneva, Gem, Rockhill, Ogallala, Arapahoe, Ozark Beauty, and Quinalt.

True day-neutral cultivars have been bred from the second group. They flower in continuous cycles throughout the year in mild climates such as coastal southern California. They differ from the everbearers in that they do not go dormant during the shortest days of the year if favorable growing temperatures prevail. The first cultivars of this type have been released in California and named Aptos, Brighton, and Hecker.

As with many other temperate zone fruit species, strawberry plants develop a rest or dormancy condition in the fall that must be overcome by the chilling temperatures of winter before vigorous growth will resume in the spring. Strawberry cultivars differ in the amount of winter chilling required. Short-day cultivars originating in California, such as Tioga, Tufts, and Toro, require little chilling and are suitable for regions with very mild winters. Most cultivars originating elsewhere, on the other hand, have a high winter chilling requirement and would not be suitable for mild winter regions. 'Midway', 'Surecrop', and 'Raritan', for example, have a high winter-chilling requirement.

Strawberries grow best on well-drained, slightly acid, sandy soils, although a range of soil types can be used by selecting cultivars adapted to them. Poorly drained heavy clay soils should be avoided. In most areas outside California, sites with a gentle slope are desirable to give good water drainage and air movement. In California, strawberries are usually grown on level sites to facilitate irrigation.

Irrigation with high-quality water (low in soluble salts) is essential for commercial strawberry production, particularly in semiarid regions. Irrigation is desirable even in areas where summer rainfall can be expected, as rains may not fall at critical times during the growth and development of the crop. Furrow or sprinkler irrigation is generally used but drip irrigation is also proving satisfactory.

Strawberry blossoms are often damaged by frost in the spring in the midwestern and eastern parts of the United States, often eliminating the entire crop. The freezing point of the opened strawberry flower is about −0.5°C (31°F). To avoid frost damage a sloping site should be selected to allow drainage of cold air to lower levels. A northern exposure retards early spring blooming and lessens the chances of frost damage. Sprinkler irrigation systems are efficient and economical in protecting strawberry blossoms against frost damage. Sprinklers should be started when the air temperature in the strawberry field at plant level drops to about 1°C (34°F). Sprinklers protect blossoms at air temperatures down to −4.5°C (24°F).

Fertilizer requirements for strawberries vary considerably with the locality, cultivar, and soil type. In California, strawberries generally respond only to nitrogen, but in Washington and Oregon phosphorus is often needed as well as potassium and sometimes sulfur, boron, and magnesium. In highly acid soils lime applications are helpful. In the eastern United States nitrogen is mostly used, but potassium and, less often, phosphorus are sometimes needed.

Different planting systems are used in the various strawberry growing regions. Planting through plastic has been suc-

Fig. 29-1 Use of clear polyethylene plastic in a strawberry planting. Plants are allowed to grow through holes in plastic, which warms the soil, promotes early plant growth and fruiting, and helps keep the berries clean.

cessful (Fig. 29-1). In California the traditional method is the double row, raised bed system with two rows (about 25 cm; 10 in apart) of plants, spaced 20 to 35 cm (8 to 14 in) in the rows, with the beds 100 to 105 cm (40 to 42 in) apart center to center. In coastal California, either a summer or winter planting system is used, often with the plants grown as annuals. Plants grown longer than this in southern California do not receive enough winter chilling and lose vigor, and their fruits are small and inferior.

Summer plantings are established from mid-July in the Central Valley (Fresno area) to late August or early September in coastal California depending upon the cultivar and location. Plants are dug from nursery fields when semidormant in January and held in cold storage at −2.2°C (28°F) packed in containers lined with thin polyethylene bags until planting time. The plants grow rapidly through the fall, become semidormant in winter, and resume growth in early spring with fruit harvested from about March in southern California and late April in northern California and continuing on as late as October in some areas. The planting is then destroyed, if it is on an annual system, and the field may be cultivated and fumigated and prepared for a winter planting.

Winter plantings are used in the coastal districts of southern and central California, which have relatively mild winters. The plants are dug from high elevation northern California nurseries from mid-October to about November 1 and planted in the fields after 10 to 14 days of cold storage at above-freezing temperatures. The newly set plants grow through the winter and early spring, and the short days stimulate fruit bud initiation. Harvest of the crop begins as early as February in southern California. If annually operated, the planting may be destroyed in time to prepare the ground for a summer planting. Modifications of the winter planting system are also used in Florida and Mexico, where California cultivars are used exclusively.

In strawberry growing regions with cold winters, such as the northwestern, midwestern, and eastern United States, the conventional matted row system is often used and the plants are grown as perennials. Plants are set out in the spring about 0.6 m

(2 ft) apart on raised beds. In many cases runners from the original plants are allowed to root until a matted row 38 to 60 cm (15 to 24 in) wide is produced. In other cases a hill system, similar to that described for California, is used. Harvest takes place in the spring, a year after planting. Such strawberry fields may be kept for several years if weeds, pests, and diseases can be controlled. In many places the red stele disease (*Phytophthora fragaria*) is the factor limiting production.

Strawberries are easily propagated vegetatively by runner plants (see Fig. 5–30). If these runners encounter loose soil and adequate moisture, they form roots, grow rapidly and, in turn, give rise to additional runner plants. A critical point in planting strawberries is to have the soil level against the crown just above the root-stem junction. Plants set too low or too high may not survive. Only high-quality vigorous plants with pest- and disease-free crowns and root systems (white or straw color) should be used. Do not use plants showing moldy crowns or roots. It is best to obtain new plants from a strawberry nursery that produces plants in fumigated soil and which are free of viral, bacterial, and fungal diseases, nematodes, insects, and other pests. Preferably the plants should be certified by state agencies as true to cultivar and disease- and pest-free.

Ripe strawberries are extremely perishable and require careful handling. They are soft with a thin tender skin, and are easily attacked by fruit decay organisms. Peak-quality berries are fresh, bright, clean, and solid red with little or no white or green showing on the surface. Fruits of some strawberry cultivars ripen slightly after they are picked but those of others do not. The fruits should be moved from the field into the shade and refrigerated immediately after harvest. Berries of some cultivars, such as Tioga, Tufts, and Aiko, store quite well if they are handled carefully. Others, such as Sequoia, do not. The ideal storage condition for strawberries is 0°C (32°F) and 90 percent relative humidity.

Much of the strawberry crop in the eastern and midwestern parts of the United States is marketed by "pick-your-own" systems, but in California the crop is moved largely through commercial fresh shipment, freezer, and preserves channels.

Strawberries are subject to many disease and insect problems. Virus susceptibility of many of the early cultivars eliminated them. Development by plant breeders of new virus and red stele resistant cultivars has been an outstanding achievement in plant science, rejuvenating an entire agricultural industry. Viruses are best controlled by planting only resistent cultivars and obtaining plants certified to be free of known viruses. *Verticillium, Rhizoctonia, Pythium*, nematodes, and weeds are best controlled by preplanting soil fumigation with registered fumigants. Chloropicrin and methyl bromide combinations are used in California and Florida. Aphids, mites, and thrips also attack strawberries and, if present, must be controlled by the proper insecticides and miticides.

Walnuts (*Juglans* spp.) JUGLANDACEAE (*26, 27, 38, 54, 57, 67*)

The walnut is a large deciduous tree bearing both male catkins and the female (pistillate) flowers at different locations on the same tree (see Fig. 2–35). The roughened nut is enclosed in a thick husk. The edible portion is the seed inside the nut.

Fifteen species of *Juglans* are indigenous to southeastern

Europe and western Asia, eastern Asia, and North and South America. The most important species, producing the Persian or English walnuts of commerce, is *Juglans regia* L. It is native to a broad area from the Carpathian Mountains eastward to southern Russia and northern India. It was probably moved by migrating populations from ancient Persia to Greece and later distributed throughout the Roman empire. There are records of it being grown in England about 1550. The early colonists from England brought seeds to America. The settlers called the resulting trees English walnuts to distinguish them from the native American black walnuts. Persian walnut is a better name than English walnut, however, since it relates more to the area where the species originated.

Another important species is *J. nigra* L., the native species of eastern and central United States. It has a tasty nut but with a thick and hard-to-crack shell. It is highly prized for its lumber, which is used in making furniture, gunstocks, and cabinets. Many cultivars of this species have been selected and propagated vegetatively for nut production.

A third important species is *J. hindsii* Jeps., native to a small area in northern California. Its value is in the use of its seedlings as rootstocks for *J. regia* cultivars in the huge Persian walnut industry in California's Central Valley.

Persian walnuts are produced commercially in several European countries including France, Italy, Yugoslavia, Poland, Germany, Czechoslovakia, and Bulgaria, as well as in Russia, China, and the United States. All the commercial U.S. production is in California, except for a small production in Oregon.

Trees of the Persian walnut cultivars grown in California withstand a winter temperature of only about −11°C to −9.5°C (12°F to 15°F). These originated from ancestors grown in such mild winter areas as southern France, Spain, and Iran. The most popular Persian walnut cultivars being grown in California are Hartley, Payne, Franquette, Eureka, Ashley, and Serr. Trees of the Carpathian type of *J. regia* grown in the eastern United States are much hardier, surviving winter temperatures as low as −37°C to −42°C (−35°F to −45°F) if they are fully dormant. These Carpathian walnuts originated from seeds brought to the eastern United States and Canada from *J. regia* trees growing in such cold winter areas as Germany and the Carpathian Mountains. A limited number of trees of several cultivars of this type are in production throughout the midwestern and middle Atlantic states of the United States. Some Carpathian walnut cultivars are Hansen, Metcalf, Fickes, Somers, and Broadview.

Trees of the mild winter type of Persian walnuts thrive and produce heavy crops in the long, hot, dry and rainless summers of California's Central Valley, where over 80,000 ha (200,000 ac) have been planted. Nuts are damaged if summer temperatures are much over 40.5°C (105°F). Late spring or summer rains can increase the chances of damage by walnut blight. Spring frosts can also damage developing flowers. Persian walnuts have a winter chilling requirement to overcome the rest or dormancy influence in the buds. With insufficient chilling shoot growth and bloom in the spring is delayed and abnormal.

Walnut trees grow best on a fertile, well-drained, alluvial loam soil 1.8m (6 ft) or more in depth. Ample water sources must be available to provide irrigation throughout the summer. Sites subject to late spring or early fall frosts should be avoided. Walnut trees require annual applications of nitrogen fertilizers and, in California, zinc deficiency often develops. This is overcome by foliar sprays of zinc sulfate.

Walnut cultivars are self-fruitful and wind pollinated, but often the male catkins are not shedding pollen at the time the pistillate, nut-bearing flowers (Fig. 2–35) are receptive (this problem is termed dichogamy). It is necessary, then, to interplant cultivars, one of which produces pollen at a time when the pistillate flowers of the principal cultivar are receptive. All walnut cultivars are cross-compatible.

In many areas of the world where Persian walnuts are grown seedling trees are used, propagated from seeds taken from individual trees with good bearing characteristics and producing large high quality nuts. This procedure, nevertheless, results in considerable variability in the resulting tree characteristics and in the nuts produced and would cause difficult problems in large-scale production and marketing. In California the cultivars are maintained by propagating all trees vegetatively, either by patch or T-budding or by whip grafting on seedling rootstocks (see Ch. 5).

The rootstock most widely used is *J. hindsii* seedlings or, in some cases, 'Paradox' seedlings, which are natural F_1 hybrids resulting from *J. hindsii* pistillate flowers being pollinated by *J. regia* pollen from nearby trees. To a much lesser extent, *J. regia* seedlings are also used as rootstocks.

Carpathian walnut cultivars are usually propagated by grafting onto *J. nigra* seedlings with the bark graft method on young established rootstock trees planted in place in the orchard.

Persian walnut trees are best trained to a modified central-leader system (see Ch. 13). This produces a strong, well-shaped tree with wide-angled scaffolds capable of bearing heavy crops without limb breakage. With this system four or five primary scaffolds, well spaced vertically and around the tree, are allowed to develop, with the lowest branch about 1.8 m (6 ft) from the ground.

In large commercial Persian walnut plantings the harvest is completely mechanized. Mechanical tree shakers remove the nuts from the trees in early fall just as soon as the hulls split open and separate from the nut easily and when at least 80 percent of the nuts on the trees will be removed. They fall on to smooth, well-prepared soil where pick-up machines immediately gather them into bins. The nuts are then dried in a dehydrator, then fumigated in closed bins en route to central receiving stations.

Walnuts are subject to a number of disease and insect pests. Crown rot fungi can attack *J. hindsii* roots, particularly where there is considerable moisture at the soil level. Crown gall, due to a bacterium, attacks most types of walnut roots and is very difficult to control. Oak root fungus attacks *J. regia* roots primarily; *J. hindsii* is resistant. Walnut blight is a bacterial disease damaging the nuts. Insect pests include the walnut husk fly, navel orange worm, codling moth, aphids, and scale, but all these can be controlled by the proper insecticide sprays. Mites and root lesion nematodes are also problems in some cases. Black-line is a breakdown of the phloem tissue at the graft union of *J. regia* cultivars on *J. hindsii* seedling rootstocks. This generally occurs after the trees are 15 to 20 years old. It does not occur when *J. regia* seedlings are used as the rootstock. The cause of this trouble is believed to be a virus to which the *J. hindsii* tissue is susceptible.

REFERENCES

1. Amerine, M. A. 1964. Wine. *Sci. Amer.* 211(2): 46–56.

2. ——, and V. L. Singleton. 1965. *Wine*. Berkeley: University of California Press.

3. ——, and G. L. Marsh. 1969. *Wine making at home*. Yountville, Calif.: Vintage Press.

4. Anon. 1975. Controlling diseases of raspberries and blackberries. USDA Farmers Bul. 2208.

5. Anon. 1975. Growing raspberries. USDA Farmers Bul 2165.

6. Anon. 1975. Growing cherries east of the Rocky Mountains. USDA Farmers Bul. 2185.

7. Anon. 1975. Growing blackberries. USDA Farmers Bul. 2160.

8. Beutel, J. A., W. J. Moller, and K. O. Roberts. 1975. Berry production. Univ. of Calif. Div. Agr. Sci. Leaflet 2779.

9. Bianchini, F., and F. Corbetta. 1975. *The complete book of fruits and vegetables*. New York: Crown.

10. Boynton, D., and G. H. Oberly. 1966. Pear nutrition. In *Nutrition of fruit crops*, ed. N. F. Childers. New Brunswick, N.J.: Horticultural Publications.

11. Brann, J. L., Jr., P. A. Arneson, and G. H. Oberly. 1975. Tree fruit production recommendations for commercial growers. New York State Col. Agr. and Life Sci. Publ. (unnumbered).

12. Brightwell, W. T. 1971. Rabbiteye blueberries. Univ. of Ga. Col. Agr. Res. Bul. 100.

13. Brown, A. G. 1975. Apples. In *Advances in fruit breeding*, eds. J. Janick and J. N. Moore. West Lafayette, Ind.: Purdue University Press.

14. Chandler, W. H. 1957. *Deciduous orchards*. 3rd ed. Philadelphia: Lea & Febiger. Ch. 16, Pome fruits.

15. Childers, N. F., ed. 1966. *The peach: varieties, culture, marketing, pest control*. New Brunswick, N.J.: Rutgers University College of Agriculture and Environmental Science.

16. ——. 1976. *Modern fruit science*. 7th ed. New Brunswick, N.J.: Horticultural Publications.

17. Cook, J. A. 1966. Grape nutrition. In *Fruit nutrition*, ed. N. F. Childers. New Brunswick, N.J.: Horticultural Publications.

18. Courter, J. W., ed. 1977. Proceedings 1977 Illinois Strawberry School. Univ. of Ill. Coop. Ext. Publ.

19. Cross, C. E., I. E. Demoranville, K. H. Deubert, R. M. Devlin, J. S. Norton, W. E. Tomlinson, and B. M. Zuckerman. 1969. Modern cultural practices in cranberry growing. Mass. Agr. Exp. Sta. Ext. Ser. Publ. 39.

20. Eck, P., and N. F. Childers, eds. 1966. *Blueberry culture*. New Brunswick, N.J.: Rutgers University Press.

21. Einset, J., and C. Pratt. 1975. Grapes. In *Advances in fruit breeding*, eds. J. Janick and J. N. Moore. West Lafayette, Ind.: Purdue University Press.

22. Fogle, H. W., H. L. Keil, W. L. Smith, S. M. Mircetich, L. C. Cochran, and H. Baker, 1974. Peach production. USDA Handbook 463.

23. Galletta, G. J. 1975. Blueberries and cranberries. In *Advances in fruit breeding*, eds. J. Janick and J. N. Moore. West Lafayette, Ind.: Purdue University Press.

24. Gerdts, M., and J. H. LaRue. 1976. Growing shipping peaches and nectarines in California. Univ. of Calif. Div. Agr. Sci. Leaflet 2851.

25. Greathead, A. S., N. Welch, W. S. Seyman, N. F. McCalley, V. Voth, and R. S. Bringhurst. 1977. Strawberry production in California. Univ. of Calif. Div. Agr. Sci. Leaflet 2959.

26. Griggs, W. H. 1953. Pollination requirements of fruits and nuts. Calif. Agr. Exp. Sta. Ext. Ser. Cir. 424.

27. ——. 1970. The status of deciduous fruit pollination. Rpt. 9th Pollination Conf., Hot Springs, Ark. Univ. Ark. Agr. Ext. Ser.

28. ——, and B. T. Iwakiri. 1954. Pollination and parthenocarpy the production of Bartlett pears in California. *Hilgardia* 22(19): 643–78.

29. ——, and B. T. Iwakiri. 1977. Asian pear varieties in California. Univ. of Calif. Div. Agr. Sci. Publ. 4068.

30. ——, and B. T. Iwakiri. 1977. Asian pears in California. *Calif. Agr.* 31(1):8–12.

31. Gould, H. P. 1938. Quince growing. USDA Leaflet 158.

32. Hall, I. V. 1969. Growing cranberries. Canada Dept. Agr. Publ. 1282.

33. ——, L. E. Aalders, L. P. Jackson, G. W. Wood, and C. L. Lockhart. 1975. Lowbush blueberry production. Canada Dept. Agr. Publ. 1477.

34. Hesse, C. O. 1952. Apricot culture in California. Calif. Agr. Exp. Sta. Ext. Ser. Cir. 412.

35. ——. 1975. Peaches. In *Advances in fruit breeding*, eds. J. Janick and J. N. Moore. West Lafayette, Ind.: Purdue University Press.

36. Hull, J., Jr. 1970. Commercial strawberry culture in Michigan. Mich. State Univ. Coop. Ext. Bul. E-682.

37. Hull, J. W. 1973. Thornless blackberries for the home garden. USDA Home and Gard. Bul. 207.

38. Jaynes, R. A., ed. 1979. *Nut tree culture in North America.*, Hamden, Conn.: Northern Nut Growers.

39. Johnson, S. and R. P. Larsen. 1971. Peach culture in Michigan. Mich. Agr. Ext. Bul. 509.

40. Johnston, S., J. Moulton, and J. Hall, Jr. 1969. Essentials of blueberry culture. Mich. State Univ. Ext. Bul. E-590.

41. Keep, E. 1975. Currants and gooseberries. In *Advances in fruit breeding*, eds. J. Janick and J. N. Moore. West Lafayette, Ind.: Purdue University Press.

42. Kester, D. E. 1979. Almonds. In *Nut tree culture in North America*, ed. R. A. Jaynes. Hamden, Conn.: Northern Nut Growers Assoc.

43. Lagerstedt, H. B. 1975. Filberts. In *Advances in fruit breeding*, eds. J. Janick and J. N. Moore. West Lafayette, Ind.: Purdue University Press.

44. Lamb, R. C., and L. J. Edgerton. 1973. Peach growing. New York State Col. Agr. and Life Sci., Plant Sci. Inf. Bul. 44.

45. LaRue, J., and M. Gerdts. 1973. Growing plums in California. Calif. Agr. Exp. Sta. Ext. Ser. Cir. 563.

46. Layne, R. E. C., and H. A. Quamme. 1975. Pears. In *Advances in fruit breeding*, eds. J. Janick and J. N. Moore. West Lafayette, Ind. Purdue University Press.

47. Ljones, B. 1966. Bush fruit nutrition. In *Fruit nutrition*, ed. N. F. Childers. New Brunswick, N.J.: Horticultural Publications.

48. Madden, G. D. 1979. Pecans. In *Nut tree culture in North America*, ed. R. A. Jaynes. Hamden, Conn.: Northern Nut Growers.

49. Madden, G. D., and H. L. Malstrom. 1974. Pecans and hickories. In *Advances in fruit breeding*, eds. J. Janick and J. N. Moore. West Lafayette, Ind.: Purdue University Press.

50. McGregor, S. E. 1976. Insect pollination of cultivated crop plants. USDA Handbook 496.

51. Micke, W., and D. E. Kester, eds. 1978. Almond orchard management. Univ. of Calif. Div. Agr. Sci. Priced Publ. 4092.

52. ———, and F. G. Mitchell. 1972. Handling sweet cherries for the fresh market. Calif. Agr. Exp. Sta. Ext. Ser. Cir. 560.

53. Mitchell, F. G., E. C. Maxie, and A. S. Greathead. 1964. Handling strawberries for fresh market. Calif. Agr. Exp. Sta. Ext. Cir. 527.

54. Moyer, W. C., ed. 1976. *The buying guide for fresh fruits, vegetables, herbs, and nuts*. Fullerton, Calif.: Blue Goose.

55. Ourecky, D. K. 1975. Brambles. In *Advances in fruit breeding*, eds. J. Janick and J. N. Moore. West Lafayette, Ind.: Purdue University Press.

56. ———. 1975. Blackberries, currants, and gooseberries. New York State Col. Agr. and Life Sci. Inform. Bul. 97.

57. O'Rourke, F. L. S. 1969. The Carpathian (Persian) walnut. In *Handbook of North American nut trees*, ed. R. A. Jaynes. Knoxville, Tenn.: Northern Nut Growers.

58. Painter, J. H. 1969. Filberts in the Northwest. In *Handbook of North American nut trees*, ed. R. A. Jaynes. Knoxville, Tenn.. Northern Nut Growers.

59. Porritt, S. W. 1974. Commercial storage of fruits and vegetables. Canada Dept. Agr. Publ. 1532.

60. Rizzi, A. D., and H. I. Forde. 1974. Pecans. Univ. Calif. Coop. Ext. AXT 382.

61. Ryall, A. L., and W. T. Pentzer. 1974. *Handling, transportation, and storage of fruits and vegetables*. vol. 2, Fruits and Tree Nuts. Westport, Conn.: AVI.

62. Savage, E. F., and V. E. Prince. 1972. Performance of peach cultivars in Georgia. USDA and Georgia Agr. Exp. Sta. Res. Bul. 114.

63. Scheer, W. P. A. 1974. Commercial raspberry production guide. Wash. State Univ. E.M. 3803.

64. Scott, D. H., A. D. Draper, and G. M. Darrow. 1973. Commercial blueberry growing. USDA Farmers Bul. 2254.

65. ———, and F. J. Lawrence. 1975. Strawberries: In *Advances in fruit breeding*, eds. J. Janick and F. N. Moore. West Lafayette, Ind.: Purdue University Press.

66. Serr, E. F., Jr. 1964. Walnut rootstocks. Univ. Calif. Agr. Ext. Ser. AXT 120.

67. ———. 1969. Persian walnuts in the western states. In *Handbook of North American nut trees*, ed. R. A. Jaynes. Knoxville, Tenn.: Northern Nut Growers.

68. Shaulis, N. J., T. D. Jordan, and J. P. Tompkins. 1973. Cultural practices for New York vineyards. New York State Col. Agr. and Life Sci. Ext. Bul 805.

69. Slate, G. L. 1969. Filberts—including varieties grown in the East. In *Handbook of North American nut trees*, ed. R. A. Jaynes. Knoxville, Tenn.: Northern Nut Growers.

70. Smith, D., D. Ricks, and W. Sherman. 1974. The Michigan and U.S. sweet cherry industry—present and future. Mich. State Univ. Res. Rpt. 218.

71. Tomkins, J. P., and D. K. Ourecky. 1972. Growing strawberries in New York State. Cornell Univ. Plant Sci. (Pomology) Inf. Bul. 15.

72. Upshall, W. H. 1970. *North American apples: varieties, rootstocks, outlook*. East Lansing, Mich.: Michigan State University Press.

73. Waldo, G. F., R. S. Bringhurst, and V. Voth. 1968. Commercial strawberry growing in the Pacific Coast states. USDA Farmers Bul. 2236.

74. Weaver, R. 1976. *Grape growing*. New York: John Wiley.

75. Weinberger, J. H. 1975. Plums. In *Advances in fruit breeding*, eds. J. Janick and J. N. Moore. West Lafayette, Ind.: Purdue University Press.

76. Weinberger, J. H. 1975. Growing nectarines. USDA Agr. Inf. Bul. 379.

77. Wilhelm, S. 1974. The garden strawberry: a study of its origin. *Amer. Sci.* 62(3):264–71.

78. Winkler, A. J., J. A. Cook, W. M. Kliewer, and L. A. Lider. 1974. *General viticulture*. 2nd ed. Berkeley: University of California Press.

79. Woodroof, J. G. 1967. *Tree nuts: production, processing, products*, vol. 1. Westport, Conn.: AVI.

Subtropical Fruit and Nut Crops

The fruit and nut crops considered in this chapter are grown at low altitudes in those parts of the temperate zones nearest the equator. Most grow in the true tropics but do not produce well there, although some types, like the West Indian race of avocados, do best in strictly tropical climates. Most mature subtropical fruit and nut trees tolerate some subfreezing temperatures but are killed or severely injured below about 9.5°C (15°F). Certain species, like the olive, require winter cold for flower initiation (11). Some species, such as avocado, citrus, date, and olive, are evergreen; others, such as the fig, persimmon, pomegranate, and pistachio, are deciduous. They are all highly heterozygous and must be propagated by vegetative methods (rather than by seed) to maintain superior cultivars (see Ch. 5).

Avocado (*Persea americana* Mill.) LAURACEAE (1, 7, 14, 15, 24)

The avocado, an evergreen tree, grows to a height of 4.5 to 13.6 m (15 to 45 ft) with two or more periods of shoot growth during the year. It may flower in winter or spring, and the flowering period may last as long as six months.

Avocados are native to southern Mexico. In Central America and the West Indies the fruit has been used as a food for centuries. Based upon these centers of origin three distinct horticultural races are recognized: Mexican, Guatemalan, and West Indian. They differ in fruit size, oil content, and low-temperature tolerance. Wild forms of avocado are found in all these areas. Trees of these races hybridize readily.

Mexico is the leading producer of avocados, followed by the United States, Brazil, Colombia, Venezuela, and Ecuador.

Avocados now grow to a limited extent in most tropical and subtropical countries of the world. U.S. production is easily the highest in monetary value. California produces about 90,000 MT per year and Florida about 30,000 MT. The development of the industry in these two states started about 1920.

Trees of the West Indian race produce well in tropical climates, but those of the other two generally fail to flower or set fruit in the tropics. On the other hand, the West Indian race sets little or no fruit in subtropical climates, such as that of southern California. In regions where minimum winter temperatures of −5.5°C to −3.5°C (22°F to 26°F) occur, only trees of the Mexican race can be expected to survive. If the proper race and cultivar are chosen, avocados thrive and produce well in climatic conditions from truly tropical to the warmer parts of the temperate zone.

Avocado trees grow well in a wide range of soil types provided the drainage is good. Adequate, but not excessive, soil nitrogen is conducive to good fruit production. A leaf nitrogen of about 1.8 percent is associated with best yields of 'Fuerte' avocados.

All commercially grown avocado cultivars originated as chance seedlings. The excellent Fuerte has long been the world's leading avocado cultivar but has now been replaced by Hass. 'Fuerte' is a Mexican-Guatemalan hybrid, with green, pear-shaped fruits that mature over a long period of time in California—from November to May. Fruits are high in oil and weigh 224 to 448 gm (8 to 16 oz). Hass, a Guatemalan-Mexican hybrid, is the chief summer-maturing cultivar grown in California. At maturity the skin of the fruit is green but gradually turns black. It weighs 168 to 336 gm (6 to 12 oz). In Florida the leading cultivars are Guatemalan-West Indian hybrids. They are 'Booth 8', 'Booth 7', 'Lulu', and 'Waldin'. The fruits are green and weigh from 280 to 700 gm (10 to 25 oz).

Florida avocados are generally larger than the California types but contain less oil. California harvests and ships avocados throughout the year, while the Florida season is from August through January.

Avocado flowers occur in panicles of several dozen to several hundred that develop on shoot terminals all over the tree. The number of flowers per tree is large. Avocado flowers are all perfect (having both male and female parts), but they exhibit an unusual behavior. Flowers may open in the morning with receptive pistils (functionally female)—but shed no pollen. Then the flower closes, not to reopen until the afternoon of the second day, when it reopens to shed pollen—but with the stigma no longer receptive. The flower finally closes permanently that night. This kind of flower behavior is termed Type A. If the flower is "female" in the afternoon, then "male" the following morning, it is termed Type B. Each cultivar is characterized as Type A or B. Flowers of a given cultivar tend to behave uniformly as Type A or B. Hence avocados sometimes yield best when cultivars are interplanted so that cross-pollination can take place. They depend upon large insects, principally honeybees, for transfer of pollen and good fruit set; 3 hives for every 2 ha (1 per ac) may be sufficient.

The avocado fruit is a berry, consisting of a leathery skin (exocarp), the fleshy, buttery mesocarp—which is eaten—and a large seed consisting mostly of two cotyledons.

Avocado cultivars must be propagated vegetatively to retain their characteristics. Various methods are used—T-budding, tip grafting (whip graft method), side veneer, cleft and bark grafting (see Ch. 5) onto seedling rootstocks. In California seedlings of the Mexican race are preferred for rootstocks, but West Indian race seedlings are used in Florida.

Fig. 30–1 Mature avocado fruits ready for harvest. They can be "stored" on the tree in this stage for several months. They remain hard and firm until picked, when they begin to soften. *Source:* Blue Anchor.

Avocado trees of all ages are pruned sparingly, mainly by pinching back upright shoot tips to prevent excessive height growth. Heavy pruning encourages strong vegetative growth, reducing yields.

Avocado fruits in California are considered mature and ready to harvest only when the oil content of the flesh reaches 8 percent and when the seed coats within the fruits change from yellowish white to dark brown. In more tropical areas fruits are mature with less oil. Cultivars of the three horticultural races differ in oil content, the Mexican race having the highest, Guatemalan race intermediate, and West Indian the lowest. The mature fruits can be "stored" on the tree, however, for several months (Fig. 30–1). The fruits remain hard as long as they stay on the tree, softening only after harvest. Mature avocado fruits, even though firm, bruise easily and must be carefully handled. Avocados can be held for about a month in cold storage—7°C (45°F) for 'Fuerte' and 4.5°C (40°F) for 'Lulu' and 'Booth 8'. The fruit softens at room temperature; softening can be hastened by wrapping the avocado in aluminum foil. Mature, soft fruits can be maintained for more than two months at 2°C (36°F) but must be utilized shortly thereafter.

The major avocado production problem in California, and most other areas of commercial production, is the susceptibility of the roots to *Phytophthora cinnamomi* fungus, which is accentuated by poorly drained soils. There is a great need for *Phytophthora*-resistant rootstocks, and considerable research is under way to develop them. Cercospora spot on fruits and leaves is the most important avocado disease in Florida.

Citrus (*Citrus* spp.) RUTACEAE (*10, 14, 15, 18, 22, 23, 26, 27, 30*)

The citrus fruits, especially oranges, are one of the world's four major fruit crops, along with grapes, bananas, and apples. Commercial citrus species are native to southeast Asia and eastern India. Most present-day cultivars have been grown for many years. The famous seedless 'Washington Navel' orange was found in Bahia, Brazil, in the early 1800s and was introduced to Washington, D.C. by the USDA in 1870 and from there sent to Riverside, California in 1873. Commercial citrus is produced at low elevations in the world's subtropical climatic zones between 20° and 40° north and south of the equator. Citrus has little cold resistance and is not grown commercially where minimum temperatures are likely to fall below −6.5°C (20°F).

World citrus production occurs in three main areas: North and Central America—36 percent; the Mediterranean region—27 percent; parts of the Southern Hemisphere and Asia—37 percent. The United States is the largest producer of citrus fruits, mainly oranges, grapefruit, and lemons. Japan and Brazil are in second and third place. About 80 percent of all citrus grown is consumed in the producing countries themselves. Oranges account for the bulk (82 percent) of the citrus produced, with lemons and grapefruit taking up just under 9 percent each. Mandarins (tangerines) make up the rest. During the past 100 years world citrus production has increased from less than 1 million to over 44 million MT.

Citrus production in the United States by crop and state is shown in Table 30–1.

Table 30–1 Estimated U.S. Production of Citrus by Species and State 1976–77. 1000 Boxes (1000 Metric Tons in Parentheses)

Species	Arizona	California	Florida	Texas	Total
Oranges	3950	46,600	186,800	6900	244,250
	(134)	(1586)	(7626)	(266)	(9612)
Grapefruit	3000	7600	51,500	12,400	74,500
	(87)	(225)	(1986)	(450)	(2748)
Lemons	5000	20,600	——	——	25,600
	(172)	(710)			(882)
Mandarins	650	1820	3300	——	5770
(tangerines)	(22)	(62)	(142)		(226)

Florida far overshadows all other citrus-producing states, especially in orange and grapefruit production.

The common and scientific names and the important citrus cultivars grown in the United States are given below:

Common Name	Scientific Name	Important Cultivars
Grapefruit	Citrus × paradisi Macf.	Redblush, Marsh, Duncan, Thompson, Burgundy, Ruby Red
Lemon	C. limon (L.) Burm. f.	Eureka, Lisbon
Lime	C. aurantifolia (Christm.) Swingle	Tahiti (Persian), Key (Mexican or West Indian), Bearss (Persian)
Orange (sweet)	C. sinensis (L.) Osbeck	Valencia, Washington Navel, Hamlin, Pineapple, Parson Brown
Mandarins	C. reticulata (Blanco)	Orlando, Dancy, Temple, Kinnow, Wilking, Murcott, Robinson, Nova

Citrus species interbreed easily, and a number of interspecific and intergeneric hybrids have been developed. Some of these are listed below, as well as some minor citrus species sometimes used as rootstocks.

Common Name	Scientific Name
Calamondin	× Citrofortunella mitis Blanco
Citrange	× Citroncirus webberi Ing. and Moore
Citrangequat	P. trifoliata × sinensis × Fortunella spp.
Citron	Citrus medica L.
Cleopatra mandarin	C. reticulata Blanco
Kumquat	Fortunella spp.
Meyer lemon	Citrus limon (L.) Burm. F. 'Meyer'
Pummelo (Shaddock)	C. maxima [Burm.] Merrill
Rough lemon	C. limon (L.) Burm. F. 'Rough'
Sour Orange	C. aurantium L.
Trifoliate orange	Poncirus trifoliata (L.) Raf.

A deep, well-drained fertile soil is optimal for growing citrus, but many kinds of soils are used. Soils with low fertility can be made more productive by adding fertilizers. Citrus generally requires enough added nitrogen fertilizers to maintain a leaf nitrogen of about 2.5 percent dry weight. California soils usually have adequate phosphorus and potassium for citrus, but magnesium is occasionally deficient and may require magnesium nitrate sprays. Zinc and manganese deficiency often appears in California citrus and is corrected with zinc sulfate or manganese sulfate sprays. In alkaline or highly saline soils iron deficiency appears and the trees require iron chelate sprays. In Florida, with its less fertile soils, the fertilizer program for citrus includes nitrogen, potassium, magnesium, and possibly phosphorus as well as such micronutrient elements as boron, iron, copper, manganese, zinc, and molybdenum.

Some areas where citrus grows have long, dry periods that make irrigation mandatory. All types of irrigation are used: furrow, basin, sprinkler, and drip.

Since much of the citrus crop is on the trees during the winter months, frost damage is a real hazard. In selecting the site for the grove low-lying frost pockets should be avoided. Oil burning heaters or wind machines are often installed in bearing orchards to protect against freeze damage to blossoms, fruits, and trees. Usually heater fires are lit when orchard thermometers drop to a reading of −2°C or −3°C (27°F or 28°F) and are turned off at 0°C (32°F); 87 to 150 heaters per ha (35 to 60 per ac) may be required. Wind machines are operated at −1°C (30°F) and below except when there is no temperature inversion (see Ch. 10). Where water is available for flood or furrow irrigation, it may be applied for heat release in cold weather.

Most commercial kinds of citrus set adequate crops without cross-pollination. A few of the citrus hybrids do, however, require cross-pollination. Bees work citrus flowers, and hives are placed in citrus groves for collection of honey.

In subtropical regions with cool winters most citrus species bloom once a year in the spring. Flower initiation takes place in the buds about three months earlier. In the tropics and warm-winter areas the flowering period may be prolonged or it may occur several times during the year. Lemons grown in the mild southern California coastal regions and in southern Florida bloom and fruit the year round.

'Navel' oranges from California are available in the markets from November through June, whereas 'Valencias' are harvested from mid-March to mid-November. Florida 'Valencias' are on the markets from March through July and the Florida "early mid-season" orange cultivars (Pineapple, Temple, Hamlin, and Parson Brown) are marketed from October to April. Grapefruit harvest periods are: Florida—September through July; Texas—October through April; California—December through October; and Arizona—November through August. Lemons in the United States are produced mostly in California with much smaller amounts in Arizona and Florida. California lemons are on the market year round. Arizona lemons are available from October through February. Florida lemons are almost all used in processed forms.

Seed-propagated citrus trees produce acceptable fruit, but superior cultivars must be propagated by vegetative methods. In the early days of orange production in Florida, seedling trees were grown. In modern times, however, most citrus is propagated by T-budding on seedling rootstocks (see Ch. 5). Citrus cuttings root fairly easily, but this method of propagation is little used commercially.

Seeds of most citrus species produce nucellar embryos by apomixis (see Ch. 5); in addition to the sexual embryo, the nucellar embryos are the same genotype as the female parent and thus maintain the maternal clone. These asexual nucellar seedlings can be separated from sexual embryos in the nursery by their greator vigor and uniformity of character; this permits rootstock uniformity. The type of rootstock used in citrus can strongly influence fruit quality, yield, and tree size of the fruiting cultivar, as well as other horticultural characteristics.

Rootstocks generally used are seedlings of rough lemon, sour orange, 'Troyer' citrange, trifoliate orange, 'Cleopatra' mandarin, and sweet orange. Because of susceptibility to tristeza (quick decline), sour orange is no longer used as a rootstock for oranges in California but still is used to some extent in Florida. Sweet orange cultivars on sour orange roots are susceptible to the tristeza virus. This combination can be used in Florida, however, because of an apparently less virulent form of the virus. Sweet orange, 'Cleopatra' mandarin, and trifoliate orange roots give trees that produce high-quality fruits. However, trifoliate and trifoliate hybrid rootstocks are very susceptible to the exocortis virus and infected trees are dwarfed to some extent, depending upon the virus's intensity. Trees on rough lemon roots tend to produce coarse-textured fruits low in solids and acids.

All citrus cultivars and rootstocks are subject to a number of viral diseases. The best control is to use only propagating material or nursery trees produced under conditions free of such viruses. Most citrus-producing countries have set up elaborate certification programs to produce virus-free, true-to-type nursery stock. Citrus trees produce inferior mutations frequently, so propagating material should be taken only from mother trees with a history of producing high-quality, true-to-type fruits.

Pruning young citrus trees delays bearing and should be only extensive enough to develop a trunk and strong scaffold system. Bearing orange and grapefruit trees require but little pruning. On the other hand, bearing lemon trees need heavier pruning to facilitate orchard operations and limit their height.

Citrus fruits store best on the tree but they can be held for a time under refrigeration. Florida oranges may be kept for about 12 weeks at 0°C (32°F) and 90 percent relative humidity. California oranges store best slightly above 4.5°C (40°F). California and Arizona grapefruit keep for six weeks at 15.5°C (60°F), but Texas and Florida grapefruit require 10°C (50°F), all with 90 percent relative humidity. Lower storage temperatures cause fruit deterioration in grapefruit. Fully matured and colored lemons can be held for several weeks at 0° to 4.5°C (32° to 40°F), but for prolonged storage—four to six months—they should be picked dark green and held at 14.5°C to 15.5°C (58°F to 60°F).

Most California oranges are marketed fresh but in Florida about 90 percent are processed, mostly as frozen concentrate juice. About two-thirds of Florida's grapefruit are marketed in a processed form. Production of Florida frozen concentrated orange juice has been one of the outstanding examples of the development of a new industry by modern technology. In 1972 almost 513 million liters (135 million gal) of frozen orange concentrate was produced in Florida.

Many insect pests attack citrus. Some important ones are citrus red mite, citrus thrips, citrus mealy bug, red scale, yellow scale, snow scale, purple scale, citrus whitefly, and aphids. In addition, certain species of nematodes attack citrus roots.

Citrus disease problems are more devastating than insect pests and must be controlled for citrus growing to be successful. Virus diseases include tristeza, exocortis, xyloporosis, vein enation, and yellow vein. These are all transmitted by budding and grafting with infected wood, and some are distributed by insect vectors. Consequently, it is best to avoid infected propagating material and susceptible rootstocks. A disease caused by a mycoplasm-like organism (see p. 252) called stubborn is an important citrus disease in California. The only known control is disease-free propagating material. Fungal diseases attacking citrus are brown rot gummosis due to *Phytophthora*, brown rot of fruit, *Septoria* spot, and *Armillaria* root rot. Bacterial diseases are citrus blast and citrus canker. A disease of unknown origin called blight is causing serious tree losses in Florida, mostly of trees on rough lemon rootstock.

Date (*Phoenix dactylifera* L.) PALMAE (*14, 15, 16*)

The date palm is a tall, graceful, monocotyledenous evergreen tree growing to a height of 15 m (50 ft) or more, much prized for its nutritious fruits and its ornamental value. The species is dioecious, with male and female flowers borne on separate plants.

There is evidence that the date was cultivated in Mesopotamia (present-day Iraq) as early as 3000 B.C., and it was a principal food crop for the ancient eastern Mediterranean civilizations. It later spread across North Africa. The early Spanish missionaries brought the date to the Western Hemisphere where it later became established as a crop in the hot, dry interior valleys of southern California, southern Arizona, and northern Mexico. Starting about 1900, plant explorers of the USDA visited the date-growing regions of Iraq, Egypt, Tunisia, Algeria, and Morocco and brought back offshoots[1] of most of the best cultivars in each country. These were set out in experimental plantings in the Coachella Valley in California and the Salt River Valley in Arizona. The United States Date and Citrus Station was established by the USDA near Indio, California in 1904 to study the cultural problems of the date in the United States.

[1]Plants arising from axillary shoots, usually near the base of the palm. Detaching and replanting these offshoots is the principal means of propagating date palms.

Egypt is the world's leading date-producing country, closely followed by Iran and Iraq, which are the principal date-exporting countries. Commercial quantities of dates are also grown in Algeria, Tunisia, Saudi Arabia, Morocco, Israel, and Libya, with minor production in other suitable areas from India to Mauritania. In the United States, dates are grown on about 1600 ha (4000 ac) in California and some scattered plantings occur in southwestern Arizona and Texas.

The date palm withstands some winter cold, but is injured at temperatures below −7°C (20°F). To produce high-quality fruit, long, hot, dry summers with low humidity are required, as well as ample irrigation. The trees are grown as ornamentals in the climatic regions where the fruit produced is of poor quality.

Date palms grow on a wide range of soil types; a deep, well-drained, sandy loam is best. They tolerate soils more alkaline and saline than most other crop species, but do not produce the best tree growth and crops under such conditions.

The stem of the date tree has a single growing point, the terminal shoot tip, which gives the height increase. The long, 3 to 6 m (10 to 20 ft) leaves live for three to seven years and are shed slowly after they die, hanging for many years around the trunk. Under cultivation, dead leaves are cut off, leaving a whorl of 100 or more green leaves around the top; seven to eight leaves are required to develop each bunch of pollinated fruit.

Although the date palm is naturally wind-pollinated, pollen must be transferred artificially to the female flowers to ensure good fruit set. The 0.6 to 1.2 m (2 to 4 ft) long male inflorescence (spadix) produces hundreds of flowers and an abundance of pollen that can be collected easily by cutting the recently opened inflorescence and drying the flowers where bees cannot rob the pollen. Most date growers keep one good male tree for every 30 to 50 females and collect pollen as required. Pollen is dried in the shade and stored at about −18°C (0°F) for at least one year.

Female flowers are borne in a somewhat smaller inflorescence. When the spathe opens to expose the spadix, the female flowers are dusted either manually or mechanically with pollen. In California, most of the pollination is done in the period from late February to late April.

Fruit is thinned to improve fruit size and quality and to avoid severe alternate bearing. Usually about one-third of the spadix tip is removed at the time of pollination. When pollination is assured and the fruits are developed to perhaps 1 cm (0.5 in) in diameter, some center strands are removed. Out of a total of 8000 to 10,000 female flowers per spadix, 1000 to 1200 fruits are allowed to develop on Deglet Noor, the principal California cultivar.

The fruit stalk is carefully bent and tied to an adjacent leaf stalk to mitigate wind damage and help support the ripening fruit. When the fruit begins to change color from green to yellow or red, bunches are usually covered with paper wrappers, open at the lower end, to protect the fruit from rain and birds.

Many hundreds of date cultivars are grown in the Old World. Cultivars are classed by fruit type as soft, semidry, or dry. Different date-growing regions have developed and grown certain cultivars for centuries. Some of the most important, by country, are: Iraq—Zahidi, Sayer, Khadrawy, Halawy; Egypt—Saidy, Samani, Hayami, Zagloul; Algeria—Deglet Noor, Rhars, Mech Degla; United States—Deglet Noor, Medjool (originally from Morocco), Zahidi, Khadrawy.

In the United States dates are usually eaten only as ripe fruit. However, in the Old World date-growing areas several cultivars with low tannin content in the firm, colored (khalal) stage prior to softening are much appreciated as crisp, fresh fruit. A large part of the crop of 'Barhee', 'Samany', 'Hayany', 'Braim', and others is consumed fresh. Green and cull fruit at all stages of development is used as livestock feed.

Date cultivars are propagated only by cutting away and replanting the offshoots, which usually grow out from the main trunk near the soil level; above-ground offshoots root poorly unless girdled around the base. Neither cuttings nor grafts can be used with this monocotyledonous plant. Seed propagation is not feasible since the characteristics of the mother tree are not maintained in the female seedlings; about one-half of the seedlings are males.

Date palms are pruned only to remove the old flower stalks and leaves when they become brown and interfere with pollination and harvest operations. In the United States, the thorny spines are removed from the leaf bases to facilitate pollination and other operations but not in most Old World date-growing areas.

Manual harvesting lasts from several weeks to several months, depending upon the cultivar, as all of the fruits on a bunch do not mature at the same time and local microclimates affect ripening. Dates are usually left on the tree until they pass from the red colored stage to the amber-dark brown color of most mature dates, in order to allow full development of sugars and the loss of astringency. With care, fruit can be removed in the late khalal stage and ripened artificially. Keeping quality is best when the fruits have lost their watery consistency and have become pliable but not tough.

Mechanical harvesting, as practiced in the United States and Israel for the semidry cultivars Deglet Noor and Zahidi, requires that the fruit be left on the tree until fruit moisture is below 18 percent, when whole bunches can be removed in one or two harvests.

For home gardens, freshly harvested fruits are partially dried indoors with the drying completed in the sun. These fruits can then be stored for several years if protected from insects; storage in a home freezer is recommended. Commercially, dates are fumigated with methyl bromide immediately after harvest, cleaned by water sprays and roller brushes, and then dried in warm air currents. Some soft cultivars are only brushed or toweled. They are graded to remove culls and placed into uniform lots of ripeness, size, and appearance. If the fruits are not fully ripe, they can be placed in heated rooms at 27°C to 49°C (80°F to 120°F) for several hours or days to complete ripening. Following this, dates may be dehydrated by warm, circulating air, after which they will keep for many months without refrigeration. Fresh, nondehydrated dates can be stored for several weeks in a household refrigerator.

In the United States, Bank's grass mite is a serious pest of dates whose control requires two or more applications of sulfur dust. Nitidulid beetles and certain moths are controlled with malathion dust in which a fungicide is incorporated to control fruit rotting fungi, applied once or twice during the early harvest period. The paper wraps used to protect fruit bunches from rain prevents most fruit rot damage.

Fig (*Ficus carica* L.) MORACEAE (*4, 5, 14, 15, 28*)

The edible fig is a deciduous tree or bush. There are almost 2000 species in the genus *Ficus,* most of them evergreen and used as ornamentals.

The fig apparently was first brought into cultivation in the southern part of the Arabian peninsula by at least 3000 B.C. It later spread into what is now Iraq, Syria, and Turkey and on into all the Mediterranean countries. Along with the date, vinifera grape, and olive, the fig was an important food crop for the ancient civilizations of the eastern Mediterranean region. During the age of exploration following the discovery of America by Columbus the fig was taken to most subtropical areas of the Western Hemisphere. Spain is now the leading fig-producing country followed by Italy, Turkey, Greece, Portugal, and the United States. About 80 percent of U.S. production comes from California with small amounts grown in the Gulf states and extending to Virginia, often as home garden trees. About 85 percent of California's production is marketed as dried figs, 12 percent as canned, and 3 percent as fresh fruit. The United States imports about 3000 MT of figs annually from both Spain and Portugal.

Mature trees withstand winter temperatures of $-12°C$ to $-9.5°C$ (10°F to 15°F) depending on the cultivar, but young trees are not as cold resistant and may have to be protected by wrapping during the winter. For vigorous shoot growth to take place in the spring, buds of most *F. carica* cultivars require some winter chilling.

Fig trees grow well in a wide range of soils but do best in deep, nonalkaline clay loams. They respond to nitrogen fertilizers. In semiarid regions summer irrigation is required.

Some types of figs produce two crops a year. In the first or early summer crop, the fruits develop from latent flower buds on shoots produced the previous summer. This is termed the "breba" crop. In the second or late summer main crop, the fruits develop in the axils of leaves on shoots produced that same summer.

The edible fig is a strange "fruit." Fig. 30–2 helps explain its structure. Botanically it consists of vegetative peduncle tissue called a **syconium.** The true fruits are the tiny drupelets inside the cavity of the fused peduncles. There are four horticultural types of figs: (1) common, (2) San Pedro, (3) Smyrna—all producing only long-styled pistillate or female flowers—and (4) the inedible *caprifig* (producing both short-styled pistillate and staminate or male flowers).

In the common fig, the fruits are persistent, developing without the stimulation of pollination and fertilization. Consequently, they are apparently seedless. Some cultivars of this type are Kadota (Dottato), Mission, Adriatic, Brown Turkey, Celeste, and Conadria.

The San Pedro type produces the breba crop without pollination and fertilization of the flowers, but the second (late summer) crop develops only if the flowers have been pollinated—as described below for the Smyrna-type fig. San Pedro, King, and Gentile are cultivars of this type grown in California.

In the Smyrna-type fig the breba crop is usually not produced; the second crop develops only if the pistillate flowers

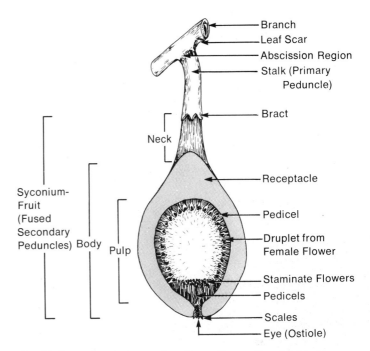

Fig. 30–2 Longitudinal section through a caprifig syconium showing the various parts. The short-styled female flowers line the inner wall of the syconium. The staminate flowers, shown here, near the ostiole are typical of the male caprifig. The edible fig syconium is similar to this but has only long-styled female flowers. *Source:* Adapted from Storey, W. B. Figs. In *Advances in fruit breeding,* eds. J. Janick and J. N. Moore. West Lafayette, Ind.: Purdue University Press.

within the syconium are pollinated with pollen carried from the male flowers of the caprifig syconium by the tiny *Blastophaga* wasp. When this is done, hundreds of tiny fruits with viable seed and a brittle endocarp form inside the syconium of the Smyrna-type fig. The 'Calimyrna' ('Lob Injir') fig is of this type, grown on about half the 6800 ha (17,000 ac) of figs in California. There are many more cultivars of the Smyrna type grown in the Mediterranean area. To attain pollination, fruit setting, and development of the edible syconia of the Smyrna-type fig, pollination (caprification) from the male caprifig by the *Blastophaga* wasp is necessary. Flowers of all edible figs produce no pollen. Pollen is obtained only from within the syconia of the inedible caprifigs, which are borne on caprifig trees, usually grown separately from the fruiting Smyrna-type trees. Pollen is actually transferred by the small wasp (*Blastophaga psenes*), which overwinters in the pollen-producing caprifig. These caprifigs (with the wasps inside) are gathered and placed in small bags or wire baskets that are hung in the fruiting Smyrna-type trees. The emerging wasps, covered with pollen, enter the Smyrna fruits and pollinate the long-styled pistillate flowers inside. Thus, for fruit setting of the Smyrna-type fig, caprifig trees are necessary as well as the *Blastophaga* wasp. For home gardens the common fig cultivars are preferred rather than the Smyrna-type fig cultivars with their complex pollination problems.

The fig is so easily propagated by hardwood cuttings that this is the usual method although all types of budding and grafting as well as air layering, are successful (see Ch. 5). Hardwood cuttings of two or three year wood 20 to 30 cm (8 to 12 in) long are best taken in later winter, treated with the root-promoting indolebutyric acid (see p. 100), then stored in moist packing material, like sawdust, at room temperature for about four weeks, then planted in the nursery with just the top bud showing.

Figs can be pruned to most any system since the second (main) crop is produced in the leaf axils of current season's shoots. Heavy dormant pruning reduces the first (breba) crop and may reduce the total crop, especially with the Smyrna type. Trees of some cultivars, if not kept pruned, can grow to a huge size with a spread of 30 m (100 ft) or more. In order to facilitate fruit harvesting, trees of others, like the 'Kadota', in California are kept small, low, and flat-topped, with a height of only 1.5 to 1.8 m (5 to 6 ft). Figs can easily be trained to an attractive espalier form against a wall.

For best flavor, figs grown in the home garden should not be picked until the fruits are soft and "wilt" at the neck, hanging down from their own weight. They are then fully mature and ripe and ready to eat. Milky latex exuding from the stem when the fruit is pulled off indicates the fruit is still immature. Fresh figs are extremely perishable and can be held only about a week at 0°C (32°F) with a 90 percent humidity. Fully matured figs can be either frozen or dried and still retain their flavor and color. For best drying allow the figs to become completely mature on the tree, with maximum sugar content. Complete the drying on trays in the sun, turning frequently.

Figs are susceptible to root knot nematodes, viruses, and endosepsis, a fruit rot in the Smyrna-type fig carried by the pollinating wasps. Birds feed on the developing fruits, and bees are attracted to the sweet juices from the fig "eye."

Kiwifruit (Chinese Gooseberry) (*Actinidia chinensis* Planch.) ACTINIDIACEAE (*2, 8, 20, 25*)

The kiwifruit is a native of south central China. The plants grow naturally as deciduous fruiting vines along the forest edges of the Yangtze Valley of China. Seeds were taken to New Zealand in 1906 where the plant was named the Chinese gooseberry. It became a commercial export crop in the 1950s. It was renamed the kiwifruit because of its resemblance to the native bird, the kiwi. New Zealand is the leading kiwifruit producer with fruits on the market from May through November. There is a growing interest in the kiwifruit as a new crop both in Europe and in California.

The kiwifruit vine is grown on 1.8 m (6 ft) trellises, much like a grapevine. They are very vigorous and are usually planted in rows 4.5 m (15 ft) apart with the plants set 6 m (20 ft) apart in the rows. Full bearing 10-year-old vines can yield 17 to 22 MT of fruit per ha (7 to 9 MT per ac) (Fig. 30–3).

The kiwifruit requires frequent irrigation throughout the summer. A deep, well-drained soil is best. Mature plants need about 188 kg of nitrogen fertilizer per ha (150 lb per ac) each year. Wind protection for the plants and trellises is needed to prevent broken shoots and scarred fruit.

Flowers, fruits, and shoots of the kiwifruit plant in active growth are damaged by temperatures of −1.5°C (29°F), but dormant, leafless canes of mature vines in winter withstand

Fig. 30–3 Good crop of kiwifruits on a trellised vine. Fruits are about 5 cm (2 in) in length. *Source:* Blue Anchor.

temperatures as low as −12°C (10°F). Kiwifruits can generally be grown wherever citrus is cultivated in the temperate zones. Kiwifruit requires some winter cold (300 to 500 hours below 7°C; 45°F), so it does not grow well in the tropics.

The kiwifruit is dioecious (male and female flowers borne on separate plants); about one male plant for every nine female plants—both blooming at the same time—is required for pollination. Pollen is transferred by insects, chiefly bees.

In both New Zealand and California the most popular fruiting cultivar is Hayward. In California the vines bloom in May and the fruits are harvested in November. The fruit, which is a matured ovary, is about the size of a large chicken egg. It has a greenish brown, rather unattractive skin, densely covered with short hairs. The firm but juicy flesh is an attractive emerald green color containing many small black edible seeds. The taste is difficult to describe; it is somewhat tart but with a delicate flavor seeming to blend citrus, gooseberry, strawberry, and pineapple.

The kiwifruit can be propagated by rooting leafy cuttings under mist after treating them with indolebutyric acid (see Ch. 5). They can also be propagated by T-budding in late summer or by whip or cleft grafting in the spring using one-year-old kiwifruit seedlings as rootstocks.

Vines of the kiwifruit are trained to a single trunk on the trellis with one arm, cane, or cordon in each direction (bilateral cordon) on three-wire trellises. Fruiting canes are allowed to develop every 0.3 to 0.6 m (1 to 2 ft) along the side cordons. Fruits develop from basal buds on the current season's shoots, which grew from last year's fruiting arms. Dormant pruning is required to remove old fruiting canes, leaving one- or two-year-old fruiting canes to produce the next year's crop. Summer pruning may be required to admit light to reduce excessive shading of fruiting wood.

Kiwifruits are considered ready to harvest when the soluble solids reach 8 percent. Properly protected with a fungicide, the fruits store well up to six months if cooled to 0°C (32°F) within 24 hours of harvest and if the relative humidity is held at 95 percent. Fruits are packed in trays covered with polyethylene sheets to prevent water loss and fruit shrivel during the long storage period. The fruits are usually eaten fresh but can also be preserved by canning or freezing. Kiwifruits have a very high vitamin C content—105 mg/100 gm, about double that of oranges.

In California there are a few serious insect and disease pests of kiwifruit; these are omniverous leaf roller, oak root fungus, phytophthora, and nematodes. Where nematodes occur, the soil should be fumigated before planting. In New Zealand the tortricid leaf roller caterpillar and greedy scale are the main insect pests. Botrytis and other fruit rots can be a problem in the stored fruits.

Olive (*Olea europaea* L.) OLEACEAE (*3, 6, 11, 21*)

The olive is an attractive evergreen tree with gray-green foliage. It was under cultivation long before the time of earliest recorded history, originating in the eastern Mediterranean area and providing ancient civilizations with one of their most valuable foods from the fruits and the oil. The olive was particularly valuable in those early days because it grew readily on a wide range of soils and tolerated the long, hot, rainless summers of the Mediterranean region. Its fruits are nourishing and the oil could be consumed or used as a fuel for lamps. Its ease of propagation by hardwood cuttings allowed perpetuation of superior types.

Olive trees live for many hundreds of years; if the tops die a new tree often develops from the roots. They grow in all areas of the world having a Mediterranean climate—that is, moderately cold winters and long, hot, low-humidity summers. Commercial olive production lies in those areas between 30° and 45° north and south latitudes where severe winters do not occur. Spain is the world's leading olive producer, followed by Italy, Greece, Tunisia, Turkey, and Portugal. Olives in the United States are produced only in California but this crop represents less than 1 percent of the total world production.

Olive trees are killed to the ground by temperatures below about −11°C (12°F). Most—but not all—cultivars require at least two months of winter chilling (daily fluctuating temperatures between about 1.5°C and 15.5°C (35°F and 60°F) for the flowers to initiate in the buds. The trees bloom in midspring, about eight weeks after the flower buds have been initiated.

Olive trees grow well on many different kinds of soil, from rocky shallow hillsides to deep fertile valley soils, from acid to fairly alkaline soils. They tolerate considerable salinity and boron. They do not withstand poorly drained soils, however, and quickly die if water stands around their roots for a few weeks. To obtain satisfactory tree growth and production, moderate annual nitrogen fertilizer application is required together with irrigation through the summer. In some soils olives respond to potassium and boron fertilizers.

All olive-producing countries have their own local cultivars many of which have been grown for centuries. Some leading oil cultivars are Picual, Frantojo, Cornicabra, Chem-

lali, and Souri. Prominent table olive cultivars are Manzanillo, Sevillano (Gordal), Ascolano, Conservolia, Calamata, and Galega.

Olive flowers are produced on inflorescences of about 15 flowers each that arise in the leaf axils of shoots that grew the previous summer. Most olive flowers are perfect; that is, each flower contains the pollen-producing anthers and the fruit-producing pistil. Very often, however, the pistil aborts, resulting in nonfruiting staminate flowers. The olive is wind-pollinated and trees of most cultivars set some fruit with their own pollen, but in many years fruit set is heavier if cross-pollination with trees of other cultivars is available. In some years olives tend to set so many fruits the trees cannot mature them properly. Fruit sizes are small, maturity is delayed, and usually the trees will not even bloom the next year—leading to an alternate bearing situation. In such cases fruits on overloaded trees should be thinned shortly after fruit set in the spring. This can be done by hand but spray thinning with an auxin-type material—naphthaleneacetic acid—(see Ch. 6) is more feasible.

Most olive cultivars can be propagated by cuttings, either hardwood cuttings planted directly in the nursery row or leafy, softwood cuttings rooted in mist propagating beds (see Ch. 5). Root initiation is greatly stimulated by applications of auxin-type chemicals (see p. 100). Olives can also be propagated by grafting or budding the scion cultivar onto rootstocks (seedlings or rooted cuttings) (see Ch. 5). Older trees can be easily top-worked by bark grafting to change cultivars.

Young olive trees should be pruned sparingly with the objective of establishing a central trunk with four or five well-spaced primary scaffold branches. Mature trees bear fruit laterally on shoots produced the previous summer, so moderate annual pruning is required to stimulate development of such fruiting shoots. Dead, diseased, broken, and interfering branches should be removed as required. As the trees become very old, they may lose vigor and productivity but by judicious heavy cutting back, new growth can be forced out that will again yield well.

The table olive crop is harvested in autumn when the fruits are a green to straw color. Fruits left on the tree until winter when they turn black and attain their maximum oil content are harvested for oil extraction. Olives as picked from the tree are very bitter and cannot be eaten because of a bitter glucoside in the raw fruits. This can be partially leached out with running water, or it can be neutralized by several repeat applications of a dilute alkaline solution such as 1.5 percent sodium hydroxide (lye), which must then be thoroughly washed out with water. If the olive fruits are exposed to the air during this process, phenolic compounds oxidize and the olives turn black and are sold as "black ripe" olives. If they are kept under the solution continually, they stay green and are sold as "green ripe" olives. Hot brine is added to the fruits, then they are canned and heated in a pressurized retort to a temperature of 115°C (240°F) for one hour to eliminate any toxic bacteria.

The Spanish-green fermented style of processed table olives, used primarily in the Mediterranean countries, involves a different treatment. The fruits are picked green, then treated briefly with lye to remove some of the bitterness, washed thoroughly, and transferred to barrels containing a 28° to 30° salometer brine solution. Lactic acid fermentation starts and continues for six to eight months. After this the olives are bottled in 28° salometer brine, then sealed. All types of commercial olive processing involve chemical reactions that must be carefully watched and controlled or considerable losses can occur.

Olive oil is extracted after the olives turn black on the tree in midwinter and reach their maximum oil content (20 to 30 percent). Harvested fruits are washed, then ground—skin, flesh, and pits—in crushers. The olive paste is then spread out in large mats of coconut fiber that are stacked up in layers six or eight high separated by screens and placed in a powerful hydraulic press. Several repeated slow pressings release a liquid consisting of water and olive oil, which is collected in large settling tanks. The oil rises to the top of the liquid and is drawn off. Bitterness is removed from the oil by washing with warm water, which is then separated from the oil by centrifuging. Filtering gives a final golden clear product.

Olives are subject to several insect and disease pests. In the Mediterranean countries the olive fly *(Dacus oleae)* and the olive moth *(Prays oleaellus)* are of most concern. These do not occur in California. Black scale *(Saissetia oleae)* can be severe on olives and is found in most olive-producing countries. Olives are attacked by a gall-producing bacteria *(Phytomonas savastanoi)*; they are also susceptible to two fungal diseases—verticillium wilt, which affects the tree's roots, and peacock spot *(Cycloconium oleaginum)*, which can defoliate the trees.

Persimmon (*Diospyros* spp.) EBENACEAE (*9, 19*)

There are a number of *Diospyros* species native to various parts of the world. The most important commercially is *Diospyros kaki* L.f., which originated in China and was imported into Japan about 750 A.D. Many introductions of this species were made into the United States following Commodore Perry's visit to Japan in 1853. Trees of the native American species (*D. virginiana* L.) grow naturally in the southeastern and southern Middle West. They produce small but very tasty fruits. There are some named cultivated types but most fruits are collected from wild, volunteer trees.

Cultivars of *D. kaki* are grown commercially and as home garden trees in mild subtropical or temperate climatic regions like the Mediterannean countries, Florida, and California. The trees do not survive winter temperatures below about −18°C (0°F). In Japan the persimmon is an important fruit crop, ranking second to citrus, with an annual production of about 450,000 MT. In the United States *D. kaki* cultivars are produced commercially in California, but fruit acreage has been declining from a peak reached about 1937.

The oriental persimmon is a small (6 to 9 m; 20 to 30 ft) attractive deciduous tree producing large orange-red fruits that mature in late fall. The trees grow well in a wide range of soils but do best in those that are deep and well drained. They may require nitrogen fertilization each year to maintain vegetative growth but excessive shoot growth—over 30 cm (12 in) per year—causes premature fruit drop. Irrigation is required in regions with rainless summers.

The two soft-fruited types of oriental persimmon cultivars are Hachiya, the favored one in California, and Tanenashi, mostly grown in the southern United States. Fuyu is a nonastringent, firm-fruited cultivar favored in Japan. It has flat, tomato-shaped fruits that can be eaten while still firm and buttery. 'Tanenashi' and 'Hachiya' fruits are larger and heart-shaped. *D. virginiana* fruits are small—about the size of a ping-pong ball and a dull orange when ripe.

'Hachiya' and 'Fuyu' trees generally produce only pistillate (female) flowers, but the fruits set parthenocarpically (without pollination) and are generally seedless. However, if a *D. kaki* persimmon tree with male, pollen-producing flowers is nearby, some of the female flowers of Hachiya or other cultivars may be pollinated and the resulting fruits have some seeds. Seeded fruits usually set better than the nonseeded.

D. kaki cultivars are best propagated by whip grafting on *D. kaki* seedling rootstocks, although they are easily T-budded (see Ch. 5).

Pruning and training are done to encourage formation of a structurally strong tree with wide-angled scaffold branches since the wood of *D. kaki* trees is naturally brittle and tends to break or split under heavy fruit loads. A modified leader form (see p. 304) is probably best. *D. kaki* flowers are borne on current season's growth. Sufficient annual pruning should be given to force 20 to 30 cm (8 to 12 in) of new growth each season, but excessive pruning results in long, rank shoots that are often unfruitful.

Mature fruits of all *D. virginiana* and most *D. kaki* cultivars are very astringent until properly ripened and allowed to soften. 'Hachiya' fruits, for example, are picked when the orange-red color starts to develop but when they are still firm enough to handle for market. As the fruits ripen and soften—at room temperature—the astringency disappears. It is not necessary that *D. virginiana* or *D. kaki* fruits be frosted to eliminate the astringency. Treatment of persimmon fruits with CO_2, ethylene, or vapors from alcoholic beverages promotes ripening and loss of astringency. Placing some persimmons in a plastic bag with one or two apples, ripe pears, or bananas and holding at room temperature for several days results in loss of astringency due to the ethylene released by the other fruits. Firm persimmons may be frozen whole in plastic bags and used as needed by simply thawing. When completely thawed they are soft and free of astringency. Astringency in persimmon fruits is generally due to tannin compounds. During ripening the tannins are bound into firm, insoluble particles that can no longer be tasted. Fruits of some *D. kaki* cultivars, such as Fuyu, are nonastringent when mature and can be eaten while still firm.

Freshly harvested, mature persimmon fruits can be stored for three to four months at −1°C (30°F) and 90 percent relative humidity.

Persimmon trees are remarkably free of insect and disease pests.

Pistachio (*Pistachia vera* L.) ANACARDIACEAE (*12, 17, 29*)

Pistachio is one of the most ancient nut crops. It was cultivated at least 3000 years ago in the low mountain regions of central Asia, Pakistan, and India, where wild trees can still be found. Iran, Turkey, Afghanistan, Italy, Syria, and Greece are the leading producers of pistachio nuts for export. In the United States pistachio nuts are produced commercially only in California where, in recent years, there have been many new plantings in the San Joaquin Valley. (Another species, *P. chinensis* Bunge., which originated in China, is a much larger, beautiful shade tree widely planted in subtropical zones, especially for its attractive fall leaf coloration.)

P. vera is a small to medium-size deciduous tree that can live for several hundred years. Tree growth and production are best in regions with long, hot, dry summers and moderately cold winters. The trees survive winter temperatures of $-18°C$ (0°F). Many subtropical and all tropical regions have insufficient winter cold to break the rest period of the buds, and, consequently, spring shoot growth is poor.

While pistachio trees survive on rocky, shallow soils in desert areas, they grow and yield best when planted in deep, well-drained sandy loams. They do well on highly calcareous soils and grow under conditions of alkalinity and salinity that would be detrimental to most other crops. Although pistachio trees stay alive under prolonged drought conditions, summer irrigation is necessary for good tree growth and productivity. For vigorous tree growth and good yields nitrogen fertilization is also required.

The pistachio is dioecious (male and female flowers borne on separate trees) so that in any planting some male trees must be included to provide adequate pollination (one pollinator tree for every 10 or 12 trees). Pollen is distributed by the wind. Pistachios exhibit alternate bearing—producing a heavy crop one year followed by a light or no crop the next.

In the commercial trade pistachio nuts are classified according to the country of their origin, but each producing country has a number of local cultivars, probably selected from superior seedlings and propagated vegetatively. In California, Kerman is the most widely planted female cultivar and Peters is the male cultivar most used for pollination.

P. vera cultivars are somewhat difficult to propagate, the usual method being T-budding (see p. 104) from midspring to fall with seedlings of *P. atlantica* or *P. terebenthis* as rootstocks. The rootstock seedlings must be growing vigorously and the vegetative buds should be large, taken from dark-colored budwood on bearing trees known to produce good crops.

Pistachio trees are trained to a modified leader or vase system with well-spaced lateral branches. Pistachio flowers and fruits are borne on previous season's growth, so pruning should be sufficient to force ample shoot growth each year. Small cuts should be made, thinning out weak, shaded branches or heading back excessively vigorous growth.

Pistachio nuts are drupes, like peaches or apricots, maturing in late summer or early fall. The outer "husk" is the exocarp and mesocarp (two outer layers of ovary wall). The hard thin, gray-white shell, which splits open just before nut maturity, is the endocarp. The part eaten is the embryo, consisting mainly of the two green cotyledons covered by a thin seed coat. Pistachio nuts are ready to harvest when the green or reddish husk becomes translucent and separates from the shell. The nuts are borne in clusters that can be picked up by hand but, in more rapid modern operations, machine shaking of the trees drops the nuts onto catching frames. The attached husks can be removed mechanically, and empty nuts are separated by flotation. Most nuts are marketed in the split shells.

The most troublesome disease attacking pistachios in California is due to the soil-borne fungus *Verticillium albo-atrum*. Plantings should not be made in soil previously planted to cotton, vegetables, or strawberries as it is likely to be contaminated with the *Verticillium* organism. Trees in poorly drained wet soils may become infected with a root disease caused by *Phytophthora* spp. As root knot nematodes also attack pistachios, fumigation is done before the trees are planted in infested soil. There are many serious insect pests of pistachio in the Near East countries, but few have appeared so far in California plantings.

Pomegranate (*Punica granatum* L.) PUNICACEAE (13, 14)

This deciduous shrub or small tree is one of the most ancient of fruits. It apparently originated in the region of present-day Iran and was held in great esteem for religious ceremonies by the ancient civilizations of the Middle East. It was referred to by the early Greek writers in their myths. Cultivation of pomegranates spread east to India and the Orient and west to all countries circling the Mediterranean Sea, where it became particularly popular in Spain. The city of Granada, Spain was named after the high-quality pomegranates produced there. It is now a popular fruit in the Far East, India, and in Iraq and Iran, where certain superior cultivars have been developed. Spanish missionaries brought the pomegranate to the New World shortly after Cortez conquered Mexico in 1521, then the Franciscan padres brought it to all the missions along the California coast in the 1700s.

All commercial U.S. production of pomegranates comes now from California, where about 600 ha (1500 ac) are grown. Pomegranates make handsome ornamentals because of their brilliant orange-red flowers in the spring, their shiny, bright-green leaves, and the large, red apple-shaped fruits ripening in the fall.

Pomegranates grow well on a wide range of soils and tolerate mild alkaline conditions. It is essentially a desert plant and survives long periods of drought, but for commercial production of high-quality fruits summer irrigation is required. Some nitrogen fertilization is also needed.

Local cultivars are used in the countries where the pomegranate is grown. In California the most widely planted, by far, is 'Wonderful', followed by 'Ruby Red', 'Early Red', and 'Granada', the latter two being patented. Pomegranates are apparently self-pollinated.

Pomegranates are easily propagated by cuttings, principally hardwood cuttings planted in outdoor nurseries in early spring. Leafy cuttings root easily in mist propagating beds in the summer. Seeds germinate readily, but the seedlings are variable and do not reproduce the cultivar.

The pomegranate can be allowed to grow as a bush for home garden use, but commercial growers prefer to train it as a single or multiple trunk tree. It suckers readily, so annual pruning should include sucker removal plus light thinning out of the top to encourage production of new fruiting spurs.

The pomegranate fruit is a round, apple-sized berry with a hard leathery rind that encloses many seeds. The edible part is the pulpy and juicy sac which surrounds the seed. The inner hard and stony seed coat encloses the embryo. The pulp is removed from the fruit and the red juice extracted by pressure. It can be used for flavoring or for making juice drinks or jelly.

Fruits mature in the fall and should be picked after they become full red and the juice attains a crimson color but before they split open. Often the attractive red fruits with attached calyx are just used for table decorations. Pomegranates store well and keep for about four months at 0°C (32°F) if the humidity is maintained at about 90 percent.

Pomegranates in California have few serious insect or disease problems.

REFERENCES

1. Bergh, B. O. 1975. Avocados. In *Advances in fruit breeding*, eds. J. Janick and J. N. Moore. West Lafayette, Ind.: Purdue University Press.

2. Beutel, J. A., F. H. Winter, S. C. Manners, and M. W. Miller. 1976. A new crop for California: kiwifruit. *Calif. Agr.* 30(10):5–7.

3. Chandler, W. H. 1958. *Evergreen orchards*. 2nd ed. Philadelphia: Lea & Febiger. Ch. 8, The olive.

4. Condit, I. J. 1955. Fig varieties: A monograph. *Hilgardia* 23(11):323–538.

5. ———. 1969. *Ficus: the exotic species*. Berkeley: Univ. of Calif. Div. Agr. Sci.

6. Cruess, W. V. 1958. *Commercial fruit and vegetable products*. 4th ed. New York: McGraw-Hill. Ch. 9, Pickling and canning of ripe olives.

7. Embleton, T. W., and W. W. Jones. 1966. Avocado and mango nutrition. In *Nutrition of fruit crops*, ed. N. F. Childers. New Brunswick, N.J.: Horticultural Publications.

8. Fletcher, W. A. 1971. Growing Chinese gooseberries. New Zealand Dept. Agr. Bul. 349.

9. Gould, H. P. 1942. The native persimmon. USDA Farmers Bul. 685.

10. Häfliger, E., ed. 1975. Citrus. Tech. Monograph No. 4. Basle, Switzerland: CIBA-GEIGY.

11. Hartmann, H. T., and K. W. Opitz. 1977. Olive production in California. Univ. of Calif. Div. Agr. Sci. Leaflet 2474.

12. Joley, L. E. 1979. Pistachio. In *Nut tree culture in North America*. ed. R. A. Jaynes. Hamden, Conn.: Northern Nut Growers.

13. LaRue, J. H. 1969. Growing pomegranates in California. Calif. Agr. Ext. Ser. AXT 305.

14. McGregor, S. E. 1976. Insect pollination of cultivated crop plants. USDA/ARS Handbook 496.

15. Mortesen, E., and E. T. Bullard. 1970. *Handbook of tropical and subtropical horticulture*. Agency for International Development. Washington, D.C.: U.S. Government Printing Office.

16. Nixon, R. W. 1951. Date culture in the United States. USDA Cir. 728.

17. Opitz, K. W. 1969. The pistachio nut. Univ. of Calif. Agr. Ext. Ser. AXT 315.

18. ———, and R. G. Platt. 1969. Citrus growing in California. Calif. Agr. Exp. Sta. Ext. Ser. Manual 39.

19. ———, and J. H. LaRue. 1973. Growing persimmons. Univ. of Calif. Agr. Ext. Ser. AXT 40–4.

20. ———, and J. Beutel. 1975. Kiwi propagation. *Proc. Inter. Plant Prop. Soc.* 25:63–65.

21. Philippe, J. M., and J. Humanes-Guillén. 1977. *Modern olive growing*. Rome: Food and Agricultural Organization of the United Nations.

22. Reuther, W., ed. 1967, 1968, 1973. *The citrus industry*, vols. 1–3. Berkeley: Univ. of Calif. Div. Agr. Sci.

23. ———. 1977. Citrus. In *Ecophysiology of tropical crops*, eds. P. de T. Alvim and T. T. Kozlowski, New York: Academic Press.

24. Sauls, J. W., R. L. Phillips, and L. K. Jackson, eds. 1977. The avocado: Proc. First Inter. Tropical Fruit Short Course. Gainesville: University of Florida.

25. Schroeder, C. A., and W. A. Fletcher. 1967. The Chinese gooseberry *(Actinidia chinensis)* in New Zealand. *Econ. Bot.* 21:81–92.

26. Smith, P. F. 1966. Citrus nutrition. In *Fruit nutrition*, ed. N. F. Childers. New Brunswick, N.J.: Horticultural Publications.

27. Soost, R. K., and J. W. Cameron. 1975. Citrus. In *Advances in fruit breeding*, eds. J. Janick and J. N. Moore. West Lafayette, Ind.: Purdue University Press.

28. Storey, W. B. 1974. Figs. In *Advances in fruit breeding*, eds. J. Janick and J. N. Moore. West Lafayette, Ind.: Purdue University Press.

29. Whitehouse, W. E. 1957. The pistachio nut—a new crop for the western United States. *Econ. Bot.* 11(4):281–321.

30. Ziegler, L. W., and H. S. Wolfe. 1975. *Citrus growing in Florida*. Gainesville: University Presses of Florida.

Tropical Fruit and Nut Crops

There are a great many tropical fruit and nut species. This chapter discusses the principal ones that have gained great popularity for their adaptability to many parts of the tropics, their high productivity and ease of culture, and their attractive, flavorful, easy-to-eat products. Some have become an indispensable part of the food supply in many households throughout the world.

There are other, lesser known tropical fruits and nuts that have for some reason not been brought into wide culture and distribution *(25, 33, 35)*. With sufficient research to overcome their difficulties or, perhaps, by hybridization to develop new forms, fruits of some of these other lesser known tropical species in the future will become commonplace in world markets. Some species deserving more consideration as potential tropical fruit crops, although unheard of by most people, are the durian, mangosteen, naranjilla, pejibaye, pummelo, soursop, and uvilla *(36)*. The mangosteen, for example, is often described as the world's best-flavored fruit, yet it is virtually unknown outside southeast Asia *(3)*.

Banana (*Musa acuminata* Colla.) MUSACEAE *(10, 12, 15, 37, 39, 41, 44)*

Bananas appear to have originated in southeast Asia, spreading to India, Africa, and finally to tropical America, which now supplies the bulk of the world's commercial shipments. Bananas are depicted in cave-temple wall paintings in India that can be traced back to 500 or 600 B.C., so they were cultivated at this time and probably much earlier.

Ecuador, Honduras, Costa Rica, and Panama are the leading banana-producing countries, although commercial plantings are increasing in the Philippines. The United States, Japan, West Germany, France, and the United Kingdom are the chief banana-importing countries. Bananas, along with grapes, oranges, and apples, represent the world's most important fruit crops. Bananas, both the sweet dessert cultivars and the starchy cooking plantain types (*M. paradisiasa* L.) are important food items throughout the tropics. Cooking bananas, however, seldom reach temperate zone markets. Bananas arrive at the world's markets the year around.

Bananas thrive and yield best in tropical regions where temperatures average from 27°C to 29°C (80°F to 85°F), not dropping below 15°C (60°F) nor rising above 35°C (95°F). A frost kills banana leaves and cool temperatures—10°C to 13°C (50°F to 55°F)—impair fruit quality. Bananas require constant soil moisture. If rainfall is inadequate, irrigation, preferably from high overhead sprinklers, is essential for good production. Bananas have a high nitrogen and potassium fertilizer requirement in a ratio of 1:3 to 1:5 for good yields in most soils.

The banana is a giant monocotyledenous herbaceous perennial plant with an underground, horizontal rhizome from which roots develop. This rhizome is the banana's true stem. The pseudostems, which reach a height of up to 6 m (20 ft) comprise many overlapping leaf sheath bases. New rolled leaves emerge through the center of previous overlapping leaf bases. Each individual leaf is about 2.4 m (8 ft) long and 0.6 m (2 ft) wide, making it one of the largest photosynthetic units known. After approximately 40 leaves have been produced—about nine months after planting the sucker—the plant enters a reproductive phase and the vegetative apex inside the leaf sheath changes to a floral apex. This grows rapidly pushing the inflorescence out the top of the pseudostem. Each inflorescence contains 5 to 13 groups of flowers (''hands'') with each group enclosed in a floral bract. The hands are made up of double rows of ''fingers'' (Fig. 31–1).

In the commercial edible banana cultivars there are three types of flowers borne along the inflorescence stem: (1) a large group of female flowers that result in the parthenocarpic seedless fruits (fruits that develop without fertilization of the egg); (2) beyond this, a small group of hermaphroditic flowers (having both male and female parts); and (3) male flowers only.

Fig. 31–1 *Left:* A banana fruit stalk at an early stage of development. *Right:* Cluster of mature fruits ready for harvest. The entire fruit stalk will be cut off by the sharpened chisel on the end of a pole. Note that the individual banana fruits have turned upward during their development. *Source:* United Brands Company.

After emerging from the top of the pseudostem, the inflorescence turns and hangs downward because of its weight so that the developing banana fruits are at the top of the inflorescence stalk and the nonfruiting sterile portion below. The fingers are negatively geotropic and gradually turn upward during the first week or 10 days. In cultivation the nonfruiting inflorescence tip is often removed so as not to attract insects. About 80 to 120 days or longer are required for the fruits to mature enough for harvest.

Banana harvesting begins about nine months after planting, which is considerably less than for most tree fruit crops. Although each pseudostem produces fruits but once before dying, a banana planting can exist for many years as a succession of new pseudostems arising from buds along the underground, horizontal rhizome.

The seedless edible banana cultivars must be propagated vegetatively. The best propagating material for setting out new plantations is the sword suckers 0.3 to 0.9 m (1 to 3 ft) tall, which arise from the rhizome alongside the older plants. These plus the rhizome are cut off and planted, with new roots de-

veloping from the base of the leaf sheaths. Suckers should be taken only from plantings free of burrowing nematodes and bunchy top virus.

Over the world there are about 300 named banana cultivars (many are synonyms), but the most important shipping bananas are the seedless triploid cultivars of the Cavendish subgroup, including the Valery, Giant Cavendish, and Robusta. These are resistant to fusarium wilt (Panama disease), a problem that has plagued banana producers for many years. Growing these resistant, but tender, cultivars starting in the 1950s required the shipment of the bananas in protective cartons rather than as loose bunches. Before this the fusarium-susceptible 'Gros Michel' was grown. Its compact stems withstood the long journey to market as uncrated individual bunches without bruising.

Bananas are harvested when the fruits are fully mature but still hard and solid green (Fig. 31–2). They do not ripen well if left on the plants. The bananas' ''hands'' are cut into clusters of 4 to 16 ''fingers'' for shipping to importing countries in 40 lb polyethylene-lined cartons. Upon arrival at dis-

622

Fig. 31–2 Mature banana plantation showing a tramway in action carrying fruit stalks from the farmer to the boxing station. *Source:* United Brands Company.

tributing centers the cartons first go to ripening rooms where temperatures are held between 13.5°C and 16.5°C (56°F and 62°F) with relative humidity between 85 and 95 percent. At this time low amounts, 0.1 percent (1000 ppm) of ethylene gas is introduced into the sealed rooms and left for 24 hours. One special "lecture" tube, containing 0.09 m³ (3 ft³) of ethylene, is opened into each 90 m³ (3000 ft³) of volume of ripening space. This triggers the natural ripening of the bananas, and skin color changes from green to yellow. In warm weather the bananas are moved to the retail shelves just as the yellow color appears, but in cold weather the fruit is allowed to attain a more pronounced yellow before going to the markets. Good fruit storage temperatures after ripening are 13°C to 16°C (56°F to 60°F). Bananas are ready to use when a full yellow color is attained but best flavor and nutritive value develops when flecks of brown appear on the skin surface. The banana is a highly nutritious food, higher in energy value than most fruits other than the avocado.

The most serious problem in growing bananas was the Panama disease, caused by certain *Fusarium* species, soil-borne organisms that spread from plant to plant, causing them to wilt and die. However, resistant Cavendish type cultivars are now grown. Cercospora leaf spot and bunchy top virus are also problems in some banana growing countries. Although there are few serious insect pests, the burrowing nematode can significantly reduce yields. Wind damage can be serious in banana plantations in windy areas. 'Dwarf Cavendish', a small Cavendish type, is widely grown in Hawaii, South Africa, and other places where wind is a problem.

Cacao (*Theobroma cacao* L.) STERCULIACEAE (*4, 8, 12, 25, 28, 42*)

Cacao is believed to be native to the upper Amazon region in South America and possibly to Central America. It was first cultivated by the Mayan and Aztec civilizations of tropical Central America who used the ground beans to make a cocoa beverage. Columbus, on his fourth voyage in 1502, took cacao beans back to Spain. The beverage was improved considerably by the addition of sugar. Spain kept the secret of this new drink for about 100 years, but it gradually spread over Europe and became very popular.

Cacao production has developed into a billion dollar industry of worldwide importance in the manufacture of cocoa and chocolate. Until about 1900 most cacao plantations were in Central and South America and the Caribbean islands. In 1880, however, cacao was introduced into West Africa where it started on small farms of 0.8 to 2.0 ha (2 to 5 ac) each. Production in this region increased phenomenally so that world cocoa production jumped from 100,000 MT in 1900 to over 1 million MT by 1970. Ghana is the leading producer, followed by Brazil, Nigeria, and the Ivory Coast. The United States imports 25 percent of the world production; Germany, 13 percent; and the United Kingdom, 10 percent.

Cacao trees are broad-leaved evergreens that grow to a height of 4.5 to 7.5 m (15 to 25 ft). They require a truly tropical climate, with most production areas located within 15° of the equator and at altitudes below 300 m (1000 ft). Cacao trees grow best at a mean annual temperature varying between 21°C to 27°C (70°F to 80°F) with an absolute minimum of 10°C (50°F). Production is highest in areas with high humidity and rainfall well distributed throughout the year (about 127 to 152 mm; 5 to 6 in per month) and with little or no dry season. Winds are harmful to cacoa trees—increasing water loss from the leaves and causing defoliation—so that windbreaks are often used. Cacao trees, like some other tropical crops (coffee and tea), are usually grown in the shade of taller trees, planted especially for this purpose or retained when forests are cleared for new plantings. The optimum degree of shade depends upon the fertility of the soil. On fertile or fertilized soils, no shade is needed and yields increase.

Cacao trees grow best in deep, slightly acid soils, high in organic matter, well drained but with a high water holding capacity. Heavy clay soils are unsuitable. Cacao trees respond to nitrogen, phosphorus, and potassium fertilizers when shade is reduced or removed.

Cacao plantings consist largely of seedling trees that develop a wide, branching growth habit and start bearing at two to six years of age. Some high-yielding clones have been developed that are propagated vegetatively by rooting cuttings. The flowers and fruit are borne directly on the older, leafless parts of the branches and on the trunk (Fig. 31–3). Flowering and fruiting may occur throughout the year, determined largely by the rainfall pattern, but harvest is mostly from September to March.

Cacao flowers are perfect (with both stamens and pistils) and may be self- or cross-pollinated for fruit setting. Pollen is believed to be transferred by various small insects working the flowers. Lack of adequate cross-pollination may sometimes limit crop production.

The approximately 6000 flowers forming on a mature

Fig. 31–4 A mature cacao fruit cut open to show the seeds (''beans'') inside. *Source:* USDA.

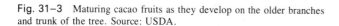

Fig. 31–3 Maturing cacao fruits as they develop on the older branches and trunk of the tree. Source: USDA.

tree develop into 20 to 40 podlike oval fruits 10 to 50 cm (4 to 12 in) long containing 20 to 60 seeds, each surrounded by a sweet, white mucilage (Fig. 31–4). A good yield is 270 kg (600 lb) of dry beans (seeds) per acre, but yields of over 1350 kg (3000 lb) per acre have been obtained from improved cultivars. The pods are harvested weekly when they change to a red or yellow color. They are cut open when fully ripe to remove the seeds (Fig. 31–4). The mucilaginous pulp around the seeds is removed by a fermentation process, which takes three to eight days and causes temperatures to rise to about 51°C (125°F). This kills the embryo in the seeds and develops certain chemical precursors that give the chocolate flavors when the beans are later sun-dried and finally roasted. Cocoa has mild stimulating properties from its theobromine and caffein.

Cacao trees, especially the pods, are attacked by *Phytophthora palmivora,* producing a disease called black pod, as well as by several other fungus pathogens, such as *Marasmius* spp., which cause a witch's broom disease. A viral disease called swollen shoot has caused great damage in West Africa. Several insect pests also attack cacao.

Cacao is the name of the plant.
Cocoa is the name of one of the products.

Cashew (*Anacardium occidentale* L.)
ANACARDIACEAE (*6, 8, 10, 12, 22, 23, 24, 31*)

The cashew is native to eastern Brazil, but it is now cultivated in all tropical areas of the world. It was taken by early Portuguese explorers to colonies in western India and East Africa about 1500. The delicious cashew is one of the most important nuts of commerce. The largest producing areas are southern India, Kenya, Tanzania and Mozambique in East Africa (where it has formed natural forests covering thousands of hectares), and northeastern Brazil. Most cashew production formerly came from volunteer seedling trees on poor land in foothill areas of southwestern India. Cashew processing installations had been built in these regions and whole cashews were formerly shipped from Africa to India for processing. Mozambique has since about 1965 surpassed India in cashew production and has become the main source of cashew nuts for the United States. Russia and its Eastern Europe neighbors lead in the importation of cashews from India.

The cashew is a good example of a species that has become an important crop in areas to which it was transplanted while receiving, until recent years, little attention in its native region. However, in every country where the cashew is a major crop and foreign exchange earner, the industry depends upon government subsidies.

The cashew is a somewhat straggly, drought-resistant, broad-leaved evergreen, ranging from a small shrub in poor, dry soils to a 12 m (40 ft) tree in fertile soil with ample moisture. Young trees are very tender to cold but when mature withstand light frosts.

Cashew flowers are borne in terminal panicles of 300 or more flowers each, having both staminate (male) and hermaphroditic (male and female) flowers in a ratio of about six to one or less. Only about 5 percent of the latter type develop into fruits. Each flower has one ovary, which contains one ovule. Flowers are self-fruitful and can be either wind or insect pollinated.

The cashew fruit (see Fig. 31–5) is attached at the end of the cashew "apple," which is actually the swollen pedicel, or fruit stem. This "apple" is 7 to 10 cm (3 to 4 in) long and about 5 cm (2 in) wide, red or yellow in color at maturity, and is eaten as a popular "fruit" by the natives where cashews are grown. The kidney-shaped cashew nut of commerce is the seed (with the seed coats removed) produced inside the true fruit, which has a two-layered ovary wall or shell. Between the two layers are cells containing a phenolic resin or oil that has valuable industrial uses but is extremely irritating to human tissues, internal and external.

Cashew trees are usually grown from seeds planted in place in the field. Two or three seedlings emerge in each position, later thinned to the most vigorous one. Seeds for planting should be taken from trees bearing large crops of high-quality nuts. Cashews can also be propagated vegetatively by approach grafting, budding, or by air layering (see Ch. 5). In Venezuela side veneer grafting has proved successful and is employed to multiply selected clones.

The cashew industry will not develop to its fullest potential until the primitive practice of cultivating variable and unproductive trees raised from seeds has been replaced by vegetative propagation methods so that the commercial plantings will consist of uniform trees giving high predictable yields of high-quality nuts.

Fig. 31–5 Group of cashews as harvested from the tree. *A:* Enlarged fleshy fruit stem or pedicel, called the cashew apple. *B:* True cashew fruit containing the seed or "nut" inside. *Source:* USDA.

The trees start bearing by the second or third year and are in full production by the tenth year. They may live for another 20 years. Yields can range from 0.5 to 45 kg (1 to 100 lb) of nuts per tree per year.

In processing, the nuts are first soaked to achieve uniform humidity, then de-oiled (roasted). In hand processing, which is still done in some regions of India, the shells are cracked by wooden hammers by skillful persons who can do this without damaging the kernel (seed) inside. The kernels are dried at about 68°C (155°F), and the seed coat is peeled off by hand. In Africa shelling is largely mechanized in factories using machines developed in Italy, Germany, and England. Such machines have also been in use since about 1970 in northeastern Brazil and more recently in Central America.

Up until about 1923 weevil infestations in transit practically prohibited shipments to distant countries. A process for replacing the air in hermetically sealed containers with carbon dioxide eliminated such losses. Now, after roasting and salting, the kernels are vacuum-packed for retail distribution.

Cashew trees are subject to several fungal diseases, chiefly anthracnose. There are also several troublesome insect pests such as thrips and capsid bugs.

Coconut (*Cocos nucifera* L.) PALMAE (*8, 10, 12, 22, 29, 46*)

The coconut is by far the most important nut crop in the world, used for its copra, from which coconut oil is extracted. It is a tall unbranched monocotyledonous tree (palm) grown throughout all the tropical regions (Fig. 31–6). The native home of the coconut is difficult to determine since over the centuries the nuts (seeds) have been so easily dispersed by early ocean voyagers and by ocean currents from island to island and continent to continent. Some believe it originated in the islands of the Malaysian Archipelago, but others believe it had a Central American origin.

It is estimated that there are about 3.4 million ha (8.5 million ac) of coconuts, of which 0.98 million are in the Philippines, 0.64 in India, 0.6 in Indonesia, 0.43 in Ceylon, and 0.24 in various South Sea islands. In the United States coconuts are grown to a limited extent in Florida and Hawaii as well as in Puerto Rico. World coconut production has been increasing at about 5 percent per year.

Although the coconut is a tropical plant with commercial production within 15° of the equator, it grows and fruits some distance from the equator, as shown by plantings in southern Florida at a latitude of 26° north. Coconuts withstand some frost. Growth and production are best under high humidity with mean annual temperatures around 26.5°C (80°F) and daily fluctuations of no more than 5°C. The coconut palm is a light-requiring tree and does not grow well under shade or in very cloudy conditions.

Coconuts need ample, well-distributed soil moisture and suffer from long, rainless periods. Annual rainfall of at least 1524 to 1778 mm (60 to 70 in) is required although irrigation can be used to supplement low rainfall. The trees grow in a wide range of soil types—beach sand, coral rock, or rich muck—provided they are at least 1.2 m (4 ft) deep. Coconuts tolerate high salt levels in the soil and salt sprays as are found along the seashores. Shallow soils with a high water table, which prevents good root development, are unsuitable since the tall palms are likely to blow over in tropical typhoons and hurricanes.

Coconut palms respond to nitrogen and potassium fertilizers and, in some soils, to phosphorus although in many naturally fertile soils no benefits have been obtained from added fertilizers. Little is known of their need for trace elements.

The coconut tree has a tall flexible trunk marked by leaf scars and topped by a crown of leaves (Fig. 31–6). Each leaf is about 6 m (20 ft) long with a central midrib and about 100 opposite leaflets. A growing point in the central crown produces new leaves and flowers. This growing point is the only bud on the palm; hence if it is killed, death of the entire palm follows. These growing points, called hearts of palm, are a

Fig. 31–6 Grove of bearing coconut palms in Hawaii. *Source:* USDA.

very nutritious and tasty food product, reminiscent of artichoke hearts. Trees of some palm species, including the coconut palm, can be grown specifically for this product, even though extracting it kills the tree.

Coconut palms start flowering about the fifth year and continue to flower throughout the year from then on. Both male and female flowers are borne on the same many-branched inflorescence arising from a leaf axil in the top of the palm. Each inflorescence can have up to 8000 male flowers along the terminal part of the inflorescence and one to 30 globular female flowers near the base. Transfer of pollen from the male to the female flowers by wind, birds, or various insects is required for nuts to develop.

The coconut fruit is classed as a drupe—just as is the fruit of the peach or apricot. The hard shell commonly seen when one buys a coconut in the stores is the inner layer of the matured ovary wall of the fruit—the endocarp. Outside of this is the husk—the mesocarp plus exocarp—which is usually removed when the nuts are harvested. Inside the shell (endocarp) is the true seed with a thin brown seed coat. The white "meat" of the coconut is part of the endosperm, a food storage tissue. The coconut "milk" is also endosperm in a liquid form. The tiny embryo is buried under one of the three "eyes" in the endosperm at the end where the fruit was attached to the plant. The coconut is mature and ready to eat about a year after pollination of the flower.

There are no named clonal cultivars of the coconut. All trees are propagated by seed since no parts of the tree can be used for vegetative propagation. The coconut palm does not produce "offsets" as does the date palm (see p. 613). Tree characteristics of the coconut are reproduced fairly well by seed, however, so that the best strategy is to select seeds for new plantings from trees that produce large crops of high-quality nuts. There are some seed-propagated cultivars where the seeds are gathered from isolated groves of trees that all have similar characteristics. There are also self-pollinating dwarfed selections that bear early and give high yields, flowering in three to four years from seed.

Coconuts (still enclosed in the husk) are usually germinated in a seedbed. Fully matured nuts (at least 12 months old) are planted flat on their sides and covered to about their depth with soil. They must be kept moist to germinate. The embryo grows out through one of the "eyes," with roots developing at the base of the sprout and growing down through the husk. After 8 to 10 leaves have formed, the new plant plus the husk is transplanted to its permanent location with trees set about 7.5 m (25 ft) apart.

The edible part of the coconut is the white endosperm, usually eaten fresh and raw, plus the liquid endosperm—the "milk." Much more important is the dried endosperm—known in the trade as copra. This is used principally as a source of coconut oil, the most widely used vegetable oil after soybean oil.

To prepare copra the husk is removed by knives that also split the nut in two. The "milk" is not saved. The open halves of the nuts are turned upward and stacked in trays to dry. After 4 to 6 days the "meat" is pried out with special spoons then further dried in the sun or artificially in heated kiln dryers until the moisture content is about 5 percent. The dried product—copra—is then chopped into uniform small pieces, sacked, and delivered to large processing plants for extraction of the oil. These may be located in overseas industrialized countries or in the cities, like Manila, of the producing countries. Fresh coconut meat contains from 35 to 50 percent oil. In general, 1000 full-sized coconuts yield 225 kg (500 lb) of copra that produce 95 l (25 gal) of oil. Dried copra can be stored under refrigeration below 10°C (50°F) for several months. The copra cake left after oil extraction is ground to a meal that is a high-protein cattle feed.

The United States imports most of the world's coconut oil, followed by West Germany and the United Kingdom. Coconut oil is one of the most widely used oils. It has a high degree of fat saturation and has good stability. Coconut oil has both edible and inedible uses. It is used in the preparation of margarines, shortenings for cooking, frying oils, and imitation dairy products. Coconut oil is also used in the manufacture of liquid and solid soaps and detergents, cosmetics, hair oil, and various lubricants.

Coconut trees are highly susceptible to various diseases. Viruses have eliminated entire plantations. Lethal yellowing, thought to be caused by a mycoplasma-like organism, is particularly severe in the Caribbean area and has killed thousands of acres of coconut palms. No control is known. A similar disease has occurred in West Africa. In the Philippines a disease called cadang-cadang has wiped out many large coconut plantations. *Phytophthora palmivora* fungus can kill the terminal growing point, leading to the death of the entire palm. Bronze leaf wilt causes death of the older leaves, working its way to the younger leaves. It is a nonpathogenic problem due to unfavorable weather conditions, often appearing after a long drought.

There are insect pests that attack coconut palms, but only a few are serious and these can generally be controlled by sanitary measures. A rhinoceros beetle, which attacks the terminal bud and thus kills the palm, is considered a serious pest in many coconut-growing areas.

Coffee (*Coffea arabica* L.) RUBIACEAE (*8, 10, 12, 19, 22, 27*)

The coffee tree is believed to be indigenous to Ethiopia in tropical East Africa, possibly to the Kaffa province. The Arabs were using coffee as a beverage as long ago as 600 A.D. and introduced it to the Mediterranean countries about 1500. It found its way into western Europe about 1630 (tea was first used there about 1610 and cocoa about 1528).

Coffee plants were brought to Brazil in 1727 and, after 40 years, it became, and still is, the world's leading coffee grower and exporter, now producing one-third of the world's coffee supply—about 1.5 million tons annually. Colombia ranks second in coffee production with about 0.5 million tons annually. The African countries of Angola, Uganda, Ivory Coast, and Madagascar together produce about 0.8 million tons annually, mostly of a different species, *C. canephora* (*C. robusta*). This is a cheaper, less flavorful coffee, but it is now in great demand for use in blending with *C. arabica* coffees and in the manufacture of instant coffees. *C. liberica* is an important species in some areas but produces an inferior coffee. Mexico, El Salvador, and Guatemala each produce about 0.1 million tons of coffee per year. Coffee is the mainstay of the economy of the Central American countries. Coffee is grown to a limited extent in Puerto Rico and Hawaii. Production of the famous Hawaiian Kona coffee has been declining in recent years because of high production costs. Young coffee seedlings are occasionally grown in the warmer parts of the United States as attractive ornamentals.

The United States consumes about one-third of the world's coffee, importing about 1.5 million tons annually, about 7.2 kg (16 lb) per person. Other heavy coffee consuming countries are West Germany, Italy, France, Sweden, the Netherlands, and Britain.

Coffee plantations are generally located in selected areas with optimal growing conditions between 21° north and south latitudes. In Colombia coffee is produced on small family farms less than 3.2 ha (8 ac) in size on mountainsides ranging from 900 to 1800 m (3000 to 6000 ft) above sea level.

C. arabica trees withstand temperatures near 0°C (32°F) for only a short period. Frost is one of the principal hazards in growing coffee. Cold-damaged trees that have been exposed to temperatures below freezing have considerable difficulty in recovering. Optimal growing temperatures are between 17°C (61°F) and 23°C (74°F). Temperatures above 27°C (80°F) tend to reduce flowering and fruiting, while temperatures below about 13°C (55°F) cause cessation of growth and tree stunting.

Coffee trees need a continual soil moisture supply. Annual rainfall of about 1650 mm (65 in) is required although supplemental irrigation can be given in drought periods.

In many countries other than Brazil and Hawaii, coffee trees are planted in the shade of other tall-growing trees. Coffee, apparently, has a low light saturation level for photosynthesis, so the trees grow adequately in the shade. However, sun-grown coffee trees give the highest yields provided all other cultural factors, particularly soil fertility, are optimal. *C. arabica* trees grown at higher elevations—900 to 1800 m (3000 to 6000 ft)—where the temperatures are somewhat cooler produce a milder type bean, from which a better drink can be prepared, than trees grown at lower and hotter elevations.

Coffee trees and their foliage are tender and are quickly torn apart by strong winds. Wherever such winds blow, rows of windbreak trees are used.

The trees grow best in a slightly acid, loamy soil at least 0.9 m (3 ft) deep with good aeration and drainage. To grow and yield well coffee trees require a high level of soil fertility. They readily show symptoms of a lack of any of the essential elements. Plantations grown without added fertilizers show a steady decline in production. Coffee growers would ideally learn to recognize deficiency symptoms and apply the proper fertilizers. Deficiency symptoms of all the essential mineral elements have appeared in coffee plantations *(27)*. Coffee yields vary considerably—from about 2240 kg/ha (2000 lb/ac) of "clean" coffee (beans removed from the fruit) in Hawaii to only 400 kg/ha (360 lb/ac) in Brazil.

Most coffee trees now in bearing are seedling trees, grown in a nursery for one year before planting in the field. *C. arabica* is self-fertile and tends to reproduce fairly true from seed so that several seed-propagated cultivars have been developed such as Mondo Novo and Caturra in Brazil, Villalobos and Hibrido in Central America, and Moko in Saudi Arabia. *C. canephora* trees are self-sterile and depend upon cross-pollination, so the seedlings vary considerably.

Coffee trees are planted about 2.4 m (8 ft) apart and are kept low—about 1.8 m (6 ft) by pruning to facilitate harvesting. They start bearing full crops on the lateral branches at about 5 years and reach full production at 15. Clusters of 2 to 20 perfect flowers (both male and female parts) are produced in the leaf axils. The white flowers are very attractive and fragrant. Pollination is accomplished by wind or insects. Fruits develop in clusters at the nodes and are ready for harvest six to seven months after bloom.

Botanically the coffee fruit is a drupe—similar to a peach or apricot—except that within each fruit is a mucilaginous pulp covering two thin, fibrous parchment-like "pits" (endocarp), each surrounding a single seed. The two greenish seeds (the coffee "beans") in each fruit consist mostly of a hard, thick, and folded endosperm food storage tissue covered with a thin silvery seed coat. The tiny embryo in the seed is embedded in one end of the endosperm. The fruits (called "cherries" by the growers) first are green, then become dark red when ripe.

Harvesting of coffee begins in Brazil in May at the end of the rainy season. In harvesting the coffee fruits, which are all picked by hand, the pickers must remove only the mature red fruits, leaving the green ones for further development (Fig. 31–7). A coffee tree may have blossoms, green fruit, and ripe fruit all at the same time on the same branch. An average coffee tree yields about 2.25 kg (5 lb) of ripe fruits (converting to about 0.5 kg; 1 lb of roasted, ground coffee). Following harvesting the pulp must be removed from the coffee "cherries" to obtain the seeds ("beans") inside. There is both a dry and a wet process for this. In the dry process the fruits are washed, then spread out on concrete slabs in the open sun to dry, being turned several times a day. Following this they are repeatedly run through fanning and hulling machines to free the coffee beans inside. In the wet process the "cherries" are run through a depulping machine that breaks them open and squeezes the beans out of the pulpy skin. They then go into large tanks for 24 to 40 hours where the jelly-like substance surrounding the beans ferments slightly. Then the beans are thoroughly washed, spread out in the sun to dry, and continually turned and mixed.

Fig. 31–7   Harvesting coffee fruits. Coffee trees are nearly five years old before they produce a usable crop. The total annual yield of the average tree amounts to only a single pound of coffee after roasting. *Source:* National Coffee Association of U.S.A.

In wet weather, drying machines are used, tumbling the beans in perforated drums through which warm air is blown.

After they are well dried, the coffee beans are inspected to remove any that are defective, then are packed into 60 kg (132 lb) bags for shipment to coffee-importing countries. Different types of coffee are often blended together by the purchasers. Roasting the green coffee beans develops the characteristic tastes and color and must be skillfully done. Coffee purchases are often based on quality as determined by taste tests by highly trained coffee tasters on sample lots of roasted and ground coffee. Millions of bags of unroasted coffee beans are shipped to the consuming countries each year for blending, roasting, grinding, and packing. Marketing of coffee produced by thousands of small farmers must necessarily be done by cooperative organizations. In Colombia, for example, the National Federation of Coffee Growers represents the growers in marketing agreements and conducts research in coffee production and processing.

Many disease and insect pests affect coffee trees. Probably the worst disease is the leaf-rust fungus (*Hemileia vastatrix*). This rust first appeared in Ceylon in 1869 and destroyed all coffee plantations throughout the island and spread to other coffee producing countries in that part of the world. Coffee planters in Ceylon dared not risk replanting coffee so turned to tea, developing Ceylon into the world's second largest tea producer (India is first). Vigorous trees well fertilized with nitrogen seem to resist coffee leaf rust, and sprays with copper compounds aid in controlling the fungus. Coffee rust appeared in Central American countries in the mid-1970s and could develop into a devastating problem for coffee growers and the economies of these countries. The coffee bean borer (*Stephanodores*) is a problem in Brazil where it is referred to as the coffee plague. The coffee leaf miner and the Mediterranean fruit fly commonly attack coffee trees in some countries.

Macadamia (*Macadamia integrifolia* Maiden & Betche) PROTEACEAE (*8, 9, 10, 22, 32, 34, 35, 40, 43*)

This attractive, nut-producing, evergreen tree is native to eastern tropical Australia where it was discovered in 1857. It was introduced into Hawaii in 1878 and used as an ornamental until the 1920s when the first commercial plantings were made. In Hawaii, which is now the leading macadamia-producing area, it has developed into an important crop where, in 1975, 4160 ha (10,400 ac) had been planted, including over 2400 ha (6000 ac) of nonbearing trees. The macadamia has become the third most important crop in Hawaii—after sugarcane and pineapples. The macadamia is also grown in Australia, southern California, Arizona, southern Florida, Mexico, Guatemala, Costa Rica, Brazil, Malawi, Zimbabwe Rhodesia, Panama, Jamaica, and South Africa. Plantings in all these areas are quite small, except Australia, Malawi, and South Africa, where sizeable acreages have been set out.

Commercial macadamia culture is suited only for subtropical to tropical frostfree localities, although mature trees in a dormant state have withstood temperatures as low as −6.5°C (20°F) for short periods without serious injury. The trees also tolerate temperatures up to 46°C (115°F) for short periods. They seem to have climatic requirements similar to the 'Fuerte' avocado. Macadamia trees tolerate a wide range of soil types

but grow best in a deep, fertile, well-drained, slightly acid soil. The trees have a definite requirement for nitrogen, phosphorus, potassium, and magnesium fertilizers, which are best applied in small amounts several times a year. Micronutrients such as iron, zinc, manganese, and boron are also needed in Hawaiian macadamia orchards under certain conditions.

Macadamia trees require ample soil moisture throughout the year from rainfall (a minimum of about 1524 mm; 60 in annually) plus supplementary irrigation in dry periods to induce flowering and good fruit set. Some of the productive orchards in Hawaii are in well-drained soils receiving as much as 3430 mm (135 in) of rainfall per year.

Macadamia trees have a shallow, poorly anchored root system and, in windy areas, should be protected by rows of windbreak trees. In Hawaii the Norfolk Island pine (*Araucaria heterophylla*) is commonly used in the wet areas.

The principal macadamia cultivars grown commercially in Hawaii are Kakea, Keauhou, Ikaika, Keaau, and Ka'u, all the smooth-shell type. These are propagated by grafting in early summer—with a side wedge or a simple splice graft (see p. 100)—onto seedlings of smooth-shell (*M. integrifolia*) or rough-shell species (*M. tetraphylla* L.) as a rootstock.

Macadamia trees usually start flowering and fruiting at five years. A full commercial crop is obtained after the seventh year. Flowering in Hawaii starts in November and December and continues through January, February, and March, with harvesting of the nuts starting in late July and continuing through March of the next year.

The tubular ivory-white perfect flowers of the smooth shell types are produced in groups of three or four on pedicels with 100 to 500 groups on a whiplike terminal or axillary pendulous cluster about 15 to 25 cm (6 to 10 in) long. Flowers of many cultivars require insects to transfer pollen from flower to flower to obtain good fruit set. Honeybees in the orchards at bloom are believed to promote fruit set. The ovary of each flower contains two ovules, and develops into a follicle (see p. 38), having a husk and shell. The husk, in most cultivars, splits open naturally to reveal the shell. Inside the shell are two seeds ("nuts"), each consisting mostly of the edible cotyledons of the embryo.

Harvesting is done by hand in small plantings, and is simply a matter of picking up the nuts as they drop. In large plantings, after the nuts drop to the ground, one special machine blows the leaves away, another sweeps the nuts into windrows, and a third pick-up machine gathers the nuts for hauling to the processing plant. Harvesting is done six or seven times a year. Mechanized harvesting is also being developed with the tree-shaking and pick-up equipment used in harvesting almonds and walnuts.

The in-shell nuts are dried to 1.5 percent moisture and then are cracked. In the Hawaiian processing plants the cracked nuts are separated electronically from the shells. The nuts are then cooked in coconut oil, cooled, inspected, salted, and vacuum-packed in cans or glass jars. Macadamia nuts, cooked and salted, are a fine specialty food, with their delicate, sweet taste and crisp bite. They are much in demand by nut fanciers and gourmets.

Blossom blight diseases caused by attacks of *Botrytis* and *Phytophthora* fungi develop on macadamias and require approved fungicide sprays. A mite attacks the flowers in all stages but is controlled by sulfur sprays and other approved miticides. Aphids and thrips damage flowers occasionally.

The mango is one of the most important fruit crops of the tropical regions. It is a broad-leaved evergreen tree with a symmetrical leafy canopy producing luscious fruits of varying shapes from oblong to round (Fig. 31–8). The trees can become very large—up to 27 m (90 ft) high with a 37 m (125 ft) spread. The mango is believed to have originated in the Indo-Burmese region of southeastern Asia. There is evidence that the mango has been under cultivation in India for over 4000 years. It has been associated with the economic, cultural, religious, and aesthetic life of the Indian people since prehistoric times. India is still, by far, the leading producer of mangoes with well over 800,000 ha (2 million ac)—75 percent of the world's production. Most of the choicest cultivars thrive in India. Mangoes are also grown extensively in Pakistan, Bangladesh, Burma, Thailand, the Philippines, Malaysia, Indonesia, Vietnam, Ceylon, China, South Africa, Australia, Mexico, Brazil, Kenya, Tanzania, Egypt, Cuba, Puerto Rico, and, in small amounts, in Hawaii and the southern coastal areas of Florida.

The mango was carried (as seeds) throughout the tropical regions by the early Spanish and Portuguese explorers, reaching the Americas in the eighteenth century. It was first introduced into Hawaii from Mexico about 1810 by Don Marin, a noted Spanish horticulturist. The mango was introduced into Florida in 1861.

Although the mango is a tropical plant, mature trees have withstood temperatures as low as −4°C (25°F) for a few hours. Young trees and actively growing shoots are likely to be killed at −1°C (30°F). Flowers and small fruits are damaged if temperatures drop below 4.5°C (40°F) for a few hours. Temperatures of 24°C to 27°C (75°F to 80°F) are considered optimal for mangos during the growing season, along with high humidity. They tolerate temperatures as high as 48°C (118°F).

Temperature affects the flowering time of the trees. A cool—or a dry—period, generally during the winter, which slows or stops growth is beneficial in inducing flowering. The mango grows in regions of both heavy (2540 mm; 100 in) or scant (254 mm; 10 in) rainfall. Precipitation of 890 to 1015 mm

(35 to 40 in) in a year, if well distributed, is best. If prolonged rainless periods occur, supplementary irrigation should be provided for good crops. In Florida fixed overhead sprinklers have been very successful in mango orchards because, in part, of their added benefit of frost protection during cold weather. Heavy rains during flowering can drastically reduce fruit set.

Mango trees grow on a wide range of soil types, but best production comes from well-drained sandy loam to loam soils at least 1.5 to 1.8 m (5 to 6 ft) deep. Little is known of the fertilizer requirements for mango. The trees are generally able to obtain sufficient mineral nutrients from the soils in which they are grown, and little experimental work has been done. Sand culture experiments have established mineral deficiency symptoms, but more field test plot work is needed to correlate mineral deficiencies with tree productivity.

There are three types, or races, of the mango:

1. The Indian race, grown in India, Pakistan, and Bangladesh, has highly flavored, brilliantly colored fruits, well suited to commercial production. These are monoembryonic[1] and must be propagated vegetatively. There are many cultivars of the Indian race. Some are 'Alfonso', 'Mulgoba,' 'Haden', and 'Tommy Atkins'. Haden is a popular cultivar in Hawaii. Tommy Atkins and the later-ripening Keitt are the principal cultivars in Florida.

2. The Indochina or Saigon race produces smaller, less attractive, fruits with a yellowish-green color and nonfibrous flesh with a delicate flavor. This type is polyembryonic and generally reproduces true by seed. Cultivars of this type are generally known by the name of the district where they originated, such as Cambodiana, Carabao, and Pico.

3. A third race consists of seedling types often grown in the Western Hemisphere and not fitting into either of the above groups. They produce fruits with skin mostly green in color and with an inferior flavor.

The mango inflorescence is a branched terminal panicle, up to 0.6 m (2 ft) long, having several hundred to several thousand flowers. A tree may have from 200 to 3000 panicles so that tremendous numbers of flowers are produced. Both male and female or perfect flowers are formed on the same panicle. Pollination is accomplished by various insects. Only a very small percentage of the flowers develop into fruits. These are classed as drupes (like peach and apricot fruits) and range in size from about 85 gm (3 oz) to over 2.3 kg (5 lb), depending upon the cultivar. The delicious fleshy part, which is eaten, is the mesocarp

Fig. 31–8 Young mango tree in Hawaii bearing a good crop of fruits. Mango trees grow to a very large size. *Source:* W. Yee.

[1]Some types of mango are apomictic (see p. 92). The seeds may contain, in addition to the usual sexual zygotic embryo, other vegetative "embryos" that are of the same genotype as the female parent. These are termed polyembryonic and will reproduce true from seed if the apomictic seedlings are used. These vegetative embryos arise from the nucellus tissue in the ovule or shoots may develop by budding from the cotyledons or the hypocotyl. Other nonapomictic types of mango are monoembryonic—having only the sexual zygotic embryo. To reproduce cultivars of this type vegetative propagation is necessary.

of the fruit (ovary wall). Masses of fibers extend from the stony pit (endocarp) into the flesh in some cultivars, making the fruit difficult to eat. Inside the stony pit is the true seed.

Mango trees tend strongly toward biennial bearing. There may be very low numbers of perfect (male and female parts) flowers, and embryo abortion after fertilization may cause the young fruits to drop. A major problem in many mango-producing areas is getting good yields regularly—obtaining good fruit set from the abundant bloom. The best approach is to plant cultivars with regular habits like Tommy Atkins, Keitt, Kent, and Pope.

Mangos can be propagated in many ways. Polyembryonic types—which come true from seed—can be propagated by seed or by one of the vegetative methods listed below. Monoembryonic types, which have only a sexually produced embryo, must be propagated vegetatively if the cultivar characteristics are to be retained. Many methods are used, such as approach grafting (used in India since ancient times), whip grafting, side grafting, and veneer grafting. T-budding, chip budding, and patch budding have also been successful. Mango is difficult to propagate by stem cuttings or layering (see Ch. 5).

The mango, like most other broad-leaved evergreen tropical and subtropical trees, requires very little pruning, although with heavy crops limbs need cutting back to prevent breakage. Young trees should be trained enough to develop a central trunk and several well-spaced primary scaffold branches to form a sturdy framework. Dead wood and crowded interfering branches should be removed from mature trees.

Mango fruits grow rapidly and are ready to harvest about 12 weeks after fruit set. In Florida and Hawaii mango harvest is from mid-May to October, depending upon the cultivar. The fruits are best picked after the green skin color changes to yellow but when the flesh is still firm. Fruits ripen three to six days after picking. If harvested too soon, the fruits of most cultivars do not develop a good flavor. Harvested fruits can be refrigerated at about 13°C (55°F) to delay ripening during shipment. Fruit ripening is best done at 21°C to 24°C (70°F to 75°F); ethylene gas treatment can be given to induce uniform ripening.

The mango is a highly esteemed tropical fruit. It is generally peeled for eating fresh, but it can also be frozen, dried, canned, or used for pies, jams, and jellies.

Mango imports into U.S. markets come mostly from Mexico with much smaller amounts received from Haiti, Taiwan, and India. Most Mexican production is in the state of Veracruz.

Mangos are subject to several disease and insect problems. Anthracnose is the most serious fungal disease causing flowers, young fruits, leaves, and twigs to turn black and drop. This is best prevented by maintaining preventive fungicide sprays on all parts of the tree. On the windward side of mountain ranges in Hawaii, which have heavy rains throughout the year, there are huge mango trees that flower but never fruit because of the *Anthracnose* fungus.

Mites, mealy bugs, scale insects, stem borers, and thrips can build up to sufficiently high levels on mango trees to cause severe damage and greatly limit fruit production. Mangos have not developed to a greater extent commercially in Hawaii because of a quarantine against importation of the fruits into mainland United States due to the mango seed weevil, which can be found in some mango seeds.

Papaya (*Cariaca papaya* L.) CARICACEAE (8, 10, 12, 16, 17, 22, 33, 48)

The papaya plant is a large, fast-growing, short-lived herbaceous perennial that bears clusters of delicious, mild-flavored large or small fruits varying in shape from spherical to pearlike.

C. papaya plants have never been found in the wild, but a close relative, *C. peltata*, grows wild in southern Mexico and Central America, leading to the supposition that *C. papaya* may have originated in this region. The early Spanish and Portuguese explorers carried the papaya to most tropical countries throughout the world.

The papaya is now grown in many places in the tropics between 32° north and south latitudes, from sea level up to about 1500 m (5000 ft). For heavy production of high-quality fruits, papayas must be grown in warm, 21°C to 26.5°C (70°F to 80°F), frost-free climates in full sun. Lower temperatures give poor results. Papayas grow on many soil types, but good aeration and drainage are necessary with, preferably, a soil pH of 6.5 to 7.0. Papaya trees need ample soil moisture at all times. If rainfall is lacking during parts of the year, irrigation is required to supplement the rain. For good plant growth and production the various mineral nutrients must be readily available in the soil. The kinds and amount of fertilizers required depend upon the soil type.

There are different types of papaya grown in the various tropical countries—some large-fruited and some small. The only commercial cultivar now being grown in Hawaii is Puna Solo, which was selected from an introduction from Barbados, West Indies, in 1911. It has small fruits of about 1/2 kg (1 lb) each. Several new papaya cultivars have been developed in Hawaii, originating from controlled crosses. Some of these are 'Waimanolo', 'Sunrise', 'Higgins', and 'Wilder'. Florida grows a type called Blue Solo, which originated as a cross of 'Solo' with a blue-stemmed plant having large fruits. The Blue Solo type is too variable, however, to be called a cultivar.

The papaya is considered dioecious but, for practical purposes, the trees are generally classified into three sex types. Three types of papaya plants can develop when seeds are planted. The first type produces only male flowers. This type is easily determined by the flower clusters borne on long peduncles arising in the axils of the leaves. These trees are generally cut out as soon as the sex can be determined since they are completely unfruitful. In a second type the trees have only female flowers, which produce fruits. These develop in the leaf axils, singly or in short clusters. Such flowers rarely have stamens. The third type of tree has hermaphroditic (perfect) flowers—with both male and female parts. Seedlings from the Solo cultivar grown in Hawaii develop into trees producing female flowers and hermaphroditic flowers on separate plants. Fruits developing from the latter type are preferred since they have a desirable pear shape, whereas those from female flowers develop into round fruits. Female 'Solo' trees are generally cut out as soon as their sex can be determined.

Papaya fruits develop in the axils of the leaves arising around the top of the tree. As the trees grow older—and taller—the fruits become difficult to harvest, so they are cut out and replaced with a younger planting.

Botanically the papaya fruit is a berry. The edible part is the soft fleshy mesocarp and endocarp of the ovary wall. The thin, leathery skin (exocarp) is not eaten. The inside of the ovary wall of the fruit is lined with great numbers of seeds surrounded by a mucilaginous material developed from the seed coats. The seeds are removed before the fruits are served for eating.

Immature fruits contain papain, a protein-digesting enzyme, which is extracted from the latex of the skin. This is obtained by scoring or injuring the fruit, then collecting and drying the latex. The papain is used as a meat tenderizer.

Papayas are propagated by seed, planted directly in the field, in seed flats, or in individual peat pots for later transplanting. Fresh seed germinates in about two weeks with adequate moisture and heat. Planting distances in the field are about 2.4 m (8 ft) in the rows and 3.3 m (11 ft) between rows. Several seedlings are planted in each place and after about five months, when flowering starts and the trees' sex can be determined, the unwanted types are cut out.

Papaya trees produce mature fruits about 10 months after planting, then bear the year around. Individual fruits are harvested when they are at a mature-green stage and show a tinge or more of yellow at the apical end. Fruits can be picked by hand when the trees are young but as they become taller the fruits cannot be reached. In Hawaii an interesting harvest method has been developed. A rubber cup, or so-called plumber's friend, is attached to a long pole and pushed up under the fruit and twisted, breaking the fruit loose if it is mature. The picker then catches the fruit as it falls to the ground. Tractor-mounted picking platforms, designed after cherry pickers, as well as other harvest aids, have added an extra year to the production life of trees, giving it four years after planting (Fig. 31–9). A yield of 22.4 to 56.0 thousand kg/ha (20 to 50 thousand lb/ac) of fruit can be obtained in Hawaii.

Before Hawaiian papayas can be shipped to the U.S. mainland they must be treated to destroy fruit flies, usually by fumigating the fruit in open field boxes with ethylene dibromide. In addition, to destroy decay organisms, the fruits are dipped in hot water (49°C; 120°F) for 20 minutes, then in cool water for 20 minutes before they are fumigated. A vapor heat treatment can be used in place of the fumigation treatment to kill the fruit flies. In the vapor heat method the temperature at the center of the fruit is brought to 47°C (117°F) at 100 percent relative humidity.

Harvested papayas can be held under refrigeration for one to three weeks at 7°C to 10°C (45°F to 50°F). Fruits are ready to eat when they turn completely yellow or feel soft to a gentle squeeze.

Most papaya fruits are consumed locally because of difficulties in long distance transportation of the tender fruits. The practice of air shipments to the U.S. mainland and to Japan, however, has given impetus to the fast-growing Hawaiian industry. Mainland air shipments increased from 2.38 million kg (5.3 million lb) in 1966 to 87.75 million kg (19.5 million lb)

Fig. 31–9 Two methods of harvesting papayas commercially in Hawaii. *Left:* Rubber suction cups on end of pole twist fruit off. *Right:* Mechanized "tree squirrel" places picker up in tree where fruit is detached by hand. *Source:* Blue Anchor, Inc.

in 1975. In 1976 fast ship service was offered, which soon handled about 20 percent of all mainland papaya movement. Most U.S. supplies of papaya come from Hawaii. Even in the warmest parts of southern California the weather is too cool in most years for papayas to ripen properly, and the industry in Florida has been hard hit by viruses and the papaya wasp.

Both fungal and viral diseases attack papayas. Anthracnose is a common fungus disease in Hawaii attacking the fruits. A *Phytophthora* blight fungus is the most important disease and attacks above-ground portions of the plant as well as the roots. Two viral diseases—papaya mosaic and papaya ringspot—occur in Hawaii and are a threat to the industry. In Florida, in fact, viral diseases appearing from 1945 to 1950 proved catastrophic and have blocked any expansion of the industry. No good control measures have yet been developed.

Mites are a serious pest on papayas but they can be controlled by sulfur sprays. The melon, oriental, and Mediterranean fruit flies attack papaya fruits in Hawaii and are the cause of the strict quarantine and fumigation requirements.

Pineapple (*Ananas comosus* [L.] Merr.)
BROMELIACEAE
(*1, 2, 5, 7, 8, 10, 12, 13, 30*)

The pineapple is a low-growing herbaceous, perennial monocotyledonous tropical plant producing tasty fruits known well and consumed widely throughout the world, principally as canned products. It originated in Brazil, Paraguay, and northern Argentina in central South America. Improved cultivars selected and propagated by the Indians in this region had become widely distributed throughout tropical America even before Columbus' discovery of the New World.

The botanical name, *Ananas,* was taken from the name *Nana* used by the American Indians. This is used as the common name in all European languages except English. Referring to the fruit's similarity to a pine cone, the Spanish word *pinas* plus *apple* led to its name in English.

The Portuguese explorers apparently disseminated the pineapple throughout the world's tropical regions in the 1500s, carrying the fruit "crowns"—which could remain viable for long periods of time—in their ships. Pineapples were first brought to Hawaii in 1813 and canning started in 1892. James Dole started his pineapple plantations in 1900.

The pineapple is now an important commercial crop in many tropical countries including Hawaii, the Philippines, Thailand, Taiwan, Malaysia, Ivory Coast, Kenya, South Africa, Mexico, Cuba, Puerto Rico, Brazil, and Australia. Prior to 1950 Hawaii produced about 70 percent of the world's processed pineapples but, because of ever-increasing production costs, this had decreased by the mid 1970s to less than 36 percent as other countries expanded their production.

The pineapple is a strictly tropical plant, showing severe leaf damage at freezing temperatures. Temperatures over 32°C (90°F) can lower fruit quality, and higher daytime temperatures can sunburn exposed fruits. As the fruits start to mature, night temperatures around 21°C (70°F) and dry weather are desirable for best quality.

A well-drained, slightly acid sandy loam is best for pineapples, but they grow on a wide range of soils provided drainage and aeration are good. Preplanting soil fumigation is essential to control nematodes where pineapples are grown on the same soil for many years. Pineapples need fertile soils and generally require added fertilizers, particularly nitrogen and potassium. In Hawaii, preplanting ground applications of nitrogen, phosphorus, and potassium at relatively high levels are made. Subsequent foliage sprays containing nitrogen, potassium, iron, and zinc are applied by ground sprayers.

Pineapple plants need ample soil moisture throughout the year—50 to 100 mm (2 to 4 in) of rain a month for good production. During rainless periods, supplementary irrigation should supply this amount of water, particularly for young plantings getting established. The pineapple plant survives very well, however, under drought conditions.

There are many pineapple cultivars, but the leading one commercially over much of the tropical region is Smooth Cayenne. In Central and South America and the Caribbean region, 'Pernambuco', 'Red Spanish', 'Monte Liro', and 'Sugar Loaf' are widely grown. 'Queen', 'Z', and 'McGregor' are grown in South Africa, with 'Natel', 'Ripley', and 'Alexandria' grown in Australia.

Pineapples are propagated vegetatively with crowns, slips, or suckers. The **crown** is the vegetative shoot on top of the fruit. **Slips** are side shoots arising from the fruiting stem just below the fruit. **Suckers** are side shoots developing from the main stem above ground level. New plants from crowns require about 24 months to fruit, from slips about 20 months, and from suckers 17 months. Plantings are generally made to coincide with periods of heavy rainfall. A double row system is used in Hawaii with plants set about 30 cm (12 in) apart in rows 50 cm (20 in) apart, with the beds 1.5 m (5 ft) apart. Sheets of black polyethylene film are often used as a mulch between rows with the propagating pieces inserted through the plastic into the soil.

Each original plant set out produces one fruit at the top of the stem. This is called the plant crop. After these fruits are harvested, one or two suckers are allowed to develop from the mother plant. Each sucker, about a year later, produces one pineapple fruit ready to harvest. This is called the ratoon crop. Sometimes a second ratoon crop is grown. However, highest yields and best quality fruits are obtained from the plant crop.

The pineapple forms in a complex fashion. At the terminal vegetative growing point of the plant a central axis core develops, bearing an inflorescence of 100 or more closely attached lavender flowers, arranged spirally, each subtended by a bract. This central axis core terminates in a crown, a rosette of small leaves. Each of the many pineapple flowers on the inflorescence consists of a calyx with three violet-colored sepals joined at their bases, three purple petals, six stamens, and a pistil having three stigmas and three carpels. All parts of each flower, together with the bract, develop into fruitlet tissue. As it develops, the entire inflorescence converts into the single pineapple fruit (botanically a sorosis) by the coalescence of the inner stem tissue and the fruitlets (developed ovaries of the flowers).

Fruits of commercial pineapple cultivars weigh from 1.4 to 2.7 kg (3 to 6 lb), but those of some types are much larger. The fibrous center tissue becomes woody and tough and is usually discarded when the fruit is eaten, as is the tough and leathery outer rind.

With solid block plantings of a single cultivar, pineapple fruits are seedless because each pineapple cultivar is self-incompatible (its own pollen does not fertilize its egg). In solid block fields where no pollen from other cultivars is present, no embryo or seed forms but, fortunately, the fruit develops anyway. Thus, it is parthenocarpic. If different cultivars were mixed in the same field so cross-pollination could take place, the fruits would have seeds.

For orderly harvesting and marketing it is important that flowering—and subsequent fruit maturation—begin at about the same time in all plants in a field. Pineapples do not do this too well on their own. Plant scientists found in the 1930s that pineapple plants treated with ethylene or acetylene start forming flowers. A common commercial practice developed from this, particularly in warm rainy areas, is to drop a few pieces of granular calcium carbide into the center of the pineapple terminal leaf cluster. In contacting the water accumulated in the center of the plant the calcium carbide reacts to release acetylene, which affects the terminal growing point in such a manner as to cause floral induction. Activity is known to be greater with applications of the calcium carbide made at night (2).

$$CaC_2 + 2H_2O \longrightarrow H—C \equiv C—H + Ca(OH)_2$$

calcium water   acetylene   calcium
carbide   hydroxide

Other chemicals, like the sodium salt of the auxin naphthaleneacetic acid, and ethephon—an ethylene-releasing material—(see Ch. 6), applied to the plants as water sprays have also been effective in inducing floral induction in some areas. These materials appear to be more effective in cool areas than in the warm, humid tropics.

Pineapple harvesting is semimechanized. A long endless belt attached to the harvesting machine stretches out over about 9 m (30 ft) of pineapple plants and moves slowly over the field. Workers follow along behind this belt in the rows, breaking off the fruits by a bending and twisting motion and placing them on the belt, which moves them to the waiting trucks for hauling to processing plants or shipment overseas.

Highest quality in pineapple fruits develops only when they are allowed to become fully ripe on the plant. They do not become sweeter if picked at an immature stage as they have no starch reserves. Much of the pineapple crop is harvested fully ripe and processed and canned immediately at local canneries as slices, wedges, crushed pulp, and as pineapple juice. With the advent of the large jet planes for shipment, more and more fresh pineapples are seen in local markets in Europe and the United States. European markets are largely supplied with fresh pineapples from Africa, while U.S. shipments originate mostly in Hawaii, Puerto Rico, and Mexico. Ripe, ready-to-eat fresh pineapples can be stored for two to four weeks at about 7°C (45°F) with 85 to 90 percent relative humidity. Temperatures below this are damaging. Fresh pineapple should never be frozen.

Numerous pests and diseases constantly confront pineapple growers. Mealy bug wilt is best controlled through elimination by insecticides of ants that are associated with the mealy bugs. *Phytophthora* fungi can cause heart rot and foot rot in the plants, particularly in poorly drained soils with high rainfall. Some diseases of the pineapple fruits are endogenous brown spot, pink disease, and fruitlet core rot. Control of nematodes by soil fumigation is necessary in some areas.

SOME MINOR TROPICAL FRUITS AND NUTS

Many tropical fruit and nut crops have found a place for themselves in certain tropical localities. For one reason or another they have not made a major impact on the world's food consumers. Flavor of the fruits may not be appealing to many, preparation for eating may be difficult, bearing may be undependable, harvesting and transportation of the crops may be difficult, or control of diseases or insect pests may be costly. Most of the plants—usually broad-leaved evergreens—are attractive, however, and are often used in landscaping, with the fruits considered a bonus.

Bread Fruit (*Artocarpus altilis* [Park]) Fusb. MORACEAE (*21, 33*)

This beautiful evergreen tree has been grown since prehistoric times throughout the South Pacific. It reaches a height of 12 to 18 m (40 to 60 ft) and usually has large, deeply pinnate, lobed, glossy green leaves. There are two types: the seeded and the more desirable seedless form, which is usually grown.

The tree produces a large warty looking fruit 10 to 20 cm (4 to 8 in) in diameter. As the fruits mature, greenish-brown or yellow spots appear on the green fruit surface. Inside the rind the fruit consists of a white, fibrous pulp. Breadfruit is high in carbohydrates but low in proteins and fat. The unripened but mature fruits are often diced and cooked as a starchy vegetable. The Polynesians cooked breadfruit over an open fire or in an underground oven before eating. Today it is baked, boiled, or steamed, resembling the sweet potato in flavor. As the mature breadfruit becomes fully ripe on the tree, its starch changes to sugar and the pulp can be mixed with coconut "milk" and made into a pudding.

Breadfruit plants were being taken from Tahiti to the West Indies in a memorable voyage in 1792 by Captain Bligh and botanist David Nelson in the ship *HMS Bounty* when the epic mutiny took place. Captain James Cook had seen breadfruit used as a food in many Pacific Islands and recommended it for feeding the incoming slaves from West Africa if it could be grown in the West Indies. While breadfruit eventually was established in Jamaica, it did not live up to expectations as the slaves preferred eating bananas and plantains.

Cherimoya (*Annona cherimola* Mill.) ANNONACEAE (*33*)

This plant grows fast for a few years, then slows down to form a tree about 4.5 m (15 ft) tall with a 6 m (20 ft) spread. The dull green leaves, about 15 cm (6 in) long, drop in late spring just as new ones are forming. The brown to yellowish fragrant flowers start appearing about the same time as the new leaves. The green fruits with bumpy scales look like pine cones. They weigh about 0.5 kg (1 lb) and are ready to pick when they turn yellowish green. The fruits should be kept under refrigeration until the skin turns brown; then they are ready to eat. The custardlike flesh has a mild flavor suggestive of bananas and pineapples. Hand pollination usually increases fruit set and improves carpel development.

Guava (*Psidium guajava* L.) MYRTACEAE (*10, 33*)

Guava is an evergreen shrub or small tree. It grows wild in Hawaii although some are under cultivation. The fruit is round, oval, or pear-shaped, about 5 cm (2 in) in diameter. The thick rind is edible, as is the soft pulp inside. Guava fruits are used mostly as a component of juice drinks or for making jams and jellies. Guavas are very high in vitamin C, containing 10 times more than tomatoes.

Another species, the strawberry guava (*P. littorale* Raddi.) is hardier than *P. guajava* and is grown in subtropical regions. It can withstand minimum temperatures as low as −6.5°C (20°F). The strawberry guava is useful in landscaping as a hedge or container plant and has attractive greenish-gray bark. The leaves, about 7.6 cm (3 in) long, are a glossy, golden-green color. The dark red fruits, which mature in the. fall or winter, have a white sweet tart flesh.

Litchi (*Litchi chinensis* Sonn.) SAPINDACEAE (*10, 33*)

The litchi is a handsome evergreen tropical tree forming a dense symmetrical rounded form and growing to a height of 12 m (40 ft). It has been cultivated in southern China for thousands of years, producing the dried litchi "nut," shipped to Chinese communities in the United States. The litchi grows well in southern Florida and has fruited in warm areas near San Diego in southern California. It bears fruits in clusters of 5 to 20 at the ends of shoots. The fruits have a rough, warty, hard shell that turns red when ripe and looking like a cluster of strawberries.

The juicy white flesh inside the brittle shell has a gelatinous consistency. The fruits are often dried, having a sweet flavor with a raisinlike texture.

Passion Fruit (Granadilla) (*Passiflora edulis* Sims.) PASSIFLORACEAE (*33, 35*)

This is a strong-growing fruitful, woody perennial evergreen vine grown commercially in Hawaii, Australia, Brazil, Philippines, Taiwan, and South Africa, adapted to the warm lowlands. The vines are grown on high wire trellises or on lattices. While the vines require considerable heat to produce fruit, they grow but do not fruit in cooler areas. The yellow fruits, which are round and about the size of a large plum, have a delicious, sprightly but acid flavor. The extracted juice is often used commercially mixed into canned fruit juices.

Surinam Cherry (*Eugenia uniflora* L.) MYRTACEAE (*33, 35*)

Native to Brazil, the Surinam cherry is grown in the southern half of Florida and in Hawaii as an ornamental shrub or hedge. It is a compact evergreen, growing up to 3 m (10 ft) in height. The creamy flowers are fragrant and the small, tomatolike fruits become edible when they change from yellow to a deep red color. The fruit is excellent for making jams, jellies, syrups, and sherbets.

REFERENCES

1. Albrigo, L. G. 1966. Pineapple nutrition. In *Fruit nutrition*, ed. N. F. Childers. New Brunswick, N.J.: Horticultural Publications.

2. Aldrich, W. W., and H. Y. Nakasone. 1975. Day vs. night application of calcium carbide for flower induction in pineapple. *J. Am. Soc. Hort. Sci.* 100(4):410–13.

3. Almeyda, N., and F. Martin. 1976. Cultivation of neglected tropical fruits with promise. Part 1. The mangosteen. USDA/ARS S-155.

4. Alvim, P. de T. 1977. Cacao. In *Ecophysiology of tropical crops*, eds. P. de T. Alvim and T. T. Kozlowski. New York: Academic Press.

5. Anon. 1973. *Pineapple in Hawaii*. Honolulu: The Pineapple Growers Association of Hawaii.

6. Argles, G. K. 1976. *Anacardium occidentale*—Cashew. In *The propagation of tropical fruit trees*, eds. R. J. Garner and S. A. Chaudri. East Malling, England: Commonwealth Agricultural Bureaux.

7. Bartholomew, D. P., and S. B. Kadzimin. 1977. Pineapple. In *Ecophysiology of tropical crops*, eds. P. de T. Alvim and T. T. Kozlowski. New York: Academic Press.

8. Brouk, B. 1975. *Plants consumed by man*. New York: Academic Press.

9. California Macadamia Society annual yearbooks.

10. Chandler, W. H. 1958. *Evergreen orchards*. 2nd ed. Philadelphia: Lea & Febiger.

11. Cobin, M. 1954. The lychee in Florida. Florida Agr. Exp. Sta. Bul. 546.

12. Cobley, L. S. 1957. *The botany of tropical crops*. London: Longmans.

13. Collins, J. L. 1960. *The pineapple*. World crops series. London: Leonard-Hill-Interscience.

14. Embleton, T., and W. W. Jones. 1966. Avocado and mango nutrition. In *Fruit Nutrition*, ed. N. F. Childers. New Brunswick, N.J.: Horticultural Publications.

15. Freiberg, S. R. 1966. Banana nutrition. In *Fruit nutrition*, ed. N. F. Childers. New Brunswick, N.J.: Horticultural Publications.

16. Harkness, R. W. 1976. Papaya growing in Florida. Florida Agr. Exp. Sta. Cir. S-180.

17. Ito, P. J. 1976. Papaya production in Hawaii. *Fruit Var. Jour.* 30(4):105–6.

18. Lynch, S. J., and M. J. Mustard. 1955. Mangos in Florida. Fla. Dept. Agri. Bul. No. 20.

19. Maestri, M., and R. S. Barros. 1977. Coffee, In *Ecophysiology of tropical crops*, eds. P. de T. Alvim and T. T. Kozlowski. New York: Academic Press.

20. Mathews, W. H. 1962. Pineapples in Florida. Univ. Fla. Agr. Ext. Ser. Cir. 195A.

21. Matsumoto, E. A. 1976. The breadfruit. *Fruit Var. Jour.* 30(4): 108–10.

22. McGregor, S. E. 1976. Insect Pollination of Cultivated Plants. USDA/ARS Handbook 496.

23. Morton, J. 1961. The cashew's brighter future. *Econ. Bot.* 15:57–78.

24. ———, and F. D. Venning. 1972. Avoid failures and losses in the cultivation of the cashew. *Econ. Bot.* 26(3):245–54.

25. Mortensen, E., and E. T. Bullard. 1970. *Handbook of tropical and subtropical horticulture.* U.S. Agency for International Development. Washington D.C.: U.S. Government Printing Office.

26. Mukherjee, S. K. 1953. The mango: its botany, cultivation, uses and future improvement. *Econ. Bot.* 7(2):130–62.

27. Müller, L. E. 1966. Coffee nutrition. In *Fruit nutrition,* ed. N. F. Childers. New Brunswick, N.J.: Horticultural Publications.

28. Murray, D. B. 1966. Cacao nutrition. In *Fruit nutrition,* ed. N. F. Childers. New Brunswick, N.J.: Horticultural Publications.

29. ———. 1977. Coconut palm. In *Ecophysiology of tropical crops,* eds. P. de T. Alvim and T. T. Kozlowski. New York: Academic Press.

30. Nakasone, H. Y. 1976. Pineapple production. *Fruit Var. Jour.* 30(4):100–4.

31. Nambiar, M. C. 1977. Cashew, In *Ecophysiology of tropical crops,* eds. P. de T. Alvim and T. T. Koslowski. New York: Academic Press.

32. Ooka, H. 1976. Macadamia nut production in Hawaii. *Fruit Var. Jour.* 30(4):110–15.

33. Popenoe, W. 1920. *Manual of tropical and sub-tropical fruits.* New York: Macmillan.

34. Rosedale, D. O. 1963. Growing macadamia nuts in California. Univ. of Calif. Agr. Ext. Ser. AXT 103.

35. Ruehle, G. D., H. Mowry, L. R. Toy, and H. S. Wolfe. 1958. Miscellaneous tropical and sub-tropical Florida fruits. Univ. Fla. Agr. Ext. Ser. Bul. 156A.

36. Ruskin, F. R., ed. *Under-exploited tropical plants with promising economic value.* Washington, D.C.: National Academy of Sciences.

37. Seelig, R. A. 1969. *Bananas: fruit & vegetable facts & pointers.* Washington, D.C.: United Fresh Fruit and Vegetable Association.

38. Shigeura, G., and R. M. Bullock. 1976. Production of guava (*Psidium guajava* L.) in Hawaii. *Fruit Var. Jour.* 30(4)98–100.

39. Simmonds, N. W. 1966. *Bananas.* 2nd ed. London: Longmans.

40. Storey, W. B. 1969. Macadamia. In *Handbook of North American nut trees,* ed. R. A. Jaynes. Knoxville, Tenn.: Northern Nut Growers.

41. Tai, E. A. 1977. Banana. In *Ecophysiology of tropical crops,* eds. P. de T. Alvim and T. T. Kozlowski. New York: Academic Press.

42. Urquhart, D. H. 1961. *Cacao.* 2nd ed. London: Longmans.

43. Warner, R. M. 1972. Propagation of tropical crop plants. *Proc. Inter. Plant Prop. Soc.* 22:181–90.

44. ———, and R. L. Fox. 1976. Effects of nitrogen and climatic factors on seasonality of banana production in Hawaii. *Proc. Inter. Plant Prop. Soc.* 26:38–47.

45. Wolfe, H. S. 1962. The mango in Florida. Fla. State Hort. Soc. Proc. 75:387–91.

46. Woodroof, J. G. 1970. *Coconuts: production, processing, products.* Westport, Conn.: AVI.

47. Yee, W. 1973. The mango in Hawaii. Univ. of Hawaii Agr. Ext. Ser. Cir. 388.

48. ———, E. K. Akamine, G. M. Aoki, R. A. Hamilton, F. H. Haramoto, R. B. Hine, O. V. Holtzmann, J. T. Ishida, J. T. Keeler, and H. Y. Nakasone. 1970. Papayas in Hawaii. Univ. of Hawaii Coop. Ext. Ser. Cir. 436.

Glossary

A horizon   The surface layer of varying thickness of a mineral soil having maximum organic matter accumulation, maximum biological activity, and/or eluviation by water of materials such as iron and aluminum oxides and silicate clays.

Abscisic acid   A plant hormone involved in abscission, dormancy, stomatal closure, growth inhibition, and other plant responses.

Abscission zone   A layer of thin-walled cells extending across the base of a petiole or peduncle, whose breakdown separates the leaf or fruit from the stem causing the leaf or fruit to drop.

Absorption   The taking up of water by assimilation or imbibition. The taking up by capillary, osmotic, chemical, or solvent action such as the taking up of water from air, or taking up of gases by water, or taking up of mineral nutrients by plant roots.

Acclimatization   The adaptation of an individual plant to a changed climate, or the adjustment of a species or a population to a changed environment, often over several generations.

Achene   A simple, dry, one-seeded indehiscent fruit with the seed attached to the ovary wall at one point only. The so-called strawberry and sunflower ''seeds'' are examples.

Acid delinting   A process used to remove the short fibers (lint) from seed cotton.

Acid soil   Soil with a reaction below pH 7; more technically, a soil having a preponderance of hydrogen ions over hydroxyl ions in solution.

Adaptation   The process of change in structure or function of an individual or population caused by environmental changes.

Adenosine diphosphate (ADP)   A nucleotide (a nitrogen-based compound) composed of adenine and ribose with two phosphate groups attached. ATP and ADP participate in metabolic reactions (both catabolic and anabolic). These molecules through the process of being phosphorylated (accepting phosphate groups) or dephosphorylated (losing phosphate groups) transfer energy within the cells to drive metabolic processes.

Adenosine triphosphate (ATP)   ATP has three phosphoric groups attached and is the phosphorylated condition of ADP. It conveys energy needed for metabolic reactions, then loses one phosphate group to become ADP (adenosine diphosphate).

Adhesion   The molecular attraction between unlike substances such as water and sand particles.

Adsorption   The attraction of ions or molecules to the surface of a solid.

Adventitious   Refers to structures arising from an unusual place; for example, buds at places other than shoot terminals or leaf axils, or roots growing from stems or leaves.

Aeration, soil   The process by which air in the soil is replaced by air from the atmosphere.

Aerobic   An environment or condition in which oxygen is not deficient for chemical, physical, or metabolic processes.

Agar   A gelatinous substance obtained from certain species of red algae; widely used as a substrate in aseptic cultures.

Aggregate (soil)   Many primary soil particles held in a single unit as a clod, crumb, block, or prism.

Agronomy   The art and science of crop production and soil management.

Air-dry   The state of dryness at equilibrium with the moisture content in the surrounding atmosphere.

Air layer   An undetached aerial portion of a plant on which roots are caused to develop commonly as the result of wounding or other stimulation.

Air porosity   The proportion of the bulk volume of soil that is filled with air at any given time or under a given condition, such as a specified moisture tension.

Albino A plant or part of a plant lacking chlorophyll. Albinism is usually lethal in higher plants.

Aleurone The outer layer of cells surrounding the endosperm of a cereal grain (caryopsis).

Alkali soil *See* Sodic soil.

Alkaline soil Any soil that has a pH greater than 7.

Alluvial soil A recently developed soil from deposited soil material that exhibits essentially no horizon development or modifications.

Alternate An arrangement of leaves or buds in which a bud or leaf grows on one side of a stem at one node and on the other side at the next node.

Alumino-silicates Compounds containing aluminum, silicon, and oxygen as main constituents. An example is microcline, $KA1Si_3O_8$.

Ambient temperature Air temperature at a given time and place; not radiant temperature.

Amendment (soil) Any substance such as lime, sulfur, gypsum or an organic material like peat moss, sawdust or bark used to alter the properties of a soil, generally to improve its physical properties.

Amino acids The fundamental building blocks of proteins. There are 20 common amino acids in living organisms, each having the basic formula NH_2-CHR-COOH.

Ammonification The biochemical process whereby ammoniacal nitrogen is released from nitrogen-containing organic compounds.

Ammonium fixation The incorporation of ammonium ions by soil fractions in such a manner that they are relatively insoluble in water and nonexchangeable by the usual methods of cation exchange.

Anaerobic An environment or condition in which molecular oxygen is deficient for chemical, physical, or biological processes.

Angiosperm One of a large group of seed-bearing plants in which the female gamete is protected within an enclosed ovary. A flowering plant.

Anion A negatively charged particle that during electrolysis is attracted to positively charged surfaces.

Annual ring The cylinder of secondary xylem added to a woody plant stem by the cambium in any one year.

Annuals Plants living one year or less. During this time the plant grows, flowers, produces seeds, and dies.

Anther In a flower the saclike structure of the stamen in which microspores (pollen grains) are produced; usually borne on a filament.

Anthesis A developmental stage in flowering at which anthers rupture and pollen is shed. A state of full bloom.

Anthocyanin A class of water-soluble pigments that account for many of the red to blue flower, leaf, and fruit colors. Anthocyanins occur in the vacuole of the cell.

Antipodal nuclei The three or more nuclei at the end of the embryo sac opposite the egg nucleus (female gamete). They are produced by mitotic divisions of the megaspore and degenerate following sexual fertilization.

Apical dominance The inhibition of lateral buds on a shoot due to auxins produced by the apical bud.

Apical meristem A mass of undifferentiated cells capable of division at the tip of a root or shoot. These cells differentiate by division, allowing the plant to grow in depth or height.

Apomixis The asexual (vegetative) production of seedlings in the usual sexual structures of the flower but without the mingling and segregation of chromosomes. Seedling characteristics are the same as those of the maternal parent.

Arable land Land suitable for the production of crops.

Asexual reproduction The production of a new plant by any vegetative means not involving meiosis and the union of gametes.

Assimilation The transformation of organic and inorganic materials into protoplasm.

Atom The smallest particle in which an element combines, either with itself or with other elements; the smallest quantity of matter possessing the properties of a particular element.

Autotrophic Plants capable of utilizing carbon dioxide or carbonates as the sole source of carbon and obtaining energy for life processes from the oxidation of inorganic elements or compounds such as iron, sulfur, hydrogen, ammonium, and nitrites or from radiant energy. (*See* Heterotrophic.)

Available nutrient That portion of an element or compound in the soil that can be readily absorbed, assimilated, and utilized by growing plants. (*Available* should not be confused with *exchangeable*.)

Available water The portion of water in a soil that can be readily absorbed by plant roots. That soil moisture held in the soil between field capacity and permanent wilting percentage (available water = F.C. − P.W.P.)

Axil The angle on the upper side of the union of a branch and main stem or of a leaf and a stem.

Axillary bud A bud formed in the axil of a leaf.

B horizon A soil layer of varying thickness (usually beneath the A horizon) that is characterized by an accumulation of silicate clays, iron and aluminum oxides, and humus, alone or in combination and/or a blocky or prismatic structure.

Backcross In breeding, a cross of a hybrid with one of its parents or with a genetically equivalent organism. In genetics, a cross of a hybrid with a homozygous recessive.

Bar A unit of pressure equal to 1 million dynes/cm². Approximately equivalent to 1 atm of pressure.

Bark The tissues of a woody stem or root from the cambium outward.

Base pair The nitrogen bases that pair in the DNA molecule—adenine with thymine, and guanine with cytosine.

Berry A simple fleshy fruit formed from a single ovary; the ovary wall fleshy and including one or more carpels and seeds. For example, fruits of the tomato and grape are botanically berries.

Biennial A plant that completes its life cycle within two seasons. For most biennial plants the two seasons are separated by an obligate degree of cold temperature sufficient to initiate flowering and fruit formation, after which the plant dies.

Binomial In biology each species is generally indicated by two names; first, the genus to which it belongs and second, the species name (e.g., *Quercus suber*, cork oak).

Biodegradable Materials readily decomposed by microorganisms such as bacteria and fungi.

Biology The science that deals with living organisms.

Bloat Excessive accumulation of gases in the rumen of some animals.

Bolting Rapid production of flower stalks in some herbaceous plants after sufficient chilling or a favorable photoperiod.

Botany The science of plants, their characteristics, functions, life cycles, and habits.

Brace root (anchor root) A type of adventitious root that grows from above-ground parts of the stem and serves to support some plants; for example, corn.

Bract A modified leaf, from the axil of which arises a flower or an inflorescence.

Breeder seed Seed (or vegetative propagating material; e.g., potato) increased by the originating, or sponsoring, plant breeder or institution and used as the source to increase foundation seed.

Broadcast Scattering seed or fertilizers uniformly over the soil surface rather than placing in rows.

Bud A region of meristematic tissue with the potential for developing into leaves, shoots, flowers, or combinations; generally protected by modified scale leaves.

Bud scar A scar left on a shoot when the bud or bud scales drop.

Bud sport A mutation arising in a bud and producing a genetically different shoot. Includes change due to gene mutation, somatic reduction, chromosome deletion or polyploidy.

Budding A form of grafting in which a single vegetative bud is taken from one plant and inserted into stem tissue of another plant so that the two will grow together. The inserted bud develops into a new shoot.

Bulb A highly compressed underground stem (basal plate) to which numerous storage scales (modified leaves) are attached. Examples are lily, onion, tulip.

Bulk density (soil) The mass of a known volume (including air space) of soil. The soil volume is determined in place, then dried in an oven to constant weight at 105° C. Bulk density (D_B) = oven dry weight of soil/volume of soil.

Bunch type grass Grass that does not spread by rhizomes or stolons.

C horizon A soil layer beneath the B layer that is relatively little affected by biological activity and pedogenesis and is lacking properties diagnostic of an A or B horizon.

C_3 cycle The Calvin-Benson cycle of photosynthesis, in which the first products after CO_2 fixation are three-carbon molecules.

C_4 cycle The Hatch-Slack cycle of photosynthesis, in which the first products after CO_2 fixation are four-carbon molecules.

Calcareous soil Soil containing sufficient calcium and/or magnesium carbonate to effervesce visibly when treated with cold 0.1 normal (0.1N) hydrochloric acid.

Calcium pectate An organic calcium compound found in the middle lamella between plant cells and serving as an intercellular cement.

Callus Mass of large, thin-walled parenchyma cells, usually developing as the result of a wound.

Calorie (gram calorie) Unit for measuring energy, defined as the heat necessary to raise the temperature of 1 g of water from 14.5° C to 15.5° C at standard pressure; 1 kilocalorie (kcal) raises the temperature of 1 kg of water 1° C. Thus 1 kcal = 1000 cal.

Calyx The collective term for the sepals.

Cambium (vascular) A thin layer of longitudinally dividing cells between the xylem and phloem that gives rise to secondary growth.

Capillary water The water held in the "capillary" or small pores of a soil, usually with a tension greater than 60 cm of water.

Capsule (botanical) A simple, dry, dehiscent fruit, with two or more carpels.

Carbohydrate Compound of carbon, hydrogen, and oxygen in the ratio of one atom each of carbon and oxygen to two of hydrogen, as in sugar, starch, and cellulose.

Carbon dioxide fixation The addition of H^+ to CO_2 to yield a chemically stable carbohydrate. The H^+ is contributed by NADPH, the reduced (hydrogen-rich) form of $NADP^+$, produced in the noncyclic phase of the light reactions of photosynthesis. The H^+ comes originally from the photolysis of water.

Carbon-nitrogen ratio The ratio of the weight of organic carbon to the weight of total nitrogen in a soil or in organic material.

Carotene Yellow plant pigments, precursors of vitamin A. Alpha, beta, and gamma carotenes are converted into vitamin A in the animal body.

Carpel Female reproductive organ of flowering plants. In some plants one or more carpels unite to form the pistil.

Caryopsis Small, one-seeded, dry fruit with a thin pericarp surrounding and adhering to the seed; the "seed" (grain) or fruit of grasses.

Casparian strip A secondary thickening that develops on the radial and end walls of some endodermal cells.

Catalyst Any substance that accelerates a chemical reaction but does not enter into the reaction itself.

Cation A positively charged ion.

Cation exchange capacity (base-exchange capacity) A measure of the total amount of exchangeable cations that a soil can hold; expressed in meq/100 g soil at pH 7.

Catkin A type of inflorescence (a spike) generally bearing either pistillate or staminate flowers. Found on walnuts and willows, for example.

Cell The basic structural and physiological unit of plants and animals.

Cell membrane The membrane that separates the cell wall and the cytoplasm and regulates the flow of material into and out of the cell.

Cell plate The precursor of the cell wall, formed as cytokinesis starts during cell division. It develops in the region of the equatorial plate and arises from membranes in the cytoplasm.

Cell wall The outermost, cellulose limit of the plant cell; the barrier that develops between nuclei during mitosis.

Cellulose A complex carbohydrate composed of long, unbranched beta-glucose molecules, which makes up 40 to 55 percent by weight of the plant cell wall.

Cenozoic The geologic era extending from about 65 million years ago to the present time.

Center of origin A geographical area in which a species is thought to have evolved through natural selection from its ancestors.

Cereal A member of the GRAMINAE family grown primarily for its mature, dry seed.

Cereal forage Cereal crop harvested when immature for hay, silage, green chop, or pasturage.

Certified seed The progeny of foundation, registered, or certified seed, produced and handled so as to maintain satisfactory genetic identity and purity, and approved and certified by an official certifying agency.

Character The expression of a gene in the phenotype.

Chelate A chemical compound in which a metallic ion is firmly combined with a molecule by multiple chemical bonds.

Chimera A plant composed of two or more genetically different tissues. Includes *periclinal chimera,* in which one tissue lies over another as a glove fits a hand; *mericlinal chimera,* where the outer tissue does not completely cover the inner tissue; and *sectorial chimera,* in which the tissues lie side by side.

Chisel (subsoil) A tillage implement with one or more cultivator-type shanks to which are attached knifelike units that shatter or break up hard, compact layers, usually in the subsoil.

Chlorophyll A complex organic molecule that traps light energy for conversion through photosynthesis into chemical energy.

Chloroplast Chlorophyll-containing cytoplasmic body, in which important reactions of sugar or starch synthesis take place during photosynthesis.

Chlorosis A condition in which a plant or a part of a plant is light green or greenish yellow because of poor chlorophyll development or the destruction of chlorophyll resulting from a disease or a mineral deficiency.

Chromosome A specific, highly organized body in the nucleus of the cell that contains DNA.

Class (soil) A group of soils having a definite range in a particular property such as acidity, degree of slope, texture, structure, land-use capability, degree of erosion, or drainage.

Classification The systematic arrangement into categories on the basis of characteristics. Broad groupings are made on the basis of general characteristics and subdivisions on the basis of more detailed differences in specific properties.

Clay (1) Soil particles less than 0.002 mm in equivalent diameter. (2) Soil material containing more than 40 percent clay, less than 45 percent sand, and less than 40 percent silt.

Claypan A compact slowly permeable layer of varying thickness and depth in the subsoil having a much higher clay content than the overlying material. Claypans are usually hard when dry, and plastic and sticky when wet.

Climax vegetation Fully developed plant community in equilibrium with its environment.

Clod A compact, coherent mass of soil produced artificially, usually by tillage operations, especially when performed on soils either too wet or too dry.

Clone The aggregate of individual organisms originating from one sexually produced individual (or from a mutation) and maintained exclusively by asexual propagation.

Clove One of a group of small bulbs produced, for example, by garlic and shallot plants.

Coenzyme A substance, usually nonprotein and of low molecular weight, necessary for the action of some enzymes.

Cohesion Holding together; a force holding a solid or liquid together, owing to attraction between like molecules.

Colchicine An alkaloid, derived from the autumn crocus, used specifically to inhibit the spindle mechanism during cell division and thus cause a doubling of chromosome number.

Cold frame An enclosed, unheated covered frame useful for growing and protecting young plants in early spring. The top is covered with glass or plastic, and sunlight provides heat.

Coleoptile A transitory membrane (first leaf) covering the shoot apex in the seedlings of certain monocots. It protects the plumule as it emerges through the soil.

Coleorhiza Sheath that surrounds the radicle of the grass embryo and through which the young developing root emerges.

Collenchyma Enlongated, parenchymatous cells with variously thickened walls, commonly at the acute angles of the cell wall.

Colloid (soil) Organic and inorganic matter with very small particle size and a correspondingly large surface area per unit of mass.

Community All the plant populations within a given habitat; usually the populations are considered to be interdependent.

Companion cells Cells associated with the sieve-tubes in the phloem.

Companion crop A crop sown with another crop and harvested separately. Small-grain cereal crops are often sown with forage crops (grasses or legumes) and harvested in the early summer, allowing the forage crop to continue to grow (e.g., oats sown as a companion crop with red clover).

Compensation point (light) The light intensity at which the rates of photosynthesis and respiration are equal.

Complete flower A flower that has pistils, stamens, petals, and sepals, all attached to a receptacle.

Compost A mixture of organic residues and soil that has been piled, moistened, and allowed to decompose biologically. Mineral fertilizers are sometimes added.

Compound leaf A leaf whose blade is divided into a number of distinct leaflets.

Cone The woody, usually elongated seed-bearing organ of a conifer, consisting of a central stem, woody scales and bracts (often not visible), and seeds.

Contact herbicide A chemical that kills plants on contact.

Cork An external, secondary tissue impermeable to water and gases produced by certain kinds of woody plants.

Cork cambium The cambium from which cork develops.

Corm A short, solid, vertical, enlarged underground stem in which food is stored; it contains undeveloped buds (leaf and flower). Examples are crocus, freesia, and gladiolus.

Corolla The collective term for all petals of a flower.

Cortex Primary tissue of a stem or root bounded externally by the epidermis and internally in the stem by the phloem and in the root by the pericycle.

Cotyledons Leaflike structures at the first node of the seedling stem. In some dicots, cotyledons contain the stored food for the young plant not yet able to photosynthesize its own food. Often referred to as seed leaves.

Cover crop A close-growing crop grown primarily for the purpose of protecting or improving soil between periods of regular crop production or between trees and vines in orchards and vineyards.

Crop residue Portion of crop plants remaining after harvest.

Crop rotation Growing crop plants in a different location in a systematic sequence to help control insects and diseases, improve the soil structure and fertility, and decrease erosion.

Cross-pollination The transfer of pollen from a stamen to the stigma of a flower on another plant, except for clones where the two plants must be in different clones.

Cross-section The surface exposed when a plant stem is cut horizontally and the majority of the cells are cut transversely.

Crown The region at the base of the stem of cereals and forage species from which tillers or branches arise. In woody plants, the root-stem junction. In forestry, the top portions of the tree.

Crumb (soils) A soft, porous, more or less rounded natural unit of structure from 1 to 5 mm in diameter.

Crust A surface layer on soils, ranging in thickness from a few millimeters to a few centimeters. It is more compact, hard, and brittle when dry than the soil beneath it.

Cubing Process of forming hay into high-density cubes to facilitate transportation, storage, and feeding.

Culm Stem of grasses and bamboos; usually hollow except at the swollen nodes.

Cultivar (derived from "*culti*vated *vari*ety") International term denoting certain cultivated plants that are clearly distinguishable from others by any characteristic and that when reproduced (sexually or asexually) retain their distinguishing characters. In the United States *variety* is considered synonomous with *cultivar*.

Cure To prepare crops for storage by drying. Dry onions, sweet potatoes, and hay crops are examples. Dehydration of fruits for storage is not considered curing.

Cuticle An impermeable surface layer on the epidermis of plant organs.

Cutin A clear or transparent waxy material on plant surfaces that tends to make the surface waterproof.

Cutting A detached leaf, stem or root that is encouraged to form new roots and shoots and develop into a new plant.

Cyme A type of inflorescence which has a broad, more or less flat-topped determinate flower cluster, with the central flower opening first.

Cytochrome A class of several electron-transport proteins serving as carriers in mitochondrial oxidation and in photosynthetic electron transport.

Cytokinesis Division of cytoplasmic constituents at cell division.

Cytokinins A group of plant growth hormones important in the regulation of nucleic acid and protein metabolism and in cell division, organ initiation, and delaying senescence.

Cytology The study of cells and their components and of the relationship of cell structure to function.

Cytoplasm The living material of the cell, exclusive of the nucleus, consisting of a complex protein matrix or gel. The part of the cell in which essential membranes and cellular organelles are found.

Damping off A pathogenic disorder causing seedlings to die soon after seed germination.

Day length Number of hours of daylight in each 24-hour cycle.

Day-neutral plants Those capable of flowering under either long or short day lengths.

DDT (Dichlorodiphenyltrichloroethane) One of the earliest insecticides of the chlorinated hydrocarbon family. No longer used in some countries because of its persistence in the environment.

Deciduous Refers to trees and shrubs that lose their leaves every fall. Distinguished from evergreens, which retain them.

Decomposition Degradation into simpler compounds; rotting or decaying.

Dehiscence The splitting open at maturity of pods or capsules along definite lines or sutures.

Dehulled seed Seed from which pods, glumes, or other outer covering have been removed, as sometimes with lespedeza and timothy. Also often ambiguously referred to as "hulled" seed.

Denitrification Biological reduction of nitrate or nitrite to gaseous nitrogen or nitrogen oxides.

Deoxyribonucleic acid (DNA) A molecule composed of repeating subunits of ribose (a sugar), phosphate, and the nitrogenous bases adenine, guanine, cytosine, and thymine. Genes, the fundamental units of inheritance on chromosomes, are sequences of DNA molecules.

Desalinization Removal of salts from saline soil or water.

Determinate (flowering) The flowering of plant species uniformly within certain time limits, allowing most of the fruit to ripen about the same time.

Diatomaceous earth A geologic deposit of fine, grayish, siliceous material composed chiefly of the remains of diatoms.

Dichogamy Maturation of male or female flowers at different times, ensuring cross-pollination. Common in maple and walnuts.

Dicotyledonae (dicots) The subclass of flowering plants that have two cotyledons.

Differentiation Development from one cell to many cells, together with a modification of the new cells for the performance of particular functions.

Diffusion The movement of molecules, and thus a substance, from a region of higher concentration of those molecules to a region of lower concentration.

Digestion The breakdown of complex foods to simpler food materials, which are more easily utilized. Digestion requires energy.

Dihybrid cross A cross between organisms differing in two characters.

Dioecious Refers to individual plants having either staminate (male) or pistilate (female) flowers, but not both. Therefore, plants of both sexes must be grown near each other to provide pollen before fruits and seed can be produced. Examples are English holly, asparagus, ginkgo, date palms.

Diploid (2n) Refers to two sets of chromosomes. Germ cells have one set and are haploid; somatic cells have two sets and are diploid (except for polyploid plants).

Disease Any change from the state of metabolism necessary for the normal development and functioning of any organism.

Disperse (1) to break up compound particles, such as aggregates, into the individual component particles. (2) To distribute or suspend fine particles, such as clay, in or throughout a dispersion medium.

Diurnal Recurring or repeated every day. Going through regular or routine changes daily.

Dominant Referring to the gene (or the expression of the character it influences) that, when present in a hybrid with a contrasting gene, completely dominates in the development of the character. In peaches, for example, white fruit is dominant over yellow.

Dormancy Lack of growth of seeds, buds, bulbs, or tubers due to unfavorable environmental conditions (external dormancy or quiescence) or to factors within the organ itself (internal dormancy or rest).

Double fertilization The process of sexual fertilization in the angiosperms in which one nucleus from the male gametophyte fertilizes the egg nucleus to form the zygote and a second nucleus from the male gametophyte fertilizes two polar nuclei to form endosperm tissue.

Drip irrigation A method of watering plants so that only soil in the plant's immediate vicinity is moistened. Water is supplied from a thin plastic tube at a low rate of flow. Sometimes called trickle irrigation.

Drupe A simple, fleshy fruit derived from a single carpel, usually one-seeded, in which the exocarp is thin, the mesocarp fleshy, and the endocarp hard.

Dry land farming The practice of crop production without irrigation.

Dry matter percentage The percent of the total fresh plant material left after water is removed. The percentage is determined by weighing a sample of fresh plant material, oven-drying the sample, then reweighing the dried sample. Dry matter percentage equals fresh weight of sample less dry weight and the difference divided by the dry weight times 100.

Earlywood (spring wood) The less dense part of the growth ring. It is made up of cells with thinner walls, a greater radial diameter, and shorter length than those formed later in the year.

Ecology The study of life in relation to its environment.

Ecosystem A living community and all the factors in its nonliving environment.

Ecotype Genetic variant within a species that is adapted to a particular environment yet remains interfertile with all other members of the species.

Edaphic Pertaining to the influence of the soil on plant growth.

Electron The elementary charge of negative electricity.

Element A substance that cannot be divided or reduced by any known chemical means to a simpler substance; 92 natural elements are known.

Eluviation The removal of soil material in suspension (or in solution) from a layer or layers of a soil. (Usually, the loss of materials in solution is described by the term *leaching*.)

Emasculate To remove the anthers from a bud or flower before pollen is shed. Emasculation is a normal preliminary step in hybridization to prevent self-pollination.

Embryo A miniature plant within a seed produced as a result of the union of a male and female gamete resulting in the development of a zygote.

Embryo sac Typically, an eight-nucleate female gametophyte. The embryo sac arises from the megaspore by successive mitotic divisions.

Endemic. Species native to a particular environment or locality.

Endocarp Inner layer of the fruit wall (pericarp).

Endodermis In roots, a single layer of cells at the inner edge of the cortex. The endodermis separates the cortical cells from cells of the pericycle.

Endogenous Produced from within. Opposite of *exogenous*.

Endoplasmic reticulum The lamellar or tubular system of the colorless cytoplasm in a cell.

Endosperm The 3n tissue of angiospermous seeds that develops from sexual fusion of the two polar nuclei of the embryo sac and a male sperm cell. The endosperm provides nutrition for the developing embryo. A food storage tissue.

Energy (kinetic) The capacity to do work. Examples are light, heat, chemical, electrical, or nuclear energy.

Enzyme Any of many complex proteins produced in living cells, that, even in very low concentrations, promotes certain chemical reactions but does not enter into the reactions itself.

Epicotyl The upper portion of the embryo axis or seedling, above the cotyledons and below the first true leaves.

Epidermis The outer layer of cells on all parts of the primary plant body: stems, leaves, roots, flowers, fruits, and seeds. It is absent from the root cap and on apical meristems.

Epigeal germination A type of seed germination in dicots in which the cotyledons rise above the soil surface. This occurs in beans, for example.

Epigyny Arrangement of flower parts in which the ovary is embedded in the receptacle so that the other parts appear to arise from the top of the ovary.

Epiphyte A plant that grows upon another plant yet is not parasitic.

Erosion The wearing away of the surface soil by wind, moving water, or other means.

Ethylene A gaseous growth hormone (C_2H_4) regulating various aspects of vegetative growth, fruit ripening, and abscission of plant parts.

Etiolation A condition involving lack of chlorophyll, increased stem elongation, and poor or absent leaf development. It occurs in plants growing under very low light intensity or complete darkness.

Evapotranspiration The total loss of water by evaporation from the soil surface and by transpiration from plants, from a given area, and during a specified period of time.

Evergreen Trees or shrubs that are never entirely leafless, as in pine or citrus.

Evolution The development of a species, genus, or other larger group of plants or animals over a long time period.

Exchange capacity The total ionic charge of the adsorption complex active in the adsorption of ions. Also called anion exchange capacity, cation exchange capacity, and base exchange capacity.

Exocarp The outermost layer of the fruit wall (pericarp).

Exogenous Produced outside of, originating from, or because of external causes. Opposite of *endogenous*.

Explant Living tissue removed from its place in a body and placed in an artificial medium for tissue culture.

F₁ First filial generation in a cross between any two parents.

F₂ Second filial generation, obtained by crossing two members of the F_1 generation, or by self-pollinating plants of the F_1 generation.

Facultative Referring to an organism having the power to live under a variety of conditions; a facultative parasite is either parasitic or saprophytic.

Fallow Cropland left idle for one or more seasons for any number of reasons, such as to accumulate moisture, destroy weeds, and allow the decomposition of crop residue.

Family In plant taxonomy, a group of genera.

Fascicle A bundle of needle-leaves of gymnosperms such as the pines.

Fatty acid Organic compound of carbon, hydrogen, and oxygen that combines with glycerol to make a fat.

Fermentation An anaerobic chemical reaction in foods, such as the production of alcohol from sugar by yeasts.

Fertilization (floral) The union of an egg and a sperm (gametes) to form a zygote.

Fertilization (soil) Application to the soil of needed plant nutrients, such as nitrogen, phosphoric acid, potash, and others.

Fertilizer Any organic or inorganic material of natural or synthetic origin added to a soil to supply elements essential to the growth of plants.

Fibers Elongated, tapering, thick-walled strengthening cells in various parts of the plant.

Field capacity (field moisture capacity) The percentage of water remaining in a soil two or three days after having been saturated and after free drainage due to gravity has practically ceased.

Fixation (soil) The process in soil by which certain chemical elements essential for plant growth convert from a soluble or exchangeable form to a much less soluble or to a nonexchangeable form.

Fleshy fruit Any fruit formed from an ovary that has fleshy or pulpy (not dried) walls at maturity. Also, those fruits that include fleshy parts of the perianth, floral tube, or the receptacle.

Flocculate To clump together individual, tiny soil particles, especially fine clay, into small granules. Opposite of *disperse*.

Flooding A method of irrigation by which water is released from field ditches and allowed to spread over the land.

Flora A collective term for all the plant types that grow in a region.

Floral incompatibility A genetic condition in which certain normal male gametes are incapable of functioning in certain pistils.

Flower Floral leaves grouped together on a stem that, in the angiosperms, are adapted for sexual reproduction.

Fodder Coarse grasses such as corn and sorghum harvested with the seed and leaves and cured for animal feed.

Follicle A simple, dry dehiscent fruit, having one carpel and splitting along one suture. Examples are milkweeds and magnolia.

Food chain The path along which food energy is transferred within a natural plant and animal community (from producers to consumers to decomposers).

Foot-candle (ft-c) A standard measure of light (English system). The light of one candle falling on a surface one foot away from the candle. 1 ft-c = 10.76 lux. *See* Lux.

Forage Vegetation used as feed for livestock, such as hay, pasture, and silage. The material is fed green or dehydrated.

Forcing A cultural manipulation used to hasten flowering or growing plants outside their natural season.

Fossil Any impression, natural or impregnated remains, or other trace of an animal or plant of past geological eras that has been preserved in the earth's crust.

Foundation seed Seed stocks increased from breeder seed, and handled to closely maintain the genetic identity and purity of a cultivar.

Friable (soil) Generally refers to a soil consistency that crumbles when handled.

Fruit A mature ovary; in some plants other flower parts are commonly included as part of the fruit, e.g., the hypanthium of the apple flower surrounds the ovary.

Fumigation Control of insects, disease-causing organisms, weeds, or nematodes by gases applied in an enclosed area such as a greenhouse or under plastic laid on the soil.

Fungicide A pesticide chemical used to control plant diseases caused by fungi.

Fungus (plural, fungi) A thallus plant unable to photosynthesize its own food (exclusive of bacteria).

Furrow Small V-shaped ditch made for planting seed or for irrigating.

Furrow irrigation A method of irrigation by which the water is applied to row crops in ditches.

Gamete An haploid-generation male sperm cell or a female egg cell capable of developing into an embryo after fusion with a germ cell of the opposite sex.

Gametophyte In a seed plant the few-celled, haploid generation arising from a meiotic division and giving rise through mitosis to the male or female gametes.

Gene A group of base pairs in the DNA molecule in the chromosome that determines or conditions one or more hereditary characters.

Genetic code The sequence of nitrogen bases in a DNA

molecule that codes for an amino acid or protein. In a broader sense, for example, the full sequence of events from the translation of chromosomal DNA to the final stage of the synthesis of an enzyme.

Genetics   The science or study of inheritance.

Genotype   The genetic makeup of a nucleus or of an individual.

Genus (plural, genera)   A group of structurally or phylogenetically related species.

Geotropism   Growth curvature in plants induced by gravity.

Germination (seed)   Sequence of events in a viable seed starting with imbibition of water that leads to growth of the embryo and development of a seedling.

Gibberellins   A group of natural growth hormones whose most characteristic effect is to increase the elongation of stems.

Glacial till   A product of glacial weathering in which rock particles varying in size from clay to boulders are deposited by the glacier on the land surface as it melts and recedes.

Glucose   A simple sugar composed of 6 carbon, 12 hydrogen, and 6 oxygen atoms ($C_6H_{12}O_6$).

Graft   To place a detached branch (scion) in close cambial contact with a rooted stem (rootstock) in such a manner that scion and rootstock unite to form a new plant.

Grain (caryopsis)   A simple, dry, indehiscent fruit with ovary walls fused to the seed. The so-called seed of cereal or grain crops such as corn, wheat, barley, and oats is actually a fruit.

Gravitational water   Water that moves into, through, or out of the soil under the influence of gravity.

Green chop   Forage that is chopped in the field while succulent and green and fed directly to livestock, made into silage, or dehydrated.

Green manure   A crop that is plowed under while still green and growing to improve the soil.

Groundwater   Water that fills all the unblocked pores of underlying material below the water table, which is the upper limit of saturation.

Growing medium (soil mix)   Soil or soil substitute prepared by combining such materials as peat moss, vermiculite, sand, or composted sawdust. Used for growing potted plants or germinating seed.

Growth   An irreversible increase in cell size and/or cell number. An increase in dry weight, regardless of cause.

Growth regulator   A synthetic or natural compound that in low concentrations controls growth responses in plants.

Growth retardant   A chemical that selectively interferes with normal hormonal promotion of plant growth, but without appreciable toxic effects.

Guard cells   Specialized epidermal cells that contain chloroplasts and surround a stoma.

Gully erosion   A process whereby water accumulates in narrow channels and, over relatively short periods, removes the soil from this narrow area to considerable depths.

Guttation   Exudation of water in liquid form from plants.

Gymnosperm   A seed plant with seeds not enclosed by a megasporophyll or pistil.

Gynoecium   The female part of a flower or pistil formed by one or more carpels and composed of the stigma, style, and ovary.

Haploid   Having only one complete set of chromosomes; referring to an individual or generation containing such a single set of chromosomes per cell.

Hardening off   Adapting plants to outdoor conditions by withholding water, lowering the temperature, or nutrient supply. This conditions plants for survival when transplanted outdoors.

Hardpan   A hardened soil layer, in the lower A horizon or in the upper B horizon, caused by the cementing of soil particles.

Hardy plants   Plants adapted to cold temperatures or other adverse climatic conditions of an area. *Half-hardy* indicates some plants may be able to take local conditions with a certain amount of protection.

Hay   Herbage of forage plants, including seed of grasses and legumes, that is harvested and dried for animal feed.

Head (botanical)   A type of inflorescence, typical of the composite family, in which the individual flowers are grouped closely together on a receptacle.

Heaving   The partial lifting of plants out of the ground, frequently breaking their roots, as a result of freezing and thawing of the surface soil during the winter.

Heavy soil   A soil with a high content of the fine separates, particularly clay, or one with a high tractor power requirement and hence difficult to cultivate.

Heeling in   Temporary storing of bare-rooted trees and shrubs by placing the roots in a trench and covering with soil or sawdust.

Helix   A spiral form; a term often used in reference to the double spiral of the DNA molecule.

Herbaceous   Refers to plants that do not develop woody tissues.

Herbarium   A collection of dried and pressed plant specimens.

Herbicide   Any chemical used to kill plants; an herbicide may work against a narrow or a wide range of plant species.

Herbivore   Animal that subsists principally or entirely on plants or plant products.

Heredity   The transmission of morphological and physiological characters from parents to their offspring.

Hermaphrodite flower   A flower having both stamens (male) and pistils (female).

Heterosis (hybrid vigor)   (1) The increased vigor, growth, size, yield, or function of a hybrid progeny over the parents that results from crossing genetically unlike organisms. (2) The increase in vigor or growth of a hybrid progeny in relation to the average of the parents.

Heterotrophic   Capable of deriving energy for life processes only from the decomposition of organic compounds and incapable of using inorganic compounds as sole sources of energy or for organic synthesis. Contrast with *autotrophic*.

Heterozygous   Having different genes of a Mendelian pair present in the same cell or organism; for instance, a tall pea plant with genes for both tallness (T) and dwarfness (t).

Hill   Raising the soil in a slight mound for planting, or setting plants some distance apart.

Hilum The scar on a dicot seed, such as a bean seed, where it was attached to the fruit.

Histology The science that deals with the microscopic structure of plant or animal tissues.

Homologous chromosomes The two members of a chromosome pair.

Homozygous Having similar genes of a Mendelian pair present in the same cell or organism; for instance, a dwarf pea plant with genes for dwarfness (tt) only.

Horizon, soil A layer of soil, approximately parallel to the soil surface, with distinct characteristics produced by soil-forming processes.

Hormone A chemical substance that is produced in one part of a plant and used in minute quantities to induce a growth response in another part. For example, auxins are one type of hormone.

Hotbed A bed of soil enclosed in a low glass or transparent plastic frame and heated with fermenting manure, electric cables, or steam pipes. Used to germinate seeds, root cuttings, and grow other plants for transplanting outside.

Hot caps Waxpaper cones, paper sacks, or cardboard boxes with bottoms removed and placed over individual plants in spring for frost and wind protection.

Humidity, relative The ratio of the weight of water vapor in a given quantity of air to the total weight of water vapor that quantity of air is capable of holding at a given temperature, expressed as a percentage.

Humus The more or less stable fraction of the soil organic matter remaining after the major portion of plant and animal residues have decomposed.

Hybrid The offspring of two plants or animals differing in one or more Mendelian characters.

Hybridization (1) The crossing of individuals of unlike genetic constitution. (2) A method of breeding new cultivars that uses crossing to obtain genetic recombinations.

Hydrologic cycle The movement of water from the atmosphere to the earth and its return to the atmosphere.

Hydrolysis A chemical reaction in which water participates as a reactant and not as a solvent. Usually, the splitting of a molecule to form smaller molecules that incorporate hydrogen and hydroxyl ions, derived from water, in their structures.

Hydroponics Growing plants in aerated water containing all the essential mineral nutrients rather than soil. Also called soilless gardening.

Hypogeal germination In dicots, a type of seed germination in which the cotyledons remain below the soil surface; for example, peas.

Hypothesis A proposition or supposition provisionally adopted to explain certain facts. Once proven by ultimate scientific investigation, it becomes a theory or a law.

Igneous rock Rock formed from the cooling and solidification of magma that has not been changed appreciably since its formation.

Illuminance The luminous flux (brightness of light) per unit area on an intercepting surface at any given point.

Imbibition The absorption of liquids or vapors into the ultramicroscopic spaces in materials like cellulose.

Immune Free from attack by a given pathogen; not subject to the disease.

Imperfect flower A flower lacking either stamens or pistils.

Impervious Resistant to penetration by fluids or by roots.

Inbred line A pure line usually originating by self-pollination and selection.

Incompatibility (floral) Failure to obtain fertilization and seed formation after pollination, usually because of slow pollen tube growth in the stylar tissue.

Incompatibility (graft) Failure of two graft components (stock and scion) to unite and develop into a successfully growing plant.

Incomplete flower A flower that is missing one or more of the following parts: sepals, petals, stamens, or pistils.

Indehiscent fruit A fruit that does not split open naturally at maturity.

Indeterminate Pertaining to growth of plants, the flowers of which are borne on lateral branches, the central stem continuing vegetative growth, with blooming continued for a long period. Examples are alfalfa and fuchsia.

Indigenous Produced or living naturally in a specific environment.

Indoleacetic acid (IAA) A natural or synthetic plant growth regulator; an auxin.

Inferior ovary An ovary that is imbedded in the receptacle, or an ovary whose base lies below the point of attachment of the perianth.

Infiltration rate The maximum velocity at which water can enter the soil under specified conditions, including the presence of an excess of water.

Inflorescence An axis bearing flowers, or a flower cluster (e.g., umbel, spike, panicle).

Inheritance The acquisition of characters or qualities by transmission from parent to offspring.

Inoculate (1) To induce a disease in a living organism by introducing a pathogen. (2) To treat seeds of leguminous plants with bacteria to induce nitrogen-fixation in the roots.

Inorganic compound A chemical compound that generally is not derived from life processes; compounds that do not contain carbon.

Insecticide Any chemical (organic or inorganic) substance that kills insects.

Integuments The tissues covering or surrounding the ovule, usually consisting of an inner and outer layer; they subsequently become the seedcoats of the mature ovule.

Intercalary growth A pattern of stem elongation typical of grasses. Elongation proceeds from the lower internodes to the upper internodes through the differentiation of meristematic tissue at the base of each internode.

Internode The region of a stem between two successive nodes.

In vitro Latin for "in glass." Living in test tubes; outside the organism or in an artificial environment.

In vivo Latin for "in living." In the living organism.

Ions Atoms, groups of atoms, or compounds that are electrically charged as a result of the loss of electrons (cations) or the gain of electrons (anions).

Irradiation In genetics and plant breeding, exposing seed, pollen, or other plant parts to X-rays or other short wavelength (gamma) radiations to increase mutation rates.

Irrigation Applying water to the soil, other than by natural rainfall.

Isolation The prevention of crossing among plant populations because of distance or geographic barriers (geographic isolation).

Lamina Blade or expanded part of a leaf.

Lateral bud A bud that grows out from the leaf axil on the side of a stem.

Latewood (summer wood) The denser part of the growth ring produced late in the season. It is made up of xylem cells with thicker walls, smaller radial diameter, and generally longer than those formed earlier in the growing season.

Latex A milky secretion produced by various kinds of plants.

Lathhouse An open structure built of wood lath or plastic screen for protecting plants from excessive sunlight or frost.

Layering A form of vegetative propagation in which an intact branch develops roots as the result of contact with the soil or another rooting medium.

Leach To remove soluble materials from soil or plant tissue with water.

Leaf mold Partially decayed leaves useful for improving soil structure and fertility.

Leggy Weak-stemmed and spindly plants with sparse foliage caused by too much heat, shade, crowding, or overfertilization. *See* Etiolation.

Legume Plant member of the family LEGUMINOSAE, with the characteristic capability to fix atmospheric nitrogen in nodules on its roots if inoculated with proper bacteria.

Lenticel An opening made up of loosely arranged cells in the periderm that permits passage of gases.

Light reactions The reactions of photosynthesis in which light energy is required: the photo (light) activation or excitement of electrons in the chlorophyll molecule, transfer of the electrons, photolysis of water, and associated reactions.

Light soil A coarse-textured sandy soil; hence easy to till.

Lignin An organic substance found in secondary cell walls that gives stems strength and hardness. Wood is composed of lignified xylem cells (about 15 to 30 percent by weight).

Lime (agricultural) A material containing the carbonates, oxides and/or hydroxides of calcium and/or magnesium. It is used to increase soil pH and to neutralize soil acidity.

Line Group of individuals from a common ancestry. When propagated by seed, it retains its characteristics. A type of cultivar.

Lipid Any of a group of fats or fatlike compounds insoluble in water but soluble in certain other solvents.

Loam A textural class for soil with prescribed amounts of sand, silt, and clay.

Lodging A condition in which plants are caused to bend for various reasons at or near the soil surface and fall more or less flat on the ground. Most frequently observed in cereals.

Lucerne A name used in Europe, Australia, and other regions for alfalfa.

Lux (lx) The amount of illumination impinging upon a surface of 1m², each point of which is at a distance of 1m away from a uniform point source of light from one candle. 1 lux = 0.093 ft-c.

Macronutrient A chemical element, like nitrogen, phosphorus, and potassium, necessary in large amounts (usually greater than 1 ppm) for the growth of plants.

Male sterility A condition in some plants in which pollen either is not formed or does not function normally, even though the stamens may appear normal.

Malthusian theory Developed by T. Malthus, a British economist (1766–1834), who speculated that the world's population would grow faster than food productivity and thus world starvation would eventually occur.

Meiosis Two successive nuclear divisions, in the course of which the diploid chromosome number is reduced to the haploid and genetic segregation occurs.

Mendel's laws A set of three laws formulated by Gregor Mendel; each is generally true but there are numerous exceptions. The laws are: (1) characters exhibit alternative inheritance, being either dominant or recessive; (2) each gamete receives one member of each pair of factors present in a mature individual; and (3) reproductive cells combine at random.

Meristem Undifferentiated tissue whose cells can divide and differentiate to form specialized tissues; such as xylem or phloem.

Mesocarp Middle layer of the fruit wall (pericarp).

Mesophyll Parenchyma tissue in leaves found between the two epidermal layers.

Mesozoic A geologic era beginning 225 million years ago and ending 65 million years ago

Messenger RNA Ribonucleic acid produced in the nucleus and capable of carrying parts of the message coded in chromosomal DNA. Messenger RNA moves from the nucleus to the ribosomes, where protein is synthesized in the cytoplasm.

Metabolism The overall physiological activities of an organism.

Metamorphic rock A rock that has been greatly altered from its previous condition through the combined action of heat and pressure.

Microclimate Atmospheric environmental conditions in the immediate vicinity of the plant, including interchanges of energy, gases, and water between atmosphere and soil.

Micronutrient A chemical element necessary in extremely small amounts (less than 1ppm) for the growth of plants. Examples are boron, chlorine, copper, iron, manganese, and zinc.

Micropyle An opening leading from the outer surface of the ovule between the edges of the two integuments inward to the surface of the nucellus.

Microspore One of the four haploid spores that originates from the meiotic division of the microspore mother cell in the anther of the flower and that gives rise to the pollen grain.

Microspore mother cell Diploid cell in the anther that gives rise, through meiosis, to four haploid microspores.

Middle lamella The pectic layer lying between the primary cell walls of adjoining cells.

Millimho (mmho) A measure of electrical conductivity, 1 mmho = 0.001 mho. The mho is the reciprocal of an ohm.

Mineral soil A soil whose makeup and physical properties are largely those of mineral matter.

Minor element *See* Micronutrient.

Mist propagation Applying water in mist form to leafy cuttings in the rooting stage to reduce transpiration.

Mitosis A form of nuclear cell division in which chromosomes duplicate and divide to yield two nuclei that are identical with the original nucleus. Usually mitosis includes cellular division (cytokinesis).

Mixed bud A bud containing both rudimentary flowers and vegetative shoots.

Moisture, dry basis A basis for representing moisture content of a product. It is calculated from the net weight of water lost by drying, divided by dried weight of the material and the answer multiplied by 100 = percent.

Mole (M) Amount of a substance that has a weight in grams numerically equal to the molecular weight of the substance. Also called gram-molecular weight.

Molecular biology A field of biology concerned with the interaction of biochemistry and genetics in the life of an organism.

Molecule A unit of matter; the smallest portion of an element or a compound that retains chemical identity with the substance in mass. A molecule usually consists of the union of two or more atoms, and some organic molecules contain hundreds of atoms.

Monocotyledonae (monocots) The subclass of flowering plants that have only a single cotyledon at the first node of the primary stem.

Monoecious A plant with separate male and female flowers on the same plant, such as corn and walnuts.

Morphology (plant) The study or science of the form, structure, and development of plants.

Muck (soil) Highly decomposed organic material in which the original plant parts are not recognizable.

Mulch Any material such as straw, sawdust, leaves, plastic film, and loose soil that is spread upon the surface of the soil to protect the soil and plant roots from the effects of rain, soil crusting, freezing, or evaporation.

Multiple fruit A cluster of matured fused ovaries produced by separate flowers; for example, pineapple.

Mutation A sudden, heritable change appearing in an individual as the result of a change in genes or chromosomes.

Mycelium The mass of hyphae forming the body of a fungus.

Mycology A branch of botany dealing with the study of fungi.

Mycorrhiza The association, usually symbiotic, of fungi with the roots of some seed plants.

Nanometer (nm) A unit of length equal to one millionth (10^{-6}) of a millimeter or one millimicron; 1 nm equals 10 angstrom units.

Natural selection Environmental effects in channeling the genetic variation of organisms along certain pathways.

Naturalized plant A plant introduced from one environment into another in which the plant has become established and more or less adapted to a given region by growing there for many generations.

Necrosis Death associated with discoloration and dehydration of all or some parts of plant organs.

Nematodes Unsegmented roundworms abundant in many soils; important because many species of them attack plants or animals.

Neutral soil A soil in which the surface layer is neither acid nor alkaline in reaction.

Nitrification The conversion of ammonium ions into nitrates through the activities of certain bacteria.

Nitrogen assimilation The incorporation of nitrogen into organic cell substances by living organisms.

Nitrogen fixation The conversion of atmospheric nitrogen (N_2) into oxidized forms that can be assimilated by plants. Certain blue-green algae and bacteria are capable of biochemically fixing nitrogen.

Nitrogenous base A nitrogen-containing compound found in DNA and RNA that in sequence, specifies precise genetic information. The nitrogenous bases in DNA are adenine, thymine, cytosine, and guanine. In RNA, they are adenine, uracil, cytosine, and guanine.

Nodes Enlarged regions of stems that are generally solid where leaves are attached and buds are located. Stems have nodes but roots do not.

Nucellus A tissue originally making up the major part of the young ovule, in which the embryo sac develops.

Nucleic acid An acid found in all nuclei; all known nucleic acids fall into two classes, DNA and RNA.

Nut A dry, indehiscent, single-seeded fruit with a hard, woody pericarp (shell), such as the walnut and pecan.

Nutrient, plant Element essential to plant growth used in the elaboration of food and tissue.

Obligate parasite An organism that must live as a parasite and cannot otherwise survive.

Obligate saprophyte An organism obliged to live only on nonliving animal or plant tissue.

Opposite An arrangement of leaves or buds on a stem. They occur in pairs on opposite sides of a single node.

Organ A part of an animal or plant body adapted by its structure for a particular function.

Organic In chemistry, the carbon compounds, many of which are associated with living organisms.

Organic soil A soil that contains a high percentage (greater than 20 percent) of organic matter.

Osmosis The diffusion of fluids through a semipermeable or selectively permeable membrane.

Ovary The basal, generally enlarged part of the pistil in which seeds are formed. The ovary, at maturity, is a fruit. It is a characteristic organ of angiospermous plants.

Ovule A rudimentary seed, containing, before fertilization, the embryo sac, including an egg cell, all being enclosed in the nucellus and one or two integuments.

Oxidation-reduction reaction A chemical reaction in which one substance is oxidized (loses electrons, or loses hydrogen ions and their associated electrons, or combines with oxygen) and a second substance is reduced (gains electrons, or gains hydrogen ions and their associated electron, or loses oxygen).

Oxidative respiration The chemical decomposition of foods (glucose, fats, and proteins) requiring oxygen as a terminal electron acceptor and yielding carbon dioxide, water, and energy. The energy is commonly stored in ATP.

Palatability Term used to describe how agreeable or attractive feed stuff is to animals or how readily they consume it.

Paleozoic A geologic era beginning about 570 million years ago and ending about 225 million years ago.

Palisade parenchyma The cell layer in leaves immediately below the upper epidermis; packed with chloroplasts. Found in dicots, but not in monocots.

Palmate Arrangement of leaflets of a compound leaf or of the veins in a leaf. Characterized by subunits arising from a common point much as fingers arise from the palm of the hand.

Panicle An inflorescence, common in the grass family, that has a branched central axis. An example is oats.

Parasite An organism obtaining its nutrients from the living body of another plant or animal.

Parenchyma A tissue composed of thin-walled, loosely packed, unspecialized cells.

Parthenocarpy Fruit development without sexual fertilization. Such fruits are seedless. Examples are the 'Navel' orange and some fig cultivars.

Particle size (soil) The effective diameter of a particle measured by sedimentation, sieving, or micrometric methods.

Parts per million (ppm) Weight units of any given substance per one million equivalent weight units; the weight units of solute per million weight units of solution (i.e., 1 ppm = 1 mg/l).

Pasture Area of domesticated forages, usually improved, on which animals are grazed.

Pathogen An organism that causes disease.

Pathology The study of diseases, their effects on plants or animals, and their treatment.

Pearl The process of grinding off the hull, bran, aleurone, and germ of barley or rice to yield a pellet of endosperm.

Peat Any unconsolidated soil mass of semicarbonized vegetable tissue formed by partial decomposition in water. An example is sphagnum peat moss.

Pectin Polysaccharide from the middle lamella of the plant cell wall; jelly-forming substance found in fruit.

Ped A unit of soil structure such as an aggregate, crumb, prism, block, or granule formed by natural processes.

Pedicel Individual flower stalk of an inflorescence.

Peduncle Flower stalk that is borne singly; or the main stem of an inflorescence.

Percolation, soil water The downward movement of water through soil.

Perennial A plant that grows more or less indefinitely from year to year and usually produces seed each year.

Perfect flower Having both stamens and pistils; an hermaphroditic flower.

Perianth The petals and sepals of a flower, collectively.

Pericarp The fruit wall, which develops from the ovary wall.

Pericycle The layer of cells immediately inside the endodermis. Branch roots arise from the pericycle.

Periderm A corky layer formed by the cork cambium at the surface of organs that are undergoing secondary growth.

Permanent wilting percentage. *See* Wilting point.

Permeable Referring to a membrane, cell, or cell system through which substances may diffuse.

Petal Part of a flower, often brightly colored.

Petiole The stalk that attaches a leaf blade to a stem.

pH (solution) A measure of acidity or alkalinity, expressed as the negative logarithm (base 10) of the hydrogen-ion concentration. pH 7 is neutral. Values less than this indicate acidity; higher values indicate alkalinity.

pH (soil) The negative logarithm of the hydrogen-ion activity of a soil.

Phellogen Cork cambium, a cambium layer giving rise externally to cork and, in some plants, internally to phelloderm.

Phenology The study of the timing of periodic phenomena such as flowering, growth initiation, or growth cessation, especially as related to seasonal changes in temperature or photoperiod.

Phenotype The external physical appearance of an organism.

Phloem A tissue through which nutritive and other materials are translocated through the plant. The phloem consists of sieve tube cells, companion cells, phloem parenchyma, and fibers.

Photoperiod That length of day or period of daily illumination required for the normal growth and sexual reproduction of some plants.

Photoperiodism Response of a plant to the relative lengths of day and night (light and dark), particularly in respect to flower initiation and bulbing.

Photophosphorylation The production of ATP by the addition of a phosphate group to ADP using the energy of light-excited electrons produced in the light reactions of photosynthesis. Photo = light, phosphorylation = adding phosphorus.

Photosynthesis The process in green plants of converting water and carbon dioxide into sugar with light energy; accompanied by the production of oxygen.

Phototropism A change in the manner of growth of a plant in response to nonuniform illumination. Usually, the response, which is auxin-regulated, is a bending toward the strongest light.

Phylum A primary division of the animal or plant kingdom.

Physiology, plant The science of the functions and activities of living plants.

Phytochrome A reversible protein pigment occurring in the cytoplasm of green plants. It is associated with the absorption of light that affects growth, development, and differentiation of a plant, independent of photosynthesis (e.g., in the photoperiodic response).

Pigments   Molecules that are colored by the light they absorb. Some plant pigments are water soluble and are found mainly in the cell vacuole.

Pinching   The removal of the terminal bud or apical meristematic growth to stimulate branching.

Pistil   The seed-bearing organ in the flower, composed of the ovary, the style, and the stigma.

Pistillate flower   A female flower having pistils but no stamens.

Pith   A region in the center of some stems and roots consisting of loosely packed, thin-walled parenchyma cells.

Placenta (plural, placentae)   The tissue within the ovary to which the ovules are attached.

Plasmolysis   The separation of the cytoplasm from the cell wall because of the removal of water from the protoplast.

Plastids   The cellular organelles in which carbohydrate metabolism is localized.

Plow layer   The surface soil layer ordinarily moved in tillage.

Plow-plant   The practice of plowing and planting a crop in one operation, with no additional seedbed preparation.

Plumule   The first bud of an embryo or that portion of the young shoot above the cotyledons.

Polar nuclei   Two centrally located nuclei in the embryo sac that unite with a second sperm cell in a triple fusion. In certain seeds the product of this fusion develops into the endosperm.

Polar transport   The directed movement within plants of compounds (usually hormones) mostly in one direction; polar transport overcomes the tendency for diffusion in all directions.

Pollen   The almost microscopic, yellow bodies that are borne within the anthers of flowers and contain the male generative (sex) cells.

Pollen mother cell   A 2n cell that divides twice (once by meiosis and once by mitosis) to form a tetrad of four pollen grains.

Pollen tube   A tubelike structure developed by the tube nucleus in the microspore that helps guide the sperm through the stigma and style of a flower to the embryo sac.

Pollination   The transfer of pollen from a stamen (or staminate cone) to a stigma (or ovulate cone).

Polyembryony   The presence of more than one embryo in a developing seed.

Polyploidy   A condition in which a plant has somatic (nonsexual) cells with more than 2n chromosomes per nucleus.

Polysaccharides   Long-chain molecules composed of units of a sugar; starch and cellulose are examples.

Pome   A simple fleshy fruit, the outer portion of which is formed by floral parts that surround the ovary (i.e., apple and pear fruits).

Pore size distribution   The volume of the various sizes of pores in a soil. It is expressed as a percentage of the bulk volume (soil plus pore space).

Porosity   That percentage of the total bulk volume of a soil not occupied by the solid particles.

Postemergence spray   A pesticide or herbicide that is applied after the crop plants have emerged from the soil.

Potting mixture (soil mix)   Combination of various ingredients such as soil, peat, sand, perlite, or vermiculite designed for starting seeds or growing plants in containers.

Pre-emergence spray   A pesticide or herbicide that is applied after planting, but before the crop plants emerge from the soil.

Primary tissue   A tissue that has differentiated from a primary meristem.

Primordium   An organ in its earliest stage of development, such as leaf primordium.

Profile (soil)   A vertical section of the soil through all its horizons and extending into the parent material.

Protein   Any of a group of nitrogen-containing compounds that yield amino acids on hydrolysis and have high molecular weights. They are essential parts of living matter and are one of the essential food substances of animals.

Proterozoic   The earliest geologic era, beginning about 4.5 to 5 billion years ago and ending 570 million years ago; also called Precambrian era.

Protoplasm   The essential, complex living substance of cells on which all vital functions of nutrition, secretion, growth, and reproduction depend.

Protoplast   The organized living unit of a single cell.

Provenance   The natural origin of a tree or group of trees. In forestry, the term is considered synonymous with geographic origin.

Pure line   Plants in which all members have descended by self-fertilization from a single homozygous individual.

Raceme   An inflorescence in which flowers on pedicels are borne on a single, unbranched main axis.

Radial face   The wood surface exposed when a stem is cut along a radius from pith to bark, and the cut parallels the long axis of the majority of the cells.

Radicle   The part of the embryonic axis that becomes the primary root. The first part of the embryo to start growth during seed germination.

Range   Land and native vegetation that is predominantly grasses, grasslike plants, or shrubs suitable for grazing by animals.

Range management   Producing maximum sustained use of range forage without detriment to other resources or uses of land.

Raphe   Ridge on seeds, formed by the stalk of the ovule, in those seeds in which the funiculus is sharply bent at the base of the ovule.

Ray   A narrow group of cells, usually parenchyma, extending radially in the wood and bark.

Reaction (soil)   *See* pH (soil).

Receptacle   The enlarged tip of a stem on which a flower is borne.

Recessive   The condition of a gene such that it does not express itself in the presence of the contrasting (dominant) gene.

Recombination The mixing of genotypes that results from sexual reproduction.

Reduction division A nuclear division in which the chromosomes are reduced from the diploid to the haploid number.

Registered seed The progeny of foundation or registered seed produced and handled so as to maintain satisfactory genetic identity and purity, and approved and certified by an official certifying agency. Registered seed is normally grown for the production of certified seed.

Replication In cell physiology, the production of a second molecule of DNA exactly like the first molecule.

Reproduction, sexual Development of new plants by seeds (except in apomixis).

Reproduction, vegetative (vegetative propagation) Reproduction by other than sexually produced seed. Includes grafting, cuttings, layering, and so forth, as well as apomixis.

Respiration The oxidation of food by plants and animals to yield energy for cellular activities.

Rest period An endogenous physiological condition of viable seeds, buds, or bulbs that prevents growth even in the presence of otherwise favorable environmental conditions. This is referred to by some seed physiologists as *dormancy*.

Rhizobium Genus of bacteria that live symbiotically in the roots of legumes and fix nitrogen that is used by plants.

Rhizome An underground stem, usually horizontal and often elongated; distinguished from a root by the presence of nodes and internodes. Capable of producing new shoots.

Ribonucleic acid, RNA A single-strand acid, formed on a DNA template, found in the protoplasm, and controlling cellular chemical activities. Whereas DNA transmits genetic information from one cell generation to the next, ribonucleic acid is an intermediate chemical translating genetic information into action.

Ribosome A protoplasmic granule containing ribonucleic acid (RNA) and believed to be the site of protein synthesis.

Ripening Chemical and physical changes in a fruit that follow maturation.

Rock The material that forms the essential part of the earth's solid crust, including loose incoherent masses such as sand and gravel, as well as solid masses of granite, limestone, and others.

Root The descending axis of a plant, usually below ground, serving to anchor the plant and absorb and conduct water and mineral nutrients.

Root cap A mass of hard cells covering the tip of a root and protecting it from mechanical injury.

Root hair An absorptive unicellular protuberance of the epidermal cells of the root.

Rooting media Materials such as peat, sand, perlite, or vermiculite in which the basal ends of cuttings are placed vertically during the development of roots.

Root pressure Pressure developed in the root as the result of osmosis and causing bleeding in stem wounds of some plants.

Rootstock (understock) The trunk or root material to which buds or scions are inserted in grafting.

Roughage Plant materials that are relatively high in crude fiber and low in digestible nutrients, such as straw.

Ruminant Cud-chewing mammals such as cattle, sheep, goats, and deer, characteristically having a stomach divided into four compartments.

Runner *See* Stolon.

Saline soil A nonsodic soil containing sufficient soluble salts to impair plant growth.

Samara A dry, indehiscent, simple fruit that has winglike appendages on both sides of the ovary. These appendages help carry the wind-borne fruit.

Sand A soil particle between 0.05 and 2.0 mm in diameter.

Saprophyte An organism deriving its nutrients from the dead body or the nonliving products of another plant or animal.

Savanna Grassland having scattered trees, either as individuals or clumps; often a transitional type between true grassland and forest.

Scarify To scratch, chip, or nick the seed coverings of certain species to enhance the passage of water and gases as an aid to seed germination.

Scientific method An approach to a problem that consists of stating the problem, establishing one or more hypotheses as solutions to the problem, testing these hypotheses by experimentation or observation, and accepting or rejecting the hypotheses.

Scion A small shoot that is inserted by grafting into a rootstock.

Scion-stock interaction The effect of a rootstock on a scion (and vice versa) in which a scion on one kind of rootstock performs differently than it would on its own roots or on a different rootstock.

Sclerenchyma Supporting or protective tissue in which the cells have hard lignified walls.

Scutellum The rudimentary leaflike structure at the first node of the (embryonic) stem (culm) of a grass plant. The single cotyledon of a monocotyledenous seedling.

Secondary phloem Phloem cells formed by activity of the vascular cambium. Secondary phloem is found in biennials and perennials, but usually not in annuals.

Secondary xylem Xylem cells formed by activity of the vascular cambium. The development of the secondary xylem accounts for the so-called annual rings seen in most trees.

Sedimentary rock Rock formed from material originally deposited as a sediment, then physically or chemically changed by compression and hardening while buried in the earth's crust.

Seed The mature ovule of a flowering plant containing an embryo, an endosperm (sometimes), and a seed coat.

Seed (breeder) Seed (or, sometimes, vegetative propagating material) directly controlled by the originator (or the sponsoring plant breeder or institution) that provides the source for the initial increases of foundation seed.

Seed (certified) Progeny of foundation, registered, or other certified seed that is so handled as to maintain satisfactory genetic identity and/or purity and that has been approved and certified by a certifying agency.

Seed (foundation) Seed stocks so handled as to maintain specific genetic identity and purity, such as may be designated by an agricultural experiment station. Foundation seed is the source of certified seed, either directly or through registered seed.

Seed (registered) Progeny of foundation or other registered seed so handled as to maintain satisfactory genetic identity and purity; approved and certified by a certifying agency.

Seedbed Soil that has been prepared for planting seeds or transplants.

Seed potatoes Pieces of potato tubers or whole tubers that are planted to produce new plants and subsequent commercial crops.

Self-fertile Capable of fertilization and producing viable seed after self-pollination.

Self-incompatibility Inability to produce viable seed following self-pollination. The inability is sometimes due to a pollen-borne gene that prevents pollen tube growth on a stigma with the same gene.

Self-pollination Transfer of pollen from the stamens to the stigma of either the same flower, other flowers on the same plant, or flowers on other plants of the same clone.

Self-sterility Failure to complete fertilization and obtain viable seed after self-pollination.

Semiarid Climate in which evaporation exceeds precipitation, a transition zone between a true desert and a humid climate. Usually annual precipitation is between 250 and 500 mm (10 and 20 in).

Senescence A physiological aging process in which tissues in an organism deteriorate and finally die.

Sepals The outermost series of floral parts; usually green, leaflike structures at the base of a flower; collectively, they form the calyx.

Sessile Used in reference to flowers, florets, leaves, leaflets, or fruits that are attached directly to a shoot and not borne on any type of a stalk.

Sexual reproduction Development of new plants by the processes of meiosis and fertilization in the flower to produce a viable embryo in a seed.

Short day plants Plants that initiate flowers only under short day (long night) conditions.

Sidedressing Applying fertilizer on a soil surface close enough to a plant that cultivating or watering carries the fertilizer to the plant's roots.

Silage Forage that is chemically changed and preserved in a succulent condition by partial fermentation in the preparation of food for livestock.

Silique A dry, one-seeded, dehiscent (infrequently indehiscent) fruit consisting of two carpels that form a bilocular ovary. Common in the CRUCIFERAE family.

Silo A structure for making and storing silage.

Silt A soil textural class consisting of particles between 0.05 and 0.002 mm in diameter.

Simple fruit A fruit derived from a single pistil.

Sod Top 3 to 7 cm (1 to 3 in) of soil permeated by and held together with grass roots or grass-legume roots.

Sodic soil A soil that contains so much exchangeable sodium (more than 15 percent) that it interferes with the growth of most crop plants. Also, if the total soluble salts is more than 4 mmho per cm^2, the soil is a saline sodic soil; if it is less than 4 mmho per cm^2, the soil is a nonsaline sodic soil.

Soil The solid portion of the earth's crust in which plants grow. It is composed of mineral material, air, water, and organic matter both living and dead.

Soil air The gaseous phase of the soil; that percentage of the total volume not occupied by solid or liquid.

Soil conservation A combination of all management and land use methods that safeguard the soil against depletion or deterioration by natural or by human-induced factors.

Soil fertilization *See* Fertilization (soil).

Soil management The total tillage operations, cropping practices, fertilizing, liming, and other treatments conducted on or applied to a soil for the production of plants.

Soil organic matter The organic fraction of the soil that includes plant and animal residues at various stages of decomposition, cells and tissues of soil organisms, and substances synthesized by the soil population.

Soil pasteurization Treating the soil with heat (usually steam at 60°C to 70°C (140°F to 160°F) to destroy most harmful pathogens, nematodes, and weed seeds. Less severe than soil sterilization.

Soil salinity The amount of soluble salts in a soil, expressed as parts per million, millimho/cm, or other convenient ratios.

Soil series The basic unit of soil classification; a subdivision of a family, comprising soils that are essentially alike in all major profile characteristics.

Soil solution The aqueous liquid phase of the soil and its solutes consisting of ions dissociated from the surfaces of the soil particles and of other soluble materials.

Soil sterilization Treating soil by gaseous fumigation, chemicals, heat (usually steam) at 100°C (212°F) to destroy all living organisms.

Soil structure The arrangement of primary soil particles into secondary particles, units, or peds that act as primary particles. The secondary units are characterized and classified on the basis of size, shape, and degree of distinctness.

Soil texture The relative percentages of sand, silt, and clay in a soil.

Soil tilth The physical condition of soil as related to its ease of tillage, fitness as a seedbed, and suitability for plant growth.

Soil type The lowest unit in the natural system of soil classification; a subdivision of a soil series.

Solute A substance dissolved in a solvent.

Solution An homogeneous mixture; the molecules of the dissolved substance (the solute) are dispersed among the molecules of the solvent.

Solvent A substance, usually a liquid, that can dissolve other substances (solutes).

Somatic tissue Nonreproductive, vegetative tissue. Tissue developed through mitosis that will not undergo meiosis.

Species A group of similar organisms capable of interbreeding and more or less distinctly different in geographic range and/or morphological characteristics from other species in the same genus.

Sperm   A male gamete.

Spermatophyte   A seed-bearing plant.

Spike   An inflorescence that has a central axis on which sessile flowers are borne. Examples are some grasses, gladioli, snapdragons.

Spongy parenchmya   The cell layer in a leaf located between the palisade parenchyma and the lower epidermis; these cells have thin cell walls and are loosely packed.

Spore   A reproductive cell that develops into a plant without union with other cells.

Sprigging   Vegetative propagation by planting stolons or rhizomes (sprigs).

Square (botanical)   An unopened flowerbud in cotton with its accompanying bracts.

Stamen   The male reproductive structure of a flower. The stamen produces pollen and is composed of a filament on which is borne an anther.

Staminate (male) flower   A flower having stamens but no pistils.

Starch   A complex polysaccharide carbohydrate. The form of food commonly stored by plants.

Stele   The vascular tissue and closely associated tissues in the axes of plants. The central cylinder of the stem.

Stem   The main body of a plant, usually the ascending axis, whether above or below ground in opposition to the descending axis or root. Stems, but not roots, produce nodes and buds.

Stigma   In a flower, the portion of the style pollen adheres to.

Stock   *See* Rootstock.

Stolon   A slender, prostrate above-ground stem. The runners of white clover, strawberry, and bermuda grass plants are examples of stolons.

Stoma (stomate) (plural, stomata, stomates)   A small opening, bordered by guard cells, in the epidermis of leaves and stems, through which gases including water vapor pass.

Stool (horticultural)   Sprouts that arise from the base of the plant below ground and become rooted. They are used for vegetative propagation.

Stool or stooling (agronomic)   Shoots that arise from below the soil at the base of a plant.

Stratification   The practice of exposing imbibed seeds to cool 2°C to 10°C (35°F to 50°F) (sometimes warm) temperatures for a period of time prior to germination in order to break dormancy. This is a standard practice in germination of seeds of many grass and woody species.

Stress (water)   Plant(s) unable to absorb enough water to replace that lost by transpiration. Results may be wilting, cessation of growth, or death of the plant or plant parts.

Strip cropping   The practice of growing crops that require different types of tillage, such as row and sod, in alternate strips along contours or across the prevailing direction of wind.

Style   Slender column of tissue that arises from the top of the ovary in the flower through which the pollen tube grows toward the ovule.

Suberin   A waxy, waterproofing substance in cork tissue.

Subirrigation   Application of water from below the soil surface, usually from a ditch or a perforated hose or pipe, or by placing a potted plant on a constantly moist surface.

Subsoil   That part of the soil below the plow layer.

Subsoiling   Breaking of compact subsoils, without inverting them, with a special knifelike instrument (chisel) that is pulled through the soil at depths usually of 30 to 60 cm (12 to 24 in) and at spacings usually of 60 to 150 cm (2 to 5 ft).

Sucrose   Table sugar ($C_{12}H_{22}O_{11}$); a carbohydrate formed by chemically joining a molecule of glucose ($C_6H_{12}O_6$) with a molecule of fructose ($C_6H_{10}O_5$).

Summer fallow   The tillage of uncropped land during the summer in order to control weeds and store moisture in the soil for the growth of a later crop.

Sunscald   High temperature injury to plant tissue due to intense sun's rays warming the trunks of trees during winter, cracking and splitting the bark. It can be prevented by shading or whitewashing tree trunks and larger branches. Sunscald also occurs on unshaded vegetable fruits (tomatoes and melons) or to houseplants exposed to direct sunlight.

Superior ovary   An ovary situated above the receptacle; all other floral parts develop below the base of the ovary.

Symbiosis   An obligate relationship between two organisms of different species living together in close association for their mutual benefit. An example is the mycelium of a fungus with roots of seed plants.

Synergids   The two nuclei within the embryo sac at the upper end in the ovule of the flower, which, with the third (the egg), constitute the egg apparatus.

Systemic   A pesticide material absorbed by plants, making them toxic to feeding insects. Also, pertaining to a disease in which an infection spreads throughout the plant.

Tangential face   The wood surface exposed when a cut is made at right angles to the rays and parallel to the long axis of the majority of cells.

Tannin   Broad class of soluble polyphenols with a common property of condensing with protein to form a leatherlike substance that is insoluble in water.

Taproot   An elongated, deeply growing primary root.

Taxon (plural, taxa)   A taxonomic group of plants of any rank such as family, genus, species, and so forth.

Taxonomy   The science dealing with describing, naming, and classifying plants and animals.

Tendril   A slender coiling modified leaf or stem arising from stems and aiding in their support.

Tension, soil-moisture   The equivalent negative pressure of water in soil. The attraction with which water is held to soil particles.

Terminal bud   A bud at the distal end of a stem.

Terrace   A level, usually narrow, plain bordering a river, lake, or the sea. Rivers sometimes are bordered by terraces at different levels. It also refers to a raised, more or less level strip of land usually constructed on a contour and designed to make the land suitable for tillage and prevent erosion.

Tetraploid   Having four sets of chromosomes per nucleus.

Texture (soil)   The relative proportions of the various-sized groups of individual soil grains in a mass of soil. It refers to the proportions of sand, silt, and clay in a given amount of soil.

Thallophytes A division of plants whose body lacks roots, stems, and leaves (e.g., mushrooms).

Thinning Removing young plants from a row to provide the remaining plants with more space to develop. Also, the removal of excess numbers of fruits from a tree so the remaining fruits will become larger.

Tile (drain) Pipe made of burned clay, concrete, or similar material, in short lengths, usually buried at the bottom of a ditch, with open joints to collect and carry excess water from the soil. The newer type polyvinyl tile is made in continuous lengths, and is perforated to allow water to enter the pipe for removal from the soil.

Tilth *See* Soil tilth.

Tissue A group of cells of similar structure that performs a special function.

Topdressing Applying materials such as fertilizer or compost to the soil surface while plants are growing.

Topsoil The layer of soil moved in cultivation.

Topworking (top-grafting) To change the cultivar of a tree by grafting the main scaffold branches.

Tracheid An elongated, tapering xylem cell with lignified pitted walls adapted for conduction and support.

Transfer RNA *See* Ribonucleic acid.

Translocation The transfer of food materials or products of metabolism throughout the plant.

Transpiration The loss of water vapor through the stomata of leaves.

Tuber An enlarged, fleshy, underground tip of a stem. The white (Irish) potato produces tubers as food storage organs.

Tuberous root An enlarged fleshy, underground root (e.g., sweet potato and dahlia).

Turgid Swollen, distended; referring to cells or tissues that are firm because of water uptake.

Turgor pressure The pressure within the cell resulting from the absorption of water into the vacuole and the imbibition of water by the protoplasm.

2,4-Dichlorophenoxyacetic acid (2,4-D) A selective auxin type herbicide that kills broad-leaved plants but not grasses.

Umbel A type of inflorescence in which flowers are borne at the end of stalks that arise like the ribs of an umbrella from one point (e.g., carrot, onion).

Unavailable water Water held by the soil so strongly that the root cannot absorb it.

Understock *See* Rootstock.

Vacuole A cavity in the plant's cell bounded by a membrane in which various plant products and byproducts are stored.

Variety (botanical) A subdivision of a species with distinct morphological characters and given a Latin name according to the rules of the International Code of Botanical Nomenclature. A taxonomic variety is known by the first validly published name applied to it so that nomenclature tends to be stable.

Variety (cultivated) *See* Cultivar.

Vascular bundle A strand of tissue containing primary xylem and primary phloem and frequently enclosed by a bundle sheath of parenchyma or fibers.

Vascular cambium A meristem that produces secondary xylem and secondary phloem cells. Vascular cambium is found in biennials and perennials.

Vector A carrier; for example, an insect that carries pathogenic organisms from plant to plant.

Vegetation The plants that cover a region; it is formed of the species that make up the flora of the area.

Vegetative Referring to asexual (stem, leaf, root) development in plants in contrast to sexual (flower, seed) development.

Vein The vascular strand of xylem and phloem in a leaf.

Vernalization In reference to flowering, the process by which floral induction in some plants is promoted by exposing the plants to chilling for a certain length of time.

Vessel A series of xylem elements in the stem and root that conduct water and mineral nutrients.

Virgin soil A soil that has not been significantly disturbed from its natural environment.

Vitamins Natural organic substances, necessary in small amounts for the normal metabolism of plants and animals.

Volatile Evaporating readily or easily dissipated in the form of a vapor.

Water potential The difference between the activity of water molecules in pure distilled water at atmospheric pressure and 3°C (standard conditions) and the activity of water molecules in any other system; the activity of these water molecules may be greater (positive) or less (negative) than the activity of the water molecules under standard conditions.

Water table The upper surface of ground water or that level below which the soil is saturated with water.

Wavelength The distance between two corresponding points on any two consecutive waves. For visible light it is very small and is generally measured in nanometers.

Weathering All physical and chemical changes produced in rocks, at or near the earth's surface, by atmospheric agents.

Weed A plant not valued for use or beauty. Any plant growing where it is not wanted.

Wilting point (Permanent Wilting Point, PWP) The moisture content of soil at which plants wilt and fail to recover even when placed in a humid atmosphere.

Windbreak A planting of trees or shrubs, usually perpendicular or nearly so to the principal wind direction, to protect soil, crops, homesteads, roads, and so on, against the effects of winds.

Windrow Hay, grain, leaves, or other material swept or raked into rows to dry.

Winter hardiness The ability of a plant to tolerate severe winter conditions.

Wood Secondary nonfunctioning xylem in a perennial shrub or tree.

Xanthophyll Yellow carotenoid pigment ($C_{40}H_{56}O_2$) found along with chlorophyll in green plants.

Xylem Specialized cells through which water and minerals move upward from the soil through a plant.

Zygote A protoplast resulting from the fusion of gametes (either isogametes or heterogametes). The beginning of a new plant in sexual reproduction.

APPENDIX

Foods, Approximate Measures, Units, and Weight (Edible Part Unless Footnotes Indicate Otherwise)		Water	Food Energy	Protein	Fat
	Gm	Per-cent	Cal-ories	Gm	Gm

FRUITS AND FRUIT PRODUCTS

Foods, Approximate Measures, Units, and Weight		Gm	Percent	Calories	Gm	Gm
Apples, raw, unpeeled, without cores:						
3¼ in diam. (about 2 per lb)	1 apple	212	84	125	Trace	1
Apricots:						
Raw, without pits (about 12 per lb with pits).	3 apricots	107	85	55	1	Trace
Dried:						
Uncooked (28 large or 37 medium halves per cup).	1 cup	130	25	340	7	1
Avocados, raw, whole, without skins and seeds:						
California, mid- and late-winter (with skin and seed, 3⅛-in diam.; wt., 10 oz).	1 avocado	216	74	370	5	37
Florida, late summer and fall (with skin and seed, 3⅝-in diam.; wt., 1 lb).	1 avocado	304	78	390	4	33
Banana without peel (about 2.6 per lb with peel).	1 banana	119	76	100	1	Trace
Blackberries, raw	1 cup	144	85	85	2	1
Blueberries, raw	1 cup	145	83	90	1	1
Cherries:						
Sweet, raw, without pits and stems.	10 cherries	68	80	45	1	Trace
Cranberry sauce, sweetened, canned, strained.	1 cup	277	62	405	Trace	1
Dates:						
Whole, without pits	10 dates	80	23	220	2	Trace
Chopped	1 cup	178	23	490	4	1
Grapefruit:						
Raw, medium, 3¾-in diam. (about 1 lb 1 oz):						
Pink or red	½ grapefruit with peel	241	89	50	1	Trace
White	½ grapefruit with peel	241	89	45	1	Trace
Grapes, European type (adherent skin), raw:						
Thompson Seedless	10 grapes	50	81	35	Trace	Trace
Lemon, raw, size 165, without peel and seeds (about 4 per lb with peels and seeds).	1 lemon	74	90	20	1	Trace
Olives, pickled, canned:						
Green	4 medium or 3 extra large or 2 giant	16	78	15	Trace	2
Ripe, Mission	3 small or 2 large	10	73	15	Trace	2
Oranges, all commercial cultivars, raw:						
Whole, 2⅝-in diam., without peel and seeds (about 2½ per lb with peel and seeds).	1 orange	131	86	65	1	Trace
Papayas, raw, ½-in cubes	1 cup	140	89	55	1	Trace
Peaches:						
Raw:						
Whole, 2½-in diam., peeled, pitted (about 4 per lb with peels and pits).	1 peach	100	89	40	1	Trace
Dried:						
Uncooked	1 cup	160	25	420	5	1
Pears:						
Raw, with skin, cored:						
Bartlett, 2½-in diam. (about 2½ per lb with cores and stems).	1 pear	164	83	100	1	1
Bosc, 2½-in diam. (about 3 per lb with cores and stems).	1 pear	141	83	85	1	1
D'Anjou, 3-in diam. (about 2 per lb with cores and stems).	1 pear	200	83	120	1	1
Pineapple: Raw, diced	1 cup	155	85	80	1	Trace
Plums:						
Raw, without pits:						
Japanese and hybrid (2⅛-in diam., about 6½ per lb with pits).	1 plum	66	87	30	Trace	Trace
Prune-type (1½-in diam., about 15 per lb with pits).	1 plum	28	79	20	Trace	Trace
Prunes, dried, "softenized," with pits: Uncooked	4 extra large or 5 large prunes	49	28	110	1	Trace
Raisins, seedless: Cup, not pressed down	1 cup	145	18	420	4	Trace
Raspberries, red: Raw, capped, whole	1 cup	123	84	70	1	1
Strawberries: Raw, whole berries, capped	1 cup	149	90	55	1	1
Tangerine, raw, 2⅜-in diam., size 176, without peel	1 tangerine	86	87	40	1	Trace

Carbo-hydrate Gm	Calcium Mg	Phos-phorus Mg	Iron Mg	Potas-sium Mg	Vitamin A Inter-national Units	Thiamin Mg	Ribo-flavin Mg	Niacin Mg	Ascorbic Acid Mg
31	15	21	.6	233	190	.06	.04	.2	8
14	18	25	.5	301	2890	.03	.04	.6	11
86	87	140	7.2	1273	14,170	.01	.21	4.3	16
13	22	91	1.3	1303	630	.24	.43	3.5	30
27	30	128	1.8	1836	880	.33	.61	4.9	43
26	10	31	.8	440	230	.06	.07	.8	12
19	46	27	1.3	245	290	0.04	0.06	0.6	30
22	22	19	1.6	117	160	.04	.09	.7	20
12	15	13	.3	129	70	.03	.04	.3	7
104	17	11	.6	83	60	.03	.03	.1	6
58	47	50	2.4	518	40	.07	.08	1.8	0
130	105	112	5.3	1153	90	.16	.18	3.9	0
13	20	20	.5	166	540	.05	.02	.2	44
12	19	19	.5	159	10	.05	.02	.2	44
9	6	10	.2	87	50	.03	.02	.2	2
6	19	12	.4	102	10	.03	.01	.1	39
Trace	8	2	.2	7	40	—	—	—	—
Trace	9	1	.1	2	10	Trace	Trace	—	—
16	54	26	.5	263	260	.13	.05	.5	66
14	28	22	.4	328	2450	.06	.06	.4	78
10	9	19	.5	202	1330	.02	.05	1.0	7
109	77	187	9.6	1520	6240	.02	.30	8.5	29
25	13	18	.5	213	30	.03	.07	.2	7
22	11	16	.4	83	30	.03	.06	.1	6
31	16	22	.6	260	40	.04	.08	.2	8
21	26	12	.8	226	110	.14	.05	.3	26
8	8	12	.3	112	160	.02	.02	.3	4
6	3	5	.1	48	80	.01	.01	.1	1
29	22	34	1.7	298	690	.04	.07	.7	1
112	90	146	5.1	1106	30	.16	.12	.7	1
17	27	27	1.1	207	160	.04	.11	1.1	31
13	31	31	1.5	244	90	0.04	0.10	0.9	88
10	34	15	.3	108	360	.05	.02	.1	27

Nutritive Values of the Edible Parts of Foods

Foods, Approximate Measures, Units, and Weight (Edible Part Unless Footnotes Indicate Otherwise)		Water	Food Energy	Protein	Fat
	Gm	Per-cent	Cal-ories	Gm	Gm

LEGUMES (DRY), NUTS, SEEDS

Almonds, shelled:						
Chopped (about 130 almonds)	1 cup	130	5	775	24	70
Beans, dry:						
Common cultivars as Great Northern, navy, and others:						
Cooked, drained:						
Great Northern	1 cup	180	69	210	14	1
Navy	1 cup	190	69	225	15	1
Red kidney	1 cup	255	76	230	15	1
Lima, cooked, drained	1 cup	190	64	260	16	1
Blackeye peas, dry, cooked (with residual cooking liquid).	1 cup	250	80	190	13	1
Brazil nuts, shelled (6-8 large kernels).	1 oz	28	5	185	4	19
Cashew nuts, roasted in oil	1 cup	140	5	785	24	64
Coconut meat, fresh:						
Piece, about 2 by 2 by ½ in	1 piece	45	51	155	2	16
Shredded or grated, not pressed down.	1 cup	80	51	275	3	28
Filberts (hazelnuts), chopped (about 80 kernels).	1 cup	115	6	730	14	72
Lentils, whole, cooked	1 cup	200	72	210	16	Trace
Peanuts, roasted in oil, salted (whole, halves, chopped).	1 cup	144	2	840	37	72
Pecans, chopped or pieces (about 120 large halves).	1 cup	118	3	810	11	84
Walnuts:						
Black:						
Chopped or broken kernels	1 cup	125	3	785	26	74
Persian or English, chopped (about 60 halves)	1 cup	120	4	780	18	77

VEGETABLES

Asparagus, green:						
Cooked, drained:						
Spears, ½-in diam. at base:						
From raw	4 spears	60	94	10	1	Trace
From frozen	4 spears	60	92	15	2	Trace
Beans:						
Lima, immature seeds, frozen, cooked, drained:						
Thick-seeded types (Fordhooks)	1 cup	170	74	170	10	Trace
Thin-seeded types (baby limas)	1 cup	180	69	210	13	Trace
Snap:						
Green:						
Cooked, drained:						
From raw (cuts and French style).	1 cup	125	92	30	2	Trace
From frozen:						
Cuts	1 cup	135	92	35	2	Trace
French style	1 cup	130	92	35	2	Trace
Yellow or wax:						
Cooked, drained:						
From raw (cuts and French style).	1 cup	125	93	30	2	Trace
From frozen (cuts)	1 cup	135	92	35	2	Trace
Canned, drained solids (cuts).	1 cup	135	92	30	2	Trace
Beets:						
Cooked, drained, peeled:						
Whole beets, 2-in diam.	2 beets	100	91	30	1	Trace
Canned, drained solids:						
Whole beets, small	1 cup	160	89	60	2	Trace
Beet greens, leaves and stems, cooked, drained.	1 cup	145	94	25	2	Trace
Broccoli, cooked, drained:						
From raw:						
Stalk, medium size	1 stalk	180	91	45	6	1
From frozen:						
Stalk, 4½ to 5 in long	1 stalk	30	91	10	1	Trace
Brussels sprouts, cooked, drained:						
From raw, 7-8 sprouts (1¼- to 1½-in diam.).	1 cup	155	88	55	7	1
From frozen	1 cup	155	89	50	5	Trace

Carbo-hydrate	Calcium	Phos-phorus	Iron	Potas-sium	Vitamin A Inter-national Units	Thiamin	Ribo-flavin	Niacin	Ascorbic Acid
Gm	Mg	Mg	Mg	Mg	Units	Mg	Mg	Mg	Mg
25	304	655	6.1	1005	0	.31	1.20	4.6	Trace
38	90	266	4.9	749	0	.25	.13	1.3	0
40	95	281	5.1	790	0	.27	.13	1.3	0
42	74	278	4.6	673	10	.13	.10	1.5	—
49	55	293	5.9	1163	—	.25	.11	1.3	—
35	43	238	3.3	573	30	.40	.10	1.0	—
3	53	196	1.0	203	Trace	.27	.03	.5	—
41	53	522	5.3	650	140	.60	.35	2.5	—
4	6	43	.8	115	0	.02	.01	.2	1
8	10	76	1.4	205	0	.04	.02	.4	2
19	240	388	3.9	810	—	.53	—	1.0	Trace
39	50	238	4.2	498	40	.14	.12	1.2	0
27	107	577	3.0	971	—	.46	.19	24.8	0
17	86	341	2.8	712	150	1.01	.15	1.1	2
19	Trace	713	7.5	575	380	.28	.14	.9	—
19	119	456	3.7	540	40	.40	.16	1.1	2
2	13	30	.4	110	540	.10	.11	.8	16
2	13	40	.7	143	470	.10	.08	.7	16
32	34	153	2.9	724	390	.12	.09	1.7	29
40	63	227	4.7	709	400	.16	.09	2.2	22
7	63	46	.8	189	680	.09	.11	.6	15
8	54	43	.9	205	780	.09	.12	.5	7
8	49	39	1.2	177	690	.08	.10	.4	9
6	63	46	.8	189	290	.09	.11	.6	16
8	47	42	.9	221	140	.09	.11	.5	8
7	61	34	2.0	128	140	.04	.07	.4	7
7	14	23	.5	208	20	.03	.04	.3	6
14	30	29	1.1	267	30	.02	.05	.2	5
5	144	36	2.8	481	7400	.10	.22	.4	22
8	158	112	1.4	481	4500	.16	.36	1.4	162
1	12	17	.2	66	570	.02	.03	.2	22
10	50	112	1.7	423	810	.12	.22	1.2	135
10	33	95	1.2	457	880	.12	.16	.9	126

Foods, Approximate Measures, Units, and Weight (Edible Part Unless Footnotes Indicate Otherwise)		Water	Food Energy	Protein	Fat
	Gm	Per- cent	Cal- ories	Gm	Gm
Cabbage:					
Common varieties:					
Raw:					
Coarsely shredded or sliced	1 cup	70	92	15	1	Trace
Finely shredded or chopped	1 cup	90	92	20	1	Trace
Cooked, drained	1 cup	146	94	30	2	Trace
Red, raw, coarsely shredded or sliced.	1 cup	70	90	20	1	Trace
Savoy, raw, coarsely shredded or sliced.	1 cup	70	92	15	2	Trace
Cabbage, celery (also called pe-tsai or wongbok), raw, 1-in pieces.	1 cup	75	95	10	1	Trace
Cabbage, white mustard (also called bokchoy or pakchoy), cooked, drained.	1 cup	170	95	25	2	Trace
Carrots:					
Raw, without crowns and tips, scraped:					
Whole, 7½ by 1⅛ in, or strips, 2½ to 3 in long.	1 carrot or 18 strips	72	88	30	1	Trace
Grated	1 cup	110	88	45	1	Trace
Canned:					
Sliced, drained solids	1 cup	155	91	45	1	Trace
Cauliflower:					
Raw, chopped	1 cup	115	91	31	3	Trace
Cooked, drained:	1 cup	125	93	30	3	Trace
Celery, Pascal type, raw:					
Stalk, large outer, 8 by 1½ in, at root end.	1 stalk	40	94	5	Trace	Trace
Collards, cooked, drained:					
From raw (leaves without stems)	1 cup	190	90	65	7	1
From frozen (chopped)	1 cup	170	90	50	5	1
Corn, sweet:					
Cooked, drained:					
From raw, ear 5 by 1¾ in	1 ear	140	74	70	2	1
From frozen:					
Ear, 5 in long	1 ear	229	73	120	4	1
Kernels	1 cup	165	77	130	5	1
Cucumber slices, ⅛ in thick (large, 2⅛-in diam.; small, 1¾-in diam.):					
With peel	6 large or 8 small slices	28	95	5	Trace	Trace
Endive, curly (including escarole), raw, small pieces.	1 cup	50	93	10	1	Trace
Kale, cooked, drained:					
From raw (leaves without stems and midribs).	1 cup	110	88	45	5	1
From frozen (leaf style)	1 cup	130	91	40	4	1
Lettuce, raw:					
Butterhead, as Boston types:					
Head, 5-in diam	1 head	220	95	25	2	Trace
Leaves	1 outer or 2 inner or 3 heart leaves.	15	95	Trace	Trace	Trace
Crisphead, as Iceberg:					
Head, 6-in diam	1 head	567	96	70	5	1
Pieces, chopped or shredded	1 cup	55	96	5	Trace	Trace
Looseleaf (bunching varieties including romaine or cos), chopped or shredded pieces.	1 cup	55	94	10	1	Trace

Carbo-hydrate	Calcium	Phos-phorus	Iron	Potas-sium	Vitamin A Inter-national Units	Thiamin	Ribo-flavin	Niacin	Ascorbic Acid
Gm	Mg	Mg	Mg	Mg		Mg	Mg	Mg	Mg
4	34	20	0.3	163	90	0.04	0.04	0.02	33
5	44	26	.4	210	120	.05	.05	.3	42
6	64	29	.4	236	190	.06	.06	.4	48
5	29	25	.6	188	30	.06	.04	.3	43
3	47	38	.6	188	140	.04	.06	.2	39
2	32	30	.5	190	110	.04	.03	.5	19
4	252	56	1.0	364	5270	.07	.14	1.2	26
7	27	26	.5	246	7930	.04	.04	.4	6
11	41	40	.8	375	12,100	.07	.06	.7	9
10	47	34	1.1	186	23,250	.03	.05	.6	3
6	29	64	1.3	339	70	.13	.12	.8	90
5	26	53	.9	258	80	.11	.10	.8	69
2	16	11	.1	136	110	.01	.01	.1	4
10	357	99	1.5	498	14,820	.21	.38	2.3	144
10	299	87	1.7	401	11,560	.10	.24	1.0	56
16	2	69	.5	151	310	.09	.08	1.1	7
27	4	121	1.0	291	440	.18	.10	2.1	9
31	5	120	1.3	304	580	.15	.10	2.5	8
1	7	8	.3	45	70	.01	.01	.1	3
2	41	27	.9	147	1650	.04	.07	.3	5
7	206	64	1.8	243	9130	.11	.20	1.8	102
7	157	62	1.3	251	10,660	.08	.20	.9	49
4	57	42	3.3	430	1580	.10	.10	.5	13
Trace	5	4	.3	40	150	.01	.01	Trace	1
16	108	118	2.7	943	1780	.32	.32	1.6	32
2	11	12	.3	96	180	.03	.03	.2	3
2	37	14	.8	145	1050	.03	.04	.2	10

Foods, Approximate Measures, Units, and Weight (Edible Part Unless Footnotes Indicate Otherwise)			Water	Food Energy	Protein	Fat
		Gm	Per-cent	Cal-ories	Gm	Gm
Muskmelons, raw, orange-fleshed (with rind and seed cavity, 5-in diam., 2⅓ lb).	½ melon with rind	477	91	80	2	Trace
Honeydew (with rind and seed cavity, 6½-in diam., 5¼ lb).	¹/₁₀ melon with rind	226	91	50	1	Trace
Mustard greens, without stems and midribs, cooked, drained.	1 cup	140	93	30	3	1
Okra pods, 3 by ⅝ in, cooked	10 pods	106	91	30	2	Trace
Onions:						
Mature:						
Raw:						
Chopped	1 cup	170	89	65	3	Trace
Sliced	1 cup	115	89	45	2	Trace
Young green, bulb (⅜ in diam.) and white portion of top.	6 onions	30	88	15	Trace	Trace
Parsley, raw, chopped	1 tbsp	4	85	Trace	Trace	Trace
Parsnips, cooked (diced or 2-in lengths).	1 cup	155	82	100	2	1
Peas, green:						
Canned:						
Whole, drained solids	1 cup	170	77	150	8	1
Frozen, cooked, drained	1 cup	160	82	110	8	Trace
Peppers, hot, red, without seeds	1 tsp	2	9	5	Trace	Trace
Peppers, sweet (about 5 per lb, whole), stem and seeds removed:						
Raw	1 pod	74	93	15	1	Trace
Potatoes, cooked:						
Baked, peeled after baking (about 2 per lb, raw).	1 potato	156	75	145	4	Trace
Boiled (about 3 per lb, raw):	1 potato	137	80	105	3	Trace
Pumpkin, canned	1 cup	245	90	80	2	1
Radishes, raw (prepackaged) stem ends, rootlets cut off.	4 radishes	18	95	5	Trace	Trace
Rhubarb, cooked, added sugar:						
From raw	1 cup	270	63	380	1	Trace
Spinach:						
Raw, chopped	1 cup	55	91	15	2	Trace
Cooked, drained:						
From raw	1 cup	180	92	40	5	1
From frozen:						
Chopped	1 cup	205	92	45	6	1
Leaf	1 cup	190	92	45	6	1
Canned, drained solids	1 cup	205	91	50	6	1
Squash, cooked:						
Summer (all varieties), diced, drained.	1 cup	210	96	30	2	Trace
Winter (all varieties), baked, mashed.	1 cup	205	81	130	4	1
Sweetpotatoes:						
Cooked (raw, 5 by 2 in; about 2½ per lb):						
Baked in skin, peeled	1 potato	114	64	160	2	1
Boiled in skin, peeled	1 potato	151	71	170	3	1
Canned:						
Solid pack (mashed)	1 cup	255	72	275	5	1
Tomatoes:						
Raw, 2³/₅-in diam. (3 per 12 oz pkg.).	1 tomato	135	94	25	1	Trace
Canned, solids and liquids	1 cup	241	94	50	2	Trace
Turnips, cooked, diced	1 cup	155	94	35	1	Trace
Turnip greens, cooked, drained:						
From raw (leaves and stems)	1 cup	145	94	30	3	Trace
From frozen (chopped)	1 cup	165	93	40	4	Trace
Watermelon, raw, 4 by 8 in wedge with rind and seeds	1 wedge with rind and seeds	926	93	110	2	1

Source: B. K. Watt, and A. L. Merrill. 1963. Composition of foods. USDA Handbook 8, and C. F. Adams, and M. Richardson. 1977. Nutritive value of foods. USDA Home and Garden Bull. No. 72.

Carbo-hydrate	Calcium	Phos-phorus	Iron	Potas-sium	Vitamin A International Units	Thiamin	Ribo-flavin	Niacin	Ascorbic Acid
Gm	Mg	Mg	Mg	Mg		Mg	Mg	Mg	Mg
20	38	44	1.1	682	9240	.11	.08	1.6	90
11	21	24	.6	374	60	.06	.04	.9	34
6	193	45	2.5	308	8120	.11	.20	.8	67
6	98	43	.5	184	520	.14	.19	1.0	21
15	46	61	.9	267	Trace	.05	.07	.3	17
10	31	41	.6	181	Trace	.03	.05	.2	12
3	12	12	.2	69	Trace	.02	.01	.1	8
Trace	7	2	.2	25	300	Trace	.01	Trace	6
23	70	96	.9	587	50	.11	.12	.2	16
29	44	129	3.2	163	1170	.15	.10	1.4	14
19	30	138	3.0	216	960	.43	.14	2.7	21
1	5	4	.3	20	1300	Trace	.02	.2	Trace
4	7	16	.5	157	310	.06	.06	.4	94
33	14	101	1.1	782	Trace	.15	.07	2.7	31
23	10	72	0.8	556	Trace	.12	.05	2.0	22
19	61	64	1.0	588	15,680	.07	.12	1.5	12
1	5	6	.2	58	Trace	.01	.01	.1	5
97	211	41	1.6	548	220	.05	.14	.8	16
2	51	28	1.7	259	4460	.06	.11	.3	28
6	167	68	4.0	583	14,580	.13	.25	.9	50
8	232	90	4.3	683	16,200	.14	.31	.8	39
7	200	84	4.8	688	15,390	.15	.27	1.0	53
7	242	53	5.3	513	16,400	.04	.25	.6	29
7	53	53	.8	296	820	.11	.17	1.7	21
32	57	98	1.6	945	8610	.10	.27	1.4	27
37	46	66	1.0	342	9230	.10	.08	.8	25
40	48	71	1.1	367	11,940	.14	.09	.9	26
63	64	105	2.0	510	19,890	.13	.10	1.5	36
6	16	33	.6	300	1110	.07	.05	.9	28
10	14	46	1.2	523	2170	.12	.07	1.7	41
8	54	37	.6	291	Trace	.06	.08	.5	34
5	252	49	1.5	—	8270	.15	.33	.7	68
6	195	64	2.6	246	11,390	.08	.15	.7	31
27	30	43	2.1	426	2510	.13	.13	.9	30

Metric Conversion Chart

	Into Metric			Out of Metric	
If You Know	Multiply By	To Get	If You Know	Multiply By	To Get

LENGTH

inches	2.54	centimeters	millimeters	0.04	inches
feet	30	centimeters	centimeters	0.4	inches
feet	0.303	meters	meters	3.3	feet
yards	0.91	meters	kilometers	0.62	miles
miles	1.6	kilometers			

AREA

sq. inches	6.5	sq. centimeters	sq. centimeters	0.16	sq. inches
sq. feet	0.09	sq. meters	sq. meters	1.2	sq. yards
sq. yards	0.8	sq. meters	sq. kilometers	0.4	sq. miles
sq. miles	2.6	sq. kilometers	hectares	2.47	acres
acres	0.4	hectares			

MASS (WEIGHT)

ounces	28	grams	grams	0.035	ounces
pounds	0.45	kilograms	kilograms	2.2	pounds
short ton	0.9	metric ton	metric tons	1.1	short tons

VOLUME

teaspoons	5	milliliters	milliliters	0.03	fluid ounces
tablespoons	15	milliliters	liters	2.1	pints
fluid ounces	30	milliliters	liters	1.06	quarts
cups	0.24	liters	liters	0.26	gallons
pints	0.47	liters	cubic meters	35	cubic feet
quarts	0.95	liters	cubic meters	1.3	cubic yards
gallons	3.8	liters			
cubic feet	0.03	cubic meters			
cubic yards	0.76	cubic meters			

PRESSURE

lbs/in²	0.069	bars	bars	14.5	lbs/in²
atmospheres	1.013	bars	bars	0.987	atmospheres
atmospheres	1.033	kg/cm²	kg/cm²	0.968	atmospheres
lbs/in²	0.07	kg/cm²	kg/cm²	14.22	lbs/in²

RATES

lbs/acre	1.12	kg/hectare	kg/hectare	0.892	lbs/acre
tons/acre	2.24	metric tons/hectare	metric tons/hectare	0.445	tons/acre

Temperature Conversion Table

Celsius temperatures have been rounded to the nearest whole number.

F	C	F	C	F	C
−26	−32	19	− 7	64	18
−24	−31	21	− 6	66	19
−22	−30	23	− 5	68	20
−20	−29	25	− 4	70	21
−18	−28	27	− 3	72	22
−17	−27	28	− 2	73	23
−15	−26	30	− 1	75	24
−13	−25	32	0	77	25
−11	−24	34	1	79	26
− 9	−23	36	2	81	27
− 8	−22	37	3	82	28
− 6	−21	39	4	84	29
− 4	−20	41	5	86	30
− 2	−19	43	6	88	31
0	−18	45	7	90	32
1	−17	46	8	91	33
3	−16	48	9	93	34
5	−15	50	10	95	35
7	−14	52	11	97	36
9	−13	54	12	99	37
10	−12	55	13	100	38
12	−11	57	14	102	39
14	−10	59	15	104	40
16	− 9	61	16	106	41
18	− 8	63	17	108	42
				212	100

Fahrenheit to Celsius: Subtract 32 from the Fahrenheit figure, multiply by 5 and divide by 9.
Celsius to Fahrenheit: Multiply the Celsius figure by 9, divide by 5 and add 32.

Index

Illustrations are indicated by boldface type.